DICTIONARY & THESAURUS

Bloomsbury Books
London

LIST OF ABBREVIATIONS

adj	adjective	*pl*	plural
adv	adverb	*poss*	possessive
def art	definite article	*prep*	preposition
demons	demonstrative	*pron*	pronoun
esp	especially	*sing*	singular
f	feminine	*vi*	intransitive verb
indic	indicative	*vt*	transitive verb
inf	informal	*vt, vi*	transitive and
n	noun		intransitive verb
per	personal	*usu*	usually

© 1994 Geddes & Grosset Ltd,
David Dale House, New Lanark, Scotland.

Reprinted 1995.

This edition published 1995 by Bloomsbury Books,
an imprint of Godfrey Cave Associates,
42 Bloomsbury Street, London, WC1B 3QJ.

ISBN 1 85471 500 3

Printed in UK

Dictionary

A

a the indefinite article, used before a consonant. *see* **an.**

aback *adv* backwards; by surprise.

abacus *n* a square slab on the top of a column; a counting frame.

abandon *vt* to forsake entirely; to desert; to give oneself up to a desire or emotion.

abandoned *adj* deserted; depraved.

abase *vt* to bring low; degrade; disgrace.

abasement *n* degradation.

abash *vt* to put to confusion; to make ashamed.

abate *vt* to lessen. * *vi* to become less.

abatement *n* reduction; decrease

abbatoir *n* a public slaughterhouse.

abbess *n* a female superior of a nunnery.

abbey *n* (*pl* **abbeys**) a monastery or convent.

abbot *n* the male superior of an abbey or monastery.

abbreviate *vt* to shorten.

abdicate *vt* to resign voluntarily; to relinquish.

abdomen *n* the lower belly.

abduct *vt* to entice; to lead away by force.

abduction *n* the unlawful carrying off of a person.

aberration *n* a wandering from the right way; derangement of the mind.

abet *vt* to aid or to encourage (in evil).

abetter, abettor *n* one who abets.

abeyance *n*: **in ~** suspense.

abhor *vt* to shrink from with horror; to detest.

abhorrence *n* detestation.

abhorrent *adj* hateful.

abide *vi* to stay in a place; to dwell. * *vt* to wait for; to tolerate; to endure.

abiding *adj* permanent.

ability *n* the power to do a thing; skill; (*pl* **abilities**) the powers of the mind.

abject *adj* mean; vile.

abjure *vt* to renounce upon oath.

ablaze *adv* on fire; in a blaze.

able *adj* capable; skilful.

ablution *n* a washing away from; a cleansing.

ably *adv* with ability.

abnormal *adj* deviating from a fixed rule; irregular.

aboard *adv*, *prep* on board; in a ship.

abode *n* residence.

abolish *vt* to destroy; to do away with.

abominable *adj* hateful.

abominate *vt* to hate extremely; to abhor.

abomination *n* hatred; the object of hatred.

aborigine *n* the original inhabitant of a country.

abortion *n* a miscarriage, usually induced.

abortive *adj* fruitless.

abound *vi* to be, or have, in great plenty.

about *prep* around; near to; concerning. * *adv* around; nearly.

above *prep* to or in a higher place than; more than. * *adv* to or in a higher place.

above board *adv* without concealment or deception.

abreast *adv* side by side.

abridge *vt* to shorten; to condense.

abridgement *n* a summary of a text without loss of meaning; a shortening.

abroad *adv* at large; in a foreign country.

abrogate *vt* to repeal; to make void.

abrupt *adj* broken off; steep; sudden; curt in manner or speech.

abruptness *n* suddenness.

abscess *n* a gathering of pus in some part of the body.

abscond *vi* to fly from justice.

absence *n* the state of being absent; inattentive.

absent[1] *adj* not present; inattention.

absent[2] *vt* to keep oneself away from.

absentee *n* one who absents himself.

absolute *adj* unlimited; despotic.

absolutely *adv* unconditionally.

absolution *n* a freeing from guilt or its punishment.

absolve *vt* to free from, as from guilt or punishment; pardon.

absorb *vt* to drink in; to soak up; to engross.

absorbent *adj* imbibing; swallowing; able to soak up moisture.

absorption *n* act or process of imbibing or swallowing up; total interest in.

abstain vi to keep back from; to refrain.

abstemious adj sparing in food or drink; temperate.

abstinence n a refraining from anything, especially from strong drink.

abstract vt to draw from; to separate and consider by itself; to summarize.

abstract adj existing in the mind only; not concrete. * n a summary.

abstracted adj lost in thought.

absurd adj contrary to reason; ridiculous.

absurdity n the quality of being absurd; that which is absurd.

abundance n great plenty.

abundant adj abounding; plentiful.

abuse vt to ill-use; to insult.

abuse n misuse; insulting words.

abusive adj insulting.

abut vi to border; to meet.

abyss n a bottomless gulf; a chasm.

academic adj belonging to an academy or university; theoretical. * n a teacher or researcher in a university.

academy n a school of arts or sciences; a society of persons for the cultivation of arts and sciences.

accede vi to assent to; to comply with.

accelerate vt to hasten; to quicken the speed of.

acceleration n increase of velocity.

accent n a stress or modulation of the voice; a manner of speaking.

accent vt to express or note the accent of.

accentuate vt to emphasize.

accept vt to receive; to admit.

acceptance n reception; approval.

access n approach; admission.

accessible adj easy of approach; affable.

accession n the act of acceding; addition; succession to a throne.

accessory adj additional. * n an accomplice.

accident n a chance or unforeseen event; a mishap.

accidental adj happening by chance.

acclaim n praise; enthusiastic approval. * vt to applaud.

acclamation n a shout of joy or approval.

acclimatize vt to accustom to a new climate; to become used to.

accolade n a high honour; strong praise.

accommodate vt to make suitable; to adjust; to provide lodging for.

accommodating adj obliging.

accommodation n lodgings; loan.

accompaniment n the music played to accompany a singer or other performer.

accompany vt to go with; to perform music along with.

accomplice n an associate, especially in a crime.

accomplish vt to fulfil.

accomplished adj elegant; having a finished education; skilled.

accomplishment npl attainments.

accord n harmony; agreement. * vt to make to agree; to grant. * vi to agree.

accordance n agreement.

accordingly adv consequently.

accordion n a small keyed wind instrument.

accost vt to speak to first; to solicit.

account n a reckoning; a bill; narration. * vt to reckon; to value. * vi to give or render reasons; to explain (with for).

accountable adj liable to be called to account; responsible.

accountant n one skilled in accounts.

accoutrements npl military dress and arms; special equipment.

accredit vt to give credit or authority to.

accredited adj authorized.

accretion n enlargement by natural growth or by external additions.

accrue vi to come to; to result from.

accumulate vt to heap up. * vi to increase.

accumulation n a heap; a collection.

accuracy n correctness.

accurate adj done with care; exact.

accursed adj lying under a curse; doomed.

accusation n a charge brought against anyone.

accusative adj, n a case in grammar.

accuse vt to charge with a crime; to blame.

accused n a person charged with a crime.

accustom vt to make familiar with by use.

accustomed adj familiar by custom; usual.

ace n a unit; a single point on cards or dice; an expert.

acerbity n sourness; bitterness.

acetic adj sour; like vinegar.

ache vi to be in pain. * n a gnawing pain.

achieve vt to accomplish; to win.

achievement n an accomplishment through effort.

acid adj sharp or sour to the taste. * n a sour substance; one that with certain other substances forms salts.

acidity n sourness.

acknowledge vt to own the knowledge of; to own or confess.

acknowledgement n recognition.

acolyte n an attendant.

acorn n the fruit of the oak.

acoustics n the science of sound; the sound properties, good or bad, of a room or hall.

acquaint vt to make to know; to inform.

acquiesce vi to rest satisfied; to comply.

acquiescence n assent.

acquiescent adj resting satisfied; submitting.

acquire vt to obtain; to gain.

acquisition n acquirement; gain.

acquisitive adj fond of getting; eager to possess things.

acquit vt to set free; to absolve.

acquittal n a setting free from a charge.

acre n a quantity of land containing 4840 square yards.

acreage n the number of acres in a piece of land

acrid adj sharp to the taste or smell.

acrimonious adj full of bitterness.

acrimony n sharpness or harshness of temper or tone of speech.

acrobat n a rope dancer; a gymnast.

acronym n a word made up of initial letters or parts of words.

across prep, adv from side to side; over; crosswise.

act vi to be in action; to exert power; to conduct oneself. * vt to do; to perform; to play on the stage; to pretend. * n a deed; power; a part of a play; law, as an act of parliament; pretence.

acting n performance of a part in a play. * adj taking someone's place for a time.

action n a deed; operation; a gesture; a lawsuit; a battle.

actionable adj furnishing grounds for an action at law.

active adj busy; quick; lively.

activity n nimbleness; an occupation,

work or leisure a person is engaged in.

actor n one who acts; a stage player.

actress n a female stage player.

actual adj real.

actuary n a specialist in insurance statistics.

actuate vt to put into action; to incite.

acumen n sharpness of perception; sagacity.

acute adj sharp; pointed; keen; sharp in sound or of hearing; intense; of supreme importance.

adage n a proverb; a maxim.

adagio adj, adv in music, slow; with grace. * n a slow movement.

adamant n any substance of impenetrable hardness; the diamond.

adapt vt to adjust or change to suit a purpose.

adaptability n the capability of being adapted.

adaptation n the result of adapting, e.g. a book for another medium.

add vt to join to; to find sum of.

addendum n (pl **addenda**) something added.

addict vt (usually passive with **to**) to be given to or dependent on. * n one addicted to something, e.g. drugs.

addition n act of adding; the thing added.

additional adj added on.

addled adj rotten; muddled.

address vt to direct; to speak to. * n verbal or written application; speech or discourse; tact; direction of a letter.

adept n, adj well skilled (person).

adequate adj sufficient; passable.

adhere vi to stick; to cling.

adherent adj sticking to. * n a follower.

adhesion n the act or state of sticking to; adherence.

adhesive adj sticking; sticky.

adieu interj farewell.

adipose adj fatty.

adjacent adj adjoining.

adjective n a word which qualifies a noun.

adjoining adj adjacent.

adjourn vt to postpone. * vi to leave off for a time.

adjournment n act of adjourning; postponement.

adjudge vt to decree.

adjudicate vt to adjudge; to determine judicially; to give a ruling on.

adjunct n something added or joined. * adj united with.

adjust vt to set right; to fit.

adjustable adj able to be adjusted.

adjustment n the act of adjusting; a settlement.

administer vt to manage; to dispense; to distribute.

administration n management; the executive part of a government.

admirable adj worthy of admiration; excellent.

admiral n the commander of a fleet or navy.

admiralty n a board for administering naval affairs.

admiration n wonder mingled with delight and respect; esteem.

admire vt to regard with delight or affection and respect.

admissible adj allowable.

admission n admittance; concession.

admit vt to allow to enter; to grant.

admittance n permission to enter; entrance; allowance; confession.

admonish vt to warn; to reprove.

admonition n gentle or solemn reproof.

adolescence n a growing up to adulthood; the age of youth.

adopt vt to take and raise as one's own (child); to embrace.

adorable adj worthy to be loved.

adoration n worship paid to God; profound reverence.

adore vt to worship; to love intensely.

adorn vt to deck with ornaments; to beautify.

adrenaline n a hormone secreted in glands in the kidney which is released by stress and increases the heart and pulse rate.

adrift adv at the mercy of circumstance; floating at random.

adroit adj skilful; clever.

adulation n servile flattery.

adult adj full-grown. * n a person grown to manhood.

adulterate vt to debase by mixture.

adulterer n a person guilty of adultery.

adultery n unfaithfulness to marriage vows.

advance vt to put forward; (in commerce) to pay beforehand. * vi to go forward. * n a going forward; progress.

advanced adj in the van of progress.

advancement n improvement; promotion in station, career, etc.

advantage n a favourable state; gain; a term in tennis.

advantageous adj profitable.

advent n arrival; the four weeks before Christmas.

adventure n a hazardous enterprise; an exciting experience. * vt, vi to risk or hazard.

adventurer n one who risks, hazards, or braves.

adventurous adj daring.

adverb n a word which modifies a verb, adjective or another adverb.

adversary n an enemy; an antagonist.

adverse adj hostile; contrary.

adversity n misfortune.

advertise vt to announce; to publish a notice of.

advertisement n information; a public notice promoting something.

advertiser n one who advertises.

advice n an opinion offered; counsel.

advisable adj fitting or proper to be done; expedient.

advise vt to counsel; to warn; to inform. * vi to deliberate or consider.

advised adj cautious; done with advice.

advisedly adv deliberately.

advocate n one who pleads for another; an intercessor. * vt to plead in favour of; to defend, esp in a law court.

adze n a kind of axe, with the edge at right angles to the handle.

aegis n protection; sponsorship.

aerate vt to put air or other gas into.

aerial adj belonging to the air; lofty. * n a device, antenna to receive and transmit radio waves.

aerie, eyrie n the nest of a bird of prey.

aeronaut n one who flies, sails or floats in the air.

aeronautics n the science of flight.

aeroplane, airplane n an aircraft with wings.

aesthetics the science or philosophy of art and the beautiful.

afar *adv* at, to or from a distance.

affability *n* geniality; friendliness.

affable *adj* courteous; accessible.

affair *n* a business matter; an event; a sexual relationship, usually temporary.

affect *vt* to act upon; to move the feelings of; to pretend.

affectation *n* an assumed air put on by a person; pretence.

affection *n* fondness; love.

affectionate *adj* tender; loving.

affidavit *n* a written declaration upon oath.

affiliate *vt* to adopt; to attach to a society or other body.

affinity *n* relation by marriage; liking; similarity; chemical attraction.

affirm *vt* to assert; to declare.

affirmation *n* a solemn declaration (instead of an oath).

affirmative *adj* positive; stating a thing to be true. * *n* that which expresses assent; the word 'yes'.

affix *vt* to fasten to. * *n* a syllable or letter added to a word.

afflict *vt* to grieve; to cause pain or sorrow.

affliction *n* distress; grief; pain.

affluence *n* abundance; wealth.

affluent *adj* wealthy; abundant.

afford *vt* to yield; to supply; to be able to spend, to grant.

affray *n* a fight; a disturbance; a tumult.

affront *vt* to insult; to offend. * *n* an insult.

afield *adv* to or in the field; far away.

afloat *adv*, *adj* floating; at sea.

afoot *adv* on foot; in motion; happening.

aforementioned *adj* mentioned before.

aforenamed *adj* named before.

aforesaid *adj* said before.

afraid *adj* struck with fear; feeling regret.

afresh *adv* anew.

aft *adj*, *adv* astern.

after *adj* later. * *prep* later in time than; behind. * *adv* later in time.

aftermath *n* the result or after effects usually of something unpleasant; a season's second crop of grass.

afternoon *n* the time from noon to evening.

afterthought *n* reflection after an act.

afterwards *adv* subsequently.

again *adv* once more.

against *prep* in opposition to; in expectation of.

agate *n* a hard quartz-like mineral.

age *n* a period of time; an epoch; the length of a person's life. * *vi*, *vt* to grow or make old; to show signs of advancing age.

agency *n* means; a specialized or specific business; the business of an agent.

agenda *npl* business to be transacted at a meeting.

agent *n* one who acts; a deputy.

agglomeration *n* a heap.

aggrandize *vt* to magnify; to increase in power, riches, etc.

aggravate *vt* to intensify; to exasperate.

aggravation *n* the act of aggravating; provocation.

aggregate *vt* to collect. * *adj* total * *n* the sum of parts.

aggression *n* the first act of hostility; attack.

aggressive *adj* inclined to attacking; prone to quarrelling.

aggressor *n* the person who starts hostilities.

aggrieve *vt* to pain; to vex.

aghast *adj*, *adv*. amazed; horrified.

agile *adj* nimble.

agility *n* nimbleness.

agitate *vt* to put in violent motion; to excite; to stir up.

agitated *adj* disturbed.

agitation *n* excitement; commotion.

agitator *n* one who excites discontent or revolt.

agnostic *n* one who disclaims any knowledge of God.

agog *adv* in eager excitement.

agonize *vi* to writhe with extreme pain.

agonizing *adj* giving extreme pain.

agony *n* extreme pain of body or mind; anguish.

agrarian *adj* relating to land and agriculture.

agree *vi* to be in concord; to suit.

agreeable *adj* suitable to; pleasing; grateful.

agreement *n* harmony; conformity; compact.

agriculture *n* the art or science of cultivating the ground.

aground *adv* stranded; on the shore.

ague *n* an intermittent fever with shivering.

ahead *adv* before; onward.

aid *vt* to help. * *n* help.

Aids *n* acronym for a complex medical condition, *a*cquired *i*mmune *d*eficiency *s*yndrome.

ail *vt* to pain. * *vi* to be in pain.

ailment *n* a pain; a disease.

aim *vi* to point with a weapon; to intend; to endeavour. * *vt* to level or direct as a firearm. * *n* intention; purpose.

aimless *adj* without aim.

air *n* the atmosphere; a light breeze; a tune; bearing (*npl*) affected manner. * *vt* to expose to the air; to dry.

air conditioning *n* a regulating system controlling temperature, freshness and humidity of air (in a building).

aircraft *n* any machine that flies in the air.

airily *adv* in an airy manner.

airing *n* an exposure to the air or to a fire; an excursion in the open air.

airline *n* a company or organization running aeroplanes for transportation.

airplane *see* **aeroplane**.

airport *n* a place where aircraft land and take off and undergo repairs.

air pump *n* a machine for pumping the air out of a vessel.

air raid *n* an attack on ground targets by military aircraft.

airtight *adj* so tight or compact as not to let air pass.

airy *adj* open to the air; fresh; casual; light-hearted.

aisle *n* a wing or side of a church; a passage in a church.

ajar *adv* partly open.

akin *adj* of the same kin; related to.

alabaster *n* a soft marble-like mineral.

alacrity *n* liveliness; eagerness.

alarm *n* a call to arms; sudden surprise; fright. * *vt* to give notice of danger.

alarming *adj* terrifying.

alarmist *n* one prone to excite alarm.

albino *n* a person with abnormally white skin and hair and pink eyes.

album *n* a book for autographs, sketches, etc; a long-playing record containing several items.

albumen *n* the white of an egg.

alchemy *n* an obsolete science, aiming at changing metals into gold, etc.

alcohol *n* pure spirit of a highly intoxicating nature produced by distilling or fermenting.

alcove *n* a recess.

alderman *n* formerly a magistrate of a town.

ale *n* a fermented malt liquor; beer.

alert *adj* vigilant; quick. * *vt* to warn.

alertness *n* briskness; activity.

algebra *n* the science of computing by symbols.

alias *adv* otherwise. * *n* (*pl* **aliases**) an assumed name.

alibi *n* the plea that one was elsewhere when a crime was committed.

alien *adj* foreign. * *n* a foreigner.

alienate *vt* to transfer to another; to estrange; to cause hostility towards.

alight *vi* to get down; to settle on.

alight *adv*, *adv*. on fire.

alike *adj* like; similar. * *adv* in the same manner.

aliment *n* nourishment; food.

alimony *n* an allowance to a woman legally separated from her husband.

alive *adj* living; lively.

alkali *n* a substance, as potash and soda, which neutralizes acids.

all *adj* every one. * *n* everything * *adv* wholly; entirely.

allay *vt* to ease; to assuage.

allegation *n* an assertion or statement made, often without having proof.

allege *vt* to assert, often without proof.

allegiance *n* loyalty.

allegorical *adj* figurative.

allegory *n* a story, etc which conveys a meaning different from the literal one.

allegro a word denoting a sprightly movement in music.

alleviate *vt* to make light; to assuage; to relieve pain.

alley *n* a narrow walk or passage.

alliance *n* state of being allied; league; the countries forming this.

allied *adj* united by treaty or marriage.

alliteration *n* the repetition of a letter at the beginning of two or more words in close succession.

allocate *vt* to distribute.

allot *vt* to give by lot; to apportion.

allow *vt* to let; to admit the truth or the possibility of; to grant.

allowance *n* a sum allotted; permission.

alloy *vt* to mix with baser metals. * *n* a mixture of metals.

allude *vi* to refer to.

allure *vt* to entice; to decoy.

allurement *n* temptation; enticement.

alluring *adj* attractive.

allusion *n* a hint; a reference.

alluvial *adj* deposited by water.

ally *vt* to unite by friendship, marriage, or treaty. * *n* an associate.

almanac *n* a calendar of days, weeks, and months, etc.

almighty *adj* omnipotent. * *n* God.

almond *n* the nut of the almond tree.

almoner *n* formerly a hospital social worker.

almost *adv* nearly.

aloft *adv* in the sky; on high.

alone *adj* solitary. * *adv* separately.

along *adv* lengthways. * *prep* by the side of.

aloof *adv* apart.

aloud *adv* loudly.

alpaca *n* a llama with long hair; cloth made from this hair.

alpha the first letter in the Greek alphabet.

alphabet *n* the letters of a language.

alpine *adj* pertaining to high mountains. * *n* a small plant growing on mountainsides.

already *adv* even now.

also *adv* likewise; too.

altar *n* an elevated stone on which sacrifices were offered; the communion table.

alter *vt* to change. * *vi* to vary.

alteration *n* partial change or variation.

altercation *n* a wrangle; an angry dispute.

alternate *adj* by turns. * *vt* to follow by turns.

alternative *n* a choice of two things.

although *conj* though.

altitude *n* height.

alto *adj* high. * *n* (in music) contralto.

altogether *adv* wholly.

altruism *n* devotion to others; unselfishness.

aluminium *n* a soft, white, light metal.

always *adv* at all times.

amalgam *n* a mixture of mercury with another metal, usually silver.

amalgamate *vt* to unite in an amalgam; to combine.

amass *vt* to form into a mass; to heap up.

amateur *n* a lover of any art or science or a participant in any sport or activity, but not a professional.

amaze *vt* to astonish.

amazement *n* wonder.

ambassador *n* a diplomatic representative of a country abroad.

amber *n* a mineralized yellow or yellow-brown fossil resin used for jewellery.

ambidextrous *adj* using both hands alike.

ambiguity *n* doubtfulness of meaning or interpretation.

ambiguous *adj* doubtful; obscure.

ambit *n* compass; scope.

ambition *n* desire for preferment or power.

ambitious *adj* aspiring.

amble *vi* to walk at a slow easy pace. * *n* an easy pace.

ambrosia *n* the imaginary food of the gods.

ambulance *n* a vehicle for transporting the sick or wounded.

ambulatory *adj* movable; walking.

ambush *n* the place or act of lying in wait in order to surprise.

ameliorate *vt* to make better.

amen *adv* so be it.

amenable *adj* easily led; co-operative; accountable.

amend *vt* to correct; to improve. * *vi* to grow better.

amendment *n* a change for the better; correction; reformation.

amends *npl* compensation; satisfaction; recompense.

amenity *n* pleasantness; agreeableness of situation.

amethyst *n* a precious stone of a bluish violet or purple colour.

amiability *n* sweetness of temper.

amiable *adj* loveable; pleasant; friendly.

amicable *adj* friendly; kind.

amid, amidst *prep* in the midst of.

amidships *adv* in or towards the middle of a ship.

amiss *adj* in error; improper. * *adv* improperly.

amity *n* friendship.

ammonia *n* volatile alkali.

ammonite *n* an extinct marine animal; its coiled shell found as a fossil.

ammunition *n* war stores and projectiles, e.g. bullets, rockets, fired from weapons; any helpful facts, etc, to be used in winning an argument.

amnesty *n* a general pardon.

amoeba *n* (*pl* **amoebae, amoebas**) a minute organism that constantly changes shape, found in fresh water.

among, amongst *prep* amidst.

amorous *adj* inclined to or showing love.

amorphous *adj* shapeless.

amount *vi* to mount up to; to result in. * *n* the sum total.

ampere *n* the unit of current in electricity.

amphibian *n* (*pl* **amphibia**) an animal able to live either on land or in water.

amphibious *adj* able to live in water or on land; (of a vehicle) built to operate on land and water.

amphitheatre *n* a building of an oval form, with rows of seats all round, rising one above the other.

ample *adj* spacious; abundant; sufficient.

amplification *n* enlargement.

amplifier *n* a device that amplifies or enlarges or makes the sound louder.

amplify *vt, vi* to enlarge; to make louder; to fill out.

amplitude *n* ampleness; extent; abundance.

amply *adv* fully; copiously.

amputate *vt* to cut off, as a limb.

amuck, amok *n, adv*: **to run ~** to attack all and sundry.

amulet *n* a charm against evils.

amuse *vt* to entertain; to beguile; to cause laughter.

amusement *n* diversion; entertainment.

amusing *adj* droll; diverting.

an *adj* the indefinite article, used before words beginning with a vowel sound.

anachronism *n* the error of assigning an event or circumstance out of its time.

anaemia *n* bloodlessness.

anaesthetic *adj* producing insensibility. * *n* a substance (drug or gas) which produces insensibility.

anagram *n* a word formed from the letters of another, e.g. rood from door.

analogous *adj* corresponding.

analogy *n* similarity.

analyse *vt* to resolve into its elements.

analysis *n* (*pl* **analyses**) a breaking up of a thing into its elements.

analyst *n* one who analyses.

anarchic *adj* without rule or government.

anarchist *n* one who opposes all forms of government.

anathema *n* an object of detestation.

anatomical *adj* relating to anatomy.

anatomy *n* the science dealing with physical structure of animals and plants; the art of dissection.

ancestor *n* a forefather.

ancestral *adj* relating or belonging to ancestors.

ancestry *n* lineage; descent.

anchor *n* an iron instrument that grips the sea or river bed and holds a ship at rest in water. * *vt* to hold fast by an anchor.

anchorage *n* a place where a ship can anchor.

ancient *adj* old; antique.

ancillary *adj* subservient or subordinate.

and *conj* a word joining words or phrases; also; in addition, consequently.

andante *adj* in music, with slow, graceful movement.

anecdote *n* a short often amusing story.

anemometer *n* an instrument for measuring the force of the wind.

aneroid *adj* a kind of barometer.

aneurysm *adj* dilatation of an artery.

anew *adv* once more.

anger *n* wrath. * *vt* to enrage.

angle *n* the inclination of two lines which meet in a point; a corner; a viewpoint.

angle *vi* to fish with hook and line.

angler n one who fishes with hook and line.

Anglican adj pertaining to the Church of England.

Anglicize vt to make English.

Anglophobia n an excessive hatred of English people, customs, etc.

angry adj full of anger; wrathful.

anguish n extreme pain, body or mind.

angular adj sharp-cornered; (of a person) thin and bony.

animal n a living being having sensation and voluntary motion.

animate vt to give life to; to enliven; to produce moving objects and figures by animation.

animated adj lively; living; (film, etc) made by animation.

animation n life; vigour; vivacity; the art of drawing objects and filming them to create moving images on film or tape.

animosity n violent hatred; active enmity.

ankle n the joint which connects the foot with the leg.

annals npl a yearly record of events.

annex vt to unite at the end; to subjoin; to take possession of.

annexation n the act of annexing.

annexe n an extension to a building, built on to it or erected nearby.

annihilate vt to reduce to nothing.

annihilation n the act of annihilating.

anniversary n a day on which some event is annually celebrated.

annotate vt to write notes upon.

announce vt to make known.

announcement n declaration.

annoy vt to hurt; to vex.

annoyance n act of annoying; state of being annoyed.

annual adj yearly; lasting a year. * n a book published yearly.

annuitant n one who receives an annuity.

annuity n a sum of money payable yearly.

annul vt to make of no effect; to repeal.

anoint vt to consecrate with oil; to rub with or apply oil to.

anomalous adj irregular; exceptional.

anomaly n irregularity.

anonymous adj nameless; unsigned.

another adj not the same.

answer vt to reply to; to suit. * n a reply; a solution.

answerable adj accountable.

antagonism n opposition; hostility.

antagonist n an opponent.

antagonistic adj hostile.

Antarctic adj of or near the South Pole.

antecedent adj going before. * n that which goes before; (pl) ancestors; a person's history.

antechamber n anteroom.

antedate vt to date before the true time.

antediluvian adj before the flood.

antelope n a kind of deer.

antemeridian adj before midday; a.m.

antenna n (pl **antennae**) one of the feelers of an insect; an aerial.

anterior adj prior.

anteroom n a room leading to another.

anthem n a piece of Scripture set to music.

anthology n a collection of poems or prose.

anthracite n a kind of coal which burns almost without flame.

antics npl buffoonery and posturing.

anticipate vt to forestall.

anticipation n act of anticipating; expectation.

anticlimax n a tame ending to a striking beginning.

anticyclone n an opposite state of atmospheric conditions to what exists in a cyclone, presaging good weather.

antidote n a remedy for poison or any evil.

antipathy n aversion; dislike.

antipodes npl the opposite side of the globe.

antiquarian adj pertaining to antiquaries.

antiquated adj old-fashioned; out of date.

antique adj old. * n an ancient relic, object of value or work of art.

antiquity n ancient times; great age; (pl **antiquities**) remains of ancient times.

antiseptic adj counteracting contamination.

antithesis n (pl **antitheses**) contrast.

antler n a branch of a stag's horn.

anvil n an iron block used by smiths.

anxiety n concern; worry.

anxious *adj* troubled; worried; eager.

any *adj* one indefinitely.

aorta *n* the artery leading from the heart.

apace *adv* fast.

apart *adj*, *adv* separate; aside; in pieces.

apartment *n* a room; a flat.

apathetic *adj* indifferent.

apathy *n* want of feeling; indifference.

ape *n* a monkey. * *vt* to mimic.

aperture *n* an opening.

apex *n* (*pl* **apexes, apices**) the summit.

apiary *n* a place where bees are kept.

apiece *adv* in a separate share.

aplomb *n* self-possession.

apocalypse *n* a disastrous happening.

apocryphal *adj* fictitious.

apologetic *adj* excusing.

apologize *vi* to make an excuse.

apology *n* that which is said in defence or as an expression of regret.

apoplexy *n* a shock involving paralysis.

apostasy *n* departure from one's faith or party.

apostate *n* one who renounces his religion or his party.

apostrophe *n* a mark (') indicating contraction of a word, or the possessive case.

apotheosis *n* a deification.

appal *vt* to dismay.

appalling *adj* causing dread or terror.

apparatus *n* (*pl* **apparatus**) tools or equipment for doing work or for a special purpose.

apparel *n* clothing. * *vt* to dress.

apparent *adv* evident; seeming.

apparition *n* a ghost or phantom.

appeal *vi*, *vt* to entreat; to carry to a higher court. * *n* entreaty.

appear *vi* to become visible; to seem.

appearance *n* act of coming into sight; semblance.

appease *vt* to pacify; to calm.

appellant *n* one who appeals.

appellation *n* a name; a title.

append *vt* to add; to attach.

appendage *n* something added; an external organ, e.g. a tail.

appendicitis *n* inflammation of the vermiform appendix of the bowels.

appendix *n* an adjunct; a supplement; a prolongation.

appertain *vi* to belong.

appetite *n* a desire or relish for food.

appetize *vt* to whet the appetite.

applaud *vt* to praise by clapping the hands.

applause *n* praise loudly expressed.

apple *n* a fruit.

appliance *n* the act of applying; the thing applied; a device or machine usually for domestic use.

applicability *n* relevance.

applicable *adj* suitable.

applicant *n* one who applies, e.g. for work.

application *n* the act of applying; perseverance; diligence.

apply *vt* to fasten or attach. * *vi* to suit; to make application.

appoint *vt* to fix; to nominate.

appointment *n* office; engagement.

apposite *adj* suitable.

appraise *vt* to fix or set a price or value on.

appreciable *adj* that may be appreciated.

appreciate *vt* to value; to be grateful to or thankful for. * *vi* to rise in value.

appreciation *n* the act of appreciating; a just valuation; approval; gratitude; a rise in value.

apprehend *vt* to take hold of; to arrest; to fear; to understand.

apprehension *n* seizure; dread.

apprehensive *adj* fearful.

apprentice *n* one who is learning a trade or occupation. * *vt* to bind as an apprentice.

apprise *vt* to inform.

approach *vt*, *vi* to come near. * *n* the act of drawing near; an avenue.

approbation *n* approval.

appropriate *vt* to take to oneself as one's own. * *adj* suitable.

appropriateness *n* peculiar fitness.

approval *n* praise; a favourable opinion.

approve *vt* to consider good; to sanction. * *vi* (with **of**) to express approbation.

approximate *adj* near; almost right or good. * *vt* to bring near. * *vi* to come near.

approximately *adv* nearly.

apricot *n* a stone fruit, allied to the plum.

April n the fourth month of the year.

apron n a garment worn in front to protect the clothes.

apt adj suitable; liable.

aptitude n natural facility.

aquarium n (pl **aquariums, aquaria**) a vessel or tank or building for aquatic plants and animals.

Aquarius n the water bearer, a sign in the zodiac.

aquatic adj living or growing in water; (pl) water sports.

aqueduct n a conduit made for conveying water.

aqueous adj watery.

aquiline adj hooked like the beak of an eagle.

Arab n a native of Arabia; an Arabian horse.

arabesque n a species of ornamentation consisting of fanciful figures in dance and music, and floral forms in art.

arable adj fit for ploughing and growing.

arbiter n an umpire.

arbitrarily adv by will or caprice only; despotically.

arbitrary adj despotic; capricious.

arbitrate vi to act as an arbiter; to decide.

arbitrator n a person chosen to decide a dispute; referee.

arboriculture n the art of cultivating trees and shrubs.

arc n a part of a circle or curve.

arcade n a covered passage containing shops.

arcane adj understood only with inside knowledge; secret; mysterious.

arch[1] adj chief; expert; roguish; sly.

arch[2] n a curved structure supporting a bridge or roof.

archaeology n the science of antiquities; knowledge of ancient art.

archaic adj antiquated; obsolete.

archbishop n a chief bishop.

archdeacon n a church dignitary, next in rank to a bishop.

archer n a person who shoots with a bow and arrow.

archery n the art of the archer.

archipelago n a sea abounding in islands.

architect n one who plans buildings.

architecture n the art or science of building.

archive n a record; (generally pl) public records.

archness n roguishness; slyness.

archway n a passage under an arch.

Arctic adj pertaining to the regions about the North Pole; frigid; cold.

ardent adj fervent; eager.

ardour n warmth; eagerness; passion.

arduous adj difficult.

arduously adv with effort.

area n any open surface; surface measurement; any enclosed or sunken space.

arena n an open space of ground for contests or games.

argue vt, vi to discuss; to dispute.

argument n a reason offered; a plea; a controversy.

argumentative adj prone to argument.

arid adj dry; parched.

Aries n the Ram, the first of the twelve signs in the zodiac.

arise vi to rise up; to come about.

aristocracy n government by the nobility; the nobility.

aristocrat n a noble.

arithmetic n the science of numbers; computation.

ark n a large floating vessel; a place of refuge.

arm n the limb from the shoulder to the hand; a weapon; (pl) war; armour; armorial bearings. * vt to furnish with arms. * vi to take up arms.

armada n a fleet of armed ships.

armament n a force armed for war; war equipment of an army, ship or vehicle.

armistice n a truce.

armorial adj relating to arms in heraldry.

armour n defensive arms.

armoury n a place for keeping arms.

armpit n the hollow place under the shoulder.

army n a body of men armed for war.

aroma n perfume.

aromatic adj fragrant.

around prep about; encircling. * adv on every side.

arouse vt to stir up.

arraign vt to indict; to censure.

arrange vt to put in order; to prepare for; to plan; to adjust a musical work for different instruments.

arrangement n orderly disposition; classification; agreement.

arrant adj downright; thorough.

array n order; apparel. * vt to draw up in order; to adorn.

arrear n (generally pl) that which remains unpaid.

arrest vt to stop; to apprehend. * n a seizure by warrant.

arrival n the act of coming to a place.

arrive vi to come; to reach; to succeed.

arrogance n haughtiness; insolent bearing.

arrogant adj haughty; overbearing; self-important.

arrow n a barbed shaft shot from a bow.

arsenal n a public establishment for making or storing weapons of war.

arsenic n a virulent mineral poison.

arson n the malicious setting on fire of a house, etc.

art n practical skill; cunning; profession of a painter, etc.

arterial adj pertaining to arteries; pertaining to a main road, railway, etc.

artery n a tube which conveys blood from the heart; a main road, etc, or means of communication.

artesian adj applied to wells made by boring.

artful adj skilful; crafty.

article n a separate item; composition (in newspaper); a part of speech, as the. * vt to bind by articles. * vi to stipulate.

articulate adj distinct; clear and intelligible. * vi to utter distinct sounds.

artifice n an artful device or deception.

artificial adj made by art; not natural.

artillery n cannon and heavy guns in general; the troops who manage them.

artist n one skilled in some art, especially the fine arts.

artistic adj characteristic of art; aesthetic.

artless adj unaffected.

as adv, conj, prep like; for example; because; in the same way; playing the part of.

asbestos n a mineral fibrous incombusti-ble substance.

ascend vi to rise. * vt to climb.

ascendancy, ascendency n controlling power; sway.

ascendant adj superior. * n superiority.

ascension n act of ascending.

ascent n rise; upward slope.

ascertain vt to make certain; to find out.

ascetic adj unduly rigid in self-denial and self-discipline.

ascribe vt to attribute.

aseptic adj not liable to putrefy; rendered free of germs.

ashamed adj affected by shame or guilt.

ashen adj made of ash; pale.

ashes npl the remains of anything burned; (fig) a dead body.

ashore adv, adj on or to the shore.

aside adv on one side; apart. * n words spoken by an actor to an audience only.

asinine adj belonging to or resembling the ass; stupid.

ask vt to request. * vi to make inquiry.

askance, askant adv awry; obliquely.

askew adv, adj awry.

asleep adj, adv. sleeping.

aspect n appearance; outlook.

asperity n roughness; harshness.

aspersion n calumny, lie; (esp pl) slander; defamation.

asphalt n a kind of pitch used for paving.

aspirant n a candidate.

aspirate vt to pronounce with an audible breath; to add an h sound to.

aspiration n ardent desire; ambition.

aspire vi to aim at high things.

ass n a long-eared animal akin to the horse.

assagai, assegai n a light African throwing spear.

assail vt to attack.

assailant n one who assails; an attacker.

assassin n one who kills by surprise or secretly.

assassinate vt to murder by surprise or treacherously.

assault n an attack. * vt to assail.

assay n proof; analysis of ores. * vt to try.

assemblage n a collection of persons or things.

assemble vt to bring together. * vi to come together.

assembly n a gathering of people to consult together; a putting together of many parts to make a whole.

assent n consent. * vi to agree.

assert vt to affirm.

assertive adj affirming confidently.

assess vt to rate; to value or estimate amount, worth, etc.

assessable adj that may be assessed.

assessment n the act of assessing; the sum levied.

asset n a useful or valuable thing.

assiduity n close application; diligence.

assiduous adj constantly diligent.

assign vt to designate; to allot; to make over to another.

assignable adj that may be assigned.

assignation n an appointment to meet; a making over by transfer of title.

assignee n one to whom an assignment is made.

assignment n an allotment or legal transfer; a task assigned to someone.

assimilate vt to make like to; to digest.

assist vt to help. * vi to lend help.

assistance n help; aid.

assistant n one who assists.

assize n an assessment court; (pl) periodical courts for administering justice.

associate vt to join in company with. * vi to keep company with. * n a companion; a business colleague or partner.

association n act of associating; union.

assort vt to arrange. * vi to suit.

assortment n a varied collection.

assuage vt to allay; to calm.

assume vt to take for granted; to usurp. * vi to claim more than is due.

assumption n act of assuming; the thing assumed.

assurance n secure confidence; impudence; insurance.

assure vt to confirm; to insure.

assuredly adv certainly.

asterisk n a star-shaped mark used in printing (*) to indicate an omission, cross-reference, footnote, etc.

astern adv in or at the hinder part of a ship.

asteroid n a small planet.

asthma n a disease marked by shortness of breath.

astigmatism n a defect in the eyes preventing proper focusing.

astir adv awake or stirring; active.

astonish vt to amaze.

astonishment n amazement.

astound vt to astonish; to stun.

astrakhan n a rough cloth with a curled pile made from lambs bred in Astrakhan.

astral adj belonging to the stars.

astray adv straying.

astride adv with the legs apart or on either side of something.

astringent n a medicine that contracts the tissues. * adj binding; constricting; harsh; sharp; bracing.

astrologer n one versed in astrology.

astrology n the art of foretelling future events from the stars.

astronomer n one versed in astronomy.

astronomical adj pertaining to astronomy; very large.

astronomy n the science of the heavenly bodies.

astute adj shrewd; crafty.

astuteness n shrewdness.

asunder adv apart; into parts.

asylum n a place of refuge; an institution for the care of the insane.

at prep denoting nearness, presence or location.

atheism n the disbelief in the existence of God.

atheist n one who disbelieves the existence of God.

athenaeum n a literary or scientific club.

athlete n one skilled in exercises of agility or strength.

athletic adj pertaining to an athlete; strong; active.

athletics npl sporting events of track and field; physical exercises.

atlas n a collection of maps.

atmosphere n the air surrounding the earth; pervading influence.

atmospheric adj pertaining to the atmosphere.

atoll n a ring-shaped coral reef or islands.

atom n a minute particle, esp of a chemical element; anything extremely small.

atomic adj pertaining to or consisting of

atoms; pertaining to atomic energy, bomb, warfare.

atone vi to make up for; to expiate.

atrocious adj abominable; very wicked.

atrocity n horrible wickedness.

atrophy n a wasting away.

attach vt to join; to affix. * vi to adhere.

attaché n one attached to the suite of an ambassador or a diplomatic mission.

attachment n fidelity; tender regard.

attack vt to assault. * n an assault; seizure by a disease.

attain vi to arrive at. * vt to reach; to gain.

attainable adj that may be attained.

attainment n accomplishment.

attempt vt to try to do. * n an essay; effort.

attend vt to wait on; to be present at. * vi to pay regard.

attendance n the act of attending; the persons attending.

attendant adj accompanying * n one who waits on or accompanies.

attention n heed; courtesy.

attentive adj heedful; courteous; diligent.

attenuate vt to make slender; to weaken.

attest vt to bear witness to.

attestation n testimony.

attic n a garret; a room or storing space under the roof of a house.

attire vt to dress. * n dress

attitude n posture; a position or viewpoint taken on some matter.

attorney n (pl **attorneys**) a law agent.

attract vt to draw to; to entice.

attraction n allurement; charm.

attractive adj having the power of attracting; enticing; pretty.

attributable adj that may be attributed.

attribute vt to ascribe, to impute. * n a quality; an adjectival word or clause.

attributive adj that attributes.

attrition n the act of wearing down by rubbing.

attune vt to put in tune; to adjust to or acclimatize.

auburn adj reddish brown.

auction n a public sale.

auctioneer n the person who sells at auction.

audacious adj daring; impudent.

audacity n daring; impudence.

audible adj that may be heard.

audience n an assembly of hearers; reception.

audit n an examination of accounts.

auditor n one who examines accounts.

auditory adj pertaining to the sense of hearing. * n an audience.

auger n a tool for boring holes.

aught n anything.

augment vt to make larger; to increase; * n increase; a prefix to a word.

augmentation n increase.

augur n one who foretold the future; a soothsayer. * vt to foretell.

august adj regal; imposing.

August n the eighth month of the year.

aunt n the sister of one's father or mother.

aureole n in art, a golden disk or halo round the head of saints.

auricle n the external ear; either of the two ear-like cavities of the heart.

aurora borealis n the northern lights or streamers.

auscultation n detecting heart conditions by listening to beats.

auspices npl omens; patronage.

auspicious adj fortunate; favourable.

austere adj stern; severe.

austerity n sternness; severity; living without luxuries.

authentic adj genuine.

authenticate vt to attest; to confirm.

authenticity n genuineness.

author n the writer of a book, etc.

authoress n a female author.

authoritative adj official; decisive.

authority n legal power or right; person exercising this power.

authorize vt to sanction.

autobiography n memoirs of a person written by himself or herself.

autocracy n absolute government by one person.

autocrat n an absolute ruler.

autograph n a signature.

automatic adj self-acting; carried out without conscious thought.

automaton n (pl **automata**) a self-moving machine, or a person acting like one.

autonomy n self-government.

autopsy n an examination of a dead body to discover the cause of death.

autumn n the third season of the year.

auxiliary adj helping. * n a person or thing that helps.

avail vt, vi. to profit. * vi to be of use. * n advantage; use.

available adj attainable.

avalanche n a vast snow slide.

avarice n greed of gain.

avaricious adj covetous; greedy.

avenge vt to take satisfaction for; to harm in retaliation.

avenue n an approach to; a broad street.

aver vt to assert.

average n medium. * adj medial; moderate; not outstanding in ability. * vi to form a mean.

averse adj disinclined.

aversion n dislike.

avert vt to turn aside or away from.

aviary n a place for keeping birds.

aviation n the art of flying.

aviator n one who flies aeroplanes.

avocation n a person's regular business or occupation.

avoid vt to shun.

avoirdupois n, adj a system of weight, in which a pound contains sixteen ounces.

avow vt to declare with confidence; to confess frankly.

avowal n an admission.

avowedly adv openly.

await vt to wait for; to expect.

awake vt to rouse from sleep. * vi to cease from sleep. * adj not sleeping.

awaken vt, vi to awake.

award vt to adjudge. * vi to make an award. * n a judgement; a reward or prize.

aware adj informed; cognizant.

away adv absent; at a distance.

awe n fear; fear mingled with reverence. * vt to strike with fear.

awful adj very bad; terrible.

awhile adv for some time.

awkward adj inexpert; inelegant; deliberately unhelpful; difficult.

awl n a tool for piercing small holes in leather.

awning n a canvas covering.

awry adj, adv. twisted; distorted; gone wrong.

axe n an instrument for hewing and chopping.

axiom n a self-evident truth.

axiomatic adj self-evident.

axis n (pl axes) the line on which a body revolves; a partnership.

axle n the pole on which a wheel turns.

azure adj sky-blue.

B

babble vi to talk idly; to prate. * n idle talk; murmur, as of a stream.

babel n confusion.

baboon n a large kind of monkey.

baby n a child just born; a young animal.

baby-sit vt, vi to look after a child during the parents' absence.

bachelor n an unmarried man; a graduate of a university or college.

bacillus n (pl bacilli) a microscopic organism; a microbe.

back n the hind or (in beasts) the upper part of the body. * vt to support; to cause to recede. * adv to the rear.

backbite vt to speak evil of secretly.

backbone n the spine; strength.

background n the ground behind; the setting of a picture or photograph; that which has taken place beforehand causing and leading up to an event, etc; social status.

backslide vi to degenerate; to relapse.

backward adj lagging behind; dull.

backwoods npl outlying forest districts.

bacon n pig's flesh cured and dried.

bacteriology n the study of bacteria.

bacteria npl microbes; germs.

bad adj wicked; immoral.

badge n a distinguishing mark or emblem.

badger n a burrowing quadruped. * vt to worry; to pester.

badminton n a game like lawn tennis played with shuttlecocks as balls.

baffle vt to frustrate; to defeat.

bag n a sack; a pouch; a purse.

bagatelle n a trifle.

baggage *n* luggage.

bagpipe *n* a musical wind instrument.

bail *vt* to liberate from custody on security for reappearance; to free (a boat) from water; to bale. * *n* security given for release; the small bar placed on the stumps in cricket.

bailliff *n* a subordinate civil officer; a landowner's or landlord's steward or agent.

bait *n* food to trap or lure animals or fish; an enticement. * *vt* to furnish with a lure; to harass, esp by verbal teasing.

bake *vt* to dry and harden by fire; to cook in an oven.

balance *n* a pair of scales; equilibrium; difference of two sums; the sum due on an account. * *vt* to bring to an equilibrium; to settle. * *vi* to hesitate.

balance sheet *n* a statement of assets and liabilities.

balcony *n* a railed or walled platform projecting from a window; an upper tier of seats in a theatre or cinema.

bald *adj* wanting hair; bare; paltry.

baldly *adv* nakedly; meanly.

baldness *n* state of being bald; meagreness.

bale *n* a bundle or package of goods. * *vt* to free a boat from water; (with out) to escape from aircraft by parachute; to bail.

baleful *adj* deadly.

balk, baulk *n* a ridge; a great beam; part of a billiard table. * *vt* to baffle.

ball *n* a round body; a bullet; a dance.

ballad *n* a narrative poem; a popular sentimental song.

ballast *n* heavy matter carried in a ship to keep it steady.

ballet *n* a theatrical dance.

balloon *n* a large bag filled with a gas which makes it float in the air.

ballot *n* a system of voting. * *vi* to vote by ballot.

balmy *adj* (of weather) pleasantly mild and calm.

balsam *n* soothing ointment.

baluster *n* a small column or pillar supporting a rail.

balustrade *n* a row of pillars joined by a rail.

bamboo *n* a tropical plant of the reed kind.

bamboozle *vt* to hoax; to confuse.

ban *n* a prohibition; an edict. * *vt* to curse; to forbid.

banal *adj* commonplace; vulgar.

banana *n* an edible plant with yellow fruit growing in hanging bunches.

band *n* that which binds; a company of people acting together, e.g. a group of musicians. * *vt* to unite in a troop.

bandage *n* a band; a cloth for a wound, etc. * *vt* to bind with a bandage.

bandit *n* a robber.

bandoleer *n* a shoulder strap for carrying cartridges.

bandy *vt* to exchange, esp words in anger; to pass to and fro.

bandy-legged *adj* having crooked legs.

baneful *adj* pernicious; poisonous.

bang *vt* to thump. * *n* a heavy blow.

bangle *n* a bracelet or anklet.

banish *vt* to drive away; to exile.

banishment *n* act of banishing; exile.

banister *n* a form of baluster that supports the uprights of a staircase.

banjo *n* a six-stringed musical instrument.

bank *n* ground rising from the side of a river, lake, etc; place where money is deposited. * *vt* to deposit in a bank.

banking *n* the business of a banker.

bankrupt *n* one who cannot pay his debts. * *adj* unable to pay debts; insolvent.

banner *n* a standard.

banns *npl* the proclamation of marriage.

banquet *n* a feast.

banter *vt* to chaff; to rally. * *n* raillery.

baptise *vt* to administer baptism to; to christen.

baptism *n* an immersing in or sprinkling with water as a religious ceremony.

baptismal *adj* pertaining to baptism.

bar *n* a bolt; obstacle; a long piece of wood or metal; a tribunal; a body of barristers; anything that prohibits or obstructs; a counter where liquors are served. * *vt* to prohibit.

barb *n* the notched tip of a fishing hook or arrow.

barbarian *adj* savage; uncivilized. * *n* a savage

barbarism *n* extreme cruelty, coarseness or ignorance; an impropriety of speech.

barbarity *n* the state or qualities of a barbarian; ferociousness.

barbarous *adj* cruel; inhuman.

barbed *adj* jagged with hooks or points.

barber *n* a hairdresser.

bare *adj* uncovered; empty; worn. * *vt* to make naked; to reveal.

barebacked *adj* unsaddled.

barefaced *adj* shameless.

barefoot *adj, adv* with the feet bare.

bargain *n* a gainful transaction; a cheap purchase. * *vi* to make a bargain.

barge *n* a flat-bottomed boat for freight used on canals and rivers; a canal pleasure boat. * *vi* to push in bodily.

bark *n* the outer rind of a tree; a barque; the noise made by a dog. * *vt* to strip bark off; to treat with bark; to make the cry of dogs.

barley *n* a species of grain used for making malt, beer, whisky, puddings, etc.

barmaid, barman *n* a woman, man who tends a bar.

barn *n* a building for storing grain, etc.

barometer *n* an instrument for measuring the weight of the atmosphere.

baron *n* a peer of the lowest rank.

baroness *n* a baron's wife.

baronet *n* the lowest order of hereditary titles.

barrack *n* (*usually pl*) buildings for housing soldiers. * *vt* to jeer loudly at.

barrage *n* a bar or dam constructed across a river; the firing of heavy artillery; a continuous onslaught as of words or blows.

barrel *n* a round wooden cask; the tube of a gun.

barren *adj* unfruitful; sterile.

barrenness *n* the state or quality of being barren.

barricade *n* a temporary fortification; a barrier. * *vt* to bar.

barrier *n* a fence; a bar.

barrister *n* a lawyer qualified to plead at the bar.

barrow *n* a small handcart; a burial mound.

barter *vi* to traffic by exchange. * *vt* to exchange in commerce. * *n* traffic by exchange.

baritone *n* a male voice between tenor and bass.

basalt *n* a dark volcanic rock, often found in columnar form.

base *adj* low; worthless. * *n* foundation; support; chief ingredient of a compound. * *vt* to place on a basis; to found.

baseball *n* an American game with four bases set in diamond shape, played with bat and ball.

baseless *adj* groundless.

basement *n* the ground floor.

baseness *n* meanness; vileness.

bashful *adj* modest; shy.

basic *adj* relating to a base; fundamental.

basil *n* an aromatic herb.

basilica *n* a hall or church with double colonnades.

basin *n* a broad shallow dish; a reservoir; a dock; the land drained by a river.

basis *n* (*pl* **bases**) a base; groundwork.

bask *vi* to lie in the sun.

basket *n* a wicker container.

bass *n* the lowest part in musical harmony; the lowest male voice.

bassoon *n* a musical wind instrument.

bastard *adj* illegitimate; not genuine. * *n* a person whose parents are unmarried.

baste *vt* to beat with a stick; to drip fat on meat while roasting; to sew with temporary stitches.

bastion *n* a fortification standing out from a rampart.

bat *n* a flying mammal like a mouse; a club used to strike the ball in cricket, etc. * *vi* to play with a bat.

batch *n* the quantity of bread baked at one time; a quantity.

bath *n* a place to bathe in; immersion in water.

bathe *vt* to immerse in water. * *vi* to take a bath.

baton *n* a staff; a truncheon; a thin stick used by a conductor of music.

battalion *n* a military body three or more companies strong.

batten *n* a board for flooring; strip of wood to fasten down the hatches; a plank. * *vt* to fasten with battens.

batter *vt* to beat with violence. * *n* a cooking mixture of flour, eggs and milk.

battery *n* a fully equipped artillery unit;

an apparatus for originating an electric current; a violent assault.

battle n encounter of two armies; a combat.

battlement n a parapet with openings to discharge missiles through.

battleship n a large warship furnished with heavy artillery.

bauble n a trifle.

bawl vi to shout; to weep loudly.

bay adj reddish-brown. * n an inlet on the shore of the sea or a lake; the laurel tree; the bark of a dog. * vt to bark at; (with at) with back to the wall.

bayonet n a dagger-like weapon fixed to a rifle.

bay window n a projecting window which forms a recess or bay within.

bazaar n a place of sale; a sale of articles for a charitable purpose.

be vi to exist; to remain.

beach n the shore of the sea. * vt to run (a vessel) on a beach.

beached pa stranded.

beacon n a flare; a signal of danger. * vt to light up.

bead n a little ball strung on a thread; a small drop of liquid; a small projection for sighting a gun.

beadle n a minor officer of a parish, church, or college.

beak n the bill of a bird.

beaker n a large drinking cup; a glass vessel.

beam n a main timber in a building; part of a balance which sustains the scales; a ray of light. * vi to shine; to smile broadly.

beaming adj emitting beams or rays; radiant.

bean n a name of several kinds of pulse or peas.

bear vt to carry; to suffer; to bring forth; to permit. * vi to suffer; to produce.

bear n a large shaggy quadruped.

beard n the hair on the chin, etc.

bearer n a carrier of anything.

bearing n manner, appearance and general behaviour.

beast n an animal; a brutal man.

beat vt to strike; to overcome. * vi to throb; to sail against the wind. * n a stroke; a

rhythmic stroke of the heart; musical rhythm; the area patrolled by a police officer.

beatify vt to make happy; to pronounce a person worthy of canonization.

beating n act of striking; defeat.

beauteous adj beautiful.

beautiful adj full of beauty.

beautify vt to make beautiful; to adorn.

beauty n loveliness; elegance; a beautiful thing or person.

becalm vt to make calm.

because conj by cause of; on this account that; since.

beckon, beck vi to make a sign to approach by nodding, etc.

become vi to come to be. * vt to suit.

becoming adj fitting; graceful.

bed n something to sleep or rest on; the channel of a river; a layer; a stratum. * vt to lay in a bed; to sow. * vi to go to bed.

bedding n the materials of a bed.

bedeck vt to adorn.

bedraggle vt to soil by drawing through the mud.

bedroom n a sleeping room.

bedsit n one room with cooking and sleeping facilities.

bedstead n a frame for supporting a bed.

beef n the flesh of an ox or cow.

beefeater n a yeoman of the royal guard.

beeline n a direct line or way.

beer n a fermented liquor made from barley and hops.

beeswax n the wax secreted by bees for their combs.

beet n a vegetable with fleshy roots, yielding sugar.

beetle n a common insect; a wooden mallet. * vi to jut; to hang over.

beetle-browed adj having prominent brows.

befall vt to happen to.

befit vt to suit.

before prep, adv in front of; earlier than; rather than; onward.

beforehand adv in advance.

befriend vt to act as a friend to.

beg vt to ask in charity; to ask earnestly; to avoid answering a question; to take for granted.

beget vt to procreate; to produce.

beggar n one who begs. * vt to reduce to poverty; to be beyond, esp description.

begin vi to commence. * vt to enter on.

beginner n one who begins; a novice.

beginning n the first stage; commencement.

begrudge vt to envy the possession of.

beguile vt to dupe; to while away; to charm.

behalf n interest; support.

behave vt to conduct (oneself). * vi to act.

behaviour n conduct.

behead vt to cut off the head.

behest n a command.

behind prep in the rear of. * adv backwards.

behold vt to look upon; to regard with attention.

beholden adj obliged.

being n existence; a creature.

belabour vt to beat soundly.

belated adj arriving or made late.

belay vt (naut) to fasten a rope by winding round something.

belch vt to cast forth violently; to expel wind through the mouth.

beleaguer vt to besiege.

belfry n a bell tower.

belie vt to represent falsely; to fail to be equal to.

belief n faith; trust; opinion.

believe vt to accept as true; think.

belittle vt to make smaller; to disparage.

bell n a metallic vessel for making ringing sounds when struck; anything in the form of a bell. * vt to put a bell on.

bellicose adj pugnacious.

belligerent adj waging war; quarrelsome. * n a nation waging war.

bellow vi to roar like a bull. * n a roar.

bellows npl an instrument for blowing fires, supplying wind to organ pipes, etc.

belly n that part of the body which contains the bowels; the abdomen. * vt, vi to swell; to bulge.

belong vi to be the property of; to appertain to; to be a member.

belongings npl personal possessions.

beloved adj greatly loved.

below prep under; beneath. * adv in a lower place.

belt n a girdle; a band; a stripe; area, e.g. of trees.

bemoan vt to lament.

bemused adj muddled.

bench n a long seat; a long work table; seat of justice; body of judges.

bend vt to curve; to direct to a certain point; to adjust for one's own purpose. * n a curve.

beneath prep, adv. below; under.

benediction n a solemn blessing.

benefactor n a person who confers a benefit.

benefice n an ecclesiastical living.

beneficent adj kind; bountiful.

beneficial adj helpful; bringing about improvement.

beneficiary n a person who is benefited or assisted or gains.

benefit n an act of kindness; a favour; something that brings improvement; an allowance from government, an employer, etc. * vt to do a service to.

benevolence n kindness; active love of mankind.

benevolent adj kind; charitable.

benign adj gracious; kind.

bent n bias of mind; aptitude; a wiry grass.

benumb vt to deprive of sensation.

benzene n a liquid used to remove grease and as an insecticide.

bequeath vt to leave by will.

bequest n a legacy.

bereave vt to deprive of someone dear by death.

bereavement n loss by death.

berry n a pulpy fruit containing seeds.

berserk adj frenzied.

berth n a place in which a moored ship lies; a place for sleeping in a train, ship, etc. * vt to moor.

beseech vt to entreat.

beseechingly adv imploringly.

beset vt to surround; to attack from every direction.

besetting adj habitual.

beside, besides prep by the side of; near. * adv moreover.

besiege vt to lay siege to.

besotted *adj* infatuated.

bespatter *vt* to spatter over.

bespeak *vt* to speak for beforehand.

best *adj* the superlative degree of 'good'. * *adv* the superlative of 'well'. * *vt* to defeat; to beat.

bestial *adj* brutish.

bestiality *n* brutish conduct.

bestir *vt* to rouse oneself to action.

bestow *vt* to gift; to present with.

bestraddle *vt* to bestride.

bestride *vt* to stride over or across; to span.

bet *n* a wager. * *vt* to wager.

betide *vi* to befall; to happen.

betoken *vt* to imply; to foreshadow.

betray *vt* to prove false to; to entrap.

betrayal *n* act of betraying.

betroth *vt* to pledge in marriage.

betrothal *n* mutual promise to marry.

better *adj* comparative of 'good'. * *adv* comparative of 'well'. * *vt* to advance; to outdo.

between *prep* in the middle.

bevel *n* an instrument for setting angles.

beverage *n* a drink.

bevy *n* a flock of birds.

bewail *vt* to lament.

beware *vi* to take care.

bewilder *vt* to perplex.

bewilderment *n* perplexity.

bewitch *vt* to enchant.

bewitching *adj* fascinating.

bewitchment *n* fascination.

beyond *prep* on the farther side of; post; not within reach. * *adv* at a distance; further on.

bias *n* weight on one side; a bent; a prejudice. * *vt* to incline to one side.

biased, biassed *adj* prejudiced.

bib *n* a cloth or plastic cover tied round the neck (of a child) to protect clothing from food spillage.

Bible *n* the Holy Scriptures of the Christian faith.

biblical *adj* pertaining to the Bible.

bibliographical *adj* pertaining to bibliography.

bibliography *n* an account, description or reference list of books on a subject.

bibliomania *n* a passion for possessing books.

bibliophile *n* a lover of books.

bibulous *adj* given to tippling.

bicentenary *n* two hundred years.

biceps *npl* muscles of the forearm.

bicker *vi* to quarrel.

bicycle *n* a two-wheeled vehicle propelled by pedals.

bicyclist *n* one who rides a bicycle.

bid *vt* to ask; to order; to offer. * *n* an offer, as at an auction.

biddable *adj* obedient.

bidding *n* an invitation; a command.

biennial *adj* lasting for two years; taking place once in two years.

biennially *adv* once in two years.

bier *n* the frame on which a corpse rests or is borne.

bifurcate(d) *adj* forked or divided into two.

big *adj* great; large.

bigamist *n* one who commits bigamy.

bigamy *n* the crime of having two wives or husbands at once.

bigot *n* a person obstinately wedded to particular ideas.

bigoted *adj* prejudiced.

bigotry *n* intolerance.

bilateral *adj* two-sided.

bile *n* the bitter secretion of the liver; ill-nature.

bilge *n* the bulging part of a cask; the breadth of a ship's bottom.

bilge water *n* dirty water in the bilge of a ship.

bilingual *adj* in two languages.

bilious *adj* affected by bile.

bill *n* the beak of a bird; an instrument for pruning; an account of money due; draft of a new law; a poster or leaflet.

billet *n* a small note in writing; lodgings; a situation. * *vt* to quarter, as soldiers.

billet-doux *n* (*pl* **billets-doux**) a love letter.

billiards *npl* a game played on a table with balls and cues.

billion *n* a million of millions.

billow *n* a great wave of the sea.

bimonthly *adj* every two months.

bin *n* a receptacle.

binary *adj* twofold.

bind *vt* to tie; to oblige; to cover (a book); to make firm; to bandage. * *vi* to grow hard, tight or stiff; to be obligatory.

binding n the cover and sewing of a book. * adj obligatory.

bingo n a gambling game with numbered cards for several people in which numbers called are covered by players until a card is full.

binocular adj adapted for both eyes. * npl field or opera glasses.

binomial adj, n. an algebraic expression with two terms.

biochemistry n the study of the chemistry of living organisms.

biogenesis n the doctrine that living matter springs only from living matter.

biographer n a writer of biography.

biography n written life of a person.

biologist n one skilled in biology.

biology n the study of the science of living organisms.

bipartite adj having two parts.

biped n an animal with two feet.

bird n a feathered, egg-laying vertebrate with wings.

birth n the act of bearing or coming into life.

birthright n any right to which a person is entitled by birth.

biscuit n a hard, flat, sweet or plain cake.

bisect vt to half.

bishop n the head of a diocese.

bishopric n the office of a bishop; a diocese.

bit n a morsel; the metal part of a bridle; a boring tool used with a brace.

bitch n a female dog or wolf.

bite vt to crush or sever with the teeth; to cause to smart; to wound by reproach, etc; to corrode. * n a wound made by biting; a mouthful.

biting adj sharp; piercingly cold; sarcastic.

bitter adj sharp to the taste; severe; painful.

bitterness n the quality of being bitter.

bitumen n a pitch-like substance.

bivalve n a two-valved animal.

bivouac n an encampment of soldiers for the night in the open air.

biweekly adj occurring every two weeks.

bizarre adj fantastic; odd; strange

black adj having no light; dark; gloomy; sullen; atrocious; wicked. * n the darkest colour. * vt to make black.

blackboard n a board for writing on with chalk.

blacken vt to make black. * vi to grow black or dark; to speak ill of.

blackguard n a scoundrel. * vt to revile.

blackleg n one who works during a strike.

blackmail n money extorted by threats. * vt to commit the crime of blackmail.

black market n illegal buying and selling when restrictions are in force.

blackout n total darkness when lighting has failed or been switched off; a loss of consciousness temporarily.

blacksmith n a smith who works in iron.

bladder n a membrane in animals containing the urine; a blister.

blade n a leaf; the cutting part of a sword, knife; the flat part of an oar.

blame vt to censure. * n censure; fault.

blameless adj free from blame.

blanch vt to make white. * vi to grow white.

blancmange n a white jelly.

bland adj mild; gentle.

blandish vt to soothe; to flatter.

blandishment n flattery.

blank adj white; empty. * n a void space.

blanket n a woollen covering.

blank verse n verse without rhyme.

blare vi to give forth a loud, harsh sound.

blarney n flattery; insincere talk.

blasé adj satiated; used up; bored.

blaspheme vt to speak irreverently of something held sacred.

blasphemous adj impious; irreverent.

blast n a gust of wind; the sound of a wind instrument; a violent explosion; harsh criticism. * vt to blight.

blatant adj noisy and loud; glaringly obvious.

blaze n a flame; a fire; brilliance. * vi to flame. * vt to noise abroad.

bleach vt to make white. * vi to grow white.

bleak adj dreary; dark and gloomy.

blear adj sore; dimmed.

blear-eyed, bleary-eyed adj sore or watery-eyed.

bleat vi to cry as a sheep. * n the cry of a sheep.

bleed vi to emit or lose blood. * vt to take blood from.

bleeding n a flow of blood; the operation of letting blood; the drawing of sap from a tree.

blemish vt to mar; to tarnish. * n a stain; dishonour.

blend vt to mix together. * n a mixture.

bless vt to make happy; to invoke a blessing.

blessed adj happy; holy.

blessing n a benediction; a prayer of thanks; good wishes.

blight n that which withers up or destroys wholesale; mildew. * vt to wither up; to blast; to cause failure.

blind adj destitute of sight; having no outlet. * n a screen; a pretext. * vt to make blind.

blindfold adj having the eyes covered.

blindly adv heedlessly.

blindness n want of sight; ignorance.

blink vi to wink; to twinkle. * vt to shut the eyes upon.

blinker n a flap to prevent a horse from seeing sideways.

bliss n perfect happiness.

blissful adj full of bliss.

blister n a watery bubble on the skin; a swelling as on paint. * vt to raise a blister; to castigate vigorously.

blithe adj joyful.

blizzard n a violent snowstorm.

bloated adj inflated.

blob n a small globe of liquid.

block n a heavy piece of wood; a lump of solid matter; a piece of wood in which a pulley is placed; buildings in a group; an obstacle. * vt to shut up; to obstruct.

blockade n a close siege by troops or ships. * vt to besiege closely.

blockhead n a stupid fellow.

blockhouse n a building used for defence.

blond, blonde adj having fair hair; of a fair complexion.

blood n the red fluid which circulates in animals; kindred. * adj pertaining to blood.

bloodless adj without blood; lifeless.

bloodshot adj inflamed.

bloodthirsty adj eager to shed blood.

blood vessel n an artery or a vein.

bloody adj stained with blood; cruel.

bloom n a blossom; a flower; state of healthy youthfulness. * vi to blossom.

blossom n the flower of a plant. * vi to bloom.

blot vt to spot; to stain; to dry. * n a spot or stain; a disgrace.

blotch n a spot or discoloured patch.

blotting paper n absorbent paper to dry up ink.

blouse n a loose upper garment.

blow vi to make a current of air; to pant; to bloom. * vt to impel by wind; to inflate. * n a blast; a blossoming; a heavy punch; a stroke; a misfortune.

blowpipe n a tube for heating flame by blowing air into it; a tube for blowing poison darts.

blubber n the fat of whales. * vi to weep noisily.

bludgeon n a short club.

blue n the colour of the sky; one of the seven primary colours; a university athletic distinction. * adj of a blue colour; sky-coloured; depressed. * vt to dye a blue colour.

blueprint n a print of plans, etc, photographed on a blue background; a plan used as a basis of future work.

bluestocking n a learned woman.

bluff adj hearty; blunt. * n a steep projecting bank. * vt, vi to persuade or deceive by a show of boldness or strength.

bluish adj slightly blue.

blunder vi to err stupidly. * n a mistake; an error.

blunt adj not sharp; unceremonious; rude; straightforward. * vt to make blunt or dull.

blur n a stain; a blot; a hazy impression. * vt to stain; to obscure.

blurt vt to utter suddenly or unadvisedly.

blush vi to redden in the face. * n a red colour in the face caused by shame, embarrassment, etc.

bluster vi to roar like wind; to swagger; to boast and bully. * n swaggering.

blustering adj noisy; windy.

boa n a large snake without fangs; a feathery or fur scarf.

boar n the male of the pig or hog.

board n a strip of timber broad and thin; a table; food; persons seated round a table; a council; a group of people in charge of a company; the deck of a ship. * vt to cover with boards; to supply with food; to enter a train, bus, ship, etc.

boarder n one who receives food and lodging at a stated charge.

boarding house n a house where board and lodging are provided for payment.

boarding school n a school where the pupils are boarders.

boast vi to brag. * vt to magnify. * n a bragging utterance.

boastful adj given to boasting.

boat n a small open vessel, usually impelled by oars; a small ship.

boatswain n a petty officer or warrant officer on board ship.

bob n something that hangs or plays loosely; a short jerking motion; a woman's short haircut. * vt to move with a short jerking motion. * vi to play to and fro or up and down; to curtsey.

bobbin n a winding pin; a reel.

bode vt to portend.

bodice n the upper part of a dress; an inner vest; a corset.

bodily adv wholly; entirely.

body n the trunk or main part of an animal or human being; matter; a person; a dead person; a group of people; any solid figure.

bodyguard n one appointed to guard the safety of another.

bog n a marsh.

bogus adj sham.

boil vi to bubble from the action of heat; to seethe. * vt to heat to a boiling state. * n a sore swelling or tumour.

boisterous adj stormy; noisy; loud and high-spirited.

bold adj daring.

boldness n courage.

bole n the body or stem of a tree.

bolster n a long pillow. * vt to hold up; to give support to a person.

bolt n an arrow; a thunderbolt; a bar of a door. * vi to leave suddenly. * vt to fas-

ten; to swallow hastily.

bomb n an explosive shell.

bombard vt to attack with continual fire and bombs; to attack with words and questions.

bombast n high-sounding words.

bombastic adj inflated; turgid; pompous.

bona fide adv, adj in good faith; genuine.

bond n that which binds; obligation; a legal deed; (pl) chains; a place where dutiable goods are stored. * vt to grant a bond in security for money; to store till duty is paid.

bondage n slavery.

bonded adj liable to pay duty.

bone n the hard part of the skeleton. * vt to take out bones from.

bonfire n an open-air fire.

bon mot n (pl **bons mots**) a witticism.

bonnet n a headdress.

bonny adj beautiful.

bonus n a premium; extra gift to shareholders; an addition to a salary.

book n a collection of printed sheets bound together. * vt to enter in a book; to reserve beforehand; to note a person's particulars for a minor offence.

booking office n an office where people buy tickets in advance.

bookish adj fond of study.

book-keeper n one who keeps accounts.

booklet n a little book.

bookmaker n a person who takes bets on events and pays out winnings.

bookseller n one who sells books.

bookworm n one who pores over books.

boom n a long pole to extend the bottom of a sail; a chain barrier across a river or harbour; a hollow roar; prosperity in commerce; in film studies, a long pole with a microphone at the end. * vi to roar; to make a loud, deep noise; to boost; to prosper.

boomerang n an Australian missile which when thrown returns to the thrower.

boon n a favour; something helpful; a plessing.

boor n a rustic; a rude, unhelpful person.

boorish adj clownish; rude.

boot n a covering for the foot.

booth n a temporary shed; a stall; a cubicle for voting or for a telephone.

booty *n* spoil; plunder.

border *n* the outer edge of anything; the boundary line between two countries. * *vi* to approach near. * *vt* to surround with a border.

bore *vt* to make a hole in; to pester; to weary by being dull, uninteresting or repetitious. * *n* the hole made by boring; the diameter of a tube; a tiresome person; a great tidal wave.

boreal *adj* northern.

born *pp of* **bear** to bring forth.

borne *pp of* **bear** to carry.

borrow *vt* to ask or receive as a loan.

bosom *n* the breast; the seat of the affections. * *adj* beloved.

boss *n* a knob; a master; a manager. * *vt* to be domineering; to be or act as a boss.

botanic, botanical *adj* pertaining to botany.

botanist *n* one skilled in botany.

botany *n* the science which treats of plants.

botch *vt* to perform clumsily.

both *adj, pron* the two. * *conj* as well.

bother *vt* to annoy. * *vi* to trouble oneself. * *n* a trouble.

bothersome *adj* causing trouble.

bottle *n* a narrow-mouthed vessel of glass or plastic; the contents of a bottle.

bottom *n* the lowest part; the ground under water; foundation. * *vt* to found or build upon.

boudoir *n* a woman's private room.

bough *n* a branch of a tree.

boulder *n* a large roundish stone or rock.

boulevard *n* a wide street planted with trees.

bounce *vi* to spring or rush out suddenly; to rebound; to boast. * *n* springiness; a boast.

bouncing *adj* big; strong; boastful.

bound *n* a boundary; a leap. * *vt* to limit. * *vi* to leap. * *adj* obliged; sure; ready; destined.

boundary *n* a bounding line; a border.

bounden *adj* obligatory.

boundless *adj* unlimited.

bounteous *adj* liberal.

bountiful *adj* generous.

bounty *n* liberality; a premium to encourage trade; a reward.

bouquet *n* a bunch of flowers; a perfume from wine.

bourgeois *n* a middle-class citizen.

bout *n* a contest; a spell.

bovine *adj* dull, stupid.

bow[1] *vt* to bend. * *vi* to make a reverence. * *n* a bending of the head or body; the curved forepart of a ship.

bow[2] *n* a weapon to shoot arrows; the rainbow; a stick for playing on violin strings; a slipknot.

bowdlerize *vt* to expurgate.

bowed *adj* bent like a bow.

bowels *npl* the lower intestines.

bower *n* an arbour.

bowl[1] *n* a ball of wood; (*pl*) the game played with such bowls. * *vi* to play with bowls; to deliver a ball at cricket.

bowl[2] *n* a large roundish dish.

bow-legged *adj* bandy-legged.

bowler[1] *n* one who plays bowls; to deliver a ball at cricket.

bowler[2] *n* a stiff felt hat.

bowling green *n* a smooth lawn for the game of bowls.

bowman *n* an archer.

bowsprit *n* a spar projecting over the bow of a ship.

bow window *n* a bay window.

box *n* a case of wood, metal, etc; a seat in a theatre; a blow; a tree or shrub. * *vt* to put in a box; to strike. * *vi* to fight with the fists.

boxer *n* a pugilist.

boy *n* a male child.

boycott *vt* to refuse dealings with.

boyhood *n* the state of being a boy.

brace *n* a support; a bandage; a couple; a boring tool; (*pl*) suspenders. * *vt* to tighten; to straighten up; to strengthen.

bracelet *n* an ornament for the wrist.

bracing *adj* invigorating.

bracken *n* a species of fern.

bracket *n* a support for something fixed to a wall; a mark–() or []–in writing or printing to enclose words. * *vt* to place within or connect by brackets; to group.

bracketing *n* grouping together.

brackish *adj* salt; saltish.

brag vi to talk big. * n a boast.

braggart adj boastful. * n a boaster.

braid vt to weave together strands of hair, thread, etc. * n a plaited band.

braided adj edged with braid.

brain n the centre of thought and sensation; the soft matter within the skull.

braise, braize vt to cook in a covered pan.

brake n a device on a wheel to reduce speed or to stop motion; a type of wagon.

bran n the husks of ground corn.

branch n the offshoot of a tree; the offshoot of anything, as of a river, family. * vi to spread in branches; (with out) to broaden or increase one's activities.

brand n a burning piece of wood; a mark made with a hot iron; a trademark; a particular make (of goods). * vt to mark with a hot iron; to denounce.

brandish vt to shake; wave.

brandy n a spirit distilled from wine or fruit such as apricot, plum, etc.

brass n a yellow alloy of copper and zinc; brass section of an orchestra or band; impudence.

brassière n a woman's undergarment protecting and supporting the breasts; a bra.

brat n an ill-behaved child.

bravado n bluster.

brave adj daring; valiant. * vt to defy.

bravery n courage.

brawl vi to quarrel noisily. * n uproar.

brawn n the flesh of a boar; muscle; strength.

brawny adj muscular.

bray vi to make a loud harsh sound, as an ass. * n the cry of an ass.

brazen adj made of brass; impudent.

brazier n a worker in brass; a portable fire.

breach n the act of breaking; quarrel. * vt to make a gap in.

bread n food made of flour or meal baked.

breadth n width.

break vt to sever by fracture; to rend; to tame; to interrupt; to dissolve any union; to tell with discretion. * vi to come to pieces; to burst forth. * n an opening; a breach; a pause; the dawn.

breakage n a breaking.

breakdown n a failure or stoppage due to mechanical malfunction; a nervous or mental collapse; an analysing and classifying of a project, etc, into its separate parts.

breaker n a large, crested wave.

breakfast n the first meal in the day.

breakneck adj dangerously fast.

breakwater n a mole or bar to break the force of the waves.

breast n the fore part of the body; the conscience; the affections. * vt to face.

breastbone n the bone of the breast.

breath n the air drawn into and expelled from the lungs; life; pause; a gentle breeze.

breathe vt, vi to take breath; to live; to utter.

breathing n respiration.

breathless adj out of breath.

bred pp of **breed**.

breech n the hinder part (of a gun, etc); (pl **breeches**) garment for men.

breed vt, vi to bring forth; to educate; to rear. * n offspring; kind.

breeding n the raising of a breed; good manners.

breeze n a light wind.

brethren npl of **brother**.

breve n a note in music.

brevity n shortness.

brew vt to prepare from malt; to concoct; to scheme. * vi to make beer; to infuse tea. * n the mixture formed by brewing.

brewery n the place where beer brewing is carried on.

bribe n a gift to corrupt the conduct or judgment. * vt to gain over by bribes.

bribery n the giving or taking of bribes.

bric-à-brac n old curios.

brick n a rectangular block of baked clay or other material used in building.

bricklayer n one who builds with bricks.

bridal n a wedding. * adj belonging to a bride or a wedding.

bride n a woman about to be or newly married.

bridegroom n a man about to be or newly married.

bridesmaid n a woman who attends on a bride during a wedding.

bridge n a roadway across a river; a structure to carry people, vehicles, railways across; something that serves to fill a gap or helps communication; a platform on a ship from which the captain issues commands; a card game like whist. * vt to build a bridge over.

bridle n the headgear of a horse; a curb; a check. * vt to put a bridle on; to restrain.

brief adj short. * n a summary of a client's case; (pl) underpants without legs.

brigade n a group of two or more regiments.

brigadier n the officer who commands a brigade.

bright adj clear; shining; lively; clever.

brighten vti to make bright.

brilliance n the state of being brilliant; splendour.

brilliant adj sparkling. * n a diamond.

brim n the rim of anything.

brimful adj full to the brim.

brindled adj marked with brown streaks.

brine n salt water.

bring vt to lead; to fetch; to produce; to cause to happen.

brink n the edge; the margin; the moment before a happening, often a disaster.

brisk adj lively.

brisket n the breast of an animal.

briskly adv actively.

bristle n a stiff hair. * vt, vi to stand on end; to show anger.

brittle adj apt to break.

broach n a roasting spit. * vt to pierce, as with a spit; to tap; to open up.

broad adj wide.

broaden vi to grow broad. * vt to make broad.

broadside n a discharge of all the guns on one side of a ship.

brocade n a silk stuff with raised pattern.

brochure n a pamphlet.

brogue n a strong shoe formerly of raw hide; the Irish accent.

broil n a brawl. * vt to cook over a fire.

broken adj crushed; ruined.

broker n an agent who buys and sells for others.

brokerage n the business of a broker.

bromide n a drug; a platitude.

bronchi npl the tubes branching from the windpipe to the lungs.

bronchial adj belonging to the air tubes.

bronchitis n inflammation of the bronchial tubes.

bronze n an alloy of copper and tin; a colour.

brooch n an ornament to pin on a dress.

brood vi to sit on eggs; to ponder anxiously. * n offspring.

brook n a small stream. * vt to bear.

broom n a shrub with yellow flowers; a brush.

broth n a meat soup with vegetables.

brother n a son of the same parents; an associate; a fellow creature; a working or lay member of a male religious order.

brotherhood n the relationship of a brother; an association.

brow n the ridge over the eye; the forehead; the edge of a cliff.

browbeat vt to bully.

brown adj dusky; tanned. * n a colour resulting from the mixture of red, black, and yellow.

brownie n a junior Guide; a small nutty, chocolate cake.

browse vt to feed upon; to read through casually.

bruise vt to crush; to injure and cause discolouration of the skin without drawing blood. * n a skin discolouration from a blow.

brunette n a woman with a dark complexion and dark hair.

brunt n the main area to bear the shock of an attack, etc.

brush n an implement with bristles for cleaning by rubbing or sweeping or for painting; a skirmish; a thicket; the tail of a fox. * vt, vi to sweep; to touch lightly.

brushwood n small trees and shrubs growing together.

brusque adj abrupt; rude.

brutal adj cruel.

brutality n savageness; cruelty.

brute adj purely physical; sheer, as in brute force. * n a beast; a brutal person.

brutish adj brutal; sensual.

bubble n a fluid film enclosing air; a swindle. * *vi* to rise in bubbles.

buccaneer *n* a pirate.

buck *n* the male of deer, goats; a lively, stylish young fellow. * *vi* to jump violently.

bucket *n* a pail.

buckle *n* a strap or belt fastener. * *vt* to fasten; to bend.

buckshot *n* lead shot for hunting big game.

bucolic *adj* pastoral; rustic.

bud *n* a young shoot or flower. * *vi* to put forth buds.

budding *n* a method of grafting buds. * *adj* promising.

budge *vt* to move; to stir.

budget *n* a financial statement; an estimate for expenditure. * *vt, vi* to put on a budget; to plan; to make a budget.

buff *n* a yellow colour; the bare skin. * *adj* light yellow. * *vt* to clean or shine by rubbing.

buffer *n* anything for deadening the shock of collision, etc.

buffet[1] *n* a sideboard; a refreshment bar; a meal where people serve themselves.

buffet[2] *n* a blow; a slap. * *vt* to box; to contend against.

buffoon *n* a clown; one who plays the fool to amuse; a fool.

buffoonery *n* the antics of a buffoon.

bugle *n* a hunting horn; a kind of trumpet.

bugler *n* one who plays the bugle.

build *vt* to construct; to establish. * *vi* to form a structure. * *n* make; form.

building *n* an edifice; the art or trade of building.

building society *n* a financial company where deposits of money are paid interest and loans are made esp for house buying and mortgages.

bulb *n* a round root.

bulbous *adj* swelling out.

bulge *n* a swelling; a rounded projection. * *vt* to swell out.

bulk *n* size; the main mass; cargo.

bulky *adj* large and awkwardly shaped.

bull *n* the male of cattle, elephant and whale; an edict of the pope.

bulldog *n* a species of dog; a never-say-

die person.

bullet *n* a metal missile shot from a firearm.

bulletin *n* an official report.

bullion *n* uncoined gold or silver.

bull's-eye *n* the centre of a target; a shot hitting this; any aim that is achieved.

bully *n* an overbearing quarrelsome fellow. * *vt* to insult and threaten.

bulwark *n* a rampart; a person or thing acting as a strong buffer.

bump *n* a heavy blow, or the noise of it; a lump produced by a blow. * *vt* to crash or knock against.

bumper *n* a full glass; a protective metal bar fixed at the front and rear of a vehicle to absorb shock.

bumptious *adj* self-assertive.

bun *n* a small cake; a round coil of hair worn at the nape of the neck.

bunch *n* a cluster.

bundle *n* a package. * *vt, vi* to tie in a bundle; to hurry off.

bungalow *n* a one-storeyed house.

bungle *vi* to botch. * *n* a clumsy performance.

bunion *n* a lump on the ball of the big toe.

bunk *n* a sleeping berth; a narrow bed.

bunker *n* a large bin; a sandpit hazard on a golf course; an underground shelter.

bunting *n* stuff of which flags are made; flags.

buoy *n* a floating navigation mark. * *vt* to keep afloat; (with **up**) to give support or encouragement to.

buoyancy *n* capacity for floating; cheerfulness; resilience.

buoyant *adj* floating; light; cheerful.

bur, burr *n* a prickly fruit, seed case or flowerhead.

burden *n* a load; something hard or wearisome to bear; a chorus. * *vt* to load; to oppress.

bureau *n* (*pl* **bureaux**) a writing table; a chest of drawers; a government office.

bureaucracy *n* government through state departments; unnecessary officialdom.

burgeon *vt, vi* to flourish; to grow rapidly and profusely.

burglar *n* a housebreaker.

burglary n the act of housebreaking.

burgundy n a red or white wine produced in Burgundy.

burial n the act of burying; interment.

burlesque adj comic. * n a caricature; a satirical play caricaturing some subject. * vt to turn into ridicule.

burly adj stout; portly; of a strong build.

burn vti to consume with fire; to be on fire; to rage fiercely. * n a hurt caused by fire; a rivulet.

burning adj fiery; vehement.

burnish vt to polish. * n polish.

burrow n a hole in the earth made by rabbits, etc. * vi to excavate.

bursar n a treasurer; a student who holds a scholarship.

bursary n a scholarship.

burst vi to fly or break open; to rush forth. * vt to break by force.

bury vt to put into a grave; to cover; to conceal.

bus n (pl **buses**) an omnibus.

bush n a shrub; a thicket.

business n occupation; concern.

busk vi to entertain for money.

bust n the bosom; the figure from head to chest in sculpture.

bustle vi to hustle. * n hurry.

busy adj occupied. * vt to employ.

busybody n a meddler.

but conj, prep, adv yet, except, only.

butcher n one who kills or sells animals for food. * vt to slaughter.

butler n a male servant in charge of a wine cellar.

butt n the end of a thing; a mark to be shot at; an object of ridicule; a cask of wine. * vt to strike with the head.

butter n the substance obtained from cream by churning. * vt to spread with butter; to flatter grossly.

buttercup n a wild yellow cup-shaped flower.

butterfly n a winged insect often brightly coloured; a showy person; a swimming stroke.

buttermilk n the milk that remains after the butter is separated.

button n a knob or disc for fastening; a badge. * vt to fasten with buttons.

buttress n a construction to support and strengthen a wall; a prop. * vt to support by a prop.

buxom adj jolly; large.

buy vt to purchase.

buzz vi to hum. * n a humming noise.

by prep, adv. used to denote the instrument, agent, or manner; at the rate of; not later than.

bye n in certain games, reaching the second round without playing an opponent in the first; a ball scoring a run in cricket without being hit by a batsman.

bygone adj past.

bylaw n a local law.

bypass n a road that skirts a town; a rechannelling, esp of blood flow into the heart. * vt to go round so as to avoid.

byre n a cow house.

bystander n a spectator.

byway n a side way.

byword n a common saying; a proverb.

C

cabal n an intrigue; a party clique. * vi to combine in plotting.

cabbage n a vegetable.

cabin n a hut; a room in a ship. * vt to confine.

cabinet n a closet; a showcase; the ministers of state.

cabinet-maker n a maker of furniture.

cable n anchor rope; a submarine telegraph wire. * vt to send by cable.

cackle vi to utter a cry (as of a hen); to chatter. * n clucking; idle talk or laughter.

cadaverous adj ghastly, deathlike.

cadence n a fall of the voice at the end of a sentence.

cadet n a younger brother; a military pupil.

cadge vt vi. to go about begging.

cadmium n a whitish metal.

Caesarean Section n the removal by surgery of a baby from the womb.

café n a small informal restaurant; a coffee bar.

cage *n* a wire frame to confine birds or beasts.

cairn *n* a heap of stones as landmark or memorial.

cairngorm *n* a yellow-brown rock crystal as a gem.

caisson *n* a structure to raise sunken vessels; a structure used in laying foundations in deep water.

cajole *vt* to wheedle; to persude by smooth words.

cake *n* baked dough in various forms; fancy bread; a flat compact mass.

calamitous *adj* disastrous.

calamity *n* misfortune; disaster.

calcareous *adj* containing lime.

calculate *vt* to count; to think out; to estimate.

calculating *adj* scheming.

calculus *n* (*math*) a method of calculation.

calendar *n* a means of calculating years, months, days; an almanac; a list of coming events.

calf *n* the young of the cow; the fleshy lower part of the leg.

calibre *n* the diameter of the bore of a gun; quality.

calico *n* a cotton cloth, usually unbleached.

call *vt* to name; to summon. * *vi* to utter a loud sound; to make a short visit. * *n* a summons; a short visit; a bird's note; a need; a demand.

calligraphy *n* the art of writing.

calling *n* a vocation.

callipers *n, npl* compasses for measuring calibre; a metal support strapped to the leg for support.

callisthenics *n* exercises for strength or grace of movement.

callous *adj* hardened; unfeeling.

callow *adj* young and immature.

calm *adj* still; quiet; windless. * *n* tranquillity. * *vt* to soothe; to pacify.

calmness *n* composure, stillness.

calorie *n* a unit of heat; a unit measuring the energy of food.

calorific *adj* causing heat.

calumnious *adj* slanderous.

calumny *n* slander; defamation.

calve *vi* to give birth to a calf.

calypso *n* a West Indian story in song to a syncopated rhythm.

camber *n* the slight curve upward towards the centre of a road surface.

cambered *adj* curved.

cambric *n* a fine white linen.

cameo *n* a precious stone carved in relief.

camera *n* an apparatus for taking photographs or cinema and television pictures; a judge's private chamber.

camisole *n* an under bodice.

camp *n* the ground on which tents are pitched; the collection of tents; those who support a cause or party.

campaign *n* the operations of an army in war.

campaigner *n* an old soldier.

campus *n* the grounds (and buildings) of a university.

can[1] *n* a metal vessel; a tin.

can[2] *vi* (*past* could) to be able.

canal *n* an artificial watercourse for boats; a duct or channel in the body.

canard *n* a false rumour.

canary *n* a light wine; a song bird.

cancel *vt* to strike out; to delete; to annul; to undo or call off.

cancer *n* one of the signs of the zodiac; a malignant growth.

candelabrum *n* (*pl* **candelabra**) a branched ornamental candlestick.

candid *adj* frank; outspoken; fair and unprejudiced.

candidate *n* an applicant for a post or office; someone worthy to be chosen; someone taking an examination.

candidly *adv* sincerely.

candle *n* a stick of wax with a wick for lighting.

candlestick *n* a candleholder.

candour *n* frankness.

candy *vt* to conserve with sugar. * *n* a sweetmeat.

cane *n* a walking stick; the stem of some plants as bamboo; a thin stick for supporting plants. * *vt* to beat with a cane.

canine *adj* pertaining to dogs.

canister *n* a small box; an explosive shell.

canker *n* an ulcer; a blight.

cannabis *n* a drug from the hemp plant.

cannibal *n* a person who eats human flesh. * *adj* relating to cannibalism.

cannon *n* a large gun mounted on a carriage; a shot in billiards when the cue ball strikes two other balls; an impact and rebound. * *vt* to collide with.

cannonade *n* a bombardment.

cannot the negative of **can**.

canny *adj* cautious; wary.

canoe *n* a skiff driven by paddles.

canon *n* a decree; a law; a rule or criterion; a list of an author's works accepted as genuine; a cathedral cleric.

cañon, canyon *n* a narrow mountain gorge.

canonize *vt* to declare a person to be a saint.

canopy *n* a covering over a throne, bed, etc.

cant *n* insincere talk; jargon.

cantankerous *adj* cross.

cantata *n* a short oratorio.

canteen *n* a restaurant within or attached to a place of work, school etc; (the box holding) a full set of cutlery; a place in camp or barracks for the sale of food and drink; a flask for water.

canter *n* a moderate gallop. * *vi* to move at a moderate gallop.

cantilever *n* a large supporting bracket; a principle applied in bridge making.

canto *n* a division of a poem.

canvas *n* a coarse cloth; sails of ships; a painting.

canvass *vt* to solicit the votes of.

canyon *n* a long, narrow mountain gorge.

cap *n* a covering for the head; a top piece. * *vt* to put a cap on; to excel; to outdo.

capability *n* a capacity; competence.

capable *adj* efficient; able.

capacious *adj* wide; roomy.

capacity *n* volume; ability.

cape *n* a headland; a sleeveless coat.

caper *vi* to skip. * *n* a leap; a prank.

capillary *adj* minute; hairlike. * *n* (*pl* **capillaries**) a small blood vessel.

capital *adj* chief; punishable with death. * *n* the top of a column; the chief city; wealth.

capitalist *n* a man of wealth.

capitalize *vt* to convert into capital.

capitation *adj, n.* per head especially of a tax.

Capitol *n* the US senate house.

capitulate *vi* to surrender on conditions.

caprice *n* a whim.

capricious *adj* fickle; unreliable.

Capricorn *n* one of the signs of the zodiac.

capsize *vt* to upset.

capstan *n* an apparatus for winding in anchors, etc.

capsule *n* a gelatin case containing a drug to be swallowed; a covering; the part of a spacecraft, often manned, that gathers information and is recovered later.

captain *n* a commander, a leader.

caption *n* a headline of a newspaper or book; the explanatory text under an illustration; a subtitle.

captivate *vt* to fascinate.

captive *n* a prisoner.

captivity *n* the state or condition of being a captive.

capture *n* arrest. * *vt* to seize.

car *n* a motor vehicle; the compartment for passengers on a train, aircraft, cable railway etc.

carafe *n* a glass water bottle.

caramel *n* burnt sugar as colouring matter; a caramel flavoured sweet.

carat *n* unit of purity for gold.

caravan *n* a company travelling together; a house on wheels.

carbide *n* a compound of carbon with a metal.

carbine *n* a cavalry rifle.

carbohydrate *n* a compund of carbon, hydrogen and oxygen found in sugar, starch etc.

carbolic *adj* an antiseptic acid obtained from coal tar.

carbon *n* pure charcoal.

carbonaceous *adj* containing carbon.

carboniferous *adj* carbon-bearing.

carbonize *vt* to convert into carbon.

carbuncle *n* a large boil.

carburettor *n* the device in an internal combustion engine making and controlling the mixture of air and fuel.

carcass *adj* the body of a dead animal.

card *n* a piece of pasteboard for various

purposes. * vt to comb wool, etc.

cardboard n a thick card.

cardiac adj pertaining to the heart.

cardigan n a knitted garment with front fastenings.

cardinal adj chief. * n a Roman Catholic dignitary.

care n solicitude; attention. * vi to be anxious; to have regard; to look after; to provide for.

career n a race; a profession. * vi to proceed rapidly and without control.

careful adj anxious; cautious.

careless adj heedless; thoughtless; carefree.

caress vt to fondle. * n an embrace.

caret n an omission mark, thus (^).

cargo n freight.

caricature n a ludicrous portrait. * vt to burlesque; to parody.

caries n bone decay; tooth decay.

carmine n a bright crimson colour.

carnage n slaughter.

carnal adj sensual; sexual; worldly.

carnally adv lustfully.

carnation n flesh-colour; a rose-pink flower.

carnival n a gala day; public merry-making; a travelling funfair.

carnivorous adj feeding on flesh.

carol n a song of joy, especially one sung at Christmas.

carotoid n one of two great arteries in the neck.

carousal n a noisy revel.

carouse vi to drink freely.

carp vi to find fault. * n a voracious fish.

carpenter n a worker in timber.

carpentry n the trade of a carpenter.

carpet n a woven cover for floors.

carpeting n cloth for carpets.

carriage n a vehicle; the price of carrying; behaviour; bearing.

carrion n putrid flesh.

carrot n a reddish vegetable of a tapering shape; something offered as a reward.

carry vt to bear; to convey; to gain; to behave.

cart n a vehicle with two wheels for carrying goods.

carte blanche n (pl **cartes blanches**) a blank paper; unconditional terms.

cartel n a challenge; a written agreement for the exchange of prisoners; a union formed to promote and achieve common aims.

cartilage n gristle.

cartography n science of making maps.

carton n a cardboard box.

cartoon n a humorous or satirical topical sketch; a comic strip often animated.

cartridge n a case containing the charge for a gun.

carve vt to cut; to engrave.

carver n one who carves; a large knife for carving.

cascade n a waterfall.

case n a box; a covering; an event; a suit in court; an ailment or disease being medically treated; the patient undergoing treatment; a form in the inflection of nouns. * vt to put in a case.

case-hardened adj callous.

casement n a hinged window.

cash n money. * vt to turn into money.

cashier n one who has charge of money. * vt to dismiss.

cashmere n a soft wool or woollen fabric woven from the hair of Kashmir goats.

casino n a gaming hall.

cask n a barrel.

casket n a jewel case.

casque n a helmet.

casserole n a covered dish for cooking; the food stewed in a casserole.

cassock n a garment worn by clerics and choristers.

cast vt to throw; to throw off; to let fall; to condemn; to model. * n a throw; a squint; a mould; a company of actors.

castaway n a shipwrecked person.

caste n social class and distinctions.

castigate vt to reprimand severely; to chastise.

casting n that which is cast in a mould; the allotting of actors to their roles.

cast iron n iron formed in moulds.

castle n a fortress; an imposing mansion.

castor n a small cruet; a small wheel.

castor oil n a medicinal oil used as a purgative.

castrate vt to geld.

casual *adj* accidental; occasional; informal; careless.

casually *adv* by chance.

casualty *n* an accident; the person injured or killed in an accident or a war.

cat *n* a domestic feline animal; a related animal such as a lion or tiger.

cataclysm *n* a deluge; an upheaval.

catacomb *n* an underground vault.

catalogue *n* a list; a register.

catapult *n* a sling.

cataract *n* a waterfall; a disease of the eye.

catarrh *n* a cold in the head, due to inflammation of a mucus membrane in the nose.

catastrophe *n* disaster; finale.

catch *vt* to lay hold on; to grasp; to entangle; to receive by contagion; to get. * *n* a grasping; a song; play on words; a type of fastening; a hidden obstacle.

catching *adj* infectious.

catechise *vt* to instruct by question and answer; to question.

catechism *n* a manual of instruction by questions and answers especially of religious tenets.

categorical *adj* positive.

categorically *adv* absolutely.

category *n* a class or order or division.

cater *vi* to provide provisions, etc.

catgut *n* a cord made from intestines of animals and used as strings for violins, harps, guitars, etc.

cathedral *n* the principal church in a diocese.

cathode *n* the negative pole of an electric current.

catholic *adj* universal; general. * *n* a member of the universal Christian Church.

catholicism *n* adherence to the Catholic Church.

cattle *npl* oxen; livestock.

caucus *n* a party organization or clique.

caulk *vt* to stop up seams of a ship.

causal *adj* implying cause.

causation *n* the relation of cause and effect.

cause *n* that which produces an effect; reason; origin; suit; an enterprise. * *vt* to bring about.

causeway, causey *n* a paved way.

caustic *adj* burning; biting; sarcastic.

caustically *adv* scathingly.

cauterize *vt* to sear or burn, especially in treating a wound.

caution *n* care; pledge. * *vt* to warn.

cautious *adj* wary; careful.

cavalcade *n* a procession of persons on horseback; a company of horsemen.

cavalier *adj* careless; haughty.

cavalry *n* mounted troops.

cave *n* an underground hollow. * *vt, vi* (with **in**) to collapse; to give in on yield.

caveat *n* a warning.

cavern *n* a large cave.

cavernous *adj* hollow.

cavity *n* a hollow place especially a hole in a tooth.

cease *vi* to leave off; to stop. * *vt* to put a stop to.

ceaseless *adj* incessant.

cede *vt* to give up.

cedilla *n* the mark (ç) of the soft c.

ceiling *n* the upper inside surface of a room.

celebrant *n* the officiating priest; one taking part in a religious ceremony.

celebrate *vt* to commemorate; to accord high praise to.

celebrated *adj* famous.

celebrity *n* fame; a famous person.

celerity *n* speed; quickness.

celestial *adj* heavenly.

celibacy *n* the unmarried state.

celibate *n* one vowed to celibacy. * *adj* unmarried.

cell *n* a small room; a cave; a unit mass in living matter.

cellar *n* an apartment underground.

cellophane *n* a thin transparent paper used as protective wrapping.

cellular *adj* consisting of cells.

cement *n* mortar; a bond of union. * *vt* to unite closely.

cemetery *n* a burial place.

cenotaph *n* a monument to one who is buried elsewhere.

censor *n* a critic; a supervisor (of books, films, etc) who advocates removal of anything obscene, treasonable etc.

censorious *adj* fault-finding.

censure *n* blame; reproof. * *vt* to judge;

to blame.

census *n* an official count of people.

cent *n* a coin worth a hundredth of a dollar.

centaur *n* a fabulous being, half man and half horse.

centenarian *n* one a hundred years old.

centenary *n* the hundredth anniversary or its commemoration.

centigrade *adj* divided into a hundred degrees.

centimetre *n* the hundredth part of a metre.

central *adj* at the centre; most important; principal.

centralize *vt* to move to the centre; to cause to be under a central jurisdiction, authority, government.

centre *n* the middle point; a nucleus. * *vt* to collect to a point. * *vi* to have as a centre.

centreboard *n* a movable keel.

centrifugal *adj* tending to fly from a centre.

century *n* a hundred years.

ceramic *adj* pertaining to pottery. * *npl* the art of pottery.

cereal *adj* pertaining to corn. * *n* a grain plant; a breakfast food from the grains of such a plant.

cerebral *adj* of the brain; requiring use of the brain.

ceremonial *adj* pertaining to ceremony. * *n* rites and their observance; form of duty.

ceremonious *adj* formal.

ceremony *n* outward rite; pomp; observance.

certain *adj* sure; particular.

certainly *adv* without doubt.

certainty *n* truth; fact.

certificate *n* a written testimony.

certify *vt* to declare; to attest.

cessation *n* stoppage.

cesspool *n* a receptacle for sewage.

chafe *vt* to warm by rubbing; to irritate (skin) by rubbing; to enrage.

chaff *n* the husk of corn; banter. * *vt* to banter; to make fun of laughingly.

chagrin *n* vexation.

chain *n* a series of links; a measure of length; (*pl*) bondage. * *vt* to confine with chains.

chair *n* a movable seat; an official seat; professorship.

chalet *n* a Swiss cottage; a ski lodge or holiday house modelled on this.

chalice *n* a cup; a communion cup.

chalk *n* a soft limestone. * *vt* to mark with chalk.

challenge *n* a defiance; a calling in question; a demand especially to fight; a task or request requiring special effort. * *vt* to defy; to call in question.

challenger *n* one who challenges.

chamber *n* an apartment; a public body.

chamberlain *n* an officer of state; a city treasurer.

chamois *n* a species of antelope; a soft leather.

champ *vt* to chew; to bite.

champagne *n* a brisk sparkling wine.

champion *n* a defender of a cause; a vindicator. * *vt* to uphold.

championship *n* state of being a champion; a contest held to find a champion.

chance *n* accident; opportunity; luck. * *vi* to happen. * *adj* casual.

chancel *n* the altar end of a church.

chancellor *n* the head of a university, court.

chancery *n* a division of the High Court.

chandelier *n* a branching lamp with many lights that hangs from a ceiling.

change *vt* to alter; to exchange. * *n* variety; small coins.

changeable *adj* variable; capricious.

channel *n* a watercourse; a narrow sea; a band of radio frequencies allotted for a purpose, such as broadcasting by a television station. * *vt* to groove; to convey; to guide.

chant *vt i.* to sing; to intone. * *n* a song.

chaos *n* disorder; total confusion.

chapel *n* a place of worship.

chaperon *n* a lady guardian or escort.

chaplain *n* an army or navy clergyman.

chapter *n* a division of a book.

char *vt* to burn. * *n* a fish.

character *n* a letter or figure; the distinguishing attributes of a person or thing; nature; quality; a part in a play.

characteristic adj distinctive.

characterize vt to describe; to mark or be characteristic of.

charade n a word puzzle acted out in syllables followed by all of the word; a travesty.

charcoal n charred wood.

char vt to blacken by fire.

charge vt to load; to fill; to price; to entrust; to accuse; to command; to attack. * n care; cost; attack; order; accusation.

chargeable adj imputable.

chargé d'affaires n an ambassador's deputy.

charger n a large dish; a warhorse.

chariot n a state carriage.

charioteer n a chariot driver.

charitable adj benevolent; generous in giving; lenient.

charity n love; benevolence; generosity to the needy; a money-raising fund or institution.

charlatan n a quack.

charm n a spell. * vt to delight.

charming adj enchanting.

charnel house n a burial vault.

chart n a map; a table of information.

charter n a warrant; a hire. * vt to hire.

chary adj careful; cautious.

chase vt to pursue; to emboss. * n pursuit; hunt; a printer's frame.

chasm n a deep cleft.

chassis n the frame of a motor vehicle.

chaste adj pure.

chasten vt to discipline by punishment; to tame; to make repentant.

chastise vt to punish.

chastity n purity; virginity.

chat vi to gossip. * n talk.

château n a castle.

chattel n (usu in pl) belongings.

chatter vi to talk idly; to jabber. * n talk.

chauffeur n one employed to drive a car.

chauvinism n jingoism.

cheap adj of a low price; common; inferior.

cheapen vt reduce in price; to belittle.

cheat vt to deceive; to swindle. * n a trick; a swindler.

check vti. to stop; to curb; to chide; to control. * n position in chess; a control.

checkmate n the winning move in chess. * vt to frustrate.

cheddar n a brand of cheese.

cheek n the side of the face; impudence.

cheer n gaiety; happiness; good spirits; a shout of joy. * vt to brighten; to gladden; to applaud.

cheerful adj happy, blithe.

cheering adj encouraging.

cheerless adj gloomy; dejected.

cheese n the curd of milk dried and pressed.

cheeseparing adj mean.

chef n a head cook.

chemical n any substance obtained by a chemical process.

chemise n an undergarment worn by females.

chemist n one skilled in chemistry; a pharmacy.

chemistry n the science of the properties and nature of substances.

cheque n an order for money.

chequer n a square pattern; (pl) draughts.

chequered, checkered adj varied; fluctuating.

cherish vt to treasure.

cheroot n a kind of cigar.

cherry n a tree and its small red fruit; a bright red colour.

chess n a game played on a squared board.

chessman n a piece used in chess.

chest n a large box; the breast.

chestnut n a tree; its edible nut; its wood; a stale joke. * adj reddish-brown.

chew vt to masticate.

chic n style. * adj stylish.

chicane, chicanery n trickery.

chick, chicken n the young of birds.

chicken-hearted adj timid.

chickenpox n an eruptive fever.

chicory n a plant with a root that when ground is used for or with coffee.

chide vti. to reprove; to scold.

chief adj first; leading. * n a leader.

chieftain n the head of a clan.

chilblain n a painful swelling on the hands or toes produced by cold.

child n an infant; offspring.

childhood n the stage between birth and adolescence.

childish adj like a child; trifling.

childlike adj innocent.

chill n a cold fit. * adj cold. * vt to discourage.

chime n a harmony of bells; (pl) a set of bells. * vi to accord.

chimerical adj fanciful.

chimney n a smoke escape.

chimpanzee n a large ape.

chin n the lower part of the face.

china n porcelain.

chink n an opening; a crack. * vt, vi to jingle as of coins.

chintz n calico, patterned and coloured.

chip n a fragment. * vt to cut into chips.

chiropody n the treatment of the feet.

chirp vi to cheep.

chisel n a cutting tool. * vt to cut or engrave.

chiselled adj clear-cut.

chivalrous adj gallant; knightly.

chivalry n knighthood; gallantry.

chloride n a chlorine compound.

chlorine n a gaseous element used in bleaching and disinfectants.

chloroform n a volatile liquid anaesthetic.

chlorophyll n the green colouring matter of plants.

chocolate n a beverage and sweet from cacao; its colour.

choice n option; selection; preference. * adj select; precious.

choir n a band of singers; the place especially in church where they sit.

choke vt to suffocate. * vi to be blocked up.

cholera n a highly infectious and deadly disease.

choleric adj bad-tempered; peevish.

choose vt to prefer; to select.

chop vt to cut to pieces. * vi to turn suddenly. * n a piece of meat.

chopsticks n two wooden sticks used to eat especially by Chinese.

choral adj belonging to, sung by or written for a choir.

chord n three or more musical notes played together.

chorister n a singer in a choir.

chorus n a company of singers; musical refrain.

chosen adj select.

Christ n Jesus of Nazareth, the Christian Messiah.

christen vt to baptize; to name.

Christendom n the whole body of Christians.

Christian n a professed follower of Christ.

Christianity n the religion of Christians.

Christmas n the festival of Christ's nativity, December 25.

chrome, chromium n a hard metal used in steel alloys and electro-plating.

chronic adj permanent.

chronicle n a diary of events; history. * vt to record.

chronological adj arranged in order of happening.

chronology n the science of time; the sequence of events and their arrangement in order.

chronometer n a timepiece.

chrysalis n the grub stage of certain insects.

chubby adj plump.

chuck vt to tap under the chin; to toss; to pitch; to give up; to throw away.

chuckle vi to laugh in the throat; to exult. * n a half-suppressed laugh.

chum n a close friend.

chunk n a short thick piece.

church n a building consecrated to the worship of God; the body of clergy.

churchyard n a cemetery.

churlish adj surly; sullen.

churn n a vessel that is vigorously turned and shaken to make butter; a milk container.

chute n a sloping channel or slide for water, rubbish, logs etc.

cicatrix, cicatrice n a scar.

cider n fermented apple juice.

cigar n a roll of tobacco leaf for smoking.

cigarette n a paper cylinder of shredded tobacco.

cinchona n a tree whose bark yields quinine.

cinder n a burned coal.

cinema n a building where films are shown; the art or industry of film-making.

cinnamon n a tree and the aromatic spice

from it; a yellow-brown colour.

cipher, cypher *n* the figure 0; any numeral; a person or thing of no importance; a secret writing.

circle *n* a round figure; a group; its bounding line; a ring; a class. * *vt, vi* to move round; to enclose.

circuit *n* area; extent; journey of judges to hold courts; a detour; the path of an electric current.

circuitous *adj* roundabout.

circular *adj* round. * *n* a notice.

circulate *vi* to move in a circle; to pass from person to person or place to place. * *vt* to spread.

circulation *n* circulating; the area centred and the number sold, of a newspaper etc; the flow of blood through the arteries and the veins; currency.

circulatory *adj* circulating.

circumcise *vt* to cut off the foreskin.

circumference *n* the bounding line of a circle.

circumflex *n* an accent (^) on vowels marking contraction, etc.

circumlocution *n* a roundabout mode of speaking.

circumlocutory *adj* diffuse.

circumnavigate *vt* to sail round.

circumscribe *vt* to enclose; to limit.

circumspect *adj* wary.

circumspection *n* caution.

circumstance *n* an event; (*pl*) state of affairs; condition.

circumstantial *adj* indirect; incidental.

circumvent *vt* to avoid by going round; to evade; to outwit.

circus *n* (*pl* **circuses**) an enclosed area or place for games etc.; a travelling show of entertainers and animals.

cirrus *n* (*pl* **cirri**) a thin, trailing cloud.

cistern *n* a water tank.

citation *n* quotation; summons.

cite *vt* to summon; to quote.

citizen *n* an inhabitant of a city.

citizenship *n* the rights of a citizen.

citrus *n* a type of tree including the orange and lemon; the fruit.

city *n* a large town.

civet *n* a civet cat; the perfume obtained from it.

civic *adj* pertaining to a city or citizen.

civil *adj* municipal; non-military; of the state; polite; internal.

civilian *n* one engaged in civil, not military pursuits.

civility *n* courtesy.

civilization *n* culture; social development; the modern world.

civilize *vt* to convert from a savage or wild state; to refine.

clad *pp* of clothe.

claim *vt* to demand as due; to assert outright to; to state one's ownership of. * *n* a formal demand; the thing claimed.

claimant *n* one who claims.

clairvoyance *n* the supposed power of seeing things not present to the senses.

clamber *vi* to scramble over.

clammy *adj* sticky; damp; moist.

clamorous *adj* noisy.

clamour *n* shouting; uproar. * *vi* to demand with shouts.

clamp *n* a gripping appliance. * *vi* to fasten or grip.

clan *n* a family; a tribe.

clandestine *adj* secret; underhand.

clang *n* a ringing noise.

clank *n* a dull metallic ring as of chains.

clannish *adj* united; belonging to a group and excluding others.

clap *vt* to strike together noisily, especially the hands; to pat. * *n* explosive sound as of thunder.

clapper *n* the tongue of a bell.

claret *n* a red wine. * *adj* claret-coloured.

clarify *vti* to make clear; to purify by heating.

clarinet *n* a reed instrument.

clarion *n* a shrill trumpet. * *adj* rousing.

clash *vi* to make a noise by collision; to be antagonistic to or incompatible. * *n* noisy collision; jarring.

clasp *n* an embrace; a hook. * *vt* to fasten; to embrace.

clasp knife *n* a knife with blades that fold into the handle.

class *n* a rank; a group; a body of students learning together, a standard or grade of worth. * *vt* to arrange in classes.

classic *adj* of the first rank. * *n* a work of the first rank in any of the arts.

classical *adj* refined; standard; pertaining to or in keeping with the great masterpieces of Greece and Rome; traditional.

classification *n* organization into classes or categories.

classify *vt* to arrange; to categorize; to restrict, especially information, to an inner group for security reasons.

clatter *vi* to make rattling noises; to talk noisily. * *n* a rattling noise.

clause *n* a part of a sentence; a single item of a treaty, contract, bill, etc.

claustrophobia *n* a morbid fear of confined spaces or being shut in.

clavicle *n* the collarbone.

claw *n* a hooked nail; a crab's pincer. * *vt* to scratch or dig with claws or nails.

clay *n* heavy soil.

claymore *n* a large two-edged sword; a basket-hilted sword.

clean *adj* free from dirt; pure. * *vt* to purify; to cleanse.

cleanliness *n* state of being clean.

cleanse *vt* to make clean or pure.

clear *adj* bright; shining; limpid; fair; plain; shrill. * *adv* manifestly. * *vt* to make clear; to free from suspicion.

clearance *n* a setting free; an emptying; a discharge.

clearing *n* the act of making clear; a settling up; land cleared of trees.

cleavage *n* a splitting or tendency to split.

cleave *vi* to stick; to adhere.

cleave *vt* to split; to sever.

cleaver *n* a butcher's axe or knife.

clef *n* a mark to show the key in music.

cleft *n* a crevice; a fissure.

clemency *n* mercy.

clench *vt* to hold tight; to close (teeth) tightly.

clergy *npl* the ministers of the Christian religion.

cleric *n* a clergyman.

clerical *n* pertaining to the clergy, or to a clerk.

clerk *n* an office employee; an official who looks after records.

clever *adj* adroit; talented.

cleverness *n* ability.

click *vi* to clink; to make a faint sharp sound.

client *n* a customer.

clientele *n* clients collectively.

cliff *n* a steep rock face.

climacteric *n* a critical period in life; the menopause.

climate *n* weather characteristics or conditions; a prevailing atmosphere, mood or feeling.

climax *n* the highest point; an ascending scale.

climb *vi, vt* to ascend; to mount.

clinch *vt* to settle finally (a deal, an argument); to fasten; to grasp. * *n* a grip hindering the use of the arms; a tight embrace.

cling *vi* to adhere; to cleave.

clinic *n* a place for the care of out patients; a private hospital; doctors practising in a group.

clinical *adj* of or pertaining to the treatment, progress and medical observation of patients; objective; detached.

clink *vt* to jingle.

clinker *n* burnt brick, or hard cinders.

clip *vt* to shear; to trim with scissors; to shorten or cut off words when speaking; to grip or fasten with a clip or clasp. * *n* a clasp to hold or fasten or hook together; an excerpt or extract from a film.

clique *n* a party; a set; an exclusive group.

cloak *n* a loose outer garment; a pretext. * *vt* to hide; to veil.

clock *n* a timepiece.

clockwork *n* the machinery of a clock; unfailing regularity.

clod *n* a lump of earth; a stupid fellow.

clog *n* a shoe with a wooden sole.

cloister *n* a monastery or convent; a covered walk there or in a college.

close *vt* to shut; to finish. * *vi* to end. * *n* the end.

close *adj* shut fast; tight; dense; near; stingy; secretive. * *n* an enclosed place; a courtyard or its entrance; the precincts of a cathedral.

close-fisted *adj* niggardly.

closet *n* a small room or recess. * *vt* to shut up.

closure *n* a stoppage; a closing.

clot *n* a curdled or coagulated mass (of blood). * *vi* to become thick.

cloth n a woven fabric.

clothe vt to attire.

clothes n dress; coverings.

cloud n a mass of visible water vapour high in the air; a crowd; gloom. * vt to darken; to obscure; to hide.

cloudless adj clear.

cloudy adj overcast; indistinct; muddy.

clove n a spice; one segment of a bulb of garlic.

clover n a three-leaved plant used as fodder.

clown n a lout; a jester; a circus entertainer.

clownish adj boorish.

cloy vt to glut; to surfeit with sweetness.

club n a cudgel; a golf stick; a society of people; their meeting place; a suit at cards; an association for some common object. * vt to beat with a club. * vi to join together.

clue n a guide or help to solve a puzzle.

clump n a thick cluster; the sound made by heavy or clumsy footsteps.

clumsy adj awkward; graceless; tactless; a collection of eggs hatched at the one time; a brood of chickens.

cluster n a bunch. * vi to keep close together.

clutch vt to seize; to grasp. * n the lever that puts an engine in or out of action.

coach n a four-wheeled close vehicle; a long-distance bus; a sports trainer.

coagulate vti to curdle; to clot; of liquid, to thicken to a semisolid state.

coal n a black mineral used as fuel.

coalesce vi to unite; to fuse; to muge.

coalition n a party union; an alliance.

coal mine n a mine containing coal.

coal tar n a black liquid got by distilling coal.

coarse adj rude; gross; crude.

coast n the seashore. * vi to sail along a shore; to travel without mechanical power, especially downhill.

coaster n a vessel which trades along the coast; a protective mat to place under a glass or bottle.

coastguard n a coast police force.

coasting adj a brakeless downhill ride.

coat n an outer garment; a covering; a layer. * vt to cover.

coax vt to wheedle; to pursuade by gentleness or flattery.

cobble vt to mend coarsely. * npl a road surfaced with rounded stones.

cobbler n a mender of shoes.

cobweb n a spider's web.

cocaine n a drug injected to deaden pain.

cochineal n an insect; the scarlet dye got from it.

cock n a male bird; a tap; the hammer of a gun. * vt to set erect.

cockney n a native of London. * adj pertaining to a cockney.

cockpit n a pit where game cocks fight; a pilot's compartment in an aeroplane.

cocktail n an alcoholic drink composed of a mixture of spirits and other ingredients.

cocoa n cacao seeds; the beverage made from them.

coconut n the fruit of the coco palm.

cocoon n the case spun by the silkworm.

coddle vt to be overprotective; to cook in water below boiling point.

code n a collection of laws, rules, or signals; letters, numbers, symblos arranged to transmit secret messages.

codicil n a supplement to a will.

codification n reducing laws to a code.

codify vt to systematize laws, rules etc.

coefficient adj cooperating. * n a factor in an expression.

coerce vt to force; to compel.

coercion n the act of compulsion; government by force.

coexecutor n a joint executor.

coexist vi to live together, especially peacefully; at the same time.

coffee n a drink made from the seeds of the coffee tree.

coffer n a chest for holding valuables.

coffin n the coffer or chest for holding a corpse.

cog n the tooth of a wheel. **cogency** n force.

cogent adj convincing.

cogitate vi to ponder.

cognac n French brandy.

cognition n perception.

cognizable adj capable of being known or perceived.

cognizance n knowledge; judicial notice.

cognizant *adj* having knowledge of.

cohabit *vi* to dwell together.

cohere *vi* to stick together.

coherent *adj* connected; intelligible, of speech; logical and consistent.

cohesion *n* the force keeping the particles of bodies together.

cohort *n* a company of soldiers.

coiffure *n* a hairstyle.

coil *vt* to wind into a ring. * *n* a ring or rings into which a rope, etc, is wound, or a spiral of a thing wound, esp. a wire for electric current.

coin *n* a piece of money. * *vt* to mint; to invent a new word or phrase.

coinage *n* coined money.

coincide *vi* to correspond in space or time; to agree exactly.

coincidence *n* concurrence; the occurrence by chance of two events at the same time.

coincident *adj* corresponding.

colander *n* a strainer for food.

cold *adj* not hot; chill; indifferent. * *n* absence of heat; an illness due to cold.

coleslaw *n* raw cabbage shredded and mixed in a dressing as a salad.

colic *n* a griping pain.

collaborator *n* an associate in literary or scientific labour; one who works against one's country in wartime.

collage *n* a picture or piece of artwork composed of random scraps of paper, material etc. pasted on a surface.

collapse *n* a breakdown; a fall; a failure. * *vi* to fall; to break down.

collar *n* a band worn round the neck; the neckband of a garment.

collate *vt* to examine and compare, as books, etc.

collateral *adj* side by side; indirect.

collation *n* the collating of texts etc.

colleague *n* an associate in office, a fellow worker.

collect *vti* to bring together; to infer; to arrange; to accumulate things as a hobby.

collect *n* a short prayer.

collected *adj* self-possessed.

collection *n* act of collecting; that which is collected; an accumulation of things of value or interest; money gathered for a purpose.

collective *adj* taken as a whole.

collectivism *n* the doctrine of the state ownership of land and all means of production.

college *n* an institution of scholars; a centre of higher learning.

collide *vi* to strike against each other.

collier *n* a coal miner; a coal ship.

colliery *n* a coal mine.

collision *n* act of striking together; conflict.

colloquial *adj* conversational; informal and non-literary of talk.

collude *vi* to connive.

collusion *n* fraud by agreement; conspiracy.

collusive *adj* fraudulently concerted.

colon *n* a mark of punctuation, thus (:); the large intestine.

colonel *n* the commander of a regiment.

colonial *adj* pertaining to a colony. * *n* a person belonging to a colony.

colonist *n* an inhabitant of a colony.

colonization *n* act of colonizing.

colonize *vt* to found a colony.

colonnade *n* a range of columns.

colony *n* a settlement in a new country.

colophon *n* the device or emblem of a publisher on a book.

colossal *adj* huge.

colour *n* the hue or appearance of a body to the eye; a pigment; complexion; pretence; (*pl*) a flag. * *vt* to tinge; to varnish; to embellish. * *vi* to blush.

colouring *n* act of giving a colour; colour applied; a false appearance.

colourist *n* a painter who excels in use of colour.

colt *n* a young horse.

column *n* a pillar; a body of troops; a section of a page; a line of figures; an article or feature appearing regularly in a newspaper etc.

coma *n* a stupor; a lengthy period of unconsciousness.

comatose *adj* torpid; deathlike.

comb *n* a toothed appliance for dressing hair, wool. etc. * *vt* to arrange hair with a comb; to search for thoroughly.

combat *vi* to fight * *vt* to oppose. * *n* a

fight; a contest.

combatant adj contending. * n a fighter.

combative adj disposed to fight.

combination n a union; an alliance of persons; numbers arranged to open the combination lock of a safe.

combine vt to join. * vi to league together. * n a machine that cuts and threshes crops.

combustible adj inflammable.

combustion n a burning.

come vi to move forward; to draw near; to arrive; to happen.

comedian n an actor of comic roles; one who entertains by telling jokes.

comedy n drama written to amuse.

comely adj good-looking; becoming.

comestible n an eatable.

comet n a heavenly body having a luminous tail.

comfort vt to console; to gladden. * n consolation.

comfortable adj contented; at ease; having adequate money to live well.

comic adj relating to comedy; amusing.

comical adj funny.

comma n a mark of punctuation, thus (,).

command vt to order; to govern; to have at one's disposal. * vi to have chief power. * n order; authority.

commandant n the military officer in charge of men or an establishment.

commandeer vt to appropriate.

commander n one who commands.

commanding adj dominating; authoritative.

commandment n a precept of the moral law.

commando n a soldier belonging to a special attacking force.

commemorate vt to celebrate the memory of someone or something.

commemoration n a solemn celebration as a memorial to.

commence vi, vt to take the first step; to begin.

commend vt to praise; to recommend.

commendable adj worthy of praise.

commendation n praise.

commensurate adj proportional.

comment vi to make remarks or criticisms. * vt to annotate. * n an explanatory note.

commentary n a book of comments or notes; a spoken explanation of events as they take place.

commentator n one who reports and explains events as on TV.

commerce n exchange of goods, trade.

commercial adj trading; pertaining to commerce; intended to be profit-making. * n an advertisement shown on TV.

commingle vt to blend.

commiserate vt to pity; to condole with.

commiseration n pity; sympathy.

commissariat n the stores department of an army; the supplies themselves.

commission n trust; warrant; a percentage; a body of commissioners; the appointment of a soldier to officer's rank; a business or task given or entrusted to someone. * vt to require the services of.

commissionaire n a porter or messenger.

commissioner n one appointed to perform some office.

commit vt to entrust; to consign especially to custody; to perpetrate.

commitment n a pledge; imprisonment.

committal n the act of committing.

committee n a body appointed to manage any matter on behalf of a larger body.

commodious adj spacious and suitable.

commodity n any article of commerce.

commodore n the commander of a squadron.

common adj general; usual; of no rank; of little value. * n an open public ground.

commonly adv usually.

commonplace adj ordinary; trite.

common sense n sound judgment.

commonwealth n the public good; the state; a republic; a federation of states.

commotion n tumult; disorder.

communal adj belonging to a community or commune; shared; common to.

commune vi to confer with privately or spiritually.

commune n a group of people living together and sharing everything.

communicable adj capable of being imparted to another.

communicant n a partaker of the Lord's

supper.

communicate vti to impart.

communication n news; a message; (pl) the passing and exchange of information, ideas etc. by means of speech, telecommunications, the media etc.

communicative adj candid; talkative.

communion n intercourse; celebration of the Lord's Supper.

communism n the doctrine of a community of property.

communist n an advocate of communism.

community n the body of the people; a body of people living in the same locality.

commutable adj exchangeable.

commutation n exchange; change; lessening.

commute vt, vi to travel a distance daily between home and work; to exchange; to lessen; to reduce the length of a prison sentence.

compact adj solid; dense. * vt to consolidate. * n an agreement.

compact disc n a disc playing recordings read by a laser beam.

companion n a comrade; a friend.

companionable adj sociable.

company n a body of guests, of traders, or of soldiers; a business; a ship's crew.

comparable adj similar.

comparative adj relative.

compare vt to examine side by side; to liken; to form degrees of comparison.

comparison n relation; simile; illustration; inflection in an adjective.

compartment n spaces divided off (in drawers, etc); one of the several divisions of a railway carriage carrying passengers; something separate; a category.

compass n a circuit; limit; range; an instrument with a magnetic needle pointing to the north; an instrument for describing circles.

compassion n sympathy.

compatible adj consistent; in keeping; able to live with agreeably; of like mind.

compatriot n one of the same country.

compel vt to drive; to urge; to force.

compendium n a summary.

compensate vt to make amends for; to

requite. * vi to atone.

compensation n recompense.

compete vi to strive (as rival); to contend.

competence n sufficiency, ability.

competent adj well qualified; fit.

competently adv adequately.

competition n rivalry; a contest; a, match.

competitor n a rival.

compilation n the act of compiling; the thing compiled.

compile vt to collect (facts, figures, etc).

complacence, complacency n satisfaction; self-satisfaction.

complacent adj pleased, with oneself.

complain vi to grumble at; to be dissatisfied with; to lament; to make a charge; to feel unwell.

complainant n a plaintiff.

complaint n a grumble; an accusation; an ailment.

complement n the full quota, allowance or number.

complementary adj completing.

complete adj finished. * vt to finish; to fulfil.

completion n the fulfilment; the finishing.

complex adj involved; difficult. * n a whole composed of many parts e.g. buildings or units.

complexion n the colour of the face; aspect.

complexity n intricacy.

compliance n concurrence; acquiescence.

compliant adj yielding; docile.

complicate vt to make complex or difficult.

complication n a complex situation; something that worsens or adds to a difficulty; a medical condition following on and arising from the original malady.

complicity n state of being an accomplice.

compliment n an expression of praise or admiration. * vt to praise; to congratulate.

comply vi to acquiesce.

component adj constituent. * n a constituent part.

compose vt to write, especially music; to calm.

composed adj calm; serene.

composer n a writer of music.

composite adj compound.

composition n a putting together; the thing composed, as a piece of music or literature; the make-up of something.

compositor n one who sets types.

composure n calmness.

compound vt, vi to put together; to mix; to adjust. * adj composed of two or more parts. * n a mass composed of two or more elements; an enclosure.

comprehend vt to understand.

comprehensible adj intelligible.

comprehension n understanding.

comprehensive adj inclusive; of wide scope. * n a secondary school accepting pupils of all abilities.

compress vt to press together. * n a soft pad to apply to a wound.

compressed adj flattened; condensed.

compression n a condensing; the increasing of pressure in an engine to compress the gases so that they explode.

comprise vt to contain; to consist of.

compromise n a settlement by agreement. * vt to settle by mutual concessions; to endanger.

comptroller n a controller.

compulsion n force; an overpowering urge.

compulsive adj compelling; acting as if forced.

compulsory adj obligatory.

compunction n remorse.

computation n reckoning.

compute vt to count; estimate.

computer n an electronic device that processes data according to instructions fed into it.

comrade n a mate; companion.

concave adj curving inwards.

conceal vt to hide.

concealment n a hiding place.

concede vt to yield; to grant.

conceit n vanity; an exaggerated opinion of oneself.

conceited adj vain.

conceivable adj thinkable; imaginable.

conceive vti to comprehend; to think; to become pregnant.

concentrate vt to collect to one point; to direct the mind solely to one aim or object; to condense in order to increase the strength of something.

concentric adj having a common centre.

concept n a general idea; an abstract idea.

conception n act of conceiving; an idea.

concern vt to interest oneself in; to apply to; to cause anxiety to. * n anxiety.

concert n agreement; harmony; a musical performance.

concerted adj planned; combined.

concertina n a musical instrument.

concerto n a musical composition for solo instrument and orchestra.

concession n a grant; the act of yielding.

conch n a marine shell.

conciliate vt to reconcile; to propitiate.

conciliatory adj persuasive.

concise adj brief; pointed.

conclave n the assembly of cardinals for the election of a pope; a close assembly.

conclude vti to end; to deduce.

conclusion n inference; the end; a final judgement or opinion.

concoct vt to devise; to plot; to produce from a mixture of ingredients; to fabricate.

concoction n a mixture; an invention.

concomitant adj accompanying. * n a connected circumstance.

concord n union; harmony.

concordance n agreement; a complete index.

concourse n a gathering; a crowd; a large area where crowds can gather.

concrete adj solid; real, not abstract. * n a mass of stones and mortar.

concretion n a compacted mass.

concur vi to unite; to agree.

concurrence n agreement; association; joint action.

concurrent adj happening at the same time; agreeing; attendant.

concussion n a violent shock especially of an explosion or heavy blow; unconsciousness due to a heavy blow to the head.

condemn vt to censure; to sentence.

condemnatory adj condemning.

condensation n act of condensing; state of being condensed; an abridgement.

condense vt to compress; to liquefy; to reduce by cutting especially of text or speech.

condenser n a chamber in which steam is condensed; a vessel for condensing or accumulating electricity.

condescend vi to stoop; to deign; to be patronizing.

condescension n graciousness; patronizing behaviour.

condiment n seasoning or spice.

condition n state; case; stipulation; illness.

conditioned adj depending; relative; displaying learned behaviour.

condole vi to sympathize.

condolence n expression of sympathy.

condone vt to pardon.

conducive adj leading to; contributing to.

conduct n behaviour; management; escort. * vt to lead; to manage; to behave; to direct an orchestra; to transmit e.g. heat or electricity.

conduction n property by which bodies transmit heat or electricity.

conductor n a leader; a director of an orchestra; one who is in charge of a train.

conduit n a channel; a subway for pipes.

cone n a pointed figure with a circular base; the fruit of firs, etc.

confection n a mixture; a sweetmeat.

confectioner n a maker of sweetmeats.

confederacy n a league.

confederate adj allied. * n an ally; a fellow conspirator. * vti to unite.

confederation n a league of states.

confer vi to consult together. * vt to give or bestow.

conference n a meeting for consultation.

confess vt to own; to admit. * vi to make a confession.

confessedly adv avowedly.

confession n the act of confessing; a creed.

confessional n the place where a priest hears confessions.

confessor n a priest who hears confession.

confidant nm **confidante** nf a trusted friend.

confide vi, vt to trust wholly; to entrust.

confidence n trust; assurance.

confidential adj private; privy to secrets.

confidently adv with assurance.

confiding adj trusting.

configuration n shape brought about by arranging of parts.

confine n a boundary. * vt to restrain; to shut up.

confinement n imprisonment; childbirth.

confirm vt to ratify; to coroborate; to admit to comminion in church.

confirmation n proof; the receiving into full communion.

confirmatory adj corroborative.

confirmed adj fixed; settled.

confiscable adj liable to forfeiture.

confiscate vt to seize as forfeit.

conflagration n a great fire.

conflict n a struggle; a fight; strife; an emotional upset. * vi to be at variance.

conflicting adj contradictory.

confluence n a flowing together; the meeting of streams.

confluent adj mingling.

conform vti to adapt; to comply.

conformation n structure.

conformity n agreement; likeness; keeping to established rules.

confound vt to confuse; to astound; to overthrow.

confront vt to face; to oppose; to challenge face to face.

confuse vt to mix together; to derange; to perplex; to embarass.

confusion n disorder.

confute vt to disprove.

congeal vt to coagulate; to thicken.

congenial adj kindred; having like natures or tastes; compatible.

congenital adj hereditary.

congested adj overcrowded; clogged with blood etc; blocked.

congestion n undue fullness (esp. of blood); overcrowding; a blockage of traffic.

conglomerate adj stuck together in a mass.

conglomeration n a mixed mass.

congratulate vt to compliment; to felicitate.

congratulatory adj complimentary.

congregate vti to meet together.

congregation n an assembly.

Congregationalism n the form of church

government where each separate church managing its own affairs.

congress n an assembly; the legislature of the United States.

congressional adj pertaining to a congress.

congruence, congruency n agreement; suitability.

congruent adj suitable; agreeing; corresponding.

congruous adj accordant; corresponding; appropriate.

conic, conical adj cone-like; cone-shaped.

coniferous adj bearing cones.

conjectural adj reading an opion by guesswork.

conjecture n supposition. * vt to surmise.

conjoin vt to unite.

conjoint adj united.

conjugal adj pertaining to marriage.

conjugate vt to inflect (a verb). * adj joined in pairs.

conjugation n the inflection of verbs.

conjunction n connexion; a connecting word.

conjunctive adj uniting

conjuncture n a crisis.

conjure vt to summon up by magic. * vi to juggle.

conjurer, conjuror n one who entertains with magic tricks and juggling.

connect vt to join; to associate; to link by telephone; to transfer from one vehicle to another to continue journey.

connective adj binding together. * n a conjunction.

connection, connexion n a relation by blood or marriage; relationship; the vehicle timed to connect with another.

connive vi to concur in a wrong.

connoisseur n an expert; a judge of fine arts.

connotation n the implied meaning; the resultant meaning.

conquer vt to gain by force; to vanquish. * vi to overcome.

conqueror n a victor.

conquest n subjugation; that which is conquered.

conscience n the sense of right and wrong.

conscientious adj high principled; regulated by conscience; thorough; diligent.

conscious adj aware; sensible of.

consciousness n awareness.

conscript n one compulsorily enrolled to serve in the army or navy.

conscription n a compulsory enrolment for military or naval service.

consecrate vt to set apart for sacred use; to dedicate.

consecutive adj following in order.

consent n concurrence; agreement; permission. * vi to assent; to acquiesce; to permit.

consequence n result; inference; importance.

consequent adj following; resulting.

consequential adj pompous.

conservancy n a board controlling a port, fishery, countryside, etc.

conservation n preservation especially of the environment and natural resources.

conservative adj averse to change. * n one opposed to political changes; a Tory.

conservatory n a greenhouse.

conserve vt to keep in a sound state; to keep safe; to preserve or pickle food.

consider vti to think on; to ponder; to weigh up; to examine.

considerable adj worth considering; fairly large.

considerate adj thoughtful of others.

consideration n serious deliberation.

considering prep in view of; allowing for; seeing that.

consign vt to hand over to another.

consignee n the person to whom goods are consigned.

consigner n one who consigns.

consignment n goods consigned.

consist vi to be composed of.

consistency n a degree of density or firmness; harmony; being true to one's previous ideas, behaviour etc.

consistent adj fixed; compatible; reliably unchanging in deed or thought.

consolation n solace; a comfort.

consolatory adj giving consolation.

console vt to comfort.

consolidate vt to make solid; to strengthen.

consonance n concord; agreement.

consonant adj accordant; consistent. * n a letter or sound that is not a vowel.

consort n a partner; a wife or husband; a companion. * vi to associate with unsuitable people; to agree; to accord.

consortium n a combining for a special purpose.

conspicuous adj outstanding; noticable.

conspiracy n a plot.

conspire vi to plot together.

constable n a policeman or woman of the lowest rank.

constabulary n the body of constables.

constancy n steadfastness.

constant adj steadfast; faithful. * n a fixed quantity.

constellation n a group of stars.

consternation n dismay.

constipation n difficulty in moving the bowels.

constituency n the body of voters; the voters of an area.

constituent adj component; being a part of a whole. * n an elector; one essential part of a whole.

constitute vt to set up; to compose; to appoint.

constitution n the condition of the body; a system of government.

constitutional adj of, pertaining to a constitution; legal. * n a walk taken for one's health.

constrain vt to force; to necessitate; to restrain; to imprison.

constrained adj forced; embarassed.

constraint n necessity; embarassment; inhibition; confinement.

constrict vt to contract; to compress; to limit free movement.

constriction n contraction; a feeling of tightness; compression.

construct vt to build; to devise.

construction n a structure; meaning; interpretation.

constructive adj having ability to construct; develop; improve.

construe vt to arrange words so as to discover the sense of a sentence; to interpret.

consul n a state agent in foreign towns.

consulate n the office or residence of a consul.

consult vi, vt to take counsel; to consider; to seek advice.

consultant n a consulting physician.

consultation n a seeking of advice from a doctor or lawyer.

consume vt, vi to eat or drink; to destroy; to use up; to squander.

consumer n one who buys goods and uses services.

consummate vt to finish, to perfect. * adj complete; perfect.

consummation n end; perfection.

consumption n expenditure.

contact n a touching together; close union; a business aquaintance; one who has been close to a person with a contagious disease. * vt to get in touch with.

contagious adj infectious, spread by touch.

contain vt to hold; to restrain.

contaminate vt to corrupt; to pollute.

contamination n pollution.

contemplate vt to meditate on; to intend.

contemplation n meditation.

contemplative adj thoughtful.

contemporaneous adj concurrent.

contemporary adj belonging to the same time. * n one who lives at the same time; a person of the same age.

contempt n scorn; disregard.

contemptible adj mean; worthy of contempt.

contemptuous adj scornful.

contend vi to strive; to vie; to dispute.

content adj satisfied. * vt to please; to satisfy. * n satisfaction; capacity; (pl) the things held by a container.

contented adj satisfied.

contention n a struggle; a quarrel.

contentious adj quarrelsome.

contest vt, vi to call in question; to strive; to contend; to emulate. * n a competition.

context n the setting (of a passage).

contiguity n the nearness.

contiguous adj touching; adjacent.

continent adj chaste; moderate; able to control urination and defecation.

continent n a large mass of land; the mainland of Europe.

contingency *n* a possible event; accident.

contingent *adj* incidental; conditional; that may happen. * *n* a quota; a detachment of troops; a possible happening.

continual *adj* incessant.

continuance *n* duration.

continue *vi* to remain; to persevere. * *vt* to prolong; to extend.

continuity *n* unbroken sequence; the whole script and scenario of a film.

continuous *adj* uninterrupted.

contort *vt* to twist; to pull out of shape.

contortion *n* a twisting out of shape.

contortionist *n* an entertainer who twists his body into unnatural positions.

contour *n* outline; form; a line on a map joining all points at the same height above sea level.

contraband *n* smuggled goods.

contract *vt* to reduce; to incur; to shorten (a word); to be affected by a disease. * *vi* to shrink; to make a mutual agreement. * *n* an agreement; abond.

contraction *n* shrinking; a shortening; tensing of a muscle.

contractor *n* a firm that arranges sale of materials or goods or manpower.

contradict *vt* to deny; to say the contrary.

contradictory *adj* inconsistent.

contralto *n* the lowest voice of a woman.

contraption *n* a devise; a gadget; an improvised or complicated contrivance.

contrary *adj* opposite; adverse; opposed; perverse. * *n* the opposite.

contrast *vt* to set in opposition; to show up the differences in. * *vi* to stand in contrast to * *n* opposition; difference.

contravene *vt* to oppose; to transgress.

contravention *n* violation.

contribute *vt* to give; to write magazine articles; to make suggestions.

contribution *n* something given; a gift.

contributor *n* one who contributes; a writer to a periodical.

contributory *adj* aiding; partly responsible for.

contrite *adj* penitent.

contrition *n* sorrow for sin; repentance.

contrivance *n* a scheme; a plan; an invention, often mechanical.

contrive *vt* to invent; to devise; to achieve, often by unusual means.

control *n* restraint; authority; a standard to compare with and check against. * *vt* to regulate; to be in command.

controller *n* a supervisor of public accounts.

controversial *adj* disputable.

controversy *n* a dispute.

contusion *n* a severe bruise.

conundrum *n* a riddle.

convalesce *vi* to recover health.

convalescence *n* gradual recovery after illness.

convalescent *n* one recovering from sickness.

convene *vi* to assemble; to call a meeting. * *vt* to convoke.

convenience *n* ease; comfort; something useful and labour saving; a public lavatory.

convenient *adj* suitable.

convent *n* a monastery; a nunnery.

convention *n* an assembly; an agreement; a recognized social custom.

conventional *adj* customary; unoriginal; following accepted rules.

converge *vi* to tend to the same point.

convergent *adj* approaching; meeting; arriving at the same point or result.

conversant *adj* familiar with; versed in.

conversation *n* easy talk.

conversationalist *n* a good talker.

conversazione *n* a social meeting.

converse *vi* to talk familiarly. * *n* conversation; the very opposite.

conversion *n* a change of religion, party, etc.; an alteration to a building.

convert *vti* to transform; to change. * *n* one who has changed his opinion, practice, or religion.

convertible *adj* transformable * *n* a car with a folding or detachable roof.

convex *adj* curved outwards.

convey *vt* to transport; to carry; to transfer especially the title of a property; to make known.

conveyance *n* any means of transport; a transference of property by deed.

convict *vt* to prove to be guilty. * *n* a criminal undergoing sentence.

conviction *n* a proving guilty; a strong

belief.

convince vt to persuade; to satisfy.

convincing adj conclusive; believable beyond doubt.

convivial adj festive; jovial; sociable.

convolute, convoluted adj rolled, coiled on itself; invloved; difficult to follow.

convolution n a winding; a spiral.

convoy vt to escort. * n a protecting force of ships or vehicles.

convulse vt to agitate violently * vi to cause spasms of helpless laughter.

convulsion n a shaking fit; a disturbance.

convulsive adj spasmodic.

cook vt to prepare food; to concoct. * n one who prepares food.

cookery n the art of preparing food.

cool adj moderately cold; self-possessed. * vt to make cool.

coolly adv with assurance.

coolness n calm assurance.

coop n a cage or pen for poultry.

cooper n one who makes barrels.

cooperage n the work or workshop of a cooper.

cooperate vi to act, work together with another.

cooperation n copartnership.

cooperative adj operating jointly; helpful.

coopt vt to elect into a body, committee etc. by vote of its members.

coordinate adj equal in rank. * vt to arrange in the same order; to integrate.

coordination n act of coordinating; harmonious movement of parts of the body.

cope vt to cover; to grapple (with); to manage something successfully.

copestone n the topmost stone.

copier, copyist n a transcriber; a machine that makes copies; an imitator.

coping n the topmost course of a wall, etc.

copious adj abundant.

copper n a reddish metal.

copperplate n an engraver's plate; the print from it; perfect handwriting.

coppersmith n one who works in copper.

coppice, copse n a thicket.

copulate vi to have sexual intercourse.

copulative adj that unites. * n a conjunction.

copy n an imitation; matter to be set up in type. * vt to imitate; to transcribe.

copyright n the sole right to publish (a book, etc).

coquetry n flirtation.

coracle n a boat made of skin-covered wickerwork.

coral n a sea rock built up from the skeletons of minute organisms.

cord n a thin rope; a band.

cordial adj hearty. * n a refreshing drink.

cordiality n heartiness.

cordon n a line or chain of police or soldiers barring entry to an area; a knight's ribbon.

corduroy n a thick cotton stuff corded or ribbed.

core n the heart; the essence; the seed-bearing centre of fruit; the centre of the earth below the mantle.

co-respondent n a joint respondent in divorce proceedings.

cork n a tree or its bark; a stopper. * vt to stop with a cork.

corm n a bulb-shaped root.

corn n grain (as wheat, oats, etc); a horny growth on the foot.

cornea n the transparent membrane over the eye.

corned adj salted.

corner n an angle; the place where two lines, sides, streets etc. meet; a difficult or dangerous position; a free kick from the corner of the pitch in football, hockey; a nook.

cornerstone n the indispensable stone, part, or basis.

cornet n a brass instrument of the trumpet family; a cone-shaped wafer for ice cream.

cornice n the upper moulding of a column, a room, a wall, etc.

cornucopia n the horn plenty full of fruit and vegetables.

corolla n the inner envelope; the petals of a flower.

corollary n an additional inference from a proved proposition.

corona n the halo round the sun in total eclipse; a circle of florets.

coronation n the ceremony of crowning.

coroner n an officer who holds an inquest in a case of sudden death.

corporal n the lowest noncommissioned officer. * adj pertaining to the body; physical; material.

corporate adj formed into a legal body; united; joint.

corporately adv in a corporate capacity.

corporation n a body corporate, empowered to act as an individual.

corporeal adj material; not spiritual.

corps n a body of troops.

corpse n the dead body of a human being.

corpulence n excessive fatness.

corpulent adj portly; fat.

corpuscle n a red or white blood cell in the body.

corpuscular adj pertaining to corpuscles.

corral n a pen for cattle; an enclosure or stockade.

correct adj right. * vt to make right; to chastise.

corrective adj intended to correct * n that which corrects; restriction.

correlate vi to be reciprocally related. * vt to determine the relations between.

correlation n reciprocal relation.

correlative adj having a mutual relation, as father and son. * n a word that relates to another word, as: either and or.

correspond vi to be like or similar; to agree; to write to.

correspondence n agreement; exchange or writing of (letters, etc).

corridor n a passage in a building or train linking rooms, compartments, etc.

corroborate vt to strengthen; to confirm.

corroboration n confirmation.

corrode vt to eat or wear away by degrees; to rust.

corrosion n wearing away through chemical action.

corrosive adj gnawing; blighting. * n a corroding agent.

corrugate vt to wrinkle; to fold into parallel ridges.

corrugated adj wrinkled; ridged.

corrupt vt to taint morally; to infect; to bribe. * vi to become debased or vitiated. * adj tainted; depraved.

corruptible adj subject to decay, destruction, debasement.

corruption n act or process of corrupting; depravity; bribery.

corset n a close-fitting undergarment supporting the lower body.

cortége n a train of attendants; a funeral procession.

cortex n the bark of a tree; a membrane.

coruscate vi to flash; to glitter.

corvette n an escort ship of war.

cosy adj snug. * n a teapot cover.

cosmetic n a skin beautifier. * adj beautifying; correcting; improving.

cosmic adj relating to the universe.

cosmography n a description of the world.

cosmology n the science of the world or the universe.

cosmonaut n a Russian astronaut.

cosmopolitan, cosmopolite n a citizen of the world; a much travelled person; someone without national prejudices. * adj unprejudiced.

cosmos n the universe and its system.

cost vt to be bought for; to set a price on; to cause. * n charge; price; trouble.

costal adj pertaining to the ribs.

costive adj constipated.

costume n an established mode of dress; garb; attire; clothing worn by actors.

costumier n a dealer in costumes.

cot n a small house; a small bed.

coterie n a small social group of people with like interests; a clique.

cottage n a small house.

cotton n a soft substance in the pods of several plants; cloth made of cotton.

cotton wool n cotton in the raw state bleached and sterilized.

couch vt to express in specific language or mode of speech. * n a bed; a sofa.

couchant adj lying down.

cough n a noisy explosion of air from the lungs. * vt, vi to make a violent effort to expel the air from the lungs.

could past tense of **can** was able.

council n an assembly; a governing or advisory body elected or appointed.

councillor n a member of a council.

counsel n deliberation; advice; design; a

barrister. * vt to advise; to recommend.

counsellor n an adviser; a barrister.

count vt to number; to judge. * vi to reckon; to rely on; to matter or be of importance; to mark time. * n reckoning.

countenance n the face; air; aspect; favour. * vt to favour.

counter n a shop table; (pl) tokens for card games. * vt to parry. * adj rival; opposite.

counteract vt to act in opposition to; to hinder; to check; to neutralize.

counterbalance vt to weigh against with an equal weight or power.

counterfeit vt, vi to forge; to copy; to feign. * adj fraudulent. * n a forgery.

counterfoil n a part of a cheque, etc, kept for reference.

countermand vt to annul a former command. * n a contrary order.

counterpane n a bedcover.

counterpart n a corresponding part or person; a duplicate.

counterpoint n the art of musical composition; the sounding or playing of two or several melodies or parts at the same time.

countersign vt to sign with an additional signature. * n a password.

countess n the wife of an earl or count.

countless adj innumerable.

country n a large tract of land; a region; a kingdom or state; the public; rural parts. * adj rural.

country dance n a folk dance usually with partners facing each other in line.

county n a shire or division of a country.

coup n a stroke or blow; a masterstroke.

coupé n a four seater closed car with two doors and a sloped back.

couple n a pair; a brace; a man and his wife. * vt, vi to unite; to copulate.

couplet n two lines that rhyme.

coupling n the links connecting railway carriages or machine parts.

coupon n a ticket entitling holder to some money, service, or privilege.

courage n bravery.

courageous adj bold; fearless.

courier n an express messenger.

course n a running; a passage; a route; career; ground run over; line of conduct; a track; a series of lectures, etc; range of subjects taught; a layer of stones in masonry; part of a meal served at one time.

court n an enclosed area; the retinue of a sovereign; judges in session; flattery. * vt to woo; to flatter; to seek.

courteous adj polite.

courtesy n politeness.

courtier n an attendant at a royal court.

courtliness n dignity mingled with graciousness.

courtly adj dignified.

court martial n (pl **courts martial**) a court to try military or naval offences.

courtship n wooing.

cousin n the child of an uncle or aunt.

cove n a small inlet.

covenant n a contract; a compact. * vi, vt to enter into a formal agreement.

cover vt to overspread; to cloak; to shelter; to defend; to wrap up; to brood on; to include; to understudy; to write a newspaper report. * n a cloak; disguise; shelter; insurance against loss etc.

coverlet n the cover of a bed.

covert adj secret; private. * n a shelter.

covet vt to desire eagerly; to envy.

covetous adj grasping; greedy.

cow n a female of domestic cattle, whale, elephant etc. * vt to terrorise; to dishearten; to intimidate.

coward n one who is not brave.

cowardice n timidity.

cower vi to crouch; to waver or tremble through fear.

cowl n a monk's hood; a covering over a chmney to aid ventilation.

cowpox n an eruption on the teats of cows from which the smallpox vaccine is obtained.

coxcomb n a fop; a vain fellow.

coxswain n the person who steers a boat or has charge of a ship's boat.

coy adj shy; reserved.

crab n a crustacean; a sign of the zodiac.

crabbed adj perverse.

crack n a chink; a sudden sharp sound; a sounding blow; a chat. * vt, vi to split; to break; to open a safe forcibly; to open a bottle; to make a joke; to decipher a code; to chat; to give in under pressure.

cracker n a small firework; a hard biscuit.

crackle vi to make small sharp noises.

cradle n an infant's bed on rockers; a framework under a ship for launching or suppporting it; a frame for a broken limb. * vt to lay or rock in a cradle.

craft n ability; guile; manual art; trade; a ship or aircraft.

craftily adv artfully; cunningly.

craftsman n an skilled worker.

crafty adj cunning.

crag n a steep rugged rock.

cram vti to stuff; to coach for an examination.

cramp n a spasmodic contraction of a muscle; a clamp. * vt to affect with spasms; to restrain; to hamper.

cramped adj restrained; restricted; of handwriting, small and hard to read.

crane n a long-legged, long-necked bird; a machine for raising heavy weights. * vi to stretch out one's neck.

cranial adj relating to the skull.

cranium n the skull.

crank n a contrivance for producing a horizontal or perpendicular motion by means of a rotary motion, or the contrary; a bend or turn; a fadist. * adj liable to be overset; loose. * vt to wind.

cranny n a chink.

crash vi to fall with a clatter; to collide with or fall violently; to gatecrash. * n a noise of breakage; a collapse esp. financial; a failure; a violent impact or descent.

crass adj gross; dense; stupid.

crate n a wooden packing case.

crater n the bowl-shaped mouth of a volcano; a hole or depression caused by a bomb or meteor explosion.

cravat n a neckcloth.

crave vt to ask earnestly; to have an intensely strong desire for.

craven n a coward. * adj cowardly.

craving n a morbid desire.

craw n the crop of fowls.

crawl vi to creep on hands and knees; to be servile towards. * n a crawling motion; slow motion; a swimming stroke.

crayon n a pencil of coloured chalk; a coloured drawing.

craze vt to shatter; to derange. * vi to become crazy. * n an inordinate desire or enthusiasm; a passing fashion.

crazy adj deranged.

creak vi to make a grating sound. * n a sharp, grating sound.

cream n the oily part of milk from which butter is made; the best of anything. * vt to take off cream from.

creamery n a place where milk is made into butter and cheese.

crease n a mark made by folding; the lines marking the batman's stance (in cricket). * vt to make creases in.

create vt to make out of nothing; to cause to be; to shape; to invent; to appoint.

creation n the universe; an original work of any kind.

creative adj original; imaginative.

creator n the Supreme Being; a producer.

creature n a human being; a mere tool.

crèche n a public nursery for children.

credence n credit; trust.

credential n warrant; voucher (pl) testimonials.

credibility n reliability.

credible adj worthy of belief.

credit n belief; reputed integrity; transfer of goods on trust; side of an account in which payment is entered; money possessed or at one's disposal; distinction given to an examinee for good marks. * vt to trust; to believe; to sell or lend in trust.

creditable adj estimable; praiseworthy.

creditor n one to whom a debt is due.

credulity n simplicity; overtrustfulness.

credulous adj easily imposed on.

creed n belief.

creek n a small bay.

creel n a fisherman's basket.

creep vi to crawl; to move stealthily; to be servile; to shiver.

creeper n a creeping plant.

cremate vt to consume by burning.

creosote n an oily liquid, antiseptic and wood preservative.

crepuscular adj pertaining to twilight.

crescent *n* a figure shaped like the new moon. * *adj* increasing.

crest *n* a tuft on the head of certain birds; the plume of feathers on a helmet; a device or symbol of a family or office; the top of a hill.

crestfallen *adj* dejected.

cretaceous *adj* chalky.

cretin *n* one afflicted with deficiency of thyroid hormone resulting in mental retardation.

crevice *n* a cleft; a fissure.

crew *n* a company; a gang; the personnel of a ship or aircraft.

crib *n* a child's bed; a small habitation; a rack; a stall for cattle; a literal translation or list of answers often used illicitly by students in examinations. * *vt* to confine; to pilfer; to copy illicitly.

crick *n* a cramp in the neck.

cricket *n* a chirping insect; a game played with bat and ball at a wicket.

crime *n* a breach of law.

criminal *adj* guilty; wicked. * *n* a malefactor; one who has broken the law.

crimp *vt* to curl; to seize; to pinch or fold together.

crimson *n* a deep red colour. * *adj* of a deep red. * *vt* to dye a deep red colour. * *vi* to blush.

cringe *vi* to fawn; to crouch.

crinkle *vi* to wrinkle. * *vt* to be corrugated or crimped. * *n* a wrinkle.

cripple *n* a lame person. * *vt* to lame; to disable.

crisis *n* (*pl* **crises**) a turning point; a critical moment; an emergency.

crisp *adj* brittle; friable; fresh and bracing. * *n* a thin potato chip.

criterion *n* (*pl* **criteria**) a standard; a rule regarded as a measure of judgment.

critic *n* a judge; a reviewer; a censor.

critical *adj* skilled in judging; crucial; exacting.

criticism *n* the art or act of judging or the exposition of it.

criticize *vi, vt* to judge critically; to censure.

critique *n* a review.

croak *vi* to make a low hoarse noise in the throat. * *n* the cry of raven or frog.

crochet *n* a type of knitting, some with a hooked needle.

crock *n* an earthen vessel; a pot.

crockery *n* china dishes; earthenware pots.

croft *n* a small plot of land with a farmhouse.

crone *n* an old woman.

crony *n* a familiar friend.

crook *n* a bend; a hooked staff; a shepherd's staff; a pastoral staff; a dishonest person; a swindler.

crooked *adj* bent; deceitful.

crop *n* the stomach or craw of birds; grain while growing; a riding whip. * *vt* to clip or cut short; to browse; to cultivate; (with **up**) to appear unexpectedly.

crop-eared *adj* having the ears cut short.

croquet *n* an open-air game played with mallets, balls and hoops.

croquette *n* a ball of mashed potato, meat or fish fried until brown.

cross *n* two straight lines crossing each other; a monument in the form of a cross; the symbol of the Christian religion; the meeting place of roads, the town centre; adversity. * *vt* to mark with a cross; to pass over; to intersect; to cancel; to vex or thwart. * *adj* peevish.

crossbow *n* a bow fixed crosswise on a stock.

crossbreed *n* a mixed breed.

cross-examination *n* the examination of a witness by the opposing lawyer.

cross-purpose *n* a contrary purpose or aim; a misunderstanding.

cross-question *vt* to cross-examine.

crossroad *n* a road that crosses another; (*pl*) the point where two roads cross.

cross section *n* a surface exposed after cutting a solid at right angles to its length; a representative group (of people) chosen at random.

crosswise *adv* transversely.

crossword *n* a word puzzle on a grid with clues in which words reading down must fit in with those reading across.

crotch *n* the part of the body where the legs fork; the area of the genitals.

crotchet *n* a note in music; a half a minim.

crotchety *adj* perverse; bad-tempered.

crouch vi to bend low; to squat.

croupier n the dealer at a gaming table.

crow n a large black bird with croaking voice; the cock's cry. * vi to make the cry of a cock; to exult.

crowbar n a bar of iron used as a lever.

crowd n a throng. * vt to press together. * vi to throng.

crown n royal headgear; a king's power and symbol of office; the completion; the top of the head; a wreath or garland; a reward; the centre of a road; the upper part of a tooth. * vt to invest with a crown; to adorn; to perfect.

crowning adj highest; final.

crow's-feet npl the wrinkles about the eyes.

crucial adj decisive; critical.

crucible n a vessel or pot for heating substances to high temperatures.

crucifix n a figure of Christ upon the cross.

Crucifixion n the death of Christ.

cruciform adj cross-shaped.

crucify vt to put to death by nailing to a cross.

crude adj raw; unripe; rough; vulgar.

cruel adj unmerciful; harsh; fierce.

cruelty n severity; barbarity.

cruet n a small bottle for holding oil, vinegar etc.

cruise vi to sail hither and thither; to travel at a moderate speed. * n a sailing to and fro; a pleasure voyage.

cruiser n a swift armed warship.

crumb n a fragment; a small piece.

crumble vti. to break into small fragments; to pulverize; to decay.

crumple vt, vi to press into wrinkles; to crease; to collapse.

crunch vt to crush between the teeth.

crusade n an enterprise or serious activity to further a cause.

crush vt to squeeze; to bruise; to overpower; to stamp out. * vi to press forward. * n a crowding; an infatuation.

crushing pa overwhelming.

crust n the hard outer coating of anything. * vt, vi to cover with a crust.

crustacea npl a general name for jointed shellfish.

crusty adj covered with a crust; surly.

crutch n a stick with armpit or arm rests to support the body and allow mobility to a lame person; the crotch.

crux n the crucial or deciding point.

cry vi to utter the loud shrill sounds of weeping, joy, etc; to weep. * vt to proclaim. * n a shriek or scream; weeping; an appeal for help; a catchword.

crypt n an underground vault used as chapel or burial place.

cryptic adj hidden; secret; mysterious.

cryptogram n secret characters or cipher.

crystal n pure transparent quartz; articles made of this; the geometrical form assumed by certain bodies in solidifying.

crystallize vti to form into crystals.

cub n the young of the bear, fox, etc; a junior boy scout.

cube n a regular solid body, with six equal square sides; the third power of a number. * vt to raise to the third power.

cubic, cubical adj cube-shaped.

cubicle n a compartment with a bed partitioned off in a dormitory.

cubism n a style of painting representing subjects from different viewpoints at the same time using geometrical shapes, cubes etc.

cud n the food which ruminants bring up to chew again.

cuddle vt to hug closely; to curl up comfortably.

cudgel n a short thick stick.

cue n the last words of an actor's speech as a sign to a following actor; catchword; hint; the straight rod used in billiards.

cuff n a blow; a slap; part of a sleeve near the hand. * vt to beat with the fist or open hand.

cuisine n style of cooking.

cul-de-sac n a blind alley.

culinary adj relating to cookery.

cull vt to gather; to reduce numbers of certain animals by killing.

culminate vi to reach the highest point.

culmination n the highest point; acme

culpability n blame; guilt.

culpable adj blameworthy.

culprit n an accused person; a criminal.

cult n a system of worship often with special or secret rites.

cultivate vt to till; to refine; to civilize.

culture n refinement; appreciation of the arts; the whole range of skills of a people at a certain period; artificial rearing of bees, bacteria, etc.

cultured adj educated; refined.

culvert n an arched waterway or drain.

cumbersome adj burdensome; awkward; heavy.

cumin, cummin n an aromatic plant.

cummerbund n a girdle or waistband.

cumulate vt to heap together.

cumulative adj growing by additions.

cumulus n (pl **cumuli**) a cloud formation resembling snowy mountains.

cuneiform adj wedge-shaped

cunning adj astute; crafty. * n craftiness.

cup n a small drinking vessel with a handle; its contents; a cup-shaped trophy often silver or ornamental.

cupboard n a shelved cabinet for crockery, food, etc.

cupidity n a longing to posess; avarice.

cur n a mongrel dog; a low fellow.

curate n an assistant clergyman.

curative adj tending to cure.

curator n a superintendent; a custodian.

curb vt to control; to check. * n a check; part of a bridle; the edge of the pavement; the kerb.

curd n coagulated milk. * vt, vi to curdle; to congeal.

curdle vti to change into curds; to thicken.

cure n healing; a remedy. * vt to heal; to preserve food by salting, pickling etc.

curfew n an evening bell rung as a signal to put out lights.

curio n a curiosity.

curious adj inquisitive; strange; singular.

curl vt to form into ringlets. * vi to go into coils; to play at the game of curling. * n a ringlet of hair; a twist.

curling n a game played on ice with large, heavy, smooth stones.

currency n circulation; circulating medium; the time when a thing is currect or prevalent; the money used in a particular country.

current adj running; circulating. * n a running; a stream; progressive motion of water, electricity, etc.

curriculum n a course of study (at school, university, etc).

curriculum vitae n a (written) statement or summary of a person's career.

curry n a highly spiced sauce; a dish spiced with this. * vt to flavour with curry; to comb a horse; to seek (favour).

curse vt to call down evil on; to blight; to torment. * vi to swear. * n an oath.

cursed adj execrable; detestable.

cursive adj running; flowing. * n running script.

cursory adj hasty; careless; superficial.

curt adj short; rude; abrupt.

curtail vt to cut short; to cut down e.g. privileges.

curtain n a screen for a window, etc; the moving screen of a theatre stage; (pl) the end; death. * vt to enclose with curtains.

curtsy, curtsey n an obeisance or bow.

curvature n a curving.

curve n a bent line; an arch. * vt, vi to bend.

cushion n a pillow for a seat; the padded rim of a snooker table; any buffer against shock. * vt to furnish with cushions; to protect against; to lessen shock or impact.

cusp n a point or sharp horn, as of moon.

custard n a mixture of milk, eggs, and sugar prepared as a pudding or sauce.

custodian n a guardian; a keeper.

custody n care; security; imprisonment.

custom n habit; fashion; business patronage; (pl) duties on merchandise imported or exported.

customary adj habitual; usual.

customer n a regular purchaser at a shop or from a business.

cut vt to divide into pieces; to mow; to clip; to reduce prices etc. * vi to make an incision; to stop filming. * adj gashed. * n a wound; act of dividing a pack of cards; form; fashion or shape of a garment; a reduction in price; a share of gains etc.

cutaneous adj pertaining to the skin.

cuticle n the skin at the base of fingernails and toenails; epidermis.

cutlass n a broad, curving sword.

cutlery *n* instruments used for eating; forks, knives and spoons.

cutlet *n* a piece of meat cut off the ribs, leg or neck; a chop.

cutter *n* a light sailing vessel; a ship's boat; one who cuts cloth.

cutting *n* a piece cut off; an incision; a passage; a piece cut off a plant for propagating; an excerpt cut from a newspaper; film editing.

cyanide *n* a poisonous compound of cyanogen and a metal.

cycle *n* a period of time; a series; a bicycle. * *vi* to ride a bicycle.

cyclic, cyclical *adj* recurring in series.

cyclist *n* one who rides a bicycle.

cyclone *n* a storm moving in a circle; a hurricane.

cylinder *n* a solid or hollow roller-shaped body.

cymbal *n* a musical instrument of two brass plates which are clashed together.

cynic *n* a sneering, censorious person.

cynic, cynical *adj* sceptical; surly; sneering; captious.

cynicism *n* surliness; heartlessness.

cypher *n see* **cipher**.

cyst *n* a sac in animal bodies containing morbid matter.

czar, tsar *n* the former emperor of Russia.

Czech *n* a native of Czech Lands; the language.

D

dab *vt* to hit lightly with something soft or moist. * *n* a gentle blow; a small mass of anything soft or moist; an adept.

dabble *vt* to wet; to sprinkle; to move hands or feet in water. * *vi* to trifle.

dado *n* the decorative border round the lower part of the walls of a room.

dagger *n* a short sharp-pointed sword.

daily *adj* happening every day. * *adv* day by day. * *n* a newspaper published every weekday

dainty *adj* nice; delicate; elegant. * *n* a delicacy.

dairy *n* a place where milk is sold, or converted into butter or cheese.

dais *n* the high table where principal guests or speakers are seated; a raised platform.

dale *n* a valley.

dalliance *n* lovemaking; trifling.

dally *vi* to trifle; to delay; to lose time by idleness.

dam *n* a mother (of a four-footed animal.); a barrier to confine water. * *vt* to confine by a dam.

damage *n* hurt; injury; money; compensation. * *vt* to injure; to harm.

damask *n* a figured cloth, usually of silk or linen. * *adj* pink or rosy colour of the **damask rose**.

dame *n* a lady.

damn *vt* to condemn; to curse; to consign to eternal punishment.

damnation *n* condemnation.

damned *adj* hateful; detestable; consigned to hell.

damp *adj* moist; humid. * *n* moist air. * *vt* to moisten; to dispirit; to stifle.

dampness *n* moisture.

damsel *n* a girl.

dance *vi* to move in time to music; to skip or leap lightly. * *n* a party for dancing; a dance performance of an artistic nature; music for dancing.

dandruff *n* scurf on the head under the hair.

dandy *n* a fop; a coxcomb.

danger *n* risk; hazard; peril.

dangle *vi* to hang loose. * *vt* to swing.

dank *adj* damp; moist.

dapper *adj* small and neat.

dappled *adj* spotted.

dare *vti* to be bold; to defy; to venture on; to challenge. * *n* a challenge.

daredevil *n* a reckless fellow. * *adj* daring; bold.

daring *adj* bold; fearless. * *n* courage.

dark *adj* without light; gloomy; secret; ignorant; having brown or black skin or hair. * *n* darkness; ignorance.

darkness *n* absence of light; gloom.

darling *adj* dearly beloved. * *n* one much beloved.

darn *vt* to mend holes in clothes.

dart n a pointed missile thrown by the hand; a sudden bound. * vt to shoot. * vi to move rapidly; (pl) an indoor game in which darts are thrown at a target.

dash vti to shatter; to rush; to frustrate. * n a violent striking; a rushing or onset; a mark in writing (—); a small quantity of something added to food; a tinge.

dashboard n an instrument panel in a car.

dashing adj spirited; showy; stylish.

data see datum.

data processing n the analysis of information stored in a computer for various uses.

date n the time when any event happened; an appointment esp. with one of the opposite sex; era; age. * vt, vi to note the time of; to have origin to affix a date to.

dative adj, n. a grammatical case.

datum n (pl data) a fact granted as basis for further inference.

daub vt to smear; to paint without skill. * n poor painting; a smear.

daughter n a female child.

daughter-in-law n a son's wife.

daunt vt to intimidate; to scare; to cow.

dauntless adj fearless.

dawdle vi to waste time; to saunter.

dawn vi to grow light. * n the break of day; first appearance.

day n the time between the rising and setting of the sun; light; time; a particular period of success or influence.

daybreak n the dawn.

daydream n a reverie.

daylight n the light of the sun; dawn; a visible gap; a sudden realization or understanding.

daytime n the time of daylight.

daze vt to stupefy; to stun; to perplex. * n confusion; bewilderment esp. produced by a blow or a shock.

dazzle vt to overpower with light or splendour. * vi to be intensely bright.

deacon n a church official.

dead adj without life; perfectly still; cold; unerring; exact. * n stillness; gloom.

deadbeat adj quite exhausted.

deaden vt to make numb; to muffle.

dead-end n a cul-de-sac; a hopeless situation; a job without prospects.

dead heat n a race in which the competitors finish at the same time.

deadline n the time or date by which a thing must be done.

deadlock n a complete standstill; a clash of interests making progress inpossible.

deadly adj mortal; implacable.

deadpan adj deliberately expressionless.

dead weight n a heavy or oppressive burden; weight of a body without its load.

deaf adj unable to hear; inattentive.

deafen vt to stun with noise.

deaf-mute n a deaf and dumb person.

deal n an indefinite quantity; a business transaction; the distribution of playing cards. * vt to distribute; to behave; to do business with; to solve.

dealer n a trader; one who deals cards; a seller of illegal drugs.

dealing n conduct; behaviour; business.

dean n the head of the chapter of a cathedral; an officer in a university.

dear adj costly; valuable; beloved.

dearth n scarcity; want.

death n extinction of life; decease; the destruction of something.

deathless adj immortal.

death rate n the proportion of deaths in a town, country, etc.

debacle n a sudden break-up; a crash; a rout.

debar vt to shut out from something.

debase vt to lower; to degrade.

debate n a discussion; a formal argument; controversy. * vt, vi to dispute; to deliberate.

debauch vt to corrupt. * vi to revel. * n excess in eating or drinking.

debauched pa profligate.

debauchery n intemperance; depraved over-indulgence; corruption; lewdness.

debenture n interest-bearing bonds in return for a loan.

debilitate vt to enfeeble.

debility n weakness.

debit n a recorded item of debt; the lefthand page or debtor side of a ledger.

debonair adj sauve; carefree; sprightly.

debris n (sing or pl) fragments; rubbish; wreckage.

debt n what is owing; an obligation.

debtor n one who owes.

début n a first appearance in public.

decade n a period of ten years.

decadence n a falling off; decay; deterioration esp. of morality.

decamp vi to leave without notice.

decant vt to pour from one vessel into another.

decanter n a stoppered bottle in which wine is brought to table.

decapitate vt to behead.

decay vi to fall away; to waste; to wither; to fail. * n decline; putrefaction.

decease n death. * vi to die.

deceased adj dead.

deceit n fraud; guile; treachery.

deceive vt to mislead; to cheat.

December n the twelfth and last month of the year.

decency n propriety.

decent adj quite good; kind; generous.

decentralize vt to transfer power from the central to the local authority.

deception n the act or state of being deceived; fraud.

deceptive adj misleading; ambiguous.

decide vti to determine; to settle; to resolve; to give a judgment on.

deciduous adj (of trees) shedding all leaves annually.

decimal adj by tens; having 10 as the basis of numeration.

decimate vt to destroy a large number.

decipher vt to decode; to solve.

decision n determination of a judgment; verdict; firmness of character.

decisive adj conclusive; absolute.

deck vt to clothe; to adorn. * n the floor of a ship, aircraft, bus or bridge; a pack of playing cards; the turntable of a record-player; the ground.

declaim vi to make a formal speech; to harangue.

declamatory adj grandiloquent.

declaration n assertion; affirmation.

declare vti to make known; to assert; to admit possession of (dutiable goods).

declared adj avowed.

declension n a falling off; a downcome; the variation in form that nouns, etc, undergo.

decline vi to bend downwards; to swerve; to fail. * vt to refuse; to inflect a noun, etc.; to diminish; to draw to an end; to deviate. * n a falling off; decay; consumption.

declivity n a downward slope.

decode vt to decipher.

decompose vt to resolve into original elements. * vi to decay.

decomposition n analysis; decay.

décor n a general decorative effect or appearance esp. of a room.

decorate vt to adorn; to deck.

decoration n ornamentation; a mark or badge of honour.

decorative adj ornamental.

decorator n one who paints houses.

decorous adj seemly; becoming.

decorum n propriety; seemliness.

decoy n an animal or bird trained to lure others into a snare; one who lures others into a trap. * vt to lure into a snare.

decrease vi, vt to become or make less. * n a diminution; a reduction.

decree n an edict; an order or law. * vt to enact; to award.

decrepit adj broken down with age.

decry vt to cry down; to disparage.

dedicate vt to consecrate; to devote (often refl); to inscribe to a friend.

dedication n consecration; inscription or address.

deduce vt to infer; to arrive at by reasoning.

deduct vt to subtract from.

deduction n inference; discount.

deductive adj that is or may be deduced from premises.

deed n an act; feat; a written agreement.

deem vt to judge. * vi to be of opinion.

deep adj being far below the surface; involved; engrossed; profound; intense; secret; artful. * n the sea.

deepfreeze n a refrigerator in which food is frozen and stored.

deeply adv at a great depth; profoundly.

deer n (pl deer) a quadruped with antlers on the males.

deerstalking n the hunting of deer.

deface vt to disfigure; to erase.

defalcation n misappropriation of funds.

defamation n slander.

defame vt to slander.

default n an omission; neglect; absence; lapse. * vi to fail to meet payment or keep contract.

defaulter n one who fails to answer a summons or to make payment due.

defeat n overthrow; loss of battle; frustration of one's plans; loss of a game, race etc. * vt to frustrate; to conquer.

defect n a want; a blemish.

defection n abandonment of a person or cause.

defective adj faulty; incomplete.

defence n a protection; fortification; vindication; apology; plea; defending the goal etc. against attacks from the opposing side; the defending players in a team.

defenceless adj unprotected.

defend vt to guard; to support; to act as defendant.

defendant n one sued at law.

defensible adj justifiable.

defer vt to postpone. * vi to yield to another's opinion, wishes, judgment.

deference n regard; respect.

deferential adj respectful.

defiance n wilful disobedience; a challenge to fight; contempt of danger.

defiant adj bold; insolent; challenging.

deficiency n want; defect; deficit.

deficient adj defective; lacking.

deficit n shortage; the amount by which a sum falls short of what is needed; an excess of expenditure over income.

defile vt to pollute. * n a narrow pass.

define vt to limit; to explain exactly.

definite adj precise; exact.

definition n an explanation or description.

definitive adj limiting; positive; final.

deflate vt to release gas or air from; to reduce in size or importance; to reduce inflation in the economy.

deflect vi to deviate. * vt to turn aside.

deflection n deviation.

deflower vt to strip of flowers; to ravish.

defoliation n the shedding of leaves.

deform vt to disfigure.

deformed adj misshapen.

defraud vt to cheat.

defray vt to bear the charges of.

deft adj apt; clever; nimble.

defunct adj deceased; no longer functioning. * n a dead person.

defuse vt to disarm an explosive by removing its fuse; to decrease tension in a crisis or other situation

defy vt to dare; to challenge; to set at nought; to resist attempts at; to elude.

degeneracy n decline in good qualities.

degenerate vi to decline in good qualities. * adj depraved; base. * n a degenerate or immoral person.

degradation n a depriving of rank; disgrace; humiliation.

degrade vt to depose; to dishonour.

degraded adj debased; dishonoured.

degree n a step; rank; grade; measure; the 360th part of the circumference of a circle; a university distinction.

dehydrate vt to remove water from. * vi to lose water esp. from body tissue.

deify vt to make a god of; to idolize.

deign vi to condescend to give or do something.

deity n a god.

deject vt to dispirit; to depress.

dejected adj cast down; discouraged.

dejection n lowness of spirits.

delay vti to defer; to retard; to stop; to linger. * n a stay; a hindrance.

delectable adj delightful.

delegate vt to send as a representative; to depute. * n a representative; an agent.

delegation n a body of delegates.

delete vt to erase; to efface.

deleterious adj hurtful.

deliberate vi, vt to weigh well; to consider; to debate. * adj cautious; well advised; intentional.

deliberation n thoughtful consideration.

delicacy n refinement of taste; tenderness; a luxurious food.

delicate adj pleasing; fine; minute; tender; not robust.

delicious adj highly delightful esp. to the taste.

delight n great joy or pleasure. * vt, vi to charm; to take great pleasure.

delightful adj charming; giving pleasure.

delineate vt to draw in outline; to sketch.

delinquency n a fault; wrongdoing; a crime.

delinquent *adj* neglecting duty. * *n* culprit; an offender, esp. a young law breaker.

delirious *adj* raving; frenzied.

delirium *n* temporary disorder of the mind.

deliver *vt* to set free; to rescue; to hand over; to carry and distribute regularly; to give birth; to launch or throw.

deliverance *n* release; rescue; a legal judgment.

delivery *n* childbirth; rescue; distribution (of letters); manner of speaking; the act of giving birth; the bowling of a ball in cricket.

dell *n* a small valley.

delta *n* the space between diverging mouths of a river; the fourth letter of the Greek alphabet.

delude *vt* to deceive; to trick.

deluge *n* a flood; the flood; heavy rain. * *vt* to inundate; to drown.

delusion *n* a mistaken idea; a fallacy.

delusive *adj* deceptive.

delve *vti* to dig.

demagogue *n* a voluble political orator deriving power from appealing to popular prejudices.

demand *vt* to claim by right; to question. * *n* a claim, often urgent; a challenging; the desire shown by consumers for particular goods or services.

demarcation *n* a boundary; a fixed limit.

demean *vt* to lower in dignity; to debase.

demeanour *n* behaviour.

demented *adj* insane; infatuated.

demise *n* death; termination.

demit *vt* to resign (an office).

demobilize *vt* to discharge from the armed forces; to disband.

democracy *n* government by the people through elected representatives; political, social or legal equality.

democrat *n* a friend to popular government.

demolish *vt* to pull down; to defeat.

demon *n* an evil spirit.

demonstrable *adj* that may be demonstrated or proved.

demonstrate *vt* to prove beyond doubt; to exhibit * *vi* to show support for a cause by public protest and parades.

demonstration *n* proof; show of feeling; a display of feeling by public protest, mass meetings etc.

demonstrative *adj* open; unreserved.

demoralization *n* corruption; loss of morale.

demoralize *vt* to corrupt; to dispirit.

demur *vi* to hesitate; to object. * *n* pause; objection.

demure *adj* affectedly modest.

demy *n* a size of paper, generally 22 x 17 inches.

den *n* a cave; a dell; a lair of a wild beast.

denial *n* contradiction; refusal of a request; reluctance to admit the truth of something.

denim *n* a hard-wearing cloth esp. for jeans. (*pl*) trousers of this.

denomination *n* class; religious sect.

denominator *n* the divisor in a vulgar fraction.

denote *vt* to indicate; to imply; to mean.

dénouement *n* the unfolding, the final outcome of the plot in a play; the issue.

denounce *vt* to threaten; to condemn; to accuse publicly.

dense *adj* thick; close.

density *n* compactness; stupidity; the ratio of mass to volume.

dent *n* a mark made by a blow or pressure. * *vt* to mark.

dental *adj* pertaining to the teeth.

dentist *n* one qualified to treat disorders of the teeth.

denude *vt* to make bare; to strip.

denunciation *n* the utterance of a threat, censure or menace.

deny *vt* to contradict; to disavow.

deodorant *n* a preparation that masks unpleasant smells.

deodorize *vt* to rid of smell.

deoxidize *vt* to deprive of oxygen.

depart *vi* to go away; to deviate; to die.

department *n* a separate part; a division; a branch; a place of activity.

department store *n* a large shop with many departments each selling different types of goods.

departure *n* act of going away; withdrawal, death.

depend vi to hang from; to be reliant on; to trust.

dependant n one who depends on another; a retainer.

dependence n reliance; trust; subordination.

dependency n a subject territory.

dependent adj relying on; contingent.

depict vt to portray; to describe.

depilate vt to strip of hair.

deplete vt to empty; to exhaust.

deplorable adj shocking; pitiable.

deplore vt to regret deeply; to deprecate.

deploy vt to open out; to distribute and position strategically (soldiers etc).

depopulate vt to reduce the population of.

deport vt to expel (an undesirable person) from a country; to conduct (one's self).

deportation n banishment from a country.

deportment n carriage; behaviour.

depose vt to dethrone; to divest of office.

deposit vt to lay down; to lodge in a place. * n something deposited; money left in a bank; money left in earnest.

deposition n affidavit; testimony; displacement.

depot n a storehouse; a warehouse; a place for storing military supplies; a military training centre; a railway or bus station.

deprave vt to corrupt.

depraved adj profligate; perverted.

deprecate vt to disapprove of.

deprecation n disapproval.

depreciate vt to lower the value of; to undervalue. * vi to fall in value.

depreciation n a fall in value, esp. of an asset through wear and tear.

depress vt to press down; to deject.

depression n dejection; an economis phase characterized by stagnation, unemployment etc.; a lowering of atmospheric pressure; a hollow.

deprivation n want; bereavement.

deprive vt to take from; to dispossess.

deprived adj lacking the essentials of life, e.g. food, housing, education.

depth n deepness; a deep place; intensity; profoundness.

deputation n persons sent to act for others.

depute vt to appoint as a substitute.

deputy n a substitute; a representative.

derange vt to displace; to disorder; to unbalance; to make insane.

deranged adj distracted.

derelict adj abandoned. * n the thing or person abandoned.

dereliction n failure; wilful neglect.

deride vt to ridicule; to jeer.

derision n mockery.

derisive adj mocking.

derivation n source or origin.

derivative adj derived. * n a derivative word; an offshoot.

derive vti to obtain; to draw; to trace to its origin; to come from.

dermatology n the study of skin and its diseases.

derogatory adj disparaging.

descant n a discourse; a melody. * vi to sing; to discourse.

descend vi, vt to climb down; to invade; to be derived; to sink morally.

descendant n an heir; offspring.

descent n act of descending; declivity; invasion; lineage.

describe vt to portray; to relate.

description n a verbal account; relation; kind; sort.

descriptive adj graphic.

desecrate vt to violate a sacred place.

desecration n profanation.

desert adj waste. * n a sandy barren region.

desert vi to leave; to quit. * vi to run away esp. from the armed forces. * n virtue; merit.

deserter n a runaway.

deserve vti to merit.

deservedly adv justly.

desiccate vt to dry.

design vt to plan; to propose; to make working drawings for. * vi to intend. * n a drawing or sketch; purpose; aim.

designate vt to point out; to name; to mark; to appoint or nominate for a position.

designation n name; title; nomination.

designedly adv purposely.

designer n one who designs; a creator of high-class fashion clothes. * adj of the latest fashion or trend.

designing *adj* artful; scheming.

desirable *adj* longed for; advisable.

desire *n* longing; craving; love. * *vt* to wish for; to covet.

desist *vi* to stop; to leave off.

desk *n* a (sloping) table designed for writer's or reader's use; the section of a newspaper responsible for a particular topic.

desolate *adj* forlorn; forsaken; waste. * *vt* to lay waste.

desolation *n* ruin; gloom; loneliness.

despair *n* hopelessness. * *vi* to give up all hope.

despatch, dispatch *vt* to send away in haste; to kill; to perform quickly. * *n* an official message; speed.

desperate *adj* reckless; hopeless; urgently needing money; extreme; dangerous.

despicable *adj* contemptible.

despise *vt* to scorn; to disdain.

despite *prep* not withstanding; in spite of.

despoil *vt* to rob; to rifle; to plunder.

despondent *adj* dejected; hopeless.

despondency *n* dejection.

despot *n* a tyrant.

despotic *adj* autocratic.

dessert *n* the fruit or sweet course at the end of a meal.

destination *n* a goal; the place to which one is going.

destiny *n* fate; a predetermined course of events.

destitute *adj* in want; forlorn.

destitution *n* want.

destroy *vt* to pull down; to overthrow; to kill.

destroyer *n* a small swift warship to destroy submarines.

destruction *n* ruin; death; slaughter.

destructive *adj* ruinous causing destruction; negative or adverse (of criticism).

desultory *adj* casual; rambling.

detach *vt* to release.

detached *adj* separate; (of a house) not joined to another; aloof; unbiassed.

detachment *n* separation; a body of troops away from the main army.

detail *vt* to recount; to particularize; to set apart. * *n* an individual fact; an item; a

small part of a picture, statue etc.; a small detachment for special duties.

detailed *adj* minute; thorough.

detain *vt* to keep back; to arrest; to place in confinement.

detect *vt* to discover; to notice.

detective *n* a police officer whose duty is to detect criminals.

detention *n* act of detaining; confinement; being kept in (school) after hours.

deter *vt* to hinder; to discourage.

detergent *adj* cleansing; purging. * *n* a cleaning agent.

deteriorate *vi* to grow worse. * *vt* to depreciate.

determination *n* firm resolution; conclusion.

determine *vt* to bound; to fix permanently; to resolve; to bring to an end.

deterrent *n* a warning; a curb; a nuclear weapon to deter attack through fear of retaliation. * *adj* detering.

detest *vt* to abhor; to loathe.

detestable *adj* odious.

dethrone *vt* to depose.

detonate *vti* to explode.

detonation *n* an explosion.

detour *n* a roundabout way.

detract *vti* to disparage; to defame.

detractor *n* a slanderer; a muscle which detracts.

detriment *n* loss; damage.

devastate *vt* to lay waste; to overwhelm.

develop *vt* to unfold; to make visible; to make to grow; to treat a photographic film or plate to reveal an image. * *vi* to grow or expand.

development *n* growth; land or property that has been improved.

deviate *vi* to stray; to wander; to diverge.

device *n* a contrivance; an emblem.

devil *n* an evil spirit; Satan; a wicked person; a difficulty. * *vt* to pepper and broil. *vi*. to drudge for another, especially a barrister.

devilment *n* mischief.

devilry *n* extreme wickedness.

devious *adj* circuitous; deceitful; underhand.

devise *vt* to plan; to contrive; to invent.

devoid *adj* destitute; free from.

devolution *n* the transfer of duties or business to another.

devolve *vt* to transfer; to depute.

devote *vt* to dedicate; to give or use for a particular activity or purpose.

devoted *adj* zealous; attached; loyal.

devotion *n* consecration; attachment; strong affection; piety.

devour *vt* to eat ravenously; to swallow up; to absorb eagerly.

devout *adj* pious; sincere.

dew *n* atmospheric vapour deposited on cool surfaces at night.

dexterity *n* adroitness; skill.

dexterous *adj* skilful; expert.

dhow *n* an Arab trading vessel.

diabolic, diabolical *adj* fiendish.

diagnose *vt* to identify a disease from symptoms.

diagnosis *n* the identification of an illness from symptoms.

diagonal *adj* applied to a line drawn from corner to corner.

diagram *n* an illustrative figure in outline.

dial *n* a time recorder; the face of a clock; the numbered disc on some telephones for connecting some calls.

dialect *n* the form of a language peculiar to a province.

dialectic, dialectical *adj* relating to dialectics; pertaining to a dialect.

dialectics *npl* the art of reasoning; logical skill.

dialogue *n* a conversation between two or more.

diameter *n* the line passing through or across the centre (esp. of a circle).

diamond *n* the most valuable of gems; a suit of playing cards; the playing field in baseball.

diaphragm *n* the midriff, a muscle separating thorax and abdomen; a disc or plate closing partly or wholly a tube; a contraceptive cap.

diarrhoea *n* looseness of the bowels.

diary *n* a daily record of events.

diastole *n* dilation of the heart in beating.

diatribe *n* a tirade.

dice *see* **die**.

dictaphone *n* an instrument for recording and reproducing speech.

dictate *vt* to read for reproduction by another person or by a recording machine; to prescribe; to order.

dictation *n* act, art, or practice of dictating; command.

dictator *n* one invested with absolute authority.

diction *n* a way of speaking or enunciating; a choice of words.

dictionary *n* a book with the words of a language arranged alphabetically, with their meanings, pronunciations etc.

didactic *adj* instructive.

diddle *vt* to trick.

die *vi* to cease to live; to expire.

die[1] *n* (*pl* **dice**) a cube with sides marked 1, 2, 3, 4, 5, 6, used in games of chance.

die[2] *n* (*pl* **dice**) a stamp.

diesel *n* a vehicle driven by a diesel engine.

diesel engine *n* an internal combustion engine where ignition is produced by the heat of highly compressed air alone.

diet *n* food; a course of feeding. * *vt*, *vi* to eat or cause to eat according to special guidelines.

differ *vi* to be unlike; to disagree.

difference *n* dissimilarity; a dispute; a disagreement; remainder (in subtraction).

different *adj* distinct; dissimilar.

differential *adj* discriminating; variable; relating to increments in given functions. * *n* an infinitesimal difference between two states of a variable quantity; the difference in wage rates for different types of labour esp. within an industry.

differentiate *vt* to mark or distinguish by a difference.

difficult *adj* arduous; perplexing; hard to please; hard to understand.

diffidence *n* want of confidence; reserve.

diffident *adj* wanting confidence; bashful.

diffuse *vt* to pour out and spread; to proclaim. * *adj* widely spread; not concise.

diffusion *n* dispersion; circulation.

dig *vt* to turn up with a spade. * *vi* to work with a spade; to excavate; to investigate; to nudge; to understand; to approve.

digest vt to assimilate; to think out; to dissolve in the stomach. * n a summary.

digestible adj capable of being digested.

digestion n process of making food assimilable.

digit n a finger; any of the figures 0 to 9.

digital adj of, using digits e.g. a clock.

dignified adj stately; grave.

dignify vt to ennoble; to grace; to exalt.

dignitary n one holding high rank.

dignity n honour; rank; formality in manner and appearance.

digress vi to depart from main subject; to deviate.

dike, dyke n a ditch; an embankment.

dilapidated adj in a ruinous condition.

dilapidation n decay; ruin.

dilation n expansion; enlargement.

dilate vti to expand; to distend.

dilatory adj tardy; putting off.

dilemma n a fix; a quandary.

diligence n application.

diligent adj industrious; persevering.

dilute vt to reduce in strength by adding water or some qualifying matter. * adj weak; diluted.

dilution n reduction in strength.

dim adj obscure; faint. * vt to dull; to make dark.

dimension n the measure of a thing, size, extent, capacity.

diminish vti to lessen; to decrease.

diminutive adj small. * n a word denoting smallness.

dimple n a small hollow on the cheek or chin.

din n a loud sound long continued. * vt to stun with noise; to teach with constant repetition.

dine vi to eat dinner.

dinghy n a small ship's boat.

dingy adj dull; faded.

dinner n the principal meal of the day.

diocese n the see of a bishop.

dip vt to plunge quickly in and out of a liquid; to immerse. * vi to incline. * n a bathe; downward slope; a mixture in which to dip something.

diphtheria n an infectious throat disease.

dipthong n the blending of two vowel sounds.

diploma n a document conferring a degree of honour.

diplomacy n the art of negotiating esp. between nations; tact.

diplomat n a diplomatist.

diplomatic adj prudent, tactful.

dire adj dreadful; urgent.

direct adj straight; express; sincere. * vt to point or aim at; to show; to conduct; to order; to instruct; to address a letter.

direction n course; guidance; command; management; address on a letter; the way in which one is pointing.

directly adv without delay; expressly.

director n a superintendent; a counsellor; one who directs the production of a stage or screen show.

directory n a book with lists of names, addresses, telephone numbers etc.

dirge n a lament.

dirt n any filthy substance; scandal.

dirty adj soiled with dirt; mean; dishonest; obscene. * vt to soil; to sully.

disable vt to deprive of power; to injure.

disabled adj handicapped physically.

disabuse vt to undeceive.

disadvantage n inconvenience; loss.

disaffect vt to estrange; to make discontented.

disaffection n disloyalty.

disagree vi to differ; to fall out; to dissent.

disagreeable adj offensive; displeasing.

disagreement n difference; discord.

disappear vi to vanish from sight.

disappearance n removal from sight.

disappoint vt to fail to fulfil the hopes of a person; to frustrate; to foil.

disapprobation n disapproval; censure.

disapproval n dislike; blame.

disapprove vt to censure as wrong; to blame.

disarm vt, vi to deprive of arms; to disband.

disarmament n the laying down of arms.

disarrange vt to derange; to upset.

disarray vt to throw into disorder. * n disorder.

disaster n a calamity; a failure.

disavowal n denial.

disband vt to disperse. * vi to break up.

disbelief n want of belief; distrust.

disbelieve vt to refuse to credit.

disburse vt to pay out.

disc, disk n the flat face of a thin, round body (e.g. coin, sun, counter, gramophone record, etc).

discard vt to throw away.

discern vti to perceive; to judge.

discerning adj sharp-sighted; acute.

discharge vt to unload; to fire; to dismiss; to perform; to acquit. * n a dismissal; release; matter coming from a sore or wound.

disciple n a learner; a follower.

disciplinarian n one who enforces discipline; a martinet.

disciplinary adj intended for discipline.

discipline n training; order; subjection to laws; punishment; correction. * vt to train; to punish to enforce discipline; tobring under control.

disclaim vt to disown, reject.

disclaimer n disavowal; denial.

disclose vt to open; to uncover; to reveal.

discoloration n stain.

discolour vt to change the colour; to stain.

discomfiture n rout; disappointment.

discomfort n uneasiness; its cause; lack of comfort.

disconcert vt to embarrass.

disconnect vt to disunite; to separate.

disconsolate adj comfortless.

discontentment n dissatisfaction.

discontinue vti to leave off; to cease.

discord n want of harmony; strife.

discordant adj harsh sounding.

discotheque n a gathering for dancing to recorded music; a club or party for this.

discount n a sum deducted from the cost. * vt to cash a bill at present worth; to take away from.

discourage vt to dishearten; to dissuade.

discourse n a speech; a treatise; a sermon. * vi to talk.

discourteous adj rude.

discover vt to lay open to view; to detect; to find or learn about for the first time.

discredit n want of credit; distrust. * vt to damage the reputation of.

discreditable adj dishonourable.

discreet adj prudent.

discrepancy n variance; a disagreement as between firgures in a total.

discretion n prudence; judgment.

discretionary adj left to one's discretion.

discriminate vt to distinguish; to select.

discrimination n discernment.

discursive adj rambling.

discus n a quoit; a disc.

discuss vt to debate; to examine by argument.

discussion n a debate.

disdain vt to scorn. * n contempt.

disdainful adj contemptuous.

disease n an ailment.

disembark vti to put or go ashore.

disembody vt to divest of the body.

disenchant vt to disillusion.

disengage vt to detach; to release; to extricate.

disentangle vt to extricate.

disfavour n want of favour.

disfiguration n defacement.

disfigure vt to mar the appearance of.

disfigurement n a blemish.

disgorge vt to vomit; to discharge; to surrender.

disgrace n shame; dishonour.

disgraceful adj shameful.

disguise vt to conceal; to dissemble; to change the appearance of. * n a make up; a pretence; a false appearance.

disgust n loathing; repugnance. * vt to offend; to sicken.

disgusting adj repulsive; sickening.

dish n an open vessel for serving food; the meat served. * vt to put in a dish.

dishearten vt to discourage.

dishevelled adj disarranged; untidy.

dishonest adj fraudulent; untrustworthy.

dishonesty n fraudulence.

dishonour n disgrace. * vt to bring shame on; to refuse payment of.

dishonourable adj base; vile.

disinclined adj unwilling.

disinfect vt to cleanse from infection.

disinfectant n a substance that destroys infectious germs.

disingenuous adj crafty; cunning.

disinherit vt to cut off from inheriting.

disintegrate vt to break up into parts.

disinter vt to take out of a grave.

disinterested *adj* impartial.

disjointed *adj* unconnected; incoherent.

disk *n* see disc.

dislike *n* aversion; distaste. * *vt* to feel aversion to.

dislocate *vt* to displace a joint; to upset the working of.

dislodge *vt* to remove; to oust.

disloyal *adj* faithless; untrustworthy

dismal *adj* dark; gloomy.

dismantle *vt* to strip; to take apart.

dismay *vt* to terrify; to appal. * *n* terror; consternation.

dismember *vt* to sever limb from limb.

dismiss *vt* to send away.

dismissal *n* discharge.

dismount *vi* to descend from a horse.

disobedience *n* neglect or refusal to obey.

disobedient *adj* failing, refusing to obey; unruly.

disobey *vt* to neglect or refuse to obey.

disobliging *adj* unaccommodating.

disorder *n* confusion; disease. * *vt* to disarrange.

disorganize *vt* to throw into confusion.

disown *vt* to repudiate; to refuse to acknowledge as one's own.

disparage *vt* to depreciate; to belittle.

disparate *adj* unlike.

disparity *n* inequality.

dispassionate *adj* cool; impartial.

dispel *vt* to scatter; to banish.

dispensary *n* a place where medicines are made up and dispensed.

dispensation *n* distribution; exemption.

dispense *vt* to deal out; to administer; to exempt.

disperse *vti* to scatter; to diffuse; to vanish.

dispirited *adj* dejected.

displace *vt* to derange; to supersede.

displacement *n* quantity of water displaced by a floating body.

display *vt* to unfold; to show; to parade. * *vi* to make a show. * *n* exhibition; parade; a computer monitor for presenting visual information.

displease *vti* to offend; to disgust.

displeased *adj* annoyed.

displeasing *adj* unpleasant.

displeasure *n* annoyance.

disport *n* pastime. * *vi* to sport; to gambol.

disposable *adj* designed to be discarded after use; available.

disposal *n* control; arrangement.

dispose *vti* to arrange; to incline; to regulate; to give, sell or transfer to another; to throw away.

disposed *adj* inclined.

disposition *n* order; character; inclination; arrangement.

dispossess *vt* to deprive of possession.

disproportion *n* inequality.

disproval *n* disproof.

disprove *vt* to prove to be wrong; to confute.

dispute *vi* to argue; to debate. * *vt* to impugn. * *n* controversy; strife.

disqualify *vt* to make ineligible through violation of rules; to incapacitate.

disquiet *n* unrest; anxiety.

disregard *n* neglect. * *vt* to slight; to ignore.

disrepair *n* neglect.

disreputable *adj* of bad character.

disrepute *n* disgrace.

disrespect *n* discourtesy.

disrobe *vt* to undress; to uncover.

disruption *n* disorder; confusion.

dissatisfaction *n* discontent.

dissatisfied *adj* discontented.

dissect *vt* to cut up; to examine minutely.

dissemble *vt, vi* to hide; to disguise.

disseminate *vt* to spread abroad esp. ideas, information etc.

dissemination *n* propagation.

dissension *n* discord.

dissent *vi* to disagree; to separate from an established church. * *n* disagreement.

dissenting *adj* disagreeing.

dissertation *n* a formal discourse or treatise.

disservice *n* an ill-service.

dissident *adj* dissenting. * *n* one who disagrees with government policies so strongly as to suffer imprisonment.

dissimilar *adj* unlike.

dissimulate *vti* to dissemble.

dissipate *vti* to scatter; to squander.

dissipated *adj* dissolute.

dissociate *vt* to disunite; to repudiate a

connection with.

dissolute *adj* profligate.

dissolution *n* melting; break up (of a parliament); death.

dissolve *vti* to liquefy; to break up legally; to annul; to be overcome with emotion.

dissuade *vt* to exhort against; to deter by argument.

distance *n* remoteness in place or time; space between two points or places; reserve. * *vt* to outstrip.

distant *adj* far off; cold; shy.

distaste *n* dislike.

distemper *n* a disordered state of mind or body; a dog disease; a method of painting on plaster without oil.

distend *vti* to stretch; to swell.

distention *n* inflation.

distil *vi, vt* to extract the essence of; to fall in drops; to rectify or purify.

distiller *n* a maker of alcoholic spirit.

distillery *n* a distilling factory.

distinct *adj* separate; clear; definite.

distinction *n* difference; eminence; honour.

distinctive *adj* distinguishing.

distinctness *n* clearness; precision.

distinguish *vti* to mark a difference; to perceive; to differentiate; to honour.

distinguished *adj* eminent; of elegant appearance.

distort *vt* to twist; to misrepresent.

distract *vt* to draw the attention aside; to bewilder; to confuse.

distracted *adj* frantic; maddened.

distraction *n* derangement; diversion; an amusement; extreme agitation.

distrain *vt* to seize, as goods, for debt.

distraught *adj* distracted; agitated.

distress *n* anguish; destitution. * *vt* to afflict with pain.

distressed *adj* afflicted; extremely agitated, pained or poor.

distressing *adj* grievous.

distribute *vt* to deal out; to apportion; to classify.

distribution *n* division; sharing.

district *n* a region marked off for some special purpose.

distrust *vt* to doubt; to suspect; * *n* doubt; suspicion.

distrustful *adj* suspicious.

disturb *vt* to throw into disorder; to agitate.

disuse *n* neglect. * *vt* to cease to use.

ditch *n* a long narrow trench.

divan *n* a sofa or bed without back or sides.

dive *vi* to plunge into water head foremost; to descend steeply (of aircraft); to submerge; to dash headlong.

diverge *vi* to deviate; to digress.

divergent *adj* diverging; dissimilar.

diverse *adj* different; unlike.

diversified *adj* varied.

diversify *vt* to vary; to invest in a broad range or securities, or in a variety of commercial operations to reduce risk or risk of loss.

diversion *n* amusement; a feigned attack.

diversity *n* variety.

divert *vt* to turn aside; to amuse.

diverting *adj* amusing.

divest *vt* to strip; to unclothe.

divide *vt* to separate into parts; to share; to sever; to estrange * *vi* to part; to vote.

dividend *n* a number to be divided; share of profit.

divider *n* a distributor; (*pl*) compasses.

divination *n* prediction.

divine *adj* of or belonging to God. * *n* a clergyman. * *vti* to foretell; to guess; to dowse.

divining rod *n* a wand used by diviners to locate underground water.

divinity *n* the science of divine things.

divisible *adj* capable of division.

division *n* act of dividing; separation; a separation into two opposing sides to vote; disunion; portion; a process in arithmetic.

divisive *adj* creating division or discord.

divisor *n* the number by which the dividend is divided.

divorce *n* a dissolution of marriage; a separation. * *vt* to dissolve a marriage.

divulge *vt* to disclose.

dizzy *adj* giddy.

do *vt, aux* to perform; to bring about; to prepare. * *vi* to act or behave; to fare in health; to cheat; to rob. * *n* a party.

docile *adj* easily taught; tractable.

dock n an enclosed basin for ships; an enclosure in court for prisoners. * vt to cut off; to put a ship in dock.

docket n a summary; a bill tied to goods. * vt to make or attach an abstract of.

dockyard n an area with docks and facilities for repairing and refitting ships.

doctor n a learned person; a physician.

doctorate n the degree of a doctor.

doctrine n a principle or belief; the teaching of a person, school, or church.

document n written evidence or proof.

dodge vt, vi to move nimbly aside; to evade a duty; to quibble. * n a trick.

dog n a domestic quadruped. * vt to follow closely.

dogged adj obstinate; relentless.

doggerel n worthless verse.

dogma n a body of opinion; authoritative belief.

dogmatic, dogmatical adj positive; overbearing.

dogmatism n assertion without proof.

doldrums npl the dumps; equatorial region of calms.

dole n money reeived from the state while unemployed; what is dealt out. * vt to deal out in small quantites.

doleful adj woeful; gloomy; sad.

doll n a child's toy in human form.

dollar n an American unit of money.

dolmen n a table-shaped ancient stone structure.

dolorous adj mournful.

dolt n a blockhead.

domain n an estate; a province; a sphere of activity etc.

dome n an arched roof; a large cupola.

domestic adj belonging to the home; tame. * n a household servant.

domesticate vt to make domestic or tame.

domicile n a habitation.

dominant adj ruling; prevailing over others; overlooking from a superior height.

dominate vt to rule.

domineer vi to lord over others.

domineering adj overbearing.

dominion n territory with one ruler or government; authority.

domino n (pl **dominoes**) a masquerade dress; a half-mask; (pl), a game played with dotted ivory or bone rectangles.

don n a fellow of a college. * vt to put on.

donate vt to bestow.

donation n a gift.

donor n one who gives something; one who donates blood, organs etc. for medical purposes..

doom n fate; ruin. * vt to condemn to failure or ruin.

door n the entrance of a house, room, carriage, etc; the frame closing it.

doric adj an order of architecture; a rustic dialect.

dormant adj sleeping; inactive.

dormitory n a sleeping room with many beds.

dorsal adj pertaining to the back.

dose n the quantity of medicine given at one time.

dot n a small point, as made with a pen, etc. * vt to mark with a dot.

dotage n the feeble-mindedness of old age.

dote vi to be excessively fond of.

double adj twice as large, as strong etc.; designed or intended for two; made of two similar parts; having two meanings, characters, etc. * adv twice; in twos. * n a number or amount that is twice as much; a person or thing identical to another. * vti to make or become twice as much or as many; to fold; to bend; to bend sharply backwards; to have an additional purpose.

double bass n the lowest-toned instrument of violin class.

double-dealing n duplicity.

double-cross vt to betray an associate; to cheat.

doubt vi to waver; to question; to suspect. * vt to believe to be uncertain. * n uncertainty; suspicion.

doubtful adj feeling doubt; uncertain; suspicious.

doubtless adv unquestionably.

douche n a jet of water applied to the body.

dough n flour moistened with water or milk and kneaded to make bread.

douse, dowse vti to plunge into water.

dovetail n a wedge-shaped joint resembling a dove's tail used in woodwork.

* *vt, vi* to join as above; to fit exactly.

dowager *n* a title given to the widow of a nobleman.

dowdy *adj* ill-dressed; not stylish.

down *n* the fine soft feathers of birds; a hill. * *adv* toward or in a lower physical position; toward or to the ground, floor, or bottom; or in a lower status or in a worse condition; in cash; to or in a state of less activity. * *adj* occupying a low position, esp. lying on the ground; depressed, dejected. * *n* a low period (as in activity, emotional life, or fortunes); (*inf*) prejudice. * *vti* to defeat; to swallow.

downcast *adj* dejected.

downfall *n* ruin.

downpour *n* a heavy fall of rain.

downright *adj* plain; blunt; utter.

downtrodden *adj* oppressed.

downward, downwards *adv* in a descending course. * *adj* descending.

dowry *n* a wife's marriage portion.

doze *vi* to be half asleep. * *n* a light sleep.

dozen *n* twelve.

drab *adj* of a dull brown colour; dull; uninteresting.

draconian *adj* very severe.

draft *n* a detachment of men or things; an order for money; the first sketch or outline of speech or other writing; conscription in U.S. * *vt* to sketch; to select.

draftsman *n see* **draughtsman**.

drag *vt* to draw along slowly and with force; to search with a dragnet or a hook. * *vi* to protract. * *n* a brake; a check.

dragnet *n* a net to be drawn along the bottom.

dragon *n* a fabulous winged monster.

dragoon *n* a cavalry man. * *vt* to harass; to persecute.

drain *vt, vi* to draw off; to filter; to flow off; to drink the entire contents of. * *n* a sewer; a channel for liquids.

drainage *n* a system of drains.

dram *n* a unit of weight; a small draught of spirits.

drama *n* a stage, radio or television play.

dramatic, dramatical *adj* pertaining to the drama; theatrical.

dramatize *vt* to turn into a drama.

drape *vt* to cover or hang with cloth.

drastic *adj* acting with strength or violence.

draught *n* the quantity drunk at once; a sketch; the depth a ship sinks in water; a current of air; (*pl*) a game on a squared board using 24 round pieces.

draughtsman *n* a designer.

draw *vt, vi* to pull along or towards; to cause to come; to attract; to sketch; to infer; to end a game with equal scores; to shrink. * *n* the act of drawing; a drawn game.

drawback *n* a defect; a hindrance or handicap.

drawbridge *n* a movable (up and down or sideways) bridge.

drawer *n* one who draws a cheque; a sliding box in a table, chest or desk; (*pl*) an undergarment.

drawing *n* a pencil sketch.

drawing room *n* a reception or living room.

drawl *vi, vt* to speak slowly with drawn-out vowel sounds. * *n* affected slowness of speech.

dread *n* fear; terror. * *adj* exciting great fear; terrible. * *vt* to fear greatly.

dreadful *adj* terrible.

dream *n* a vision in sleep; an idle fancy; an ambition. * *vt, vi* to have dreams; to fancy.

dreary *adj* cheerless.

dredge *n* a dragnet. * *vt* to scoop up, esp from the bottom of a river etc.

dredger *n* a floating vessel for dredging and deepening.

dregs *npl* lees; grounds.

drench *vt* to soak.

dress *vt* to clothe; to set in order; to decorate; to wash and bandage; to prepare food for cooking. * *n* clothes; a woman's one-piece garment; style or manner of clothing.

dresser *n* a kitchen sideboard; a surgeon's assistant.

dressing *n* a bandage, oitment etc. applied to a wound; a sauce.

dribble *vi* to trickle. * *vt* (in games) to move the ball little by little with the foot, hand, stick etc.

drift n a heap of snow, sand, etc. deposited by the wind; natural course, tendency; the general meaning or intention (of what is said); an aimless course. * vt to cause to drift. * vi to be driven or carried along by water or air currents.

drill vti to pierce a hole with a drill; to train (soldiers); to furrow; to sow in rows. * n a hole borer; a furrow; exercise; procedure; routine.

drill n a cotton cloth.

drink vi to swallow liquid. * n a beverage; alcoholic liquor.

drip vi to fall in drops. * n a liquid that falls in drops; its sound; a device for injecting a fluid slowly and continuously into a vein.

dripping n the fat from roasting meat.

drive vb (pt drove, pp driven) vt to urge, push or force onward; to convey in a vehicle; to carry through strongly; to propel (a ball) with hard blow. * vi to be forced along; to be conveyed in a vehicle. * n a trip in a vehicle; a stroke to drive a ball (in golf, etc.); a driveway; an intensive campaign; the transmission of power to machinery.

driver n one who drives; a golf club.

drizzle vi to rain in small fine drops. * n a fine rain.

droll adj comic; amusing; whimsical.

drone n the male or nonworking bee; a humming sound; monotonous speech. * vi to hum; to speak in a monotonous tone.

droop vi to hang down; to languish.

drop n a globule of any liquid; a distance to fall. * vt, vi to pour or let fall in drops; to fall; to let fall; to sink; to set down from a vehicle; to mention in passing; to give up (an idea etc.).

dropsy n an unnatural collection of water in the body.

dross n the scum of metals; refuse; rubbish.

drought n a period of very dry weather.

drove n a herd or flock in motion.

drown vt, vi to suffocate or be suffocated in water.

drowse vi to doze.

drowsy adj sleepy, heavy.

drudge vi to toil; to slave. * n a menial servant.

drudgery n distasteful toil.

drug n any substance used in medicine. * vt to dose with drugs.

drum n a sound percussion instrument; a stretched membrane in the ear. * vi, vt to beat a drum; to teach or instruct by constant repetition.

drunk adj intoxicated.

drunkard n one given to drink.

drunkenness n intoxication.

dry adj free from moisture; thirsty. * vt, vi to free from moisture; thirsty; marked by a matter-of-fact, ironic or terse manner of speech; uninteresting.

dry rot n a timber disease.

dual adj consisting of two; twofold.

dub vt to confer a knighthood on by touching with a sword.

dubiety n doubtfulness.

dubious adj wavering; uncertain; untrustworthy.

duchess n a duke's wife.

duchy n a country ruled by a duke.

duck vti to plunge in water; to bow. * n a waterfowl; a kind of canvas.

duct n a narrow tube in the body; a channel or pipe for fluids, electric cables etc.

due adj owed; owing; proper. * adv directly. * n a fee; a right; a just title.

duel n a set fight between two persons; any conflict between two people, sides, ideas etc.

duet n a piece of music for two performers.

duke n one of the highest order of nobility.

dukedom n the lands or title of a duke.

dulcet adj sweet; melodious.

dull adj stupid; drowsy; cheerless. * vt to make dull; to stupefy; to blunt; to sully.

dulse n an edible seaweed.

duly adv properly; suitably.

dumb adj mute; silent.

dumbbells n weights used for developing the muscles of the arm.

dumbfound, dumfound vt to astonish; to confuse.

dummy n a stupid person; a figure used to display clothes; the exposed hand in a game of bridge; a sham.

dump n a place for refuse; a temporary store; a thud; a dirty, dilapidated place; (pl) low spirits.

dunce n a stupid person.

dune n a sand hill on the sea coast.

dung n the excrement of animals. * vt to manure.

dungeon n an underground prison.

duodenum n the first portion of the small intestines.

dupe n one easily cheated. * vt to impose on; to deceive; to trick.

duplex adj double; twofold.

duplicate adj double. * n a copy. * vt to double; to make an exact copy.

duplicity n guile; trickery.

durable adj lasting; permanent.

duration n continuance; the period in which an event continues.

duress n constraint; imprisonment.

during prep for the time of; throughout.

dusk n twilight.

dusky adj darkish.

dust n fine dry particles of earth, etc; earth as symbolic of mortality. * vt to free from dust; to sprinkle.

duster n a cloth, etc, for removing dust.

duty n what one is bound to do; service; a tax on goods.

dux n the head of a class in a school.

dwarf n one noticeably undersized. * vt to make (or make seem) small.

dwell vi to live in a place; to continue; to focus the attention on; to think, talk, write at length about.

dwelling n habitation; abode.

dwindle vi to diminish gradually.

dye vt to stain; to give a new colour to. * n a colouring matter; tinge; hue.

dynamic adj relating to force that produces motion; forceful; energetic.

dynamics n the science of force or power.

dynamite n a powerful explosive.

dynamo n a machine for producing an electric current.

dynasty n a line of rulers of the same powerful family.

dysentery n a disorder of the intestines.

dyspepsia, dyspepsy n indigestion.

E

each adj, pron everyone separately.

eager adj keen; ardent earnest.

ear n the organ of hearing; the power of appreciating musical sounds; heed; a spike of corn.

earache n a pain in the ear.

early adv, adj before the expected time; of or occurring in the first part of a period or series; timely, soon.

earn vt to gain by labour; to deserve.

earnest adj ardent; eager; serious.

earnings npl wages.

earring n an ornament worn in the ear.

earth n the globe we inhabit; dry land; the ground; the burrow of a badger, fox etc. * vt to cover with earth.

earthenware n ware made of clay; pottery.

earthquake n a shaking or trembling of the earth.

earthwork n a rampart of earth.

earthy adj consisting of or resembling earth; crude.

earwig n an insect with a pineen-like apendage at the end of the body.

ease n freedom from toil, pain, etc; rest; comfort. * vt to calm; to alleviate; to shift a little.

easel n a stand to support pictures while they are being painted.

east n that part of the sky where the sun rises; the countries east of Europe. * adj in or towards the east.

Easter n the festival commemorating Christ's Resurrection.

easterly adj coming from the east, as winds; moving towards the east.

eastern adj belonging to the east; oriental.

easy adj free from pain or anxiety; simple; relaxed in manner; lenient; compliant; unhurried.

eat vt to chew and swallow, as food; to wear away; to corrode.

eaves npl that part of the roof overhanging the walls.

eavesdrop vi to try to hear or to listen in to a private conversation.

ebb *n* the flowing back of the tide; decline. * *vi* to flow back; to decline.

ebony *n* a hard, heavy, dark wood.

ebullient *adj* enthusiastic; exuberant; boiling.

eccentric *adj* not conforming to the usual pattern; unconventional; odd; whimsical.

eccentricity *n* oddity of conduct, dress, etc.

ecclesiastic, ecclesiastical *adj* belonging to the church or clergy. * *n* a clergyman.

echo *n* the repetition of sound by reflection of sound waves; imitation. * *vt;vi* to repeat; to resound; to imitate.

eclectic *adj* selecting the best of everything (esp. in philosophy and the arts).

eclipse *n* an obscuring of the light of the sun, moon etc, by some other body; an overshadowing. * *vt* to darken; to surpass.

economic, economical *adj* pertaining to economics or the economy; showing a profit; frugal; careful.

economics *n* the science of the application of wealth and concerned with the production, and consumption and distribution of goods and services.

economize *vti* to manage money with prudence to save.

economy *n* thrift; prudent management; the management of finances and resources of a business, industry etc; the economic system of a country.

ecstasy *n* rapture; enthusiasm.

ecstatic, ecstatical *adj* entrancing; transporting.

ecumenic, ecumenical *adj* of the whole christian church; seeking christian unity worldwide

eczema *n* a skin disease.

eddy *n* a whirling current of water or air. * *vi* to move round and round.

edge *n* the sharp side; an abrupt border or margin; keenness; force; effectiveness. * *vt* to put an edge or fringe on; to move gradually.

edged *adj* sharp; keen.

edgeways *adv* sideways.

edible *adj* eatable.

edict *n* a decree; a manifesto.

edifice *n* a large building.

edify *vt* to improve morally or mentally.

edit *vt* to prepare a text for publication; to prepare a final version of a film by selecting, cutting and arranging sequences.

edition *n* the number of copies of a book printed at one time.

editor *n* one who is responsible for the issue of a book or newspaper.

editorial *n* a leading article in a newspaper expressing the opinions of its editor or owner.

educate *vt* to train and instruct; to provide schooling.

education *n* instruction and training, as imparted in schools, colleges and universities; the theory and practice of teaching.

eerie *adj* awesome; weird.

efface *vt* to blot out; to erase; to make oneself inconspicuous through shyness, humility or false modesty.

effect *n* a result; an impression; (*pl*) belongings. * *vt* to bring about; to accomplish.

effective *adj* efficient; making a striking impression; forceful; fruitful.

effectual *adj* producing the desired result.

effeminacy *n* a display or impression of feminine qualities in a man; weakness; timidity.

effeminate *adj* womanish; unmanly.

effervesce *vi* to bubble or sparkle.

effervescent *adj* bubbling; sparkling.

effete *adj* worn out; feeble; decadent.

efficacious *adj* achieving the desired result.

efficiency *n* competence

efficient *adj* capable; competent.

effigy *n* a portrait; a sculpture or figure of a person esp. one crudely executed to ridicule or show contempt.

effluent *adj* flowing out. * *n* a stream from a river or lake; liquid waste discharged from a sewer, an industrial plant, a nuclear station etc.

effluvium *n* (*pl* **effluvia**) noisome vapour.

effort *n* exertion; strenuous endeavour.

effrontery *n* brazen impudence.

effusion *n* a pouring out; copious utterance.

effusive *adj* profuse; gushing.

egg *n* the shell-covered embryo laid by birds, snakes, insects, etc. * *vt* to urge on.

ego *n* the 'I'; the self, self-image; conceit.

egoist *n* a self-centred person.

egotism *n* self-importance; self-centredness.

egotist *n* one always talking of him or herself.

egregious *adj* conspicuously bad or flagrant.

egress *n* exit.

egret *n* a species of heron.

eiderdown *n* the down or soft feathers of the eider duck used for stuffing quilts etc.

eight *adj n* a cardinal number and its symbol (8); the crew of an eight-oared rowing boat.

eighteen *adj, n* eight and ten (18).

eighteenth *adj, n* the ordinal number of 18.

eighth *adj, n* the ordinal number of 8.

eightieth *adj, n* the ordinal number of 80.

eighty *adj* eight times ten (80).

either *adj, pron* one or the other; one of two. * *conj* used as correlative to or.

ejaculate *vt* to exclaim.

eject *vt* to throw out; to expel. * *vi* to escape from an aircraft or spacecraft using an ejecetion seat.

ejection seat *h* an escape seat, esp. in combat aircraft, that can be ejected with its occupant in an emergancy by means of explosive bolts.

eke *vt* (with **out**) supplement; to use frugally; to make a living with difficulty.

elaborate *vt* to workout; to explain in detail. * *adj* highly detailed.

elapse *vi* to by, of time.

elastic *adj* springy; rebounding; flexible.

elated *adj* exultant.

elation *n* joy; exultation.

elbow *n* the joint between the forearm and upper arm; a sharp turn or bend. * *vt* to push away with the elbow.

elder *adj* older. * *n* an older person; an office bearer in the Presbyterian Church.

elderly *adj* quite old

eldest *adj* oldest.

elect *vt* to choose by voting to select. * *adj* chosen.

election *n* the act of choosing by vote; the choice made esp.

electioneering *n* the arts used to secure the election of a candidate.

elector *n* one who has a vote in an election.

electorate *n* the body of electors.

electric, electrical *adj* containing, conveying, worked or produced by electricity.

electricity *n* the force that is developed by friction, and by chemical, thermal, or magnetic action.

electrify *vt* to charge with electricity; to thrill; to astonish.

electrocute *vt* to kill by electricity.

electrode *n* a conductor through which an electric current enters or leaves a gas discharge tube etc.

electrodynamics *n* the science which treats of electric currents.

electrolysis *n* chemical decomposition by electricity.

electromagnetic *adj* having electric and magnetic properties. * *n* electromagnetism

electron *n* a negativley charged elementary particle that forms the part of the atom outside the nucleus.

electronic *adj* of or worked by streams of electrons flowing through devices, vacuum or gas. * *adv* electronically.

electronics *n* (*sing*) the study, developemant and application of electronic devices; as (*pl*) electronic circuits.

elegance *n* beauty; refinement; grace.

elegant *adj* graceful; refined; dignified.

elegy *n* a lament.

element *n* a constiituent part; a favourable environment for a plant or animal; a wire that produces heat in a electric cooker, kettle, etc; (*pl*) atmospheric conditions (wind, rain, etc,); (*pl*) the basic principles, rudiments.

elementary *adj* basic, simple.

elevate *vt* to lift up; to raise in rank; to improve in intellectual or moral stature.

elevation *n* a raised place; the height above the earth's surface or above sea level; the angle to which a gun is raised above the horizon; a drawing that shows the front, the rear, the front view of something.

elevator n a cage or platform for moving something from one level to another; a moveable surface on the tailplane of an aircraft to produce motion up or down; a lift; a building for storing grain.

eleven adj one more than ten (11).

eleventh adj, n the ordinal number of 11..

elicit vt to draw out by inquiry.

elide vt to omit a letter or syllable at the beginning or end of a word.

eligible adj qualified; suitable.

eliminate vt to get rid of; to eradicate; to exclude a competitor from a competition by defeat.

elite n the pick; the best.

elixir n the specific sought after by alchemists to prolong life or transmute metals.

ellipse n an oval figure; a closed plane figure found by the plane section of a right-angled cone.

elocution n the art of effective speaking.

elongate vt to lengthen.

elope vi to run away secretly esp. of lovers to be married.

eloquence n skill in speaking and the use of words; persuasive speech.

else adj, adv other; besides.

elsewhere adv in some other place.

elucidate vt to make clear.

elude vt to avoid by artifice; to baffle.

elusive adj evasive; deceptive; difficult to contact.

emaciate vi, vt to become or make lean.

emanate vi to flow out; to issue.

emanation n outflowing; effluvium.

emancipate vt to free from restraint; to liberate esp. form slavery.

emasculate vt to castrate; to enfeeble.

embalm vt to preserve (corpse) with drugs, chemicals etc.

embankment n a protecting mound to hold back water or to carry a roadway.

embargo n prohibition on ships from sailing; restraint; a restriction of commerce by law; a prohibtion

embark vti to go or put on board; to be

gin an activity or enterprise.

embarrass vt to confuse; to harass; to burden; to make a person uncomfortable.

embarrassment n confusion; entanglement; trouble; abashment.

embassy n the office or residence of an ambassador.

embellish vt to adorn.

embellishment n decoration; ornament.

embers n live remains of a fire.

embezzle vt to misapply funds.

embezzlement n fraudulent use of funds.

embitter vt to make bitter.

emblem n a symbol; a heraldic device.

emblematic, emblematical adj symbolic.

embody vt to give concrete form to; to incorporate in a single book, law, system etc..

emboss vt to mould or adorn in relief.

embrace vt to clasp in the arms; to accept an idea etc. eagerly.

embroider vt to adorn with patterned needlework.

embroidery n decorative needlework.

embroil vt to involve a person in trouble.

embryo n unborn or unhatched offspring.

embryonic adj rudimentary; imperfect.

emendation n correction (in texts, etc).

emerald n a bright green precious stone, its colour. * adj bright green.

emerge vi to come forth; to issue; to be revealed as the result of investigation.

emergency n a crisis requiring immediate attention.

emetic n a medicine that induces vomiting.

emigrant n one who leaves one's country to settle in another.

emigrate vi to go to reside in another country.

eminence n a height; fame; a title for a cardinal.

eminent adj exalted; prominent.

emissary n an agent sent on a mission; a messenger.

emit vt to send or throw out; to utter.

emollient adj soothing; softening.

emolument n salary; remuneration.

emotion n a strong feeling of joy, sadness, anger, fear etc..

emperor n the sovereign of an empire.

emphasis n a particular stress placed on anything; force, vigour.

emphasize vt to lay stress on.

emphatic, emphatical adj impressive; decisive.

empire n dominion; sway; states ruled by an emperor.

empirical adj based on observation, experiment or experience.

employ vt to give work to; to keep at work

employee n one who works for an employer.

employment n occupation or profession.

emporium n (pl emporia, emporiums) a commercial centre; a large shop selling goods of all types.

empower vt to authorize.

empress n the consort of an emperor; a female ruler of an empire.

empty adj void; vacant; lacking in substance, value or reality; hungry. * vt to take everything out of.

emulate vt to strive to equal; to vie with.

emulsion n a mixture of mutually insoluble liquids in which one is dispersed in droplets throughout the other; a light-senstive substance on photographic paper or film.

enable vt to empower; to authorize.

enact vt to establish by law; to decree; to act.

enactment n a decree; an act.

enamel n an ornamental or preservative glass-like coating on metals, etc.; the hard outer layer of a tooth. * vt to cover with enamel.

enamour vt to inspire with love.

encampment n a camp.

enchant vt to charm; to fascinate.

enchanter n a sorcerer; a bewitching person.

enchanting adj charming.

enchantment n magic; fascination.

encircle vt to encompass; to embrace.

enclosure n a space fenced in; something enclosed with a letter on a parcel or envelope.

encompass vt to encircle; to sail round.

encore adv again; once more. * n a call for a performance to be repeated.

encounter n an unexpected meeting; a conflict. * vt, vi to confront; to fight against.

encourage vt to inspire with hope; to urge on; to promote the development of.

encroach vi to trespass on rights, lands, etc, of others.

encroachment n trespass; intrusion.

encrust vt to cover with a crust.

encumber vt to burden; to hamper.

encumbrance n a burden; a mortgage.

encyclopaedia, encyclopedia n a book or books of general knowledge.

end n the extreme point; the close; the stopping place; death; result; aim. * vt to bring to an end. * vi to come to an end; to result in.

endanger vt to imperil.

endear vt to make dear or more loved.

endeavour n effort; attempt. * vi to try; to strive; to aim.

endemic adj peculiar to a people or region.

endorse vt to write one's name on the back of (cheques, etc); to ratify; to support; to record an offence on a driving licence.

endorsement n a docket; signature; approval.

endow vt to settle money or property on; to enrich; to provide with special power.

endurance n fortitude; patience.

endure vi, vt to bear patiently; to tolerate; to last; to continue in existence.

enemy n one who is unfriendly; an antagonist; a hostile army; something harmful.

energetic adj forceful; vigorous; lively.

energy n power; force; vigour; capacity to do work.

enervate vt to enfeeble.

enforce vt to urge with energy; to impose; to compel compliance with threats.

enfranchise vt to give the right of voting to.

engage vt to bind by pledge; to attach; to promise to marry; to attract; to enter into; to attack. * vi to bind one's self.

engagement n a contract; a betrothal; an appointment arranged with someone; a fight.

engaging adj winning; attractive.

engender vt to breed; to occasion.

engine n a power machine; a locomotive; a contrivance.

engineer n a maker or designer or operator of machinery. * vt to plan or construct; to contrive; to plan.

engineering n the art or business of an engineer.

engrave vt to cut or carve on metal; to imprint.

engraving n a print from an engraved plate.

engross vt to absorb.

engulf vt to swallow up.

enhance vt to increase in value, importance, attractiveness.

enigma n a puzzle; a mystery.

enigmatic, enigmatical adj puzzling; obscure; mysterious.

enjoin vt to command; prescribe.

enjoy vi to take delight in; to experience.

enjoyment n pleasure; satisfaction.

enlarge vti to make large; to grow large; to speak or write.

enlighten vt to make clear; to instruct.

enlightened adj instructed; cultured.

enlist vi to enter on a list; to enrol (in army). * vt to ensure support of.

enliven vt to brighten; to gladden.

enmity n hostility; ill-will.

ennoble vt to exalt; to dignify.

enormity n great wickedness, a serious crime.

enormous adj huge.

enough adj adequate, sufficient. * n a sufficiency. * adv tolerably.

enrage vt to make very angry.

enrapture vt to fill with delight.

enrich vt to make rich; to fertilize.

enrol vt to write in a roll; to record; to admit as a member of a society.

enrolment n act of enrolling; a register; a record.

enshrine vt to enclose; to cherish.

ensign n a badge; an emblem; a flag.

enslave vt to make a slave of; to subjugate.

ensnare vt to entrap.

ensue vi to result from.

entail vt to involve as a result; to settle lands on individuals in succession so that all are really only life-renters. * n this mode of settlement.

entanglement n disorder; a relationship between a man and a woman considered to be unsuitable.

enter vi to go or come in or into; to come on stage; to begin, start; (with for) to register as an entrant. * vt to come or go into; to pierce, penetrate; (organization) to join; to insert; (proposal etc.) to submit; to record (an item) in a diary etc.

enteric adj belonging to the intestines. * n enteric fever, same as typhoid fever.

enterprise n a venture; boldness.

entertain vti to receive as a guest; to please; to amuse; to consider; to have in mind.

entertaining adj pleasing; amusing.

entertainment n entertaining; amusement; an act or show intended to amuse and interest.

enthral vt to enslave; to charm; to captivate.

enthusiasm n ardent feeling; fervent zeal; keen interest.

enthusiast n a person full of enthusiasm for something.

entice vt to tempt; to allure; to lure away by promise of reward.

enticing adj attractive; tempting; fascinating.

entire adj whole; complete.

entitle vt to give a title to; to empower.

entity n being; existence.

entomology n the science of insect life.

entrails npl the intestines.

entrance n coming or going in; the place of entry; the power or authority to enter; an admission fea.

entrance vt to enrapture; to fill with delight.

entreat vt to beg earnestly; to implore.

entreaty n urgent prayers or plea.

entrench vt to dig in; to establish oneself in a strong defensive position.

entry n act of entering; entrance; an item recorded in a diary, account or dictionary.

enumerate vt to count one by one; to list.

enunciate vt to utter; to pronounce (clearly)..

enunciation n clear utterance; statement; expression; declaration; public attestation.

envelop vt to wrap up.

envelope n a cover (of letter, etc).

enviable adj exciting envy.

environment n conditions and surroundings that influence our development and that of plants and animals.

environs npl neighbourhood.

envisage vt to picture to one's self.

envoy n one sent on a mission.

envy n jealousy; discontent caused by another's possessions, achievements etc. * vt to begrudge.

enzyme n a complex protein produced by living cells that induces or speeds chemical reactions inplants and animals.

ephemeral adj short-lived.

epic adj heroic; in the grand style. * n a heroic poem.

epidemic adj a disease affecting a whole community. * n a disease which attacks many people at the same period.

epidermis n the outer skin.

epiglottis n the valve covering larynx during swallowing.

epigram n a pointed, witty, or sarcastic saying.

epilepsy n a disorder of the nervous system marked by convulsions and loss of consiousness.

epilogue n a speech addressed to audience at the close of a play; the concluding section of a book.

episcopacy n Church government by bishops; bishops collectively.

episcopal adj relating to bishops.

episode n an incident in a sequence of events; a piece of action in a book or drama.

epistle n a letter.

epitaph n an inscription on a tomb.

epithet n a descriptive adjective.

epitome n a typical example; personification; a brief summary.

epoch n a period of time.

equable adj uniform; even; hot extreme; even tempered.

equal adj the same in all respects. * n one not inferior or superior to another. * vt to make or be equal to ; to do something equal to.

equality n sameness; evenness.

equalize vt to make equal.

equanimity n evenness of temper.

equate vt to make equal; to make, treat or regard as compatible

equation n an act of equalling; the state of being equal; (chem) an expression representing a reaction in symbols.

equator n an imaginary circle passing round the globe, equidistant from the poles.

equestrian adj on horseback. * n a horseman.

equidistant adj equally distant.

equilateral adj equal sided.

equilibrium n a state of balance, weight, power, force etc.

equine adj pertaining to a horse.

equinox n the two times at which the sun crosses the equator and day and night are equal.

equip vt to furnish; to provide with all necessary tools, supplies etc.

equipment n everything needed for a particular task, expedition etc.

equitable adj fair; just.

equity n fairness; just dealing; (pl) ordinary shares in a company.

equivalent adj, n equal in value amount, force, meaning etc; virtually identical, esp. in function as effect. * n an equivalent thing.

equivocal adj ambiguous; questionable.

equivocate vi to quibble.

era n a fixed reckoning date; a period of time.

eradicate vt to root out; to obliterate.

erase vt to rub out; to remove a recording from magnetic tape; to remove data froma computer memory or storage medium.

erect adj upright;sex organs, rigid from sexual stimulation. * vt to build.

erection n act of erecting; formation; anything erected; structure; a swelling and rigidity of the penis due to sexual excitement.

erode vt to eat or wear away gradually.

erosion n a wearing away (as of sea cliffs).

erotic adj of sexual love; amatory.

err vi to wander; to stray.

errand n a message; a short journey to carry out a task.

errant adj roving; wandering.

erratic adj irregular; eccentric; unreliable.

erratum n (pl **errata**) an error in printing, etc.

erroneous adj wrong; mistaken.

error n a mistake; a fault.

erudite adj deeply read; learned.

erupt vi to burst out; to break out into a rash; to explode ejecting ash and lava from a volcano.

eruption n a bursting forth; a breaking out.

escapade n a mad prank.

escape vti to get out of the way of; to avoid; to be free. * n a getting away by flight; a leakage e.g. of gas etc.; a temporary respite.

escarpment n the steep side of a hill, rock, or rampart.

eschew vt to shun; to avoid.

escort n a guard; an attendant. * vt to attend and guard.

esoteric adj private; select; understood only by elite minority.

especial adj distinct; chief.

espionage n spying.

esplanade n a seaside terrace or promenade.

espouse vt to marry; to adopt a cause etc.

espy vt to catch sight of.

essay vt to try. * n an endeavour or experiment; a short literary composition.

essence n the nature or being of anything; a substance extracted from another without the loss of the qualities of the origional; perfume.

essential adj vital; indispensable; volatile (oil).

establish vt to fix firmly; to institute; to set up (a business etc.) permanently to settle a person in a position; to have generally accepted; to place beyond doubt.

established adj legally confirmed (church); assured.

establishment n household staff; a place of business; (cap) those in power whose aim is to preserve the status quo.

estate n landed property; a large area of residential or industrial developement; a person's total possessions, esp. at their death; a social or political class.

estate agent n a person whose business is selling and leasing property.

esteem vt to value on; to regard highly; to prize. * n judgment; estimation; regard.

estimable adj worthy; respected.

estimate vt to calculate; to appraise. * n valuation; an approximate calculation; a judgement or opinion.

estrangement n withdrawal of friendship.

estuary n the mouth of a river; a firth.

etch vt to portray on metal plates by use of acids.

etching n the impression taken from an etched plate.

eternal adj everlasting.

eternity n infinite time; future life.

ether n a volatile liquid used as an anaesthetic or solvent.

ethereal adj airy; heavenly; aerial; intangible.

ethic, ethical adj moral.

ethics n the science of morals; principles.

ethnic, ethnical adj of races or large groups of people classed accordingly to common traits and customs.

etiquette n code of manners; decorum.

etymology n the study of the history and development of words.

eugenics n the science which treats of racial improvement.

eulogize vt to praise; to extol.

eulogy n praise; panegyric.

euphemism n the use of a mild for a harsh term ('fairy tale' for 'lie'.)

euphonic adj pleasing to the ear.

euthanasia n the act or practice of killing painlessly, esp. to relieve incurable suffering.

evacuate vt to make empty; to quit; to move people from a danger to a safe area; to discharge wastes from the body.

evade vt to avoid; to escape from.

evaluate vt to assess; to determine the value carefully.

evangelist n a preacher of the gospel.

evaporate vi to change into vapour; to remove water from; to disappear.

evasion n avoidance; an equivocal reply

or excuse.

evasive *adj* shuffling; equivocating.

eve, even *n* evening; the evening before as (Christmas Eve).

even *adj* level; smooth; equal; divisible by 2. * *vt* to equalize; to make even; to balance (debts etc.) * *adv* just; exactly; fully; quite; at the very time..

evening *n* the close of the day.

event *n* an incident; a happening; contingency; an item or contest; an itenm or contect in a sports programme.

eventful *adj* memorable.

eventuality *n* a possible result.

ever *adv* always; at any time; in any case.

evergreen *n* a tree or plant always in leaf. * *adj* always green.

everlasting *adj* eternal; never ending.

every *adj* each of all.

everybody *n* every person.

everyday *adj* happening daily; commonplace; worn or used every day.

everything *pnon* all things; all; of the greatest inportance.

everywhere *adv* in every place.

evict *vt* to dispossess by law; to expel.

eviction *n* expulsion (of tenant).

evidence *n* testimony; proof.

evident *adj* clear; plain; understandable.

evil *adj* wicked; bad. * *n* sin; harm.

evince *vt* to show; to prove.

eviscerate *vt* to disembowel.

evoke *vt* to call forth.

evolution *n* a process of change in a particular direction; the process by which something attains its distinctive characteristics; a theory thta existing types of plants and animals have developed from earlier forms. * *adj* evolutionary.

evolve *vti* to unfold; to open out; to develop.

exacerbate *vt* to aggravate; to make something worse.

exact *adj* accurate; precise. * *vt* to compel payment.

exacting *adj* severe; greatly demanding; requiring close attention and precision.

exactly *adv* in an exact manner; precisely. * *interj* quite so! indeed!

exaggerate *vt* to overstate.

exalt *vt* to raise in power, rank, etc; to extol.

examination *n* an interrogation; a testing by set questions.

examine *vt* to scrutinize; to inquire into; to question (witness); to test.

example *n* a sample; pattern; model; a warning to others.

exasperate *vt* to enrage; to annoy intensely.

excavate *vt* to hollow out by digging; to unearth; to expose to view (remains etc.) by digging.

exceed *vt* to surpass; to overstep (the limit).

excel *vt* to surpass. * *vi* to be preeminent.

excellent *adj* of high quality; choice.

except *vt* to omit; to exclude. * *vi* to object. * *prep* without.

excepting *prep* excluding; except.

exceptional *adj* unusual; rare; superior.

excerpt *n* an extract. * *vt* to extract from a book, etc.

excess *n* surplus; intemperance.

excessive *adj* undue; extreme.

exchange *vt* to give and take (one thing in return for another). * *n* the conversion of money from one currency to another; a place where things and services are exchanged, esp. a marketplace for securities; a centre or device in which telephone lines are interconnected

excision *n* a cutting out.

excitable *adj* easily agitated.

excite *vt* to arouse the feelings of, esp. to generate feelings of pleasurable anticipation; to cause to experience strong emotion; to rouse to activity; to stimulate a response, eg. in a bodily organ.

excitement *n* strong pleasurable emotion; agitation; commotion.

exclaim *vi, vt* to call out; to declare loudly, suddenly and with emotion.

exclamation *n* a loud outcry; an emotional utterance; an interjection.

exclude *vt* to shut out.

exclusion *n* a shutting out; a ban; omission.

exclusive *adj* excluding all else; reserved for particular persons; snobbishly aloof; fashionable; high-class, expensive; unobtainable or unpublished elsewhere; sole, undivided.

excommunicate *vt* to bar from church privileges and rites.

excrement *n* waste matter discharged from the body.

excretion *n* ejection of waste matter.

excruciating *adj* intensley painful or distressful.

excursion *n* a pleasure trip.

excuse *vt* to let off; to forgive; to overlook. * *n* an apology; that which excuses; a reason or explanation of.

execrable *adj* hateful; detestable.

execute *vt* to perform; to carry out; to put to death; to make valid.

execution *n* the act or manner of performing; skill in music; capital punishment.

executive *n* a person or group concerned with administration or management of a business or organization. * *adj* having the power to execute decisions, laws, decrees etc.

executor *n* one who carries out provisions of will.

exemplary *adj* model; worthy of imitation.

exemplify *vt* to show by example.

exempt *vt* to free from; excuse. * *adj* free; immune.

exemption *n* release; immunity.

exercise *n* the use or application of a power or right; regular physical or mental exertion; something performed to develope or test a specific ability or skill. * *vt* to use, exert, employ; to engage in regular physical activity; to engage the attention of; to perplex.

exert *vt* to put forth strength etc; to strive.

exertion *n* effort.

exhale *vti* to breathe out.

exhaust *vt* to use up; to make empty; to use up; tire out; (subject) to deal with or develope completely. * the escape of waste gas or steam from an engine.

exhaustion *n* extreme weariness.

exhaustive *adj* full; thorough.

exhibit *vt* to display, esp in public; to present to a court in legal form. * *n* an act or instance of exhibiting, something exhibited; something produced and identified in court for use as evidence.

exhibition *n* display; any public show.

exhilarate *vt* to elate; to enliven.

exhort *vt* to encourage; to warn.

exhume *vt* to disinter.

exigence *n* pressing necessity; urgency.

exile *n* banishment; the person banished. * *vt* to banish from one's country.

exist *vi* to be; to live; to manage one's life with difficulty.

existent *adj* being; existing.

exit *n* a going out; a way out.

exonerate *vt* to free from blame.

exorbitant *adj* excessive esp. of prices.

exorcise *vi* to drive out evil spirits.

exotic *adj* foreign; excitingly different or unusual.

expand *vt,vi* to spread out; to swell; to describe in fuller detail; to become more friendly and genial.

expanse *n* a wide area.

expansion *n* enlargement; increase.

expansive *adj* wide; genial.

expatiate *vi* to speak or write about at lenght.

expatriate *vt* to exile oneself or banish another. * *n* (a person) living in another country, or self-exiled or banished.

expect *vt* to anticipate, to regard as likely to arrive or happen; to consider necessary, reasonable or due; to suppose.

expectancy *n* hope; expectation.

expectant *adj* awaiting; anxious; hopeful.

expectation *n* something that is expected to happen; (*pl*) prospects for the future, esp of inheritance.

expectorate *vt* to spit or cough out.

expediency *n* fitness; suitability under the circumstances.

expedient *adj* suitable for the present time or circumstances. * *n* device; a means to an end; a means used for want of a better.

expedite *vt* to accelerate.

expedition *n* promptness; an enterprise or those who undertake it.

expeditious *adj* speedy; prompt.

expel *vt* to drive out; to banish.

expend *vt* to spend; to use up; to consume.

expenditure *n* outlay; cost.

expense *n* cost; charge; price.

expensive *adj* costly; lavish.

experience *n* personal trial; knowledge

gained from contact with life or work; an effecting event. * *vt* to try; meet with.

experiment *n* a trial; a practical test; a controlled procedure carried out to discover, test or demonstrate something.* *vi* to carry out experiments.

experimental *adj* of, derived from, or proceeding by experiment; provisional.

expert *adj* skilful; knowledgeable throughtraining and experience. * *n* a specialist.

expertise *n* expert knowledge or skill.

expiate *vt* to atone for.

expire *vt* to breathe out; to exhale. * *vi* to die; to end.

explain *vt* to make clear; to expound. * *vi* to account for.

explanation *n* interpretation; reason.

explanatory *adj* serving to explain.

expletive *n* an oath.

explicable *adj* explainable.

explicit *adj* definite; expressly or frankly stated.

explode *vti* to burst with a loud noise; to expose; discredit.

exploit *n* a brilliant deed; a bold achievement. * *vt* to make use of; to take unfair advantage of.

exploitation *n* successful application of industry to any object, as land, mines, etc.

explore *vt* to search; to examine closely; to travel through for the purpose of discovery.

explorer *n* a traveller in unknown regions.

explosion *n* a violent detonation; an outburst (of feeling).

explosive *adj* liable to explode. * *n* material that explodes.

exponent *n* a person who explains or interprets something.

export *vt* to send goods abroad for sale. * *n* the commodity exported.

expose *vt* to deprive of protection or shelter; to uncover; to display; to endanger.

exposed *adj* unmasked; unsheltered.

exposition *n* explanation; exhibition.

exposure *n* a laying open to view or weather or danger; the time during which light reaches and acts on a photographic film, paper or plate; publicity.

expound *vt* to explain.

express *vt* to declare; to utter; to make known; to squeeze out. * *adj* swift, special; explicit; plain. * *n* a swift messenger, service, or conveyance; an express train. * *adv* with haste; at high speed; by express service.

expression *n* a phrase or mode of speech; facial look; taste and feeling (music); terms or collection saving to express something in mathematics.

expressive *adj* striking; full of expression.

expressly *adv* of set purpose; explicity.

expulsion *n* ejection; discharge.

expunge *vt* to blot out; to erase.

expurgate *vt* to purify (from sin, etc); cut out offensive passages from (books, etc).

exquisite *adj* beautiful; incomparable; acutely felt, as pain or pleasure.

extend *vti* to stretch out; to prolong in time; to spread; to accord; to reach; to hold out, eg the hand.

extension *n* extent, scope; an added part, eg to a building; an extra period; a programme of extramural teaching provided by a college, etc; an additional telephone connected to the principal line.

extensive *adj* far-reaching; large.

extent *n* compass; size; range; scope.

extenuate *vt* to make excuses for.

extenuation *n* mitigation.

exterior *adj* external; outside.

exterminate *vt* to destroy utterly.

external *adj* on the outside; visible.

extinct *adj* dead; extinguished; no longer existing or active.

extinction *n* destruction.

extinguish *vt* to put out; quench.

extinguisher *n* a device for putting out a fire.

extol *vt* to exalt; glorify.

extort *vt* to exact by force, eg money, promises.

extortionate *adj* exorbitant; harsh.

extra *adj, adv* additional. * something additional; a specialedition of a newspaper; one who plays a non-speaking part in a film.

extract *vt* to take or pull out by force; to withdraw by chemical or physical

means; to abstract. * *n* the essence of a
substance obtained by extraction; a passage taken from a book, play, film etc.

extraction *n* lineage; a drawing out.

extradite *vt* to give up foreign criminals
to police of their own country.

extradition *n* the handing over of fugitive foreign criminals.

extramural *adj* connected with a university but not as regular students.

extraneous *adj* foreign; irrelevant; ines-
sential.

extraordinary *adj* unusual; remarkable.

extravagance *n* excess; over-spending;
flamboyance; wastefulness.

extravagant *adj* lavish in spending; excessively, high of prices; unrestrained;
wasteful; profuse.

extravaganza *n* a fantastic literary or
musical composition.

extreme *adj* of the highest degree or intensity; excessive, immoderate,
unwarranted; very severe, stringent;
outermost. * *n* the highest or furthest
limit or degree.

extremely *adv* in the utmost degree.

extremist *n* a supporter of extreme measures.

extremity *n* the farthest point; the utmost
need (*pl*) the hands or feet..

extricate *vt* to set free; to disentangle.

exuberance *n* high spirits.

exuberant *adj* high-spirited; lively.

exude *vti* to ooze out.

exult *vi* to rejoice exceedingly; to triumph.

exultant *adj* jubilant.

eye *n* the organ of vision; mind; perception; a small hole; a catch; a shoot. * *vt*
to regard closely.

eyebrow *n* the hairy arch above the eye.

eyelash *n* the hair that edges the eyelid.

eyelid *n* the cover of the eye.

eyesight *n* power of sight.

eyesore *n* something offensive to the sight.

eye-witness *n* a person who sees an event.

eyrie *n* an eagle's nest.

F

fable *n* a short story with a moral; a falsehood.

fabled *adj* legendary.

fabric *n* frame of anything; a building;
texture; cloth.

fabricate *vt* to fashion; to invent.

fabrication *n* construction; forgery.

fabulous *adj* incredible; mythical.

façade *n* front view of an edifice.

face *n* the front part of the head; the countenance; aspect; assurance; dial of a
watch. * *vt* to front; to oppose.

facet *n* one of many sides (of gems).

facetious *adj* humorous.

facilitate *vt* to make easy.

facility *n* ease; dexterity.

facsimile *n* an exact copy.

fact *n* a deed; event; truth.

faction *n* an unscrupulous and self-inter-
ested party; discord.

factor *n* an agent; a land steward; an essential element; a measure of a number.

factory *n* a building where goods are
made.

faculty *n* capacity; power; special aptitude; a department of a university.

fad *n* personal habit on idiosyncrasy.

fade *vt, vi* to (cause to) lose vigour or
brightness or intensity gradually; to vanish gradually.

fail *vi* to weaken; to fade away; to stop
operating; to become bankrupt; not to
succeed; to miss; *vt* to disappoint the
expectations on hope.

failure *n* failing, non-performance, lack
of success; an unsuccessful person or
thing.

faint *vi* to become feeble; to swoon. * *adj*
dim., indistinct; weak; feeble. * *n* a
swoon.

fair *adj* pleasing to the eye; light in colour; just; favourable (weather); moderately good or large; average * *adv* justly.
* *n* a regular market or gathering for sale
of goods

fairly *adv* honestly, justly; moderately.

fairy *n* an elf; a sprite.

faith *n* belief; trust; religious conviction;

system of beliefs; fidelity to one's promises.

faithful *adj* loyal; trusty; accurate.

faithless *adj* false; unfaithful.

fake *vt* to disguise and so cheat; to pretend; to simulate.* *n* a faked article; a forgery; an impostor.

fall *vi* to drop down; to descend; to collapse; to sin; to lose power, status, office; to be injured or die in battle; to happen. * *n* a drop; a decrease; a decline in status or position; overthrow.

fallacious *adj* deceitful; misleading.

fallacy *n* a false argument or idea.

fallible *adj* liable to err; make mistakes.

fall-out *n* a deposit of radioactive dust from a nuclear explosion; a by-product.

fallow *adj* left uncultivated for one or more seasons; yellowish-brown.

false *adj* not true; forged; treacherous; deceitful; artificial.

falsehood *n* untruth; a lie.

falsetto *n* an unnaturally high-pitched voice.

falsification *n* wilful misrepresentation.

falsify *vt* to make false by altering in order to deceive.

falter *vi* to hesitate; to waver; to move unsteadily.

fame *n* reputation; renown.

familiar *adj* well-acquainted; friendly; common; well-known; presumptuous. * *n* an intimate; a spirit supposed to assist a witch.

familiarity *n* intimacy; presumptuous.

family *n* parents and their children; a set of relatives; the descendants of a common ancestor; a group of related plants or animals.

famine *n* extreme scarcity of food.

famish *vt,vi* to starve; to suffer extreme hunger.

famous *adj* renowned.

fan[1] *n* an instrument or device for creating a current of air; to cool by moving; to ventilate; to stir up or excite; to spread out like a fan.* *vt* the air.

fan[2] *n* an enthusiastic follower of a person, a sport or a hobby .

fanatic *adj* frenzied, bigoted. * *n* a zealot; an over enthusiastic person.

fancy *n* imagination; caprice; whim; delusion. * *vt, ti* to imagine; to like. * *adj* elegant; unreal.

fancy dress *n*

fanfare *n* a flourish of trumpets.

fang *n* a long, sharp, pointed tooth.

fanlight *n* a window over a door.

fantastic *adj* unrealistic; fanciful; unbelievable; imaginative.

fantasy *n* imagination; a product of this; an imaginative poem, play or novel.

far *adj* remote; extreme in political views. * *adv* very distant in space, time or degree; very much.

farce *n* a ludicrous situation.

farcical *adj* droll; ludicrous.

fare *vi* to be in a specified condition. * *n* food; the cost of a journey.

farewell *interj, n* goodbye.

farinaceous *adj* starchy; mealy.

farm *n* land (with buildings) on which crops and animals are raised. * *vt,vi* to cultivate; to lease out; to subcontract.

farmer *n* one who manages and operates a farm.

farther *adj, comp* more remote. * *adv* to a greater degree.

farthest *adj super* most distant. * *adv* at the greatest distance.

fascia *n* the instrument panel of a motor vehicle, the dash-board; the flat surface above a shop front with the name etc.

fascinate *vt* to charm; to captivate.

fascination *n* charm; spell.

fashion *n* a current style of dress, conduct, speech etc; the manner of form of appearance or action. * *vt* to make in a particular form; to suit or adapt.

fashionable *adj* stylish; in keeping with the prevailing fashion.

fast *adj* firm; fixed; steadfast; swift; lasting. * *vt* to abstain from food. * *n* a period of doing without food.

fasten *vt,vi* to fix firmly; to become fixed.

fastidious *adj* hard to please; over-refined.

fat *adj* plump; oily; rich; fertile. * *n* oily substance in animal bodies; the richest or best point of anything.

fatal *adj* deadly; disastrous.

fatalist *n* one who holds all things are predetermined.

fatality n a fatal occurrence; a death caused by disaster or accident; a person so killed.

fate n destiny; necessity; death; doom; lot.

fateful adj having important, often unpleasant, consequences.

father n a male parent; an ancestor; name given to R.C. priests. * vt to adopt; to found; to originate.

fatherhood n state of being a father.

father-in-law n the father of one's husband or wife.

fatherland n one's native country.

fathom n a nautical measure of length (6 ft/1.83m) * vt to try the depth of; to sound; to comprehend.

fatigue n tiredness from physical or mental effort; the tendency of a material to break under repeated stress. *vt, vi to make or become tired.

fatten vt to make fat.

fatuous adj foolish; idiotic.

fault n a slight offence; a flaw; a break of strata; an incorrect stroke in tennis.

faulty adj defective; imperfect.

fauna n a collective term for the animals of a region or specific environment.

favour n goodwill; kindness; leave; a token of goodwill; a gift presented at a party. * vt to befriend; to show support for; to oblige with; to facilitate.

favourable adj kindly disposed; propitious; conductive to.

favoured adj regarded with favour.

favourite n a person habitually preferred; a darling; a competitor expected to win; a minion. * adj preferred; beloved.

favouritism n showing undue partiality.

fawn n a young deer. * vi to cringe or flatter to gain favour. * adj light brown.

fax see **facsimile**.

fear n dread; terror; awe; anxiety. * vt, vi to dread; to hesitate; to reverence.

feasibility n practicability.

feasible adj practicable; possible.

feast n a sumptuous meal; a periodic religious celebration. * vi, vt to have or take part in a feast; to entertain with a feast.

feat n an exploit; a notable act.

feather n any of the light outgrowths forming the covering of a bird, a hollow central shaft with a vane of fine barbs on each side. * vt to ornament with feathers.

feature n any of the part of the face; a characteristic trait of something; a special attraction or distinctive quality of something; a prominent newspaper article etc. * vt, vi to make or be a feature of (something).

February n the second month in the year.

fecund adj fruitful; prolific.

federal adj united in a league for national purposes, but each partner having independent powers in local affairs.

federation n a union of independent bodies or states to take common action on certain matters.

fee n a reward for services; a payment; charge. * vt to pay a fee to.

feeble adj weak; infirm.

feed vt to give food to; to fatten. * vi to take food; to eat; to graze. * n food for animals; material fed into a machine.

feedback n a return to the input of part of the output of a system; information about a product, service etc. returned to the supplier for evaluation.

feel n the sense of touch; feeling; a quality as revealed by touch. * vt, vi to perceive or explore by the touch; to find one's way by cautious trail; to be conscious of, experience; to be affected by; to convey a certain sensation when touched.

feeler n an organ of touch in insects, &c.; remark, &c., made to probe a situation.

feeling adj sensitive; sympathetic. * n the sense of touch; emotion; sympathy; a belief; an opinion arising from emotion (pl) emotions; sensibilities.

feign vt, vi to pretend; to invent.

feint n a pretence (of doing); a sham blow.

felicitate vt to congratulate.

felicitous adj happy; apt.

felicity n happiness; aptness.

feline adj cat-like.

fell adj cruel; savage. * n a skin; a stony hill. * vt to strike down.

fellow n a partner; one of a pair; a man; a member of the governing body in some colleges and universities; a member of a learned society.

fellowship *n* companionship; an association; the status of a college fellow.

felon *n* a criminal.

felony *n* a serious crime.

felt *n* a fabric made of wool.

female *n* a girl or woman. *adj of the sex that produces young.

feminine *adj* womanly; womanish.

feminism *n* the movement to win political, economic and social equality for women.

femoral *adj* belonging to the thigh.

femur *n* the thigh bone.

fen *n* a marsh; a bog.

fence *n* a barrier put round land to mark a boundary, or prevent animals, etc from escaping; a receiver of stolen goods. * *vt, vi* to surround a fence; to keep (out) as by a fence; to make evasive answers; to act as a fence for stolen goods.

fencing *n* the practice of sword play; material for fences.

fend *vt* to keep or ward off; (with **for**) to provide a livelihood for.

fender *n* a hearth guard; a buffer along a ship's side; the part of a car body over the wheel.

ferment *n* that which causes fermentation, as yeast; tumult; agitation. * *vt, vi* to cause or subject to fermentation; to cause agitation or excitement.

fermentation *n* the breakdown of complex molecules in organic components caused by the influence of yeast or other substances.

ferocious *adj* fierce; savage.

ferocity *n* savagery; fury.

ferret *n* a species of weasel. * *vt* to drive out (rabbits); to search out (secrets).

ferry *n* a boat used for ferrying; a ferrying service; the location of a ferry. * *vt* to convey (passengers etc) over a stretch of water; to transport from one place to another, esp along a regular route.

fertile *adj* fruitful; inventive.

fertilize *vt* to enrich (soil) by adding nutrients; to impregnate.

fertilizer *n* natural organic or artificial substances used to enrich the soil.

fervent *adj* burning; ardent; passionate.

fervid *adj* zealous; eager.

fervour *n* zeal; earnestness.

fester *vi* to suppurate; to rankle.

festival *n* a feast; a gala day; performances of music, plays etc. Given periodically.

festive *adj* joyous; merry.

festivity *n* festive gaiety.

fetch *vt* to go and bring back; to heave.

fête *n* a festival. * *vt* to honour; to make much of.

fetid *adj* stinking; offensive.

fetish *n* anything excessively reverenced.

fetter *n* a shackle for feet; restraint. * *vt* to hobble; to restrict.

feu *n* land held in fee.

feud *n* a quarrel esp. between individuals, families, clans.

feudalism *n* the holding of land in return for military service.

fever *n* a disease marked by high temperature; restless excitement.

few *adj* not many; a small number.

fiancé, fiancée *n* a man, woman engaged to be married.

fiasco *n* an ignominious failure.

fibre *n* a natural or synthetic thread, e.g. from cotton, nylon, which is spun into yarn; a material composed of such yarn; texture; strength or character; roughage.

fibreglass *n* a glass composed of fibres often bonded with plastic used in making various products.

fickle *adj* vacillating; inconstant.

fickleness *n* inconstancy.

fiction *n* a made-up story; novels; plays collectively.

fictitious *adj* imaginary; false.

fiddle *n* a violin. *vt* to play the violin; to swindle.

fidelity *n* faithfulness; loyalty.

fidget *vi* to be restless. * *n* a restless person.

field *n* land suitable for tillage or pasture; range; sports ground; an area affected by electrical, magnetic or gravitational influence etc; the area visible through an optical lens; all competitors in a contest; in a computer; a section of a record in a database. * *vt, vi* to catch and return the ball in cricket etc; to handle (e.g. questions) successfully.

field marshal *n* an army officer of the highest rank.

fiend *n* a demon; a cruel person; an avid fan.

fiendish *adj* like a fiend.

fierce *adj* wild; savage; violent; intense.

fiery *adj* burning; passionate; irascible.

fight *vi, vt* to contend; to strive for victory. * *n* a struggle; a battle.

fighter *n* a person who fights; a person who does not yield easily; an aircraft designed to destroy enemy aircraft.

figment *n* a fiction; a falsehood.

figuration *n* shape; form.

figurative *adj* using figures of speech; metaphorical.

figure *n* form; outline; diagram; pattern; person; statue; symbol; price; digit; a set of steps on movements (*pl*) arithmetic. * *vt, vi* to represent in a diagram or outline to imagine; to estimate; to appear.

figurehead *n* the carved figure on the bow of ships; a nominal head or leader.

filament *n* a slender thread; the fine wire in a light bulb.

filch *vt* to pilfer; to steal.

file *n* a container for holding papers; an orderly arrangement of papers; a line of persons or things; in computer, a collection of related data under a specific name; a smoothing or polishing or grinding tool. * *vt, vi* to put on public records, to march in file; to wear down.

filial *adj* of or relating to a son or daughter.

filigree *n* delicate tracery in gold or silver.

filings *npl* particles rubbed off by a file.

fill *vt, vi* to make or become full; to pervade; to hold; to satisfy.

fillet *n* a thin boneless strip of fish or meat. * *vt* to bone meat, &c.

filling *n* a substance used to fill a tooth cavity; the contents of a sandwich, pie etc. *adj* substantial (of a meal).

filly *n* a female colt.

film *n* a fine, thin skin, coating etc; a flexible cellulose material covered with a light-sensitive substance used in photography; a haze or blur; a motion picture.

filter *n* a device or substance straining out solid particles, impurities etc; a traffic signal that allows cars to turn left or right while the main lights are red. * *vt, vi* to pass through or as through a filter, to remove with a filter.

filth *n* dirt; pollution; obscenity.

filthy *adj* dirty; foul; obscene.

filtrate *vt* to filter.

fin *n* an organ by which a fish etc. steers itself and swims; any fin-shaped object used as a stabilizer, as on an aircraft or rocket.

final *adj* last; conclusive. *n* (often *pl*) the last of a series of contests; a final examination.

finale *n* the last piece; end, esp. of any public performance; the last section in a musical composition.

finance *n* the management of money. * *vt* to supply or raise money for.

financier *n* one skilled in finance.

find *vt* to come upon; to discover; to have; to supply; to declare. * *n* a discovery.

finding *n* a verdict; a discovery.

fine *adj* slender; minute; keen; delicate. * *n* a money penalty. * *vt* to punish by a fine.

finery *n* showy apparel or jewellery.

finesse *n* delicacy or subtlety of performance; skilfulness, diplomacy in handling a situation. * *vt* to achieve by finesse.

finger *n* one of the five digits of the hand usually excluding the thumb; anything finger-shaped. * *vt* to touch.

fingerprint *n* the impression of the ridges on a fingertip, esp as used for purposes of identification.

finish *n* the last part, the end; anything used to finish a surface; the finished effect; means or manner of completion or perfecting; polished manners, speech etc. *vt, vi* to bring to an end, to come to the end of; to consume entirely; to perfect; to give a desired surface effect to.

finite *adj* limited; bounded.

fiord, fjord *n* an inlet of the sea.

fire *n* the flame, heat and light of combustion

fire alarm *n* a device that uses a bell, hooter etc, to warn of a fire.

firearm n a gun or rifle.

firebrand n a flaming piece of wood; one who causes mischief or disturbance.

fire brigade n an organisation of men and women trained to extinguish fires.

fire escape n a means of exit from a building, esp. a stairway, for use in case of fire.

fireplace n a place for a fire, esp a recess in a wall; the surrounding area.

fireproof adj incombustible.

fireside n the hearth; home.

firework n a device packed with explosive and combustible material used to produce noisy and colourful displays.

firing squad n a detachment with the task of firing a salute at a military funeral or carrying out an execution.

firm adj steady; strong; hard; resolute. * n a business partnership.

firmament n the sky or heavens.

first n an person or thing that is first; the beginning; the winning place, as in a race; the highest award in a university degree. *adj before all others in a series; foremost, as in rank, equality etc. * adv before anyone or anything else.

first aid n emergency treatment for an injury etc., before regular medical aid is available.

first-class adj, n of the highest quality, as in accommodation, travel.

firsthand adj obtained directly.

first-rate adj, adv of the best quality; (inf) excellent.

firth n a wide river mouth.

fiscal adj relating to public finance. * n a public prosecutor.

fish n a cold-blooded animal living in water, having backbones, gills and fins. *vi to catch or try to catch fish.

fisherman n one who fishes for a living or for sport.

fishery n the business of fishing; fishing ground.

fishing n the art of catching fish.

fishmonger n a dealer in fish; his shop.

fishy adj like a fish in odour, taste etc; creating doubt or suspicion.

fission n a split or cleavage; the splitting of the atomic nucleus resulting in the release of energy, nuclear fission.

fissure n a cleft; a chasm.

fist n the hand clenched.

fit n a spasm; convulsion; right size; caprice. * adj suitable; proper; healthy. * vt, vi to make fit; to suit; to adapt; to equip.

fitful adj spasmodic; uncertain.

fitment n a piece of equipment, esp fixed furniture.

fitter n one who fits; one who puts the parts of machinery together.

fitting adj becoming; appropriate. * npl fixtures.

five adj, n one more than four; the symbol for this (5, V, v).

fix vt, vi to make fast or firm; to settle; to appoint; to direct one's eyes steadily at something; to repair; to arrange or influence a result. * n a dilemma.

fixed adj firm; fast.

fixture n what is fixed to anything, as to land or to a house; a fixed article of furniture; a firmly established person or thing; a fixed or appointed time or event.

fizz vi to make a hissing sound.

flabby adj soft; limp.

flaccid adj flabby.

flag n a standard; ensign; a flat paving stone. * vi to droop; to languish.

flagellate vt to whip.

flagellation n a scourging.

flagon n a jug-shaped metal or pottery vessel.

flagrant adj glaring; shameful; notorious.

flail n a hand-threshing implement.

flair n natural ability; aptitude; discernment; stylishness.

flake n a scale; a fleecy particle (snow). * vi to peel off. * vt to form into flakes.

flamboyant adj florid; flaming; strikingly elaborate; dashing; exuberant.

flame n a sheet of fire; a blaze; passion. * vi to blaze; to become red in the face with emotion.

flan n an open case of pastry or sponge cake with a sweet or savoury filling.

flange n a raised edge on wheel.

flank n the fleshy part of the side; from the ribs to the hip; the side of (army, mountain, &c.). * vt to be at the side of;

to menace on the side.

flannel n a soft woollen cloth, a small cloth for washing the face; nonsense; equivocation. (pl) flannel trousers.

flap n the beat of wings or a similar sound; anything hanging loose (esp. part of a garment); vi, vt to move like wings; to flutter; agitation; panic, to panic.

flare n a sudden flash; a bright light used as a signal or illumination; a widened part or shape. * vi to burn with a sudden, bright, unsteady flame; to widen our gradually.

flash n a sudden gleam; a brief moment, display, news item. * vi, vt to shine out suddenly; to signal.

flashback n an interruption in the continuity of a story etc, by telling or showing an earlier episode.

flashbulb n a small bulb giving an intense light used in photography.

flashlight n a torch.

flash point n the ignition point.

flashy adj gaudy; showy.

flask n a kind of bottle; a vacuum flask.

flat adj level; prostrate; tasteless; below pitch; deflated; dull; tedious; (of battery) drained of electric current. * n a storey or set of rooms in a house.

flatten vt to make flat.

flatter vt to praise unduly or insincerely.

flattery n undeserved praise.

flatulence n wind in the stomach.

flaunt vi, vt to show off.

flavour n distinctive taste. * vt to season; to give flavour to.

flaw n a crack; a defect.

flax n a plant cultivated for its fibres.

flaxen adj of or like flax; fair; pale yellow.

flay vt to strip off (skin).

flea n a jumping, bloodsucking insect.

fleck n a spot; a streak. * vt to streak.

fledgling n a young bird; a trainee.

flee vi to run away from danger etc; to disappear.

fleece n a sheep's coat. * vt to shear the wool from; to rob; to defraud.

fleet n a squadron of ships; navy; a group of cars, ships, buses under one management. * adj swift; nimble.

fleeting adj transient; passing.

flesh n the soft part of the body; the pulpy part of fruits and vegetables; meat; the body and its appetites.

fleshy adj plump; fat.

flex vt to bend.

flexible adj pliable; supple; adaptable.

flick n a touch with a whip; a flip. * vt to flip; to strike with a flick.

flicker vi to burn unsteadily. * n an unsteady light; a flickering movement.

flight[1] n the act, manner, or power of flying; distance flown; an aircraft scheduled to fly a certain trip; a set of stairs, as between landings.

flight[1] n an act or instance of fleeing.

flighty adj fickle; giddy.

flimsy adj thin; slight; weak; light and thin; unconvincing * n copying paper.

flinch vi to shrink; to quail; to drawback.

fling vt to hurl; to scatter. * vi to kick out violently; to move quickly or impetuously. * n a throw; a Highland dance.

flint n a hard stone; a pebble.

flinty adj hard; cruel.

flip n a flick. * vt to flick; to flick with the thumb.

flippancy n undue levity; frivolity.

flippant adj saucy; heedless; frivolous.

flirt vt, vi to throw or jerk; to make insincere amorous approaches; to trifle or toy e.g. with an idea. * n one who toys amorously with the opposite sex.

flit vi to fly or dart ; to vacate premises.

float n a cork or other device used on a fishing line to signal that the bait has been taken; a low flat vehicle decorated for exhibit in a parade; a small sum of money available for cash expenditures. * vt, vi to rest on the surface of or be suspended in liquid; to put into circulation.

floe n floating ice.

flog vt to whip; to thrash.

flood n a deluge; a river; abundance. * vt to overflow; to deluge.

floodgate n a gate or lock in a waterway.

floodlight n a strongbeam of light used to illuminate a stage, sports field, stadium etc. * vt (pt **floodlit**) to illuminate with floodlights.

floodmark n high-water mark.

floodtide n the rising tide.

floor n the inside bottom surface of a room; the bottom surface of anything; as the ocean; a storey in a building; the lower limit, the base. * vt to provide with a floor; (inf) to defeat; (inf) to shock, to confuse.

flop vi (pt **flopped**) to sway or bounce loosely; to move in a heavy, clumsy or relaxed manner; (inf) to fail. * n a flopping movement; a collapse; (inf) a complete failure.

floppy adj limp; hanging loosely.

floppy disk n a disk of flexible material for storing data in a computer.

flora n the plant life of a region or district.

floral adj pertaining to flowers.

florid adj flowery; ruddy of complexion.

florist n a cultivator or seller of flowers.

flotation n the act or process of floating; a launching of a business venture.

flotilla n a small fleet.

flotsam n floating wreckage.

flounce[1] vi, to move in an emphatic or impatient manner.

flounce[2] n a frill of material sewn to the skirt of a dress. * vt to add flounces to.

flounder n a flat fish. * vi to move awkwardly and with difficulty; to be clumsy in thinking and in speaking.

flour n the meal of grain.

flourish vi to grow luxuriantly; to thrive; to live and work at a specified period. * vt to brandish. * n showy expression; fanciful stroke of the pen; brandishing.

flout vt to disobey openly; to treat with contempt.

flow vi to move, as water; to issue; to glide smoothly; to hang loose; to circulate; to be plentiful. * n a stream; current.

flow chart n a diagram representing the sequence of and relationships between different steps or procedures in a complex process, e.g. manufacturing.

flower n the blossom of plants; youth; the prime. * vi to blossom; to bloom.

flowery adj full of or decorated with flowers; figurative; elaborate of language.

fluctuate vi (of prices) to be continually varying in an irregular way; to waver; to be unstable.

fluctuating adj varying.

flu u influenza.

flue n a smoke vent.

fluent adj flowing; voluble; able to speak and write a foreign language with ease; articulate; graceful.

fluff n light down or nap; a mistake.

fluid adj capable of flowing. * n that which flows, as water or air.

fluke n the barb of an anchor; a lucky stroke; a flat fish; a flattened parasitic worm.

fluoride n any of various compounds of fluoride.

flurry n a sudden gust of wind, rain or snow; bustle; hurry. vt, vi to (cause to) become flustered.

flush[1] n a rapid flow, as of water; sudden, vigorous growth; a sudden excitement; a blush. *vt, vi to cause to blush; to excite; to flow rapidly.

flush[2] vt to make game birds fly away suddenly.

flush[3] n (poker, etc) a hand of cards all of the same suit.

fluster vt to agitate; to confuse.

flute n an orchestral woodwind instrument with finger holes and keys held horizontally and played through a hole located near one end; a decorative groove. * vi to play or make sounds like a flute.

flutist, flautist n a flute player.

flutter vi to flap; to quiver; to beat irregularly or spasmodically (of the heart) * n a tremor; stir; nervous excitement; commotion; a small bet.

fly[1] n a two-winged insect; a natural or imitation fly attached to a fish-hook as bait.

fly[2] vb (pt **flew**, pp **flown**) vi, vt to move through the air, esp on wings; to travel in an aircraft; to control an aircraft; to take flight, as a kite; to escape, flee from; to pass quickly; (inf) to depart quickly). * n a flap that hides buttons.

fly[3] adj (inf) sly, astute.

flying adj capable of flight; fleeing; fast-moving. * n the act of flying an aircraft.

flying start n a start in a race when the

competitor is already moving at the starting line; a promising start.

flyleaf n (pl **flyleaves**) a blank leaf at the beginning or end of a book.

flyover n a bridge that carries a road or railway over another; a fly-past.

fly-past n a processional flight of aircraft.

foal n young of horse, ass.

foam n froth or fine bubbles on the surface of liquid. * vi to cause or emit foam.

fob n a watch pocket in a trouser waistband. *vt (with **off**) to cheat; to put off; to palm off.

focal adj belonging to a focus.

focus n point in which reflected rays converge; correct adjustment of the eye or lens to form a clear image; a centre of activity or interest. * vt to concentrate; the centre.

fodder n food for cattle.

foe n an enemy.

foetus n the unborn young of an animal, esp. in later stages; in humans, the offspring in the womb from the fourth month until birth.

fog n a thick mist; cloudiness on a developed photograph.

foible n a weakness or failing; an idiosyncrasy.

foil vt to frustrate; to baffle. * n defeat; a sword used in fencing; a leaf of metal; a background to set things off.

foist vt to palm off.

fold[1] vt, vi to cover by bending or doubling over so that one part covers another; to interlace (one's arms); to incorporate (an ingredient) into a food mixture by gentle overturning. * n something folded, as a piece of cloth; a crease or hollow made by folding.

fold[2] n a pen for sheep. * vt to pen in a fold.

foliage n leaves.

folio n a sheet once folded; a leaf in a ledger; a book of largest size.

folk n people in general; folk music.

folklore n popular tales, songs, &c. of a people.

follow vt, vi to go or come after; to pursue; to accompany; to succeed; to result from; to understand; to practise; to be occupied with.

follower n a disciple or adherent; a person who imitates another.

following n a body of followers, adherents or believers. * adj succeeding; next after; now to be stated.

folly n foolishness; madness; an extravagant or fanciful building serving no practical purpose.

foment vt to stir up strife or agitation.

fond adj tender; loving; doting.

fondle vt to caress.

font n the receptacle for baptismal on holy water; set of type.

food n nourishment; provisions.

fool n a simpleton; a clown; a jester; a cold pudding of whipped cream and fruit purée. * vi to trifle. * vt to deceive.

foolhardy adj rash; venturesome.

foolproof adj proof against failure; easy to understand; easy to use.

foolscap n a size of paper.

foot n (pl **feet**) that upon which anything stands; the lower end of the leg; the lower part or edge of something; the bottom; a measure of 12 inches, a group of syllables serving as a unit of metre in verse. * vt to pay; to walk; to dance.

football n a large ball; game played with it by two teams.

foothold n a ledge etc, for placing the foot when climbing etc; a place from which further progress may be made.

footing n foothold; basis; status.

footlights n a row of lights in front of the stage floor.

foot-path n a narrow path for pedestrians.

footprint n impression of the foot.

footsore adj having painful feet from excessive walking.

footstep n a track; a footprint.

for prep, because of, as a result of; as the price of, or recompense of; in order to be, to serve as; to quest of; in the direction of; on behalf of; in place of; in favour of; with respect to; in spite of; to the extent of; throughout the space of; during. * conj because.

forage n fodder. * vt to collect or go in search of provisions.

foray vt to pillage. * n a sudden raid.

forbear vi to endure; to avoid. * vt to hold oneself back from.

forbearance n patience; restraint.

forbid vt to prohibit; to oppose.

forbidding adj unfriendly; solemn; strict; repulsive.

force n strength, power, effort; (physics) (the intensity of) an influence that causes movement of a body or other effects; a body of soldiers, police etc. prepared for action; effectiveness; violence, compulsion. * vt to compel by physical effort, superior strength etc; to achieve by force; to press or drive against resistance; to produce with effort; to break open; to impose, inflict.

forced adj affected; overstrained.

forceful adj powerful, effective.

forceps n an instrument for grasping and holding firmly, or exerting traction upon objects, esp by jewellers and surgeons.

ford n a crossing place in a river. * vt to wade across.

fore adj in front of; prior. * adv before.

forearm n the arm from elbow to wrist.

forearm vt to arm beforehand.

forebode vt to foretell; to portend.

forecast vt to foresee; to predict events, weather etc. through national analysis. * n a prediction.

foreclose vt to preclude; to stop.

forecourt n an enclosed space in front of a building, as in a filling station.

forefathers pl n ancestors.

forefront n the foremost part.

foregoing adj preceding.

foregone adj past; inevitable; preceding.

foreground n the front part of a picture.

forehead n the brow.

foreign adj alien; native belonging to another country; introduces from outside.

foreman n an overseer; the spokesman in a jury.

foremost adj first; chief; most advanced.

forensic adj belonging to or used in courts of law.

forensic medicine n the application of medical expertise to legal and criminal investigations.

forerunner n a herald; precursor.

foresee vt (pt **foresaw**, pp **foreseen**) to be aware of beforehand.

foreshadow vt to prophesy; to augur.

foreshore n the shore between high- and low-water marks.

foresight n forethought; provision for the future.

forest n an extensive wood.

forestall vt to anticipate.

forestry n the science of planting and cultivating forests.

foretaste n a taste beforehand.

forever adv always; eternally.

foreword n a preface to a book.

forfeit vt to lose by fault; to be penalized by forfeit. * n a penalty.

forge n a furnace; a smithy. * vt, vi to shape by heating and hammering; to falsify; to counterfeit a signature etc.

forgery n fraudulently copying; a forged copy.

forget vt to cease to remember.

forgetful adj apt to forget; inattentive.

forget-me-not n a small blue flower.

forgive vt to pardon; to stop feeling resentment. * vi to be merciful or forgiving.

forgiving adj compassionate.

forgo vt to go without; to abstain from.

fork n a small, usu metal, instrument with two or more thin prongs set in a handle, used in eating and cooking; anything that divides into prongs or branches; the point of separation. (* vt, vi to divide into branches; to follow a branch of a fork in the road etc.

fork-lift truck n a vehicle with power-operated prongs for raising and lowering loads.

forlorn adj deserted; hopeless.

form n general structure; the figure of a person or animal; arrangement; a printed document with blanks to be filled in; a class in school; condition of mind or body; changed appearance of a word to show inflection. * vt, vi to shape; to train; to develop (habits); to constitute; to be formed.

formal adj in conformity with established rules or habits; regular; relating to outward appearance only; ceremonial;

punctilious; stiff.

formality n in accordance with custom.

format n the size, form, shape in which books, etc are issued; the general style or presentation of something; (*comput*) the arrangement of data on magnetic disk etc of access and storage. * vt to arrange in a particular form, esp for a computer.

formative adj pertaining to formation and development; shaping.

former adj comp deg past; preceding.

formidable adj terrifying; difficult.

formula n (pl **formulas, formulae**) a set of symbols expressing the composition of a substance; a general expression in algebraic form for solving a problem; a prescribed form; a fixed method according to which something is to be done.

formulate vt to express clearly or in a formula.

forsake vt to abandon; to renounce.

fort n a fortress.

forte adv loudly (*mus*). * n a person's strong point.

forth adv forward; abroad.

forthcoming adj about to appear.

forthright adv frank; straightforward; outspoken.

forthwith adv without delay.

fortification n the act of fortifying; defensive works.

fortify vt to strengthen; to erect defences; to add alcohol to.

fortitude n endurance; courage; patience.

fortnight n two weeks.

fortress n a stronghold; a castle.

fortuitous adj chance; accidental.

fortunate adj lucky; prosperous.

fortune n chance; luck; fate; vast wealth; prosperity.

fortune-teller n a person who claims to foretell a person's future.

forum n an assembly or meeting to discuss topics of public concern; a medium for public debate, as a magazine.

forward adv towards the front. * adj in advance, ready; bold; pert. * n a first-line player. * vt to hasten; to advance; to send on .

fossil adj petrified and preserved in rocks.

* n petrified remains of plants and animals; an out-of-date person or thing.

foster vt to nourish; to promote; to bring up a child not one's own.

foul adj dirty; filthy; stormy; impure; obscene; contrary to rules. * vt, vi to defile; to dirty; to strike against. * n unfair play.

found vt to lay the base of; to establish; to institute; to cast (in a mould). * vi to rest on.

foundation n an endowment for an institution; such an institution; the base of a house, wall etc; an underlying principle etc.

founder n an originator; an endower; a moulder of metals. * vi, vt to fill with water and sink; to fall ; to collapse.

foundry n a workshop for casting metal.

fount n a set of printing type on characters of one style and size; a source.

fountain n a spring; an artificial jet; source.

fowl n a bird; poultry.

fox n a dog-like animal, red-furred and bushy-tailed; a sly person. *vt to deceive by cunning.

fracas n an uproar.

fraction n a small part, amount etc; (*math*) a quantity less than a whole, expressed as a decimal or with a numerator and denominator. * adj **fractional**. * adv **fractionally**.

fractious adj snappish; peevish.

fracture n a break; breaking of a bone. * vt to break.

fragile adj easily broken; frail; delicate.

fragment n a part broken off. *vt, vi to break or cause to break into fragments.

fragmentary adj disjointed.

fragrance, fragrancy n a perfume.

fragrant adj sweet-smelling.

frail adj easily broken; weak; fragile.

frame vt to form according to a pattern; to construct; to put into words; to enclose (a picture) in a border; (*sl*) to falsify evidence against (an innocent person). * n something composed of parts fitted together and united; the physical make-up of an animal esp a human body; the case enclosing a window, door etc;

an ornamental border, as round a picture; (*snooker*) a single game. *n* **framer**.

franc *n* a French coin.

franchise *n* the right to vote in public elections; authorization to sell the goods of a manufacturer in a particular area. * *vt* to grant a franchise.

frank *adj* free and direct in expressing oneself; honest, open. * *vt* to mark letters etc with a mark denoting free postage. * *n* a mark indicating free postage. *n* **frankness**.

frankincense *n* incense; perfume.

frantic *adj* mad; distracted; furious; wild.

fraternal *adj* of or belong to a brother or a fraternity; brotherly; friendly.

fraternity *n* brotherly feeling; a society of people with common interests.

fraternize *vi* to associate as brothers.

fratricide *n* murder of a brother.

fraud *n* criminal deception; a deceitful person; an impostor.

fraudulent *adj* dishonest.

fraught *adj* full of; loaded with.

fray *n* an affray; a fight. * *vt, vi* to wear away or become worn.

freak *n* an unusual happening; (*inf*) a person who dresses or acts in a notably unconventional manner. * *adj* **freakish**.

freakish *adj* grotesque.

freckle *n* a brownish spot on the skin.

free *adj* (**freer, freest**) not under the control or power of another; having social and political liberty; independent; able to move in any direction; not exact; generous; frank; with no cost or charge; clear of obstruction. * *adj* without cost; in a free manner. * *vt* (*pt* **freed**) to set free.

freedom *n* liberty; privilege; frankness; undue familiarity.

freehand *adj* drawn by hand.

freehanded *adj* generous.

freehold *n* land with no burdens except taxes.

freelance *n* a person who pursues a profession without long-term commitment to any employer * *vt* to work as a freelance. also **freelancer**.

Freemason *n* a member of the secretive fraternity dedicated to mutual aid.

free trade *n* trade based on the unrestricted international exchange of goods with tariffs used only as a source of revenue. *n* **freetrader**.

freeway *n* in North America, a fast road, a motorway.

freewheel *vi* to ride a bicycle with the gear disconnected; to drive a car with the gear in neutral. * *n* **freewheeler**.

free will *n* freedom of human beings to make choices that are not determined by prior causes or by divine intervention.

freeze *vi, vt* to be formed into, or become covered by ice; to become motionless; to be made speechless by strong emotion; to become formal and unfriendly; to convert from a liquid to a solid with cold.

freezer *n* a container that freezes and preserves food for long periods.

freezing point *n* the temperature at which a liquid solidifies.

freight *n* cargo (ship); load (train); the cost of transport.

freighter *n* a ship or aircraft carrying freight.

French fries, french fries *npl* thin strips of potato fried in oil etc, chips.

French windows, French doors *npl* a pair of floor-length casement windows in an outside wall, opening on to a patio, garden etc.

frenzied *adj* distracted; maddened.

frenzy *n* madness; passion; wild excitement.

frequent *adj* coming, happening often; numerous; common. * *vt* to visit often.

frequency *n* repeated occurrence; the number of occurrences, cycles etc, in a given period.

fresco *n* a painting on plaster while wet or fresh.

fresh *adj* new; brisk; unfaded; not salt; not stale; pure; cool.

freshen *vt* to make fresh. * *vi* to grow fresh.

freshman *n* a novice; newcomer; a student in the first year at a university etc.

fret *vt* to eat into; to vex. * *vi* to be vexed. * *n* irritation; peevishness; one of a series of ridges along the fingerboard of a guitar, banjo etc. used as a guide for depressing the strings.

fretful adj peevish; petulant.

fretwork n ornamental and perforated woodwork.

friable adj easily crumbled.

friar n a member of certain RC religious orders.

fricassé n a dish of white meat highly seasoned.

friction n a rubbing together; resistance offered to moving bodies; unpleasantness; conflict between differing opinions, ideas etc.

Friday n the sixth day of the week.

fridge n a refrigerator.

friend n a close companion; one warmly attached to another; a Quaker.

friendly adj kind; well-disposed; favourable. * n a sporting game played for fun, not in a competition.

friendship n mutual attachment.

frieze n a decorative band round the upper part of room walls.

frigate n a warship smaller than a destroyer used for escort, anti-submarine, and patrol duties.

fright n sudden fear; a shock; something unsightly or ridiculous in appearance.

frighten vt to strike with fear; to terrify.

frightful adj dreadful; fearful; very bad.

frigid adj cold; stiff; formal.

frill n a ruffle; a fringe; an affectation.

fringe n a decorative border of hanging threads; an outer edge; a marginal or minor part. * vt to be or make a fringe fore. * adj at the outer edge; additional; minor; unconventional.

frisk vi to dance, skip, gambol. * vt to search (a person) by feeling or looking for concealed weapons etc.

frisky adj jumping with gaiety; lively.

fritter n fried batter with fruit; a pancake. * vt to trifle away; to waste.

frivolity n levity; trifling act, thought or action.

frivolous adj trivial; trifling; irresponsible.

frizzle vi to curl; to grill with hissing noise.

fro adv from; back; backward.

frock n an outer garment; dress.

frogman n a person who wears a rubber suit, flippers, oxygen supply etc and is trained in working underwater.

frolic adj joyous; frisky. * n a lively party or game; merriment; a merry prank. * vi to gambol.

frolicsome adj given to pranks.

from prep beginning at, starting with; out of; originating with; out of the possibility or use of.

frond n the leaf of a fern.

front n outward behaviour; (inf) an appearance of social standing etc; the part facing forward; the first part; the promenade of a seaside resort; the advanced battle area in warfare; a person or group used to hid another's activity

frontage n the front of a building.

frontal adj of or belonging to the front; of the forehead. * n a decorative covering for the front of an altar.

frontier n the border between two countries; the limit of existing knowledge of a subject.

frontispiece n picture facing the title page of a book.

frost n a temperature at or below freezing point; a coating of powdery ice particles; coldness of manner. * vt to cover (as if) with frost or frosting; to give a frost-like opaque surface to (glass).

frostbite n injury or deadening of sensation to a part of the body by excessive cold.

froth n foam; bubbles; empty talk; frivolity.

frown vi to scowl; to concentrate or look displeased by contracting the brow. * n a stern look.

frozen see **freeze**.

frugal adj careful; thrifty; meagre.

frugality n thrift.

fruit n the produce of plants; offspring; the outcome or result of any action.

fruitful adj producing much fruit; very productive.

fruition n fulfilment; realization.

frump n a dowdy woman.

frustrate vt to balk; to foil; to prevent from achieving a goal or gratifying a desire.

frustration n disappointment.

fry vt to cook over direct heat in hot fat * n young fish.

fuddle vt to stupefy with drink.

fudge n a soft sweet made of butter, milk, sugar, flavouring etc. * vt, vi to fake; to fail to come to grips with; to refuse to commit oneself; to cheat.

fuel n material burned to supply heat and power, or as a source of nuclear energy; anything that serves to intensify strong feelings. * vt, vi (pt fuelled) to supply with fuel.

fugitive adj fleeting; transient. * n a runaway; a refugee.

fugue n a piece of music in which the theme is taken up by the parts in succession.

fulcrum n (pl fulcra, fulcrums) the point of support of a lever.

fulfil vt to carry into effect; to carry out a promise; to satisfy; to bring to an end; complete.

fulfilment n accomplishment.

full adj having or holding all that can be contained; having eaten all one wants; having a great number (of); complete; having reached to greatness size, extent etc. *adj completely, directly, exactly.

full-blown adj fully developed or expanded.

full stop n the punctuation mark (.) at the end of a sentence.

full time n the finish of a match.

full-time adj working or lasting the whole time.

fulminate vi, vt to thunder; to explode.

fulsome adj insincere; excessively, flattering.

fumble vi to grope; to handle clumsily.

fume n (often pl) smoke; vapour; rage. * vi to emit smoke; to rage.

fumigate vt to purify, disinfect by fumes.

fun n merriment; sport; amusement.

function n office; duty; work; occupation; an official ceremony or social entertainment. * vi to perform work; to act; to operate.

functional adj of a function or functions; practical, not ornamental.

fund n a stock; money set apart for a special object; a supply. * (pl) ready money.

* vt to provide money for; to invest.

fundamental adj basic; essential. * n an essential part.

funeral n the ceremony associated with the burial or cremation of the dead; a procession accompanying a coffin to a burial.

funereal adj dark; dismal.

fungus n (pl fungi, funguses) any of a major group of lower plants, as mildews, mushrooms, yeasts etc, that lack chlorophyll and reproduce by spores.

funicular adj made of ropes. * n a cable railway.

funnel n a utensil for conveying liquids into bottles; an air or smoke shaft; a metal chimney for the escape of smoke, steam etc. * vt, vi to (cause to) pour through a funnel.

funny adj droll; comical; puzzling; unwell.

fur n the short soft hair of certain animals; a coating.

furious adj full of rage; violent.

furl vt to roll up a sail.

furlong n the eighth of a mile.

furlough n leave of absence esp. for military personnel.

furnace n a fire chamber where powerful heat can be raised.

furnish vt to provide a room with furniture; to supply; to equip.

furnishing n pl furniture, carpets etc.

furniture n household effects.

furore n excitement; stir.

furrow n a trench made by a plough; a wrinkle. * vt to groove; to wrinkle.

further adv besides; farther; in addition. * adj more distant; additional. * vt to advance; to promote.

furthermore adv moreover; besides.

furthermost adj most remote.

furthest adj, adv farthest.

furtive adj sly; stealthy.

fury n rage; frenzy.

fuse n a tube or wick filled with combustible material for setting off an explosive charge; a piece of thin wire that melts and breaks when an electric current exceeds a certain level. * vt to join or become joined by melting.

fuselage n the body of an aircraft.

fusilade n a general discharg of rifles.

fusion n act of melting; a blending; union; partnership; nuclear fusion.

fuss n excited activity; bustle; anxious state. * vt to worry over.

fusty n musty; mildewed.

futile adj serving no useful end; ineffective.

futility n uselessness.

future adj forthcoming. * n time to come; future events; likelihood of eventual success.

futuristic adj forward-looking in design, appearance, intention etc.

fuzz n fluff.

fuzzy adj like fuzz; fluffy; blurred.

G

gab vi to chatter. * n idle talk.

gabble vt, vi to talk or utter rapidly or incoherently; to utter inarticulate or animal sounds. * n **gabbler**.

gable n the top of end wall of a house.

gadfly n a cattle-biting fly.

gadget n a small, often ingenious, mechanical or electronic tool or device.

gag vt to stop the mouth; to silence. *vi to retch; to tell jokes * n something thrust into mouth, any restraint.

gaiety n mirth; high spirits, liveliness.

gain vti to obtain, earn, esp by effort; to win in a contest; to attract; to get as an addition (esp profit or advantage); to make an increase in; to reach. * vi to make progress, to increase in weight. * n an increase esp in profit or advantage; an acquisition.

gainful adj profitable. * adv **gainfully**.

gainsay vt to contradict; to deny; to dispute.

gait n a manner of walking.

gala n a celebration; a festival; a festive season.

galaxy n any of the systems of stars in the universe; any splendid assemblage; the Milky Way.

gale n a strong wind; an outburst.

gall n bile; rancour; spite; nut-like growth on oaks. * vt to fret; annoy intensely.

gallant adj brave; courteous; dignified.

gallantry n bravery; courtesy.

gall bladder n a membranous sac attached to the liver in which bile is stored.

galleon n a Spanish warship.

gallery n a long, usu low, ship of ancient or medieval times, propelled by oars; the kitchen of a sip, aircraft; (print) a shallow tray for holding type; proofs printed from such type. Also **galley proof**.

galley n a long, low vessel with sails and oars; a shallow tray for type; a proof sheet printed from such type; a ship's kitchen.

galling adj bitter; provoking.

gallon n measure holding 2,77.42 cubic inches.

gallop vi to go at full speed. * n a horse's fastest pace.

gallows n sing (pl **gallows**) a wooden frame for hanging criminals.

gallstone n a small solid mass in the gall bladder.

galore n abundance; plenty.

galvanize vt to electrify; to electroplate; to stimulate into action.

galvanometer n an instrument for measuring electric force.

gambit n any action to gain an advantage.

gamble vi to play games of chance for money.

gambol vi to skip; to frisk. * n a frolic.

game n sport of any kind; a contest; a scheme; animals and birds hunted for sport or food. * adj brave; plucky; willing.

gamekeeper n a person who breeds and takes car of game birds and animals, as on an estate.

gaming n gambling.

gammon n a lower part of cured or smoked ham; flitch of bacon; nonsense.

gamut n the musical scale; the entire range of emotions etc.

gang n.a group of persons, esp labourers, working together; a group of person acting or associating together, esp for illegal purposes. * vt, vi to form into or act as a gang.

ganglion *n* an enlargement in the course of a nerve; any centre of activity or energy.

gangrene *n* death of body tissue when the blood supply is obstructed.

gangster *n* a member of a criminal gang.

gangway *n* a passageway, esp an opening in a ship's side for loading etc; a gangplank.

gaol *see* **jail**.

gap *n* an opening; a breach in a wall, fence etc; an interruption in continuity; an interval; a mountain pass; divergence.

gape *vi* to open the mouth wide; to stare wide-eyed and open-mouthed in astonishment; to yawn.

garage *n* an enclosed shelter for motor vehicles; a place where motor vehicles are repaired and services, and fuel sold. * *vt* to put or keep in a garage.

garb *n* dress; clothes.

garbage *n* waste matter; offal; rubbish

garble *vt* to tell a confused or jumbled story; to tell only part of truth.

garden *n* an area of ground for growing herbs, fruits, flowers, or vegetables, usu attached to a house; a public park or recreation area, usu laid-out with plants and trees. * *vi* to make, or work in, a garden. *n* **gardener, gardening.**

gargle *vt, vi* to rinse the throat by breathing air from the lungs through liquid held in the mouth. * *n* a liquid for this purpose; the sound made by gargling.

gargoyle *n* a grotesquely carved face as a gutter spout.

garish *adj* gaudy; showy.

garland *n* a wreath of flowers.

garlic *n* a bulbous strong-smelling herb.

garment *n* any article of clothing.

garner *vt* to store up.

garnet *n* a precious stone.

garnish *vt* to adorn; to decorate (food).

garret *n* an attic.

garrison *n* the soldiers in a fortress. * *vt* to man with troops.

garrotte, garrote *vt* to throttle or strangle.

garrulous *adj* very talkative.

garter *n* an elasticated band to hold up a stocking or sock.

gas *n* (*pl* **gases**) an air-like substance with the capacity to expand indefinitely and not liquefy or solidify at ordinary temperatures; (*inf*) empty talk; gasoline. * *vt* (*pt* **gassed**) to poison or disable with gas; (*inf*) to talk idly.

gash *vt* to slash; to cut. * *n* a deep cut.

gasket *n* a piece or ring of rubber, metal etc sandwiched between metal surfaces to act as a seal.

gasp *vi* to labour for breath; to pant. * *vt* to utter breathlessly.

gastric *adj* belonging to the stomach.

gastronomy *n* the art of good eating.

gate *n* a movable structure controlling passage through an opening in a fence or wall; a device (as in a computer) that outputs a signal when specified input conditions are met. * *vt* to supply with a gate.

gate-crash *vt* to arrive at a party etc. uninvited.

gather *vt, vi* to bring together in one place or group; to collect (as taxes); to harvest; to draw (parts) together; to come together in a body; to cluster around a focus of attention.

gathering *n* an assembly; folds made in a garment by gathering; an abscess.

gauche *adj* socially inept; graceless; tackless.

gaudy *adj* showy; flashy.

gauge *vt* to measure. * *n* a measuring rod; a measure; distance between rails of a railway; calibre.

gaunt *adj* emaciated; lean.

gauze *n* a light transparent cloth; a surgical dressing.

gavotte *n* a sprightly dance.

gay *adj* merry; frolicsome; colourful; homosexual.

gaze *vi* to stare; to contemplate. * *n* a fixed look.

gazette *n* a newspaper, especially an official one.

gazetteer *n* a geographical dictionary.

gazump *vt, vi* to force up a price (esp of a house) after a price has been agreed. *n* **gazumper**.

gear *n* clothing; equipment, esp for some task or activity; a toothed wheel for meshing with another; a specific adjustment of such a system. * vt to connect by or furnish with gears; to adapt (one thing) to confirm with another.

gearbox n a metal case enclosing a system of gears.

gear lever n a lever used to engage or change gear, esp in a motor vehicle.

gelatine n a tasteless, odourless substance extracted by boiling bones, hoofs etc and used in food, medicines etc.

gelding n a castrated male horse.

gem n a precious stone.

gemini npl the Twins, a sign of the zodiac.

gender n sex, male or female; words, masculine or feminine.

genealogy n family descent; lineage.

general adj not local, special, or specialized; of or for a whole genus, relating to or covering all instances or individuals of a class or group; widespread, common to many; not specific or precise; holding superior rank, chief.

general election n a national election to choose parliamentary representatives in every constituency.

generalize vt, vi to form general conclusions from specific instances; to talk (about something) in general terms. * n **generalization**.

generally adv in general; popularly; usually.

general practitioner n a non-specialist doctor who treats all types of illnesses in the community.

generate vt to beget; to produce.

generation n the act or process of generating; a single succession in natural descent; people of the same period.

generator n one who or that which generates; a machine that changes mechanical energy to electrical energy.

generic adj pertaining to a genus.

generosity n liberality.

generous adj noble; bountiful.

genesis n origin.

genetic adj relating to origin, development or production; of relating to genes.

genial adj cordial; cheerful; pleasing; warm.

genitals, genitalia npl the external sexual organs.

genius n (pl **geniuses**) outstanding capacity; disposition; one gifted with extraordinary mental power.

genius n (pl **genii**) demon; spirit of place.

genre n portrayal of scenes from ordinary life; a sort or category of work esp. literary or autistic.

genteel adj affectedly refined or polite.

gentility n refinement; gentle birth.

gentle adj well-born; refined, mild; hot rough or rude.

gentleman n a man of good birth; a courteous, honourable man.

gentry n well-born people.

genuflection, genuflexion n a bending of the knee.

genuine adj real; true; sincere.

genus n (pl **genera**) a kind; race; class containing several species.

geography n the science of the physical nature of the earth, such as land and sea masses, climate, vegetation etc, and their interaction with the human population; the physical features of a region. * n **geographer, geographic, geographical**.

geology n the science relating to the history and the structure of the earth.

geometric, geometrical adj pertaining to geometry.

geometry n the branch of mathematics dealing with the properties, measurement, and relationships of points, lines, planes and solids.

germ n any microscopic, disease-causing organism; an origin or foundation capable of growing and developing.

germane adj closely allied; relevant.

germinate vi to sprout; to start developing.

gerrymander vt to manipulate in one's own or party interests.

gerund n a verbal noun.

gestate vt to carry (young) in the womb during pregnancy; to develop (a plan, etc) gradually in the mind. * n **gestation**.

gesticulate vi, vt to make gestures when speaking.

gesture *n* an expressive movement of the body or limbs.

get *vt, vi* to obtain: to gain; to reach; to become; to catch; to persuade; to cause to be; to prepare; to kill; to understand; to come; to go; to arrive; to manage.

geyser *n* a hot-water spring; a water heater.

ghastly *adj* deathlike; hideous.

ghetto *n* (*pl* **ghettos**) a section of a city in which members of a minority group live, esp because of social, legal or economic pressure.

ghost *n* a spirit; an apparition; a faint trace or suggestion. * *vt* to ghost write; to write on behalf of another who then gets the credit.

ghoul *n* a spirit said to prey on corpses.

giant *n* a huge legendary being of great strength; a person or thing of great size, strength, intellect etc. * *adj* incredibly large.

gibberish *n* inarticulate talk; nonsense..

gibe *vt* to taunt; to sneer. * *n* a taunt.

giddy *adj* dizzy; fickle; frivolous; flightly.

gift *n* a present; talent; natural ability. * *vt* to endow; to present.

gifted *adj* talented.

gigantic *adj* huge; colossal; immense.

giggle *n* to snigger.

gild *vt* to cover with gold; to illuminate.

gill, gil *n* the organ of respiration in fishes.

gill *n* a quarter of a pint.

gilt *pp of* **gild** overlaid with gold.

gimlet *n* a boring tool with screw point.

gimmick *n* a trick or device for attracting notice, advertising or promoting a person, product or service. * *n* **gimmickry**.

gin *n* a spirit flavoured with juniper berries; a pile-driving machine; a snare.

ginger *n* a hot spice; vigour; a reddish-brown.

gingerbread *n* a cake flavoured with ginger.

gingerly *adv* cautiously.

gingham *n* a striped or checked cotton cloth.

gipsy *see* **gypsy**

girder *n* a large steel beam for supporting joists, the framework of a building etc.

girdle *n* a belt. * *vt* to encompass.

girl *n* a female child.

girlfriend *n* a female friend, esp with whom one is romantically involved.

girth *n* a saddle strap; the thickness round the waist etc.

gist *n* the essence; the substance of anything.

give *vt* to bestow; to hand over; to deliver; to yield; to utter; to pledge; to act as host.

gizzard *n* the muscular stomach of a bird.

glacial *adj* icy, frozen.

glacier *n* a slowly moving mass of ice on a mountain side.

glad *adj* pleased; cheerful.

gladden *vti* to make or become glad.

glade *n* a clear space in wood.

gladiator *n* a combatant in Roman arenas.

glamour *n* charm; allure; attractiveness; beauty.

glance *vi* to strike obliquely and go off at an angle; to flash; to look quickly.

gland *n* an organ that separates substances from the blood and synthesizes them for further use in, or for elimination from, the body. * *adj* **glandular**.

glare *n* a dazzling light; a fixed , fierce stare. * *vi* to shine brightly; to look fiercely and angrily.

glass *n* a hard brittle substance, usu transparent; glassware; a glass article, as a drinking vessel; (*pl*) spectacles or binoculars.

glasshouse *n* a large greenhouse for the commercial cultivation of plants.

glassware *n* objects made of glass, esp drinking vessels.

glassy *adj* smooth; expressionless, lifeless.

glaucoma *n* an eye disease.

glaze *vt, vi* to provide (windows etc) with glass; to give a hard glossy finish to (pottery etc); to cover (foods, etc) with a glossy surface.

glazier *n* one whose business is to set window glass.

gleam *n* a ray. * *vi* to flash.

glean *vt, vi* to gather (after reapers); to pick up.

glee *n* joy and gaiety; a song in parts for three or more male voices.

glen *n* a narrow valley.

glib *adj* speaking or spoken smoothly, to

the point of insincerity.

glide *vt, vi* to move smoothly and effortlessly; to descend in an aircraft or glider with little or no engine power.

glider *n* an engineless aircraft carried along by air currents.

glimmer *vi* to give a faint, flickering light; to appear faintly.

glimpse *n* a brief, momentary view. * *vt* to catch a glimpse of.

glint *n* a brief flash of light; a brief indication. * *vt, vi* to (cause to) gleam brightly.

glisten *vi* to shine, as light reflected from a wet surface.

glitter *vi* to sparkle; (*usu with* **with**) to be brilliantly attractive. * *n* a sparkle; showiness, glamour; tiny pieces of sparkling material used for decoration.

gloaming *n* twilight.

gloat *vi* to feast one's eyes on with evil feelings of satisfaction.

globe *n* a sphere; a planet; a star; the earth.

globule *n* a small globe-like particle; a droplet of liquid.

gloom *n* darkness; deep sadness.

gloomy *adj* dark; dismal; depressed.

glorify *vt* to extol; to magnify the worth or importance.

glory *n* praise; honour; renown; splendour. * *vi* to rejoice; to exult.

gloss *n* the lustre of a polished surface; a superficially attractive appearance. * *vt* to give a shiny surface; (*with* **over**) to hide (an error etc) or make seem right or inconsequential.

glossary *n* a list of specialized or technical words and their definitions.

glossy *adj* smooth and shining; highly polished; superficial; lavishly produced (of magazines).

glove *n* a cover for the hand.

glow *vi* to shine (as if) with an intense heat; to emit a steady light without flames; to be full of life and enthusiasm. * *n* a light emitted due to intense heat; a steady, even light without flames.

glower *vi* to scowl; to stare sullenly or angrily.

glowworm *n* a beetle that units a greenish luminous light.

glucose *n* a crystalline sugar occurring naturally in fruits, honey etc.

glue *n* a sticky substance used as an adhesive. * *vt* to join with glue.

glum *adj* sullen; moody.

glut *vt* to over supply (the market); to stuff; to gorge. * *n* over abundance.

glutinous *adj* gluey; viscous.

glutton *n* a voracious eater; a person with a great capacity for e.g. work.

gluttony *n* excess in eating.

glycerine *n* a colourless sweet liquid obtained from fats.

gnarl *n* a knot in wood.

gnarled *adj* full of knots; rough and weather-beaten (of hands).

gnash *vt* to grind (the teeth).

gnat *n* a biting insect.

gnaw *vt, vi* to nibble; to bite away bit by bit; to torment as by pain or guilt.

gnome *n* a sprite; a dwarf dwelling in the earth.

go *vi, vt* to move on a course; to proceed; to work properly; to act, sound, as specified; to result; to become; to be accepted or valid; to leave, to depart; to die; to be allotted or sold; to be able to pass (through); to fit (into); to be capable of being divided (into); to undertake (duties etc); to fall asleep; to take place as planned.

goad *n* a spiked stick to prick cattle; a spur; a stimulus to action.

goal *n* the winning post; an objective; an aim.

gobble *vt* to gulp; to bolt; to read eagerly.

go-between *n* a messenger, an intermediary.

goblet *n* a drinking cup without handle; a saucepan.

goblin *n* a mischievous or evil sprite.

god *n* any of various beings conceived of as supernatural and immortal, esp a male deity; an idol; a person or thing deified. (*with cap*) in monotheistic religions, the creator and ruler of the universe.

goddess *n* a female deity.

godfather *n* a male sponsor for a child at baptism. (Also **godmother, -son, -daughter**.)

god-forsaken *adj* desolate, wretched.

godliness *n* piety.

godsend *n* anything that comes unexpectedly when needed or desired.

goggle *vi* to roll the eyes; to stare with bulging eyes. * *adj* bulging. * *npl* large spectacles.

gold *n* a precious yellow metal; coins; jewellery made of this, money; wealth.

golden *adj* made of or relating to fold; bright yellow; priceless; flourishing.

gold leaf *n* gold beaten out thin.

goldsmith *n* a worker in gold.

golf *n* an outdoor game in which the player attempts to hit a small ball with clubs around a turfed course into a succession of holes in the smallest number of strokes.

golf course, links *n* a tract of land laid out for playing golf.

gondola *n* a long narrow, black boat used on the canals of Venice; an enclosed car suspended from a cable used to transport passengers, esp skiers up a mountain.

gondolier *n* a person who rows a gondola.

gong *n* a disk-shaped percussion instrument struck with a usu padded hammer; (*sl*) a medal.

good *adj* having the right or proper qualities; valid; healthy or sound; virtuous, honourable; enjoyable, pleasant etc. * *n* something good; benefit; something that has economic utility.

goodness *n* quality of being good.

good sense *n* sound judgment.

good-tempered *adj* good-natured.

goodwill *n* benevolence; the established custom and reputation of a business.

gore *n* (clotted) blood; a gusset in material to shape a garment. * *vt* to wound with tusk or horn.

gorge *n* the throat; a very narrow pass. * *vt* to eat greedily and overmuch.

gorgeous *adj* splendid; strikingly attractive; brightly coloured.

gory *adj* bloody.

gospel *n* one who chatters idly about others; such talk. * *vi* to take part in or spread gossip.

gossamer *n* cobweb-like threads in the air or on bushes; any very flimsy material.

gossip *n* a tattler; idle talk about others. * *vt* to tattle.

Gothic *adj* in the pointed-arch style of architecture of the Middle Ages; dark, supernatural, grotesque of a certain style of literature.

gouge *n* a chisel with a grooved blade. * *vt* to scoop out.

gourd *n* a general name for melon-like plants; a drinking vessel.

gourmand *n* a glutton.

gourmet *n* a fastidious eater.

gout *n* a disease affecting joints, esp. the big toe.

govern *vt* to rule; to regulate; to influence the action of.

government *n* the exercise of authority over a state, organization etc; a system of ruling, political administration etc; those who direct the affairs of a state etc.

governor *n* a person appointed to govern a province etc; the elected head of any state of the US.

gown *n* a loose outer garment, specifically a woman's formal dress, a nightgown, a long, flowing robe worn by clergymen, judges, university teachers etc; a type of overall worn int he operating room.

grab *vt* to seize; to snatch; to catch the interest or attention.

grace *n* favour; kindness; divine influence; mercy; a title; beauty of form or movement; ease of manner; short prayer before meals. * *vt* to adorn; to dignify.

graceful *adj* elegant.

gracious *adj* having or showing kindness, courtesy etc; compassionate; polite to supposed inferiors.

gradation *n* arrangement step by step.

grade *n* a stage or step in a progression; a group of people of the same rank, merit etc; the degree of slope; a sloping part; a mark or rating in an examination.

gradient *n* degree of ascent or descent, in a road; a sloping road or railway.

gradual *adj* slow and regular.

graduate *vt, vi* to mark off into degrees; to receive a university degree. * *n* a recipient of a degree.

graduation *n* act of marking with degrees;

the conferring or receiving of university degrees.

graft n a shoot inserted in another plant; the transplanting of skin, bone etc. * vt to insert such a shoot; to join organically.

grain n the seed of any cereal plant, as wheat, corn etc; cereal plants; a tiny, solid particle, as of salt or sand; the arrangement of fibres, layers etc of wood, leather etc.

grammar n the study of the correct use of language; the rules for speaking and writing a language; a grammar textbook.

gramme n the French unit of weight.

gramophone n an instrument that recorded and reproduced sounds; forerunner of the record player.

granary n a storehouse for grain.

grand adj noble; magnificent; imposing; important; illustrious; comprehensive.

grandeur n greatness; splendour.

grandfather n a father's or mother's father.

grandiloquence n pompous language.

grandiose adj imposing; bombastic.

grandmother n a mother's or father's mother.

grand piano n a large piano with a horizontal harp-shaped case.

granite n a hard igneous rock; firmness and endurance.

grant vt to bestow; to confer on; to admit as true; to cede. * n a gift; money or a gift granted for a particular purpose; a conveyance in writing.

granular adj consisting of grains.

granulate vti to form into grains.

granule n a little grain.

grape n the juicy purple or green berry fruit of the vine growing in clusters.

graph n a diagram representing successive changes int he value of a variable quantity of quantities.

graphic, graphical adj described in realistic detail; pertaining to a graph, lettering, drawing, painting etc.

grapple vt, vi to seize; to wrestle.

grasp vt, vi to grip; to lay hold of; to understand. * n a grip; reach; comprehension.

grasping adj avaricious; greedy.

grass n any of a large family of plants with jointed stems and long narrow leaves including cereals, bamboo etc; such plants grown as lawn; pasture.

grate n a frame of metal bars for holding fuel in a fireplace; a grating * vt to grind into particles by scraping; to rub against (an object) or grind (the teeth) together with a harsh sound; to irritate.

grateful adj pleasing; gratifying; appreciative.

grater n a grinding-down utensil.

gratification n pleasure; enjoyment.

gratify vt to please; delight; to indulge.

grating n a frame of bars. * adj harsh; irritating.

gratis adv without charge.

gratitude n thankfulness for favours, gifts received.

gratuitous adj free of charge; unjustified.

gratuity n a free gift; a tip.

grave vt to engrave; to impress deeply. * n a tomb. * adj weighty; serious; solemn; sombre.

gravel n small pebble; a disease of the kidneys.

gravitate vt, vi to tend towards the centre.

gravity n the force drawing bodies towards the centre of the earth; seriousness.

gravy n meat juice.

graze vti to rub lightly; to scrape (the skin) slightly; to scratch; to eat grass; to supply grass.

grease n fat in a soft state. * vt to smear with grease; to lubricate.

great adj large; eminent; noble; chief; intense; excellent; skilful.

greatness n eminence; grandeur.

greed n avarice; excessive hunger or desire for food, money etc.

greedy adj ravenous; grasping; voracious.

green adj grass-coloured; fresh; not ripe; in experienced; naive; environmentally conscious; jealous. * n a grassy plot; the colour of grass; a mixture of blue and yellow.

greengrocer n a dealer in vegetables and fruit.

greenhouse n a glass house for rearing plants.

greenroom n a theatre retiring room.

greet vt to salute; to welcome; to address in a friendly way.

gregarious adj living in flocks; sociable; fond of company.

grenade n a small bomb thrown manually or projected (as by a rifle or special launcher).

grey n a neutral colour between black and white; something, esp. an animal of a grey colour. * adj of a grey colour; grey-haired; dreary; vague; indeterminate.

grid n a gridiron, a grating; an electrode for controlling the flow of electrons in an electron tube; a network of squares on a map used for easy reference; a national network of transmission lines, pipes etc for electricity, water, gas etc.

griddle n a flat iron plate for baking scones etc.

grief n sorrow; deep distress.

grievance n injustice; hardship; a cause for complaint.

grieve vti to deplore; to mourn.

grievous adj heavy; distressing.

grill vt to cook by direct heat using a grill or gridiron (inf) to question relentlessly. * n a device on a cooker that radiates heat downward for grilling; a gridiron; grilled food; a grille; a grillroom.

grille,grill n an open grate forming a screen.

grillroom n a restaurant that specializes in grilled food.

grim adj stern; unyielding; forbidding.

grimace n a contortion of the face.

grime n soot, dirt. * vt to dirty; to soil or befoul.

grimy adj foul; dirty.

grin vi to laugh through the teeth. * n a broad, friendly smile.

grind vb (pt **ground**) vt to reduce to powder or fragments by crushing; to wear down, sharpen, or smooth by friction.

grip n a grasp; a handle. * vti to grasp, clutch.

gripe vt, vi to grasp; to pinch; to complain. * n a clutch.

grisly adj dreadful; terrifying.

gristle n cartilage esp. in meat.

grit n coarse particles of sand; stubborn or resolute courage or firmness. * vt to clench or grind the teeth; to spread grit esp. on icy roads.

grizzled adj greyish.

groan vi to moan. * n a deep moan.

grocer n a merchant who deals in food and household supplies.

grog n a mixture of spirits and cold water.

groggy adj dazed and unsteady.

groin n the junction of the trunk and thighs in front.

groom n one who tends horses; a bridegroom. * vt to clean and care for animals; to make heat and tidy; to train someone for a specific purpose.

groove n a long hollow; a rut, a spiral track in a gramophone record for the stylus; a settle routine. * vt to furrow or to make a groove in.

grope vi to search about blindly as in the dark; to search uncertainly for a solution to a problem. * vt to find by feeling; (sl) to fondle sexually.

gross adj thick; coarse; obscene; shameful; whole. * n twelve dozen; the whole; the total without deduction.

grotesque adj distorted or fantastic in appearance, shape etc; absurdly incongruous.

grotto n a picturesque cave.

ground n the solid surface of the earth; soil; the connection of an electrical conductor with the earth.

grounding n basic general knowledge of a subject.

groundwork n basis; foundation.

group n a number of persons or things considered as a collective unit; two or more figures forming one artistic design.

grouse n a gamebird. * vt to complain.

grout n coarse meal; mortar.

grove n a small wood.

grovel vi to crawl; to prostrate or abase oneself.

groveller n an abject wretch.

grow vi to increase; to make progress; to become; to develop; to accrue. * vt to produce; to raise; to cultivate.

growl vi to snarl; to make a rumbling noise as an angry animal. * vt to speak in a growling voice. * n a growling sound; a grumble.

grown-up adj adult.

growth n the act or process of growing; progressive increase, development; something that grows or has grown; an abnormal formation of tissue, as a tumour.

grub vi, vt to dig; to root out; to work hard. * n the larva of an insect.

grubby adj dirty, soiled.

grudge vi, vt to envy; to give unwillingly. * n ill-will; envy; resentment.

gruel n food made by boiling meal in water.

gruelling adj severely testing; exhausting.

gruesome adj repulsive; causing horror.

gruff adj surly; harsh; hoarse.

grumble vi to mutter with discontent.

grumpy adj surly; gruff; bad-tempered.

grunt vi to make a noise like a hog.

guarantee n a pledge or security for another's debt or obligation; a pledge to replace something substandard etc; an assurance that something will be done as specified.

guarantor n a person who gives a guaranty or guarantee.

guard vti to watch over; to defend. * n defence; protector; sentinel; attention.

guarded adj circumspect; discreet.

guardian n a custodian; a person legally in charge of a minor or someone incapable of taking care of their own affairs.

guerrilla n a member of a force of irregular soldiers, usually biased politically, in conflict with regulars on police etc.

guess vt to form an opinion of or state with little or no factual knowledge; to judge correctly by doing this; to sur or suppose. * n an estimate based on guessing.

guest n a person entertained at the home, club etc of another; any paying customer of a hotel, restaurant; a performer appearing by special invitation.

guesthouse n a private home or boarding-house offering accommodation.

guide vt to point out the way for; to lead; to direct the course of; to control. * n a person who leads or directs others.

guidebook n a book containing directions and information for tourists.

guided missile n a military missile whose course is controlled by radar or internal instruments etc.

guide dog n a dog trained to guide people who are blind.

guild, gild n a society for mutual aid.

guile n wiliness; deceit.

guillotine n an instrument for beheading persons; a machine for cutting paper.

guilt n the fact of having done a wrong or committed an offence; a feeling of self-reproach from believing one has done a wrong.

guilty adj criminal; wicked; feeling guilt.

guinea pig n a person or thing subject to an experiment.

guise n an external appearance, aspect; an assumed appearance, pretence.

guitar n a musical instrument having six strings and is plucked with the fingers.

gulf n an arm of the sea; a bay; a chasm.

gull n a long-winged sea bird.

gullet n the throat; the food passage from the mouth.

gully n watercourse cut out by heavy rain.

gulp vt to swallow eagerly. * n a mouthful.

gum n the firm tissue surrounding the teeth; the sticky substance found in some trees.

gumption n shrewd good sense.

gun n a weapon with a metal tube from which a projectile is discharged by an explosive.

gunman n an armed gangster; a hired killer.

gunmetal n an alloy of copper and tin formerly used for cannon.

gunner n a soldier etc, who helps fire artillery; a naval warrant officer in charge of a ship's gun.

gunpowder n an explosive mixture used for blasting etc.

gunwale, gunnel n the upper edge of a ship's side.

gurgle vi to flow with a bubbling sound; to utter this sound.

gush vi to rush out; to be effusively sentimental in speech or writing.

gushing adj rushing forth; effusive.

gusset n a triangular piece of cloth inserted

in a garment to strengthen or widen.

gust n a sudden blast fo wind; an outburst.

gut n the intestine; (pl) entrails.; courage; daring * vt to remove entrails.

gutter n a water channel below eaves or at the roadside. * (candle) to melt unevenly.

gutter press n news-papers that concentrate on the sensational in their coverage.

guttural adj throaty. * n a throat sound, as g.

guy n a rope to steady anything; an effigy of Guy Fawkes; a man or boy.

guzzle vi, vt to swallow greedily.

gymnasium n (pl **gymnasia, gymnasiums**) a place for athletic exercises.

gymnast n a gymnastic expert.

gymnastics npl athletic exercises; training in these.

gynaecology n the branch of medicine dealing with disorders of the female reproductive system.

gypsy n (with cap) a member of a travelling people, orig from India.

gyrate vi to rotate, to whirl.

gyration n a whirling round.

gyroscope, gyrostat n an apparatus for illustrating laws of rotation.

H

haberdasher n a draper.

habit n usage; custom; a distinctive costume or dress.

habitable adj that may be inhabited.

habitat n the natural abode.

habitation n abode; residence.

habitual adj customary; usual.

habituate vt to accustom; to inure.

habitué n a regular frequenter.

hack n a hired horse; a worn-out horse; a mediocre writer; a coach for hire. * vt to gash; to kick; to ride a horse crosscountry. * adj banal; hackneyed.

hackneyed adj much used; trite.

haemorrhage n the escape of blood from a blood vessel; heavy bleeding. * vi to bleed heavily.

haemorrhoids npl piles.

haft n the handle of an axe etc.

hag n an ugly old woman.

haggard adj wild-looking; gaunt.

haggis n a dish of heart, liver, etc, of sheep minced and boiled in the stomach sac.

haggle vt to drive a hard bargain; to barter.

hail n frozen rain; a call. * vi, vt to rain hail; to call to; to greet or welcome with approval; to acclaim; to originate from.

hair n a thread-like covering on the skin of mammals; a mass of hair growing on the human head etc.

hairdresser n a person who cuts, styles, colours, etc hair.

hairpiece n an additional piece of hair attached to a person's real hair.

hairpin bend n a sharply curving bend in a road etc.

hair-raising adj terrifying, shocking.

hair's-breadth n a minute distance.

hairsplitting n making fine distinctions.

hairstyle n an arrangement of the hair in a certain way.

hairy adj covered in hair; difficult; dangerous.

halcyon adj calm; peaceful.

hale adj sound; robust. * vt to drag by force.

half n (pl **halves**) one of two equal parts.

half-brother n a brother by one parent only.

half-caste n one born of parents of different races.

half-hearted adj lukewarm.

half-sister n a sister by one parent only.

hall n a large public room; the entrance passage of house.

hallmark n a mark used on gold, silver or platinum articles to signify a standard of purity; a characteristic feature. * vt to stamp with a hallmark.

hallucination n the apparent perception of sights, sounds etc that are not actually present; something perceived in this manner.

halo n circle of light round sun or moon; a symbolic disc round the head of a saint.

halt vi, vt to hesitate; to stop; to cease marching. * n a limp; stoppage on a march; a minor station on a railway line.

halter n a rope or headgear for a horse.

halve vt to divide into two equal parts.

halyard n a line for handling sails.

ham n the thigh of a pig salted and dried; an actor who overacts; a licensed amateur radio operator.

hamburger n ground beef; a cooked patty of such meat, often in a bread roll.

hamlet n a small village.

hammer n a tool for driving nails, etc. * vt,v i to beat or forge; to defeat utterly.

hammock n a swinging bed of cloth or netting suspended by the ends.

hamper n a large basket. * vt to hinder; to interfere; to encumber.

hand n the part of the arm below the wrist, used for grasping; a side or direction; control; applause; help; a hired worker; a pointer on a clock; the breadth of a hand, four inches when measuring the height of a horse.

handbook n a textbook; a manual.

handcuff n a fetter; a manacle.

handful n as much as the hand will hold; a small quantity or number; a person difficult to control.

handicap n an allowance in sporting contests to make the chances more equal for the competitors; a mental or physical impairment.

handicraft n manual skill.

handiwork n product of one's own labour.

handkerchief n a cloth for blowing the nose.

handle vt to feel, use, or hold with the hand; to deal with; to manage; to buy and sell goods. * n the part of anything designed to be held by the hand.

handsome adj good-looking; dignified; genius.

handwriting n manner of writing.

handy adj expert; convenient; ready; near.

hang vt, vi to suspend; to attach by hinges to allow to swing freely; to execute.

hangar n a shelter for aircraft.

hanger n a device on which something is hung, e.g. clothes.

hanger-on n a dependent; a parasite.

hangman n a public executioner.

hangover n the unpleasant after-effects of excessive consumption of alcohol.

hang-up n an emotional preoccupation with something.

hanker vi to desire longingly.

haphazard adj chance; random.

hapless adj unlucky; unhappy.

happen vi to take place; to occur.

happy adj pleased; lucky; joyous.

harangue n a speech; a tirade.

harass vt to plague; to vex; to imitate.

harbour n a shelter; a haven; an inlet for anchoring ships. * vt to shelter; to nurse in the mind secretly.

hard adj firm; solid; difficult to understand, accomplish, bear; painful; unfeeling; harsh; grasping; alcoholic (of drink). * adv fast; with difficulty; earnestly.

hardboard n a stiff board made of compressed wood chips.

hard cash n payment in coins and notes as opposed to cheque etc.

harden vt, vi to make hard; to inure; to be unfeeling.

hardhearted adj pitiless.

hardly adv scarcely; barely; with difficulty; not to be expected.

hard sell n an aggressive selling technique.

hardship n privation; injustice.

hardware n common metal articles, e.g. tools etc; the mechanical and electronic components that make up a computer system.

hardy adj bold; intrepid; able to withstand exposure or emotional hardship.

harebrained adj giddy; heedless.

harelip n a deformity of the upper lip in the form of a vertical fissure.

hark vi to listen.

harlequin n a well-known comic pantomime figure; a comic; a buffoon.

harlot n a prostitute.

harm n hurt; damage; evil. * vt to injure.

harmful adj hurtful.

harmless adj not likely to cause harm.

harmonic, harmonical adj pertaining to harmony; musical. * n a secondary tone.

harmonica n a small wind instrument.

harmonious adj melodious; friendly.

harmonize vi, vt to be in, or bring into, or sing in harmony.

harmony n musical concord; accord; agreement in action, ideas etc.

harness n device by which a horse is fastened to a vehicle, plough etc. * vt to put a harness on; to control so as to use the power of.

harp n a stringed musical instrument.

harpoon n a barbed whaling spear.

harpsichord n a stringed instrument with keyboard resembling a grand piano.

harridan n a bad-tempered hag; a nag.

harrow n a large rake for breaking ploughed ground * vt to draw a harrow over; to cause mental distress to.

harrowing adj distressing.

harry vt to harass; to worry; pillage; plunder.

harsh adj grating; rough; jarring on the senses or feeling; rigourous, cruel.

harvest n the reaping season; the crop reaped; the fruit of labour.

hash vt to chop; to mince. * n a dish of minced meat.

hashish n resin derived from the leaves and shoots of the hemp plant, smoked or chewed as an intoxicant.

hasp n a clasp for a staple.

hassock n a footstool.

haste n speed; hurry. * vt to hurry.

hasten vt, vi to haste; to accelerate.

hasty adj speedy; rash; precipitate.

hat n a head covering.

hatch vt to produce (young) from eggs; to contrive; to devise. * n a brood; a trap door; a door or opening on an aircraft.

hatchback n a sloping rear end on a car with a door; a car of this design.

hatchet n a small axe.

hatchway n an opening in a ship's deck.

hate vt to detest; to abhor. * n great dislike; the person or thing hated.

hateful adj odious.

hatred n great dislike.

haughty adj proud and disdainful; arrogant.

haul vt to pull; to drag. * n a catch (of fish, etc); the distance over which something is transported.

haulage n the transport of commodities; the charge for hauling.

haunch n the hip; the thigh.

haunt vt to frequent; to recur repeatedly to; to appear habitually as a ghost. * n a resort; a place often visited.

haunted adj visited by apparitions.

have vt (pres t **has**, pr p **having**, pt **had**) to have in one's possession; to possess as an attribute; to experience; to allow, or tolerate; to engage in; to cause, compel, or require to be; to be obliged.

haven n a harbour; a shelter.

havoc n widespread destruction or disorder; devastation.

hawk n a bird of prey; an aggressive or ruthless person. * vt to hunt with hawks.

hawser n a small cable.

hay n grass cut and dried for fodder.

hazard n risk; venture; obstacle on the golf course. * n to risk.

hazardous adj perilous; risky.

haze n vapour; mist; smoke; slight vagueness.

hazy adj obscure; dim; vague.

he pron of the third person. * n a male person.

head n the part of an animal or human body containing the brain, eyes, ears, nose and mouth; the top part of anything; the chief person; (pl) mind; pressure of water, steam etc; the source of a river etc; froth, as on beer.

headache n pain in the head.

headgear n covering for the head.

heading n something forming the head, top or front; the title, topic etc of a chapter etc; the direction in which a vehicle is moving.

headlight n a light at the front of a vehicle.

headline n printed lines at the top of a newspaper article giving the topic.

headlong adj with the head first; with uncontrolled speed or force; rashly.

head-on adj with the head or front foremost; without compromise.

headquarters n the centre of operations of one in command, as in an army; the main office in any organization.

headstrong adj obstinate; determined to do as one pleases.

headway n progress or success.

heady adj rash; hasty.

heal vt to make sound or healthy; to cure.

health n a sound state of body or mind.

healthy adj hale; sound; beneficial.

heap n a mass; a pile. * vt to amass.

hear vt, vi to perceive by the ear; to listen; to learn; to conduct a legal hearing.

hearing n one of the five senses; attention; opportunity to be heard.

hearing aid n an electronic amplifier worn behind the ear to improve hearing.

hearsay n report; rumour.

hearse n a car for conveying a coffin.

heart n the organ which propels the blood; the centre of life; spirit; strength; courage; (pl) a suit of playing cards marked with a heart-shaped symbol.

heartache n sorrow; anguish.

heartbeat n the rhythmic contraction and dilation of the heart.

heartbreak n overwhelming sorrow or grief.

heartburn n a burning sensation in the lower chest.

hearten vt to encourage.

hearth n the floor of the fireplace; the fireside; home.

heartless adj unfeeling.

hearty adj warm; cordial; keen; unrestrained, as laughter; healthy; plentiful.

heat n energy produced by molecular agitation; the quality of being hot; hot weather or climate; strong feeling, esp anger etc; the period of sexual excitement and readiness for mating in female animals.

heath n a waste or shrub-covered tract of land; heather.

heathen n a pagan an irreligious or uncivilized person.

heating n a system of providing heat.

heatwave n a prolonged period of hot weather.

heave vt, vi to lift; to move upward; to utter; to swell; to come to a stop (of ship).

heaven n the sky; bliss.

heaviness n weight; gloom.

heavy adj weighty; sad; drowsy; hard to do; clumsy; dull; serious; grievous.

heavyweight n a professional boxer weighing more than 175 pounds (29 kg); (inf) a very influential or important individual.

heckle n vt to harass a speaker with questions or taunts.

hectic adj vt, vi feverish.

hector n a bully; involving intense excitement on activity; to bluster; to bully.

hedge n a fence consisting of a dense line of bushes or small trees; an evasive or non-committal answer or statement. * vt to surround or enclose with a hedge; to place secondary bets as a precaution.

hedonism n the doctrine that pleasure is the chief good.

heed vt to attend to; to notice. * n care; attention.

heedless adj inattentive; negligent.

heel n the hind part of the foot; the part of a sock or shoe covering the heel. * vt to add a heel to; to list or tilt (of ships).

hefty adj heavy; large and strong; big.

height n the distance from top to bottom.

heighten vt to raise higher or more intense.

heinous adj flagrant.

heir n one who inherits.

heiress n a female heir.

heirloom n any possession which descends from generation to generation.

helicopter n a kind of aircraft lifted and moved, or kept hovering, by large rotary blades mounted horizontally.

helium n a gaseous element.

helix n (pl **helices**) a wire coil.

hell n the abode of the wicked after death; any place or state of extreme misery or pain.

hello interj an expression of greeting. * n the act of saying 'hello'.

helm n a rudder, the steering wheel on a ship; management; authority.

helmet n head armour.

helmsman n the man who steers a ship.

help vt to make things better or easier for; to aid; to assist; to remedy; to keep from; to serve or wait on. * n the action of helping; aid; assistance; a remedy.

helpful adj giving help; useful.

helpless adj unable to manage alone, dependent on others; weak and defenceless.

hem n the border of a garment. * vt to form a hem; (with **in**) to enclose; to confine.

hemisphere n a half sphere; half the earth.

hen n a female bird.

hence adv from this place; time, reason.

henceforth adv from now on.

henchman n a trusted supporter.

heptagon n a seven-sided figure.

her pron the possessive and objective case of she.

herald n a person who conveys news or messages; a forerunner. * vt to proclaim.

heraldry n the study of genealogies and coats of arms; ceremony; pomp.

herb n any plant used medicinally or as seasoning.

herbaceous adj descriptive of fleshy as opposed to woody plants.

herbal n a book treating of herbs.

herbalist n one skilled in herbs.

herbarium n (pl **herbariums, herbaria**) a collection of dried plants.

herbivorous adj herb-eating.

herd n a large number of animals, esp cattle, living and feeding together. * vt, vi to assemble or move animals together.

here adv in this place; now; on earth.

hereabout adv about this place.

hereafter adv after this time. * n (with the) the future; life after death.

hereby adv by this means; near.

hereditary adj transmitted to offspring.

heredity n the transmission of genetic material that determines physical and mental characteristics from one generation on to another.

heresy n a belief contrary to accepted beliefs or doctrines.

heretic n one guilty of heresy.

heritable adj transmissible.

heritage n something inherited at birth; anything deriving from the past.

hermaphrodite adj being of both sexes.

hermetic, hermetical adj airtight.

hermit n a recluse.

hernia n a rupture esp. of part of the intestine.

hero n a brave man; the chief character in a play or novel or film.

heroine n a woman with the attributes of a hero; the leading female character in a play, novel etc.

heroism n the qualities or conduct of a hero; magnanimity; bravery; valour.

hers pron possessive used only when no noun follows; belonging to her.

herself pron emphatic and reflexive form of she and her.

hesitancy n a hesitating.

hesitate vi to pause; to be uncertain or undecided; to falter; to stammer.

hew vi to cut; chop; hack; to shape.

hexagon n a rectilinear figure of six sides.

heyday n a period of greatest success or happiness; bloom; prime.

hiatus n a gap; a break.

hibernate vt to pass the winter in sleep; to be inactive.

hide vt, vi to conceal; to screen; to lie hidden. * n the skin of an animal; camouflaged place of concealment used by hunters, bird-watchers etc.

hidebound adj bigoted; narrow-minded.

hideous adj frightful; ugly; horrifying.

hiding n concealment; a thrashing.

hierarchy n a group of people or things arranged in order of rank, grade etc.

hieroglyph, hieroglyphic n picture writing; writing hard to decipher.

high adj elevated; dear; (of price); not fresh (of food); intoxicated. * adv greatly; in on to a high degree, rank etc. * n a high level, place etc; a euphoric state induced by drugs or alcohol.

highborn adj of noble birth.

highbrow n, adj an intellectual.

high-flyer n an ambitious person; a person of great ability in any profession.

high-handed adj overbearing.

highland n a mountainous region; (pl)

highlight n the lightest area of a painting etc; the most interesting or important feature; (pl) lightening of areas of the hair using a bleach. * vt to bring to special attention; to give highlights to.

high-minded adj proud; having honourable pride.

highness n a title of honour given to royalty; the state or quality of being high.

high-rise adj, n (a building) with multiple storeys.

highroad n main road.

high school n a secondary school.

highway n a public road; a major road.

hike vi to take a long walk. * vt to pull up.
* n a long walk; a tramp.

hilarious adj very amusing.

hilarity n laughter; jollity.

hill n a rise in the land lower than a mountain; a slope in a road.

hillock n a small hill.

hilt n a handle, particularly of a sword.

him pron the objective case of **he.**

himself pron the emphatic and reflexive form of **he** and **him.**

hind n a female stag; a rustic. * adj situated at the back.

hinder vt to prevent; to thwart.

hindmost adj farthest behind; last.

hindrance n a check; an obstruction; an obstacle.

hinge n a joint or flexible part on which a door, lid, etc turns; a natural joint, as of a clam. * vt, vi to attach or hang by a hinge; to depend.

hint vt, vi to suggest indirectly; to insinuate. * n an indirect or subtle suggestion; a slight mention; a little piece of advice.

hip n the joint of the thigh; the fruit of dog the rose. * adj stylish; up-to-date.

hire vt to engage for wages; to lease out.
* n wages; payment for the temporary use of something.

hirsute adj hairy; shaggy.

his pron possessive case of **he.**

hiss vt to make a sound like that of letters.

histology n the study of tissues, animal or vegetable.

historian n a writer of history.

history n a record or account of past events; the study, analysis of past events.

histrionic, histrional adj theatrical.

histrionics n theatricals; exaggerated behaviour.

hit vt, vi to strike; not to miss; to reach; to affect strongly. * n a stroke; a blow; a collision; a successful and popular song.

hitch vt, vi to move, pull etc with jerks; to fasten with a hook, knot etc; to obtain a ride by hitchhiking.

hitchhike vct to travel by asking for free lifts from motorists along the way.

hive n a shelter for a colony of bees; a beehive; a scene of great activity.

hoard n a hidden stock or accumulation

of money stored away for future use.
* vt, vi to collect; to store secretly.

hoarding n a large board for pasting advertisements on.

hoarse adj rough-voiced; grating.

hoary adj white or grey with age.

hoax n a practical joke. * vt to deceive; to trick.

hob n a flat surface on a cooker with hot plates or burners.

hobble vi to limp; to shackle (a horse).

hobby n a favourite spare time pursuit.

hobbyhorse n a wooden horse for children; a favourite or obsessive subject.

hobgoblin n a goblin; an imp.

hobnob vi to socialize.

hockey n game played with a ball and curved stick between two teams of eleven players each.

hod n a trough on a pole for carrying mortar and bricks.

hoe n a garden tool with a long handle.

hog n a castrated male pig raised for its meat; a selfish, greedy or dirty person.
* vt to take more than one's share; to hoard greedily.

hoist vt to heave up. * n an elevator; lift.

hold vt, vi to have one's grasp; to confine; to keep; to maintain; to contain; to possess; to occupy; to support; to regard; to believe; to consider. * n a grasp; possession; a dominance over; lowermost inside part of a ship.

holding n a small rented farm with land; (often pl) property, esp. land, stocks and bonds.

hole n a hollow place; an aperture; cavity; a den; a small dirty place; a difficult situation; a small bound hollow to receive a golf ball; a fairway plus tee in golf.

holiday n a day or period away from work etc; a time for rest or amusement.

holiday-maker n a person on holiday.

holiness n sanctity.

hollow adj not solid; empty; false. * n a depression; a cavity; a valley. * vt to excavate.

holocaust n the mass murder of Jews in Europe by Nazis.

holograph n a document in one's own

handwriting.

holster n a pistol case attached to a belt.

holy adj sinless; consecrated.

homage n duty; fealty; a demonstration of respect or honour.

home n one's own abode; residence; native place; a household; an institution.

homeland n the country where a person was born.

homely adj simple; plain; everyday.

home-made adj made or looking as if made at home.

homesick adj affected with homesickness; longing for home.

homespun adj coarse; rough; unsophisticated. * n a home-made cloth.

homestead n a house with the grounds and buildings attached; native seat.

homeward adv towards home.

homework n work, esp piecework, done at home; schoolwork to be done outside the classroom; preliminary study for a project.

homicidal adj murderous.

homicide n manslaughter; a person who kills.

homily n a sermon; sound advice.

homoeopathy, homeopathy n curing disease by producing similar symptoms, 'like curing like'.

homogeneous adj of the same kind; of uniform structure.

homonym n a word alike in form or sound, but not in meaning, as here, hear.

honest adj free from fraud; upright; truthful; trustworthy; frank.

honesty n uprightness; truth.

honey n a sweet sticky yellowish substance juice collected by bees from flowers and made into a food.

honeycomb n the waxy storage cells of bees.

honeymoon n the holiday spent together by a newly married couple.

honeysuckle n a sweet-smelling climbing plant.

honorary adj unpaid; conferring honour; voluntary.

honour n glory; good name; fame; integrity; distinction; a title of respect; (pl) university distinctions. * vt to esteem; exalt; pay (bill) when due.

honourable adj worthy of honour; distinguished; just.

hood n a cowl; a head covering.

hoof n the horny part of an animal's foot.

hook n a piece of metal bent so as to catch or hold; a sickle. * vt to catch with a hook; to ensnare; to drive a ball to the left (golf). * vi to bend; to be curving.

hoop n the band of a cask; a ring; anything so shaped.

hoot vi to shout in contempt; to cry as an owl; to blow a whistle etc.

hooter n something that makes a hooting sound e.g. a car horn; a nose.

hop n a leap on one leg; a spring; a short trip by air. * vi to leap; to skip.

hope vt to desire and expect. * vi to trust. * n expectation and desire; the object of this.

hopeful adj filled with hope; inspiring hope or promise of success.

hopeless adj without hope; despondent.

hopper n a contrivance for passing grain into a mill; a barge for dredgings.

horde n a crowd; a throng; a rabble.

horizon n the apparent junction of the earth and sky; the limit of a person's knowledge; interest etc.

horizontal adj level; parallel to the plane of the horizon.

hormone n a product of living cells formed in one part of the organism and carried to another part, where it takes effect; a synthetic compound having the same purpose.

horn n a hard pointed growth on the heads of some animals; anything horn-like; a wind instrument esp. the French horn; a device blown or sounded as a warning.

horology n the science of clockmaking.

horoscope n a chart of the signs and positions of planets etc, by which astrologers profess to predict future events.

horrible adj dreadful; frightful; very unpleasant.

horrid adj shocking; hideous.

horrify vt to shock; to appal.

horror n dread; intense fear; a person or thing inspiring horror.

horse n four-legged, solid-hoofed her-

horseman *n* a skilful rider.

horseplay *n* rough, rude conduct.

horseshoe *n* a flat, U-shaped plate nailed to a horse's hoof.

horticulture *n* the art or science of growing flowers, fruit and vegetables.

hose *n sing or pl* stockings; breeches; a flexible tube for conveying water etc.

hosiery *n* stockings and socks.

hospice *n* a nursing home for the care of the terminally ill.

hospitable *adj* generous and welcoming; kind.

hospital *n* an institution for the care of the sick.

hospitality *n* kindness, generosity to guests and strangers.

host[1] *n* a person who receives or entertains; an animal or plant on or in which another lives; a compere.

hostage *n* a person kept as a pledge to secure the performance of conditions.

hostel *n* a lodging house.

hostess *n* a female host.

hostile *adj* unfriendly.

hostility *n* enmity; (*pl*) warfare.

hot *adj* (**hotter, hottest**) of high temperature; very warm; giving or feeling heat; causing a burning sensation on the tongue; following closely.

hot *adj* having heat; burning; passionate; pungent; eager.

hot-blooded *adj* high-spirited.

hotel *n* a commercial establishment providing lodging and meals for travellers etc.

hotelier *n* the owner or manager of a hotel.

hothead *n* an impetuous person. * *adj* **hotheaded**.

hothouse *n* a heated greenhouse for raising plants; an environment that encourages rapid growth.

hound *n* a hunting dog. * *vt* to urge on.

hour *n* a period of 60 minutes, a 24th part of a day; the time.

hourly *adj* occuring every hour; done during an hour; frequent. * *adj* at every hour; frequently.

house *n* a building to live in, esp by one person or family; a household; the audience in a theatre; a legislative assembly.

house arrest *n* detention in one's own house, as opposed to prison.

housebreaker *n* a burglar; one employed to demolish buildings.

household *n* inmates of a house. * *adj* domestic; pertaining to house and family.

housekeeper *n* a person who runs a home, esp one hired to do so.

housekeeping *n* the daily running of a household.

house warming *n* a party given to celebrate moving into a new house.

housing *n* houses collectively; the provision of accommodation; a casing enclosing a piece of machinery etc.

hovel *n* a small mean dwelling.

hover *vi* to hang in the air; to linger.

hovercraft *n* a land or water vehicle that travels supported on a cushion of air.

how *adv* in what manner.

however *adv* in whatever manner. * *conj* yet; though.

howl *vt, vi* to utter the long, wailing cry of wolves, dogs etc; to shout or laugh in pain, amusement etc.

hub *n* the centre part of a wheel; a centre of activity.

hubbub *n* tumult; noise.

huddle *vi, vt* to crowd together.

hue *n* colour; tint; an outcry.

huff *n* a state of smouldering resentment. * *vi* to blow; to puff.

hug *vt* to embrace; to keep close to; to squeeze tightly. * *n* a close embrace.

huge *adj* immense; enormous.

hulk *n* the body of an old ship; a large, clumsy person.

hulking *adj* unwieldly; bulky.

hull *n* the outer covering of anything, as nut, grain; the framework of a ship. * *vt* to strip off covering.

hum *vb* (*pt* **hugged**) *vt, vi* to make a low continuous vibrating sound.

human *adj* of or relating to human beings.

humane *adj* merciful; compassionate.

humanity *n* the human race; philanthropy;

kindness.

humble adj lowly; modest; meek; servile. * vt to lower in condition or rank; to humiliate.

humdrum adj commonplace; dull.

humid adj moist; damp (of air).

humidity n moisture; (a measure of) the dampness in the air.

humiliate vt to humble; to mortify; to lower the pride or dignity.

humility n modesty; meekness.

hummock n a rounded knoll.

humorist n a wit; a humorous writer.

humorous adj jocular; funny; amusing.

humour n disposition; mood; caprice; jocularity; temperament; state of mind. * vt to gratify; to indulge.

hump n a protuberance.

humpback n a species of whale.

humus n vegetable mould.

hunch n a hump; an intuitive feeling. *vt to arch into a hump. * vt to move forward jerkily.

hundred adj ten times ten.

hundredweight n 112 lb.; 1/20 ton.

hunger n a craving for food; any strong desire.

hungry adj longing for food; craving something.

hunt vt, vi to chase; to search for; to drive away. * n hunting; the chase; a party organised for hunting.

hurdle n a portable frame of bars for temporary fences or for jumping over.

hurl vt to throw with force.

hurrah interj an exclamation of joy.

hurricane n a violent tropical storm.

hurried adj hasty; performed quickly.

hurry vt, vi to act; move; drive with haste. * n rush; urgency; haste.

hurt n a wound; an injury; harm. * vt to pain; bruise; harm; injure; damage.

hurtful adj harmful.

hurtle vi to move or throw with great speed and force.

husband n a man who has a wife. * vt to manage frugally; to conserve.

hush n stillness. * vt, vi to silence.

husk n the outer dry covering of certain fruits and seeds.

husky adj dry; hoarse; harsh; hefty; strong. * n an Arctic sled dog.

hussy n a shameless girl.

hustle vt, vi to jostle; to push or force hurriedly; to obtain by rough means..

hut n a small crude house or cabin..

hutch n a pen or coop for small animals.

hybrid n the offspring of two plants or animals of different species; a mongrel. * adj crossbred.

hydrant n a large pipe with a valve for drawing water from a main.

hydraulic adj operated by water or other liquid.

hydraulics n the science dealing with the mechanical properties of liquids.

hydrogen n a flammable, colourless, odourless, tasteless, gaseous chemical element, the lightest substance known.

hydrometer n an instrument for finding specific gravity of liquids.

hydrophobia n a disease caused by the bite of an infected animal and marked by dread of water; rabies.

hydrostatic adj relating to hydrostatics.

hydrostatics n the science which treats of the reactions of fluids at rest.

hygiene n principles and practice of health and cleanliness.

hymn n a song of praise.

hyperbole n an exaggeration for effect or emphasis.

hypercritical adj overcritical.

hyphen n a mark (-) joining syllables or words.

hypnosis n (pl hypnoses) a relaxed state resembling sleep in which the mind responds to external suggestion.

hypnotism n the act of inducing hypnosis; the study and use of hypnosis.

hypnotize vt to put in a state of hypnosis; to fascinate.

hypochondria n needless and anxiety about one's health.

hypocrisy n a falsely pretending to possess virtues, beliefs etc; an example of this. * n **hypocritical**.

hypodermic adj introduced beneath the skin (injection).

hypotenuse n the side opposite the right angle of a right-angled triangle.

hypothesis n (pl hypotheses) something

assumed for the purpose of argument.

hysteria *n* a mental disorder marked by excitability, anxiety, imaginary organic disorders etc; frenzied emotion.

hysteric *n* a hysterical person.

hysterical *adj* caused by hysteria; suffering from hysteria; (*inf*) extremely funny.

I

I *pron* pronoun, the first person who is speaking or writing used in referring to himself or herself.

ice *n* frozen water; ice cream or water ice. **vt, vi* to freeze; to cool with ice; to cover with icing.

iceberg *n* a floating mass of ice.

icebound *adj* surrounded with ice.

ice cream *n* a sweet frozen food.

ice floe *n* a sheet of floating ice.

icicle *n* a hanging taper of ice formed by frozen dripping water.

icy *adj* like ice; chilling.

idea *n* a mental impression or notion; an opinion or belief.

ideal *adj* perfect. * *n* perfect type; a standard for attainment or imitation; an aim or principle.

idealism *n* the doctrine that ideas are the sole reality.

idealist *n* a visionary.

idealize *vt* to represent as ideal.

identical *adj* exactly the same.

identification *n* act of identifying.

identify *vt* to consider to be the same; to establish the identity of; to associate closely.

identity *n* the state of being exactly alike; the distinguishing characteristics of a person, personality; the state of being the same as a specified person or thing.

ideology *n* the doctrines, opinions or beliefs of an individual, social class, political party etc.

idiocy *n* mental deficiency; stupidity.

idiom *n* an accepted expression with a different meaning from the literal.

idiosyncrasy *n* a personal peculiarity; a quirk; eccentricity.

idiot *n* (*inf*) a foolish person.

idiotic *adj* stupid; senseless.

idle *adj* doing nothing; lazy; not occupied; out of work; useless; worthless **vt* to waste or spend time uselessly **vi* to move aimlessly; (*of an engine*) to operate without transmitting power.

idleness *n* inaction; sloth.

idly *adv* lazily; carelessly.

idol *n* a graven image or anything worshipped.

idolatry *n* the worship of idols.

idolize *vt* to love excessively.

idyl, idyll *n* a romantic or a pastoral poem.

idyllic *adj* describing an idyll; charmingly picturesque.

if *conj* on condition that; in the event that; supposing that; even though; whenever.

igneous *adj* descriptive of rocks formed from solidified magma or lava.

ignite *vt, vi* to kindle; to set fire to; to burn or cause to burn.

ignition *n* an act or instance of igniting; the starting of an internal combustion engine.

ignoble *adj* mean; base.

ignominious *adj* shameful; base.

ignominy *n* public disgrace; shame.

ignoramus *n* (*pl* **ignoramuses**) an ignorant person.

ignorance *n* want of knowledge.

ignorant *adj* uninformed; uneducated.

ignore *vt* to disregard.

ill *adj* bad or evil; crabbed; sick; ugly. * *n* evil; pain. * *adv* not well; badly.

ill-bred *adj* not polite; rude.

illegal *adj* contrary to law.

illegible *adj* unreadable.

illegitimate *adj* born out of wedlock.

illicit *adj* improper; unlawful.

illiterate *adj* not able to read or write; ignorant.

ill-judged *adj* injudicious; unwise.

ill-mannered *adj* rude; boorish.

ill-natured *adj* bad-tempered; spiteful.

illness *n* sickness.

illogical *adj* not logical.

ill-tempered *adj* cross; morose.

ill-treat *vt* to treat unkindly, unfairly etc.

illuminate *vt* to light up; to adorn; to enlighten.

illumination n a brightening up with colours or lights.

illuminative adj enlightening.

illusion n a false notion; an unreal or misleading image or appearance; deception.

illusionist n a conjuror; a magician.

illusive adj deceptive.

illusory adj fallacious.

illustrate vt to make clear by explanation or drawing.

illustration n an example, a picture, or drawing; esp in a book.

illustrative adj explanatory.

illustrious adj renowned; distinguished.

ill-will n hatred; malice.

image n a likeness; an idol; a mental picture; the visual impression of something in a lens, mirror etc.

imagery n picturesque language.

imaginary adj not real; visionary.

imagination n fancy; the creative faculty.

imagine vt,vi to fancy; to conceive; to believe falsely.

imbecile adj weak-minded; foolish.*n an adult with a mental age of a three to eight-year-old child; a silly person.

imbibe vt to drink in; to absorb.

imitate vt to copy; to mimic; to impersonate.

imitation n a counterfeit; a copy; an act of impersonation or mimicking.

imitative adj given to imitation.

immaculate adj spotless; pure; morally unblemished.adj inherent; all pervading.

immaterial adj unimportant.

immature adj unripe; not mature.

immeasureable adj immense.

immediate adj acting or occuring without delay; next, nearest, without intervening agency; next in relationship; in close proximity, near to.

immediately adv instantly; directly; near.

immemorial adj ancient beyond memory.

immense adj immeasurable; huge; vast.

immensity n infinity; vastness.

immerse vt to plunge into (esp. water).

immersion heater n an electric element for heating liquids.

immigrant n one who settles in a country not his own.

immigrate vi to enter a country as a settler.

imminent adj impending; about to happen; threatening.

immobile adj fixed; stable.

immoderate adj excessive; intemperate.

immodest adj indelicate.

immoral adj depraved; wicked; corrupt.

immortal adj eternal; living forever; having lasting fame *n an immortal being or person.

immortality n endless life or fame.

immortalize vt to make famous for ever.

immovable adj steadfast; unalterable.

immune adj not susceptible to a specified disease through innoculation or natural resistance; confering immunity.

immunity n freedom from (disease, service, &c); exemption.

immunize vt to make immune, esp against infection.

immutable adj unchangeable.

imp n a mischievous child.

impact n a collision; a blow.

impair vt to make worse; to weaken.

impale vt to transfix with a sharp pointed instrument.

impalpable adj intangible; not easily understood.

impart vt to give; to bestow; to confer.

impartial adj just; fair; unbiased.

impartiality n freedom from bias.

impassable adj incapable of being travelled over or through.

impasse n a deadlock.

impassioned adj moved by passion.

impassive adj unmoved; apathetic.

impatience n intolerance of delay; restlessness; short temper.

impatient adj fretful; intolerant; restless.

impeach vt to question a person's honesty; to charge with a crime.

impeachment n an indictment.

impeccable adj faultless.

impecunious adj penniless.

impede vt to hamper; to obstruct.

impediment n an obstruction; a physical defect, e.g. a stammer.

impel vt to drive or urge forward.

impend vi to hang over; to threaten.

impenetrable adj impervious; unable to be passed through.

impenitent adj unrepentant; obdurate.

imperative adj commanding; obligatory; designating or of the mood of a verb that expresses a command, entreaty etc.

imperceptible adj minute; not easily grasped or detected by the senses.

imperfect adj incomplete; faulty; designating a verb tense that indicates a past action or state as incomplete or continuous.

imperfection n the state or quality of being imperfect; a defect, fault.

imperial adj pertaining to an empire.

imperil vt to endanger.

imperious adj commanding; arrogant.

imperishable adj indestructible.

impermeable adj impervious; impenetrable by liquids.

impersonal adj without reference to a particular person; cold; unfeeling; (of a verb) occuring only in the third person singular

impersonate vt to assume the character of another for entertainment or for fraud.

impertinence n insolence; irrelevance; rudeness.

impertinent adj saucy; pert; rude; irelevant.

imperturbable adj serene; unmoved.

impervious adj impassable; not receptive to or affected by.

impetuous adj hasty; thoughtless.

impetus n the force with which a body moves against resistance; driving force or motive.

impinge vi to collide; to clash; to encroach.

impious adj profane; irreverent.

impish adj mischievous.

implacability n pitilessness; relentlessness.

implacable adj not to be appeased; inexorable; unrelenting.

implant vt to plant; to instil.

implement n a tool, utensil, or instrument. * vt to fulfil; to carry out.

implicate vt to involve; to incriminate.

implication n entanglement; inference; deduction.

implicit adj implied; not stated; unquestioning.

implore vti to beseech, to entreat.

imply vt to suggest; to suggest indirectly.

impolite adj rude; uncivil.

impolitic adj inexpedient.

imponderable adj without weight; *n something difficult to measure or assess.

import vt to bring from abroad; to signify; to imply.

importance n significance; a high place in public estimation; high self-esteem.

important adj momentous; serious; powerful and authoritative.

importunate adj urgent; persistent.

importune vt to press urgently; to crave.

impose vt to lay on as a tax; to inflict oneself on others; to cheat; to lay pages of type or film and secure them.

imposing adj impressive; stately.

imposition vt, vi an unfair obligation.

impossibility n state or character of being impossible; that which cannot be, or cannot be done.

impossible adj not possible; inconceivable; unendurable.

impostor, imposter n a deceiver.

impotence, impotency n powerlessness; inability to engage in sexual intercourse.

impotent adj feeble; incompetent; sexually impotent.

impound vt to confine; to seize legally.

impoverish vt to make poor; to exhaust.

impracticable adj not feasible; unmanageable; unattainable.

impractical adj not practical; not competent in practical skills.

impregnable adj invincible; secure against attack.

impregnate vt to cause to become prgnant; to fertilize; to saturate; to pervade.

impresario n the manager of an opera, concert series, etc.

impress vt to press into; to stamp; to fix deeply and favourably (on the mind).

impression n the effect produced in the mind by an experience; a mark produced by imprinting; a vague idea, notion; the number of copies of a book printed at one time; an impersonation.

impressionable adj susceptible; easily influenced.

impressionism n a movement in art giving more attention to general effect and impressions than to details.

impressionist n an artist who aims at broad effects; a mimic or impersonator.

impressive adj imposing; striking; arousing admiration.

imprint vt to impress; to stamp. * n a printer's and publisher's name, address etc.

imprison vt to confine in prison.

improbability n unlikelihood.

improbable adj unlikely to be true or to happen.

impromptu n an unprepared remark, poem, etc; a short, unrehearsed musical composition* adj extempore.

improper adj lacking propriety; indecent; erroneous; unsuitable.

impropriety n an unbecoming act.

improve vt, vi to better; to grow better; to use to good purpose.

improvement n advance; betterment; an alteration that enhances the value of something.

improvidence n wastefulness.

improvident adj thriftless; careless.

improvise vt to compose and recite, etc, without preparation. to do or use whatever is at hand.

imprudence n rashness, indiscretion.

imprudent adj indiscreet; heedless.

impudent adj impertinent; saucy.

impugn vt to challenge; to contradict.

impulse n a thrust; a motive; a sudden determination to act.

impulsive adj impetuous; hasty.

impunity n freedom from punishment.

impure adj foul; obscene; adulterated.

impurity n pollution; adulteration.

impute vt to attribute; ascribe.

in prep, adv within; not out; during; being a member of; wearing.

inability n lack of ability.

inaccessible adj unattainable.

inaccuracy n uncorrectness; error.

inaccurate adj incorrect; not exact.

inaction n idleness; rest.

inactive adj idle; indolent.

inadequacy n insufficiency.

inadequate adj defective; not capable.

inadmissible adj not allowable.

inadvertent adj heedless; careless.

inadvisable adj not advisable; inexpedient.

inalienable adj incapable of being transferred.

inane adj silly; senseless.

inanimate adj lifeless; spiritless.

inanity n silliness.

inapplicable adj inappropriate.

inapposite adj not to the point.

inappropriate adj unsuitable.

inapt adj unapt; unfit.

inaptitude n unfitness.

inarticulate adj not expressed in words; incapable of coherent or effective expression of ideas, feelings, etc.

inattention n want of attention; neglect.

inattentive adj not attending; thoughtless.

inaudible adj unable to be heard.

inaugural adj introductory.

inaugurate vt to introduce, to install into office; to open a building etc. formally to the public; to initiate.

inauguration n a formal opening or start.

inauspicious adj ill-omened.

inborn adj innate; inherent.

inbred adj innate; produced by inbreeding

inbreed vt,vi to breed by continual mating of individuals or closely related stocks.

incalculable adj numberless; very great; uncertain.

incandescent adj white or glowing with heat.

incantation n recital of words containing a magic spell.

incapable adj unfit to perform an activity.

incapacitate vt to render unfit; to disable.

incapacity n unfitness; disqualification.

incarceration n imprisonment.

incarnate vt to embody in flesh. * adj endowed with a human body.

incarnation n embodiment in human form.

incautious adj unwary; imprudent.

incendiary n one who wilfully sets fire to property; an arsonist *adj inflammatory; seditious; (of bomb) design to start fires.

incense *n* perfume of spices burnt in religious rites.

incense *vt* to inflame; to provoke.

incentive *adj* inciting. * *n* an inducement.

inception *n* the initial stage.

incessant *adj* unceasing; constant.

incessantly *adv* continually.

incest *n* intercourse between close blood relations.

incestuous *adj* guilty of incest.

inch *n* the twelfth part of a foot in length; * *vt,vi* to move very slowly or by degrees.

incidence *n* the degree or range of occurence or effect.

incident *n* a distinct event; a minor event.

incidental *adj* casual; occasional; happening by the way; (*pl*) miscellaneous items.

incidentally *adv* in passing; as an aside.

incinerate *vt* to burn to ashes.

incinerator *n* a furnace for burning.

incipient *adj* beginning to be or appear.

incise *vt* to cut in or into; to carve.

incision *n* a cut, esp by a surgeon into a body.

incisive *adj* sharp; biting; trenchant.

incisor *n* a front cutting tooth.

incite *vt* to urge on; to stir up.

incitement *n* a motive; encouragement.

inclemency *n* harshness, severity (of the weather).

inclement *adj* not clement; stormy.

inclination *n* a propensity or disposition, esp a liking; a deviation from the horizontal or vertical; a slope.

incline *vi* to lean, to slope; to be disposed towards an opinion or action. * *vt* to cause to bend forwards; to cause to deviate. * *n* a slope

inclined *adj* sloping; disposed.

include *vt* to enclose; to comprise; to contain.

inclusive *adj* including; comprising.

incoherence *n* rambling, inarticulate speech or thought; unconnected.

incoherent *adj* confused; unintelligible.

incombustible *adj* not able to be burned.

income *n* all moneys coming in for work or investments etc.

incoming *adj* coming; accruing; *n the*

act of coming in; that which comes in; income.

incommunicative *adj* reserved; unsocial.

incomparable *adj* matchless.

incompatible *adj* irreconcilable; unable to exist together in harmony.

incompetence, incompetency *n* unfitness; incapacity; lack of skill or ability.

incompetent *adj* not competent; incapable; unskilful; an incompetent person.

incomplete *adj* imperfect; defective; unfinished.

incomprehensible *adj* unintelligible; inconceivable.

inconceivable *adj* unimaginable.

inconclusive *adj* indecisive; uncertain as to result or outcome.

incongruity *n* inconsistency; absurdity.

incongruous *adj* discordant; inconsistent; lacking harmony or agreement of parts.

inconsequential, inconsequent *adj* not following logically; irrelevant.

inconsiderable *adj* unimportant; insignificant.

inconsiderate *adj* thoughtless; unkind.

inconsistency *n* incongruity; want of agreement; irregularity; fickleness.

inconsistent *adj* not consistent; variable.

inconsolable *adj* grieved beyond measure.

inconspicuous *adj* not easily noticed; undistinguished.

incontestable *adj* unquestionable.

incontinence *n* lack of self-restraint; inability to control excretion of bodily wastes.

incontinent *adj* suffering from incontinence; unrestrained.

incontrovertible *adj* certain; indisputable.

inconvenience *n* annoyance; awkwardness; that which incommodes.

inconvenient *adj* awkward.

incorporate *vt* to unite in one body.

incorporation *n* a union.

incorrect *adj* faulty; untrue; improper.

incorrigible *adj* incurable; hopeless.

incorruptible *adj* incapable of physical corruption, decay or dissolution; incapable of being bribed.

increase *vi* to become greater; to augment. * *vt* to add to. * *n* a growing larger; addition; profit; interest.

incredible *adj* unbelievable.

incredulity *n* doubt; scepticism.

incredulous *adj* sceptical; doubting.

increment *n* the amount of an increase.

incriminate *vt* to involve in an accusation; to accuse.

incubate *vi* to sit on eggs; to hatch.

incubator *n* an apparatus in which eggs are hatched by artificial heat; an apparatus for nurturing premature babies.

inculcate *vt* to teach; to implant.

incumbent *n* holder of a church living.

incumbrance *see* **encumbrance**.

incur *vt* to bring upon oneself.

incurable *adj* hopeless; past cure.

incursion *n* a raid; an inroad.

indebted *n* beholden; obliged; owing.

indebtedness *n* amount of debt owed.

indecency *n* immodesty; impurity.

indecent *adj* unseemly; obscene.

indecipherable *adj* incapable of being deciphered.

indecision *n* inability to take a decision.

indecisive *adj* wavering; vacillating.

indecorous *adj* unseemly; improper.

indeed *adv* truly; certainly **interj* expressing irony, disbelief, surprise, etc.

indefatigable *adj* untiring; unremitting.

indefensible *adj* untenable; inexcusable.

indefinable *adj* vague; difficult to explain clearly.

indefinite *adj* uncertain; unlimited; vague.

indelible *adj* not able to be erased.

indelicacy *n* immodesty; coarseness.

indelicate *adj* improper; coarse.

indemnify *vt* to make good a loss; to insure against loss, damage, etc.

indemnity *n* compensation for loss.

indent *vt* to notch; to indicate a paragraph by leaving a space at the margin. ** n* an order for supplies.

indentation *n* a notch; a small bay.

indenture *n* a written contract between two parties.

independence *n* the state of being independent.

independent *adj* free; unrestrained.

indescribable *adj* unutterable; inexpressible; too beautiful, etc for words.

indestructible *adj* imperishable.

indeterminate *adj* uncertain.

index *n* an alphabetical list of names, subjects, items, etc mentioned in a printed book, usually listed alphabetically at the end of the text; any indication or sign.

index finger *n* the forefinger.

index-linked *adj* anything linked directly to changes in the cost of living index.

indicate *vt* to point out; to show; to be a sign or symptom of; to state briefly; to suggest.

indicative *adj* pointing out; affirming; serving as a sign of.

indicator *n* a thing that indicates or points; an instument showing the operating condition of a piece of machinery.

indict *vt* to charge with a crime.

indictment *n* a formal charge or accusation of a crime.

indifference *n* unconcern; apathy.

indifferent *adj* unconcerned; heedless; uninterested; average; mediocre.

indigenous *adj* native; existing naturally in a particular country, region or enviroment.

indigestible *adj* not easily digested.

indigestion *n* pain caused by difficulty in digesting food.

indignant *adj* angry; scornful.

indignation *n* wrath and scorn; annoyance; esp at an injustice.

indignity *n* humiliation; an insult.

indigo *n* a blue vegetable dye.

indirect *adj* roundabout.

indiscreet *adj* tactless; imprudent.

indiscretion *n* imprudence; a thoughtless act; rashness.

indiscriminate *adj* not making any distinction; general; confused; random.

indispensable *adj* necessary; vital.

indisposed *adj* disinclined; unwell.

indisposition *n* a slight ailment.

indisputable *adj* unquestionable.

indistinct *adj* faint; confused.

indistinguishable *adj* incapable of being distinguished.

individual *adj* existing as a seperate thing or being; of, by, for, or relating to a single person. ** n* a single thing or being.

individualist *n* a person who thinks or behaves with marked independence.

individuality n seperate or distinct existence; personality.

individually adv separately.

indivisible adj not able to be divided.

indoctrinate vt to instruct systematically in a doctrine, idea or belief.

indolence n laziness; idleness.

indolent adj lazy; idle.

indomitable adj unyielding; invincible.

indoors adv within house.

indorse, etc see endorse, etc.

indubitable adj certain; evident.

induce vt to persuade; to draw(a conclusion) from particular facts; to bring on.

inducement n an incentive; a motive.

induct vt to install; to introduce.

induction n introduction to office; a prologue; magnetic influence.

indulge vt to gratify; to humour. * vi to give way to one's desire.

indulgence n favour; intemperance; tolerance.

indulgent adj forbearing; yielding; lenient.

industrial adj pertaining to industry.

industrialist n a person who owns or manages an industrial enterprise.

industrious adj diligent; active.

industry n organised production or manufacture of goods.

inebriated adj drunken.

inedible adj not fit to be eaten.

ineffable adj indescribable.

ineffective adj useless; impotent.

ineffectual adj fruitless; futile.

inefficacy n failure to produce effect.

inefficient adj incapable; ineffective.

inelegant adj plain; ungraceful; uncouth.

ineligibility n state or quality of being ineligible.

ineligible adj not qualified; unsuitable.

inept adj unsuitable; awkward; clumsy.

ineptitude n unfitness; silliness.

inequality n lack of equality; unevenness of surface.

inequitable adj unfair; unjust.

inert adj lifeless; sluggish; inactive; dull with few or no properties.

inertia n inactivity; tendency of matter to remain in existing state of rest (or continue in a fixed direction) unless acted on by an outside force.

inestimable adj invaluable; priceless.

inevitable adj unavoidable.

inexact adj not exactly true or correct.

inexcusable adj indefensible.

inexhaustible adj unfailing.

inexorable adj inflexible; relentless.

inexpedient adj not advisable; injudicious.

inexpensive adj cheap.

inexperienced adj unskilled; raw.

inexplicable adj unaccountable.

inexpressible adj unspeakable.

inextricable adj that cannot be disentangled, solved, or escaped from.

infallibility n freedom from liability to error; perfection.

infallible adj incapable of errors; reliable.

infamous adj scandalous; notorious.

infamy n public disgrace; ignominy.

infancy n early childhood; the early stages of anything.

infant n a very young child.

infanticide n child murder.

infantile adj childish; weak.

infantry n foot soldiers.

infatuate vt to inspire with foolish or short-lived passion.

infatuated adj besotted.

infect vt to taint with disease; to corrupt.

infection n an infecting or being infected; an infectious disease; a diseased condition.

infectious adj able to be transmitted.

infer vt to conclude, to deduce.

inference n conclusion; deduction.

inferior adj subordinate. * n a person lower in rank, degree, quality.

inferno n hell; intense heat; a devastating fire.

infernal adj diabolical; fiendish; extremely irritating.

infertility n barrenness.

infest vt to overrun in large numbers, usu to be harmful; to be parasitic in or on.

infidelity n want of faith; dishonesty; unfaithfulness esp in marriage.

infighting n intense competition within an organisation.

infiltrate vt, vi to filter or pass gradualy through or into; to permeate; to penetrate gradually or stealthily, e.g. as spies.

infinite *adj* limitless; vast.

infinitesimal *adj* microscopic; minute.

infinitive *n* the form of a verb without reference to person, number or tense.

infinitude *n* infinity.

infinity *n* immensity; a countless number, quantity or time period.

infirm *adj* weak; sickly.

infirmary *n* a hospital.

infirmity *n* physical weakness; fault; disease.

inflame *vt* to kindle; to excite; to incense. * *vt* to grow hot.

inflammable *adj* combustible.

inflammation *n* a condition of the body marked by heat, swelling, and pain.

inflammatory *adj* tending to excite passion.

inflate *vt* to fill up with air or gas; distend; to increase beyond what is normal, esp the supply of money or credit.

inflated *adj* puffed up; elated.

inflation *n* an increase in the currency in circulation or a marked expansion of credit, resulting in a fall in currency value and a sharp rise in prices.

inflection *n* modulation of voice; changes in word forms.

inflexible *adj* unbending; rigid.

inflict *vt* to impose as a penalty.

inflorescence *n* a flowering.

influence *n* moving or directing power; sway; effect. * *vt* to move; to persuade.

influential *adj* exerting influence; possessing power.

influenza *n* contagious, feverish viral disease marked by muscular pain and inflamation of the respitory system.

influx *n* a flowing in of people or things to a place.

inform *vt* to tell; to enlighten; to teach; to give information to the police etc, in accusing another.

informal *adj* without ceremony; unofficial; casual.

information *n* intelligence; news; data stored in, or retrieved from a computer.

informative *adj* instructive.

informer *n* one who informs; a spy.

infraction *n* a violation; a breach.

infrequent *adj* uncommon; rare.

infringe *vt* to break; to transgress.

infringement *n* a breach, esp of the law.

infuriate *vt* to madden; to enrage.

infuse *vt* to pour in; to instil; to steep.

infusion *n* process of infusion; liquor (as tea) so obtained.

ingenious *adj* inventive, original; resourceful.

ingenuity *n* inventiveness.

ingenuous *adj* open, original or candid.

inglorious *adj* unhonoured; humiliating.

ingot *n* a bar of metal got from a mould.

ingrate *n* an ungrateful person.

ingratiate *vt* to get into another's favour.

ingratitude *n* thanklessnes.

ingredient *n* something included with others in a mixture; a component.

ingress *n* entrance.

inhabit *vt,vi* to live in; to dwell; to reside.

inhabitable *adj* habitable.

inhabitant *n* a resident.

inhale *vt* to draw into the lungs.

inhaler *n* a respirator; an apparatus for inhaling vapours.

inharmonious *adj* discordant.

inherent *adj* inborn; ingrained.

inherit *vt,vi* to come into possession of as an heir.

inheritance *n* a heritage; something inherited.

inhibit *vt* to restrain; to forbid.

inhibition *n* restraint; embargo.

inhospitable *adj* unfriendly and ungenerous to strangers; barren.

inhuman *adj* cruel; merciless.

inhumanity *n* cruelty.

inimical *adj* unfriendly; hostile.

inimitable *adj* matchless; peerless.

iniquitous *adj* wicked; criminal.

iniquity *n* wickedness; injustice.

initial *adj* primary; of or at the beginning. * *n* the first letters of a person's name (*pl.*). * *vt* to mark or sign with initials.

initiate *vt* to begin; to originate; to admit as a member of a club etc.

initiation *n* formal introduction or admittance.

initiative *n* first step; lead; power of originating.

inject *vt* to force (fluid into the body) esp

with a syringe.

injudicious *adj* unwise; indiscreet.

injunction *n* a command; exhortation; advice; a legal writ restraining or ordering.

injure *vt* to hurt; to damage.

injurious *adj* harmful; wrongful.

injury *n* physical damage; harm.

injustice *n* wrong; unfairness.

ink *n* a coloured liquid used for writing, printing etc. *vt* to cover, mark, or colour with ink.

inkling *n* a vague notion; a hint.

inland *adj* interior; remote from the sea; domestic; *n* an inland region.

inlay *vt* to decorate a surface by inserting pieces of metal, wood, etc.

inlet *n* a narrow strip of water extending into a body of land; an opening.

inmate *n* a resident; an occupant, esp of a prison or other institution.

inn *n* a small hotel; a public house.

innate *adj* inborn; natural; instinctive.

inner *adj* interior. * *n* the part of a target adjoining the bull's eye.

innings *n sing* (*pl* innings) the batting period of each side (cricket).

innocence *n* purity; simplicity; without guilt or guile.

innocent *adj* not guilty of a particular crime; free from sin; blameless.

innocuous *adj* harmless.

innovate *vi* to introduce new methods, ideas, etc; to make changes.

innovation *n* novelty; change.

innuendo *n* an indirect hint; a sly remark, often derogatory.

innumerable *adj* countless.

inoculate *vt* to inject a serum or a vaccine into, esp in order to create an immunity; to protect as if by inoculation.

inopportune *adj* untimely; inconvenient.

inordinate *adj* excessive; extravagant.

inorganic *adj* not having the structure or characteristics of living organisms.

inpatient *n* a patient being treated while remaining in hospital.

inquest *n* a judicial inquiry held by a coroner; esp into a case of violent or unexplained death.

inquire *vi* to ask about; to question; to investigate.

inquiring *adj* questioning; curious.

inquiry, enquiry *n* research; a question; an investigation.

inquisition *n* an inquiry; a formal search; a tribunal for trial.

inquisitive *adj* prying; inquiring; curious.

inroad *n* a raid; a foray; an encroachment or advance.

insane *adj* not sane; mentally ill.

insanity *n* lunacy; derangement of the mind; mania.

insatiable *adj* rapacious; greedy.

inscribe *vt* to mark or engrave on a surface; to add (a person's name) to a list; to dedicate (a book) to someone.

inscription *n* words engraved on stone or metal.

inscrutable *adj* hard to understand; incomprehensible; enigmatic.

insect *n* any of a class of small anthropods with three pairs of legs, a head, thorax, and abdomen and two or four wings.

insecticide *n* an insect killer.

insectivorous *adj* insect-eating.

insecure *adj* unsafe; risky; feel anxiety; not dependable.

insecurity *n* unsteadiness; peril; risk; lack of confidence; instability; something insecure.

insensibility *n* want of feeling; apathy.

insensible *adj* unconscious; unaware; indifferent; imperceptible.

insensitive *adj* not sensitive; callous.

inseparable *adj* never apart; closely attached, as romantically.

insert *vt* to put, fit, or set in.

insertion *n* a thing inserted (as advertisement); lace, etc, worked into cloth.

inset *vt* to set in; to implant. * *n* an insertion.

inshore *adj, adv.* near or towards the shore.

inside *n* the inner side, surface, or part; internal; known only to insiders; secret. * *adv* on or in the inside; within; indoors; (*prep*) in or within.

insider *n* a person within a place or group; a person with access to confidential information.

insidious *adj* treacherous; stealthy.

insight n discernment; penetration.

insignia npl badges of office or honour.

insignificance n littleness; triviality.

insignificant adj trifling; mean.

insincere adj faithless; deceitful.

insincerity n hypocrisy.

insinuate vt to introduce slowly, by degrees, etc.; to hint.

insipid adj tasteless; flat; uninteresting.

insist vi to urge or press strongly.

insistence n urgency.

insobriety n intemperance.

insolence n rudeness; impudence.

insolent adj overbearing; insulting.

insoluble adj incapable of being dissolved; impossible to solve or explain.

insolvency n bankruptcy.

insolvent adj not able to pay debts.

insomnia n abnormal sleeplessness.

inspect vt to examine; to scan carefully.

inspection n careful survey; examination.

inspector n an official who inspects in order to ensure compliance with regulations, etc.

inspectorate n a body of examiners.

inspiration n an inspiring; any stimulus to creative thought.

inspire vt to stimulate, as to some creative effort; to motivate by divine influence; to arouse (a thought or feeling) in (someone); to cause.

instability n inconstancy; fickleness.

install vt to invest with office; to settle in a position or state.

installation n machinery, equipment, etc that has been installed.

instalment n a sum of money to be paid at regular specified times.

instance n an example; a step in proceeding. * vt to give as an example

instant adj immediate; (food) concentrated or precooked for quick preparation. * n a moment; a particular moment.

instantaneous adj done in an instant.

instead adv in place of.

instep n the upper part or arch of the foot.

instigate vt to spur on; to urge; to initiate.

instigation n incitement; prompting.

instil vt to put (an idea etc) in or into (the mind) gradually.

instinct n a natural impulse; a knack.

instinctive adj spontaneous.

institute vt to set up; to found; to begin; to originate. * n an organization for the promotion of science, art etc.

institution n an established law, custom etc; an organization having a social, educational, or religious purpose; the building housing it; (inf) a long-established person or thing.

instruct vt to teach; to advise; to give instruction.

instruction n information; education; knowledge imparted; (pl) orders, directions; detailed guidance.

instructive adj educational; informative.

instrument n a thing by means of which something is done; any of various devices for indicating, controlling, measuring etc; any of various devices producing musical sound; a formal document.

instrumental adj serving as a means of doing something; helpful; of, performed on, or written for a musical instrument or instruments.

instrumentalist n a person who plays a musical instrument.

insubordinate adj disobedient; mutinous.

insubordination n revolt; disobedience.

insufferable adj intolerable.

insufficiency n inadequacy; unfitness.

insufficient adj not enough; inadequate.

insular adj pertaining to an island; narrow-minded.

insulate vt to set apart; to isolate; to cover with a non-conducting material in order to prevent the escape of, heat, sound, etc.

insulin n a hormone that controls absorption of sugar by the body.

insult n a gross affront; indignity. * vt, vi to treat with insolence; to offend.

insuperable adj insurmountable.

insupportable adj intolerable.

insurance n a contract purchased to guarantee compensation for a specified loss by fire, death, etc.

insure vt to contract against loss, damage, etc.

insurgent adj rebellious. * n a rebel.

insurmountable adj insuperable.

insurrection n a revolt; a rebellion.

intact adj untouched; unimpaired; whole.

intangible adj that cannot be touched, incorporeal; indefinable. * n something that is intangible.

integer n a whole; a whole number.

integral adj necessary for completeness; whole or complete; made up of parts forming a whole.

integrate vt to make up a whole; to complete; to bring parts together into a whole.

integrity n uprightness; honesty.

intellect n the ability to reason or understand; high intelligence; a very intelligent person.

intellectual adj of, involving, or appealing to the intellect; requiring intelligence. * n an intellectual person.

intelligence n the ability to learn or understand; the ability to cope with information; those involved with gathering secret, esp military, information.

intelligent adj quick of mind; acute; well informed.

intelligible adj comprehensible; clear.

intemperance n excess of any kind.

intemperate adj immoderate; unrestrained; extreme (weather).

intend vt to design; to have in mind as an aim or purpose.

intense adj strained; extreme; severe; passionate; emotional.

intensely adv in a high degree.

intensify vt to deepen; to augment.

intensity n vehemence; keenness; ardour; strength; the force or energy of any physical agent.

intensive adj strained; concentrated; describing the special and extensive care give to patients after serious surgery.

intent adj set; bent. * n purpose.

intention n purpose; design.

intentionally adv on purpose.

inter vt to bury.

interact vi to act reciprocally.

interaction n mutual or reciprocal action.

intercede vi to mediate; to plead for.

intercept vt to take or stop in its course; to obstruct; to cut off.

interception n act of intercepting.

intercession n mediation.

interchange vt to give and receive one thing for another

intercom n (inf) a system of intercommunication, as in an aircraft.

intercommunication n interchange of ideas and means for securing it.

intercourse n communion; fellowship; sexual intercourse.

interdict vt to forbid; to veto.

interest n a feeling of concern about something; anything in which one has a share; benefit; money paid for the use of money; *vt to excite the attention of; to cause to have a share in; to concern oneself with.

interested adj concerned; biased.

interesting adj engaging; intriguing; attractive.

interfere vi to clash; to interpose; to meddle; to obstruct.

interference n intermeddling; clashing; (radio,T.V) the interruption of reception by atmospherics or by unwanted signals.

interim n the meantime; an intervening period of time; * adj temporary.

interior adj internal; inland.

interject vt to throw in between; to insert; to interrupt

interjection n a word thrown in abruptly.

interlace vti to weave together.

interleave vt to insert blank leaves between other leaves.

interlock vi, vt to clasp together.

interloper n an intruder; a meddler.

interlude n an interval.

intermediary n a go-between; a mediator.

intermediate adj intervening; middle.

interment n burial.

interminable adj endless; boundless.

intermingle vt to mingle together.

intermission n a pause between parts of a performance; a rest.

intermittent adj coming and going; ebbing and flowing; periodic.

intern vt to confine prisoners, etc, in a prescribed area.

internal adj of or on the inside; inward.

international adj between or among nations; concerned with the relationship between nations; for the use of all nations; of or for people in various nations.

internecine *adj* deadly; bloody; mutually destructive.

interpolate *vt* to interrupt speech etc. with comments; to insert a passage into a text.

interpose *vt* to place between.

interpret *vt* to explain; to translate; to construe; to give one's own conception of; * *vi* to translate between speakers of different languages.

interpretation *n* an explanation.

interpreter *n* one who interprets; a translator.

interrogate *vt* to question.

interrogation *n* a questioning; a mark of questioning, (?).

interrogative *adj* denoting a question.

interrupt *vi* to break in upon.

interruption *n* a hindrance; a stoppage; a break in continuity, by passing through or crossing.

intersect *vt* to divide; to cross mutually.

intersection *n* a cutting; crossing of two lines; the point of crossing.

intersperse to scatter; to mingle.

interstellar *adj* among the stars.

intertwine *vt* to weave or twist together.

interval *n* time or distance between; the difference of pitch between two sounds.

intervene *vi* to interpose or interfere; to settle or hinder a matter etc.

intervention *n* a coming between; interference; mediation.

interview *n* a meeting in which a person is asked about his or her views, etc; a meeting at which a candidate for a job is questioned and assessed for a job.

interweave *vt* to intertwine.

intestate *adj* dying without having made a will.

intestinal *adj* pertaining to the intestines.

intestine *n* the part of the alimentary canal between the stomach and the anus.

intimacy *n* close friendship; familiarity; close friendship.

intimate *adj* most private or personal; very close or familiar, esp sexually. * *n* a close friend. * *vt* to make known.

intimation *n* a hint; an announcement.

intimidate *vt* to overawe; to cow.

into *prep* expressing motion towards the inside; to a particular condition.

intolerable *adj* insufferable; unbearable.

intolerance *n* bigotry; narrow-mindedness; inability to endure.

intolerant *adj* illiberal; bigoted.

intonation *n* a modulation of the voice.

intone *vi* to chant in a slow monotone.

intoxicant *n* an alcoholic drink etc.

intoxicate *vt* to make drunk; to stir up.

intoxication *n* drunkenness; frenzy; great excitement.

intractable *adj* ungovernable; headstrong; difficult to solve (of problem) or alleviate (of illness).

intransigent *adj* irreconcilable; unwilling to compromise.

intransitive *adj* of a verb whose action is limited to subject.

intrepid *adj* undaunted; fearless.

intricacy *n* entanglement; complexity.

intricate *adj* involved; detailed.

intrigue *n* an underhand plot. * *vi* to plot secretly; to rouse curiosity.

intriguing *adj* scheming; crafty; interesting; attractive.

intrinsic, intrinsical *adj* in itself; belonging to the real nature of a person or thing; inherent.

introduce *vt* to present; to insert; to begin; to make known; to bring into use.

introduction *n* an introducing or being introduced; the presentation of one person to another; preliminary statement; preface; presentation.

introductory *adj* prefatory; preliminary.

introspection *n* self-examination.

introvert *n* a person who is more interested in his or her own thoughts, feelings, etc than in external objects or events. **adj* characterized by introversion (*also* **introverted**)

intrude *vi* to trespass; meddle. * *vt* to thrust in; to force oneself on others.

intrusion *n* encroachment; trespass.

intrusive *adj* jutting in; forward.

intuition *n* insight; instinctive perception apprehension of the truth of something.

intuitive *adj* natural; apprehended instinctively.

inundate *vt* to flow over; to flood.

inundation *n* a flood; a deluge.

inure *vt* to harden by use.

invade vt to enter as an enemy; to attack; to encroach upon.

invalid[1] adj void; illegal.

invalid[2] n a person who is ill or disabled. * vt to cause to become an invalid; to disable; to cause to retire from the armed forces because of ill-health or injury.

invalidate vt to render of no effect; no legal use.

invalidity n ineffectiveness.

invaluable adj priceless.

invariable adj constant; unchangeable.

invasion n hostile entrance; encroachment; intrusion.

invective n a tirade; vituperation. * adj abusive.

inveigh vi to rail against.

inveigle vt to beguile; to decoy.

invent vt to originate; to devise; to concoct; to fabricate (a lie etc.).

invention n a new contrivance; ingenuity.

inventive adj ingenious; skilled in invention.

inventory n an itemized list of goods, property etc, as of a business. *vt to make an inventory of; to enter in an inventory.

inverse adj opposite; reversed; contrary.

inversion n reversal; complete turn about.

invert vt to turn upside down; to reverse in order, position or relationship.

invertebrate adj without backbone; n an animal without a backbone..

inverted adj turned upside down etc.

invest vt to commit (money) to property, stocks and shares etc, for profit; to devote effort, time, etc on a particular activity; to install in office with ceremony; to furnish with power, authority, etc. *vi to invest money.

investigate vt to search into; to examine; to inquire into.

investiture n the act or right of giving legal possession; the ceremony of investing a person with an office, robes, title, etc.

investment n the act of investing money productively; the amount invested; an activity in which time, effort or money has been invested.

inveteracy n confirmed obstinacy.

inveterate adj deep-rooted; confirmed.

invidious adj envious; causing ill-will.

invigorate vt to strengthen; to enliven; to refresh.

invincible adj unconquerable.

inviolable adj sacred; not to be broken.

inviolate adj virgin; stainless; intact.

invisible adj unseen; imperceptible.; hidden.

invitation n a bidding to come or do something.

invite vt to ask to come somewhere or do something; to ask for; to give reason for; to tempt; to entice.

inviting pa attractive; enticing.

invocation n a prayer to God for help; an appeal to muse for aid; a summons.

invoice n a list of goods supplied, with prices; a bill. * vt to make out a bill (for goods).

invoke vt to call upon (God etc.); to address in prayer; to resort to (law etc.) as pertinent; to implore.

involuntary adj done without power to choose; instinctive.

involve vt to roll up; include; to implicate; to complicate; to make busy.

invulnerable adj not able to be hurt; secure.

inward adj situated within or directed to the inside; relating to or in the mind or spirit. *adv inwards.

inwardly adv within; in the mind or spirit; towards the inside or centre.

inwards adv towards the inside or interior; in the mind or spirit.

iodine n a nonmetallic element got from seaweed.

Ionic adj one of orders of Greek architecture.

iota n the ninth letter of the Greek alphabet; a jot; a very small quantity.

ipecacuanha n a medicinal plant and medicine got from it.

irascibility n anger; testiness.

irascible adj easily angered; irritable.

irate adj angry; enraged.

ire n anger; wrath; rage.

iridescence n display of colours like the rainbow.

iridescent *adj* shimmering with rainbow colours.

iris *n* (*pl* **irises, irides**) the round pigmented membrane surrounding the pupil of the eye; a perennial herbaceous plant with sword shaped leaves and brightly coloured flowers.

irk *vt* to weary; to vex; to annoy.

irksome *adj* wearisome; tedious.

iron *n* a metallic element, the most common of all metals; a tool, etc of this metal; a heavy implement with a heated flat undersurface for pressing cloth; (*pl*) shackles of iron; firm strength; power; any of certain golf clubs with angled metal heads. * *adj* of iron; like iron, strong and firm. * *vt, vi* to press with a hot iron.

ironic, ironical *adj* satirical; sarcastic.

ironmonger *n* a dealer in hardware; metal goods, tools etc.

irony *n* a form of sarcasm in which the sense is opposite to the words.

irradiate *vt* to illuminate; to enlighten.

irradiation *n* illumination.

irrational *adj* void of reason; senseless; absurd.

irreconcilable *adj* inconsistent; implacable; incompatible.

irredeemable *adj* hopelessly lost; inconvertible.

irrefutable *adj* unanswerable; unable to deny or disprove.

irregular *adj* not regular; crooked; not conforming to the rules; imperfect; not belonging to the regular armed forces.

irrelevance, irrelevancy *n* inaptness; lack of point.

irrelevant *adj* not to the point.

irreligious *adj* not religious; profane.

irremediable *adj* without remedy.

irreparable *adj* irremediable; not able to be repaired, rectified or made good.

irrepressible *adj* uncontrollable.

irreproachable *adj* faultless.

irresistible *adj* overwhelming; resistless; fascinating.

irresolute *adj* undecided; wavering.

irresolution *n* indecision.

irrespective *adj* making no exceptions; regardless of.

irresponsible *adj* lacking a sense of responsibility; flighty.

irretrievable *adj* irreparable; hopeless.

irreverence *n* disrespect; impiety.

irreverent *adj* not paying due respect.

irreversible *adj* irrevocable.

irrevocable *adj* unalterable.

irrigate *vt* to water land artificially; (medicine) to wash out a cavity, wound etc.

irrigation *n* supplying land with water.

irritability *n* hastiness of temper.

irritable *adj* short-tempered; touchy.

irritant *adj* irritating; galling. * *n* an irritating agent; a stimulant.

irritate *vt* to provoke; to inflame.

irritating *adj* annoying.

irritation *n* annoyance.

irruption *n* an invasion; inroad.

irruptive *adj* rushing in or upon.

is 3rd per. sing. pres. indic. verb to *be*.

Islam *n* the religion of Mohammed; the Moslem world.

island *n* land surrounded by water.

isle *n* an island.

islet *n* a little isle.

isobar *n* a line on a map joining places with equal atmospheric pressure.

isolate *vt* to cut off; to set apart from others; to quarantine; to seperate a constituent subject from a compound.

isolation *n* detachment; loneliness.

isometric *adj* pertaining to equality of measure or dimension.

isosceles *adj* having two sides equal.

isotherm *n* a line on a map joining places with equal temperature.

isotope *n* any of two or more forms of an element having the same atomic number but different atomic weights.

issue *n* an outgoing; an outlet; a result; offspring; a point under dispute; a sending or giving out; all that is put forth at one time (an issue of bonds, a priodical etc.)* *vi* to go or flow out; to result (from) or end (in); to be published. * *vt* to let out; to discharge; to give or deal out, as supplies; to publish.

isthmus *n* a narrow neck of land; connecting two larger bodies of land.

it *pron* 3rd. per. neuter.

italic *adj* the name of a printing type in

which the letters slant upwards to the right *pl* ; italic type (*italic*).

italicize *vt* to print in italics.

itch *n* an irritating sensation on the surface of the skin causing a need to scratch; an insistent desire;* *vt* to have or feel an irritating sensation in the skin; to feel a restless desire.

item *n* an article; a unit; a seperate thing; a bit of news or information; (*inf*) a couple having an affair.

itemize *vt* to specify the terms of; to set down by items.

iterate *vt* to repeat.

iteration *n* repetition.

itinerant *adj* travelling from place to place; *n* a traveller.

itinerary *n* a travel route; a record or detailed plan of a journey.

its *pron* 3rd per. possessive of it.

itself *n* the neuter reflexive pronoun.

ivory *n* a hard bony substance forming tusks of elephants, etc; a creamy white colour; * *adj* of or like ivory; creamy white.

ivy *n* a climbing or creeping plant with a woody stem and evergreen leaves.

J

jab *vt, vi* (*pt*) to poke or thrust roughly; to punch with short, straight blows.

jabber *vi* to gabble; to speak or say rapidly, incoherently, or foolishly.

jack *n* any of various mechanical or hydraulic devices used to lift something heavy; * *vt* to raise by means of a jack.

jacket *n* a short outer garment; an outer covering.

jackknife *n* a pocket-knife. * *vi* (articulated lorry) to lose control so that the cab and trailer swing against each other.

jackpot *n* the accumulated stakes in certain games, as poker.

jade *n* a hard, semiprecious stone; it's light green colour.

jaded *adj* tired, exhausted; satiated.

jag *vt* to notch; to prick. * *n* a point.

jagged *adj* ragged; notched.

jail *n* a prison; a gaol.

jam *n* a preserve made of boiled fruit and sugar; * *vt* to press into a confined space; to crowd full of people or things; to cause interference to a radio signal rendering it unintelligable.

jangle *vi* to make a harsh or discordant sound, as bells. * *vt* to cause to jangle.

janitor *n* a caretaker.

January *n* the first month of the year.

jar *vi* to clash; to grate. * *n* a harsh sound; a vase or jug; a jolt.

jargon *n* the specialised or technical vocabulary of a science, profession, etc; obscure and usu pretentious language.

jaundice *n* a disease marked by yellowness of the eyes and skin.

jaundiced *adj* disillusioned.

jaunt *vi* to go from place to place.

jauntily *adv* briskly; sprightly.

jaunty *adj* sprightly.

javelin *n* a spear for throwing.

jaw *n* one of the bones which hold the teeth.

jaywalk *vi* to walk across a street carelessly without obeying traffic rules.

jazz *n* a general term for American popular music, characterized by syncopated rhythms.

jealous *adj* suspicious of a rival; envious.

jealousy *n* suspicion; envy.

jeans *npl* trousers made from denim.

jeep *n* a small robust vehicle with heavy duty tyres and four-wheel drive.

jeer *vi* to laugh derisively; to mock.

jelly *n* the juice of fruit boiled with sugar to a glutinous state.

jemmy *n* a burglar's crowbar.

jeopardize *vt* to hazard.

jeopardy *n* hazard; risk.

jerk *vt, vi* to give a sudden pull, thrust, or push to. * *n* a sudden thrust; a quick pull.

jerky *adj* moving by jerks.

jersey *n* a knitted woollen garment; a sweater.

jest *n* a joke; pleasantry. * *vi* to joke.

jet *n* a spouting forth; a nozzle for emission of fluid or gas; a hard black mineral that when polished is used for jewellery.

jet-black *adj* of the deepest black.

jetsam, jetson *n* cargo thrown overboard

to lighten a ship; this cargo when washed ashore.

jettison v. to throw goods overboard.

jetty n a small pier.

jewel n a precious stone; highly prized.

jeweller n a dealer in jewels.

jewellery n jewels in general, e.g. rings, necklaces, brooches etc.

jib n the triangular foremost sail of a ship; the arm of a crane.

jib vt, vi to shift a sail; to turn aside.

jibe vt to taunt; to scoff at; gibe. * n a taunt; a sneer.

jig n a lively dance or tune. * vi to dance.

jigsaw n a picture on wood or board cut into irregular shapes for re-assembling for amusement.

jilt vt to discard a lover.

jingle vi, vt to clink, or tinkle. * n a tinkling sound, as of bells; a catchy verse.

jingoism n belligerent patriotism.

jinx n someone or something thought to bring bad luck.

jitter vi to feel nervous. *npl a nervous feeling of panic.

job n a piece of work done for pay; a task; a duty; the thing or material being worked on; work; employment.

jobber n a carriage hirer; a stockjobber.

jockey n a professional racehorse rider. * vt to manoeuvre for a better position.

jocular adj joking; full of jokes.

jocularity n merriment.

jog vt to give a slight shake or nudge to; to rouse, as the memory. * vi to run at a slow pace for exercise. * n a slight shake or push; a nudge; a slow walk or trot.

join vt, vi to bring and come together (with); to connect; to unite; to unite; to become a part or member of (a club, etc.); to participate in; * n a joining; a place of joining.

joiner n a worker in wood.

joint n a place where, or way in which, two things are joined; the part where two bones move on one another in an animal. * adj common to two or more; sharing with another. * vt to connect by a joint or joints; to divide (an animal carcass) into parts for cooking.

jointly adv together; in common.

joist n a beam supporting floorboards.

joke n something said or done to cause laughter; a thing said or done merely in fun.

jolly adj merry; jovial; full of fun.

jolt vi, vt to shake with sudden jerks; to surprise or shock suddenly.

jostle vti to knock against; to hustle; to elbow for position.

jot n an iota. * vt to note down briefly.

jotter n a notebook.

jotting n a memorandum.

journal n a daily record of happenings, as a diary; a newspaper or periodical.

journalism n the work of gathering news for, or producing a newspaper, magazine or broadcast.

journalist n a newspaper contributor.

journey n a travelling; the distance travelled; a tour * vi to travel.

jovial adj gay; merry; jolly.

jowl n the jaw. *cheek by jowl*, side by side.

joy n delight; gladness.

joyful adj filled with, expressing, or causing joy.

joyous adj full of joy.

jubilant adj rejoicing greatly; triumphant.

jubilation n the joy of triumph.

jubilee n a 25th or 50th anniversary of an event.

Judaism n the religion of the Jews; Jewish modes of thought.

judge n a public official with authority to hear and decide cases in a court of law. * vt, vi to hear and pass judgement on the relative worth of anything.

judgment n act of judging; a legal decision; an opinion; good sense; discernment; censure.

judicial adj pertaining to judges or courts of justice; impartial.

judiciary adj relating to courts of justice * n judges collectively.

judicious adj possessing prudence; characterized by sound judgement.

jug n a vessel for holding and pouring liquids; a pitcher.

juggernaut n a terrible, irresistable force; a large heavy truck.

juggle vi to conjure; to manipulate.

juggler n a conjuror.

K

jugular *adj* pertaining to the throat.

juice *n* fluid of fruits, vegetables and meat.

July *n* the seventh month of the year.

jumble *vt,vi* to mix in a confused mass * *n* a muddle; articles for a jumble sale.

jumbo *n* something very large of its kind.

jump *vi* to spring or leap from the ground, a height, etc; to jerk; a sudden transition; an obstacle; a nervous start.

jumper *n* a knitted pullover.

junction *n* a point of union; a railway centre.

juncture *n* where lines meet; link or cross each other.

June *n* the sixth month of the year.

jungle *n* an area overgrown with dense tropical trees and other vegetation, etc.

junior *adj* younger in age; of more recent or lower status; of juniors.

junk *n* discarded rubbish or useless articles; any narcotic drug; Chinese floating vessel.

jurisdiction *n* judicial authority, its range or extent.

jurisprudence *n* the science or philosophy of law; a division of the law.

jurist *n* one versed in law.

juror *n* one who serves on a jury.

jury *n* a number of men and women sworn to hear evidence and deliver a verdict on a case; a panel.

just *adj* fair, impartial; deserved, merited; proper, exact; conforming strictly with the facts. *adv* exactly; nearly; only.

justice *n* justness, fairness; the use of authority to maintain what is just; the administration of law; a judge.

justiciary, justiciar *n* an administrator of justice.

justifiable *adj* that may be justified.

justification *n* a defence; vindication; remission of sin.

justify *vt* to prove right; to vindicate.

justly *adv* rightly; properly.

jut *vi* to project.

juvenile *adj* young; youthful; immature.

juxtaposition *n* a placing near or side by side.

kail, kale *n* a kind of cabbage.

kaleidoscope *n* a small tube containing bits of coloured glass reflected by mirrors to form symmetrical patterns as the tube is rotated.

keel *n* the backbone of a ship. * *vt, vi* to (cause to) turn over.

keen *adj* shrewd; sharp; eager; low (of prices) as to be competative.

keep *vt* to hold; to preserve; to guard; to detain; to continue any state, course, or action; to obey; to perform * *vi* to endure; not to perish or be impaired * *n* care; guard; a strong tower.

keeper *n* one who guards.

keeping *n* care, charge; observance.

keepsake *n* a gift treasured because of the giver.

keg *n* a small cask or barrel.

kennel *n* a small shelter for dogs; (*pl*) a place where dogs are bred or kept.

kerb *n* stone edging to pavement.

kernel *n* the core (esp. of nut).

kerosene *n* a fuel oil distilled from petrol.

kettle *n* a metal vessel with spout for boiling water.

kettledrum *n* a drum made of a hollow metal body with a parchment head.

key *n* a device for locking and unlocking something; a thing that explains or solves, as the legend of a map, a code etc.

keyboard *n* a set of levers on which the fingers press on a piano, computer, etc.

keynote *n* the basic note of a musical scale; the basic idea or ruling principle.

keystone *n* the top stone of an arch, keeping whole together.

khaki *adj* dull yellowish-brown.

kick *vt, vi* to strike with the foot; to recoil * *n* a blow with the foot or feet; recoil; a thrill; an intoxicating effect.

kidnap *vt* to carry off a person by force and hold to ransom.

kidney *n* one of two glands that secrete urine an animal's kidney as food.

kill *vt* to cause the death of; to destroy. * *n* the act of killing; an animal or animals killed.

kiln n a stone furnace for baking or hardening lime, bricks, pottery etc.

kilogram, kilogramme n a measure of weight (2.204 lbs).

kilometre n a measure of length, 1000 metres or 0.62 mile.

kin n family; kindred; relatives.

kind n race; genus; variety; nature * adj humane; friendly; sympathetic.

kindle vt, vi to set on fire; to light; to arouse.

kindly adj friendly; genial; kind; gracious.

kindness n goodness; helpfulness; benevolence.

kindred n kinship; blood relations * adj related; akin; similar.

kinetic adj causing motion; of motion in relation to force.

kinetics n the science of motion in relation to force.

king n the man who rules a country and its people; a man with the title of ruler, but with limited power to rule.

kingdom n a state; a realm, a country headed by a king; any of the three divisions of the natural world: animal, vegetable, mineral.

kink n a tight twist or curl in a piece of string, rope, hair etc; a painful cramp in the neck, back, etc; an eccentricity of personality. * vt, vi to form or cause to form a kink or kinks.

kiosk n a light open structure for sale of papers, sweets, etc; a public telephone booth.

kipper n a herring split open, salted, and dried.

kirk n a church.

kiss vt, vi to touch with the lips as an expression of love, affection or in greeting. * n an act of kissing; a light, gentle touch.

kit n an outfit; equipment e.g. tools etc.; a set of parts for assembly.

kitchen n a place where food is prepared.

kite n a light paper-covered frame for flying in air.

kith n relatives and friends.

kleptomania n an irresistible impulse to steal.

knack n dexterity; a trick; a habit.

knapsack n a backpack.

knead vt to work dough; to squeeze and press with the hands.

knee n the joint between the thigh and the lower part of the human leg; anything shaped like a bent knee. * vt (pt **kneed**) to hit or touch with the knee.

kneel vi to go down and remain on the knees.

knell n the sound of a bell (esp. funeral bell). * vi to toll.

knickers npl an undergarment covering the lower body and having separate leg holes, worn by women and girls.

knife n a cutting instrument. * vt to cut or stab with a knife.

knight n a rank conferring title Sir; a chessman shaped like a horse's head.

knighthood n the rank or dignity of a knight.

knit vb (pt **knitted** or **knit**) vt, vi to form (fabric or a garment) by interlooping yarn using knitting needles or a machine.

knitting n the thing being knitted.

knob n a rounded lump or protuberance; a boss or stud or handle (of a door).

knock vt, vi to strike; to strike against; to rap on a door; to criticize. * n a blow; a rap.

knocker n the device hinged against a door for knocking.

knockout n a punch or blow that produces unconsciousness.

knoll n a little round hill.

knot n a lump in a thread, etc formed by a tightened loop or tangling; a fastening made by tying lengths of rope, etc. * vt, vi (pt **knotted**) to make or form a knot (in); to entangle or become entangled.

know vt to be aware that; to be sure that; to understand; to be acquainted with. * vi to have knowledge.

knowing adj well informed; shrewd; implying a secret understanding.

knowledge n acquaintance with; learning; information.

knuckle n the joint of a finger.

Koran n the sacred book of Muslims.

kudos n glory; fame; renown.

L

label *n* a slip of paper, cloth, metal etc attached to anything to provide information about its nature, contents.

laboratory *n* a building where scientific work and research is carried out.

laborious *adj* arduous; laboured; hard-working.

labour *n* exertion; toil; workers collectively; the process of childbirth * *vi* to work; to be burdened; to give unnecessary details.

labourer *n* a worker; esp doing heavy or manual work.

labyrinth *n* a place full of winding paths; a maze.

lac *n* a resin yielding shellac.

lace *n* a cord, etc used to draw together and fasten parts of a shoe, a corset etc.

lacerate *vt* to tear to torture.

lack *vt* to want; to need. * *vi* to be in want. * *n* want; failure deficiency.

lackadaisical *adj* languid; showing lack of energy or interest.

lackey *n* footman; flunkey.

laconic *adj* concise; brief; using few words.

lacquer *n* n varnish; lacquered ware * *vt* to varnish; to gloss.

lactic *adj* related to or procured from milk.

lad *n* a boy; a young man.

ladder *n* a portable metal or wooden framework for climbing up and down.

laden *adj* loaded; burdened.

lading *n* cargo; freight.

ladle *n* a large long-handled spoon.

lady *n* a woman of rank; a title.

lag * *vi* to loiter; to fall behind; to insulate pipes with insulating material.

lager *n* a light beer.

laggard *adj* slow * *n* a dawdler.

lagging *n* insulating material.

lagoon *n* a shallow saltwater lake cut off from the sea by a coral reef.

laisser faire *n* non-interference; freedom of action (esp. in commerce, etc).

laity *n* lay people, as distinguished from the clergy.

lake *n* water wholly surrounded by land; a purplish-red pigment.

lame *adj* crippled; limping.

lament *vi* to weep; to grieve * *vt* to bewail * *n* a mournful song or tune.

lamentable *adj* distressing; deplorable.

lamentation *n* mourning; sorrow.

lamp *n* any device producing light, either by electricity, gas or by burning oil etc.

lance *n* a long spear * *vt* to cut or pierce with a lancet.

land *n* the solid part of the earth's surface; ground, soil; a country and its people; property in land. * *vt,vi* to go ashore from a ship; to come to port; to arrive at a specified place; to come to rest.

landing *n* act or place of disembarking; a platform or flat area at the top of a flight of stairs; the floor between flights of stairs.

landlady *n* the mistress of an inn or boarding house; a woman who rents property.

landlocked *adj* enclosed by land.

landlord *n* owner of land or houses; owner or host of an inn, etc.

landlubber *n* one with little experience of the sea and sailing.

landmark *n* a prominent feature that serves as a guide or distinguishes a locality; an important event or turning point.

landowner *n* a person who owns land.

landscape *n* an expanse of natural scenery seen in one view; a picture of natural, inland scenery. * *vt* to make (a plot of ground) more attractive.

landslip, landslide *n* the sliding of a mass of soil or rocks down a slope; an overwhelming victory esp in an election.

lane *n* a narrow road, path etc; a path or strip specifically designated for ships, aircraft, cars etc.

language *n* human speech; speech peculiar to a nation.

languid *adj* faint; listless; weak.

languish *vi* to be or become faint; to droop; to pine.

languishing *pa* pining, spiritless.

languor *n* faintness; listlessness.

lank *adj* tall and thin; long an limp.

lanky *adj* (**lankier, lankiest**) lean, tall and ungainly.

lanoline n a soothing ointment.

lantern n a portable transparent case for holding a light.

lap n the seat formed by knees and thighs in sitting posture; one round of a course in a race.

lapel n the folded back part of coat etc. continuous with the cotton.

lapse n a small error; a decline or drop to a lower condition, degree, or state; a moral decline.

larceny n theft of goods.

lard n melted and clarified pig fat. * vt to embellish.

larder n a store cupboard for provisions.

large adj great in size, number; big, bulky.

largely adv widely; copiously; mainly.

largess n a present; bounty.

largo n adv slow (in music).

lark n a frolic; a prank.

larva n (pl **larvae**) an insect in grub state.

larynx n the upper part of the windpipe containing the vocal cords.

lascivious adj lewd; lecherous.

lash n the thong of a whip; a stroke with a whip * vt to whip; to bind.

lassitude n faintness; weariness.

last adj coming after all the others; latest; final. * adv the last time. * vi to endure; to continue. * n a shaped block on which shoes are made; a foot mould.

lasting adj durable; permanent.

latch n the catch of a door, gate etc. * vt, vi to fasten with a latch.

late adj behind time; long delayed; deceased * adv at a late time; recently.

latent adj not yet apparent; dormant.

lateral adj of, at, from, towards; on the side.

lath n a long narrow slip of wood to support plaster, etc.

lathe n a machine for shaping wood or iron.

lather n froth of soap and water; frothy.

Latin adj of ancient Rome, its people, their language etc.

latitude n breadth; width; scope; freedom from restriction on action or opinions; distance north or south of the equator.

latter adj later; coming after; modern; being the last mentioned of two.

lattice n a network of crossed laths; a trellis; a window so formed.

laudable adj praiseworthy.

laudatory adj expressing praise.

laugh vi to make the sound expressive of mirth; to be gay, mirthful * n the sound or act of laughing.

laughable adj amusing; comical.

laughing stock n an object of ridicule.

laughter n the act or sound of laughing.

launch vt to throw; to propel and slide (into water). * vi to initiate; to put into action. * n the act of launching; a large open motorboat.

launder vt, vi to wash and iron clothes.

launderette n an establishment equipped with coin-operated washing machines.

laundry n place where clothes are washed and ironed.

laureate adj decked with laurel leaves as a mark of honour. * a poet laureate, the official court poet.

lava n molten volcanic rocks.

lavatory n a place for washing hands, urinating etc.

lavish adj profuse; generous; abundant; extravagant * vt to give or spend generously.

law n all the rules of conduct in an organized community as upheld by authority.

law-abiding adj obeying the law.

lawbreaker n a person who violates the law.

lawful adj legal; rightful.

lawgiver n a legislator.

lawless adj not regulated by law; not in conformity with law, illegal.

lawn n a smooth level grass plot; a fine linen.

lawsuit n a suit between private parties in a law court.

lawyer n a person whose profession is advising others in matters of law or representing them in a court of law.

lax adj loose; slack; vague; not strict.

laxative adj purging * n a gentle purgative.

laxity n slackness; carelessness.

lay vt to cause to lie; to place; to impose; to allay, to bring forth eggs; to wager. * n a song; a poem. * adj not clerical, or expert.

layer *n* a stratum; a single thickness; a coat, as of paint. * *vt* to separate into layers.

layman *n* one not a clergyman; a non-specialist or professional.

layout *n* the manner in which anything is laid out.

laziness *n* indolence; sloth.

lazy *adj* slothful; indolent.

lea *n* a meadow.

lead *n* a soft and heavy metal; a stick of graphite.

lead *vt, vi* to guide or conduct; to direct; to precede; to entice; to influence; to be first * *n* guidance; the role of a leader; the amount or distance ahead; a clue; the leading role in a play etc.

leaden *adj* heavy; dull; like lead; gloomy.

leader *n* a guide; a captain; an editorial article; the first violin in an orchestra.

leading *adj* chief; principal.

leaf *n* one of the thin parts of a plant growing from the skin; a sheet of paper or metal; two pages of a book.

leaflet *n* a little leaf; a sheet of printed information or advertising matter.

league *n* a union for mutual help; an alliance; a treaty; an association of sports club that organizes matches between members.

leak *n* a hole which admits water or gas; confidential information made public deliberately or accidentally * *vi* to let water in or out; to disclose.

leakage *n* a leaking.

lean *vi* to slope; to incline; to rest against; to rely on.

lean *adj* thin; barren; meagre.

leaning *n* inclination, tendency.

leap *vi, vt* to jump; to bound * *n* a spring.

learn *vt, vi* to gain knowledge or skill; to find out; to realize.

learning *n* knowledge; scholarship.

lease *n* a letting for a term of years * *vt* to let or lease.

leasehold *adj* held by lease * *n* tenure by lease.

leaseholder *n* a tenant under a lease.

leash *n* a thong or strap for leading animals. * *vt* to hold or restrain on a leash.

least *adj* smallest. * *adv* in the smallest degree. * *n* the smallest amount.

leather *n* tanned and dressed hide.

leave *n* permission; farewell; the period allowed for absence. * *vt* to let remain; to bequeath; to quit; to deposit.

lecherous *adj* lustful; lewd.

lectern *n* a reading desk in a church.

lecture *n* a discourse; a reprimand * *vi* to deliver a lecture * *vt* to reprove.

ledge *n* a narrow shelf; a ridge; a layer.

ledger *n* an account book.

leech *n* a bloodsucking worm; a person who clings to or uses another.

leer *n* a sly or lewd glance. * *vi* to give a leer.

lees *npl* dregs; sediment.

leeward *adj* pertaining to the lee. * *adv* towards the lee.

leeway *n* the drift of a ship to leeward * to make up leeway, to make up lost time.

left *adj* denoting opposite to the right; towards the west when facing north. * *n* the left side; the left hand; the left wing in politics.

left-wing *adj* of or relating to the liberal faction of a political party.

leg *n* one of the limbs on which humans and animals support themselves and walk; any of a series of games or matches in a competition.

legacy *n* money, property etc. left to someone in a will.

legal *adj* of or based on law; permitted by law; of or for lawyers. * *vt* to make lawful.

legality *n* conformity to law.

legalize *vt* to make lawful; to sanction.

legatee *n* one to whom a legacy is left.

legend *n* a story handed down from the past; a notable person or the stories of his or her exploits.

legendary *adj* fabulous; mythical.

leggings *npl* protective outer covering for the lower leg; a leg-hugging fashion garment for women.

legible *adj* able to be read.

legion *n* a great number.

legislate *vi* to make or pass laws.

legislative *adj* capable of enacting laws.

legislator *n* one who makes laws.

legislature *n* the lawmaking body in a state.

legitimate *adj* legal; born in wedlock; genuine; valid.

leguminous *adj* pertaining to pod-bearing plants, e.g. peas, pulse, beans, etc.

leisure *n* spare time; freedom from business; relaxation.

leisurely *adj* not hasty; relaxed. * *adv* slowly.

lend *vt* to grant use of a thing temporarily; to provide money at interest.

length *n* extent from end to end; duration; extension; a long expanse; a piece of specified length cut from a longer piece.

lengthen *vt* to make long; to extend.

lengthwise *adv* in the direction of the length.

lenience, leniency *n* quality of being lenient; mildness.

lenient *adj* merciful; forbearing; not harsh.

lens *n* (*pl* **lenses**) a curved piece of transparent glass, plastic etc used in optical instruments to form an image; a similar transparent part of the eye that focuses light rays on the retina.

Leo *n* the Lion, fifth sign of zodiac.

leotard *n* a skintight one-piece garment worn by dancers and others engaged in strenuous exercise.

leper *n* one affected with leprosy.

leprosy *n* disease of the skin.

lesbian *n* a female homosexual. * *adj* of or characteristic of lesbians.

lesion *n* an injury; a wound.

less *adj* smaller. * *adv* in a lower degree; to a smaller extent. * *n* a smaller quantity.

lessee *n* the holder of a lease.

lessen *vt, vi* to make or become less.

lesser *adj* less; smaller.

lesson *n* something to be learned or studied; an example.

lest *conj* for fear that.

let *vt* to permit; to allow; to lease; to rent.

let-down *n* a disappointment.

lethal *adj* deadly; fatal.

lethargic *adj* drowsy; dull.

lethargy *n* a drowsy state.

letter *n* a symbol representing a phonetic value in a written language; a character of the alphabet; a written or printed message.

letter box *n* a slit in the doorway of a house or building through which letters are delivered; a postbox.

lettering *n* the act or process of inscribing with letters; letters collectively; a title; an inscription.

lettuce *n* a leafy plant used in salads.

leukaemia, leukemia *n* a chronic disease characterized by an abnormal increase in the number of white blood cells.

level *n* an instrument for determining the horizontal; a horizontal line or surface; an even surface. * *adj* horizontal; even; flat * *vt, vi* to make level; to flatten.

level-headed *adj* having an even temper and sound judgment.

lever *n* a bar for raising weights; a means to an end; a device used to operate machinery.

leverage *n* power gained by use of a lever; power; influence.

levity *n* lightness; frivolity; lack of seriousness.

levy *vt* to collect (taxes) by the force or authority. * *n* the amount levied.

lewd *adj* lustful; sensual; obscene.

lexicographer *n* a dictionary compiler.

lexicon *n* a dictionary.

liability *n* an obligation; debt; a handicap; a disadvantage. *pl* debts; obligations.

liable *adj* responsible; subject to; likely to do.

liaison *n* intercommunication as between units of a military force; an illicit love affair.

liar *n* one who tells lies.

libel *n* a defamatory or damaging writing.

libellous *adj* slanderous; defamatory.

liberal *adj* generous; ample; profuse; not too strict; free; of education, contributing to a general broadening of the mind.

liberality *n* generosity; breadth of view.

liberate *vt* to free; to deliver.

liberator *n* one who liberates.

libertine *n* a profligate; a rake * *adj* licentious.

libertinism *n* depravity.

liberty *n* state of being free esp from slavery; captivity etc.; privilege; license;

undue familiarity; impertinence.

libidinous *adj* lustful.

Libra *n* the Balance, the seventh sign in zodiac.

librarian *n* the keeper of a library.

library *n* a collection of books or the place in which they are kept.

lice *npl of* **louse**.

licence *n* authority given to do something specified; a certificate or document giving permission; excess of liberty *

license *vt* to grant a licence to.

licensee *n* one to whom a licence is granted.

licentious *adj* profligate; morally unrestrained.

lichen *n* a kind of moss, alga or fungus.

licit *adj* lawful; legal.

lick *vt* to pass tongue over; to lap; to flicker round of flames; to thrash; to defeat.

lid *n* a removable cover of a box, vessel, etc., an eyelid.

lie *vi* to speak untruthfully. * *n* an untrue statement.

lie *vi* to stretch out or rest in a horizontal position; to be in a specified condition; to be situated; to exist. * *n* relative position of objects.

lieu *n* place; stead.

lieutenant *n* a deputy; a chief assistant; an army officer ranking below a captain.

life *n* the state of living or being alive; existence; spirit; vigour; vivacity.

lifeboat *n* a small rescue boat carried by a ship; a specially designed and equipped rescue vessel that helps those in distress along the coastline.

life buoy *n* a buoyant object for keeping persons afloat.

lifeguard *n* an expert swimmer employed to prevent drownings.

lifeless *adj* dead; dull; heavy.

lifelike *adj* true to life in appearance.

lifelong *adj* lasting through life.

lift *vt, vi* to raise up; to hoist; to cheer; to steal; to disperse (of fog); to rise * *n* a hoist; an elevation of mood; a ride in a vehicle.

liftoff *n* the vertical thrust of a space-craft etc, at launching; the time of this.

ligament *n* band of tough tissue joining bones at joints.

ligature *n* a tie for blood vessels in operations.

light *n* the agent by which objects are made visible to the eye; day; that which gives or admits light; illumination of mind. * *adj* bright; clear; not heavy; active; slight. * *vt* to give light to; to enlighten; to ignite. * *vi* to brighten; to alight.

lighten *vi* to shine; to flash * *vt* to illuminate; to make less heavy; to alleviate; to cheer.

lighter *n* a flat-bottomed boat for loading and unloading ships; a small device producing a flame to light cigarettes.

light-footed *adj* nimble; active.

light-headed *adj* giddy.

light-hearted *adj* merry; carefree.

lighthouse *n* a tower with a light to guide ships.

lightly *adv* easily; nimbly.

lightning *n* the vivid flash of electricity that precedes thunder.

lightweight *adj* of less than average weight; trivial, unimportant.

light year *n* the distance light travels in one year.

lignite *n* fossil wood.

like *adj* equal; similar; resembling * *adv, prep* similarly * *vt, vi* to be fond of; to be pleased; to approve. * *n* a like; a counterpart.

likelihood *n* probability.

likely *adj* probable; suitable.

liken *vt* to compare.

likewise *adv* in like manner; also.

liking *n* inclination; fondness; affection.

limb *n* the arm or leg; a large branch of a tree.

limber *adj* flexible * *n* the detachable front of a gun carriage.

limbo *n* a kind of purgatory; an intermediate stage between extremes.

lime *n* a substance got by heating limestone, and with sand and water forming cement.

limelight *n* intense publicity.

limerick *n* a humorous doggerel verse of five lines.

limestone *n* a rock composed mainly of

calcium carbonate of lime.

limit n boundary; utmost extent; restraint.
* vt to bound; to restrict.

limited adj narrow; restricted; lacking imagination.

limp vi to walk lamely * n a lameness in walking. * adj not firm; flabby; lethargic.

limpid adj clear; crystal.

linchpin n a pin fastening a wheel to the axle; a person or thing vital to the success of an enterprise.

line n a length of cord, rope, or wire; a cord for measuring, making level; a system of conducting fluid, electricity etc; edge, limit, boundary; border, outline, contour, a row of persons or things, as printed letters across a page.

lineage n race; descent.

lineal adj straight; direct; hereditary.

lineament n a facial feature; form.

linear adj of, made of, or using a line or lines; narrow and long.

linen n cloth made of flax; household articles made of linen, e.g. sheets.

liner n a large passenger ship or aircraft.

linesman n an assistant referee.

linger vi to delay; to loiter; to remain in the mind.

linguist n one skilled in languages.

linguistics adj the science of language.

lining n an inner covering of a garment etc..

link n a single loop or ring of a chain; a person or thing acting as a connection, as in a communication system. * vt, vi to connect or become connected.

links npl flat sandy ground; a golf course, esp by the seaside.

linoleum n a floor covering of coarse fabric backing with a smooth, hard decorative coating.

linseed n flaxseed.

lint n linen specially prepared as a dressing for wounds; fluff.

lintel n the upper bar of a doorway or a window.

lion n a beast of prey; king of the beasts; sign in zodiac (Leo); a celebrity.

lion-hearted adj courageous.

lip n either of the front edges of the mouth;

the edge or rim of a jug etc; insolent talk.

lipstick n a small stick of cosmetic for colouring the lips; the cosmetic itself.

liquefy vt to melt; to dissolve.

liqueur n a sweet, many-flavoured alcoholic drink..

liquid adj fluid; smooth. * n any fluid. adj in liquid form; clear; limpid; readily convertible into cash (of assets).

liquidate vt to settle the accounts of; to wind up a bankrupt business; to convert into cash; to kill; to eliminate.

liquidation n the winding up of a bankrupt estate.

liquor n a drink (esp alcoholic).

liquorice n a black extract from the root of a plant, used in medicine and confectionery; a liquorice flavoured sweet.

lisp vi to pronounce imperfectly (esp. 's'). * n lisping speech.

lissom, lissome adj supple.

list n a series of names, numbers written in order.

listen vi to try to hear; to give heed.

listener n a person who listens.

listless adj languid; weary; unenthusiastic.

litany n a series of petitions in a prayer book; any tedious recital.

literacy n the ability to read and write.

literal adj exact; word for word.

literary adj versed in letters and literature.

literate adj able to read and write; educated.

literature n the writings of a period or country.

lithe adj pliant; flexible.

lithesome adj supple; nimble.

lithograph vt to imprint on stone and transfer to paper.

litigant n one engaged in a lawsuit.

litigate vt, vi to go to law; to contest points of law.

litigious adj contentious.

litre n a unit of capacity in metric system, 1.76 pints.

litter n a portable bed; scattered rubbish; young produced at one birth. * vt, vi to strew carelessly; to make tidy.

little adj small; short * adv in a small degree; less; slightly; not in the least. * *n* small in amount, degree etc.

liturgy *n* a ritual for public worship.

live *vi* to exist; to dwell; to conduct one's self in life; to subsist; to gain a livelihood. * *vt* to lead; to spend; to pass.

live *adj* alive; having life; not exploded; carrying electric current.

livelihood *n* means of living.

lively *adj* vivacious; spirited.

liver *n* the organ which secretes bile; animal liver as food.

livestock *n* (farm) animals raised for use or sale.

livid *adj* of a leaden colour; very angry.

living *n* livelihood; benefice of a clergyman; a way of living.

living room *n* a room in a house used for general entertainment and relaxation.

load *vt* to charge with a load; to burden; to oppress; to put film in a camera; to install a program in a computer memory; to charge, as a gun. * *n* a burden; cargo; a large amount.

loading *n* a cargo; a burden.

loaf *n* a shaped mass of bread. * *vi* to idle about.

loam *n* a rich clayey soil.

loan *n* lending; something lent, esp money. * *vt*, *vi* to lend.

loath, loth *adj* reluctant.

loathe *vt*, *vi* to hate; abhor.

loathsome *adj* disgusting.

lob *n* a slow, high-pitched ball (cricket, etc). * *vt* to bowl slowly.

lobby *n* an entrance hall; a person or group who try to influence (legislators) to support a cause etc.

lobe *n* the lower part of the ear; a division of the brain, lungs, etc.

local *adj* pertaining to or serving the interests of a particular place; of or for a particular part of the body. * *n* an inhabitant of a specific place; a local pub.

locale *n* a locality.

locality *n* a place; a neighbourhood.

locate *vt* to place the position of something.

loch *n* a Scottish lake.

lock *n* a fastening device operated by a key; the part of a canal dock in which

the level of the water can be changed by the operation of gates.

locker *n* a small cupboard, chest etc.

locket *n* a small gold case worn round the neck.

locksmith *n* a maker of locks.

locomotive *n* a railway engine.

locum (tenens) *n* a temporary deputy.

locust *n* a type of destructive grasshopper; a hardwood leguminous tree.

lode *n* a vein of mineral ore.

lodge *n* a small house at the entrance to a park or stately home. * *vt*, *vi* to live in a place for a time; to live as a paying guest.

lodger *n* a person who lives in a rented room in another's home.

lodging *n* a temporary abode; rented accommodation.

loft *n* the space or room under the rafters; a gallery. * *vt* to lift into the air.

lofty *adj* high; haughty; stately.

log *n* a section cut from a felled tree; a device for measuring the speed of ships; a written record, esp one kept on a ship's voyage or aircraft's flight.

logarithms *n* a mathematical system for facilitating calculations.

logbook *n* an official record of a ship's or aircraft's voyage or flight; an official document containing details of a vehicle's registration.

logic *n* the science of reasoning.

logical *adj* conforming to the rules of logic; capable of reasoning; consistent.

logistics *n* the planning and organization of any complex activity.

loin *n* the lower part of the back.

loiter *vi* to hang about; to linger.

loll *vi* to lean idly; to hang out (tongue).

lone *adj* solitary; single; isolated.

lonesome *adj* solitary.

long *adj* not short; protracted; late; tedious; slow; far-reaching; well supplied. * *vt* to desire earnestly. * *adv* for a long time; from start to finish.

long-distance *adj* travelling or communicating over long distances.

longevity *n* great length of life.

longhand *n* ordinary handwriting, as opposed to shorthand.

longing *n* an intense desire.

longitude n length; distance east or west of fixed meridian.

longitudinal adj running lengthwise.

long-suffering adj patient.

long-term adj of or extending over a long time.

long-winded adj tedious.

look vi to direct the eye so as to see; to gaze; to consider; to expect; to heed; to appear. * n gaze; a glance; aspect; appearance.

lookout n a watching for; a watching post; a watcher.

loom n a weaving machine. * vi to come into view indistinctly, large or threateningly.

loop n a figure made by a curved line crossing itself; an intra-uterine contraceptive device.

loophole n a narrow slit for outlook, etc; a way of escape or evading obligation etc.

loose adj untied; free; vague; careless; not firm, tight or compact. * vt to untie; to set free; to discharge a bullet.

loosen vt to make loose. * vi to become loose.

loot n booty; plunder; money.

lop vt to cut off.

lopsided adj leaning to one side.

loquacious adj talkative.

lord n a master; a ruler; a nobleman.

lordly adj proud; haughty.

lore n learning, esp of a traditional kind, e.g. folklore.

lose vb (pt **lost**) vt, vi to have taken from one by death, accident, removal, etc; to be unable to find.

loss n a losing or being lost; the damage, trouble caused by losing; the person, thing, or amount lost.

lot n a part or share; fate which falls to one; a considerable quantity; the thing drawn at random to decide something.

loth adj see **loath.**

lotion n a healing or cleansing or cosmetic liquid.

lottery n a system of raising money by selling numbered tickets that offer the chance of winning a prize.

lotus n a legendary plant causing forget-fulness to the eater; a kind of lily.

loud adj easily audible; noisy; showy; obtrusive.

lounge vi to loiter; to loll; to spend time idly. * n a comfortable room.

louse n (pl **lice**) a parasitic insect.

lousy adj infested with lice.

lout n an awkward, rude fellow.

love vt to regard with affection; to like; to delight in. * vi to be in love. * n warm affection; the passionate affection for another; a word of endearment.

lovely adj beautiful; charming.

lover n a person in love with another; a person having an extramarital sexual relationship.

loving adj fond; kind.

low adj situated below any given surface; not high; deep; mean.

lower vt to let down; to abase.

lower vi to frown; to threaten a storm.

lowering adj threatening a storm.

lowing n the bellowing of cattle.

lowland n comparatively low or level country.

lowly adj humble; meek.

loyal adj faithful; true.

loyalist n one who is true to his country.

loyalty n fidelity; constancy.

lubber n a clumsy fellow.

lubricant n a substance for oiling or greasing.

lubricate vt to smear with oil to lessen friction; to make smooth, slippery, greasy.

lucent adj shining; resplendent.

lucid adj easily understood; sane.

luck n chance; fortune; success.

lucky adj fortunate; auspicious.

lucrative adj paying; gainful.

ludicrous adj laughable; droll; absurd.

lug vt to haul. * n the ear.

luggage n a traveller's baggage.

lugubrious adj sad; doleful.

lukewarm adj moderately warm; indifferent.

lull vt to calm; to send to sleep; to allay (fears etc) usually by deception. * n a calm interval.

lullaby n a cradle song.

lumbago n rheumatism in the lower back.

lumbar *n* pertaining to the lower back.

lumber *n* useless articles; rubbish; felled timber.

luminary *n* an enlightening, influential or famous person.

luminous *adj* shining; clear.

lump *n* a small shapeless mass; an abnormal swelling; a stupid or boring person.

lunacy *n* mental derangement; utter folly.

lunar *adj* pertaining to the moon.

lunatic *adj* insane. * *n* a madman.

lunch, luncheon *n* a midday meal.

lung *n* either of the two organs of respiration.

lunge *n* a sword thrust; a plunge forward.

lurch *vi* to roll or sway to one side. * *n* a sudden roll.

lure *n* a bright fishing bait; something that tempts or entices. * *vt* to entice.

lurid *adj* vivid; glaring; sensational; ghastly pale; wan.

lurk *vi* to lie hidden in wait; to loiter furtively.

luscious *adj* very sweet; delicious.

lush *adj* luxuriant; juicy.

lust *n* longing desire; sensual appetite * *vi* to desire eagerly; to feel lust.

lustily *adv* stoutly; vigorously.

lustre *n* brightness; renown; a glossy surface.

lustrous *adj* bright; shining.

lusty *adj* vigorous; robust.

luxuriant *adj* profuse; abundant.

luxuriate *vi* to give oneself up to luxury.

luxurious *adj* given to luxury.

luxury *n* indulgence and pleasure in sumptuous things; *pl* something costly and enjoyable but not a necessity.

lymph *n* colourless fluid in the body contained in and collected from the tissues.

lynch *vt* to put to death by mob law.

lyre *n* an ancient stringed instrument re lated to the harp.

lyric, lyrical *adj* of the nature of song.

M

macaroni *n* pasta rolled into tubes.

macaroon *n* a cake or biscuit of ground almonds.

mace *n* a spiked club; an ensign of office; an aromatic spice made from the outside covering of the nutmeg.

machine *n* a structure of fixed and moving parts, for doing useful work; an organization functioning like a machine; the controlling group in a political party.

machine gun *n* an automatic gun.

machinery *n* machines in general; mechanism.

machinist *n* one who works a machine.

machismo *n* excessive masculine pride.

macrocosm *n* great world or the universe regarded as a whole.

mad *adj* insane; crazy; frantic; angry.

madam *n* a polite form of address a woman; a woman in charge of a brothel.

madcap *n*, *adj* (a) frolicsome girl, reckless, lively (person).

madden *vt* to make mad.

madman (madwoman) *n* an insane person.

madness *n* insanity; folly.

maelstrom *n* a whirlpool.

magazine *n* a storehouse; a munition depot; a periodical publication containing feature articles, fiction etc.; a supply chamber as in a camera, a rifle etc.

magenta *n* a bright purplish-crimson dye or colour.

maggot *n* a worm like grub.

magic *n* the use of charms, spells etc. to supposedly influence events by supernatural means; any mysterious power; the art of producing illusions by sleight of hand, etc.

magical *adj* marvellous.

magician *n* a conjurer.

magistrate *n* a public officer who administrates justice.

magnanimity *n* greatness of soul or mind; noble and generous conduct.

magnanimous *adj* noble and generous; unselfish.

magnate *n* a man of rank, wealth or influence.

magnesium *n* a white malleable metal.

magnet *n* a piece of iron or steel that has the property of attracting iron.

magnetic *adj* of magnetism or a magnet.

magnetism *n* the science which treats of

magnetic phenomena; personal charm.

magnificence n grandeur; pomp.

magnificent adj imposing; splendid; superb.

magnify vt to enlarge; to extol; to glorify; to exaggerate.

magnitude n greatness; importance.

mahogany n a hard reddish wood much used for furniture; a reddish-brown colour.

maid n a young girl; a female servant.

maiden n a young unmarried woman; a runless over in cricket.

mail n letters etc. conveyed and delivered by the post office; a postal system.

maim vt to mutilate; to disable.

main adj chief; leading. * n strength; the greater part; the ocean.

mainland n the land, other than islands.

mainstay n the chief support.

maintain vt, vi to keep up; to sustain.

maintenance n upkeep; the support (esp financial) given to a spouse after divorce.

maize n corn; a light yellow colour.

majestic adj august; stately.

majesty n grandeur; nobility; dignity.

major adj the greater in number, quantity, or extent; very serious; life-threatening; (music) higher than the corresponding minor by half a tone. * n an army officer; below lieutenant colonel.

majority n the greater number.

make vt, vi to create; to construct; to produce; to cause to be; to perform; to force; to act or do; to earn; to reach. * n style; brand or origin; manner of production.

make-believe n pretence; sham.

makeshift n a temporary substitute.

maladjustment n poor adaptation, esp to social environment.

maladministration n bad management.

malady n illness; disease.

malaise n a feeling of discomfort.

malaria n an infectious disease.

malcontent n a discontented person.

male n a man or boy; an animal or plant of that sex. * adj of the sex of a man.

malefactor n a criminal; a felon.

malevolent adj spiteful; malicious.

malformation n deformity.

malfunction n faulty functioning.

malice n spite; ill will.

malicious adj spiteful; intentionally destructive.

malign adj harmful; evil; malignant.

malignant adj malevolent; virulent.

malinger vi to feign illness.

mall n an avenue; an area of shops.

malleable adj capable of being beaten out by hammering; pliable.

mallet n a wooden hammer.

malnutrition n lack of nutrition.

malpractice n evil practice; misconduct.

malt n barley prepared by various processes for brewing and distilling.

maltreat vt to abuse.

mammal n an animal of the class Mammalia; a warm-blooded vertebrate that suckle their young.

mammoth n an extinct species of elephant. * adj gigantic.

man n a human being; a male adult; mankind; a male servant; a husband; an ordinary soldier; a member of a team.

manacle n a handcuff * vt to fetter.

manage vt to wield; to conduct or direct.

manageable adj able to be managed; tractable.

management n direction; the directors of a business, organization etc.

manager n a person who manages a company, organization etc.; an agent who looks after the business affairs of an actor, writer etc..

mandarin n any high-ranking official; (with cap) the Beijing dialect that is the official pronunciation of the Chinese language.

mandate n a command; written authority to act for another.

mandatory adj compulsory.

mandible n an animal's jaw.

mandolin n a stringed instrument.

mane n the long hair on the neck of the horse, lion etc.

manequin a woman who models fashion clothes.

manful adj bold; energetic.

mange n a skin disease of dogs, etc.

mangle vt to mutilate; to smooth; to press.

manhole n a hole giving entrance.

manhood n virility; manliness.

mania n great enthusiasm; a craze.

maniac n a madman; an enthusiast.

manicure n the fingernails and care of the hands.

manifest adj clearly visible; evident. * vt to display. * n a list of a ship's or aircraft's cargo.

manifestation n evidence; revelation.

manifestly adv evidently.

manifesto n a public declaration of policy issued by a government or a party.

manifold adj numerous and various.

manipulate vt to handle; to manage skilfully or craftily.

mankind n the human race.

manly adj brave; hardy.

man-made adj manufactured or created by man; artificial, synthetic.

manner n the mode in which anything is done; bearing or conduct; pl behaviour.

mannerism n a personal peculiarity.

manoeuvre n a tactical movement; a planned and controlled movement of troops, ships etc.; a stratagem.

manor n the land or house belonging to a lord.; a police district.

mansion n a large imposing house.

manslaughter n the killing of a person without malice.

mantel, mantelpiece n the ornamental work round a fireplace; the shelf above.

mantle n a loose sleeveless cloak.

manual adj done by the hand. * n a textbook; a book of instructions.

manufacture n the making of goods on large scale.

manure n dung or other substance for fertilizing soil. * vt to treat with manure.

manuscript n a paper written with the hand.

many adj numerous.

map n a plan of any part of the earth's surface. * vt to make a map; to plan.

mar vt to injure; impair; to spoil.

marauder n a robber; a rover.

marble n a valuable building and monumental stone; a small ball of stone, etc.

march vi to walk in step * vt to cause to march. * n a measured or military walk; a distance walked; a musical composi-

tion; a boundary; (cap) the third month of a year.

mare n the female of the horse.

margarine n a butter substitute made from vegetable and animal fats, etc.

margin n an edge; the blank border of a printed page; surplus; the difference between the cost and the selling price.

marginal adj written in the margin; situated at the margin or border; close to the lower limit of acceptability; very slight, insignificant.

marina n a harbour for pleasure craft.

marine adj pertaining to the sea; naval.

mariner n a seaman.

marionette n a puppet.

marital adj pertaining to marriage.

maritime adj relating to the sea or ships; bordering on or living near the sea.

mark n a visible sign or stamp; eminence; token; aim; a cross made instead of a signature; a symbol, e.g. a punctuation mark; a grade for academic work; impression; influence; the basic monetary unit of Germany.

marked adj pre-eminent; obvious.

market n a meeting of people for buying and selling merchandise; a space or building in which a market is held; the chance to sell or buy; demand for (goods, etc.); a region where goods can be sold.

marketable adj fit for sale.

marketing n all the processes involved in moving goods from the producer to the consumer.

marksman n one skilled at shooting.

marmalade n a preserve made from oranges, sugar and water.

maroon n a brownish-crimson colour; a distress rocket. * vt to abandon esp on a desert island.

marquee n a large tent used for entertainment.

marquetry n inlaid work.

marriage n wedlock; a wedding; a union.

marrow n a soft substance in cavities of bones; a kind of gourd eaten as a vegetable.

marry vt, vi to unite in wedlock.

marsh n a swamp; boggy land.

marshal n one who is in charge of ceremonies etc.; a military officer of the highest rank. * vt to arrange in order.

marsupial adj, n (an animal) carrying its young in a pouch.

martial adj warlike; military.

martyr n one who is tortured and suffers death for his faith.

martyrdom n the death of a martyr; torture.

marvel n a wonder. * vi to feel astonishment; to be filled with wonder.

marvellous adj wonderful; miraculous; astonishing.

mascot n a charm; someone or something thought to bring good luck.

masculine adj, n male; manly; robust.

mash n a soft thick mixture of ingredients, esp as food for horses and cattle; mashed potatoes.

mask n a covering to conceal or protect the face; a moulded likeness of the face; anything that conceals or disguises; a respirator placed over the nose and mouth to aid or prevent inhalation of a gas; (photog) a screen used to cover part of a sensitive surface to prevent exposure by light.

mason n a worker or builder in stone.

masonry n stonework; the craft of freemasons.

masquerade n a fancy-dress ball at which masks are worn; a pretence; false show.

mass n a lump; magnitude; a large quantity; bulk; size; the main part; in physics, the property of a body expressed as a measure of the amount of material contained in it; pl the common people; cap the celebration of the Eucharist.

massacre n ruthless slaughter. * vt to slaughter.

massage n the rubbing and kneading of parts of body.

masseur, masseuse n one who gives massage professionally.

massive adj bulky and heavy; solid.

mast n an upright on which a ship's sails are set.

master n one who rules or directs; an employer; an owner; a ship's captain; a teacher; an expert of craftsman; a writer, painter etc. regarded as pre-eminent; an original from which copies are made; a holder of an advanced academic degree.

masterful adj imperious; headstrong.

masterly adj skilful; expert.

masterpiece n an artist's greatest work; any extraordinary piece of work.

masterstroke n a supremely able act.

mastery n command; ascendancy.

masticate vt to chew and prepare for swallowing.

masturbate vi to manually stimulate one's sexual organs to achieve orgasm without sexual intercourse.

mat n a fabric of plaited fibre, straw, etc., for protection purpose.

match n any person or thing which goes with another; an equal; a contest; a marriage; a strip of wood or cardboard tipped with a chemical that ignites when struck.

matchless adj unrivalled.

mate n an associate; an animal's sexual partner; a companion; a husband or wife; four as a pair; a ship's officer.

material n consisting of matter; important; not spiritual; essential. * n the substance of which anything is made; a person suitable for a task, a position etc.

materialism n the doctrine of materialists.

materialist n one whose interest lies in acquiring possessions.

materialize vt to give concrete form to.

maternal adj of, like a mother.

maternity n motherhood. * adj relating to pregnancy.

mathematician n one concerned with mathematics.

mathematics n the science dealing with quantities, forms, space, etc. and their relationships by use of numbers and symbols.

matin n morning; (pl) morning prayers.

matinée n an afternoon performance.

matriarch n a woman who rules.

matricide n the killing of a mother; the person guilty of it.

matriculate vt, vi to enrol or be enrolled.

matrimonial adj pertaining to marriage.

matrimony n marriage.

matrix n a mould.

matron n a woman in charge of domestic and nursing arrangements.

matted adj entangled.

matter n what a thing is made of; material; whatever occupies space and is perceptible to the senses.

matting n a course material, such as woven straw or hemp.

mattress n a casing of strong cloth filled with cotton, foam rubber, springs, etc.

mature adj ripe; fully developed; due payable. * vt, vi to make or become ripe.

maturity n ripeness; perfection.

maul vt to handle roughly; to paw.

mausoleum n a large tomb.

mauve n a shade of pale purple.

maxim n an established principle.

maximum n the greatest quantity.

May n the fifth month of the year; hawthorn blossom. * v aux used to imply possibility, desire, etc.

maybe adv perhaps.

mayhem n violent destruction, confusion.

mayonnaise n a salad dressing.

mayor, mayoress n the chief administrative officer of a municipality.

maze n a labyrinth; a perplexity.

me pers pron the objective case of I.

meadow n a piece of land where grass is grown for hay.

meagre adj thin; scanty.

meal n the food taken at one time; any edible ground grain.

mean adj selfish; ungenerous; despicable; base; middle; moderate. * n the middle; average; pl resources; measures. * vt, vi to intend; to signify.

meander n a winding course. * vi to wind about; to wander aimlessly.

meaning adj significant. * n significance.

meantime adv during the intervening time; at the same time.

meanwhile adv, n meantime.

measles n (used as sing) an acute, contagious viral disease.

measurable adj that may be measured.

measure n the extent, capacity or magnitude of a thing; a standard; an instrument for measuring; just degree; a course of action; a legislative proposal; a musical time. metre.

measured adj set, marked off by a standard; rhythmical; regular; deliberate; stately.

measurement n dimensions.

meat n food in general; animal flesh as food; the essence of something.

mechanic n a person skilled in operating, maintaining, repairing machines.

mechanical adj of or using machinery or tools; produced or operated by machinery; done as if by a machine, lacking thought or emotion.

mechanics n the science of motion and force; knowledge of machinery; the technical aspects of something.

mechanism n the working parts of a machine; any system of interrelated parts.

medal n a piece of metal struck to celebrate an event; a reward of merit.

medallist n a winner of a medal.

meddle vi to interfere in another's affairs.

meddlesome adj interfering.

mediate vi to try to reconcile; to intercede.

mediation n intercession for another.

mediator n an intercessor; an advocate.

medical adj pertaining to medicine.

medicament, medication n a medicine.

medicinal adj healing.

medicine n the science of preventing, treating or curing disease; any healing substance.

medieval, mediaeval adj pertaining to the Middle Ages.

mediocre adj of moderate quality.

mediocrity n moderate skill, ability, etc.

meditate vi to think deeply; reflect.

meditation n reflection; contemplation of spiritual or religious matters.

meditative adj thoughtful.

medium n (pl media, mediums) the middle state or condition; a substance for transmitting an effect; any intervening means, instrument, or agency; (pl media) a means of communicating information (e.g.) newspapers, television, radio); (pl mediums) a person claiming to act as an intermediary between the living and the dead.

medley n (pl medleys) a miscellany; a

musical piece made up of various tunes.

meek adj patient, submissive.

meet vt, vi to come face to face; to encounter; to light on; to receive; to satisfy; to assemble.

meeting n an assembly; an encounter.

melancholy n mental depression; dejection; sadness. * adj dejected.

mellifluent, mellifluous adj sweet; honeyed.

mellow adj soft and ripe; matured (of wine); genial; kind hearted.

melodious adj tuneful; pleasing to the ear.

melodrama n a sensational drama, film.

melodramatic adj over-emotional.

melody n a tuneful composition.

melon n a large juicy fruit.

melt vt, vi to liquefy; to soften; to dissolve; to fade; to disappear.

member n a limb; one of a society or company; a representative in parliament etc.

membership n the members of a body.

membrane n a thin flexible sheet or film.

memento n a souvenir.

memoir n a biography or autobiography.

memorabilia npl things worthy of record; objects, souvenirs of famous people.

memorable adj worthy to be remembered; easy to remember; famous.

memorandum n (pl **memorandums, memoranda**) a note to help the memory; a communication in writing.

memorial adj bringing to memory. * n a monument; a remembrance.

memorize vt to commit to memory.

memory n the faculty of remembering; the sum of the things remembered; an individual recollection.

menace n a threat. * vt to threaten.

mend vt to repair; to improve.

mendacious adj lying; false.

mendacity n deceit.

menial adj low; servile descriptive of work of little skill.

meningitis n inflammation of the membranes enveloping the brain.

menopause n the time of life during which a woman's menstrual cycle ceases.

menstrual adj monthly.

menstruation n the monthly discharge of blood from the uterus.

mental adj pertaining to the mind; occuring or performed in the mind; having a psychiatric disorder; crazy; stupid.

mention n a brief reference or notice; an official recognition or citation.

mentor n a wise adviser.

menu n a bill of fare; a list of options.

mercantile adj relating to trade.

mercenary adj hired; grasping. * n a soldier hired for service in a foreign army.

merchandise n goods; trade.

merchant n a trader on a large scale; a retailer.

merchant navy n commercial shipping.

merciful adj compassionate; tender.

merciless adj pitiless; cruel.

mercurial adj volatile; sprightly.

mercury n a heavy silvery liquid metallic element used in thermometers etc.

mercy n pity; compassion; pardon.

mere adj sole; simple; nothing more than.

meretricious adj gaudy; insincere.

merge vt to absorb; to blend.

merit n excellence; worth; pl the rights and wrongs (of a case); desert. * vt to deserve; to be worthy of.

meritorious adj praiseworthy.

merriment n mirth; noisy gaiety.

merry adj joyous; jovial, cheerful.

mesh n the wires of a screen etc; engagement of geared wheels.

mesmeric adj hypnotic.

mesmerism n the power by exercise of will to control the actions of another.

mesmerize vt to subject to mesmerism; to hypnotize; to hold spellbound.

mesozoic adj belonging to one of the geological periods or formations.

mess n a state of disorder or untidiness, esp if dirty; a building where service personnel dine.

message n a communication; an errand; the chief idea a writer, artist etc. seeks to communicate in a work.

messenger n one who bears a message.

messy adj dirty; confused; untidy.

metabolism n the total processes in living organisms by which tissue is formed, energy produced and waste product eliminated.

metal n any of a class of chemical ele-

ments which are often lustrous, ductile solids, and are good conductors of heat, electricity, etc, such as gold, iron, copper, etc.

metallurgy n the science of extracting metals from their ores.

metamorphic adj altered in structure.

metamorphosis n (pl **metamorphoses**) a complete change of form.

metaphor n a figure of speech in which a word or phrase is used for another of which it is an image.

metaphoric, metaphorical adj figurative.

metaphysical adj pertaining to metaphysics; abstract.

metaphysics n the branch of philosophy dealing with the nature of being and reality.

mete vt to dole out or distribute.

meteor n a small particle of matter which travels at great speeds through space.

meteoric adj brilliant but transitory.

meteorite n a spent meteor.

meteorology n the study of the atmosphere and of weather-forecasting.

meter n an instrument for registering consumption of gas, water, time etc.

method n mode of procedure; system; orderliness of thought or arrangement.

methodical adj systematic; orderly.

methylated spirit n a form of alcohol, used as a solvent.

meticulous adj over careful; precise about small details.

metre n pattern in verse or music.

metre n the basic unit of length in the metric system (39.37 in.).

metric adj pertaining to the decimal system.

metrication n conversion of an existent system of units into the metric system.

metric system n a decimal system of weights and measures.

metronome n an instrument that beats musical tempo.

metropolitan adj belonging to a metropolis.

mettle n spirit; courage.

mezzanine n an intermediate storey between others; a theatre balcony.

mezzo adj in music, middle; mean.

mezzoprano n a female voice, singer with a range between soprano and contralto.

mice npl of mouse.

microbe n a germ; a bacillus.

microcosm n man as an epitome of the universe or macrocosm; a very small copy.

microfilm n film on which documents, etc, are recorded in reduced scale.

microphone n an instrument for transforming sound waves into electric signals, esp for transmission, or recording.

microscope n an optical instrument for magnifying.

microscopic, microscopical adj minute; visible only through a microscope.

mid adj middle; intervening.

midday n the middle of the day; noon.

middle adj equally distant from the extremes.

middle age n the time between youth and old age.

Middle Ages npl the period of European history between about AD500 and 1500.

middle class n people between the working classes and the aristocracy.

midnight n twelve o'clock at night.

midriff n the diaphragm.

midst n the middle. * prep amidst; among.

midsummer n the middle of summer.

midway n halfway.

midwife n a woman that assists women in childbirth.

might n power; strength.

mighty adj strong; powerful; large.

migrant n a person or animal who migrates.

migrate vi to remove from one region or country to another.

migratory adj roving; wandering.

mild adj gentle; merciful; soft.

mildew n a mouldy deposit or coating caused by fungus.

mile n 1760 yards or 1.61 km.

mileage n distance in miles.

milestone n a stone or post marking each mile of a road; an important event in life.

militancy n aggressiveness.

militant adj warring; combative.

militarism n military spirit; reliance on force.

military adj pertaining to soldiers.

militate vi (with against) to influence, to have an adverse effect on.

militia n an army composed of civilians.

milk n a fluid secreted by female mammals to feed their young. * vt to draw milk from; to extract money etc. from; to exploit.

mill n a machine for grinding corn, etc; a factory. * vt to grind.

millennium n a period of 1000 years.

milligram(me) n the thousandth part of a gram(me).

millimetre n the thousandth part of a metre.

million n a thousand thousands; 1,000,000.

millionaire n a person worth a million pounds; one who is extremely rich.

millstone n a stone used in grinding corn.

mime n a drama enacted through gestures.

mimic adj imitative. * n one who imitates; an actor skilled in mimicry.

mimicry n imitation.

mince vt, vi to chop into small pieces; to act or walk affectedly; to clip (words).

mincemeat n a mixture of chopped apples, raisins, etc used as a pie filling.

mind n the intellectual faculty or power; intellect; reason; understanding; inclination; opinion; memory. * vt to heed; to pay attention to; to obey; to take care of; to care about; to object.

mindful adj attentive; heedful.

mine pron my; belonging to me. * n an excavation from which minerals are dug; an explosive device concealed in the water or ground to destroy enemy ships, personnel, or vehicles that pass over or near them; a rich supply or source.

minefield n an area in which explosive mines are laid; a situation containing hidden problems.

miner n a person who works in a mine.

mineral n an inorganic substance found in or on the earth.

mineralogist n an expert on mineralogy.

mineralogy n the science of minerals.

mingle vt to mix together; to blend.

miniature n a small-scale portrait; a reduced copy.

minim n a note in music; the smallest liquid measure; a single drop.

minimize vt to estimate at the lowest; to disparage.

minimum n the smallest amount.

minister n a member of a government heading a department; a diplomat; a clergyman serving a church. * vt to give help to. * vi to perform a service.

ministration n service; a giving of aid; the work of a minister of the church.

ministry n service; office of a minister; clergy; a government department headed by a minister.

minor adj lesser; smaller; petty. * n a person under full legal age.

minority n the state of a minor; the smaller of two parties voting; any smaller group.

minstrel n a bard; a travelling musician of the Middle Ages.

mint n the place where money is coined; a large amount of money; an aromatic plant with leaves used for flavouring. * vt to coin. * adj in perfect condition.

minuet n a slow graceful dance; the music played for it.

minus adj less. * n the sign of subtraction (-).

minute adj very small; precise: exact.

minute n the sixtieth part of an hour or a degree; pl a summary of proceedings; an official record of a meeting. * vt to record, summarize the proceedings (of).

minutiae npl small details.

miracle n a marvel; a supernatural event.

miraculous adj marvellous; supernatural.

mirage n an optical illusion caused by light reflection from hot air.

mire n wet, muddy soil; mud.

mirror n a looking glass; a faithful depiction.

misadventure n a mishap; bad luck.

misalliance n an unsuitable marriage.

misanthrope, misanthropist n a hater of mankind.

misapply vt to apply wrongly.

misapprehend vt to misunderstand.

misapprehension n a mistake.

misappropriate vt to appropriate dishonestly; to embezzle.

misbehave vi to behave badly.

miscalculate vt to reckon wrongly.

miscarriage n a failure; mismanagement; the premature expulsion of a foetus.

miscellaneous adj mixed; diverse.

mischance n ill luck; mishap.

mischief n wayward, prankish behaviour.

mischievous adj troublesome; hurtful.

misconduct n immoral or bad behaviour.

misconstrue vt to interpret wrongly.

miscount vt, vi to make an error in counting; a wrong counting.

misdeed n an evil action.

misdemeanour n a minor offence.

miser n a skinflint; a hoarder of money.

miserable adj wretched; despicable.

misery n wretchedness; sorrow; poverty.

misfit n a bad fit; a maladjusted person.

misfortune n ill fortune; calamity.

misgiving n a doubt; mistrust.

misguided adj foolish; mistaken.

mishap n a slight or unfortunate accident.

misinform vt to give wrong information to.

misinterpret vt to interpret wrongly.

misjudge vt to judge erroneously.

mislay vt to lose temporarily; to put down in the wrong place.

mislead vt to deceive; to misinform.

mismanage vt to manage badly.

misnomer n an incorrect or unsuitable name for someone or something.

misogynist n a woman-hater.

misplace vt to put out of place.

misprint n a mistake in printing.

mispronounce vt, vi to pronounce wrongly.

misquote vt to quote incorrectly.

misrepresent vt to represent falsely.

misrule n misgovernment.

miss vt to fail to hit, find, meet, etc.; to lose; to omit; to fail to take advantage of; to feel the loss of. * n a failure to hit; loss; want; an unmarried woman; a girl.

misshapen adj ill-formed.

missile n an object, a a rock, spear, rocket.

missing adj lost; absent.

mission n a group of people sent by a church, government, etc to carry out a special duty or task.

missionary n one sent to a foreign country to propagate religion.

missive n an official letter.

misspell vt to spell wrongly.

misspend vt to squander; to waste.

mist n a mass of visible water vapour.

mistake vt to misunderstand or misinterpret. * vi to err. * n a blunder, an error of judgment; a misunderstanding.

mistaken adj erroneous; ill-judged.

mistress n the feminine of master; a woman with whom a man is having a prolonged affair.

mistrust n suspicion. * vt to suspect; to doubt.

misunderstand vt to take the wrong meaning from.

misuse vt to use for wrong purpose; to abuse. * n improper use.

mite n a minute parasitic animal; a very small object or person.

mitigate vt to lessen, to abate, to moderate.

mitre n the headdress of a bishop; a diagonal joint between two pieces of wood to form a corner.

mitten n a fingerless glove.

mix vt, vi to unite or blend; to mingle; to join; to combine (ingredients etc.).

mixed adj blended; assorted; of different kinds, classes, races etc.; confused.

mixture n a compound; a medley; a jumble.

mix-up n a mistake; confusion, muddle.

mnemonics n art of memory; rules for assisting memory.

moan vi to utter a mournful sound.

moat n a ditch round a castle or fort.

mob n a crowd; a rabble; a gang of animals.

mobile adj movable, not fixed; easily changing; characterized by ease in change of social status; capable of moving freely and quickly; having transport.

mobilize vt to organize troops in readiness for service.

moccasin n a deerskin shoe; any soft flexible shoe.

mock vt to imitate or ridicule; to behave with scorn; to defy; (with up) to make a model of. * n ridicule; an object of scorn. * adj false, sham, counterfeit.

mockery n derision; a sham.

mock-up n a full-scale working model of a machine, etc.

mode n way of acting, doing, existing; manner; fashion; (music) any of the scales used in composition; (statistics) the predominant item in a series of items; a mood in grammar.

model n a pattern; an ideal; a standard worth imitating; a representation on a smaller scale, usu three-dimensional; a person who sits for an artist or photographer; a person who displays clothes by wearing them.

moderate vt to restrain from excess; to temper, to lessen. * vi to preside over.

moderation n temperance; restraint.

modern adj of the present or recent times; contemporary; up-to-date.

modernism n modern thought or practice.

modernize vt to make modern.

modest adj retiring; bashful; diffident; moderate.

modesty n bashful reserve; chastity.

modicum n a small quantity.

modification n the act of modifying.

modify vt to change slightly; to lessen the severity of; to limit in meaning.

modulate vt to measure; to vary (the voice) in tone.

module n a unit of measurement; a self-contained unit, esp in a space-craft.

moist adj slightly wet; damp.

moisten vt to make damp or moist.

moisture n dampness; humidity.

moisturize vt to add moisture to the skin, air etc. with various preparations.

mole n a dark spot on human skin; a break-water; a spy within an organization.

molecular adj belonging to or consisting of molecules.

molecule n the simplest unit of a substance; a small particle.

molest vt to annoy; to vex; to assault esp sexually.

mollify vt to soften; to appease; to tone down.

mollusc n a soft-bodied invertebrate animal with a hard shell (e.g. oyster, etc.).

molten adj melted by heat.

moment n an indefinitely brief period of time; importance; gravity.

momentary adj lasting only for a moment.

momentous adj important; weighty.

momentum n (pl **momenta**) the force possessed by a moving body.

monarch n a sovereign ruling by hereditary right.

monarchy n government headed by a monarch; a kingdom.

monastery n the residence of monks.

monastic adj of monks or monasteries.

monasticism n the monastic life or system.

Monday n the second day of the week.

monetary adj relating to money.

money n current coin or its equivalent in bank notes, etc.

moneyed adj wealthy.

mongrel adj of mixed or unknown breed.

monitor n a prefect; any device for regulating the performance of a machine, aircraft etc. * vt, vi to check on; to regulate, control a machine etc.

monk n a male member of a religious order in a monastery.

monkey n (pl **monkeys**) any of the primates except man and the lemurs, esp the smaller, long-tailed primates; a mischievous child.

monocle n a single eyeglass.

monogamy n marriage to one wife or husband only.

monogram n letters (esp initials) interwoven in one design.

monograph n an essay on one subject.

monolith n a standing stone or pillar.

monologue n a soliloquy.

monopolize vt to obtain entire control of.

monopoly n an exclusive trading privilege; exclusive use or possession.

monosyllable n a word of one syllable.

monotone n speaking without inflection; a sameness of style, colour etc.

monotonous adj unvarying; tedious.

monotony n an irksome sameness.

monsoon n a seasonal wind of Southern Asia.

monster n a huge frightsome creature.

monstrosity n an unnatural, misshapen creature or thing.

monstrous adj unnatural; horrible.

montage *n* the art or technique or assembling various elements.

month *n* any of the twelve divisions of the year; a calendar month; a period corresponding to the moon's revolution.

monthly *adj* continuing for a month; done, happening, payable etc, every month.

monument *n* a tomb, pillar, statue etc, erected as a memorial.

monumental *adj* of, like, or serving as a monument; colossal; lasting.

mood *n* a temporary state of mind; (grammar) the form of the verb indicating mode of action.

moody *adj* in low spirits; temperamental.

moon *n* the natural satellite that revolves around the earth and shines by reflected sunlight; any natural satellite of another planet; something shaped like the moon.

moonbeam *n* a ray of light from the moon.

moonlight *n* the light of the moon. * *vi* to have a secondary (usu night-time) job.

moor *n* a heath; wasteland. * *vt* to secure a ship by cable or anchor.

mooring *n* the anchors, buoys, etc, by which or to which a boat is moored.

moot *adj* debatable; hypothetical.

mop *n* a rag, sponge etc.fixed to a handle for washing floors or dishes, a thick, unruly head of hair.

mope *vi* to be downcast and uninterested.

moral *adj* of or relating to character and human behaviour, particularly as regards right and wrong; virtuous, esp in sexual conduct; capable of distinguishing right from wrong.

morale *n* the tone, spirit, or mental condition prevailing with regard to courage, discipline, confidence etc.

morality *n* the doctrine of moral duties; ethics; virtue; an old form of drama.

moralize *vt, vi* to reflect on, moral questions.

morass *n* a marsh; a bog; a fen.

moratorium *n* legal permission to defer payments due; a temporary stoppage.

morbid *adj* diseased; sickly; gruesome.

more *adj comp* of much and many greater in amount, extent, etc. * *adv* in a greater degree.

moribund *adj* in a dying state.

morning *n* the first part of the day.

morose *adj* surly; sullen; glum.

morphia, morphine *n* an alkaloid derived from opium.

morsel *n* a bite; a small piece.

mortal *adj* subject to death; deadly; fatal; human. * *n* a human being.

mortality *n* the state of being mortal; the death rate.

mortar *n* a bowl in which substances are pounded with a pestle; an artillery piece that fires shells at low velocities and high trajectories; a cement.

mortgage *n* a conveyance of property as security for loan; the deed of conveyance. * *vt* to pledge as security.

mortification *n* gangrene; humiliation.

mortify *vt, vi* to affect with gangrene; to shame.

mortifying *adj* humiliating.

mortise lock *n* a lock set into a mortise in a door.

mortuary *n* a place for temporary storage of dead bodies; a morgue.

mosaic *n* inlaid work of marble, precious stones, etc.

Moslem, Muslim *n* a Mohammedan; an adherent of Islam.

mosque *n* a Moslem place of worship.

moss *n* a very small green plant that grows in clusters on rocks, moist ground, etc.

mossy *adj* overgrown with moss.

most *adj superl* of **more** greatest in any way. * *adv* in the greatest degree.

motel *n* an hotel for motorists with adjacent parking.

moth *n* a nocturnal insect allied to the butterfly.

mother *n* a female parent; source or origin; the head of a nunnery, etc. * *adj* of, like a mother; native. * *vt* to be or care for as a mother.

mother-in-law *n* the mother of one's spouse.

motherly *adj* of, proper to a mother.

motion *n* activity, movement; a formal suggestion made in a meeting, law court, or legislative assembly; evacuation of the bowels. * *vt, vi* to signal or direct by a gesture.

motionless *adj* not moving; still.

motion picture *n* a film, movie.

motive *n* something (as a need or desire) that causes a person to act.

motley *adj* composed of diverse element.

motor *n* anything that produces motion; a machine for converting electrical energy into mechanical energy; a motor car. * *adj* producing motion; of or powered by a motor; of, by or for motor vehicles. * *vi* to travel by car.

motorbike *n* a motorcycle.

motorboat *n* a boat propelled by an engine or motor.

motorist *n* a person who drives a car.

motorway *n* a road with controlled access for fast-moving traffic.

mottled *adj* marked with blotches of various colours.

motto *n* (*pl* **mottoes**) a short saying adopted as a maxim or ideal.

mould *n* a fungus producing a furry growth on the surface of organic matter; a hollow form in which something is cast. * *vt* to make in or on a mould; to form, to shape, to guide.

moulder *vt, vi* to decay; to crumble.

moulding *n* anything cast in a mould; ornamental contour along an edge.

moult *vi* to shed or cast the hair, horns, skin, etc.

mound *n* an artificial elevation of earth or stones; a rampart; a hillock.

mount *n* a hill; a mountain; a setting for photographs, etc; a backing; a horse. * *vi* to rise; to get on horseback; to provide with horses; to amount. * *vt* to climb; to fix, place in position.

mountain *n* a high hill, a vast number.

mountaineer *n* a mountain climber.

mourn *vi* to sorrow. * *vt* to grieve for.

mournful *adj* expressing grief or sorrow.

mourning *n* lamentation; clothes worn by mourners.

mouse *n* (*pl* **mice**) a small rodent with a pointed snout, long body and slender tail; a timid person; a hand-held device used to position the cursor and control software on a computer screen.

moustache *n* the hair on the upper lip.

mouth *n* the opening in the head through which food is eaten, sound uttered or words spoken; the lips; opening, entrance, as of a bottle, etc. * *vt* to say, esp insincerely; to form words with the mouth without uttering sound. * *vi* to utter pompously; to grimace.

mouthpiece *n* the part of a musical instrument or tobacco pipe placed between the lips; a spokesman for others.

mouthwatering *adj* appetizing; tasty.

movable *adj* portable. * *npl* furniture; belongings; personal property.

move *vt* to cause to change place; to set in motion; to affect; to rouse; to prevail on; to make a motion. * *vi* to stir; to go from one place to another; to walk; to change residence.

movement *n* motion; change of position; a gesture; joint action; the policy of a group; a trend; a division of a musical work.

movies *npl* the cinema.

moving *adj* touching; pathetic.

mow *vt, vi* to cut down; to cut grass.

much *adj* (*comp* **more**, *superl* **most**) great in quantity. * *adv* considerably.

mucous, mucose *adj* slimy. * **mucous membrane**, a membrane lining the nose and other cavities of the body.

mucus *n* a viscid fluid secreted by mucous membrane.

mud *n* moist soft earth; mire.

muddle *vt* to make a mess of; to mix up; to confuse. * *n* a mess; confusion.

muddy *adj* like, covered in mud; confused; not bright; unclear.

muff *n* a fur cover for both hands.

muffin *n* a baked roll.

muffle *vt* to wrap up close; to conceal; to deaden sound.

muffler *n* a long scarf; the silencer of a motor vehicle.

mug *n* a large cup. * *vt* to assault (and rob).

mule *n* the offspring of a male donkey and a female horse; an obstinate person.

mull *vt* to heat, sweeten, and spice (as wine, etc); to ponder.

multifarious *adj* many and varied.

multilateral *adj* many-sided.

multiple *adj* manifold; various; complex.

* n a number which contains another an exact number of times.

multiplication n the act or process of multiplying.

multiplicity n great number or variety.

multiply vt, vi to make or become many; to increase; to find the product of by multiplication.

multipurpose adj able to be used for many tasks or functions.

multistorey adj, n (building) with many storeys.

multitude n a crowd; a throng; the populace.

mumble vi, vt to mutter; to speak indistinctly.

mummify vi to embalm as a mummy.

mummy n an embalmed human body, esp an embalmed corpse of ancient Egypt.

mumps n a contagious disease.

munch vt, vi to chew steadily.

mundane adj routine; everyday; banal.

municipal adj of or concerning a city, town, etc or its local government.

municipality n the corporation or governing body of a town.

munificent adj bountiful; generous.

mural adj pertaining to a wall. * n a picture or design painted onto a wall.

murder n unlawful and intentional manslaughter. * vt to kill (with malice aforethought); to mar.

murderous adj cruel; savage.

murky adj dark; gloomy; obscure.

murmur n a low continuous, indistinct sound; an abnormal sound made by the heart.

muscle n fibrous tissue that contracts and relaxes, producing body movement; strength; power.

muscular adj brawny; sinewy.

muse n poetic inspiration. * vi, vt to ponder; to meditate.

museum n a building housing a collection of curios, works of art, etc.

mushroom n an edible fungus. * vi to gather mushrooms; to spread rapidly.

music n melody or harmony; the art of producing musical compositions featuring vocal or instrumental sounds having rhythm, harmony, melody.

musical adj melodious; harmonious; having an interest in or talent for music. * n a play or film incorporating story, song and dance.

musician n one skilled in music.

musing n meditation.

Muslim see **Moslem.**

muslin n a fine cotton cloth.

must aux vb expressing necessity or certainty. * n something that must be done or possessed.

mustard n a plant with pungent seeds; the condiment got from them; a brownish-yellow colour.

muster vt to collect, as troops. * vi to assemble. * n an assembling of troops.

musty adj mouldy; stale; damp.

mutable adj changeable; unstable.

mutation n change; alteration.

mute adj silent; dumb; not pronounced. * n a person who cannot speak.

mutilate vt to cut off a part; to maim.

mutineer n one guilty of mutiny.

mutinous adj rebellious.

mutiny n a revolt against authority in military service. * vi to rise in revolt.

mutter vi to mumble; to murmur to grumble. * n indistinct speech.

mutual adj reciprocal; shared alike; having the same feelings one for the other.

muzzle n the projecting mouth and nose of an animal; the open end of a gun; a strap fitted over an animal's jaws to prevent biting. * vt to gag.

muzzy adj bewildered; tipsy.

my pron the possessive case sing of I.

myopia n short-sightedness.

myriad n a countless number.

myself pron emphatic and reflexive form of I; in my normal state.

mysterious adj very obscure; incomprehensible; secret.

mystery n something beyond human intelligence; something unexplained; a secret; an old form of drama.

mystic adj having a meaning beyond normal human understanding; magical.

mystify vt to perplex; to bewilder.

myth n a tradition or fable embodying the primitive ideas of a people.

mythology n the study of myths.

N

nab vt to catch; to seize or arrest.

nadir n the lowest point.

nag n a horse; a person who nags. * vt ,vi to plague; to pester; to scold constantly.

nail n a horny substance covering the tip of the finger or toe; a metal spike. * vt to fasten, secure or hang with nails.

naïve adj ingenuous; unsophisticated.

naïveté n lack of sophistication.

naked adj bare; nude; destitute.

name n the word by which a person or thing is designated; title; reputation; a family. * vt to give a name to.

nameless adj unknown; unspeakable.

namely adv that is to say.

namesake n one named after, or with the same name as another.

nap n the woolly substance on the surface of cloth, etc; a short sleep.

napalm n a substance added to petrol to form a jelly-like compound used in fire-bombs and flame-throwers.

nape n the back of the neck.

napery n table and household linen.

naphtha n a volatile oil distilled from coal.

napkin n a serviette; a small square of cloth or paper used at table to protect clothes or wipe the mouth and fingers.

nappy n a piece of absorbent material wrapped around a baby to absorb or retain its excreta.

narcotic n a sedative; a drug often addictive used to induce sleep or relieve pain.

narrate vt to tell or relate.

narration n a narrative; a story.

narrative adj pertaining to narration. * n a history or tale spoken or written.

narrow adj of little breadth; very limited; not liberal; near. * vt, vi to make or become narrow.

narrow-minded adj illiberal; prejudiced.

nasal adj pertaining to or sounded through the nose. * n a sound made through the nose.

nascent adj budding; dawning; opening.

nasty adj filthy; indecent; disagreeable.

natal adj pertaining to birth.

nation n people living under the same government and of common descent, culture, language and history.

nationalist n one who supports a policy of independence or Home Rule.

nationality n national character; patriotism; a nation or national group.

nationalize vt to convert land, mines, etc, into state property.

native adj pertaining to the place of one's birth; indigenous; inborn. * n a person both in the place indicated; a local inhabitant; an indigenous plant or animal; an indigenous inhabitant.

nativity n birth; time, place, manner of birth.

natural adj pertaining to nature; native; inborn; normal; unaffected; simple; naïve; (music) not sharp or flat.

natural history n the study of nature, esp the animal, mineral and vegetable world.

naturalist n a person who studies natural history.

naturalization n the giving of citizen rights to one of foreign birth.

naturalize vt to acclimatize; to confer.

naturally adv in a natural manner, by nature; of course.

nature n the phenomena of physical like not dominated by man; the entire material world as a whole, or forces observable in it; the essential character of anything.

naught n nought; nothing.

naughty adj bad; mischievous; titillating.

nausea n sickness; disgust.

nauseate vt, vi to arouse feelings of disgust or revulsion.

nauseous adj loathsome; disgusting.

nautical adj pertaining to ships.

naval adj pertaining to ships or to a navy.

nave n the central part of a church.

navel n a depression in the centre of the abdomen.

navigable adj affording passage to ships.

navigate vi, vt to guide the course of a ship, aeroplane, etc; to sail.

navigation n the method of calculating the position of a ship, aircraft etc.

navvy n a labourer, who works on roads.

navy n the warships of a nation with their

crews and equipment.

near adj not distant; intimate; closely related; approximate; narrow (of escape etc.). * prep close to. * adv almost; close by. * vt, vi to approach.

nearly adv almost; closely.

near-sighted adj short-sighted.

neat adj trim; (of alcohol) undiluted.

nebula n (pl **nebulae**) celestial objects like white clouds, generally clusters of stars.

nebulous adj cloudy; hazy; indistinct.

necessary adj indispensable; essential. * n a proved need, pl essential needs.

necessitate vt to compel; to constrain.

necessity n urgent need; compulsion.

neck n the part of body connecting the head and shoulders; an isthmus; the narrowest part of a bottle.

necklace n a string of beads worn round the neck.

necropolis n cemetery.

nectar n the fabled drink of the gods; a delicious drink; the honey of flowers.

need n want; necessity; poverty. * vt, vi to lack; to require; to be obliged.

needful adj needy; necessary.

needle n a small steel instrument for sewing; an indicator on a dial; the thin, short leaf of trees such as the pine or spruce.

needy adj indigent; very poor.

negation n a denial; a saying no.

negative adj expressing denial or refusal; the opposite of positive. * n a photographic print from which positive prints are taken. * vt to veto; to contradict.

neglect vt to disregard; to slight; to pay no attention to; to leave uncared for; omit. * n want of care.

neglectful adj heedless; careless.

negligé n a woman's loose dressing gown.

negligence n carelessness.

negotiable adj capable of being negotiated or transferred.

negotiate vi to treat; to bargain in order to reach an agreement or settlement.

negotiation n bargaining.

neigh vi to whinny. * n the cry of a horse.

neighbour n a person living near; a fellow human being. * vt to adjoin.

neighbourhood n a particular area, district or community; the vicinity.

neighbouring adj adjoining.

neighbourly adj friendly.

neither pron, adj not either. * conj not either; also not.

nephew n the son of a brother or sister.

nepotism n favouritism to relatives shown by influential people.

nerve n one of the fibrous threads which convey messages to and from brain; courage; audacity. * vt to strengthen.

nervous adj timid; excitable; forcible.

nest n a bird's hatching place.

nestle vi to lie close and snug.

net n a meshwork of cord, twine, etc; a piece of this used to catch fish, to divide a tennis court etc.; a snare. * vt to snare; to twine.

net, nett adj clear of deductions, allowances or changes; the opposite of gross.

netball n a game for two teams, in which points are scored by putting a ball through an elevated horizontal ring.

nether adj lower.

netting n a piece of network.

nettle n a weed with stinging hairs. * vt to irritate.

network n an interconnecting arrangement of lines; a group cooperating with each other; a chain of interconnected operations, computers etc.

neuralgia n pain in a nerve.

neuritis n inflammation of nerve.

neurology n the study of nerves.

neurosis n (pl **neuroses**) a mental disorder with symptoms such as anxiety.

neurotic adj suffering from neurosis; highly strung.

neuter adj (of nouns) neither masculine nor feminine; (biol) having no sex organs. * vt to castrate or spay.

neutral adj nonaligned; not taking sides with either party in a dispute or war; having no distinctive characteristics; (chem) neither acid nor alkaline. * n a position of a gear mechanism in which power is not transmitted.

neutralize vt to render neutral.

never adv at no time; in no case.

nevertheless adv for all that; notwithstanding.

new adj recent; novel; fresh; unused.

news *npl* current events; recent happenings; the mass media's coverage of such events.

newsagent *n* a retailer of newspapers.

newspaper *n* a paper published periodically giving latest news.

next *adj* nearest; immediately preceding or following; adjacent. * *adv* in the nearest time, place, rank, etc; on the first subsequent occasion.

nexus *n* tie; connexion.

nibble *vt, vi* to bite little by little.

nice *adj* fastidious; pleasant; dainty.

nicety *n* precision; exactness.

niche *n* a recess in a wall for a statue, etc.

nick *n* a notch; a score; a critical moment; a police station. * *vt* to make a small cut in; to wound superficially.

nickname *n* a name given to an individual in jest or ridicule. * *vt* to give a nickname to.

nicotine *n* a poisonous alkaloid present in tobacco.

niece *n* the daughter of one's brother or sister.

nigh *adj* near. * *prep.* near to.

night *n* the period from sunset to sunrise.

nightcap *n* a cap worn in bed; an alcoholic drink taken just before bedtime.

nightclub *n* a place of entertainment for drinking, dancing, etc, at night.

nightdress *n* a loose garment worn in bed by women and girls.

nightfall *n* evening.

nightly *adj* done or happening by night or every night; nocturnal.

nightmare *n* a frightening dream; any horrible experience.

nil *n* nothing.

nimble *adj* active; agile.

nine *adj, n* cardinal number; one more than eight, (9 or IX).

nineteen *adj, n* nine and ten (19 or XIX).

ninety *adj, n* nine times ten (90 or C).

ninth *adj, n* next after eighth; one of nine equal parts of a thing.

nip *vt* to pinch; to snip. * *n* a pinch; a small bite from a dog; frost or cold.

nippers *npl* small pincers.

nipple *n* the small protuberance on a breast or udder through which the milk passes, a teat; a teat-like rubber part on the cap of a baby's bottle.

nitrogen *n* a gaseous element forming nearly 78 per cent of air.

nitrogenous *adj* pertaining to nitrogen.

nitroglycerine *n* a powerful explosive.

no *adv* expressing negation. * *n* a denial; a refusal; a negative vote or voter. * *adj* none.

noble *adj* of high rank; famous; lofty in character; stately. * *n* a peer; a person of high rank.

nobleman *n* a noble; a peer.

nobody *n* no one; a person of no importance.

nocturnal *adj* nightly; by night.

nod *vi, vt* to make a slight bow, to incline the head quickly in assent or greeting.

node *n* a knot; a knob; the joint of a stem.

nodule *n* a little knot or lump.

noise *n* a din; clamour; a harsh sound. * *vt* to make public.

noisome *adj* noxious; offensive.

nomad *n* a wanderer; one of a people or tribe who travel in search of pasture.

nomenclature *n* a system of names; vocabulary of scientific terms.

nominal *adj* formal; existing in name only; having only token worth.

nominate *vt* to name; to designate; to appoint to an office or post; to propose someone as a candidate (for election).

nominee *n* a person nominated for office, etc.

nonchalance *n* indifference; coolness.

noncommittal *adj* not revealing one's opinion.

nonconductor *n* a substance which does not conduct heat, electricity, etc.

nonconformist *n* one who does not conform to the established church.

nondescript *adj* hard to classify, indeterminate; lacking individual characteristics. * *n* a nondescript person of thing.

none *n, pron* not one; not any.

nonentity *n* a person of no significance.

nonsense *n* words without meaning.

nonstop *adj* making no intermediate stops (of train etc.). * *adv* never ceasing; never stopping or pausing.

noodle *pl* pasta in thin strips.

noon *n* twelve o'clock in the day.

noose *n* a loop on a running knot; a lasso.

nor *conj* and not; not either.

norm *n* a rule; a pattern; a standard.

normal *adj* according to a rule; regular.

north *n* the cardinal point opposite the midday sun. * *adj* in, of, towards, from the north. * *adv* in or towards the north.

northeast *n* the point midway between north and east.

northward *adv, adj* towards the north.

northwest *n* the point midway between the north and west.

nose *n* the part of the face above the mouth, used for breathing and smelling, having two nostrils; the sense of smell. * *vt* to discover as by smell. * *vi* to sniff for; to inch forwards; to pry.

nostalgia *n* yearning for past times or places.

nostalgic *adj* feeling or expressing nostalgia; longing for one's youth.

nostril *n* one of the two apertures of the nose for breathing and smelling.

not *adv* expressing denial, refusal or negation.

notable *adj* worthy of being noted or remembered; distinguished; memorable.

notation *n* act of recording anything by symbols.

notch *n* an incision; nick. * *vt* to indent.

note *n* a mark, a sign or token; an explanation; an epistle; a musical sound or its symbol; the sound of a bird's call. * *vt* to mark down; to observe.

noted *adj* famous; celebrated.

notepaper *n* paper for writing down notes.

nothing *n* not anything; a trifle; a zero; thing of no importance or value. * *adv* in no way; not at all.

notice *n* heed; regard; intimation; warning; information. * *vt* to observe.

noticeable *adj* worthy of notice; remarkable; easily seen or noticed.

notice board *n* a board on which notices are pinned for public information.

notification *n* intimation; warning.

notify *vt* to make known; to inform.

notion *n* a concept; an idea; an opinion.

notoriety *n* publicity (esp discreditable).

notorious *adj* widely known, esp unfavourably.

notwithstanding *prep, conj* in spite of; nevertheless; although.

nougat *n* a chewy sweet consisting of sugar paste and nuts.

nought *n* not anything; a zero.

noun *n* the name of anything.

nourish *vt* to feed; to foster; to encourage the growth of; to raise.

nourishment *n* food, nutriment.

novel *adj* new and striking. * *n* a fictitious story or narrative in book form.

novelty *n* a new or strange thing; *pl* cheap, small objects for sale.

November *n* the eleventh month of the year.

novice *n* a beginner; a person in a religious order before taking vows.

now *adv*, at the present time. * *conj* since; seeing that.

nowhere *adv* not in, at, or to anywhere.

noxious *adj* hurtful; pernicious.

nozzle *n* the projecting spout of something; e.g. a nose or pipe.

nuance *n* a fine shade; a delicate distinction of meaning etc.

nuclear *adj* of or relating to a nucleus; using nuclear energy.

nuclear energy *n* energy released as a result of nuclear fission or fusion.

nuclear fission *n* the splitting of a nucleus of an atom either spontaneously or by bombarding it with particles.

nuclear fusion *n* the combining of two nuclei into a heavier nucleus.

nuclear power *n* electrical or motive power produced by a nuclear reactor.

nuclear reactor *n* a device in which nuclear fission is maintained and harnessed to produce energy.

nucleus *n* (*pl* **nuclei, nucleuses**) the central part of core around which something may develop, or be grouped or concentrated; the centrally positively charged portion of an atom.

nude *adj* naked; bare. * *n* a naked human figure esp in a work of art; nakedness.

nudge *n* a light jog with the elbow. * *vt* to jog with the elbow; to remind.

nugget *n* a lump, as of gold.

nuisance *n* that which annoys.

null *adj* of no force; void; invalid.

nullify *vt* to render null; to cancel out.

numb *adj* benumbed; having no feeling through shock or cold. * *vt* to deaden.

number *n* a symbol or word indicating how many; a numeral identifying a person or thing by its position in a series. * *vt, vi* to count; to give a number to; to include or be included as one of a group; to limit the number of; to total.

numberplate *n* a plate on the front or rear of a motor vehicle that displays its registration number.

numeral *adj* pertaining to number. * *n* a figure or symbol representing a number.

numerate *adj* able to use and understand numbers and arithmetic.

numerical *adj* denoting number; consisting of numbers.

numerous *adj* many.

numismatics *n* the study of coins and medals.

nun *n* woman belonging to a religious order.

nuncio *n* an ambassador of the Pope.

nunnery *n* a convent.

nuptials *npl* marriage.

nurse *n* one trained to care for the sick, or infirm. * *vt* to tend; to suckle; to foster.

nursery *n* a place where children may be left in temporary care; a place where young trees and plants are raised for transplanting.

nursery rhyme *n* a short traditional poem or song for children.

nursery school *n* a school for young children, usu under five.

nursery slope *n* a gently inclined slope for novice skiers.

nursing *n* the profession of a nurse.

nursing home *n* an establishment providing care for convalescent, chronically ill, or disabled people.

nurture *n* upbringing; education; nourishment. * *vt* to nourish; to educate.

nut *n* a fruit containing a kernel in a hard covering; a screw fastening a bolt.

nutcracker *n* an instrument for cracking nuts; a bird with speckled plumage.

nutmeg *n* the aromatic kernel produced by a tree, grated and used as a spice.

nutriment *n* food; nourishment.

nutritious *adj* nourishing; health-giving.

nylon *n* any of numerous tough, synthetic materials used esp in plastics.

nymph *n* the larva of the dragonfly, mayfly etc.

O

oaf *n* a lout; a stupid clumsy person.

oak *n* a tree with a hard durable wood, having acorns as fruits.

oar *n* a pole with a flat blade for rowing.

oarsman *n* one who rows at the oar.

oasis *n* (*pl* **oases**) a fertile tract in a desert.

oast *n* a kiln to dry hops or malt.

oats *npl* a cereal grass widely cultivated for its edible grain; the seeds.

oath *n* a solemn affirmation.

oatmeal *n* ground oats; porridge or this.

obdurate *adj* unrelenting.

obedience *n* the doing of what is commanded.

obedient *adj* submissive; dutiful; complaint.

obeisance *n* a bow or curtsy; an act of respect.

obese *adj* very stout; corpulent.

obesity *n* excessive fatness.

obey *vt, vi* to do as commanded; to yield to; to comply with.

obfuscate *vt* to darken; to confuse.

obituary *n* an announcement of a person's death, often with a short biography.

object *n* the end aimed at; a purpose; anything present to the senses. * *vt, vi* to oppose; to disapprove.

objection *n* the act of objecting; a ground for; or expression of, disapproval.

objectionable *adj* causing an objection; disagreeable.

objective *adj* not influenced by opinions or feelings; impartial; having an independent existence of it sown, real. * *n* the thing or placed aimed at.

obligation *n* the binding power of a promise, contract or law.

obligatory *adj* binding; compulsory.

oblige *vt* to constrain; to compel; to do or favour; to gratify.

obliging *adj* civil; kind; agreeable.

oblique *adj* slanting; indirect; allusive.

obliterate *vt* to blot out; to destroy.

oblivion *n* the state of forgetting or being utterly forgotten.

oblivious *adj* forgetful; unaware.

oblong *adj* rectangular and longer than broad. * *n* an oblong figure.

obnoxious *adj* odious; unpopular.

oboe *n* a wind instrument of wood with a mouthpiece with a double reed.

obscene *adj* indecent; vile; offensive to a moral standard.

obscure *adj* darkened; dim; abstruse; unimportant; humble. * *vt* to darken; to hide from view; to confuse; to make unclear.

obscurity *n* darkness; dimness; an obscure thing or person.

obsequious *adj* cringing; fawning.

observance *n* the observing of a rule or practice; the performance of rites, etc.

observant *adj* attentive; watchful.

observation *n* the act or faculty of observing; a comment or remark.

observatory *n* a building for astronomical observations.

observe *vt, vi* to take notice of; to remark; to keep religiously; to celebrate.

observer *n* a person who observes; a delegate who attends a formal meeting but may not take part; an expert analyst and commentator in a particular field.

obsess *vt* to possess or haunt the mind of.

obsession *n* the complete capture of the mind by some idea; a persistent preoccupation.

obsolescent *adj* going out of date.

obsolete *adj* antiquated; out of date.

obstacle *n* an obstruction; a hindrance.

obstetrics *n* the branch of medicine concerned with the care and treatment of women during pregnancy and childbirth.

obstinate *adj* stubborn; self-willed.

obstreperous *adj* unruly; disorderly.

obstruct *vt* to block up; to impede; to hinder; to keep light from.

obstructive *adj* causing delay; preventing.

obtain *vt* to acquire; to gain; to earn. * *vi* to prevail; to hold good.

obtrusive *adj* forward; interfering; pushy.

obtuse *adj* blunt; stupid; greater than a right angle.

obvious *adj* plain; evident.

occasion *n* an occurrence; an incident; an opportunity; a cause; a juncture.

occasional *adj* casual; happening now and then; incidental.

occult *adj* hidden; mysterious; belonging to the supernatural arts; mystic.

occupancy *n* tenancy.

occupation *n* possession; tenure; business; vocation; employment.

occupy *vt* to take possession of; to fill; to employ; to engage; to engross.

occur *vi* to happen.

occurrence *n* an event, an incident.

ocean *n* the vast body of water surrounding the land or one of its divisions.

octagon *n* a plane figure having eight angles and sides.

octave *n* in music, the eighth full tone above or below a given tone, the interval of eight degrees between a tone and either of its octaves.

octavo *n* a book with eight leaves to a sheet, abbreviated 8vo.

October *n* the tenth month of the year.

ocular *adj* pertaining to the eye; visual.

oculist *n* one skilled in diseases of the eyes.

odd *adj* eccentric; peculiar; occasional; not divisible by two; extra or left over.

oddity *n* the state of being odd; an odd thing or person; peculiarity.

oddment *n* a remnant esp of fabric.

odds *n, sing, pl* inequality; excess; difference in favour of one; advantage.

ode *n* a lyric poem of exalted tone.

odious *adj* hateful; offensive; disgusting.

odium *n* hatred; dislike; blame.

odorous *adj* fragrant.

odour *n* any scent or smell; reputation.

oesophagus *n* the gullet.

of *prep* denoting source, cause, etc.

off *adv* away; distant; detached; out of condition. * *adj* cancelled; having gone bad (of food). * *prep* away from; not on.

offence *n* injury; insult; displeasure; crime; law; misdemeanour.

offend *vt* to displease; to affront; to shock.

* *vi* to break the law.

offensive *adj* causing offence; disgusting; impertinent; aggressive. * *n* an attack.

offer *vt* to present for acceptance or rejection; to tender; to bid. * *vi* to present itself * *n* a bid; a proposal.

offering *n* a gift; a sacrifice.

offhand *adv* without thinking. * *adj* inconsiderate; curt; brusque.

office *n* duty; public employment; function; service; place of business.

officer *n* the holder of an office; one who has a commission in the army or navy.

official *adj* pertaining to an office properly authorized; formal. * *n* an officer; one holding public office.

officious *adj* fussy; meddling; interfering.

offing *n* the near or foreseeable future.

off-licence *n* a licence to sell alcohol for consumption off the premises.

off-peak *adj* denoting use of a service, etc., in a period of lesser demand.

offset *n* a method of printing in which an image is transferred form a plate to a rubber surface and then to paper.

offshoot *n* a shoot; a sprout.

offshore *adv* at sea some distance from the shore.

offside *adj, adv* illegally in advance of the ball.

offspring *n, sing, pl* children; progeny.

offstage *adj, adv* out of sight of the audience; behind the scenes.

often *adv* frequently; many times.

ogle *vt, vi* to gape at; to look at lustfully.

ohm *n* the unit of electric resistance.

oil *n* a greasy liquid, often inflammable, got from animal, vegetable, and mineral sources.

oilskin *n* waterproof cloth; a garment of this.

oil slick *n* a mass of oil floating on the surface of water.

oil well *n* a well from which petroleum is extracted.

oily *adj* like or covered with oil; greasy; too suave or smooth, unctuous.

ointment *n* a fatty substance for applying to skin for healing or cosmetic purposes.

old *adj* aged; not new or fresh; out of date; former; not modern; worn out.

old-fashioned *adj* out of date.

olfactory *adj* pertaining to sense of smell.

oligarchy *n* rule by a small select body.

olive *n* an evergreen tree; its edible fruit yielding oil; a greenish colour.

olympiad *n* a four-year period, being the term between successive Olympic games.

omega *n* the last letter of Greek alphabet.

omelette, omelet (US) *n* eggs beaten and cooked flat in a pan.

omen *n* a sign of a future event.

ominous *adj* foreboding; ill-omened.

omission *n* a failure to do something; a leaving out of something.

omit *vt* to neglect; to leave out.

omnipotence *n* unlimited power.

omnipotent *adj* all-powerful.

omniscience *n* the faculty of knowing all things; universal knowledge.

omniscient *adj* all-knowing.

omnivorous *adj* all-devouring.

on *prep* in contact with the upper surface of; supported by, attached to, or covering; at the time of; concerning, about; immediately after; using. * *adv* (so as to be) covering or in contact with something; forward; (device) switched on; continuously in progress; due to take place; (actor) on stage; on duty.

once *adv* on the occasion only; formerly; at some time. * *conj* a soon as. * *n* one time.

oncoming *adj* approaching.

one *adj* single; undivided; united; the same; of a certain unspecified time. * *n* the figure I; unity; unit. * *pron.* any single person; any individual; anything.

onerous *adj* burdensome; heavy.

one-sided *adj* partial; unfair.

one-way *adj* requiring no reciprocal action or obligation.

ongoing *adj* progressing, continuing.

onion *n* an edible bulb with a pungent taste and odour.

onlooker *n* a spectator.

only *adj* single; sole. * *adv* for one purpose; merely; just; not more than. * *conj* but; except that.

onomatopoeia *n* forming words by imitation of sounds, as *hiss*.

onrush n a rapid onset.

onset n an attack; an assault; a beginning.

onslaught n a fierce attack.

onus n a burden; a duty; a responsibility.

onward adj advancing.

onwards adv forward; ahead.

ooze n soft mud or slime. * vi to issue gently; to percolate; to seep.

opal n a precious stone, remarkable for its changing colours.

opaque adj not transparent.

open adj not shut; uncovered; accessible; unfenced; treeless; public; candid; clear. * vt, vi to begin; to declare open. * n a sporting competition that any player can enter.

open-hearted adj frank; generous.

opening adj beginning. * n a way in or out; a breach; a vacancy; a chance.

opera n a musical drama.

operate vt, vi to work; to act; to produce an effect; to treat surgically; to control.

operation n action; process; procedure; surgical treatment; military action.

operative adj effective; functioning; in force. * n a workman; factory hand.

operetta n a light musical drama.

ophthalmology n the branch of medicine dealing with the eyes.

opiate n a narcotic drug containing opium.

opinion n a belief; a notion; a judgement; an evaluation; expert advice.

opium n a drug obtained from poppies.

opponent n an adversary.

opportune adj timely; convenient.

opportunist n a person who seizes opportunities for his or her benefit.

opportunity n a fit or convenient time.

oppose vt, vi to act against; to resist; to obstruct; to bar.

opposed adj adverse; hostile.

opposite adj facing; adverse; contrary.

opposition n the act of opposing; contradiction; antagonism; contrast; the party opposing the government.

oppress vt to treat harshly; to subjugate; to weigh down in the mind.

oppression n cruelty; severity; persecution; physical or mental distress.

oppressive adj burdensome; tyrannical; sultry, close of weather.

opt vi to chose or exercise an option.

optical adj of or relating to the eye or light; optic; aiding or correcting vision; visual.

optician n one who makes or sells optical aids.

optics n the science of light and sight.

optimism n the tendency to take the most hopeful and cheerful view.

optimist n a sanguine person.

option n choice; free choice; the right to buy, sell or lease at a fixed price within a specified time.

optional adj voluntary; left to choice.

opulence n wealth; riches; luxury.

or conj denoting; an alternative.

oracle n a very wise person.

oral adj spoken; of the mouth; taken by mouth. * n a spoken examination.

orange n a juicy, a trees fruit; its tree; its colour, reddish-yellow.

oration n a public speech.

oratory n eloquence in public speaking.

orb n a sphere, esp one ornamented and surmounted by a cross as part of royal insignia.

orbit n the path of a planet; the eye socket; the path of an electron around the nucleus of an atom. * vt, vi to put (a satellite) into orbit; to circle round.

orchard n an area planted with fruit trees.

orchestra n a group of musicians playing together under a conductor.

orchestral adj suitable for or performed by an orchestra.

ordain vt to consecrate (for ministry).

ordeal n a severe trial or test.

order n arrangement; method; relative position; sequence; tidiness; rules of procedure; a religious fraternity; an honour of decoration; an instruction or command. * vt, vi to arrange; to command.

orderly adj in good order; well-behaved; methodical. * n a hospital attendant; a soldier attending an officer.

ordinal adj, n a number showing position in a series.

ordinance n a statute; an edict.

ordinary adj regular; usual; normal; commonplace; unexceptional.

ordination n the act of ordaining or being ordained; admission to the ministry.

ore *n* rock substance containing metal.

organ *n* a complex musical wind instrument with pipes, stops, and a keyboard; a part of an animal or plant that performs a vital or natural function.

organic *adj* pertaining to or affecting a bodily organ; of the class of compounds that are formed from carbon; (vegetables etc.) grown without the use of artificial fertilizers or pesticides.

organism *n* anything living; an organized body.

organization *n* suitable arrangements for effective work; system; structure.

organize *vt* to put in working order; to establish; to institute; to arrange for.

orgasm *n* the climax of sexual excitement.

orgy *n* a wild party, with excessive drinking and indiscriminate sexual activity.

orient, orientate *vt, vi* to adjust (one-self) to a particular situation.

oriental *adj* of the Orient.

orifice *n* an opening or mouth of a cavity.

origin *n* a source; a beginning; ancestry or parentage.

original *adj* relating to the origin or beginning; novel; unusual; inventive, creative. * *n* an original work, as of art; something from which copies are made.

originality *n* initiative; freshness and independence of thought.

originate *vt, vi* to bring into being.

ornament *n* decoration. * *vt* to beautify.

ornamental *adj* decorative, not useful.

ornate *adj* richly ornamented; highly.

ornithology *n* the study of birds.

orphan *n, adj* a child without parents.

orphanage *n* an institution for the care of orphans.

orthodox *adj* conforming with established behaviour or opinions; not heretical.

orthopaedics *n* the study and surgical treatment of bone and joint disorders.

oscillate *vi* to swing back and forth as a pendulum.

ossification *n* the formation of bone.

ossify *vt, vi* to change into bone; (of habits etc.) to become rigid and inflexible.

ostensible *adj* apparent; pretended.

ostentation *n* a showing off.

ostentatious *adj* showy; pretentious.

osteopathy *n* the treatment of disease by manipulation of the bones and muscles.

ostracize *vt* to exclude; to banish from society.

other *adj, pron* not the same.

ought *vi* to be bound; to be obliged.

ounce *n* a unit of weight, equal to one sixteenth of a pound or 28.34 grams.

our *adj, pron* pertaining or belonging to us.

ourselves *pron* emphatic and reflexive form of we.

oust *vt* to eject, expel, esp by underhand means; to remove forcibly.

out *adv* not in; outside; in the open air; beyond bounds; ruled out, no longer considered; on strike; at an end; extinguished; into the open; published. * *prep* out of; out through; outside. * *adj* external; outward. * *n* means of escape.

outbid *vt* to bid more than another.

outboard *n* an engine attached to the outside of a boat.

outbreak *n* a sudden eruption of anger, war, disease, etc.

outburst *n* an explosion of anger etc.

outcast *n* a person rejected by society.

outclass *vt* to surpass or excel greatly.

outcome *n* the issue; the result.

outcrop *n* the exposure of strata at the surface.

outcry *n* clamour; protest.

outdistance *vt* to get ahead of.

outdo *vt* to excel; to surpass.

outdoors *adv* in or into the open air.

outer *adj* external.

outer space *n* any region of space beyond the earth's atmosphere.

outfit *n* the equipment used in an activity; clothes worn together, an ensemble.

outfitter *n* a supplier of clothes.

outgoing *adj* departing; sociable, forthcoming. * *n* an outlay; *pl* expenditure.

outgrow *vt* to surpass in growth; to grow too large for (clothes); to change one's ideas, habits etc. as one develops.

outhouse *n* a small building.

outing *n* a short excursion for pleasure.

outlandish *adj* strange; unconventional.

outlaw *vt* to declare illegal. * *n* an outlawed person; a notorious criminal.

outlay *n* expenditure.

outlet *n* an opening.

outline *n* a profile; a draft.

outlive *vt* to live longer than; to outlast.

outlook *n* a view; a prospect; a viewpoint.

outlying *adj* detached; remote, distant.

outmanoeuvre *vt* to surpass in strategy.

outmoded *adj* old-fashioned.

outnumber *vt* to exceed in number.

outpatient *n* a non-resident hospital patient.

outpost *n* a military post or detachment at a distance from a main force.

output *n* the quantity (of goods, etc.) produced, esp over a given period; information delivered by a computer; esp to a printer.

outrage *vt* to injure; to ravish. * *n* a gross offence, injury or insult.

outright *adv* completely; utterly.

outset *n* the beginning.

outside *n* the external surface; the exterior. * *adj* outer; outdoor; slight (of a chance). * *adv* on or to the outside.

outsider *n* a person or thing not included in a set, group, etc., a non-member; a contestant not thought to have a chance in a race.

outsize *adj* of a larger than usual size.

outskirts *npl* districts remote from the centre, as of a city.

outspoken *adj* frank; candid; blunt.

outstanding *adj* excellent; distinguished, prominent; unpaid; unresolved.

outstrip *vt* to outrun; to excel.

outward *adj* directed towards the outside; external.

outweigh *vt* to count for more than, to exceed in value, weight, or importance.

outwit *vt* to defeat by cunning.

oval *adj* egg-shaped.

ovary *n* one of the two female reproductive organs producing eggs.

ovation *n* enthusiastic applause.

oven *n* an enclosed cooking or baking compartment.

over *prep* higher than; on top of; across; to the other side of; above; more than; concerning. * *adv* above; across; in every part; completed; up and down; in addition; too. * *adj* upper; excessive; surplus; finished; remaining.

overact *vt, vi* to act in an exaggerated manner, to overdo a part.

overall *adj* including everything. * *adv* as a whole; generally. * *n* a loose protective garment.

overawe *vt* to restrain by awe; to daunt.

overbalance *vt* to lose balance and fall.

overbearing *adj* haughty; domineering.

overboard *adv* over the side of a ship; to extremes of enthusiasm.

overburden *vt* to overload; to oppress.

overcast *adj* clouded over.

overcharge *vt* to charge too much; of battery, to overload; to fill to excess.

overcoat *n* a warm topcoat.

overcome *vt* to subdue; to conquer; to get the better of; to render helpless or powerless, as by tears, laughter etc.

overdo *vt* to do to excess; to overcook.

overdose *n* too great a dose.

overdraft *n* an overdrawing, an amount overdrawn, at a bank.

overdue *adj* past the time fixed or due.

overestimate *vt* to set too high an estimate on or for.

overflow *vt, vi* to flood; to abound (with emotion etc.). * *n* surplus; excess; an outlet for surplus water etc.

overflowing *adj* abundant, copious.

overgrown *adj* grown beyond the normal size; rank; ungainly.

overhang *vt, vi* to project over.

overhaul *vt* to examine thoroughly with a view to repairs; to overtake.

overhead *adj, adv* above the head; in the sky. * *n* (often *pl*) the continuing costs of a business, as of rent, light, etc.

overhear *vt* to hear by accident.

overjoyed *adj* highly delighted.

overland *adj, adv* by on or across land.

overlap *vt* (*pt* **overlapped**) to extend over so as to coincide in part.

overlay *vt* to coat; to smother.

overload *vt* to overburden.

overlook *vt* to superintend; to pardon; to fail to notice.

overnight *adv* for, through or during the night.

overpass *n* a road crossing another road, path, etc., at a higher level.

overpower vt to overcome; to subdue.

overpowering adj overwhelming.

overrate vt to rate or assess too highly.

overreach vt to fail by attempting too much or going too far.

override vt to nullify; to prevail.

overrule vt prevail over.

overrun vt to ravage; to outrun, to swarm over. * vi to overflow.

overseas adj, adv across or beyond the sea; abroad.

overseer n an inspector; a superintendent.

overshadow vt to throw a shadow over; to cast into the shade; to outdo.

overshoot vt (pt **overshoot**) to shoot or send beyond (a target, etc.); (aircraft) to fly or taxi beyond the end of a runway when landing or taking off.

oversight n a mistake; an omission.

oversleep vi (pt **overslept**) to sleep beyond the intended time.

overstate vt to exaggerate.

overstep vt to exceed.

overt adj public; openly done; unconcealed; deliberate.

overtake vt to come up with and pass; to catch.

overtax vt to overstrain oneself.

overthrow vt to overturn; to defeat. * n ruin; defeat.

overtime n time beyond the regular hours; (payment for) extra time work.

overtone n an additional subtle meaning; an implicit quality; (music) an instrumental introduction to an opera, etc.

overture n a proposal; an offer; a musical introduction to an opera, etc.

overturn vt to capsize; to overthrow.

overweight adj weighing more than the proper amount. * n excess weight.

overwhelm vt to submerge; to overpower.

overwhelming adj irresistible; uncontrollable; vast; vastly superior; extreme.

overwork vt to work beyond one's strength or too long.

overwrought adj overexcited.

owe vt to be indebted to; to feel the need to do or give out of gratitude.

own adj belonging to oneself or itself. * vt to possess by right; to avow; to concede.

owner n one who owns or possesses, a proprietor.

oxide n a compound of oxygen with another element.

oxtail n the tail of an ox, esp skinned and used for stews, soups, etc.

oxygen n a colourless, odourless, tasteless, highly reactive gaseous element forming part of air, water, etc., and essential to life and combustion.

oxygen mask n an apparatus worn over the nose and mouth through which oxygen passes from a storage tank.

oxygen tent n a canopy over a hospital bed, etc., within which a supply of oxygen is maintained.

ozone n a condensed form of oxygen.

ozone layer n a layer of ozone in the upper atmosphere that absorbs ultraviolet rays from the sun.

P

pace n the measure of a single stride; gait; rate of progress. * vi to step; to walk slowly. * vt to walk up and down; to determine the pace in a race.

pacific adj peaceable; calm.

pacify vt to calm; to allay; to restore peace to.

pack n a set of cards; a set of hounds; a gang. * vt to make up into a bundle; to fill; to stuff; to crowd; to dismiss. * vi to form into a hard mass, to assemble.

package n a parcel; a wrapped bundle.

packet n a small box.

packet n a small parcel; a mailboat.

pack ice n ice masses packed together.

packing n wrapping material; stuffing.

pact n a contract; an agreement.

pad n a peice of stuffing, esp absorbant material; block of writing paper.

padding n anything added to achieve length or amount, esp in a book.

paddle vi to wade in shallow water; to row. * vt to propel by an oar or paddle. * n a broad short oar.

paddock n a grassy enclosure for horses.

paddy n threshed, unmilled rice; a rice field.

padlock n a detachable lock. * vt to secure with a padlock.

pagan n a person who has no religion.

page n an attendant at a formal function; a sheet of paper in a book, newspaper.

pageant n a spectacular procession, etc.

pageantry n a spectacular display.

pagoda n an Eastern temple.

pail n a bucket.

pain n bodily suffering; distress; ; labour; effort. * vt to cause pain to.

painstaking adj laborious and careful.

paint vt to coat with colour; to portray. * vi to make a picture. * n a pigment.

painter n one whose occupation is to paint; an artist in colour; a rope for fastening a small boat.

painting n the act or art of painting.

pair n two things of like kind; a couple; a man and his wife. * vi to join in pairs.

palace n a royal residence.

palaeography n the art of deciphering ancient writing.

palaeontology n the science of fossil organic remains.

palatable adj having a pleasant taste; pleasant and acceptable.

palate n the roof of the mouth; taste.

palatial adj spacious; magnificent.

pale n a pointed stake; a boundary. * vi to grow pale. * adj light in colour.

palette n an artist's mixing board.

paling n a fence formed with stakes.

pall n a mantle, as of smoke; covering on a coffin. * vi to shroud.

pallet n a portable platform used in bulk storage.

palliate vt to alleviate; to excuse.

palliative adj mitigating. * n something that eases pain, sorrow, etc.

pallid adj pale; wan.

pallor n paleness.

palm n the underside of hand; a tropical tree; symbol of victory.

palmistry n fortune-telling by lines on the hand.

palpable adj perceptible by the touch; plain; obvious.

palpitate vi to throb; to tremble.

palpitation n violent pulsation of the heart.

paltry adj mean; trifling.

pamper vt to indulge to excess; to spoil.

pamphlet n a small unbound book.

pan n a broad shallow vessel for cooking, the bowl of a lavatory.

panacea n a remedy for all ills.

panache n stylish behaviour.

pancake n a thin cake of cooked batter.

pancreas n a fleshy gland secreting digestive juice.

pandemonium n chaos; scene of disorder and noise.

pander vi to gratify or exploit the weaknesses of others.

pane n a plate of glass in a window.

panegyric n a eulogy.

panel n a rectangular section of door, ceiling, etc; a group of selected persons; a board for instruments or controls.

pang n a sudden pain or feeling.

panic n a sudden blind fear.

panoply n splendid display.

panorama n a complete view.

pant vi to gasp; to long for.

pantomime n a Christmas theatrical show.

pantry n a small cupboard for provisions.

papacy n the office of the pope.

paper n thin sheets used for writing, printing, etc, a newspaper; an essay. * adj made of paper. * vt to cover with paper.

papyrus n (pl **papyri**) reed from which the ancients made paper.

par n state of equality; original, normal, or face value of shares.

parable n a religious allegory; a story with a moral lesson.

parachute n a fabic canopy used to retard speed of fall from an aircraft.

parade n display; show, muster; a promenade. * vt, vi to show off; to marshal; to walk up and down.

paradise n the garden of Eden; heaven; supreme bliss.

paradox n something containing seeming contradictory qualities or phrases.

paraffin n a distilled oil used as fuel.

paragon n a model of excellence.

paragraph n a subdivision in a piece of writing, marked by a new line.

parallax n the apparent change of position of object when viewed from different points.

parallel adj equidistant at all points; corresponding. * n a circle of latitude.

parallelogram n a quadrilateral, whose opposite sides are parallel and of equal length.

paralyse vt to affect with paralysis; to render helpless.

paralysis n the loss of sensation and movement in any part of the body.

parapet n a wall breast-high.

paraphernalia npl belongings; trappings.

paraphrase n an interpretation of a passage of the sake of clarity. * vt to interpret.

parasite n a hanger-on; a plant or animal that lives on another.

parasol n a sun shade.

parboil vt to boil partly.

parcel n a small bundle or packet. * vt to divide into portions.

parch vt to become hot, dry or thirsty; to scorch.

parchment n a skin prepared for writing on.

pardon vt to forgive; to excuse. * n forgiveness; remission of penalty.

pardonable adj excusable.

pare vt to trim by cutting; to peel.

parent n a father or mother; a progenitor; a source.

parentage n extraction; birth.

parenthesis n (pl **parentheses**) a written explanatory 'aside', usually in brackets thus ().

pariah n an outcast.

parish n a district served by one clergyman. * adj parochial.

parity n equality; a likeness.

park n a recreation field; a glebe; a grass field; artillery and ground occupied by it; a stance for motors. * vt to enclose; to store.

parlance n conversation; talk.

parley vi to confer, to discuss. * n conference, esp with an enemy during cessation of hostilities.

parliament n a legislative assembly made up of representatives of a nation.

parlour n a sitting room.

parochial adj provincial in outlook; narrow-minded.

parody n a humorous imitation of a literary or musical work or style.

parole n word of honour; conditional release of a prisoner.

paroxysm n a fit (of rage, grief, etc).

parquet n wood flooring.

parse vt to tell the parts of speech and their relations in a sentence.

parsimonious adj miserly.

parsimony n excessive economy; stinginess.

parson n a parish minister; a clergyman.

part n a portion; a section; a share; a role. pl ability; a region. * vi to divide; share; break; separate; depart.

partake vi, vt to get a share of; to have or take a share in a meal.

partial adj only; incomplete; biased.

participate vi, vt to share in.

participle n a word partly verb and partly adjective.

particle n an atom; a word that cannot be used alone; a prefix; a suffix.

particular adj single; special; careful; fastidious. * n a detail; a single item.

parting adj separating; final. * n departure; a division; a shed of the hair.

partisan adj biased; one-sided.

partition n division; a dividing wall or screen. * vt to divide up.

partner n a sharer in business, etc; either of a couple, married or unmarried.

partnership n fellowship; joint interest; the state of being a partner.

party n a company; faction; a social entertainment; a side; a political group.

pass vi to go past; to change; to die; to elapse; to be enacted; to succeed at examination; to cross; to utter; to become law. * n an approval; passport; an uninvited sexual approach.

passable adj allowable; fairly good.

passage n a way through; transit; road; channel; journey; part of book.

passenger n a traveller in a conveyance.

passing adj current; fleeting.

passion n strong feeling; great suffering; anger; love.

passionate adj moved by passion; hasty.

passive adj submissive; inert; acted on.

passport n a licence to travel abroad; ticket of admission or acceptance.

password n a secret word which gives ready entrance.

past adj gone by; spent; ended. * n former time. * prep. beyond. * adv by.

paste n a plastic mass of varied materials.

pastel n a crayon drawing.

pasteurize vt to inoculate; to sterilize (milk, etc).

pastime n recreation; play.

pastor n a minister of a church.

pastoral adj rustic; rural; relating to a pastor. * n a poem of rural life.

pastry n crust of pies, tarts, etc.

pasture n grass for cattle; grass land. * vi to graze.

pasty adj like paste; pallid apperance.

pat n a tap; a small lump. * vt to tap. * adj apt; glib.

patch n a repair piece; a small piece of ground. * vt to mend.

patchwork n something made of various bits, esp in needlework.

patella n the kneecap.

patent n grant of sole right to make or sell patented article. * adj open; obvious; secured by patent. * vt to obtain patent for.

paternal adj fatherly; hereditary.

paternity n fatherhood; origin; descent.

path n a footway; a track; a course; a direction.

pathetic adj inspiring pity.

pathologist n a medical specialist in pathology.

pathology n the study of diseases.

pathos n expression or exciting deep feeling of pity.

patience n endurance; composure under trial; a card game.

patient adj uncomplaining; calm * an invalid.

patriarch n the chief of a tribe or family.

patrician adj high born; aristocratic. * n a nobleman.

patriot n a lover of his country.

patriotism n love of country.

patrol n a unit of persons, esp employed for security; their going of the rounds. * vti to go the rounds, inspect, etc.

patron n one who encourages, helps, or protects.

patronage n support; conferring of favours or benefits.

patronize vt to act as patron of; to favour; to treat with condescension.

patter vi to make a sound like that of rain or hail, or feet; to mumble; n chatter.

pattern n a model; a design.

paucity n fewness; poverty.

paunch n the belly; esp of a potbelly.

pauper n a very poor person.

pause n a temporary stop; suspense. * vi to stop; hesitate.

pave vt to make a smooth roadway with blocks, flags, etc.

pavement n paved path for walkers.

pavilion n a large tent; a clubhouse; temporary building for exhibitions.

paw n the foot of animals with claws. * vt to scrape with the forefoot.

pawn n a security; pledge; piece of least value (chess). * vt to give in pledge.

pawnbroker n a person licensed to lend money on pledged goods.

pay vt, vi to give money for goods, service, etc; to reward; to bestow (attention, etc). * n wages; salary; reward.

payable adj due on a certain date.

payee n one to whom money is to be paid.

payment n act of paying; what is paid.

peace n quiet; calm; freedom from war or disorder; a treaty ending a war.

peaceable adj disposed to peace.

peaceful adj quiet; calm; mild.

peacemaker n one who restores good feeling; a reconciler.

peak n pointed top of hill; projection on cap; highest point.

peal n a loud clash; a clang; chime; loud laughter. * vi to ring out.

pearl n a lustrous gem found in oyster.

peasant n a rural labourer.

peasantry n peasants; country people.

peat n partly carbonized turf used as fuel.

pebble n small water-worn stone.

peccable adj liable to sin.

peccadillo n a petty fault or sin.

peck n a quick kiss. * vi, vt to strike or pick up with the beak.

peckish adj hungry.

pectoral *adj* pertaining to the breast.

peculiar *adj* one's own; particular; special; odd.

peculiarity *n* a characteristic; an oddity.

pecuniary *adj* financial; relating to money.

pedal *adj* pertaining to a foot. * *n* foot lever in cycle, etc. * *vt, vi* to work a pedal; to cycle.

pedant *n* one who parades his knowledge esp of insignificant details.

pedantry *n* a vain display of learning.

peddle *vi, vt* to sell small items from place to place.

pedestal *n* the base of a column, etc.

pedestrian *adj* going on foot; commonplace. * *n* a person who walks.

pedigree *n* lineage; ancestry.

pedlar *n* one who sells small goods from place to place.

peel *vt* to strip off skin, esp of fruit; to bare. * *vi* to lose the skin, bark, or rind. * *n* the skin or rind.

peep *vi* to chirp; to begin to appear; to look through a slit. * *n* a furtive or hurried glance.

peer *n* an equal; a nobleman. * *vi* to peep out; to look closely or with difficulty.

peerage *n* the rank or title of a peer.

peerless *adj* matchless.

peevish *adj* fretful; querulous.

peg *n* a wooden nail, pin, or bolt.

pellet *n* a little ball; a pill; small shot.

pelt *n* a raw hide; a blow. * *vti* to assault (with stones, etc); to fall heavily (as rain); to hurry; to rush.

pelvis *n* the bony framework which joins the lower limbs to the body.

pen *n* an instrument for writing, drawing, etc; enclosure for livestock. * *vt* to write; to coop up.

penal *adj* involving punishment.

penalty *n* due punishment; a fine.

penance *n* punishment imposed for sin.

pence *n* plural of penny.

penchant *n* bias; liking.

pencil *n* an instument for drawing; a fine paintbrush.

pendant *n* a hanging ornament.

pendent *adj* hanging; pendulous.

pending *p.a* in suspense. * *prep* during.

pendulous *adj* hanging; swinging.

pendulum *n* a weight suspended and swinging (as in clock).

penetrate *vti* to enter or pierce; to discern.

penetrating *adj* sharp; discerning.

peninsula *n* land almost surrounded by water.

penitence *n* repentance; sorrow.

penitent *adj* repentant; contrite.

pennant *n* a long pointed flag at masthead.

penny *n* (*pl* **pennies** or **pence**: pennies denotes the number of coins; pence the value) a low value coin .

pension *n* a periodic payment for past services or old age; a boarding house.

pensioner *n* one in receipt of a pension.

pensive *adj* thoughtful; grave.

pentagon *n* a plane figure having five sides.

pentameter *n* a verse of five feet.

penthouse *n* a top floor apartment.

penultimate *adj* the last but one.

penury *n* poverty; want.

people *n* human beings; a nation; a race; a person's family. *pl* persons; the masses. * *vt* to populate.

pepper *n* a seasoning; fruit of the pepper plant.

peptic *adj* promoting digestion.

perambulate *vt* to walk up and down.

perceive *vt* to apprehend; understand.

percentage *n* the duty, rate, etc, on each hundred.

perceptible *adj* discernible.

perch *n* a freshwater fish; a roost for fowls; an elevated position.

percolate *vt* to filter through.

percolator *n* a strainer or filter.

percussion *n* collision; impact; sounding (medical); musical instruments usu played with sticks or hammers.

perdition *n* entire ruin; eternal death.

peremptory *adj* urgent; insistent; dictatorial.

perennial *adj* lasting through the year; never-ending.

perfect *adj* finished; complete; faultless. * *vt* to make perfect.

perfection *n* great excellence; flawlessness.

perfidious adj treacherous.

perfidy n treachery.

perforate vt to bore through; to pierce.

perform vt to accomplish; to do. * vi to act a part; to play a musical instrument.

performance n achievement; deed; entertainment (musical, etc).

performer n an actor, musician, etc.

perfume n a pleasant scent; fragrance. * vt to scent.

perfunctory adj careless; half-hearted; indifferent.

perhaps adv it may be; possibly.

peril n risk; danger.

perimeter n the total measurement round any figure; a boundary around.

period n a portion of time; an age; full stop (.); menstruation; a stage in life.

periodic adj regular.

periodical n a publication issued weekly, monthly, etc.

periphery n the boundary line of a figure.

periscope n an instrument by which observer in trench or submarine can see objects on surface.

perish vi to die; to decay.

perjure vt to bear false witness; to commit perjury.

perjury n false evidence on oath.

permanence n duration; fixedness.

permanent adj lasting; abiding.

permeable adj allowing the passage of fluid, gases, etc.

permeate vt to pass through the pores; to pervade.

permissible adj allowable.

permission n leave; consent.

permissive adj allowing but not compelling.

permit vt , i.to allow; to grant; to concede. * n permit. a written permission.

permutation n interchange; in mathematics, all the possible variations of a series.

pernicious adj injurious; deadly; noxious.

perpend vt to consider; to ponder.

perpendicular adj upright; at right angles. * n a line at right angles to another.

perpetrate vt to commit.

perpetration n commission.

perpetual adj unending; eternal.

perpetuate vt to make lasting.

perpetuity n endless duration; an annuity payable forever.

perplex vt to confuse; to puzzle.

perplexity n bewilderment.

perquisite n a reward or benefit, other than salary, attaching to an office; a gratuity.

persecute vt to harass with unjust punishment; to ill-treat; to oppress, esp minority group, race, etc.

persevere vi to pursue steadily any design.

persevering adj constant in purpose.

persist vi to persevere; stand firm.

persistence, persistency n steadfastness; obstinacy.

persistent adj persisting; steady.

person n a human being; the body; a verb inflexion.

personal adj individual; private; one's own; unkind (remarks).

personality n one's individual characteristics; a celebrity; a person with distinct qualities.

personification n embodiment; a metaphor ascribing life to inanimate objects.

personify vt to embody; to endow with human qualities.

personnel n the staff.

perspective n the art of representing objects on a flat surface as they are to the eye; objectivity.

perspicacity n acuteness of mind.

perspicuity n clearness; lucidity.

perspiration n sweat.

perspire vi to sweat.

persuade vt to influence by argument, etc; to induce.

persuasive adj convincing; winning.

pert adj lively; saucy; forward.

pertain vi to belong; to concern.

pertinent adj to the point.

perturb vt to disturb; to disquiet.

perturbation n uneasiness; disquiet.

perusal n reading; study.

peruse vt to read through; to examine carefully.

pervade vt to permeate; to spread throughout.

perverse adj obstinate in being wrong; stubborn; contrary.

perversion n corruption; misuse; an abnormal way of obtaining sexual satisfaction.

perversity n obstinacy; wickedness; a perverse act.

pervert vt to corrupt; to misapply. * n a person who is sexually perverted.

pervious adj penetrable.

pessimism n tendency to make or expect the worst of everything.

pessimist n one who takes a gloomy view of life.

pest n a plague; a nuisance.

pestilence n a deadly epidemic.

pestilential adj destructive; hurtful.

pestle n an instrument for grinding material.

pet n a darling; a favourite; a domestic animal kept as a companion. * adj cherished. * vt to fondle.

petal n a flower leaf.

petite adj tiny; dainty.

petition n an entreaty; a written demand for government action etc. signed by many. * vt to ask humbly for; to present a petition.

petrify vt to turn into stone; to paralyse or stupefy with terror.

petrol n refined petroleum.

petroleum n natural mineral oil.

petrology n the study of rocks.

petty adj small; trivial; small minded.

petulance n peevishness; ill-humour.

petulant adj irritable; fretful.

pew n a seat in a church.

pewter n an alloy of tin and lead.

phantom n an apparition; a spectre.

pharmaceutic, pharmaceutical adj pertaining to the dispensing of drugs.

pharmacy n the preparation and dispensing of drugs; a drug store.

phase n a stage; an aspect; apparent shape (moon).

phenomenal adj astounding.

phenomenon n (pl **phenomena**) an appearance; anything visible; a remarkable thing or person.

phial n a small glass bottle.

philander vi to flirt.

philanthropic, philanthropical adj benevolent.

philanthropy n the love of mankind; benevolence; charitable actions.

philatelist n a collector of postage stamps.

philately n stamp collecting.

philologist n one versed in philology.

philology n the study of language, linguistic science.

philosopher n a person who studies philosophy.

philosophically adv calmly; wisely; serenely.

philosophy n the science of mind, conduct, and phenomena; a particular system of ethics.

phlegm n the secretion of the mucous membrane discharged in coughing, etc; lack of emotion.

phlegmatic adj sluggish; unemotional.

phoenix n a fabled bird, said to burn itself and rise again from its own ashes; emblem of immortality.

phone n contraction for telephone.

phonetic adj pertaining to vocal sound.

phonetics npl the science of sounds of human voice and their representation.

phonograph n an instrument for reproducing sounds.

phosphate n a salt of phosphoric acid.

phosphorescence n emission of light without heat as from fish in the dark.

phosphorescent adj luminous.

phosphorus n a nonmetallic element, luminous in dark.

photograph n a picture obtained by photography. * vt to take or produce a photograph.

photography n the art of recording images permanently and visibly by action of light on prepared plates.

phrase n a related group of words; diction; style.

phrenetic adj frantic.

phrenology n theory that intelligence is related to shape of skull.

phylloxera n an insect which attacks vines.

physical adj relating to matter and energy, the human body, or natural science. *n a general medical examination.

physician n a doctor of medicine.

physicist n a specialist in physics.

physics n the science of matter in relation to force.

physiognomy n reading character from study of facial expression.

physiology n the science of bodily structures, organs, and functions.

physique n physical frame.

pianist n a performer on the piano.

piano n a large stringed keyboard instrument.

piazza n a square surrounded by colonnades.

pica n a standard printing type, equal to twelve points.

picaresque adj describing the fortunes of adventurers.

piccolo n a small flute.

pick vti to strike with something sharp; to pick at; to pluck; to choose; to nibble. * n an excavating axe; choice.

pickaxe n a pick.

picket n a pointed stake; a military guard; a preventive guard against strikebreakers. * vt to post (soldiers, etc); to tether.

pickle n brine; vegetables preserved in vinegar; plight. * vt to preserve in pickle.

picnic n an informal meal taken on an outing and eaten outdoors.

pictorial adj illustrated by pictures.

picture n a painting, drawing, likeness, etc; mental image; vivid description; motion picture * vt to portray.

picturesque adj striking, vivid, usually pleasing.

pie n meat or fruit with paste covering baked; unsorted type.

piece n a portion; a distinct part; a short composition or writing; a picture; a coin.

piecemeal adv in or by pieces.

piecework n work paid by quantity, not by time.

pied adj of various colours.

pier n stone column supporting arch, etc; a wharf or landing stage.

pierce vt to thrust through; to perforate.

piercing adj penetrating; cutting.

pierrot n a humorous entertainer in clown-like dress.

piety n religious devoutness.

pig n a hog; a bar of smelted iron.

pigeon n a bird with a small head and a large body.

pigeonhole n a compartment in a desk for papers.

pig-headed adj stupidly obstinate.

pigment n colouring matter.

pigtail n a plait of hair hanging down back.

pile n a heap; a large amount; a massive building; a supporting pillar driven into the ground. * vt to heap.

piles npl a swelling of the rectum veins.

pilfer vi to steal on a small scale.

pilgrim n a person who makes a pilgrimage.

pilgrimage n a journey, esp to a holy place.

pill n a medicine in a tablet form; an oral contraceptive.

pillage n plunder; spoil. * vt to plunder.

pillar n a supporting column.

pillion n a cushion on back of saddle for second rider.

pillory n the stocks or frame once used for punishment of offenders. * vt to expose to ridicule.

pillow n a cushion for the head while sleeping; something which supports and distributes pressure.

pilot n a person who operates a ship or an aircraft; a guide. * vt to direct the course of; to act as a pilot; to guide.

pimp n a prostitute's agent.

pimple n a small red swelling on skin.

pin n a short pointed piece of metal for fastening clothes; a peg; a bolt. * vt to fasten.

pinafore n a sleeveless garment worn over a dress, blouse, etc..

pincers npl nippers; gripping claws.

pinch vt to cramp; to be sparing. * n a nip; distress; need; small portion.

pine n a coniferous tree. * vi to languish.

pinfold n a pen; enclosure for cattle.

pinion n the outer joint of a bird's wing. * vt to restrain; to bind arms to sides.

pink n a garden flower; a pale red colour; excellence. * vt to stab.

pinnace n a boat with oars and sails.

pinnacle n a turret; pointed peak; the highest point; climax.

pint n a liquid measure equal to one eighth of a gallon.

pioneer n a person who initiates or explores new areas of enterprise, research, etc; an explorer; an ealy settler. * vt ti initiate; to explore; to act as a pioneer.

pious adj devout; religious; sanctimonious.

pip n the seed of a fleshy fruit; spot on cards, dice, etc.

pipe n a musical instrument; long tube conveying gas, water, etc; shrill voice; tobacco-smoking apparatus. * vt (musical) to play on a pipe.

piping adj giving out a whistling sound. * n sound of pipes; system of pipes.

piquant adj sharp; pungent.

pique n irritation; resentment. * vti to cause resentment in; to offend.

piracy n a person who commits robbery at sea; infringement of copyright.

pirate n a sea robber; an infringer of copyright.

pirouette n spinning round on toe in ballet.

piscatorial adj of or relating to fish or fishing.

Pisces npl the Fishes, a sign in the zodiac.

pistil n the seed-bearing organ of a flower.

pistol n a small firearm fired with one hand.

piston n a metal plug which slides to and fro in the hollow cylinder of an engine, pump, etc.

pit n a hollow in the earth; shaft of a mine; a depression in skin; orchestra space in a theatre. * vt to mark with little hollows; to set in competition.

pitch vt to fix in ground; to set; to throw; to set the keynote of; to set in array. * vi to fall headlong; to encamp; to rise and fall, as a ship. * n a throw; highest rise; elevation of a note; a thick dark substance obtained from tar.

pitcher n a vessel for carrying liquids.

pitchfork n a fork for pitching hay.

piteous adj arousing pity.

pitfall n concealed danger; a trap.

pith n the soft centre of stem of plant; marrow; essence.

pitiable adj deserving pity.

pittance n a small quantity or allowance of money.

pity n sympathy or compassion. * vt to grieve for.

pivot n that on which something turns or depends.

placard n a poster or notice for public display.

placate vt to appease.

place n an open space in a town; a locality; position; room; passage in book; rank; office. * vt to put or set; to locate.

placid adj calm; tranquil.

plagiarism n the stealing words or ideas of another.

plague n a deadly epidemic; pestilence; nuisance.

plaid n a large woollen shawl-like wrap; cloth with tartan or checkered pattern.

plain adj smooth; level; clear; simple; evident; unflavoured. * n a tract of level land.

plaint n a lamentation; formal statement of grievance.

plaintiff n a person who brings a lawsuit against another.

plaintive adj mournful.

plait n a fold; a braid, as of hair, etc. * vt to fold; to braid.

plan n the ground shape of an object; scheme; process; method. * vt to scheme; to design.

plane adj level; flat. * n smooth surface; joiner's smoothing tool; an aeroplane. * vt to make smooth.

planet n a celestial body moving round sun or other star.

planetary adj under the influence of one of the planets; wandering.

plank n a flat broad piece of timber.

plant n a vegetable organism; an herb; a shoot; industrial machinery and equipment. * vt to set in ground; to implant; to establish.

plantation n a cultivated planting of trees; a tropical estate.

plaque n an ornamental plate; a film of mucus on the teeth that harbours bacteria.

plasma n the colourless liquid part of blood, milk or lymph.

plaster n a cement for covering walls; a preparation for casts, etc; adhesive dressing for wounds or relief of pain.

plastic adj easily shaped or moulded; any of various non-metallic compounds, syntheticaly produced.

plasticine n a modelling clay.

plate n a flat piece of metal, glass, etc; a shallow dish for meals. * vt to coat with gold, etc.

plateau n a flat, elevated piece of land; a stable period.

platform n a raised structure for speaking from, entering trains, etc; a statement of political policy.

plating n the art of covering articles with metal.

platinum n a heavy metal very difficult to fuse.

platitude n a dull truism; a commonplace remark.

platonic adj free from physical desire.

platoon n a military unit divided into squads or sections.

platter n a large, oval serving dish.

plaudit n a commendation (usu pl).

plausibility n quality of being plausible; speciousness.

plausible adj apparently truthful or reasonable.

play vi, vt to sport; frolic; gamble; act; engage in games; perform upon. * n free movement; a game; sport; gaming; a drama.

player n an actor; musician; sportsman, sportswoman.

playful adj full of fun, humorous, sportive.

playhouse n a theatre; a small house for children to play in.

playschool n a nursery for pre-school children.

plaything n a toy; a thing or person treated as a toy.

playwright n a writer of plays.

plea n an answer to a charge; an entreaty; a request.

plead vi, vt to argue for or against; to answer to a charge; to urge; to beg earnestly; to urge in excuse.

pleading n statement of facts for or against a claim.

pleasance n pleasure; a shady grove.

pleasant adj pleasing; agreeable.

pleasantry n a polite or amusing remark.

please vti to satisfy; to give pleasure to; to be willing. * adv a word to express politeness or emphasis in a request; an expression of polite affirmation.

pleasing adj agreeable; giving pleasure.

pleasure n enjoyment; recreation; preference.

plebian adj, n relating to the common people; base; vulgar.

plebiscite n a vote of the whole electorate on a political issue.

plectrum n a thin piece of metal, etc for plucking strings of guitar, etc.

pledge n something given in security; a surety; a toast. * vt to pawn; to toast; to bind by solemn promise.

plenary adj full; complete; attended by all members.

plenitude n fullness; abundance.

plentiful adj ample; abundant.

plenty n abundance; more than enough. * adj plentiful.

plethora n overabundance; a glut; (med) an excess of red corpuscles in the blood.

pleura n (pl pleurae) membrane enveloping the lungs.

pleurisy n an inflammation of the pleura.

pliable adj supple; easily persuaded; pliant.

pliant adj pliable; flexible.

pliers npl a hand tool for cutting, shaping wire.

plight vt to pledge (word, honour, etc). * n a pledge; predicament.

plinth n square slab forming base of column.

plod vi to work or walk laboriously.

plot n a small piece of ground; a plan; a conspiracy; the story of a play, novel, etc. * vt to devise; to conspire; to mark on a map.

plough, plow n an implement for turning up the soil. * vt, vi to furrow; to work at laboriously.

pluck vt to pick or gather; to snatch; to strip off feathers. * n courage or spirit.

plug n a stopper used for filling a hole; a

device for connecting an appliance to an electrical supply; a cake of tobacco. * *vt* to stop with a plug.

plumage *n* the feathers of a bird.

plumb *n* a lead weight attached to a line used to determine depth or true vertical. * *adj* true vertical * *adv* vertically. * *vt* to supply or install as plumbing; to test with a plumb line.

plumber *n* a person who installs and repairs water or gas pipes.

plumbing *n* the system of pipes used in water or gas supply, or drainage.

plume *n* a bird's feather; an ornament of feathers in hat, etc. * *vt* to preen.

plummet *n* a plumb. * *vt* to fall in a perpendicular manner; to drop abruptly.

plump *adj* rounded; chubby * *vti* to make plump; to favour or give support. * *adv* staight down, straight ahead; suddenly.

plunder *vt* to stel goods by force; to loot. * *n* plundering; booty.

plunge *vt* to thrust into water; to immerse; to penetrate quickly. * *vi* to dive into water, etc; to rush into. * *n* a dive.

plunger *n* a large rubber suction cup used to free clogged drains.

plural *adj* denoting more than one. * *n* (*gram*) the form referring to more than one person or thing.

plurality *n* a majority; being plural; a large number.

plus *prep* added to; in addition to. **n* the sign (+) of addition.

plush *n* a velvety fabric; * *adj* (*inf*) luxurious.

plutocracy *n* the power or rule of wealth.

ply *vti* to work at; to wield skilfully; to press hard; to voyage or journey regularly; (goods)to sell. * *n* a layer or thickness

pneumatic *adj* concerning wind, air or gas; operated by or filled with compressed air.

pneumonia *n* an acute inflammation of the lungs.

poach *vt* to cook (eggs) by breaking into boiling water. * *vi* take game illegally; to trespass; to encroach upon.

pocket *n* a small pouch in a garment, etc; a deposit, as of gas, minerals, etc; an iso-

lated or closed area. * *vt* to put in one's pocket; to take dishonestly.

pod *n* the seed vessel of plants; a detachable compartment on a spacecraft; a protective container.

poem *n* an imaginative arrangement of words, esp in meter, often ryhmed.

poet *n* the author of a poem.

poetry *n* the art of writing poems; poems collectively; poetic spirt or quality.

pogrom *n* an organized extermination of a minority group.

poignant *adj* incisive; deeply moving.

point *n* the sharp end of anything; a headland; a dot; a moment in time; exact spot; purpose; a place in a cycle, scale or course; essence; feature; railway switch; a unit in printing equal to one seventy-second of an inch * *vti* to indicate; to sharpen; to aim.

point-blank *adj* aimed straight at a mark; direct, blunt.

pointed *adj* sharp; personal.

pointer *n* an indicator; a rod for pointing with; a dog trained to point out game.

poise *n* a balanced state; bearing; carriage * *vt* to balance; to put into readiness; * *vi* to hover.

poison *n* a substance which when absorbed is fatal or injurious to an organism; any corrupt influence. * *vt* to give poison to; to taint; to corrupt.

poke *n* a bag or sack; a prod or nudge. * *vt* to prod; to hit. * *vi* to pry or search (about or around)..

poker *n* an iron rod for poking a fire; a card game.

polar *adj* of or near the North or South pole; of a pole; having positive and negative electricity; directly opposite.

polarity *n* the condition of being polar; the magnet's property of pointing north; diametrical opposition.

pole *n* a long slender piece of wood, metal, etc; either end of an axis, esp of the earth; either of two opposed forces, parts, etc, as the ends of a magnet.

polemic *n* a controversy or argument over doctrine; strong criticism. * *adj* involving dispute, controversial.

pole star *n* a star near North Pole; a lodestar.

police n the government department for maintaining public order, detecting crime, law enforcement, etc. *vt to control, protect, etc with police or similar body.

policy n system or manner of government; principle or course of action; an insurance contract.

polish vti to make smooth and glossy; to refine. * n gloss; elegance.

polite adj polished in manners; refined; elegant.

politic adj prudent; astute.

political adj relating to politics or govenment.

politician n a person engaged in politics.

politics n the science and art of government; political activities; factional scheming for power.

polka n a lively dance.

poll n a counting, listing, etc of persons; the number of votes recorded; an opinion survey. * vt to cast a vote.

pollen n the fine, powder-like material found in the anthers of flowers.

pollinate vt to fertilize by uniting pollen with seed.

pollute vt to contaminate with harmful substances; to make corrupt; to profane.

pollution n the act of polution; contamination by chemicals, noise, etc.

polo n a game resembling hockey, played on horseback.

polygamy n the practice of being married to more than one person at a time.

polyglot adj having command of many languages; composed of several languages. * n a person who speaks several languages.

polygon n a plane figure of three or more sides.

polygraph n an instrument used for measuring involuntary changes in blood pressure, breathing, etc, often used as a lie detector.

polystyrene n a rigid plastic material used for packing insulating, etc.

polysyllable n a word of more syllables than three.

polytechnic n an institution that provides instruction in many aplied sciences and technical subjects.

polyurethane n any of various polymers that are used esp in flexible and rigid foams, resins, etc.

pommel n a knob or ball, as on sword hilt, saddle bow. * vt to pummel.

pomposity n the state of being pompous; a pompous act or utterance.

pompous adj pretentious; self-important.

pond n a body of standing water smaller than a lake.

ponder vt to consider carefully.

ponderous adj heavy; awkward; dull.

pontiff n the Pope; a bishop.

pontifical adj of a pontiff; pompous.

pontoon n a boat or float forming a support for a bridge.

pony n a small horse.

pool n a small pond; a swimming pool; a puddle; a combination of resources for a common purpose; a form of billiards.

poop n the stern of a ship.

poor adj having little money; needy; unfortunate; deficient; inferior; disappointing. *n those who have little.

pop n a short, explosive sound; any carbonated beverage; a shot. * adj in a popular modern style.

pope n the head of the Roman Catholic church.

populace n the common people; all the peaple in a country, region, etc.

popular adj well-liked; common; prevalent.

population n the inhabitants; total number of people in an area.

populous adj densely inhabited.

porcelain n the variety of ceramic ware.

porch n a covered entry to a building.

pore n a minute opening in the skin; a small interstice. * vi to examine or study with care.

pork n the flesh of a pig, used as food.

pornography n pictues, films, etc, intended primarly to arouse sexual desire, and usu considered obscene.

porridge n a food made from oatmeal boiled in water or milk.

port n a harbour; a gate; a porthole; the left side of a ship; a circuit in a computer for the transferring of data

port *n* a fortified red wine.

portable *adj* able to be carried; not heavy.

portal *n* a door or gate; the main entrance.

portcullis *n* a sliding or falling grating at portal of a castle.

portend *vt* to give warning of; to foreshadow.

portent *n* an omen; a warning.

porter *n* a doorkeeper; a carrier; a dark brown beer.

portfolio *n* a case for drawings, papers, etc; office of minister of state; a list of stocks, shares, etc.

portico *n* a covered walkway.

portion *n* a part; a share; fate. * *vt* to divide.

portly *adj* dignified; stout.

portrait *n* a picture of a person; a vivid description.

portray *vt* to make a portrait of; to depict.

pose *n* attitude or position. * *vi*, *vt* to strike an attitude; to assert; to sit for a painting, photograph, etc..

poser *n* a difficult problem; a person who poses.

position *n* place; situation; posture; rank; a job; point of view.

positive *adj* explicit; absolute; confident; affirmative; noting the simple form of an adjective; a form of electricity; greater than zero.

possess *vt* to have and hold; to own.

possession *n* ownership; occupancy.

possessive *adj* denoting possession. * *n* the possessive case.

possible *adj* that may be or exist; practicable.

post *n* a piece of timber, etc, set upright; a place assigned; a military or other station; office or employment; a letter carrier; the postal system * *vti* to place in letter box; to enter in ledger; to travel by post horses.

postage *n* the charge for conveyance by post.

postal *adj* relating to the carrying of mails.

postcard *n* a letter card.

poster *n* a large printed bill for advertising.

posterior *adj* later or subsequent. * *n* the buttocks.

posterity *n* descendants; future generations.

postern *n* a back or private entrance.

postgraduate *n* a person persuing further study after a degree.

posthaste *adv* with all speed.

posthumous *adj* (child) born after the father's death; given or occurring after one's death.

postman *n* a mail carrier.

postmortem *adj* an autopsy; after death..

post office *n* a place where postal business is conducted ;the public department in charge of postal service.

postpone *vt* to delay; defer.

postscript *n* an addition to a letter after signature.

postulate *n* self-evident truth; assumption. * *vt* to state; assume.

posture *n* an attitude; a body position; a stand.

pot *n* a vessel for holding or boiling liquids; vessel for holding plants; frame for catching fish, lobsters, etc. * *vt* to plant in pot; to shoot.

potash *n* potassium carbonate.

potassium *n* the metallic element.

potato *n* a tuber eaten as a vegetable.

potency *n* power; force.

potentate *n* one who possesses great power; a monarch.

potential *adj* possible. * unrealized ability.

potion *n* a mixture of liquids.

potpourri *n* a mixture of scented, dried flowers;a medley.

pottery *n* earthenware; workshop where it is made.

pouch *n* a pocket; a small bag.

poultice *n* a moist dressing applied to sore parts of the body.

poultry *n* domestic birds kept for meat or eggs.

pounce *n* to fall on suddenly.

pound *n* a monetary unit; a place of confinement or temporary holding. * *vt* to beat; to pulverize. * *vi* to strike repeatedly; to throb; to work hard.

pour *vi* to flow continuously; to rain heavily; to serve liquid refreshment.

pout vi to thrust out the lips; to look sulky. * n a sullen look.

poverty n want; the condition of being poor.

powder n fine particles; dust; gunpowder. * vti to reduce to, or sprinkle with, powder; to salt.

powdery adj dusty; friable.

power n ability to act or do; strength; influence; talent; command; authority; a state or government; warrant; a mechanical advantage or effect.

practicable adj feasible; possible.

practical adj skilful in work; useful; handy.

practice n custom; habit; exercise of any profession; training; drill.

practise vti to do frequently or habitually; to exercise, as any profession; to commit; to form a habit.

practitioner n one who practises a profession (esp. medicine).

pragmatic adj practical; testing all concepts by their practical results.

prairie n an extensive tract of grassy land.

praise vti to express approval of; to commend; to worship. * n commendation.

pram n four-wheeled carriage for a baby.

prance vi to spring on the hind legs; to swagger.

prank n a mischievous trick or joke.

prattle vi to talk much and idly; to prate. * n trifling talk.

pray vi, vt to beg or implore; to ask reverently.

prayer n supplication; entreaty; praise or thanks to God.

preach vi to deliver a sermon; to give earnest advice. * vt to proclaim.

preamble n introductory part of a story, speech, etc.

precarious adj uncertain; insecure.

precaution n a preventative measure; careful foresight.

precede vt to go before; to preface.

precedence n priority; order according to rank.

precedent n a parallel case serving as example.

precept n rule of conduct; maxim; mandate.

precinct n a bounding line; an urban area where traffic is prohibited. pl neighbourhood; environs.

precious adj of great worth or value; very fastidious; affected.

precipice n a cliff or overhanging rock face.

precipitate vti to hurl headlong; to hasten rashly; to sink to the bottom of a vessel; to bring down (moisture). * adj headlong; overhasty. * n a deposit from a liquid.

precipitation n rash haste; rain, snow, etc.

precipitous adj very steep.

précis n a summary; abstract.

precise adj exact; definite; punctilious; particular.

precision n exactness; accuracy.

preclude vt to shut out; to prevent; to make impossible.

precocious adj prematurely ripe; forward.

precocity n too early development.

preconceive vt to form an opinion beforehand.

preconcerted adj pre-arranged.

precursor n a forerunner; omen.

precursory adj forerunning.

predator n a person who preys, plunders or devours.

predecessor n one who was in office before another.

predestinate vt to foreordain. * adj foreordained.

predetermine vti to determine beforehand.

predicament n a quandary; critical position.

predicate vti to affirm one thing of another. * n that which is affirmed.

predict vt to foretell.

prediction n a prophecy.

predilection n a previous preference.

predispose vt to incline beforehand.

predominant adj outstanding; superior.

preen vt (birds) to trim and trim the feathers; to groom oneself.

preface n an introduction; foreword. * vt to introduce by preliminary remarks.

prefect n person placed in authority over others; a student monitor in a school.

prefer vt to like better; to promote or advance.

preferable adj more desirable.

preference n choice; favour; prior claim.

preferential adj implying preference.

preferment n promotion.

prefix vt to put at the beginning. * n a letter or syllable put at beginning of a word.

pregnant adj having a fetus in the womb; significant; fulled with.

prehistoric adj prior to time of written records.

prejudge vt to condemn beforehand.

prejudice n bias; prejudgment; intolerance. * vt to affect or injure through prejudice.

preliminary adj introductory. * n preface.

prelude vt to preface. * n a musical introduction.

premature adj too early; untimely; hasty.

premeditate vti to plan beforehand.

premier adj first; principal * n the prime minister.

premiere n the first public performance of a play, film, etc.

premise n a proposition on which reasoning is based; something assumed.

premises n a building and its adjuncts.

premium n a reward; a bonus; sum paid for insurance; increase in value.

premonition n a foreboding; a feeling that something is about to happen.

preoccupied adj engrossed; lost on thought.

preparartory adj introductory.

prepare vti to make ready.

preponderance n superiority of weight, influence, etc; ascendancy.

preponderant adj superior in power, influence, etc..

preposition n a word used before a noun or pronoun to show its relation to another part of the sentence.

prepossess vt to influence in advance; to prejudice.

prepossessing adj attractive.

prepossession n preconceived opinion; prejudice.

preposterous adj absurd; utterly ridiculous.

prerogative n a prior claim; an exclusive privilege; hereditary right.

presage n a presentiment; omen. * vti to betoken; to forebode.

prescience n foreknowledge.

prescribe vti to lay down authoritatively; to direct medically; to appoint.

prescription n a written direction for preparing a medicine; a claim or title based on long use.

prescriptive adj based on and acquired by long use.

presence n state of being visible; appearance; personality; something (as a spirit) felt or believed to be present.

present adj being at hand, in view; now existing; ready at hand; quick. * n present time; a gift; pl law term for document itself (these presents).

present vt to introduce; to show; to give or bestow; to nominate to a benefice; to point or aim.

presentable adj suitable for presenting.

presentation n act of presenting; thing presented; a gift; a display or exhibition.

presently adv in a short while; soon; now.

preservation n the act of preserving.

preservative adj tending to preserve. * n something that preserves, esp a food additive.

preserve vt to save from injury; to keep in a sound state; to maintain; to restrict the hunting of, as game. * n fruit, vegetables, etc, treated with a preservative; jam; a restricted area.

preside vi to direct or control (a meeting); to take the chair.

presidency n office of president.

president n highest officer in a republic; chairman.

press vt to weigh down; to urge; to enforce; to emphasize; to embrace. * vi to push with force. * n a pressing; a crowd; a machine for crushing or squeezing; a printing machine; printing; newspapers.

pressing adj urgent.

pressure n a weighing down; force; influence; urgency.

prestige n influence based on character or conduct.

presume vti to take for granted; to infer; to act in a forward way.

presumption n arrogance; supposition.

presumptuous adj over-confident; arrogant.

presuppose vt to take for granted.

pretence n act of pretending; pretext; false claim.

pretend vti to claim, represent, or assert falsely; to feign.

pretentious adj claiming great importance; ostentatious.

pretext n a pretence; excuse.

pretty adj attractive; pleasing. * adv moderately; fairly.

prevail vi to overcome; to be in force; to succeed; to persuade.

prevalence n superior strength or influence; general diffusion.

prevalent adj prevailing; dominant; widespread.

prevaricate vi to make evasive or misleading statements.

prevent vt to stop or impede.

prevention n hindrance; obstruction.

previous adj antecedent; prior.

prey n a victim; animal killed for food by another. * vi to victimize.

price n the value of a commodity; cost; worth.

priceless adj invaluable.

prick n a sharp point; puncture or piercing. * vt to puncture.

pride n self-esteem; conceit; delight. * vt to be proud of.

priest n in various churches, a person authorized to perform sacred rites.

priesthood n the office of a priest; the order of priests.

priggish adj conceited; affected.

prim adj formal; demure.

primacy n the office of primate or archbishop.

prima donna n the chief female singer in an opera; (inf) a temperamental and affected person.

primal adj primary; primitive; fundamental.

primary adj first; chief; elementary; first in order of time.

primate n any of the highest order of mammals, including man..

prime adj original; not divisible by any smaller number; best quality.

primer n child's first reader; first coat of paint; a detonating device.

primeval adj primitive; original.

primitive adj original; antiquated; primary.

primordial adj first of all; original.

prince n the son of a king or emperor.

princely adj noble; august; magnificent.

principal adj first; chief; most important. * n head of a school, firm, etc; chief in authority; capital sum lent at interest.

principality n sovereignty; territory of a prince.

principally adv chiefly; mainly.

principle n cause or origin; a general truth; a fundamental law; a rule of conduct; uprightness.

print vt to mark by pressure; to stamp; to copy by pressure. * vi to publish. * n a mark made by pressure; an engraving, etc; a newspaper; printed calico.

printing n the art or process of making impressions on paper, cloth, etc; typography.

prior adj preceding; earlier. * n a monk next in dignity to an abbot.

priority n precedence; first claim.

priory n a religious house ruled by a prior(ess).

prise vt to force up.

prism n a solid whose ends are any similar, equal, and parallel plane figures; a kind of lens for decomposing light.

prison n a place of confinement; a jail. * vt to imprison.

pristine adj original; first.

privacy n seclusion; secrecy.

private adj separate from others; solitary; personal; secret. * n a common soldier.

privation n destitution; hardship.

privilege n a prerogative, benefit, or right. * vt to authorize; to exempt.

privy adj private; clandestine; admitted to the knowledge of (with to).

prize n that which is seized from an enemy; a reward of merit. * vt to value highly.

prizefight n a boxing match for a prize.

probability n likelihood.

probable adj likely; credible.

probate n the official proof of a will; confirmation.

probation n proof; trial; period of trial.

probe n a surgeon's instrument for examining a wound. * vt to explore; to examine carefully.

probity n uprightness; honesty.

problem n a question for solution; a knotty point.

proboscis n the trunk of an elephant, etc; the sucking tube of insects.

procedure n mode of conducting business; conduct.

proceed vi to go forward; to issue; to take legal action.

proceeding n transaction; procedure.

proceeds npl money brought in by a transaction.

process n progressive course; method of operation; lapse; legal proceedings; a writ.

procession n a body of people on the march.

processional adj relating to a procession. * n a service book as guide for religious processions.

proclaim vt to announce publicly; to publish.

proclamation n an official public announcement.

proclivity n inclination; tendency.

procrastinate vti to put off; to postpone unduly.

procreation n the begetting of young.

procurator n the manager of another's affairs; legal agent or prosecutor.

procure vt to obtain; to cause.

prod n a goad; a nudge; a stab. * vt to goad.

prodigal adj lavish; wasteful. * n a waster; a spendthrift.

prodigious adj portentous; enormous.

prodigy n a gifted child; an extraordinary person, thing or act.

produce vti to bring forward; to exhibit; to bear, yield; to cause; to extend. * n outcome; yield.

product n result; effect.

production n fruit; product; performance.

productive adj fertile; fruitful.

profane adj not sacred; secular; blasphemous; impure. * vt to treat with irreverence; to pollute.

profanity n profane language or conduct.

profess vt to avow; to acknowledge; to pretend. * ni to declare openly.

profession n open avowal; vocation; calling; members of a profession.

professional adj pertaining to a profession. * n one who makes his living by arts, sports, etc, as distinguished from an amateur.

professor n a university teacher of highest rank.

professorship n the office of a professor.

proffer vt to offer for acceptance.

proficiency n expertness; degree of advancement.

proficient adj fully versed; competent. * n an adept or expert.

profile n an outline; the side face or outline of it.

profit n any advantage, benefit, or gain. * vt to benefit. * vi to derive profit; to improve.

profitable adj yielding profit;lucrative; useful.

profligacy n depravity; vicious course of life.

profligate adj dissolute; openly vicious. * n a depraved man.

profound adj deep; deep in skill or knowledge; far-reaching.

profundity n depth.

profuse adj lavish; exuberant.

progeny n offspring; descendants.

prognosis n a forecast of the course of a disease.

prognosticate vt to foretell; to predict.

programme n a plan of proceedings; list of items at concert, etc; policy of political party.

progress n a going forward; a journey of state; advance. * vi to advance; to improve.

progressive adj forward; liberal; increasing by degrees; relating to whist drive where some players move forward.

prohibit vt to forbid; to prevent.

prohibition n an interdict; veto on sale of intoxicants.

prohibitive adj excessive.

project vti to hurl; to scheme; to delineate; to jut. * n a scheme, plan.

projectile adj throwing forward. * n a missile; a bullet or shell.

projection n a prominence; plan or outline on a plane surface.

projector n a company promoter; schemer.

prolapse n a displacement of an internal organ.

proletariate n the lower classes.

prolific adj fruitful.

prologue n introduction; speech, usually in verse, introducing a drama.

prolong vt to lengthen out.

promenade n a walk for pleasure; a public walk. * vi to walk up and down.

prominence n a projection; distinction.

prominent adj jutting out; eminent.

promiscuous adj indiscriminate, esp in sexual relations.

promise n an undertaking to do or not do something; pledge. * vti to give one's word; to show promise of.

promissory adj containing a promise. * a signed promise to pay.

promontory n a headland.

promote vt to forward; to encourage; to exalt; to form (a company).

promotion n advancement; furtherance.

prompt adj ready; unhesitating. * vt to incite to action; to whisper (words to actor, etc).

promulgate vt to publish.

prone adj lying face-downwards; inclined; apt.

prong n a spike, as of a fork.

pronominal adj of the nature of a pronoun.

pronoun n a word used instead of a noun.

pronounce vti to articulate; to utter; to affirm.

pronouncement n a definite statement of policy.

pronunciation n articulation.

proof n trial; convincing evidence; argument; test; standard strength (spirit); print copy for revision. * adj impenetrable; able to resist.

prop n a support. * vt to hold up; to sustain.

propaganda n methods or system of spreading beliefs, doctrines, etc.

propagandist n a popularizer of special doctrines; a missionary.

propagate vt to multiply; to diffuse. * vi to have young.

propel vt to drive or thrust forward.

propeller n a screw for propelling steamboats, etc.

propensity n natural tendency.

proper adj one's own; peculiar; correct; real.

property n a quality or attribute; characteristic; ownership; goods; estate; a stage requisite.

prophecy n a prediction; inspired utterance.

prophet n a seer; inspired preacher.

prophylactic adj, n preventive of disease.

propitious adj favourable; merciful.

proportion n comparative relation; symmetry; equal share; lot; ratio.

proposal n proposition; offer (esp of marriage).

propose vt to offer for consideration. * vi to make a proposal; to purpose.

proposition n a proposal; offer of terms; a statement or assertion; a problem or theorem for solution.

propound vt to propose; to put, as a question.

proprietary adj belonging to a proprietor.

proprietor n an owner.

propriety n fitness; justness.

propulsion n the driving forward (as of an engine).

prosaic adj like prose; commonplace.

proscribe vt to outlaw; to forbid.

proscription n outlawry; vetoing.

prose n ordinary speech.

prosecute vti to carry on; to pursue at law.

prosecution n a suit at law; the party prosecuting.

prosecutor n one who prosecutes.

proselyte n a convert.

proselytize vti to make or seek to make converts.

prospect n a distant view; scene; outlook; expectation. * vti to search, explore (for metals, oil, etc).

prospective *adj* looking forward; probable.

prospectus *n* a statement or outline of some enterprise.

prosper *vi, vt* to thrive or cause to thrive.

prosperity *n* success; a thriving state; good fortune.

prostitute *n* a person who performs sex acts for money.

prostitution *n* the act or activity of being a prostitute; to corrupt for unworthy purposes.

prostrate *adj* lying flat; lying at mercy. * *vt* to lie flat, to humble oneself.

protagonist *n* chief actor in a drama; the principal leader in an affair.

protean *adj* assuming different shapes; changeable.

protect *vt* to shield from danger, loss, etc.

protection *n* defence; shelter; taxation of foreign goods to protect home products.

protégé (*m*), **protégée** (*f*) *n* one under the care of another.

protein *n* an essential element in food of animals.

protest *vi* to affirm with solemnity. * *vt* to assert; to mark for nonpayment, as a bill. * *n* a formal declaration of dissent.

protestation *n* a solemn affirmation; a strong protest.

protocol *n* first draft of a treaty; ceremonial etiquette.

protoplasm *n* the life germ of animals and plants.

prototype *n* model; pattern.

protozoa *npl* the lowest class of animal life.

protract *vt* to prolong; to delay.

protractor *n* an instrument for measuring or plotting angles.

protrude *vti* to thrust forward; to project.

protrusion *n* a sticking out.

protuberance *n* a prominence; a knob.

proud *adj* haughty; arrogant; high-spirited.

prove *vti* to test; to establish the truth of; to demonstrate; to obtain probate of; to turn out to be.

proverb *n* a popular saying; an adage; a maxim.

proverbial *adj* well-known; notorious.

provide *vti* to make ready beforehand; to prepare; to supply.

provided *conj* on condition.

providence *n* foresight; divine foresight and care.

provident *adj* foreseeing; prudent; frugal.

providential *adj* due to divine providence.

province *n* a division of a country; sphere of action.

provincial *adj* rustic; countrified.

provision *n* preparation; stores provided; proviso; *pl* food.

provisional *adj* temporary.

proviso *n* a stipulation; condition.

provisory *adj* conditional.

provocation *n* cause of resentment.

provocative *adj* inciting; rousing.

provoke *vti* to incite; to irritate.

prow *n* the forepart of a ship.

prowess *n* bravery; skill.

prowl *vi, vt* to sneak around.

proximate *adj* nearest; next.

proximity *n* nearness.

proxy *n* agency of a substitute; a deputy; a warrant to act or vote for another.

prude *n* a person who affects excessive modesty.

prudence *n* caution; discretion.

prudent *adj* provident; cautious; discreet.

prune *vt* to trim; to lop off * *n* a dried plum.

prurience, pruriency *n* a lustful craving.

prurient *adj* lustful; filthy-minded.

pry *vi* to scan closely; to peer.

psalm *n* a sacred song or hymn.

pseudo *pref* signifying false or spurious.

pseudonym *n* a name assumed by a writer.

psychiatry *n* treatment of mental disease.

psychic *adj* belonging to the soul; spiritualistic.

psychology *n* the science concerned with the human mind aand behaviour.

puberty *n* beginning of manhood and womanhood; sex maturity.

pubescent *adj* arriving at puberty.

public *adj* not private; pertaining to a whole community; open to all; common. * *n* the people. * In public, in open view.

publican *n* keeper of a public house.

publication *n* act of publishing; book, etc, published.

publicity *n* any information or action that brings a person or cause to public notice; work concerned with such matters.

publish *vt* to make public; to proclaim; to print and offer for sale.

pucker *vti* to wrinkle. * *n* a fold or wrinkle.

pudding *n* a dessert dish.

puddle *n* a small pool of dirty water; clay impervious to water.

puddling *n* process of working clay so as to be impervious or of converting cast iron into wrought iron.

puerile *adj* boyish; childish.

puff *n* whiff of wind or breath; a puffball; light pastry; undeserved praise. * *vti* to breathe hard; to praise overmuch.

pugilism *n* the practice of boxing.

pugnacious *adj* quarrelsome.

pugnacity *n* aggressiveness; quarrelsomeness.

pull *vti* to draw towards one; to tug; to rend; to pluck; to gather. * *n* act of pulling; an effort.

pulley *n* a grooved wheel with running cord for raising weights.

pulmonary *adj* pertaining to the lungs.

pulp *n* the fleshy part of fruit, etc; soft substance obtained by mashing down cloth, wood, etc.

pulpit *n* preacher's raised desk or platform.

pulsate *vi* to beat or throb.

pulse *n* the beating of heart or artery; vibration; beans, pease, etc.

pulverize *vi* to reduce to dust.

pumice *n* a porous stone, used for polishing.

pummel *vt* to strike with fists.

pump *n* a machine for raising water or extracting air; a shoe used in dancing. * *vi* to work a pump. * *vt* to raise with a pump; to quiz.

pun *n* a play upon words. * *vi* to make puns.

punch *n* a tool for perforating; a blow; a spirituous beverage; a puppet show figure. * *vt* to stamp or perforate; to strike.

punctilious *adj* formal; precise.

punctual *adj* exact; prompt.

punctuality *n* scrupulous exactness.

punctuate *vt* to mark with points or stops.

punctuation *n* the art of inserting stops in sentence.

puncture *n* hole made by sharp point. * *vt* to pierce.

pungent *adj* biting; acrid; caustic.

punish *vt* to inflict pain as a penalty; to chastise.

punishment *n* pain, loss, or penalty.

punitive *adj* penal; designed to punish.

punt *n* a flat-bottomed boat.

puny *adj* small and weak.

pup *n* a young dog, seal, fox, etc.

pupa *n* (*pl* **pupae**) the chrysalis form of an insect.

pupil *n* a learner; a scholar; opening in centre of eye.

puppet *n* a mechanical figure moved by strings; a person who is a mere tool.

purchase *vt* to buy; to acquire. * *n* buying; thing bought; leverage.

pure *adj* clean; clear; unmixed; chaste.

purgative *adj* cleansing. * *n* an aperient or purging medicine.

purge *vti* to make pure or clean; to clear from accusation.

purification *n* a cleansing from guilt.

purify *vt* to make pure or clear.

puritan *n* one very strict in religious and moral matters.

purity *n* cleanness; innocence; chastity; freedom from adulteration.

purl *n* gentle murmur of a stream; a stitch in knitting. * *vi* to ripple.

purloin *vt* to steal or pilfer.

purple *n* a colour; red and blue blended; purple robe or the imperial rank denoted by it; regal power. * *adj* blood-red; royal.

purport *n* meaning. * *vt* to signify; to intend.

purpose *n* end or aim; design; intention. * *vt* to propose.

purse *n* a small pouch for money; funds. * *vt* to pucker.

purser *n* the ship's officer in charge of accounts.

pursuance *n* the carrying out (of a design).

pursuant *adj* agreeable; conformable to.

pursue *vti* to follow for some end; to chase.

pursuit *n* chase; quest; business occupation.

purvey *vti* to provide; to supply provisions.

purveyor *n* a caterer.

purview *n* the scope; limit; sphere.

pus *n* yellow matter of a sore.

push *vti* to press against with force; to shove; to urge. * *n* vigorous effort; emergency.

pusillanimous *adj* cowardly; timid.

pustule *n* a small blister or pimple.

put *vt* to place or set; to ask; to apply; to state.

put, putt *vt* to throw (a heavy stone) from the shoulder; in golf, to play the ball into the hole.

putative *adj* supposed; reputed.

putrefaction *n* decay; rottenness.

putrefy *vt* to render putrid. * *vi* to decay; to rot.

putrescence *n* a putrid state.

putrid *adj* rotten; corrupt.

putter *n* a kind of golfing club.

putty *n* a paste made of whiting and linseed oil. * *vt* to cement with putty.

puzzle *vt* to perplex. * *vi* to be bewildered. * *n* perplexity.

pyjamas *npl* sleeping clothes.

pylon *n* a tower like structure supporting electric power lines.

pyramid *n* a solid body having triangular sides meeting in a point at the top.

pyre *n* a funeral pile.

pyrotechnics *n* the art of making or the use of fireworks.

pyrrhic *n* a metrical foot of two syllables.

Q

qua *adv* in the quality of; as.

quack *vi* to cry like a duck. * *n* the cry of a duck; an untrained person who practices medicine faudulently. * *adj* sham.

quad *n* a quadrangle or court.

quadragesima *n* lent.

quadrangle *n* a plane figure, having four angles and sides; an inner square of a building.

quadrant *n* the fourth part of a circle or its circumference; an instrument for taking altitudes; a sextant.

quadratic *adj* in algebra, involving the square of an unknown quantity.

quadrennial *adj* lasting or occurring once in four years.

quadrilateral *n* a plane figure having four sides and angles.

quadrille *n* a dance for four couples, each forming side of a square.

quadruped *n* an animal with four feet.

quadruple *adj* fourfold. * *vt* to make fourfold. * *vi* to become fourfold.

quaff *vti* to drink deep.

quaggy *adj* boggy.

quagmire *n* wet boggy ground.

quaich *n* a silver or wooden drinking cup.

quail *vi* to flinch; to cower. * *n* a bird allied to partridge.

quaint *adj* attractive or pleasant in an old-fashioned style.

quaintly *adv* oddly; whimsically.

quake *vi* to shake; to tremble, esp with fear or cold.

Quaker *n* a member of the Society of Friends.

qualification *n* quality which fits a person for office or occupation; ability; capability; restriction.

qualified *adj* competent; limited.

qualify *vt* to render or to become fit for office, etc; to modify or limit.

qualitative *adj* determining the nature of the component parts of bodies.

quality *n* sort, kind, or character; attribute; high rank.

qualm *n* a sudden fit of nausea; a scruple.

quandary *n* a state of perplexity; a predicament.

quantitative *adj* relating to the size or amount.

quantity *n* bulk; measure; amount; large portion.

quantum *n* a quantity; a sufficient amount.

quarantine *n* isolation period imposed to prevent the spread of disease.

quarrel *n* an angry dispute; a brawl. * *vi* to dispute violently.

quarrelsome *adj* apt to quarrel; contentious.

quarry *n* an excavation for the extraction

of stone, slate, etc; a place from which stone is excavated; a source of information, etc. * vti to excavate (from) a quarry; to research.

quart n 2 pints or one-fourth of a gallon.

quarter n the fourth part of anything; any point of the compass; a district; locality; one of four divisions of heraldic shield; proper position; mercy to a beaten foe; pl shelter or lodging. * vt to divide into four equal parts; to cut to pieces; lodge.

quarterly adj recurring each quarter. * adv once in a quarter. * n a periodical published quarterly.

quartermaster n a petty officer in charge of steering, signals, etc (navy); an officer in charge of stores, rations, etc (army).

quartet, quartette n a musical composition in four parts; the four performers.

quarto n a page size, approx 9 by 12 inches (23 by 30.5mm).

quartz n silica in crystalline form.

quash vt to quell; to suppress; to make void.

quasi. pref meaning sort of, sham, almost, as quasi-religious.

quassia n a medicinal bark with bitter taste.

quatercentenary n a four-hundredth anniversary.

quatrain n a stanza of four lines rhyming alternately.

quaver vi, vt to shake; to tremble; to quiver. * n a voice tremor; half a crotchet.

quay n a landing stage for vessels; wharf.

queasy adj squeamish.

queen n the wife of a king; a female sovereign.

queenly adj royal; gracious.

queer adj odd; droll; peculiar.

quell vt to subdue; to allay.

quench vt to put out, as fire; to slake, as thirst.

querulous adj complaining; peevish.

query n a question; the mark of interrogation (?). * vi to ask questions. * vt to question.

quest n search; pursuit; inquiry.

question n an interrogation; inquiry; discussion. * vi to ask a question; to doubt. * vt to interrogate.

questionable adj doubtful.

questionnaire n a series of questions designed to collect statistical information.

queue n a line of people, vehicles, etc awaiting entry, a turn etc.

quibble n a minor objection or criticism. * vi to evade the question by play on words; to prevaricate.

quick adj alive; brisk; swift; keen; living. * n the living flesh.

quicken vti to give life to; to vivify; to cheer; to speed up.

quicklime n lime burned but unslaked.

quicksand n a sandbank yielding under pressure, therefore dangerous.

quicksilver n mercury.

quickstep n a ballroom dance in quicktime.

quidnunc n one always on the alert for news; a newsmonger.

quiescent adj resting; still; tranquil.

quiet adj at rest; calm; peaceful; secluded. * n rest; peace. * vt to calm; to lull; to allay.

quietism n tranquillity; resignation; a form of mysticism.

quill n the hollow stem of a feather; anything made of this as a pen; the spine of a porcupine. * vt to plait.

quilt n a padded bedcover.

quince n pear-shaped fruit used for preserves.

quincentenary n a five-hundredth anniversary.

quinine n a bitter drug from bark of cinchona tree, used as an anti-malarial.

quinquennial adj lasting for, or occurring once every five years.

quinquennium n the space of five years.

quinsy n inflammation of tonsils or throat.

quintessence n purest form of a substance; vital part.

quintet, quintette n a musical composition in five parts.

quintuple adj fivefold.

quintuplet adj one of five offspring produced at one birth.

quip n a gibe; retort.

quire n twenty-four sheets of paper.

quirk n an unexpected turn or twist; a peculiarity of mannerism.

quit adj discharged; free. * vti to discharge; to depart; to acquit.

quite adv completely; wholly.

quiver n a sheath for arrows. * vi to shake; to shiver.

quixotic adj romantic or chivalrous to extravagance.

quiz n a short written or oral test; a form of entertainment where players are asked questions of general knowledge.

quoit n a flattish ring of iron, thrown at a mark.

quondam adj former.

quorum n minimum number needed to constitute a meeting.

quota n share assigned to each.

quotation n passage quoted; estimated price.

quote vt to cite (from writings or speeches); to give prices of articles.

quotient n the answer to a division sum.

R

rabbi n (pl **rabbis**) the religious and spiritual leader of a Jewish congregation.

rabble n a noisy crowd; a mob.

rabid adj infected with rabies; fanatical.

rabies n an acute viral disease transmitted by the bite of an infected animal.

race n any of the divisions of human kind; a contest in speed; a course or career; a rapid current. * vt to run swiftly; to compete in speed.

racecourse n a track on which races are run.

racehorse n a horse bred for racing.

raceme n a flower cluster on common stem.

racial adj characteristic of race.

rack vt to stretch unduly; to torture. * n a frame for holding or stretching articles; a frame for setting up snooker balls for play, anguish; instrument of torture.

racket n a din; clamour; the bat in tennis, etc; (pl) a game like tennis.

racy adj strongly flavoured; risqué.

radial adj branching from a common centre.

radiance n brilliancy; lustre.

radiant adj emitting rays; brilliant; beaming.

radiate vi, vt to emit rays; to broadcast; to spread; to shine.

radiation n emission of rays.

radiator n apparatus for warming a room.

radical adj pertaining to the root; original; fundamental; inherent. * n a root; a political reformer.

radically adv root and branch; thoroughly.

radicle n the first rootlet of a seed.

radioactivity adj giving off radiant energy in the form of particles or rays caused by the disintegration of atomic nuclei.

radiograph n image given by rays.

radiography n process of taking pictures by X-rays for use in medicine.

radium n a metallic element which is highly radioactive.

radius n (pl **radii, radiuses**) distance from the centre of a circle to the circumference; a bone of the forearm.

raffle n a kind of lottery. * vi to engage in a raffle. * vt to dispose of by raffle.

raft n logs fastened together and floated; a floating structure.

rafter n one of several sloping beams supporting a roof.

rag n a tattered cloth; a shred; a sensational newspaper.

rage n violent anger; fury. * vi to be furious with anger.

ragged adj tattered.

ragwort n a common weed.

raid n a hostile incursion; a sudden foray. * vt to make a raid on.

rail n a bar of wood or metal; a connected series of posts; a railway. * vt, vi to enclose with rails; to scold; to jeer.

railing n a fence.

raillery n banter; chaff.

railroad n a railway.

railway n a road or track with parallel lines of rails along which vehicles travel.

rain n moisture falling in drops. * vi to fall in drops.

rainbow n a many-coloured bow that often appears in the sky during sunshine and showers containing the colours of the spectrum.

raise vt to cause to rise; to lift upward; to excite; to stir up; to levy; to breed; to abandon (siege).

rake n a toothed implement for scraping ground or for gleaning; a dissolute person. * vt to glean; to gather.

rakish adj dissolute; sloping, as masts; jaunty.

rally vt to reunite, as disordered troops; to collect; a large gathering of people. * vi to recover strength. * n a stand; recovery of health, morale, etc.

ram n a male sheep; sign (Aries) of Zodiac; a battering engine; pile-driving machine. * vt to batter; to charge.

ramble vi to roam about; to talk incoherently. * n an aimless walk.

rambler n a climbing plant; a person who rambles.

rambling adj unsettled; disconnected.

ramification n a branching; a network of parts; a consequence.

ramify vti to subdivide; to branch out.

ramp n a sloping walk or runway.

rampage vi to prance; to rage and storm.

rampant adj in heraldry, standing on hind legs; unchecked; unrestrained.

rampart n a defensive earthwork.

ramshackle adj broken-down; shaky.

ranch n a large cattle or sheep farm.

rancid adj rank; tainted.

rancorous adj spiteful; virulent.

rancour n deep-seated hatred.

random n chance; at random, without aim * adj haphazard.

range vti to set in a row; to place in order; to roam over; to rank. * n a row; a series of mountains; compass or extent; a place for gun practice.

ranger n a park warden.

rank n a row; a line; a social class; dignity. * vti to classify; to place in line. * adj overgrown; tainted.

rankle vi, vt to grow bitter; to irritate.

ransack vt to plunder; to search thoroughly.

ransom n release from captivity by payment; price paid for release. * vt to re-

deem.

rant vi to rave, declaim * n bombast.

rap n a smart blow; a knock. * vi, vt to strike smartly; (inf) talk, conversation.

rapacious adj greedy of plunder; grasping.

rapacity n excessive greed; extortion.

rape n the act of forcing a woman to have sexual intercourse against her will; a plundering. *vt to commit rape (upon)

rapid adj very swift; speedy. * n a swift current.

rapier n a long narrow sword.

rapt adj transported; enraptured.

rapture n extreme joy; ecstasy.

rapturous adj ecstatic; enthusiastic; intense joy.

rare adj sparse; uncommon; infrequent; precious; underdone.

rarefy vti to make or become less dense.

rarity n scarceness; thinness; a rare article.

rascal n a scoundrel; a rogue.

rase vt to wipe out; to destroy; to level to the ground.

rash adj precipitate; hasty. * n an eruption on the skin.

rasher n a thin slice of bacon.

rasp vt to rub with something rough; to grate. * n a coarse file; a raspberry.

ratchet n a catch which checks a toothed wheel and moves only one way.

rate n proportion; standard; degree of speed; price; a tax; assessment. * vt to fix the value, rank, etc, of; to reprove. * vi to classify.

rather adv more readily; preferably.

ratification n sanction; confirmation.

ratify vt to approve and sanction.

ratio n proportion of two classes of objects to each other.

ration n a fixed amount allowed.

rational adj endowed with reason; wise; judicious.

rationale n exposition of reasons for any opinion or action.

rattan n a walking stick or cane.

rattle vi, vt to clatter; to chatter. * n a clattering noise; a toy which makes a clatter.

raucous adj hoarse; harsh; loud.

ravage n havoc; devastation. * vt to lay waste.

rave vi to be delirious; to dote.

ravenous adj excessively hungry.

ravine n a gorge or pass.

ravish vt to carry off by force; to captivate; to rape.

ravishing adj enchanting.

raw adj uncooked; in natural state; crude; unripe; cold and damp; sore.

ray n a line of light; a gleam of intelligence; a radius; a flatfish.

rayon n a textile fibre made from a cellulose solution; a fabric of such fibres.

raze vt to blot out; to demolish.

razor n an instrument for shaving off hair.

reach vt to extend; to hand; to stretch out; to arrive at; to gain. * vi to extend. * n extent; scope.

react vi, vt to act in return; to return an impulse.

reaction n an action in response to a stimulus;(chem.) an action set up by one substance in another.

reactionary adj retrograde. * n one who opposes progress.

read vt to peruse; to utter aloud; to explain. * vi to peruse; to study; to stand written or printed; to make sense. * adj well-informed.

reader n a person who reads; a proof corrector; a university lecturer.

readily adv promptly; cheerfully.

reading adj bookish; studious. * n perusal; study of books; interpretation; rendering.

ready adj prepared; prompt; willing.

real adj actual; true; genuine; in law, applied to things fixed as land, houses, etc.

real estate n property; land.

realism n doctrine that the things of sense are the only reality; truth to nature in art; the practical as opposed to the ideal.

realist n one who believes in realism.

realistic adj life-like; vivid.

reality n fact; truth.

realize vt to make real; to convert into money; to make tangible; to gain.

really adv actually; in truth; positively.

realm n kingdom; domain; sphere.

realty n real property.

ream n 20 quires or 480 sheets of paper.

reap vti to harvest; to gather in; to receive as a reward.

rear n the part behind; the part of army or fleet behind van. * vti to raise; to educate; to breed, as cattle; to stand on hind legs.

rearguard n troops guarding the rear.

reason n mental faculty; power of thinking; a motive or cause; justice; moderation. * vi, vt to use reason; to argue.

reasonable adj rational; just; moderate.

reasoning n the exercise of faculty of reason; arguments used.

reassure vt to give confidence.

rebate n abatement in price; deduction; discount.

rebel n one who refuses to cooperate with lawful authority. *adj rebellious. * vi to revolt; to act as rebel.

rebellion n a rising up against authority.

rebound n a recoil;vi to spring back; to bounce back.

rebuff n a check; a repulse. * vt to check; snub.

rebuke vt to reprimand. * n a reproof.

recalcitrant adj obstinate.

recall vt to call back; to revive in memory.

recant vti to withdraw or retract; to abjure.

recantation n withdrawal of previous statements or beliefs.

recapitulate vt to summarize; to go over chief points.

recapitulation n a summary.

recast vt to mould anew.

recede vi to go back; to grow less. * vt to give back.

receipt n a written acknowledgment of something received. * vt to discharge, as an account.

receive vt to take, as a thing offered; to accept; to welcome; to take in.

receiver n a person who receives; one who knowingly takes stolen goods from a thief; equipment that receives electronic signals; (law) a person appointed to manage or hold in trust property in bankruptcy or lawsuit.

recent adj new; late; fresh.

receptacle n a place or vessel for holding

articles.

reception n welcome; a formal receiving of guests; admission.

receptionist n a person employed to receive visitors in an office, hospital, hotel, etc.

receptive adj quick to absorb knowledge.

receptivity n power of absorbing ideas or knowledge.

recess n withdrawal; a nook or alcove; holiday.

recession n a time of severe economic downturn.

recipe n a list of ingredients and directions for preparing food; a method for achieving an end.

recipient n a person who receives.

reciprocal adj mutual; alternating.

reciprocate vi to move backward and forward; to give in return. * vt to interchange.

reciprocity n interchange on even terms; equality of tariffs; fair trade.

recital n a narration; musical entertainment, esp. by one performer.

recite vti to repeat aloud from memory; to relate.

reckless adj heedless; rash; incaution.

reckon vti to count; consider; to calculate.

reckoning n calculation; a statement of accounts.

recline vti to lean backwards; to lean down on one side.

recluse adj retired; solitary. * n a hermit.

recognition n the act of recognizing; identification; acknowledgement; admission.

recognize vt to know again; to acknowledge.

recoil vi to start back; to shrink; to rebound. * n a rebound, as of a gun.

recollect vt to remember.

recommend vt to praise to another; to advise.

recommendation n a favourable notice; repute.

recompense vt to compensate; to reward. * n compensation; amends.

reconcile vt to make friendly again; to harmonize; to settle.

reconciliation n act of reconciling; renewal of friendship.

recondition vt to repair and restore to good working order.

reconnaissance n a survey for military purposes.

reconnoitre vti to survey or spy out an area or position.

reconsider vt to consider again.

reconstruct vt to rebuild.

record vt to preserve in writing; to chronicle. * n a written memorial; a register; best result in contests; gramophone disc.

recorder n an official registrar; a device that records; a tape recorder.

recount vt to relate in detail; to count again.

recoup vt to make good; to indemnify.

recourse n a going to for help or protection.

recover vt to get back; to regain; to revive; to obtain as compensation. * vi to grow well.

recovery n restoration from sickness, etc; a winning back.

recreant adj craven; cowardly. * n a coward; renegade.

recreate vt to revive; to amuse.

recreation n relaxation after toil; amusement or sport.

recrimination n mutual accusations.

recrudescence n renewed outbreak.

recruit vt to enlist new soldiers. * vi to gain new supplies. * n a soldier newly enlisted; a beginner.

rectangle n a four sided geometric figure having all its angles right angles.

rectangular adj right-angled.

rectification n refining by distillation; adjustment.

rectify vt to set right; to correct or redress.

rectitude n uprightness; honesty.

rector n a ruler; a clergyman in charge of a parish; a headmaster.

recumbent adj leaning; reclining.

recuperate vti to recover health.

recuperative adj healing; strengthening.

recur vi to return; to happen again and again.

recurrence n a happening occuring again and again.

recurrent adj returning repeatedly.

red adj blood-coloured. * n a primary colour.

redeem vt to buy back; to ransom; to save; to atone for; to perform (a promise).

redemption n ransom; release.

redolent adj fragrant; reminiscent.

redoubtable adj formidable; valiant.

redress vt to set right; to adjust; to relieve. * n relief; compensation.

reduce vt to bring down; to decrease; to degrade; to subdue.

reduction n act of reducing; diminution; conversion into another state or form; subjugation.

redundant adj superfluous to requirements; deprived of one's job as being no longer necessary.

reduplicate vti to double again; to repeat.

reed n a tall grass with jointed hollow stem; a pastoral pipe.

reedy adj harsh and thin, as a voice.

reef n a fold in a sail; a low line of rocks in sea; a vein of ore * vt to reduce sail.

reek n vapour; smoke. * vi to smoke; to exhale.

reel n a bobbin; an appliance for winding a fishing line; a lively dance; a length of film. * vt to wind upon a reel; to stagger.

refectory n a dining hall of a college.

refer vt to trace back; to submit (a matter) to another person; to assign. * vi to appeal; to allude.

referee n an umpire; a judge.

reference n allusion; relation; scope.

referendum n the settling of a national question by a direct vote of the people.

refine vti to purify; to polish; to become purer.

refinement n fineness of manners or taste; an improvement; a fine distinction..

refinery n a place for refining sugar, metals,oil, etc.

refit vti to fit anew; to repair. * n repair.

reflect vti to throw back, esp. rays of light or heat; to mirror; to meditate; to consider; to cast reproaches on.

reflection n act of reflecting; meditation; reproach; a reflected image.

reflective adj thoughtful; meditating.

reflector n a polished surface for reflecting light, etc.

reflex adj bent or directed back; involuntary response to a stimulus. * n a reflex action.

reflexive adj in grammar, referring back to subject.

reform vti to improve; to better; to amend; to form anew. * n a beneficial change; amendment.

reformer n one who effects reforms in religion, politics, etc..

refract vt to bend back sharply; to deflect (a ray of light).

refraction n deflection of rays on passing from one medium to another.

refrain vt to restrain. * vi to forbear. * n the recurring phrase or chorus of a song.

refresh vt to revive; to freshen.

refreshment n that which refreshes, as food and drink.

refrigerate vt to cool.

refrigerator n an apparatus for keeping things cool or for making ice.

refuge n protection from danger or distress; a retreat; a shelter; a plea.

refugee n one who seeks refuge in another land; to escape persecution.

refund vt to repay.

refusal n rejection; option.

refuse vti to deny what is asked.

refuse adj worthless. * n waste matter; rubbish.

refutation n disproof.

refute vt to disprove; to rebut.

regain vt to recover possession of; to reach again.

regal adj royal; relating to a king or queen.

regale vti to entertain sumptuously.

regalia npl ensigns of royalty, as crown, sceptre, etc.

regard vt to notice carefully; to observe; to heed; to consider; to value. * n look or gaze; respect; deference; attention; (pl) good wishes.

regarding prep. respecting; concerning.

regardless adj heedless; careless.

regatta n a yacht (or boat) race.

regency n government of a regent.

regenerate vt to produce anew; to produce again in the original form.

regent *adj* ruling. * *n* a ruler; one who governs during minority, illness, or absence of a king.

regime *n* mode or system of government; administration.

regimen *n* orderly government; regulation of diet, exercise, etc.

regiment *n* a miltary unit smaller than a division; *vt* to organize in a strict manner.

region *n* a tract of land; country.

register *n* an official record; a roll of voters; a recording machine; a meter.

registrar *n* official keeper of records.

registration *n* act of registering; enrolment.

registry *n* place where a register is kept.

regret *n* grief; remorse; penitence. * *vt* to grieve at; lament.

regrettable *adj* deplorable; unwelcome.

regular *adj* according to rule, law, etc; normal; constant; uniform * *n* a soldier.

regulate *vt* to adjust by rule; to direct.

regulation *n* a rule; order.

regurgitate *vti* to pour or cause to surge back.

rehabilitate *vt* to put back in good condition.

rehearsal *n* a trial performance.

rehearse *vt* to repeat; to recite; to perform (by way of practice).

reign *vi* to be sovereign; to rule; to prevail. * *n* royal authority; duration of kingship.

reimburse *vt* to refund.

rein *n* the strap of a bridle; restraint. * *vt* to govern by a bridle; * *vi* to obey the reins.

reinforce *vt* to supply with fresh strength or assistance.

reinstate *vt* to restore to a former position.

reissue *vt* to issue a second time. * *n* a second issue.

reiterate *vt* to repeat again and again.

reject *vt* to cast off; to discard; to forsake; to decline; to refuse to accept.

rejoice *vi*, *vt* to be glad; to exult; to cheer.

rejuvenate *vt* to make young again.

relapse *vi* to fall back into a worse state. * *n* a falling back into bad health; a backsliding.

relate *vt* to tell; to narrate. * *vi* to refer.

related *adj* connected by blood or by some common bond.

relation *n* act of relating; account; connection; kindred; a relative; proportion.

relationship *n* kinship.

relative *adj* comparative; pertinent; relating to a word, clause, etc. * *n* a kinsman; a relating word, esp. relative pronoun.

relax *vt* to slacken; to unbend. * *vi* to become feeble or languid.

relaxation *n* recreation; the condition of being relaxed.

relay *n* supply of horses to relieve jaded ones; fresh supply of men or materials; a relayed broadcast. * *vt* to broadcast signals.

release *vt* to set free; to deliver from; to allow cinema film to be shown. * *n* liberation from; discharge from.

relegate *vt* to send away; to move to an inferior position; to demote.

relent *vi* to relax severity; to grow milder.

relentless *adj* unmerciful; pitiless.

relevance, relevancy *n* pertinence; pointedness; applicability.

relevant *adj* applicable; to the purpose.

reliable *adj* trustworthy; dependable.

reliance *n* trust; confidence.

reliant *adj* confident; self-reliant.

relic *n* something treasured for connection with a saint or hero; a memento; (*pl*) bones of saints.

relief *n* ease of pain; remedy; redress; assistance given to the needy or victims of a disaster; raised design in sculpture; prominence; relief from duty by another person.

relieve *vt* to ease or lessen pain; to succour; to release from duty; to give variety to.

religion *n* a system of faith or worship; a belief in God or gods.

relinquish *vt* to give up; to renounce.

relish *vt* to enjoy the taste of; to have a taste for. * *vi* to have a pleasing taste. * *n* taste; flavour; savour.

reluctance *n* unwillingness.

reluctant *adj* loath; averse.

rely *vt* to depend upon; to trust in.

remain vi to continue in a place; to survive; to be left; to last. * npl a dead body.

remainder n residue; remnant.

remand vt to recommit to jail for further enquiries.

remark n notice; a comment * vt to observe; to note; to utter.

remarkable adj noteworthy; uncommon; striking.

remediable adj curable; correcting.

remedy n a cure; redress; a specific. * vt to cure; to repair; to put right..

remember vti to recollect; recall; observe; bear in mind.

remembrance n memory; recollection; memorial; keepsake.

remind vt to put in mind.

reminder n a jog to memory.

reminisce vi to write, think or talk about past events.

reminiscence n recollections; what is recalled to mind; (pl) personal memories.

reminiscent adj recalling the past.

remiss adj careless; heedless.

remission n pardon; abatement.

remit vt to send payment; to relinquish; to forgive; to transmit. * vi to slacken.

remittance n sum of money remitted.

remnant n a scrap; fragment.

remonstrance n a protest against something; expostulation.

remonstrate vi to protest against; to warn.

remorse n sorrow for a fault; compunction; bitter regret.

remorseless adj ruthless; merciless.

remote adj distant; foreign; slight; inconsiderable.

remount vti to mount again. * n a fresh horse.

removable adj able to be removed.

removal n change of place; dismissal.

remove vti to move from its place; to take away; to dismiss. * n a removal; departure; a stage in gradation.

remuneration n pay for service; reward.

remunerative adj profitable; lucrative.

renaissance n revival.

renal adj pertaining to the kidneys.

renascent adj becoming active again.

rend vti to tear away and apart; to split; to rive.

render vt to give in return; to give back; to afford; to furnish; to translate; to interpret; to boil down.

rendering n translation; interpretation.

rendezvous n appointed meeting place.

renegade n a deserter; a person who is faithless to a principle, party, religion, or cause.

renounce vt to disown; to forsake. * vi to revoke.

renovate vt to renew; to make like new.

renovation n act of renovating; renewal.

renown n fame; glory; celebrity.

renowned adj famous; eminent.

rent n money paid for use of lands or houses; a tear; a schism * vt to let or hire for rent.

rental n rent; rent roll.

renunciation n act of disowning or rejecting; disavowal.

reorganize vt to organize anew.

repair vt to restore; to mend; to retrieve. * vi to betake one's self; to resort. * n return to good condition; renovation.

reparation n amends; compensation.

repartee n a witty retort.

repatriate vt to restore to one's own country.

repay vt to pay back; to refund; to requite.

repayment n act of repaying; money repaid.

repeal vt to revoke; to annul; to abrogate. * n a cancelling; revocation.

repeat vt to do or utter again; to recite; to recapitulate. * n repetition.

repel vti to drive back; to repulse; to shock.

repellent adj repulsive; unattractive.

repent vi, vt to feel regret for one's conduct; to be penitent.

repentance n penitence; sorrow for wrong-doing.

repentant adj feeling or showing sorrow.

repercussion n reverberation; echo; a far-reaching, often indirect reaction to an event.

repertoire n actor's or company's stock of plays, etc.

repetition n repeating; saying from memory; recitation.

replace vt to put back in place; substitute; supersede.

replenish vt to fill again; to stock anew.

replete adj filled up; stuffed; gorged.

repletion n surfeit; plethora.

replica n an exact copy; a reproduction.

replication n an answer; echo; plaintiff's answer to defendant's plea.

reply vt, vi to answer; to respond. * n an answer; a rejoinder.

report vti to bring back as answer; to relate; to take down speaker's exact words; to give account of; to inform against. * n an official statement; account; rumour; loud noise.

reporter n one who reports for newspaper, radio or television.

repose vt to lay at rest. * vti lie at rest; to rely. * n sleep; quiet; composure; serenity.

repository n a storehouse; warehouse.

reprehend vt to reprove; to censure.

reprehensible adj deserving censure; culpable.

reprehension n reproof; blame.

represent vt to show; to typify; to describe; to act part of; to stand for; to be entitled to speak for (constituency).

representation n an image or likeness; dramatic performance; a remonstrance; the representing of a constituency.

representative adj typical; representing; acting as delegate. * n a member of parliament; an agent, delegate.

repress vt to check; to quell; to keep under control.

repression n check; restraint.

repressive adj tending to repress.

reprieve vt to grant a respite to; suspension of punishment of a criminal; respite.

reprimand n a severe reproof * vt to rebuke sharply.

reprint vt to print again. * n a new edition.

reprisal n something done by way of retaliation.

reproach vt to reprove, rebuke. * n censure; blame; disgrace.

reproachful adj abusive; upbraiding.

reprobate adj dissolute; profligate. * n a hardened sinner. * vt to condemn strongly; to cast off.

reproduce vt to generate, as offspring; to make copies of.

reproduction n a copy; a facsimile.

reproductive adj generative; producing again (as seed).

reproof n rebuke; censure.

reprove vt to censure; to reprimand.

reptile adj creeping; grovelling. * n any of a class of cold-blooded, air-breathing vertebrates with horny scales or plates; a grovelling or despised person.

reptilian adj like reptiles.

republic n a state governed by rulers popularly elected.

republican adj pertaining to a republic. * n one who favours republican government.

repudiate vt to reject; to disown; to deny.

repudiation n rejection; disavowal.

repugnance n aversion; reluctance.

repugnant adj offensive; highly distasteful.

repulse n a check or defeat; a refusal; a rebuff * vt to repel.

repulsion n aversion; the tendency of certain bodies to repel each other.

repulsive adj forbidding; disgusting.

reputable adj held in esteem; respectable.

reputation n good name; repute; character.

repute vt to estimate; to deem * n reputation; character.

reputed adj supposed; seeming.

request n an expressed desire; a petition. * vt to ask; to beg.

requiem n a mass for the dead; music for this mass.

require vt to ask as of right; to demand; to exact.

requirement n demand; an essential condition.

requisite adj necessary; essential.

requisition n a demand, esp. for supplies.

requite vt to repay; to reward; to avenge.

rescind vt to annul; to revoke.

rescue vt to free from danger or harm. * n deliverance.

research n careful investigation; a scientific study.

resemblance n likeness.

resemble vt to be like; to compare.

resent vt to be indignant about; to begrudge; to take badly.

resentment n deep sense of injury; indignation.

reservation n something kept back; doubt; scepticism; land reserved for special purpose, as big game, etc; a proviso.

reserve vt to keep in store; to retain. * n that which is retained; stiffness of manner; caution; limitation; shyness; (pl) emergency troops.

reserved adj shy; distant.

reservoir n a place where water is stored for use.

reside vi to dwell; to live.

residence n abode; dwelling.

residential adj pertaining to or suitable for residence.

residual adj left after part is taken.

residue n remainder; part of estate left after paying all charges.

resign vt to give up; to renounce; to submit calmly.

resignation n calm submission; giving up of office.

resigned adj submissive; patient.

resilient adj rebounding; elastic.

resin n a sticky substance that oozes from trees and plants etc.

resist vti to withstand; to oppose.

resistance n opposition; stopping power or effect.

resolute adj determined; bold.

resolution n firmness of purpose; formal decision; the picture definition on a television.

resolve vti to split up into elements; analyse; solve; determine. * n fixed purpose.

resonance n power of sending back or intensifying sound.

resonant adj resounding; ringing.

resort vi to have recourse; to go. * n recourse; a popular holiday destination.

resource n any source of aid; an expedient; (pl) funds; means.

respect vt to regard; to esteem; to concern. * n regard; deference; reference to.

respectable adj worthy of respect; decent; moderate.

respectably adv worthily; pretty well.

respectful adj civil; courteous.

respective adj relating severally each to each.

respiration n act of breathing.

respiratory adj pertaining to breathing.

respite n temporary intermission; a delay; interval; reprieve. * vt to reprieve.

resplendent adj very bright; glittering.

respond vi to answer.

respondent adj answering; corresponding. * n defendant in a lawsuit, esp. in divorce.

response n an answer; to reply.

responsibility n liability; charge; trust.

responsible adj answerable; liable; important.

responsive adj responding; sensitive to influence or stimulus; sympathetic.

rest n cessation of action; peace; sleep; a pause; remainder. * vi to cease from action; to repose; to die; to remain. * vt to lean or place for support.

restaurant n a place where meals can be bought or eaten.

restful adj giving rest; quiet; peaceful.

restitution n a giving back; reparation; amends.

restless adj always on the move; uneasy; anxious.

restoration n act of restoring; renewal; repair.

restorative adj having power to renew strength.

restore vt to make strong again; to cure; to give back.

restrain vt to hold back; to curb; to check.

restraint n the ability to hold back; something that restrains; control of emotions, impulses, etc.

restrict vt to limit; to curb.

result vi to follow as a consequence; to ensue; to end. * n consequence; outcome.

resultant adj following as a result or consequence.

resume vt to begin again; to continue after stopping.

resumé n a recapitulation; a summary.

resumption n act of resuming.

resurgent adj rising again.

resurrection n a rising again.

resuscitate vti to revive.

resuscitation n recovering from seeming death.

retail vt to sell directly to the consumer in small quantities. * n the sale of goods in small quantities; used also as adj.

retain vt to hold back; to keep in possession; to engage (a barrister) for a law case.

retainer n a follower; a dependant; a retaining or preliminary fee paid to barrister for his services.

retaliate vi, vt to return like for like; to take revenge.

retaliation n the return of like for like.

retard vt to render slower; to impede; to delay.

retch vi to strain in vomiting.

retention n a holding back; power of retaining (ideas); memory.

retentive adj good at remembering.

reticence n silence; reserve.

reticent adj uncommunicative; reserved.

retina n inner part of eye where visual nerves are.

retinue n a body of attendants.

retiral n act of retiring.

retire vi, vt to go back; to withdraw from active working life; to go to bed.

retired adj secluded; private; withdrawn from business.

retirement n retired life; seclusion.

retiring adj reserved; unobtrusive; shy.

retort vt to retaliate; to make a smart reply. * n a ready answer; a repartee; a vessel used in distilling.

retract vti to take back; to recant; to unsay.

retraction n act of drawing back; recantation.

retreat n seclusion; a shelter; the retiring of an army from an enemy. * vi to draw back; to retire from an enemy.

retribution n just punishment; requital for evil done.

retrievable adj that may be retrieved or recovered.

retrieve vt to recover; to regain.

retrograde adj going backwards; declining morally.

retrogressive adj declining; backward.

retrospect n a review of the past.

return vi to come or go back. * vt to send back; to report officially; to elect. * n repayment; yield on investment; election of representative; official report; (pl) tabulated statistics.

reunion n a social gathering, esp. of old associates.

reveal vt to disclose; to divulge.

revel n a noisy feast. * vi to carouse; to make merry.

revelation n act of making known; an illuminating experience.

revelry n noisy festivity; jollity.

revenge vti to take vengeance for; to avenge. * n retaliation; vindictive feeling.

revenue n income from lands, etc; yearly income of a state; produced by taxation.

reverberate vti to return, as sound; to echo.

revere vt to regard with awe and respect.

reverence n awe combined with respect; veneration; a title of the clergy. * vt to revere; to pay reverence to.

reverent adj expressing reverence.

reverie n a daydream.

reversal n the act of reversing.

reverse vt to alter to the opposite; to annul; to move backwards. * n a defeat; a set back; a check; the back surface (of coin, medal, etc). * adj opposite.

reversible adj able to be reversed, turned outside in, etc.

reversion n a return to a former condition or type; right to future possession.

revert vt to go back; * vi to return to a former position, habit, etc.

review vt to re-examine; reconsider; inspect. * vi to write reviews. * n a survey; retrospect; a criticism; a magazine which reviews books; official inspection of troops.

revile vt to vilify; to abuse.

revise vt to go over carefully and correct. * n a second proof sheet in printing.

revival n a reawakening; a religious awakening.

revive vi to recover new vigour. * vt to refresh; to reproduce (a play, etc).

revoke vt to repeal; to annul. * vi in card playing, to neglect to follow suit.

revolt *vi* to rebel; to be disgusted; with at * *vt* to shock. * *n* rebellion; mutiny.

revolting *adj* exciting extreme disgust; shocking.

revolution *n* act of revolving; rotation; circuit; a radical change in government as from a monarchy to a republic.

revolutionary *adj* involving radical changes. * *n* a revolutionist.

revolutionize *vt* to bring about a complete change in.

revolve *vi*, *vt* to turn round an axis or centre; to consider attentively.

revolver *n* a pistol capable of firing several shots without reloading.

revue *n* a topical play usually interspersed with music.

revulsion *n* disgust; aversion.

reward *n* recompense. * *vt* to repay.

rhapsody *n* an enthusiastic speech or writing;(mus) an irregular instrumental composition of an epic.

rhetoric *n* the art of speaking or writing correctly and effectively; eloquence; declamation.

rheum *n* watery fluid secreted by mucous glands of the nose, eyes, etc.

rheumatism *n* a painful disease of the muscles and joints.

rhombus *n* a parallelogram with equal sides but angles not right angles.

rhomboid *n* a quadrilateral whose opposite sides only are equal, and whose angles are not right angles.

rhyme *n* the repetition of like endings in words or verse lines; poetry; verse. * *vt* to make rhymes; to put into rhyme.

rhythm *n* regular recurrence of accent in music and poetry.

rib *n* one of the curved bones springing from the backbone; something resembling a rib, as in an umbrella.

ribald *adj* irreverant; humorously vulgar.

ribbon *n* a narrow band of silk, satin, etc.

rice *n* a cereal extensively cultivated in hot countries.

rich *adj* wealthy; costly; fertile; plentiful; bright; mellow; highly flavoured.

rickets *npl* a disease of children marked by softening and distortion of the bones.

rickety *adj* ramshackle; shaky.

ricochet *n* a rebounding from a surface.

rid *vt* to free (from something objectionable); to disencumber. * *adj* free; clear.

riddance *n* deliverance; clearance.

riddle *n* a puzzling question; an enigma; a coarse sieve. * *vt* ; to sift; to perforate with shot.

ride *vi* to be borne on horseback, in a vehicle, etc; to practise horsemanship; to be at anchor. * *vt* to sit on, so as to be carried; to domineer over. * *n* an excursion on horseback, or in a vehicle.

ridge *n* a narrow elevation as crest of hill, or edge of roof.

ridicule *n* laughter with contempt; mockery. * *vt* to make sport of.

ridiculous *adj* absurd; laughable.

riding *adj* used in riding (a riding habit).

rife *adj* abundant; prevalent; widespread.

rifle *n* a shoulder gun with a grooved barrel. * *vt* to plunder; to groove a gun barrel.

rift *n* an opening; a cleft; a split.

rig *vt* to manipulate fraudulently; to fit with tackling. * *n* style of masts and cut of sails of a ship.

rigging *n* a ship's spars, ropes, etc.

right *adj* straight; upright; just; correct; opposite of left; perpendicular. * *adv* justly; very; to the right hand. * *n* uprightness; truth; justice. * *vti* to put right; to do justice; to make erect.

righteous *adj* moral; virtuous; just.

rightful *adj* lawful.

rightly *adv* properly; fitly; justly.

rigid *adj* stiff; unyielding; stern.

rigidity *n* stiffness; harshness.

rigmarole *n* confused or disconnected talk.

rigor *n* a sudden chill attended with severe shivering.

rigorous *adj* severe; stringent.

rigour *n* stiffness; austerity; severity.

rim *n* border; edge; margin.

rind *n* outer coat of fruits, trees, etc; bark.

ring *n* anything in the form of a circle; a gold hoop for finger; a circular area for contests, a group with mutual interests; sound of bell. * *vt* to encircle; to cause to sound. * *vi* to sound.

ringleader *n* the leader of a faction.

rink n a space on the ice reserved for curling; a place for roller-skating.

rinse vt to flush under clean water to remove soap.

riot n an uproar; a tumult; noisy revelry. * vi to engage in a riot; to revel.

riotous adj noisy; turbulent; disorderly.

rip vt to tear or cut open. * n a rent; a scamp.

ripe adj ready for harvest; mature.

ripple n a little wave on the surface of water.

rise vi to ascend; to stand up; to swell; to slope upwards; to rebel. * n ascent; elevation; source; increase (in price).

risible adj prone to laugh; laughable.

rising adj increasing in power, etc; approaching. * n a mounting up; an insurrection; a prominence.

risk n hazard; jeopardy. * vt to hazard; to venture.

risky adj dangerous; full of risk.

rite n a solemn religious act; form; ceremony.

ritual n a fixed (religious) ceremony.

rival n a competitor for the same goal. * adj competing. * vt to emulate; to strive to excel.

rivalry n competition; emulation.

river n a large running stream of water.

rivet n a fastening bolt clinched by hammering. * vt to clinch; to fasten firmly.

rivulet n a small stream.

road n a public way for travellers, vehicles, etc; a highway;a surfaced track for travelling.

roam vi to wander; to travel.

roan adj of mixed colour, red predominating. * n a horse of roan colour.

roar vi to cry with a loud voice; to bellow. * n the full loud cry of large animal; a shout.

roaring adj boisterous; noisy; brisk.

roast vt to cook with little or no moisture; to expose to great heat. * n roasted meat, or meat for roasting.

rob vt to take by force; to steal from.

robbery n theft with violence.

robe n a gown, or long, loose garment. * vt to invest with robes.

robot n a mechanical device that acts in a seemingly human; a mechanism guided by automatic controls.

robust adj sturdy; healthy and strong.

rock vt to move to and fro; to swing. * vi to reel. * n a large mass of stone; a reef; a sweetmeat.

rockery n an artificial mound of earth and stones for growing ferns, etc, on.

rocket n any device driven forward by gases escaping through a rear vent. *vi to move in or like a rocket; to soar.

rococo n, adj a florid style of decoration prevalent in 18th century.

rod n a straight slender stick; a wand; a fishing rod.

rodent adj gnawing. * n an animal that gnaws, as the rat.

rodeo n the rounding up of cattle; a display of cowboy skill.

roe n the spawn of fishes.

rogue n a knave; a rascal.

roguery n trickery; fraud; mischievousness.

roister vt to bluster; to swagger.

roll n a scroll; anything wound into cylindrical form; a list or register; a rolling movement; a small cake of bread; an undulation; the sound of thunder; the beating of drumsticks. *vti to move by turning over or from side to side; to move like a wheel; to press with a roller.

roller n a cylinder for smoothing, crushing, etc; a long, swelling wave.

rolling adj revolving; undulating.

romance n a tale in prose or verse; a novel of adventures; a love story; a love affair.

romantic adj imaginative; fanciful; picturesque.

romp n a noisy game; a frolic. * vi to play boisterously.

rood n a cross or crucifix.

roof n the cover of any building; a canopy; an upper limit.

rook n a kind of crow; a cheat; a piece in chess.

rookery n a nesting place for crows.

room n space; scope; opportunity; stead; apartment in a house.

roost n a bird's perch or sleeping place.

root n that part of a plant which fixes itself in the ground foundation; origin; a form from which words are derived.

rooted adj fixed; deep; radical.

rope n a stout cord; a series of things connected; a cable. * vi, vt to fasten with a rope; to curb.

rosary n a string of beads for keeping count of prayers.

rose n a plant and its flower, of many species; knot of ribbons; a perforated nozzle. * adj rose colour.

rosette n an ornamental knot of ribbons.

roster n a list showing order in which officers, etc, are to take up certain duties (army).

rostrum n a platform for public speaking.

rot vi, vt to decompose; to decay. * n putrid decay; a fatal sheep disease; nonsense.

rota n a turn in succession; a list or roster of duties.

rotary adj turning on an axle.

rotate vi to revolve round a centre or axis; to act in turn.

rotation n motion round a centre or axis; regular succession (as of crops).

rote n repetition without understanding.

rotten adj decomposed; decayed.

rotund adj round; spherical; plump.

rouble n Russian monetary unit.

rouge n a red cosmetic for tinting cheeks and lips.

rough adj not smooth; rugged; harsh; rude; uneven; ill-mannered.

round adj circular; spherical; plump; curved; not minutely accurate, as a number. * n rung of a ladder; a circular course; circuit made by one on duty; a vocal composition in parts; ammunition for firing once; a turn or bout. * vt to make round; to encircle. * vi to make a circuit. * adv in a circle; around. * prep about; around.

roundabout adj indirect; circuitous. * n a merry-go-round.

rouse vt to arouse; to awaken. * vi to awake.

rout n a noisy crowd; a disorderly retreat. *vti to grub up, as a pig; to make a furrow.

route n a course or way.

routine n regular habit or practice.

rove vi to roam; to wander.

row n a line of objects; a rank; a line of seats.* vt to impel by oars, as a boat.

row n a noisy disturbance; a riot.

rowdy n a turbulent fellow; a rough. * adj disreputable.

royal adj regal; relating to a king or queen.

royalist n an adherent of a king or queen.

royalty n state of being royal; a royal personage; share paid to a superior, inventor, or author.

rub vti to move one thing along surface of another with pressure or friction; to scour; to chafe. * n impediment; friction; pinch; gibe.

rubber n that which rubs; an eraser; in card playing, winning two out of three games.

rubbish n refuse; debris; trash; nonsense.

rubble n broken stones of irregular shapes.

ruby n a valuable gem of various shades of red.

rucksack n a bag worn on the back by hikers.

rudder n the steering apparatus of a ship.

ruddy adj reddish; a healthy red.

rude adj rough-hewn; uncivilized; ill-mannered; vulgar.

rudiments npl the origin, first principle, or germ of anything, esp. learning, art, etc.

rudimentary adj undeveloped; primitive.

rue vt to feel remorse for.

rueful adj woeful; piteous; remorseful.

ruff n a plaited collar or frill; a ruffle; act of trumping at cards. * vt to trump at cards.

ruffian n a brutal lawless person.

ruffle vt to rumple; to derange. * vi to bluster. * n a frill for the neck or wrist; agitation.

rug n a heavy fabric used as a mat or coverlet.

rugged adj rough; uncouth; rocky.

rugby n a football game for two teams of fifteen players played with an oval ball.

ruin n destruction; fall; overthrow; (pl) remains of old buildings. * vt to destroy; to impoverish.

rule *n* a ruler or measure; a guiding principle; a precept, law, maxim; government; method. * *vti* to govern; to manage; to mark with lines; to decide; to reign.

ruling *adj* reigning; predominant. * *n* a point settled by a judge, chairman, etc.

rum *n* spirit distilled from molasses.

rumble *vi* to make a dull, continued sound. * *n* a low, continued sound.

ruminant *n* an animal that chews the cud.

ruminate *vi* to regurgitate food after it has been swallowed; to meditate.

rummage *vt* to search narrowly but roughly; to ransack. * *n* a careful search.

rumour *n* an unconfirmed report. * *vt* to spread abroad.

rump *n* end of an animal's backbone; buttocks.

rumple *vt* to wrinkle; to ruffle.

rumpus *n* a great disturbance; a din.

run *vi* to move rapidly; to take part in a race; to flee; to spread or flow. * *vt* to incur; to smuggle; to melt. * *n* act of running; course run; trip; general demand; distance sailed or travelled.

rung *n* the round or step of a ladder.

runner *n* a messenger; an athlete; a creeping plant; that on which anything slides.

rupture *n* a break; fracture; breach; disagreement; quarrel; hernia.

rural *adj* pertaining to the country; rustic.

ruse *n* artifice; trick; deception.

rush *vi* to dash forward. * *n* a headlong advance; hurry; a reed; an unedited film print.

rusk *n* a light hard cake or biscuit.

rust *n* the red oxide formed on iron exposed to moisture; a parasite fungus.* *vi* to contract rust; to degenerate in idleness.

rustic *adj* rural; homely; unpolished.

rustle *vi*, *vt* to make a sound as of rubbing of dry leaves. * *n* the crinkling sound of blown leaves.

rusty *adj* covered with rust; impaired by inaction.

rut *n* the track of a wheel; a groove; routine.

ruthless *adj* cruel; pitiless.

rye *n* a cereal plant and its seed; a whiskey made from rye.

S

sabbath *n* a day of rest and worship, observed on a Saturday by Jews, Sunday by Christians and Friday by Muslims.

sabbatical *n* a year's leave from a teaching post, often paid, for research or travel.

sabotage *n* a deliberate damage of machinery, or disruption of public services, by enemy agents, disgruntled employees, etc, to prevent their effective operation. *vt* to practise sabotage on; to spoil, disrupt.

saccharin *n* a non-fattening sugar substitute.

sachet *n* a small bag for perfume, etc.

sack *n* a bag made of coarse cloth used as a container; pillage of a town. * *vt* to pillage, as a town; to dismiss.

sacrament *n* a solemn religious ordinance; a sacred symbol or pledge.

sacred *adj* set apart for a holy purpose; consecrated; religious.

sacrifice *n* something given up in the interests of another; loss; the thing offered up. * *vt* to give up.

sacrum *n* the bone at base of vertebral column.

sad *adj* sorrowful; gloomy.

sadden *vt* to make sad. * *vi* to become sad.

saddle *n* a seat for a rider on a horse or bicycle. * *vt* to put a saddle on.

sadism *n* sexual pleasure obtained by inflicting cruelty on another; extreme cruelty.

safe *adj* secure; free from danger; trustworthy. * *n* a strong box for securing valuables; a burglar-proof chamber; a cupboard.

safeguard *n* a defence; protection. * *vt* to guard.

safety *n* freedom from danger, hurt, or loss.

safety belt *n* a belt worn by a person working at great height to prevent falling; a seatbelt in a car.

safety valve *n* a valve which opens when pressure of steam in boiler becomes too great.

sag *vi* to sink in the middle; to droop.

sagacity *n* shrewdness; high intelligence.

sage *adj* wise; grave. * *n* a wise man; an aromatic plant.

Sagittarius *n* the archer, a sign of the zodiac.

sail *n* a canvas spread to catch the wind; a voyage in a sailing vessel. * *vi*, *vt* to move by means of sails; to glide; to navigate.

sailor *n* a seaman; a mariner.

saint *n* one eminent for piety.

sake *n* behalf; purpose; benefit; interest.

salad *n* raw herbs as lettuce, cress, etc, dressed.

salary *n* a fixed, regular payment for work.

sale *n* act of selling; market; auction.

salesman *n* one employed to sell goods.

salience *n* projection; protrusion.

salient *adj* springing; projecting; conspicuous.

saline *adj* consisting of salt; salt.

saliva *n* the fluid secreted by glands of mouth that aids digestion.

sallow *adj* having a sickly, yellowish colour. * *n* a kind of willow.

sally *n* a sudden attack or outburst; a lively remark, a quip.

salon *n* a reception room; a gallery.

saloon *n* a spacious apartment; main cabin of a steamer.

salt *n* a substance for seasoning and preserving food; a compound produced by the combination of a base with an acid; savour; an old sailor. * *vt* to sprinkle with salt.

saltire *n* a cross (X) dividing heraldic shield into four parts.

salubrious *adj* healthful.

salutary *adj* beneficial, wholesome.

salutation *n* a greeting; a salute.

salute *vt* to greet; to welcome; to greet with a bow; kiss, etc. * *vi* to make a salute.

salvable *adj* that may be saved.

salvage *n* the saving of a ship or its cargo at sea; the saving of property from fire; payment for such service.

salvation *n* redemption of man from sin.

salve *n* a healing ointment; remedy. * *vt* to apply salve to.

salver *n* a small tray.

salvo *n* a salute of guns; a sudden burst.

same *adj* identical; exactly similar; unchanged; uniform; monotonous.

sample *n* a specimen; a small part representative of the whole.

sanatorium *n* an establishment for the treatment of convalescents or the chronically ill.

sanctification *n* a purifying from sin; consecration.

sanctified *adj* made holy; consecrated.

sanctify *vt* to make holy.

sanctimonious *adj* making a show of sanctity; hypocritical.

sanction *n* permission; authority; a penalty by which a law is enforced. * *vt* to ratify; to authorize.

sanctity *n* saintliness; holiness.

sanctuary *n* a sacred place; part of a church where the altar is placed; a sure refuge.

sanctum *n* a sacred place; a private room.

sand *n* fine particles of stone; *pl* tracts of sand on the seashore, etc.

sandal *n* a shoe consisting of a sole strapped to the foot.

sandpaper *n* paper coated with sand for smoothing and polishing.

sandstone *n* a stone composed of compressed sand.

sandwich *n* slices of bread, with meat or savoury between. * *vt* to fit between two other pieces.

sane *adj* sound in mind; sensible.

sanguine *adj* full of blood; cheerful; hopeful.

sanitary *adj* healthful; hygienic.

sanitation *n* measures for securing good health in a community; hygiene; drainage and disposal of sewage.

sanity *n* soundness of mind.

sanskrit *n*, *adj* the ancient language of Hindus.

sap *vti* to undermine. * *n* a trench; vital juice of plants.

sapient *adj* wise; sage; discerning.

sapling n a young tree.

sapphire n a precious stone of a rich blue colour.

sarcasm n a bitter cutting jest; gibe.

sarcastic adj biting; taunting; satirical.

sarcophagus n (pl sarcophagi) a coffin of stone.

sardonic adj bitter; mocking; grimly jocular.

sartorial adj pertaining to a tailor.

sash n a long band or scarf worn for ornament; a window frame.

satan n the devil; the adversary of God.

satchel n a little bag for carrying books, papers, etc.

sate vt to satisfy the appetite of; to glut.

satellite n a small planet revolving round a larger; a man-made object orbiting the earth to gather scientific information, etc.

satiate vt to satisfy fully; to surfeit. * adj glutted.

satin n a glossy close-woven silk cloth.

satire n a composition in prose or verse, ridiculing or censuring manners and customs of the time.

satirize vt to ridicule; to hold up to scorn.

satisfaction n pleasure; contentment; atonement; payment.

satisfactory adj adequate; up to expectation.

satisfy vti to gratify fully; to convince.

saturate vt to soak thoroughly.

saturation n state of being soaked or filled with another substance to utmost limit.

Saturday n the seventh day of the week.

saturn n a planet.

sauce n a liquid relish or seasoning for food.

saucepan n a deep cooking pan with a handle and a lid.

saucer n a curved plate in which cup is set.

saucy adj pert;impudent; rude.

saunter vi to stroll about idly. * n a stroll.

sausage n minced seasoned meat, esp pork, packed into animal gut or other casing.

savage adj wild; barbarous; brutal. * n a barbarian.

savagery n cruelty; barbarity.

save vt to preserve; to protect; to rescue; to spare. * vi to be economical. * prep except.

saving adj thrifty; preserving; excepting. * n what is saved. * prep excepting.

saviour n a preserver; rescuer.

savour n taste; flavour; a distinctive quality. * vi to have a particular taste.

savoury adj tasty; palatable; spicy not sweet.

saw n a cutting instrument with toothed edge; a maxim * vti to cut with a saw.

sawdust n small fragments of wood produced in sawing.

sawmill n a mill for sawing timber.

say vti to utter in words; to speak; to declare; to relate.

saying n a proverb; maxim.

scab n crust formed over a sore on healing; itch; mange.

scabbard n the sheath of a sword.

scabies n contagious itching skin disease.

scaffolding n a framework to aid in building houses, etc.

scald vt to burn with hot liquid. * n a burn from hot liquid or steam; scurf.

scale n a thin flake on skin of animals; instrument for weighing; series of steps; gradation; a measure; rank; series of musical notes. * vt to weigh; to strip of scales; to climb. * vi to peel.

scallop n an edible shellfish; a curving or indentation on edge. * vt to indent or curve edges.

scalp n the skin and hair of top of head. * vt to cut off scalp.

scalpel n a short, thin, very sharp knife.

scamp n a knave; rogue.

scamper vi to scurry. * n a hurried run.

scan vt to look through quickly; to examine with a radiological device; to mark the rhythm of verse.

scandal n a disgraceful event or action; a feeling of moral outrage; shame.

scandalous adj shameful; disgraceful.

scant adj limited; meagre. * vt to stint; to grudge. * adv scarcely.

scapegoat n one who bears the blame of others.

scapula n the shoulder blade.

scar n the mark of a wound; a blemish; a

cliff; a steep bare bank. * vt to form a scar; to wound.

scarab n egyptian beetle; a gem cut in the form of a beetle.

scarce adj rare; deficient; hard to find.

scarcity n dearth; deficiency.

scare vt to terrify; to scare. * n a causeless alarm; panic.

scarecrow n anything set up to scare away birds.

scarf n a broad band or sash for neck wear; a joint in timber.

scarify vt to make small incision in the skin; to shock; to criticize savagely.

scarlet n, adj a bright red colour.

scarp n a precipitous slope.

scathing adj severe; bitterly critical; withering.

scatter vt to disperse; to throw loosely about, to occur at random. * vi to straggle apart.

scatterbrain n a giddy, thoughtless person.

scattered adj thinly spread; dispersed.

scenario n summary of leading incidents in a play.

scene n a stage; a distinct part of a play; a painted device on the stage; place of action; a view; display of emotion.

scenery n the painted scenes and hangings of the stage; landscape; view.

scenic adj relating to natural scenery.

scent n an odour left by an animal, by which it can be tracked , a perfume; sense of smell; . * vt to discern by smell.

sceptic n a doubter; disbeliever.

sceptical adj doubting; doubting truth of revelation.

scepticism n doubt; incredulity.

sceptre n the rod borne by a ruler as a symbol of power.

schedule n a timetable; a list or inventory. * vt to plan.

scheme n a plan of proceedings; a system; a project. * vti to plan; project; plot.

schism n a separation; a disruption.

scholar n a school pupil; a learned person.

scholarship n learning; an annual grant to a student, usu won by competitve examination.

school n a place of instruction; a body of pupils; disciples; sect or body; a shoal (of fishes). * vt to instruct; to train.

schooner n a vessel with two masts.

sciatica n neuralgia of the sciatic nerve.

science n knowledge; knowledge reduced to a system; study of natural laws and principles; trained skill.

scientific adj skilled in science.

scientist n a specialist in a branch of science.

scimitar n a short curved sword.

scintillate vi to sparkle; to twinkle.

scion n a cutting; a young shoot; a descendant.

scissors npl a cutting instrument of two blades, whose edges slide past each other.

sclerosis n a hardening of tissue.

scoff n an expression of scorn; a gibe. * vi to jeer; to mock. * vt to mock at.

scold vi, vt to rebuke angrily; to find fault with harshly; to tell off.

scoop n a short-handled shovel for grain, etc; a coal scuttle; a hollowing out spoon or gouge for cheese, etc. * vt to hollow out.

scooter n a child's two wheeled vehicle with a footboard and steering handle; a motor scooter.

scope n an aim or end; range; opportunity.

scorch vti to singe; parch; shrivel; to drive at reckless speed.

score n a notch; a line; a furrow; an account or reckoning; runs, points, etc, made in games; twenty; reason; copy of concerted musical piece. * vt to mark; record; register.

scorn n extreme contempt. * vt to disdain; to deride. * vi to feel or show scorn.

scornful adj disdainful; mocking; contemptuous.

scotch vt to stamp out.

scoundrel n a rogue, rascal.

scour vti to clean by rubbing; to purge violently; to pass swiftly over.

scourge n a lash; a whip; a grievous affliction; a plague. * vt to lash; to afflict sorely.

scout n an exploring or reconnoitering

messenger; a person employed to find new talent. * vi to act as scout.

scowl vi to frown in anger. * n a sullen frowning look.

scraggy adj lean and bony; gaunt.

scramble vi to clamber on all fours; to push rudely; to break and stir eggs; to make unintelligible in transit. * n a pushing and struggling for something.

scrambling adj irregular; straggling.

scrap n a small piece; a fragment; a cut-out picture.

scrape vti to rub with something hard; to grate; to erase; to gather money laboriously; to make a grating noise. * n a rasping sound; serious trouble.

scratch vti to tear or mark with something sharp; to tear with nails; to erase or cancel * n a slight mark or wound; starting line; competitor without start. * adj haphazard.

scrawl vti to scribble. * n slovenly writing.

scream vi to shriek. * n a shrill cry.

screen n a shield from draughts, heat, etc; a partition in a church; a sieve; a sheet on which pictures are projected; an electronic display. * vt to shelter; to conceal; to sift.

scree npl debris of rocks; shingle.

screw n a cylinder with a spiral ridge; a screw propeller; a twist or turn. * vt to fasten by a screw; to twist; to oppress.

screwdriver n an instrument for turning screw nails.

screw nail n a nail grooved like a screw.

scribble vti to write carelessly. * n a scrawl.

scribe n a writer; copyist.

scrimp vt to make too small or short. * adj scanty.

script n handwriting; type imitating handwriting; the text of a play or a film.

scripture n any sacred writing.

scroll n a roll of paper; a first draft; a spiral design.

scrotum n the bag which contains the testicles.

scrounge vti to seek or obtain (something) for nothing.

scrub vt to rub hard; to make clean or bright. * n a stunted tree or bush; a mean person.

scrubby adj stunted; niggardly.

scruple n (usu pl) a moral principle or belief causing one to doubt or hesitate about a course of action. *vt, vi to hesitate owing to scruples.

scrupulous adj conscientious; exact.

scrutinize vti to examine closely; to investigate.

scrutiny n close search; careful investigation.

scuffle n a confused struggle. vi to strive confusedly at close quarters.

scull n a short oar, used in pairs. * vt to propel by sculls.

scullery n a back kitchen where dishes, etc, are washed.

sculptor n an artist in stone, wood, clay, etc.

sculpture n the art of carving wood or stone into images; an image in stone, etc.

scum n impurities which rise to the surface of liquids; offscourings.

scupper n hole to carry off water from ship's deck; to sink deliberately.

scurrilous adj foul-mouthed; abusive.

scurry vt to hurry. * n hurry; haste.

scurvily adv basely; shabbily.

scurvy n a disease caused by insufficiency of vitamin C. * adj vile; mean.

scuttle n a pail for coals; a hatchway; a short run; a quick race. * vt to sink by making holes in (a ship). * vi to scurry.

scythe n an implement for mowing grass, etc.

sea n an expanse of salt water; ocean or part of it; a vast quantity; a great wave.

seagoing adj applied to vessels going to foreign ports.

seal n a stamp or die with motto or device; wax with stamp impression; guarantee; carnivorous marine animal. * vt to set a seal to; to confirm; to close.

sea level n the level of the sea's surface.

seam n the joining line of edges of cloth; a vein of metal; a scar.

seamy adj sordid; disagreeable; shabby.

séance n to try to communicate with the dead; a meeting of spiritualists.

seaport n a town on the sea or estuary

accesible to oceangoing ships.

sear vt to brand; to burn; to deaden.

search vt to look or rummage for; to explore, examine. * n quest; pursuit; inquiry.

searching adj penetrating; severe; testing.

seashore n land beside the sea or between high and low water marks.; the beach.

seasick adj affected with sickness by rolling of ship.

seaside n the seacoast.

season n a division of the year; a suitable time; time of greatest activity. * vt to accustom; to acclimatize; to flavour.

seasonable adj opportune; timely.

seasoning n salt, spices, etc used to enhance the flavour of food.

seat n that on which one sits; a chair, stool, etc; place of sitting; a right to sit; residence; station; manner of sitting. * vt to place on a seat; to settle.

seaward adj, adv toward the sea.

seaweed n a mass of plants growing in or under water; a sea plant, esp a marine alga.

sebaceous adj containing fatty matter.

secede vi to withdraw from fellowship.

secession n disruption; withdrawal from membership.

secluded adj retired; remote; private.

seclusion n solitude; privacy.

second adj next after the first; inferior; other. * n one who comes next after first; one who supports another; to place in temporary service elsewhere; sixtieth part of a minute. * vt to support.

secondary adj subordinate; not elementary; inferior.

secrecy n concealment; seclusion; habit of keeping secrets.

secret adj not made public; concealed from others; hidden; private; remote. * n something hidden; a mystery; a hidden cause.

secretariat n an administrative office or staff, as in a government.

secretary n a person employed to deal with correspondence, filing, answering telephone calls etc; head of a state department; executive officer of company.

secrete vt to hide; to produce and release

(a substance) out of blood or sap.

secretion n act or process of secreting; matter secreted, as bile, etc.

secretive adj given to secrecy; reticent.

sect n a body of persons united in doctrine; a denomination.

sectarian adj pertaining to a sect; bigoted. * n member of a sect.

section n a cutting; part cut off; subdivision of chapter, etc; slice; distinct part; the plane figure formed when solid is cut through.

sectional adj made up of sections; partial.

sector n part of circle between two radii; a mathematical instrument.

secular adj worldly; temporal; not sacred.

secularize vt to free from religious influence; to hand over church property to state.

secure adj free from care or danger; safe; confident. * vt to make safe; to seize and confine; to guarantee; to fasten.

security n safety; confidence; protection; a guarantee; a surety; pl bonds, stocks, etc.

sedate adj staid; sober; calm; composed.

sedately adv calmly; tranquilly.

sedative adj soothing. * n an opiate; a soothing drug.

sedentary adj inactive; requiring much sitting.

sediment n that which settles to bottom of liquids; matter deposited by water or wind.

sedition n action or speech against law and order.

seditious adj inciting to rebellion; inflammatory.

seduce vt to lead astray; to corrupt.

seduction n allurement; temptation; attraction.

seductive adj enticing; alluring.

sedulous adj assiduous; diligent.

see vt to perceive by the eye; to notice; to understand. * vi to have the power of sight. * interj Look! * n diocese or sphere of a bishop.

seed n the small hard part of a plant from which a new plant grows; descendant. * vti to sow; to produce seed.

seedling n a plant reared from the seed.

seedy adj abounding with seeds; shabby; out of sorts.

seeing n vision, sight. *adj having sight; observant. *conj in view of the fact that; since.

seek vti to search for; to ask for; to resort to.

seem vi to appear; to look as if; to pretend.

seemingly adv apparently.

seemly adj becoming; decent.

seer n a prophet.

seesaw n a swinging movement up and down; a children's game on balanced plank; vacillation.

seethe vi to be very angry outwardly.

segment n a section; part of circle cut off by straight line; a portion.

segregate vt to set apart or separate from others; to isolate.

seismic adj pertaining to earthquakes.

seismology n the science of earthquakes.

seize vti to lay hold of forcibly; to apprehend; to attack, as fear, illness, etc.

seizure n act of seizing; a sudden attack of illness.

seldom adv rarely; not often.

select vt to choose; to pick out. * adj chosen.

selection n process of choosing; things chosen.

self n (pl selves) one's individual person or interest. * adj or pron same; uniform.

self-conscious adj thinking about one's self overmuch; shy.

self-defence n the act of defending oneself.

self-denial n the forbearing to gratify one's desires; unselfishness.

self-esteem n high opinion of one's self; vanity.

self-evident adj obvious; needing no proof.

self-important adj pompous.

self-imposed adj voluntarily undertaken.

selfish adj absorbed in one's self; ungenerous.

self-respect n proper pride.

self-righteous adj stressing one's own goodness; pharisaical.

self-seeking adj selfish.

self-sufficient adj needing no help.

sell vt to give for a price; to betray. * vi to practise selling; to be sold.

semaphore n a system of visual signalling using the operators arms, flags etc.

semblance n similarity; appearance.

semibreve n a musical note = 2 minims.

semicircle n a half circle.

semicolon n the point (;) marking a longer pause than a comma.

seminal adj pertaining to seed; germinal.

seminar n a group of students engaged in research or study under supervision; any group meeting to pool and discuss ideas.

seminary n a school, academy, or college.

semiquaver n half a quaver in music.

semitic adj hebrew.

semolina n granular flour.

senate n a legislative or deliberative council; governing body in some universities.

senator n a member of a senate.

send vt to cause to go or be carried; to transmit; to dispatch.

senile adj aged; doting; tottering.

senility n a state of being mentally weakened by old age.

senior adj older; higher in rank or standing. * n one older in age or office.

seniority n priority in rank or office.

sensation n perception through the senses; feeling; a thrill.

sensational adj causing excited feeling; emotional.

sense n one of the five senses, sight, hearing, taste, smell, touch; understanding; good judgment; discernment; meaning.

senseless adj stupid; foolish; meaningless; purposeless.

sensibility n acuteness of perception; delicacy of feeling.

sensible adj having good sense; judicious; reasonable; appreciable.

sensitive adj susceptible to impressions; easily affected; touchy; tender.

sensitize vt to make (paper) susceptible to rays of light.

sensory adj relating to the sensorium; conveying sensation.

sensual adj bodily, relating to the senses

rather than the mind; arousing sexual desire.

sensuous *adj* giving pleasure to the body or the mind through the senses.

sentence *n* opinion; judgment of a court; a number of words containing complete sense. * *vt* to pass sentence upon; to condemn.

sententious *adj* abounding in maxims; terse; judicial.

sentient *adj* making use of the senses.

sentiment *n* tenderness of feeling; thought prompted by emotion; a toast.

sentimental *adj* apt to be swayed by feelings; romantic.

sentinel *n* a guard; sentry.

sentry *n* a soldier on guard to give warning of danger.

separable *adj* that may be separated; capable of separation.

separate *vt* to put or set apart; to sever; to divide apart. * *vi* to go apart. * *adj* detached; distinct.

separation *n* the act of separating or the state of being seperate; a formal arrangement of husband and wife to live apart.

separatist *n* one who advocates separation; a seceder.

sepia *n* a brown pigment.

September *n* the ninth month of the year.

septenary *adj* consisting of or proceeding by sevens; lasting seven years.

septennial *adj* occuring every, or lasting seven years.

septic *adj* promoting or causing putrefaction.

septicaemia *n* blood poisoning.

septuagenarian *n* a person seventy years of age.

septum *n* (*pl* septa) a membrane separating organs or cavities.

sepulchral *adj* grave; hollow, as a voice.

sepulchre *n* a tomb. * *vt* to bury.

sequel *n* that which follows; a consequence; issue.

sequence *n* a coming after; succession; series.

sequester *vt* to set apart; to withdraw; to seize goods till debt is paid; to confiscate.

sequestrate *vt* to seize and dispose of

goods for benefit of creditors.

sequestration *n* confiscation of debtor's goods in interest of creditors.

serenade *n* music played at night under a person's window, esp by a lover. * *vti* to perform such music.

serene *adj* clear; bright; calm; unruffled.

serenity *n* calmness; peace; equanimity.

sergeant *n* a noncommissioned officer above corporal in the army etc; a police officer.

serial *adj* appearing periodically. * *n* a story issued in parts.

series *n* a succession of things; sequence.

serious *adj* grave; earnest; attended with danger; important; critical.

sermon *n* a religious discourse; an admonition.

serpentine *adj* spiral; winding; crafty. * *n* a mineral.

serrated *adj* notched; toothed.

serum *n* the watery part of bodily fluid, esp liquid that seperates out from the blood when it coagulates; such fluid taken from the blood of an animal immune to a disease, used as an anti-toxin.

servant *n* a domestic; an attendant.

serve *vt* to work for and meet the needs of; to minister to; to deliver or execute; to supply with (food). * *vi* to be a servant; to suit.

service *n* work of servant; employment; kindness; official duties; public worship; liturgy; table dishes; the services, army, navy, etc.

serviceable *adj* useful; beneficial.

serviette *n* a table napkin.

servile *adj* slavish; fawning; subservient.

servility *n* meanness of spirit; excessive deference.

servitude *n* slavery; bondage.

sessile *adj* stalkless; growing direct from stem.

session *n* the meeting of a court; a series of such meetings; aperiod of study; a university year.

set *vt* to place in position; to fix; to appoint; to regulate or adjust; to fit to music; to adorn; to spread (sails). * *vi* to sink below horizon; to solidify; to tend; to point out game; to apply one's self.

* *n* direction; tendency; attitude; bent; collection of things used together; a group of games; persons associated.

settee *n* a short sofa.

setting *n* descent below horizon; hardening of plaster; the mounting of a gem; fitting to music; a background scene; enviroment.

settle *vt, vi* to fix permanently; to quiet; to decide; to pay; to agree; to subside; to become calm; to clarify; to take up residence.

settled *adj* established; steadfast.

settlement *n* an arrangement; a newly established colony; subsidence (of buildings).

settler *n* a colonist.

seven *adj* one more than six.

sevenfold *adj* seven times.

seventeenth *adj, n* the ordinal of seventeen.

seventh *adj* the ordinal of seven.

seventieth *adj, n* the ordinal of seventy.

seventy *adj, n* seven times ten.

sever *vt* to seperate; to divide into parts; to break off.

several *adj* separate; more than two; but not very many.

severally *adv* separately.

severance *n* separation.

severe *adj* serious; grave; harsh; searching; austere.

severity *n* harshness; cruel treatment; intensity.

sew *vti* to make by needle and thread.

sewage *n* waste matter carried off by sewers.

sewer *n* a subterranean drain, to carry off water, filth, etc.

sewerage *n* the system of sewers; sewage.

sex *n* the characteristics that distinguish male and female organisms on the basis of their reproductive function.

sexagenarian *n* a person sixty years of age.

sexism *n* discrimination on the basis of sex.

sextant *n* instrument for measuring angles and altitudes.

sextuple *adj* sixfold.

sexual *adj* pertaining to sex.

sexual intercourse *n* the act of copulation.

sexuality *n* state of being sexual.

shabbily *adv* in a shabby manner; with shabby clothes; meanly.

shabby *adj* threadbare; mean; stingy.

shackle *n* a fetter; a manacle. ***** *vt* to fetter; hamper.

shade *n* interception of light; obscurity; darkness; a shady place; a screen; dimness; gradation of light; a ghost.

shading *n* light and shade in a picture.

shadow *adj* a figure projected by interception of light; shade; an inseparable companion; a spirit. ***** *vt* to shade; to cloud; to follow closely.

shadowy *adj* faint; dim; unsubstantial.

shady *adj* abounding in shade; of doubtful character.

shaft *n* the handle of a tool, etc; body of a column; pole of carriage; a critical remark or attack; well-like entrance to mine.

shaggy *adj* long and unkempt; rough; untidy.

shake *vt* to move quickly to and fro; to agitate. ***** *vi* to tremble. ***** *n* a tremor; shock; a trill.

shaky *adj* unsteady; feeble.

shale *n* a clay rock having a slaty structure.

shall *vb aux* in first person it is a future tense; in the second and third it implies authority.

shallow *adj* not deep; superficial; simple. ***** *n* a shoal.

sham *n* a pretence; a fraud. ***** *adj* false. ***** *vti* to feign; pretend.

shambles *npl* a place of great disorder.

shambling *adj* walking with awkward, unsteady gait.

shame *n* a painful emotion excited by guilt, disgrace, etc. ***** *vt* to make ashamed; to disgrace.

shameful *adj* disgraceful; infamous.

shameless *adj* immodest; unblushing.

shampoo *n* a liquid cleansing agent for washing the hair. ******vt* to wash the hair with shampoo.

shandy *n* beer diluted with a nonalchoholic drink (as lemonade).

shank n the leg; the shinbone; the stem or shaft of tool, anchor, etc.

shanty n a hut or mean dwelling; sailors' song.

shape vt to form; to mould. * vi to suit. * n form or figure; make; a model.

shapely adj well-proportioned.

shard n a fragment of pottery.

share n a part, lot, or portion; ploughshare; one of equal parts of company's capital. * vti to divide; to apportion among others; to have part.

shareholder n owner of shares in company.

shark n a voracious sea fish; a swindler.

sharp adj having a cutting edge or point; keen; shrewd; piercing; biting; barely honest. * n a note raised a semitone.

sharpen vt to make sharp; to whet.

sharpshooter n an expert shot; a sniper.

shatter vti to break in pieces; to smash.

shave vt to cut hair close with razor; to pare; to miss narrowly; to graze; to fleece. * n a cutting off of the beard; a narrow escape.

shaving n a thin slice pared off.

shawl n a loose covering for the shoulders.

she pron nominative third person sing. feminine.

sheaf n (pl **sheaves**) a bundle of stalks of wheat, etc; a collection of papers tied in a bundle.

shear vti to clip or eat through; to remove (a sheep's fleece) by clipping; to break off.

shears npl a large kind of scissors.

sheath n a close fitting cover; a condom.

sheathe vt to put into sheath; to protect by a casing.

sheathing n covering of metal to protect ship's bottom.

shed vti to cast off; to diffuse; to let fall in drops; to spill. * n a watershed; a hut; a roofed shelter.

sheen n brightness; gloss.

sheer adj mere; downright; precipitous. * vi to swerve; to shy.

sheet n a broad, thin piece of anything; broad expanse; bed linen; a single piece

of paper; a newspaper.

shelf n (pl **shelves**) a horizontal board fixed in position to support books, etc; a ledge.

shell n hard outer crust or case; an explosive projectile. * vt to strip off shell; to fire shells.

shellfish n an aquatic animal with a shell covering.

shelter n a protection; asylum; refuge. * vt to protect. * vi to take shelter.

shelve vt to place on a shelf; to defer consideration. * vi to slope.

shelving n shelves collectively.

shepherd n a person who looks after sheep.

sheriff n chief law officer or judge of a county.

sherry n a fortified wine of southern Spain.

shield n a protective covering or guard; a piece of armour carried for defence on the left arm. * vt to protect; to screen.

shieling n see Shealing.

shift vi to change; to move; to contrive; to manage; *n a change; expedient; a dodge; relay time.

shiftless adj improvident; useless; without resource.

shifty adj unreliable; changeable; tricky.

shillyshally vi to wobble; to vacillate.

shimmer vi to glisten softly. * n a flicker.

shin n the front of lower leg.

shine vi to emit light; to beam; to be bright, lively, conspicuous.

shingle n thin wood used in roofing; loose gravel. *vt to roof with shingles.

shingles n a viral disease marked by a painful rash of red spots.

shining adj bright; illustrious.

shinty n a form of hockey.

ship n a large seagoing vessel; *vti to put or take on board; to transport for service in a ship; to fix in place.

shipmate n a fellow sailor.

shipment n a consignment; goods shipped.

shipper n one who exports or imports goods by sea.

shipping n ships in general; the business of transporting goods.

shipshape *adj* in seamanlike fashion; trim.

shipwreck *n* the wreck of a ship; the loss of a vessel at sea.

shipyard *n* a shipbuilding establishment.

shirk *vti* to try to evade a duty.

shirt *n* a sleeved garment of cotton etc for the upper body.

shiver *vti* to shatter. * *vi* to tremble, as from cold; to shudder. * *n* a splinter; shaking fit.

shoal *n* a large number of fish swimming together.

shock *n* a violent collision; a sudden emotional disturbance; the effect of an electrical charge on the body. * *vt* to horrify; to disgust.

shocking *adj* dreadful; offensive.

shoddy *n* made of inferior quality. *adj* made of shoddy; trashy.

shoe *n* outer covering for foot; metal plate on hoof of horse; a drag for a wheel.

shoehorn *n* a curved piece of horn (or metal) to aid in putting on shoe.

shoot *vt* to discharge with force; to hit or kill with missile; to propel quickly.* *vi* to dart along; to sprout. * *n* a young branch or bud; a chute.

shooting *n* killing game; land rented to shoot over.

shop *n* a place where goods are sold by retail; a workshop. * *vi* to visit shops.

shore *n* land along edge of sea; coast; a prop. * *vt* to prop up.

short *adj* not long or tall; scanty; concise; curt; brittle. *npl* short trousers. * *in* short, briefly.

shortage *n* a deficit.

shortcoming *n* a defect.

shorten *vt* to make short; to reduce amount.

shorthand *n* abbreviated writing.

short-sighted *n* unable to see far; wanting foresight.

shortwave. *n* a radio wave sixty metres or less in length.

shot *n* act of shooting; a projectile; a bullet; range or reach; a marksman.

shoulder *n* the joint connecting arm, foreleg, or wing to body; a projection. *vt* to jostle; to put on shoulder.

shout *vi* to utter a loud cry. * *n* a loud cry.

shove *vti* to push forward; to jostle. * *n* a push.

shovel *n* a kind of spade with slightly curved blade.

show *vt* to display to view; to let be seen; to prove. * *vi* to appear. * *n* display; pageant; pretence; a theatrical performance.

shower *n* a brief fall of rain, etc; a copious supply. * *vti* to rain; to pour down; to bestow liberally.

showroom *n* a room in which goods are exhibited.

shrapnel *n* an artillery shell filled with small pieces of metal that scatter on impact.

shred *vt* to tear into small pieces. * *n* a fragment or scrap.

shrew *n* a scold; a kind of mouse.

shrewd *adj* astute; clever.

shrewish *adj* given to scolding.

shriek *vi* to scream * *n* a shrill cry.

shrill *adj* piercing in sound; strident.

shrine *n* a hallowed place; an altar; a tomb.

shrink *vi* to contract; to shrivel; to flinch.

shrive *vt* to confess and absolve.

shrivel *vi, vt* to shrink into wrinkles; to wither up.

shroud *n* a burial cloth; anything that covers or conceals.

shrub *n* a bush with separate stems from same root.

shrubbery *n* a plantation of shrubs.

shrug *vti* to raise one's shoulders in surprise, doubt, indifference, etc.

shudder *vi* to tremble with fear; to quake. * *n* a tremor.

shuffle *vt* to shove one way and the other; to confuse; to mix cards. * *vi* to quibble; to drag one's feet. *n* an evasion; a shuffling gait or step.

shuffling *adj* moving with irregular gait; evasive.

shun *vt* to avoid; to refrain from.

shunt *vi, vt* in railways, to switch from one track to another.

shut *vti* to close or stop up; to bar.

shutter *n* a movable screen for a window.

shuttle *n* a boat-shaped contrivance for shooting cross threads in loom; an aircraft, spacecraft, etc, making back-and-forth trips over a given route..

shuttlecock n a cork stuck with feathers, used in game of badminton.

shy adj timid; retiring; very self-conscious; coy. * vi, vt to start aside, as horse; to throw. * n a throw.

shyness n reserve; coyness.

sibilant adj hissing. * n a letter uttered with a hissing as s and z.

sic adv thus; it is so; usually written (sic).

sick adj ill; disgusted; uhealthy; vomiting.

sicken vt to make sick; to disgust. * vi to become sick.

sickening adj disgusting.

sickle n a reaping hook.

sickness n disease; ill-health.

side n the broad or long surface of a body; edge, border; slope (of hill); bias (of ball). * vi to support; espouse (a cause). * adj oblique.

sideboard n a piece of furniture used to hold dining utensils, etc.

sidelong adv indirect. * adj oblique.

sidetrack vt to prevent action by diversionary tactics; to shunt aside.

sideways adv see Sidewise.

sidewise adv toward one side; on one side.

siding n a short line of rails for shunting purposes.

siege n the surrounding of a fortified place to cut off supplies and compel its surrender; the act of beseiging; a continued attempt to gain something.

sienna n a reddish-brown pigment.

siesta n a nap in hottest part of day.

sieve n a strainer; sifter.

sift vt to separate coarser parts from finer with a sieve.

sifter n a sieve.

sigh vi to draw a deep and audible breath, as in grief, weariness or relief. * n a long and deep breath.

sight n act or power of seeing; view; visibility; estimation; a show. * vt to see.

sightless adj blind.

sightseeing n the visiting of interesting places.

sign n a mark, token, stamp, or symbol; an emblem; indication; gesture. * vti to affix signature; to make a sign.

signal n a sign to give information, orders, etc, at a distance. * adj notable. * vti to convey by signs.

signally adv remarkably; notably.

signatory n party to signing a treaty or other agreement.

signature n one's name written by oneself; a printed sheet when folded before being used.

signboard n a board marked with person's name or business.

significant adj weighty; important; highly expressive; momentous.

signify vt to make known; to mean; to imply.

silence n quiet; secrecy; stillness; absence of sound. * vt to still; to cause to be quiet.

silent adj mute; taciturn; making no noise.

silhouette n a shadow outline of a shape against light.

silicon n nonmetallic element whose oxide is silica.

silk n the fine thread produced by silkworm; cloth made of silk.

silky adj like silk; smooth and glossy.

sill n the timber or stone at foot of window.

silly adj foolish; unwise; frivolous; being stunned or dazed.

silo n a pit or tower for storage (fodder).

silt n sediment from moving water.

silver n a ductile, malleable, precious metal of a white colour used in jewellery, cutlery etc.. * vti to coat with silver.

silvering n coating with silver or quicksilver.

silversmith n a worker or dealer in silver.

silver-tongued adj persuasive; musical.

similar adj like; resembling.

similarity n likeness; resemblance.

simile n a figure of speech containing a comparison.

similitude n likeness; resemblance.

simmer vi to boil gently.

simper vi to smile in a silly manner. * n an affected smile.

simple adj not complex; single; artless; plain; silly; easy to understand or solve * n a medicinal herb.

simplicity n sincerity; artlessness; innocence; folly.

simplify vt to make simple.

simulate vt to pretend to have or feel; to feign.

simulation n reproducing specific conditions or conduct.

simultaneous adj taking place at the same time.

sin n a transgression of the divine law; iniquity; a wicked act; an offence. * vi to do wrong.

since adv from that time; ago. * prep after. * conj because that.

sincere adj genuine, real, not pretended; honest; straightforward.

sincerity n honesty of mind; freedom from pretence.

sinecure n a paid office with few, if any, duties.

sinew n the fibrous cord which joins muscle to bone.

sinful adj wicked; erring.

sing vi, vt to utter melodious sounds; to celebrate in song.

singe vt to burn surface. * n a slight burn.

single adj being one or a unit; individual; unmarried; sincere. * vt to select individually (with out).

singly adv one by one; sincerely.

singular adj denoting only one person or thing; remarkable; quaint; rare. * n singular number.

singularly adv peculiarly; remarkably.

sinister adj left; evil; malevolent; ominous.

sink vi to fall below surface (water); to subside; to fall in value, strength, etc. * vt to immerse; to dig (shaft); to degrade. * n a drain or receptacle to carry off dirty water.

sinking adj depressing, as in feeling.

sinner n a transgressor; offender; a person who sins.

sinuate vt to wind. * adj winding.

sinuosity n a wavy line; a bend.

sinuous adj winding; curved; tortuous.

sinus n an air cavity in the skull that opens in the nasal cavities.

sip vt to drink in small quantities. * n a drop; a taste.

siphon n a bent tube for drawing off liquids.

sir n a word of respect used to men; a title.

siren n a device producing a loud wailing sound as a warning signal; a sea nymph who lured sailors to destruction; an alluring, dangerous woman.

sirloin n the upper part of loin of beef.

sirocco n a hot wind blowing over southern Europe from south.

sister n a female born of the same parents; a member of a religious sisterhood.

sister-in-law n a husband or wife's sister.

sit vi to rest oneself on the buttocks, as on a chair, to perch (birds); to incubate; to have a seat (in Parliament); to suit; to take an examination.

site n situation; a building plot; the scene of something.

sitter n one who sits for his portrait.

sitting n a session, as of a court.

situated adj placed; located; circumstanced.

situation n position; station; post.

six adj, n one more than five.

sixfold adj, adv six times.

sixteen adj, n six and ten.

sixteenth adj ordinal of sixteen.

sixth adj ordinal of six.

sixtieth adj, n ordinal of sixty.

sixty adj, n six times ten.

size n magnitude; the dimensions or proportions of something; a thin pasty glue used by painters to glaze paper, etc. * vt to arrange according to size; to cover with size.

skate n a steel bar fastened to boot for moving on ice; a coarse flat fish. * vt to go on skates.

skateboard n a short, oblong board with two wheels at each end for standing on and riding.

skein n a small hank of thread.

skeleton n the bony framework of an animal; outline.

sketch n an outline; a first rough draught quickly made. * vt to draw; to outline.

skewer n a pin for fastening meat.

ski n (pl skis) a long narrow runner of wood, metal or plastic that is fastened to a boot to enable movement across snow. * vi to travel on skis.

skid vti to slide without rotating; to slip sideways as cycle, aeroplane, etc. * n a drag to reduce speed.

skiff n a small light boat.

skilful adj skilled; dexterous; adroit.

skill n ability; expertness; aptitude; proficiency.

skim vt to remove the scum from the surface of; to glance over (book). * vi to glide along (water).

skin n the natural outer coating of animals; a hide; rind. * vt to strip the skin from; flay.

skin-deep adj superficial.

skinflint n a stingy person.

skinny adj very thin.

skip vi to leap; to bound; to spring. * vt to omit. * n a light leap; captain of curling or bowling team.

skipper n the captain of a ship.

skirmish n a minor fight in a war. * vi to fight when reconnoitering.

skirt n lower part of a coat; woman's garment that hangs from the waist; border. * vti to border; to pass along edge.

skit n a short humorous sketch.

skittish adj excitable; frisky; fickle.

skulk vi to lurk; to keep out of sight; to shirk duty.

skull n the bony case which contains the brain; the cranium.

sky n the vault of heaven.

skylight n a window in a roof.

skyward adj, adv toward the sky.

slab n a flat piece of stone, wood, etc. * adj thick and slimy.

slack adj loose; easy-going; not busy; relaxed. * n loose part of a rope, etc. * vti to idle; less active; to slacken.

slacken vi to become slack; * vt to relax; to reduce; to loosen.

slag n fused dross of metal; clinkers.

slake vt to quench; to mix (lime) with water.

slam vti to shut with a bang. * n a bang; winning of all tricks at bridge.

slander n a false and injurious report. * vt to vilify; to defame.

slang n, adj expressions in common use but not approved as good English; jargon.

slant adj sloping. * vti to slope; to incline; to tell in such a way as to have a bias.* n a slope.

slap n a blow with the open hand. * vt to strike with the open hand.

slapdash adv carelessly; at random.

slash vti to strike at wildly with knife, sword, etc; to slit, as a sleeve. * n a long cut; slit.

slate n rock which splits into thin layers; a thin roofing slab; a writing plate. * vt to cover with slates; to criticize harshly.

slater n one who slates buildings.

slating n the roof or roofing; harsh criticism.

slaughter n a slaying; carnage; massacre. * vt to slay; to kill for market.

slave n a person without freedom or personal rights.

slaver n saliva dripping from mouth. * vti to let saliva drip; to fawn upon.

slavery n bondage; drudgery.

slavish adj servile; oppressively laborious.

slay vt to kill by violence; to murder.

sledgehammer n a large, heavy hammer for two hands.

sledge n a vehicle on runners used over snow; a sleigh.

sleek adj smooth and glossy; plausible.

sleep vi, vt to rest with mind and body inactive; to slumber; to lie dormant. * n slumber; repose; death.

sleeper n one who sleeps; a beam for support joists, floors, rails, etc; a sleeping car (railway).

sleepy adj drowsy; sluggish; not alert.

sleet n hail or snow mingled with rain.

sleeve n part of a garment enclosing arm.

sleight n manual dexterity; **sleight of hand** jugglery.

slender adj thin; slim; scanty.

slice vt to cut into thin pieces; a stroke that makes the ball curl to th right (golf). * n a thin broad piece cut off.

slide vi, vt to slip or glide over surface, as ice. * n a slope or track for sliding on.

slight adj small; trifling; frail. * n intentional disregard. * vt to treat as of no account.

slim adj slight; slender; cunning.

slime n oozy sticky mud; mucus.

sling vt to hurl; to suspend; to place in a sling. * n a contrivance for hurling stones; a hanging bandage for injured limb.

slink vt to steal away.

slip vi to move smoothly along; to glide; to miss one's foothold; to let go (anchor); to err; to escape (memory). * n act of slipping; omission; error; leash; narrow strip (paper, etc); incline on which ships are built.

slipper n a light soft shoe for household wear.

slippery adj causing to slip; unreliable.

slipshod adj down at heels; slovenly.

slit vt to cut lengthwise. * n a long cut or opening.

sliver n a splinter.

slobber vi, vt to drool; to run at the mouth.

slogan n a catchy phrase used in advertising or as a motto by a political party etc.

sloop n a sailing vessel with one mast.

slop vt to spill. * n unappetising; semi-liquid food; spilled water; poor liquor; (pl) dirty or waste water.

slope n a slant.* vti to incline.

sloppy adj careless; untidy; slovenly.

slot n a long narrow opening; a slit. *vt to fit into a slot.

sloth n indolence; laziness; a slow-moving mammal.

slouch n to sit or move in a drooping or ungainly manner * vi, vt to move with drooping gait.

slouching adj awkward; crouching.

slough n cast skin of snake. * vi, vt to cast or come off (skin).

slovenly adj untidy; dirty; careless.

slow adj not rapid; tardy; dull; stupid.

sludge n mire; soft mud; sediment.

sluggish adj lazy; slothful; slow.

sluice n a gate for regulating flow of water in canal, etc. * vti to scour with water.

slum n an overcrowded area.

slumber vi to sleep; to doze. * n a light sleep.

slump n sudden fall in value or slacking in demand. * vt to lump together; to fall heavily (shares).

slur vt to pronounce or speak indistinctly; to run together (words). * n a stain, stigma.

slush n sludge or soft mud; half-melted snow.

slut n a slovenly or immoral woman; a slattern.

sly adj cunning; crafty; wily.

smack vi to make a sharp noise with lips; to taste. * vt to slap. * n a loud kiss; a slap; a taste; a fishing vessel.

small adj little; petty; short; narrow-minded; mean.

small arms npl rifles, pistols, etc, as distinguished from artillery.

smallpox n a contagious disease, now rare, marked by pustules on skin.

small talk n light, social talk.

smart n a quick, keen pain. * adj keen;clever; quick; brisk; witty; spruce. * vi to feel a sharp pain.

smarten vt to make smart.

smash vt to dash or go to pieces. * n a crash; ruin; failure.

smattering n a superficial knowledge.

smear vt to daub with anything greasy.

smell vti to perceive by the nose; to give out an odour. * n sense of smell; scent; odour.

smelt vt to melt, as ore. * n a small fish allied to salmon.

smile vi to show joy by the features of the face. * n a look of pleasure.

smirk vi to smile affectedly. * n an inane smile; simper.

smite vti to strike; to slay; to afflict.

smock n a chemise; a smock frock.

smocking n a fancy stitch in sewing.

smoke n sooty vapour from burning substance; vapour; act of smoking (pipe, etc). * vi, vt to emit smoke; to use tobacco; to fumigate.

smoking n the use of tobacco. * adj emitting smoke.

smoky adj giving out smoke; filled with smoke.

smooth adj even on the surface; glossy; pleasant. * vt to make smooth; to level.

smother n to cover over quickly * vti to stifle; to suffocate.

smoulder vi to burn and smoke without flame.

smudge *vt* to stain with dirt. * *n* a stain; a smear.

smug *n* complacent; self-satisfied.

smuggle *vt* to import or export secretly without paying duty.

smuggling *n* the importing or exporting goods without paying duty.

smut *n* a spot or stain; a flake of soot; obscene language.

smutty *adj* soiled with smut; obscene.

snack *n* a light meal between regular meals.

snag *n* a short projecting stump; a knot; a stumbling block.

snake *n* a limbless, scaly reptile with a long tapering body, often with salivery glands modified to produce venom.

snap *vti* to bite or seize suddenly; to break with a sharp sound. * *n* a sudden bite; spring catch; sharp noise.

snapshot *n* a hasty shot at a moving animal; an instantaneous photograph.

snare *n* a running noose for catching animals; a pitfall; a trap. * *vt* to catch in snare; to trap.

snarl *vi* to growl with bared teeth, as an angry dog; to speak rudely; to become entangled. * *n* a growl.

snarling *adj* snappish; peevish.

snatch *vt* to seize abruptly or without permission. * *vi* to grasp (at). * *n* a sudden seizing; a small portion.

sneak *vi, vt* to go slyly; to steal off; to behave meanly. * *n* a telltale; a mean wretch.

sneer *vi* to show contempt by a look; to jeer. * *n* a scoff; a jeer.

sneeze *vi* to emit air violently and audibly through nose.

snick *vt* to cut; to clip; to snip.

sniff *vi* to smell; to inhale through the nose audibly.

snigger *vi* to giggle; to laugh in sly fashion. * *n* a partly suppressed laugh.

snip *vt* to cut off at a stroke. * *n* a single cut; small piece; a certainty.

snipe *vt* to lie in wait and pick off enemy by rifle fire.

snippet *n* a small part cut off; *pl* odds and ends.

snivelling *adj* whining; tearful.

snob *n* a person who wishes to be associated with those of a higher social status, whilst acting condescendingly to those whom he or she regards as inferior.

snooze *n* a short sleep. * *vi* to take a short nap.

snore *vi* to breathe noisily in sleep; noisy breathing in sleep.

snorkel *n* a breathing tube extending above the water, used in swimming just below the surface. * *vi* to swim using a snorkel.

snort *vi* to eject air violently through nose, as horses. * *n* an explosive breath sound.

snout *n* animal's nose or muzzle.

snow *n* vapour frozen in the air and falling in flakes.

snowball *n* a ball of snow pressed together for throwing.

snowdrift *n* a bank of drifted snow.

snowdrop *n* an early spring flower.

snowplough *n* an implement for clearing snow from roads.

snub *vt* to humiliate with words or look; to slight. * *n* a check; rebuke.

snuff *vti* to sniff; to smell; to take snuff; to crop or trim (wick). * *n* charred part of wick; powdered tobacco.

snuffle *vi* to speak through the nose. * *n* a nasal twang; cant; *pl* cold in the head.

snug *adj* neat; trim; cosy.

snuggle *vi* to lie close for warmth; to nestle.

so *adv* in this or that manner; to that degree; thus; very. * *conj* provided that; therefore.

soak *vti* to become saturated; to wet thoroughly.

soap *n* a compound of fat with an alkali, used in washing. * *vt* to rub with soap.

soar *vi* to fly upwards; to tower.

sob *vi* to weep convulsively. * *n* a short choking sigh.

sober *adj* temperate; not drunk; staid; grave; thoughtful.

sobriety *n* temperance; saneness; gravity.

sobriquet *n* a nickname.

soccer *n* a football game played on a field by two teams of eleven players with a round inflated ball.

sociable *adj* fond of companions; social.

social adj living or organized in a community, not solitary; genial; affable.

socialism n a theory of social organization aiming at co-operative action and the nationalization of capital and land.

socialist n one who advocates socialism.

social security n financial assistance for the unemployed, the disabled, etc to alleviate economic distress.

society n the social relationship between human beings or animals organized collectively.

sociologist n one versed in social science.

sociology n the science of the history, nature, etc, of human society; social science.

sock n a short stocking covering the foot and lower leg.

socket n a cavity into which anything is fitted.

sod n small square piece of turf.

soda n the alkali, carbonate of sodium.

sodden adj saturated; soaked and soft.

sofa n a couch with cushioned seat, back, and arms.

soft adj yielding easily to pressure; delicate; smooth; not harsh; quiet.

soften vti to make or become soft; to tone down; to melt; to relent.

softly adv gently; tenderly.

soil vti to make dirty; to tarnish. * n dirt; top layer of earth; mould; country.

sojourn vi to reside for a time. * n a temporary stay.

solace vt to cheer or console. * n consolation; comfort.

solar adj pertaining to or proceeding from sun; sunny.

solder vt to unite metals by a metal alloy. *n an alloy capable when fused of cementing metals together.

soldier n a person in military service.

sole n the under side of the foot; the bottom of a shoe; a flatfish. * vt to furnish with a sole. * adj single; only; alone.

solecism n a grammatical error; a breach of rules of syntax.

solely adv singly; alone; only.

solemn adj grave; formal; impressive; awe inspiring.

solemnity n gravity; a solemn ceremony.

solicit vti to ask earnestly; to invite.

solicitation n supplication; entreaty.

solicitor n a lawyer.

solicitous adj anxious; very concerned.

solid adj resisting pressure; not liquid or gaseous; not hollow; compact; firm; strongly constructed. * n a compact body.

solidarity n unity of interest and action.

solidity n density; firmness.

soliloquy n the act of talking to oneself.

solitaire n a gem in a single setting; a stud; a game for one player.

solitary adj being alone; lonely; unfrequented. * n a recluse.

solitude n loneliness; a lonely place.

solo n a tune or air for a single performer. vi to perform by oneself.

soloist n a solo singer or performer.

solstice n the time when the sun is farthest north or south of equator, 21st June and 21st Dec. respectively.

solubility n quality of being soluble.

soluble adj capable of being dissolved in a fluid; capable of solution, as a problem.

solution n the dissolving of a solid in a liquid; explanation; result.

solve vt to explain; to make clear; to unravel.

solvency n ability to pay debts.

solvent adj having the power of dissolving; able to pay all debts. * n a fluid that dissolves another substance.

sombre adj dark; gloomy; dismal.

some adj an indefinite number; considerable; more or less. * pron an indefinite part, quantity, or number; certain individuals.

somebody n some person; a person of importance.

somehow adv one way or another.

somersault n a leap in which the heels turn over the head.

something n a thing unspecified; part or portion. * adv to some degree.

sometime adv once; by and by. * adj former.

sometimes adv now and then; at times.

somewhat n more or less. * adv in some degree.

somewhere adv in some place.

somnambulism n the act of walking in sleep.

somnolence n sleepiness.

somnolent adj sleepy; drowsy.

son n a male child or descendant.

song n that which is sung; vocal music; a lyric; the call of certain birds.

sonic adj of, producing, or involving sound waves.

son-in-law n a daughter's husband.

sonnet n a poem of fourteen pentameter lines with varying rhymes.

sonorous adj resonant; deep-toned.

soon adv in a short time; quickly; readily.

soot n a black substance formed from burning matter.

sooth adj true. * n truth; reality.

soothe vt to calm; to comfort; to relieve pain.

soothsayer n one who foretells the future.

sop n something dipped in broth or liquid food; bribe given to pacify.

sophism n false reasoning but with appearance of truth.

soporific adj causing sleep. * n a drug that induces sleep.

soprano n the highest female voice; a singer with such a voice.

sorcerer n a wizard; a person who uses magic powers.

sorceress n a female sorcerer.

sorcery n magic; enchantment; witchcraft.

sordid adj mean; vile; base; squalid.

sore adj painful; tender. * n an ulcer, wound, etc.

sorely adv seriously; grievously.

sorrow n grief; distress of mind; sadness; regret. * vi to grieve.

sorrowful adj full of sorrow.

sorry adj feeling sorrow or pity; grieved; wretched.

sort n nature or character; kind; species; a set. * vt to arrange in order; to sort.

soufflé n a light dish of baked egg whites.

soul n the spiritual element in man; conscience; essence; a person.

sound adj whole; firm; healthy; orthodox; just. * n a narrow channel of water; a strait; that which is heard; noise. * vti to measure the depth of; to examine medi-

cally; to try to discover the opinion, etc, of; to make a noise; to probe; to pronounce; to be spread or published.

sounding adj resounding. * n the ascertaining depth of water.

soundings npl the depths of water in rivers, harbours, etc.

soundtrack n the sound accompanying a film; the area on cinema film that carries the sound recording.

soup n a kind of broth.

sour adj acid to the taste; tart; peevish; distasteful or unpleasant. * vt to make sour; to embitter.

source n that from which anything rises; the fountainhead; origin.

souse n pickle; to plunge into water.

south n one of four compass points; position of sun at noon. * adj being in or toward the south.

southeast n the point midway between south and east. * adj pertaining to or from the southeast.

southerly adj lying toward the south; coming from the south.

southern adj belonging to the south; southerly.

southward adv, adj toward the south.

southwest n the point midway between south and west. * adj pertaining to or from the southwest.

souvenir n a keepsake; a momento.

sovereign adj supreme in power; chief * n a monarch; a ruler.

sovereignty n supreme power; dominion.

sow vti to scatter seed over; to spread abroad.

spa n a resort for medicinal water.

space n the limitless three-dimensional expanse within which all objects exist; outer space; a specific area; an interval; empty area; room; an unoccupied area or seat. * vt to arrange at intervals.

spacious adj roomy; capacious.

spade n an instrument for digging; one of the suits of cards.

span n reach or space from thumb to extended little finger; nine inches; short space of time; spread of arch. * vt to extend across; to measure with the fingers extended.

spank vt to slap with the flat of the hand, esp on the buttocks.

spanner n a tool with a hole or jaws to grip and turn nuts or bolts.

spar n a long piece of timber; a pole; a crystalline mineral; boxing match. * vi to box; to bandy words.

spare adj scanty; thin; held in reserve. * vti to use frugally; to dispense with; to be saving; to forbear; to have mercy on.

sparing adj frugal; economical.

spark n a particle of burning matter; a flash of light from an electrical discharge. * vi to emit fiery particles.

sparkle n a little spark; lustre. * vi to emit sparks; to glitter.

sparkling adj glittering; lively.

sparse adj thinly scattered; scanty.

spartan adj rigorously severe.

spasm n a violent contraction of muscles; a convulsive fit.

spasmodic adj intermittently.

spastic n a person who suffers from cerebral palsy. *adj affected by muscle spasm.

spate n a sudden heavy flood; a large amount.

spatial adj pertaining to space.

spatter vt to scatter a liquid on; to sprinkle.

spatula n a broad thin blade, used in spreading plasters, paints, etc.

spawn n the eggs or ova of fish, etc. * vti to deposit spawn.

speak vi, vt to utter words; to talk; to deliver a speech; to pronounce.

speaker n one who speaks; the presiding official in a legislative assembly.

spear n a long, pointed weapon; a lance. * vt to pierce with a spear.

special adj particular; distinctive; uncommon.

specialist n one who devotes himself to some particular subject; an expert.

speciality n special characteristic; something made or sold exclusively by certain traders. * specialty n special characteristic; a special pursuit; a special product.

specialize vti to apply one's self to a particular subject.

species n sing, pl a kind, sort, or variety; a class of plants or animals; subdivision of a genus.

specific adj pertaining to a species; definite; precise. * n a remedy for a special disease; a sure remedy.

specifically adv definitely; precisely.

specification n a requirement; detailed statement of particulars for carrying out contracts, etc.

specify vt to make specific; to state in detail.

specimen n a sample; a part to typify the whole.

specious adj superficially correct; plausible.

speck n a small spot; a flaw; a particle.

speckled adj spotted.

spectacle n a show; an exhibition; a pageant; pl glasses to assist vision.

spectacular adj impressive; astounding.

spectator n an onlooker.

spectral adj shadowy; ghostly.

spectre n an apparition; a ghost.

spectroscope n the instrument employed in decomposition of rays of light.

spectrum n (pl spectra) the coloured bands produced by passing light through a prism.

speculate vi to theorize; to conjecture; to gamble in stocks, land, etc.

speculation n act of speculating; theory; hazardous financial transactions.

speculative adj risky; contemplative.

speculator n one who takes undue risks in business.

speech n the faculty of speaking; language; talk; a formal discourse; oration.

speechless adj silent; unable to speak.

speed n success; velocity; haste. * vi, vt to make haste; to prosper; to fare.

speedometer n indicator for showing speed of motors, cycles, etc.

spell n a charm; fascination; a period of work. * vt to give in correct order the letters of words.

spend vti to pay out, as money; to squander; to pass, as time; to exhaust of force.

spendthrift n, adj a prodigal; wasteful.

spent adj wearied; exhausted.

sperm n semen; the male reproductive cell.

spew vti to vomit; to flow or gush forth.

sphere n an orb; a ball; a sun, star, or planet; extent of motion, action, etc.

spheric, spherical adj globular.

spheroid n a body like a sphere, as earth, orange, etc.

sphincter n a ring-like muscle closing an opening an orifice.

sphinx n a fabled monster, half human, half lion.

spicate adj spiked; pointed.

spice n an aromatic seasoning for food; relish; flavour. * vt to flavour; to season.

spicy adj pungent; piquant; racy.

spider n a small wingless creature (arachnid) with eight legs, and abdominal spinnerets for spinning silk threads to make webs.

spike n a piece of pointed iron; an ear of corn, etc. * vt to fasten with spikes; to transfix; to plug a hole (cannon).

spill vti to let run out or overflow; to shed. * n a piece of wood or twisted paper for lighting candle, etc; a fall.

spin vti to draw out and twist into threads; to protract; to whirl; to rotate swiftly. * n a rapid run.

spinach n a plant with large green edibble leaves

spinal adj pertaining to the spine.

spinal cord n the cord of nerves enclosed by the spinal column.

spindle n a tapering rod on which thread is wound; an axis; a yarn measure; a slender stalk.

spine n a prickle; a pointed spike in animals; the backbone.

spinnaker n a triangular sail used in running before wind.

spinster n an unmarried woman.

spiral adj winding like thread of screw. * n a helix or coil.

spirally adv in spiral fashion.

spire n a cone-like structure; a steeple.

spirit n the breath of life; the soul; a spectre; vivacity; courage; mood; essence; a volatile liquid; pl alcoholic liquor.

spirited adj lively; animated.

spiritless adj dejected; depressed.

spirit level n an instrument for testing when a thing is horizontal.

spiritual adj not material; mental; holy; divine.

spiritualism n the doctrine that soul, spirit, is only reality; belief that communication can be obtained with the dead.

spiritualist n one who believes in spiritualism.

spirituality n quality of being spiritual; spiritual nature.

spit n a prong on which meat is roasted; low land running into the sea. * vt to put on a spit; to pierce.

spit vti to eject from the mouth, as saliva.

spite n ill-will; rancour; malice.

spiteful adj malignant; malicious.

spittle n saliva.

spittoon n a vessel to receive discharges of spittle.

splash vti to bespatter with liquid matter. * n water or mud thrown on anything; noise of heavy body striking water; a spot of mud.

splay vt to slope or form with an angle. * adj turned outward, as a person's feet.

spleen n a large lymphatic organ in the upper left part of the abdomen which modifies the blood structure; spitefulness; ill humour.

splendid adj brilliant; showy; famous.

splendour n brilliancy; magnificence; grandeur.

splenetic adj morose; sullen; spiteful.

splice vt to unite, by interweaving, as ropes, or overlapping, as timber. * n union by interweaving or joining.

splint n a rigid structure to keep a broken limb in position.

splinter n a piece of wood split off * vt to split into small pieces.

split vti to cleave; to rend; to burst; to separate. * n a rent; fissure; breach. * adj divided; rent.

splutter n a confused noise; a stir. * vi to speak incoherently; to spit when speaking.

spoil n pillage; booty; plunder. * vt to plunder; to impair; to over indulge a child. * vi to grow useless; to decay.

spoke n one of bars or rays of a wheel; rung (of ladder). * vi pret of speak.

spoken adj oral; speaking (as in fair-spoken).

spokesman n one who speaks on behalf of others.

sponge n a plantlike marine animal with an internal skeleton of elastic interlacing horny fibres; a piece of natural or manmade sponge for washing or cleaning. *vi (inf) to wipe with a sponge. *vi (inf) to scrounge.

sponger n one who lives on others; a parasite.

sponsor n a person or organization that pays the expenses connected with an artistic production or sports event in return for advertising; in US, a business firm, etc that pays for a radio or TV programme advertising its product. *vt to act as sponsor for.

spontaneity n voluntary action; readiness.

spontaneous adj arising naturally; instinctive.

spook n a ghost; an apparition. *vt to frighten.

spool n a reel, esp to wind thread or yarn on.

spoon n a domestic utensil used in feeding or cooking.

spoor n the track or trail of an animal.

sporadic adj scattered; occurring here and there.

spore n the reproductive body of a flowerless plant.

sport n a game; good humoured joking; out-of-door recreation; jest. * vti to play; to trifle; to wear publicly.

sporting adj indulging in sport; belonging to sport.

spot n a speck, a blemish; a flaw; a locality. * vt to stain; to note.

spotless adj blameless; stainless.

spouse n a husband or wife.

spout n a nozzle; projecting mouth of a vessel; a waterspout. * vti to gush forth; to mouth one's words.

sprain vt to overstrain as muscles or ligaments of a joint. * n a violent strain of a joint.

sprawl vi to spread the limbs untidily.

spray n a twig; collection of small branches; windblown water. * vt to sprinkle with a fluid.

spread vti to stretch or expand; to distribute; to apply a coating; to emit; to diffuse. * n extent; a meal or banquet.

spree n a merry frolic; a carousal.

sprig n a small shoot or spray; a twig with leaves on it.

sprightly adj lively; gay.

spring vi to leap; to start up; to dart; to warp. * vt to cease to operate suddenly; to start or rouse. * n a leap; resilience; elastic spiral; an issue of water; source of supply; season of the year.

springboard n an flexible board used in vaulting, etc.

spring-clean vi to clean (a house, etc) thoroughly.

sprinkle vti to scatter; in small drops.

sprint n a short foot race; a spurt.

sprit n a small spar to extend and raise sail.

sprite n a spirit; a goblin; a dainty person.

sprout vi to bud; to push out new shoots. * n a shoot of a plant; pl brussels sprouts.

spruce adj neat; trim * n a pine tree yielding valuable timber.

spry adj nimble; active; lively.

spume n froth; foam; surf. *vi to froth.

spur n a goad or rowel worn on horsemen's heels; a stimulus; an incentive; an outgrowth; a ridge running off from main range. * vt to prick with a spur; to incite.

spurious adj counterfeit; false.

spurn vt to drive away, as with the foot; to reject or treat with disdain.

spurred adj wearing spurs.

spurt vti to spirt; to exert one's whole strength (in a race). * n a gush of liquid; a special effort.

sputter vi to emit saliva in speaking; to speak hastily and indistinctly.

sputum n spittle.

spy vt to gain sight of; to explore. * vi to pry. * n a secret agent; an informer.

squabble vi to wrangle; to quarrel noisely. * n a scuffle; a brawl.

squad n a small group of soldiers.

squadron n a unit of cavalry or of a fleet.

squalid adj sordid; wretched; dirty.

squall vi to scream loudly. * n a loud scream; a violent gust of wind.

squalor n wretchedness; foulness.

squander vt to spend lavishly; to waste.

square adj having four equal sides and four right angles; forming a right angle; just; honest. * n a parallelogram having four equal sides and right angles; an area with houses in form of square; an instrument for drawing right angles; product of a number multiplied by itself * vti to make square; to adjust; to settle (accounts); to suit.

squash vt to crush; to beat into pulp.

squat vi to crouch down on the heels ; to crouch; to settle on land without authority.

squatter n one who settles on land or property without a title.

squawk vi to cry with a harsh voice; as of a bird.

squeak vi to utter a high pitched sound. * n a high pitched sound.

squeal vi to cry with a sharp, shrill voice. * n a shrill, sharp cry.

squeeze vt to subject to pressure; to hug. * vi to press; to crowd. * n pressure; an embrace.

squint adj looking obliquely. * n an oblique look. * vi to half close or cross the eyes.

squire n an attendant on a knight; a country gentleman. * vt to escort.

squirm vi to wriggle; to writhe.

squirrel n a rodent with a long bushy tail.

squirt vt to throw out in jets. * vi to spirt. * n a syringe; a jet.

stab vti to pierce with a pointed weapon; to pain suddenly and sharply. * n a thrust with dagger, etc; a secret injury.

stability n steadiness; firmness.

stable adj firm; steadfast. * n a building for horses, etc. * vt to put or keep in a stable.

stabling n accommodation for horses.

staccato adj in music, a sign for separate emphasis on each note.

stack n a large, regularly built pile of hay, records, papers, etc; a chimney head; a tall chimney. * vt to pile together.

stadium n an arena.

staff n (pl **staves, staffs**) a stick or rod; a prop or support; a baton; the five parallel lines on which musical notes are written; the officers assisting generals, etc;

in any body of assistants, e.g. in schools.

stag n a full grown male deer.

stage n a raised platform, esp. for actors; a theatre; a halting place; distance between two halting places; field of action; degree of progress. * vt to put on the stage.

stagger vi to reel; to totter; to amaze. * n a lurch; an involuntary swaying of body.

staging n scaffolding.

stagnant adj not flowing; motionless; with a foul smell; sluggish.

stagnate vi to cease to flow; to become foul.

stagnation n state of being motionless; sluggishness.

staid adj sober; grave; sedate.

stain vt to discolour; to soil; to disgrace; to dye. * n a discoloration; disgrace.

stainless adj untarnished; pure.

stair n a series of connected steps.

staircase n a flight of stairs; space occupied by stairs.

stake n a sharpened piece of wood; a post; that which is pledged or wagered; hazard (preceded by at). * vt to mark with stakes; to pledge; to wager.

stalactite n a mass of calcareous matter hanging from roof of cave.

stalagmite n a spike-like calcareous mass rising from floor of cave.

stale adj not fresh; musty; trite. * vt to make stale.

stalemate n a draw in chess through one player not being able to make any move except one that puts his king in check; a deadlock.

stalk n the stem of a plant; a strut. * vi, vt to walk in stately fashion; to follow game warily.

stalker n one who hunts (stalks) deer.

stall n a compartment in a stable; a bench or shed where goods are exposed for sale; a seat near orchestra in theatre; seat in chancel or choir of church. *vti to play for time; to postpone.

stallion n a male horse for breeding purposes.

stalwart adj stout-hearted; tall and strong.

stamen n the organ of flower that produces pollen.

stamina n staying power; strength.

stammer vi, vt to stutter; to halt in speech. * n a stutter.

stamp vti to strike by thrusting foot down; to impress; to imprint; to affix a postage stamp to; to coin. * n an instrument for crushing or for making impressions; mark imprinted; a postage stamp; character; sort.

stampede n a sudden panicky rush (esp. of cattle). * vi, vt to make or cause a sudden rush.

stance n posture; the attitude taken in a particular situation.

stanchion n a supporting prop or post.

stand vi, vt to be erect; stop; endure; be on end; become a candidate; not to fail; pay for. * n a halt; station; small table; booth for exhibiting; tiered platform for spectators.

standard n a flag; an ensign; a rule or measure; a test; a grade; an upright.

stand-in n a substitute.

standing adj upright; erect; permanent; stagnant. * n rank; position.

standpoint n point of view; opinion.

stanza n a verse or connected number of lines of poetry.

staple n a principle commodity of trade or industry of a region, etc; a main constituent; a U-shaped thin piece of wire for fastening. *vt to fasten with a staple.

star n a celestial body other than sun or moon; a figure with radiating points; a badge of honour; an asterisk; thus *; an outstanding artiste. * vt to adorn with stars; to bespangle. * vi to shine as a star; to be pre-eminent.

starboard n, adj the right-hand side of a ship.

starch n a vegetable substance, employed for stiffening linen, etc.

starched adj stiffened with starch; precise; formal.

stare vi to look fixedly. * vt to affect or abash by staring. * n a fixed look.

stargazer n an astronomer; an astrologer.

stark adj bare; plain; blunt. * adv wholly.

starless adj having no stars visible.

starlight n the light from the stars.

starry adj abounding with stars; like stars.

start vi, vt to spring up; to set out; to begin; to wince; to startle. * n a sudden movement; a jump; a handicap; outset.

starter n a device for starting motor engine; one who gives signal for setting off; the first course in a meal.

startle vi to move suddenly. * vt to frighten.

startling adj surprising; alarming.

starvation n state of being starved.

starve vi to suffer or die through lack of food. *vt deprive (a person) of food; to deprive (of) anything necessary.

state n condition; situation; rank; pomp; a nation; civil power. * adj national; public. * vt to narrate.

statecraft n skill in managing affairs of state.

stated adj fixed; regular.

stately adj imposing; dignified; lofty.

statement n something stated; narrative.

statesman n a well-known and experienced politician.

static adj fixed; stationary; at rest. *n electrical interference causing noise on radio or TV.

station n position; situation; rank; class; a stopping place for trains, etc. * vt to assign a position to.

stationary adj fixed; not moving.

stationery n paper, pens, etc.

statistic n a fact expressed in numbers.

statistician n one versed in statistics.

statue n an image of a human figure or animal in marble, bronze, etc. that is moulded.

statuesque n statue-like.

statuette n a small statue.

stature n height; tallness.

status n social position; rank; state of affairs.

statute n a law enacted by parliament.

statutory n enacted by statute.

staunch adj loyal, dependable. *vt to stop from running (as blood).

stave n a pole; one of segments in side of cask; a stanza, in music, the staff * vt to make a hole in. *to stave off, to put off; to delay.

stay vt to prop; to stop; to delay; * vt to remain; to reside. * n sojourn; stop; obstacle; a prop; support; in place.

steadfast *adj* firm; constant; resolute.

steady *adj* firm; constant; regular. * *vt* to make or keep firm.

steak *n* a slice of beef or fish for grilling or frying.

steal *vti* to gain secretly; to take from someone.

stealth *n* a manner of moving quietly and secretly.

steam *n* the vapour of boiling water; energy (*fig*.) * *vti* to emit steam; to expose to steam.

steamy *adj* damp; misty; full of condensation.

steel *n* iron hardened by addition of carbon; a knife sharpener; sternness. * *adj* made of steel; hard. * *vt* to harden; to temper.

steep *adj* sloping greatly; precipitous. * *n* a cliff * *vt* to soak.

steepen *vi* to become steep.

steeple *n* a spire; a pointed tower; usu of a church.

steeplechase *n* a race over obstacles, esp cross-country.

steer *vti* to direct and govern, as a ship; to guide. * *n* a young ox; a bullock.

stellar *adj* pertaining to stars; starry.

stem *n* the stalk of a tree, shrub, etc; stock of a family; the prow of a vessel. * *vt* to dam up; to check.

stench *n* a foul smell.

stencil *n* a thin plate with a pattern cut through it, used for marking surface beneath. * *vt* to paint by means of a stencil.

stenographer *n* one who is skilled at writing in shorthand.

stentorian *adj* loud-voiced.

step *vi* to walk. * *vt* to measure by steps; to fix a mast. * *n* a pace; a grade; a degree; a rise; footprint; rung of ladder; (*prefix*) related by remarriage of a spouse or partner.

stepladder *n* a portable self-supporting ladder.

stepping stone *n* a stone to raise the feet above a stream or mud; a means of advancement.

stereo *n* a hi-fi or record player with two loudspeakers; stereophonic sound. *adj stereophonic sound.

stereophonic *adj* (*sound reproduction system*) using two seperate channels for recording and transmission to create a spatial effect.

stereotype *n* a fixed general image of a person or thing shared by many people.

sterile *adj* barren; unfruitful; free from bacteria.

sterility *n* barrenness; unfruitfulness; free from bacteria.

sterilize *vt* to make sterile; to rid of bacteria by boiling, etc.

sterling *adj* genuine; pure; denoting standard British money.

stern *adj* austere; harsh. * *n* the hind part of a ship.

sternum *n* the breastbone.

stertorous *adj* marked by laboured and noisy breathing.

stethoscope *n* an instrument for sounding the chest, lungs, etc.

stevedore *n* one who loads or unloads vessels.

stew *vt* to boil slowly in a closed vessel. * *vi* to be cooked slowly. * *n* meat stewed; state of anxiety.

steward, stewardess *n* one who manages affairs for another; one who helps to manage a public function; an attendant on ship or aeroplane passengers.

stick *vti* to pierce or stab; to fasten; to fix; to adhere. * *n* a rod or wand; a staff.

stickler *n* a person who is scrupulous or obstinate about something.

sticky *adj* adhesive; gluey.

stiff *adj* rigid; formal in manner; stubborn; difficult; not flexible or supple.

stiffening *n* substance used to make anything stiff.

stifle *vti* to suffocate; to suppress; to smother.

stigma *n* (*pl* **stigmas, stigmata**) a mark or brand; a mark of infamy; top of pistil of a flower.

stigmatize *vt* to hold up to reproach.

stiletto *n* a small dagger; a pointed instrument for making eyelet holes. a shoe with a long pointed heel.

still *adj* at rest; calm; silent; not carbonated. * *vt* to make still; to appease or allay. * *adv* to this time; yet * *n* a distilling apparatus.

stillborn *adj* dead at birth.

still life *n* a painting of inanimate objects such as fruits, flowers, etc; objects without life.

stilt *n* either of a pair of poles, with a rest for the foot on which one can walk.

stilted *adj* pompous; unnaturally formal.

stimulant *adj* energizing. * *n* a drug that increases energy for a time; an intoxicant.

stimulate *vt* to rouse up; to incite; to spur on.

stimulating *adj* rousing; invigorating.

stimulus *n* (*pl* **stimuli**) an incentive to action; a spur; a response in a living organism.

sting *vt* to pierce, as wasps; to prick, as a nettle. * *n* a sharp-pointed defensive organ of certain animals; secreting poison (plants); any acute mental or physical pain.

stinging *adj* sharp; keen; painful.

stingy *adj* very niggardly; scanty; mean.

stink *vi* to emit a strong offensive smell. * *n* a foul smell.

stint *vt* to restrict. * *vi* to cease. * *n* limit; restriction.

stipend *n* yearly allowance; salary.

stipple *vt* to engrave by means of dots.

stipulate *vi* to specify as terms of an agreement.

stipulation *n* a condition; item in a contract.

stir *vt* to set in motion; to agitate; to rouse. * *vi* to be in motion; to be up and doing. * *n* bustle; noise.

stirring *adj* rousing; exciting.

stirrup *n* a foot support in riding.

stitch *n* a sharp pain; movement of a needle in sewing. * *vti* to join by stitches.

stoat *n* a kind of weasel, valuable for its fur.

stock *adj* a post; stem of a tree; wooden piece of a rifle; lineage; capital; shares in state funds; goods in hand; cattle; a thick gravy for soups; a garden plant; *pl* an old instrument of torture for offenders; shares; frame on which a ship is built. * *adj* standing; permanent.

stockade *n* an area fenced round for protection; an enclosure.

stockbroker *n* one who deals in stocks and shares.

stockbroking *n* the business of a stockbroker.

stockholder *n* an owner of shares.

stocking *n* a close-fitting covering for foot and leg.

stock market, stock exchange *n* place where shares are bought and sold.

stockpile *n* a reserve supply of essentials.

stocktaking *n* a periodical valuation of goods in a shop, etc.

stodgy *adj* damp; heavy; indigestible.

stoic *n* one indifferent to pleasure or pain; one imperturbable and serene whatever fortune brings.

stoicism *n* impassiveness; serenity of spirit.

stoke *vt* to stir and keep supplied with fuel, as a fire.

stole *n* a vestment worn round neck and with hanging ends.

stolid *adj* dull; unresponsive.

stomach *n* the principal organ of digestion; appetite.

stone *n* a hard mass of earthy or mineral matter; a pebble; concretion in the kidneys or bladder; the nut of a fruit; a measure of 14 lbs/6.35kg. * *vt* to pelt with stones; to free from stones.

stony *adj* abounding in or like stone; hard; frigid; unfeeling.

stool *n* a portable seat, without a back, for one person; matter evacuated from the bowels.

stoop *vi* to bend forward and downward; to yield; to condescend. * *n* a downward bend of body; a veranda; a flagon.

stop *vti* to halt; to hinder or check; to suspend; to close up; to stay; * *n* pause; punctuation mark; device for regulating musical sounds.

stopcock *n* a tap to regulate flow of water, gas, etc.

stopgap *n* a temporary expedient.

stoppage *n* a halt.

stopper *n* that which closes a small vent or hole.

stopwatch n a watch that can be started and stopped instantaneously.

storage n act of storing; charge for storing goods; the storage of goods in a computer memory.

store n a large quantity for supply; a warehouse; abundance. * vt to amass; to hoard up.

storeroom n a room for reception of stores.

storey n a floor of a building, also story.

stork n a large heron-like bird.

storm n a heavy fall of rain, snow etc. with strong winds; tempest; a tumult. * vti to assail; to take by assault; to rage.

stormy adj tempestuous; violent.

story n a narrative; a tale; a fiction; a falsehood.

stout adj bold; valiant; corpulent. * n a dark-brown malt liquor.

stove n an apparatus for warming a room, cooking, etc.

stow vt to store; to pack closely.

stowaway n one who hides himself on a ship to avoid paying the fare.

straddle vt to have one leg or support on either side of something.

straggle vi to stray; to be scattered.

straggler n one who wanders from main body; a laggard.

straight adj continuing in one direction, not curved or bent; not crooked; upright.

straighten vt to make straight.

straightforward adj honest; open.

strain vti to stretch tightly; to exert to the utmost; to sprain; to filter. * n violent effort; tenor; theme; a poem; tune; race.

strained adj overstretched; forced or unnatural.

strainer n a filter or sieve.

strait adj confined; narrow; strict. * n a narrow passage of water; distress (often pl).

straiten vt to make narrow; to embarrass; to distress.

straitjacket n a strong garment used to bind arms of violent people to their bodies.

strait-laced adj puritanical; strict in morals.

strand n the shore; beach; a single peice

of thread or wire twisted to make a rope or cable. * vti to drive or be driven ashore; to leave helpless without transport or money.

strange adj foreign; wonderful; odd.

stranger n a foreigner; an alien; a visitor.

strangle vt to choke; to throttle.

strangulate vt to strangle; to stop circulation by pressure.

strangulation n compression of the windpipe; constriction.

strap n a narrow band of leather, metal, cloth, etc; a razor strop. * vt to fasten with strap.

strapping adj tall and well made.

stratagem n a device or plan to deceive an enemy; a ruse.

strategic, strategical adj pertaining to strategy.

strategy n the planning and conduct of war; a political, economic, or business policy.

stratification n arrangement in layers.

stratify vt to form or deposit in strata.

stratum n (pl **strata**) a layer of rock, earth, etc.

stratus n a low horizontal layer of clouds.

straw n the stalk of threshed grain, pulse, etc.

stray vi to wander; to err. * adj strayed; straggling.

streak n a long mark of contrasting colour; a stripe. * vt to mark with streaks.

stream n a small river or brook; a current. * vi, vt to move in a stream; issue forth.

streamer n a banner; a long decorative ribbon.

streamline vt to shape (a car, boat etc.) in a way that lessens resistance through air or water; to make more efficient; to simplify.

street n a road in a town, village or city lined with trees.

strength n force or energy; power; numbers of an army, fleet, etc. * On the strength of, in reliance upon.

strenuous adj earnest; energetic; vigorous.

stress vt to emphasize. * n pressure; mental or physical tension; emphasis.

stretch vti to draw out tight; to extend; to strain; to exaggerate. * n strain; scope; expanse.

stretcher n a portable frame for carrying sick or wounded.

strew vt to spread by scattering; to scatter loosely.

stricken pp of **strike**; smitten; afflicted, as by something painful.

strickle n a hone; a grindstone.

strict adj rigid in enforcing rules; exact; severe.

stricture n an unnatural contraction of throat, intestines, etc; censure.

stride vi to walk with long steps. * n a long step.

strident adj harsh; grating.

strife n conflict; discord; quarrel.

strike vi to hit with force; to sound (clock); to cease work to enforce a demand for better conditions. * vt to smite; to mint; to come sharply against; to lower (flag); to take down (tent). * n a cessation of work; a military attack.

striking adj surprising; impressive.

string n a slender cord; twine; a series; cord or wire of musical instrument. * vt to thread on a string.

stringency n severity; pressure.

stringent adj strict; severe; binding.

strip vt to lay bare; to skin. * vi to undress. * n a long narrow piece.

stripe n a streak; a band; a lash; a weal.

stripper n a striptease artist; device or solvent that removes paint.

strive vi to endeavour; to struggle; to vie.

stroke n a blow; calamity; attack; striking of a clock; touch; a line; a gentle rub; the sweep of an oar; the aft-most rower who sets time to others. * vt to rub gently with hand.

stroll vi to ramble; to saunter. * n a short leisurely walk.

strong adj powerful; robust; firm; forcible; ardent.

stronghold n a fort; a keep; a centre of strength or support.

strongroom n a room where valuables are kept.

strop n a strip of leather for sharpening razors, etc.

structural adj pertaining to structure.

structure n a building of any kind; manner of building; make; form; organization.

struggle vi to strive; to contend. * n a violent effort; contest; strife.

strum vi, vt to play noisily on a stringed instrument.

strut vi to walk with affected dignity. * n a pompous gait; a support for a rafter or framework.

strychnine n a highly poisonous alkaloid.

stubble n the stumps of cornstalks left after reaping.

stubborn adj obstinate; wilful; mulish; dogged.

stucco n a fine plaster; work made of stucco.

stuck-up adj giving one's self airs; proud; pompous.

stud n a post; a nail with a large head; an ornamental button; a set of breeding horses.

student n a scholar; one given to study.

studied adj deliberate; well-considered.

studio n the workplace of a painter or sculptor; a building or room where motion pictures are made or TV and radio programmes are recorded.

studious adj given to study; earnest.

study n application to learning; subject studied; room set apart for study; thought, reflexion. * vti to apply mind to; to investigate; to reflect on.

stuff n material; textile fabrics; trash. * vti to pack; to cram.

stuffing n padding; seasoning packed into meat, fowls, etc, in cooking.

stuffy adj close; stifling; poorly ventilated.

stultify vi, vt to make ineffectual or foolish.

stumble vi to trip; to err; to light on by chance. * n a stagger; trip.

stump n part of felled tree left standing; part of limb left after amputation; a wicket (cricket). * vt to lop; to dismiss batsman off his ground; to pay (up).

stun vt to make senseless; to stupefy; to amaze.

stunning adj strikingly attractive.

stunt vt to dwarf * n a check in growth; a

showy turn; a feat of strength or skill.

stunted *adj* dwarfed.

stupefaction *n* insensibility; amazement.

stupefy *vt* to astound; to dull the senses.

stupendous *adj* immense; awe-inspiring.

stupid *adj* foolish; dull-witted.

stupidity *n* dullness of mind; folly.

stupor *n* torpor; insensibility.

sturdy *adj* stout; strong; hardy.

stutter *vi* to stammer. * *n* a stammer.

sty *n* a pen for swine; a foul place.

sty, stye *n* a small swelling on edge of eyelid.

style *n* manner of doing anything; title; fashion. * *vt* to designate; to term.

stylish *adj* fashionable.

stylist *n* a master of style.

stylus *n* the component in a record player which contacts with the grove of a record and transmits sound to the amplifier.

suave *adj* gracious in manner; pleasant.

sub *n* (*inf*) a submarine; a sustitute; a subscription; a subeditor. **prefix* under, below; subordinate, next in rank to.

subconscious *adj* happening without one's awareness. **n* the part of the mind that is active without one's conscious awareness.

subcutaneous *adj* immediately below the skin.

subdivide *vt* to divide into smaller parts.

subduce, subduct *vt* to take away; to subtract.

subdue *vt* to overcome; to overpower; to tone down.

subeditor *n* an under or assistant editor.

subject *adj* ruled by another; liable. * *n* one who owes allegiance to a ruler or government; theme; topic; the nominative of a verb. * *vt* to subdue; to expose.

subjection *n* authority; control.

subjective *adj* relating to the conscious subject; opposed to objective.

subjugate *vt* to subdue; to conquer.

subjunctive *adj, n* the mood of a verb which expresses condition, hypothesis, doubt.

sublet *vt* to let to another person what oneself holds as tenant.

sublime *adj* awe-inspiring; noble; majestic. * The sublime, the awe-inspiring in the works of nature or of art, as opposed to the beautiful.

subliminal *adj* under the threshold of consciousness; subconscious.

sublimity *n* loftiness of style or feeling; grandeur.

submarine *adj* being under surface of the sea. * *n* a submersible boat.

submerge *vti* to put under water; to sink.

submersed *adj* being or growing under water.

submersible *adj* capable of being submerged and propelled under water. * *n* a submarine.

submission *n* surrender; obedience; resignation.

submissive *adj* humble, compliant.

submit *vti* to yield or surrender; to refer to another's judgment; to suffer without complaint.

subordinate *adj* secondary; lower in rank. * *n* one who ranks below another. * *vt* to place in a lower rank.

subordination *n* inferiority of rank; subjection.

subpoena *n* a summons to give evidence in law court.

subscribe *vti* to pay to receive regular copies (of a magazine, etc.); to donate money (to a charity, campaign); to support or agree with (an opinion, faith).

subscriber *n* a contributor.

subscript *adj* written below.

subscription *n* sum subscribed to receive copies (of a magazine) or to be a member of a club.

subsection *n* a division of a section.

subsequent *adj* following; next.

subserviencen servility; obseqiousness.

subservient *adj* serving to further some end; helpful; servile; inferior.

subside *vi* to sink or fall to the bottom; to abate; to settle.

subsidence *n* a sinking down of land or sea; a landslip.

subsidiary *adj* minor; subordinate; supplementary.

subsidize *vt* to assist with money; to purchase help by a subsidy.

subsidy *n* government financial aid to a private person or company to assist an enterprise.

subsist *vi* to have existence; to live.

subsistence *n* existence; livelihood.

subsoil *n* the stratum of earth just below surface.

substance *n* that of which a thing consists; material; a body; essence.

substantial *adj* of considerable value or style; real; solid; strong.

substantiate *vt* to give proof for; to verify.

substantive *adj* expressing existence; real. * *n* a noun.

substitute *vt* to put in the place of another; to exchange. * *n* a deputy.

substructure *n* a foundation; basis.

subterfuge *n* an artifice; evasion.

subterranean *adj* underground.

subtile *adj* subtle; thin; fine.

subtitle *n* an explanatory, usu secondary, title of a book; a printed translation superimposed on a foreign language film.

subtle *adj* thin; acute; sly; artful.

subtlety *n* nicety of distinction.

subtract *vt* to take from; to deduct.

subtraction *n* the taking of a number from a greater.

suburb *n* an outlying residential part of a city.

suburban *adj* situated in the suburbs.

subvention *n* a government grant; a subsidy.

subversion *n* the act of undermining the authority of a government or institution.

subversive *adj* destructive.

subvert *vt* to ruin utterly; to overturn.

subway *n* an underground passage.

succeed *vt* to follow in order; to come after. * *vi* to ensue; to become heir; to accomplish what is attempted.

success *n* favourable result; good fortune.

successful *adj* prosperous; fortunate.

succession *n* a following in order; lineage.

successive *adj* coming in succession; consecutive.

successor *n* one who succeeds or follows another.

succinct *adj* brief; concise.

succour *vt* to help when in difficulty; to aid. * *n* aid; help.

succulent *adj* full of sap; juicy.

succumb *vi* to yield; to submit.

such *adj* of like kind or degree; similar.

suck *vti* to draw (liquid, etc) into the mouth. * *n* milk drawn from breast.

sucker *n* a person who is easily taken in or deceived.

suckle *vt* to nurse at the breast.

suckling *n* an unweaned child or animal.

suction *n* act of sucking; the sucking up of a fluid by exhaustion of air.

sucrose *n* sugar.

sudden *adj* happening without warning; abrupt.

sue *vt* to bring a legal action against.

suet *n* white, solid fat in animal tissue, used in cooking.

suffer *vt* to endure; to permit. * *vi* to undergo pain.

sufferance *n* endurance of pain; passive consent.

suffering *n* the bearing of pain; distress.

suffice *vi* to be sufficient. * *vt* to satisfy.

sufficiency *n* an ample supply; competence.

sufficient *adj* adequate; enough.

suffix *n* a letter or syllable affixed to the end of a word.

suffocate *vti* to stifle; to choke; to be stifled.

suffrage *n* a vote; right of voting; the franchise.

suffuse *vt* to spread over or fill, as with colour or light.

sugar *n* a sweet granular substance, manufactured from sugar cane, maple, beet, etc. * *vt* to sweeten.

sugary *adj* sweet; flattering.

suggest *vt* to hint; to propose; to intimate.

suggestion *n* a hint; a tentative proposal.

suggestive *adj* hinting at; stimulating; prompting thought; rather indecent; risqué.

suicidal *adj* fatal; self-destructive.

suicide *n* self-murder or self-murderer.

suit *n* a petition; a courtship; an action at law; a set of matching garments. * *vti* to adapt; to fit; to satisfy.

suitable *adj* fitting; appropriate; becoming.

suite *n* a retinue; a set, as of rooms.

suitor *n* a wooer.

sulk vi to be sullen or pettish.

sulky adj sullen; morose.

sullen adj ill-natured; morose; sour; dismal.

sully vti to soil; to tarnish.

sulphur n brimstone; a yellow nonmetallic element.

sulphurous adj impregnated with sulphur; like sulphur.

sultry adj very hot; oppressive.

sum n the whole; aggregate; essence; substance; quantity of money; arithmetical problem vt to add up; to review main facts.

summarize vt to set forth main facts; to make an abstract or outline.

summary adj concise; brief; dispensing with formalities. * n an abridged account; an abstract.

summation n addition; aggregate.

summer n the warmest season of year; between spring and autumn.

summit n the top; highest point.

summon vt to call by authority; to cite to appear in court.

summons n a notice to appear, esp. in court; an earnest call.

sumptuous adj very costly; magnificent.

sun n the star around which the earth and other planets revolve which gives light and heat to the solar system; the sunshine. *vt to expose oneself to the sun's rays.

sunbeam n a ray of the sun.

sunburn vt inflamation of the skin from exposure to the sun.

Sunday n the day after Saturday; the Christian day of worship; the Christian Sabbath.

sunder vt to part; to separate.

sundial n an instrument to show time by shadow cast by sun.

sundry adj miscellaneous; various.

sunglasses npl tinted glasses to protect the eyes from sunlight.

sunlit adj lit by the sun.

sunny adj like the sun; brilliant; bright or cheerful.

sunrise n first appearance of sun in morning.

sunset n descent of sun below horizon.

sunshine n the light of the sun; warmth; brightness.

sunstroke n acute illness caused by over exposure to sun's rays.

sup vt to sip; to imbibe. * vi to take supper. * n a sip; a small mouthful.

superadj (inf) fantastic; excellent; (inf) a superintendent, as in the police. *n a variety of high octane fuel.

superannuation n regular contributions from employee's wages towards a pension scheme.

superb adj magnificent; grand; of the highest quality.

supercilious adj haughty; scornful; disdainful.

superficial adj being on the surface; shallow.

superfluous adj needless; redundant.

superhuman adj more than human.

superimpose vt to lay upon something else.

superintend vt to supervise; direct; manage.

superior adj higher; better; preferable. * n one higher in rank; head of monastery, convent.

superiority n pre-eminence.

superlative adj highest in degree; supreme. * n the highest degree of adjectives or adverbs.

supermarket n a large, self-service shop selling food and household goods.

supernatural adj that which cannot be explained by nature.

superpowern a nation with great economic and military strength.

superscribe vt to write upon or over.

supersede vt to set aside; displace; supplant.

supersensitive adj oversensitive.

supersonicadj faster than the speed of sound.

superstition n credulity in regard to the supernatural; a belief without reason.

superstitious adj credulous.

superstructure n anything resting on a foundation; a building.

supervise vt to oversee and direct; to superintend.

supervision n oversight.

supine adj lying on the back; indolent. * n a part of the Latin verb.

supper n the evening meal.

supplant vt to supersede; to oust, esp. by craft.

supple adj pliant; flexible.

supplement n an addition; appendix. * vt to make additions to.

supplicant adj suppliant. * n one who begs earnestly for some favour.

supplication n earnest prayer; entreaty.

supply vt to furnish; to satisfy. * n store; pl stores; money provided for government expenses; a substitute.

support vt to uphold; to prop; to maintain; to endure; to back up. * n a prop; aid; maintenance.

supporter n a defender; adherent; prop.

suppose vt to assume; to imagine; to imply; to expect.

supposition n assumption; surmise.

suppress vt to put down; to quell; to conceal; to crush.

suppression n concealment; stoppage.

suppressive adj tending to suppress.

suppurate vi to form or discharge pus.

suppuration n a gathering of pus.

supremacy n supreme authority.

supreme adj highest in authority; sovereign; paramount.

surcharge vt to overload. * n an excessive load; an overcharge; unauthorized expenditure of public bodies and charged against members.

sure adj certain; positive; unfailing; stable.

surety n security against loss, etc; guarantee; bail.

surf n the swell of sea breaking on shore.

surface n the outside part of anything; external appearance.

surfeit n an excess of food or drink; satiety. * vti to feed to excess.

surge n the swelling of a wave; a billow. * vi to swell; to heave.

surgeon n a medical man skilled in surgery.

surgery n the operative branch of medical practice; a doctor's consulting room.

surgical adj pertaining to surgery.

surly adj morose; churlish.

surmise n a supposition; conjecture. * vt to guess; to suspect.

surmount vt to rise above; to overcome.

surname n the family name of an individual.

surpass vt to go beyond; to excel.

surplus n, adj excess beyond what is required; balance.

surprise n act of taking unawares; astonishment. * vt to take unawares; to startle; to astonish.

surprising adj amazing; remarkable.

surrender vt to deliver up; to resign; to cede. * n a yielding or giving up. * vt to yield.

surreptitious adj done by stealth; underhand.

surrogate n a person or thing substituting for another person or thing, esp bearing a child.

surround vt to encompass.

surrounding n an environment; generally in pl.

surveillance n a keeping watch over; oversight.

survey vt to oversee; to inspect; to measure and value as land, etc. * n a general view; examination; plan.

surveying n the art or practice of measuring land.

surveyor n a measurer; an inspector.

survival n a living or continuing longer; a relic or custom of the past.

survive vt to outlive; to outlast; to endure.

susceptible adj easily affected; sensitive.

suspect vt to mistrust; to conjecture. * n a suspected person.

suspend vt to hang; to postpone; to discontinue; to debar tempoarily from a privelege, etc.

suspender n a supporting strap or brace.

suspense n uncertainty; anxiety.

suspension n abeyance; temporary cessation of office; postponement; (chem) a dispersion of fine particles in a liquid.

suspension bridge n a bridge suspended by cables anchored to towers at either end.

suspensory adj giving support.

suspicion n act of suspecting; mistrust; a belief held or formed without sure proof;

a trace.

suspicious adj mistrustful; doubtful.

sustain vt to hold up or support; maintain; endure.

sustenance n nourishment.

suture n a seam; the line of junction of bones of skull; the stitching of a wound.

swab n a wad of aborbant material, usu cotton, used to clean wounds, take specimens, etc; a mop. * vt to clean with a swab.

swaddle vt to swathe; to bind tight with clothes.

swagger vt to strut; to bluster. * n swinging gait.

swallow vt to receive through the gullet into the stomach; to engulf; to accept without question. * n a well-known migratory bird; gullet.

swamp n a bog; a fen. * vt to overwhelm; to capsize, as a boat.

swap vt to barter; to exchange.

swarm n a multitude, esp. of insects. * vi to throng together; to leave hive in a body; to climb a tree, etc.

swarthy adj tawny; dark-complexioned.

swashbuckler n an adventurous person.

swath n a line of mown grass or grain; sweep of a scythe.

swathe vt to wrap around, as with a bandage.

sway vi to move backwards and forwards; to vacillate in judgement or opinion * n influence; control.

swear vi, vt to make a solemn declaration; to curse; to use obscene language.

sweat n perspiration; labour. * vi, vt to emit moisture through pores.

sweater n a knitted pullover.

sweaty adj moist with sweat.

sweep vt to remove(rubbish, dirt) with a brush; to carry along. * vi to pass with swiftness or pomp; to move with a long reach. * n reach; range; rapid survey; one who sweeps chimneys.

sweeping adj comprehensive.

sweepstake n a gamble in which the stakes go to drawers of winning horses, etc.

sweet adj agreeable to the taste; having taste of honey or sugar; fragrant; melodious; kind; gentle. * n a dessert; pl confectionery.

sweetheart n a lover.

swell vi to grow larger; to heave; to bulge out. * vt to expand. * n gradual increase; a rise of ground; a wave of surge.

swelling adj inflamation.

swelter vi to be overcome with heat; to perspire.

swerve vi to turn aside; to alter course suddenly.

swift adj speedy; fleet; prompt. n a species of swallow.

swig n a long drink, esp from a bottle.

swill vi to drink greedily; to rinse with a large amount of water.* n a liquid refuse fed to pigs.

swim vi to float; to move through water; to be dizzy. * vt to pass by swimming. * n act of swimming.

swimmingly adv smoothly; with great success.

swindle vt to cheat. * n a gross fraud.

swindler n a cheat.

swine n sing, pl a pig; pl pigs collectively.

swing vi to move to and fro; to turn round at anchor; to change opinion or preference. * vt to achieve; to bring about. * n sweep of a scythe; rhythm; apparatus for swinging on; free course; a form of jazz music.

swipe vti to strike with sweeping blow. * n a sweeping blow.

swirl vi to turn with a whirling motion.

swish vt to move with a soft, whistling sound.* n swishing sound.

switch n a sudden change; a swap; a device for changing the course of an electric current. * vt to change.

swivel n a coupling that permits parts to rotate. * vt to turn as if on a pivot.

swoon vi to faint.

swoop vi to dart upon prey from a height. * n the pounce or dart as of a hawk.

sword n a weapon with a long blade and a handle at one end.

sworn adj bound by oath.

sycophant n a person who flatters to win favor.

syllable n a sound or combination of sounds uttered with one effort.

syllabus n an outline or summary, esp of a course of study.

sylph n a slender, graceful female.

sylviculture n forestry.

symbol n a sign; an emblem; a type; a figure.

symbolism n the lavish use of symbolic language.

symbolize vt to represent by a symbol; to typify.

symmetry n the corresponding arrangement of one part to another in size, shape and position.

sympathetic adj compassionate; showing sympathy.

sympathy n fellow feeling; compassion.

symphonist n a composer of symphonies.

symphony n unison of sound; an orchestral piece of music.

symposium n (pl **symposia**) a discussion (oral or written) on some subject by experts.

symptom n a bodily sensation indicative of a particular disease; an indication.

symptomatic adj indicative; relating to symptoms.

synagogue n a place where Jews assemble for worship and religious study.

synchronize vi, vt to agree or make to agree in time.

synchronous adj happening at the same time; simultaneous.

syncopate vt to contract words by omission of middle letters; in music, to pass from one bar to another by a slur.

syncopation n word shortening; interruption of musical rhythm.

syndicate n a company formed for a special purpose.

synonym n a word having same meaning as another.

synonymous adj of similar meaning; interchangeable.

synopsis n a summary.

syntax n correct arrangement of words in sentences.

synthesis n the combining of parts to make a whole.

synthetic adj inflectional; artificially produced.

syringe n a hollow tube with a plunger and a sharp needle at either end by which liquids are injected or withdrawn, esp in medicine. * vt to inject or cleanse with a syringe.

syrup n a thick sweet substance made by boiling sugar with water; the concentrated juice of a fruit or plant.

system n a method of working or organizing by following a set of rules; the body as a functional unity; a plan; method.

T

tab n a small flap; a tag.

table n an article of furniture with flat surface set on legs; fare; persons round the table; a list or index. * vt to lay on a table.

tableau n (pl **tableaux**) a picture; a striking group or dramatic scene.

table d'hôte n dinner served in hotel or restaurant at fixed price.

tableland n a plateau; a region of elevated flat land.

tablet n a set of ivory or paper slips for memoranda; a slab bearing an inscription; a small cake, as of soap, etc.

tabloid n a small format newspaper.

taboo n a ban or prohibition. * vt to forbid approach to or use of.

tabular adj in form of a table; flat.

tacit adj implied, but not expressed; silent.

taciturn adj of few words; silent.

tack n a small nail; a stitch; course of a ship as regards the wind. * vt to fasten by tacks; to attach slightly. * vi to change course of a ship to catch the wind.

tackle n gear or apparatus; pulleys, ropes, rigging. * vt to grapple with; to seize.

tact n fineness of touch; judgment; taste; adroitness.

tactical adj pertaining to tactics.

tactics npl stratagem; ploy; the science and art of military manoeuvring.

tactile adj having the sense of touch.

tactless adj lacking tact.

taffeta n a silk fabric.

tag n a metallic point to end of a lace; an appendage; a catchword.

tail n appendage to hinder part of animal's body; hinder part; reverse of a coin.

tailor n a maker of clothes, esp.. for men.

taint vt to defile; to infect. * vi to be infected. * n infection; a stain.

take vti to receive or accept; to capture; to understand; to employ; to be infected; to bear; to conduct.

taking adj alluring; attracting.

talc n a smooth mineral used in ceramics and talcum powder.

talent n any innate or special aptitude.

talisman n a charm; a mascot.

talk vi to utter words; to converse. * vt to discuss. * n familiar conversation; rumour; discussion.

talkative adj garrulous; fond of talking.

tall adj high in stature; lofty.

talon n the claw of a bird of prey.

tambourine n a percussion instrument.

tame adj domesticated; spiritless; insipid. * vt to make tame; to subdue.

tamper vi to meddle or interfere; to use bribery.

tampon n a plug of absorbent material inserted in the vagina during menstruation.

tan vt to convert into leather, as skins; to make sunburnt. * n bark used for tanning.

tandem adv one behind another. * n a pair of horses yoked single file; a bicycle with riders single file.

tang n a taste; characteristic flavour; part of tool which fits into handle.

tangent n a straight line touching a circle but not cutting it.

tangible adj perceptible to touch; real; actual.

tangle vt to interweave; to involve. * n a knot; a muddle; complication.

tango n a Latin American ballroom dance.

tank n a large cistern; a reservoir; a covered armoured car with caterpillar wheels and containing men and weaponry.

tankard n a large drinking vessel with a lid.

tannery n a place for tanning leather.

tanning n process of converting hides into leather.

tantalize vt to torment by raising false hopes.

tantamount adj equal; equivalent.

tantrum n a fit of bad temper.

tap n pipe for drawing off liquor; a spigot; a stopper or plug; a touch. * vti to broach; to strike lightly.

tape n a narrow band of linen; magnetic tape, as in an audio cassette or videotape.

taper n a long wick coated with wax. * adj narrowing to a point. * vt to narrow to a point.

tapestry n rich woven hangings of wool and silk, with pictorial representations.

tapeworm n a long tape-like worm found sometimes in intestines.

taproot n main root of a plant.

tar n a thick, dark, viscous substance obtained from pine, coal, etc; a sailor. * vt to smear with tar.

tarantella n a lively Italian dance.

tardily adv slowly.

tardy adj slow; late; backward.

target n a circular shield; a shooting mark or butt.

tariff n a schedule of dutiable goods; a scale of charges.

tarnish vti to sully; to dim.

tarpaulin n canvas covered with tar.

tarry vi to stay; to delay. * vt to wait for.

tart adj sharp to the taste; acid; snappish. * n a small fruit pie.

tartan n a woollen checkered cloth of many colours.

task n a piece of work imposed by another; lesson to be learned; toil. * vt to burden.

tassel n a small ornament with hanging threads.

taste vti to perceive flavour of by tongue or palate; to partake slightly of; to experience; to have a flavour. * n flavour; trial; sample; discernment; good style.

tasteful adj showing good taste.

tasteless adj stale; void of taste.

tasty adj savoury; palatable.

tatter n a loose hanging rag.

tattle vi to talk idly; to gossip. * n idle talk.

tattoo *n* military call to quarters; military exhibition. * *vt* to prick ink into skin.

taunt *vt* to reproach; to upbraid. * *n* a bitter reproach.

Taurus *n* the Bull, one of twelve signs of zodiac.

taut *adj* tight; stretched.

tautology *n* repetition of same meaning in different words.

tavern *n* an inn.

tawdry *adj* showy but inelegant.

tawny *adj* tan-coloured; yellowish-brown.

tax *n* a charge made by government on property, income, etc; a burdensome duty. * *vt* to place tax on; to accuse.

taxation *n* act of levying taxes; the aggregate of taxes.

taxidermy *n* the art of stuffing animals.

tea *n* dried leaves of an Eastern shrub; beverage made from them.

teach *vti* to instruct; to inform; to give instruction.

teacher *n* one who teaches; a schoolmaster.

teaching *n* act or business of instructing.

teak *n* an Indian tree producing hard durable timber.

team *n* a brood; a litter; two or more draught animals harnessed together; a side in a game, match, etc.

tear *n* a drop of water appearing in, or falling from, the eye.

tear *vti* to pull in pieces; to wound; to pull with violence. * *n* a rent.

tease *vt* to pull apart fibres of; to torment.

teat *n* the nipple.

technical *adj* pertaining to arts, crafts, or sciences.

technicality *n* something peculiar to a special art, craft, etc.

technique *n* manner of artistic execution; manipulative skill.

technology *n* the science of the industrial arts.

techy, tetchy *adj* peevish; fretful.

tedious *adj* tiresome; fatiguing.

tedium *n* irksomeness.

tee *n* the target in quoits, curling, etc; the starting place for each hole in golf.

teem *vi* to pour (with rain); to be prolific.

teeming *adj* fruitful; prolific.

teens *npl* the years of one's age having ending teen.

teeth *npl* of tooth.

teethe *vi* to cut one's first teeth.

teetotal *adj* totally abstaining from intoxicants.

telegram *n* a telegraphic message.

telegraph *n* a contrivance for sending messages to a distance, esp.. by electricity, and with or without wires. * *vt* to send a telegraph.

telepathy *n* the transference of thought from mind to mind without aid of senses.

telephone *n* an instrument transmitting sound to a distance by electricity. * *vti* to transmit by telephone.

telescope *n* an optical instrument for viewing distant objects.

television *n* the transmission of visual images and sound via electrical and sound waves; a television receiving set; television broadcasting.

tell *vti* to number; to relate; to explain; to report; to inform; to bid.

teller *n* a bank clerk in charge of cash; one appointed to count votes.

telling *adj* very effective.

telltale *adj* revealing; informative. * *n* a blabber; a betrayer of secrets.

temerity *n* contempt of danger; rashness.

temper *vt* to mix in due proportion; to moderate; to harden. * *n* due mixture; disposition of mind; passion; mood; quality.

temperament *n* disposition; nature.

temperance *n* moderation, esp. in regard to alchoholic drink.

temperate *adj* moderate; calm.

temperature *n* degree of heat or cold.

tempered *adj* disposed; hardened, as steel.

tempest *n* a violent storm.

tempestuous *adj* very stormy; violent.

temple *n* a place of worship; a church; side of head above either cheekbone.

tempo *n* musical time.

temporal *adj* pertaining to time; secular; worldly; civil, secular.

temporarily *adv* for a time only; provisionally.

temporary *adj* lasting but for a time; provisional.

temporize vi to hedge; to wait and see; to trim.

tempt vt to entice; to put to test; to allure into evil.

temptation n enticement to evil.

tempting adj attractive; alluring.

ten adj, n the number next after nine.

tenable adj able to be held; defensible; sound.

tenacious adj holding fast; unyielding; tough; stubborn.

tenacity n doggedness; toughness.

tenancy n a holding land, etc, as a tenant.

tenant n an occupier who pays rent.

tend vi to incline; trend; aim * vt to attend; guard; to look after.

tendency n inclination; bias; proneness.

tender n a small vessel carrying stores, etc, to larger one; the part of a locomotive carrying fuel and water; an offer; an estimate. * vt to offer or present; to send in an estimate. * adj fragile; delicate; sensitive; compassionate; weak.

tendon n a sinew; fibrous band joining muscles to bones.

tendril n a slender, twining shoot by which some plants cling or climb.

tenebrous adj dark;gloomy.

tenement n block of buildings divided into separate houses.

tenet n a doctrine, opinion, or dogma.

tenfold adj ten times more.

tennis n a game with balls and rackets.

tenon n the end of piece of wood shaped to fit into mortise or hole in another piece.

tenor n a prevailing course; purport; drift; higher of two kinds of men's voices; one with tenor voice.

tense n verbal inflection to express time. * adj stretched tight; strained.

tensile adj of or relating to tension; stretchable.

tension n act of stretching; tightness; strain; anxiety.

tensor n a muscle that extends or tightens a part.

tent n a portable shelter of canvas.

tentacle n a thread-like organ of various animals, serving as limb or feeler.

tentative adj experimental.

tenterhook n one of hooks on cloth-stretching frame. *(with on) in a state of anxiety or suspense.

tenth adj ordinal number of 10.

tenuity n thinness; rarity.

tenuous adj thin; slender.

tenure n a holding or conditions of holding land, office etc.

tepid adj lukewarm.

tercentenary adj comprising three hundred years. * n the three-hundredth anniversary.

term n a limit; boundary; period of session, etc; rent day; a word; pl conditions. * vt to name; to call.

terminable adj capable of being ended or bounded.

terminal adj pertaining to the end. * n an extremity; the clamping screw at each end of a voltaic battery; computer keyboard and monitor.

terminate vti to bound; to limit; to end.

terminology n the terms special to science, art, etc.

terminus n (pl termini) a boundary; a limit; end of a transport line.

terrace n a raised level bank of earth; a row of houses.

terracotta n a reddish-brown pottery or its colour.

terrestrial adj pertaining to the earth; worldly.

terrible adj awful; terrifying.

terrific adj terrifying; dreadful.

terrify vt to scare; to affright.

territory n a large tract of land; a region.

terror n extreme fear; dread.

terrorism n the use of violence to intimide.

terrorize vt to intimidate by means of terror.

terse adj concise; pointed.

tertiary adj third; applied to a geological formation.

tessellated adj resembling mosaic.

test n a putting to the proof; examination; trial. * vt to try.

testament n in law, a person's will; (with cap.) one of two divisions of Bible.

testamentary adj bequeathed by will.

testator (f **testatrix**) n one who leaves a will at death.

testicle *n* one of two semen producing glands.

testify *vi, vt* to bear witness; to affirm on oath.

testimonial *n* a recommendation of one's character or abilities.

testimony *n* evidence; declaration.

testy *adj* fretful; peevish.

tête-à-tête *adv* face to face. * *n* a private talk.

tether *n* a rope confining animal within certain limits. * *vt* to confine with a tether.

tetragon *n* a plane figure having four angles.

tetrahedron *n* a solid body having four equal triangles as its faces.

text *n* a main part of a printed work; a topic; a textbook.

textbook *n* a standard book of instruction; a manual.

textile *adj* woven. * *n* a fabric made by weaving.

texture *n* the grain or feel of a thing.

thallus *n* a plant showing little difference between leaf, stem, and root.

than *conj* introduces second member of comparison.

thank *n* almost always in *pl* expression of gratitude. * *vt* to give thanks to.

thanksgiving *n* act of giving thanks, esp.. to God.

that *adj, demons pron* (*pl* those) pointing out a person or thing at a distance; the farther of two. * *rel pron; sing, pl* equivalent to who or which. * *conj* introducing noun clause; in order that.

thatch *n* straw used as cover for roofs or stacks. * *vt* to put thatch on.

thaw *vi, vt* to melt, as ice or snow; to become genial. * *n* the melting of ice or snow.

the *def art* denoting particular person or thing.

theatre *n* a playhouse; an operating room; sphere of action.

theatrical *adj* artificial; showy; pompous.

theft *n* act of stealing.

their *poss.adj, pron* belonging to them * theirs possessive case of they, used without noun.

theism *n* belief in gods.

them *per pron* the objective case of they.

theme *n* a subject or topic.

themselves *per pron pl* of himself, herself, etc.

then *adv* at that time. * *conj* from that place or time; therefore.

thenceforth *adv* from that time.

thenceforward *adv* from that time onward.

theocracy *n* direct government by God; a state so governed.

theologian *n* a person well versed in theology.

theology *n* the study of religious doctrine and divine things.

theorem *n* a proposition capable of being proved.

theoretical *adj* not practical; hypothetical.

theorize *vi* to conjecture; to speculate.

theory *n* speculation; hypothesis to explain something.

therapeutic *adj* pertaining to the healing art; curative.

there *adv* in or at that place.

thereafter *adv* after that; accordingly.

thereby *adv* by that means.

therefore *adv, conj* for that or this reason; consequently.

thereupon *adv* upon that or this; immediately.

therewith *adv* with that or this.

thermal *adj* pertaining to heat; warm; hot.

thermodynamics *npl* the science of heat as a force.

thermometer *n* an instrument for measuring degree of temperature.

thermos *n* a vacuum flask used to keep liquids warm.

thermostat *n* an appliance for regulating steam pressure and temperature.

thesaurus *n* a reference book of synonyms and antonyms.

these *pronominal adj pl* of **this**.

thesis *n* (*pl* theses) a subject for discussion; a theme; an essay.

thespian *adj* relating to dramatic acting.

they *per pron pl* the plural of he, she or it.

thick *adj* dense; close; foggy; crowded; dull.

thicket n a copse; a tangle of shrubs.
thickset adj thickly planted; stumpy.
thief n (pl **thieves**) a person who steals.
thieve vi, vt to steal.
thigh n the leg above the knee.
thimble n a metal cover for finger in sewing.
thin adj not thick; sparse; slim; lean; poor. * vti to make or become thin.
thing n an inanimate object; any separate entity; pl clothes; baggage, etc.
think vi, vt to have the mind working; to reflect; to judge; to believe.
third adj ordinal of three.
thirst n the desire or distress occasioned by want of water; eager desire after anything. * vi to feel thirst; to desire vehemently.
thirteen adj, n ten and three.
thirty adj, n thrice ten.
this adj, pron (pl **these**) that which is near or present.
thong n a strap of hide or leather.
thorax n the human chest.
thorn n a prickly tree or shrub.
thorough adj complete; entire.
thoroughbred adj of pure stock.
thoroughfare n a public or open road.
thoroughgoing adj downright; extreme.
those adj, pron pl of that.
though conj notwithstanding.
thought n the power of thinking; opinion; judgment; care.
thousand adj, n ten hundred.
thrash, thresh vt to beat out grain from husk; to flog.
thread n a fine cord; any fine filament; spiral part of a screw; general purpose. * vt to pass thread through; to make one's way through.
threadbare adj worn out; trite.
threat n declaration of intention to punish or hurt.
threaten vt to use threats towards.
threatening adj impending; menacing.
three adj, n the number next after two.
threescore adj three times a score; sixty.
thresh vt to beat out grain from husks.
threshold n a door sill; entrance.
thrice adv three times.
thrift n frugality; a plant.

thriftless adj wasteful.
thrifty adj frugal; saving.
thrill vti to send a quiver through. * n a quiver; a tingling feeling.
thrilling adj exciting.
thrive vi to prosper; to flourish.
throat n the opening downward at back of mouth.
throb vi to beat, as the heart; to palpitate.
throe n extreme pain; agony.
throne n a royal seat.
throng n a crowd. * vi, t. to crowd together.
throttle n the windpipe; the gullet; engine's steam or petrol regulator.
through prep from end to end of; by means of * adj, adv from end to end.
throughout prep quite through. * adv in every part.
throw vti to fling or cast; to propel; to twist or wind; to utter; a cast at dice, etc; a venture.
thrum n coarse yarn. * vti to drum; to strum.
thrush n a singing bird; an oral fungal infection.
thrust vti to push with force; to shove; to stab; to intrude. * n a violent push; a stab.
thumb n the short thick finger of hand. * vt to soil with fingers.
thump n a dull, heavy blow. * vti to strike with something heavy.
thunder n the sound which follows lightning; any loud noise. * vi to make a loud noise.
thunderbolt n a shaft of lightning.
thunderclap n a peal of thunder.
thundering adj resounding.
thunderstruck adj amazed.
thursday n the fifth day of the week.
thus adv in this manner.
thwart adj transverse. * vt to cross; to frustrate. * n rowers' seat athwart boat.
thyme n a small aromatic herb or shrub.
tiara n a diadem for head.
tibia n the shin bone.
tick n the beat of watch or clock; a tapping; a dot. * n insect. * vti to mark with a dot; to sound, as watch.
ticket n a label; a piece of cardboard giving right of entry, travel, etc.

tickle *vi, vt* to touch lightly in certain places and cause involuntary laughter; to please; to puzzle.

ticklish *adj* difficult; critical.

tidal *adj* pertaining to tides.

tide *n* time; season; the ebb and flow of sea.

tidings *npl* news; information.

tidy *adj* clean and orderly; neat; trim * *vt* to make tidy.

tie *vt* to fasten; to constrain; * *n* a fastening; a necktie; bond; an equality in numbers.

tier *n* a row; a rank.

tiff *n* a slight quarrel.

tiffany *n* a gauze or very thin silk.

tight *adj* compact; well-knit; fitting close or too close; scarce, as money; tipsy.

tights *npl* a one-piece garment covering the legs and lower body.

tile *n* a slab of baked clay for roofing, flooring, etc; a drain pipe. * *vt* to cover with tiles.

till *n* a money drawer in shop counter. * *prep*. until. * *vt* to cultivate; to plough and prepare for seed.

tiller *n* the handle of a rudder.

tilt *vi* to joust; to lean or slope. * *n* a slant; a joust; an awning for cart or boat.

timber *n* wood for building purposes.

timbre *n* characteristic quality of musical note.

time *n* the measure of duration; a point of duration; occasion; season; epoch; present life; rhythm * *vt* to regulate or measure.

timely *adj* opportune. * *adv* early.

timeous *adj* timely.

timetable *n* a table of school hours and classes; a schedule.

timid *adj* fearful; shy.

timorous *adj* full of fear.

tin *n* a malleable white metal.

tincture *n* a tinge, tint, or shade; flavour; extract or solution of drug in alcohol. * *vt* to tinge.

tinder *n* an inflammable substance used for kindling fire from a spark.

tine *n* a prong; tooth of harrow, etc.

tinge *vt* to tint; to imbue. * *n* a tint; a slight colour.

tingle *vi* to feel a thrilling sensation.

tinker *n* a mender of kettles, etc. * *vti* to mend; to patch up.

tinkle *vi* to make small, sharp sounds; to clink. * *n* a sharp, ringing sound.

tinplate *n* thin sheet iron coated with tin.

tinsel *n* glittering thread or foil; something gaudy but of little value; mere glitter.

tint *n* a tinge; hue. * *vt* to tinge.

tintinnabulation *n* a jingling, as of bells.

tiny *adj* very small; puny.

tip *n* a small end or point; a tap; a gratuity; a dump; a hint. * *vt* to cant, as a cart; to put tip on; to give gratuity to.

tipple *vi, vt* to drink strong liquors frequently; to imbibe often.

tipsy *adj* mildly intoxicated.

tiptoe *vi* to walk very quietly.

tiptop *adj* excellent; first-rate.

tirade *n* a violent speech, denunciation.

tire *n* band or hoop of iron or rubber round wheels; headdress. * *vt* to fatigue; to weary; to attire.

tiresome *adj* wearisome; tedious.

tissue *n* delicate fabric; thin paper sheet; substance (muscle, fat, etc) composing parts of animals and plants; a fabrication.

titanic *adj* huge; gigantic.

titbit *n* a tasty morsel.

titillation *n* a pleasant feeling, a teasing, esp. sexual.

title *n* an inscription; heading; name; appellation of dignity; a right.

titled *adj* having a title.

title deed *n* the legal document proving right to property.

title page *n* the page of book containing its name, author, etc.

titter *vi* to giggle. * *n* a half-suppressed laugh.

titular *adj* nominal.

to *prep*. denoting motion towards.

toadstool *n* a mushroom-like fungus.

toady *n* a base sycophant; a sponger. * *vt* to fawn upon.

toast *vt* to dry and brown before the fire; to drink health of * *n* toated bread; person or sentiment whose health is drunk.

tobacco *n* a narcotic plant whose leaves when dried are used for smoking or snuff.

toboggan n a snow sledge

toddle vi to walk with uncertain steps, as a child.

toddy n a mixture of spirit, hot water, and sugar.

toe n one of the five extremities of the foot.

toffee n a sweetmeat made of butter and sugar.

toga n a loose robe.

together adv in company.

toil vi to labour; to drudge. * n hard work; a snare.

toilet n the lavatory; the act of washing and dressing oneself.

toilsome adj laborious.

token n a mark; symbol; keepsake.

tolerable adj passable; middling.

tolerance n forbearance.

tolerant adj indulgent; broad-minded.

tolerate vt to allow or permit; to put up with.

toll n a tax charged for use of road, bridge, etc; sound of a bell. * vi to ring bell slowly.

tomb n a grave; burial vault.

tombstone n a stone erected over a grave.

tome n a volume; a large book.

tomfoolery n nonsense; silly acts.

tomorrow n the day after the present.

tone n sound or character of sound; timbre; temper; colour scheme. * vti to tone down, to soften.

tongs npl an appliance for lifting coal, sugar, etc.

tongue n the organ of speech and taste; speech; language; clapper of bell.

tonic adj strengthening; bracing. * n a bracing medicine; keynote.

tonight n the present night.

tonnage n weight of ship's freight; duty on ships.

tonne n a metric ton, 1,000 kg.

tonsil n one of glands on each side of throat.

tonsillitis n inflammation of tonsils.

too adv over; as well; also.

tool n an instrument to work with.

tooling n skilled work with a tool.

tooth n (pl **teeth**) one of the bony projections from gums used for chewing.

toothache n a pain in teeth.

toothed adj jagged; indented.

top n the highest part; summit; toy for spinning. * vi, t. to excel; to be at top.

top-heavy adj overweighted above and apt to fall over.

topic n a theme or text.

topical adj local; full of allusions.

topography n scientific description of a district; local geography.

topple vi to fall over; overbalance.

torch n a light to be carried in the hand.

toreador n a Spanish bullfighter.

torment n torture; anguish. * vt to torture; to tease.

tornado n (pl **tornadoes**) a hurricane.

torpedo n (pl **torpedoes**) a kind of electric eel; a self-propelled explosive submarine projectile.

torpid adj numb; inactive.

torpor n apathy; numbness.

torrent n a rushing stream.

torrid adj parched; violently hot.

torsion n act of twisting; amount or force of twist.

torso n a headless, limbless trunk, esp. of statue.

tort n wrong; injury.

tortuous adj crooked; winding.

torture n extreme pain; agony. * vt to rack; to harass.

toss vti to throw upward; to jerk, as head; to roll about. * n a throw; a fall.

tot n anything small; a sum in addition. * vt to add.

total adj, n whole; complete.

totem n a tribal emblem.

totter vi to stagger; to reel.

touch vti to come in contact with; to handle lightly; to reach; to move feelings of * n contact; feeling; skill in some art.

touching adj affecting. * prep. concerning.

touchstone n a stone for testing purity of gold and silver; a test or criterion.

touchy adj irritable; sensitive.

tough adj flexible; tenacious; stubborn.

tour n a long trip, esp for pleaasure. * vt to make a tour.

tourist n one who makes a tour.

tournament n a contest in which individuals or sides are pitted against one another.

tourniquet *n* an appliance for stopping flow from cut artery.

tousle *vt* to ruffle; to disarrange.

tout *vi* to seek for custom openly; to canvas obtrusively. * *n* a shameless canvasser.

tow *vt* to haul by a rope. * *n* haulage; fibres of flax or hemp.

toward, towards *prep* in the direction of * *adv* at hand.

towel *n* a cloth for drying.

tower *n* a lofty narrow building; a fortress. * *vi* to soar.

towering *adj* lofty; violent.

town *n* an urban centre, smaller than a city and larger than a village.

toxic *adj* poisonous.

toxin *n* a poisonous substance.

toy *n* a plaything; a trifle. * *vi* to dally; to trifle.

trace *n* a mark left by anything; footstep; track; one of straps by which a carriage is drawn. * *vt* to track out; to copy by marking over.

trachea *n* the windpipe.

track *n* a footprint; rut made by wheel; beaten path; course. * *vt* to trace; to follow step by step.

trackless *adj* pathless; untrodden.

tract *n* wide region; a short treatise.

tractable *adj* docile; manageable.

traction *n* act of drawing, esp.. vehicles.

trade *n* employment; commerce; traffic. * *vi*, *vt* to buy and sell.

trademark *n* a distinctive mark put by manufacturer on his goods.

trades union *n* a union of workers in a trade to protect their interests.

tradition *n* knowledge handed down orally; a custom.

traduce *vt* to slander; defame.

traffic *n* trade; commerce; intercourse; conveyance of passengers or goods on railways, roads, etc. * *vi* to trade.

tragedy *n* an elevated drama with fatal ending; any dreadful event.

tragic, tragical *adj* fatal; disastrous.

trail *n* a track or scent. * *vt* to drag along the ground; to hang downwards.

trailer *n* a climbing plant; a vehicle towed by another.

train *vt* to draw along; to drill; to exercise; to teach; to take aim * *n* something drawn along; a series of railway carriages coupled with engine; trailing part of skirt; a retinue; process.

training *n* exercise; education; practice.

trait *n* a distinguishing feature.

traitor *n* one guilty of treason.

trajectory *n* the path of a moving body, as bullet, comet, etc.

tram *n* a tramway line; a tramcar.

trammel *n* a net for birds or fishes; a shackle; a handicap; a hindrance. * *vt* to impede.

tramp *vti* to tread under foot; travel on foot. * *n* a journey on foot; a vagrant.

trample *vt* to tread on heavily; to ride roughshod over.

trance *n* a state of insensibility; a swoon.

tranquil *adj* calm; serene.

transact *vti* to carry through.

transaction *n* management; performance; *pl* report of proceedings of societies.

transcend *vt* to rise above; to surpass.

transcendent *adj* of surpassing merit; pre-eminent; supernatural.

transcribe *vt* to copy.

transcript *n* a written copy.

transcription *n* act of transcribing; a copy.

transfer *vt* to convey from one place or person to another. * *n* conveyance of titles, etc, from one to another; a design that can be printed off on another surface.

transfigure *vt* to change in form or shape.

transfix *vt* to piece through.

transform *vt* to change the form of; to convert.

transformation *n* a complete change of appearance or nature.

transfuse *vt* to transfer, as blood, from one person to another.

transgress *vt* to break or violate. * *vi* to do wrong.

transgression *n* fault; offence.

transient *adj* passing quickly; fleeting.

transit *n* a passing across; passage of planet across sun's disc or of star across meridian of a place; conveyance.

transition *n* passage from one place or state to another.

transitive adj in grammar, said of action passing from subject to object.

transitory adj fleeting.

translate vt to remove from one place to another; to render into another language.

translation n removal; a turning into another language; a version.

translucent adj semi-transparent.

translucid adj translucent.

transmissible adj able to be passed through or along.

transmission n a passing through; act of sending.

transmit vt to convey or effect conveyance of news, light, etc; to hand down.

transmogrify vt to transform; to change.

transmute vt to change from one form into another.

transom n a strengthening cross beam over door or window.

transparency n clearness; obviousness; picture visible only when light passes through.

transparent adj clear; not opaque; frank.

transpiration n emission of vapour or moisture through pores.

transpire vt to emit through pores of skin. * vt to exhale; to become known.

transplant vt to remove and plant in another place.

transport vt to carry from one place to another; to banish; to enrapture. * n conveyance for goods; a ship for carrying troops, etc; rapture.

transpose vt to change the order of things.

transposition n change in order of words for effect.

transubstantiate vt to change to another substance.

transude vi to pass through pores.

transversal adj lying across. * n line cutting other straight lines.

transverse adj lying across; crosswise.

trap n a contrivance for catching animals; an ambush; a contrivance in drains to prevent foul air rising; a light uncovered vehicle; an igneous rock. * vti to snare; to take unawares; to set trap for.

trap door n a door in a floor or ceiling or roof.

trapeze n a swing for gymnastic exercises.

trapezium n (pl **trapezia**) a plane four-sided figure of which no two sides are parallel.

trappings npl finery; adornment, esp.. for horses.

trash n rubbish; refuse.

travail vi to labour; to toil. * n toil and pain; childbirth.

travel n journey to a distant country. * vi to journey.

traverse adj transverse. * n a crosspiece; denial of a plea in lawsuit; barrier across a trench. * vt to cross; to journey through; to deny. * adv athwart; crosswise.

travesty n a wilful misrepresentation.

trawl vi to fish by trailing a net. * n a large net for deep-sea fishing.

trawler n a fishing vessel with a trawl net.

tray n a broad, flat, rimmed utensil for carrying dishes, etc.

treacherous adj faithless; deceitful.

treachery n betrayal of trust; perfidy; treason.

treacle n the syrup obtained in the refining of sugar.

tread vi to step or walk. * vt to trample; dance. * n step; the part of a shoe, tyre, etc that touches the ground.

treason n treachery; disloyalty to king or country.

treasonable adj involving treason.

treasure n great wealth; something greatly valued. * vt to prize highly.

treasurer n one who has the charge of funds.

treasury n place where public money is stored; government department that controls finance.

treat vti to handle; to act towards; to discourse on. * n an entertainment; a rare pleasure.

treatise n an essay; pamphlet.

treatment n mode of dealing with.

treaty n an agreement between nations.

treble adj threefold. * n highest part in music; soprano.

tree n a woody plant with trunk and branches.

trefoil n a three-leaved plant, as clover; a sculptured tracery like clover.

trek vi to migrate by wagon.

trellis n a lattice-work structure.

tremble vi to shake; to quiver.

tremendous adj terrible; huge.

tremor n an involuntary trembling; a shivering.

tremulous adj trembling; quavering.

trench vti to dig a ditch in; to turn over and mix, as soil. * n a long narrow cutting; a deep ditch with rampart.

trenchant adj cutting; severe.

trend vi to incline towards. * n direction; tendency.

trepidation n consternation; fear.

trespass vi to intrude on another's land; to transgress; to sin. * n a sin; offence; intrusion on another's property.

tress n a lock of hair.

trestle n a frame for supporting things.

trial n a putting to the test; ordeal; attempt; hardship.

triangle n a figure having three sides and three angles.

triangular adj having form of triangle.

tribe n a division of a people; family; race.

tribulation n deep affliction; suffering.

tribunal n a court of justice.

tributary adj paying tribute; subordinate. * n a stream flowing into another.

tribute n merited praise.

trice n an instant.

trick n an artifice; fraud; a knack; a habit; a prank. * vt to deceive; to cheat.

trickery n cheating; fraud.

trickle vi to fall in drops.

trickster n a knave; cheat.

tricycle n three-wheeled cycle.

trident n three-pronged sceptre.

tried adj approved; reliable.

triennial adj happening every three years.

trifle n thing of little value; a confection or pudding. * vi, t. to toy; to idle.

trifling adj trivial; frivolous.

trigger n the catch by which a gun is fired.

trigonometry n the science dealing with measurement of triangles and ratios of their angles.

trilateral adj three-sided.

trill n a tremor of voice in singing. * vt to warble.

trilogy n a series of three connected dramas, poems, etc.

trim vt to put in order; to prune; to adjust (cargo). * adj spruce; neat. * n readiness; good condition.

trimming n an embellishment, esp.. of garment; pl accessories; parings.

trinity n a union of three in one.

trinket n a trifling ornament.

trio n a set of three; composition for three performers.

trip vi to step lightly; to skip; to stumble. * vt to cause to stumble. * n a stumble; an excursion or jaunt.

tripartite adj divided into three; made between three parties.

tripe n stomach of sheep, cow, etc, prepared as food.

triple adj threefold; treble.

triplet n three of a kind; pl three children at one birth.

triplicate adj threefold.

tripod n a three-legged stand.

tripper n a day excursionist.

trisect vt to cut into three equal parts.

trisyllable n a word consisting of three syllables.

trite adj commonplace; well-worn.

triumph n a rejoicing for victory; a great victory. * vi to gain a victory; to exult.

triumphal adj pertaining to a triumph.

triumphant adj victorious; exultant.

triumvirate n a coalition of three men in office.

trivet n a tripod for kettle, etc.

trivial adj common; trifling.

trod, trodden v. past and p.p. of tread.

troglodyte n a cave dweller.

troll vti to sing in chorus or succession; to fish by trailing bait. * n a part song; a fishing reel; a dwarfish elf.

trolley, trolly n a small truck.

trollop n a slattern.

trombone n a deep-toned wind instrument.

troop n a collection of people or animals; a cavalry company; pl soldiers in general. * vi to gather in large numbers.

trooper n a cavalryman; a mounted policeman.

troopship n a ship used for transport of military forces.

trophy n a token or memorial of victory.

tropic n one of the two parallel lines of latitude on either side of the equator; (pl) the regions lying between these lines.

tropical adj excessively hot; relating to the tropics.

trot vi to run with small steps. * n a medium pace.

troth n truth; faith.

trouble vt to disturb; to distress. * n distress; affliction.

troublesome adj annoying; tiresome.

trough n a long shallow drinking vessel; a hollow.

trounce vt to beat severely.

troupe n a company of performers.

trousers npl a garment for men, covering legs.

trousseau n a bride's outfit.

trowel n a hand tool for spreading mortar, etc.

truant n one who stays from school without leave.

truce n a temporary stoppage of fighting; armistice.

truck n a heavy motor vehicle for transporting goods. *vt to convey by truck. * vi to drive a truck.

truculence n ferocity.

truculent adj aggressive; overbearing.

trudge vi to walk, esp.. with heavy steps.

true adj conformable to fact; genuine; loyal; honest; exact.

truffle n an edible fungus growing underground.

truism n a self-evident truth.

truly adv really; according to truth.

trump n a winning card; one of the favoured suit for time being; a real good fellow. * vt to take with a trump card; to concoct (with up).

trumpet n a metal wind instrument. * vt to proclaim; to sound.

truncate vt to cut off; to lop.

truncated adj cut short.

truncheon n a short staff; a baton of authority.

trundle vi to roll or bowl. * n a little wheel.

trunk n the stem of a tree; body of an animal; chest for containing clothes, etc; proboscis of an elephant, etc.

trunk line n main line of railway, telephone, etc.

truss n a bundle, as of hay; a bandage; crossbeams to support roof * vt to tie up (fowl) for cooking; to strengthen; to bind firmly.

trust n reliance; confidence; hope; credit; a business combine; money or property entrusted to individuals (trustees) for use in specified ways. * vti to rely upon; to credit; to entrust.

trustee n one appointed to hold property for benefit of others.

trustworthy adj faithful; honest.

trusty adj reliable; staunch.

truth n conformity to fact or reality; integrity; constancy; reality.

try vt to test; to afflict; to examine judicially; to attempt.

trying adj severe; searching.

tryst n an appointment to meet; a rendezvous.

tub n an open wooden vessel; a small bath.

tube n a pipe; a hollow cylinder.

tuber n an underground fleshy stem or root.

tuberculosis n a disease marked by presence of tubercles in tissues; consumption.

tubing n material for tubes series of tubes.

tubular adj like a tube; consisting of tubes.

tuck vt to gather in a fold. * n fold in garment; roll of drum; eatables.

tuesday n the second work day of the week.

tuft n a cluster; clump.

tug vti to pull with effort. * n a strong pull; steam towing vessel.

tuition n instruction; business of teaching.

tulle n a thin silk fabric.

tumble vi to roll about; to fall. * vt to overturn. * n a fall.

tumbler n an acrobat; a drinking glass.

tumid adj swollen; bombastic.

tumour n an abnormal growth of tissue in any part of the body.

tumult n uproar; riot.

tumultuous adj turbulent; disorderly.

tundra n flat, treeless arctic plain.

tune *n* a short air or melody; harmony; correct intonation; frame of mind; mood. * *vt* to put into tune; to adapt.

tunic *n* a loose garment sometimes worn by both sexes; a military jacket; a covering membrane.

tuning fork *n* a two-pronged fork which when struck gives a standard musical note.

tunnel *n* an arched underground passage, esp on railways.

turban *n* a headdress.

turbid *adj* muddy; dense.

turbine *n* a horizontal water wheel; a rotary motor driven by steam, water, etc.

turbulence *n* disorder; tumult.

turbulent *adj* disorderly; riotous.

tureen *n* a large deep dish for soup.

turf *n* the grassy layer on surface of ground; a sod. * the turf, the business of horse racing.

turgid *adj* swelling; bombastic.

turmeric *n* an E. Indian plant whose root is used as a dye, a drug, and a flavour.

turmoil *n* uproar; disorder.

turn *vt* to cause to move round; to shape by a lathe; to alter course; to reverse; to change. * *vi* to revolve; to bend or curve; to become sour. * *n* a revolution; a bend; a short walk; purpose; short spell.

turncoat *n* one who deserts his party or principles.

turning *n* a turn; bend; art of shaping articles on a lathe.

turnstile *n* a revolving barrier that serves as entrance gate.

turpentine *n* resin got from certain trees; oil distilled from this.

turpitude *n* baseness; depravity.

turquoise *n* a greenish blue precious stone.

turret *n* a little tower forming part of a building; rotary iron tower to protect guns and gunners on warship.

tusk *n* a long pointed tooth projecting from mouth as in elephant, boar.

tussle *n* a struggle; scuffle.

tussock *n* a clump of grass.

tutelage *n* guardianship.

tutelar *adj* protecting.

tutor *n* a teacher.

twaddle *vi* to prate; to chatter. * *n* silly talk.

twang *vi* to pluck a taut string or wire. * *n* sound of a taut string plucked.

tweak *vt* to pinch; twist.

tweed *n* a twilled woollen fabric.

tweezers *npl* small pincers to pluck out hairs, etc.

twelfth *adj* the ordinal of twelve

twelve *adj, n* ten and two.

twentieth *adj* the ordinal of twenty.

twenty *adj, n* twice ten.

twice *adv* two times.

twiddle *vti* to twirl idly.

twig *n* a small shoot or branch.

twilight *n* the faint light after sunset and before dawn.

twill *n* a textile fabric with parallel ribs.

twin *n* one of two born at a birth. * *adj* double.

twine *n* strong thread or cord. * *vti* to twist; to coil.

twinge *n* a sudden darting pain.

twinkle *vi* to sparkle; to blink. * *n* a sparkle.

twirl *vti* to turn round rapidly; to rotate. * *n* a curl; a flourish.

twist *n* something twined, as a thread; roll of tobacco; a wrench; a turn. * *vti* to twine; to writhe; to pervert.

twitch *vt* to pluck; to jerk. * *n* a quick pull; a muscular jerk.

two *adj, n* the number next above one.

tymbal *n* a kettledrum.

tympanum *n* (*pl* **tympana**) the drum of the ear.

type *n* a distinguishing mark; emblem; model; letter used in printing; such letters collectively.

typewriter *n* a machine for producing printed letters by inked type.

typhoid *n* enteric fever; a low fever with acute intestinal pain.

typhoon *n* a violent hurricane.

typhus *n* a dangerous fever.

typical *adj* characteristic; symbolic.

typify *vt* to represent; exemplify.

typography *n* the art of printing.

tyrannical *adj* despotic; overbearing.

tyrannize *vi* to act the tyrant; to oppress.

tyranny *n* oppressive government; despotism.

tyrant *n* a despot; an oppressor.

tyre *n* a protective ring, usu rubber round the rim of a wheel.

tyro *n* a novice, a beginner.

U

ubiquitous *adj* existing everywhere; omnipresent.

udder *n* the milk gland of cows, sheep, etc.

ugly *adj* unattractive; unsightly; repulsive; ill-tempered.

ulcer *n* a festering sore.

ulceration *n* an ulcerous condition.

ulster *n* a long loose overcoat.

ulterior *adj* not evident;on further side; (motives) hidden .

ultimate *adj* utmost; final.

ultimatum *n* a last or final offer.

ultra *pref, adj* beyond; extreme.

ultramarine *n* a vivid blue pigment.

ululate *vi* to howl, as with pain.

umbilical *adj* pertaining to the navel.

umbra *n* the dark central part of a shadow.

umbrage *n* resentment; offence.

umbrella *n* a folding frame with handle and covering covering, etc, as protection from rain; general protection.

umpire *n* a judge or referee.

un- *pref* the addition of this prefix negatives or reverses the original meaning, as untrue, not true.

The sense of these 'u' words is in most cases self-evident, and only those in common use are given below, together with a fairly complete list of those whose meaning is less obvious.

unable *adj* not able; unequal to some task.

unacceptable *adj* unwelcome.

unaccountable *adj* not responsible.

unaccustomed *adj* unusual.

unacknowledged *adj* ignored.

unacquainted *adj* not familiar with.

unadorned *adj* plain; simple.

unadvisable *adj* not prudent.

unaffected *adj* simple; sincere; unmoved.

unaided *adj* without aid.

unalterable *adj* unchangeable.

unanimity *n* complete agreement. the 'un' here stands for 'unus', one.

unanimous *adj* being of one mind.

unanswerable *adj* conclusive.

unappreciated *adj* not duly prized.

unapproachable *adj* inaccessible.

unarmed *adj* defenceless.

unassailable *adj* impregnable.

unassuming *adj* modest.

unattended *adj* solitary; alone.

unattractive *adj* uninteresting.

unauthorized *adj* unwarranted.

unavailing *adj* of no avail.

unaware *adj, adv* unconscious; ignorant.

unawares *adv* unexpectedly.

unbearable *adj* intolerable.

unbecoming *adj* unseemly.

unbend *vi* to make straight.

unbiased *adj* impartial; just.

unbounded *adj* boundless, vast.

unbridled *adj* unrestrained.

unburden *vt* to rid of a load or burden.

uncanny *adj* weird; mysterious.

unceasing *adj* continual.

uncertain *adj* doubtful; variable.

unchallenged *adj* unopposed.

unchanging *adj* constant; immutable.

uncharitable *adj* harsh; ungenerous.

uncivil *adj* rude; discourteous.

uncivilized *adj* barbarous.

uncle *n* the brother of one's father or mother.

unclean *adj* dirty; impure.

uncomfortable *adj* ill at ease.

uncommunicative *adj* reserved; taciturn.

uncompromising *adj* unyielding.

unconditional *adj* unqualified.

unconnected *adj* separate; rambling.

unconscionable *adj* inordinate.

unconscious *adj* insensible; unaware.

unconstitutional *adj* not according to the principles of the constitution.

uncontrollable *adj* headstrong.

unconventional *adj* free and easy.

unconverted *adj* unchanged.

uncouple *vt* to set loose, as dogs on leash.

uncouth *adj* odd in appearance.

uncover *vt* to divest of a cover.

unctuous *adj* oily; greasy.

uncultivated *adj* not tilled; boorish.

undaunted *adj* intrepid; fearless.

undecided adj wavering; irresolute.

undemonstrative adj reserved; placid.

undeniable adj indisputable; true.

under prep. below; beneath; subject to; inferior. * adv in a lower condition or degree. * adj lower; subordinate.

underclothes n clothes worn under others or next skin.

undercurrent n a current below another.

undergo vt to bear; to suffer.

undergraduate n a student who has not taken his degree.

undergrowth n shrubs growing among large ones; copsewood.

underhand adj sly; dishonest.

underline vt to mark with a line underneath for emphasis.

undermine vt to sap; to injure by underhand means.

underrate vt to undervalue.

undersized adj dwarfish; small.

understand vti to comprehend.

understanding n comprehension; discernment; knowledge; agreement.

understudy n one who gets up a theatrical part to be ready as substitute.

undertake vti to take in hand.

undertaker n one who manages funerals.

undertaking n a task; project; promise.

undertone n an undercurrent of feeling.

undertow n the backward suction of a wave breaking on shore; undercurrent.

underwear n underclothes.

underworld n the world of criminals.

underwrite vt to sign one's name as answerable for a certain amount of insurance.

undisguised adj open; candid.

undisturbed adj calm; tranquil.

undo vt to reverse what has been done.

undoing n reversal; ruin.

undoubted adj certain; unquestionable.

undress vt vi to take off one's clothes.

undue adj unnecessary; excessive.

undulation n a waving motion; a gentle slope; vibratory motion.

undulatory adj wave-like.

unearned adj unmerited; (income) not earned by labour or skill.

unearth vt to discover; to reveal.

unearthly adj weird; ghostly.

uneasy adj restless; awkward; anxious.

unendurable adj intolerable.

unequable adj changeful; fitful.

unequal adj ill-matched.

unequivocal adj undoubted; clear.

uneven adj unequal; rough; odd.

unexceptionable adj irreproachable.

unexpected adj unlooked for; sudden.

unexplored adj unvisited.

unfading adj ever fresh.

unfailing adj sure.

unfair adj unjust; biassed.

unfaithful adj disloyal; false.

unfamiliar adj strange; unaccustomed.

unfasten vt to loose; to unfix.

unfavourable adj adverse.

unfeeling adj devoid of feeling; harsh.

unfit adj unsuitable; incompetent.

unflinching adj resolute; firm.

unfold vti to open the folds of; to display.

unforeseen adj unexpected; sudden.

unforgiving adj relentless; implacable.

unfortunate adj unlucky; unhappy.

unfounded adj false; groundless.

unfrequented adj rarely visited; solitary.

unfurl vt to spread out (sail, flag, etc)

unfurnished adj without furniture.

ungainly adj clumsy; awkward.

ungenerous adj stingy; mean.

ungovernable adj headstrong; unruly.

ungraceful adj inelegant.

ungrammatical adj not according to grammar.

ungrateful adj not thankful; irksome.

ungrudging adj generous; hearty.

unguent n an ointment.

unhappily adv unfortunately.

unhappy adj miserable; sad; unlucky.

unhealthy adj sickly; unwholesome.

unheeded adj ignored; disregarded.

unheeding adj careless.

unhesitating adj instant; prompt.

unhinge vt to loosen; to derange.

unholy adj profane; wicked.

uniform adj regular; unvarying. * n regulation dress of certain persons.

uniformity n sameness; agreement; conformity to one type.

unify vt to form into one.

unimpaired adj uninjured.

unimpeachable *adj* irreproachable.

uninhabited *adj* deserted; desolate.

unintelligent *adj* dull; stupid.

unintelligible *adj* incapable of being understood; meaningless.

unintentional *adj* accidental.

uninteresting *adj* tedious; wearisome.

uninterrupted *adj* continuous; unbroken.

uninviting *adj* unattractive.

union *n* concord; a league; a trade union.

unionist *n* a trade unionist.

unique *adj* being the only one of its kind.

unison *n* harmony; concord.

unit *n* a single thing or person; an individual; a standard quantity.

unite *vti* to combine; to connect.

unity *n* harmony; oneness; the number 1.

universal *adj* all-embracing, total.

universe *n* the whole creation; the world.

university *n* educational institution for higher learning.and research.

unjust *adj* unfair; bad; biassed.

unkempt *adj* uncombed; rough.

unknowingly *adv* unwittingly.

unlace *vt* to unfasten.

unlawful *adj* illegal.

unless *conj* if it be not that.

unlicensed *adj* without legal permission.

unlike *adj* different; dissimilar.

unlimited *adj* unbounded; limitless.

unlooked-for *adj* unexpected.

unlucky *adj* unfortunate; ill-fated.

unmanageable *adj* beyond control.

unmannerly *adj* rude; ill-bred.

unmask *vt* to strip off mask; to expose.

unmeasured *adj* excessive; boundless.

unmerciful *adj* ruthless; cruel.

unmerited *adj* undeserved.

unmitigated *adj* unqualified; absolute.

unnatural *adj* inhuman; affected.

unnavigable *adj* incapable of being navigated.

unnerve *vt* to unman; to deprive of power.

unobtrusive *adj* retiring; modest.

unoccupied *adj* empty; at leisure.

unopposed *adj* meeting with no opposition.

unorthodox *adj* unconventional.

unpack *vt* to empty a pack, trunk, etc.

unpalatable *adj* unpleasant to taste.

unparalleled *adj* unequalled; matchless.

unpardonable *adj* inexcusable.

unpleasant *adj* disagreeable.

unpractised *adj* raw; unskilful.

unprecedented *adj* unparalleled.

unpretentious *adj* modest.

unprincipled *adj* immoral; wicked.

unproductive *adj* barren.

unprofessional *adj* contrary to professional etiquette.

unprofitable *adj* fruitless; futile.

unqualified *adj* untrained; incompetent.

unquestionable *adj* indisputable.

unravel *vt* to disentangle; to solve.

unreadable *adj* illegible.

unreal *adj* sham; visionary.

unreasonable *adj* immoderate; absurd.

unrecorded *adj* not placed on record.

unrelenting *adj* hard; pitiless.

unreliable *adj* untrustworthy.

unremitting *adj* ceaseless; constant.

unrequited *adj* unrewarded.

unreserved *adj* frank; full; open.

unrest *n* disquiet; uneasiness.

unrestrained *adj* unbridled; loose.

unripe *adj* immature.

unrivalled *adj* peerless.

unroll *vti* to unfold; to display.

unruffled *adj* calm; composed.

unruly *adj* disorderly.

unsatisfactory *adj* not up to expectation.

unsavoury *adj* insipid; unpleasing.

unscathed *adj* uninjured.

unscrupulous *adj* unprincipled.

unseemly *adj* unbecoming; improper.

unsentimental *adj* matter-of-fact.

unserviceable *adj* useless.

unsettle *vt* to upset; to derange.

unshaken *adj* firm; resolute.

unshapely *adj* ill-formed.

unsightly *adj* ugly; repulsive.

unsociable *adj* reserved; solitary.

unsolicited *adj* unsought.

unsophisticated *adj* natural; artless.

unsound *adj* diseased; faulty.

unspeakable *adj* unutterable.

unstable *adj* unsteady; fickle.

unsteady *adj* changeable; unsafe.

unstinted *adj* lavish; generous.

unsubstantial *adj* visionary; flimsy.

unsuitable *adj* unfit; unbecoming.

unsullied *adj* pure; stainless.

unsung *adj* not celebrated in song or poetry.

unsurpassed *adj* unexcelled.

unsuspecting *adj* free from suspicion.

unswerving *adj* steadfast; straight.

untenable *adj* not fit to be occupied.

unthinkable *adj* inconceivable.

unthinking *adj* careless; heedless.

untidy *adj* slovenly; careless.

untie *vt* to loosen; to undo.

until *prep, conj* up to the time that; till.

untimely *adj* ill-timed; unseasonable.

untiring *adj* unwearied.

unto *prep* to.

untold *adj* countless; vast; unrecorded.

untouched *adj* unscathed; unmoved.

untoward *adj* unseemly; unfavourable.

untried *adj* not attempted; inexperienced.

untroubled *adj* calm; unruffled.

untrue *adj* incorrect; faithless.

untrustworthy *adj* unreliable; false.

unusual *adj* rare; peculiar.

unutterable *adj* unspeakable.

unvarnished *adj* plain; unadorned.

unvarying *adj* uniform.

unveil *vt* to uncover; to disclose to view.

unwarrantable *adj* unjustifiable; illegal.

unwavering *adj* steady; staunch.

unwearied *adj* tireless; incessant.

unwieldy *n* huge; cumbersome.

unwilling *adj* reluctant; loath.

unwind *vt* to wind off.

unwitting *adj* ignorant; unaware.

unworthy *adj* base; worthless.

unwritten *adj* understood though not expressed; traditional.

unyielding *adj* stubborn; unbending.

up *adv* aloft; in or to a higher position; upright; out of bed. * *prep.* from below to.

upbraid *vt* to reproach; to taunt.

upbringing *n* training; breeding.

upheaval *n* great social or political changes.

uphold *vt* to support; to sustain.

upholster *vt* to furnish (chairs, sofas, etc) with springs, stuffing, etc.

upkeep *n* maintenance.

upon *prep* up and on; on.

upper *adj* higher in place or rank.

uppish *adj* snobbish.

upright *adj* erect; trustworthy.

uproar *n* a great tumult.

uproarious *adj* noisy; boisterous.

uproot *vt* to tear up by roots.

upset *vt* to overturn; to discompose. * *n* act of upsetting. * *adj* fixed.

upshot *n* final issue; end.

upstairs *adj, adv* in or towards upper story of building; house, etc.

upstart *n* one who has suddenly risen in position; an arrogant person.

urban *adj* belonging to a city.

urbane *adj* sophisticated; polite.

urchin *n* a small mischievous boy.

urge *vt* to press to do something.

urgent *adj* pressing; imperative.

urine *n* fluid excreted from kidneys and bladder.

urn *n* a kind of vase.

us *pron* the objective case of we.

usage *n* treatment; customary practice.

use *n* employment practice; need. * *vt* to put to use; to avail one's self of; to employ.

user *n* one who uses

useful *adj* helpful; serviceable.

usher *n* a doorkeeper; an assistant.

usual *adj* customary; common.

usurer *n* one who takes exorbitant interest.

usurp *vt* to seize and hold without right.

usury *n* extortionate interest for loan.

utensil *n* a kitchen implement.

utility *n* usefulness; profit.

utilize *vt* make use of.

utmost *adj* the highest degree.

utopia *n* an ideal state or government.

utopian *adj* ideally perfect; visionary.

utter *adj* complete; total. * *vt* to speak; pronounce; spread abroad.

uvula *n* small fleshy body hanging from back palate.

V

vacancy n empty space; an unfilled post.

vacant adj empty; unfilled; silly.

vacate vt to quit possession of.

vacation n holiday time.

vaccinate vt to inoculate against small-pox.

vaccine n inoculating lymph.

vacillate vi to waver; to be undecided.

vacuous adj empty; void; vacant.

vacuum n a space void of air; empty space; a vacuum cleaner.

vagabond adj roaming; idling. * n a tramp.

vagrant adj wandering. * n a tramp; a sturdy beggar.

vague adj indefinite; hazy.

vain adj empty; fruitless; conceited. * In vain, to no purpose.

vale n a valley.

valedictory n farewell.

valentine n a love gift or missive sent on Valentine's day (14th February).

valet n a manservant.

valiant adj brave; heroic.

valid adj well grounded; sound.

validity n justness; soundness.

valley n the low ground between hills.

valour n bravery; courage.

valuable adj of great worth. * npl precious belongings.

valuator n an appraiser or valuer.

value n worth; importance; price. * vt to estimate; to prize; to appraise.

valve n a lid or flap for an opening, giving passage in one direction only.

vampire n a fabled bloodsucking creature; a person who preys on others; a bat.

van n a covered motor vehicle.

vandal n a barbarian; a person who willfully damages property.

vane n a weathercock; blade of a wind-mill, etc.

vanguard n front part of an army; the leading position of any movement.

vanilla n a flavouring prepared from tropical orchid.

vanish vi to disappear; to pass away.

vanity n idle show; craving for praise; emptiness; conceit.

vanquish vt to conquer; overcome.

vapid adj spiritless; flat; dull.

vaporize vt to convert or pass off into vapour.

vapour n a gas or fume given off by a body when sufficiently heated.

variable adj fickle; changeable.

variance n dispute; quarrel.

variant n an alternative form.

variation n change; alteration.

varicose adj enlarged, said of veins.

varied adj diverse; various.

variegated pp diversified in colour.

variety n diversity; change in assortment; a species.

various adj different; several.

varnish n a resinous solution used to give gloss to wood, paper, etc; a gloss; a sham.

vary vti to change; to alter; to differ; to disagree.

vascular adj pertaining to vessels, ducts, etc, of organic bodies.

vase n a jar-shaped vessel for ornament or use.

vast adj of great extent; immense.

vat n a huge tub or tank for holding liquors.

vaudeville n a light comedy with dances and songs.

vault n an arched roof; cellar; a leap. * vi to leap.

vaunt vi, vt to brag; to exult. * n a boast.

veal n the flesh of a calf.

veer vi to change direction.

vegetable adj, n a plant grown for food.

vegetarian n a person who consumes a diet that excludes meat and fish.

vegetate vi to live a plant's life; to lead an aimless life.

vegetation n plants in general.

vehement adj ardent; forcible.

vehicle n any kind of land carriage; a medium.

veil n a screen; a face shade; a disguise. * vt to conceal.

vein n a blood vessel which returns blood to heart; sap tube or rib in leaves; a seam of ore; disposition; mood; streak.

velocity n rate of motion; speed.

velvet n a rich soft fabric.

venal adj base; corrupt.

vend vt to sell.

vendetta n a feud.

veneer n a thin facing of fine wood glued on a less valuable sort; a gloss. * vt to overlay with veneer; to gloss.

venerable adj worthy of respect and admiration.

venerate vt to revere; honour.

vengeance n punishment in return for an injury.

venial adj pardonable; slight.

venison n the flesh of deer.

venom n poison; spite; malice.

venomous adj poisonous; spiteful.

venous adj pertaining to a vein.

vent n an outlet; a flue; expression. * vt to emit; utter.

ventilate vt to give air to; to discuss freely.

ventral adj abdominal.

ventricle n a small cavity in body, esp. one of those in heart or brain.

ventriloquist n one able to disguise his voice so that it seems to come from another speaker.

venture n a risky undertaking. * vi to dare. * vt to risk.

venturesome adj bold; hazardous.

venue n the appointed place of trial (law); meeting place.

veracious adj truthful; accurate.

veracity n truthfulness.

veranda, verandah n a portico or balcony along front of house.

verb n the predicative word in a sentence.

verbal adj spoken; oral.

verbally adv by word of mouth.

verbatim adv word for word.

verbiage n the use of too many words.

verbosity n superabundance of words; wordiness.

verdant adj green; simple; gullible.

verdict n the finding of a jury; considered opinion.

verdigris n the green rust of copper.

verdure n green vegetation.

verge n border; margin; brink. * vi to incline; to border.

verification n a proving true.

verify vt to prove to be true; to confirm.

verisimilitude n the appearance of truth; probability.

veritable adj true; real; actual.

verity n truth.

vermicular adj worm-like.

vermilion n a beautiful red colour.

vermin n noxious animals or insects as rats, lice, etc.

verminous adj infested by vermin.

vernacular adj native. * n mother tongue.

vernal adj pertaining to the spring.

versatile adj readily turning; variable; many-sided.

verse n a line of poetry; metre; poetry; a stanza; a short division of any composition.

versed adj conversant; skilled, with in.

version n a translation; rendering.

versus against.

vertebra n (pl **vertebrae**) one of bones of spine; pl the spine.

vertebrate adj having a backbone.

vertex n ; pl ^texes or tices. the highest point; apex; zenith.

vertical adj upright; plumb.

vertigo n giddiness.

verve n spirit; energy.

very adj true; real. * adv truly.

vesicle n a small bladder or blister.

vessel n a hollow utensil for holding things; a ship.

vest n a waistcoat; an undergarment. * vi to furnish with (power, property, etc). * vt to invest.

vestal adj virgin; pure. * n a nun.

vested adj robed; established.

vestibule n lobby or hall of house.

vestige n footprint; mark or trace.

vestment n a garment, esp. priestly garment.

vestry n room where clerical vestments are kept.

vesture n dress; clothing.

veteran adj long experienced, esp. in war.

veterinary adj pertaining to diseases of domestic animals.

veto n the right to reject or forbid. * vt to refuse assent to.

vexatious adj annoying; troublesome.

vexed adj annoyed; much disputed.

via prep by way of.

viaduct *n* an arched bridge over a valley.

vial *n* a small glass bottle.

vibrant *adj* vibrating; tremulous.

vibrate *vti* to wave to and fro; to swing; to quiver.

vibratory *adj* causing to vibrate.

vicarious *adj* acting for, or on behalf of, another.

vice *n* a blemish; moral failing; profligacy; an instrument for gripping things firmly.

vice *prefix* denoting depute or one who acts in the place of another, e.g. vice-president.

vicinity *n* neighbourhood.

vicious *adj* malicious; bad-tempered.

vicissitude *n* one of ups and downs of life.

victim *n* a person who has suffered injury; a dupe.

victimize *vt* to make a victim of.

victor *n* conqueror; winner.

victory *n* defeat of enemy or rival; triumph.

victual *n* food provided; provisions; usu. in *pl* * *vt* to supply with food or stores.

vide see; refer to.

vie *vi* to contend; to compete.

view *n* a look; inspection; survey; range of vision; scene; intention. * *vti* to see; to survey; to consider.

vigil *n* a watching, esp. devotional.

vigilance *n* watchfulness.

vigilant *adj* watchful.

vignette *n* an engraving on title page, etc., without definite border; a picture without definite edges.

vigorous *adj* full of vigour.

vigour *n* energy; force; strength.

vile *adj* base; depraved.

villify *vt* to slander.

villa *n* a country or suburban house.

village *n* a collection of houses smaller than a town.

villain *n* a criminal; a scoundrel.

villainous *adj* base; vile; wicked.

vim *n* vigour; energy.

vinaigrette *n* a salad dressing of oil, vinegar and seasoning.

vindicate *vt* to justify; uphold.

vindictive *adj* revengeful.

vine *n* a plant that bears grapes.

vinegar *n* a liquid containing acetic acid, used as a condiment and preserve.

vineyard *n* a plantation of vines.

vintage *n* the yearly produce of vine; wine of particular year.

vintner *n* a wine seller.

viola *n* a large violin; genus of plants including violet, pansy, etc.

violate *vt* to injure; to outrage.

violation *n* infringement.

violence *n* great force; injury.

violent *adj* vehement; furious.

violin *n* a four-stringed musical instrument.

virago *n* a bad tempered woman.

virescent *adj* slightly green.

virgin *n* a person who has never had sexual intercourse. * *adj* untouched; pure.

virginal *adj* of or pertaining to a virgin. * *n* a kind of spinet.

virile *adj* sexually potent; strong.

virtual *adj* in effect, but not in name.

virtue *n* moral goodness; admirable quality.

virtuoso *n* a person highly skilled, esp in playing a musical instrument.

virtuous *adj* moral; upright.

virulent *adj* poisonous; malignant.

virus *n* a microorganism capable of causing ill-health; illness caused by a virus.

visa *n* an endorsement on a passport allowing the holder to travel in the country of the government issuing it.

visage *n* the face or countenance.

vis-à-vis *adv* face to face.

viscera *npl* the entrails.

viscid *adj* sticky or adhesive.

viscous *adj* glutinous; viscid.

visible *adj* perceivable by the eye.

vision *n* sight; object of sight; a dream.

visionary *adj* imaginary; fanciful. * *n* an unpractical person.

visit *vt* to call upon; to afflict. * *vi* to make calls. * *n* a call.

visor, vizor *n* the movable faceguard of a helmet.

vista *n* an extended view.

vital *adj* mortal; essential.

vitality *n* vital force; energy.

vitals *npl* parts essential to life.

vitamin *n* an essential element in diet.

vitiate *vt* to make faulty; to impair.

vitreous *adj* glassy.

vitrify *vt* to convert into glass.

vitriol *n* sulphuric acid.

vituperate *vt* to abuse; to revile.

vivacious *adj* lively; sprightly.

vivid *adj* bright; striking.

vivify *vt* to animate.

viviparous *adj* giving birth to live young.

vivisection *n* act of experimenting on a living animal.

vixen *n* a female fox; a shrew.

vocabulary *n* a list of words with definitions; an individual's command or use of words.

vocal *adj* pertaining to the voice.

vocalist *n* a singer.

vocation *n* a calling; occupation.

vocative *n* the vocative case.

vociferous *adj* clamorous; noisy.

vogue *n* temporary fashion.

voice *n* the sound uttered by the mouth; utterance; speech; sound emitted; vote; a form of verb inflection. * *vt* to utter or express.

void *adj* empty; null. * *n* an empty space. * *vt* to make vacant; to nullify.

volatile *adj* readily passing off in vapour; flighty.

volcano *n* a mountain formed by ejections of lava, ashes, etc through an opening in the earth's crust.

volition *n* will; power of choice.

volley *n* a simultaneous discharge of missiles.

volleyball *n* a team game played by hitting an inflated ball over a net with the hands; the ball used.

volt *n* unit of electromotive force.

volubility *n* fluency of speech.

voluble *adj* over fluent; glib.

volume *n* an amount of space; mass or bulk; a book.

volumetric *adj* pertaining to measurement by volume.

voluminous *adj* bulky; copious.

voluntary *adj* acting of one's own free will; without remuneration; deliberate.

volunteer *n* a person who undertakes military or other service of his own free will. * *vi* to offer one's services.

voluptuous *adj* fond of bodily pleasures; a sensualist.

vomit *vi, vt* to throw up from stomach; to eject; matter ejected from stomach.

voracious *adj* greedy; ravenous.

vortex *n* (*pl* **vortices, vortexes**) a whirling motion as in whirlpool, whirlwind.

vote *n* the recording of opinion for or against proposal; suffrage. * *vi, vt* to give a vote. * *vt* to grant by vote.

votive *adj* promised by vow.

vouch *vt* to attest; to guarantee.

voucher *n* a written record of a transaction; a token that can be exchanged for something else.

vouchsafe *vt* to condescend to grant.

vow *n* a solemn promise; an oath. * *vt* to promise solemnly.

vowel *n* a simple vocal sound; letter denoting it.

voyage *n* a journey, esp by ship.

vulcanite *n* a rubber hardened by treating with sulphur.

vulgar *adj* coarse in manners.

vulgarity *n* rudeness of manners.

vulnerable *adj* liable to injury.

vulpine *adj* crafty; foxy.

vulture *n* a large bird of prey; a rapacious person.

W

wad *n* a fibrous mass; a bundle of paper money.

wadding *n* any soft material for use in packing, padding, etc.

waddle *vi* to walk with rolling gait.

wade *vi* to walk through water; to walk with difficulty.

wafer *n* a thin crisp cracker or biscuit.

waft *vt* to sail or bear along gently.

wag *vti* to shake up and down or to and fro. * *n* a wit; joker.

wage *vt* to stake; to carry on, esp war; * *n* salary; hire; usu. in *pl*

wager *n* a bet; subject of bet. * *vt* to stake.

wagon, waggon *n* a four-wheeled cart; a truck.

waif *n* a homeless, neglected child.

wail vi to lament; to cry aloud. * n a moaning cry.

waist n part of body from ribs to hips.

waistcoat n a sleeveless undercoat; a vest.

wait vi to stay in expectation; to attend; to serve at table. * n period of waiting.

waiter n a servant in attendance at table.

waive vt to forgo; give up.

wake vi to be awake. * vt to arouse. * n vigil over dead; track left by ship.

waken vti to arouse; wake.

walk vi to advance step by step. * n a ramble; a road, path; sphere of life.

wall n a rigid vertical structure for enclosing, dividing or protecting.

wallet n a flat pocketbook for paper money, cards, etc.

wallow vi to roll in mud, to indulge oneself in emotion.

waltz n a whirling dance and its music.

wand n a magician's rod.

wander vi to ramble; to roam; to err.

wane vt to grow less; to decline.

want n need; longing; dearth; poverty. * vti to lack; need.

wanton adj frisky; lustful. * n a lewd person.

war n a fight between nations; enmity; a contest.

warble vti to sing like a bird; to trill.

ward vt to guard; to fend off * n guard; custody; one under a guardian; a division of a town or country; apartment of an hospital.

warden n a guardian; head of college or hostel.

warder n a guard; a keeper.

wardrobe n a cabinet or closet for keeping clothes; one's stock of clothes.

ware n merchandise; goods, usu. in pl * adj wary.

warehouse n a building for storing wares, goods.

warfare n military service; war.

warm adj moderately hot; zealous; excited; lively. * vti to make or become warm or animated.

warmth n gentle heat; cordiality.

warn vt to caution; to advise.

warning n caution; previous notice.

warp vti to twist; to pervert. * n lengthwise threads in loom; a twist.

warped adj twisted by shrinking; perverted.

warrant vt to guarantee; to authorize; to justify. * n a guarantee; writ or summons; voucher.

warranty n warrant; guarantee.

warrior n a gallant soldier.

wart n a hard dry growth on skin.

wary adj cautious; prudent.

was vb past tense of to be.

wash vti to cleanse with water; to colour lightly. * n flow or dash of water; a lotion; thin coat of colour.

washer n a ring of metal, rubber, etc, for tightening nut on screw.

washing n clothes washed; a cleansing.

wasp n a stinging winged insect.

waspish adj like a wasp; venomous; irritable; snappish.

wastage n lost by use or waste.

waste vti to ravage; to damage; to squander; to grow less. * adj unused; devastated. * n a wilderness; useless spending; decrease; refuse.

waste pipe n a pipe to carry off waste water.

watch n a guard; vigilance; sentry; a timepiece. * vti to guard; to observe carefully; to await.

watchful adj vigilant; cautious.

watchmaker n one who makes or repairs watches.

watchword n a password; a slogan; a motto.

water n the commonest of liquids, clear and transparent when pure. * vti to supply with water; to irrigate; to dilute; to take in water.

watercolour n a pigment ground up with water and gum instead of oil; a picture painted with watercolours.

watercourse n a channel for water.

waterfall n a stream falling over rocks; a cascade.

waterlogged adj soaked or filled with water.

waterproof adj impervious to water. * n cloth so made.

watershed n dividing ridge between river systems.

waterspout n a column of water sucked up by whirlwind.

watery adj like water; tasteless.

wave vi, vt to move up and down, or to and fro; to brandish; to beckon. * n a rising motion on surface of water, etc; a waving of hand as signal.

waved adj undulating.

waver vi to move to and fro; falter; flicker.

wax n secretion by bees; anything like wax. * vt to rub with wax; to grow larger.

waxwork n modelling in wax; pl figures in wax.

way n a track, path, or road; distance traversed; direction; condition; method; course.

wayfarer n a traveller.

waylay vt to lie in wait for; to accost.

wayside n the side of a road.

wayward adj wilful; perverse.

we pron plural of I.

weak adj feeble; frail; foolish; vacillating.

weaken vti to make or become weak.

weakling n a weak creature.

weal n a raised mark on skin.

wealth n riches; abundance.

wean vt to break off from any habit; to discontinue giving mother's milk.

weapon n any instrument of offence or defence.

wear vt to have on, as clothes; to waste by rubbing; to exhibit. * vi to last; to exhaust.

wearisome adj tiresome; tiring.

weary adj tired; jaded. * vt to wear out strength or patience; to become weary.

weather n the general atmospheric conditions at any particular time. * vt to affect by weather, as rocks; to bear up against (storms, etc).

weathercock n a vane turning with wind.

weatherglass n a barometer.

weave vt to form by interlacing threads; to compose or fabricate.

web n woven cloth; tissue or texture; film; membrane between toes of waterfowl.

webbed adj having the toes united by a membrane.

webbing n a strong narrow band used for girths, etc.

wed vti to marry; unite together.

wedding n marriage; nuptials.

wedge n a block sloping to thin edge at one end. * vt to cleave, fix, or fasten with wedge.

wedlock n marriage.

Wednesday n fourth day of week.

weed n a useless plant; tobacco; * vt to remove weeds.

week n seven consecutive days.

weep vi, vt to shed tears; to mourn.

weft n cross-threads of web.

weigh vt to find heaviness of; to reflect on; to raise anchor. * vi to have weight; to bear heavily.

weight n heaviness; gravity; heavy mass; pressure.

weir n a dam across a stream.

weird n fate. * adj unearthly; queer.

welcome adj pleasing. * n a kind reception.

weld vt to fuse together, esp metal; to unite.

welfare n well-being; state provision of financial aid to the unemployed, sick, etc.

well n a spring; a pit sunk for water; staircase or lift space. * vi to bubble up; to issue forth.

well adv rightly; smartly. * adj hale; hearty.

wellington n a high waterproof boot.

welter vi to wallow; to roll. * n a confused mass.

went past tense of go.

west n one of the four compass points; sun's setting place.

western adj in or from west.

wet adj covered with water; moist; rainy. * n water; rain. * vt to make wet.

whale n largest of sea animals.

whaler n a ship employed in whale fishery.

wharf n (pl **wharfs**, **wharves**) a loading place for ships; quay.

wheat n a cereal from which flour is obtained.

wheaten adj made from wheat.

wheel n a round spoked frame turning on axis; anything like a wheel. * vti to revolve or cause to revolve.

wheelbarrow *n* a hand carriage with one wheel.

wheelwright *n* a maker of wheels and carts.

wheeze *vi* to breathe hard and audibly.

whelk *n* a shellfish; a periwinkle.

when *adv, conj* at what or which time; while; whereas.

whence *adv, conj* from what place.

where *adv, conj* at or in what place.

whereas *conj* that being so.

whereby *adv, conj* by which or what.

wherefore *adv, conj* for which reason; why.

whereon *adv, conj* on which or on what.

whereupon *adv* upon which.

wherever *adv* at whatever place.

whet *vt* to sharpen; edge; stimulate.

whether *pron* which of two. * *conj, adv* which of two or more.

whetstone *n* a sharpening stone.

which *pron* an interrogative pronoun; a relative pronoun, the neuter of who.

whiff *n* a puff of air, smoke, smell.

while *n* short space of time. * *conj* during that time that. * *vt* to pass (time) pleasantly.

whilst *adv* while.

whim *n* a sudden fancy.

whimper *vi* to whine. * *n* a pathetic cry.

whimsical *adj* fantastic; odd.

whine *vi* utter plaintive cry. * *n* a wail.

whip *vt* to lash; flog; beat into froth.

whippersnapper *n* a forward but insignificant person.

whir *vi* to fly with buzzing sound.

whirl *vti* to revolve rapidly.

whirlpool *n* a whirling eddy of water.

whirlwind *n* a whirling eddy of air.

whisk *vt* to stir or move rapidly. * *n* a jerking motion; small brush; an egg-beater.

whisker *n* hair on cheeks.

whisky, whiskey *n* spirit distilled from barley, etc.

whisper *vti* to speak very softly. * *n* a low voice.

whist *interj* hush! * *n* a game of cards.

whistle *vi* to make a shrill sound with lips or instrument. * *n* a shrill sound; a small wind instrument.

white *adj* snow-coloured; pure.

whitewash *n* lime and water for whitening walls, etc; to coneal the truth.

whither *adv* to what or which place.

whittle *vt* to pare down.

who *pron, rel, interr* referring to persons only.

whole *adj* hale and sound. * *n* the total; all.

wholesale *n* sale of goods in large quantities. * *adj* extensive.

wholesome *adj* healthy; salutary.

wholly *adv* entirely.

whoop *n* a loud shout.

whooping cough *n* see Hooping cough.

whose *pron* the possessive case of who or which.

why *adv, conj* for what reason.

wick *n* the thread of a lamp or candle.

wicked *adj* bad; sinful; roguish.

wicket *n* a small gate; the three upright stumps in cricket.

wide *adj* broad; extensive.

widen *vti* to make or grow wide.

widow *n* a woman whose husband is deceased.

widower *n* a man whose wife is deceased.

width *n* breadth.

wield *vt* to handle; to exercise.

wife *n* ; *pl* wives. a married woman.

wig *n* an artificial head of hair.

wigwam *n* a North American Indian domed shelter.

wild *adj* in a state of nature; untamed; stormy.

wilderness *n* a desert; waste.

wildfire *n* sheet lightning.

wile *n* fraud; trick. * *vt* to entice.

wilful *adj* stubborn; headstrong.

will *vb aux* expressing futurity or resolve. * *vti* to determine by choice; to wish; to bequeath. * *n* wish; choice; determination; purpose; last testament; feeling.

willing *adj* ready; instant; ungrudging.

willow *n* a tree or shrub, valuable for basket-making, etc; a cricket bat.

wily *adj* cunning; sly.

win *vt* to gain; to allure. * *vi* to gain victory.

wince *vi* to shrink, as from pain.

winch *n* crank of wheel or axle; a windlass.

wind *n* a current of air; breath; flatulence. * *vt* to blow, as a horn. * *vt* to put out of breath; to rest.

wind *vt* to twist; to coil. * *vi* to twine; to meander.

windfall *n* fruit blown down; an unexpected financial gain.

winding *adj* bending; twisting. * *n* a turn; a bend.

windlass *n* a kind of hoisting machine; a winch.

windmill *n* a mill driven by wind.

window *n* a glazed opening in wall for light.

windpipe *n* the air passage to lungs; trachea.

windward *n* the point from which the wind blows.

wine *n* the fermented juice of grapes.

winepress *n* an apparatus for pressing juice from grapes.

wing *n* organ of flight; side extension of building, army, etc; side. * *vt* to fly; to wound.

wink *vi* to shut and open eyelids; to give hint by eyelids; to connive. * *n* a winking or hint given by it.

winning *adj* attractive; charming.

winnow *vt* to fan chaff from grain; to sift.

winsome *adj* attractive; winning.

winter *n* the cold season of year. * *vi* to pass the winter.

wipe *vt* to clean by gentle rubbing; to efface.

wire *n* a thread of metal; a telegram * *vt* to bind with wire. * *vi* to telegraph.

wiry *adj* wire-like; sinewy.

wisdom *n* sound judgment and knowledge; prudence.

wise *adj* learned; judging rightly.

wish *vi* to have a desire; to long. * *vt* to express desire. * *n* a desire.

wisp *n* a small bundle of straw, etc; anything slender.

wistful *adj* pensive; yearning.

wit *vti* to know; to be aware. * to wit, namely; that is to say. * *n* understanding; humour; a humorist.

witch *n* a woman who practices magic and is considered to have dealings with the devil.

witchcraft *n* the practice of magic.

with *prep* expressing nearness or connection; among; possessing.

withdraw *vt* to draw back; to retract. * *vi* to retire.

wither *vi* to fade or shrivel.

withers *npl* ridge between shoulder bones of horse.

withhold *vt* to hold back; not to grant.

within *prep* inside. * *adv* inwardly.

without *prep*, *adv* outside.

withstand *vti* to oppose; to resist.

witness *n* testimony; evidence; one who gives sworn evidence. * *vti* to see; to attest; to sign as witness.

witticism *n* a witty remark.

witty *adj* humorous; smart and droll.

wizard *n* a magician; conjuror.

wizen, wizened *adj* shrivelled.

wobble *vi* to sway from side to side.

woe *n* grief; misery.

woebegone *adj* grief-stricken.

wolf *n* ; *pl* wolves. a wild animal of the dog family.

woman *n* ; an adult female; female sex. *pl* women.

womanhood *n* the state or qualities of a woman.

won *pret*, *pp* of **win**.

wonder *n* something very strange; a marvel; feeling excited by something strange. * *vi* to be struck with wonder; to marvel.

woo *vt* to court with a view to marriage.

wood *n* a collection of growing trees; timber.

wooden *adj* made of wood; stiff.

woodwork *n* carpentry.

wool *n* the fleece of sheep, goats, etc.

woolgathering *n* idle dreaming.

woollen *adj* made of wool. * *n* cloth made of wool.

word *n* an articulate sound expressing an idea; information; a saying; motto; promise; *pl* wrangel.

wording *n* the mode of expressing in words.

wordy *adj* using many words; verbose.

work *n* effort; employment; a task; achievement; a book or other composition; a factory * *vi* to labour, toil; to be employed; to ferment. * vt to bring about; to influence; to fashion.

working class n people who work for wages, esp manual workers.

workman n an artisan; a skilled worker.

workmanship n skill of a worker or quality of his work.

workshop n a place where some craft is carried on.

world n the whole creation; the earth; mankind; the public.

worldly adj relating to this world or this life.

worm n a small creeping animal; thread of screw; spiral pipe in a condenser. * vi to work slowly and secretly. * vt to undermine; to extract.

worn pp of **wear**.

worry vt to harass; to fret. * n anxiety.

worse adj bad or ill in greater degree; inferior.

worship n religious service; adoration; reverence; title of honour. * vt to adore; to perform religious service.

worshipful adj honourable.

worst adj bad or evil in highest degree. * vt to defeat.

worsted n woollen yarn used in knitting.

worth adj equal in value to; deserving of * n value; price.

worthy adj deserving; befitting. * n a notable person.

would-be adj wishing to be; pretended.

wound n a cut or stab, etc; injury. * vti to inflict a wound; to pain.

wove pret of **weave**.

wrack n seaweed generally; wreck; a thin flying cloud.

wrangle vi to dispute angrily. * n a dispute.

wrap vt to fold or roll; to envelop. * n a shawl or rug.

wrapper n a loose morning gown; cover for postal packets, as books, etc.

wrath n violent anger; rage.

wreak vt to inflict, execute (vengeance, etc).

wreath n a garland.

wreathe vt to entwine; to encircle.

wreck n ruin; destruction of ship at sea. * vt to ruin; destroy.

wreckage n remains of wrecked ship.

wrench n a violent twist; tool for screwing nuts, etc. * vt to pull with a twist.

wrest vt to twist; to distort.

wrestle vi to contend by grappling and trying to throw down.

wretch n a miserable person; base creature.

wretched adj unhappy; worthless.

wriggle vi, vt to twist about.

wright n an artisan; a carpenter.

wring vt to twist and squeeze; to extort.

wrinkle n a crease in skin; furrow; hint. * vti to crease.

wrist n the joint uniting hand to arm.

writ n a written court order.

write vti to form by a pen, etc; to set down in words; to communicate by letter; to compose.

writer n an author; a clerk; a law agent.

writhe vti to turn and twist, as in pain.

wrong adj not right; false. * n an injury. * vt to treat unjustly.

wrongful adj injurious; unjust.

wry adj contorted; twisted; ironic.

wynd n a narrow alley; a lane.

X

xanthic adj yellowish; of or relating to xanthine.

xenophobia n fear or dislike of foreigners or strangers.

xerography n photocopying by using light to form an electrostatic image.

X-ray, x-ray n a radiation of very short wavelengths, capable of penetrating solid bodies. * vt to photograph by x-rays.

xylophone n a musical instrument of wooden bars freely suspended and vibrating when struck.

Y

yacht n a light sailing vessel for pleasure or racing.

yahoo n a rude brutish or crude person.

yak *n* a Tibetan ox.

yam *n* a tropical plant and its edible root.

yap *vi* to talk constantly.

yard *n* a standard measure of 3 feet; an enclosure; a spar hung across a mast to support a sail.

yardarm *n* either end of a ship's yard.

yarn *n* any spun thread; a spun-out story.

yaw *vi* to swerve suddenly in sailing.

yawl *n* a ship's small boat; a small yacht.

yawn *vi* to open the jaws involuntarily, as from drowsiness.* *n* act of yawning.

year *n* the period of earth's complete revolution round sun; 12 months; 365 or 366 days.

yearling *n* a one-year-old animal.

yearn *vi* to be filled with longing, love, or pity for.

yeast *n* fermenting substance for raising bread; barm.

yell *vi* to scream * *n* a shrill cry.

yellow *adj, n* a bright golden colour.

yelp *vi* to utter a sharp bark.

yesterday *n* the day before the present.

yet *adv* in addition; still. * *conj* nevertheless.

yew *n* a large evergreen tree.

yield *vt* to produce in return for labour, etc; to afford; to give up. * *vi* to submit. * *n* product; crop.

yodel *vti* to sing with changes from natural to falsetto voice.

yoga *n* a system of exercises for attaining bodily and spiritual control and well-being.

yoke *n* a neckpiece of wood binding oxen together in drawing; a pair of draught oxen; a bond or link. * *vt* to couple.

yokel *n* a country person regarded as unsophisticated.

yolk *n* the yellow part of an egg.

yonder *adv* over there.

you *pron* the 2nd person singular and plural, the person or persons spoken to.

young *adj* not old; youthful. * *n* offspring; young persons.

youngster *n* a boy; young person.

youth *n* period from childhood to manhood; a young man; young people.

yule *n* Christmas.

zany *adj* comical; eccentric.

zeal *n* eagerness; ardour; fanaticism.

zealot *n* an extreme partisan; a fanatic.

zebra *n* a striped wild animal related to the horse.

zenith *n* the point of heavens right overhead; highest point.

zephyr *n* the west wind; any soft breeze.

zeppelin *n* a rigid, cigar-shaped airship.

zero *n* a cipher; nothing; point from which marking of a scale begins.

zest *n* relish; keen enjoyment.

zigzag *adj* a line with short sharp turns. * *vi* to turn sharply this way and that.

zinc *n* a soft bluish white metal.

zither *n* a flat, stringed musical instrument.

zodiac *n* the tract in the heavens within which the apparent path of sun, moon, and planets is confined, and containing the twelve constellations, or signs of zodiac.

zone *n* a girdle or belt; one of the five great belts of the earth; any well-defined tract.

zoolite *n* a fossil animal.

zoology *n* the science of animal life.

zoophyte *n* a plant-like animal, as sponge, coral.

zoroastrian *n* a believer in religion of zoroaster, founder of Parseeism, or fire worship.

zymotic *adj* caused by or relating to an infection or an infectious disease; producing fermentation.

zymurgy *n* the chemistry of fermentation in brewing, etc.

Thesaurus

A

abandon *vb* abdicate, abjure, desert, drop, evacuate, forsake, forswear, leave, quit, relinquish, yield; cede, forgo, give up, let go, renounce, resign, surrender, vacate, waive. * *n* careless freedom, dash, impetuosity, impulse, wildness.

abandoned *adj* depraved, derelict, deserted, discarded, dropped, forsaken, left, outcast, rejected, relinquished; corrupt, depraved, dissolute, lost, profligate, reprobate, shameless, sinful, unprincipled.

abate *vb* diminish, decrease, lessen, lower, moderate, reduce, relax, remove, slacken; deduct, mitigate, rebate, remit; allay, alleviate, appease, assuage, blunt, calm, compose, dull, mitigate, moderate, mollify, pacify, qualify, quiet, quell, soften, soothe, tranquillize.

abbreviate *vb* abridge, compress, condense, contract, cut, curtail, epitomize, reduce, retrench, shorten.

abbreviation *n* abridgment, compression, condensation, contraction, curtailment, cutting, reduction, shortening

abdicate *vb* abandon, cede, forgo, forsake, give up, quit, relinquish, renounce, resign, retire, surrender.

aberration *n* departure, deviation, divergence, rambling, wandering; abnormality, anomaly, eccentricity, irregularity, peculiarity, singularity, unconformity; delusion, disorder, hallucination, illusion, instability.

abhor *vb* abominate, detest, disgust, execrate, hate, loathe, nauseate.

abhorrent *adj* hateful, horrifying, horrible, loathsome, nauseating, odious, offensive, repellent, repugnant, repulsive.

abide *vb* lodge, rest, sojourn, stay, wait; dwell, inhabit, live, reside; bear, continue, persevere, persist, remain; endure, last, suffer, tolerate; (*with* by) conform to, discharge, fulfil, keep, persist in.

abiding *adj* changeless, constant, continuing, durable, enduring, lasting, permanent, stable, unchangeable.

ability *n* ableness, adroitness, aptitude, aptness, cleverness, dexterity, efficacy, efficiency, facility, ingenuity, knack, power, readiness, skill, strength, talent, vigour; competency, qualification; calibre, capability, capacity, faculty.

able *adj* accomplished, adroit, apt, clever, expert, ingenious, practical, proficient, qualified, quick, skilful, talented, versed; competent, effective, efficient, fitted, quick; capable, gifted, mighty, powerful, talented.

abnormal *adj* aberrant, anomalous, divergent, eccentric, exceptional, idiosyncratic, irregular, odd, peculiar, singular, strange, unnatural, unusual, weird.

abolish *vb* abrogate, annul, cancel, eliminate, invalidate, nullify, quash, repeal, rescind, revoke; annihilate, destroy, end, eradicate, extirpate, extinguish, obliterate, overthrow, suppress, terminate.

abominable *adj* accursed, contemptible, cursed, damnable, detestable, execrable, hellish, horrid, nefarious, odious; abhorrent, detestable, disgusting, foul, hateful, loathsome, nauseous, obnoxious, shocking, revolting, repugnant, repulsive; shabby, vile, wretched.

abortive *adj* immature, incomplete, futile, fruitless, idle, ineffectual, inoperative, nugatory, profitless, unavailing, unsuccessful, useless, vain.

about *prep* around, encircling, surrounding, round; near; concerning, referring to, regarding, relating to, relative to, respecting, touching, with regard to, with respect to; all over, over, through. * *adv* around, before; approximately, near, nearly.

above *adj* above-mentioned, aforementioned, aforesaid, foregoing, preceding, previous, prior. * *adv* aloft, overhead; before, previously; of a higher rank. * *prep* higher than, on top of; exceeding, greater than, more than, over; beyond, superior to.

aboveboard *adj* candid, frank, honest, open, straightforward, truthful, upright. * *adv* candidly, fairly, openly, sincerely.

abrupt *adj* broken, craggy, jagged, rough,

rugged; precipitous, steep; hasty, ill-timed, precipitate, sudden, unanticipated, unexpected; blunt, brusque, curt, discourteous; cramped, harsh, jerky, stiff.

absence *n* nonappearance, nonattendance; abstraction, distraction, inattention, musing, preoccupation, reverie; default, defect, deficiency, lack, privation.

absent *adj* abroad, away, elsewhere, gone, not present; abstracted, dreaming, inattentive, lost, musing, napping, preoccupied.

absolute *adj* complete, ideal, independent, perfect, supreme, unconditional, unconditioned, unlimited, unqualified, unrestricted; arbitrary, authoritative, autocratic, despotic, dictatorial, imperious, irresponsible, tyrannical, tyrannous; actual, categorical, certain, decided, determinate, genuine, positive, real, unequivocal, unquestionable, veritable.

absolutely *adv* completely, definitely, unconditionally; actually, downright, indeed, indubitably, infallibly, positively, really, truly, unquestionably.

absolution *n* acquittal, clearance, deliverance, discharge, forgiveness, liberation, pardon, release, remission, shrift, shriving.

absorb *vb* appropriate, assimilate, drink in, imbibe, soak up; consume, destroy, devour, engorge, engulf, exhaust, swallow up, take up; arrest, engage, engross, fix, immerse, occupy, rivet.

absorbent *adj* absorbing, imbibing, penetrable, porous, receptive.

abstain *vb* avoid, cease, deny oneself, desist, forbear, refrain, refuse, stop, withhold.

abstemious *adj* abstinent, frugal, moderate, self-denying, sober, temperate.

abstinence *n* abstemiousness, avoidance, fast, moderation, restraint, self-denial, sobriety, teetotalism, temperance.

abstract *vb* detach, disengage, dissociate, disunite, isolate, separate; appropriate, purloin, seize, steal, take; abbreviate, abridge, epitomize. * *adj* isolated, separate, simple, unrelated; abstracted, occult, recondite, refined, subtle, vague; nonobjective, nonrepresentational. * *n*

abridgment, condensation, digest, excerpt, extract, précis, selection, summary, synopsis.

abstracted *adj* absent, absent-minded, dreaming, inattentive, lost, musing, preoccupied; abstruse, refined, subtle.

absurd *adj* extravagant, fantastic, fatuous, foolish, idiotic, incongruous, ill-advised, ill-judged, irrational, ludicrous, nonsensical, nugatory, preposterous, ridiculous, self-annulling, senseless, silly, stupid, unreasonable.

abundant *adj* abounding, affluent, ample, bountiful, copious, exuberant, fertile, flowing, full, good, large, lavish, luxuriant, rich, liberal, much, overflowing, plentiful, plenteous, replete, teeming, thick.

abuse *vb* betray, cajole, deceive, desecrate, dishonour, misapply, misemploy, misuse, pervert, pollute, profane, prostitute, violate, wrong; harm, hurt, ill-use, illtreat, injure, maltreat, mishandle; berate, blacken, calumniate, defame, disparage, lampoon, lash, malign, revile, reproach, satirize, slander, traduce, upbraid, vilify. * *n* desecration, dishonour, ill-use, misuse, perversion, pollution, profanation; ill-treatment, maltreatment, outrage; malfeasance; aspersion, defamation, disparagement, insult, invective, obloquy, opprobrium, railing, rating, reviling, ribaldry, rudeness, scurrility, upbraiding, vilification, vituperation.

abusive *adj* calumnious, carping, condemnatory, contumelious, denunciatory, injurious, insolent, insulting, offensive, opprobrious, reproachful, reviling, ribald, rude, scurrilous, vituperative.

academic *adj* collegiate, lettered, scholastic. * *n* academician, classicist, doctor, fellow, pundit, savant, scholar, student, teacher.

accelerate *vb* dispatch, expedite, forward, hasten, hurry, pick up, precipitate, press on, quicken, speed, step up, urge on.

accentuate *vb* accent, emphasize, mark, point up, punctuate, stress; highlight, overemphasize, underline, underscore.

accept *vb* acquire, derive, get, gain, obtain, receive, take; accede to, acknowledge, acquiesce in, admit, agree to, approve, assent to, avow, embrace; estimate, construe, interpret, regard, value.

acceptable *adj* agreeable, gratifying, pleasant, pleasing, pleasurable, welcome.

access *vb* broach, enter, open, open up. * *n* approach, avenue, entrance, entry, passage, way; admission, admittance, audience, interview; addition, accession, aggrandizement, enlargement, gain, increase, increment; (*med*) attack, fit, onset, recurrence.

accession *n* addition, augmentation, enlargement, extension, increase; succession.

accessory *adj* abetting, additional, additive, adjunct, aiding, ancillary, assisting, contributory, helping, subsidiary, subordinate, supplemental. * *n* abettor, accomplice, assistant, associate, confederate, helper; accompaniment, attendant, concomitant, detail, subsidiary.

accident *n* calamity, casualty, condition, contingency, disaster, fortuity, incident, misadventure, miscarriage, mischance, misfortune, mishap; affection, alteration, chance, contingency, mode, modification, property, quality, state.

accidental *adj* casual, chance, contingent, fortuitous, undesigned, unintended; adventitious, dispensable, immaterial, incidental, nonessential.

acclimatize *vb* accustom, adapt, adjust, condition, familiarize, habituate, inure, naturalize, season.

accommodate *vb* contain, furnish, hold, oblige, serve, supply; adapt, fit, suit; adjust, compose, harmonize, reconcile, settle.

accompany *vb* attend, chaperon, convoy, escort, follow, go with.

accomplice *n* abettor, accessory, ally, assistant, associate, confederate, partner.

accomplish *vb* achieve, acquire, attain, bring about, carry, carry through, complete, compass, consummate, do, effect, execute, fulfil, perform, perfect; conclude, end, finish, terminate.

accomplished *adj* achieved, completed, done, effected, executed, finished, fulfilled, realized; able, adroit, apt, consummate, educated, experienced, expert, fin-

ished, instructed, practised, proficient, qualified, ripe, skilful, versed; elegant, fashionable, fine, polished, polite, refined.

accord *vb* admit, allow, concede, deign, give, grant, vouchsafe, yield; agree, assent, concur, correspond, harmonize, quadrate, tally. * *n* accordance, agreement, concord, concurrence, conformity, consensus, harmony, unanimity, unison.

accordingly *adv* agreeably, conformably, consistently, suitably; consequently, hence, so, thence, therefore, thus, whence, wherefore.

account *vb* assess, appraise, estimate, evaluate, judge, rate; (*with* for) assign, attribute, explain, expound, justify, rationalize, vindicate. * *n* inventory, record, register, score; bill, book, charge; calculation, computation, count, reckoning, score, tale, tally; chronicle, detail, description, narration, narrative, portrayal, recital, rehearsal, relation, report, statement, tidings, word; elucidation, explanation, exposition; consideration, ground, motive, reason, regard, sake; consequence, consideration, dignity, distinction, importance, note, repute, reputation, worth.

accountable *adj* amenable, answerable, duty-bound, liable, responsible.

accumulate *vb* agglomerate, aggregate, amass, bring together, collect, gather, grow, heap, hoard, increase, pile, store.

accurate *adj* careful, close, correct, exact, faithful, nice, precise, regular, strict, true, truthful.

accuse *vb* arraign, charge, censure, impeach, indict, tax.

ace *n* (*cards, dice*) one spot, single pip, single point; atom, bit, grain, iota, jot, particle, single, unit, whit; expert, master, virtuoso. * *adj* best, expert, fine, outstanding, superb.

achieve *vb* accomplish, acquire, attain, complete, consummate, do, effect, execute, finish, fulfil, perform, realize; acquire, gain, get, obtain, win.

acid *adj* pungent, sharp, sour, stinging, tart, vinegary.

acknowledge *vb* recognize; accept, admit,

accept, allow, concede, grant; avow, confess, own, profess.

acquaint vb familiarize; announce, apprise, communicate, enlighten, disclose, inform, make aware, make known, notify, tell.

acquaintance n companionship, familiarity, fellowship, intimacy, knowledge; associate, companion, comrade, friend.

acquire vb achieve, attain, earn, gain, gather, get, have, obtain, procure, realize, secure, win; accomplish, learn thoroughly, master.

acquit vb absolve, clear, discharge, exculpate, excuse, exonerate, forgive, liberate, pardon, pay, quit, release, set free, settle.

acrimonious adj abusive, acrid, bitter, caustic, censorious, churlish, crabbed, harsh, malignant, petulant, sarcastic, severe, sharp, spiteful, testy, venomous, virulent.

act vb do, execute, function, make, operate, work; enact, feign, perform, play. * n achievement, deed, exploit, feat, performance, proceeding, turn; bill, decree, enactment, law, ordinance, statute; actuality, existence, fact, reality.

acting adj interim, provisional, substitute, temporary. * n enacting, impersonation, performance, portrayal, theatre; counterfeiting, dissimulation, imitation, pretence.

action n achievement, activity, agency, deed, exertion, exploit, feat; battle, combat, conflict, contest, encounter, engagement, operation; lawsuit, prosecution.

active adj effective, efficient, influential, living, operative; assiduous, bustling, busy, diligent, industrious, restless; agile, alert, brisk, energetic, lively, nimble, prompt, quick, smart, spirited, sprightly, supple; animated, ebullient, fervent, vigorous.

actual adj certain, decided, genuine, objective, real, substantial, tangible, true, veritable; perceptible, present, sensible, tangible; absolute, categorical, positive.

acumen n acuteness, astuteness, discernment, ingenuity, keenness, penetration, sagacity, sharpness, shrewdness.

acute adj pointed, sharp; astute, bright, discerning, ingenious, intelligent, keen, quick, penetrating, piercing, sagacious, sage, sharp, shrewd, smart, subtle; distressing, fierce, intense, piercing, pungent, poignant, severe, violent; high, high-toned, sharp, shrill; (med) sudden, temporary, violent.

adapt vb accommodate, adjust, conform, coordinate, fit, qualify, proportion, suit, temper.

add vb adjoin, affix, annex, append, attach, join, tag; sum, sum up, total.

addict vb accustom, apply, dedicate, devote, habituate. * n devotee, enthusiast, fan; head, junkie, user.

addition n augmentation, accession, enlargement, extension, increase, supplement; adjunct, appendage, appendix, extra.

address vb accost, apply to, court, direct. * n appeal, application, entreaty, invocation, memorial, petition, request, solicitation, suit; discourse, oration, lecture, sermon, speech; ability, adroitness, art, dexterity, expertness, skill; courtesy, deportment, demeanour, tact.

adequate adj able, adapted, capable, competent, equal, fit, requisite, satisfactory, sufficient, suitable.

adhere vb cling, cleave, cohere, hold, stick; appertain, belong, pertain.

adherent adj adhering, clinging, sticking. * n acolyte, dependant, disciple, follower, partisan, supporter, vassal.

adhesive adj clinging, sticking; glutinous, gummy, sticky, tenacious, viscous. * n binder, cement, glue, paste.

adjacent adj adjoining, bordering, contiguous, near, near to, neighbouring, touching.

adjourn vb defer, delay, postpone, procrastinate; close, dissolve, end, interrupt, prorogue, suspend.

adjunct n addition, advantage, appendage, appurtenance, attachment, attribute, auxiliary, dependency, help.

adjust vb adapt, arrange, dispose, rectify; regulate, set right, settle, suit; compose, harmonize, pacify, reconcile, settle; accommodate, adapt, fit, suit.

administer vb contribute, deal out, dispense, supply; conduct, control, direct, govern, manage, oversee, superintend.

admirable adj astonishing, striking, surprising, wonderful; excellent, fine, rare, superb.

admiration n affection, approbation, approval, astonishment, delight, esteem, pleasure, regard.

admire vb approve, esteem, respect; adore, prize, cherish, revere, treasure.

admissible adj allowable, lawful, permissible, possible.

admission n access, admittance, entrance, introduction; acceptance, acknowledgement, allowance, assent, avowal, concession.

admit vb let in, receive; agree to, accept, acknowledge, concede, confess; allow, bear, permit, suffer, tolerate.

adopt vb appropriate, assume; accept, approve, avow, espouse, maintain, support; affiliate, father, foster.

adore vb worship; esteem, honour, idolize, love, revere, venerate.

adult adj grownup, mature, ripe, ripened. * n grownup person.

adulterate vb alloy, contaminate, corrupt, debase, deteriorate, vitiate.

advance adj beforehand, forward, leading. * vb propel, push, send forward; aggrandize, dignify, elevate, exalt, promote; benefit, forward, further, improve, promote; adduce, allege, assign, offer, propose, propound; augment, increase; proceed, progress; grow, improve, prosper, thrive. * n march, progress; advancement, enhancement, growth, promotion, rise; offer, overture, proffering, proposal, proposition, tender; appreciation, rise.

advantage n ascendancy, precedence, preeminence, superiority, upper-hand; benefit, blessing, emolument, gain, profit, return; account, behalf, interest; accommodation, convenience, prerogative, privilege.

advantageous adj beneficial, favourable, profitable.

advent n accession, approach, arrival, coming, visitation.

adventure vb dare, hazard, imperil, peril, risk, venture. * n chance, contingency, experiment, fortuity, hazard, risk, venture; crisis, contingency, event, incident, occurrence, transaction.

adventurous adj bold, chivalrous, courageous, daring, doughty; foolhardy, headlong, precipitate, rash, reckless; dangerous, hazardous, perilous.

adversary n antagonist, enemy, foe, opponent.

adverse adj conflicting, contrary, opposing; antagonistic, harmful, hostile, hurtful, inimical, unfavourable, unpropitious; calamitous, disastrous, unfortunate, unlucky, untoward.

advertise vb advise, announce, declare, inform, placard, proclaim, publish.

advice n admonition, caution, counsel, exhortation, persuasion, suggestion, recommendation; information, intelligence, notice, notification; care, counsel, deliberation, forethought.

advisable adj advantageous, desirable, expedient, prudent.

advise vb admonish, counsel, commend, recommend, suggest, urge; acquaint, apprise, inform, notify; confer, consult, deliberate.

adviser n counsellor, director, guide, instructor.

advocate vb countenance, defend, favour, justify, maintain, support, uphold, vindicate. * n apologist, counsellor, defender, maintainer, patron, pleader, supporter; attorney, barrister, counsel, lawyer, solicitor.

affable adj accessible, approachable, communicative, conversable, cordial, easy, familiar, frank, free, sociable, social; complaisant, courteous, civil, obliging, polite, urbane.

affair n business, circumstance, concern, matter, office, question; event, incident, occurrence, performance, proceeding, transaction; battle, combat, conflict, encounter, engagement, skirmish.

affect vb act upon, alter, change, influence, modify, transform; concern, interest, regard, relate; improve, melt, move, overcome, subdue, touch; aim at, aspire to, crave, yearn for; adopt, assume, feign.

affectation *n* affectedness, airs, artificiality, foppery, pretension, simulation.

affection *n* bent, bias, feeling, inclination, passion, proclivity, propensity; accident, attribute, character, mark, modification, mode, note, property; attachment, endearment, fondness, goodwill, kindness, partiality, love.

affectionate *adj* attached, devoted, fond, kind, loving, sympathetic, tender.

affirm *vb* allege, assert, asseverate, aver, declare, state; approve, confirm, establish, ratify.

affliction *n* adversity, calamity, disaster, misfortune, stroke, visitation; bitterness, depression, distress, grief, misery, plague, scourge, sorrow, trial, tribulation, wretchedness, woe.

affluent *adj* abounding, abundant, bounteous, plenteous; moneyed, opulent, rich, wealthy.

afford *vb* furnish, produce, supply, yield; bestow, communicate, confer, give, grant, impart, offer; bear, endure, support.

affray *n* brawl, conflict, disturbance, feud, fight, quarrel, ruffle, struggle.

affront *vb* abuse, insult, outrage; annoy, chafe, displease, fret, irritate, offend, pique, provoke, vex. * *n* abuse, contumely, insult, outrage, vexation, wrong.

afraid *adj* aghast, alarmed, anxious, apprehensive, frightened, scared, timid.

after *prep* later than, subsequent to; behind, following; about, according to; because of, in imitation of. * *adj* behind, consecutive, ensuing, following, later, succeeding, successive, subsequent; aft, back, hind, rear, rearmost, tail.* *adv* afterwards, later, next, since, subsequently, then, thereafter.

again *adv* afresh, anew, another time, once more; besides, further, in addition, moreover.

against *prep* adverse to, contrary to, resisting; abutting, close to, facing, fronting, off, opposite to, over; in anticipation of, for, in expectation of; in compensation for, to counterbalance, to match.

age *vb* decline, grow old, mature. * *n* aeon, date, epoch, period, time; decline, old age, senility; antiquity, oldness.

agent *n* actor, doer, executor, operator, performer; active element, cause, force; attorney, broker, commissioner, deputy, factor, intermediary, manager, middleman.

aggravate *vb* heighten, increase, worsen; colour, exaggerate, magnify, overstate; enrage, irritate, provoke, tease.

aggressive *adj* assailing, assailant, assaulting, attacking, invading, offensive; pushing, self-assertive.

aggrieve *vb* afflict, grieve, pain; abuse, illtreat, impose, injure, oppress, wrong.

aghast *adj* appalled, dismayed, frightened, horrified, horror-struck, panic-stricken, terrified; amazed, astonished, startled, thunderstruck.

agile *adj* active, alert, brisk, lively, nimble, prompt, smart, ready.

agitate *vb* disturb, jar, rock, shake, trouble; disquiet, excite, ferment, rouse, trouble; confuse, discontent, flurry, fluster, flutter; canvass, debate, discuss, dispute, investigate.

agitation *n* concussion, shake, shaking, succession; commotion, convulsion, disturbance, ferment, jarring, storm, tumult, turmoil; discomposure, distraction, emotion, excitement, flutter, perturbation, ruffle, tremor, trepidation; controversy, debate, discussion.

agony *n* anguish, distress, pangs.

agree *vb* accord, concur, harmonize, unite; accede, acquiesce, assent, comply, concur, subscribe; bargain, contract, covenant, engage, promise, undertake; compound, compromise; chime, cohere, conform, correspond, match, suit, tally.

agreement *n* accordance, compliance, concord, harmony, union; bargain, compact, contract, pact, treaty.

aid *vb* assist, help, serve, support; relieve, succour; advance, facilitate, further, promote. * *n* assistance, cooperation, help, patronage; alms, subsidy, succour, relief.

ailment *n* disease, illness, sickness.

aim *vb* direct, level, point, train; design, intend, mean, purpose, seek. * *n* bearing, course, direction, tendency; design, object, view, reason.

air vb expose, display, ventilate. * n atmosphere, breeze; appearance, aspect, manner; melody, tune.

alarm vb daunt, frighten, scare, startle, terrify. * n alarm-bell, tocsin, warning; apprehension, fear, fright, terror.

alert adj awake, circumspect, vigilant, watchful, wary; active, brisk, lively, nimble, quick, prompt, ready, sprightly, spry. * vb alarm, arouse, caution, forewarn, signal, warn. * n alarm, signal, warning.

alien adj foreign, not native; differing, estranged, inappropriate, remote, unallied, separated. * n foreigner, stranger.

alike adj akin, analogous, duplicate, identical, resembling, similar. * adv equally.

alive adj animate, breathing, live; aware, responsive, sensitive, susceptible; brisk, cheerful, lively, sprightly.

allay vb appease, calm, check, compose; alleviate, assuage, lessen, moderate, solace, temper.

allege vb affirm, assert, declare, maintain, say; adduce, advance, assign, cite, plead, produce, quote.

allegiance n duty, homage, fealty, fidelity, loyalty, obligation.

alliance n affinity, intermarriage, relation; coalition, combination, confederacy, league, treaty, union; affiliation, connection, relationship, similarity.

allow vb acknowledge, admit, concede, confess, grant, own; authorize, grant, let, permit; bear, endure, suffer, tolerate; grant, yield, relinquish, spare; approve, justify, sanction; abate, deduct, remit.

allure vb attract, beguile, cajole, coax, entice, lure, persuade, seduce, tempt. * n appeal, attraction, lure, temptation.

ally vb combine, connect, join, league, marry, unite. * n aider, assistant, associate, coadjutor, colleague, friend, partner.

almighty adj all-powerful, omnipotent.

alone adj companionless, deserted, forsaken, isolated, lonely, only, single, sole, solitary.

along adv lengthways, lengthwise; forward, onward; beside, together, simultaneously.

alter vb change, conform, modify, shift, turn, transform, transmit, vary.

alternate vb fluctuate, oscillate, vacillate, vary, waver, wobble; change, exchange, interchange, reciprocate; intermit, revolve; relieve, spell, take turns. * adj intermittent, periodic; alternative, equivalent, substitute; reciprocal. * n deputy, alternative, proxy, replacement, representative, substitute.

alternative adj another, different, second, substitute. * n choice, option, preference.

although conj albeit, even if, for all that, notwithstanding, though.

altitude n elevation, height, loftiness.

altogether adv completely, entirely, totally, utterly.

always adv continually, eternally, ever, evermore, perpetually, unceasingly.

amass vb accumulate, aggregate, collect, gather, heap, scrape together.

amaze vb astonish, astound, bewilder, confound, confuse, dumbfound, perplex, stagger, stupefy.

ambiguous adj dubious, doubtful, enigmatic, equivocal, uncertain, indefinite, indistinct, obscure, vague.

ambitious adj aspiring, avid, eager, intent.

amenable adj acquiescent, agreeable, persuadable, responsive, susceptible; accountable, liable, responsible.

amend vb better, correct, improve, mend, redress, reform.

amends npl atonement, compensation, expiation, indemnification, recompense, reparation, restitution.

amiable adj attractive, benign, charming, genial, good-natured, harmonious, kind, lovable, lovely, pleasant, pleasing, sweet, winning, winsome.

amicable adj amiable, cordial, friendly, harmonious, kind, kindly, peaceable.

amiss adj erroneous, inaccurate, incorrect, faulty, improper, wrong. * adv erroneously, inaccurately, incorrectly, wrongly.

amorous adj ardent, enamoured, fond, longing, loving, passionate, tender; erotic, impassioned.

amount n aggregate, sum, total.

ample adj broad, capacious, extended, extensive, great, large, roomy, spacious; abounding, abundant, copious, generous, liberal, plentiful; diffusive, unrestricted.

amuse vb charm, cheer, divert, enliven, entertain, gladden, relax, solace; beguile, cheat, deceive, delude, mislead.

analysis n decomposition, dissection, resolution, separation.

anarchy n chaos, confusion, disorder, misrule, lawlessness, riot.

ancestor n father, forebear, forefather, progenitor.

ancestry n family, house, line, lineage; descent, genealogy, parentage, pedigree, stock.

anchor vb fasten, fix, secure; cast anchor, take firm hold. * n (naut) ground tackle; defence, hold, security, stay.

ancient adj old, primitive, pristine; antiquated, antique, archaic, obsolete.

angelic adj adorable, celestial, cherubic, heavenly, saintly, seraphic; entrancing, enrapturing, rapturous, ravishing.

anger vb chafe, displease, enrage, gall, infuriate, irritate, madden. * n choler, exasperation, fury, gall, indignation, ire, passion, rage, resentment, spleen, wrath.

angry adj chafed, exasperated, furious, galled, incensed, irritated, nettled, piqued, provoked, resentful.

anguish n agony, distress, grief, pang, rack, torment, torture.

animate vb inform, quicken, vitalize, vivify; fortify, invigorate, revive; activate, enliven, excite, heat, impel, kindle, rouse, stimulate, stir, waken; elate, embolden, encourage, exhilarate, gladden, hearten. * adj alive, breathing, live, living, organic, quick.

animosity n bitterness, enmity, grudge, hatred, hostility, rancour, rankling, spleen, virulence.

annex vb affix, append, attach, subjoin, tag, tack; connect, join, unite.

annihilate vb abolish, annul, destroy, dissolve, exterminate, extinguish, kill, obliterate, raze, ruin.

announce vb advertise, communicate, declare, disclose, proclaim, promulgate, publish, report, reveal, trumpet.

annoy vb badger, chafe, disquiet, disturb, fret, hector, irk, irritate, molest, pain, pester, plague, trouble, vex, worry, wound.

annul vb abolish, abrogate, cancel, countermand, nullify, overrule, quash, repeal, recall, reverse, revoke.

anoint vb consecrate, oil, sanctify, smear.

anonymous adj nameless, unacknowledged, unsigned.

answer vb fulfil, rejoin, reply, respond, satisfy. * n rejoinder, reply, response, retort; confutation, rebuttal, refutation.

answerable adj accountable, amenable, correspondent, liable, responsible, suited.

antagonism n contradiction, discordance, disharmony, dissonant, incompatibility, opposition.

anterior adj antecedent, foregoing, preceding, previous, prior; fore, front.

anticipation n apprehension, contemplation, expectation, hope, prospect, trust; expectancy, forecast, foresight, foretaste, preconception, presentiment.

antipathy n abhorrence, aversion, disgust, detestation, hate, hatred, horror, loathing, repugnance.

antique adj ancient, archaic, bygone, old, old-fashioned.

anxiety n apprehension, care, concern, disquiet, fear, foreboding, misgiving, perplexity, trouble, uneasiness, vexation, worry.

anxious adj apprehensive, restless, solicitous, uneasy, unquiet, worried.

apathetic adj cold, dull, impassive, inert, listless, obtuse, passionless, sluggish, torpid, unfeeling.

aplomb n composure, confidence, equanimity, self-confidence.

apologetic adj exculpatory, excusatory; defensive, vindictive.

apology n defence, justification, vindication; acknowledgement, excuse, explanation, plea, reparation.

apostle n angel, herald, messenger, missionary, preacher; advocate, follower, supporter.

appal vb affright, alarm, daunt, dismay,

frighten, horrify, scare, shock.

apparent *adj* discernible, perceptible, visible; conspicuous, evident, legible, manifest, obvious, open, patent, plain, unmistakable; external, ostensible, seeming, superficial.

apparition *n* appearance, appearing, epiphany, manifestation; being, form; ghost, phantom, spectre, spirit, vision.

appeal *vb* address, entreat, implore, invoke, refer, request, solicit. * *n* application, entreaty, invocation, solicitation, suit.

appear *vb* emerge, loom; break, open; arise, occur, offer; look, seem, show.

appearance *n* advent, arrival, apparition, coming; form, shape; colour, face, fashion, feature, guise, pretence, pretext; air, aspect, complexion, demeanour, manner, mien.

append *vb* attach, fasten, hang; add, annex, subjoin, tack, tag.

appetite *n* craving, desire, longing, lust, passion; gusto, relish, stomach, zest; hunger.

applaud *vb* acclaim, approve, cheer, clap, commend, compliment, encourage, extol, magnify.

application *n* emollient, lotion, ointment, poultice, wash; appliance, exercise, practice, use; appeal, petition, request, solicitation, suit; assiduity, constancy, diligence, effort, industry.

apply *vb* bestow, lay upon; appropriate, convert, employ, exercise, use; addict, address, dedicate, devote, direct, engage.

appoint *vb* determine, establish, fix, prescribe; bid, command, decree, direct, order, require; allot, assign, delegate, depute, detail, destine, settle; constitute, create, name, nominate; equip, furnish, supply.

appreciate *vb* appreciate, esteem, estimate, rate, realize, value.

apprehend *vb* arrest, capture, catch, detain, seize, take; conceive, imagine, regard, view; appreciate, perceive, realize, see, take in; fear, forebode; conceive, fancy, hold, imagine, presume, understand.

approach *vb* advance, approximate, come

close; broach; resemble. * *n* advance, advent; approximation, convergence, nearing, tendency; entrance, path, way.

appropriate *vb* adopt, arrogate, assume, set apart; allot, apportion, assign, devote; apply, convert, employ, use. * *adj* adapted, apt, befitting, fit, opportune, seemly, suitable.

approve *vb* appreciate, commend, like, praise, recommend, value; confirm, countenance, justify, ratify, sustain, uphold.

approximate *vb* approach, resemble. * *adj* approaching, proximate; almost exact, inexact, rough.

apt *adj* applicable, apposite, appropriate, befitting, fit, felicitous, germane; disposed, inclined, liable, prone, subject; able, adroit, clever, dextrous, expert, handy, happy, prompt, ready, skilful.

aptitude *n* applicability, appropriateness, felicity, fitness, pertinence, suitability; inclination, tendency, turn; ability, address, adroitness, quickness, readiness, tact.

arbitrary *adj* absolute, autocratic, despotic, domineering, imperious, overbearing, unlimited; capricious, discretionary, fanciful, voluntary, whimsical.

arch *adj* cunning, knowing, frolicsome, merry, mirthful, playful, roguish, shrewd, sly; consummate, chief, leading, pre-eminent, prime, primary, principal.

ardent *adj* burning, fiery, hot; eager, earnest, fervent, impassioned, keen, passionate, warm, zealous.

ardour *n* glow, heat, warmth; eagerness, enthusiasm, fervour, heat, passion, soul, spirit, warmth, zeal.

arduous *adj* high, lofty, steep, uphill; difficult, fatiguing, hard, laborious, onerous, tiresome, toilsome, wearisome.

area *n* circle, circuit, district, domain, field, range, realm, region, tract.

argue *vb* plead, reason upon; debate, dispute; denote, evince, imply, indicate, mean, prove; contest, debate, discuss, sift.

arise *vb* ascend, mount, soar, tower; appear, emerge, rise, spring; begin, originate; rebel, revolt, rise; accrue, come, emanate, ensue, flow, issue, originate, proceed, result.

arm vb array, equip, furnish; clothe, cover, fortify, guard, protect, strengthen.

army n battalions, force, host, legions, troops; host, multitude, throng, vast assemblage.

around prep about, encircling, encompassing, round, surrounding. * adv about, approximately, generally, near, nearly, practically, round, thereabouts.

arouse vb animate, awaken, excite, incite, kindle, provoke, rouse, stimulate, warm, whet.

arrange vb array, class, classify, dispose, distribute, group, range, rank; adjust, determine, fix upon, settle; concoct, construct, devise, plan, prepare, project.

array vb arrange, dispose, place, range, rank; accoutre, adorn, attire, decorate, dress, enrobe, embellish, equip, garnish, habit, invest. * n arrangement, collection, disposition, marshalling, order; apparel, attire, clothes, dress, garments; army, battalions, soldiery, troops.

arrest vb check, delay, detain, hinder, hold, interrupt, obstruct, restrain, stay, stop, withhold; apprehend, capture, catch, seize, take; catch, engage, engross, fix, occupy, secure, rivet. * n check, checking, detention, hindrance, interruption, obstruction, restraining, stay, staying, stopping; apprehension, capture, detention, seizure.

arrive vb attain, come, get to, reach.

arrogance n assumption, assurance, disdain, effrontery, haughtiness, loftiness, lordliness, presumption, pride, scornfulness, superciliousness.

art n business, craft, employment, trade; address, adroitness, aptitude, dexterity, ingenuity, knack, sagacity, skill; artfulness, artifice, astuteness, craft, deceit, duplicity, finesse, subtlety.

artful adj crafty, cunning, disingenuous, insincere, sly, tricky, wily.

article n branch, clause, division, head, item, member, paragraph, part, point, portion; essay, paper, piece; commodity, substance, thing.

artificial adj counterfeit, sham, spurious; assumed, affected, constrained, fictitious, forced, laboured, strained.

artless adj ignorant, rude, unskilful, untaught; natural, plain, simple; candid, fair, frank, guileless, honest, plain, unaffected, simple, sincere, truthful, unsuspicious.

ascend vb arise, aspire, climb, mount, soar, tower.

ascertain vb certify, define, determine, establish, fix, settle, verify; discover, find out, get at.

ashamed adj abashed, confused.

ask vb interrogate, inquire, question; adjure, beg, conjure, crave, desire, dun, entreat, implore, invite, inquire, petition, request, solicit, supplicate, seek, sue.

aspect n air, bearing, countenance, expression, feature, look, mien, visage; appearance, attitude, condition, light, phase, position, posture, situation, state, view; angle, direction, outlook, prospect.

asperity n ruggedness, roughness, unevenness; acrimony, causticity, corrosiveness, sharpness, sourness, tartness; acerbity, bitterness, churlishness, harshness, sternness, sullenness, severity, virulence.

aspersion n abuse, backbiting, calumny, censure, defamation, detraction, slander, vituperation, reflection, reproach.

aspiration n aim, ambition, craving, desire, hankering, hope, longing.

assassinate vb dispatch, kill, murder, slay.

assault vb assail, attack, charge, invade. * n aggression, attack, charge, incursion, invasion, onset, onslaught; storm.

assemble vb call, collect, congregate, convene, convoke, gather, levy, muster; congregate, forgather.

assembly n company, collection, concourse, congregation, gathering, meeting, rout, throng; caucus, congress, conclave, convention, convocation, diet, legislature, meeting, parliament, synod.

assent vb accede, acquiesce, agree, concur, subscribe, yield. * n accord, acquiescence, allowance, approval, approbation, consent.

assertion n affirmation, allegation, asseveration, averment, declaration, position, predication, remark, statement, word; defence, emphasis, maintenance, pressing, support, vindication.

assess *vb* appraise, compute, estimate, rate, value; assign, determine, fix, impose, levy.

assign *vb* allot, appoint, apportion, appropriate; fix, designate, determine, specify; adduce, advance, allege, give, grant, offer, present, show.

assist *vb* abet, aid, befriend, further, help, patronize, promote, second, speed, support, sustain; aid, relieve, succour; alternate with, relieve, spell.

associate *vb* affiliate, combine, conjoin, couple, join, link, relate, yoke; consort, fraternize, mingle, sort. * *n* chum, companion, comrade, familiar, follower, mate; ally, confederate, friend, partner, fellow.

association *n* combination, company, confederation, connection, partnership, society.

assort *vb* arrange, class, classify, distribute, group, rank, sort; agree, be adapted, consort, suit.

assume *vb* take, undertake; affect, counterfeit, feign, pretend, sham; arrogate, usurp; beg, hypothesize, imply, postulate, posit, presuppose, suppose, simulate.

assurance *n* assuredness, certainty, conviction, persuasion, pledge, security, surety, warrant; engagement, pledge, promise; averment, assertion, protestation; audacity, confidence, courage, firmness, intrepidity; arrogance, brass, boldness, effrontery, face, front, impudence.

astonish *vb* amaze, astound, confound, daze, dumbfound, overwhelm, startle, stun, stupefy, surprise.

astute *adj* acute, cunning, deep, discerning, ingenious, intelligent, penetrating, perspicacious, quick, sagacious, sharp, shrewd.

athletic *adj* brawny, lusty, muscular, powerful, robust, sinewy, stalwart, stout, strapping, strong, sturdy.

atom *n* bit, molecule, monad, particle, scintilla.

atonement *n* amends, expiation, propitiation, reparation, satisfaction.

atrocity *n* depravity, enormity, flagrancy, ferocity, savagery, villainy.

attach *vb* affix, annex, connect, fasten, join, hitch, tie; charm, captivate, enamour, endear, engage, win; (*legal*) distress, distrain, seize, take.

attack *vb* assail, assault, charge, encounter, invade, set upon, storm, tackle; censure, criticise, impugn. * *n* aggression, assault, charge, offence, onset, onslaught, raid, thrust.

attain *vb* accomplish, achieve, acquire, get, obtain, secure; arrive at, come to, reach.

attempt *vb* assail, assault, attack; aim, endeavour, seek, strive, try. * *n* effort, endeavour, enterprise, experiment, undertaking, venture; assault, attack, onset.

attend *vb* accompany, escort, follow; guard, protect, watch; minister to, serve, wait on; give heed, hear, harken, listen; be attendant, serve, tend, wait.

attention *n* care, circumspection, heed, mindfulness, observation, regard, watch, watchfulness; application, reflection, study; civility, courtesy, deference, politeness, regard, respect; addresses, courtship, devotion, suit, wooing.

attentive *adj* alive, awake, careful, civil, considerate, courteous, heedful, mindful, observant, watchful.

attire *vb* accoutre, apparel, array, clothe, dress, enrobe, equip, rig, robe. * *n* clothes, clothing, costume, dress, garb, gear, habiliment, outfit, toilet, trapping, vestment, vesture, wardrobe.

attitude *n* pose, position, posture; aspect, conjuncture, condition, phase, prediction, situation, standing, state.

attract *vb* draw, pull; allure, captivate, charm, decoy, enamour, endear, entice, engage, fascinate, invite, win.

attribute *vb* ascribe, assign, impute, refer. * *n* characteristic, mark, note, peculiarity, predicate, property, quality.

audacity *n* boldness, courage, daring, fearlessness, intrepidity; assurance, brass, effrontery, face, front, impudence, insolence, presumption, sauciness.

audience *n* assemblage, congregation; hearing, interview, reception.

austere *adj* ascetic, difficult, formal, hard, harsh, morose, relentless, rigid, rigorous, severe, stern, stiff, strict, uncompromising, unrelenting.

authentic *adj* genuine, pure, real, true, unadulterated, uncorrupted, veritable; accurate, authoritative, reliable, true, trustworthy.

authority *n* dominion, empire, government, jurisdiction, power, sovereignty; ascendency, control, influence, rule, supremacy, sway; authorization, liberty, order, permit, precept, sanction, warranty; testimony, witness; connoisseur, expert, master.

authorize *vb* empower, enable, entitle; allow, approve, confirm, countenance, permit, ratify, sanction.

auxiliary *adj* aiding, ancillary, assisting, helpful, subsidiary. * *n* ally, assistant, confederate, help.

available *adj* accessible, advantageous, applicable, beneficial, profitable, serviceable, useful.

avenge *vb* punish, retaliate, revenge, vindicate.

averse *adj* adverse, backward, disinclined, indisposed, opposed, unwilling.

aversion *n* abhorrence, antipathy, disgust, dislike, hate, hatred, loathing, reluctance, repugnance.

avid *adj* eager, greedy, voracious.

avoid *vb* dodge, elude, escape, eschew, shun; forebear, refrain from.

awaken *vb* arouse, excite, incite, kindle, provoke, spur, stimulate; wake, waken; begin, be excited.

award *vb* adjudge, allot, assign, bestow, decree, grant. * *n* adjudication, allotment, assignment, decision, decree, determination, gift, judgement.

aware *adj* acquainted, apprised, conscious, conversant, informed, knowing, mindful, sensible.

away *adv* absent, not present. * *adj* at a distance; elsewhere; out of the way.

awe *vb* cow, daunt, intimidate, overawe. * *n* abashment, fear, reverence; dread, fear, fearfulness, terror.

awful *adj* august, awesome, dread, grand, inspired; abashed, alarming, appalled, dire, frightful, portentous, tremendous.

awkward *adj* bungling, clumsy, inept, maladroit, unskilful; lumbering, unfit, ungainly, unmanageable; boorish; inconvenient, unsuitable.

B

baby *vb* coddle, cosset, indulge, mollycoddle, pamper, spoil. * *adj* babyish, childish, infantile, puerile; diminutive, doll-like, miniature, pocket, pocket-sized, small-scale. * *n* babe, brat, child, infant, suckling, nursling; chicken, coward, milksop, namby-pamby, sad sack, weakling; miniature; innocent.

back *vb* abet, aid, countenance, favour, second, support, sustain; go back, move back, retreat, withdraw. * *adj* hindmost. * *adv* in return, in consideration; ago, gone, since; aside, away, behind, by; abaft, astern, backwards, hindwards, rearwards. * *n* end, hind part, posterior, rear.

backward *adj* disinclined, hesitating, indisposed, loath, reluctant, unwilling, wavering; dull, slow, sluggish, stolid, stupid. * *adv* aback, behind, rearward.

bad *adj* baleful, baneful, detrimental, evil, harmful, hurtful, injurious, noxious, pernicious, unwholesome, vicious; abandoned, corrupt, depraved, immoral, sinful, unfair, unprincipled, wicked; unfortunate, unhappy, unlucky, miserable; disappointing, discouraging, distressing, sad, unwelcoming; abominable, mean, shabby, scurvy, vile, wretched; defective, inferior, imperfect, incompetent, poor, unsuitable; hard, heavy, serious, severe.

badge *n* brand, emblem, mark, sign, symbol, token.

badger *vb* annoy, bait, bother, hector, harry, pester, persecute, tease, torment, trouble, vex, worry.

baffle *vb* balk, block, check, circumvent, defeat, foil, frustrate, mar, thwart, un-

bait vb harry, tease, worry. * n allurement, decoy, enticement, lure, temptation.

balance vb equilibrate, pose, (naut) trim; compare, weigh; compensate, counteract, estimate; adjust, clear, equalize, square. * n equilibrium, liberation; excess, remainder, residue, surplus.

bald adj bare, naked, uncovered, treeless; dull, inelegant, meagre, prosaic, tame, unadorned, vapid.

ban vb anathematize, curse, execrate; interdict, outlaw. * n edict, proclamation; anathema, curse, denunciation, execration; interdiction, outlawry, penalty, prohibition

band[1] vb belt, bind, cinch, encircle, gird, girdle; ally, associate, combine, connect, join, league; bar, marble, streak, stripe, striate, vein. * n crew, gang, horde, society, troop; ensemble, group, orchestra.

band[2] n ligament, ligature, tie; bond, chain, cord, fetter, manacle, shackle, trammel; bandage, belt, binding, cincture, girth, tourniquet.

bandit n brigand, freebooter, footpad, gangster, highwayman, outlaw, robber.

bang vb beat, knock, maul, pommel, pound, strike, thrash, thump; slam; clatter, rattle, resound, ring. * n clang, clangour, whang; blow, knock, lick, thump, thwack, whack.

bank[1] vb incline, slope, tilt; embank. * n dike, embankment, escarpment, heap, knoll, mound; border, bound, brim, brink, margin, rim, strand; course, row, tier.

bank[2] vb deposit, keep, save. * n depository, fund, reserve, savings, stockpile.

banner n colours, ensign, flag, standard, pennon, standard, streamer.

bar vb exclude, hinder, obstruct, prevent, prohibit, restrain, stop. * n grating, pole, rail, rod; barricade, hindrance, impediment, obstacle, obstruction, stop; bank, sand bar, shallow, shoal, spit; (legal) barristers, counsel, court, judgement, tribunal.

barbaric adj barbarous, rude, savage, uncivilized, untamed; capricious, coarse,

gaudy, riotous, showy, outlandish, uncouth, untamed, wild.

bare vb denude, depilate, divest, strip, unsheathe; disclose, manifest, open, reveal show. * adj denuded, exposed, naked, nude, stripped, unclothed, uncovered, undressed, unsheltered; alone, mere, sheer, simple; bald, meagre, plain, unadorned, uncovered, unfurnished; empty, destitute, indigent, poor.

bargain vb agree, contract, covenant, stipulate; convey, sell, transfer. * n agreement, compact, contract, covenant, convention, indenture, transaction, stipulation, treaty; getting, proceeds, purchase, result.

barren adj childless, infecund, sterile; (bot) acarpous, sterile; bare, infertile, poor, sterile, unproductive; ineffectual, unfruitful, uninstructive.

barricade vb block up, fortify, protect, obstruct. * n barrier, obstruction, palisade, stockade.

barrier n bar, barricade, hindrance, impediment, obstacle, obstruction, stop.

barter vb bargain, exchange, sell, trade, traffic.

base[1] adj cheap, inferior, worthless; counterfeit, debased, false, spurious; baseborn, humble, lowly, mean, nameless, plebeian, unknown, untitled, vulgar; abject, beggarly, contemptible, degraded, despicable, low, menial, pitiful, servile, sordid, sorry, worthless.

base[2] vb establish, found, ground. * n foundation, fundament, substructure, underpinning; pedestal, plinth, stand; centre, headquarters, HQ, seat; starting point; basis, cause, grounds, reason, standpoint; bottom, foot, foundation, ground.

bashful adj coy, diffident, shy, timid.

basis n base, bottom, foundation, fundament, ground, groundwork.

bastard adj adulterated, baseborn, counterfeit, false, illegitimate, sham. * n love child.

batch vb assemble, bunch, bundle, collect, gather, group. * n amount, collection, crowd, lot, quantity.

bathe vb immerse, lave, wash; cover, enfold, enwrap, drench, flood, infold, suffuse. * n bath, shower, swim.

batter¹ vb beat, pelt, smite; break, bruise, demolish, destroy, shatter, shiver, smash; abrade, deface, disfigure, indent, mar; incline, recede, retreat, slope. * n batsman, striker.

batter² n dough, goo, goop, gunk, paste, pulp.

battle vb contend, contest, engage, fight, strive, struggle. * n action, affair, brush, combat, conflict, contest, engagement, fight, fray.

bawl vb clamour, cry, hoot, howl, roar, shout, squall, vociferate, yell.

beam vb beacon, gleam, glisten, glitter, shine. * n balk, girder, joist, scanting, stud; gleam, pencil, ray, streak.

bear vb support, sustain, uphold; carry, convey, deport, transport, waft; abide, brook, endure, stand, suffer, tolerate, undergo; carry on, keep up, maintain; cherish, entertain, harbour; produce; cast, drop, sustain; endure, submit, suffer; act, operate, work. * n growler, grumbler, moaner, snarler; speculator.

bearing n air, behaviour, demeanour, deportment, conduct, carriage, conduct, mien, port; connection, dependency, relation; endurance, patience, suffering; aim, course, direction; bringing forth, producing; bed, receptacle, socket.

beastly adj abominable, brutish, ignoble, low, sensual, vile.

beat vb bang, baste, belabour, buffet, cane, cudgel, drub, hammer, hit, knock, maul, pommel, pound, punch, strike, thrash, thump, thwack, whack, whip; bray, bruise, pound, pulverize; batter, pelt; conquer, defeat, overcome, rout, subdue, surpass, vanquish; pulsate, throb; dash, strike. * adj baffled, bamboozled, confounded, mystified, nonplused, perplexed, puzzled, stumped; dead-beat, done, dog-tired, exhausted, tired out, worn out; beaten, defeated, licked, worsted. * n blow, striking, stroke; beating, pulsation, throb; accent, metre, rhythm; circuit, course, round.

beautiful adj charming, comely, fair, fine, exquisite, handsome, lovely, pretty.

beautify vb adorn, array, bedeck, deck, decorate, embellish, emblazon, garnish, gild, grace, ornament, set.

beauty n elegance, grace, symmetry; attractiveness, comeliness, fairness, loveliness, seemliness; belle.

become vb change to, get, go, wax; adorn, befit, set off, suit.

becoming adj appropriate, congruous, decent, decorous, fit, proper, right, seemly, suitable; comely, graceful, neat, pretty.

bed vb embed, establish, imbed, implant, infix, inset, plant; harbour, house, lodge. * n berth, bunk, cot, couch; channel, depression, hollow; base, foundation, receptacle, support, underlay; accumulation, layer, seam, stratum, vein.

befool vb bamboozle, beguile, cheat, circumvent, delude, deceive, dupe, fool, hoax, hoodwink, infatuate, stupefy, trick.

befriend vb aid, benefit, countenance, encourage, favour, help, patronize.

beg vb adjure, ask, beseech, conjure, crave, entreat, implore, importune, petition, pray, request, solicit, supplicate.

begin vb arise, commence, enter, open; inaugurate, institute, originate, start.

beginning n arising, commencement, dawn, emergence, inauguration, inception, initiation, opening, outset, start, rise; origin, source.

behaviour n air, bearing, carriage, comportment, conduct, demeanour, deportment, manner, manners, mien, port.

behind prep abaft, after, following. * adv abaft, aft, astern, rearward. * adj arrested, backward, checked, detained, retarded; after, behind. * n afterpart, rear, stern, tail; back, back side, reverse; bottom, buttocks, posterior, rump.

behold vb consider, contemplate, eye, observe, regard, see, survey, view.

being n actuality, existence, reality, subsistence; core, essence, heart, root.

belief n assurance, confidence, conviction, persuasion, trust; acceptance, assent, credence, credit, currency; creed, doctrine, dogma, faith, opinion, tenet.

bellow vb bawl, clamour, cry, howl, vociferate, yell.

bend vb bow, crook, curve, deflect, draw; direct, incline, turn; bend, dispose, influence, mould, persuade, subdue; (naut) fasten, make fast; crook, deflect, deviate, diverge, swerve; bow, lower, stoop; condescend, deign, stoop. * n angle, arc, arcuation, crook, curvature, curve, elbow, flexure, turn.

beneath prep below, under, underneath; unbecoming, unbefitting, unworthy. * adv below, underneath.

beneficial adj advantageous, favourable, helpful, profitable, salutary, serviceable, useful, wholesome.

benefit vb befriend, help, serve; advantage, avail, profit. * n favour, good turn, kindness, service; account, advantage, behalf, gain, good, interest, profit, utility.

benevolent adj altruistic, benign, charitable, generous, humane, kind, kindhearted, liberal, obliging, philanthropic, tender, unselfish.

benign adj amiable, amicable, beneficent, benevolent, complaisant, friendly, gentle, good, gracious, humane, kind, kindly, obliging.

bent adj angled, angular, bowed, crooked, curved, deflected, embowed, flexed, hooked, twisted; disposed, inclined, prone, minded; (with **on**) determined, fixed on, resolved, set on. * n bias, inclination, leaning, partiality, penchant, predilection, prepossession, proclivity, propensity

beside, besides adv additionally, also, further, furthermore, in addition, more, moreover, over and above, too, yet.

besiege vb beset, blockade, encircle, encompass, environ, invest, surround.

best vb better, exceed, excel, predominate, rival, surpass; beat, defeat, outdo, worst. * adj chief, first, foremost, highest, leading, utmost. * adv advantageously, excellently; extremely, greatly. * n choice, cream, flower, pick.

bet vb gamble, hazard, lay, pledge, stake, wage, wager. * n gamble, hazard, stake, wager.

betray vb be false to, break, violate; blab, discover, divulge, expose, reveal, show, tell; argue, betoken, display, evince, expose, exhibit, imply, indicate, manifest, reveal; beguile, delude, ensnare, lure, mislead; corrupt, ruin, seduce, undo.

better vb advance, amend, correct, exceed, improve, promote, rectify, reform. * adj bigger, fitter, greater, larger, less ill, preferable. * n advantage, superiority, upper hand, victory; improvement, greater good.

beware vb avoid, heed, look out, mind.

bewilder vb confound, confuse, daze, distract, embarrass, entangle, muddle, mystify, nonplus, perplex, pose, puzzle, stagger.

bewitch vb captivate, charm, enchant, enrapture, entrance, fascinate, spellbind, transport.

beyond prep above, before, farther, over, past, remote, yonder.

bias vb bend, dispose, incline, influence, predispose, prejudice. * n bent, inclination, leaning, partiality, penchant, predilection, prepossession, proclivity, propensity, slant, tendency, turn.

bicker vb dispute, jangle, quarrel, spar, spat, squabble, wrangle; play, quiver, tremble, vibrate.

bid vb charge, command, direct, enjoin, order, require, summon; ask, call, invite, pray, request, solicit; offer, propose, proffer, tender. * n bidding, offer, proposal.

big adj bumper, bulking, bulky, great, huge, large, massive, monstrous; important, imposing; distended, inflated, full, swollen, tumid; fecund, fruitful, productive, teeming.

bigoted adj dogmatic, hidebound, intolerant, obstinate, narrow-minded, opinionated, prejudiced.

bill vb charge, dun, invoice; programme, schedule; advertise, boost, plug, promote, publicize. * n account, charges, reckoning, score; advertisement, banner, hoarding, placard, poster; playbill, programme, schedule; bill of exchange, certificate, money; account, reckoning, statement.

billow vb surge, wave; heave, roll, surge, swell. * n roller, surge, swell, wave.

bind vb confine, enchain, fetter, restrain,

restrict; bandage, tie up, wrap; fasten, lash, pinion, secure, tie, truss; engage, hold, oblige, obligate, pledge; contract, harden, shrink, stiffen.

birth *n* ancestry, blood, descent, extraction, lineage, race; being, creation, creature, offspring, production, progeny.

bit *n* crumb, fragment, morsel, mouthful, piece, scrap; atom, grain, jot, mite, particle, tittle, whit; instant, minute, moment, second.

bite *vb* champ, chew, crunch, gnaw; burn, make smart, sting; catch, clutch, grapple, grasp, grip; bamboozle, cheat, cozen, deceive, defraud, dupe, gull, mislead, outwit, overreach, trick. * *n* grasp, hold; punch, relish, spice, pungency, tang, zest; lick, morsel, sip, taste; crick, nip, pain, pang, prick, sting.

bitter *adj* acrid; dire, fell, merciless, relentless, ruthless; harsh, severe, stern; afflictive, calamitous, distressing, galling, grievous, painful, poignant, sore, sorrowful.

black *adj* dark, ebony, inky, jet, sable, swarthy; dingy, dusky, lowering, murky, pitchy; calamitous, dark, depressing, disastrous, dismal, doleful, forbidding, gloomy, melancholy, mournful, sombre, sullen.

blacken *vb* darken; deface, defile, soil, stain, sully; asperse, besmirch, calumniate, defame, malign, revile, slander, traduce, vilify.

blame *vb* accuse, censure, condemn, disapprove, reflect upon, reprehend, reproach, reprove, upbraid. * *n* animadversion, censure, condemnation, disapproval, dispraise, disapprobation, reprehension, reproach, reproof; defect, demerit, fault, guilt, misdeed, shortcoming, sin, wrong.

bland *adj* balmy, demulcent, gentle, mild, soothing, soft; affable, amiable, complaisant, kindly, mild, suave.

blank *adj* bare, empty, vacuous, void; amazed, astonished, confounded, confused, dumbfounded, nonplussed; absolute, complete, entire, mere, perfect, pure, simple, unabated, unadulterated, unmitigated, unmixed, utter, perfect.

blare *vb* blazon, blow, peal, proclaim, trumpet. * *n* blast, clang, clangour, peal.

blasphemy *n* impiousness, sacrilege; cursing, profanity, swearing.

blast *vb* annihilate, blight, destroy, kill, ruin, shrivel, wither; burst, explode, kill. * *n* blow, gust, squall; blare, clang, peal; burst, discharge, explosion.

blaze *vb* blazon, proclaim, publish; burn, flame, glow. * *n* flame, flare, flash, glow, light.

bleak *adj* bare, exposed, unprotected, unsheltered, storm-beaten, windswept; biting, chill, cold, piercing, raw; cheerless, comfortless, desolate, dreary, uncongenial.

blemish *vb* blur, injure, mar, spot, stain, sully, taint, tarnish; asperse, calumniate, defame, malign, revile, slander, traduce, vilify. * *n* blot, blur, defect, disfigurement, fault, flaw, imperfection, soil, speck, spot, stain, tarnish; disgrace, dishonour, reproach, stain, taint.

blend *vb* amalgamate, coalesce, combine, commingle, fuse, mingle, mix, unite. * *n* amalgamation, combination, compound, fusion, mix, mixture, union.

bless *vb* beatify, delight, gladden; adore, celebrate, exalt, extol, glorify, magnify, praise.

blind *vb* blear, darken, deprive of sight; blindfold, hoodwink. * *adj* eyeless, sightless, stone-blind, unseeing; benighted, ignorant, injudicious, purblind, undiscerning, unenlightened; concealed, confused, dark, dim, hidden, intricate, involved, labyrinthine, obscure, private, remote; careless, headlong, heedless, inconsiderate, indiscriminate, thoughtless; blank, closed, shut. * *n* cover, curtain, screen, shade, shutter; blinker; concealment, disguise, feint, pretence, pretext, ruse, stratagem, subterfuge.

blink *vb* nictate, nictitate, wink; flicker, flutter, gleam, glitter, intermit, twinkle; avoid, disregard, evade, gloss over, ignore, overlook, pass over. * *n* glance, glimpse, sight, view, wink; gleam, glimmer, sheen, shimmer, twinkle.

bliss *n* beatification, beatitude, blessedness, blissfulness, ecstasy, felicity, happiness, heaven, joy, rapture, transport.

block *vb* arrest, bar, blockade, check, choke, close, hinder, impede, jam, obstruct, stop; form, mould, shape; brace, stiffen. * *n* lump, mass; blockhead, dunce, fool, simpleton; pulley, tackle; execution, scaffold; jam, obstruction, pack, stoppage.

blood *n* children, descendants, offspring, posterity, progeny; family, house, kin, kindred, line, relations; consanguinity, descent, kinship, lineage, relationship; courage, disposition, feelings, mettle, passion, spirit, temper.

bloom *vb* blossom, blow, flower; thrive, prosper. * *n* blossom, blossoming, blow, efflorescence, florescence, flowering; delicacy, delicateness, flush, freshness, heyday, prime, vigour; flush, glow, rose.

blot *vb* cancel, efface, erase, expunge, obliterate, rub out; blur, deface, disfigure, obscure, spot, stain, sully; disgrace, dishonour, tarnish. * *n* blur, erasure, blemish, blur, spot, stain; disgrace, dishonour.

blow¹ *n* bang, beat, buffet, dab, impact, knock, pat, punch, rap, slam, stroke, thump, wallop, buffet, impact; affliction, calamity, disaster, misfortune, setback.

blow² *vb* breathe, gasp, pant, puff; flow, move, scud, stream, waft. * *n* blast, gale, gust, squall, storm, wind.

blue *adj* azure, cerulean, cobalt, indigo, sapphire, ultramarine; ghastly, livid, pallid; dejected, depressed, dispirited, downcast, gloomy, glum, mopey, melancholic, melancholy, sad.

bluff¹ *adj* abrupt, blunt, blustering, coarse, frank, good-natured, open, outspoken; abrupt, precipitous, sheer, steep. * *n* cliff, headland, height.

bluff² *vb* deceive, defraud, lie, mislead. * *n* deceit, deception, feint, fraud, lie.

blunder *vb* err, flounder, mistake; stumble. * *n* error, fault, howler, mistake, solecism.

blunt *adj* dull, edgeless, obtuse, pointless, unsharpened; insensible, stolid, thickwitted; abrupt, bluff, downright, plainspoken, outspoken, unceremonious, uncourtly. * *vb* deaden, dull, numb, weaken.

blur *vb* bedim, darken, dim, obscure; blemish, blot, spot, stain, sully, tarnish. * *n* blemish, blot, soil, spot, stain, tarnish; disgrace, smear.

blush *vb* colour, flush, glow, redden. * *n* bloom, flush, glow, colour, reddening, suffusion.

boast *vb* bluster, brag, crack, flourish, crow, vaunt. * *n* blustering, boasting, bombast, brag, braggadocio, bravado, bombast, swaggering, vaunt.

bodily *adj* carnal, corporeal, fleshly, physical. * *adv* altogether, completely, entirely, wholly.

body *n* carcass, corpse, remains; stem, torso, trunk; aggregate, bulk, corpus, mass; being, individual, mortal creature, person; assemblage, association, band, company, corporation, corps, coterie, force, party, society, troop; consistency, substance, thickness.

boil *vb* agitate, bubble, foam, froth, rage, seethe, simmer. * *n* ebullience, ebullition.

boisterous *adj* loud, roaring, stormy; clamouring, loud, noisy, obstreperous, tumultuous, turbulent.

bold *adj* adventurous, audacious, courageous; brave, daring, dauntless, doughty, fearless, gallant, hardy, heroic, intrepid, mettlesome, manful, manly, spirited, stouthearted, undaunted, valiant, valorous; assured, confident, self-reliant; assuming, forward, impertinent, impudent, insolent, pushing, rude, saucy; conspicuous, projecting, prominent, striking; abrupt, precipitous, prominent, steep.

bolt *vb* abscond, flee, fly. * *n* arrow, dart, missile, shaft; thunderbolt

bond *vb* bind, connect, fuse, glue, join. * *adj* captive, enslaved, enthralled, subjugated. * *n* band, cord, fastening, ligament, ligature, link, nexus; bondage, captivity, chains, constraint, fetters, prison, shackle; attachment, attraction, connection, coupling, link, tie, union; compact, obligation, pledge, promise.

bonus *n* gift, honorarium, premium, reward, subsidy.

book *vb* bespeak, engage, reserve; programme, schedule; list, log, record, register. * n booklet, brochure, compendium, handbook, manual, monograph, pamphlet, textbook, tract, treatise, volume, work.

booty n loot, pillage, plunder, spoil.

border vb bound, edge, fringe, line, march, rim, skirt, verge; abut, adjoin, butt, conjoin, connect, neighbour. * n brim, brink, edge, fringe, hem, margin, rim, skirt, verge; boundary, confine, frontier, limit, march, outskirts.

bore[1] vb annoy, fatigue, plague, tire, trouble, vex, weary, worry. * n bother, nuisance, pest, worry.

bore[2] vb drill, perforate, pierce, sink, tunnel. * n calibre, hole, shaft, tunnel.

borrow vb take and return, use temporarily; adopt, appropriate, imitate; dissemble, feign, simulate.

boss vb command, direct, employ, run. * n employer, foreman, master, overseer, superintendent.

bother vb annoy, disturb, harass, molest, perplex, pester, plague, tease, trouble, vex, worry. * n annoyance, perplexity, plague, trouble, vexation.

bottom vb build, establish, found. * adj base, basic, ground, lowermost, lowest, nethermost, undermost. * n base, basis, foot, foundation, groundwork; dale, meadow, valley; buttocks, fundament, seat; dregs, grounds, lees, sediment.

bounce vb bound, jump, leap, rebound, recoil, spring. * n knock, thump; bound, jump, leap, spring, vault.

bound[1] adj assured, certain, decided, determined, resolute, resolved; confined, hampered, restricted, restrained; committed, contracted, engaged, pledged, promised; beholden, duty-bound, obligated, obliged.

bound[2] vb border, delimit, circumscribe, confine, demarcate, limit, restrict, terminate. * n boundary, confine, edge, limit, march, margin, periphery, term, verge.

bound[3] vb jump, leap, spring. * n bounce, jump, leap, spring, vault.

boundary n border, bourn, circuit, circumference, confine, limit, march, periphery, term, verge.

boundless adj endless, immeasurable, infinite, limitless, unbounded, unconfined, undefined, unlimited, vast.

bow[1] n (naut) beak, prow, stem.

bow[2] vb arc, bend, buckle, crook, curve, droop, flex, yield; crush, depress, subdue; curtsy, genuflect, kowtow, submit. * n arc, bend, bilge, bulge, convex, curve, flexion; bob, curtsy, genuflection, greeting, homage, obeisance; coming out, debut, introduction; curtain call, encore.

box[1] vb fight, hit, mill, spar. * n blow, buffet, fight, hit, spar.

box[2] vb barrel, crate, pack, parcel. * n case, chest, container, crate, portmanteau, trunk.

boy n lad, stripling, youth.

brace vb make tight, tighten; buttress, fortify, reinforce, shore, strengthen, support, truss. * n couple, pair; clamp, girder, prop, shore, stay, support, tie, truss.

branch vb diverge, fork, bifurcate, ramify, spread. * n bough, offset, limb, shoot, sprig, twig; arm, fork, ramification, spur; article, department, member, part, portion, section, subdivision.

brand vb denounce, stigmatize, mark. * n firebrand, torch; bolt, lightning flash; cachet, mark, stamp, tally; blot, reproach, stain, stigma.

brave vb dare, defy. * adj bold, courageous, fearless, heroic, intrepid, stalwart.

bravery n courage, daring, fearlessness, gallantry, valour.

brawl vb bicker, dispute, jangle, quarrel, squabble. * n broil, dispute, feud, fracas, fray, jangle, quarrel, row, scuffle, squabble, uproar, wrangle.

brawny adj athletic, lusty, muscular, powerful, robust, sinewy, stalwart, strapping, strong, sturdy.

breach n break, chasm, crack, disruption, fissure, flaw, fracture, opening, rent, rift, rupture; alienation, difference, disaffection, disagreement, split.

break vb crack, disrupt, fracture, part, rend, rive, sever; batter, burst, crush, shatter, smash, splinter; cashier, degrade, discard, discharge, dismiss; disobey, infringe, transgress, violate; intermit, in-

terrupt, stop; disclose, open, unfold. * *n*
aperture, breach, chasm, fissure, gap,
rent, rip, rupture; break-up, crash, debacle.

breath *n* exhaling, inhaling, pant, sigh,
respiration, whiff; animation, existence,
life; pause, respite, rest; breathing space,
instant, moment.

breathe *vb* live, exist; emit, exhale, give
out; diffuse, express, indicate, manifest,
show.

breed *vb* bear, beget, engender, hatch,
produce; bring up, foster, nourish, nurture, raise, rear; discipline, educate, instruct, nurture, rear, school, teach, train;
generate, originate. * *n* extraction, family, lineage, pedigree, progeny, race,
strain.

brevity *n* briefness, compression, con-
ciseness, curtness, pithiness, shortness,
terseness, transiency.

bribe *vb* buy, corrupt, influence, pay off,
suborn. * *n* allurement, corruption, enticement, graft, pay-off, subornation.

bridle *vb* check, curb, control, govern, restrain. * *n* check, control, curb.

brief *vb* give directions, direct, instruct;
capsulate, summarize, delineate, describe, draft, outline, sketch; (*law*) retain. * *adj* concise, curt, inconsiderable,
laconic, pithy, short, succinct, terse;
fleeting, momentary, short, temporary,
transient. * *n* abstract, breviary, brief-
ing, epitome, compendium, summary,
syllabus; (*law*) precept, writ.

bright *adj* blazing, brilliant, dazzling,
gleaming, glowing, light, luminous, radiant, shining, sparkling, sunny; clear,
cloudless, lambent, lucid, transparent;
famous, glorious, illustrious; acute, discerning, ingenious, intelligent, keen;
auspicious, cheering, encouraging, exhilarating, favourable, inspiring, promising, propitious; cheerful, genial, happy, lively, merry, pleasant, smiling, vivacious.

brilliant *adj* beaming, bright, effulgent,
gleaming, glistening, glittering, lustrous, radiant, resplendent, shining,
sparkling splendid; admirable, celebrated, distinguished, famous, glorious, il-

lustrious, renowned; dazzling, decided,
prominent, signal, striking, unusual.

brim *n* border, brink, edge, rim, margin,
skirt, verge; bank, border, coast, margin, shore.

bring *vb* bear, convey, fetch; accompany, attend, conduct, convey, convoy,
guide, lead; gain, get, obtain, procure,
produce.

brisk *adj* active, alert, agile, lively, nimble, perky, quick, smart, spirited, spry.

brittle *adj* brash, breakable, crisp, crumbling, fragile, frangible, frail, shivery.

broad *adj* ample, expansive, extensive,
large, spacious, sweeping, vast, wide;
enlarged, hospitable, liberal, tolerant;
diffused, open, spread; coarse, gross, indecent, indelicate, unrefined, vulgar.

broken *adj* fractured, rent, ruptured, separated, severed, shattered, shivered,
torn; exhausted, feeble, impaired, shak-
en, shattered, spent, wasted; defective,
halting, hesitating, imperfect, stammering, stumbling; contrite, humble, lowly, penitent; abrupt, craggy, precipitous,
rough.

brook *vb* abide, bear, endure, suffer, tolerate. * *n* burn, beck, creek, rill, rivulet,
run, streamlet.

brotherly *adj* affectionate, amicable, cordial, friendly, kind.

bruise *vb* contuse, crunch, squeeze; batter, break, maul, pound, pulverize; batter, deface, indent. * *n* blemish, contusion, swelling.

brush *vb* buff, clean, polish, swab, sweep,
wipe; curry, groom, rub down; caress,
flick, glance, graze, scrape, skim, touch.
* *n* besom, broom; action, affair, collision, contest, conflict, encounter, engagement, fight, skirmish.

brutal *adj* barbaric, barbarous, brutish,
cruel, ferocious, inhuman, ruthless, savage; bearish, brusque, churlish, gruff,
impolite, harsh, rude, rough, truculent,
uncivil.

brute *n* barbarian, beast, monster, ogre,
savage; animal, beast, creature. * *adj*
carnal, mindless, physical; bestial,
coarse, gross.

bubble *vb* boil, effervesce, foam. * *n*

bead, blob, fluid, globule; bagatelle, trifle; cheat, delusion, hoax.

bud vb burgeon, germinate, push, shoot, sprout, vegetate. * n burgeon, gem, germ, gemmule, shoot, sprout.

budget vb allocate, cost, estimate. * n account, estimate, funds, resources; bag, bundle, pack, packet, parcel, roll; assortment, batch, collection, lot, set, store.

build vb construct, erect, establish, fabricate, fashion, model, raise, rear. * n body, figure, form, frame, physique; construction, shape, structure.

bulk n dimension, magnitude, mass, size, volume; amplitude, bulkiness, massiveness; body, majority, mass.

bully vb browbeat, bulldoze, domineer, haze, hector, intimidate, overbear. * n blusterer, browbeater, bulldozer, hector, swaggerer, roisterer, tyrant.

bump vb collide, knock, strike, thump. * n blow, jar, jolt, knock, shock, thump; lump, protuberance, swelling.

bunch vb assemble, collect, crowd, group, herd, pack. * n bulge, bump, bundle, hump, knob, lump, protuberance; cluster, hand, fascicle; assortment, batch, collection, group, lot, parcel, set; knot, tuft.

bundle vb bale, pack, package, parcel, truss, wrap. * n bale, batch, bunch, collection, heap, pack, package, packet, parcel, pile, roll, truss.

burden vb encumber, grieve, load, oppress, overlay, overload, saddle, surcharge, try. * n capacity, cargo, freight, lading, load, tonnage, weight; affliction, charge, clog, encumbrance, impediment, grievance, sorrow, trial, trouble; drift, point, substance, tenor, surcharge.

burn[1] n beck, brook, gill, rill, rivulet, runnel, runlet, stream. water

burn[2] vb blaze, conflagrate, enflame, fire, flame, ignite, kindle, light, smoulder; cremate, incinerate; scald, scorch, singe; boil, broil, cook, roast, seethe, simmer, stew, swelter, toast; bronze, brown, sunburn, suntan, tan; bake, desiccate, dry, parch, sear, shrivel, wither; glow, incandesce, tingle, warm. * n scald, scorch, singe; sunburn.

burst vb break open, be rent, explode, shatter, split open. * adj broken, kaput, punctured, ruptured, shattered, split. * n break, breakage, breach, fracture, rupture; blast, blowout, blowup, discharge, detonation, explosion; spurt; blaze, flare, flash; cloudburst, downpour; bang, crack, crash, report, sound; fusillade, salvo, spray, volley, outburst, outbreak flare-up, blaze, eruption.

bury vb entomb, inearth, inhume, inter; conceal, hide, secrete, shroud.

business n calling, employment, occupation, profession, pursuit, vocation; commerce, dealing, trade, traffic; affair, concern, engagement, matter, transaction, undertaking; duty, function, office, task, work.

bustle vb fuss, hurry, scurry. * n ado, commotion, flurry, fuss, hurry, hustle, pother, stir, tumult.

busy vb devote, employ, engage, occupy, spend, work. * adj employed, engaged, occupied; active, assiduous, diligent, engrossed, industrious, sedulous, working; agile, brisk, nimble, spry, stirring; meddling, officious.

but conj except, excepting, further, howbeit, moreover, still, unless, yet. * adv even, notwithstanding, still, yet.

butchery n massacre, murder, slaughter.

butt[1] vb bunt, push, shove, shunt, strike; encroach, impose, interfere, intrude, invade, obtrude. * n buck, bunt, push, shove, shunt, thrust.

butt[2] n aim, goal, mark, object, point, target; dupe, gull, victim.

butt[3] vb abut, adjoin, conjoin, connect, neighbour. * n end, piece, remainder, stub, stump; buttocks, posterior, rump.

C

cackle vb giggle, laugh, snicker, titter; babble, chatter, gabble, palaver, prate, prattle, titter. * n babble, chatter, giggle, prate, prattle, snigger, titter.

cage vb confine, immure, imprison, incarcerate. * n coop, pen, pound.

calamity n adversity, affliction, blow, casualty, cataclysm, catastrophe, disaster, distress, downfall, evil, hardship, mischance, misery, misfortune, mishap, reverse, ruin, stroke, trial, visitation.

calculate vb cast, compute, count, estimate, figure, rate, reckon, weigh; tell.

calculating adj crafty, designing, scheming, selfish; careful, cautious, circumspect, far-sighted, politic, sagacious, wary.

calibre n bore, capacity, diameter, gauge; ability, capacity, endowment, faculty, gifts, parts, scope, talent.

call vb christen, denominate, designate, dub, entitle, name, phrase, style, term; bid, invite, summons; assemble, convene, convoke, muster; cry, exclaim; arouse, awaken, proclaim, rouse, shout, waken; appoint, elect, ordain. * n cry, outcry, voice; appeal, invitation, summons; claim, demand, summons; appointment, election, invitation.

callous adj hard, hardened, indurated; apathetic, dull, indifferent, insensible, inured, obdurate, obtuse, sluggish, torpid, unfeeling, unsusceptible.

calm vb allay, becalm, compose, hush, lull, smooth, still, tranquillize; alleviate, appease, assuage, moderate, mollify, pacify, quiet, soften, soothe, tranquillize. * adj halcyon, mild, peaceful, placid, quiet, reposeful, serene, smooth, still, tranquil, unruffled; collected, cool, composed, controlled, impassive, imperturbable, sedate, self-possessed, undisturbed, unperturbed, unruffled, untroubled. * n lull; equanimity, peace, placidity, quiet, repose, serenity, stillness, tranquillity.

camp¹ vb bivouac, encamp, lodge, pitch, tent. * n bivouac, encampment, laager; cabal, circle, clique, coterie, faction, group, junta, party, ring, set.

camp² adj affected, artificial, effeminate, exaggerated, mannered, theatrical.

canal n channel, duct, pipe, tube.

cancel vb blot, efface, erase, expunge, obliterate; abrogate, annul, countermand, nullify, quash, repeal, rescind, revoke.

candid adj fair, impartial, just, unbiased, unprejudiced; artless, frank, free, guileless, honest, honourable, ingenuous, naive, open, plain, sincere, straightforward.

candidate n applicant, aspirant, claimant, competitor, probationer.

candour n fairness, impartiality, justice; artlessness, frankness, guilelessness, honesty, ingenuousness, openness, simplicity, sincerity, straightforwardness, truthfulness.

canon n catalogue, criterion, formula, formulary, law, regulation, rule, standard, statute.

canvass vb agitate, debate, discuss, dispute; consider, examine, investigate, scrutinize, sift, study. * n debate, discussion, dispute; examination, scrutiny, sifting.

cap vb cover, surmount; complete, crown, finish; exceed, overtop, surpass, transcend; match, parallel, pattern. * n beret, head-cover, head-dress; acme, chief, crown, head, peak, perfection, pitch, summit, top.

capable adj adapted, fitted, qualified, suited; able, accomplished, clever, competent, efficient, gifted, ingenious, intelligent, sagacious, skilful.

capacious adj ample, broad, comprehensive, expanded, extensive, large, roomy, spacious, wide.

capacity n amplitude, dimensions, magnitude, volume; aptitude, aptness, brains, calibre, discernment, faculty, forte, genius, gift, parts, power, talent, turn, wit; ability, capability, calibre, cleverness, competency, efficiency, skill; character, charge, function, office, position, post, province, service, sphere.

capital adj cardinal, chief, essential, important, leading, main, major, pre-eminent, principal, prominent; fatal; excellent, first-class, first-rate, good, prime, splendid. * n chief city, metropolis, seat; money, estate, investments, shares, stock.

capsize vb overturn, upset.

captain vb command, direct, head, lead, manage, officer, preside. * n chief, chieftain, commander, leader, master, officer, soldier, warrior.

captivate *vb* allure, attract, bewitch, catch, charm, enamour, enchant, enthral, fascinate, gain, hypnotize, infatuate, win.

captivity *n* confinement, durance, duress, imprisonment; bondage, enthralment, servitude, slavery, subjection, thraldom, vassalage.

capture *vb* apprehend, arrest, catch, seize. * *n* apprehension, arrest, catch, catching, imprisonment, seizure; bag, prize.

cardinal *adj* capital, central, chief, essential, first, important, leading, main, preeminent, primary, principal, vital.

care *n* anxiety, concern, perplexity, trouble, solicitude, worry; attention, carefulness, caution, circumspection, heed, regard, vigilance, wariness, watchfulness; charge, custody, guardianship, keep, oversight, superintendence, ward; burden, charge, concern, respon∑sibility.

careful *adj* anxious, solicitous, concerned, troubled, uneasy; attentive, heedful, mindful, regardful, thoughtful; cautious, canny, circumspect, discreet, leery, vigilant, watchful.

careless *adj* carefree, nonchalant, unapprehensive, undisturbed, unperplexed, unsolicitous, untroubled; disregardful, heedless, inattentive, incautious, inconsiderate, neglectful, negligent, regardless, remiss, thoughtless, unobservant, unconcerned, unconsidered, unmindful, unthinking.

caress *vb* coddle, cuddle, cosset, embrace, fondle, hug, kiss, pet. * *n* cuddle, embrace, fondling, hug, kiss.

caricature *vb* burlesque, parody, take off, travesty. * *n* burlesque, farce, parody, representation, take-off, travesty.

carriage *n* conveyance, vehicle; air, bearing, behaviour, conduct, demeanour, deportment, front, mien, port.

carry *vb* bear, convey, transfer, transmit, transport; impel, push forward, urge; accomplish, compass, effect, gain, secure; bear up, support, sustain; infer, involve, imply, import, signify.

carve *vb* chisel, cut, divide, engrave, grave, hack, hew, indent, incise, sculpture; fashion, form, mould, shape.

case[1] *vb* cover, encase, enclose, envelop, protect, wrap; box, pack. * *n* capsule, covering, sheathe; box, cabinet, container, holder, receptacle.

case[2] *n* condition, plight, predicament, situation, state; example, instance, occurrence; circumstance, condition, contingency, event; action, argument, cause, lawsuit, process, suit, trial.

cast *vb* fling, hurl, pitch, send, shy, sling, throw, toss; drive, force, impel, thrust; lay aside, put off, shed; calculate, compute, reckon; communicate, diffuse, impart, shed, throw. * *n* fling, throw, toss; shade, tinge, tint, touch; air, character, look, manner, mien, style, tone, turn; form, mould.

caste *n* class, grade, lineage, order, race, rank, species, status.

castigate *vb* beat, chastise, flog, lambaste, lash, thrash, whip; chaste, correct, discipline, punish; criticize, flagellate, upbraid.

castle *n* citadel, fortress, stronghold.

casual *adj* accidental, contingent, fortuitous, incidental, irregular, occasional, random, uncertain, unforeseen, unintentional, unpremeditated.

casualty *n* chance, contingency, fortuity, mishap; accident, catastrophe, disaster, mischance, misfortune.

catalogue *vb* alphabetize, categorize, chronicle, class, classify, codify, file, index, list, record, tabulate. * *n* enumeration, index, inventory, invoice, list, record, register, roll, schedule.

catastrophe *n* conclusion, consummation, denouement, end, finale, issue, termination, upshot; adversity, blow, calamity, cataclysm, debacle, disaster, ill, misfortune, mischance, mishap, trial, trouble.

catch *vb* clutch, grasp, gripe, nab, seize, snatch; apprehend, arrest, capture; overtake; enmesh, ensnare, entangle, entrap, lime, net; bewitch, captivate, charm, enchant, fascinate, win; surprise, take unawares. * *n* arrest, capture, seizure; bag, find, haul, plum, prize; drawback, fault, hitch, obstacle, rub, snag; captive, conquest.

categorical *adj* absolute, direct, downright, emphatic, explicit, express, positive, unconditional, unqualified, unreserved.

category n class, division, head, heading, list, order, rank, sort.

cater vb feed, provide, purvey.

cause vb breed, create, originate, produce; effect, effectuate, occasion, produce. * n agent, creator, mainspring, origin, original, producer, source, spring; account, agency, consideration, ground, incentive, incitement, inducement, motive, reason; aim, end, object, purpose; action, case, suit, trial.

caustic adj acrid, cathartic, consuming, corroding, corrosive, eating, erosive, mordant, virulent; biting, bitter, burning, cutting, sarcastic, satirical, scalding, scathing, severe, sharp, stinging.

caution vb admonish, forewarn, warn. * n care, carefulness, circumspection, discretion, forethought, heed, heedfulness, providence, prudence, wariness, vigilance, watchfulness; admonition, advice, counsel, injunction, warning.

cautious adj careful, chary, circumspect, discreet, heedful, prudent, wary, vigilant, wary, watchful.

cease vb desist, intermit, pause, refrain, stay, stop; fail; discontinue, end, quit, terminate.

ceaseless adj continual, continuous, incessant, unceasing, unintermitting, uninterrupted, unremitting; endless, eternal, everlasting, perpetual.

celebrate vb applaud, bless, commend, emblazon, extol, glorify, laud, magnify, praise, trumpet; commemorate, honour, keep, observe; solemnize.

celebrated adj distinguished, eminent, famed, famous, glorious, illustrious, notable, renowned.

celebrity n credit, distinction, eminence, fame, glory, honour, renown, reputation, repute; lion, notable, star.

cement vb attach, bind, join, combine, connect, solder, unite, weld; cohere, stick. * n glue, paste, mortar, solder.

cemetery n burial-ground, burying-ground, churchyard, god's acre, graveyard, necropolis.

censor vb blue-pencil, bowdlerize, cut,

edit, expurgate; classify, kill, quash, squash, suppress. * n caviller, censurer, faultfinder.

censure vb abuse, blame, chide, condemn, rebuke, reprehend, reprimand, reproach, reprobate, reprove, scold, upbraid. n animadversion, blame, condemnation, criticism, disapprobation, disapproval, rebuke, remonstrance, reprehension, reproach, reproof, stricture.

ceremonious adj civil, courtly, lofty, stately; formal, studied; exact, formal, punctilious, precise, starched, stiff.

ceremony n ceremonial, etiquette, form, formality, observance, solemnity, rite; parade, pomp, show, stateliness.

certain adj absolute, incontestable, incontrovertible, indisputable, indubitable, positive, inevitable, undeniable, undisputed, unquestionable, unquestioned; assured, confident, convinced, sure, undoubting; infallible, never-failng, unfailing; actual, existing, real; constant, determinate, fixed, settled, stated.

certify vb attest, notify, testify, vouch; ascertain, determine, verify, show.

chafe vb rub; anger, annoy, chagrin, enrage, exasperate, fret, gall, incense, irritate, nettle, offend, provoke, ruffle, tease, vex; fret, fume, rage.

chaff vb banter, deride, jeer, mock, rally, ridicule, scoff. * n glumes, hulls, husks; refuse, trash, waste.

chain vb bind, confine, fetter, manacle, restrain, shackle, trammel; enslave. * n bond, fetter, manacle, shackle, union.

challenge vb brave, call out, dare, defy, dispute; demand, require. * n defiance, interrogation, question; exception, objection.

champion vb advocate, defend, uphold. * n defender, promoter, protector, vindicator; belt-holder, hero, victor, warrior, winner.

chance vb befall, betide, happen, occur. * adj accidental, adventitious, casual, fortuitous, incidental, unexpected, unforeseen. * n accident, cast, fortuity, fortune, hap, luck; contingency, possibility; occasion, opening, opportunity; contingency, fortuity, gamble, peradventure, uncertainty; hazard, jeopardy, peril, risk.

change *vb* alter, fluctuate, modify, vary; displace, remove, replace, shift, substitute; barter, commute, exchange. * *n* alteration, mutation, revolution, transition, transmutation, turning, variance, variation; innovation, novelty, variety, vicissitude.

changeable *adj* alterable, inconstant, modifiable, mutable, uncertain, unsettled, unstable, unsteadfast, unsteady, variable, variant; capricious, fickle, fitful, flighty, giddy, mercurial, vacillating, volatile, wavering.

channel *vb* chamfer, cut, flute, groove. * *n* canal, conduit, duct, passage; aqueduct, canal, chute, drain, flume, furrow; chamfer, groove, fluting, furrow, gutter.

chant *vb* carol, sing, warble; intone, recite; canticle, song.

chaos *n* anarchy, confusion, disorder.

character *n* emblem, figure, hieroglyph, ideograph, letter, mark, sign, symbol; bent, constitution, cast, disposition, nature, quality; individual, original, person, personage; reputation, repute; nature, traits; eccentric, trait.

characteristic *adj* distinctive, peculiar, singular, special, specific, typical. * *n* attribute, feature, idiosyncrasy, lineament, mark, peculiarity, quality, trait.

charge *vb* burden, encumber, freight, lade, load; entrust; ascribe, impute, lay; accuse, arraign, blame, criminate, impeach, inculpate, indict, involve; bid, command, exhort, enjoin, order, require, tax; assault, attack bear down. * *n* burden, cargo, freight, lading, load; care, custody, keeping, management, ward; commission, duty, employment, office, trust; responsibility, trust; command, direction, injunction, mandate, order, precept; exhortation, instruction; cost, debit, expense, expenditure, outlay; price, sum; assault, attack, encounter, onset, onslaught.

charitable *adj* beneficial, beneficent, benignant, bountiful, generous, kind, liberal, open-handed; candid, considerate, lenient, mild.

charity *n* benevolence, benignity, fellow-feeling, good-nature, goodwill, kind-heartedness, kindness, tenderheartedness; beneficence, bounty, generosity, humanity, philanthropy. liberality.

charm *vb* allure, attract, becharm, bewitch, captivate, catch, delight, enamour, enchain, enchant, enrapture, enravish, fascinate, transport, win. * *n* enchantment, incantation, magic, necromancy, sorcery, spell, witchery; amulet, talisman; allurement, attraction, attractiveness, fascination.

chase *vb* follow, hunt, pursue, track; emboss. * *n* course, field-sport, hunt, hunting.

chaste *adj* clean, continent, innocent, modest, pure, pure-minded, undefiled, virtuous; chastened, pure, simple, unaffected, uncorrupt.

chasten *vb* correct, discipline, humble; purify, refine, render, subdued.

chastise *vb* castigate, correct, flog, lash, punish, whip; chasten, correct, discipline, humble, punish, subdue.

chastity *n* continence, innocence, modesty, pure-mindedness, purity, virtue; cleanness, decency, purity; chasteness, purity, refinement, restrainedness, simplicity, sobriety, unaffectedness.

chat *vb* babble, chatter, confabulate, gossip, prate, prattle. * *n* chit-chat, confabulation, conversation, gossip, prattle.

chatter *vb* babble, chat, confabulate, gossip, prate, prattle. * *n* babble, chat, gabble, jabber, patter, prattle.

cheap *adj* inexpensive, low-priced; common, indifferent, inferior, mean, meretricious, paltry, poor.

cheat *vb* cozen, deceive, dissemble, juggle, shuffle; bamboozle, befool, beguile, cajole, circumvent, deceive, defraud, chouse, delude, dupe, ensnare, entrap, fool, gammon, gull, hoax, hoodwink, inveigle, jockey, mislead, outwit, overreach, trick. * *n* artifice, beguilement, blind, catch, chouse, deceit, deception, fraud, imposition, imposture, juggle, pitfall, snare, stratagem, swindle, trap, trick, wile; counterfeit, deception, delusion, illusion, mockery, paste, sham, tinsel; beguiler, charlatan, cheater, cozener, impostor, jockey, knave, mountebank, trickster, rogue, render, sharper, seizer, shuffler, swindler, taker, tearer.

check vb block, bridle, control, counteract, curb, hinder, obstruct, repress, restrain; chide, rebuke, reprimand, reprove. * n bar, barrier, block, brake, bridle, clog, control, curb, damper, hindrance, impediment, interference, obstacle, obstruction, rebuff, repression, restraint, stop, stopper.

cheer vb animate, encourage, enliven, exhilarate, gladden, incite, inspirit; comfort, console, solace; applaud, clap. * n cheerfulness, gaiety, gladness, glee, hilarity, jollity, joy, merriment, mirth; entertainment, food, provision, repast; acclamation, hurrah, huzza.

cheerful adj animated, airy, blithe, buoyant, cheery, gay, glad, gleeful, happy, joyful, jocund, jolly, joyous, light-hearted, lightsome, lively, merry, mirthful, sprightly, sunny; animating, cheering, cheery, encouraging, enlivening, glad, gladdening, gladsome, grateful, inspiriting, jocund, pleasant.

cheerless adj dark, dejected, desolate, despondent, disconsolate, discouraged, dismal, doleful, dreary, forlorn, gloomy, joyless, low-spirited, lugubrious, melancholy, mournful, rueful, sad, sombre, spiritless, woe-begone.

cherish vb comfort, foster, nourish, nurse, nurture, support, sustain; treasure; encourage, entertain, indulge, harbour.

chew vb crunch, manducate, masticate, munch; bite, champ, gnaw; meditate, ruminate.

chief adj first, foremost, headmost, leading, master, supereminent, supreme, top; capital, cardinal, especial, essential, grand, great, main, master, paramount, prime, principal, supreme, vital. * n chieftain, commander; head, leader.

child n babe, baby, bairn, bantling, brat, chit, infant, nursling, suckling, wean; issue, offspring, progeny.

childish adj infantile, juvenile, puerile, tender, young; foolish, frivolous, silly, trifling, weak.

childlike adj docile, dutiful, gentle, meek,

obedient, submissive; confiding, guileless, ingenuous, innocent, simple, trustful, uncrafty.

chill vb dampen, depress, deject, discourage, dishearten. * adj bleak, chilly, cold, frigid, gelid. * n chilliness, cold, coldness, frigidity; ague, rigour, shiver; damp, depression

chip vb flake, fragment, hew, pare, scrape. * n flake, fragment, paring, scrap.

choice adj excellent, exquisite, precious, rare, select, superior, uncommon, unusual, valuable; careful, chary, frugal, sparing. * n alternative, election, option, selection; favourite, pick, preference.

choose vb adopt, co-opt, cull, designate, elect, pick, predestine, prefer, select.

chop vb cut, hack, hew; mince; shift, veer. * n slice; brand, quality; chap, jaw.

christen vb baptise; call, dub, denominate, designate, entitle, name, style, term, title.

chronic adj confirmed, continuing, deep-seated, inveterate, rooted.

chronicle vb narrate, record, register. * n diary, journal, register; account, annals, history, narration, recital, record.

chuckle vb crow, exult, giggle, laugh, snigger, titter. * n giggle, laughter, snigger, titter.

churlish adj brusque, brutish, cynical, harsh, impolite, rough, rude, snappish, snarling, surly, uncivil, waspish; crabbed, ill-tempered, morose, sullen; close, close-fisted, illiberal, mean, miserly, niggardly, penurious, stingy.

circle vb compass, encircle, encompass, gird, girdle, ring; gyrate, revolve, rotate, round, turn. * n circlet, corona, gyre, hoop, ring, rondure; circumference, cordon, periphery; ball, globe, orb, sphere; compass, enclosure; class, clique, company, coterie, fraternity, set, society; bounds, circuit, compass, field, province, range, region, sphere.

circuit n ambit, circumambience, circumambiency, cycle, revolution, turn; bounds, compass, district, field, province, range, region, space, sphere, tract; boundary, compass; course, detour, perambulation, round, tour.

circuitous adj ambiguous, devious, indirect, roundabout, tortuous, turning, winding.

circulate *vb* diffuse, disseminate, promulgate, propagate, publish, spread.

circumference *n* bound, boundary, circuit, girth, outline, perimeter, periphery.

circumscribe *vb* bound, define, encircle, enclose, encompass, limit, surround; confine, restrict.

circumspect *adj* attentive, careful, cautious, considerate, discreet, heedful, judicious, observant, prudent, vigilant, wary, watchful.

circumstance *n* accident, incident; condition, detail, event, fact, happening, occurrence, position, situation.

circumstantial *adj* detailed, particular; indirect, inferential, presumptive.

citizen *n* burgess, burgher, denizen, dweller, freeman, inhabitant, resident, subject, townsman.

civil *adj* civic, municipal, political; domestic, intestine; accommodating, affable, civilized, complaisant, courteous, courtly, debonair, easy, gracious, obliging, polished, polite, refined, suave, urbane, well-bred, well-mannered.

civility *n* affability, amiability, complaisance, courteousness, courtesy, goodbreeding, politeness, suavity, urbanity.

civilize *vb* cultivate, educate, enlighten, humanize, improve, polish, refine.

claim *vb* ask, assert, challenge, demand, exact, require. * *n* call, demand, lien, requisition; pretension, privilege, right, title.

clamour *vb* shout, vociferate. * *n* blare, din, exclamation, hullabaloo, noise, outcry, uproar, vociferation.

clandestine *adj* concealed, covert, fraudulent, furtive, hidden, private, secret, sly, stealthy, surreptitious, underhand.

clap *vb* pat, slap, strike; force, slam; applaud, cheer. * *n* blow, knock, slap; bang, burst, explosion, peal, slam.

clarify *vb* cleanse, clear, defecate, depurate, purify, strain.

clash *vb* collide, crash, strike; clang, clank, clatter, crash, rattle; contend, disagree, interfere. * *n* collision; clang, clangour, clank, clashing, clatter, crash, rattle; con-

tradiction, disagreement, interference, jar, jarring, opposition.

clasp *vb* clutch, entwine, grasp, grapple, grip, seize; embrace, enfold, fold, hug. * *n* buckle, catch, hasp, hook; embrace, hug.

class *vb* arrange, classify, dispose, distribute, range, rank. * *n* form, grade, order, rank, status; group, seminar; breed, kind, sort; category, collection, denomination, division, group, head.

classical *adj* first-rate, master, masterly, model, standard; Greek, Latin, Roman; Attic, chaste, elegant, polished, pure, refined.

classify *vb* arrange, assort, categorize, class, dispose, distribute, group. pigeonhole, rank, systematize, tabulate.

clatter *vb* clash, rattle; babble, clack, gabble, jabber, prate, prattle. * *n* clattering, clutter, rattling.

clean *vb* cleanse, clear, purge, purify, rinse, scour, scrub, wash. wipe. * *adj* immaculate, spotless, unsmirched, unsoiled, unspotted, unstained, unsullied, white; clarified, pure, purified, unadulterated, unmixed; adroit, delicate, dextrous, graceful, light, neat, shapely; complete, entire, flawless, faultless, perfect, unabated, unblemished, unimpaired, whole; chaste, innocent, moral, pure, undefiled. * *adv* altogether, completely, entirely, perfectly, quite, thoroughly, wholly.

cleanse *vb* clean, clear, elutriate, purge, purify, rinse, scour, scrub, wash, wipe.

clear *vb* clarify, cleanse, purify, refine; emancipate, disenthral, free, liberate, loose; absolve, acquit, discharge, exonerate, justify, vindicate; disembarrass, disengage, disentangle, extricate, loosen, rid; clean up, scour, sweep; balance; emancipate, free, liberate. * *adj* bright, crystalline, light, limpid, luminous, pellucid, transparent; pure, unadulterated, unmixed; free, open, unencumbered, unobstructed; cloudless, fair, serene, sunny, unclouded, undimmed, unobscured; net; distinct, intelligible, lucid, luminous, perspicuous; apparent, conspicuous, distinct, evident, indisputable, manifest, obvious, palpable, unambiguous, undeniable, unequivocal, unmistakable, unquestionable, visible; clean, guiltless, immaculate, innocent, irreproachable, sinless, spotless, unblemished, undefiled, unspotted, unsullied; unhampered, unimpeded, unobstructed; euphonious, fluty, liquid, mellifluous, musical, silvery, sonorous.

clemency n mildness, softness; compassion, fellow-feeling, forgivingness, gentleness, kindness, lenience, leniency, lenity, long-suffering, mercifulness, mercy, mildness, tenderness.

clench vb confirm, establish, fasten, fix, rivet, secure.

clever adj able, apt, gifted, talented; adroit, capable, dextrous, discerning, expert, handy, ingenious, knowing, quick, ready, skilful, smart, talented.

climax vb consummate, crown, culminate, peak. * n acme, consummation, crown, culmination, head, peak, summit, top, zenith.

clinch vb clasp, clench, clutch, grapple, grasp, grip; fasten, secure; confirm, establish, fix. * n catch, clutch, grasp, grip; clincher, clamp, cramp, holdfast.

cling vb adhere, clear, stick; clasp, embrace, entwine.

clink vb, n chink, jingle, ring, tinkle; chime, rhyme.

clip vb cut, shear, snip; curtail, cut, dock, pare, prune, trim. * n cutting, shearing; blow, knock, lick, rap, thump, thwack, thump.

cloak vb conceal, cover, dissemble, hide, mask, veil. * n mantle, surcoat; blind, cover, mask, pretext, veil.

clock vb mark time, measure, stopwatch. * n chronometer, horologue, timekeeper, timepiece, timer, watch.

clog vb fetter, hamper, shackle, trammel; choke, obstruct; burden, cumber, embarrass, encumber, hamper, hinder, impede, load, restrain, trammel. * n dead-weight, drag-weight, fetter, shackle, trammel; check, drawback, encumbrance, hindrance, impediment, obstacle, obstruction.

close¹ adj closed, confined, snug, tight; hidden, private, secret; incommunica-

tive, reserved, reticent, secretive, taciturn; concealed, retired, secluded, withdrawn; confined, motionless, stagnant; airless, oppressive, stale, stifling, stuffy, sultry; compact, compressed, dense, form, solid, thick; adjacent, adjoining, approaching, immediately, near, nearly, neighbouring; attached, dear, confidential, devoted, intimate; assiduous, earnest, fixed, intense, intent, unremitting; accurate, exact, faithful, nice, precise, strict; churlish, close-fisted, curmudgeonly, mean, illiberal, miserly, niggardly, parsimonious, penurious, stingy, ungenerous. * n courtyard, enclosure, grounds, precinct, yard.

close² vb occlude, seal, shut; choke, clog, estop, obstruct, stop; cease, complete, concede, end, finish, terminate; coalesce, unite; cease, conclude, finish, terminate; clinch, grapple; agree. * n cessation, conclusion, end, finish, termination.

clothe vb apparel, array, attire, deck, dress, rig; cover, endow, endow, envelop, enwrap, invest with, swathe.

clothes n apparel, array, attire, clothing, costume, dress, garb, garments, gear, habiliments, habits, raiment, rig, vestments, vesture.

cloud vb becloud, obnubilate, overcast, overspread; befog, darken, dim, obscure, shade, shadow. * n cirrus, cumulus, fog, haze, mist, nebulosity, scud, stratus, vapour; army, crowd, horde, host, multitude, swarm, throng; darkness, eclipse, gloom, obscuration, obscurity.

cloudy adj clouded, filmy, foggy, hazy, lowering, lurid, murky, overcast; confused, dark, dim, obscure; depressing, dismal, gloomy, sullen; clouded; blurred, dimmed, lustreless, muddy.

clown n churl, clod-breaker, clodhopper, countryman, hind, husbandman, lubber, peasant, ploughman, rustic, swain; boor, bumpkin, churl, fellow, lout; blockhead, dolt, clodpoll, dunce, dunderhead, numskull, simpleton, thickhead; buffoon, droll, farceur, fool, harlequin, jack-a-dandy, jack-pudding, jester, merry-andrew, mime, pantaloon, pickle-herring, punch, scaramouch, zany.

club *vb* combine, unite; beat, bludgeon, cudgel. * *n* bat, bludgeon, cosh, cudgel, hickory, shillelagh, stick, truncheon; association, company, coterie, fraternity, set, society, sodality.

clump *vb* assemble, batch, bunch, cluster, group, lump; lumber, stamp, stomp, stump, trudge. * *n* assemblage, bunch, cluster, collection, group, patch, tuft.

clumsy *adj* botched, cumbrous, heavy, ill-made, ill-shaped, lumbering, ponderous, unwieldy; awkward, blundering, bungling, elephantine, heavy-handed, inapt, mal adroit, unhandy, unskilled.

cluster *vb* assemble, batch, bunch, clump, collect, gather, group, lump, throng. * *n* agglomeration, assemblage, batch, bunch, clump, collection, gathering, group, throng.

clutch *vb* catch, clasp, clench, clinch, grab, grapple, grasp, grip, grapple, hold, seize, snatch, squeeze. * *n* clasp, clench, clinch, grasp, grip, hold, seizure, squeeze.

clutches *npl* claws, paws, talons; hands, power.

clutter *vb* confuse, disarrange, disarray, disorder, jumble, litter, mess, muss; clatter. * *n* bustle, clatter, clattering, racket; confusion, disarray, disorder, jumble, litter, mess, muss.

coagulate *vb* clot, congeal, concrete, curdle, thicken.

coalesce *vb* amalgamate, blend, cohere, combine, commix, incorporate, mix, unite; concur, fraternize.

coalition *n* alliance, association, combination, compact, confederacy, confederation, conjunction, conspiracy, co-partnership, federation, league, union.

coarse *adj* crude, impure, rough, unpurified; broad, gross, indecent, indelicate, ribald, vulgar; bearish, bluff, boorish, brutish, churlish, clownish, gruff, impolite, loutish, rude, unpolished; crass, inelegant.

coast *vb* flow, glide, roll, skim, sail, slide, sweep. * *n* littoral, seaboard, sea-coast, seaside, shore, strand; border.

coat *vb* cover, spread. * *n* cut-away, frock, jacket; coating, cover, covering; layer.

coax *vb* allure, beguile, cajole, cog, entice, flatter, persuade, soothe, wheedle.

cobble *vb* botch, bungle; mend, patch, repair, tinker.

coercion *n* check, curb, repression, restraint; compulsion, constraint, force.

coexistent *adj* coetaneous, coeval, simultaneous, synchronous.

coherence *n* coalition, cohesion, connection, dependence, union; agreement, congruity, consistency, correspondence, harmony, intelligibility, intelligible, meaning, rationality, unity.

coil *vb* curl, twine, twirl, twist, wind. * *n* convolution, curlicue, helix, knot, roll, spiral, tendril, twirl, volute, whorl; bustle, clamour, confusion, entanglements, perplexities, tumult, turmoil, uproar.

coincide *vb* cohere, correspond, square, tally; acquiesce, agree, harmonize, concur.

cold *adj* arctic, biting, bleak, boreal, chill, chilly, cutting, frosty, gelid, glacial, icy, nipping, polar, raw, wintry; frost-bitten, shivering; apathetic, cold-blooded, dead, freezing, frigid, indifferent, lukewarm, passionless, phlegmatic, sluggish, stoical, stony, torpid, unconcerned, unfeeling, unimpressible, unresponsive, unsusceptible, unsympathetic; dead, dull, spiritless, unaffecting, uninspiring, uninteresting. * *n* chill, chilliness, coldness.

collapse *vb* break down, fail, fall. * *n* depression, exhaustion, failure, faint, prostration, sinking, subsidence.

colleague *n* aider, ally, assistant, associate, auxiliary, coadjutor, collaborator, companion, confederate, confrere, cooperator, helper, partner.

collect *vb* assemble, compile, gather, muster; accumulate, aggregate, amass, garner.

collected *adj* calm, composed, cool, placid, self-possessed, serene, unperturbed.

collection *n* aggregation, assemblage, cluster, crowd, drove, gathering, group, pack; accumulation, congeries, conglomeration, heap, hoard, lot, mass, pile, store; alms, contribution, offering, offertory.

collision *n* clash, concussion, crash, encounter, impact, impingement, shock; conflict, crashing, interference, opposition.

collusion n connivance, conspiracy, coven, craft, deceit.

colossal adj Cyclopean, enormous, gigantic, Herculean, huge, immense, monstrous, prodigious, vast.

colour vb discolour, dye, paint, stain, tinge, tint; disguise, varnish; disguise, distort, garble, misrepresent, pervert; blush, colour, flush, redden, show. * n hue, shade, tinge, tint, tone; paint, pigment, stain; redness, rosiness, ruddiness; complexion; appearance, disguise, excuse, guise, plea, pretence, pretext, semblance.

colourless adj achromatic, uncoloured, untinged; blanched, hueless, livid, pale, pallid; blank, characterless, dull, expressionless, inexpressive, monotonous.

comatose adj drowsy, lethargic, sleepy, somnolent, stupefied.

comb vb card, curry, dress, groom, rake, unknot, untangle; rake, ransack, rummage, scour, search. * n card, hatchel, ripple; harrow, rake.

combat vb contend, contest, fight, struggle, war; battle, oppose, resist, struggle, withstand. * n action, affair, battle, brush, conflict, contest, encounter, fight, skirmish.

combative adj belligerent, contentious, militant, pugnacious, quarrelsome.

combination n association, conjunction, connection, union; alliance, cartel, coalition, confederacy, consolidation, league, merger, syndicate; cabal, clique, conspiracy, faction, junta, ring; amalgamation, compound, mixture.

combine vb cooperate, merge, pool, unite; amalgamate, blend, incorporate, mix.

come vb advance, approach; arise, ensue, flow, follow, issue, originate, proceed, result; befall, betide, happen, occur.

comely adj becoming, decent, decorous, fitting, seemly, suitable; beautiful, fair, graceful, handsome, personable, pretty, symmetrical.

comfort vb alleviate, animate, cheer, console, encourage, enliven, gladden, inspir-

it, invigorate, refresh, revive, solace, soothe, strengthen. * n aid, assistance, countenance, help, support, succour; consolation, solace, encouragement, relief; ease, enjoyment, peace, satisfaction.

comfortable adj acceptable, agreeable, delightful, enjoyable, grateful, gratifying, happy, pleasant, pleasurable, welcome; commodious, convenient, easeful, snug; painless.

comical adj amusing, burlesque, comic, diverting, droll, farcical, funny, humorous, laughable, ludicrous, sportive, whimsical.

coming adj approaching, arising, arriving, ensuing, eventual, expected, forthcoming, future, imminent, issuing, looming, nearing, prospective, ultimate; emergent, emerging, successful; due, owed, owing. * n advent, approach, arrival; forthcomingness, imminence, imminency, nearness; apparition, appearance, disclosure, emergence, manifestation, materialization, occurrence, presentation, revelation, rising.

command vb bid, charge, direct, enjoin, order, require; control, dominate, govern, lead, rule, sway; claim, challenge, compel, demand, exact. * n behest, bidding, charge, commandment, direction, hest, injunction, mandate, order, requirement, requisition; ascendency, authority, dominion, control, government, power, rule, sway, supremacy.

commander n captain, chief, chieftain, commandment, head, leader.

commence vb begin, inaugurate, initiate, institute, open, originate, start.

commend vb bespeak, recommend, regard for; commit, entrust, yield; applaud, approve, eulogize, extol, laud, praise.

comment vb animadvert, annotate, criticize, explain, interpret, note, remark. * n annotation, elucidation, explanation, exposition, illustration, commentary, note, gloss; animadversion, observation, remark.

commentator n annotator, commentator, critic, expositor, expounder, interpreter.

commerce n business, exchange, dealing, trade, traffic; communication, communion, intercourse.

commercial adj mercantile, trading.

commission vb authorize, empower; delegate, depute. * n doing, perpetration; care, charge, duty, employment, errand, office, task, trust; allowance, compensation, fee, rake-off.

commit vb confide, consign, delegate, entrust, remand; consign, deposit, lay, place, put, relegate, resign; do, enact, perform, perpetrate; imprison; engage, implicate, pledge.

commodity n goods, merchandise, produce, wares.

common adj collective, public; general, useful; commonplace, customary, everyday, familiar, frequent, habitual, usual; banal, hackneyed, stale, threadbare, trite; indifferent, inferior, low, ordinary, plebeian, popular, undistinguished, vulgar.

commotion n agitation, disturbance, ferment, perturbation, welter; ado, bustle, disorder, disturbance, hurly-burly, pother, tumult, turbulence, turmoil.

communicate vb bestow, confer, convey, give, impart, transmit; acquaint, announce, declare, disclose, divulge, publish, reveal, unfold; commune, converse, correspond.

communication n conveyance, disclosure, giving, imparting, transmittal; commence, conference, conversation, converse, correspondence, intercourse; announcement, dispatch, information, message, news.

communicative adj affable, chatty, conversable, free, open, sociable, unreserved.

community n commonwealth, people, public, society; association, brotherhood, college, society; identify, likeness, participacy, sameness, similarity.

compact¹ vb agreement, arrangement, bargain, concordant, contract, covenant, convention, pact, stipulation, treaty.

compact² vb compress, condense, pack, press; bind, consolidate, unite. * adj close, compressed, condensed, dense, firm, solid; brief, compendious, concise,

laconic, pithy, pointed, sententious, short, succinct, terse.

companion n accomplice, ally, associate, comrade, compeer, confederate, consort, crony, friend, fellow, mate; partaker, participant, participator, partner, sharer.

companionable adj affable, conversable, familiar, friendly, genial, neighbourly, sociable.

company n assemblage, assembly, band, bevy, body, circle, collection, communication, concourse, congregation, coterie, crew, crowd, flock, gang, gathering, group, herd, rout, set, syndicate, troop; party; companionship, company, fellowship, guests, society, visitor, visitors; association, copartnership, corporation, firm, house, partnership.

compare vb assimilate, balance, collate, parallel; liken, resemble.

comparison n collation, compare, estimate; simile, similitude.

compass vb embrace, encompass, enclose, encircle, environ, surround; beleaguer, beset, besiege, block, blockade, invest; accomplish, achieve, attain, carry, consummate, effect, obtain, perform, procure, realize; contrive, devise, intend, meditate, plot, purpose. * n bound, boundary, extent, gamut, limit, range, reach, register, scope, stretch; circuit, round.

compassion n clemency, commiseration, condolence, fellow-feeling, heart, humanity, kind-heartedness, kindness, kindliness, mercy, pity, rue, ruth, sorrow, sympathy, tenderheartedness, tenderness.

compassionate adj benignant, clement, commiserative, gracious, kind, merciful, pitying, ruthful, sympathetic, tender.

compatible adj accordant, agreeable to, congruous, consistent, consonant, reconcilable, suitable.

compel vb constrain, force, coerce, drive, necessitate, oblige; bend, bow, subdue, subject.

compensation n pay, payment, recompense, remuneration, reward, salary; amends, atonement, indemnification, indemnity, reparation, requital, satisfaction; balance, counterpoise, equalization, offset.

compete vb contend, contest, cope, emulate, rival, strive, struggle, vie.

competence n ability, capableness, capacity, fitness, qualification, suitableness; adequacy, adequateness, enough, sufficiency.

competent adj able, capable, clever, equal, endowed, qualified; adapted, adequate, convenient, fit, sufficient, suitable.

competition n contest, emulation, rivalry, rivals.

competitor n adversary, antagonist, contestant, emulator, opponent.

compile vb compose, prepare, write; arrange, collect, select.

complain vb bemoan, bewail, deplore, grieve, groan, grouch, growl, grumble, lament, moan, murmur, repine, whine.

complaint n grievance, grumble, lament, lamentation, plaint, murmur, wail; ail, ailment, annoyance, disease, disorder, illness, indisposition, malady, sickness; accusation, charge, information

complete vb accomplish, achieve, conclude, consummate, do, effect, effectuate, end, execute, finish, fulfil, perfect, perform, realize, terminate. * adj clean, consummate, faultless, full, perfect, form, thorough; all, entire, integral, total, unbroken, undiminished, undivided, unimpaired, whole; accomplished, achieved, completed, concluded, consummated, ended, finished.

completion n accomplishing, accomplishment, achieving, conclusion, consummation, effecting, effectuation, ending, execution, finishing, perfecting, performance, termination.

complex adj composite, compound, compounded, manifold, mingled, mixed; complicate, complicated, entangled, intricate, involved, knotty, mazy, tangled. * n complexus, complication, involute, skein, tangle, tangle; entirety, integration, network, totality, whole; compulsion, fixation, obsession, preoccupation, prepossession; prejudice.

complexity n complication, entanglement, intricacy, involution.

complicate vb confuse, entangle, interweave, involve.

complication n complexity, confusion, entanglement, intricacy; combination, complexus, mixture.

compliment vb commend, congratulate, eulogize, extol, flatter, laud, praise. * n admiration, commendation, courtesy, encomium, eulogy, favour, flattery, honour, laudation, praise, tribute.

complimentary adj commendatory, congratulatory, encomiastic, eulogistic, flattering, laudatory, panegyrical.

component adj composing, constituent, constituting. * n constituent, element, ingredient, part.

compose vb build, compact, compound, constitute, form, make, synthesize; contrive, create, frame, imagine, indite, invent, write; adjust, arrange, regulate, settle; appease, assuage, calm, pacify, quell, quiet, soothe, still, tranquillize.

composed adj calm, collected, cool, imperturbable, placid, quiet, sedate, self-possessed, tranquil, undisturbed, unmoved, unruffled.

composite adj amalgamated, combined, complex, compounded, mixed; integrated, unitary. * n admixture, amalgam, blend, combination, composition, compound, mixture, unification.

composition n constitution, construction, formation, framing, making; compound, mixture; arrangement, combination, conjunction, make-up, synthesize, union; invention, opus, piece, production, writing; agreement, arrangement, compromise.

composure n calmness, coolness, equanimity, placidity, sedateness, quiet, self-possession, serenity, tranquillity.

compound vb amalgamate, blend, combine, intermingle, intermix, mingle, mix, unite; adjust, arrange, compose, compromise, settle. * adj complex, composite. * n combination, composition, mixture; farrago, hodgepodge, jumble, medley, mess, olio.

comprehend vb comprise, contain, embrace, embody, enclose, include, involve; apprehend, conceive, discern, grasp, know, imagine, mentally, perceive, see, understand.

comprehension n comprising, embracing, inclusion; compass, domain, embrace, field, limits, province, range, reach, scope, sphere, sweep; connotation, depth, force, intention; conception, grasp, intelligence, understanding; intellect, intelligence, mind, reason, understanding.

comprehensive adj all-embracing, ample, broad, capacious, compendious, extensive, full, inclusive, large, sweeping, wide.

compression n abbreviation, condensation, confining, constriction, contraction, pinching, pressing, squeezing; brevity, pithiness, succinctness, terseness.

comprise vb comprehend, contain, embody, embrace, enclose, include, involve.

compromise vb adjust, arbitrate, arrange, compose, compound, settle; imperil, jeopardize, prejudice; commit, engage, implicate, pledge; agree, compound. * n adjustment, agreement, composition, settlement.

compulsion n coercion, constraint, force, forcing, pressure, urgency.

compulsory adj coercive, compelling, constraining; binding, enforced, imperative, necessary, obligatory, unavoidable.

compute vb calculate, count, enumerate, estimate, figure, measure, number, rate, reckon, sum.

comrade n accomplice, ally, associate, chum, companion, compatriot, compeer, crony, fellow, mate, pal.

conceal vb bury, cover, screen, secrete; disguise, dissemble, mask.

concede vb grant, surrender, yield; acknowledge, admit, allow, confess, grant.

conceit n belief, conception, fancy, idea, image, imagination, notion, thought; caprice, illusion, vagary, whim; estimate, estimation, impression, judgement, opinion; conceitedness, egoism, self-complacency, priggishness, priggery, self-conceit, self-esteem, self-suf-

ficiency, vanity; crochet, point, quip, quirk.

conceited adj egotistical, opinionated, opinionative, overweening, self-conceited, vain.

conceivable adj imaginable, picturable; cogitable, comprehensible, intelligible, rational, thinkable.

conceive vb create, contrive, devise, form, plan, purpose; fancy, imagine; comprehend, fathom, think, understand; assume, imagine, suppose; bear, become pregnant.

concern vb affect, belong to, interest, pertain to, regard, relate to, touch; disquiet, disturb, trouble. * n affair, business, matter, transaction; concernment, consequence, importance, interest, moment, weight; anxiety, care, carefulness, solicitude, worry; business, company, establishment, firm, house.

concession n acquiescence, assent, cessation, compliance, surrender, yielding; acknowledgement, allowance, boon, confession, grant, privilege.

concise adj brief, compact, compendious, comprehensive, compressed, condensed, crisp, laconic, pithy, pointed, pregnant, sententious, short, succinct, summary, terse.

conclude vb close, end, finish, terminate; deduce, gather, infer, judge; decide, determine, judge; arrange, complete, settle; bar, hinder, restrain, stop; decide, determine, resolve.

conclusion n deduction, inference; decision, determination, judgement; close, completion, end, event, finale, issue, termination, upshot; arrangement, closing, effecting, establishing, settlement.

conclusive adj clinching, convincing, decisive, irrefutable, unanswerable; final, ultimate.

concrete vb cake, congeal, coagulate, harden, solidify, thicken. * adj compact, consolidated, firm, solid, solidified; agglomerated, complex, conglomerated, compound, concreted; completely, entire, individualized, total. * n compound, concretion, mixture; cement.

concur vb accede, acquiesce, agree, approve, assent, coincide, consent, harmonize; combine, conspire, cooperate, help.

condemn vb adjudge, ban, convict, doom, judge, penalize, sentence; disapprove, proscribe, reprobate; blame, censure, damn, deprecate, disapprove, reprehend, reprove, upbraid.

condense vb compress, concentrate, consolidate, densify, thicken; abbreviate, abridge, contract, curtail, diminish, epitomize, reduce, shorten, summarize; liquefy.

condescend vb deign, vouchsafe; descend, stoop, submit.

condescension n affability, civility, courtesy, deference, favour, graciousness, obeisance.

condition vb postulate, specify, stipulate; groom, prepare, qualify, ready, train; acclimatize, accustom, adapt, adjust, familiarize, habituate, naturalize; attune, commission, fix, overhaul, prepare, recondition, repair, service, tune. * n case, circumstances, plight, predicament, situation, state; class, estate, grade, rank, station; arrangement, consideration, provision, proviso, stipulation; attendant, necessity, postulate, precondition, prerequisite.

condole vb commiserate, compassionate, console, sympathize.

conducive adj conducting, contributing, instrumental, promotive, subservient, subsidiary.

conduct vb convoy, direct, escort, lead; administer, command, govern, lead, preside, superintend; manage, operate, regulate; direct, lead. * n administration, direction, guidance, leadership, management; convoy, escort, guard; actions, bearing, behaviour, career, carriage, demeanour, deportment, manners.

confer vb advise, consult, converse, deliberate, discourse, parley, talk; bestow, give, grant, vouchsafe.

confess vb acknowledge, admit, avow, own; admit, concede, grant, recognize; attest, exhibit, manifest, prove, show; shrive.

confession n acknowledgement, admission, avowal.

confide vb commit, consign, entrust, trust.

confidence n belief, certitude, dependence, faith, reliance, trust; aplomb, assurance, boldness, cocksureness, courage, firmness, intrepidity, self-reliance; secrecy.

confident adj assured, certain, cocksure, positive, sure: bold, presumptuous. sanguine, undaunted.

confidential adj intimate, private, secret; faithful, trustworthy.

confine vb restrain, shut in, shut up; immure, imprison, incarcerate, impound, jail, mew; bound, circumscribe, limit, restrict. * n border, boundary, frontier, limit.

confinement n restraint; captivity, duress, durance, immurement, imprisonment, incarceration; childbed, childbirth, delivery, lying-in, parturition.

confirm vb assure, establish, fix, settle; strengthen; authenticate, avouch, corroborate, countersign, endorse, substantiate, verify; bind, ratify, sanction.

confirmation n establishment, settlement; corroboration, proof, substantiation, verification.

confiscate vb appropriate, forfeit, seize.

conflict vb clash, combat, contend, contest, disagree, fight, interfere, strive, struggle. * n battle, collision, combat, contention, contest, encounter, fight, struggle; antagonism, clashing, disagreement, discord, inconsistency, inharmony, interference, opposition.

conform vb accommodate, adapt, adjust; agree, comport, correspond, harmonize, square, tally.

conformation n accordance, agreement, compliance, conformity; configuration, figure, form, manner, shape, structure.

confound vb confuse; baffle, bewilder, embarrass, flurry, mystify, nonplus, perplex, pose; amaze, astonish, astound, bewilder, dumfound, paralyse, petrify, startle, stun, stupefy, surprise; annihilate, demolish, destroy, overthrow, overwhelm, ruin; abash, confuse, discompose, disconcert, mortify, shame.

confront vb face; challenge, contrapose, encounter, oppose, threaten.

confuse *vb* blend, confound, intermingle, mingle, mix; derange, disarrange, disorder, jumble, mess, muddle; darken, obscure, perplex; befuddle, bewilder, embarrass, flabbergast, flurry, fluster, mystify, nonplus, pose; abash, confound, discompose, disconcert, mortify, shame.

confusion *n* anarchy, chaos, clutter, confusedness, derangement, disarrangement, disarray, disorder, jumble, muddle; agitation, commotion, ferment, stir, tumult, turmoil; astonishment, bewilderment, distraction, embarrassment, fluster, fuddle, perplexity; abashment, embarrassment, mortification, shame; annihilation, defeat, demolition, destruction, overthrow, ruin.

congratulate *vb* compliment, felicitate, gratulate, greet, hail, salute.

congregate *vb* assemble, collect, convene, convoke, gather, muster; gather, meet, swarm, throng.

congress *n* assembly, conclave, conference, convention, convocation, council, diet, meeting.

congruous *adj* accordant, agreeing, compatible, consistent, consonant, suitable; appropriate, befitting, fit, meet, proper, seemly.

conjecture *vb* assume, guess, hypothesis, imagine, suppose. surmise, suspect; dare say, fancy, presume. * *n* assumption, guess, hypothesis, supposition, surmise, theory.

conjure *vb* adjure, beg, beseech, crave, entreat, implore, invoke, pray, supplicate; bewitch, charm, enchant, fascinate; juggle.

connect *vb* associate, conjoin, combine, couple, hyphenate, interlink, join, link, unite; cohere, interlock.

connection *n* alliance, association, dependence, junction, union; commerce, communication, intercourse; affinity, relationship; kindred, kinsman, relation, relative.

conquer *vb* beat, checkmate, crush, defeat, discomfit, humble, master, overcome, overpower, overthrow, prevail, quell, reduce, rout, subdue, subjugate, vanquish; overcome, surmount.

conquest *n* defeat, discomfiture, mastery, overthrow, reduction, subjection, subjugation; triumph, victor; winning.

conscientious *adj* careful, exact, fair, faithful, high-principled, honest, honourable, incorruptible, just, scrupulous, straightforward, uncorrupt, upright.

conscious *adj* intelligent, knowing, percipient, sentient; intellectual, rational, reasoning, reflecting, self-conscious, thinking; apprised, awake, aware, cognizant, percipient, sensible; self-admitted, self-accusing.

consecutive *adj* following, succeeding.

consent *vb* agree, allow, assent, concur, permit, yield; accede, acquiesce, comply. * *n* approval, assent, concurrence, permission; accord, agreement, consensus, concord, cooperation, harmony, unison; acquiescence, compliance.

consequence *n* effect, end, event, issue, result; conclusion, deduction, inference; concatenation, connection, consecution; concern, distinction, importance, influence, interest, moment, standing, weight.

consequential *adj* consequent, following, resulting, sequential; arrogant, conceited, inflated, pompous, pretentious, self-important, self-sufficient, vainglorious.

conservation *n* guardianship, maintenance, preservation, protection

conservative *adj* conservatory, moderate, moderationist; preservative; reactionary, unprogressive. * *n* die-hard, reactionary, redneck, rightist, right-winger; moderate; preservative.

conserve *vb* keep, maintain, preserve, protect, save, sustain, uphold. * *n* comfit, confection, jam, preserve, sweetmeat.

consider *vb* attend, brood, contemplate, examine, heed, mark, mind, ponder, reflect, revolve, study, weigh; care for, consult, envisage, regard, respect; cogitate, deliberate, mediate, muse, ponder, reflect, ruminate, think; account, believe, deem, hold, judge, opine.

considerate *adj* circumspect, deliberate, discrete, judicious, provident, prudent, serious, sober, staid, thoughtful; charitable, forbearing, patient.

consideration *n* attention, cogitation, contemplation, deliberation, notice, heed, meditation, pondering, reflection, regard; consequence, importance, important, moment, significant, weight; account, cause, ground, motive, reason, sake, score.

consistency n compactness, consistence, density, thickness; agreement, compatibility, conformableness, congruity, consonance, correspondence, harmony.

consistent adj accordant, agreeing, comfortable, compatible, congruous, consonant, correspondent, harmonious, logical.

consolation n alleviation, comfort, encouragement, relieve, solace.

console vb assuage, calm, cheer, comfort, encourage, solace, relieve, soothe.

consolidate vb cement, compact, compress, condense, conduce, harden, solidify, thicken; combine, conjoin, fuse, unite.

conspicuous adj apparent, clear, discernible, glaring, manifest, noticeable, perceptible, plain, striking, visible; celebrated, distinguished, eminent, famed, famous, illustrious, marked, noted, outstanding, pre-eminent, prominent, remarkable, signal.

conspiracy n cabal, collusion, confederation, intrigue, league, machination, plot, scheme.

conspire vb concur, conduce, cooperate; combine, compass, contrive, devise, project; confederate, contrive, hatch, plot, scheme.

constant adj abiding, enduring, fixed, immutable, invariable, invariant, permanent, perpetual, stable, unalterable, unchanging, unvaried; certain, regular, stated, uniform; determined, firm, resolute, stanch, steadfast, steady, unanswering, undeviating, unmoved, unshaken, unwavering; assiduous, diligent, persevering, sedulous, tenacious, unremitting; continual, continuous, incessant, perpetual, sustained, unbroken, uninterrupted; devoted, faithful, loyal, true, trusty.

consternation n alarm, amazement, awe, bewilderment, dread, fear, fright, horror, panic, terror.

constituent adj component, composing, constituting, forming; appointing, electoral. * n component, element, ingredient, principal; elector, voter.

constitute vb compose, form, make; appoint, delegate, depute, empower; enact, establish, fix, set up.

constitution n establishment, formation, make-up, organization, structure; character, characteristic, disposition, form, habit, humour, peculiarity, physique, quality, spirit, temper, temperament.

constitutional adj congenital, connate, inborn, inbred, inherent, innate, natural, organic; lawful, legal, legitimate. * n airing, exercise, promenade, stretch, walk.

constrain vb coerce, compel, drive, force; chain, confine, curb, enthral, hold, restrain; draw, impel, urge.

constriction n compression, constraint, contraction.

construct vb build, fabricate, erect, raise, set up; arrange, establish, form, found, frame, institute, invent, make, organize, originate.

construction n building, erection, fabrication; configuration, conformation, figure, form, formation, made, shape, structure; explanation, interpretation, rendering, version.

consult vb advise, ask, confer, counsel, deliberate, interrogate, question; consider, regard.

consume vb absorb, decay, destroy, devour, dissipate, exhaust, expend, lavish, lessen, spend, squander, vanish, waste.

consummate[1] vb accomplish, achieve, compass, complete, conclude, crown, effect, effectuate, end, execute, finish, perfect, perform.

consummate[2] adj complete, done, effected, finished, fulfilled, perfect, supreme.

consumption n decay, decline, decrease, destruction, diminution, expenditure, use, waste; atrophy, emaciation.

contact vb hit, impinge, touch; approach, be heard, communicate with, reach. * n approximation, contiguity, junction, juxtaposition, taction, tangency, touch.

contain vb accommodate, comprehend,

comprise, embody, embrace, enclose, include; check, restrain

contaminate vb corrupt, defile, deprave, infect, poison, pollute, soil, stain, sully, taint, tarnish, vitiate.

contemplate vb behold, gaze upon, observe, survey; consider, dwell on, meditate on, muse on, ponder, reflect upon, study, survey, think about; design, intend, mean, plan, purpose.

contemplation n cogitation, deliberation, meditation, pondering, reflection, speculation, study, thought; prospect, prospective, view; expectation.

contemporary adj coetaneous, coeval, coexistent, coexisting, coincident, concomitant, concurrent, contemporaneous, current, present, simultaneous, synchronous; advanced, modern, modernistic, progressive, up-to-date. * n coeval, coexistent, compeer, fellow.

contempt n contumely, derision, despite, disdain, disregard, misprision, mockery, scorn, slight.

contemptible adj abject, base, despicable, haughty, insolent, insulting, low, mean, paltry, pitiful, scurvy, sorry, supercilious, vile, worthless.

contemptuous adj arrogant, contumelious, disdainful, haughty, insolent, insulting, scornful, sneering, supercilious.

contend vb battle, combat, compete, contest, fight, strive, struggle, vie; argue, debate, dispute, litigate; affirm, assert, calm, maintain.

content[1] n essence, gist, meaning, meat, stuff, substance; capacity, measure, space, volume.

content[2] vb appease, delight, gladden, gratify, humour, indulge, please, satisfy, suffice. * adj agreeable, contented, happy, pleased, satisfied. * n contentment, ease, peace, satisfaction.

contest vb argue, contend, controvert, debate, dispute, litigate, question; strive, struggle; compete, cope, fight, vie. * n altercation, contention, controversy, difference, dispute, debate, quarrel; affray, battle, bout, combat, conflict, encounter, fight, match, scrimmage, struggle, tussle; competition, contention, rivalry.

continual adj constant, constant, perpetual, unceasing, uninterrupted, unremitting; endless, eternal, everlasting, interminable, perennial, permanent, perpetual, unending; constant, oft-repeated.

continuance n abiding, continuation, duration, endurance, lasting, persistence, stay; continuation, extension, perpetuation, prolongation, protraction; concatenation, connection, sequence, succession; constancy, endurance, perseverance, persistence.

continue vb endure, last, remain; abide, linger, remain, stay, tarry; endure, persevere, persist, stick; extend, prolong, perpetuate, protract.

continuous adj connected, continued, extended, prolonged, unbroken, unintermitted, uninterrupted.

contract vb abbreviate, abridge, condense, confine, curtail, diminish, epitomize, lessen, narrow, reduce, shorten; absorb, catch, incur, get, make, take; constrict, shrink, shrivel, wrinkle; agree, bargain, covenant, engage, pledge, stipulate. * n agreement, arrangement, bargain, bond, compact, concordat, covenant, convention, engagement, pact, stipulation, treaty.

contradict vb assail, challenge, controvert, deny, dispute, gainsay, impugn, traverse; abrogate, annul, belie, counter, disallow, negative, contravene, counteract, oppose, thwart.

contradictory adj antagonistic, contrary, incompatible, inconsistent, negating, opposed, opposite, repugnant.

contrary adj adverse, counter, discordant, opposed, opposing, opposite; antagonistic, conflicting, contradictory, repugnant, retroactive; forward, headstrong, humoursome, obstinate, refractory, stubborn, unruly, wayward, perverse. * n antithesis, converse, obverse, opposite, reverse.

contrast vb compare, differentiate, distinguish, oppose. * n contrariety, difference, opposition; comparison, distinction.

contravene vb abrogate, annul, contradict, counteract, countervail, cross, go against, hinder, interfere, nullify, oppose, set aside, thwart, transgress, traverse, violate.

contribute vb bestow, donate, give, grant, subscribe; afford, aid, furnish, supply; concur, conduce, conspire, cooperate, minister, serve, tend.

contribution n bestowal, bestowment, grant; donation, gift, offering, subscription.

contrive vb arrange, brew, concoct, design, devise, effect, form, frame, hatch, invent, plan, project; consider, plan, plot, scheme; manage, make out.

control vb command, direct, dominate, dominate, govern, manage, oversee, sway, regulate, rule, superintend; bridle, check, counteract, curb, check, hinder, repress, restrain. * n ascendency, command, direction, disposition, dominion, government, guidance, mastery, oversight, regiment, regulation, rule, superintendence, supremacy, sway.

controversy n altercation, argument, contention, debate, discussion, disputation, dispute, logomachy, polemics, quarrel, strife; lawsuit.

convenience n fitness, propriety, suitableness; accessibility, accommodation, comfort, commodiousness, ease, handiness, satisfaction, serviceability, serviceableness.

convenient adj adapted, appropriate, fit, fitted, proper, suitable, suited; advantageous, beneficial, comfortable, commodious, favourable, handy, helpful, serviceable, timely, useful.

convention n assembly, congress, convocation, meeting; agreement, bargain, compact, contract, pact, stipulation, treaty; custom, formality, usage.

conventional adj agreed on, bargained for, stipulated; accustomed, approved, common, customary, everyday, habitual, ordinary, orthodox, regular, standard, traditional, usual, wonted.

conversation n chat, colloquy, communion, confabulation, conference, converse, dialogue, discourse, intercourse, interlocution, parley, talk.

converse¹ vb commune; chat, confabulate, discourse, gossip, parley, talk. * n commerce, communication, intercourse; colloquy, conversation, talk.

converse² adj adverse, contradictory, contrary, counter, opposed, opposing, opposite; n antithesis, contrary, opposite, reverse.

conversion n change, reduction, resolution, transformation, transmutation; interchange, reversal, transposition.

convert vb alter, change, transform, transmute; interchange, reverse, transpose; apply, appropriate, convince. * n catechumen, disciple, neophyte, proselyte.

convey vb bear, bring, carry, fetch, transmit, transport, waft; abalienate, alienate, cede, consign, deliver, demise, devise, devolve, grant, sell, transfer.

convict vb condemn, confute, convince, imprison, sentence. * n criminal, culprit, felon, malefactor, prisoner.

convoy vb accompany, attend, escort, guard, protect. * n attendance, attendant, escort, guard, protection.

convulse vb agitate, derange, disorder, disturb, shake, shatter.

convulsion n cramp, fit, spasm; agitation, commotion, disturbance, shaking, tumult.

cook vb bake, boil, broil, fry, grill, microwave, roast, spit-roast, steam, stir-fry; falsify, garble.

cool vb chill, ice, refrigerate; abate, allay, calm, damp, moderate, quiet, temper. * adj calm, collected, composed, dispassionate, placid, sedate, self-possessed, quiet, staid, unexcited, unimpassioned, undisturbed, unruffled; cold-blooded, indifferent, lukewarm, unconcerned; apathetic, chilling, freezing, frigid, repellent; bold, impertinent, impudent, self-possessed, shameless. * n chill, chilliness, coolness; calmness, composure, coolheadedness, countenance, equanimity, poise, self-possession, self-restraint.

cooperate vb abet, aid, assist, co-act, collaborate, combine, concur, conduce, conspire, contribute, help, unite.

cooperation n aid, assistance, co-action, concert, concurrence, collaboration, synergy.

coordinate vb accord, agree, arrange, equalize, harmonize, integrate, methodize, organize, regulate, synchronize, systematize. * adj coequal, equal, equivalent, tantamount; coincident, synchronous. * n complement, counterpart, like, pendant; companion, fellow, match, mate.

cope vb combat, compete, contend, encounter, engage, strive, struggle, vie.

copious adj abundant, ample, exuberant, full, overflowing, plenteous, plentiful, profuse, rich.

copy vb duplicate, reproduce, trace, transcribe; follow, imitate, pattern. * n counterscript, duplicate, facsimile, offprint, replica, reproduction, transcript; archetype, model, original, pattern; manuscript, typescript.

cordial adj affectionate, ardent, earnest, heartfelt, hearty, sincere, warm, warmhearted; grateful, invigorating, restorative, pleasant, refreshing. * n balm, balsam, elixir, tisane, tonic; liqueur.

core n centre, essence, heart, kernel.

corner vb confound, confuse, nonplus, perplex, pose, puzzle. * n angle, bend, crutch, cusp, elbow, joint, knee; niche, nook, recess, retreat.

corps n band, body, company, contingent, division, platoon, regiment, squad, squadron, troop.

corpse n body, carcass, corse, remains; ashes, dust.

correct vb adjust, amend, cure, improve, mend, reclaim, rectify, redress, reform, regulate, remedy; chasten, discipline, punish. * adj accurate, equitable, exact, faultless, just, precise, proper, regular, right, true, upright.

correction n amendment, improvement, redress; chastening, discipline, punishment.

correspond vb accord, agree, answer, comport, conform, fit, harmonize, match, square, suit, tally; answer, belong, correlate; communicate.

correspondence n accord, agreement, coincidence, concurrence, conformity, congruity, fitness, harmony, match; correlation, counterposition; communication, letters, writing.

corrode vb canker, erode, gnaw; consume, deteriorate, rust, waste; blight, embitter, envenom, poison.

corrosive adj acrid, biting, consuming, cathartic, caustic, corroding, eroding, erosive, violent; consuming, corroding, gnawing, mordant, wasting, wearing; blighting, cankerous, carking, embittering, envenoming, poisoning.

corrupt vb putrefy, putrid, render; contaminate, defile, infect, pollute, spoil, taint, vitiate; degrade, demoralize, deprave, pervert, vitiate; adulterate, debase, falsify, sophisticate; bribe, entice. * adj contaminated, corrupted, impure, infected, putrid, rotten, spoiled, tainted, unsound; abandoned, debauched, depraved, dissolute, profligate, reprobate, vicious, wicked; bribable, buyable.

corruption n putrefaction, putrescence, rottenness; adulteration, contamination, debasement, defilement, infection, perversion, pollution, vitiation; demoralization, depravation, depravity, immorality, laxity, sinfulness, wickedness; bribery, dishonesty.

cost vb absorb, consume, require. * n amount, charge, expenditure, expense, outlay, price; costliness, preciousness, richness, splendour, sumptuousness; damage, detriment, loss, plain, sacrifice, suffering.

costly adj dear, expensive, high-priced; gorgeous, luxurious, precious, rich, splendid, sumptuous, valuable.

cosy adj comfortable, easy, snug; chatty, conversable, social, talkative.

couch vb lie, recline; crouch, squat; bend down, stoop; conceal, cover up, hide; lay, level. * n bed, davenport, divan, lounge, seat, settee, settle, sofa.

council n advisers, cabinet, ministry; assembly, congress, conclave, convention, convocation, diet, husting, meeting, parliament, synod.

counsel vb admonish, advise, caution, recommend, warm. * n counsel; admonition, advice, caution, instruction, opinion, recommendation, suggestion; deliberation, forethought; advocate, barrister, counsellor, lawyer.

count vb enumerate, number, score; calculate, cast, compute, estimate, reckon; account, consider, deem, esteem, hold, judge, regard, think; tell. * n reckoning, tally.

countenance vb abet, aid, approve, assist, befriend, encourage, favour, patronize, sanction, support. * n aspect, look, men; aid, approbation, approval, assistance, encouragement, favour, patronage, sanction, support.

counteract vb check, contravene, cross, counter, defeat, foil, frustrate, hinder, oppose, resist, thwart, traverse; annul, countervail, counterbalance, destroy, neutralize, offset.

counterfeit vb forge, imitate; fake, feign, pretend, sham, simulate; copy, imitate. * adj fake, forged, fraudulent, spurious, supposititious; false, feigned, hypocritical, mock, sham, simulated, spurious; copies, imitated, resembling. * n copy, fake, forgery, sham.

counterpart n copy, duplicate; complement, correlate, correlative, reverse, supplement; fellow, mate, match, tally, twin.

country n land, region; countryside; fatherland, home, kingdom, state, territory; nation, people, population. * adj rural, rustic; countrified, rough, rude, uncultivated, unpolished, unrefined.

couple vb pair, unite; copulate, embrace; buckle, clasp, conjoin, connect, join, link, pair, unite, yoke. * n brace, pair, twain, two; bond, coupling, lea, link, tie.

courage n audaciousness, audacity, boldness, bravery, daring, derring-do, dauntlessness, fearlessness, firmness, fortitude, gallantry, hardihood, heroism, intrepidity, manhood, mettle, nerve, pluck, prowess, resolution, spirit, spunk, valorousness, valour.

courageous adj audacious, brave, bold, chivalrous, daring, dauntless, fearless, gallant, hardy, heroic, intrepid, lion-hearted, mettlesome, plucky, resolute, reliant, staunch, stout, undismayed, valiant, valorous.

course vb chase, follow, hunt, pursue, race, run. * n career, circuit, race, run; road, route, track, way; bearing, direc-

tion, path, tremor, track; ambit, beat, orbit, round; process, progress, sequence; order, regularity, succession, turn; behaviour, conduct, deportment; arrangement, series, system.

court vb coddle, fawn, flatter, ingratiate; address, woo; seek, solicit; invite, solicit, woe. * n area, courtyard, patio, quadrangle; addresses, civilities, homage, respects, solicitations; retinue, palace, tribunal.

courteous adj affable, attentive, ceremonious, civil, complaisant, courtly, debonair, elegant, gracious, obliging, polished, polite, refined, respected, urbane, well-bred, well-mannered.

cover vb overlay, overspread; cloak, conceal, curtain, disguise, hide, mask, screen, secrete, shroud, veil; defend, guard, protect, shelter, shield; case, clothe, envelop, invest, jacket, sheathe; comprehend, comprise, contain, embody, embrace, include. * n capsule, case, covering, integument, tegument, top; cloak, disguise, screen, veil; guard, defence, protection, safeguard, shelter, shield; shrubbery, thicket, underbrush, undergrowth, underwood, woods.

covetous adj acquisitive, avaricious, close-fisted, grasping, greedy, miserly, niggardly, parsimonious, penurious, rapacious.

cow vb abash, break, daunt, discourage, dishearten, frighten, intimidate, overawe, subdue.

coward adj cowardly, timid. * n caitiff, craven, dastard, milksop, poltroon, recreant, skulker, sneak, wheyface.

cowardly adj base, chicken-hearted, coward, craven, dastardly, faint-hearted, fearful, lily-livered, mean, pusillanimous, timid, timorous, white-livered, yellow.

cower vb bend, cringe, crouch, fawn, shrink, squat, stoop.

coy adj backward, bashful, demure, diffident, distant, evasive, modest, prim, reserved, retiring, self-effacing, shrinking, shy, timid; affected, arch, coquettish.

crabbed adj acrid, rough, sore, tart; acrimonious, cantankerous, captious, caustic, censorious, churlish, cross, growling, harsh, ill-tempered, morose, peevish, petulant, snappish, snarling, splenetic, surly, testy, touchy, waspish; difficult, intractable, perplexing, tough, trying, unmanageable.

crack vb break; chop, cleave, split; snap; craze, madden; boast, brag, bluster, crow, gasconade, vapour, vaunt. * adj capital, excellent, first-class, first-rate, tip-top. * n breach, break, chink, cleft, cranny, crevice, fissure, fracture, opening, rent, rift, split; burst, clap, explosion, pop, report; snap.

craft n ability, aptitude, cleverness, dexterity, expertness, power, readiness, skill, tact, talent; artifice, artfulness, cunning, craftiness, deceitfulness, deception, guile, shrewdness, subtlety; art, avocation, business, calling, employment, handicraft, trade, vocation; vessel.

crafty adj arch, artful, astute, cunning, crooked, deceitful, designing, fraudulent, guileful, insidious, intriguing, scheming, shrewd, sly, subtle, tricky, wily.

craggy adj broken, cragged, jagged, rough, rugged, scraggy, uneven

cram vb fill, glut, gorge, satiate, stuff; compress, crowd, overcrowd, press, squeeze; coach, grind.

cramp vb convulse; check, clog, confine, hamper, hinder, impede, obstruct, restrain, restrict. * n convulsion, crick, spasm; check, restraint, restrict, obstruction

crash vb break, shatter, shiver, smash, splinter. * adj emergency, fast, intensive, rushed, speeded-up. * n clang, clash, collision concussion, jar.

crave vb ask, beg, beseech, entreat, implore, petition, solicit, supplicate; desire, hanker after, long for, need, want, yearn for.

craven adj coward, dastard, milk-sop, poltroon, recreant.

craving n hankering, hungering, longing, yearning.

craze vb bewilder, confuse, dement, derange, madden; disorder, impair, weaken. * n fashion, mania, mode, novelty.

crazy adj broken, crank, rickety, shaky, shattered, tottering; crack-brained, delirious, demented, deranged, distracted, idiotic, insane, lunatic, mad, silly.

create vb originate, procreate; cause, design, fashion, form, invent, occasion, produce; appoint, constitute, make.

creation n formation, invention, origination, production; cosmos, universe; appointment, constitution, establishment, nomination.

creator n author, designer, inventor, fashioner, maker, originator; god.

creature n animal, beast, being, body, brute, man, person; dependant, hanger-on, minion, parasite, retainer, vassal; miscreant, wretch.

credit vb accept, believe, trust; loan, trust. * n belief, confidence, credence, faith, reliance, trust; esteem, regard, reputableness, reputation; influence, power; honour, merit; loan, trust.

creditable adj creditable, estimable, honourable, meritorious, praiseworthy, reputable, respectable.

creed n belief, confession, doctrine, dogma, opinion, profession, tenet.

creep vb crawl; steal upon; cringe, fawn, grovel, insinuate. * n crawl, scrabble, scramble; fawner, groveller, sycophant, toady.

crest n comb, plume, topknot, tuft; apex, crown, head, ridge, summit, top; arms, badge, bearings.

crestfallen adj chap-fallen, dejected, depressed, despondent, discouraged, disheartened, dispirited, downcast, down-hearted, low-spirited, melancholy, sad.

crew n company, complement, hands; company, corps, gang, horde, mob, party, posse, set, squad, team, throng.

crick vb jar, rick, wrench, wrick. * n convulsion, cramp, jarring, spasm, rick, wrench, wrick.

crime n felony, misdeed, misdemeanour, offence, violation; delinquency, fault, guilt, iniquity, sin, transgression, unrighteousness, wickedness, wrong.

criminal adj culpable, felonious, flagitious, guilty, illegal, immoral, iniquitous, nefarious, unlawful, vicious, wicked, wrong. * n convict, culprit, delinquent, felon, malefactor, offender, sinner, transgressor.

cringe vb bend, bow, cower, crouch, fawn, grovel, kneel, sneak, stoop, truckle.

cripple vb cramp, destroy, disable, enfeeble, impair, lame, maim, mutilate, paralyse, ruin, weaken.

crisis n acme, climax, height; conjuncture, emergency, exigency, juncture, pass, pinch, push, rub, strait, urgency.

criterion n canon, gauge, measure, principle, proof, rule, standard, test, touchstone.

critic n arbiter, caviller, censor, connoisseur, judge, nit-picker, reviewer

critical adj accurate, exact, nice; captious, carping, caviling, censorious, exacting; crucial, decisive, determining, important, turning: dangerous, dubious, exigent, hazardous, imminent, momentous, precarious, ticklish.

criticism n analysis, animadversion, appreciation, comment, critique, evaluation, judgement, review, strictures.

criticize vb appraise, evaluate, examine, judge.

croak vb complain, groan, grumble, moan, mumble, repine; die.

crony n ally, associate, chum, friend, mate, mucker, pal.

crook vb bend, bow, curve, incurvate, turn, wind. * n bend, curvature, flexion, turn; artifice, machination, trick; criminal, thief, villain

crooked adj angular, bent, bowed, curved, winding, zigzag; askew, aslant, awry, deformed, disfigured, distorted, twisted, wry; crafty, deceitful, devious, dishonest, dishonourable, insidious, intriguing, knavish, tricky, unfair, unscrupulous.

crop vb gather, mow, pick, pluck, reap; browse, nibble; clip, curtail, lop, reduce, shorten. * n harvest, produce, yield.

cross vb intersect, pass over, traverse; hinder, interfere, obstruct, thwart; interbred, intermix. * adj transverse; cantankerous, captious, crabbed, churlish, crusty, cynical, fractious, fretful, grouchy, ill-natured, ill-tempered, irascible, irritable, morose, peevish, pettish,

petulant, snappish, snarling, sour, spleeny, splenetic, sulky, sullen, surly, testy, touchy, waspish. * n crucifix, gibbet, rood; affliction, misfortune, trial, trouble, vexation; cross-breeding, hybrid, intermixture.

crouch vb cower, cringe, fawn, truckle; crouch, kneel, stoop, squat.

crow vb bluster, boast, brag, chuckle, exult, flourish, gasconade, swagger, triumph, vapour, vaunt.

crowd vb compress, cram, jam, pack, press; collect, congregate, flock, herd, huddle, swarm. * n assembly, company, concourse, flock, herd, horde, host, jam, multitude, press, throng; mob, pack, populace, rabble, rout.

crown vb adorn, dignify, honour; recompense, requite, reward; recompense, requite, reward; cap, complete, consummate, finish, perfect. * n bays, chaplet, coronal, coronet, garland, diadem, laurel, wreath; monarchy, royalty, sovereignty; diadem; dignity, honour, recompense, reward; apex, crest, summit, top.

crucial adj intersecting, transverse; critical, decisive, searching, severe, testing, trying.

crude adj raw, uncooked, undressed, unworked; harsh, immature, rough, unripe; crass, course, unrefined; awkward, immature, indigestible, rude, uncouth, unpolished, unpremeditated.

cruel adj barbarous, blood-thirsty, dire, fell, ferocious, inexorable, hard-hearted, inhuman, merciless, pitiless, relentless, ruthless, sanguinary, savage, truculent, uncompassionate, unfeeling, unmerciful, unrelenting; bitter, cold, hard, severe, sharp, unfeeling.

crumble vb bruise, crush, decay, disintegrate, perish, pound, pulverize, triturate.

crumple vb rumple, wrinkle.

crush vb bruise, compress, contuse, squash, squeeze; bray, comminute, crumble, disintegrate, mash; demolish, raze, shatter; conquer, overcome, overpower, overwhelm, quell, subdue.

crust n coat, coating, incrustation, outside, shell, surface.

crusty adj churlish, crabbed, cross, cynical, fretful, forward, morose, peevish, pettish, petulant, snappish, snarling, surly, testy, touchy, waspish; friable, hard, short.

cry *vb* call, clamour, exclaim; blubber, snivel, sob, wail, weep, whimper; bawl, bellow, hoot, roar, shout, vociferate, scream, screech, squawk, squall, squeal, yell; announce, blazon, proclaim, publish. * *n* acclamation, clamour, ejaculation, exclamation, outcry; crying, lament, lamentation, plaint, weeping; bawl, bellow, howl, roar, scream, screech, shriek, yell; announcement, proclamation, publication.

cuddle *vb* cosset, nestle, snuggle, squat; caress, embrace, fondle, hug, pet. * *n* caress, embrace, hug,.

cue *vb* intimate, prompt, remind, sign, signal. * *n* catchword, hint, intimation, nod, prompting, sign, signal, suggestion.

cuff *vb* beat, box, buffet, knock, pommel, punch, slap, smack, strike, thump. * *n* blow, box, punch, slap, smack, strike, thump.

culmination *n* acme, apex, climax, completion, consummation, crown, summit, top, zenith.

culpable *adj* blameable, blameworthy, censurable, criminla, faulty, guilty, remiss, reprehensible, sinful, transgressive, wrong.

culprit *n* delinquent, criminal, evil-doer, felon, malefactor, offender.

cultivate *vb* farm, fertilize, till, work; civilize, develop, discipline, elevate, improve, meliorate, refine, train; investigate, prosecute, pursue, search, study; cherish, foster, nourish, patronize, promote.

culture *n* agriculture, cultivation, farming, husbandry, tillage; cultivation, elevation, improvement, refinement.

cumbersome *adj* burdensome, clumsy, cumbrous, embarrassing, heavy, inconvenient, oppressive, troublesome, unmanageable, unwieldy, vexatious.

cunning *adj* artful, astute, crafty, crooked, deceitful, designing, diplomatic, foxy, guileful, intriguing, machiavellian, sharp, shrewd, sly, subtle, tricky, wily; curious, ingenious. * *n* art, artful-

ness, artifice, astuteness, craft, shrewdness, subtlety; craftiness, chicanery, deceit, deception, intrigue, slyness.

curb *vb* bridle, check, control, hinder, moderate, repress, restrain. * *n* bridle, check, control, hindrance, rein, restraint.

cure *vb* alleviate, correct, heal, mend, remedy, restore; kipper, pickle, preserve. * *n* antidote, corrective, help, remedy, reparative, restorative, specific; alleviation, healing, restorative.

curiosity *n* interest, inquiringness, inquisitiveness; celebrity, curio, marvel, novelty, oddity, phenomenon, rarity, sight, spectacle, wonder.

curious *adj* interested, inquiring, inquisitive, meddling, peering, prying, scrutinizing; extraordinary, marvellous, novel, queer, rare, singular, strange, unique, unusual; cunning, elegant, fine, finished, neat, skilful, well-wrought.

curl *vb* coil, twist, wind, writhe; bend, buckle, ripple, wave. * *n* curlicue, lovelock, ringlet; flexure, sinuosity, undulation, wave, waving, winding.

current *adj* common, general, popular, rife; circulating, passing; existing, instant, present, prevalent, widespread. * *n* course, progression, river, stream, tide, undertow currently. * *adv* commonly, generally, popularly, publicly.

curse *vb* anathematize, damn, denounce, execrate, imprecate, invoke, maledict; blast, blight, destroy, doom; afflict, annoy, harass, injure, plague, scourge, torment, vex; blaspheme. * *n* anathema, ban, denunciation, execration, fulmination, imprecation, malediction, malison; affliction, annoyance, plague, scourge, torment, trouble, vexation; ban, condemnation, penalty, sentence.

cursory *adj* brief, careless, desultory, hasty, passing, rapid, slight, summary, superficial, transient, transitory.

curt *adj* brief, concise, laconic, short, terse; crusty, rude, snappish, tart.

curtail *vb* abridge, dock, lop, retrench, shorten; abbreviate, contract, decrease, diminish, lessen.

curve *vb* bend, crook, inflect, turn, twist, wind. * *n* arcuation, bend, bending, camber, crook, curve, flexure, incurvation.

cushion *vb* absorb, damp, dampen, deaden, dull, muffle, mute, soften, subdue, suppress; cradle, pillow, support. * *n* bolster, hassock, pad, pillow, woolsack.

custodian *n* curator, guardian, keeper, sacristan, superintendent, warden.

custody *n* care, charge, guardianship, keeping, safe-keeping, protection, watch, ward; confinement, durance, duress, imprisonment, prison.

custom *n* consuetude, convention, fashion, habit, manner, mode, practice, rule, usage, use, way; form, formality, observation; patronage; duty, impost, tax, toll, tribute.

customary *adj* accustomed, common, consuetudinary, conventional, familiar, fashionable, general, habitual, gnomic, prescriptive, regular, usual, wonted.

cut *vb* chop, cleave, divide, gash, incise, lance, sever, slice, slit, wound; carve, chisel, sculpture; hurt, move, pierce, touch, wound; ignore, slight; abbreviate, abridge, curtail, shorten. * *n* gash, groove, incision, nick, slit; channel, passage; piece, slice; fling, sarcasm, taunt; fashion, form, shape, style.

cutting *adj* keen, sharp; acid, biting, bitter, caustic, piercing, sarcastic, sardonic, satirical, severe, trenchant, wounding.

cycle *n* age, circle, era, period, revolution, round.

cynical *adj* captious, carping, censorious, churlish, crabbed, cross, crusty, fretful, ill-natured, ill-tempered, morose, peevish, pettish, petulant, sarcastic, satirical, snappish, snarling, surly, testy, touchy, waspish; contemptuous, derisive, misanthropic, pessimistic, scornful.

D

dab *vb* box, slap, strike. * *adj* adept, expert, proficient; pat. * *n* lump, mass, pat.

dabble *vb* dip, moisten, soak, spatter, splash, sprinkle, wet; meddle, tamper, trifle.

daft *adj* absurd, delirious, foolish, giddy, idiotic, insane, silly, simple, stupid, witless; frolicsome, merry, mirthful, playful, sportive.

dainty *adj* delicate, delicious, luscious, nice, palatable, savoury, tender, toothsome; beautiful, charming, choice, delicate, elegant, exquisite, fine, neat; fastidious, finical, finicky, over-nice, particular, scrupulous, squeamish. * *n* delicacy, tidbit, titbit.

damage *vb* harm, hurt, impair, injure, mar. * *n* detriment, harm, hurt, injury, loss, mischief.

damn *vb* condemn, doom, kill, ruin. * *n* bean, curse, fig, hoot, rap, sou, straw.

damnable *adj* abominable, accursed, atrocious, cursed, detestable, hateful, execrable, odious, outrageous.

damp *vb* dampen, moisten; allay, abate, check, depress, discourage, hinder, impede, moderate, repress, restrain; chill, cool, deaden, deject, depress, dispirit. * *adj* dank, humid, moist, wet. * *n* dampness, dank, fog, mist, moisture, vapour; chill, dejection, depression.

danger *n* jeopardy, insecurity, hazard, peril, risk, venture.

dangerous *adj* critical, hazardous, insecure, perilous, risky, ticklish, unsafe.

dank *adj* damp, humid, moist, wet.

dare *vb* challenge, defy, endanger, hazard, provoke, risk. * *n* challenge, defiance, gage.

daring *adj* adventurous, bold, brave, chivalrous, courageous, dauntless, doughty, fearless, gallant, heroic, intrepid, valiant, valorous. * *n* adventurousness, boldness, bravery, courage, dauntlessness, doughtiness, fearlessness, intrepidity, undauntedness, valour.

dark *adj* black, cloudy, darksome, dim, dusky, inky, lightless, lurid, moonless, murky, opaque, overcast, pitchy, rayless, shady, shadowy, starless, sunless, swart, tenebrous, umbrageous, unenlightened, unilluminated; abstruse, cabbalistic, enigmatical, incomprehensible, mysterious, mystic, mystical, obscure, occult, opaque, recondite, transcendental, unillumined, unintelligible; cheerless, despondent, discouraging, dismal, disheartening, funereal, gloomy, joyless; benighted, darkened, ignorant, rude, unlettered, untaught; atrocious, damnable, infamous, flagitious, foul, horrible, infernal, nefarious, vile, wicked; private, secret. * *n* darkness, dusk, murkiness, obscurity; concealment, privacy, secrecy; blindness, ignorance.

darken *vb* cloud, dim, eclipse, obscure, shade, shadow; chill, damp, depress, gloom, sadden; benight, stultify, stupefy; obscure, perplex; defile, dim, dull, stain, sully.

darling *adj* beloved, cherished, dear, loved, precious, treasured. * *n* dear, favourite, idol, love, sweetheart.

dart *vb* ejaculate, hurl, launch, propel, sling, throw; emit, shoot; dash, rush, scoot, spring.

dash *vb* break, destroy, disappoint, frustrate, ruin, shatter, spoil, thwart; abash, confound, disappoint, surprise; bolt, dart, fly, run, speed, rush. * *n* blow, stroke; advance, onset, rush; infusion, smack, spice, sprinkling, tincture, tinge, touch; flourish, show.

dashing *adj* headlong, impetuous, precipitate, rushing; brilliant, gay, showy, spirited.

date *n* age, cycle, day, generation, time; epoch, era, period; appointment, arrangement, assignation, engagement, interview, rendezvous, tryst; catch, steady, sweetheart.

dawdle *vb* dally, delay, fiddle, idle, lag, loiter, potter, trifle.

dawn *vb* appear, begin, break, gleam, glimmer, open, rise. * *n* daybreak, dawning, cockcrow, sunrise, sun-up.

day *n* daylight, sunlight, sunshine; age, epoch, generation, lifetime, time.

daze *vb* blind, dazzle; bewilder, confound, confuse, perplex, stun, stupefy. * *n* bewilderment, confusion, discomposure, perturbation, pother; coma, stupor, swoon, trance.

dazzle *vb* blind, daze; astonish, confound, overpower, surprise. * *n* brightness, brilliance, splendour.

dead *adj* breathless, deceased, defunct, departed, gone, inanimate, lifeless; apathetic, callous, cold, dull, frigid, indifferent, inert, lukewarm, numb, obtuse, spiritless, torpid, unfeeling; flat, insipid, stagnant, tasteless, vapid; barren, inactive, sterile, unemployed, unprofitable, useless. * *adv* absolutely, completely, downright, fundamentally, quite; direct, directly, due, exactly, just, right, squarely, straight. * *n* depth, midst; hush, peace, quietude, silence, stillness.

deaden *vb* abate, damp, dampen, dull, impair, muffle, mute, restrain, retard, smother, weaken; benumb, blunt, hebetate, obtund, paralyse.

deadly *adj* deleterious, destructive, fatal, lethal, malignant, mortal, murderous, noxious, pernicious, poisonous, venomous; implacable, mortal, rancorous, sanguinary.

deal *vb* allot, apportion, assign, bestow, dispense, distribute, divide, give, reward, share; bargain, trade, traffic, treat with. * *n* amount, degree, distribution, extent, lot, portion, quantity, share; bargain, transaction.

dear *adj* costly, expensive, high-priced; beloved, cherished, darling, esteemed, precious, treasured. * *n* beloved, darling, deary, honey, love, precious, sweet, sweetie, sweetheart.

dearth *n* deficiency, insufficiency, scarcity; famine, lack, need, shortage, want.

deathless *adj* eternal, everlasting, immortal, imperishable, undying; boring, dull, turgid.

debase *vb* adulterate, alloy, depress, deteriorate, impair, injure, lower, pervert, reduce, vitiate; abase, degrade, disgrace, dishonour, humble, humiliate, mortify, shame; befoul, contaminate, corrupt, defile, foul, pollute, soil, taint.

debate *vb* argue, canvass, contest, discuss, dispute; contend, deliberate, wrangle. * *n* controversy, discussion, disputation; altercation, contention, contest, dispute, logomachy.

debonair *adj* affable, civil, complaisant, courteous, easy, gracious, kind, obliging, polite, refined, urbane, well-bred.

debris *n* detritus, fragments, remains, rubbish, ruble, ruins, wreck, wreckage.

debt *n* arrears, debit, due, liability, obligation; fault, misdoing, offence, shortcoming, sin, transgression, trespass.

decay *vb* decline, deteriorate, disintegrate, fail, perish, wane, waste, wither; decompose, putrefy, rot. * *n* caducity, decadence, declension, decline, decomposition, decrepitude, degeneracy, degeneration, deterioration, dilapidation, disintegration, fading, failing, perishing, putrefaction, ruin, wasting, withering.

deceit *n* artifice, cheating, chicanery, cozenage, craftiness, deceitfulness, deception, double-dealing, duplicity, finesse, fraud, guile, hypocrisy, imposition, imposture, pretence, sham, treachery, tricky, underhandedness, wile.

deceitful *adj* counterfeit, deceptive, delusive, fallacious, hollow, illusive, illusory, insidious, misleading; circumventive, cunning, designing, dissembling, dodgy, double-dealing, evasive, false, fraudulent, guileful, hypocritical, insincere, tricky, underhanded, wily.

deceive *vb* befool, beguile, betray, cheat, chouse, circumvent, cozen, defraud, delude, disappoint, double-cross, dupe, ensnare, entrap, fool, gull, hoax, hoodwink, humbug, mislead, outwit, overreach, trick.

decent *adj* appropriate, becoming, befitting, comely, seemly, decorous, fit, proper, seemly; chaste, delicate, modest, pure; moderate, passable, respectable, tolerable.

deception *n* artifice, cheating, chicanery, cozenage, craftiness, deceitfulness, deception, double-dealing, duplicity, finesse, fraud, guile, hoax, hypocrisy, imposition, imposture, pretence, sham, treachery, tricky, underhandedness, wile; cheat, chouse, ruse, stratagem, wile.

deceptive *adj* deceitful, deceiving, delusive, disingenuous, fallacious, false, illusive, illusory, misleading.

decide *vb* close, conclude, determine, end, settle, terminate; resolve; ajudge, adjudicate, award.

decided *adj* determined, firm, resolute, unhesitating, unwavering; absolute, cat-

egorical, positive, unequivocal; certain, clear, indisputable, undeniable, unmistakable, unquestionable.

decision *n* conclusion, determination, judgement, settlement; adjudication, award, decree, pronouncement, sentence; firmness, resolution.

decisive *adj* conclusive, determinative, final.

declaration *n* affirmation, assertion, asseveration, averment, averment, avowal, protestation, statement; announcement, proclamation, publication.

declare *vb* advertise, affirm, announce, assert, asseverate, aver, blazon, bruit, proclaim, promulgate, pronounce, publish, state, utter.

decline *vb* incline, lean, slope; decay, droop, fail, flag, languish, pine, sink; degenerate, depreciate, deteriorate; decrease, diminish, dwindle, fade, ebb, lapse, lessen, wane; avoid, refuse, reject; inflect, vary. * *n* decadence, decay, declension, declination, degeneracy, deterioration, diminution, wane; atrophy, consumption, marasmus, phthisis; declivity, hill, incline, slope.

decomposition *n* analysis, break-up, disintegration, resolution; caries, corruption, crumbling, decay, disintegration, dissolution, putrescence, rotting.

decorate *vb* adorn, beautify, bedeck, deck, embellish, enrich, garnish, grace, ornament.

decoration *n* adorning, beautifying, bedecking, decking, enriching, garnishing, ornamentation, ornamenting; adornment, enrichment, embellishment, ornament.

decorous *adj* appropriate, becoming, befitting, comely, decent, fit, suitable, proper, sedate, seemly, staid.

decoy *vb* allure, deceive, ensnare, entice, entrap, inveigle, lure, seduce, tempt. * *n* allurement, lure, enticement.

decrease *vb* abate, contract, decline, diminish, dwindle, ebb, lessen, subside, wane; curtail, diminish, lessen, lower, reduce, retrench. * *n* abatement, contraction, declension, decline, decrement, diminishing, diminution, ebb, ebbing, lessening, reduction, subsidence, waning.

decree vb adjudge, appoint, command, decide, determine, enact, enjoin, order, ordain. * n act, command, edict, enactment, fiat, law, mandate, order, ordinance, precept, regulation, statute.

decrepit adj feeble, effete, shattered, wasted, weak; aged, crippled, superannuated.

dedicate vb consecrate, devote, hallow, sanctify; address, inscribe.

deduce vb conclude, derive, draw, gather, infer.

deduction n removal, subtraction, withdrawal; abatement, allowance, defalcation, discount, rebate, reduction, reprise; conclusion, consequence, corollary, inference.

deed n achievement, act, action, derring-do, exploit, feat, performance; fact, truth, reality; charter, contract, document, indenture, instrument, transfer.

deep adj abysmal, profound; abstruse, difficult, hard, intricate, knotty, mysterious, profound, recondite, unfathomable; astute, cunning, designing, discerning, intelligent, insidious, penetrating, sagacious, shrewd; absorbed, engrossed; bass, grave, low; entire, great, heartfelt, thorough. * n main, ocean, water, sea; abyss, depth, profound; enigma, mystery, riddle; silence, stillness.

deeply adv profoundly; completely, entirely, profoundly, thoroughly; affectingly, distressingly, feelingly, mournfully, sadly.

defeat vb beat, checkmate, conquer, discomfit, overcome, overpower, overthrow, repulse, rout, ruin, vanquish; baffle, balk, block, disappoint, disconcert, foil, frustrate, thwart. * n discomfiture, downfall, overthrow, repulse, rout, vanquishment; bafflement, checkmate, frustration.

defect vb abandon, desert, rebel, revolt. * n default, deficiency, destitution, lack, shortcoming, spot, taint, want; blemish, blotch, error, flaw, imperfection, mistake; failing, fault, foible.

defective adj deficient, inadequate, incomplete, insufficient, scant, short; faulty, imperfect, marred.

defence n defending, guarding, holding, maintaining, maintenance, protection; buckler, bulwark, fortification, guard, protection, rampart, resistance, shield; apology, excuse, justification, plea, vindication.

defend vb cover, fortify, guard, preserve, protect, safeguard, screen, secure, shelter, shield; assert, espouse, justify, maintainer, plead, uphold, vindicate.

defer[1] vb adjourn, delay, pigeonhole, procrastinate, postpone, prorogue, protract, shelve, table.

defer[2] vb abide by, acknowledge, bow to, give way, submit, yield; admire, esteem, honour, regard, respect.

deference n esteem, homage, honour, obeisance, regard, respect, reverence, veneration; complaisance, consideration; obedience, submission.

deferential adj respectful, reverential.

defiance n challenge, daring; contempt, despite, disobedience, disregard, opposition, spite.

defiant adj contumacious, recalcitrant, resistant; bold, courageous, resistant.

deficiency n dearth, default, deficit, insufficiency, lack, meagreness, scantiness, scarcity, shortage, shortness, want; defect, error, failing, falling, fault, foible, frailty, imperfection, infirmity, weakness.

define vb bound, circumscribe, designate, delimit, demarcate, determine, explain, limit, specify.

definite adj defined, determinate, determined, fixed, restricted; assured, certain, clear, exact, explicit, positive, precise, specific, unequivocal.

definitive adj categorical, determinate, explicit, express, positive, unconditional; conclusive, decisive, final.

deformity n abnormality, crookedness, defect, disfigurement, distortion, inelegance, irregularity, malformation, misproportion, misshapenness, monstrosity, ugliness.

defraud vb beguile, cheat, chouse, circumvent, cozen, deceive, delude, diddle, dupe, embezzle, gull, overreach, outwit, pilfer, rob, swindle, trick.

deft *adj* adroit, apt, clever, dab, dextrous, expert, handy, ready, skilful.

defy *vb* challenge, dare; brave, contemn, despise, disregard, face, flout, provoke, scorn, slight, spurn.

degree *n* stage, step; class, grade, order, quality, rank, standing, station; extent, measure; division, interval, space.

dejected *adj* bloomy, chap-fallen, crest-fallen, depressed, despondent, disheartened, dispirited, doleful, downcast, down-hearted, gloomy, low-spirited, miserable, sad, wretched.

delay *vb* defer, postpone, procrastinate; arrest, detain, check, hinder, impede, retard, stay, stop; prolong, protract; dawdle, linger, loiter, tarry. * *n* deferment, postponement, procrastination; check, detention, hindrance, impediment, retardation, stoppage; prolonging, protraction; dallying, dawdling, lingering, tarrying, stay, stop.

delegate *vb* appoint, authorize, mission, depute, deputize, transfer; commit, entrust. * *n* ambassador, commissioner, delegate, deputy, envoy, representative.

delete *vb* cancel, efface, erase, expunge, obliterate, remove.

deliberate *vb* cogitate, consider, consult, meditate, muse, ponder, reflect, ruminate, think, weigh. * *adj* careful, cautious, circumspect, considerate, heedful, purposeful, methodical, thoughtful, wary; well-advised, well-considered; aforethought, intentional, premeditated, purposed, studied.

deliberation *n* caution, circumspection, cogitation, consideration, coolness, meditation, prudence, reflection, thought, thoughtfulness, wariness; purpose.

delicacy *n* agreeableness, daintiness, deliciousness, pleasantness, relish, savouriness; bonne bouche, dainty, tidbit, titbit; elegance, fitness, lightness, niceness, nicety, smoothness, softness, tenderness; fragility, frailty, slenderness, slightness, tenderness, weakness; carefulness, daintiness, discrimination, fastidiousness, finesse, nicety, scrupulousness, sensitivity, subtlety, tact; purity, refinement, sensibility.

delicate *adj* agreeable, delicious, pleasant, pleasing, palatable, savoury; elegant, exquisite, fine, nice; careful, dainty, discriminating, fastidious, scrupulous; fragile, frail, slender, slight, tender, delicate; pure, refined.

delicious *adj* dainty, delicate, luscious, nice, palatable, savory; agreeable, charming, choice, delightful, exquisite, grateful, pleasant.

delight *vb* charm, enchant, enrapture, gratify, please, ravish, rejoice, satisfy, transport. * *n* charm, delectation, ecstasy, enjoyment, gladness, gratification, happiness, joy, pleasure, rapture, ravishment, satisfaction, transport.

delightful *adj* agreeable, captivating, charming, delectable, enchanting, enjoyable, enrapturing, rapturous, ravishing, transporting.

delinquent *adj* negligent, offending. * *n* criminal, culprit, defaulter, malefactor, miscreant, misdoer, offender, transgressor, wrong-doer.

deliver *vb* emancipate, free, liberate, release; extricate, redeem, rescue, save; commit, give, impart, transfer; cede, grant, relinquish, resign, yield; declare, emit, promulgate, pronounce, speak, utter; deal, discharge.

deliverance *n* emancipation, escape, liberation, redemption, release.

delivery *n* conveyance, surrender; commitment, giving, rendering, transference, transferral, transmission; elocution, enunciation, pronunciation, speech, utterance; childbirth, confinement, labour, parturition, travail.

delusion *n* artifice, cheat, clap-trap, deceit, dodge, fetch, fraud, imposition, imposture, ruse, snare, trick, wile; deception, error, fallacy, fancy, hallucination, illusion, mistake, mockery, phantasm.

demand *vb* challenge, exact, require; claim, necessitate, require; ask, inquire. * *n* claim, draft, exaction, requirement, requisition; call, want; inquiry, interrogation, question.

demolish *vb* annihilate, destroy, dismantle, level, over-throw, overturn, pulverize, raze, ruin.

demon n devil, fiend, kelpie, goblin, troll.

demonstrate vb establish, exhibit, illustrate, indicate, manifest, prove, show.

demonstration n display, exhibition, manifestation, show.

demonstrative adj affectionate, communicative, effusive, emotional, expansive, expressive, extroverted, open, outgoing, passionate, sentimental, suggestive, talkative, unreserved; absolute, apodictic, certain, conclusive, probative; exemplificative, illustrative.

denial n contradiction, controverting, negation; abjuration, disavowal, disclaimer, disowning; disallowance, refusal, rejection.

dense adj close, compact, compressed, condensed, thick; dull, slow, stupid.

dent vb depress, dint, indent, pit. * n depression, dint, indentation, nick, notch.

deny vb contradict, gainsay, oppose, refute, traverse; abjure, abnegate, disavow, disclaim, disown, renounce; disallow, refuse, reject, withhold.

depart vb absent, disappear, vanish; abandon, decamp, go, leave, migrate, quit, remove, withdraw; decease, die; deviate, diverge, vary.

department n district, division, part, portion, province; bureau, function, office, province, sphere, station; branch, division, subdivision.

departure n exit, leaving, parting, removal, recession, removal, retirement, withdrawal; abandonment, forsaking; death, decease, demise, deviation, exit.

depend vb hang, hinge, turn.

dependant n client, hanger-on, henchman, minion, retainer, subordinate, vassal; attendant, circumstance, concomitant, consequence, corollary.

dependent adj hanging, pendant; conditioned, contingent, relying, subject, subordinate.

deplorable adj calamitous, distressful, distressing, grievous, lamentable, melancholy, miserable, mournful, pitiable, regrettable, sad, wretched.

depose vb break, cashier, degrade, dethrone, dismiss, displace, oust, reduce; avouch, declare, depone, testify.

deposit vb drop, dump, precipitate; lay, put; bank, hoard, lodge, put, save, store; commit, entrust. * n diluvium, dregs, lees, precipitate, precipitation, sediment, settlement, settlings, silt; money, pawn, pledge, security, stake.

depraved adj abandoned, corrupt, corrupted, debased, debauched, degenerate, dissolute, evil, graceless, hardened, immoral, lascivious, lewd, licentious, lost, perverted, profligate, reprobate, shameless, sinful, vicious, wicked.

depreciate vb underestimate, undervalue, underrate; belittle, censure, decry, degrade, disparage, malign, traduce.

depress vb bow, detrude, drop, lower, reduce, sink; abase, abash, degrade, debase, disgrace, humble, humiliation; chill, damp, dampen, deject, discourage, dishearten, dispirit, sadden; deaden, lower.

depression n cavity, concavity, dent, dimple, dint, excavation, hollow, hollowness, indentation, pit; blues, cheerlessness, dejection, dejectedness, despondency, disconsolateness, disheartenment, dispiritedness, dole, dolefulness, downheartedness, dumps, gloom, gloominess, hypochondria, melancholy, sadness, vapours; inactivity, lowness, stagnation; abasement, debasement, degradation, humiliation.

deprive vb bereave, denude, despoil, dispossess, divest, rob, strip.

depth n abyss, deepness, drop, profundity; extent, measure; middle, midst, stillness; astuteness, discernment, penetration, perspicacity, profoundness, profundity, sagacity, shrewdness.

deputation n commission, delegation; commissioners, deputies, delegates, delegation, embassies, envoys, legation.

deputy adj acting, assistant, vice, subordinate. * n agent, commissioner, delegate, envoy, factor, legate, lieutenant, proxy, representative, substitute, viceregent.

derelict adj abandoned, forsaken, left, relinquished; delinquent, faithless, guilty, neglectful, negligent, unfaithful. * n castaway, castoff, outcast, tramp, vagrant, wreck, wretch.

derision n contempt, disrespect, insult, laughter, mockery, ridicule, scorn.

derisive adj contemptuous, contumelious, mocking, ridiculing, scoffing, scornful.

derivation n descent, extraction, genealogy; etymology; deducing, deriving, drawing, getting, obtaining; beginning, foundation, origination, source.

derive vb draw, get, obtain, receive; deduce, follow, infer, trace.

descend vb drop, fall, pitch, plunge, sink, swoop; alight, dismount; go, pass, proceed, devolve; derive, issue, originate.

descendants npl offspring, issue, posterity, progeny.

descent n downrush, drop, fall; descending; decline, declivity, dip, pitch, slope; ancestry, derivation, extraction, genealogy, lineage, parentage, pedigree; assault, attack, foray, incursion, invasion, raid.

describe vb define, delineate, draw, illustrate, limn, sketch, specify, trace; detail; depict, explain, narrate, portray, recount, relate, represent; characterize.

description n delineation, tracing; account, depiction, explanation, narration, narrative, portrayal, recital, relation, report, representation; class, kind, sort, species.

desert[1] n due, excellence, merit, worth; punishment, reward.

desert[2] vb abandon, abscond, forsake, leave, quit, relinquish, renounce, resign, quit, vacate.

desert[3] adj barren, desolate, forsaken, lonely, solitary, uncultivated, uninhabited, unproductive, untilled, waste, wild.

deserve vb earn, gain, merit, procure, win.

design vb brew, concoct, contrive, devise, intend, invent, mean, plan, project, scheme; intend, mean, purpose; delineate, describe, draw, outline, sketch, trace. * n aim, device, drift, intent, intention, mark, meaning, object, plan, proposal, project, purport, purpose, scheme, scope; delineation, draught, drawing, outline, plan, sketch; adaptation, artifice, contrivance, invention, inventiveness.

designing adj artful, astute, crafty, crooked, cunning, deceitful, insidious, intriguing, Machiavellian, scheming, sly, subtle, treacherous, trickish, tricky, unscrupulous, wily.

desirable adj agreeable, beneficial, covetable, eligible, enviable, good, pleasing, preferable.

desire vb covet, crave, desiderate, fancy, hanker after, long for, lust after, want, wish, yearn for; ask, entreat, request, solicit. * n eroticism, lasciviousness, libidinousness, libido, lust, lustfulness, passion; eagerness, fancy, hope, inclination, mind, partiality, penchant, pleasure, volition, want, wish.

desolate vb depopulate, despoil, destroy, devastate, pillage, plunder, ravage, ruin, sack. * adj bare, barren, bleak, desert, forsaken, lonely, solitary, unfrequented, uninhabited, waste, wild; companionable, lonely, lonesome, solitary; desolated, destroyed, devastated, ravaged, ruined; cheerless, comfortless, companionless, disconsolate, dreary, forlorn, forsaken, miserable, wretched.

desolation n destruction, devastation, havoc, ravage, ruin; barrenness, bleakness, desolateness, dreariness, loneliness, solitariness, solitude, wildness; gloom, gloominess, misery, sadness, unhappiness, wretchedness.

despair vb despond, give up, lose hope. * n dejection, desperation, despondency, disheartenment, hopelessness.

desperate adj despairing, despondent, desponding, hopeless; forlorn, hopeless, irretrievable; extreme; audacious, daring, despairing, foolhardy, frantic, furious, headstrong, precipitate, rash, reckless, violent, wild, wretched; extreme, great, monstrous, prodigious, supreme.

desperation n despair, hopelessness; fury, rage.

despicable adj abject, base, contemptible, degrading, low, mean, paltry, pitiful, shameful, sordid, vile, worthless.

despise vb contemn, disdain, disregard, neglect, scorn, slight, spurn, undervalue.

despite n malevolence, malice, malignity, spite; contempt, contumacy, defiance. * prep notwithstanding.

despondent adj blue, dejected, depressed,

discouraged, disheartened, dispirited, gloomy, low-spirited, melancholy, sad.

despotic *adj* absolute, arrogant, autocratic, dictatorial, imperious; arbitrary, oppressive, tyrannical, tyrannous.

destination *n* appointment, decree, destiny, doom, fate, foreordainment, foreordination, fortune, lot, ordination, star; aim, design, drift, end, intention, object, purpose, scope; bourne, goal, harbour, haven, journey's end, resting-place, terminus.

destitute *adj* distressed, indigent, moneyless, necessitous, needy, penniless, penurious, pinched, poor, reduced, wanting.

destroy *vb* demolish, overthrow, overturn, subvert, raze, ruin; annihilate, dissolve, efface, quench; desolate, devastate, devour, ravage, waste; eradicate, extinguish, extirpate, kill, uproot, slay.

destruction *n* demolition, havoc, overthrow, ruin, subversion; desolation, devastation, holocaust, ravage; annihilation, eradication, extinction, extirpation, ruin; death, massacre, murder, slaughter.

destructive *adj* baleful, baneful, deadly, deleterious, detrimental, fatal, hurtful, injurious, lethal, mischievous, noxious, pernicious, ruinous; annihilatory, eradicative, exterminative, extirpative.

detach *vb* disengage, disconnect, disjoin, dissever, disunite, divide, part, separate, sever, unfix; appoint, detail, send.

detail *vb* delineate, depict, describe, enumerate, narrate, particularize, portray, recount, rehearse, relate, specify; appoint, detach, send. * *n* account, narration, narrative, recital, relation; appointment, detachment; item, part.

details *npl* minutiae, particulars, parts.

detain *vb* arrest, check, delay, hinder, hold, keep, restrain, retain, stay, stop; confine.

detect *vb* ascertain, catch, descry, disclose, discover, expose, reveal, unmask.

deter *vb* debar, discourage, frighten, hinder, prevent, restrain, stop, withhold.

deteriorate *vb* corrupt, debase, degrade, deprave, disgrace, impair, spoil, vitiate; decline, degenerate, depreciate, worsen.

determination *n* ascertainment, decision, deciding, determining, fixing, settlement, settling; conclusion, decision, judgement, purpose, resolution, resolve, result; direction, leaning, tendency; firmness, constancy, grit, persistence, stamina, resoluteness, resolution; definition, limitation, qualification.

determine *vb* adjust, conclude, decide, end, establish, fix, resolve, settle; ascertain, certify, check, verify; impel, incline, induce, influence, lead, turn; decide, resolve; condition, define, limit; compel, necessitate.

detest *vb* abhor, abominate, despise, execrate, hate, loathe, nauseate, recoil from.

detestable *adj* abhorred, abominable, accursed, cursed, damnable, execrable, hateful, odious; disgusting, loathsome, nauseating, offensive, repulsive, sickening, vile.

detract *vb* abuse, asperse, belittle, calumniate, debase, decry, defame, depreciate, derogate, disparage, slander, traduce, vilify; deprecate, deteriorate, diminish, lessen.

devastation *n* despoiling, destroying, harrying, pillaging, plundering, ravaging, sacking, spoiling, stripping, wasting; desolation, destruction, havoc, pillage, rapine, ravage, ruin, waste.

develop *vb* disentangle, disclose, evolve, exhibit, explicate, uncover, unfold, unravel; cultivate, grow, mature, open, progress.

development *n* disclosure, disentanglement, exhibition, unfolding, unravelling; growth, increase, maturation, maturing; evolution, growth progression; elaboration, expansion, explication.

deviate *vb* alter, deflect, digress, diverge, sheer off, slew, tack, turn aside, wheel, wheel about; err, go astray, stray, swerve, wander; differ, diverge, vary.

device *n* contraption, contrivance, gadget, invention; design, expedient, plan, project, resort, resource, scheme, shift; artifice, evasion, fraud, manoeuvre, ruse, stratagem, trick, wile; blazon, emblazonment, emblem, sign, symbol, type.

devious *adj* deviating, erratic, roundabout,

wandering; circuitous, confusing, crooked, labyrinthine, mazy, obscure; crooked, disingenuous, misleading, treacherous.

devise *vb* brew, compass, concert, concoct, contrive, dream up, excogitate, imagine, invent, plan, project, scheme; bequeath, demise, leave, will.

devote *vb* appropriate, consecrate, dedicate, destine; set apart; addict, apply, give up, resign; consign, doom, give over.

devoted *adj* affectionate, attached, loving; ardent, assiduous, earnest, zealous.

devotion *n* consecration, dedication; devotedness, devoutness, godliness, holiness, piety, religion, religiousness, saintliness, sanctity; adoration, devoutness, prayer, worship; affection, attachment, love; ardour, devotedness, eagerness, earnestness, zeal.

devour *vb* engorge, gorge, gulp down, raven, swallow eagerly, wolf; annihilate, consume, destroy, expend, spend, swallow up, waste.

devout *adj* devotional, godly, holy, pious, religious, saint-like, saintly; earnest, grave, serious, sincere, solemn.

dexterity *n* ability, address, adroitness, aptitude, aptness, art, cleverness, expertness, facility, knack, quickness, readiness, skilfulness, skill, tact.

diabolic, diabolical *adj* atrocious, barbarous, cruel, devilish, fiendish, hellish, impious, infernal, malevolent, malign, malignant, satanic, wicked.

dialogue *n* colloquy, communication, conference, conversation, converse, intercourse, interlocution; playbook, script, speech, text, words.

dictate *vb* bid, direct, command, decree, enjoin, ordain, order, prescribe, require. * *n* bidding, command, decree, injunction, order; maxim, precept, rule.

dictator *n* autocrat, despot, tyrant.

dictatorial *adj* absolute, unlimited, unrestricted; authoritative, despotic, dictatory, domineering, imperious, overbearing, peremptory, tyrannical.

dictatorship *n* absolutism, authoritarianism, autocracy, despotism, iron rule, totalitarianism, tyranny.

die *vb* decease, demise, depart, expire, pass on; decay, decline, fade, fade out, perish, wither; cease, disappear, vanish; faint, fall, sink.

differ *vb* deviate, diverge, vary; disagree, dissent; bicker, contend, dispute, quarrel, wrangle.

difference *n* contrariety, contrast, departure, deviation, disagreement, disparity, dissimilarity, dissimilitude, divergence, diversity, heterogeneity, inconformity, nuance, opposition, unlikeness, variation; alienation, altercation, bickering, breach, contention, contest, controversy, debate, disaccord, disagreement, disharmony, dispute, dissension, embroilment, falling out, irreconcilability, jarring, misunderstanding, quarrel, rupture, schism, strife, variance, wrangle; discrimination, distinction.

different *adj* distinct, nonidentical, separate, unlike; contradistinct, contrary, contrasted, deviating, disagreeing, discrepant, dissimilar, divergent, diverse, incompatible, incongruous, unlike, variant, various; divers, heterogeneous, manifold, many, sundry, various.

difficult *adj* arduous, exacting, hard, Herculean, stiff, tough, uphill; abstruse, complex, intricate, knotty, obscure, perplexing; austere, rigid, unaccommodating, uncompliant, unyielding; dainty, fastidious, squeamish.

difficulty *n* arduousness, laboriousness; bar, barrier, crux, deadlock, dilemma, embarrassment, emergency, exigency, fix, hindrance, impediment, knot, obstacle, obstruction, perplexity, pickle, pinch, predicament, stand, standstill, thwart, trial, trouble; cavil, objection; complication, controversy, difference, embarrassment, embroilment, imbroglio, misunderstanding.

diffident *adj* distrustful, doubtful, hesitant, hesitating, reluctant; bashful, modest, over-modest, sheepish, shy, timid.

dig *vb* channel, delve, excavate, grub, hollow out, quarry, scoop, tunnel. * *n* poke, punch, thrust.

dignified *adj* august, courtly, decorous, grave, imposing, majestic, noble, stately.

dignify *vb* advance, aggrandize, elevate, ennoble, exalt, promote; adorn, grace, honour.

dignity *n* elevation, eminence, exaltation, excellent, glory, greatness, honour, place, rank, respectability, standing, station; decorum, grandeur, majesty, nobleness, stateliness; preferment; dignitary, magistrate; elevation, height.

dilapidated *adj* decadent, decayed, ruined, run down, wasted.

dilemma *n* difficulty, fix, plight, predicament, problem, quandary, strait.

diligent *adj* active, assiduous, attentive, busy, careful, constant, earnest, hardworking, indefatigable, industrious, laborious, notable, painstaking, persevering, persistent, sedulous, tireless.

dim *vb* blur, cloud, darken, dull, obscure, sully, tarnish. * *adj* cloudy, dark, dusky, faint, ill-defined, indefinite, indistinct, mysterious, obscure, shadowy; dull, obtuse; clouded, confused, darkened, faint, obscured; blurred, dull, dulled, sullied, tarnished.

diminish *vb* abate, belittle, contract, decrease, lessen, reduce; abate, contract, curtail, cut, decrease, dwindle, lessen, melt, narrow, shrink, shrivel, subside, taper off, weaken.

din *vb* beat, boom, clamour, drum, hammer, pound, repeat, ring, thunder. * *n* bruit, clamour, clash, clatter, crash, crashing, hubbub, hullabaloo, hurly-burly, noise, outcry, racket, row, shout, uproar.

dingy *adj* brown, dun, dusky; bedimmed, colourless, dimmed, dulled, faded, obscure, smirched, soiled, sullied.

dip *vb* douse, duck, immerse, plunge, souse; bail, ladle; dive, duck, pitch, plunge; bend, incline, slope. * *n* decline, declivity, descent, drop, fall; concavity, depression, hole, hollow, pit, sink; bathe, dipping, ducking, sousing, swim.

diplomat *n* diplomatist, envoy, legate, minister, negotiator.

dire *adj* alarming, awful, calamitous, cruel, destructive, disastrous, dismal, dreadful, fearful, gloomy, horrible, horrid, implacable, inexorable, portentous, shocking, terrible, terrific, tremendous, woeful.

direct *vb* aim, cast, level, point, turn; advise, conduct, control, dispose, guide, govern, manage, regulate, rule; command, bid, enjoin, instruct, order; guide, lead, point, show; address, superscribe. * *adj* immediate, straight, undeviating; absolute, categorical, express, plain, unambiguous; downright, earnest, frank, ingenuous, open, outspoken, plain, sincere, straightforward, unequivocal.

direction *n* aim; tendency; bearing, course; administration, conduct, control, government, management, oversight, superintendence; guidance, lead; command, order, prescription; address, superscription.

directly *adv* absolutely, expressly, openly, unambiguously; forthwith, immediately, instantly, quickly, presently, promptly, soon, speedily.

dirty *vb* befoul, defile, draggle, foul, pollute, soil, sully. * *adj* begrimed, defiled, filthy, foul, mucky, nasty, soiled, unclean; clouded, cloudy, dark, dull, muddy, sullied; base, beggarly, contemptible, despicable, grovelling, low, mean, paltry, pitiful, scurvy, shabby, sneaking, squalid; disagreeable, foul, muddy, nasty, rainy, sloppy, uncomfortable.

disability *n* disablement, disqualification, impotence, impotency, inability, incapacity, incompetence, incompetency, unfitness, weakness.

disable *vb* cripple, enfeeble, hamstring, impair, paralyse, unman, weaken; disenable, disqualify, incapacitate, unfit.

disadvantage *n* disadvantageousness, inconvenience, unfavourableness; damage, detriment, disservice, drawback, harm, hindrance, hurt, injury, loss, prejudice.

disaffected *adj* alienated, disloyal, dissatisfied, estranged.

disaffection *n* alienation, breach, disagreement, dislike, disloyalty, dissatisfaction, estrangement, repugnance, ill will, unfriendliness.

disagree *vb* deviate, differ, diverge, vary; dissent; argue, bicker, clash, debate, dispute, quarrel, wrangle.

disagreeable *adj* contrary, displeasing, distasteful, nasty, offensive, unpleasant, unpleasing, unsuitable.

disagreement *n* deviation, difference, discrepancy, dissimilarity, dissimilitude, divergence, diversity, incongruity, unlikeness; disaccord, dissent; argument, bickering, clashing, conflict, contention, dispute, dissension, disunion, disunity, jarring, misunderstanding, quarrel, strife, variance, wrangle.

disappear *vb* depart, fade, vanish; cease, dissolve.

disappoint *vb* baffle, balk, deceive, defeat, delude, disconcert, foil, frustrate, mortify, tantalize, thwart, vex.

disappointment *n* baffling, balk, failure, foiling, frustration, miscarriage, mortification, unfulfilment.

disapprove *vb* blame, censure, condemn, deprecate, dislike, displeasure; disallow, reject.

disarrange *vb* confuse, derange, disallow, dishevel, dislike, dislocate, disorder, disturb, jumble, reject, rumple, tumble, unsettle.

disaster *n* accident, adversity, blow, calamity, casualty, catastrophe, misadventure, mischance, misfortune, mishap, reverse, ruin, stroke.

disastrous *adj* adverse, calamitous, catastrophic, destructive, hapless, ill-fated, ill-starred, ruinous, unfortunate, unlucky, unpropitious, unprosperous, untoward; disaster, dismissal, foreboding, gloomy, portending, portentous. threatening.

discard *vb* abandon, cast off, lay aside, reject; banish, break, cashier, discharge, dismiss, remove, repudiate.

discern *vb* differentiate, discriminate, distinguish, judge; behold, descry, discover, espy, notice, observe, perceive, recognize, see.

discharge *vb* disburden, unburden, unload; eject, emit, excrete, expel, void; cash, liquidate, pay; absolve, acquit, clear, exonerate, free, release, relieve; cashier, discard, dismiss, sack; destroy, remove; execute, perform, fulfil, observe; annul, cancel, invalidate, nullify,

rescind. * *n* disburdening, unloading; dismissal, displacement, ejection, emission, evacuation, excretion, expulsion, vent, voiding; blast, burst, explosion, firing; execution, fulfilment, observance, fulfilment; annulment, clearance, liquidation, payment, satisfaction, settlement; exemption, liberation, release; flow, flux, execration.

disciple *n* catechumen, learner, pupil, scholar, student; adherent, follower, partisan, supporter.

discipline *vb* breed, drill, educate, exercise, form, instruct, teach, train; control, govern, regulate, school; chasten, chastise, punish. * *n* culture, drill, drilling, education, exercise, instruction, training; control, government, regulation, subjection; chastisement, correction, punishment.

disclose *vb* discover, exhibit, expose, manifest, uncover; bare, betray, blab, communicate, divulge, impart, publish, reveal, show, tell, unfold, unveil, utter.

discomfiture *n* confusion, defeat, frustration, overthrow, rout, vexation.

discomfort *n* annoyance, disquiet, distress, inquietude, malaise, trouble, uneasiness, unpleasantness, vexation.

discompose *vb* confuse, derange, disarrange, disorder, disturb, embroil, jumble, unsettle; agitate, annoy, chafe, displease, disquiet, fret, harass, irritate, nettle, plague, provoke, ruffle, trouble, upset, vex, worry; abash, bewilder, disconcert, embarrass, fluster, perplex.

disconcert *vb* baffle, balk, contravene, defeat, disarrange, frustrate, interrupt, thwart, undo, upset; abash, agitate, bewilder, confuse, demoralize, discompose, disturb, embarrass, faze, perplex, perturb, unbalance, worry.

disconnect *vb* detach, disengage, disjoin, dissociate, disunite, separate, sever, uncouple, unlink.

disconsolate *adj* brokenhearted, cheerless, comfortless, dejected, desolate, forlorn, gloomy, heartbroken, inconsolable, melancholy, miserable, sad, sorrowful, unhappy, woeful, wretched.

discontent *n* discontentment, displeasure,

dissatisfaction, inquietude, restlessness, uneasiness.

discord *n* contention, difference, disagreement, dissension, opposition, quarrelling, rupture, strife, variance, wrangling; cacophony, discordance, dissonance, harshness, jangle, jarring.

discount *vb* allow for, deduct, lower, rebate, reduce, subtract; disregard, ignore, overlook. * *n* abatement, drawback; allowance, deduction, rebate, reduction.

discourage *vb* abase, awe, damp, daunt, deject, depress, deject, dismay, dishearten, dispirit, frighten, intimidate; deter, dissuade, hinder; disfavour, discountenance.

discouragement *n* disheartening; dissuasion; damper, deterrent, embarrassment, hindrance, impediment, obstacle, wet blanket.

discover *vb* communicate, disclose, exhibit, impart, manifest, show, reveal, tell; ascertain, behold, discern, espy, see; descry, detect, determine, discern; contrive, invent, originate.

discredit *vb* disbelieve, doubt, question; depreciate, disgrace, dishonour, disparage, reproach. * *n* disbelief, distrust; disgrace, dishonour, disrepute, ignominy, notoriety, obloquy, odium, opprobrium, reproach, scandal.

discreet *adj* careful, cautious, circumspect, considerate, discerning, heedful, judicious, prudent, sagacious, wary, wise.

discrepancy *n* contrariety, difference, disagreement, discordance, dissonance, divergence, incongruity, inconsistency, variance, variation.

discretion *n* care, carefulness, caution, circumspection, considerateness, consideration, heedfulness, judgement, judicious, prudence, wariness; discrimination, maturity, responsibility; choice, option, pleasure, will.

discrimination *n* difference, distinction; acumen, acuteness, discernment, insight, judgement, penetration, sagacity.

discriminatory *adj* characteristic, characterizing, discriminating, discriminative, distinctive, distinguishing.

discuss *vb* agitate, argue, canvass, consider, debate, deliberate, examine, sift, ventilate.

disdainful *adj* cavalier, contemptuous, contumelious, haughty, scornful, supercilious.

disease *n* affection, affliction, ail, ailment, complaint, disorder, distemper, illness, indisposition, infirmity, malady, sickness.

disengage *vb* clear, deliver, discharge, disembarrass, disembroil, disencumber, disentangle, extricate, liberate, release; detach, disjoin, dissociate, disunite, divide, separate; wean, withdraw.

disentangle *vb* loosen, separate, unfold, unravel, untwist; clear, detach, disconnect, disembroil, disengage, extricate, liberate, loose, unloose.

disfigurement *n* blemishing, defacement, deforming, injury, marring, spoiling; blemish, defect, deformity, injury, spot, stain.

disgrace *vb* degrade, humble, humiliate; abase, debase, defame, discredit, disfavour, dishonour, disparage, reproach, stain, sully, taint, tarnish. * *n* abomination, disrepute, humiliation, ignominy, infamy, mortification, shame, scandal.

disgraceful *adj* discreditable, dishonourable, disreputable, ignominious, infamous, opprobrious, scandalous, shameful.

disguise *vb* cloak, conceal, cover, dissemble, hide, mask, muffle, screen, secrete, shroud, veil. * *n* concealment, cover, mask, veil; blind, cloak, masquerade, pretence, pretext, veneer.

disgust *vb* nauseate, sicken; abominate, detest, displease, offend, repel, repulse, revolt. * *n* disrelish, distaste, loathing, nausea; abhorrence, abomination, antipathy, aversion, detestation, dislike, repugnance, revulsion.

dish *vb* deal out, give, ladle, serve; blight, dash, frustrate, mar, ruin, spoil. * *n* bowl, plate, saucer, vessel.

dishearten *vb* cast down, damp, dampen, daunt, deject, depress, deter, discourage, dispirit.

dishevelled *adj* disarranged, disordered, messed, tousled, tumbled, unkempt, untidy, untrimmed.

dishonest adj cheating, corrupt, crafty, crooked, deceitful, deceiving, deceptive, designing, faithless, false, falsehearted, fraudulent, guileful, knavish, perfidious, slippery, treacherous, unfair, unscrupulous.

dishonour vb abase, defame, degrade, discredit, disfavour, dishonour, disgrace, disparage, reproach, shame, taint. * n abasement, basement, contempt, degradation, discredit, disesteem, disfavour, disgrace, dishonour, disparagement, disrepute, ignominy, infamy, obloquy, odium, opprobrium, reproach, scandal, shame.

dishonourable adj discreditable, disgraceful, disreputable, ignominious, infamous, scandalous, shameful; base, false, falsehearted, shameless.

disinfect vb cleanse, deodorize, fumigate, purify, sterilize.

disintegrate vb crumble, decompose, dissolve, disunite, pulverize, separate.

disinterested adj candid, fair, high-minded, impartial, indifferent, unbiased, unselfish, unprejudiced; generous, liberal, magnanimous, unselfish.

disjointed adj desultory, disconnected, incoherent, loose.

dislike vb abominate, detest, disapprove, disrelish, hate, loathe. * n antagonism, antipathy, aversion, disapproval, disfavour, disgust, disinclination, displeasure, disrelish, distaste, loathing, repugnance.

dislocate vb disarrange, displace, disturb; disarticulate, disjoint, luxate, slip.

dislodge vb dismount, dispel, displace, eject, expel, oust, remove.

disloyal adj disaffected, faithless, false, perfidious, traitorous, treacherous, treasonable, undutiful, unfaithful, unpatriotic, untrue.

dismal adj cheerless, dark, dreary, dull, gloomy, lonesome; blue, calamitous, doleful, dolorous, funereal, lugubrious, melancholy, mournful, sad, sombre, sorrowful.

dismantle vb divest, strip, unrig.

dismay vb affright, alarm, appal, daunt, discourage, dishearten, frighten, horrify, intimidate, paralyse, scare, terrify. * n

affright, alarm, consternation, fear, fright, horror, terror.

dismiss vb banish, cashier, discard, discharge, disperse, reject, release, remove.

disobey vb infringe, transgress, violate.

disorder vb confound, confuse, derange, disarrange, discompose, disorganize, disturb, unsettle, upset. * n confusion, derangement, disarrangement, disarray, disorganization, irregularity, jumble, litter, mess, topsy-turvy; brawl, commotion, disturbance, fight, quarrel, riot, tumult; riotousness, tumultuousness, turbulence; ail, aliment, complaint, distemper, illness, indisposition, malady, sickness.

disorderly adj chaotic, confused, intemperate, irregular, unmethodical, unsystematic, untidy; lawless, rebellious, riotous, tumultuous, turbulent, ungovernable, unmanageable, unruly.

disown vb disavow, disclaim, reject, renounce, repudiate; abnegate, deny, disallow.

disparage vb belittle, decry, depreciate, derogate from, detract from, doubt, question, run down, underestimate, underpraise, underrate, undervalue; asperse, defame, inveigh against, reflect on, reproach, slur, speak ill of, traduce, vilify.

disparity n difference, disproportion, inequality; dissimilarity, dissimilitude, unlikeness.

dispassionate adj calm, collected, composed, cool, imperturbable, inexcitable, moderate, quiet, serene, sober, staid, temperate, undisturbed, unexcitable, unexcited, unimpassioned, unruffled; candid, disinterested, fair, impartial, neutral, unbiased.

dispatch, despatch vb assassinate, kill, murder, slaughter, slay; accelerate, conclude, dismiss, expedite, finish, forward, hasten, hurry, quicken, speed. * n dispatching, sending; diligence, expedition, haste, rapidity, speed; completion, conduct, doing, transaction; communication, document, instruction, letter, message, missive, report.

dispel vb banish, disperse, dissipate, scatter.

dispensation *n* allotment, apportioning, apportionment, dispensing, distributing, distribution; administration, stewardship; economy, plan, scheme, system; exemption, immunity, indulgence, licence, privilege.

dispirited *adj* chapfallen, dejected, depressed, discouraged, disheartened, down-cast, down-hearted.

display *vb* expand, extend, open, spread, unfold; exhibit, show; flaunt, parade. * *n* exhibition, manifestation, show; flourish, ostentation, pageant, parade, pomp.

displease *vb* disgruntle, disgust, disoblige, dissatisfy, offend; affront, aggravate, anger, annoy, chafe, chagrin, fret, irritate, nettle, pique, provoke, vex.

disposal *n* arrangement, disposition; conduct, control, direction, disposure, government, management, ordering, regulation; bestowment, dispensation, distribution.

dispose *vb* arrange, distribute, marshal, group, place, range, rank, set; adjust, determine, regulate, settle; bias, incline, induce, lead, move, predispose; control, decide, regulate, rule, settle; arrange, bargain, compound; alienate, convey, demise, sell, transfer.

disposed *adj* apt, inclined, prone, ready, tending.

disposition *n* arrangement, arranging, classification, disposing, grouping, location, placing; adjustment, control, direction, disposure, disposal, management, ordering, regulation; aptitude, bent, bias, inclination, nature, proneness, predisposition, proclivity, proneness, propensity, tendency; character, constitution, humour, native, nature, temper, temperament, turn; inclination, willingness; bestowal, bestowment, dispensation, distribution.

disproportion *n* disparity, inadequacy, inequality, insufficiency, unsuitableness; incommensurateness.

disputatious *adj* argumentative, bickering, captious, caviling, contentious, dissentious, litigious, polemical, pugnacious, quarrelsome.

dispute *vb* altercate, argue, debate, litigate, question; bicker, brawl, jangle, quarrel, spar, spat, squabble, tiff, wrangle; agitate, argue, debate, ventilate; challenge, contradict, controvert, deny, impugn; contest, struggle for. * *n* controversy, debate, discussion, disputation; altercation, argument, bickering, brawl, disagreement, dissension, spat, squabble, tiff, wrangle.

disqualify *vb* disable, incapacitate, unfit; disenable, incapacitate, preclude, prohibit.

disregard *vb* contemn, despise, disdain, disobey, disparage, ignore, neglect, overlook, slight. * *n* contempt, ignoring, inattention, neglect, oversight, slight; disesteem, disfavour, indifference.

disreputable *adj* derogatory, discreditable, dishonourable, disgraceful, infamous, opprobrious, scandalous, shameful; base, contemptible, low, mean, vicious, vile, vulgar.

disrespect *n* disesteem, disregard, irreverence, neglect, slight; discourteousness, impertinence, impolite, incivility, rudeness.

dissect *vb* analyse, examine, explore, investigate, scrutinize, sift.

dissemble *vb* cloak, conceal, cover, disguise, hide; counterfeit, dissimulate, feign, pretend.

disseminate *vb* circulate, diffuse, disperse, proclaim, promulgate, propagate, publish, scatter, spread.

dissent *vb* decline, differ, disagree, refuse. * *n* difference, disagreement, nonconformity, opposition, recusancy, refusal.

disservice *n* disadvantage, disfavour, harm, hurt, ill-turn, injury, mischief.

dissidence *n* disagreement, dissent, nonconformity, sectarianism.

dissimilar *adj* different, divergent, diverse, heterogeneous, unlike, various.

dissimulation *n* concealment, deceit, dissembling, double-dealing, duplicity, feigning, hypocrisy, pretence.

dissipate *vb* dispel, disperse, scatter; consume, expend, lavish, spend, squander, waste; disappear, vanish.

dissolute *adj* abandoned, corrupt, debauched, depraved, disorderly, dissipated, graceless, lax, lewd, licentious, loose, profligate, rakish, reprobate, shameless, vicious, wanton, wild.

dissolve vb liquefy, melt; disorganize, disunite, divide, loose, separate, sever; destroy, ruin; disappear, fade, scatter, vanish; crumble, decompose, disintegrate, perish.

distance vb excel, outdo, outstrip, surpass. * n farness, remoteness; aloofness, coldness, frigidity, reserve, stiffness, offishness; absence, separation, space.

distant adj far, far-away, remote; aloof, ceremonious, cold, cool, frigid, haughty, reserved, stiff, uncordial; faint, indirect, obscure, slight.

distasteful adj disgusting, loathsome, nauseating, nauseous, unpalatable, unsavoury; disagreeable, displeasing, offensive, repugnant, repulsive, unpleasant.

distinct adj definite, different, discrete, disjunct, individual, separate, unconnected; clear, defined, definite, manifest, obvious, plain, unconfused, unmistakable, well-defined.

distinction n discernment, discrimination, distinguishing; difference; account, celebrity, credit, eminence, fame, name, note, rank, renown, reputation, repute, respectability, superiority.

distinctive adj characteristic, differentiating, discriminating, distinguishing.

distinguish vb characterize, mark; differentiate, discern, discriminate, perceive, recognize, see, single out, tell; demarcate, divide, separate; celebrate, honour, signalize.

distinguished adj celebrated, eminent, famous, illustrious, noted; conspicuous, extraordinary, laureate, marked, shining, superior, transcendent.

distort vb contort, deform, gnarl, screw, twist, warp, wrest; falsify, misrepresent, pervert.

distract vb divert, draw away; bewilder, confound, confuse, derange, discompose, disconcert, disturb, embarrass, harass, madden, mystify, perplex, puzzle.

distress vb afflict, annoy, grieve, harry, pain, perplex, rack, trouble; distrain, seize, take. * n affliction, calamity, dis-

aster, misery, misfortune, adversity, hardship, perplexity, trial, tribulation; agony, anguish, dolour, grief, sorrow, suffering; gnawing, gripe, griping, pain, torment, torture; destitution, indigence, poverty, privation, straits, want.

distribute vb allocate, allot, apportion, assign, deal, dispense, divide, dole out, give, mete, partition, prorate, share; administer, arrange, assort, class, classify, dispose.

distribution n allocation, allotment, apportionment, assignment, assortment, dispensation, dispensing; arrangement, disposal, disposition, classification, division, dole, grouping, partition, sharing.

district n circuit, department, neighbourhood, province, quarter, region, section, territory, tract, ward.

distrust vb disbelieve, discredit, doubt, misbelieve, mistrust, question, suspect. * n doubt, misgiving, mistrust, question, suspicion.

disturb vb agitate, shake, stir; confuse, derange, disarrange, disorder, unsettle, upset; annoy, discompose, disconcert, disquiet, distract, fuss, incommode, molest, perturb, plague, trouble, ruffle, vex, worry; impede, interrupt, hinder.

disturbance n agitation, commotion, confusion, convulsion, derangement, disorder, perturbation, unsettlement; annoyance, discomposure, distraction, excitement, fuss; hindrance, interruption, molestation; brawl, commotion, disorder, excitement, fracas, hubbub, riot, rising, tumult, turmoil, uproar.

disunite vb detach, disconnect, disjoin, dissever, dissociate, divide, part, rend, separate, segregate, sever, sunder; alienate, estrange.

disuse n desuetude, discontinuance, disusage, neglect, nonobservance.

ditch vb canalize, dig, excavate, furrow, gouge, trench; abandon, discard, dump, jettison, scrap. * n channel, drain, fosse, moat, trench.

dive vb explore, fathom, penetrate, plunge, sound. * n drop, fall, header, plunge; bar, den, dump, joint, saloon.

diverge vb divide, radiate, separate; divaricate, separate; deviate, differ, disagree, vary.

diverse *adj* different, differing, disagreement, dissimilar, divergent, heterogeneous, multifarious, multiform, separate, unlike, variant, various, varying.

diversion *n* deflection, diverting; amusement, delight, distraction, enjoyment, entertainment, game, gratification, pastime, play, pleasure, recreation, sport; detour, digression.

diversity *n* difference, dissimilarity, dissimilitude, divergence, unlikeness, variation; heterogeneity, manifoldness, multifariousness, multiformity, variety.

divert *vb* deflect, distract, disturb; amuse, beguile, delight, entertain, exhilarate, gratify, recreate, refresh, solace.

divest *vb* denude, disrobe, strip, unclothe, undress; deprive, dispossess, strip.

divide *vb* bisect, cleave, cut, dismember, dissever, disunite, open, part, rend, segregate, separate, sever, shear, split, sunder; allocate, allot, apportion, assign, dispense, distribute, dole, mete, portion, share; compartmentalize, demarcate, partition; alienate, disunite, estrange.

divine *vb* foretell, predict, presage, prognosticate, vaticinate, prophesy; believe, conjecture, fancy, guess, suppose, surmise, suspect, think. * *adj* deiform, godlike, superhuman, supernatural; angelic, celestial, heavenly, holy, sacred, seraphic, spiritual; exalted, exalting, rapturous, supreme, transcendent. * *n* churchman, clergyman, ecclesiastic, minister, parson, pastor, priest.

division *n* compartmentalization, disconnection, disjunction, dismemberment, segmentation, separation, severance; category, class, compartment, head, parcel, portion, section, segment; demarcation, partition; alienation, allotment, apportionment, distribution; breach, difference, disagreement, discord, disunion, estrangement, feud, rupture, variance.

divorce *vb* disconnect, dissolve, disunite, part, put away, separate, sever, split up, sunder, unmarry. * *n* disjunction, dissolution, disunion, division, divorcement, parting, separation, severance.

divulge *vb* communicate, declare, disclose, discover, exhibit, expose, impart, proclaim, promulgate, publish, reveal, tell, uncover.

dizzy *adj* giddy, vertiginous; careless, heedless, thoughtless.

do *vb* accomplish, achieve, act, commit, effect, execute, perform; complete, conclude, end, finish, settle, terminate; conduct, transact; observe, perform, practice; translate, render; cook, prepare; cheat, chouse, cozen, hoax, swindle; serve, suffice. * *n* act, action, adventure, deed, doing, exploit, feat, thing; banquet, event, feast, function, party.

docile *adj* amenable, obedient, pliant, teachable, tractable, yielding.

dock[1] *vb* clip, curtail, cut, deduct, truncate; lessen, shorten.

dock[2] *vb* anchor, moor; join, meet. * *n* anchorage, basin, berth, dockage, dockyard, dry dock, harbour, haven, marina, pier, shipyard, wharf.

doctor *vb* adulterate, alter, cook, falsify, manipulate, tamper with; attend, minister to, cure, heal, remedy, treat; fix, mend, overhaul, repair, service. * *n* general practitioner, GP, healer, leech, medic, physician; adept, savant.

doctrine *n* article, belief, creed, dogma, opinion, precept, principle, teaching, tenet.

dodge *vb* equivocate, evade, prevaricate, quibble, shuffle. * *n* artifice, cavil, evasion, quibble, subterfuge, trick.

dogged *adj* cantankerous, headstrong, inflexible, intractable, mulish, obstinate, pertinacious, perverse, resolute, stubborn, tenacious, unyielding, wilful; churlish, morose, sour, sullen, surly.

dogma *n* article, belief, creed, doctrine, opinion, precept, principle, tenet.

dogmatic *adj* authoritative, categorical, formal, settled; arrogant, confident, dictatorial, imperious, magisterial, opinionated, oracular, overbearing, peremptory, positive; doctrinal.

domain *n* authority, dominion, jurisdiction, province, sway; dominion, empire, realm, territory; lands, estate; branch, department, province, realm, region.

domestic n charwoman, help, home help, maid, servant. * adj domiciliary, family, home, household, private; domesticated; internal, intestine.

domesticate vb tame; adopt, assimilate, familiarize, naturalize.

domicile vb domiciliate, dwell, inhabit, live, remain, reside. * n abode, dwelling, habitation, harbour, home, house, residence.

dominant adj ascendant, ascending, chief, controlling, governing, influential, outstanding, paramount, predominant, preeminent, preponderant, presiding, prevailing, ruling.

dominate vb control, rule, sway; command, overlook, overtop, surmount.

domineer vb rule, tyrannize; bluster, bully, hector, menace, swagger, swell, threaten.

dominion n ascendency, authority, command, control, domain, domination, government, jurisdiction, mastery, rule, sovereignty, supremacy, sway; country, kingdom, realm, region, territory.

donation n alms, benefaction, boon, contribution, dole, donative, gift, grant, gratuity, largesse, offering, present, subscription.

done adj accomplished, achieved, effected, executed, performed; completed, concluded, ended, finished, terminated; carried on, transacted; rendered, translated; cooked, prepared; cheated, cozened, hoaxed, swindled; (with for) damned, dished, hors de combat, ruined, shelved, spoiled, wound up.

double vb fold, plait; duplicate, geminate, increase, multiply, repeat; return. * adj binary, coupled, geminate, paired; dual, twice, twofold; deceitful, dishonest, double-dealing, false, hollow, insincere, knavish, perfidious, treacherous, two-faced. * adv doubly, twice, twofold. * n doubling, fold, plait; artifice, manoeuvre, ruse, shift, stratagem, trick, wile; copy, counterpart, twin.

doubt vb demur, fluctuate, hesitate, vacillate, waver; distrust, mistrust, query, question, suspect. * n dubiety, dubiousness, dubitation, hesitance, hesitancy, hesitation, incertitude, indecision, irresolution, question, suspense, uncertainty, vacillation; distrust, misgiving, mistrust, scepticism, suspicion.

doubtful adj dubious, hesitating, sceptical, undecided, undetermined, wavering; ambiguous, dubious, enigmatical, equivocal, hazardous, obscure, problematical, unsure; indeterminate, questionable, undecided, unquestioned.

doubtless adv certainly, unquestionably; clearly, indisputably, precisely.

dowdy adj awkward, dingy, ill-dressed, shabby, slatternly, slovenly; old-fashioned, unfashionable.

downcast adj chapfallen, crestfallen, dejected, depressed, despondent, discouraged, disheartened, dispirited, downhearted, low-spirited, sad, unhappy.

downfall n descent, destruction, fall, ruin.

downhearted adj chapfallen, crestfallen, dejected, depressed, despondent, discouraged, disheartened, dispirited, downcast, low-spirited, sad, unhappy.

downright adj absolute, categorical, clear, explicit, plain, positive, sheer, simple, undisguised, unequivocal; above-board, artless, blunt, direct, frank, honest, ingenuous, open, sincere, straightforward, unceremonious.

doze vb drowse, nap, sleep, slumber. * n drowse, forty-winks, nap.

dozy adj drowsy, heavy, sleepy, sluggish.

draft vb detach, select; commandeer, conscript, impress; delineate, draw, outline, sketch. * n conscription, drawing, selection; delineation, outline, sketch; bill, cheque, order.

drag vb draw, haul, pull, tow, tug; trail; linger, loiter. * n favour, influence, pull; brake, check, curb, lag, resistance, retardation, scotch, skid, slackening, slack-off, slowing.

drain vb milk, sluice, tap; empty, evacuate, exhaust; dry. * n channel, culvert, ditch, sewer, sluice, trench, watercourse; exhaustion, withdrawal.

draw vb drag, haul, tow, tug, pull; attract; drain, suck, syphon; extract, extort; breathe in, inhale, inspire; allure, engage, entice, induce, influence, lead, move, persuade; extend, protract, stretch; delineate, depict, sketch; deduce, derive, infer; compose, draft, formulate, frame, prepare; blister, vesicate, write.

drawback *n* defect, deficiency, detriment, disadvantage, fault, flaw, imperfection, injury; abatement, allowance, deduction, discount, rebate, reduction.

dread *vb* apprehend, fear. * *adj* dreadful, frightful, horrible, terrible; awful, venerable. * *n* affright, alarm, apprehension, fear, terror; awe, veneration.

dreadful *adj* alarming, appalling, awesome, dire, direful, fearful, formidable, frightful, horrible, horrid, terrible, terrific, tremendous; awful, venerable.

dream *vb* fancy, imagine, think. * *n* conceit, day-dream, delusion, fancy, fantasy, hallucination, illusion, imagination, reverie, vagary, vision.

dreamer *n* enthusiast, visionary.

dreamy *adj* absent, abstracted, fanciful, ideal, misty, shadowy, speculative, unreal, visionary.

dreary *adj* cheerless, chilling, dark, depressing, dismal, drear, gloomy, lonely, lonesome, sad, solitary, sorrowful; boring, dull, monotonous, tedious, tiresome, uninteresting, wearisome.

drench *vb* dowse, drown, saturate, soak, souse, steep, wet; physic, purge.

dress *vb* align, straighten; adjust, arrange, dispose; fit, prepare; accoutre, apparel, array, attire, clothe, robe, rig; adorn, bedeck, deck, decorate, drape, embellish, trim. * *n* apparel, attire, clothes, clothing, costume, garb, guise, garments, habiliment, habit, raiment, suit, toilet, vesture; bedizenment, bravery; frock, gown, rob.

dressy *adj* flashy, gaudy, showy.

drift *vb* accumulate, drive, float, wander. * *n* bearing, course, direction; aim, design, intent, intention, mark, object, proposal, purpose, scope, tendency; detritus, deposit, diluvium; gallery, passage, tunnel; current, rush, sweep; heap, pile.

drill *vb* bore, perforate, pierce; discipline, exercise, instruct, teach, train. * *n* borer; discipline, exercise, training.

drink *vb* imbibe, sip, swill; carouse, indulge, revel, tipple, tope; swallow, quaff; absorb. * *n* beverage, draught, liquid, potation, potion; dram, nip, sip, snifter, refreshment.

drip *vb* dribble, drop, leak, trickle; distil, filter, percolate; ooze, reek, seep, weep. * *n* dribble, drippings, drop, leak, leakage, leaking, trickle, tricklet; bore, nuisance, wet blanket.

drive *vb* hurl, impel, propel, send, shoot, thrust; actuate, incite, press, urge; coerce, compel, constrain, force, harass, oblige, overburden, press, rush; go, guide, ride, travel; aim, intend. * *n* effort, energy, pressure; airing, ride; road.

drivel *vb* babble, blether, dote, drool, slaver, slobber. * *n* balderdash, drivelling, fatuity, nonsense, prating, rubbish, slaver, stuff, twaddle.

drizzle *vb* mizzle, rain, shower, sprinkle. * *n* haar, mist, mizzle, rain, sprinkling.

drone *vb* dawdle, drawl, idle, loaf, lounge; hum. * *n* idler, loafer, lounger, sluggard.

droop *vb* fade, wilt, wither; decline, fail, faint, flag, languish, sink, weaken; bend, hang.

drop *vb* distil, drip, shed; decline, depress, descend, dump, lower, sink; abandon, desert, forsake, forswear, leave, omit, relinquish, quit; cease, discontinue, intermit, remit; fall, precipitate. * *n* bead, droplet, globule, gutta; earring, pendant.

drought *n* aridity, drouth, dryness, thirstiness.

drown *vb* deluge, engulf, flood, immerse, inundate, overflow, sink, submerge, swamp; overcome, overpower, overwhelm.

drowse *vb* doze, nap, sleep, slumber, snooze. * *n* doze, forty winks, nap, siesta, sleep, snooze.

drowsy *adj* dozy, sleepy; comatose, lethargic, stupid; lulling, soporific.

drudge *vb* fag, grub, grind, plod, slave, toil, work. * *n* fag, grind, hack, hard worker, menial, plodder, scullion, slave, toiler, worker.

drug *vb* dose, medicate; disgust, surfeit. * *n* medicine, physic, remedy; poison.

drunk *adj* boozed, drunken, inebriated,

intoxicated, maudlin, soaked, tipsy; ablaze, aflame, delirious, fervent, suffused. * n alcoholic, boozer, dipsomaniac, drunkard, inebriate, lush, soak; bacchanal, bender, binge.

dry vb dehydrate, desiccate, drain, exsiccate, parch. * adj desiccated, dried, juiceless, sapless, unmoistened; arid, droughty, parched; drouthy, thirsty; barren, dull, insipid, jejune, plain, pointless, tame, tedious, tiresome, unembellished, uninteresting, vapid; cutting, keen, sarcastic, severe, sharp, sly.

dub vb call, christen, denominate, designate, entitle, name, style, term.

dubious adj doubtful, fluctuating, hesitant, uncertain, undecided, unsettled, wavering; ambiguous, doubtful, equivocal, questionable, uncertain.

duck vb dip, dive, immerse, plunge, submerge, souse; bend, bow, dodge, stoop.

duct n canal, channel, conduit, pipe, tube; blood-vessel.

due adj owed, owing; appropriate, becoming, befitting, bounden, fit, proper, suitable, right. * adv dead, direct, directly, exactly, just, right, squarely, straight. * n claim, debt, desert, right.

dull vb blunt; benumb, besot, deaden, hebetate, obtund, paralyse, stupefy; dampen, deject, depress, discourage, dishearten, dispirit; allay, alleviate, assuage, mitigate, moderate, quiet, soften; deaden, dim, sully, tarnish. * adj blockish, brutish, doltish, obtuse, stolid, stupid, unintelligent; apathetic, callous, dead, insensible, passionless, phlegmatic, unfeeling, unimpassioned, unresponsive; heavy, inactive, inanimate, inert, languish, lifeless, slow, sluggish, torpid; blunt, dulled, hebetate, obtuse; cheerless, dismal, dreary, gloomy, sad, sombre; dim, lacklustre, lustreless, matt, obscure, opaque, tarnished; dry, flat, insipid, irksome, jejune, prosy, tedious, tiresome, uninteresting, wearisome.

duly adv befittingly, decorously, fitly, properly, rightly; regularly.

dumb adj inarticulate, mute, silent, soundless, speechless, voiceless.

dumbfound vb amaze, astonish, astound,

bewilder, confound, confuse, nonplus, pose.

dupe vb beguile, cheat, chouse, circumvent, cozen, deceive, delude, gull, hoodwink, outwit, overreach, swindle, trick. * n gull, simpleton.

duplicate vb copy, double, repeat, replicate, reproduce. * adj doubled, twofold. * n copy, counterpart, facsimile, replica, transcript.

duplicity n artifice, chicanery, circumvention, deceit, deception, dishonesty, dissimulation, double-dealing, falseness, fraud, guile, hypocrisy, perfidy.

durable adj abiding, constant, continuing, enduring, firm, lasting, permanent, persistent, stable.

duration n continuance, continuation, permanency, perpetuation, prolongation; period, time.

duress n captivity, confinement, constraint, durance, hardship, imprisonment, restraint; compulsion.

dutiful adj duteous, obedient, submissive; deferential, respectful, reverential.

duty n allegiance, devoirs, obligation, responsibility, reverence; business, engagement, function, office, service; custom, excise, impost, tariff, tax, toll.

dwell vb abide, inhabit, live, lodge, remain, reside, rest, sojourn, stay, stop, tarry, tenant.

dwindle vb decrease, diminish, lessen, shrink; decay, decline, deteriorate, pine, sink, waste away.

dye vb colour, stain, tinge. * n cast, colour, hue, shade, stain, tinge, tint.

dying adj expiring; mortal, perishable. * n death, decease, demise, departure, dissolution, exit.

dynasty n dominion, empire, government, rule, sovereignty.

E

eager adj agog, avid, anxious, desirous, fain, greedy, impatient, keen, longing, yearning; animated, ardent, earnest, enthusiastic, fervent, fervid, forward, glowing, hot, impetuous, sanguine, vehement, zealous.

ear *n* attention, hearing, heed, regard.

early *adj* opportune, seasonable, timely; forward, premature; dawning, matutinal. * *adv* anon, beforehand, betimes, ere, seasonably, shortly, soon.

earn *vb* acquire, gain, get, obtain, procure, realize, reap, win; deserve, merit.

earnest *adj* animated, ardent, eager, cordial, fervent, fervid, glowing, hearty, impassioned, importune, warm, zealous; fixed, intent, steady; sincere, true, truthful; important, momentous, serious, weighty. * *n* reality, seriousness, truth; foretaste, pledge, promise; handsel, payment.

earnings *npl* allowance, emoluments, gettings, income, pay, proceeds, profits, remuneration, reward, salary, stipend.

earth *n* globe, orb, planet, world; clay, clod, dirt, glebe, ground, humus, land, loam, sod, soil, turf; mankind, world.

earthly *adj* terrestrial; base, carnal, earthborn, low, gross, grovelling, sensual, sordid, unspiritual, worldly; bodily, material, mundane, natural, secular, temporal.

earthy *adj* clayey, earth-like, terrene; earthly, terrestrial; coarse, gross, material, unrefined.

ease *vb* disburden, disencumber, pacify, quiet, relieve, still; abate, allay, alleviate, appease, assuage, diminish, mitigate, soothe; loosen, release; facilitate, favour. * *n* leisure, quiescence, repose, rest; calmness, content, contentment, enjoyment, happiness, peace, quiet, quietness, quietude, relief, repose, satisfaction, serenity, tranquillity; easiness, facility, readiness; flexibility, freedom, liberty, lightness, naturalness, unconcern, unconstraint; comfort, elbowroom.

easy *adj* light; careless, comfortable, contented, effortless, painless, quiet, satisfied, tranquil, untroubled; accommodating, complaisant, compliant, complying, facile, indolent, manageable, pliant, submissive, tractable, yielding; graceful, informal, natural, unconstrained; flowing, ready, smooth, unaffected; gentle,

lenient, mild, moderate; affluent, comfortable, loose, unconcerned, unembarrassed.

eat *vb* chew, consume, devour, engorge, ingest, ravage, swallow; consume, corrode, demolish, erode; breakfast, dine, feed, lunch, sup.

eatable *adj* edible, esculent, harmless, wholesome.

ebb *vb* abate, recede, retire, subside; decay, decline, decrease, degenerate, deteriorate, sink, wane. * *n* refluence, reflux, regress, regression, retrocedence, retrocession, retrogression, return; caducity, decay, decline, degeneration, deterioration, wane, waning; abatement, decrease, decrement, diminution.

eccentric *adj* decentred, parabolic; aberrant, abnormal, anomalous, cranky, erratic, fantastic, irregular, odd, outlandish, peculiar, singular, strange, uncommon, unnatural, wayward, whimsical. * *n* crank, curiosity, original.

eccentricity *n* ellipticity, flattening, flatness, oblateness; aberration, irregularity, oddity, oddness, peculiarity, singularity, strangeness, waywardness.

echo *vb* reply, resound, reverberate, ring; re-echo, repeat. * *n* answer, repetition, reverberation; imitation.

eclipse *vb* cloud, darken, dim, obscure, overshadow, veil; annihilate, annul, blot out, extinguish. * *n* clouding, concealment, darkening, dimming, disappearance, hiding, obscuration, occultation, shrouding, vanishing, veiling; annihilation, blotting out, destruction, extinction, extinguishment, obliteration.

economize *vb* husband, manage, save; retrench.

economy *n* frugality, husbandry, parsimony, providence, retrenchment, saving, skimping, stinginess, thrift, thriftiness; administration, arrangement, management, method, order, plan, regulation, system; dispensation.

ecstasy *n* frenzy, madness, paroxysm, trance; delight, gladness, joy, rhapsody, rapture, ravishment, transport.

edge *vb* sharpen; border, fringe, rim. * *n* border, brim, brink, border, bound, crest, fringe, hem, lip, margin, rim, verge; animation, intensity, interest, keenness, sharpness, zest; acrimony, bitterness, gall, sharpness, sting.

edible *adj* eatable, esculent, harmless, wholesome.

edict *n* act, command, constitution, decision, decree, law, mandate, manifesto, notice, order, ordinance, proclamation, regulation, rescript, statute.

edify *vb* educate, elevate, enlightenment, improve, inform, instruct, nurture, teach, upbuild.

educate *vb* breed, cultivate, develop, discipline, drill, edify, exercise, indoctrinate, inform, instruct, mature, nurture, rear, school, teach, train.

education *n* breeding, cultivation, culture, development, discipline, drilling, indoctrination, instruction, nurture, pedagogics, schooling, teaching, training, tuition.

eerie *adj* awesome, fearful, frightening, strange, uncanny, weird.

effect *vb* cause, create, effectuate, produce; accomplish, achieve, carry, compass, complete, conclude, consummate, contrive, do, execute, force, negotiate, perform, realize, work. * *n* consequence, event, fruit. issue. outcome, result; efficiency, fact, force, power, reality; validity, weight; drift, import, intent, meaning, purport, significance, tenor.

effective *adj* able, active, adequate, competent, convincing, effectual, sufficient; cogent, efficacious, energetic, forcible, potent, powerful.

effects *npl* chattels, furniture, goods, movables, property.

effectual *adj* operative, successful; active, effective, efficacious, efficient.

efficacious *adj* active, adequate, competent, effective, effectual, efficient, energetic, operative, powerful.

efficient *adj* active, capable, competent, effective, effectual, efficacious, operative, potent; able, energetic, ready, skilful.

effigy *n* figure, image, likeness, portrait, representation, statue.

effort *n* application, attempt, endeavour, essay, exertion, pains, spurt, strain, strife, stretch, struggle, trial, trouble.

effrontery *n* assurance, audacity, boldness, disrespect, hardihood, impudence, incivility,, insolence, presumption, rudeness, sauciness, shamelessness.

effusion *n* discharge, efflux, emission, gush, outpouring; shedding, spilling, waste; address, speech, talk, utterance.

egotistic, egotistical *adj* bumptious, conceited, egoistical, opinionated, self-asserting, self-admiring, self-centred, self-conceited, self-important, self-loving, vain.

eject *vb* belch, discharge, disgorge, emit, evacuate, puke, spew, spit, spout, spurt, void, vomit; bounce, cashier, discharge, dismiss, disposes, eliminate, evict, expel, fire, oust; banish, reject, throw out.

elaborate *vb* develop, improve, mature, produce, refine, ripen. * *adj* complicated, decorated, detailed, dressy, laboured, laborious, ornate, perfected, studied.

elastic *adj* rebounding, recoiling, resilient, springy; buoyant, recuperative.

elbow *vb* crowd, force, hustle, jostle, nudge, push, shoulder. * *n* angle, bend, corner, flexure, joining, turn.

elder *adj* older, senior; ranking, senior; ancient, earlier, olden. * *n* ancestor, senior; presbyter, prior, senator, senior.

elect *vb* appoint, choose, cull, designate, pick, prefer, select. * *adj* choice, chosen, picked, selected; appointed, elected; predestinated, redeemed.

election *n* appointment, choice, preference, selection; alternative, choice, freedom, freewill, liberty; predestination.

elector *n* chooser, constituent, selector, voter.

electrify *vb* charge, galvanize; astonish, enchant, excite, rouse, startle, stir, thrill.

elegant *adj* beautiful, chaste, classical, dainty, graceful, fine, handsome, neat, symmetrical, tasteful, trim, well-made, well-proportioned; accomplished, courtly, cultivated, fashionable, genteel, polished, polite, refined.

element *n* basis, component, constituent, factor, germ, ingredient, part, principle, rudiment, unit; environment, milieu, sphere.

elementary *adj* primordial, simple, uncombined, uncomplicated, uncompounded; basic, component, fundamental, initial, primary, rudimental, rudimentary.

elevate vb erect, hoist, lift, raise; advance, aggrandize, exalt, promote; dignify, ennoble, exalt, greaten, improve, refine; animate, cheer, elate, excite, exhilarate, rouse.

eligible adj desirable, preferable; qualified, suitable, worthy.

eliminate vb disengage, eradicate, exclude, expel, eradicate, remove, separate; ignore, omit, reject.

elope vb abscond, bolt, decamp, disappear, leave.

eloquence n fluency, oratory, rhetoric.

else adv besides, differently, otherwise.

elucidate vb clarify, demonstrate, explain, expound, illuminate, illustrate, interpret, unfold.

elusive adj deceptive, deceitful, delusive, evasive, fallacious, fraudulent, illusory; equivocatory, equivocating, shuffling.

emancipate vb deliver, discharge, disenthral, enfranchise, free, liberate, manumit, release, unchain, unfetter, unshackle.

embargo vb ban, bar, blockade, debar, exclude, prohibit, proscribe, restrict, stop, withhold. * n ban, bar, blockade, exclusion, hindrance, impediment, prohibition, prohibitory, proscription, restraint, restriction, stoppage.

embark vb engage, enlist.

embarrass vb beset, entangle, perplex; annoy, clog, bother, distress, hamper, harass, involve, plague, trouble, vex; abash, confound, confuse, discomfit, disconcert, dumbfounded, mortify, nonplus, pose, shame.

embellish vb adorn, beautify, bedeck, deck, decorate, emblazon, enhance, enrich, garnish, grace, ornament.

embezzle vb appropriate, defalcate, filch, misappropriate, peculate, pilfer, purloin, steal.

embitter vb aggravate, envenom, exacerbate; anger, enrage, exasperate, madden.

emblem n badge, cognizance, device, mark, representation, sign, symbol, token, type.

embody vb combine, compact, concentrate, incorporate; comprehend, comprise, contain, embrace, include; codify, methodize, systematize.

embrace vb clasp; accept, seize, welcome; comprehend, comprise, contain, cover, embody, encircle, enclose, encompass, enfold, hold, include. * n clasp, fold, hug.

emerge vb rise; emanate, escape, issue; appear, arise, outcrop.

emergency n crisis, difficulty, dilemma, exigency, extremity, necessity, pass, pinch, push, strait, urgency; conjuncture, crisis, juncture, pass.

emigration n departure, exodus, migration, removal.

eminence n elevation, hill, projection, prominence, protuberance; celebrity, conspicuousness, distinction, exaltation, fame, loftiness, note, preferment, prominence, reputation, repute, renown.

eminent adj elevated, high, lofty; celebrated, conspicuous, distinguished, exalted, famous, illustrious, notable, prominent, remarkable, renowned.

emit vb breathe out, dart, discharge, eject, emanate, exhale, gust, hurl, jet, outpour, shed, shoot, spurt, squirt.

emotion n agitation, excitement, feeling, passion, perturbation, sentiment, sympathy, trepidation.

emphasis n accent, stress; force, importance, impressiveness, moment, significance, weight.

emphatic adj decided, distinct, earnest, energetic, expressive, forcible, impressive, intensive, positive, significant, strong, unequivocal.

empire n domain, dominion, sovereignty, supremacy; authority, command, control, government, rule, sway.

employ vb busy, devote, engage, engross, enlist, exercise, occupy, retain; apply, commission, use. * n employment, service.

employment n avocation, business, calling, craft, employ, engagement, occupation, profession, pursuit, trade, vocation, work.

empower vb authorize, commission, permit, qualify, sanction, warrant; enable.

empty vb deplete, drain, evacuate, exhaust; discharge, disembogue; flow, embogue. * *adj* blank, hollow, unoccupied, vacant, vacuous, void; deplete, destitute, devoid, hungry; unfilled, unfurnished, unsupplied; unsatisfactory, unsatisfying, unsubstantial, useless, vain; clear, deserted, desolate, exhausted, free, unburdened, unloaded, waste; foolish, frivolous, inane, senseless, silly, stupid, trivial, weak.

enable *vb* authorize, capacitate, commission, empower, fit, permit, prepare, qualify, sanction, warrant.

enact *vb* authorize, command, decree, establish, decree, ordain, order, sanction; act, perform, personate, play, represent.

enchant *vb* beguile, bewitch, charm, delude, fascinate; captivate, catch, enamour, win; beatify, delight, enrapture, rapture, ravish, transport.

enchanting *adj* bewitching, blissful, captivating, charming, delightful, enrapturing, fascinating, rapturous, ravishing.

enchantment *n* charm, conjuration, incantation, magic, necromancy, sorcery, spell, witchery; bliss, delight, fascination, rapture, ravishment, transport.

enclose *vb* circumscribe, corral, coop, embosom, encircle, encompass, environ, fence in, hedge, include, pen, shut in, surround; box, cover, encase, envelop, wrap.

encounter *vb* confront, face, meet; attack, combat, contend, engage, strive, struggle. * *n* assault, attack, clash, collision, meeting, onset; action, affair, battle, brush, combat, conflict, contest, dispute, engagement, skirmish.

encourage *vb* animate, assure, cheer, comfort, console, embolden, enhearten, fortify, hearten, incite, inspirit, instigate, reassure, stimulate, strengthen; abet, aid, advance, approve, countenance, favour, foster, further, help, patronize, promote, support.

encumbrance *n* burden, clog, deadweight, drag, embarrassment, hampering, hindrance, impediment, incubus, load; claim, debt, liability, lien.

end *vb* abolish, close, conclude, discontinue, dissolve, drop, finish, stop, terminate; annihilate, destroy, kill; cease, terminate. * *n* extremity, tip; cessation, close, denouement, ending, expiration, finale, finis, finish, last, period, stoppage, wind-up; completion, conclusion, consummation; annihilation, catastrophe, destruction, dissolution; bound, limit, termination, terminus; consequence, event, issue, result, settlement, sequel, upshot; fragment, remnant, scrap, stub, tag, tail; aim, design, goal, intent, intention, object, objective, purpose.

endanger *vb* commit, compromise, hazard, imperil, jeopardize, peril, risk.

endear *vb* attach, bind, captivate, charm, win.

endearment *n* attachment, fondness, love, tenderness; caress, blandishment, fondling.

endeavour *vb* aim, attempt, essay, labour, seek, strive, struggle, study, try. * *n* aim, attempt, conatus, effort, essay, exertion, trial, struggle, trial.

endless *adj* boundless, illimitable, immeasurable, indeterminable, infinite, interminable, limitless, unlimited; dateless, eternal, everlasting, never-ending, perpetual, unending; deathless, ever-enduring, eternal, ever-living, immortal, imperishable, undying.

endorse *vb* approve, back, confirm, guarantee, indorse, ratify, sanction, superscribe, support, visé, vouch for, warrant; superscribe.

endow *vb* bequeath, clothe, confer, dower, endue, enrich, gift, indue, invest, supply.

endowment *n* bequest, boon, bounty, gift, grant, largesse, present; foundation, fund, property, revenue; ability, aptitude, capability, capacity, faculty, genius, gift, parts, power, qualification, quality, talent.

endurance *n* abiding, bearing, sufferance, suffering, tolerance, toleration; backbone, bottom, forbearance, fortitude, guts, patience, resignation.

endure *vb* bear, support, sustain; experience, suffer, undergo, weather; abide, brook, permit, pocket, swallow, tolerate, stomach, submit, withstand; continue, last, persist, remain, wear.

enemy n adversary, foe; antagonist, foeman, opponent, rival.

energetic adj active, effective, efficacious, emphatic, enterprising, forceful, forcible, hearty, mettlesome, potent, powerful, strenuous, strong, vigorous.

energy n activity, dash, drive, efficacy, efficiency, force, go, impetus, intensity, mettle, might, potency, power, strength, verve, vim; animation, life, manliness, spirit, spiritedness, vigour, zeal.

enforce vb compel, constrain, exact, force, oblige, require, urge.

engage vb bind, commit, obligate, pledge, promise; affiance, betroth, plight, promise; book, brief, employ, enlist, hire, retain; arrest, allure, attach, draw, entertain, fix, gain, win; busy, employ, engross, occupy; attack, encounter; combat, contend, contest, fight, interlock, struggle; embark, enlist; agree, bargain, promise, stipulate, undertake, warrant.

engagement n appointment, assurance, contract, obligation, pledge, promise, stipulation; affiancing, betrothal, plighting; avocation, business, calling, employment, enterprise, occupation; action, battle, combat, encounter, fight.

engine n invention, machine; agency, agent, device, implement, instrument, means, method, tool, weapon.

engrave vb carve, chisel, cut, etch, grave, hatch, incite, sculpture; grave, impress, imprint, infix.

engross vb absorb, engage, occupy, take up; buy up, forestall, monopolize.

enhance vb advance, aggravate, augment, elevate, heighten, increase, intensify, raise, swell.

enigma n conundrum, mystery, problem, puzzle, riddle.

enigmatic adj ambiguous, dark, doubtful, equivocal, hidden, incomprehensible, mysterious, mystic, obscure, occult, perplexing, puzzling, recondite, uncertain, unintelligible.

enjoyment n delight, delectation, gratification, happiness, indulgence, pleasure, satisfaction; possession.

enlarge vb amplify, augment, broaden, extend, dilate, distend, expand, increase, magnify, widen; aggrandize, engreaten, ennoble, expand, greaten; descant, dilate, expiate; expand, extend, increase, swell.

enlighten vb illume, illuminate, illumine; counsel, educate, civilize, inform, instruct, teach.

enlist vb enrol, levy, recruit, register; enrol, list; embark, engage.

enliven vb animate, invigorate, quicken, reanimate, rouse, wake; exhilarate, cheer, brighten, delight, elate, gladden, inspire, inspirit, rouse.

enmity n animosity, aversion, bitterness, hate, hatred, hostility, ill-will, malevolence, malignity, rancour.

enormity n atrociousness, atrocity, depravity, flagitiousness, heinousness, nefariousness, outrageousness, villainy, wickedness.

enormous adj abnormal. exceptional, inordinate, irregular; colossal, Cyclopean, elephantine, Herculean, huge, immense, monstrous, vast, gigantic, prodigious, titanic, tremendous.

enough adj abundant, adequate, ample, plenty, sufficient. * adv satisfactorily, sufficiently. * n abundance, plenty, sufficiency.

enrage vb anger, chafe, exasperate, incense, inflame, infuriate, irritate, madden, provoke.

enrich vb endow; adorn, deck, decorate, embellish, grace, ornament.

enrol vb catalogue, engage, engross, enlist, list, register; chronicle, record.

enslave vb captivate, dominate, master, overmaster, overpower, subjugate.

ensnare vb catch, entrap; allure, inveigle, seduce; bewilder, confound, embarrass, encumber, entangle, perplex.

entangle vb catch, ensnare, entrap; confuse, enmesh, intertwine, intertwist, interweave, knot, mat, ravel, tangle; bewilder, embarrass, encumber, ensnare, involve, nonplus, perplex, puzzle.

enterprise n adventure, attempt, cause, effort, endeavour, essay, project, undertaking, scheme, venture; activity, adventurousness, daring, dash, energy, initiative, readiness, push.

enterprising adj adventurous, audacious, bold, daring, dashing, venturesome; active, adventurous, alert, efficient, energetic, prompt, resourceful, smart, spirited, stirring, strenuous, zealous

entertain vb fete, receive, regale, treat; cherish, foster, harbour, hold, lodge, shelter; admit, consider; amuse, cheer, divert, please, recreate.

entertainment n hospitality; banquet, collation, feast, festival, reception, treat; amusement, diversion, pastime, recreation, sport.

enthusiasm n ecstasy, exaltation, fanaticism; ardour, earnestness, devotion, eagerness, fervour, passion, warmth, zeal.

enthusiast n bigot, devotee, fan, fanatic, zealot; dreamer, visionary.

entice vb allure, attract, bait, cajole, coax, decoy, inveigle, lure, persuade, prevail on, seduce, tempt, wheedle, wile.

entire adj complete, integrated, perfect, unbroken, undiminished, undivided, unimpaired, whole; complete, full, plenary, thorough, unalloyed; mere, pure, sheer, unalloyed, unmingled, unmitigated, unmixed.

entitle vb call, characterize, christen, denominate, designate, dub, name style; empower, enable, fit for, qualify for.

entrance¹ n access, approach, avenue, incoming, ingress; adit, avenue, aperture, door, doorway, entry, gate, hallway, inlet, lobby, mouth, passage, portal, stile, vestibule; beginning, commencement, debut, initiation, introduction; admission, entrée.

entrance² vb bewitch, captivate, charm, delight, enchant, enrapture, fascinate, ravish, transport.

entreaty n adjuration, appeal, importunity, petition, prayer, request, solicitation, suit, supplication.

entrust vb commit, confide, consign.

entwine vb entwist, interlace, intertwine, interweave, inweave, twine, twist, weave; embrace, encircle, encumber, interlace, surround.

enumerate vb calculate, cite, compute, count, detail, mention, number, numerate, reckon, recount, specify, tell.

envelop vb enfold, enwrap, fold, pack, wrap; cover, encircle, encompass, enfold, enshroud, fold, hide, involve, surround.

envelope n capsule, case, covering, integument, shroud, skin, wrapper, veil, vesture, wrap.

envoy n ambassador, legate, minister, plenipotentiary; courier, messenger.

envy vb hate; begrudge, grudge; covet, emulate, desire. * n enviousness, hate, hatred, ill-will, jealousy, malice, spite; grudge, grudging.

ephemeral adj brief, diurnal, evanescent, fleeting, flitting, fugacious, fugitive, momentary, occasional, short-lived, transient, transitory.

epidemic adj general, pandemic, prevailing, prevalent. * n outbreak, pandemia, pestilence, plague, spread, wave.

epigrammatic adj antithetic, concise, laconic, piquant, poignant, pointed, pungent, sharp, terse.

epitome n abbreviation, abridgement, abstract, breviary, brief, comment, compendium, condensation, conspectus, digest, summary, syllabus, synopsis.

epitomize vb abbreviate, abridge, abstract, condense, contract, curtail, cut, reduce, shorten, summarize.

equable adj calm, equal, even, even-tempered, regular, steady, uniform, serene, tranquil, unruffled.

equal vb equalize, even, match. * adj alike, coordinate, equivalent, like, tantamount; even, level, equable, regular, uniform; equitable, even-handed, fair, impartial, just, unbiased; co-extensive, commensurate, corresponding, parallel, proportionate; adequate, competent, fit, sufficient. * n compeer, fellow, match, peer; rival.

equanimity n calmness, composure, coolness, peace, regularity, self-possession, serenity, steadiness.

equip vb appoint, arm, furnish, provide, rig, supply; accoutre, array, dress.

equipment n accoutrement, apparatus, baggage, equipage, furniture, gear, outfit, rigging.

equitable adj even-handed, candid, honest, impartial, just, unbiased, unprejudiced, upright; adequate, fair, proper, reasonable, right.

equity *n* just, right; fair play, fairness, impartiality, justice, rectitude, reasonableness, righteousness, uprightness.

equivalent *adj* commensurate, equal, equipollent, tantamount; interchangeable, synonymous. * *n* complement, coordinate, counterpart, double, equal, fellow, like, match, parallel, pendant, quid pro quo.

era *n* age, date, epoch, period, time.

eradicate *vb* extirpate, root, uproot; abolish, annihilate, destroy, obliterate.

erase *vb* blot, cancel, delete, efface, expunge, obliterate, scrape out.

erasure *n* cancellation, cancelling, effacing, expunging, obliteration.

erect *vb* build, construct, raise, rear; create, establish, form, found, institute, plant. * *adj* standing, unrecumbent, uplifted, upright; elevated, vertical, perpendicular, straight; bold, firm, undaunted, undismayed, unshaken, unterrified.

erode *vb* canker, consume, corrode, destroy, eat away, fret, rub.

erotic *adj* amorous, amatory, arousing, seductive, stimulating, titillating.

err *vb* deviate, ramble, rove, stray, wander; blunder, misjudge, mistake; fall, lapse, nod, offend, sin, stumble, trespass, trip.

errand *n* charge, commission, mandate, message, mission, purpose.

erratic *adj* nomadic, rambling, roving, wandering; moving, planetary; abnormal, capricious, deviating, eccentric, irregular, odd, queer, strange.

erroneous *adj* false, incorrect, inaccurate, inexact, mistaken untrue, wrong.

error *n* blunder, fallacy, inaccuracy, misapprehension, mistake, oversight; delinquency, fault, iniquity, misdeed, misdoing, misstep, obliquity, offence, shortcoming, sin, transgression, trespass, wrongdoing.

erudition *n* knowledge, learning, lore, scholarship.

eruption *n* explosion, outbreak, outburst; sally; rash.

escape *vb* avoid, elude, evade, flee from, shun; abscond, bolt, decamp, flee, fly; slip. * *n* flight; release; passage, passing; leakage.

escort *vb* convey, guard, protect; accompany, attend, conduct. * *n* attendant, bodyguard, cavalier, companion, convoy, gallant, guard, squire; protection, safe conduct, safeguard; attendance, company.

especial *adj* chief, distinguished, marked, particular, peculiar, principal, special, specific, uncommon, unusual. especial, discovery, notice, observation.

espouse *vb* betroth, plight, promise; marry, wed; adopt, champion, defend, embrace, maintain, support.

essay[1] *vb* attempt, endeavour, try. * *n* aim, attempt, effort, endeavour, exertion, struggle, trial.

essay[2] *n* article, composition, disquisition, dissertation, paper, thesis.

essence *n* nature, quintessence, substance; extract, part; odour, perfume, scent; being, entity, existence, nature.

essential *adj* fundamental, indispensable, important, inward, intrinsic, necessary, requisite, vital; diffusible, pure, rectified, volatile.

establish *vb* fix, secure, set, settle; decree, enact, ordain; build, constitute, erect, form, found, institute, organize, originate, pitch, plant, raise; ensconce, ground, install, place, plant, root, secure; approve, confirm, ratify, sanction; prove, substantiate, verify.

estate *n* condition, state; position, rank, standing; division, order; effects, fortune, possessions, property; interest.

esteem *vb* appreciate, estimate, rate, reckon, value; admire, appreciate, honour, like, prize, respect, revere, reverence, value, venerate, worship; account, believe, consider, deem, fancy, hold, imagine, suppose, regard, think. * *n* account, appreciation, consideration, estimate, estimation, judgement, opinion, reckoning, valuation; credit, honour, regard, respect, reverence.

estimable *adj* appreciable, calculable, computable; admirable, credible, deserving, excellent, good, meritorious, precious, respectful, valuable, worthy.

estimate *vb* appraise, appreciate, esteem, prise, rate, value; assess, calculate, compute, count, gauge, judge, reckon. * *n* estimation, judgement, valuation; calculation, computation.

estimation *n* appreciation, appeasement, estimate, valuation; esteem, estimate, judgement, opinion; honour, regard, respect, reverence.

estrange *vb* withdraw, withhold; alienate, divert; disaffect, destroy.

eternal *adj* absolute, inevitable, necessary, self-active, self-existent, self-originated; abiding, ceaseless, endless, ever-enduring, everlasting, incessant, interminable, never-ending, perennial, perpetual, sempiternal, unceasing, unending; deathless, immortal, imperishable, incorruptible, indestructible, never-dying, undying; immutable, unchangeable; ceaseless, continual, continuous, incessant, persistent, unbroken, uninterrupted.

eulogy *n* discourse, eulogium, panegyric, speech; applause, encomium, commendation, eulogium, laudation, praise.

evacuate *vb* empty; discharge, clean out, clear out, eject, excrete, expel, purge, void; abandon, desert, forsake, leave, quit, relinquish, withdraw.

evade *vb* elude, escape; avoid, decline, dodge, funk, shun; baffle, elude, foil; dodge, equivocate, fence, palter, prevaricate, quibble, shuffle.

evaporate *vb* distil, volatilize; dehydrate, dry, vaporize; disperse, dissolve, fade, vanish.

evasion *n* artifice, avoidance, bluffing, deceit, dodge, equivocation, escape, excuse, funking, prevarication, quibble, shift, subterfuge, shuffling, sophistical, tergiversation.

evasive *adj* elusive, elusory, equivocating, prevaricating, shuffling, slippery, sophistical.

even *vb* balance, equalize, harmonize, symmetrize; align, flatten, flush, level, smooth, square. * *adj* flat, horizontal, level, plane, smooth; calm, composed, equable, equal, peaceful, placid, regular,

steady, uniform, unruffled; direct, equitable, fair, impartial, just, straightforward. * *adv* exactly, just, verily; likewise. * *n* eve, evening, eventide, vesper.

evening *n* dusk, eve, even, eventide, nightfall, sunset, twilight.

event *n* circumstance, episode, fact, happening, incident, occurrence; conclusion, consequence, end, issue, outcome, result, sequel, termination; adventure, affair.

eventful *adj* critical, important, memorable, momentous, remarkable, signal, stirring.

eventual *adj* final, last, ultimate; conditional, contingent, possible. ever *adv* always, aye, constantly, continually, eternally, evermore, forever, incessantly, perpetually, unceasingly.

everlasting *adj* ceaseless, constant, continual, endless, eternal, ever-during, incessant, interminable, never-ceasing, never-ending, perpetual, unceasing, unending, unintermitting, uninterrupted; deathless, ever-living, immortal, imperishable, never-dying, undying.

evermore *adv* always, constantly, continually, eternally, ever, forever, perpetually.

everyday *adj* accustomed, common, commonplace, customary, habitual, routine, usual, wonted.

evict *vb* dispossess, eject, thrust out.

evidence *vb* evince, manifest, prove, show, testify, vouch. * *n* affirmation, attestation, confirmation, corroboration, deposition, grounds, indication, proof, testimony, token, trace, voucher, witness.

evident *adj* apparent, bald, clear, conspicuous, distinct, downright, incontestable, indisputable, manifest, obvious, open, overt, palpable, patent, plain, unmistakable.

evil *adj* bad, ill; bad, base, corrupt, malicious, malevolent, malign, nefarious, perverse, sinful, vicious, vile, wicked, wrong; bad, deleterious, baleful, baneful, destructive, harmful, hurtful, injurious, mischievous, noxious, pernicious; adverse, bad, calamitous, disastrous, unfortunate, unhappy, unpropitious, woeful. * n calamity, disaster, ill, misery, misfortune, pain, reverse, sorrow, suffering, woe; badness, baseness, corruption, depravity, malignity, sin, viciousness, wickedness; bale, bane, blast, canker, curse, harm, ill, injury, mischief, wrong.

evolve vb develop, educe, exhibit, expand, open, unfold, unroll.

exact vb elicit, extort, mulch, require, squeeze; ask, claim, compel, demand, enforce, requisition, take. * adj rigid, rigorous, scrupulous, severe, strict; diametric, express, faultless, precise, true; accurate, close, correct, definite, faithful, literal, undeviating; accurate, critical, delicate, fine, nice, sensitive; careful, methodical, precise, punctilious, orderly, punctual, regular.

exacting adj critical, difficult, exactive, rigid, extortionary.

exaggerate vb enlarge, magnify, overcharge, overcolour, overstate, romance, strain, stretch.

exalted adj elated, elevated, high, highflown, lofty, lordly, magnificent, prove.

examination n inspection, observation; exploration, inquiry, inquisition, investigation, perusal, research, search, scrutiny, survey; catechism, probation, review, test, trial.

examine vb inspect, observe; canvass, consider, explore, inquire, investigate, scrutinize, study, test; catechize, interrogate.

example n archetype, copy, model, pattern, piece, prototype, representative, sample, sampler, specimen, standard; exemplification, illustration, instance, precedent, warning.

exasperate vb affront, anger, chafe, enrage, incense, irritate, nettle, offend, provoke, vex; aggravate, exacerbate, inflame, rouse.

exasperation n annoyance, exacerbation, irritation, pro vocation; anger, fury, ire, passion, rage, wrath; aggravation, heightening, increase, worsening.

exceed vb cap, overstep, surpass, transcend; excel, outdo, outstrip, outvie, pass, surpass.

excel vb beat, eclipse, outdo, outrival, outstrip, outvie, surpass; cap, exceed, surpass, transcend.

excellence n distinction, eminence, preeminence, superiority, transcendence; fineness, fitness, goodness, perfection, purity, quality, superiority; advantage; goodness, probity, purity, uprightness, virtue, worth.

excellent adj admirable, choice, crack, eminent, first-rate, prime, sterling, superior, tiptop, transcendent; deserving, estimable, praiseworthy, virtuous, worthy.

except vb exclude, leave out, omit, reject. * conj unless. * prep bar, but, excepting, excluding, save.

exceptional adj aberrant, abnormal, anomalous, exceptive, irregular, peculiar, rare, special, strange, superior, uncommon, unnatural, unusual.

excess adj excessive, unnecessary, redundant, spare, superfluous, surplus. * n disproportion, fulsomeness, glut, oversupply, plethora, redundance, redundancy, surfeit, superabundance, superfluity; overplus, remainder, surplus; debauchery, dissipation, dissoluteness, intemperance, immoderation, overindulgence, unrestraint; extravagance, immoderation, overdoing.

excessive adj disproportionate, exuberant, superabundant, superfluous, undue; extravagant, enormous, inordinate, outrageous, unreasonable; extreme, immoderate, intemperate; vehement, violent.

exchange vb barter, change, commute, shuffle, substitute, swap, trade. truck; bandy, interchange. * n barter, change, commutation, dealing, shuffle, substitution, trade, traffic; interchange, reciprocity; bazaar, bourse, fair, market.

excise[1] n capitation, customs, dues, duty, tariff, tax, taxes, toll.

excise[2] vb cancel, cut, delete, edit, efface, eradicate, erase, expunge, extirpate, remove, strike out.

excision n destruction, eradication, extermination, extirpation.

excitable adj impressible, nervous, sensitive, susceptible; choleric, hasty, hot-headed, hot-tempered, irascible, irritable, passionate, quick-tempered.

excite vb animate, arouse, awaken, brew, evoke, impel, incite, inflame, instigate, kindle, move, prompt, provoke, rouse, spur, stimulate; create, elicit, evoke, raise; agitate, discompose, disturb, irritate, provoke.

excitement n excitation, exciting; incitement, motive, stimulus; activity, agitation, bustle, commotion, disturbance, ferment, flutter, perturbation, sensation, stir, tension; choler, heat, irritation, passion, violence, warmth.

exclaim vb call, cry, declare, ejaculate, shout, utter, vociferate.

exclude vb ban, bar, blackball, debar, ostracize, preclude, reject; hinder, prevent, prohibit, restrain, withhold; except, omit; eject, eliminate, expel, extrude.

exclusive adj debarring, excluding; illiberal, narrow, narrow-minded, selfish, uncharitable; aristocratic, choice, clannish, cliquish, fastidious, fashionable, select, snobbish; only, sole, special.

excursion n drive, expedition, jaunt, journey, ramble, ride, sally, tour, trip, voyage, walk; digression, episode.

excusable adj allowable, defensible, forgivable, justifiable, pardonable, venial, warrantable.

excuse vb absolve, acquit, exculpate, exonerate, forgive, pardon, remit; extenuate, justify; exempt, free, release; overlook. * n absolution, apology, defence, extenuation, justification, plea; colour, disguise, evasion, guise, pretence, pretext, makeshift, semblance, subterfuge.

execute vb accomplish, achieve, carry out, complete. consummate, do, effect, effectuate, finish, perform, perpetrate; administer, enforce, seal, sign; behead, electrocute, guillotine, hang.

executive adj administrative, commanding, controlling, directing, managing, ministerial, officiating, presiding, ruling. * n administrator, director, manager.

exemplary adj assiduous, close, exact, faithful, punctual, punctilious, rigid, rigorous, scrupulous; commendable, correct, good, estimable, excellent, praise-

worthy, virtuous; admonitory, condign, monitory, warning.

exempt vb absolve, except, excuse, exonerate, free, release, relieve. * adj absolved, excepted, excused, exempted, free, immune, liberated, privileged, released.

exercise vb apply, busy, employ, exert, praxis, use; effect, exert, produce, wield; break in, discipline, drill, habituate, school, train; practise, prosecute, pursue, use; task, test, try; afflict, agitate, annoy, burden, pain, trouble, try. * n appliance, application, custom, employment, operation, performance, play, plying, practice, usage, use, working; action, activity, effort, exertion, labour, toil, work; discipline, drill, drilling, schooling, training; lesson, praxis, study, task, test, theme.

exert vb employ, endeavour, exercise, labour, strain, strive, struggle, toil, use, work.

exertion n action, exercise, exerting, use; attempt, effort, endeavour, labour, strain, stretch, struggle, toil, trial.

exhaust vb drain, draw, empty; consume, destroy, dissipate, expend, impoverish, lavish, spend, squander, waste; cripple, debilitate, deplete, disable, enfeeble, enervate, overtire, prostrate, weaken.

exhaustion n debilitation, enervation, fatigue, lassitude. weariness.

exhibit vb demonstrate, disclose, display, evince, expose, express, indicate, manifest, offer, present, reveal, show; offer, present, propose.

exhibition n demonstration, display, exposition, manifestation, representation, spectacle, show; exposition; allowance, benefaction, grant, pension, scholarship.

exhilarate vb animate, cheer, elate, enliven, gladden, inspire, inspirit, rejoice, stimulate.

exhilaration n animating, cheering, elating, enlivening, gladdening, rejoicing, stimulating; animation, cheer, cheerfulness, gaiety, gladness, glee, good spirits, hilarity, joyousness.

exile vb banish, expatriate, expel, ostracize, proscribe. * n banishment, expatriation, expulsion, ostracism, proscription, separation; outcast, refugee.

exist vb be, breathe, live; abide, continue, endure, last, remain.

existence n being, subsisting, subsistence, subsisting; being, creature, entity, essence, thing; animation, continuation, life.

exit vb depart, egress, go, leave. * n departure, withdrawal; death, decrease, demise, end; egress, outlet.

exorbitant adj enormous, excessive, extravagant, inordinate, unreasonable.

exorcise vb cast out, drive away, expel; deliver, purify; address, conjure.

exotic adj extraneous, foreign; extravagant.

expand vb develop, open, spread, unfold, unfurl; diffuse, enlarge, extend, increase, stretch; dilate, distend, enlarge.

expanse n area, expansion, extent, field, stretch.

expansion n expansion, opening, spreading; diastole, dilation, distension, swelling; development, diffusion, enlargement, increase; expanse, extent, stretch.

expect vb anticipate, await, calculate, contemplate, forecast, foresee, hope, reckon, rely.

expectancy n expectance, expectation; abeyance, prospect.

expectation n anticipation, expectance, expectancy, hope, prospect; assurance, confidence, presumption, reliance, trust.

expedient adj advisable, appropriate, convenient, desirable, fit, proper, politic, suitable; advantageous, profitable, useful. * n contrivance, device, means, method, resort, resource, scheme, shift, stopgap, substitute.

expedite vb accelerate, advance, dispatch, facilitate, forward, hasten, hurry, precipitate, press, quicken, urge.

expedition n alacrity, alertness, celerity, dispatch, haste, promptness quickness, speed; enterprise, undertaking; campaign, excursion, journey, march, quest, voyage.

expel vb dislodge, egest, eject, eliminate, excrete; discharge, eject, evacuate, void; bounce, discharge, exclude, exscind,

fire, oust, relegate, remove; banish, disown, excommunicate, exile, expatriate, ostracize, proscribe, unchurch.

expenditure n disbursement, outlay, outlaying, spending; charge, cost, expenditure, outlay.

expensive adj costly, dear, high-priced; extravagant, lavish, wasteful.

experience vb endure, suffer; feel, know; encounter, suffer, undergo. * n endurance, practice, trial; evidence, knowledge, proof, test, testimony.

experienced adj able, accomplished, expert, instructed, knowing, old, practised, qualified, skilful, trained, thoroughbred, versed, veteran, wise.

experiment vb examine, investigate, test, try. * n assay, examination, investigation, ordeal, practice, proof, test, testimony, touchstone, trial.

expert adj able, adroit, apt, clever, dextrous, proficient, prompt, quick, ready, skilful. * n adept, authority, connoisseur, crack, master, specialist.

expertise n adroitness, aptness, dexterity, facility, promptness, skilfulness, skill.

expire vb cease, close, conclude, end, stop, terminate; emit, exhale; decease, depart, die, perish.

explain vb demonstrate, elucidate, expound, illustrate, interpret, resolve, solve, unfold, unravel; account for, justify, solve, warrant.

explanation n clarification, description, elucidation, exegesis, explication, exposition, illustration, interpretation; account, answer, deduction, justification, key, meaning, secret, solution, warrant.

explicit adj absolute, categorical, clear, definite, determinate, exact, express, plain, positive, precise, unambiguous, unequivocal, unreserved

explode vb burst, detonate, discharge, displode, shatter, shiver; contemn, discard, repudiate, scorn, scout.

exploit vb befoul, milk, use, utilize. * n achievement, act, deed, feat.

explore vb examine, fathom, inquire, inspect, investigate, prospect, scrutinize, seek.

explosion n blast, burst, bursting, clap,

crack, detonation, discharge, displosion, fulmination, pop.

exponent *n* example, illustration, index, indication, specimen, symbol, type; commentator, demonstrator, elucidator, expounder, illustrator, interpreter.

expose *vb* bare, display, uncover; descry, detect, disclose, unearth; denounce, mask; subject; endanger, jeopardize, risk, venture.

exposé *n* exhibit, exposition, manifesto; denouncement, divulgement, exposure, revelation.

expound *vb* develop, present, rehearse, reproduce, unfold; clear, elucidate, explain, interpret.

express *vb* air, assert, asseverate, declare, emit, enunciate, manifest, utter, vent, signify, speak, state, voice; betoken, denote, equal, exhibit, indicate, intimate, present, represent, show, signify, symbolize. * *adj* categorical, clear, definite, determinate, explicit, outspoken, plain, positive, unambiguous; accurate, close, exact, faithful, precise, true; particular, special; fast, nonstop, quick, rapid, speedy, swift. * *n* dispatch, message.

expression *n* assertion, asseveration, communication, declaration, emission, statement, utterance, voicing; language, locution, phrase, remark, saying, term, word; air, aspect, look, mien.

expressive *adj* indicative, meaningful, significant; demonstrative, eloquent, emphatic, energetic, forcible, lively, strong, vivid; appropriate, sympathetic, well-modulated.

expulsion *n* discharge, eviction, expelling, ousting; elimination, evacuation, excretion; ejection, excision, excommunication, extrusion, ostracism, separation.

exquisite *adj* accurate, delicate, discriminating, exact, fastidious, nice, refined; choice, elect, excellent, precious, rare, valuable; complete, consummate, matchless, perfect; acute, keen, intense, poignant. * *n* beau, coxcomb, dandy, fop, popinjay.

extant *adj* existent, existing, present, surviving, undestroyed, visible.

extend *vb* reach, stretch; continue, elongate, lengthen, prolong, protract, widen; augment, dilate, distend, enlarge, expand, increase; diffuse, spread; give, impart, offer, yield; lie, range, reach, spread, stretch.

extension *n* augmentation, continuation, delay, dilatation, dilation, distension, enlargement, expansion, increase, prolongation, protraction.

extensive *adj* broad, capacious, comprehensive, expanded, extended, far-reaching, large, wide, widespread.

extent *n* amplitude, expanse, expansion; amount, bulk, content, degree, magnitude, size, volume; compass, measure, length, proportions, reach, stretch; area, field, latitude, range, scope; breadth, depth, height, width.

exterior *adj* external, outer, outlying, outside, outward, superficial, surface; extrinsic, foreign. * *n* outside, surface; appearance.

exterminate *vb* abolish, annihilate, destroy, eliminate, eradicate, extirpate, uproot.

extinct *adj* extinguished, quenched; closed, dead, ended, lapsed, terminated, vanished.

extinction *n* death, extinguishment; abolishment, abolition, annihilation, destruction, excision, extermination, extirpation.

extinguish *vb* choke, douse, put out, quell, smother, stifle, suffocate, suppress; destroy, nullify, subdue; eclipse, obscure.

extol *vb* celebrate, exalt, glorify, laud, magnify, praise; applaud, commend, eulogize, panegyrize.

extort *vb* elicit, exact, extract, force, squeeze, wrench, wrest, wring.

extortion *n* blackmail, compulsion, demand, exaction, oppression, overcharge, rapacity, tribute; exorbitance.

extortionate *adj* bloodsucking, exacting, hard, harsh, oppressive, rapacious, rigorous, severe; exorbitant, unreasonable.

extra *adj* accessory, additional, auxiliary, collateral; another, farther, fresh, further, more, new, other, plus, ulterior; side, spare, supernumerary, supplemental, supplementary, surplus; extraordinary, extreme, unusual. * *adv* additionally, also, beyond, farthermore, furthermore, more, moreover, plus. * *n* accessory, appendage, collateral, nonessential, special, supernumerary, supplement; bonus, premium; balance, leftover, remainder, spare, surplus.

extract *vb* extort, pull out, remove, withdraw; derive, distil, draw, express, squeeze; cite, determine, derive, quote, select. * *n* citation, excerpt, passage, quotation, selection; decoction, distillation, essence, infusion, juice.

extraction *n* drawing out, derivation, distillation, elicitation, essence, pulling out; birth, descent, genealogy, lineage, origin, parentage.

extraordinary *adj* abnormal, amazing, distinguished, egregious, exceptional, marvellous, monstrous, particular, peculiar, phenomenal, prodigious, rare, remarkable, signal, singular, special, strange, uncommon, unprecedented, unusual, unwonted, wonderful.

extravagant *adj* excessive, exorbitant, inordinate, preposterous, unreasonable; absurd, foolish, irregular, wild; lavish, prodigal, profuse, spendthrift, useful.

extreme *adj* farthest, outermost, remotest, utmost, uttermost; greatest, highest; final, last, ultimate; drastic, egregious, excessive, extravagant, immoderate, intense, outrageous, radical, unreasonable. * *n* end, extremity, limit; acme, climax, degree, height, pink; danger, distress.

extremity *n* border, edge, end, extreme, limb, termination, verge.

extricate *vb* clear, deliver, disembarrass, disengage, disentangle, liberate, release, relieve.

exuberant *adj* abounding, abundant, copious, fertile, flowing, luxuriant, prolific, rich; excessive, lavish, overabundant, overflowing, over-luxuriant, profuse, rank, redundant, superabounding, superabundant, wanton.

exult *vb* gloat, glory, jubilate, rejoice, transport, triumph, taunt, vault.

eye *vb* contemplate, inspect, ogle, scrutinize, survey, view, watch. * *n* estimate, judgement, look, sight, vision, view; inspection, notice, observation, scrutiny, sight, vigilance, watch; aperture, eyelet, peephole, perforation; bud, shot.

F

fable *n* allegory, legend, myth, parable, story, tale; fabrication, falsehood, fiction, figment, forgery, untruth.

fabric *n* building,, edifice, pile, structure; conformation, make, texture, workmanship; cloth, material, stuff, textile, tissue, web.

fabulous *adj* amazing, apocryphal, coined, fabricated, feigned, fictitious, forged, imaginary, invented, legendary, marvellous, mythical, romancing, unbelievable, unreal.

face *vb* confront; beard, buck, brave, dare, defy, front, oppose; dress, level, polish, smooth; cover, incrust, veneer. * *n* cover, facet, surface; breast, escarpment, front; countenance, features, grimace, physiognomy, visage; appearance, expression, look, semblance; assurance, audacity, boldness, brass, confidence, effrontery, impudence.

facile *adj* easy; affable, approachable, complaisant, conversable, courteous, mild; compliant, ductile, flexible, fluent, manageable, pliable, pliant, tractable, yielding; dextrous, ready, skilful.

facilitate *vb* expedite, help.

facility *n* ease, easiness; ability, dexterity, expertness, knack, quickness, readiness; ductility, flexibility, pliancy; advantage, appliance, convenience, means, resource; affability, civility, complaisance, politeness.

facsimile *n* copy, duplicate, fax, reproduction.

fact *n* act, circumstance, deed, event, incident, occurrence, performance; actuality, certainty, existence, reality, truth.

faculty *n* ability, capability, capacity, endowment, power, property, quality; ableness, address, adroitness, aptitude, aptness, capacity, clearness, competency, dexterity, efficiency, expertness, facility, forte, ingenuity, knack, power, quickness, readiness, skill, skilfulness, talent, turn; body, department, profession; authority, power, prerogative, license, privilege, right.

fade *vb* disappear, die, evanesce, fall, faint, perish, vanish; decay, decline, droop, fall, languish, wither; bleach, blanch, pale; disperse, dissolve.

fail *vb* break, collapse, decay, decline, fade, sicken, sink, wane; cease, disappear; fall, miscarry, miss; neglect, omit; bankrupt, break.

failing *adj* deficient, lacking, needing, wanting; declining, deteriorating, fading, flagging, languishing, sinking, waning, wilting; unsuccessful. * *prep* lacking, needing, wanting. * *n* decay, decline; failure, miscarriage; defect, deficiency, fault, foible, frailty, imperfection, infirmity, shortcoming, vice, weakness; error, lapse, slip; bankruptcy, insolvency.

failure *n* defectiveness, deficiency, delinquency, shortcoming; fail, miscarriage, negligent, neglect, nonobservance, nonperformance, omission, slip; abortion, botch, breakdown, collapse, fiasco, fizzle; bankruptcy, crash, downfall, insolvency, ruin; decay, declension, decline, loss.

faint *vb* swoon; decline, fade, fail, languish, weaken. * *adj* swooning; drooping, exhausted, feeble, languid, listless, sickly, weak; gentle, inconsiderable, little, slight, small, soft, thin; dim, dull, indistinct, perceptible, scarce, slight; cowardly, dastardly, faint-hearted, fearful, timid, timorous; dejected, depressed, discouraged, disheartened, dispirited. * *n* blackout, swoon.

fair¹ *adj* spotless, unblemished, unspotted, unstained, untarnished; blond, light, lily, white; beautiful, comely, handsome, shapely; clear, cloudless, pleasant, unclouded; favourable, prosperous; hopeful, promising, propitious; clear, distinct, open, plain, unencumbered, unobstructed; candid, frank, honest, honourable, impartial, ingenuous, just, open, unbiased, upright; equitable, proper, equita-

ble, just; average, decent, indifferent, moderate, ordinary, passable, reasonable, respectful, tolerable.

fair² *n* bazaar, carnival, exposition, festival, fete, funfair, gala, kermess.

faith *n* assurance, belief, confidence, credence, credit, dependence, reliance, trust; creed, doctrines, dogmas, persuasion, religion, tenets; constancy, faithfulness, fidelity, loyalty, truth, truthfulness.

faithful *adj* constant, devoted, loyal, staunch, steadfast, true; honest, upright, reliable, trustworthy, trusty; reliable, truthful; accurate, close, conscientiousness, exact, nice, strict.

fall *vb* collapse, depend, descend, drop, sink, topple, tumble; abate, decline, decrease, depreciate, ebb, subside; err, lapse, sin, stumble, transgress, trespass, trip; die, perish; befall, chance, come, happen, occur, pass; become, get; come, pass. * *n* collapse, comedown, descent, downcome, downfall, dropping, falling, flop, plop, tumble; cascade, cataract, waterfall; death, destruction, downfall, overthrow, ruin, surrender; comeuppance, degradation; apostasy, declension, failure, lapse, slip; decline, decrease, depreciation, diminution, ebb, sinking, subsidence; cadence, close, sinking; declivity, inclination, slope.

fallible *adj* erring, frail, ignorant, imperfect, uncertain, weak.

false *adj* lying, mendacious, truthless, untrue, unveracious; dishonest, dishonourable, disingenuous, disloyal, double-faced, double-tongued, faithless, false-hearted, perfidious, treacherous, unfaithful; fictitious, forged, made-up, unreliable, untrustworthy; artificial, bastard, bogus, counterfeit, factitious, feigned, forged, hollow, hypocritical, make-believe, pretended, pseudo, sham, spurious, supposititious; erroneous, improper, incorrect, unfounded, wrong; deceitful, deceiving, deceptive, disappointing, fallacious. misleading.

falsehood *n* falsity; fabrication, fib, fiction, lie, untruth; cheat, counterfeit, imposture, mendacity, treachery.

falsify *vb* alter, adulterate, belie, cook, counterfeit, doctor, fake, falsely, garble, misrepresent, misstate, represent; disprove; violate.

falter *vb* halt, hesitate, lisp, quaver, stammer, stutter; fail, stagger, stumble, totter, tremble, waver; dodder, hesitate.

fame *n* bruit, hearsay, report, rumour; celebrity, credit, eminence, glory, greatness, honour, illustriousness, kudos, lustre, notoriety, renown, reputation, repute.

familiar *adj* acquainted, aware, conversant, well-versed; amicable, close, cordial, domestic, fraternal, friendly, homely, intimate, near; affable, accessible, companionable, conversable, courteous, civil, friendly, kindly, sociable, social; easy, free and easy, unceremonious, unconstrained; common, frequent, well-known. * *n* acquaintance, associate, companion, friend, intimate.

familiarity *n* acquaintance, knowledge, understanding; fellowship, friendship, intimacy; closeness, friendliness, sociability; freedom, informality, liberty; disrespect, overfreedom, presumption; intercourse.

familiarize *vb* accustom, habituate, inure, train, use.

family *n* brood, household, people; ancestors, blood, breed, clan, dynasty, kindred, house, lineage, race, stock, strain, tribe; class, genus, group, kind, subdivision.

famine *n* dearth, destitution, hunger, scarcity, starvation.

famish *vb* distress, exhaust, pinch, starve.

famous *adj* celebrated, conspicuous, distinguished, eminent, excellent, fabled, famed, far-famed, great, glorious, heroic, honoured, illustrious, immortal, notable, noted, notorious, remarkable, renowned, signal.

fan[1] *vb* agitate, beat, move, winnow; blow, cool, refresh, ventilate; excite, fire, increase, rouse, stimulate. * *n* blower, cooler, punkah, ventilator.

fan[2] *n* admirer, buff, devotee, enthusiast, fancier, follower, pursuer, supporter.

fanatic *n* bigot, devotee, enthusiast, visionary, zealot.

fanatical *adj* bigoted, enthusiastic, frenzied, mad, rabid, visionary, wild, zealous.

fanciful *adj* capricious, crotchety, imaginary, visionary, whimsical; chimerical, fantastical, ideal, imaginary, wild.

fancy *vb* apprehend, believe, conjecture, imagine, suppose, think; conceive, imagine. * *adj* elegant, fine, nice, ornament; extravagant, fanciful, whimsical. * *n* imagination; apprehension, conceit, conception, impression, idea, image, notion, thought; approval, fondness, inclination, judgement, liking, penchant, taste; caprice, crochet, fantasy, freak, humour, maggot, quirk, vagary, whim, whimsy; apparition, chimera, daydream, delusion, hallucination, megrim, phantasm, reverie, vision.

fantastic *adj* chimerical, fanciful, imaginary, romantic, unreal, visionary; bizarre, capricious, grotesque, odd, quaint, queer, strange, whimsical, wild.

far *adj* distant, long, protracted, remote; farther, remoter; alienated, estranged, hostile. * *adv* considerably, extremely, greatly, very much; afar, distantly, far away, remotely.

farcical *adj* absurd, comic, droll, funny, laughable, ludicrous, ridiculous.

fare *vb* go, journey, pass, travel; happen, prosper, prove; feed, live, manage, subsist. * *n* charge, price, ticket money; passenger, traveller; board, commons, food, table, victuals, provisions; condition, experience, fortune, luck, outcome.

farewell *n* adieu, leave-taking, valediction; departure, leave, parting, valedictory.

farther *adj* additional; further, remoter, ulterior. * *adv* beyond, further; besides, furthermore, moreover.

fascinate *vb* affect, bewitch, overpower, spellbind, stupefy, transfix; absorb, captivate, catch, charm, delight, enamour, enchant, enrapture, entrance.

fascination *n* absorption, charm, enchantment, magic, sorcery, spell, witchcraft, witchery.

fashion *vb* contrive, create, design, forge, form, make, mould, pattern, shape; accommodate, adapt, adjust, fit, suit. * *n* appearance, cast, configuration, conformation, cut, figure, form, make, model, mould, pattern, shape, stamp; manner, method, sort, wake; conventionalism, conventionality, custom, fad, mode, style, usage, vogue; breeding, gentility; quality.

fashionable adj modish, stylish; current, modern, prevailing, up-to-date; customary, usual; genteel, well-bred.

fast[1] adj close, fastened, firm, fixed, immovable, tenacious, tight; constant, faithful, permanent, resolute, staunch, steadfast, unswerving, unwavering; fortified, impregnable, strong; deep, profound, sound; fleet, quick, rapid, swift; dissipated, dissolute, extravagant, giddy, reckless, thoughtless, thriftless, wild. * adv firmly, immovably, tightly; quickly, rapidly, swiftly; extravagantly, prodigally, reckless, wildly.

fast[2] vb abstain, go hungry, starve. * n abstention, abstinence, diet, fasting, starvation.

fasten vb attach, bind, bolt, catch, chain, cleat, fix, gird, lace, lock, pin, secure, strap, tether, tie; belay, bend; connect, hold, join, unite.

fat adj adipose, fatty, greasy, oily, oleaginous, unctuous; corpulent, fleshy, gross, obese, paunchy, portly, plump, pudgy, pursy; coarse, dull, heavy, sluggish, stupid; lucrative, profitable, rich; fertile, fruitful, productive, rich. * n adipose tissue, ester, grease, oil; best part, cream, flower; corpulence, fatness, fleshiness, obesity, plumpness, stoutness.

fatal adj deadly, lethal, mortal; baleful, baneful, calamitous, catastrophic, destructive, mischievous, pernicious, ruinous; destined, doomed, foreordained, inevitable, predestined.

fate n destination, destiny, fate; cup, die, doom, experience, lot, fortune, portion, weird; death, destruction, ruin.

fatherly adj benign, kind, paternal, protecting, tender.

fathom vb comprehend, divine, penetrate, reach, understand; estimate, gauge, measure, plumb, probe sound.

fatigue vb exhaust, fag, jade, tire, weak-

en, weary. * n exhaustion, lassitude, tiredness, weariness; hardship, labour, toil.

fault n blemish, defect, flaw, foible, frailty, imperfection, infirmity, negligence, obliquity, offence, shortcoming, spot, weakness; delinquency, error, indiscretion, lapse, misdeed, misdemeanour, offence, peccadillo, slip, transgression, trespass, vice, wrong; blame, culpability.

faulty adj bad, defective, imperfect, incorrect; blameable, blameworthy, censurable, culpable, reprehensible.

favour vb befriend, countenance, encourage, patronize; approve; ease, facilitate; aid, assist, help, oblige, support; extenuate, humour, indulge, palliate, spare. * n approval, benignity, countenance, esteem, friendliness, goodwill, grace, kindness; benefaction, benefit, boon, dispensation, kindness; championship, patronage, popularity, support; gift, present, token; badge, decoration, knot, rosette; leave, pardon, permission; advantage, cover, indulgence, protection; bias, partiality, prejudice.

favourable adj auspicious, friendly, kind, propitious, well-disposed, willing; conductive, contributing, propitious; adapted, advantage, beneficial, benign, convenient, fair, fit, good, helpful, suitable.

favourite adj beloved, darling, dear; choice, fancied, esteemed, pet, preferred.

fear vb apprehend, dread; revere, reverence, venerate. * n affright, alarm, apprehension, consternation, dismay, dread, fright, horror, panic, phobia, scare, terror; disquietude, flutter, perturbation, palpitation, quaking, quivering, trembling, tremor, trepidation; anxiety, apprehension, concern, misdoubt, misgiving, qualm, solicitude; awe, dread, reverence, veneration.

fearful adj afraid, apprehensive, haunted; chicken-hearted, chicken-livered, cowardly, faint-hearted, lily-livered, nervous, pusillanimous, timid, timorous; dire, direful, dreadful, frightful, ghastly, horrible, shocking, terrible.

fearless *adj* bold, brave, courageous, daring, dauntless, doughty, gallant, heroic, intrepid, unterrified, valiant, valorous.

feast *vb* delight, gladden, gratify, rejoice. * *n* banquet, carousal, entertainment, regale, repast, revels, symposium, treat; celebration, festival, fete, holiday; delight, enjoyment, pleasure.

feat *n* accomplishment, achievement, act, deed, exploit, performance, stunt, trick.

feature *vb* envisage, envision, picture, visualize imagine; specialize; appear in, headline, star. * *n* appearance, aspect, component; conformation, fashion, make; characteristic, item, mark, particularity, peculiarity, property, point, trait; leader, lead item, special; favour, expression, lineament; article, film, motion picture, movie, story; highlight, high spot.

federation *n* alliance, allying, confederation, federating, federation, leaguing, union, uniting; alliance, coalition, combination, compact, confederacy, entente, federacy, league, copartnership.

fee *vb* pay, recompense, reward. * *n* account, bill, charge, compensation, honorarium, remuneration, reward, tip; benefice, fief, feud.

feeble *adj* anaemic, debilitated, declining, drooping, enervated, exhausted, frail, infirm, languid, languishing, sickly; dim, faint, imperfect, indistinct.

feed *vb* contribute, provide, supply; cherish, eat, nourish, subsist, sustain. * *n* fodder, food, foodstuff, forage, provender.

feel *vb* apprehend, intuit, perceive, sense; examine, handle, probe, touch; enjoy, experience, suffer; prove, sound, test, try; appear, look, seem, sound; believe, conceive, deem, fancy, infer, opine, suppose, think. * *n* atmosphere, feeling, quality; finish, surface, texture.

feeling *n* consciousness, impression, notion, perception, sensation, sense, sentience, touch; affecting, emotion, heartstrings, impression, passion, sensibility, sentiment, soul, sympathy; sensibility, sentiment, susceptibility, tenderness; attitude, impression, opinion.

fell *vb* beat, knock down, level, prostrate; cut, demolish, hew.

fellow *adj* affiliated, associated, joint, like, mutual, similar, twin. * *n* associate, companion, comrade; compeer, equal, peer; counterpart, mate, match, partner; member; boy, character, individual, man, person.

fellowship *n* brotherhood, companionship, comradeship, familiarity, intimacy; participation; partnership; communion, converse, intercourse; affability, kindliness, sociability, sociableness.

feminine *adj* affectionate, delicate, gentle, graceful, modest, soft, tender, womanish, womanly; effeminateness, effeminacy, softness, unmanliness, weakness, womanliness.

fence *vb* defend, enclose, fortify, guard, protect, surround; circumscribe, evade, equivocate, hedge, prevaricate; guard, parry. * *n* barrier, hedge, hoarding, palings, palisade, stockade, wall; defence, protection, guard, security, shield; fencing, swordplay, swordsmanship; receiver.

ferocious *adj* ferine, fierce, rapacious, ravenous, savage, untamed, wild; barbarous, bloody, bloodthirsty, brutal, cruel, fell, inhuman, merciless, murderous, pitiless, remorseless, ruthless, sanguinary, truculent, vandalistic, violent.

fertile *adj* bearing, breeding, fecund, prolific; exuberant, fruitful, luxuriant, plenteous, productive, rich, teeming; female, fruit-bearing, pistillate.

fervent *adj* burning, hot, glowing, melting, seething; animated, ardent, earnest, enthusiastic, fervid, fierce, fiery, glowing, impassioned. intense, passionate, vehement, warm, zealous.

festival *n* anniversary, carnival, feast, fete, gala, holiday, jubilee; banquet, carousal, celebration, entertainment, treat.

festive *adj* carnival, convivial, festal, festival, gay, jolly, jovial, joyful, merry, mirthful uproarious.

festivity *n* conviviality, festival, gaiety, jollity, joviality, joyfulness, joyousness, merrymaking, mirth.

fetch *vb* bring, elicit, get; accomplish, achieve, effect, perform; attain, reach. * *n* artifice, dodge, ruse, stratagem, trick.

feud *vb* argue, bicker, clash, contend, dispute, quarrel. * *n* affray, argument, bickering, broil, clashing, contention, contest, discord, dissension, enmity, fray, grudge, hostility, jarring, quarrel, rupture, strife, vendetta.

fever *n* agitation, excitement, ferment, fire, flush, heat, passion.

fibre *n* filament, pile, staple, strand, texture, thread; stamina, strength, toughness.

fickle *adj* capricious, changeable, faithless, fitful, inconstant, irresolute, mercurial, mutable, shifting, unsettled, unstable, unsteady, vacillating, variable, veering, violate, volatile, wavering.

fiction *n* fancy, fantasy, imagination, invention; novel, romance; fable, fabrication, falsehood, figment, forgery, invention, lie.

fictitious *adj* assumed, fabulous, fanciful, feigned, imaginary, invented, mythical, unreal; artificial, counterfeit, dummy, false, spurious, suppositious.

fiddle *vb* dawdle, fidget, interfere, tinker, trifle; cheat, swindle, tamper. * *n* fraud, swindle; fiddler, violin, violinist.

fidelity *n* constancy, devotedness, devotion, dutifulness, faithfulness, fealty, loyalty, true-heartedness, truth; accuracy, closeness, exactness, faithfulness, precision.

fidget *vb* chafe, fret, hitch, twitch, worry. * *n* fidgetiness, impatience, restlessness, uneasiness.

field *n* clearing, glebe, meadow; expanse, extent, opportunity, range, room, scope, surface; department, domain, province, realm, region.

fierce *adj* barbarous, brutal, cruel, fell, ferocious, furious, infuriate, ravenous, savage; fiery, impetuous, murderous, passionate, tearing, tigerish, truculent, turbulent, uncurbed, untamed, vehement, violent.

fiery *adj* fervent, fervid, flaming, heated, hot, glowing, lurid; ardent, fervent, fervid, fierce, flaming, glowing, impassioned, impetuous, inflamed, passionate, vehement.

fight *vb* battle, combat, contend, war; contend, contest, dispute, oppose, strive, struggle, wrestle; encounter, engage; handle, manage, manoeuvre. * *n* affair, affray, action, battle, brush, combat, conflict, contest, duel, encounter, engagement, melée, quarrel, struggle, war; brawl, broil, riot, row, skirmish; fighting, pluck, pugnacity, resistance, spirit, struggle, temper.

figure *vb* adorn, diversify, ornament, variegate; delineate,, depict, represent, signify, symbolize, typify; conceive, image, imagine, picture, represent; calculate, cipher, compute; act, appear, perform. * *n* configuration, conformation, form, outline, shape; effigy, image, likeness, representative; design, diagram, drawing, pattern; image, metaphor, trope; emblem, symbol, type; character, digit, number, numeral.

file¹ *vb* order, pigeonhole, record, tidy. * *n* data, dossier, folder, portfolio; column, line, list, range, rank, row, series, tier.

file² *vb* burnish, furbish, polish, rasp, refine, smooth.

fill *vb* occupy, pervade; dilate, distend, expand, stretch, trim; furnish, replenish, stock, store, supply; cloy, congest, content, cram, glut, gorge, line, pack, pall, sate, satiate, satisfy, saturate, stuff, suffuse, swell; engage, fulfil, hold, occupy, officiate, perform.

film *vb* becloud, cloud, coat, cover, darken, fog, mist, obfuscate, obscure, veil; photograph, shoot, take. * *n* cloud, coating, gauze, membrane, nebula, pellicle, scum, skin, veil; thread.

filter *vb* filtrate, strain; exude, ooze, percolate, transude. * *n* diffuser, colander, riddle, sieve, sifter, strainer.

filth *n* dirt, nastiness, ordure; corruption, defilement, foulness, grossness, impurity, obscenity, pollution, squalor, uncleanness, vileness.

filthy *adj* defiled, dirty, foul, licentious, nasty, obscene, pornographic, squalid, unclean; corrupt, foul, gross, impure, unclean; miry, mucky, muddy.

final *adj* eventual, extreme, last. latest, terminal, ultimate; conclusive, decisive, definitive, irrevocable.

finale n conclusion, end, termination.

finances npl funds, resources, revenues, treasury; income, property.

find vb discover, fall upon; gain, get, obtain, procure; ascertain, discover, notice, observe, perceive, remark; catch, detect; contribute, furnish, provide, supply. * n acquisition, catch, discovery, finding, plum, prize, strike.

fine[1] vb filter, purify, refine. * adj comminuted, little, minute, small; capillary, delicate, small; choice, light; exact, keen, sharp; attenuated, subtle, tenuous, thin; exquisite, fastidious, nice, refined, sensitive, subtle; dandy, excellent, superb, superior; beautiful, elegant, handsome, magnificent, splendid; clean, pure, unadulterated.

fine[2] vb amerce, mulct, penalize, punish. * n amercement, forfeit, forfeiture, mulct, penalty, punishment.

finish vb accomplish, achieve, complete, consummate, execute, fulfil, perform; elaborate, perfect, polish; close, conclude, end, terminate. * n elaboration, elegance, perfection, polish; close, end, death, termination, wind-up.

fire vb ignite, kindle, light; animate, enliven, excite, inflame, inspirit, invigorate, rouse, stir up; discharge, eject, expel, hurl. * n combustion; blaze, conflagration; discharge, firing; animation, ardour, enthusiasm, fervour, fervency, fever, force, heat, impetuosity, inflammation, intensity, passion, spirit, vigour, violence; light, lustre, radiance, splendour; imagination, imaginativeness, inspiration, vivacity; affliction, persecution, torture, trouble.

firm[1] adj established, coherent, confirmed, consistent, fast, fixed, immovable, inflexible, rooted, secure, settled, stable; compact, compressed, dense, hard, solid; constant, determined, resolute, staunch, steadfast, steady, unshaken; loyal, robust sinewy, stanch, stout, sturdy, strong.

firm[2] n association, business, company, concern, corporation, house, partnership.

first adj capital, chief, foremost, highest,

leading, prime, principal; earliest, eldest, original; maiden; elementary, primary, rudimentary; aboriginal, primal, primeval, primitive, pristine. * adv chiefly, firstly, initially, mainly, primarily, principally; before, foremost, headmost; before, rather, rather than, sooner, sooner than. * n alpha, initial, prime.

fit[1] vb adapt, adjust, suit; become, conform; accommodate, equip, prepare, provide, qualify. * adj capacitated, competent, fitted; adequate, appropriate, apt, becoming, befitting, consonant, convenient, fitting, good, meet, pertinent, proper, seemly, suitable.

fit[2] n convulsion, fit, paroxysm, qualm, seizure, spasm, spell; fancy, humour, whim; mood, pet, tantrum; interval, period, spell, turn.

fitful adj capricious, changeable, convulsive, fanciful, fantastic, fickle, humoursome, impulsive, intermittent, irregular, odd, spasmodic, unstable, variable, whimsical; checkered, eventful.

fitness n adaptation, appropriateness, aptitude, aptness, pertinence, propriety, suitableness; preparation, qualification.

fix vb establish, fasten, place, plant, set; adjust, repair; attach, bind, clinch, connect, fasten, lock, rivet, stay, tie; appoint, decide, define, determine, limit, seal, settle; consolidate, harden, solidify; abide, remain, rest, settle; congeal, harden, solidify, stiffen. * n difficulty, dilemma, pickle, plight, predicament.

flabby adj feeble, flaccid, inelastic, limp, soft, week, yielding.

flag[1] vb droop, hang, loose; decline, droop, fail, faint, lag, languish, pine, sink, succumb, weaken, weary; stale, pall.

flag[2] vb indicate, mark, semaphore, sign, signal. * n banner, colours, ensign, gonfalon, pennant, pennon, standard, streamer.

flagrant adj burning, flaming, glowing, raging; crying, enormous, flagitious, glaring, monstrous, nefarious, notorious, outrageous, shameful, wanton, wicked.

flamboyant adj bright, gorgeous, ornate, rococo.

flame vb blaze, shine; burn, flash, glow,

warm. * n blaze, brightness, fire, flare, vapour; affection, ardour, enthusiasm, fervency, fervour, keenness, warmth.

flap vb beat, flutter, shake, vibrate, wave. * n apron, fly, lap, lappet, tab; beating, flapping, flop, flutter, slap, shaking, swinging, waving.

flare vb blaze, flicker, flutter, waver; dazzle, flame, glare; splay, spread, widen. * n blaze, dazzle, flame, glare.

flash vb blaze, glance, glare, glisten, light, shimmer, scintillate, sparkle, twinkle. * n instant, moment, twinkling.

flashy adj flaunting, gaudy, gay, loud, ostentatious, pretentious, showy, tawdry, tinsel.

flat adj champaign, horizontal; level; even, plane, smooth, unbroken; low, prostrate, overthrow; dull, frigid, jejune, lifeless, monotonous, pointless, prosaic, spiritless, tame, unanimated, uniform, uninteresting; dead, flashy, insipid, mawkish, stale, tasteless, vapid; absolute, clear, direct, downright, peremptory, positive. * adv flatly, flush, horizontally, level. * n bar, sandbank, shallow, shoal, strand; champaign, lowland, plain; apartment, floor, lodging, storey.

flatter vb compliment, gratify, praise; blandish, blarney, butter up, cajole, coax, coddle, court, entice, fawn, humour, inveigle, wheedle.

flattery n adulation, blandishment, blarney, cajolery, fawning, obsequiousness, servility, sycophancy, toadyism.

flavour n gust, gusto, relish, savour, seasoning, smack, taste, zest; admixture, lacing, seasoning; aroma, essence, soul, spirit.

flaw n break, breach, cleft, crack, fissure, fracture, gap, rent, rift; blemish, defect, fault, fleck, imperfection, speck, spot.

fleck vb dapple, mottle, speckle, spot, streak, variegate. * n speckle, spot, streak.

flee vb abscond, avoid, decamp, depart, escape, fly, leave, run, skedaddle.

fleece vb clip, shear; cheat, despoil, pluck, plunder, rifle, rob, steal, strip.

fleeting adj brief, caducous, ephemeral, evanescent, flitting, flying, fugitive, passing, short-lived, temporary, transient, transitory.

flesh n food, meat; carnality, desires; kindred, race, stock; man, mankind, world.

fleshly adj animal, bodily, carnal, lascivious, lustful, lecherous, sensual.

fleshy adj corpulent, fat, obese, plump, stout.

flexible adj flexible, limber, lithe, pliable, pliant, supple, willowy; affable, complaisant, ductile, docile, gentle, pliable, pliant, tractable, tractile, yielding.

flight[1] n flying, mounting, soaring, volition; shower, flight; steps, stairs.

flight[2] n departure, fleeing, flying, retreat, rout, stampede; exodus, hegira.

flighty adj capricious, deranged, fickle, frivolous, giddy, light-headed, mercurial, unbalanced, volatile, wild, whimsical.

flimsy adj slight, thin, unsubstantial; feeble, foolish, frivolous, light, puerile, shallow, superficial, trashy, trifling, trivial, weak; insubstantial, sleazy.

flinch vb blench, flee, recoil, retreat, shirk, shrink, swerve, wince, withdraw.

fling vb cast, chuck, dart, emit, heave, hurl, pitch, shy, throw, toss; flounce, wince. * n cast, throw, toss.

flippant adj fluent, glib, talkative, voluble; bold, forward, frivolous, glib, impertinent, inconsiderate, irreverent, malapert, pert, saucy, trifling.

flirt vb chuck, fling, hurl, pitch, shy, throw, toss; flutter, twirl, whirl, whisk; coquet, dally, philander. * n coquette, jilt, philanderer; jerk.

flirtation n coquetry, dalliance, philandering.

flit vb flicker, flutter, hover; depart, hasten, pass.

float vb drift, glide, hang, ride, sail, soar, swim, waft; launch, support.

flock vb collect, congregate, gather, group, herd, swarm, throng. * n collection, group, multitude; bevy, company, convoy, drove, flight, gaggle, herd, pack, swarm, team, troupe; congregation.

flog vb beat, castigate, chastise, drub, flagellate, lash, scourge, thrash, whip.

flood vb deluge, inundate, overflow, submerge, swamp. * n deluge, freshet, inundation, overflow, tide; bore, downpour, eagre, flow, outburst, spate, rush; abundance, excess.

floor vb deck, pave; beat, confound, conquer, overthrow, prevail, prostrate, puzzle; disconcert, nonplus; florid. * n storey; bottom, deck, flooring, pavement, stage.

flounder vb blunder, flop, flounce, plunge, struggle, toss, tumble, wallow.

flourish vb grow, thrive; boast, bluster, brag, gasconade, show off, vaunt, vapour; brandish, flaunt, swing, wave. * n dash, display, ostentation, parade, show; bombast, fustian, grandiloquence; brandishing, shake, waving; blast, fanfare, tantivy.

flout vb chaff, deride, fleer, gibe, insult, jeer, mock, ridicule, scoff, sneer, taunt. * n gibe, fling, insult, jeer, mock, mockery, mocking, scoff, scoffing, taunt.

flow vb pour, run, stream; deliquesce, liquefy, melt; arise, come, emanate, follow, grow, issue, proceed, result, spring; glide, float, undulate, wave, waver; abound, run. * n current, discharge, flood, flux, gush, rush, stream, trickle; abundance, copiousness.

flower vb bloom, blossom, effloresce; develop. * n bloom, blossom; best, cream, elite, essence, pick; freshness, prime, vigour.

flowery adj bloomy, florid; embellished, figurative, florid, ornate, overwrought.

fluent adj current, flowing, gliding, liquid; smooth; affluent, copious, easy, facile, glib, ready, talkative, voluble.

fluff vb blunder, bungle, forget, fumble, mess up, miscue, misremember, muddle, muff. * n down, flew, floss, flue, fur, lint, nap; cobweb, feather, gossamer, thistledown; blunder, bungle, fumble, muff.

flurry vb agitate, confuse, disconcert, disturb, excite, fluster, hurry, perturb. * n gust, flaw, squall; agitation, bustle, commotion, confusion, disturbance, excitement, flutter, haste, hurry, hurry-scurry, perturbation, ruffle, scurry.

flush¹ vb flow, rush, start; glow, mantle, redden; animate, elate, elevate, erect,

excite; cleanse, drench. * adj bright, fresh, glowing, vigorous; abundant, affluent, exuberant, fecund, fertile, generous, lavish, liberal, prodigal, prolific, rich, wealthy, well-supplied; even, flat, level, plane. * adv evenly, flat, level; full, point-blank, right, square, squarely, straight. * n bloom, blush, glow, redness, rosiness, ruddiness; impulse, shock, thrill.

flush² vb disturb, rouse, start, uncover.

flutter vb flap, hover; flirt, flit; beat, palpitate, quiver, tremble; fluctuate, oscillate, vacillate, waver. * n agitation, tremor; agitation, hurry, commotion, confusion, excitement, flurry, fluster, hurryscurry, perturbation, quivering, tremble, tumult, twitter.

fly¹ vb aviate, hover, mount, soar; flap, float, flutter, play, sail, soar, undulate, vibrate, wave; burst, explode; abscond, decamp, depart, flee, vanish; elapse, flit, glide, pass, slip.

fly² adj alert, bright, sharp, smart, wideawake; astute, cunning, knowing, sly; agile, fleet, nimble, quick, spry.

foam vb cream, froth, lather, spume; boil, churn, ferment, fume, seethe, simmer, stew. * n bubbles, cream, froth, scum, spray, spume, suds.

foe n adversary, antagonist, enemy, foeman, opponent.

fog vb bedim, bemist, blear, blur, cloud, dim, enmist, mist; addle, befuddle, confuse, fuddle, muddle. * n blear, blur, dimness, film, fogginess, haze, haziness, mist, smog, vapour; befuddlement, confusion, fuddle, maze, muddle.

foggy adj blurred, cloudy, dim, dimmed, hazy, indistinct, misty, obscure; befuddled, bewildered, confused, dazed, muddled, muddy, stupid.

foible n defect, failing, fault, frailty, imperfection, infirmity, penchant, weakness.

foil¹ vb baffle, balk, check, checkmate, circumvent, defeat, disappoint, frustrate, thwart.

foil² n film, flake, lamina; background, contrast.

foist vb impose, insert, interpolate, introduce, palm off, thrust.

fold¹ vb bend, cover, double, envelop, wrap; clasp, embrace, enfold, enwrap, gather, infold, interlace; collapse, fail. * n double, doubling, gather, plait, plicature.

fold² n cot, enclosure, pen.

folk n kindred, nation, people.

follow vb ensue, succeed; chase, dog, hound, pursue, run after, trail; accompany, attend; conform, heed, obey, observe; cherish, cultivate, seek; practise, pursue; adopt, copy, imitate; arise, come, flow, issue, proceed, result, spring.

follower n acolyte, attendant, associate, companion, dependant, retainer, supporter; adherent, admirer, disciple, partisan, pupil; copier, imitator.

folly n doltishness, dullness, fatuity, foolishness, imbecility, levity, shallowness; absurdity, extravagance, fatuity, foolishness, imprudence, inanity, indiscretion, ineptitude, nonsense, senseless; blunder, faux pas, indiscretion, unwisdom.

fond adj absurd, baseless, empty, foolish, senseless, silly, vain, weak; affectionate, amorous, doting, loving, overaffectionate, tender.

fondle vb blandish, caress, coddle, cosset, dandle, pet.

food n aliment, board, bread, cheer, commons, diet, fare, meat, nourishment, nutriment, nutrition, pabulum, provisions, rations, regimen, subsistence, sustenance, viands, victuals; feed, fodder, forage, provender.

fool vb jest, play, toy, trifle; beguile, cheat, circumvent, cozen, deceive, delude, dupe, gull, hoodwink, overreach, trick. * n blockhead, dolt, driveller, idiot, imbecile, nincompoop, ninny, nitwit, simpleton, wilting; antic, buffoon, clown, droll, harlequin, jester, merry-andrew, punch, scaramouch, zany; butt, dupe.

foolery n absurdity, folly, foolishness, nonsense; buffoonery, mummery, tomfoolery.

foolhardy adj adventurous, bold, desperate, harebrained, headlong, hot-headed, incautious, precipitate, rash, reckless, venturesome, venturous.

foolish adj brainless, daft, fatuous, idiot-ic, inane, inept, insensate, irrational, senseless, shallow, silly, simple, thick-skulled, vain, weak, witless; absurd, ill-judged, imprudent, indiscreet, nonsensical, preposterous, ridiculous, unreasonable, unwise; childish, contemptible, idle, puerile, trifling, trivial, vain.

footing n foothold, purchase; basis, foundation, groundwork, installation; condition, grade, rank, standing, state, status; settlement, establishment.

footman n footboy, menial, lackey, runner, servant.

footstep n footmark, footprint, trace, track; footfall, step, tread; mark, sign, token, trace, vestige.

forage vb feed, graze, provender, provision, victual; hunt for, range, rummage, search, seek; maraud, plunder, raid. * n feed, fodder, food, pasturage, provender; hunt, rummage, search

foray n descent, incursion, invasion, inroad, irruption, raid.

forbid vb ban, debar, disallow, embargo, enjoin, hinder, inhibit, interdict, prohibit, proscribe, taboo, veto.

forbidding adj abhorrent, disagreeable, displeasing, odious, offensive, repellant, repulsive, threatening, unpleasant.

force vb coerce, compel, constrain, necessitate, oblige; drive, impel, overcome, press, urge; ravish, violate. * n emphasis, energy, head, might, pith, power, strength, stress, vigour, vim; agency, efficacy, efficiency, cogency, potency, validity, virtue; coercion, compulsion, constraint, enforcement, vehemence, violence; army, array, battalion, host, legion, phalanx, posse, squadron, troop.

forcible adj all-powerful, cogent, impressive, irresistible, mighty potent, powerful, strong, weighty; impetuous, vehement, violent, unrestrained; coerced, coercive, compulsory; convincing, energetic, effective, efficacious, telling, vigorous.

fore adj anterior, antecedent, first, foregoing, former, forward, preceding, previous, prior; advanced, foremost, head, leading.

foreboding n augury, omen, prediction,

premonition, presage, presentiment, prognostication.

forecast vb anticipate, foresee, predict; calculate, contrive, devise, plan, project, scheme. * n anticipation, foresight, forethought, planning, prevision, prophecy, provident.

foregoing adj antecedent, anterior, fore, former, preceding, previous, prior.

foregone adj bygone, former, past, previous.

foreign adj alien, distant, exotic, exterior, external, outward, outlandish, remote, strange, unnative; adventitious, exterior, extraneous, extrinsic, inappropriate, irrelevant, outside, unnatural, unrelated.

foremost adj first, front, highest, leading, main, principal.

forerunner n avant-courier, foregoer, harbinger, herald, precursor, predecessor; omen, precursor, prelude, premonition, prognosticate, sign.

foresight n foreknowledge, prescience, prevision; anticipation, care, caution, forecast, forethought, precaution, providence, prudence.

foretaste n antepast, anticipation, forestalling, prelibation.

foretell vb predict, prophesy; augur, betoken, forebode, forecast, foreshadow, foreshow, portend, presage, presignify, prognosticate, prophesy.

forever adv always, constantly, continually, endlessly, eternally, ever, evermore, everlastingly, perpetually, unceasingly.

forfeit vb alienate, lose. * n amercement, damages, fine, forfeiture, mulct, penalty.

forge vb beat, fabricate, form, frame, hammer; coin, devise, frame, invent; counterfeit, fabricate, falsify, feign. * n furnace, ironworks, smithy.

forgery n counterfeit, fake, falsification, imitation.

forgetful adj careless, heedless, inattentive, mindless, neglectful, negligent, oblivious, unmindful.

forgive vb absolve, acquit, condone, excuse, exonerate, pardon, remit.

forgiveness n absolution, acquittal, amnesty, condoning, exoneration, pardon, remission, reprieve.

forgiving adj absolutory, absolvatory, ac-

quitting, clearing, excusing, pardoning, placable, releasing.

forlorn adj abandoned, deserted, forsaken, friendless, helpless, lost, solitary; abject, comfortless, dejected, desolate, destitute, disconsolate, helpless, hopeless, lamentable, pitiable, miserable, woebegone, wretched.

form vb fashion model, mould, shape; build, conceive, construct, create, fabricate, make, produce; contrive, devise, frame, invent; compose, constitute, develop, organize; discipline, educate, teach, train. * n body, build, cast, configuration, conformation, contour, cut, fashion, figure, format, mould, outline, pattern, shape; formula, formulary, method, mode, practice, ritual; class, kind, manner, model, order, sort, system, type; arrangement, order, regularity, shapeliness; ceremonial, ceremony, conventionality, etiquette, formality, observance, ordinance, punctilio, rite, ritual; bench, seat; class, rank; arrangement, combination, organization.

formal adj explicit, express, official, positive, strict; fixed, methodical, regular, rigid, set, stiff; affected, ceremonious, exact, precise, prim, punctilious, starch, starched; constitutive, essential; external, outward, perfunctory; formative, innate, organic, primordial.

formative adj creative, determinative, plastic, shaping; derivative, inflectional, nonradical.

former adj antecedent, anterior, earlier, foregoing, preceding, previous, prior; late, old-time, quondam; by, bygone, foregone, gone, past, previous.

forsake vb abandon, desert, leave, quit; drop, forgo, forswear, relinquish, renounce, surrender, yield.

fortify vb brace, encourage, entrench, garrison, protect, reinforce, stiffen, strengthen; confirm, corroborate.

fortitude n braveness, bravery, courage, determination, endurance, firmness, hardiness, patience, pluck, resolution, strength, valour.

fortuitous adj accidental, casual, chance, contingent, incidental.

fortunate *adj* favoured, happy, lucky, prosperous, successful; advantageous, auspicious, favourable, happy, lucky, propitious.

fortune *n* accident, casualty, chance, contingency, fortuity, hap, luck; estate, possessions, property, substance; affluence, felicity, opulence, prosperity, riches, wealth; destination, destiny, doom, fate, lot, star; event, issue, result; favour, success.

forward *vb* advance, aid, encourage, favour, foster, further, help, promote, support; accelerate, dispatch, expedite, hasten, hurry, quicken, speed; dispatch, post, send, ship, transmit. * *adj* ahead, advanced, onward; anterior, front, fore, head; prompt, eager, earnest, hasty, impulsive, quick, ready, willing, zealous; assuming, bold, brazen, brazen-faced, confident, flippant, impertinent, pert, presumptuous, presuming; advanced, early, premature. * *adv* ahead, onward.

foster *vb* cosset, feed, nurse, nourish, support, sustain; advance, aid, breed, cherish, cultivate, encourage, favour, foment, forward, further, harbour, patronize, promote, rear, stimulate.

foul *vb* besmirch, defile, dirty, pollute, soil, stain, sully; clog, collide, entangle, jam. * *adj* dirty, fetid, filthy, impure, nasty, polluted, putrid, soiled, stained, squalid, sullied, rank, tarnished, unclean; disgusting, hateful, loathsome, noisome, odious, offensive; dishonourable, underhand, unfair, sinister; abominable, base, dark, detestable, disgraceful, infamous, scandalous, scurvy, shameful, wile, wicked; coarse, low, obscene, vulgar; abusive, foul-mouthed, foul-spoken, insulting, scurrilous; cloudy, rainy, rough, stormy, wet; feculent, muddy, thick, turbid; entangled, tangled.

found *vb* base, fix, ground, place. rest, set; build, construct, erect, raise; colonize, establish, institute, originate, plant; cast, mould.

foundation *n* base, basis, bed, bottom, footing, ground, groundwork, substructure, support; endowment, establishment, settlement.

fountain *n* fount, reservoir, spring, well; jet, upswelling; cause, fountainhead, origin, original, source.

fracture *vb* break, crack, split. * *n* breaking, rupture; breach, break, cleft, crack, fissure, flaw, opening, rift, rent.

fragile *adj* breakable, brittle, delicate, frangible; feeble, frail, infirm, weak.

fragility *n* breakability, breakableness, brittleness, frangibility, frangibleness; feebleness, frailty, infirmity, weakness.

fragment *vb* atomize, break, fracture, pulverize, splinter. * *n* bit, chip, fraction, fracture, morsel, part, piece, remnant, scrap.

fragrant *adj* ambrosial, aromatic, balmy, odoriferous, odorous, perfumed, redolent, spicy, sweet, sweet-scented, sweet-smelling.

frail *adj* breakable, brittle, delicate, fragile, frangible, slight; feeble, fragile, infirm, weak.

frame *vb* build, compose, constitute, construct, erect, form, make, mould, plan, shape; contrive, devise, fabricate, fashion, forge, invest, plan. * *n* body, carcass, framework, framing, shell, skeleton; constitution, fabric, form, structure, scheme, system; condition, humour, mood, state, temper.

frank *adj* artless, candid, direct, downright, frank-hearted, free, genuine, guileless, ingenuous, naive, open, outspoken, outright, plain, plainspoken, point-blank, sincere, straightforward, truthful, unequivocal, unreserved, unrestricted.

frantic *adj* crazy, distracted, distraught, frenzied, furious, infuriate, mad. outrageous, phrenetic, rabid, raging, raving, transported, wild.

fraud *n* artifice, cheat, craft, deception, deceit, duplicity, guile, hoax, humbug, imposition, imposture, sham, stratagem, treachery, trick, trickery, wile.

fraudulent *adj* crafty, deceitful, deceptive, dishonest, false, knavish, treacherous, trickish, tricky, wily.

freak *adj* bizarre, freakish, grotesque, monstrous, odd, unexpected, unforeseen. * *n* caprice, crotchet, fancy, humour, maggot, quirk, vagary, whim, whimsey; antic, caper, gambol; abnormality, abortion, monstrosity.

free *vb* deliver, discharge, disenthral, emancipate, enfranchise, enlarge, liberate, manumit, ransom, release, redeem, rescue, save; clear, disencumber, disengage, extricate, rid, unbind, unchain, unfetter, unlock; exempt, immunize, privilege. * *adj* bondless, independent, loose, unattached, unconfined, unentangled, unimpeded, unrestrained, untrammelled; autonomous, delivered, emancipated, freeborn, liberated, manumitted, ransomed, released, self-governing; clear, exempt, immune, privileged; allowed, open, permitted; devoid, empty, open, unimpeded, unobstructed, unrestricted; affable, artless, candid, frank, ingenuous, sincere, unreserved; bountiful, charitable, free-hearted, generous, hospitable, liberal, munificent, openhanded; immoderate, lavish, prodigal; eager, prompt, ready, willing; available, gratuitous, spontaneous, willing; careless, lax, loose; bold, easy, familiar, informal, overfamiliar, unconstrained. * *adv* openly, outright, unreservedly, unrestrainedly, unstintingly; freely, gratis, gratuitously.

freedom *n* emancipation, independence, liberation, liberty, release; elbowroom, margin, play, range, scope, swing; franchise, immunity, privilege; familiarity, laxity, license, looseness.

freeze *vb* congeal, glaciate, harden, stiffen; benumb, chill.

frenzy *n* aberration, delirium, derangement, distraction, fury, insanity, lunacy, madness, mania, paroxysm, rage, raving, transport.

frequent *vb* attend, haunt, resort, visit. * *adj* iterating, oft-repeated; common, customary, everyday, familiar, habitual, persistent, usual; constant, continual, incessant.

fresh *adj* new, novel, recent; new, renewed, revived; blooming, flourishing, green, undecayed, unimpaired, unfaded, unobliterated, unwilted, unwithered, well-preserved; sweet; blooming, delicate, fair, fresh-coloured, ruddy, rosy;

florid, hardy, healthy, vigorous, strong; active, energetic, unexhausted, unfatigued, unwearied, vigorous; keen, lively, unabated, undecayed, unimpaired, vivid; additional, further; uncured, undried, unsalted, unsmoked; bracing, health-giving, invigorating, refreshing, sweet; brink, stiff, strong; inexperienced, raw, uncultivated, unpracticed, unskilled, untrained, unused.

freshen *vb* quicken, receive, refresh, revive.

fretful *adj* captious, cross, fractious, ill-humoured, ill-tempered, irritable, peevish, pettish, petulant, querulous, short-tempered, snappish, spleeny, splenetic, testy, touchy, uneasy, waspish.

friend *adj* benefactor, chum, companion, comrade, crony, confidant, intimate; adherent, ally, associate, confrere, partisan; adherent, advocate, defender, encourager, favourer, patron, supporter, well-wisher.

friendly *adj* affectionate, amiable, benevolent, favourable, kind, kind-hearted, kindly, well-disposed; amicable, cordial, fraternal, neighbourly; conciliatory, peaceable, unhostile.

friendship *n* affection, attachment, benevolence, fondness, goodness, love, regard; fellowship, intimacy; amicability, amicableness, amity, cordiality, familiarity, fellowship, fraternization, friendliness, harmony.

fright *n* affright, alarm, consternation, dismay, funk, horror, panic, scare, terror.

frighten *vb* affright, alarm, appal, daunt, dismay, intimidate, scare, stampede, terrify.

frightful *adj* alarming, awful, dire, direful, dread, dreadful, fearful, horrible, horrid, shocking, terrible, terrific; ghastly, grim, grisly, gruesome, hideous.

fringe *vb* border, bound, edge, hem, march, rim, skirt, verge. * *n* border, edge, edging, tassel, trimming. * *adj* edging, extra, unofficial.

frisky *adj* frolicsome, coltish, lively, playful, sportive.

frivolous *adj* childish, empty, flighty, flimsy, flippant, foolish, giddy, idle, light, paltry. petty, puerile, silly, trashy, trifling, trivial, unimportant, vain, worthless.

frolic vb caper, frisk, gambol, lark, play, romp, sport. * n escapade, gambol, lark, romp, skylark, spree, trick; drollery, fun, play, pleasantry, sport.

front vb confront, encounter, face, oppose. * adj anterior, forward; foremost, frontal, headmost. * n brow, face, forehead; assurance, boldness, brass, effrontery, face, impudence; breast, head, van, vanguard; anterior, face, forepart, obverse; facade, frontage.

frontier n border, boundary, coast, confine, limits, marches.

frosty adj chill, chilly, cold, icy, stinging, wintry; cold, cold-hearted, frigid, indifferent, unaffectionate, uncordial, unimpassioned, unloving; cold, dull-hearted, lifeless, spiritless, unanimated; frosted, grey-hearted, hoary, white.

froth vb bubble, cream, foam, lather, spume. * n bubbles, foam, lather, spume; balderdash, flummery, nonsense, trash, triviality.

frown vb glower, lower, scowl.

frugal adj abstemious, careful, chary, choice, economical, provident, saving, sparing, temperate, thrifty, unwasteful.

fruit n crop, harvest, produce, production; advantage, consequence, effect, good, outcome, product, profit, result; issue, offspring, young.

fruitful adj abounding, productive; fecund, fertile, prolific; abundant, exuberant, plenteous, plentiful, rich, teeming.

fruitless adj acarpous, barren, sterile, infecund, unfertile, unfruitful, unproductive, unprolific; abortive, barren, bootless, futile, idle, ineffectual, profitless, unavailing, unprofitable, useless, vain.

frustrate vb baffle, baulk, check, circumvent, defeat, disappoint, disconcert, foil, thwart; check, cross, hinder, outwit.

fugitive adj escaping, fleeing, flying; brief, ephemeral, evanescent, fleeting, flitting, flying, fugacious, momentary, short, short-lived, temporal, temporary, transient, transitory, uncertain, unstable, volatile. * n émigré, escapee, evacuee, fleer, outlaw, refugee, runaway.

fulfil vb accomplish, complete, consummate, effect, effectuate, execute, realize; adhere, discharge, do, keep, obey, observe, perform; answer, fill, meet, satisfy.

full adj brimful, filled, flush, replete; abounding, replete, well-stocked; bagging, flowing, loose, voluminous; cloyed, crammed, glutted, gorged, overflowing, packed, sated, satiated, saturated, soaked, stuffed, swollen; adequate, complete, entire, mature, perfect; abundant, ample, copious, plenteous, plentiful, sufficient; clear, deep, distinct, loud, rounded, strong; broad, large, capacious, comprehensive, extensive, plump; circumstantial, detailed, exhaustive. * adv completely, fully; directly, exactly, precisely.

fully adv abundantly, amply, completely, copiously, entirely, largely, plentifully, sufficiently.

fumble vb bungle, grope, mismanage, stumble; mumble, stammer, stutter.

fume vb reek, smoke, vaporize. * n effluvium exhalation, reek, smell, smoke, steam, vapour; agitation, fret, fry, fury, passion, pet, rage, storm.

fun adj amusing, diverting, droll, entertaining. * n amusement, diversion, drollery, frolic, gaiety, humour, jesting, jocularity, jollity, joy, merriment, mirth, play, pranks, sport, pleasantry, waggishness.

function vb act, discharge, go, operate, officiate, perform, run, serve, work. * n discharge, execution, exercise, operation, performance, purpose, use; activity, business, capacity, duty, employment, occupation, office, part, province, role; ceremony, rite; dependant, derivative.

fund vb afford, endow, finance, invest, provide, subsidise, support; garner, hoard, stock, store. * n accumulation, capital, endowment, reserve, stock; store, supply; foundation.

fundamental adj basal, basic, bottom, cardinal, constitutional, elementary, essential, indispensable, organic, principal, primary, radical. * n essential, principal, rule.

funereal adj dark, dismal, gloomy, lugubrious, melancholy, mournful, sad, sepulchral, sombre, woeful.

funny *adj* amusing, comic, comical, diverting, droll, facetious, farcical, humorous, jocose, jocular, laughable, ludicrous, sportive, witty; curious, odd, queer, strange. * *n* jest, joke; cartoon, comic.

furious *adj* angry, fierce, frantic, frenzied, fuming, infuriated, mad, raging, violent, wild; boisterous, fierce, impetuous, stormy, tempestuous, tumultuous, turbulent, vehement.

furnish *vb* appoint, endow, provide, supply; decorate, equip, fit; afford, bestow, contribute, give, offer, present, produce, yield.

furniture *n* chattels, effects, household goods, movables; apparatus, appendages, appliances, equipment, fittings, furnishings; decorations, embellishments, ornaments.

further *vb* advance, aid, assist, encourage, help, forward, promote, succour, strengthen. * *adj* additional. * *adv* also, besides, farther, furthermore, moreover.

furtive *adj* clandestine, hidden, secret, sly, skulking, sneaking, sneaky, stealthy, stolen, surreptitious.

fury *n* anger, frenzy, fit, furore, ire, madness, passion, rage; fierceness, impetuosity, turbulence, turbulency, vehemence; bacchant, bacchante, bedlam, hag, shrew, termagant, virago, vixen.

fuse *vb* dissolve, melt, liquefy, smelt; amalgamate, blend, coalesce, combine, commingle, intermingle, intermix, merge, unite. * *n* match.

fuss *vb* bustle, fidget; fret, fume, worry. * *n* ado, agitation, bother, bustle, commotion, disturbance, excitement, fidget, flurry, fluster, fret, hurry, pother, stir, worry.

futile *adj* frivolous, trifling, trivial; bootless, fruitless, idle, ineffectual, profitless, unavailing, unprofitable, useless, vain, valueless, worthless.

future *adj* coming, eventual, forthcoming, hereafter, prospective, subsequent. * *n* hereafter, outlook, prospect.

G

gag¹ *n* jape, jest, joke, stunt, wisecrack.

gag² *vb* muffle, muzzle, shackle, silence, stifle, throttle; regurgitate, retch, throw up, vomit; choke, gasp, pant. * *n* muzzle.

gaiety *n* animation, blithesomeness, cheerfulness, glee, hilarity, jollity, joviality, merriment, mirth, vivacity.

gain *vb* achieve, acquire, earn, get, obtain, procure, reap, secure; conciliate, enlist, persuade, prevail, win; arrive, attain, reach; clear, net, profit. * *n* accretion, addition, gainings, profits, winnings; acquisition, earnings, emolument, lucre; advantage, benefit, blessing, good, profit.

gainful *adj* advantageous, beneficial, profitable; lucrative, paying, productive, remunerative.

galaxy *n* assemblage, assembly, cluster, collection, constellation, group.

gale *n* blast, hurricane, squall, storm, tempest, tornado, typhoon.

gallant *adj* fine, magnificent, showy, splendid, well-dressed; bold, brave, chivalrous, courageous, daring, fearless, heroic, high-spirited, intrepid, valiant, valorous; chivalrous, fine, honourable, high-minded, lofty, magnanimous, noble. * *n* beau, blade, spark; lover, suitor, wooer.

gallantry *n* boldness, bravery, chivalry, courage, courageousness, fearlessness, heroism, intrepidity, prowess, valour; courtesy, courteousness, elegance, politeness.

galling *adj* chafing, irritating, vexing.

gamble *vb* bet, dice, game, hazard, plunge, speculate, wager. * *n* chance, risk, speculation; bet, punt, wager.

gambol *vb* caper, cut, frisk, frolic, hop, jump, leap, romp, skip. * *n* frolic, hop, jump, skip.

game¹ *vb* gamble, sport, stake. * *n* amusement, contest, diversion, pastime, play, sport; adventure, enterprise, measure, plan, project, scheme, stratagem, undertaking; prey, quarry, victim.

game² *adj* brave, courageous, dauntless,

fearless, gallant, heroic, intrepid, plucky, unflinching, valorous; enduring, persevering, resolute, undaunted; ready, eager, willing.

game⁴ adj crippled, disabled, halt, injured, lame.

gang n band, cabal, clique, company, coterie, crew, horde, party, set, troop.

gap n breach, break, cavity, chasm, chink, cleft, crack, cranny, crevice, hiatus, hollow, interval, interstice, lacuna, opening, pass, ravine, rift, space, vacancy.

gape vb burst open, dehisce, open, stare, yawn.

garish adj bright, dazzling, flashy, flaunting, gaudy, glaring, loud, showy, staring, tawdry.

garment n clothes, clothing, dress, habit, vestment.

garnish vb adorn, beautify, bedeck, decorate, deck, embellish, grace, ornament, prank, trim. * n decoration, enhancement, ornament, trimming.

gasp vb blow, choke, pant, puff. * n blow, exclamation, gulp, puff.

gather vb assemble, cluster, collect, convene, group, muster, rally; accumulate, amass, garner, hoard, huddle, lump; bunch, crop, cull, glean, pick, pluck, rake, reap, shock, stack; acquire, gain, get, win; conclude, deduce, derive, infer; fold, plait, pucker, shirr, tuck; condense, grow, increase, thicken.

gathering n acquisition, collecting, earning, gain, heap, pile, procuring; assemblage, assembly, collection, company, concourse, congregation, meeting, muster; abscess, boil, fester, pimple, pustule, sore, suppuration, tumour, ulcer.

gaudy adj bespangled, brilliant, brummagem, cheap, flashy, flaunting, garish, gimcrack, glittering, loud, ostentatious, overdecorated, sham, showy, spurious, tawdry, tinsel.

gauge vb calculate, check, determine, weigh; assess, estimate, guess, reckon. * n criterion, example, indicator, measure, meter, touchstone, yardstick; bore, depth, height, magnitude, size, thickness, width.

gaunt adj angular, attenuated, emaciated, haggard, lank, lean, meagre, scraggy, skinny, slender, spare, thin.

gear vb adapt, equip, fit, suit, tailor. * n apparel, array, clothes, clothing, dress, garb; accoutrements, appliances, appointments, appurtenances, array, harness, goods, movables, subsidiaries; harness, rigging, tackle, trappings; apparatus, machinery, mechanics.

general adj broad, collective, generic, popular, universal, widespread; catholic, ecumenical; common, current, ordinary, usual; inaccurate, indefinite, inexact, vague.

generate vb beget, breed, engender, procreate, propagate, reproduce, spawn; cause, form, make, produce.

generation n creation, engendering, formation, procreation, production; age, epoch, era, period, time; breed, children, family, kind, offspring, progeny, race, stock.

generosity n disinterestedness, highmindedness, magnanimity, nobleness; bounteousness, bountifulness, bounty, charity, liberality, openhandedness.

generous adj high-minded, honourable, magnanimous, noble; beneficent, bountiful, charitable, free, hospitable, liberal, munificent, openhanded; abundant, ample, copious, plentiful, rich.

genius n aptitude, aptness, bent, capacity, endowment, faculty, flair, gift, talent, turn; brains, ingenuity, inspiration, intellect, invention, parts, sagacity, wit; adeptness, master, master hand, proficiency; character, disposition, naturalness, nature; deity, demon, spirit.

gentle adj amiable, bland, clement, compassionate, humane, indulgent, kind, lenient, meek, merciful, mild, moderate, soft, tender, tender-hearted, docile, pacific, peaceable, placid, quiet, tame, tractable; bland, easy, gradual, light, mild, moderate, slight, soft; high-born, noble, well-born; chivalrous, courteous, cultivated, polished, refined, well-bred.

genuine adj authentic, honest, proper, pure, real, right, true, unadulterated, unalloyed, uncorrupted, veritable; frank, native, sincere, unaffected.

gesture vb indicate, motion, signal, wave.
* n action, attitude, gesticulation, gesturing, posture, sign, signal.

get vb achieve, acquire, attain, earn, gain, obtain, procure, receive, relieve, secure, win; finish, master, prepare; beget, breed, engender, generate, procreate.

ghastly adj cadaverous, corpse-like, death-like, deathly, ghostly, lurid, pale, pallid, wan; dismal, dreadful, fearful, frightful, grim, grisly, gruesome, hideous, horrible, shocking, terrible.

ghost n soul, spirit; apparition, phantom, revenant, shade, spectre, spook, sprite, wraith.

giant adj colossal, enormous, Herculean, huge, large, monstrous, prodigious, vast.
* n colossus, cyclops, Hercules, monster.

gibe, jibe vb deride, fleer, flout, jeer, mock, ridicule, scoff, sneer, taunt. * n ridicule, sneer, taunt.

giddy adj dizzy, head-spinning, vertiginous; careless, changeable, fickle, flighty, frivolous, hare-brained, headlong, heedless, inconstant, irresolute, light-headed, thoughtless, unsteady, vacillating, wild.

gift n alms, allowance, benefaction, bequest, bonus, boon, bounty, contribution, donation, dowry, endowment, favour, grant, gratuity, honorarium, largesse, legacy, offering, premium, present, prize, subscription, subsidy, tip; faculty, talent.

gifted adj able, capable, clever, ingenious, intelligent, inventive, sagacious, talented.

gild vb adorn, beautify, bedeck, brighten, decorate, embellish, grace, illuminate.

gird vb belt, girdle; begird, encircle, enclose, encompass, engird, environ, surround; brace, support. * n band, belt, cincture, girdle, girth, sash, waistband.

girl n damsel, lass, lassie, maiden, miss, virgin.

gist n basis, core, essence, force, ground, marrow, meaning, pith, point, substance.

give vb accord, bequeath, bestow, confer, devise, entrust, present; afford, contribute, donate, furnish, grant, proffer, spare, supply; communicate, impart; deliver,

exchange, pay, requite; allow, permit, vouchsafe; emit, pronounce, render, utter; produce, yield; cause, occasion; addict, apply, devote, surrender; bend, sink, recede, retire, retreat, yield.

glad adj delighted, gratified, happy, pleased, rejoiced, well-contented; animated, blithe, cheerful, cheery, elated, gladsome, happy, jocund, joyful, joyous, light, light-hearted, merry, playful; animating, bright, cheering, exhilarating, gladdening, gratifying, joyful, joyous, pleasing.

gladden vb bless, cheer, delight, elate, enliven, exhilarate, gratify, please, rejoice.

glamour n bewitchment, charm, enchantment, fascination, spell, witchery.

glance vb coruscate, gleam, glisten, glister, glitter, scintillate, shine; dart, flit; gaze, glimpse, look, view. * n gleam, glitter; gleam, look, view.

glare vb dazzle, flame, flare, gleam, glisten, glitter, sparkle; frown, gaze, glower. * n flare, glitter.

gleam vb beam, coruscate, flash, glance, glimmer, glitter, shine, sparkle. * n beam, flash, glance, glimmer, glimmering, glow, ray; brightness, coruscation, flashing, gleaming, glitter, glittering, lustre, splendour.

glean vb collect, cull, gather, get, harvest, pick, select.

glee n exhilaration, fun, gaiety, hilarity, jocularity, jollity, joviality, joy, liveliness, merriment, mirth, sportiveness, verve.

glib adj slippery, smooth; artful, facile, flippant, fluent, ready, talkative, voluble.

glide vb float, glissade, roll on, skate, skim, slide, slip; flow, lapse, run, roll.
* n gliding, lapse, sliding, slip.

glimmer vb flash, flicker, gleam, glitter, shine, twinkle. * n beam, gleam, glimmering, ray; glance, glimpse.

glimpse vb espy, look, spot, view. * n flash, glance, glimmering, glint, look, sight.

glitter vb coruscate, flare, flash, glance, glare, gleam, glisten, glister, scintillate, shine, sparkle. * n beam, beaming, brightness, brilliancy, coruscation, gleam, glister, lustre, radiance, scintillation, shine, sparkle, splendour.

gloat vb exult, gaze, rejoice, stare, triumph.

gloomy adj dark, dim, dusky, obscure; cheerless, dismal, lowering, lurid; crestfallen, dejected, depressed, despondent, disheartened, dispirited, downcast, downhearted, glum, melancholy, morose, sad, sullen; dark, depressing, disheartening, dispiriting, heavy, melancholy, sad, saddening.

glorify vb adore, bless, celebrate, exalt, extol, laud, magnify, worship; adorn, brighten, elevate, ennoble, exalt, make bright.

glorious adj celebrated, conspicuous, distinguished, eminent, excellent, famed, famous, illustrious, pre-eminent, renowned; brilliant, bright, grand, magnificent, radiant, resplendent, splendid; consummate, exalted, excellent, high, lofty, noble, supreme.

glory vb boast, exult, vaunt. * n celebrity, distinction, eminence, fame, honour, illustriousness, praise, renown; brightness, brilliancy, effulgence, lustre, pride, resplendence, splendour; exaltation, exceeding, gloriousness, greatness, grandeur, nobleness; bliss, happiness.

glow vb incandesce, radiate, shine; blush, burn, flush, redden. * n blaze, brightness, brilliance, burning, incandescence, luminosity, reddening; ardour, bloom, enthusiasm, fervency, fervour, flush, impetuosity, vehemence, warmth.

glower vb frown, glare, lower, scowl, stare. * n frown, glare, scowl.

glum adj churlish, crabbed, crest-fallen, cross-grained, crusty, depressed, frowning, gloomy, glowering, moody, morose, sour, spleenish, spleeny, sulky, sullen, surly.

glut vb block up, cloy, cram, gorge, satiate, stuff. * n excess, saturation, surfeit, surplus.

glutton n gobbler, gorger, gourmand, gormandizer, greedy-guts, lurcher, pig.

go vb advance, move, pass, proceed, repair; act, operate; be about, extravagate, fare, journey, roam, travel, walk, wend;

depart, disappear; elapse, extend, lead, reach, run; avail, concur, contribute, tend, serve; eventuate, fare, turn out; accept, approve, bear, endure, swallow, tolerate; afford, bet, risk, wager. * n action, business, case, chance, circumstance, doings, turn; custom, fad, fashion, mode, vague; energy, endurance, power, stamina, inter, avaunt, begone, be off.

goal n bound, home, limit, mark, mete, post; end, object; aim, design, destination.

gobble vb bolt, devour, gorge, gulp, swallow.

goblin n apparition, elf, bogey, demon, gnome, hobgoblin, phantom, spectre, sprite.

god n almighty, creator, deity, divinity, idol, Jehovah, omnipotence, providence.

godsend n fortune, gift, luck, present, windfall.

golden adj aureate, brilliant, bright, gilded, resplendent, shining, splendid; excellent, precious; auspicious, favourable, opportune, propitious; blessed, delightful, glorious, halcyon, happy.

good adj advantageous, beneficial, favourable, profitable, serviceable, useful; adequate, appropriate, becoming, convenient, fit, proper, satisfactory, suitable, well-adapted; decorous, dutiful, honest, just, pious, reliable, religious, righteous, true, upright, virtuous, well-behaved, worthy; admirable, capable, excellent, genuine, healthy, precious, sincere, sound, sterling, valid, valuable; benevolent, favourable, friendly, gracious, humane, kind, merciful, obliging, well-disposed; fair, honourable, immaculate, unblemished, unimpeachable, unimpeached, unsullied, untarnished; cheerful, companionable, lively, genial, social; able, competent, dextrous, expert, qualified, ready, skilful, thorough, well-qualified; competent, credit-worthy; agreeable, cheering, gratifying, pleasant. * n advantage, benefit, boon, favour, gain, profit, utility; interest, prosperity, welfare, weal; excellence, righteousness, virtue, worth.

goodbye n adieu, farewell, parting.

goodness n excellence, quality, value, worth; honesty, integrity, morality, principle, probity, righteousness, uprightness, virtue; benevolence, beneficence, benignity, good-will, humaneness, humanity, kindness.

goodwill n benevolence, kindness, good nature; ardour, earnestness, heartiness, willingness, zeal; custom, patronage.

gorgeous adj bright, brilliant, dazzling, fine, glittering, grand, magnificent, resplendent, rich, shining, showy, splendid, superb.

gory adj bloody, ensanguined, sanguinary.

gospel n creed, doctrine, message, news, revelation, tidings.

gossip vb chat, cackle, clack, gabble, prate, prattle, tattle. * n babbler, busybody, chatterer, gadabout, gossipmonger, newsmonger, quidnunc, tale-bearer, tattler, tell-tale; cackle, chat, chitchat, prate, prattle, tattle.

gourmet n connoisseur, epicure, epicurean.

govern vb administer, conduct, direct, manage, regulate, reign, rule, superintend, supervise; guide, pilot, steer; bridle, check, command, control, curb, restrain, rule, sway.

government n autonomy, command, conduct, control, direction, discipline, dominion, guidance, management, regulation, restraint, rule, rulership, sway; administration, cabinet, commonwealth, polity, sovereignty, state.

governor n commander, comptroller, director, head, headmaster, manager, overseer, ruler, superintendent, supervisor; chief magistrate, executive, guardian, instructor, tutor.

grab vb capture, clutch, seize, snatch.

grace vb adorn, beautify, deck, decorate, embellish; dignify, honour. * n benignity, condescension, favour, good-will, kindness, love; devotion, efficacy, holiness, love, piety, religion, sanctity, virtue; forgiveness, mercy, pardon, reprieve; accomplishment, attractiveness, charm, elegance, polish, propriety, refinement; beauty, comeliness, ease, gracefulness, symmetry; blessing, petition, thanks.

graceful adj beautiful, becoming, comely, easy, elegant; flowing, natural, rounded, unlaboured; appropriate; felicitous, happy, tactful.

gracious adj beneficent, benevolent, benign, benignant, compassionate, condescending, favourable, friendly, gentle, good-natured, kind, kindly, lenient, merciful, mild, tender; affable, civil, courteous, easy, familiar, polite.

grade vb arrange, classify, group, order, rank, sort. * n brand, degree, intensity, stage, step, rank; gradient, incline, slope.

gradual adj approximate, continuous, gentle, progressive, regular, slow, successive.

graduate vb adapt, adjust, proportion, regulate. * n alumna, alumnus, laureate, postgraduate.

grand adj august, dignified, elevated, eminent, exalted, great, illustrious, lordly, majestic, princely, stately, sublime; fine, glorious, gorgeous, magnificent, pompous, lofty, noble, splendid, sublime, superb; chief, leading, main, pre-eminent, principal, superior.

grandeur n elevation, greatness, immensity, impressiveness, loftiness, vastness; augustness, dignity, eminence, glory, loftiness, magnificence, majesty, nobility, pomp, splendour, state, stateliness.

grant vb accord, admit, allow, cede, concede, give, impart, indulge; bestow, confer, deign, invest, vouchsafe; convey, transfer, yield. * n admission, allowance, benefaction, bestowal, boon, bounty, concession, donation, endowment, gift, indulgence, largesse, present; conveyance, cession.

graphic adj descriptive, diagrammatic, figural, figurative, forcible, lively, pictorial, picturesque, striking, telling, vivid, well-delineated, well-drawn.

grapple vb catch, clutch, grasp, grip, hold, hug, seize, tackle, wrestle.

grasp vb catch, clasp, clinch, clutch, grapple, grip, seize; comprehend understand. * n clasp, grip, hold; comprehension, power, reach, scope, understanding.

grasping adj acquisitive, avaricious, covetous, exacting, greedy, rapacious, sordid, tight-fisted.

grate vb abrade, rub, scrape, triturate; comminute, rasp; creak, fret, grind, jar, rasp, vex. * n bars, grating, latticework, screen; basket, fire bed.

grateful adj appreciative, beholden, indebted, obliged, thankful; acceptable, agreeable, charming, delightful, gratifying, pleasant, pleasing, satisfactory, satisfying, welcome; cordial, delicious, invigorating, luscious, nice, palatable, refreshing, savoury; alleviating, comforting, soothing.

gratify vb delight, gladden, please; humour, fulfil, grant, indulge, requite, satisfy.

gratitude n goodwill, gratitude, indebtedness, thankfulness.

grave adj cogent, heavy, important, momentous, pressing, serious, weighty; dignified, sage, sedate, serious, slow, solemn, staid, thoughtful; dull, plain, quiet, sober, sombre, subdued; cruel, hard, harsh, severe; dire, dismal, gross, heinous, infamous, outrageous, scandalous, shameful, shocking; heavy, hollow, low, low-pitched, sepulchral.

gravity n heaviness, weight; demureness, sedateness, seriousness, sobriety, thoughtfulness; importance, moment, momentousness, seriousness, weightiness.

graze vb brush, glance, scrape, scratch, shave, skim; browse, crop, feed, pasture. * n abrasion, bruise, scrape, scratch.

great adj ample, big, bulky, Cyclopean, enormous, gigantic, Herculean, huge, immense, large, pregnant, vast; decided, excessive, high, much, pronounced; countless, numerous; chief, considerable, grand, important, leading, main, preeminent, principal, superior, weighty; celebrated, distinguished, eminent, exalted, excellent, famed, famous, farfamed, illustrious, noted, prominent, renowned; august, dignified, elevated, exalted, grand, lofty, majestic, noble, sublime; chivalrous, generous, high-minded, magnanimous; fine, magnificent, rich, sumptuous.

greatness n bulk, dimensions, largeness, magnitude, size; distinction, elevation, eminence, fame, importance, renown; augustness, dignity, grandeur, majesty, loftiness, nobility, nobleness, sublimity; chivalrous, disinterestedness, generosity, magnanimity, spirit.

greed, greediness n gluttony, hunger, omnivorousness, ravenousness, voracity; avidity, covetousness, desire, eagerness, greed, longing; avarice, cupidity, graspingness, grasping, rapacity, selfishness.

greedy adj devouring, edacious, gluttonous, insatiable, insatiate, rapacious, ravenous, voracious; desirous, eager; avaricious, grasping, rapacious, selfish.

green adj aquamarine, emerald, olive, verdant, verdure, viridescent, viridian; blooming, flourishing, fresh, undecayed; fresh, new, recent; immature, unfledged, unripe; callow, crude, inexpert, ignorant, inexperienced, raw, unskilful, untrained, verdant, young; raw, unseasoned. * n common, grass plot, lawn, sward, turf, verdure.

greet vb accost, address, complement, hail, receive, salute, welcome.

greeting n compliment, salutation, salute, welcome.

grief n affliction, agony, anguish, bitterness, distress, dole, heartbreak, misery, regret, sadness, sorrow, suffering, tribulation, woe; distress, grievance, sorrow, trial, woe; disaster, failure, mishap.

grievance n burden, complaint, hardship, injury, oppression, wrong; affliction, distress, grief, sorrow, trial, woe.

grieve vb afflict, aggrieve, agonize, discomfort, distress, hurt, oppress, pain, sadden, wound; bewail, deplore, mourn, lament, regret, sorrow, suffer.

grievous adj afflicting, afflictive, burdensome, deplorable, distressing, heavy, lamentable, oppressive, painful, sad, sorrowful; baleful, baneful, calamitous, destructive, detrimental, hurtful, injurious, mischievous, noxious, troublesome; aggravated, atrocious, dreadful, flagitious, flagrant, gross, heinous, iniquitous, intense, intolerable, severe, outrageous, wicked.

grim *adj* cruel, ferocious, fierce, harsh, relentless, ruthless, savage, stern, unyielding; appalling, dire, dreadful, fearful, frightful, grisly, hideous, horrid, horrible, terrific.

grimace *vb, n* frown, scowl, smirk, sneer.

grimy *adj* begrimed, defiled, dirty, filthy, foul, soiled, sullied, unclean.

grind *vb* bruise, crunch, crush, grate, grit, pulverize, rub, triturate; sharpen, whet; afflict, harass, oppress, persecute, plague, trouble. * *n* chore, drudgery, labour, toil.

grip *vb* clasp, clutch, grasp, hold, seize. * *n* clasp, clutch, control, domination, grasp, hold.

grit *vb* clench, grate, grind. * *n* bran, gravel, pebbles, sand; courage, decision, determination, firmness, perseverance, pluck, resolution, spirit.

groan *vb* complain, lament, moan, whine; creak. * *n* cry, moan, whine; complaint; grouse, grumble.

gross *vb* accumulate, earn, make. * *adj* big, bulky, burly, fat, great, large; dense, dull, stupid, thick; beastly, broad, carnal, coarse, crass, earthy, impure, indelicate, licentious, low, obscene, unbecoming, unrefined, unseemly, vulgar, rough, sensual; aggravated, brutal, enormous, flagrant, glaring, grievous, manifest, obvious, palpable, plain, outrageous, shameful; aggregate, entire, total, whole. * *n* aggregate, bulk, total, whole.

grotesque *adj* bizarre, extravagant, fanciful, fantastic, incongruous, odd, strange, unnatural, whimsical, wild; absurd, antic, ludicrous, ridiculous.

ground *vb* fell, place; base, establish, fix, found, set; instruct, train. * *n* area, clod, distance, earth, loam, mould, sod, soil, turf; country, domain, land, region, territory; acres, estate, field, property; base, basis, foundation, groundwork, support; account, consideration, excuse, gist, motive, opinion, reason.

groundless *adj* baseless, causeless, false, gratuitous, idle, unauthorized, unwarranted, unfounded, unjustifiable, unsolicited, unsought, unwarranted.

grounds *npl* deposit, dregs, grouts, lees, precipitate, sediment, settlings; accounts, arguments, considerations, reasons, support; campus, gardens, lawns, premises, yard.

group *vb* arrange, assemble, dispose, order. * *n* aggregation, assemblage, assembly, body, combination, class, clump, cluster, collection, order.

grow *vb* enlarge, expand, extend, increase, swell; arise, burgeon, develop, germinate, shoot, sprout, vegetate; advance, extend, improve, progress, swell, thrive, wax; cultivate, produce, raise.

growl *vb* complain, croak, find fault, gnarl, groan, grumble, lament, murmur, snarl. * *n* croak, grown, snarl; complaint.

growth *n* augmentation, development, expansion, extension, growing, increase; burgeoning, excrescence, formation, germination, pollution, shooting, sprouting, vegetation; cultivation, produce, product, production; advance, advancement, development, improvement, progress; adulthood, maturity

grudge *vb* begrudge, envy, repine; complain, grieve, murmur. * *n* aversion, dislike, enmity, grievance, hate, hatred, ill-will, malevolence, malice, pique, rancour, resentment, spite, venom.

grumble *vb* croak, complain, murmur, repine; gnarl, growl, snarl; roar, rumble. * *n* growl, murmur, complaint, roar, rumble.

grumpy *adj* crabbed, cross, glum, moody, morose, sour, sullen, surly.

guarantee *vb* assure, insure, pledge, secure, warrant. * *n* assurance, pledge, security, surety, warrant, warranty.

guard *vb* defend, keep, patrol, protect, safeguard, save, secure, shelter, shield, watch. * *n* aegis, bulwark, custody, defence, palladium, protection, rampart, safeguard, security, shield; keeper, guardian, patrol, sentinel, sentry, warden, watch, watchman; conduct, convoy, escort; attention, care, caution, circumspection, heed, watchfulness.

guarded *adj* careful, cautious, circumspect, reserved, reticent, wary, watchful.

guardian *n* custodian, defender, guard,

keeper, preserver, protector, trustee, warden.

guess vb conjecture, divine, mistrust, surmise, suspect; fathom, find out, penetrate, solve; believe, fancy, hazard, imagine, reckon, suppose, think. * n conjecture, divination, notion, supposition, surmise.

guide vb conduct, escort, lead, pilot; control, direct, govern, manage, preside, regulate, rule, steer, superintend, supervise. * n conductor, director, monitor, pilot; adviser, counsellor, instructor, mentor; directory, index, key, thread; guidebook, itinerary, landmark.

guile n art, artfulness, artifice, craft, cunning, deceit, deception, duplicity, fraud, knavery, ruse, subtlety, treachery, trickery, wiles, wiliness.

guilt n blame, criminality, culpability, guiltless; ill-desert, iniquity, offensiveness, wickedness, wrong; crime, offence, sin, wrong.

guilty adj criminal, culpable, evil, sinful, wicked, wrong.

guise n appearance, aspect, costume, dress, fashion, figure, form, garb, manner, mode, shape; air, behaviour, demeanour, mien; custom, disguise, habit, manner, mode, pretence, practice.

gullible adj confiding, credulous, naive, overtrustful, simple, unsophisticated, unsuspicious.

gush vb burst, flood, flow, pour, rush, spout, stream; emotionalize, sentimentalize. * n flow, jet, onrush, rush, spurt, surge; effusion, effusiveness, loquacity, loquaciousness, talkativeness.

gusty adj blustering, blustery, puffy, squally, stormy, tempestuous, unsteady, windy.

guzzle vb carouse, drink, gorge, gormandize, quaff, swill, tipple, tope.

H

habit vb accoutre, array, attire, clothe, dress, equip, robe. * n condition, constitution, temperament; addiction, custom, habitude, manner, practice, rule,

usage, way, wont; apparel, costume, dress, garb, habiliment.

habitual adj accustomed, common, confirmed, customary, everyday, familiar, inveterate, ordinary, regular, routine, settled, usual, wonted.

hackneyed adj banal, common, commonplace, overworked, pedestrian, stale, threadbare, trite.

haggard adj intractable, refractory, unruly, untamed, wild, wayward; careworn, emaciated, gaunt, ghastly, lank, lean, meagre, raw, spare, thin, wasted, worn.

haggle vb argue, bargain, cavil, chaffer, dispute, higgle, stickle; annoy, badger, bait, fret, harass, tease, worry.

hail[1] vb acclaim, greet, salute, welcome; accost, address, call, hallo, signal. * n greeting, salute.

hail[2] vb assail, bombard, rain, shower, storm, volley. * n bombardment, rain, shower, storm, volley.

hale adj hardy, healthy, hearty, robust, sound, strong, vigorous, well.

hallow vb consecrate, dedicate, devote, revere, sanctify, solemnize; enshrine, honour, respect, reverence, venerate.

hallowed adj blessed, holy, honoured, revered, sacred.

hallucination n blunder, error, fallacy, mistake; aberration, delusion, illusion, phantasm, phantasy, self-deception, vision.

halo n aura, aureole, glory, nimbus.

halt[1] vb cease, desist, hold, rest, stand, stop. * n end, impasse, pause, standstill, stop.

halt[2] vb hesitate, pause, stammer, waver; falter, hobble, limp. * adj crippled, disabled, lame. * n hobble, limp.

hammer vb beat, forge, form, shape; excogitate, contrive, invent.

hamper vb bind, clog, confine, curb, embarrass, encumber, entangle, fetter, hinder, impede, obstruct, prevent, restrain, restrict, shackle, trammel. * n basket, box, crate, picnic basket; embarrassment, encumbrance, fetter, handicap, impediment, obstruction, restraint.

hand vb deliver, give, present, transmit; conduct, guide, lead. * n direction, part, side; ability, dexterity, faculty, skill, tal ent; course, management, turn; agency, intervention, participation, share; control, possession, power; artisan, craftsman, employee, labourer, operative, workman; index, indicator, pointer; chirography, handwriting.

handful n fistful, maniple, smattering.

handicap vb encumber, hamper, hinder, restrict. * n disadvantage, encumbrance, hampering, hindrance, restriction.

handle vb feel, finger, manhandle, paw, touch; direct, manage, manipulate, use, wield; discourse, discuss, treat. * n haft, helve, hilt, stock.

handsome adj admirable, comely, fine-looking, stately, well-formed, well-proportioned; appropriate, suitable, becoming, easy, graceful; disinterested, generous, gracious, liberal, magnanimous, noble; ample, large, plentiful, sufficient.

handy adj adroit, clever, dextrous, expert, ready, skilful, skilled; close, convenient, near.

hang vb attach, swing; execute, truss; decline, drop, droop, incline; adorn, drape; dangle, depend, impend, swing, suspend; depend, rely; cling, loiter, rest, stick; float, hover, pay

hanker vb covet, crave, desire, hunger, long, lust, want, yearn.

haphazard adj aimless, chance, random.

hapless adj ill-fated, ill-starred, luckless, miserable, unfortunate, unhappy, unlucky, wretched.

happen vb befall, betide, chance, come, occur.

happiness n brightness, cheerfulness, delight, gaiety, joy, light-heartedness, merriment, pleasure; beatitude, blessedness, bliss, felicity, enjoyment, welfare, well-being.

happy adj blessed, blest, blissful, cheerful, contented, joyful, joyous, light-hearted, merry; charmed, delighted, glad, gladdened, gratified, pleased, rejoiced; fortunate, lucky, prosperous, successful; able, adroit, apt, dextrous, expert, ready, skilful; befitting, felicitous, opportune, pertinent, seasonable, well-timed; auspicious, bright, favourable, propitious.

harangue vb address, declaim, spout. * n address, bombast, declamation, oration, rant, screed, speech, tirade.

harass vb exhaust, fag, fatigue, jade, tire, weary; annoy, badger, distress, gall, heckle, disturb, harry, molest, pester, plague, tantalize, tease, torment, trouble, vex, worry.

harbour vb protect, lodge, shelter; cherish, entertain, foster, indulge. * n asylum, cover, refuge, resting place, retreat, sanctuary, shelter; anchorage, destination, haven, port.

hard adj adamantine, compact, firm, flinty, impenetrable, marble, rigid, solid, resistant, stony, stubborn, unyielding; difficult, intricate, knotty, perplexing, puzzling; arduous, exacting, fatiguing, laborious, toilsome, wearying; austere, callous, cruel, exacting, hard-hearted, incorrigible, inflexible, insensible, insensitive, obdurate, oppressive, reprobate, rigorous, severe, unfeeling, unkind, unsusceptible, unsympathetic, unyielding, untender; calamitous, disagreeable, distressing, grievous, painful, unpleasant; acid, alcoholic, harsh, rough, sour; excessive, intemperate. * adv close, near; diligently, earnestly, energetically, incessantly, laboriously; distressfully, painfully, rigorously, severely; forcibly, vehemently, violently.

harden vb accustom, discipline, form, habituate, inure, season, train; brace, fortify, indurate, nerve, steel, stiffen, strengthen.

hardened adj annealed, case-hardened, tempered, indurated; abandoned, accustomed, benumbed, callous, confirmed, deadened, depraved, habituated, impenitent, incorrigible, inured, insensible, irreclaimable, lost, obdurate, reprobate, seared, seasoned, steeled, trained, unfeeling.

hardly adv barely, scarcely; cruelly, harshly, rigorously, roughly, severely, unkindly.

hardship n fatigue, toil, weariness; affliction, burden, calamity, grievance, hardness, injury, misfortune, privation, suffering, trial, trouble.

hardy adj enduring, firm, hale, healthy, hearty, inured, lusty, rigorous, robust, rugged, sound, stout, strong, sturdy, tough; bold, brave, courageous, daring, heroic, intrepid, manly, resolute, stout-hearted, valiant.

harm vb damage, hurt, injure, scathe; abuse, desecrate, ill-use, ill-treat, maltreat, molest. * n damage, detriment, disadvantage, hurt, injury, mischief, misfortune, prejudice, wrong.

harmful adj baneful, detrimental, disadvantageous, hurtful, injurious, mischievous, noxious, pernicious, prejudicial.

harmless adj innocent, innocuous, innoxious; inoffensive, safe, unoffending.

harmonious adj concordant, consonant, harmonic; dulcet, euphonious, mellifluous, melodious, musical, smooth, tuneful; comfortable, congruent, consistent, correspondent, orderly, symmetrical; agreeable, amicable, brotherly, cordial, fraternal, friendly, harmonious, neighbourly.

harmonize vb adapt, attune, reconcile, unite; accord, agree, blend, chime, comport, conform, correspond, square, sympathize, tally, tune.

harmony n euphony, melodiousness, melody; accord, accordance, agreement, chime, concord, concordance, consonance, order, unison; adaptation, congruence, congruity, consistency, correspondence, fairness, smoothness, suitableness; amity, friendship, peace.

harry vb devastate, pillage, plunder, raid, ravage, rob; annoy, chafe, disturb, fret, gall, harass, harrow, incommode, molest, pester, plague, molest, tease, torment, trouble, vex, worry.

harsh adj acid, acrid, astringent, biting, caustic, corrosive, crabbed, hard, rough, sharp, sour, tart; cacophonous, discordant, grating, jarring, metallic, raucous, strident, unmelodious; abusive, austere, crabbed, crabby, cruel, disagreeable, hard, ill-natured, ill-tempered, morose, rigorous, severe, stern, unfeeling; bearish, bluff, blunt, brutal, gruff, rude, uncivil, ungracious.

harvest vb gather, glean, reap. * n crops,
produce, yield; consequence, effect, issue, outcome, produce, result.

haste n alacrity, celerity, dispatch, expedition, nimbleness, promptitude, quickness, rapidity, speed, urgency, velocity; flurry, hurry, hustle, impetuosity, precipitateness, precipitation, press, rashness, rush, vehemence.

hasten vb haste, hurry; accelerate, dispatch, expedite, precipitate, press, push, quicken, speed, urge.

hasty adj brisk, fast, fleet, quick, rapid, speedy, swift; cursory, hurried, passing, rapid, slight, superficial; ill-advised, rash, reckless; headlong, helter-skelter, pell-mell, precipitate; abrupt, choleric, excitable, fiery, fretful, hot-headed, irascible, irritable, passionate, peevish, peppery, pettish, petulant, testy, touchy, waspish.

hatch vb brew, concoct, contrive, excogitate, design, devise, plan, plot, project, scheme; breed, incubate.

hate vb abhor, abominate, detest, dislike, execrate, loathe, nauseate. * n abomination, animosity, antipathy, detestation, dislike, enmity, execration, hatred, hostility, loathing.

hateful adj malevolent, malicious, malign, malignant, rancorous, spiteful; abhorrent, abominable, accursed, damnable, detestable, execrable, horrid, odious, shocking; abhorrent, disgusting, foul, loathsome, nauseous, obnoxious, offensive, repellent, repugnant, repulsive, revolting, vile.

hatred n animosity, enmity, hate, hostility, ill-will, malevolence, malice, malignity, odium, rancour; abhorrence, abomination, antipathy, aversion, detestation, disgust, execration, horror, loathing, repugnance, revulsion.

haughty adj arrogant, assuming, contemptuous, disdainful, imperious, insolent, lofty, lordly, overbearing, overweening, proud, scornful, snobbish, supercilious.

haul vb drag, draw, lug, pull, tow, trail, tug. * n heaving, pull, tug; booty, harvest, takings, yield.

haunt vb frequent, resort; follow, importune; hover, inhabit, obsess. * n den, resort, retreat.

have vb cherish, exercise, experience, keep, hold, occupy, own, possess; acquire, gain, get, obtain, receive; accept, take.

havoc n carnage, damage, desolation, destruction, devastation, ravage, ruin, slaughter, waste, wreck.

hazard vb adventure, risk, venture; endanger, imperil, jeopardize. * n accident, casualty, chance, contingency, event, fortuity, stake; danger, jeopardy, peril, risk, venture.

hazardous adj dangerous, insecure, perilous, precarious, risky, uncertain, unsafe.

hazy adj foggy, misty; cloudy, dim, nebulous, obscure; confused, indefinite, indistinct, uncertain, vague.

head vb command, control, direct, govern, guide, lead, rule; aim, point, tend; beat, excel, outdo, precede, surpass. * adj chief, first, grand, highest, leading, main, principal; adverse, contrary. * n acme, summit, top; beginning, commencement, origin, rise, source; chief, chieftain, commander, director, leader, master, principal, superintendent, superior; intellect, mind, thought, understanding; branch, category, class, department, division, section, subject, topic; brain, crown, headpiece, intellect, mind, thought, understanding; cape, headland, point, promontory.

headlong adj dangerous, hasty, heady, impulsive, inconsiderate, perilous, precipitate, rash, reckless, ruinous, thoughtless; perpendicular, precipitous, sheer, steep. * adv hastily, headfirst, helter-skelter, hurriedly, precipitately, rashly, thoughtlessly.

headstrong adj cantankerous, crossgrained, dogged, forward, headless, heady, intractable, obstinate, self-willed, stubborn, ungovernable, unruly, violent, wayward.

heady adj hasty, headlong, impetuous, impulsive, inconsiderate, precipitate, rash, reckless, rushing, stubborn, thoughtless; exciting, inebriating, inflaming, intoxicating, spirituous, strong.

heal vb amend, cure, remedy, repair, re-

store; compose, harmonize, reconcile, settle, soothe.

health n healthfulness, robustness, salubrity, sanity, soundness, strength, tone, vigour.

healthy adj active, hale, hearty, lusty, sound, vigorous, well; bracing, healthful, health-giving, hygienic, invigorating, nourishing, salubrious, salutary, wholesome.

heap vb accumulate, augment, amass, collect, overfill, pile up, store. * n accumulation, collection, cumulus, huddle, lot, mass, mound, pile, stack.

hear vb eavesdrop, hearken, heed, listen, overhear; ascertain, discover, gather, learn, understand; examine, judge.

heart n bosom, breast; centre, core, essence, interior, kernel, marrow, meaning, pith; affection, benevolence, character, disposition, feeling, inclination, love, mind, passion, purpose, will; affections, ardour, emotion, feeling, love; boldness, courage, fortitude, resolution, spirit.

heartbroken adj broken-hearted, cheerless, comfortless, desolate, disconsolate, forlorn, inconsolable, miserable, woebegone, wretched.

hearten vb animate, assure, cheer, comfort, console, embolden, encourage, enhearten, incite, inspire, inspirit, reassure, stimulate.

heartfelt adj cordial, deep, deep-felt, hearty, profound, sincere, warm.

heartless adj brutal, cold, cruel, hard, harsh, merciless, pitiless, unfeeling, unsympathetic; spiritless, timid, timorous, uncourageous.

hearty adj cordial, deep, earnest, heartfelt, profound, sincere, true, unfeigned, warm; active, animated, earnest, energetic, vigorous, warm, zealous; hale, hearty, robust, sound, strong, warm; abundant, full, heavy; nourishing, nutritious, rich.

heat vb excite, flush, inflame; animate, rouse, stimulate, stir. * n calorie, caloricity, torridity, warmth; excitement, fever, flush, impetuosity, passion, vehemence, violence; ardour, earnestness, fervency, fervour, glow, intensity, zeal; exasperation, fierceness, frenzy, rage.

heave vb elevate, hoist, lift, raise; breathe, exhale, raise; cast, fling, hurl, send, throw, toss; breathe, dilate, expand, pant, rise, swell; retch, throw up; strive, struggle.

heaven n empyrean, firmament, sky, welkin; bliss, ecstasy, elysium, felicity, happiness, paradise, rapture, transport.

heavenly adj celestial, empyreal, ethereal; angelic, beatific, beatified, cherubic, divine, elysian, glorious, god-like, sainted, saintly, seraphic; beatific, blissful, celestial, delightful, divine, ecstatic, enrapturing, enravishing, glorious, golden, rapturous, ravishing, seraphic, transporting.

heavy adj grave, hard, onerous, ponderous, weighty; afflictive, burdensome, crushing, cumbersome, grievous, oppressive, severe, serious; dilatory, dull, inactive, inanimate, indolent, inert, lifeless, sleepy, slow, sluggish, stupid, torpid; chapfallen, crestfallen, crushed, depressed, dejected, despondent, disconsolate, downhearted, gloomy, low-spirited, melancholy, sad, sobered, sorrowful; difficult, hard, laborious, onerous, tedious, tiresome, wearisome, weary; burdened, encumbered, loaded; clammy, clayey, cloggy, ill-raised, miry, muddy, oppressive, soggy; boisterous, deep, energetic, loud, roaring, severe, stormy, strong, tempestuous, violent; cloudy, dark, dense, gloomy, lowering, overcast.

hectic adj animated, excited, fevered, feverish, flushed, heated, hot.

hedge vb block, encumber, hinder, obstruct, surround; enclose, fence, fortify, guard, protect; disappear, dodge, evade, hide, skulk, temporize. * n barrier, hedgerow, fence, limit.

heed vb attend, consider, mark, mind, note, notice, observe, regard. * n attention, care, carefulness, caution, circumspection, consideration, heedfulness, mindfulness, notice, observation, regard, wariness, vigilance, watchfulness.

heedful adj attentive, careful, cautious, circumspect, mindful, observant, observing, provident, regardful, watchful, wary.

heedless adj careless, inattentive, neglectful, negligent, precipitate, rash, reckless, thoughtless, unmindful, unminding, unobserving, unobservant.

height n altitude, elevation, tallness; acme, apex, climax, eminence, head, meridian, pinnacle, summit, top, vertex, zenith; eminence, hill, mountain; dignity, eminence, exaltation, grandeur, loftiness, perfection.

heighten vb elevate, raise; ennoble, exalt, magnify, make greater; augment, enhance, improve, increase, strengthen; aggravate, intensify.

help vb relieve, save, succour; abet, aid, assist, back, cooperate, second, serve, support, sustain, wait; alleviate, ameliorate, better, cure, heal, improve, remedy, restore; control, hinder, prevent, repress, resist, withstand; avoid, forbear, control. * n aid, assistance, succour, support; relief, remedy; assistant, helper, servant.

helper adj aider, abettor, ally, assistant, auxiliary, coadjutor, colleague, helpmate, partner, supporter.

helpful adj advantageous, assistant, auxiliary, beneficial, contributory, convenient, favourable, kind, profitable, serviceable, useful.

helpless adj disabled, feeble, imbecile, impotent, infirm, powerless, prostrate, resourceless, weak; abandoned, defenceless, exposed, unprotected; desperate, irremediable, remediless.

hem vb border, edge, skirt; beset, confine, enclose, environ, surround, sew; hesitate. * n border, edge, trim.

herald vb announce, proclaim, publish. * n announcer, crier, proclaimer, publisher; harbinger, precursor, proclaimer.

herd vb drive, gather, lead, tend; assemble, associate, flock. * n drover, herder, shepherd; crowd, multitude, populace, rabble; assemblage, assembly, collection, crowd, drove, flock, multitude.

heresy n dissent, error, heterodoxy, impiety, recusancy, unorthodoxy.

heretic n dissenter, dissident, nonconformist, recusant, schismatic, sectarian, sectary, separatist, unbeliever.

heretical *adj* heterodox, impious, schismatic, schismatical, sectarian, unorthodox.

heritage *n* estate, inheritance, legacy, patrimony, portion.

hermit *n* anchoress, anchoret, anchorite, ascetic, eremite, monk, recluse, solitary.

heroic *adj* bold, brave, courageous, daring, dauntless, fearless, gallant, illustrious, intrepid, magnanimous, noble, valiant; desperate, extravagant, extreme, violent.

heroism *n* boldness, bravery, courage, daring, endurance, fearlessness, fortitude, gallantry, intrepidity, prowess, valour.

hesitate *vb* boggle, delay, demur, doubt, pause, scruple, shilly-shally, stickle, vacillate, waver; falter, stammer, stutter.

hesitation *n* halting, misgiving, reluctance; delay, doubt, indecision, suspense, uncertainty, vacillation; faltering, stammering, stuttering.

hidden *adj* blind, clandestine, cloaked, close, concealed, covered, covert, enshrouded, latent, masked, occult, private, secret, suppressed, undiscovered, veiled; abstruse, cabbalistic, cryptic, dark, esoteric, hermetic, inward, mysterious, mystic, mystical, obscure, occult, oracular, recondite.

hide *vb* bury, conceal, cover, secrete, suppress, withhold; cloak, disguise, eclipse, hoard, mask, screen, shelter, suppress, veil.

hideous *adj* abominable, appalling, awful, dreadful, frightful, ghastly, ghoulish, grim, grisly, horrible, horrid, repulsive, revolting, shocking, terrible, terrifying.

high *adj* elevated, high-reaching, lofty, soaring, tall, towering; distinguished, eminent, pre-eminent, prominent, superior; admirable, dignified, elevated, exalted, lofty, great, noble; arrogant, haughty, lofty, lordly, proud, supercilious; boisterous, strong, tumultuous, turbulent, violent; costly, dear, pricey; acute, high-pitched, high-toned, piercing, sharp, shrill. * *adv* powerfully, profoundly; eminently, loftily; luxuriously, richly.

hilarious *adj* boisterous, cheerful, convivial, exhilarated, happy, jolly, jovial, joyful, merry, mirthful, noisy.

hilarity *n* cheerfulness, conviviality, exhilarated, gaiety, glee, jollity, joviality, joyousness, merriment, mirth.

hinder *vb* bar, check, clog, delay, embarrass, encumber, impede, interrupt, obstruct, oppose, prevent, restrain, retard, stop, thwart.

hindrance *n* check, deterrent, encumbrance, hitch, impediment, interruption, obstacle, obstruction, restraint, stop, stoppage.

hint *vb* allude, glance, hint, imply, insinuate, intimate, mention, refer, suggest. * *n* allusion, implication, innuendo, insinuation, intimation, mention, reminder, suggestion, trace.

hire *vb* buy, rent, secure; charter, employ, engage, lease, let. * *n* allowance, bribe, compensation, pay, remuneration, rent, reward, salary, stipend, wages.

hiss *vb* shrill, sibilate, whistle, whir, whiz; condemn, damn, ridicule. * *n* fizzle, hissing, sibilant, sibilation, sizzle.

history *n* account, autobiography, annals, biography, chronicle, genealogy, memoirs, narration, narrative, recital, record, relation, story.

hit *vb* discomfit, hurt, knock, strike; accomplish, achieve, attain, gain, reach, secure, succeed, win; accord, fit, suit; beat, clash, collide, contact, smite. * *n* blow, collision, strike, stroke; chance, fortune, hazard, success, venture.

hitch *vb* catch, impede, stick, stop; attach, connect, fasten, harness, join, tether, tie, unite, yoke. * *n* catch, check, hindrance, impediment, interruption, obstacle; knot, noose.

hoard *vb* accumulate, amass, collect, deposit, garner, hive, husband, save, store, treasure. * *n* accumulation, collection, deposit, fund, mass, reserve, savings, stockpile, store.

hoarse *adj* discordant, grating, gruff, guttural, harsh, husky, low, raucous, rough.

hoax *vb* deceive, dupe, fool, gammon, gull, hoodwink, swindle, trick. * *n* canard, cheat, deception, fraud, humbug, imposition, imposture, joke, trick, swindle.

hoist *vb* elevate, heave, lift, raise, rear. * *n* elevator, lift.

hold *vb* clasp, clinch, clutch, grasp, grip, seize; have, keep, occupy, possess, retain; bind, confine, control, detain, imprison, restrain, restrict; bind, connect, fasten, fix, lock; arrest, check, stay, stop, suspend, withhold; continue, keep up, maintain, manage, prosecute, support, sustain; cherish, embrace, entertain; account, believe, consider, count, deem, entertain, esteem, judge, reckon, regard, think; accommodate, admit, carry, contain, receive, stow; assemble, conduct, convene; continue, endure, last, persist, remain; adhere, cleave, cling, cohere, stick. * *n* anchor, bite, clasp, control, embrace, foothold, grasp, grip, possession, retention; prop, stay, support; claim, footing, vantage point; castle, fort, fortification, fortress, stronghold, tower; locker, storage, storehouse.

hole *n* aperture, opening, perforation; abyss, bore, cave, cavern, cavity, chasm, depression, excavation, eye, hollow, pit, pore, void; burrow, cover, den, lair, retreat; den, hovel, kennel.

holiday *n* anniversary, celebration, feast, festival, festivity, fete, gala, recess, vacation.

holiness *n* blessedness, consecration, devotion, devoutness, godliness, piety, purity, religiousness, righteousness, sacredness, saintliness, sanctity, sinlessness.

hollow *vb* dig, excavate, groove, scoop. * *adj* cavernous, concave, depressed, empty, sunken, vacant, void; deceitful, faithless, false, false-hearted, hollow-hearted, hypocritical, insincere, pharisaical, treacherous, unfeeling; deep, low, muffled, reverberating, rumbling, sepulchral. * *n* basin, bowl, depression; cave, cavern, cavity, concavity, dent, dimple, dint, depression, excavation, hole, pit; canal, channel, cup, dimple, dig, groove, pocket, sag.

holocaust *n* carnage, destruction, devastation, genocide, massacre.

holy *adj* blessed, consecrated, dedicated, devoted, hallowed, sacred, sanctified; devout, godly, pious, pure, religious, righteous, saintlike, saintly, sinless, spiritual.

homage *n* allegiance, devotion, fealty, fidelity, loyalty; court, deference, duty, honour, obeisance, respect, reverence, service; adoration, devotion, worship.

home *adj* domestic, family; close, direct, effective, penetrating, pointed. * *n* abode, dwelling, seat, quarters, residence.

homely *adj* domestic, familiar, house-like; coarse, commonplace, homespun, inelegant, plain, simple, unattractive, uncomely, unpolished, unpretentious.

honest *adj* equitable, fair, faithful, honourable, open, straightforward; conscientious, equitable, fair, faithful, reliable, sound, square, true, trustworthy, trusty, uncorrupted, upright, virtuous; faithful, genuine, thorough, unadulterated; creditable, decent, honourable, proper, reputable, respectable, suitable; chaste, decent, faithful, virtuous; candid, direct, frank, ingenuous, open, sincere, unreserved.

honesty *n* equity, fairness, faithfulness, fidelity, honour, integrity, justice, probity, trustiness, trustworthiness, uprightness; truth, truthfulness, veracity; faithfulness, genuineness, thoroughness; candour, frankness, ingenuousness, openness, sincerity, truth, truthfulness, unreserve.

honorary *adj* formal, nominal, titular, unofficial, unpaid.

honour *vb* dignify, exalt, glorify, grace; respect, revere, reverence, venerate; adore, hallow, worship; celebrate, commemorate, keep, observe. * *n* civility, deference, esteem, homage, respect, reverence, veneration; dignity, distinction, elevation, nobleness; consideration, credit, esteem, fame, glory, reputation; high-mindedness, honesty, integrity, magnanimity, probity, uprightness; chastity, purity, virtue; boast, credit, glory, ornament, pride.

honourable *adj* elevated, famous, great, illustrious, noble; admirable, conscientious, fair, honest, just, magnanimous, true, trustworthy, upright, virtuous, worshipful; creditable, esteemed, estimable, equitable, proper, respected, reputable, right.

hoodwink vb blind, blindfold; cloak, conceal, cover, hide; cheat, circumvent, cozen, deceive, delete, dupe, fool, gull, impose, overreach, trick.

hoot vb boo, cry, jeer, shout, yell; condemn, decry, denounce, execrate, hiss. * n boo, cry, jeer, shout, yell.

hop vb bound, caper, frisk, jump, leap, skip, spring; dance, trip; halt, hobble, limp. * n bound, caper, dance, jump, leap, skip, spring.

hope vb anticipate, await, desire, expect, long; believe, rely, trust. * n confidence, belief, faith, reliance, sanguineness, sanguinity, trust; anticipation, desire, expectancy, expectation.

hopeful adj anticipatory, confident, expectant, fond, optimistic, sanguine; cheerful, encouraging, promising.

hopeless adj abject, crushed, depressed, despondent, despairing, desperate, disconsolate, downcast, forlorn, pessimistic, woebegone; abandoned, helpless, incurable, irremediable, remediless; impossible, impracticable, unachievable, unattainable.

horde n clan, crew, gang, troop; crowd, multitude, pack, throng.

horrid adj alarming, awful, bristling, dire, dreadful, fearful, frightful, harrowing, hideous, horrible, horrific, horrifying, rough, terrible, terrific; abominable, disagreeable, disgusting, odious, offensive, repulsive, revolting, shocking, unpleasant, vile.

horrify vb affright, alarm, frighten, shock, terrify, terrorize.

horror n alarm, awe, consternation, dismay, dread, fear, fright, panic; abhorrence, abomination, antipathy, aversion, detestation, disgust, hatred, loathing, repugnance, revulsion; shuddering.

hospitable adj attentive, bountiful, kind; bountiful, cordial, generous, liberal, open, receptive, sociable, unconstrained, unreserved.

host[1] n entertainer, innkeeper, landlord, master of ceremonies, presenter, propri-

etor, owner, receptionist.

host[2] n array, army, legion; assemblage, assembly, horde, multitude, throng.

hostile adj inimical, unfriendly, warlike; adverse, antagonistic, contrary, opposed, opposite, repugnant.

hot adj burning, fiery, scalding; boiling, flaming, heated, incandescent, parching, roasting, torrid; heated, oppressive, sweltering, warm; angry, choleric, excitable, furious, hasty, impatient, impetuous, irascible, lustful, passionate, touchy, urgent, violent; animated, ardent, eager, fervent, fervid, glowing, passionate, vehement; acrid, biting, highly flavoured, highly seasoned, peppery, piquant, pungent, sharp, stinging.

house vb harbour, lodge, protect, shelter. * n abode, domicile, dwelling, habitation, home, mansion, residence; building, edifice; family, household; kindred, race, lineage, tribe; company, concern, firm, partnership; hotel, inn, public house, tavern.

hover vb flutter; hang; vacillate, waver.

however adv but, however, nevertheless, notwithstanding, still, though, yet.

howl vb bawl, cry, lament, ululate, weep, yell, yowl. * n cry, yell, ululation.

huddle vb cluster, crowd, gather; crouch, curl up, nestle, snuggle. * n confusion, crowd, disorder, disturbance, jumble, tumult.

hue n cast, colour, complexion, dye, shade, tinge, tint, tone.

huff vb blow, breathe, exhale, pant, puff. * n anger, fume, miff, passion, pet, quarrel, rage, temper, tiff.

hug vb clasp, cling, cuddle, embrace, grasp, grip, squeeze; cherish, nurse, retain. * n clasp, cuddle, embrace, grasp, squeeze.

huge adj bulky, colossal, Cyclopean, elephantine, enormous, gigantic, herculean, immense, stupendous, vast,

hum vb buzz, drone, murmur; croon, sing.

humane adj accommodating, benevolent, benign, charitable, clement, compassionate, gentle, good-hearted, kind, kindhearted, lenient, merciful, obliging, tender, sympathetic; cultivating, elevating, humanizing, refining, rational, spiritual.

humanity n benevolence, benignity, charity, fellow-feeling, humaneness, kind-heartedness, kindness, philanthropy, sympathy, tenderness; humankind, mankind, mortality.

humanize vb civilize, cultivate, educate, enlighten, improve, polish, reclaim, refine, soften.

humble vb abase, abash, break, crush, debase, degrade, disgrace, humiliate, lower, mortify, reduce, sink subdue. * adj meek, modest, lowly, simple, submissive, unambitious, unassuming, unobtrusive, unostentatious, unpretending; low, meek, obscure, mean, plain, poor, small, undistinguished, unpretending.

humdrum adj boring, dronish, dreary, dry, dull, monotonous, prosy, stupid, tedious, tiresome, wearisome.

humid adj damp, dank, moist, wet.

humiliate vb abase, abash, debase, degrade, depress, humble, mortify, shame.

humiliation n abasement, affront, condescension, crushing, degradation, disgrace, dishonouring, humbling, indignity, mortification, self-abasement, submissiveness, resignation.

humility n diffidence, humbleness, lowliness, meekness, modesty, self-abasement, submissiveness.

humorous adj comic, comical, droll, facetious, funny, humorous, jocose, jocular, laughable, ludicrous, merry, playful, pleasant, sportive, whimsical, witty.

humour vb favour, gratify, indulge. * n bent, bias, disposition, predilection, prosperity, temper, vein; mood, state, temper; caprice, crochet, fancy, freak, maggot, vagary, whim, whimsey, wrinkle; drollery, facetiousness, fun, jocoseness, jocularity, pleasantry, wit; fluid, moisture, vapour.

hunch vb arch, jostle, nudge, punch, push, shove. * n bunch, hump, knob, protuberance; nudge, punch, push, shove; feeling, idea, intuition, premonition.

hungry adj covetous, craving, desirous, greedy; famished, starved, starving; barren, poor, unfertile, unproductive.

hunt vb chase, drive, follow, hound, pursue, stalk, trap, trail; poach, shoot; search, seek. * n chase, field-sport, hunting, pursuit.

hurl vb cast, dart, fling, pitch, project, send, sling, throw, toss.

hurly-burly n bustle, commotion, confusion, disturbance, hurl, hurly, uproar, tumult, turmoil.

hurricane n cyclone, gale, storm, tempest, tornado, typhoon.

hurried adj cursory, hasty, slight, superficial.

hurry vb drive, precipitate; dispatch, expedite, hasten, quicken, speed; haste, scurry. * n agitation, bustle, confusion, flurry, flutter, perturbation, precipitation; celerity, haste, dispatch, expedition, promptitude, promptness, quickness.

hurt vb damage, disable, disadvantage, harm, impair, injure, harm, mar; bruise, pain, wound; afflict, grieve, offend; ache, pain, smart, throb. * n damage, detriment, disadvantage, harm, injury, mischief; ache, bruise, pain, suffering, wound.

hurtful adj baleful, baneful, deleterious, destructive, detrimental, disadvantageous, harmful, injurious, mischievous, noxious, pernicious, prejudicial, unwholesome.

hush vb quiet, repress, silence, still, suppress; appease, assuage, calm, console, quiet, still. * n quiet, quietness, silence, stillness.

hypocrite n deceiver, dissembler, impostor, pretender.

hypocritical adj deceiving, dissembling, false, insincere, spurious, two-faced.

hysterical adj frantic, frenzied, overwrought, uncontrollable; comical uproarious.

I

icy adj glacial; chilling, cold, frosty; cold-hearted, distant, frigid, indifferent, unemotional.

idea n archetype, essence, exemplar, ideal, model, pattern, plan, model; fantasy, fiction, image, imagination; apprehension, conceit, conception, fancy, illusion, impression, thought; belief, judgement, notion, opinion, sentiment, supposition.

ideal adj intellectual, mental; chimerical, fancied, fanciful, fantastic, illusory, imaginary, unreal, visionary, shadowy; complete, consummate, excellent, perfect; impractical, unattainable, utopian. * n criterion, example, model, standard.

identical adj equivalent, same, selfsame, tantamount.

identity n existence, individuality, personality, sameness.

idiot n blockhead, booby, dunce, fool, ignoramus, imbecile, simpleton.

idiotic adj fatuous, foolish, imbecile, irrational, senseless, sottish, stupid.

idle adj inactive, unemployed, unoccupied, vacant; indolent, inert, lazy slothful, sluggish; abortive, bootless, fruitless, futile, groundless, ineffectual, unavailing, useless, vain; foolish, frivolous, trashy, trifling, trivial, unimportant, unprofitable. * vb dally, dawdle, laze, loiter, potter, waste; drift, shirk, slack.

idol n deity, god, icon, image, pagan, simulacrum, symbol; delusion, falsity, pretender, sham; beloved, darling, favourite, pet.

idolize vb canonize, deify; adore, honour, love, reverence, venerate.

ignoble adj base-born, low, low-born, mean, peasant, plebeian, rustic, vulgar; contemptible, degraded, insignificant, mean, worthless; disgraceful, dishonourable, infamous, low, unworthy.

ignominious adj discreditable, disgraceful, dishonourable, disreputable, infamous, opprobrious, scandalous, shameful; base, contemptible, despicable, infamous.

ignorance n benightedness, darkness, illiteracy, nescience, rusticity; blindness, unawareness.

ignorant adj blind, illiterate, nescient, unaware, unconversant, uneducated, unenlightened, uninformed, uninstructed, unlearned, unread, untaught, untutored, unwitting.

ignore vb disregard, neglect, overlook, reject, skip.

ill adj bad, evil, faulty, harmful, iniquitous, naughty, unfavourable, unfortunate, unjust, wicked; ailing, diseased, disordered, indisposed, sick, unwell, wrong; crabbed, cross, hateful, malicious, malevolent, peevish, surly, unkind, ill-bred; ill-favoured, ugly, unprepossessing. * adv badly, poorly, unfortunately. * n badness, depravity, evil, mischief, misfortune, wickedness; affliction, ailment, calamity, harm, misery, misfortune, pain, trouble.

illegal adj contraband, forbidden, illegitimate, illicit, prohibited, unauthorized, unlawful, unlicensed.

illegible adj indecipherable, obscure, undecipherable, unreadable.

illegitimate adj bastard, misbegotten, natural.

illiberal adj close, close-fisted, covetous, mean, miserly, narrow, niggardly, parsimonious, penurious, selfish, sordid, stingy, ungenerous; bigoted, narrow, narrow-minded, uncharitable, ungentlemanly, vulgar.

illicit adj illegal, illegitimate, unauthorized, unlawful, unlegalized, unlicensed; criminal, guilty, forbidden, improper, wrong.

illiterate adj ignorant, uneducated, uninstructed, unlearned, unlettered, unstructured, untaught, untutored.

illness n ailing, ailment, complaint, disease, disorder, distemper, indisposition, malady, sickness.

illogical adj absurd, fallacious, inconsistent, inconclusive, inconsequent, incorrect, invalid, unreasonable, unsound.

illuminate vb illume, illumine, light; adorn, brighten, decorate, depict, edify, enlighten, inform, inspire, instruct, make wise.

illusion n chimera, deception, delusion, error, fallacy, false appearance, fantasy, hallucination, mockery, phantasm.

illusive, illusory adj barmecide, deceitful, deceptive, delusive, fallacious, imaginary, make-believe, mock, sham, unsatisfying, unreal, unsubstantial, visionary, tantalizing.

illustrate vb clarify, demonstrate, elucidate, enlighten, exemplify, explain;

illustration 367 **immoral**

adorn, depict, draw.

illustration n demonstration, elucidation, enlightenment, exemplification, explanation, interpretation; adornment, decoration, picture.

illustrious adj bright, brilliant, glorious, radiant, splendid; celebrated, conspicuous, distinguished, eminent, famed, famous, noble, noted, remarkable, renowned, signal.

image n idol, statue; copy, effigy, figure, form, imago, likeness, picture, resemblance, representation, shape, similitude, simulacrum, statue, symbol; conception, counterpart, embodiment, idea, reflection.

imaginable adj assumable, cogitable, conceivable, conjecturable, plausible, possible, supposable, thinkable.

imaginary adj chimerical, dreamy, fancied, fanciful, fantastic, fictitious, ideal, illusive, illusory, invented, quixotic, shadowy, unreal, utopian, visionary, wild; assumed, conceivable, hypothetical, supposed.

imagination n chimera, conception, fancy, fantasy, invention, unreality; position; contrivance, device, plot, scheme.

imaginative adj creative, dreamy, fanciful, inventive, poetical, plastic, visionary.

imagine vb conceive, dream, fancy, imagine, picture, pretend; contrive, create, devise, frame, invent, mould, project; assume, suppose, hypothesize; apprehend, assume, believe, deem, guess, opine, suppose, think.

imbecile adj cretinous, drivelling, fatuous, feeble, feeble-minded, foolish, helpless, idiotic, imbecilic, inane, infirm, witless. * n dotard, driveller.

imitate vb copy, counterfeit, duplicate, echo, emulate, follow, forge, mirror, reproduce, simulate; ape, impersonate, mimic, mock, personate; burlesque, parody, travesty.

imitation adj artificial, fake, man-made, mock, reproduction, synthetic. * n aping, copying, imitation, mimicking, parroting; copy, duplicate, likeness, resemblance; mimicry, mocking; burlesque, parody, travesty.

imitative adj copying, emulative, imitating, mimetic, simulative; apeish, aping, mimicking.

immaculate adj clean, pure, spotless, stainless, unblemished, uncontaminated, undefiled, unpolluted, unspotted, unsullied, untainted, untarnished; faultless, guiltless, holy, innocent, pure, saintly, sinless, stainless.

immaterial adj bodiless, ethereal, extramundane, impalpable, incorporeal, mental, metaphysical, spiritual, unbodied, unfleshly, unsubstantial; inconsequential, insignificant, nonessential, unessential, unimportant.

immature adj crude, green, imperfect, raw, rudimental, rudimentary, unfinished, unformed, unprepared, unripe, unripened, youthful; hasty, premature, unseasonable, untimely.

immediate adj close, contiguous, near, next, proximate; intuitive, primary, unmeditated; direct, instant, instantaneous, present, pressing, prompt.

immediately adv closely, proximately; directly, forthwith, instantly, presently, presto, pronto.

immense adj boundless, illimitable, infinite, interminable, measureless, unbounded, unlimited; colossal, elephantine, enormous, gigantic, huge, large, monstrous, mountainous, prodigious, stupendous, titanic, tremendous, vast.

immerse vb baptise, bathe, dip, douse, duck, overwhelm, plunge, sink, souse, submerge; absorb, engage, involve, sink.

imminent adj close, impending, near, overhanging, threatening; alarming, dangerous, perilous.

immobile adj fixed, immovable, inflexible, motionless, quiescent, stable, static, stationary, steadfast; dull, expressionless, impassive, rigid, stiff, stolid.

immoderate adj excessive, exorbitant, extravagant, extreme, inordinate, intemperate, unreasonable.

immoral adj antisocial, corrupt, loose, sinful, unethical, vicious, wicked, wrong; bad, depraved, dissolute, profligate, unprincipled, vicious; abandoned, depraved, dissolute, indecent, licentious, unprincipled.

immortal *adj* deathless, ever-living, imperishable, incorruptible, indestructible, indissoluble, never-dying, undying, unfading; ceaseless, continuing, eternal, endless, everlasting, never-ending, perpetual, sempiternal; abiding, enduring, lasting, permanent. * *n* god, goddess; genius, hero.

immovable *adj* firm, fixed, immobile, stable, stationary; impassive, steadfast, unalterable, unchangeable, unshaken, unyielding.

immunity *n* exemption, exoneration, freedom, release; charter, franchise, liberty, license, prerogative, privilege, right.

imp *n* demon, devil, elf, flibbertigibbet, hobgoblin, scamp, sprite; graft, scion, shoot.

impact *vb* collide, crash, strike. * *n* brunt, impression, impulse, shock, stroke, touch; collision, contact, impinging, striking.

impair *vb* blemish, damage, deface, deteriorate, injure, mar, ruin, spoil, vitiate; decrease, diminish, lessen, reduce; enervate, enfeeble, weaken

impale *vb* hole, pierce, puncture, spear, spike, stab, transfix.

impart *vb* bestow, confer, give, grant; communicate, disclose, discover, divulge, relate, reveal, share, tell.

impartial *adj* candid, disinterested, dispassionate, equal, equitable, even-handed, fair, honourable, just, unbiased, unprejudiced, unwarped.

impassable *adj* blocked, closed, impenetrable, impermeable, impervious, inaccessible, pathless, unattainable, unnavigable, unreachable.

impassioned *adj* animated, ardent, burning, excited, fervent, fervid, fiery, glowing, impetuous, intense, passionate, vehement, warm, zealous.

impassive *adj* calm, passionless; apathetic, callous, indifferent, insensible, insusceptible, unfeeling, unimpressible, unsusceptible.

impatience *n* disquietude, restlessness, uneasiness; eagerness, haste, impetuosity, precipitation, vehemence; heat, irritableness, irritability, violence.

impatient *adj* restless, uneasy, unquiet; eager, hasty, impetuous, precipitate, vehement; abrupt, brusque, choleric, fretful, hot, intolerant, irritable, peevish, sudden, vehement, testy, violent.

impeach *vb* accuse, arraign, charge, indict; asperse, censure, denounce, disparage, discredit, impair, impute, incriminate, lessen.

impeccable *adj* faultless, immaculate, incorrupt, innocent, perfect, pure, sinless, stainless, uncorrupt.

impede *vb* bar, block, check, clog, curb, delay, encumber, hinder, interrupt, obstruct, restrain, retard, stop, thwart.

impediment *n* bar, barrier, block, check, curb, difficulty, encumbrance, hindrance, obstacle, obstruction, stumbling block.

impel *vb* drive, push, send, urge; actuate, animate, compel, constrain, embolden, incite, induce, influence, instigate, move, persuade, stimulate.

impend *vb* approach, menace, near, threaten.

impenetrable *adj* impermeable, impervious, inaccessible; cold, dull, impassive, indifferent, obtuse, senseless, stolid, unsympathetic; dense, proof.

impenitent *adj* hardened, hard-hearted, incorrigible, irreclaimable, obdurate, recusant, relentless, seared, stubborn, uncontrite, unconverted, unrepentant.

imperative *adj* authoritative, commanding, despotic, domineering, imperious, overbearing, peremptory, urgent; binding, obligatory.

imperceptible *adj* inaudible, indistinguishable, invisible, undiscerning; fine, impalpable, inappreciable, gradual, minute.

imperfect *adj* abortive, crude, deficient, garbled, incomplete, poor; defective, faulty, impaired.

imperfection *n* defectiveness, deficiency, faultiness, incompleteness; blemish, defect, fault, flaw, lack, stain, taint; failing, foible, frailty, limitation, vice, weakness.

imperial *adj* kingly, regal, royal, sovereign; august, consummate, exalted, grand, great, kingly, magnificent, majestic, noble, regal, royal, queenly, supreme, sovereign, supreme, consummate.

imperil vb endanger, expose, hazard, jeopardize, risk.

imperious adj arrogant, authoritative, commanding, compelling, despotic, dictatorial, domineering, haughty, imperative, lordly, magisterial, overbearing, tyrannical, urgent, compelling.

impersonate vb act, ape, enact, imitate, mimic, mock, personate; embody, incarnate, personify, typify.

impersonation n incarnation, manifestation, personification; enacting, imitation, impersonating, mimicking, personating, representation.

impertinence n irrelevance, irrelevancy, unfitness, impropriety; assurance, boldness, brass, brazenness, effrontery, face, forwardness, impudence, incivility, insolence, intrusiveness, presumption, rudeness, sauciness, pertness.

impertinent adj inapplicable, inapposite, irrelevant; bold, forward, impudent, insolent, intrusive, meddling, officious, pert, rude, saucy, unmannerly.

imperturbable adj calm, collected, composed, cool, placid, sedate, serene, tranquil, unmoved, undisturbed, unexcitable, unmoved, unruffled.

impetuous adj ardent, boisterous, brash, breakneck, fierce, fiery, furious, hasty, headlong, hot, hot-headed, impulsive, overzealous, passionate, precipitate, vehement, violent.

impetus n energy, force, momentum, propulsion.

implacable adj deadly, inexorable, merciless, pitiless, rancorous, relentless, unappeasable, unforgiving, unpropitiating, unrelenting.

implement vb effect, execute, fulfil. * n appliance, instrument, tool, utensil.

implicate vb entangle, enfold; compromise, concern, entangle, include, involve.

implication n entanglement, involvement, involution; connotation, hint, inference, innuendo, intimation; conclusion, meaning, significance.

implicit adj implied, inferred, understood; absolute, constant, firm, steadfast, unhesitating, unquestioning, unreserved, unshaken.

implore vb adjure, ask, beg, beseech, entreat, petition, pray, solicit, supplicate.

imply vb betoken, connote, denote, import, include, infer, insinuate, involve, mean, presuppose, signify.

impolite adj bearish, boorish, discourteous, disrespectful, ill-bred, insolent, rough, rude, uncivil, uncourteous, ungentle, ungentlemanly, ungracious, unmannerly, unpolished, unrefined.

import vb bring in, introduce, transport; betoken, denote, imply, mean, purport, signify. * n goods, importation, merchandise; bearing, drift, gist, intention, interpretation, matter, meaning, purpose, sense, signification, spirit, tenor; consequence, importance, significance, weight.

importance n concern, consequence, gravity, import, moment, momentousness, significance, weight, weightiness; consequence, pomposity, self-importance.

important adj considerable, grave, material, momentous, notable, pompous, ponderous, serious, significant, urgent, valuable, weighty; esteemed, influential, prominent, substantial; consequential, pompous, self-important.

importune vb ask, beset, dun, ply, press, solicit, urge.

importunity n appeal, beseechment, entreaty, petition, plying, prayer, pressing, suit, supplication, urging; contention, insistence; urgency.

impose vb lay, place, put, set; appoint, charge, dictate, enjoin, force, inflict, obtrude, prescribe, tax; (with **on, upon**) abuse, cheat, circumvent, deceive, delude, dupe, exploit, hoax, trick.

imposing adj august, commanding, dignified, exalted, grand, grandiose, impressive, lofty, magnificent, majestic, noble, stately, striking.

impossible adj hopeless, impracticable, infeasible, unachievable, unattainable; self-contradictory, inconceivable, unthinkable.

impostor n charlatan, cheat, counterfeiter, deceiver, double-dealer, humbug, hypocrite, knave, mountebank, pretender, quack, rogue, trickster.

impotent adj disabled, enfeebled, feeble, frail, helpless, incapable, incapacitated, incompetent, inefficient, infirm, nerveless, powerless, unable, weak; barren, sterile.

impoverish vb beggar, pauperize, ruin; deplete, exhaust, ruin.

impracticability n impossibility, impracticableness, impracticality, infeasibility, unpracticability.

impracticable adj impossible, infeasible; intractable, obstinate, recalcitrant, stubborn, unmanageable, thorny; impassable, insurmountable.

impracticality n impossibility, impracticableness, impractibility, infeasibility, unpracticability; irrationality, unpracticalness, unrealism, unreality, unreasonableness.

impregnable adj immovable, invincible, inviolable, invulnerable, irrefrangible, secure, unconquerable, unassailable.

impregnate vb fecundate, fertilize, fructify; dye, fill, imbrue, imbue, infuse, permeate, pervade, saturate, soak, tincture, tinge.

impress vb engrave, imprint, print, stamp; affect, move, strike; fix, inculcate; draft, enlist, levy, press, requisition. * n impression, imprint, mark, print, seal, stamp; cognizance, device, emblem, motto, symbol.

impression n edition, imprinting, printing, stamping; brand, dent, impress, mark, stamp; effect, influence, sensation; fancy, idea, instinct, notion, opinion, recollection.

impressive adj affecting, effective, emphatic, exciting, forcible, moving, overpowering, powerful, solemn, speaking, splendid, stirring, striking, telling, touching.

imprison vb confine, jail, immure, incarcerate, shut up.

imprisonment n captivity, commitment, confinement, constraint, durance, duress, incarceration, restraint.

improbable adj doubtful, uncertain, unlikely, unplausible.

impromptu adj extempore, improvised, offhand, spontaneous, unpremeditated, unprepared, unrehearsed. * adv extemporaneously, extemporarily, extempore, offhand, ad-lib.

improper adj immodest, inapposite, inappropriate, irregular, unadapted, unapt, unfit, unsuitable, unsuited; indecent, indecorous, indelicate, unbecoming, unseemly; erroneous, inaccurate, incorrect, wrong.

improve vb ameliorate, amend, better, correct, edify, meliorate, mend, rectify, reform, correct, edify; cultivate; gain, mend, progress; enhance, increase, rise.

improvement n ameliorating, amelioration, amendment, bettering, improving, meliorating, melioration; advancement, amelioration, amendment, betterment, melioration, proficiency, progress.

improvident adj careless, heedless, imprudent, incautious, inconsiderate, negligent, prodigal, rash, reckless, shiftless, thoughtless, thriftless, unthrifty, wasteful.

improvisation n ad-libbing, contrivance, extemporaneousness, extemporariness, extemporization, fabrication, invention; (mus) extempore, impromptu.

imprudent adj careless, heedless, ill-advised, ill-judged, improvident, incautious, inconsiderate, indiscreet, rash, unadvised, unwise.

impudence n assurance, audacity, boldness, brashness, brass, bumptiousness, cheek, cheekiness, effrontery, face, flippancy, forwardness, front, gall, impertinence, insolence, jaw, lip, nerve, pertness, presumption, rudeness, sauciness, shamelessness.

impudent adj bold, bold-faced, brazen, brazen-faced, cool, flippant, forward, immodest, impertinent, insolent, insulting, pert, presumptuous, rude, saucy, shameless.

impulse n force, impetus, impelling, momentum, push, thrust; appetite, inclination, instinct, passion, proclivity; incentive, incitement, influence, instigation, motive, instigation.

impulsive *adj* impelling, moving, propulsive; emotional, hasty, heedless, hot, impetuous, mad-cap, passionate, quick, rash, vehement, violent.

impunity *n* exemption, immunity, liberty, licence, permission, security.

impure *adj* defiled, dirty, feculent, filthy, foul, polluted, unclean; bawdy, coarse, immodest, gross, immoral, indelicate, indecent, lewd, licentious, loose, obscene, ribald, smutty, unchaste, unclean; adulterated, corrupt, mixed.

impute *vb* ascribe, attribute, charge, consider, imply, insinuate, refer.

inability *n* impotence, incapacity, incapability, incompetence, incompetency, inefficiency; disability, disqualification.

inaccuracy *n* erroneousness, impropriety, incorrectness, inexactness; blunder, defect, error, fault, mistake.

inaccurate *adj* defective, erroneous, faulty, incorrect, inexact, mistaken, wrong.

inactive *adj* inactive; dormant, inert, inoperative, peaceful, quiet, quiescent; dilatory, drowsy, dull, idle, inanimate, indolent, inert, lazy, lifeless, lumpish, passive, slothful, sleepy, stagnant, supine.

inactivity *n* dilatoriness, idleness, inaction, indolence, inertness, laziness, sloth, sluggishness, supineness, torpidity, torpor.

inadequate *adj* disproportionate, incapable, insufficient, unequal; defective, imperfect, inapt, incompetent, incomplete.

inadmissible *adj* improper, incompetent, unacceptable, unallowable, unqualified, unreasonable.

inadvertently *adv* accidently, carelessly, heedlessly, inconsiderately, negligently, thoughtlessly, unintentionally.

inane *adj* empty, fatuous, vacuous, void; foolish, frivolous, idiotic, puerile, senseless, silly, stupid, trifling, vain, worthless.

inanimate *adj* breathless, dead, extinct; dead, dull, inert, lifeless, soulless, spiritless.

inapplicable *adj* inapposite, inappropriate, inapt, irrelevant, unfit, unsuitable, unsuited.

inattentive *adj* absent-minded, careless, disregarding, heedless, inadvertent, inconsiderate, neglectful, remiss, thoughtless, unmindful, unobservant.

inaugurate *vb* induct, install, introduce, invest; begin, commence, initiate, institute, originate.

inauspicious *adj* bad, discouraging, ill-omened, ill-starred, ominous, unfavourable, unfortunate, unlucky, unpromising, unpropitious, untoward.

incalculable *adj* countless, enormous, immense, incalculable, inestimable, innumerable, sumless, unknown, untold.

incandescent *adj* aglow, candent, candescent, gleaming, glowing, luminous, luminant, radiant.

incapable *adj* feeble, impotent, incompetent, insufficient, unable, unfit, unfitted, unqualified, weak.

incapacitate *vb* cripple, disable; disqualify, make unfit.

incapacity *n* disability, inability, incapability, incompetence; disqualification, unfitness.

incarnation *n* embodiment, exemplification, impersonation, manifestation, personification.

incautious *adj* impolitic, imprudent, indiscreet, uncircumspect, unwary; careless, headlong, heedless, inconsiderate, negligent, rash, reckless, thoughtless.

incense[1] *vb* anger, chafe, enkindle, enrage, exasperate, excite, heat, inflame, irritate, madden, provoke.

incense[2] *n* aroma, fragrance, perfume, scent; admiration, adulation, applause, laudation.

incentive *n* cause, encouragement, goad, impulse, incitement, inducement, instigation, mainspring, motive, provocation, spur, stimulus.

inception *n* beginning, commencement, inauguration, initiation, origin, rise, start.

incessant *adj* ceaseless, constant, continual, continuous, eternal, everlasting, never-ending, perpetual, unceasing, unending, uninterrupted, unremitting.

incident n circumstance, episode, event, fact, happening, occurrence. * adj happening; belonging, pertaining, appertaining, accessory, relating, natural; falling, impinging.

incidental adj accidental, casual, chance, concomitant, contingent, fortuitous, subordinate; adventitious, extraneous, nonessential, occasional.

incipient adj beginning, commencing, inchoate, inceptive, originating, starting.

incision n cut, gash, notch, opening, penetration.

incisive adj cutting; acute, biting, sarcastic, satirical, sharp; acute, clear, distinct, penetrating, sharp-cut, trenchant.

incite vb actuate, animate, arouse, drive, encourage, excite, foment, goad, hound, impel, instigate, prod, prompt, provoke, push, rouse, spur, stimulate, urge.

incivility n discourteousness, discourtesy, disrespect, ill-breeding, ill-manners, impoliteness, impudence, inurbanity, rudeness, uncourtliness, unmannerliness.

inclement adj boisterous, harsh, rigorous, rough, severe, stormy; cruel, harsh, severe, unmerciful.

inclination n inclining, leaning, slant, slope; trending, verging; aptitude, bent, bias, disposition, penchant, predilection, predisposition, proclivity, proneness, propensity, tendency, turn, twist; desire, fondness, liking, taste, partiality, predilection, wish; bow, nod, obeisance.

incline vb lean, slant, slope; bend, nod, verge; tend; bias, dispose, predispose, turn; bend, bow. * n ascent, descent, grade, gradient, rise, slope.

include vb contain, hold; comprehend, comprise, contain, cover, embody, embrace, incorporate, involve, take in.

incoherent adj detached, loose, nonadhesive, noncohesive; disconnected, incongruous, inconsequential, inconsistent, uncoordinated; confused, illogical, irrational, rambling, unintelligible, wild.

income n earnings, emolument, gains, interest, pay, perquisite, proceeds, profits, receipts, rents, return, revenue, salary, wages.

incommode vb annoy, discommode, disquiet, disturb, embarrass, hinder, inconvenience, plague, trouble, upset, vex.

incomparable adj matchless, inimitable, peerless, surpassing, transcendent, unequalled, unparalleled, unrivalled.

incompatible adj contradictory, incongruous, inconsistent, inharmonious, irreconcilable, unadapted, unsuitable.

incompetent adj incapable, unable; inadequate, insufficient; disqualified, incapacitated, unconstitutional, unfit, unfitted.

incomplete adj defective, deficient, imperfect, partial; inexhaustive, unaccompanied, uncompleted, unexecuted, unfinished.

incomprehensible adj inconceivable, inexhaustible, unfathomable, unimaginable; inconceivable, unintelligible, unthinkable.

inconceivable adj incomprehensible, incredible, unbelievable, unimaginable, unthinkable.

inconclusive adj inconsequent, inconsequential, indecisive, unconvincing, illogical, unproved, unproven.

incongruous adj absurd, contradictory, contrary, disagreeing, discrepant, inappropriate, incoherent, incompatible, inconsistent, inharmonious, unfit, unsuitable.

inconsequent adj desultory, disconnected, fragmentary, illogical, inconclusive, inconsistent, irrelevant, loose.

inconsiderable adj immaterial, insignificant, petty, slight, small, trifling, trivial, unimportant.

inconsiderate adj intolerant, uncharitable, unthoughtful; careless, heedless, giddy, hare-brained, hasty, headlong, imprudent, inadvertent, inattentive, indifferent, indiscreet, light-headed, negligent, rash, thoughtless.

inconsistent adj different, discrepant, illogical, incoherent, incompatible, incongruous, inconsequent, inconsonant, irreconcilable, unsuitable; contradictory, contrary; changeable, fickle, inconstant, unstable, unsteady, vacillating, variable.

inconstant adj capricious, changeable, faithless, fickle, fluctuating, mercurial, mutable, unsettled, unsteady, vacillating, variable, varying, volatile, wavering;

mutable, uncertain, unsettled, unstable, variable.

inconvenience vb discommode; annoy, disturb, molest, trouble, vex. * n annoyance, disadvantage, disturbance, molestation, trouble, vexation; awkwardness, cumbersomeness, incommodiousness, unwieldiness; unfitness, unseasonableness, unsuitableness.

inconvenient adj annoying, awkward, cumbersome, cumbrous, disadvantageous, incommodious, inopportune, troublesome, uncomfortable, unfit, unhandy, unmanageable, unseasonable, unsuitable, untimely, unwieldy, vexatious.

incorporate vb affiliate, amalgamate, associate, blend, combine, consolidate, include, merge, mix, unite; embody, incarnate. * adj incorporeal, immaterial, spiritual, supernatural; blended, consolidated, merged, united.

incorrect adj erroneous, false, inaccurate, inexact, untrue, wrong; faulty, improper, mistaken, ungrammatical, unbecoming, unsound.

incorrigible adj abandoned, graceless, hardened, irreclaimable, lost, obdurate, recreant, reprobate, shameless; helpless, hopeless, irremediable, irrecoverable, irreparable, irretrievable, irreversible, remediless.

increase vb accrue, advance, augment, enlarge, extend, grow, intensify, mount, wax; multiply; enhance, greaten, heighten, raise, reinforce; extend, prolong; aggravate, prolong. * n accession, accretion, accumulation, addition, augmentation, crescendo, development, enlargement, expansion, extension, growth, heightening, increment, intensification, multiplication, swelling; gain, produce, product, profit; descendants, issue, offspring, progeny.

incredible adj absurd, inadmissible, nonsensical, unbelievable.

incredulous adj distrustful, doubtful, dubious, sceptical, unbelieving.

increment n addition, augmentation, enlargement, increase.

incriminate vb accuse, blame, charge, criminate, impeach.

inculcate vb enforce, implant, impress, infix, infuse, ingraft, inspire, instil.

incumbent adj binding, devolved, devolving, laid, obligatory; leaning, prone, reclining, resting. * n holder, occupant.

incur vb acquire, bring, contract.

incurable adj cureless, hopeless, irrecoverable, remediless; helpless, incorrigible, irremediable, irreparable, irretrievable, remediless.

incursion n descent, foray, raid, inroad, irruption.

indebted adj beholden, obliged, owing.

indecent adj bold, improper, indecorous, offensive, outrageous, unbecoming, unseemly; coarse, dirty, filthy, gross, immodest, impure, indelicate, lewd, nasty, obscene, pornographic, salacious, shameless, smutty, unchaste.

indecipherable adj illegible, undecipherable, undiscoverable, inexplicable, obscure, unintelligible, unreadable.

indecision n changeableness, fickleness, hesitation, inconstancy, irresolution, unsteadiness, vacillation.

indecisive adj dubious, hesitating, inconclusive, irresolute, undecided, unsettled, vacillating, wavering.

indecorous adj coarse, gross, ill-bred, impolite, improper, indecent, rude, unbecoming, uncivil, unseemly.

indeed adv absolutely, actually, certainly, in fact, in truth, in reality, positively, really, strictly, truly, verily, veritably. * interj really! you don't say! is it possible!

indefatigable adj assiduous, never-tiring, persevering, persistent, sedulous, tireless, unflagging, unremitting, untiring, unwearied.

indefeasible adj immutable, inalienable, irreversible, irrevocable, unalterable.

indefensible adj censurable, defenceless, faulty, unpardonable, untenable; inexcusable, insupportable, unjustifiable, unwarrantable, wrong.

indefinite adj confused, doubtful, equivocal, general, imprecise, indefinable, indecisive, indeterminate, indistinct, inexact, inexplicit, lax, loose, nondescript, obscure, uncertain, undefined, undetermined, unfixed, unsettled, vague.

indelible *adj* fast, fixed, ineffaceable, ingrained, permanent.

indelicate *adj* broad, coarse, gross, indecorous, intrusive, rude, unbecoming, unseemly; broad, coarse, foul, gross, immodest, indecent, lewd, obscene, unchaste, vulgar.

indemnify *vb* compensate, reimburse, remunerate, requite, secure.

indent *vb* bruise, jag, notch, pink, scallop, serrate; bind, indenture.

independence *n* freedom, liberty, self-direction; distinctness, nondependence, separation; competence, ease.

independent *adj* absolute, autonomous, free, self-directing, uncoerced, unrestrained, unrestricted, voluntary; (*person*) self-reliant, unconstrained. unconventional.

indescribable *adj* ineffable, inexpressible, nameless, unutterable.

indestructible *adj* abiding, endless, enduring, everlasting, fadeless, imperishable, incorruptible, undecaying.

indeterminate *adj* indefinite, uncertain, undetermined, unfixed.

index *vb* alphabetize, catalogue, codify, earmark, file, list, mark, tabulate. * *n* catalogue, list, register, tally; indicator, lead, mark, pointer, sign, signal, token; contents, table of contents; forefinger; exponent.

indicate *vb* betoken, denote, designate, evince, exhibit, foreshadow, manifest, mark, point out, prefigure, presage, register, show, signify, specify, tell; hint, imply, intimate, sketch, suggest.

indication *n* hint, index, manifestation, mark, note, sign, suggestion, symptom, token.

indicative *adj* significant, suggestive, symptomatic; (*gram*) affirmative, declarative.

indict *vb* (*law*) accuse, charge, present.

indictment *n* (*law*) indicting, presentment; accusation, arraignment, charge, crimination, impeachment.

indifference *n* apathy, carelessness, coldness, coolness, heedlessness, inattention, insignificance, negligence, unconcern, unconcernedness, uninterestedness; disinterestedness, impartiality, neutrality.

indifferent *adj* apathetic, cold, cool, dead, distant, dull, easy-going, frigid, heedless, inattentive, incurious, insensible, insouciant, listless, lukewarm, nonchalant, perfunctory, regardless, stoical, unconcerned, uninterested, unmindful, unmoved; equal; fair, medium, middling, moderate, ordinary, passable, tolerable; mediocre, so-so; immaterial, unimportant; disinterested, impartial, neutral, unbiased.

indigent *adj* destitute, distressed, insolvent, moneyless, necessitous, needy, penniless, pinched, poor, reduced.

indignant *adj* angry, exasperated, incensed, irate, ireful, provoked, roused, wrathful, wroth.

indignation *n* anger, choler, displeasure, exasperation, fury, ire, rage, resentment, wrath.

indignity *n* abuse, affront, contumely, dishonour, disrespect, ignominy, insult, obloquy, opprobrium, outrage, reproach, slight.

indirect *adj* circuitous, circumlocutory, collateral, devious, oblique, roundabout, sidelong, tortuous; deceitful, dishonest, dishonorable, unfair; mediate, remote, secondary, subordinate.

indiscreet *adj* foolish, hasty, headlong, heedless, imprudent, incautious, inconsiderate, injudicious, rash, reckless, unwise.

indiscretion *n* folly, imprudence, inconsiderateness, rashness; blunder, faux pas, lapse, mistake, misstep.

indiscriminate *adj* confused, heterogeneous, indistinct, mingled, miscellaneous, mixed, promiscuous, undiscriminating, undistinguishable, undistinguishing.

indispensable *adj* essential, expedient, necessary, needed, needful, requisite.

indisposed *adj* ailing, ill, sick, unwell; averse, backward, disinclined, loath, reluctant, unfriendly, unwilling.

indisputable *adj* certain, evident, incontestable, incontrovertible, obvious, undeniable, indubitable, unquestionable.

indissoluble *adj* abiding, enduring, firm, imperishable, incorruptible, indestructible, lasting, stable, unbreakable.

indistinct *adj* ambiguous, doubtful, uncertain; blurred, dim, dull, faint, hazy, misty, nebulous, obscure, shadowy, vague; confused, inarticulate, indefinite, indistinguishable, undefined, undistinguishable.

indistinguishable *adj* imperceptible, indiscernible, unnoticeable, unobservable; chaotic, confused, dim, indistinct, obscure, vague.

individual *adj* characteristic, distinct, identical, idiosyncratic, marked, one, particular, personal, respective, separate, single, singular, special, unique; peculiar, personal, proper, singular; decided, definite, independent, positive, self-guided, unconventional, unique. * *n* being, character, party, person, personage, somebody, someone; type, unit.

individuality *n* definiteness, indentity, personality; characterfulness, originality, self-direction, self-determination, singularity, uniqueness.

indivisible *adj* incommensurable, indissoluble, inseparable, unbreakable, unpartiable.

indoctrinate *vb* brainwash, imbue, initiate, instruct, teach.

indolent *adj* easy, easy-going, inactive, inert, lazy, listless, lumpish, otiose, slothful, sluggish, supine.

indomitable *adj* invincible, unconquerable, unyielding.

indubitable *adj* certain, evident, incontestable, incontrovertible, indisputable, sure, undeniable, unquestionable.

induce *vb* actuate, allure, bring, draw, drive, entice, impel, incite, influence, instigate, move, persuade, prevail, prompt, spur, urge; bring on, cause, effect, motivate, lead, occasion, produce.

inducement *n* allurement, draw, enticement, instigation, persuasion; cause, consideration, impulse, incentive, incitement, influence, motive, reason, spur, stimulus.

induct *vb* inaugurate, initiate, instal, institute, introduce.

indulge *vb* gratify, license, revel, satisfy, wallow, yield to; coddle, cosset, favour, humour, pamper, pet, spoil; allow, cherish, foster, harbour, permit, suffer.

indulgent *adj* clement, easy, favouring, forbearing, gentle, humouring, kind, lenient, mild, pampering, tender, tolerant.

industrious *adj* assiduous, diligent, hard-working, laborious, notable, operose, sedulous; brisk, busy, persevering, persistent.

industry *n* activity, application, assiduousness, assiduity, diligence; perseverance, persistence, sedulousness, vigour; effort, labour, toil.

ineffectual *adj* abortive, bootless, fruitless, futile, inadequate, inefficacious, ineffective, inoperative, useless, unavailing, vain; feeble, inefficient, powerless, impotent, weak.

inefficient *adj* feeble, incapable, ineffectual, ineffective, inefficacious, weak.

ineligible *adj* disqualified, unqualified; inexpedient, objectionable, unadvisable, undesirable.

inept *adj* awkward, improper, inapposite, inappropriate, unapt, unfit, unsuitable; null, useless, void, worthless; foolish, nonsensical, pointless, senseless, silly, stupid.

inequality *n* disproportion, inequitableness, injustice, unfairness; difference, disparity, disproportion, dissimilarity, diversity, imparity, irregularity, roughness, unevenness; inadequacy, incompetency, insufficiency.

inequitable *adj* unfair, unjust.

inert *adj* comatose, dead, inactive, lifeless, motionless, quiescent, passive; apathetic, dronish, dull, idle, indolent, lazy, lethargic, lumpish, phlegmatic, slothful, sluggish, supine, torpid.

inertia *n* apathy, inertness, lethargy, passiveness, passivity, slothfulness, sluggishness.

inevitable *adj* certain, necessary, unavoidable, undoubted.

inexact *adj* imprecise, inaccurate, incorrect; careless, crude, loose.

inexcusable *adj* indefensible, irremissible, unallowable, unjustifiable, unpardonable.

inexhaustible *adj* boundless, exhaustless, indefatigable, unfailing, unlimited.

inexorable *adj* cruel, firm, hard, immovable, implacable, inflexible, merciless, pitiless, relentless, severe, steadfast, unbending, uncompassionate, unmerciful, unrelenting, unyielding.

inexperienced *adj* callow, green, raw, strange, unacquainted, unconversant, undisciplined, uninitiated, unpractised, unschooled, unskilled, untrained, untried, unversed, young.

inexpert *adj* awkward, bungling, clumsy, inapt, maladroit, unhandy, unskilful, unskilled.

inexplicable *adj* enigmatic, enigmatical, incomprehensible, inscrutable, mysterious, strange, unaccountable, unintelligible.

inexpressible *adj* indescribable, ineffable, unspeakable, unutterable; boundless, infinite, surpassing.

inexpressive *adj* blank, characterless, dull, unexpressive.

inextricable *adj* entangled, intricate, perplexed, unsolvable.

infallible *adj* certain, indubitable, oracular, sure, unerring, unfailing.

infamous *adj* abominable, atrocious, base, damnable, dark, detestable, discreditable, disgraceful, dishonorable, disreputable, heinous, ignominious, nefarious, odious, opprobrious, outrageous, scandalous, shameful, shameless, vile, villainous, wicked.

infancy *n* beginning, commencement; babyhood, childhood, minority, nonage, pupillage.

infant *n* babe, baby, bairn, bantling, brat, chit, minor, nursling, papoose, suckling, tot.

infantile *adj* childish, infantine, newborn, tender, young; babyish, childish, weak; babylike, childlike.

infatuate *vb* befool, besot, captivate, delude, prepossess, stultify.

infect *vb* affect, contaminate, corrupt, defile, poison, pollute, taint, vitiate.

infection *n* affection, bane, contagion, contamination, corruption, defilement, pest, poison, pollution, taint, virus, vitiation.

infectious *adj* catching, communicable, contagious, contaminating, corrupting, defiling, demoralizing, pestiferous, pestilential, poisoning, polluting, sympathetic, vitiating.

infelicitous *adj* miserable, unfortunate, unhappy, wretched; inauspicious, unfavourable, unpropitious; ill-chosen, inappropriate, unfitting, unhappy.

infer *vb* collect, conclude, deduce, derive, draw, gather, glean, guess, presume, reason.

inference *n* conclusion, consequence, corollary, deduction, generalization, guess, illation, implication, induction, presumption.

inferior *adj* lower, nether; junior, minor, secondary, subordinate; bad, base, deficient, humble, imperfect, indifferent, mean, mediocre, paltry, poor, secondrate, shabby.

inferiority *n* juniority, subjection, subordination, mediocrity; deficiency, imperfection, inadequacy, shortcoming.

infernal *adj* abominable, accursed, atrocious, damnable, dark, demoniacal, devilish, diabolical, fiendish, fiendlike, hellish, malicious, nefarious, satanic, Stygian.

infertility *n* barrenness, infecundity, sterility, unfruitfulness, unproductivity.

infidel *n* agnostic, atheist, disbeliever, heathen, heretic, sceptic, unbeliever.

infidelity *n* adultery, disloyality, faithlessness, treachery, unfaithfulness; disbelief, scepticism, unbelief.

infiltrate *vb* absorb, pervade, soak.

infinite *adj* boundless, endless, illimitable, immeasurable, inexhaustible, interminable, limitless, measureless, perfect, unbounded, unlimited; enormous, immense, stupendous, vast; absolue, eternal, self-determined, self-existent, unconditioned.

infinitesimal *adj* infinitely small.

infinity *n* absoluteness, boundlessness, endlessness, eternity, immensity, infiniteness, infinitude, interminateness, self-determination, self-existence, vastness.

infirm *adj* ailing, debilitated, enfeebled, feeble, frail, weak, weakened; faltering, irresolute, vacillating, wavering; insecure, precarious, unsound, unstable.

inflame vb animate, arouse, excite, enkindle, fire, heat, incite, inspirit, intensify, rouse, stimulate; aggravate, anger, chafe, embitter, enrage, exasperate, incense, infuriate, irritate, madden, nettle, provoke.

inflammable adj combustible, ignitible; excitable.

inflammatory adj fiery, inflaming; dissentious, incendiary, seditious.

inflate vb bloat, blow up, distend, expand, swell, sufflate; elate, puff up; enlarge, increase.

inflation n enlargement, increase, overenlargement, overissue; bloatedness, distension, expansion, sufflation; bombast, conceit, conceitedness, self-conceit, self-complacency, self-importance, self-sufficiency, vaingloriousness, vainglory.

inflection n bend, bending, crook, curvature, curvity, flexure; (gram) accidence, conjugation, declension, variation; (mus) modulation.

inflexible adj rigid, rigorous, stiff, unbending; cantankerous, cross-grained, dogged, headstrong, heady, inexorable, intractable, obdurate, obstinant, pertinacious, refractory, stubborn, unyielding, wilful; firm, immovable, persevering, resolute, steadfast, unbending.

inflict vb bring, impose, lay on.

infliction n imposition, inflicting; judgment, punishment.

influence vb affect, bias, control, direct, lead, modify, prejudice, prepossess, sway; actuate, arouse, impel, incite, induce, instigate, move, persuade, prevail upon, rouse. * n ascendancy, authority, control, mastery, potency, predominance, pull, rule, sway; credit, reputation, weight; inflow, inflowing, influx; magnetism, power, spell.

influential adj controlling, effective, effectual, potent, powerful, strong; authoritative, momentous, substantial, weighty.

inform vb animate, inspire, quicken; acquaint, advise, apprise, enlighten, instruct, notify, teach, tell, tip, warn.

informal adj unceremonious, unconventional, unofficial; easy, familiar, natural, simple; irregular, nonconformist, unusual.

informality n uncremoniousness; unconventionality; ease, familiarity, naturalness, simplicity; noncomformity, irregularity, unusualness.

informant n advertiser, adviser, informer, intelligencer, newsmonger, notifier; relator; accuser, complainant, informer.

information n advice, intelligence, knowledge, notice; advertisement, advice, enlightenment, instruction, message, tip, word, warning; accusation, complaint, denunciation.

informer n accuser, complainant, informant.

infrequent adj rare, uncommon, unfrequent, unusual; occasional, rare, scant, scarce, sporadic.

infringe vb break, contravene, disobey, intrude, invade, transgress, violate.

infringement n breach, breaking, disobedience, infraction, nonobservance, transgression, violation.

infuriated adj angry, enraged, furious, incensed, maddened, raging, wild.

infuse vb breathe into, implant, inculcate, ingraft, insinuate, inspire, instil, introduce; macerate, steep.

ingenious adj able, adroit, artful, bright, clever, fertile, gifted, inventive, ready, sagacious, shrewd, witty.

ingenuity n ability, acuteness, aptitude, aptness, capacity, capableness, cleverness, faculty, genius, gift, ingeniousness, inventiveness, knack, readiness, skill, turn.

ingenuous adj artless, candid, childlike, downright, frank, generous, guileless, honest, innocent, naive, open, openhearted, plain, simple-minded, sincere, single-minded, straightforward, transparent, truthful, unreserved.

ingratitude n thanklessness, ungratefulness, unthankfulness.

ingredient n component, constituent, element.

inhabit vb abide, dwell, live, occupy, people, reside, sojourn.

inhabitant n citizen, denizen, dweller, inhabiter, resident.

inhale vb breathe in, draw in, inbreathe, inspire.

inherent adj essential, immanent, inborn, inbred, indwelling, ingrained, innate, inseparable, intrinsic, native, natural, proper; adhering, sticking.

inherit vb get, receive.

inheritance n heritage, legacy, patrimony; inheriting.

inhibit vb bar, check, debar, hinder, obstruct, prevent, repress, restrain, stop; forbid, interdict, prohibit.

inhibition n check, hindrance, impediment, obstacle, obstruction, restraint; disallowance, embargo, interdict, interdiction, prevention, prohibition.

inhospitable adj cool, forbidding, unfriendly, unkind; bigoted, illiberal, intolerant, narrow, prejudiced, ungenerous, unreceptive; barren, wild.

inhuman adj barbarous, brutal, cruel, fell, ferocious, merciless, pitiless, remorseless, ruthless, savage, unfeeling; nonhuman.

inhumanity n barbarity, brutality, cruelty, ferocity, savageness; hard-heartedness, unkindness.

inimical adj antagonistic, hostile, unfriendly; adverse, contrary, harmful, hurtful, noxious, opposed, pernicious, repugnant, unfavourable.

inimitable adj incomparable, matchless, peerless, unequalled, unexampled, unmatched, unparagoned, unparalleled, unrivalled.

iniquitous adj atrocious, criminal, flagitious, heinous, inequitable, nefarious, sinful, wicked, wrong, unfair, unjust, unrighteous.

initial adj first; beginning, commencing, incipient, initiatory, introductory, opening, original; elementary, inchoate, rudimentary.

initiate vb begin, commence, enter upon, inaugurate, introduce, open; ground, indoctrinate, instruct, prime, teach.

initiation n veginning, commencement, inauguration, opening; admission, entrance, introduction; indoctrinate, instruction.

initiative n beginning; energy, enterprise.

inject vb force in, interject, insert, introduce, intromit.

injunction n admonition, bidding, command, mandate, order, precept.

injure vb damage, disfigure, harm, hurt, impair, mar, spoil, sully, wound; abuse, aggrieve, wrong; affront, dishonour, insult.

injurious adj baneful, damaging, deadly, deleterious, destructive, detrimental, disadvantageous, evil, fatal, hurtful, mischievous, noxious, pernicious, prejudicial, ruinous; inequitable, iniquitous, unjust, wrongful; contumelious, detractory, libellous, slanderous.

injury n evil, ill, injustice, wrong; damage, detriment, harm, hurt, impairment, loss, mischief, prejudice.

injustice n inequity, unfairness; grievance, iniquity, injury, wrong.

inkling n hint, intimation, suggestion, whisper.

innate adj congenital, constitutional, inborn, inbred, indigenous, inherent, inherited, instinctive, native, natural, organic.

inner adj interior, internal.

innermost adj deepest, inmost.

innocence n blamelessness, chastity, guilelessness, guiltlessness, purity, simplicity, sinlessness, stainlessness; harmlessness, innocuousness, innoxiousness, inoffensiveness.

innocent adj blameless, clean, clear, faultless, guiltless, immaculate, pure, sinless, spotless, unfallen, upright; harmless, innocuous, innoxious, inoffensive; lawful, legitimate, permitted; artless, guileless, ignorant, ingenuous, simple. * n babe, child, ingénue, naif, naive, unsophisticate.

innocuous adj harmless, innocent, inoffensive, safe.

innovation n change, introduction; departure, novelty.

innuendo n allusion, hint, insinuation, intimation, suggestion.

innumerable adj countless, numberless.

inoffensive adj harmless, innocent, innocuous, innoxious, unobjectionable, unoffending.

inoperative adj inactive, ineffectual, inefficacious, not in force.

inopportune adj ill-timed, inexpedient, infelicitous, mistimed, unfortunate, unhappy, unseasonable, untimely.

inordinate adj excessive, extravagant, immoderate, intemperate, irregular.

inquest n inquiry, inquisition, investigation, quest, search.

inquire vb ask, catechize, interpellate, interrogate, investigate, query, question, quiz.

inquiry n examination, exploration, investigation, research, scrutiny, study; interrogation, query, question, quiz.

inquisition n examination, inquest, inquiry, investigation, search.

inquisitive adj curious, inquiring, scrutinizing; curious, meddlesome, peeping, peering, prying.

inroad n encroachment, foray, incursion, invasion, irruption, raid.

insane adj abnormal, crazed, crazy, delirious, demented, deranged, distracted, lunatic, mad, maniacal, unhealthy, unsound.

insanity n craziness, delirium, dementia, derangement, lunacy, madness, mania, mental aberration, mental alienation.

insatiable adj greedy, rapacious, voracious; insatiate, unappeasable.

inscribe vb emblaze, endorse, engrave, enroll, impress, imprint, letter, mark, write; address, dedicate.

inscrutable adj hidden, impenetrable, incomprehensible, inexplicable, mysterious, undiscoverable, unfathomable, unsearchable.

insecure adj risky, uncertain, unconfident, unsure; exposed, ill-protected, unprotected, unsafe; dangerous, hazardous, perilous; infirm, shaking, shaky, tottering, unstable, weak, wobbly.

insecurity n riskiness, uncertainty; danger, hazardousness, peril; instability, shakiness, weakness, wobbliness.

insensible adj imperceivable, imperceptible, undiscoverable; blunted, brutish, deaf, dull, insensate, numb, obtuse,

senseless, sluggish, stolid, stupid, torpid, unconscious; apathetic, callous, phlegmatic, impassive, indifferent, insensitive, insentient, unfeeling, unimpressible, unsusceptible.

inseparable adj close, friendly, intimate, together; indissoluble, indivisible, inseverable.

insert vb infix, inject, intercalate, interpolate, introduce, inweave, parenthesize, place, put, set.

inside adj inner, interior, internal, intimate. * prep in, in the interior of, within. * n inner part, interior; nature.

insidious adj creeping, deceptive, gradual, secretive; arch, artful, crafty, crooked, cunning, deceitful, designing, diplomatic, foxy, guileful, intriguing, machiavellian, sly, sneaky, subtle, treacherous, trickish, tricky, wily.

insight n discernment, intuition, penetration, perception, perspicuity, understanding.

insignificant adj contemptible, empty, immaterial, inconsequential, inconsiderable, inferior, meaningless, paltry, petty, small, sorry, trifling, trivial, unessential, unimportant.

insincere adj deceitful, dishonest, disingenuous, dissembling, dissimulating, double-faced, double-tongued, duplicitous, empty, faithless, false, hollow, hypocritical, pharisaical, truthless, uncandid, untrue.

insinuate vb hint, inculcate, infuse, ingratiate, instil, intimate, introduce, suggest.

insipid adj dead, dull, flat, heavy, inanimate, jejune, lifeless, monotonous, pointless, prosaic, prosy, spiritless, stupid, tame, unentertaining, uninteresting; flat, gustless, mawkish, savourless, stale, tasteless, vapid.

insist vb demand, maintain, urge.

insistence n importunity, solicitousness, urging, urgency.

insolence n impertinence, impudence, malapertness, pertness, rudeness, sauciness; contempt, contumacy, contumely, disrespect, frowardness, insubordination.

insolent adj abusive, contemptuous, contumelious, disrespectful, domineering, insulting, offensive, overbearing, rude, supercilious; cheeky, impertinent, impudent, malapert, pert, saucy; contumacious, disobedient, froward, insubordinate.

insoluble adj indissoluble, indissolvable, irreducible; inexplicable, insolvable.

insolvable adj inexplicable.

insolvent adj bankrupt, broken, failed, ruined.

inspect vb examine, investigate, look into, pry into, scrutinize; oversee, superintend, supervise.

inspector n censor, critic, examiner, visitor; boss, overseer, superintendent, supervisor.

inspire vb breathe, inhale; infuse, instil; animate, cheer, enliven, inspirit; elevate, exalt, stimulate; animate, enliven, fill, imbue, impart, inform, quicken.

instability n changeableness, fickleness, inconstancy, insecurity, mutability.

install vb inaugurate, induct, introduce; establish, place, set up.

installation n inauguration, induction, instalment, investiture.

instalment n earnest, payment, portion.

instance vb adduce, cite, mention, specify. * n case, example, exemplification, illustration, occasion; impulse, incitement, instigation, motive, prompting, request, solicitation.

instant adj direct, immediate, instantaneous, prompt, quick; current, present; earnest, fast, imperative, importunate, pressing, urgent; ready cooked. * n flash, jiffy, moment, second, trice, twinkling; hour, moment, time.

instantaneous adj abrupt, immediate, instant, quick, sudden.

instead adv in lieu, in place, rather.

instigate vb actuate, agitate, encourage, impel, incite, influence, initiate, move, persuade, prevail upon, prompt, provoke, rouse, set on, spur on, stimulate, stir up, tempt, urge.

instigation n encouragement, incitement, influence, instance, prompting, solicitation, urgency.

instil vb enforce, implant, impress, inculcate, ingraft; impart, infuse, insinuate.

instinct n natural impulse.

instinctive adj automatic, inherent, innate, intuitive, involuntary, natural, spontaneous; impulsive, unreflecting.

institute[1] n academy, college, foundation, guild, institution, school; custom, doctrine, dogma, law, maxim, precedent, principle, rule, tenet.

institute[2] vb begin, commence, constitute, establish, found, initial, install, introduce, organize, originate, start.

institution n enactment, establishment, foundation, institute, society; investiture; custom, law, practice.

instruct vb discipline, educate, enlighten, exercise, guide, indoctrinate, inform, initiate, school, teach, train; apprise, bid, command, direct, enjoin, order, prescribe to.

instruction n breeding, discipline, education, indoctrination, information, nurture, schooling, teaching, training, tuition; advice, counsel, precept; command, direction, mandate, order.

instructor n educator, master, preceptor, schoolteacher, teacher, tutor.

instrument n appliance, apparatus, contrivance, device, implement, musical instrument, tool, utensil; agent, means, medium; charter, deed, document, indenture, writing.

instrumental adj ancillary, assisting, auxiliary, conducive, contributory, helpful, helping, ministerial, ministrant, serviceable, subservient, subsidiary.

insubordinate adj disobedient, disorderly, mutinous, refractory, riotous, seditious, turbulent, ungovernable, unruly.

insufferable adj intolerable, unbearable, unendurable, insupportable; abominable, detestable, disgusting, execrable, outrageous.

insufficient adj deficient, inadequate, incommensurate, incompetent, scanty; incapable, incompetent, unfitted, unqualified, unsuited.

insular adj contracted, illiberal, limited, narrow, petty, prejudiced, restricted; isolated, remote.

insulate vb detach, disconnect, disengage, disunite, isolate, separate.

insult *vb* abuse, affront, injure, offend, outrage, slander, slight. * *n* abuse, affront, cheek, contumely, indignity, insolence, offence, outrage, sauce, slight.

insuperable *adj* impassable, insurmountable.

insupportable *adj* insufferable, intolerable, unbearable, unendurable.

insuppressible *adj* irrepressible, uncontrollable.

insure *vb* assure, guarantee, indemnify, secure, underwrite.

insurgent *adj* disobedient, insubordinate, mutinous, rebellious, revolting, revolutionary, seditious. * *n* mutineer, rebel, revolter, revolutionary.

insurmountable *adj* impassable, insuperable.

insurrection *n* insurgence, mutiny, rebellion, revolt, revolution, rising, sedition, uprising.

intact *adj* scathless, unharmed, unhurt, unimpaired, uninjured, untouched; complete, entire, integral, sound, unbroken, undiminished, whole.

intangible *adj* dim, impalpable, imperceptible, indefinite, insubstantial, intactile, shadowy, vague; aerial, phantom, spiritous.

integral *adj* complete, component, entire, integrant, total, whole.

integrity *n* goodness, honesty, principle, probity, purity, rectitude, soundness, uprightness, virtue; completeness, entireness, entirety, wholeness.

intellect *n* brains, cognitive faculty, intelligence, mind, rational faculty, reason, reasoning, faculty, sense, thinking principle, understanding.

intellectual *adj* cerebral, intelligent, mental, scholarly, thoughtful. * *n* academic, highbrow, pundit, savant, scholar.

intelligence *n* acumen, apprehension, brightness, discernment, imagination, insight, penetration, quickness, sagacity, shrewdness, understanding, wits; information, knowledge; advice, instruction, news, notice, notification, tidings; brains, intellect, mentality, sense, spirit.

intelligent *adj* acute, alert, apt, astute, brainy, bright, clear-headed, clear-sighted, clever, discerning, keen-eyed, keen-sighted, knowing, long-headed, quick, quick-sighted, sagacious, sensible, sharp-sighted, sharp-witted, shrewd, understanding.

intelligible *adj* clear, comprehensible, distinct, evident, lucid, manifest, obvious, patent, perspicuous, plain, transparent, understandable.

intemperate *adj* drunken; excessive, extravagant, extreme, immoderate, inordinate, unbridled, uncontrolled, unrestrained; luxious, self-indulgent.

intend *vb* aim at, contemplate, design, determine, drive at, mean, meditate, propose, purpose, think of.

intense *adj* ardent, earnest, fervid, passionate, vehement; close, intent, severe, strained, stretched, strict; energetic, forcible, keen, potent, powerful, sharp, strong, vigorous, violent; acute, deep, extreme, exquisite, grievous, poignant.

intensify *vb* aggravate, concentrate, deepen, enhance, heighten, quicken, strengthen, whet.

intensive *adj* emphatic, intensifying.

intent *adj* absorbed, attentive, close, eager, earnest, engrossed, occupied, preoccupied, zealous; bent, determined, decided, resolved, set. * *n* aim, design, drift, end, import, intention, mark, meaning, object, plan, purport, purpose, purview, scope, view.

intention *n* aim, design, drift, end, import, intent, mark, meaning, object, plan, purport, purpose, purview, scope, view.

intentional *adj* contemplated, deliberate, designed, intended, preconcerted, predetermined, premeditated, purposed, studied, voluntary, wilful.

intercede *vb* arbitrate, interpose, mediate; entreat, plead, supplicate.

intercept *vb* cut off, interrupt, obstruct, seize.

intercession *n* interposition, intervention, mediation; entreaty, pleading, prayer, supplication.

interchange *vb* alternate, change, exchange, vary. * *n* alternation.

intercourse *n* commerce, communication, communion, connection, converse, correspondence, dealings, fellowship, truck; acquaintance, intimacy.

interdict vb debar, forbid, inhibit, prohibit, prescribe, proscribe, restrain from. * n ban, decree, interdiction, prohibition.

interest vb affect, concern, touch; absorb, attract, engage, enlist, excite, grip, hold, occupy. * n advantage, benefit, good, profit, weal; attention, concern, regard, sympathy; part, participation, portion, share, stake; discount, premium, profit.

interested adj attentive, concerned, involved, occupied; biassed, patial, prejudiced; selfish, self-seeking.

interesting adj attractive, engaging, entertaining, pleasing.

interfere vb intermeddle, interpose, meddle; clash, collide, conflict.

interim n intermediate time, interval, meantime.

interior adj inmost, inner, internal, inward; inland, remote; domestic, home. * n inner part, inland, inside.

interject vb comment, inject, insert, interpose.

intermediary n go-between, mediator.

intermediate adj interjacent, interposed, intervening, mean, median, middle, transitional.

interminable adj boundless, endless, illimitable, immeasurable, infinite, limitless, unbounded, unlimited; long-drawn-out, tedious, wearisome.

intermingle vb blend, commingle, commix, intermix, mingle, mix.

intermission n cessation, interruption, interval, lull, pause, remission, respite, rest, stop, stoppage, suspension.

intermittent adj broken, capricious, discontinuous, fitful, flickering, intermitting, periodic, recurrent, remittent, spasmodic.

internal adj inner, inside, interior, inward; incorporeal, mental, spiritual; deeper, emblematic, hidden, higher, metaphorical, secret, spiritual, symbolical, under; genuine, inherent, intrinsic, real, true; domestic, home, inland, inside, interior.

international adj cosmopolitan, universal.

interpolate vb add, foist, insert, interpose; (math) intercalate, introduce.

interpret vb decipher, decode, define, elucidate, explain, expound, solve, unfold, unravel; construe, render, translate.

interpretation n meaning, sense, signification; elucidation, explanation, explication, exposition; construction, rendering, rendition, translation, version.

interpreter n expositor, expounder, translator.

interrogate vb ask, catechize, examine, inquire of, interpellate, question.

interrogation n catechizing, examination, examining, interpellation, interrogating, questioning; inquiry, interrogatory, query, question.

interrupt vb break, check, disturb, hinder, intercept, interfere with, obstruct, pretermit, stop; break, cut, disconnect, disjoin, dissever, dissolve, disunite, divide, separate, sever, sunder; break off, cease, discontinue, intermit, leave off, suspend.

interruption n hindrance, impediment, obstacle, obstruction, stop, stoppage; cessation, discontinuance, intermission, pause, suspension; break, breaking, disconnecting, disconnection, disjunction, dissolution, disunion, disuniting, division, separation, severing, sundering.

intersect vb cross, cut, decussate, divide, interrupt.

intersperse vb intermingle, scatter, sprinkle; diversify, interlard, mix.

interval n interim, interlude, interregnum, pause, period, recess, season, space, spell, term; interstice, skip, space.

intervene vb come between, interfere, mediate; befall, happen, occur.

intervention n interference, interposition; agency, mediation.

interview n conference, consultation, parley; meeting.

intimacy n close acquaintance, familiarity, fellowship, friendship; closeness, nearness.

intimate[1] adj close, near; familiar, friendly; bosom, chummy, close, dear, homelike, special; confidential, personal, private, secret; detailed, exhaustive, firsthand, immediate, penetrating, profound; cosy, friendly, warm. * n chum, confidant, companion, crony, friend.

intimate[2] vb allude to, express, hint, impart, indicate, insinuate, signify, suggest, tell.

intimation *n* allusion, hing, innuendo, insinuation, suggestion.

intimidate *vb* abash, affright, alarm, appal, browbeat, bully, cow, daunt, dishearten, dismay, frighten, overawe, scare, subdue, terrify, terrorize.

intolerable *adj* insufferable, insupportable, unbearable, unendurable.

intolerant *adj* bigoted, narrow, proscriptive; dictatorial, impatient, imperious, overbearing, supercilious.

intonation *n* cadence, modulation, tone; musical recitation.

intoxication *n* drunkenness, ebriety, inebriation, inebriety; excitement, exhilaration, infatuation.

intractable *adj* cantankerous, contrary, contumacious, cross-grained, dogged, froward, headstrong, indocile, inflexible, mulish, obdurate, obstinate, perverse, pig-headed, refractory, restive, stubborn, tough, uncontrollable, ungovernable, unmanageable, unruly, unyielding, wilful.

intrepid *adj* bold, brave, chivalrous, courageous, daring, dauntless, doughty, fearless, gallant, heroic, unappalled, unawed, undaunted, undismayed, unterrified, valiant, valorous.

intricacy *n* complexity, complication, difficulty, entanglement, intricateness, involution, obscurity, perplexity.

intricate *adj* complicated, difficult, entangled, involved, mazy, obscure, perplexed.

intrigue *vb* connive, conspire, machinate, plot, scheme; beguile, bewitch, captivate, charm, fascinate. * *n* artifice, cabal, conspiracy, deception, finesse, Machiavelianism, machination, manoeuvre, plot, ruse, scheme, stratagem, wile; amour, liaison, love affair.

intriguing *adj* arch, artful, crafty, crooked, cunning, deceitful, designing, diplomatic, foxy, Machiavelian, insidious, politic, sly, sneaky, subtle, tortuous, trickish, tricky, wily.

intrinsic *adj* essential, genuine, real, sterling, true; inborn, inbred, ingrained, in-

herent, internal, inward, native, natural.

introduce *vb* bring in, conduct, import, induct, inject, insert, lead in, usher in; present; begin, broach, commence, inaugurate, initiate, institute, start.

introduction *n* exordium, preface, prelude, proem; introducing, ushering in; presentation.

introductory *adj* precursory, prefatory, preliminary, proemial.

introspection *n* introversion, self-contemplation.

intrude *vb* encroach, impose, infringe, interfere, interlope, obtrude, trespass.

intrusion *n* encroachment, infringement, intruding, obtrusion.

intrusive *adj* obtrusive, trespassing.

intuition *n* apprehension, cognition, insight, instinct; clairvoyance, divination, presentiment.

intuitive *adj* instinctive, intuitional, natural; clear, distinct, full, immediate.

inundate *vb* deluge, drown, flood, glut, overflow, overwhelm, submerge.

inure *vb* accustom, discipline, familiarize, habituate, harden, toughen, train, use.

inutile *adj* bootless, ineffectual, inoperative, unavailing, unprofitable, useless.

invade *vb* encroach upon, infringe, violate; attack, enter in, march into.

invalid¹ *adj* baseless, fallacious, false, inoperative, nugatory, unfounded, unsound, untrue, worthless; (*law*) null, void.

invalid² *adj* ailing, bedridden, feeble, frail, ill, infirm, sick, sickly, valetudinary, weak, weakly. * *n* convalescent, patient, valetudinarian.

invalidate *vb* abrogate, annul, cancel, nullify, overthrow, quash, repeal, reverse, undo, unmake, vitiate.

invalidity *n* baselessness, fallaciousness, fallacy, falsity, unsoundness.

invaluable *adj* inestimable, priceless.

invariable *adj* changeless, constant, unchanging, uniform, unvarying; changeless, immutable, unalterable, unchangeable.

invasion *n* encroachment, incursion, infringement, inroad; aggression, assault, attack, foray, raid.

invective *n* abuse, censure, contumely, denunciation, diatribe, railing, reproach, sarcasm, satire, vituperation.

inveigle *vb* contrive, devise; concoct, conceive, create, design, excogitate, frame, imagine, originate; coin, fabricate, forge, spin.

invent *vb* concoct, contrive, design, devise, discover, fabricate, find out, frame, originate.

invention *n* creation, discovery, ingenuity, inventing, origination; contrivance, design, device; coinage, fabrication, fiction, forgery.

inventive *adj* creative, fertile, ingenious.

inventor *n* author, contriver, creator, originator.

inversion *n* inverting, reversing, transposal, transposition.

invert *vb* capsize, overturn; reverse, transpose.

invest *vb* put at interest; confer, endow, endue; (*mil*) beset, besiege, enclose, surround; array, clothe, dress.

investigate *vb* canvass, consider, dissect, examine, explore, follow up, inquire into, look into, overhaul, probe, question, research, scrutinze, search into, search out, sift, study.

investigation *n* examination, exploration, inquiry, inquisition, overhauling, research, scrutiny, search, sifting, study.

investiture *n* habilitation, induction, installation, ordination.

investment *n* money invested; endowment; (*mil*) beleaguerment, siege; clothes, dress, garments, habiliments, robe, vestment.

inveterate *adj* accustomed, besetting, chronic, confirmed, deep-seated, habitual, habituated, hardened, ingrained, long-established, obstinate.

invidious *adj* disagreeable, envious, hateful, odious, offensive, unfair.

invigorate *vb* animate, brace, energize, fortify, harden, nerve, quicken, refresh, stimulate, strengthen, vivify.

invincible *adj* impregnable, indomitable, ineradicable, insuperable, insurmountable, irrepressible, unconquerable, unsubduable, unyielding.

inviolable *adj* hallowed, holy, inviolate, sacramental, sacred, sacrosanct, stainless.

inviolate *adj* unbroken, unviolated; pure, stainless, unblemished, undefiled, unhurt, uninjured, unpolluted, unprofaned, unstained; inviolable, sacred.

invisible *adj* impalpable, imperceptible, indistinguishable, intangible, unapparent, undiscernable, unperceivable, unseen.

invitation *n* bidding, call, challenge, solicitation, summons.

invite *vb* ask, bid, call, challenge, request, solicit, summon; allure, attract, draw on, entice, lead, persuade, prevail upon.

inviting *adj* alluring, attractive, bewitching, captivating, engaging, fascinating, pleasing, winning; prepossessing, promising.

invoke *vb* adjure, appeal to, beseech, beg, call upon, conjure, entreat, implore, importune, pray, pray to, solicit, summon, supplicate.

involuntary *adj* automatic, blind, instinctive, mechanical, reflex, spontaneous, unintentional; compulsory, reluctant, unwilling.

involve *vb* comprise, contain, embrace, imply, include, lead to; complicate, compromise, embarrass, entangle, implicate, incriminate, inculpate; cover, envelop, enwrap, surround, wrap; blend, conjoin, connect, join, mingle; entwine, interlace, intertwine, interweave, inweave.

invulnerable *adj* incontrovertible, invincible, unassailable, irrefragable.

inward *adj* incoming, inner, interior, internal; essential, hidden, mental, spiritual; private, secret.

inwards *adv* inwardly, towards the inside, within.

iota *n* atom, bit, glimmer, grain, jot, mite, particle, scintilla, scrap, shadow, spark, tittle, trace, whit.

irascible *adj* choleric, cranky, hasty, hot, hot-headed, impatient, irritable, nettlesome, peevish, peppery, pettish, petulant, quick, splenetic, snappish, testy, touchy, waspish.

irate *adj* angry, incensed, ireful, irritated, piqued.

irksome *adj* annoying, burdensome, humdrum, monotonous, tedious, tiresome, wearisome, weary, wearying.

ironic, ironical *adj* mocking, sarcastic.

irony *n* mockery, raillery, ridicule, sarcasm, satire.

irradiate *vb* brighten, illume, illuminate, illumine, light up, shine upon.

irrational *adj* absurd, extravagant, foolish, injudicious, preposterous, ridiculous, silly, unwise; unreasonable, unreasoning, unthinking; brute, brutish; aberrant, alienated, brainless, crazy, demented, fantastic, idiotic, imbecilic, insane, lunatic.

irreclaimable *adj* hopeless, incurable, irrecoverable, irreparable, irretrievable, irreversible, remediless; abandoned, graceless, hardened, impenitent, incorrigible, lost, obdurate, profligate, recreant, reprobate, shameless, unrepentant.

irreconcilable *adj* implacalbe, inexorable, inexpiable, unappeasable; incompatible, incongruous, inconsistent.

irrecoverable *adj* hopeless, incurable, irremediable, irreparable, irretrievable, remediless.

irregular *adj* aberrant, abnormal, anomalistic, anomalous, crooked, devious, eccentric, erratic, exceptional, heteromorphous, raged, tortuous, unconformable, unusual; capricious, changeable, desultory, fitful, spasmodic, uncertain, unpunctual, unsettled, variable; disordered, disorderly, improper, uncanonical, unparliamentary, unsystematic; asymmetric, uneven, unsymmetrical; disorderly, dissolute, immoral, loose, wild. * *n* casual, freelance, hireling, mercenary.

irrelevant *adj* extraneous, foreign, illogical, impertinent, inapplicable, inapposite, inappropriate, inconsequent, unessential, unrelated.

irreparable *adj* irrecoverable, irremediable, irretrievable, remediless.

irreproachable *adj* blameless, faultless, inculpable, innocent, irreprehensible, irreprovable, unblamable..

irresistible *adj* irrefragable, irrepressible, overpowering, overwhelming, resistless.

irresolute *adj* changeable, faltering, fickle, hesitant, hesitating, inconstant, mutable, spineless, uncertain, undecided, undetermined, unsettled, unstable, unsteady, vacillating, wavering.

irrespective *adj* independent, regardless.

irresponsible *adj* unaccountable; untrustworthy.

irretrievable *adj* incurable, irrecoverable, irremediable, irreparable, remediless.

irreverent *adj* blasphemous, impious, irreligious, profane; disrespectful, slighting.

irrevocable *adj* irrepealable, irreversible, unalterable, unchangeable.

irritable *adj* captious, choleric, excitable, fiery, fretful, hasty, hot, irascible, passionate, peppery, peevish, pettish, petulant, snappish, splenetic, susceptible, testy, touchy, waspish.

irritate *vb* anger, annoy, chafe, enrage, exacerbate, exasperate, fret, incense, jar, nag, nettle, offend, provoke, rasp, rile, ruffle, vex; gall, tease; (*med*) excite, inflame, stimulate.

irritation *n* irritating; anger, exacerbation, exasperation, excitement, indignation, ire, passion, provocation, resentment, wrath; (*med*) excitation, inflammation, stimulation; burn, itch, etc.

isolate *vb* detach, dissociate, insulate, quarantine, segregate, separate, set apart.

isolation *n* detachment, disconnection, insulation, quarantine, segregation, separation; loneliness, solitariness, solitude.

issue *vb* come out, flow out, flow forth, gush, run, rush out, spout, spring, spurt, well; arise, come, emanate, ensue, flow, follow, originate, proceed, spring; end, eventuate, result, terminate; appear, come out, deliver, depart, debouch, discharge, emerge, emit, put forth, send out; distribute, give out; publish, utter. * *n* conclusion, consequence, consummation, denouement, end, effect, event, finale, outcome, result, termination, upshot; antagonism, contest, controversy; debouchment, delivering, delivery, discharge, emergence, emigration, emission, issuance; flux, outflow, outpouring, stream; copy, edition, number; egress, exit, outlet, passage out, vent, way out; escape, sally, sortie; children, offspring, posterity, progeny.

itch *vb* tingle. * *n* itching; burning, importunate craving, teasing desire, uneasy hankering.

itching *n* itch; craving, longing, craving, teasing desire, uneasy hankering.

item *adv* also, in like manner. * *n* article, detail, entry, particular, point.

itinerant *adj* nomadic, peripatetic, roaming, roving, travelling, unsettled, wandering.

J

jabber *vb* chatter, gabble, prate, prattle.

jaded *adj* dull, exhausted, fatigued, satiated, tired, weary.

jagged *adj* cleft, divided, indented, notched, serrated, ragged, uneven.

jam *vb* block, crowd, crush, press. * *n* block, crowd, crush, mass, pack, press.

jangle *vb* bicker, chatter, dispute, gossip, jar, quarrel, spar, spat, squabble, tiff, wrangle. * *n* clang, clangour, clash, din, dissonance.

jar[1] *vb* clash, grate, interfere, shake; bicker, contend, jangle, quarrel, spar, spat, squabble, tiff, wrangle; agitate, jolt, jounce, shake. * *n* clash, conflict, disaccord, dicord, jangle, dissonance; agitation, jolt, jostle, shake, shaking, shock, start.

jar[2] *n* can, crock, cruse, ewer.

jargon *n* gabble, gibberish, nonsense, rigmarole: argot, cant, lingo, slang: chaos, confusion, disarray, disorder, jumble

jaundiced *adj* biased, envious, prejudiced.

jaunt *n* excursion, ramble, tour, trip.

jaunty *adj* airy, cheery, garish, gay, fine, fluttering, showy, sprightly, unconcerned.

jealous *adj* distrustful, envious, suspicious; anxious, apprehensive, intolerant, solicitous, zealous.

jealousy *n* envy, suspicion, watchfulness.

jeer *vb* deride, despise, flout, gibe, jape, jest, mock, scoff, sneer, spurn, rail, ridicule, taunt. * *n* abuse, derision, mockery, sneer, ridicule, taunt.

jeopardize *vb* endanger, hazard, imperil, risk, venture.

jeopardy *n* danger, hazard, peril, risk, venture.

jerk *vb, n* flip, hitch, pluck, tweak, twitch, yank.

jest *vb* banter, joke, quiz. * *n* fun, joke, pleasantry, raillery, sport.

jiffy *n* instant, moment, second, twinkling, trice.

jilt *vb* break, coquette, deceive, disappoint, discard, flirt. * *n* coquette, flirt, light-o'-love.

jingle *vb* chink, clink, jangle, rattle, tinkle. * *n* chink, clink, jangle, rattle, tinkle; chorus, ditty, melody, song.

join *vb* add, annex, append, attach; cement, combine, conjoin, connect, couple, dovetail, link, unite, yoke; amalgamate, assemble, associate, confederate, consolidate, meagre, unite.

joint *vb* fit, join, unite. * *adj* combined, concerted, concurrent, conjoint. * *n* connection, junction, juncture, hinge, splice.

joke *vb* banter, jest, frolic, rally. * *n* crank, jest, quip, quirk, witticism.

jolly *adj* airy, blithe, cheerful, frolicsome, gamesome, facetious, funny, gay, jocular, jocund, jovial, joyous, merry, mirthful, jocular, jocund, playful, sportive, sprightly, waggish; bouncing, chubby, lusty, plump, portly, stout.

jolt *vb* jar, jolt, shake, shock. * *n* jar, jolting, jounce, shaking.

jostle *vb* collide, elbow, hustle, joggle, shake, shoulder, shove.

jot *n* ace, atom, bit, corpuscle, iota, grain, mite, particle, scrap, whit.

journey *vb* ramble, roam, rove, travel: fare, go, proceed. * *n* excursion, expedition, jaunt, passage, pilgrimage, tour, travel, trip, voyage.

jovial *adj* airy, convivial, festive, jolly, joyous, merry, mirthful

joy *n* beatification, beatitude, delight, ecstasy, exultation, gladness, glee, mirth, pleasure, rapture, ravishment, transport, beatification, beatitude; bliss, felicity, happiness.

joyful *adj* blithe, blithesome, buoyant, delighted, elate, elated, exultant, glad, hap-

py, jocund, jolly, joyous, merry, rejoicing.

jubilant *adj* exultant, exulting, rejoicing,
triumphant.

judge *vb* conclude, decide, decree, determine, pronounce; adjudicate, arbitrate,
condemn, doom, sentence, try, umpire;
account, apprehend, believe, consider,
decide, deem, esteem, guess, hold, imagine, measure, reckon, regard, suppose,
think; appreciate, estimate. * *n* adjudicator, arbiter, arbitrator, bencher, justice,
magistrate, moderator, referee, umpire,
connoisseur, critic.

judgment, judgement *n* brains, ballast,
circumspection, depth, discernment, discretion, discrimination, intelligence, judiciousness, penetration, prudence, sagacity, sense, sensibility, taste, understanding, wisdom, wit; conclusion, consideration, decision, determination, estimation, notion, opinion, thought;
adjudication, arbitration, award, censure, condemnation, decree, doom, sentence.

judicious *adj* cautious, considerate, cool,
critical, discriminating, discreet, enlightened, provident, politic, prudent, rational, reasonable, sagacious, sensible, sober, solid, sound, staid, wise.

juicy *adj* lush, moist, sappy, succulent,
watery; entertaining, exciting, interesting, lively, racy, spicey.

jumble *vb* confound, confuse, disarrange,
disorder, mix, muddle. * *n* confusion,
disarrangement, disorder, medley, mess,
mixture, muddle.

jump *vb* bound, caper, clear, hop, leap,
skip, spring, vault. * *n* bound, caper, hop,
leak, skip, spring, vault; fence, hurdle,
obstacle; break, gap, interruption, space;
advance, boost, increase, rise; jar, jolt,
shock start, twitch.

junction *n* combination, connection, coupling, hook-up, joining, linking, seam,
union; conjunction, joint, juncture.

just *adj* equitable, lawful, legitimate, reasonable, right, rightful; candid, even-
handed, fair, fair-minded, impartial;
blameless, conscientious, good, honest,
honourable, pure, square, straightfor-

ward, virtuous; accurate, correct, exact,
normal, proper, regular, true; condign,
deserved, due, merited, suitable.

justice *n* accuracy, equitableness, equity,
fairness, honesty, impartiality, justness,
right; judge, justiciary.

justifiable *adj* defensible, fit, proper, right,
vindicable, warrantable.

justification *n* defence, exculpation, excuse, exoneration, reason, vindication,
warrant.

justify *vb* approve, defend, exculpate, excuse, exonerate, maintain, vindicate,
support, warrant.

justness *n* accuracy, correctness, fitness,
justice, precision, propriety.

juvenile *adj* childish, immature, puerile,
young, youthful. * *n* boy, child, girl,
youth.

juxtaposition *n* adjacency, contiguity,
contact, proximity.

K

keen[1] *adj* ardent, eager, earnest, fervid, intense, vehement, vivid; acute, sharp; cutting; acrimonious, biting, bitter, caustic,
poignant, pungent, sarcastic, severe; astute, discerning, intelligent, quick, sagacious, sharp-sighted, shrewd.

keen[2] *vb* bemoan, bewail, deplore, grieve,
lament, mourn, sorrow, weep. * *n* coronach, dirge, elegy, lament, lamentation,
monody, plaint, requiem, threnody.

keep *vb* detain, hold, retain; continue, preserve; confine, detain, reserve, restrain,
withhold; attend, guard, preserve, protect; adhere to, fulfil; celebrate, commemorate, honour, observe, perform,
solemnize; maintain, support, sustain;
husband, save, store; abide, dwell, lodge,
stay, remain; endure, last. * *n* board,
maintenance, subsistence, support; don-
jon, dungeon, stronghold, tower.

keeper *n* caretaker, conservator, curator,
custodian, defender, gaoler, governor,
guardian, jailer, superintendent, warden,
warder, watchman.

keeping *n* care, charge, custody, guard,

possession; feed, maintenance, support; agreement, conformity, congruity, consistency, harmony.

key *adj* basic, crucial, essential, important, major, principal. * *n* lock-opener, opener; clue, elucidation, explanation, guide, solution, translation; (*mus*) keynote, tonic; clamp, lever, wedge.

kick *vb* boot, punt; oppose, rebel, resist, spurn. * *n* force, intensity, power, punch, vitality; excitement, pleasure, thrill.

kidnap *vb* abduct, capture, carry off, remove, steal away.

kill *vb* assassinate, butcher, dispatch, destroy, massacre, murder, slaughter, slay.

kin *adj* akin, allied, cognate, kindred, related. * *n* affinity, consanguinity, relationship; connections, kindred, kinsfolk, relations, relatives, siblings.

kind[1] *adj* accommodating, amiable, beneficent, benevolent, benign, bland, bounteous, brotherly, charitable, clement, compassionate, complaisant, gentle, good, good-natured, forbearing, friendly, generous, gracious, humane, indulgent, lenient, mild, obliging, sympathetic, tender, tender-hearted.

kind[2] *n* breed, class, family, genus, race, set, species, type; brand, character, colour, denomination, description, form, make, manner, nature, persuasion, sort, stamp, strain, style,

kindle *vb* fire, ignite, inflame, light; animate, awaken, bestir, exasperate, excite, foment, incite, provoke, rouse, stimulate, stir, thrill, warm.

kindly *adj* appropriate, congenial, kindred, natural, proper; benevolent, considerate, friendly, gracious, humane, sympathetic, well-disposed. * *adv* agreeably, graciously, humanely, politely, thoughtfully.

kindness *n* benefaction, charity, favour; amiability, beneficence, benevolence, benignity, charity, clemency, generosity, goodness, grace, humanity, kindliness, mildness, philanthropy, sympathy, tenderness,

kindred *adj* akin, allied, congenial, connected, related, sympathetic. * *n* affinity, consanguinity, flesh, relationship;

folks, kin, kinsfolk, kinsmen, relations, relatives.

king *n* majesty, monarch, sovereign.

kingdom *n* dominion, empire, monarchy, rule, sovereignty, supremacy; region, tract; division, department, domain, province, realm.

kingly *adj* imperial, kinglike, monarchical, regal, royal, sovereign; august, glorious, grand, imperial, imposing, magnificent, majestic, noble, regal, royal, splendid.

kink *n* cramp, crick, curl, entanglement, knot, loop, twist; crochet, whim, wrinkle.

kinsfolk *n* kin, kindred, kinsmen, relations, relatives.

knack *n* ability, address, adroitness, aptitude, aptness, dexterity, dextrousness, expertness, facility, quickness, readiness, skill.

knell *vb* announce, peal, ring, toll. * *n* chime, peal, ring, toll.

knife *vb* cut, slash, stab. * *n* blade, jackknife, lance.

knit *vb* connect, interlace, join, unite, weave.

knob *n* boss, bunch, hunch, lump, protuberance, stud.

knock *vb* clap, cuff, hit, rap, rattle, slap, strike, thump; beat, blow, box, cuff, rap, slap. * *n* blow, slap, smack, thump; blame, criticism, rejection, setback.

knot *vb* complicate, entangle, gnarl, kink, tie, weave. * *n* complication, entanglement; connection, tie; joint, node, knag; bunch, rosette, tuft; band, cluster, clique, crew, gang, group, pack, set, squad.

knotty *adj* gnarled, hard, knaggy, knurled, knotted, rough, rugged; complex, difficult, hard, harassing, intricate, involved, perplexing, troublesome.

know *vb* apprehend, comprehend, cognize, discern, perceive, recognize, see, understand; discriminate, distinguish.

knowing *adj* accomplished, competent, experienced, intelligent, proficient, qualified, skilful, well-informed; aware, conscious, intelligent, percipient, sensible, thinking; cunning, expressive, significant.

knowingly *adv* consciously, intentionally, purposely, wittingly.

knowledge *n* apprehension, command, comprehension, discernment, judgment, perception, understanding, wit; acquaintance, acquirement, attainments, enlightenment, erudition, information, learning, lore, mastery, scholarship, science; cognition, cognizance, consciousness, information, ken, notice, prescience, recognition.

knowledgeable *adj* aware, conscious, experienced, well-informed; educated, intelligent, learned, scholarly.

L

laborious *adj* assiduous, diligent, hardworking, indefatigable, industrious, painstaking, sedulous, toiling; arduous, difficult, fatiguing, hard, Herculean, irksome, onerous, tiresome, toilsome, wearisome.

labour *vb* drudge, endeavour, exert, strive, toil, travail, work. * *n* drudgery, effort, exertion, industry, pains, toil, work; childbirth, delivery, parturition.

lace *vb* attach, bind, fasten, intertwine, tie, twine. * *n* filigree, lattice, mesh, net, netting, network, openwork, web.

lack *vb* need, want. * *n* dearth, default, defectiveness, deficiency, deficit, destitution, insufficiency, need, scantiness, scarcity, shortcoming, shortness, want.

laconic *adj* brief, compact, concise, pithy, sententious, short, succinct, terse.

lad *n* boy, schoolboy, stripling, youngster, youth.

lag *vb* dawdle, delay, idle, linger, loiter, saunter, tarry.

lair *n* burrow, couch, den, form, resting place.

lame *vb* cripple, disable, hobble. * *adj* crippled, defective, disabled, halt, hobbling, limping; feeble, insufficient, poor, unsatisfactory, weak.

lament *vb* complain, grieve, keen, moan, mourn, sorrow, wail, weep; bemoan, bewail, deplore, regret. * *n* complaint, lamentation, moan, moaning, plaint, wailing; coronach, dirge, elegy, keen, monody, requiem, threnody.

lamentable *adj* deplorable, grievous, lamented, melancholy, woeful; contemptible, miserable, pitiful, poor, wretched.

land *vb* debark, disembark. * *n* earth, ground, soil; country, district, province, region, reservation, territory, tract, weald.

language *n* dialect, speech, tongue, vernacular; conversation, speech; expression, idiom, jargon, parlance, phraseology, slang, style, terminology; expression, utterance, voice.

languid *adj* drooping, exhausted, faint, feeble, flagging, languishing, pining, weak; dull, heartless, heavy, inactive, listless, lukewarm, slow, sluggish, spiritless, torpid.

languish *vb* decline, droop, fade, fail, faint, pine, sicken, sink, wither.

languor *n* debility, faintness, feebleness, languidness, languishment, weakness; apathy, ennui, heartlessness, heaviness, lethargy, listlessness, torpidness, torpor, weariness.

lank *adj* attenuated, emaciated, gaunt, lean, meagre, scraggy, slender, skinny, slim, starveling, thin.

lap¹ *vb* drink, lick, mouth, tongue; plash, ripple, splash, wash; quaff, sip, sup, swizzle, tipple. * *n* draught, dram, drench, drink, gulp, lick, swig, swill, quaff, sip, sup, suck; plash, splash, wash.

lap² *vb* cover, enfold, fold, turn, twist, swaddle, wrap; distance, pass, outdistance, overlap. * *n* fold, flap, lappet, lapel, ply, plait; ambit, beat, circle, circuit, cycle, loop, orbit, revolution, round, tour, turn, walk.

lapse *vb* glide, sink, slide, slip; err, fail, fall. * *n* course, flow, gliding; declension, decline, fall; error, fault, indiscretion, misstep, shortcoming, slip.

large *adj* big, broad, bulky, colossal, elephantine, enormous, heroic, great, huge, immense, vast; broad, expanded, extensive, spacious, wide; abundant, ample, copious, full, liberal, plentiful; capacious, comprehensive.

lash¹ *vb* belay, bind, strap, tie; fasten, join, moor, pinion, secure.

lash² *vb* beat, castigate, chastise, flagellate, flail, flay, flog, goad, scourge, swinge, thrash, whip; assail, castigate, censure, excoriate, lampoon, satirize, trounce. * *n* scourge, strap, thong, whip; cut, slap, smack, stroke, stripe.

last¹ *vb* abide, carry on, continue, dwell, endure, extend, maintain, persist, prevail, remain, stand, stay, survive.

last² *adj* hindermost, hindmost, latest; conclusive, final, terminal, ultimate; eventual, endmost, extreme, farthest, ultimate; greatest, highest, maximal, maximum, most, supreme, superlative, utmost; latest, newest; aforegoing, foregoing, latter, preceding; departing, farewell, final, leaving, parting, valedictory. * *n* conclusion, consummation, culmination, end, ending, finale, finis, finish, termination.

last³ *n* cast, form, matrix, mould, shape, template.

lasting *adj* abiding, durable, enduring, fixed, perennial, permanent, perpetual, stable.

lastly *adv* conclusively, eventually, finally, ultimately.

late *adj* behindhand, delayed, overdue, slow, tardy; deceased, former; recent. * *adv* lately, recently, sometime; tardily.

latent *adj* abeyant, concealed, hidden, invisible, occult, secret, unseen, veiled.

latitude *n* amplitude, breadth, compass, extent, range, room, scope; freedom, indulgence, liberty; laxity.

latter *adj* last, latest, modern, recent.

laugh *vb* cackle, chortle, chuckle, giggle, guffaw, snicker, snigger, titter. * *n* chortle, chuckle, giggle, guffaw, laughter, titter.

laughable *adj* amusing, comical, diverting, droll, farcical, funny, ludicrous, mirthful, ridiculous.

laughter *n* cackle, chortle, chuckle, glee, giggle, guffaw, laugh, laughing.

launch *vb* cast, dart, dispatch, hurl, lance, project, throw; descant, dilate, enlarge, expiate; begin, commence, inaugurate, open, start.

lavish *vb* dissipate, expend, spend, squander, waste. * *adj* excessive, extravagant, generous, immoderate, overliberal, prodigal, profuse, thriftless, unrestrained, unstinted, unthrifty, wasteful.

law *n* act, code, canon, command, commandment, covenant, decree, edict, enactment, order, precept, principle, statute, regulation, rule; jurisprudence; litigation, process, suit.

lawful *adj* constitutional, constituted, legal, legalized, legitimate; allowable, authorized, permissible, warrantable; equitable, rightful, just, proper, valid.

lawless *adj* anarchic, anarchical, chaotic, disorderly, insubordinate, rebellious, reckless, riotous, seditious, wild.

lax *adj* loose, relaxed, slow; drooping, flabby, relaxed, soft; neglectful, negligent, remiss; dissolute, immoral, licentious, seditious, wild.

lay¹ *vb* deposit, establish, leave, place, plant, posit, put, set, settle, spread; arrange, dispose, locate, organize, position; bear, deposit, produce; advance, lodge, offer, submit; allocate, allot, ascribe, assign, attribute, charge, impute; concoct, contrive, design, plan, plot, prepare; apply, burden, encumber, impose, saddle, tax; bet, gamble, hazard, risk, stake, wager; allay, alleviate, appease, assuage, calm, relieve, soothe, still, suppress; disclose, divulge, explain, reveal, show, unveil; acquire, grab, grasp, seize; assault, attack, beat up; discover, find, unearth; bless, confirm, consecrate, ordain. * *n* arrangement, array, form, formation; attitude, aspect, bearing, direction, lie, pose, position, posture, set.

lay² *adj* amateur, inexpert, nonprofessional; civil, laic, laical, nonclerical, nonecclesiastical, nonreligious, secular, temporal, unclerical.

lay³ *n* ballad, carol, ditty, lied, lyric, ode, poem, rhyme, round, song, verse.

layer *n* bed, course, lay, seam, stratum.

lazy *adj* idle, inactive, indolent, inert, slack, slothful, slow, sluggish, supine, torpid.

lead *vb* conduct, deliver, direct, draw, escort, guide; front, head, precede; advance, excel, outstrip, pass; allure, entice, induce, persuade, prevail; conduce, contribute, serve, tend. * adj chief, first, foremost, main, primary, prime, principal. * n direction, guidance, leadership; advance; precedence, priority.

leader n conductor, director, guide; captain, chief, chieftain, commander, head; superior, dominator, victor.

leadership n conduct, direction, guidance, lead; headship, hegemony, predominance, primacy, supremacy.

leading adj governing, ruling; capital, chief, first, foremost, highest, principal, superior.

league vb ally, associate, band, combine, confederate, unite. * n alliance, association, coalition, combination, combine, confederacy, confederation, consortium, union.

leak vb drip, exude, ooze, pass, percolate. * n chink, crack, crevice, hole, fissure, hole, oozing; leakage, leaking, percolation.

lean¹ adj bony, emaciated, gaunt, lank, meagre, poor, skinny, thin; dull, barren, jejune, meagre, tame; inadequate, pitiful, scanty, slender; bare, barren, infertile, unproductive.

lean² vb incline, slope; bear, recline, repose, rest; confide, depend, rely, trust.

leaning n aptitude, bent, bias, disposition, inclination, liking, predilection, proneness, propensity, tendency.

leap vb bound, clear, jump, spring, vault; caper, frisk, gambol, hop, skip. * n bound, jump, spring, vault; caper, frisk, gambol, hop, skip.

learn vb acquire, ascertain, attain, collect, gain, gather, hear, memorize.

learned adj erudite, lettered, literate, scholarly, well-read; expert, experienced, knowing, skilled, versed, well-informed.

learner n beginner, novice, pupil, student, tyro.

learning n acquirements, attainments, culture, education, information, knowledge, lore, scholarship, tuition.

least adj meanest, minutest, smallest, tiniest.

leave¹ vb abandon, decamp, go, quit, va-

cate, withdraw; desert, forsake, relinquish, renounce; commit, consign, refer; cease, desist from, discontinue, refrain, stop; allow, cease, let, let alone, permit; bequeath, demise, desist, will.

leave² n allowance, liberty, permission, licence, sufferance; departure, retirement, withdrawal; adieu, farewell, goodbye.

leavings npl bits, dregs, fragments, leftovers, pieces, relics, remains, remnants, scraps.

lecture vb censure, chide, reprimand, reprove, scold, sermonize; address, harangue, teach. * n censure, lecturing, lesson, reprimand, reproof, scolding; address, discourse, prelection.

left adj larboard, leftward, sinistral.

leg n limb, prop.

legacy n bequest, gift, heirloom; heritage, inheritance, tradition.

legal adj allowable, authorized, constitutional, lawful, legalized, legitimate, proper, sanctioned.

legalize vb authorize, legitimate, legitimatize, legitimize, permit, sanction.

legend n fable, fiction, myth, narrative, romance, story, tale.

legendary adj fabulous, fictitious, mythical, romantic.

legible adj clear, decipherable, fair, distinct, plain, readable; apparent, discoverable, recognizable, manifest.

legion n army, body, cohort, column, corps, detachment, detail, division, force, maniple, phalanx, platoon; squad; army, horde, host, multitude, number, swarm, throng. * adj many, multitudinous, myriad, numerous.

legislate vb enact, ordain.

legitimate adj authorized, lawful, legal, sanctioned; genuine, valid; correct, justifiable, logical, reasonable, warrantable, warranted.

leisure n convenience, ease, freedom, liberty, opportunity, recreation, retirement, vacation.

lend vb advance, afford, bestow, confer, furnish, give, grant, impart, loan, supply.

lengthen vb elongate, extend, produce, prolong, stretch; continue, protract.

lengthy adj diffuse, lengthened, long, long-drawn, prolix, prolonged, protracted.

lenient adj assuasive, lenitive, mitigating, mitigative, softening, soothing; clement, easy, forbearing, gentle, humouring, indulgent, long-suffering, merciful, mild, tender, tolerant.

less adj baser, inferior, lower, smaller; decreased, fewer, lesser, reduced, smaller, shorter; * adv barely, below, least, under; decreasingly. * prep excepting, lacking, minus, sans, short of, without.

lessen vb abate, abridge, contract, curtail, decrease, diminish, narrow, reduce, shrink; degrade, lower; dwindle, weaken.

lesson n exercise, task; instruction, precept; censure, chiding, lecture, lecturing, rebuke, reproof, scolding.

let¹ vb admit, allow, authorize, permit, suffer; charter, hire, lease, rent.

let² vb hinder, impede, instruct, prevent. * n hindrance, impediment, interference, obstacle, obstruction, restriction.

lethal adj deadly, destructive, fatal, mortal, murderous.

lethargic adj apathetic, comatose, drowsy, dull, heavy, inactive, inert, sleepy, stupid, stupefied, torpid.

letter n epistle, missive, note.

lettered adj bookish, educated, erudite, learned, literary, versed, well-read.

level vb equalize, flatten, horizontalize, smooth; demolish, destroy, raze; aim, direct, point. * adj equal, even, flat, flush, horizontal, plain, plane, smooth. * n altitude, degree, equality, evenness, plain, plane, smoothness; deck, floor, layer, stage, storey, tier.

levity n buoyancy, facetiousness, fickleness, flightiness, flippancy, frivolity, giddiness, inconstancy, levity, volatility.

levy vb collect, exact, gather, tax; call, muster, raise, summon. * n duty, tax.

liability n accountableness, accountability, duty, obligation, responsibility, tendency; exposedness; debt, indebtedness, obligation.

liable adj accountable, amenable, answerable, bound, responsible; exposed, likely, obnoxious, subject.

libel vb calumniate, defame, lampoon, sat-

irize, slander, vilify. * n calumny, defamation, lampoon, satire, slander, vilification, vituperation.

liberal adj beneficent, bountiful, charitable, disinterested, free, generous, munificent, open-hearted, princely, unselfish; broad-minded, catholic, chivalrous, enlarged, high-minded, honourable, magnanimous, tolerant, unbiased, unbiassed, unbigoted; abundant, ample, bounteous, full, large, plentiful, unstinted; humanizing, liberalizing, refined, refining.

liberate vb deliver, discharge, disenthral, emancipate, free, manumit, ransom, release.

liberty n emancipation, freedom, independence, liberation, self-direction, self-government; franchise, immunity, privilege; leave, licence, permission.

licence n authorization, leave, permission, privilege, right; certificate, charter, dispensation, imprimatur, permit, warrant; anarchy, disorder, freedom, lawlessness, laxity, liberty.

license vb allow, authorize, grant, permit, warrant; suffer, tolerate.

ick vb beat, flog, spank, thrash; lap, taste. * n blow, slap, stroke; salt-spring.

lie¹ vb couch, recline, remain, repose, rest; consist, pertain.

lie² vb equivocate, falsify, fib, prevaricate, romance. * n equivocation, falsehood, falsification, fib, misrepresentation, prevarication, untruth; delusion, illusion.

life n activity, alertness, animation, briskness, energy, sparkle, spirit, sprightliness, verve, vigour, vivacity; behaviour, conduct, deportment; being, duration, existence, lifetime; autobiography, biography, curriculum vitae, memoirs, story.

lifeless adj dead, deceased, defunct, extinct, inanimate; cold, dull, flat, frigid, inert, lethargic, passive, pulseless, slow, sluggish, tame, torpid.

lift vb elevate, exalt, hoist, raise, uplift. * n aid, assistance, help; elevator.

light¹ vb alight, land, perch, settle. * adj porous, sandy, spongy, well-leavened; loose, sandy; free, portable, unburdened, unencumbered; inconsiderable, moderate, negligible, slight, small, trifling, trivial, unimportant; ethereal, feathery, flimsy, gossamer, insubstantial, weightless; easy, effortless, facile; fickle, frivolous, unsettled, unsteady, volatile; airy, buoyant, carefree, light-hearted, lightsome; unaccented, unstressed, weak.

light² vb conflagrate, fire, ignite, inflame, kindle; brighten, illume, illuminate, illumine, luminate, irradiate, lighten. * adj bright, clear, fair, lightsome, luminous, pale, pearly, whitish. * n dawn, day, daybreak, sunrise; blaze, brightness, effulgence, gleam, illumination, luminosity, phosphorescence, radiance, ray; candle, lamp, lantern, lighthouse, taper, torch; comprehension, enlightenment, information, insight, instruction, knowledge; elucidation, explanation, illustration; attitude, construction, interpretation, observation, reference, regard, respect, view.

lighten¹ vb allay, alleviate, ease, mitigate, palliate; disburden, disencumber, relieve, unburden, unload.

lighten² vb brighten, gleam, shine; light, illume, illuminate, illumine, irradiate; enlighten, inform; emit, flash.

like¹ vb approve, please; cherish, enjoy, love, relish; esteem, fancy, regard; choose, desire, elect, list, prefer, select, wish. * n liking, partiality, preference.

like² adj alike, allied, analogous, cognate, corresponding, parallel, resembling, similar; equal, same; likely, probable. * adv likely, probably. * n counterpart, equal, match, peer, twin.

likelihood n probability, verisimilitude.

likely adj credible, liable, possible, probable; agreeable, appropriate, convenient, likable, pleasing, suitable, well-adapted, well-suited. * adv doubtlessly, presumably, probably.

likeness n appearance, form, parallel, resemblance, semblance, similarity, similitude; copy, counterpart, effigy, facsimile, image, picture, portrait, representation.

liking n desire, fondness, partiality, wish; appearance, bent, bias, disposition, inclination, leaning, penchant, predisposition, proneness, propensity, tendency, turn.

limit vb bound, circumscribe, define; check, condition, hinder, restrain, restrict. * n bound, boundary, bourn, confine, frontier, march, precinct, term, termination, terminus; check, hindrance, obstruction, restraint, restriction.

limitation n check, constraint, restraint, restriction.

limp¹ vb halt, hitch, hobble, totter. * n hitch, hobble, shamble, shuffle, totter.

limp² adj drooping, droopy, floppy, sagging, weak; flabby, flaccid, flexible, limber, pliable, relaxed, slack, soft.

limpid adj bright, clear, crystal, crystalline, lucid, pellucid, pure, translucent, transparent.

line vb align, line up, range, rank, regiment; border, bound, edge, fringe, hem, interline, march, rim, verge; seam, stripe, streak, striate, trace; carve, chisel, crease, cut, crosshatch; define, delineate, describe. * n mark, streak, stripe; cable, cord, rope, string, thread; rank, row; ancestry, family, lineage, race, succession; course, method; business, calling, employment, job, occupation, post, pursuit.

linger vb dally, dawdle, delay, idle, lag, loiter, remain, saunter, stay, tarry, wait.

link vb bind, conjoin, connect, fasten, join, tie, unite. * n bond, connection, connective, copula, coupler, joint, juncture; division, member, part, piece.

liquefy vb dissolve, fuse, melt, thaw.

liquid adj fluid; clear, dulcet, flowing, mellifluous, mellifluent, melting, soft. * n fluid, liquor.

list¹ vb alphabetize, catalogue, chronicle, codify, docket, enumerate, file, index, inventory, record, register, tabulate, tally; enlist, enroll; choose, desire, elect, like, please, prefer, wish. * n catalogue, enumeration, index, inventory, invoice, register, roll, schedule, scroll, series, table, tally; border, bound, limit; border, edge, selvedge, strip, stripe; fillet, listel.

list² vb cant, heel, incline, keel, lean, pitch, tilt, tip. * n cant, inclination, incline, leaning, pitch, slope, tilt, tip.

listen vb attend, eavesdrop, hark, hear, hearken, heed, obey, observe.

listless adj apathetic, careless, heedless, impassive, inattentive, indifferent, indolent, languid, vacant, supine, thoughtless, vacant.

literally adv actually, really; exactly, precisely, rigorously, strictly.

literary adj bookish, book-learned, erudite, instructed, learned, lettered, literate, scholarly, well-read.

lithe adj flexible, flexile, limber, pliable, pliant, supple.

litter vb derange, disarrange, disorder, scatter, strew; bear. * n bedding, couch, palanquin, sedan, stretcher; confusion, disarray, disorder, mess, untidiness; fragments, rubbish, shreds.

little adj diminutive, infinitesimal, minute, small, tiny, wee; brief, short, small; feeble, inconsiderable, insignificant, moderate, petty, scanty, slender, slight, trivial, unimportant, weak; contemptible, illiberal, mean, narrow, niggardly, paltry, selfish, stingy. * n handful, jot, modicum, pinch, pittance, trifle, whit.

live[1] vb be, exist; continue, endure, last, remain, survive; abide, dwell, reside; fare, feed, nourish, subsist, support; continue, lead, pass.

live[2] adj alive, animate, living, quick; burning, hot, ignited; bright, brilliant, glowing, lively, vivid; active, animated, earnest, glowing, wide-awake.

livelihood n living, maintenance, subsistence, support, sustenance.

lively adj active, agile, alert, brisk, energetic, nimble, quick, smart, stirring, supple, vigorous, vivacious; airy, animated, blithe, blithesome, buoyant, buxom, frolicsome, gleeful, jocund, jolly, merry, spirited, sportive, sprightly, spry; bright, brilliant, clear, fresh, glowing, strong, vivid; energetic, forcible, glowing, impassioned, keen, nervous, piquant, racy, sparkling, strong, vigorous.

living adj alive, breathing, existing, live, organic, quick; active, lively, quickening. * n livelihood, maintenance, subsistence, support; estate, keeping; benefice.

load vb freight, lade; burden, cumber, encumber, oppress, weigh. * n burden, freightage, pack, weight; cargo, freight, lading; clog, deadweight, encumbrance, incubus, oppression, pressure.

loathe vb abhor, abominate, detest, dislike, hate, recoil.

loathsome adj disgusting, nauseating, nauseous, offensive, palling, repulsive, revolting, sickening; abominable, abhorrent, detestable, execrable, hateful, odious, shocking.

local adj limited, neighbouring, provincial, regional, restricted, sectional, territorial, topical.

locality n location, neighbourhood, place, position, site, situation, spot.

locate vb determine, establish, fix, place, set, settle.

lock[1] vb bolt, fasten, padlock, seal; confine; clog, impede, restrain, stop; clasp, embrace, encircle, enclose, grapple, hug, join, press. * n bolt, fastening, padlock; embrace, grapple, hug.

lock[2] n curl, ringlet, tress, tuft.

lodge vb deposit, fix, settle; fix, place, plant; accommodate, cover, entertain, harbour, quarter, shelter; abide, dwell, inhabit, live, reside, rest; remain, rest, sojourn, stay, stop. * n cabin, cot, cottage, hovel, hut, shed; cave, den, haunt, lair; assemblage, assembly, association club, group, society.

lofty adj elevated, high, tall, towering; arrogant, haughty, proud; elevated, exalted, sublime; dignified, imposing, majestic, stately.

logical adj close, coherent, consistent, dialectical, sound, valid; discriminating, rational, reasoned.

loiter vb dally, dawdle, delay, dilly-dally, idle, lag, linger, saunter, stroll, tarry.

lonely adj apart, dreary, isolated, lonesome, remote, retired, secluded, sequestrated, solitary; alone, lone, companionless, friendless, solitary, unaccompanied; deserted, desolate, dreary, forlorn, forsaken.

long[1] vb anticipate, await, expect; aspire, covet, crave, desire, hanker, lust, pine, wish, yearn.

long² *adj* drawn-out, extended, extensive, far-reaching, lengthy, prolonged, protracted, stretched; diffuse, lengthy, long-winded, prolix, tedious, wearisome; backward, behindhand, dilatory, lingering, slack, slow, tardy.

longing *n* aspiration, coveting, craving, desire, hankering, hunger, pining, yearning.

look *vb* behold, examine, notice, see, search; consider, examine, inspect, investigate, observe, study, contemplate, gaze, regard, scan, survey, view; anticipate, await, expect; consider, heed, mind, watch; face, front; appear, seem. * *n* examination, gaze, glance, peep, peer, search; appearance, aspect, complexion; air, aspect, manner, mien.

loose *vb* free, liberate, release, unbind, undo, unfasten, unlash, unlock, untie; ease, loosen, relax, slacken; detach, disconnect, disengage. * *adj* unbound, unconfined, unfastened, unsewn, untied; disengaged, free, unattached; relaxed, slack; diffuse, diffusive, prolix, rambling, unconnected; ill-defined, indefinite, indeterminate, indistinct, vague; careless, heedless, negligent, lax, slack; debauched, dissolute, immoral, licentious, unchaste, wanton.

loosen *vb* liberate, relax, release, separate, slacken, unbind, unloose, untie.

loot *vb* pillage, plunder, ransack, rifle, rob, sack. * *n* booty, plunder, spoil.

lordly *adj* aristocratic, dignified, exalted, grand, lofty, majestic, noble; arrogant, despotic, domineering, haughty, imperious, insolent, overbearing, proud, tyrannical; large, liberal, noble.

lordship *n* authority, command, control, direction, domination, dominion, empire, government, rule, sovereignty, sway; manor, domain, seigneury, seigniory.

lose *vb* deprive, dispossess, forfeit, miss; dislodge, displace, mislay, misspend, squander, waste; decline, fall, succumb, yield.

loss *n* deprivation, failure, forfeiture, privation; casualty, damage, defeat, destruction, detriment, disadvantage, inju-

ry, overthrow, ruin; squandering, waste.

lost *adj* astray, missing; forfeited, missed, unredeemed; dissipated, misspent, squandered, wasted; bewildered, confused, distracted, perplexed, puzzled; absent, absentminded, abstracted, dreamy, napping, preoccupied; abandoned, corrupt, debauched, depraved, dissolute, graceless, hardened, incorrigible, irreclaimable, licentious, obdurate, profligate, reprobate, shameless, unchaste, wanton; destroyed, ruined.

lot *n* allotment, apportionment, destiny, doom, fate; accident, chance, fate, fortune, hap, haphazard, hazard; division, parcel, part, portion.

loud *adj* high-sounding, noisy, resounding, sonorous; deafening, stentorian, strong, stunning; boisterous, clamorous, noisy, obstreperous, tumultuous, turbulent, uproarious, vociferous; emphatic, impressive, positive, vehement; flashy, gaudy, glaring, loud, ostentatious, showy, vulgar.

love *vb* adore, like, worship. * *n* affection, amity, courtship, delight, fondness, friendship, kindness, regard, tenderness, warmth; adoration, amour, attachment, passion; devotion, fondness, inclination, liking; benevolence, charity, goodwill.

lovely *adj* beautiful, charming, delectable, delightful, enchanting, exquisite, graceful, pleasing, sweet, winning; admirable, adorable, amiable.

low¹ *vb* bellow, moo.

low² *adj* basal, depressed, profound; gentle, grave, soft, subdued; cheap, humble, mean, plebeian, vulgar; abject, base, base-minded, degraded, dirty, grovelling, ignoble, low-minded, menial, scurvy, servile, shabby, slavish, vile; derogatory, disgraceful, dishonourable, disreputable, unbecoming, undignified, ungentlemanly, unhandsome, unmanly; exhausted, feeble, reduced, weak; frugal, plain, poor, simple, spare; humble, lowly, reverent, submissive; dejected, depressed, dispirited.

lower *vb* depress, drop, sink, subside; debase, degrade, disgrace, humble, humiliate, reduce; abate, decrease, diminish, lessen. * adj baser, inferior, less, lesser, shorter, smaller; subjacent, under.

lowly adj gentle, humble, meek, mild, modest, plain, poor, simple, unassuming, unpretending, unpretentious; lowborn, mean, servile.

loyal adj constant, devoted, faithful, patriotic, true.

loyalty n allegiance, constancy, devotion, faithfulness, fealty, fidelity, patriotism.

luck n accident, casualty, chance, fate, fortune, hap, haphazard, hazard, serendipity, success.

lucky adj blessed, favoured, fortunate, happy, successful; auspicious, favourable, fortunate, propitious, prosperous.

lucrative adj advantageous, gainful, paying, profitable, remunerative.

ludicrous adj absurd, burlesque, comic, comical, droll, farcical, funny, laughable, odd, ridiculous, sportive.

lukewarm adj blood-warm, tepid, thermal; apathetic, cold, dull, indifferent, listless, unconcerned, torpid.

lull vb calm, compose, hush, quiet, still, tranquillize; abate, cease, decrease, diminish, subside. * n calm, calmness, cessation.

luminous adj effulgent, incandescent, radiant, refulgent, resplendent, shining; bright, brilliant, clear; clear, lucid, lucent, perspicuous, plain.

lunacy n aberration, craziness, crack, derangement, insanity, madness, mania.

lunatic adj crazy, deranged, insane, mad. * n madman, maniac, psychopath.

lurch vb appropriate, filch, pilfer, purloin, steal; deceit, defeat, disappoint, evade; ambush, lurk, skulk; contrive, dodge, shift, trick.

lure vb allure, attract, decoy, entice, inveigle, seduce, tempt. * n allurement, attraction, bait, decoy, enticement, temptation.

lurid adj dismal, ghastly, gloomy, lowering, murky, pale, wan; glaring, sensational, startling, unrestrained.

lurk vb hide, prowl, skulk, slink, sneak, snoop.

luscious adj delicious, delightful, grateful, palatable, pleasing, savoury; cloying, honeyed, sugary; fulsome, rank, nauseous, unctuous.

lush adj fresh, juicy, luxuriant, moist, sappy, succulent, watery.

lust vb covet, crave, desire, hanker, need, want, yearn. * n cupidity, desire, longing; carnality, concupiscence, lasciviousness, lechery, lewdness, lubricity, salaciousness, salacity, wantonness.

lustful adj carnal, concupiscent, hankering, lascivious, lecherous, licentious, libidinous, lubricious, salacious.

lustre n brightness, brilliance, brilliancy, splendour.

lusty adj healthful, lively, robust, stout, strong, sturdy, vigorous; bulky, burly, corpulent, fat, large, stout.

luxuriant adj exuberant, plenteous, plentiful, profuse, superabundant.

luxuriate vb abound, delight, enjoy, flourish, indulge, revel.

luxurious adj epicurean, opulent, pampered, self-indulgent, sensual, sybaritic, voluptuous.

luxury n epicureanism, epicurism, luxuriousness, opulence, sensuality, voluptuousness; delight, enjoyment, gratification, indulgence, pleasure; dainty, delicacy, treat.

lyrical adj ecstatic, enthusiastic, expressive, impassion; dulcet, lyric, mellifluous, mellifluent, melodic, melodious, musical, poetic.

M

macabre adj cadaverous, deathlike, deathly, dreadful, eerie, frightening, frightful, ghoulish, grim, grisly, gruesome, hideous, horrid, morbid, unearthly, weird.

machine n instrument, puppet, tool; machinery, organization, system; engine.

mad adj crazed, crazy, delirious, demented, deranged, distracted, insane, irrational, lunatic, maniac, maniacal; enraged, furious, rabid, raging, violent; angry, enraged, exasperated, furious, incensed, provoked, wrathful; distracted, infatuated, wild; frantic, frenzied, raving.

madden vb annoy, craze, enrage, exasperate, inflame, infuriate, irritate, provoke.

madness n aberration, craziness, derangement, insanity, lunacy, mania; delirium, frenzy, fury, rage.

magic adj bewitching, charming, enchanting, fascinating, magical, miraculous, spellbinding. * n conjuring, enchantment, necromancy, sorcery, thaumaturgy, voodoo, witchcraft; char, fascination, witchery.

magician n conjurer, enchanter, juggler, magus, necromancer, shaman, sorcerer, wizard.

magisterial adj august, dignified, majestic, pompous; authoritative, despotic, domineering, imperious, dictatorial.

magnanimity n chivalry, disinterestedness, forbearance, high-mindedness, generosity, nobility.

magnificent adj elegant, grand, majestic, noble, splendid, superb; brilliant, gorgeous, imposing, lavish, luxurious, pompous, showy, stately, superb.

magnify vb amplify, augment, enlarge; bless, celebrate, elevate, exalt, extol, glorify, laud, praise; exaggerate.

magnitude n bulk, dimension, extent, mass, size, volume; consequence, greatness, importance; grandeur, loftiness, sublimity.

maim vb cripple, disable, disfigure, mangle, mar, mutilate. * n crippling, disfigurement, mutilation; harm, hurt, injury, mischief.

main[1] adj capital, cardinal, chief, leading, principal; essential, important, indispensable, necessary, requisite, vital; enormous, huge, mighty, vast; pure, sheer; absolute, direct, entire, mere. * n channel, pipe; force, might, power, strength, violence.

main[2] n high seas, ocean; continent, mainland.

maintain vb keep, preserve, support, sustain, uphold; hold, possess; defend, vindicate, justify; carry on, continue, keep up; feed, provide, supply; allege, assert, declare; affirm, allege, aver, contend, declare, hold, say.

maintenance n defence, justification, preservation, support, sustenance, vindication; bread, food, livelihood, provisions, subsistence, sustenance, victuals.

majestic adj august, dignified, imperial, imposing, lofty, noble, pompous, princely, stately, regal, royal; grand, magnificent, splendid, sublime.

majority n bulk, greater, mass, more, most, plurality, preponderance, superiority; adulthood, manhood.

make vb create; fashion, figure, form, frame, mould, shape; cause, construct, effect, establish, fabricate, produce; do, execute, perform, practice; acquire, gain, get, raise, secure; cause, compel, constrain, force, occasion; compose, constitute, form; go, journey, move, proceed, tend, travel; conduce, contribute, effect, favour, operate; estimate, judge, reckon, suppose, think. * n brand, build, constitution, construction, form, shape, structure.

maker n creator, god; builder, constructor, fabricator, framer, manufacturer; author, composer, poet, writer.

malady n affliction, ail, ailment, complaint, disease, disorder, illness, indisposition, sickness.

malevolent adj evil-minded, hateful, hostile, ill-natured, malicious, malignant, mischievous, rancorous, spiteful, venomous, vindictive.

malice n animosity, bitterness, enmity, grudge, hate, ill will, malevolence, maliciousness, malignity, pique, rancour, spite, spitefulness, venom, vindictiveness.

malicious adj bitter, envious, evil-minded, ill-disposed, ill-natured, invidious, malevolent, malignant, mischievous, rancorous, resentful, spiteful, vicious.

malign vb abuse, asperse, blacken, calumniate, defame, disparage, revile, scandalize, slander, traduce, vilify. * adj malevolent, malicious, malignant, ill-disposed; baneful, injurious, pernicious, unfavourable, unpropitious.

malignant adj bitter, envious, hostile, inimical, malevolent, malicious, malign, spiteful, rancorous, resentful, virulent; heinous, virulent, pernicious; ill-boding, unfavourable, unpropitious; dangerous, fatal, virulent.

mammoth adj colossal, enormous, gigantic, huge, immense, vast.

man vb crew, garrison, furnish; fortify, reinforce, strengthen. * n adult, being, body, human, individual, one, person, personage, somebody, soul; humanity, humankind, mankind; attendant, butler, dependant, liege, servant, subject, valet, vassal; employee, workman.

manage vb administer, conduct, direct, guide, handle, operate, order, regulate, superintend, supervise, transact, treat; control, govern, guide, rule; handle, manipulate, train, wield; contrive, economize, husband, save.

manageable adj controllable, docile, easy, governable, tamable, tractable.

management n administration, care, charge, conduct, control, direction, disposal, economy, government, guidance, superintendence, supervision, surveillance, treatment.

manager n comptroller, conductor, director, executive, governor, impresario, overseer, superintendent, supervisor.

mandate n charge, command, commission, edict, injunction, order, precept, requirement.

mangle¹ vb hack, lacerate, mutilate, rend, tear; cripple, crush, destroy, maim, mutilate, mar, spoil.

mangle² vb calender, polish, press, smooth.

mania n aberration, craziness, delirium, dementia, derangement, frenzy, insanity, lunacy, madness; craze, desire, enthusiasm, fad, fanaticism.

manifest vb declare, demonstrate, disclose, discover, display, evidence, evince, exhibit, express, reveal, show. * adj apparent, clear, conspicuous, distinct, evident, glaring, indubitable, obvious, open, palpable, patent, plain, unmistakable, visible.

manifold adj complex, diverse, many, multifarious, multiplied, multitudinous, numerous, several, sundry, varied, various.

manipulate vb handle, operate, work.

manner n fashion, form, method, mode, style, way; custom, habit, practice; degree, extent, measure; kind, kinds, sort, sorts; air, appearance, aspect, behaviour, carriage, demeanour, deportment, look, mien; mannerism, peculiarity, style; behaviour, conduct, habits, morals; civility, deportment.

mannerly adj ceremonious, civil, complaisant, courteous, polite, refined, respectful, urbane, well-behaved, well-bred.

manners npl conduct, habits, morals; air, bearing, behaviour, breeding, carriage, comportment, deportment, etiquette.

manoeuvre vb contrive, finesse, intrigue, manage, plan, plot, scheme. * n evolution, exercise, movement, operation; artifice, finesse, intrigue, plan, plot, ruse, scheme, stratagem, trick.

manufacture vb build, compose, construct, create, fabricate, forge, form, make, mould, produce, shape. * n constructing, fabrication, making, production.

many adj abundant, diverse, frequent, innumerable, manifold, multifarious, multifold, multiplied, multitudinous, numerous, sundry, varied, various. * n crowd, multitude, people.

map vb chart, draw up, plan, plot, set out, sketch. * n chart, diagram, outline, plot, sketch.

mar vb blot, damage, harm, hurt, impair, injure, ruin, spoil, stain; deface, deform, disfigure, maim, mutilate, spoil.

march vb go, pace, parade, step, tramp, walk. * n hike, tramp, walk; parade, procession; gait, step, stride; advance, evolution, progress.

margin n border, brim, brink, confine, edge, limit, rim, skirt, verge; latitude, room, space, surplus.

marital adj connubial, conjugal, matrimonial.

mark vb distinguish, earmark, label; betoken, brand, characterize, denote, designate, engrave, impress, imprint, indicate, print, stamp; evince, heed, note, notice, observe, regard, remark, show, spot. * n brand, character, characteristic, impression, impress, line, note, print, sign, stamp, symbol, token, race; evidence, indication, proof, symptom, token, trace, track, vestige; badge, sign; footprint, trace, track, vestige; bull's-eye, butt, object, target; consequence, distinction, eminence, fame, importance, position, preeminence.

marked adj conspicuous, distinguished, eminent, notable, noted, outstanding, prominent, remarkable.

marriage n espousals, nuptials, spousals, wedding; matrimony, wedlock; union; alliance, association, confederation.

marshal vb arrange, array, dispose, gather, muster, range, order, rank; guide, herald, lead. * n conductor, director, master of ceremonies, regulator; harbinger, herald, pursuivant.

martial adj brave, heroic, military, soldier-like, warlike.

marvel vb gape, gaze, goggle, wonder. * n miracle, prodigy, wonder; admiration, amazement, astonishment, surprise.

marvellous adj amazing, astonishing, extraordinary, miraculous, prodigious, strange, stupendous, wonderful, wondrous; improbable, incredible, surprising, unbelievable.

masculine adj bold, hardy, manful, manlike, manly, mannish, virile; powerful, robust, strong; bold, coarse, forward, mannish.

mask vb cloak, conceal, cover, disguise, hide, screen, shroud, veil. * n blind, cloak, disguise, screen, veil; evasion, pretence, plea, pretext, ruse, shift, subterfuge, trick; masquerade; bustle, mummery, masquerade.

mass vb accumulate, amass, assemble, collect, gather, rally, throng. * adj extensive, general, large-scale, widespread. * n cake, clot, lump; assemblage, collection, combination, congeries, heap; bulk, dimension, magnitude, size; accumulation, aggregate, body, sum, total, totality, whole.

massacre vb annihilate, butcher, exterminate, kill, murder, slaughter, slay. * n annihilation, butchery, carnage, extermination, killing, murder, pogrom, slaughter.

massive adj big, bulky, colossal, enormous, heavy, huge, immense, ponderous, solid, substantial, vast, weighty.

master vb conquer, defeat, direct, govern, overcome, overpower, rule, subdue, subjugate, vanquish; acquire, learn. * adj cardinal, chief, especial, grand, great, main, leading, prime, principal; adept, expert, proficient. * n director, governor, lord, manager, overseer, superintendent, ruler; captain, commander; instructor, pedagogue, preceptor, schoolteacher, teacher, tutor; holder, owner, possessor, proprietor; chief, head, leader, principal.

masterly adj adroit, clever, dextrous, excellent, expert, finished, skilful, skilled; arbitrary, despotic, despotical, domineering, imperious.

mastery n command, dominion, mastership, power, rule, supremacy, sway; ascendancy, conquest, leadership, preeminence, superiority, supremacy, upperhand, victory; acquisition, acquirement, attainment; ability, cleverness, dexterity, proficiency, skill.

match vb equal, rival; adapt, fit, harmonize, proportion, suit; marry, mate; combine, couple, join, sort; oppose, pit; correspond, suit, tally. * n companion, equal, mate, tally; competition, contest, game, trial; marriage, union.

matchless adj consummate, excellent, exquisite, incomparable, inimitable, peerless, perfect, surpassing, unequalled, unmatched, unparalleled, unrivalled.

mate vb marry, match, wed; compete, equal, vie; appal, confound, crush, enervate, subdue, stupefy. * n associate, companion, compeer, consort, crony, friend, fellow, intimate; companion, equal, match; assistant, subordinate; husband, spouse, wife.

material adj bodily, corporeal, nonspiritual, physical, temporal; essential, important, momentous, relevant, vital, weighty. * n body, element, stuff, substance.

maternal adj motherlike, motherly.

matrimonial adj conjugal, connubial, espousal, hymeneal, marital, nuptial, spousal.

matter *vb* import, signify, weigh. * *n* body, content, sense, substance; difficulty, distress, trouble; material, stuff; question, subject, subject matter, topic; affair, business, concern, event; consequence, import, importance, moment, significance; discharge, purulence, pus.

mature *vb* develop, perfect, ripen. * *adj* complete, fit, full-grown, perfect, ripe; completed, prepared, ready, well-considered, well-digested.

maze *vb* amaze, bewilder, confound, confuse, perplex. * *n* intricacy, labyrinth, meander; bewilderment, embarrassment, intricacy, perplexity, puzzle, uncertainty.

meagre *adj* emaciated, gaunt, lank, lean, poor, skinny, starved, spare, thin; barren, poor, sterile, unproductive; bald, barren, dry, dull, mean, poor, prosy, feeble, insignificant, jejune, scanty, small, tame, uninteresting, vapid.

mean[1] *vb* contemplate, design, intend, purpose; connote, denote, express, imply, import, indicate, purport, signify, symbolize.

mean[2] *adj* average, medium, middle; intermediate, intervening. * *n* measure, mediocrity, medium, moderation; average; agency, instrument, instrumentality, means, measure, method, mode, way.

mean[3] *adj* coarse, common, humble, ignoble, low, ordinary, plebeian, vulgar; abject, base, base-minded, beggarly, contemptible, degraded, dirty, dishonourable, disingenuous, grovelling, low-minded, pitiful, rascally, scurvy, servile, shabby, sneaking, sorry, spiritless, unfair, vile; illiberal, mercenary, miserly, narrow, narrow-minded, niggardly, parsimonious, penurious, selfish, sordid, stingy, ungenerous, unhandsome; contemptible, despicable, diminutive, insignificant, paltry, petty, poor, small, wretched.

meaning *n* acceptation, drift, import, intention, purport, purpose, sense, signification

means *npl* instrument, method, mode, way; appliance, expedient, measure, resource, shift, step; estate, income, property, resources, revenue, substance, wealth, wherewithal.

measure *vb* mete; adjust, gauge, proportion; appraise, appreciate, estimate, gauge, value. * *n* gauge, meter, rule, standard; degree, extent, length, limit; allotment, share, proportion; degree; means, step; foot, metre, rhythm, tune, verse.

meddle *vb* interfere, intermeddle, interpose, intrude.

meddlesome *adj* interfering, intermeddling, intrusive, officious, prying.

mediation *n* arbitration, intercession, interposition, intervention.

mediator *n* advocate, arbitrator, interceder, intercessor, propitiator, umpire.

mediocre *adj* average, commonplace, indifferent, mean, medium, middling, ordinary.

meditate *vb* concoct, contrive, design, devise, intend, plan, purpose, scheme; chew, contemplate, ruminate, study; cogitate, muse, ponder, think.

meditation *n* cogitation, contemplation, musing, pondering, reflection, ruminating, study, thought.

meditative *adj* contemplative, pensive, reflective, studious, thoughtful.

medium *adj* average, mean, mediocre, middle. * *n* agency, channel, intermediary, instrument, instrumentality, means, organ; conditions, environment, influences; average, means.

medley *n* confusion, farrago, hodgepodge, hotchpotch, jumble, mass, melange, miscellany, mishmash, mixture.

meek *adj* gentle, humble, lowly, mild, modest, pacific, soft, submissive, unassuming, yielding.

meet *vb* cross, intersect, transact; confront, encounter, engage; answer, comply, fulfil, gratify, satisfy; converge, join, unite; assemble, collect, convene, congregate, forgather, muster, rally. * *adj* adapted, appropriate, befitting, convenient, fit, fitting, proper, qualified, suitable, suited.

meeting *n* encounter, interview; assemblage, assembly, audience, company, concourse, conference, congregation, convention, gathering; assignation, encounter, introduction, rendezvous; confluence, conflux, intersection, joining, junction, union; collision.

melancholy adj blue, dejected, depressed, despondent, desponding, disconsolate, dismal, dispirited, doleful, downcast, downhearted, dumpish, gloomy, glum, hypochondriac, low-spirited, lugubrious, moody, mopish, sad, sombre, sorrowful, unhappy; afflictive, calamitous, unfortunate, unlucky; dark, gloomy, grave, quiet, sad. * n blues, dejection, depression, despondency, dismals, dumps, gloom, gloominess, hypochondria, sadness, vapours.

mellow vb mature, ripen; improve, smooth, soften, tone; pulverize; perfect. * adj mature, ripe; dulcet, mellifluous, mellifluent, silver-toned, rich, silvery, smooth, soft; delicate, rich, soft; genial, good-humoured, jolly, jovial, matured, softened; mellowy, loamy, rich, softened, unctuous; perfected, well-prepared; disguised, fuddled, intoxicated, tipsy.

melodious adj arioso, concordant, dulcet, euphonious, harmonious, mellifluous, mellifluent, musical, silvery, sweet, tuneful.

melt vb dissolve, fuse, liquefy, thaw; mollify, relax, soften, subdue; dissipate, waste; blend, pass, shade.

member n arm, leg, limb, organ; component, constituent, element, part, portion; branch, clause, division, head.

memento n memorial, remembrance, reminder, souvenir.

memoir n account, autobiography, biography, journal, narrative, record, register.

memorable adj celebrated, distinguished, extraordinary, famous, great, illustrious, important, notable, noteworthy, remarkable, signal, significant.

memorandum n minute, note, record.

memorial adj commemorative, monumental. * n cairn, commemoration, memento, monument, plaque, record, souvenir; memorandum, record, remembrance.

memory n recollection, remembrance, reminiscence; celebrity, fame, renown,

reputation; commemoration, memorial.

menace vb alarm, frighten, intimidate, threaten. * n danger, hazard, peril, threat, warning; nuisance, pest, troublemaker.

mend vb darn, patch, rectify, refit, repair, restore, retouch; ameliorate, amend, better, correct, emend, improve, meliorate, rectify, reform; advance, help, improve; augment, increase.

mendacious adj deceitful, deceptive, fallacious, false, lying, untrue, untruthful.

menial adj base, low, mean, servile, vile. * n attendant, bondsman, domestic, flunkey, footman, lackey, serf, servant, slave, underling, valet, waiter.

mental adj ideal, immaterial, intellectual, psychiatric, subjective.

mention vb acquaint, allude, cite, communicate, declare, disclose, divulge, impart, inform, name, report, reveal, state, tell. * n allusion, citation, designation, notice, noting, reference.

mentor n adviser, counsellor, guide, instructor, monitor.

mercantile adj commercial, marketable, trading.

mercenary adj hired, paid, purchased, venal; avaricious, covetous, grasping, mean, niggardly, parsimonious, penurious, sordid, stingy. * n hireling, soldier.

merchandise n commodities, goods, wares.

merchant n dealer, retailer, shopkeeper, trader, tradesman.

merciful adj clement, compassionate, forgiving, gracious, lenient, pitiful; benignant, forbearing, gentle, gracious, humane, kind, mild, tender, tender-hearted.

merciless adj barbarous, callous, cruel, fell, hard-hearted, inexorable, pitiless, relentless, remorseless, ruthless, savage, severe, uncompassionate, unfeeling, unmerciful, unrelenting, unrepenting, unsparing.

mercurial adj active, lively, nimble, prompt, quick, sprightly; cheerful, light-hearted, lively; changeable, fickle, flighty, inconstant, mobile, volatile.

mercy n benevolence, clemency, compassion, gentleness, kindness, lenience, leniency, lenity, mildness, pity, tenderness;

blessing, favour, grace; discretion, disposal; forgiveness, pardon.

mere *adj* bald, bare, naked, plain, sole, simple; absolute, entire; pure, sheer, unmixed. * *n* lake, pond, pool.

merge *vb* bury, dip, immerse, involve, lose, plunge, sink, submerge.

merit *vb* deserve, earn, incur; acquire, desert, gain, profit, value. * *n* claim, right; credit, desert, excellence, goodness, worth, worthiness.

merry *adj* agreeable, brisk, delightful, exhilarating, lively, pleasant, stirring; airy, blithe, blithesome, buxom, cheerful, comical, droll, facetious, frolicsome, gladsome, gleeful, hilarious, jocund, jolly, jovial, joyous, light-hearted, lively, mirthful, sportive, sprightly, vivacious.

mess *n* company, set; farrago, hodgepodge, hotchpotch, jumble, medley, mass, melange, miscellany, mishmash, mixture; confusion, muddle, perplexity, pickle, plight, predicament.

message *n* communication, dispatch, intimation, letter, missive, notice, telegram, wire, word.

metaphorical *adj* allegorical, figurative, symbolic, symbolical.

method *n* course, manner, means, mode, procedure, process, rule, way; arrangement, classification, disposition, order, plan, regularity, scheme, system.

methodical *adj* exact, orderly, regular, systematic, systematical.

mettle *n* constitution, element, material, stuff; character, disposition, spirit, temper; ardour, courage, fire, hardihood, life, nerve, pluck, spirit, sprightliness, vigour.

mettlesome *adj* ardent, brisk, courageous, fiery, frisky, high-spirited, lively, spirited, sprightly.

microscopic *adj* infinitesimal, minute, tiny.

middle *adj* central, halfway, mean, medial, mid; intermediate, intervening. * *n* centre, halfway, mean, midst.

might *n* ability, capacity, efficacy, efficiency, force, main, power, prowess, puissance, strength.

mighty *adj* able, bold, courageous, potent,

powerful, puissant, robust, strong, sturdy, valiant, valorous, vigorous; bulky, enormous, huge, immense, monstrous, stupendous, vast.

mild *adj* amiable, clement, compassionate, gentle, indulgent, kind, merciful, pacific, tender; bland, gentle, pleasant, soft, suave; calm, gentle, kind, placid, pleasant, soft, tranquil; assuasive, demulcent, emollient, lenitive, mollifying, soothing.

militant *adj* belligerent, combative, contending, fighting.

military *adj* martial, soldier, soldierly, warlike. * *n* army, militia, soldiers.

mill *vb* comminute, crush, grate, grind, levigate, powder, pulverize. * *n* factory, manufactory; grinder; crowd, throng.

mimic *vb* ape, counterfeit, imitate, impersonate, mime, mock, parody. * *adj* imitative, mock, simulated. * *n* imitator, impersonator, mime, mocker, parodist, parrot.

mince[1] *vb* chop, cut, hash, shatter. * *n* forcemeat, hash, mash, mincemeat.

mince[2] *vb* attenuate, diminish, extenuate, mitigate, palliate, soften; pose, sashay, simper, smirk.

mind[1] *vb* attend, heed, mark, note, notice, regard, tend, watch; obey, observe, submit; design, incline, intend, mean; recall, recollect, remember, remind; beware, look out, watch out. * *n* soul, spirit; brains, common sense, intellect, reason, sense, understanding; belief, consideration, contemplation, judgement, opinion, reflection, sentiment, thought; memory, recollection, remembrance; bent, desire, disposition, inclination, intention, leaning, purpose, tendency, will.

mind[2] *vb* balk, begrudge, grudge, object, resent.

mindful *adj* attentive, careful, heedful, observant, regardful, thoughtful.

mindless *adj* dull, heavy, insensible, senseless, sluggish, stupid, unthinking; careless, forgetful, heedless, neglectful, negligent, regardless.

mine *vb* dig, excavate, quarry, unearth; sap, undermine, weaken; destroy, ruin. * *n* colliery, deposit, lode, pit, shaft.

mingle vb blend, combine, commingle, compound, intermingle, intermix, join, mix, unite.

miniature adj bantam, diminutive, little, small, tiny.

minister vb administer, afford, furnish, give, supply; aid, assist, contribute, help, succour. * n agent, assistant, servant, subordinate, underling; administrator, executive; ambassador, delegate, envoy, plenipotentiary; chaplain, churchman, clergyman, cleric, curate, divine, ecclesiastic, parson, pastor, preacher, priest, rector, vicar.

ministry n agency, aid, help, instrumentality, interposition, intervention, ministration, service, support; administration, cabinet, council, government.

minor adj less, smaller; inferior, junior, secondary, subordinate, younger; inconsiderable, petty, unimportant, small.

mint vb coin, stamp; fabricate, fashion, forge, invent, make, produce. * adj fresh, new, perfect, undamaged. * n die, punch, seal, stamp; fortune, (inf) heap, million, pile, wad.

minute¹ adj diminutive, fine, little, microscopic, miniature, slender, slight, small, tiny; circumstantial, critical, detailed, exact, fussy, meticulous, nice, particular, precise.

minute² n account, entry, item, memorandum, note, proceedings; record; instant, moment, second, trice, twinkling.

miracle n marvel, prodigy, wonder.

miraculous adj supernatural, thaumaturgic, thaumaturgical; amazing, extraordinary, incredible, marvellous, supernatural, unaccountable, unbelievable, wondrous.

mirror vb copy, echo, emulate, reflect, show. * n looking-glass, reflector, speculum; archetype, exemplar, example, model, paragon, pattern, prototype.

mirth n cheerfulness, festivity, frolic, fun, gaiety, gladness, glee, hilarity, festivity, jollity, joviality, joyousness, laughter, merriment, merry-making, rejoicing, sport.

misadventure n accident, calamity, catastrophe, cross, disaster, failure, ill-luck,

infelicity, mischance, misfortune, mishap, reverse.

miscellaneous adj confused, diverse, diversified, heterogeneous, indiscriminate, jumbled, many, mingled, mixed, promiscuous, stromatic, stromatous, various.

miscellany n collection, diversity, farrago, gallimaufry, hodgepodge, hotchpotch, jumble, medley, mishmash, melange, miscellaneous, mixture, variety.

mischief n damage, detriment, disadvantage, evil, harm, hurt, ill, injury, prejudice; ill-consequence, misfortune, trouble; devilry, wrong-doing.

mischievous adj destructive, detrimental, harmful, hurtful, injurious, noxious, pernicious; malicious, sinful, vicious, wicked; annoying, impish, naughty, troublesome, vexatious.

misconduct vb botch, bungle, misdirect, mismanage. * n bad conduct, ill-conduct, misbehaviour, misdemeanour, rudeness, transgression; ill-management, mismanagement.

misconstrue vb misread, mistranslate; misapprehend, misinterpret, mistake, misunderstand.

miser n churl, curmudgeon, lickpenny, money-grabber, niggard, pinch-fist, screw, scrimp, skinflint.

miserable adj afflicted, broken-hearted, comfortless, disconsolate, distressed, forlorn, heartbroken, unhappy, wretched; calamitous, hapless, ill-starred, pitiable, unfortunate, unhappy, unlucky, wretched; poor, valueless, worthless; abject, contemptible, despicable, low, mean, worthless.

miserly adj avaricious, beggarly, close, close-fisted, covetous, grasping, mean, niggardly, parsimonious, penurious, sordid, stingy, tight-fisted.

misery n affliction, agony, anguish, calamity, desolation, distress, grief, heartache, heavy-heartedness, misfortune, sorrow, suffering, torment, torture, tribulation, unhappiness, woe, wretchedness.

misfortune n adversity, affliction, bad luck, blow, calamity, casualty, catastrophe, disaster, distress, hardship, harm, ill, infliction, misadventure, mischance, mishap, reverse, scourge, stroke, trial, trouble, visitation.

misgiving *n* apprehension, distrust, doubt, hesitation, suspicion, uncertainty.

mishap *n* accident, calamity, disaster, ill luck, misadventure, mischance, misfortune.

mislead *vb* beguile, deceive, delude, misdirect, misguide.

misrepresent *vb* belie, caricature, distort, falsify, misinterpret, misstate, pervert.

miss¹ *vb* blunder, err, fail, fall short, forgo, lack, lose, miscarry, mistake, omit, overlook, trip; avoid, escape, evade, skip, slip; feel the loss of, need, want, wish. * *n* blunder, error, failure, fault, mistake, omission, oversight, slip, trip; loss, want.

miss² *n* damsel, girl, lass, maid, maiden.

mission *n* commission, legation; business, charge, commission, duty, errand, office, trust; delegation, deputation, embassy.

mist *vb* cloud, drizzle, mizzle, smog. * *n* cloud, fog, haze; bewilderment, obscurity, perplexity.

mistake *vb* misapprehend, miscalculate, misconceive, misjudge, misunderstand; confound, take; blunder, err. * *n* misapprehension, miscalculation, misconception, mistaking, misunderstanding; blunder, error, fault, inaccuracy, oversight, slip, trip.

mistaken *adj* erroneous, inaccurate, incorrect, misinformed, wrong.

mistrust *vb* distrust, doubt, suspect; apprehend, fear, surmise, suspect. * *n* doubt, distrust, misgiving, suspicion.

misty *adj* cloudy, clouded, dark, dim, foggy, obscure, overcast.

misunderstanding *n* error, misapprehension, misconception, mistake; difference, difficulty, disagreement, discord, dissension, quarrel.

misuse *vb* desecrate, misapply, misemploy, pervert, profane; abuse, ill-treat, maltreat, ill-use; fritter, squander, waste. * *n* abuse, perversion, profanation, prostitution; ill-treatment, ill-use, ill-usage, misusage; misapplication, solecism.

mitigate *vb* abate, alleviate, assuage, diminish, lessen, moderate, palliate, relieve; allay, appease, calm, mollify, pacify, quell, quiet, soften, soothe; moderate, temper; diminish, lessen.

mix *vb* alloy, amalgamate, blend, commingle, combine, compound, incorporate, interfuse, interlard, mingle, unite; associate, join, unite. * *n* alloy, amalgam, blend, combination, compound, mixture.

mixture *n* admixture, association, intermixture, union; compound, farrago, hash, hodgepodge, hotchpotch, jumble, medley, melange, mishmash; diversity, miscellany, variety.

moan *vb* bemoan, bewail, deplore, grieve, groan, lament, mourn, sigh, weep. * *n* groan, lament, lamentation, sigh, wail.

mob *vb* crowd, jostle, surround, swarm, pack, throng. * *n* assemblage, crowd, rabble, multitude, throng, tumult; dregs, canaille, populace, riffraff, scum.

mobile *adj* changeable, fickle, expressive, inconstant, sensitive, variable, volatile.

mock *vb* ape, counterfeit, imitate, mimic, take off; deride, flout, gibe, insult, jeer, ridicule, taunt; balk, cheat, deceive, defeat, disappoint, dupe, elude, illude, mislead. * *adj* assumed, clap-trap, counterfeit, fake, false, feigned, make-believe, pretended, spurious. * *n* fake, imitation, phoney, sham; gibe, insult, jeer, scoff, taunt.

mockery *n* contumely, counterfeit, deception, derision, imitation, jeering, mimicry, ridicule, scoffing, scorn, sham, travesty.

model *vb* design, fashion, form, mould, plan, shape. * *adj* admirable, archetypal, estimable, exemplary, ideal, meritorious, paradigmatic, praiseworthy, worthy. * *n* archetype, design, mould, original, pattern, protoplast, prototype, type; dummy, example, mould; copy, facsimile, image, imitation, representation.

moderate *vb* abate, allay, appease, assuage, blunt, dull, lessen, soothe, mitigate, mollify, pacify, quell, quiet, reduce, repress, soften, still, subdue; diminish, qualify, slacken, temper; control, govern, regulate. * *adj* abstinent, frugal, sparing, temperate; limited, mediocre, abstemious, sober; calm, cool, judicious, mild, reasonable, steady; gentle, mild, temperate.

moderation n abstemiousness, forbearance, frugality, restraint, sobriety, temperance; calmness, composure, coolness, deliberateness, equanimity, mildness, sedateness.

modern adj fresh, late, latest, new, novel, present, recent, up-to-date.

modest adj bashful, coy, diffident, humble, meek, reserved, retiring, shy, unassuming, unobtrusive, unostentatious, unpretending, unpretentious; chaste, proper, pure, virtuous; becoming, decent, moderate.

modification n alteration, change, qualification, reformation, variation; form, manner, mode, state.

modify vb alter, change, qualify, reform, shape, vary; lower, moderate, qualify, soften.

modish adj fashionable, stylish; ceremonious, conventional, courtly, genteel.

modulate vb attune, harmonize, tune; inflect, vary; adapt, adjust, proportion.

molest vb annoy, badger, bore, bother, chafe, discommode, disquiet, disturb, harass, harry, fret, gull, hector, incommode, inconvenience, irritate, oppress, pester, plague, tease, torment, trouble, vex, worry.

mollify vb soften; appease, calm, compose, pacify, quiet, soothe, tranquillize; abate, allay, assuage, blunt, dull, ease, lessen, mitigate, moderate, relieve, temper; qualify, tone down.

moment n flash, instant, jiffy, second, trice, twinkling, wink; avail, consequence, consideration, force, gravity, importance, significance, signification, value, weight; drive, force, impetus, momentum.

momentous adj grave, important, serious, significant, vital, weighty.

monarch n autocrat, despot; chief, dictator, emperor, king, potentate, prince, queen, ruler, sovereign.

monastic adj coenobitic, coenobitical, conventual, monkish, secluded.

moneyed, monied adj affluent, opulent, rich, well-off, well-to-do.

monitor vb check, observe, oversee, supervise, watch. * n admonisher, admonitor, adviser, counsellor, instructor, mentor, overseer.

monopolize vb control, dominate, engross, forestall.

monotonous adj boring, dull, tedious, tiresome, undiversified, uniform, unvaried, unvarying, wearisome.

monotony n boredom, dullness, sameness, tedium, tiresomeness, uniformity, wearisomeness.

monster adj enormous, gigantic, huge, immense, mammoth, monstrous. * n enormity, marvel, prodigy, wonder; brute, demon, fiend, miscreant, ruffian, villain, wretch.

monstrous adj abnormal, preternatural, prodigious, unnatural; colossal, enormous, extraordinary, huge, immense, prodigious, stupendous, vast; marvellous, strange, wonderful; dreadful, flagrant, frightful, hateful, hideous, horrible, shocking, terrible.

monument n memorial, record, remembrance, testimonial; cairn, cenotaph, gravestone, mausoleum, memorial, pillar, tomb, tombstone.

mood n disposition, humour, temper, vein.

moody adj capricious, humoursome, variable; angry, crabbed, crusty, fretful, ill-tempered, irascible, irritable, passionate, pettish, peevish, petulant, snappish, snarling, sour, testy; cross-grained, dogged, frowning, glowering, glum, intractable, morose, perverse, spleeny, stubborn, sulky, sullen, wayward; abstracted, gloomy, melancholy, pensive, sad, saturnine.

moral adj ethical, good, honest, honourable, just, upright, virtuous; abstract, ideal, intellectual, mental. * n intent, meaning, significance.

morals npl ethics, morality; behaviour, conduct, habits, manners.

morbid adj ailing, corrupted, diseased, sick, sickly, tainted, unhealthy, unsound, vitiated; depressed, downcast, gloomy, pessimistic, sensitive.

moreover adv, conj also, besides, further, furthermore, likewise, too.

morning n aurora, daybreak, dawn, morn, morningtide, sunrise.

morose adj austere, churlish, crabbed, crusty, dejected, desponding, downcast, downhearted, gloomy, glum, melancholy, moody, sad, severe, sour, sullen, surly.

morsel n bite, mouthful, titbit; bit, fragment, morceau, part, piece, scrap.

mortal adj deadly, destructive, fatal, final, human, lethal, perishable, vital. * n being, earthling, human, man, person, woman.

mortality n corruption, death, destruction, fatality.

mortify vb annoy, chagrin, depress, disappoint, displease, disquiet, dissatisfy, harass, humble, plague, vex, worry; abase, abash, confound, humiliate, restrain, shame, subdue; corrupt, fester, gangrene, putrefy.

mostly adv chiefly, customarily, especially, generally, mainly, particularly, principally.

motherly adj affectionate, kind, maternal, paternal, tender.

motion vb beckon, direct, gesture, signal. * n action, change, drift, flux, movement, passage, stir, transit; air, gait, port; gesture, impulse, prompting, suggestion; proposal, proposition.

motive adj activating, driving, moving, operative. * n cause, consideration, ground, impulse, incentive, incitement, inducement, influence, occasion, prompting, purpose, reason, spur, stimulus.

mould¹ vb carve, cast, fashion, form, make, model, shape. * n cast, character, fashion, form, matrix, pattern, shape; material, matter, substance; matrix, pattern.

mould² n blight, mildew, mouldiness, must, mustiness, rot; fungus, lichen, mushroom, puffball, rust, smut, toadstool; earth, loam, soil.

mouldy adj decaying, fusty, mildewed, musty.

mount¹ n hill, mountain, peak.

mount² vb arise, ascend, climb, rise, soar, tower; ascend, climb, escalate, scale;

embellish, ornament; bestride, get upon. * n charger, horse, ride, steed.

mountain n alp, height, hill, mount, peak; abundance, heap, mound, stack.

mourn vb bemoan, bewail, deplore, grieve, lament, sorrow, wail.

mournful adj afflicting, afflictive, calamitous, deplorable, distressed, grievous, lamentable, sad, woeful; doleful, heavy, heavy-hearted, lugubrious, melancholy, sorrowful, tearful.

mouth vb clamour, declaim, rant, roar, vociferate. * n chaps, jaws; aperture, opening, orifice; entrance, inlet; oracle, mouthpiece, speaker, spokesman.

move vb dislodge, drive, impel, propel, push, shift, start, stir; actuate, incite, instigate, rouse; determine, incline, induce, influence, persuade, prompt; affect, impress, stir, touch, trouble; agitate, awaken, excite, incense, irritate, rouse; propose, recommend, suggest; go, march, proceed, walk; act, live; flit, remove. * n action, motion, movement.

movement n change, move, motion, passage; emotion, motion; crusade, drive.

moving adj impelling, influencing, instigating, persuading, persuasive; affecting, impressive, pathetic, touching.

muddle vb confuse, disarrange, disorder; fuddle, inebriate, stupefy; muff, mull, spoil. * n confusion, disorder, mess, plight, predicament.

muddy vb dirty, foul, smear, soil; confuse, obscure. * adj dirty, foul, impure, slimy, soiled, turbid; bothered, confused, dull, heavy, stupid; confused, incoherent, obscure, vague.

muffle vb cover, envelop, shroud, wrap; conceal, disguise, involve; deaden, soften, stifle, suppress.

multiply vb augment, extend, increase, spread.

multitude n numerousness; host, legion; army, assemblage, assembly, collection, concourse, congregation, crowd, horde, mob, swarm, throng; commonality, herd, mass, pack, populace, rabble.

mundane adj earthly, secular, sublunary, temporal, terrene, terrestrial, worldly.

murder vb assassinate, butcher, destroy,

dispatch, kill, massacre, slaughter, slay; abuse, mar, spoil. * n assassination, butchery, destruction, homicide, killing, manslaughter, massacre.

murderer n assassin, butcher, cut-throat, killer, manslaughterer, slaughterer, slayer.

murderous adj barbarous, bloodthirsty, bloody, cruel, fell, sanguinary, savage.

murky adj cheerless, cloudy, dark, dim, dusky, gloomy, hazy, lowering, lurid, obscure, overcast.

murmur vb croak, grumble, mumble, mutter, rapine; hum, whisper. * n complaint, grumble, mutter, plaint, whimper; hum, undertone, whisper.

muscular adj sinewy; athletic, brawny, powerful, lusty, stalwart, stout, strong, sturdy, vigorous.

muse vb brood, cogitate, consider, contemplate, deliberate, dream, meditate, ponder, reflect, ruminate, speculate, think. * n abstraction, musing, revelry.

music n harmony, melody, symphony.

musical adj dulcet, harmonious, melodious, sweet, sweet-sounding, symphonious, tuneful.

musing adj absent-minded, meditative, preoccupied. * n absent-mindedness, abstraction, contemplation, daydreaming, meditation, muse, reflection, reverie, rumination.

muster vb assemble, collect, congregate, convene, convoke, gather, marshal, meet, rally, summon. * n assemblage, assembly, collection, congregation, convention, convocation, gathering, meeting, rally.

musty adj fetid, foul, fusty, mouldy, rank, sour, spoiled; hackneyed, old, stale, threadbare, trite; ill-favoured, insipid, stale, vapid; dull, heavy, rusty, spiritless.

mutable adj alterable, changeable, variable; changeful, fickle, inconstant, irresolute, mutational, unsettled, unstable, unsteady, vacillating, variable, wavering.

mute vb dampen, lower, moderate, muffle, soften. * adj dumb, voiceless; silent, speechless, still, taciturn.

mutilate vb cripple, damage, disable, disfigure, hamstring, injure, maim, mangle, mar.

mutinous adj contumacious, insubordinate, rebellious, refractory, riotous, tumultuous, turbulent, unruly; insurgent, seditious.

mutiny vb rebel, revolt, rise, resist. * n insubordination, insurrection, rebellion, revolt, revolution, riot, rising, sedition, uprising.

mutter vb grumble, muffle, mumble, murmur.

mutual adj alternate, common, correlative, interchangeable, interchanged, reciprocal, requited.

myriad adj innumerable, manifold, multitudinous, uncounted. * n host, million(s), multitude, score(s), sea, swarm, thousand(s).

mysterious adj abstruse, cabbalistic, concealed, cryptic, dark, dim, enigmatic, enigmatical, hidden, incomprehensible, inexplicable, inscrutable, mystic, mystical, obscure, occult, puzzling, recondite, secret, sphinx-like, unaccountable, unfathomable, unintelligible, unknown.

mystery n enigma, puzzle, riddle, secret; art, business, calling, trade.

mystical adj abstruse, cabbalistic, dark, enigmatical, esoteric, hidden, inscrutable, mysterious, obscure, occult, recondite, transcendental; allegorical, emblematic, emblematical, symbolic, symbolical.

mystify vb befog, bewilder, confound, confuse, dumbfound, embarrass, obfuscate, perplex, pose, puzzle.

myth n fable, legend, tradition; allegory, fiction, invention, parable, story; falsehood, fancy, figment, lie, untruth.

mythical adj allegorical, fabled, fabulous, fanciful, fictitious, imaginary, legendary, mythological.

N

nab vb catch, clutch, grasp, seize.

nag[1] vb carp, fuss, hector, henpeck, pester, torment, worry. * n nagger, scold, shrew, tartar.

nag[2] n bronco, crock, hack, horse, pony, scrag.

naive *adj* artless, candid, ingenuous, natural, plain, simple, unaffected, unsophisticated.

naked *adj* bare, nude, uncovered; denuded, unclad, unclothed, undressed; defenceless, exposed, open, unarmed, unguarded, unprotected; evident, manifest, open, plain, stark, unconcealed, undisguised; bare, mere, sheer, simple; bare, destitute, rough, rude, unfurnished, unprovided; plain, uncoloured, unexaggerated, unvarnished.

name *vb* call, christen, denounce, dub, entitle, phrase, style, term; mention; denominate, designate, indicate, nominate, specify. * *n* appellation, cognomen, denomination, designation, epithet, nickname, surname, sobriquet, title; character, credit, reputation, repute; celebrity, distinction, eminence, fame, honour, note, praise, renown.

narrate *vb* chronicle, describe, detail, enumerate, recite, recount, rehearse, relate, tell.

narrow *vb* confine, contract, cramp, limit, restrict, straiten. * *adj* circumscribed, confined, contracted, cramped, incapacious, limited, pinched, scanty, straitened; bigoted, hidebound, illiberal, ungenerous; close, near.

nasty *adj* defiled, dirty, filthy, foul, impure, loathsome, polluted, squalid, unclean; gross, impure, indecent, indelicate, lewd, loose, obscene, smutty, vile; disagreeable, disgusting, nauseous, odious, offensive, repulsive, sickening; aggravating, annoying, pesky, pestering, troublesome.

nation *n* commonwealth, realm, state; community, people, population, race, stock, tribe.

native *adj* aboriginal, autochthonal, autochthonous, domestic, home, indigenous, vernacular; genuine, intrinsic, natural, original, real; congenital, inborn, inbred, inherent, innate, natal, natural. * *n* aborigine, autochthon, inhabitant, national, resident.

natural *adj* indigenous, native, original; characteristic, essential, native; legitimate, normal, regular; artless, genuine,

ingenious, unreal, simple, spontaneous, unaffected; bastard, illegitimate.

nature *n* universe, world; character, constitution, essence; kind, quality, species, sort; disposition, grain, humour, mood, temper; being, intellect, intelligence, intelligent, mind.

naughty *adj* bad, corrupt, mischievous, perverse, worthless.

nauseous *adj* abhorrent, disgusting, distasteful, loathsome, offensive, repulsive, revolting, sickening.

naval *adj* marine, maritime, nautical.

navigate *vb* cruise, direct, guide, pilot, plan, sail, steer.

near *vb* approach, draw close. * *adj* adjacent, close, contiguous, neighbouring, nigh; approaching, forthcoming, imminent, impending; dear, familiar, intimate; close, direct, immediate, short, straight; accurate, close, literal; close, narrow, parsimonious.

nearly *adv* almost, approximately, wellnigh; closely, intimately, pressingly; meanly, parsimoniously, penuriously, stingily.

neat *adj* clean, cleanly, orderly, tidy, trim, unsoiled; nice, smart, spruce, trim; chaste, pure, simple; excellent, pure, unadulterated; adroit, clever, exact, finished; dainty, nice.

nebulous *adj* cloudy, hazy, misty.

necessary *adj* inevitable, unavoidable; essential, expedient, indispensable, needful, requisite; compelling, compulsory, involuntary. * *n* essential, necessity, requirement, requisite.

necessitate *vb* compel, constrain, demand, force, impel, oblige.

necessitous *adj* destitute, distressed, indigent, moneyless, needy, penniless, pinched, poor; destitute, narrow, pinching.

necessity *n* inevitability, inevitableness, unavoidability, unavoidableness; compulsion, destiny, fatality, fate; emergency, urgency; exigency, indigence, indispensability, indispensableness, need, needfulness, poverty, want; essentiality, essentialness, requirement, requisite.

need *vb* demand, lack, require, want. * *n*

emergency, exigency, extremity, necessity, strait, urgency, want; destitution, distress, indigence, neediness, penury, poverty, privation.

needless adj superfluous, unnecessary, useless.

needy adj destitute, indigent, necessitous, poor.

negation n denial, disavowal, disclaimer, rejection, renunciation.

neglect vb condemn, despise, disregard, forget, ignore, omit, overlook, slight. * n carelessness, default, failure, heedlessness, inattention, omission, remissness; disregard, disrespect, slight; indifference, negligence.

negligence n carelessness, disregard, heedlessness, inadvertency, inattention, indifference, neglect, remissness, slackness, thoughtlessness; defect, fault, inadvertence, omission, shortcoming.

negligent adj careless, heedless, inattentive, indifferent, neglectful, regardless, thoughtless.

negotiate vb arrange, bargain, deal, debate, sell, settle, transact, treat.

neighbourhood n district, environs, locality, vicinage, vicinity; adjacency, nearness, propinquity, proximity.

neighbourly adj attentive, civil, friendly, kind, obliging, social.

nerve vb brace, energize, fortify, invigorate, strengthen. * n force, might, power, strength, vigour; coolness, courage, endurance, firmness, fortitude, hardihood, manhood, pluck, resolution, self-command, steadiness.

nervous adj forcible, powerful, robust, strong, vigorous; irritable, fearful, shaky, timid, timorous, weak, weakly.

nestle vb cuddle, harbour, lodge, nuzzle, snug, snuggle.

nettle vb chafe, exasperate, fret, harass, incense, irritate, provoke, ruffle, sting, tease, vex.

neutral adj impartial, indifferent; colourless, mediocre.

neutralize vb cancel, counterbalance, counterpoise, invalidate, offset.

nevertheless adv however, nonetheless, notwithstanding, yet.

new adj fresh, latest, modern, novel, recent, unused; additional, another, further; reinvigorated, renovated, repaired.

nice adj accurate, correct, critical, definite, delicate, exact, exquisite, precise, rigorous, strict; dainty, difficult, exacting, fastidious, finical, punctilious, squeamish; discerning, discriminating, particular, precise, scrupulous; neat, tidy, trim; fine, minute, refined, subtle; dainty, delicate, delicious, luscious, palatable, savoury, soft, tender; agreeable, delightful, good, pleasant.

nicety n accuracy, exactness, niceness, precision, truth, daintiness, fastidiousness, squeamishness; discrimination, subtlety.

nimble adj active, agile, alert, brisk, lively, prompt, quick, speedy, sprightly, spry, swift, tripping.

noble adj dignified, elevated, eminent, exalted, generous, great, honourable, illustrious, magnanimous, superior, worthy; choice, excellent; aristocratic, gentle, high-born, patrician; grand, lofty, lordly, magnificent, splendid, stately. * n aristocrat, grandee, lord, nobleman, peer.

noise vb bruit, gossip, repeat, report, rumour. * n ado, blare, clamour, clatter, cry, din, fuss, hubbub, hullabaloo, outcry, pandemonium, racket, row, sound, tumult, uproar, vociferation.

noisy adj blatant, blustering, boisterous, brawling, clamorous, loud, uproarious, riotous, tumultuous, vociferous.

nomadic adj migratory, pastoral, vagrant, wandering.

nominal adj formal, inconsiderable, minimal, ostensible, pretended, professed, so-called, titular.

nominate vb appoint, choose, designate, name, present, propose.

nonchalant adj apathetic, careless, cool, indifferent, unconcerned.

nondescript adj amorphous, characterless, commonplace, dull, indescribable, odd, ordinary, unclassifiable, uninteresting, unremarkable.

nonentity n cipher, futility, inexistence, inexistency, insignificance, nobody, nonexistence, nothingness.

nonplus vb astonish, bewilder, confound, confuse, discomfit, disconcert, embarrass, floor, gravel, perplex, pose, puzzle.

nonsensical adj absurd, foolish, irrational, senseless, silly, stupid.

norm n model, pattern, rule, standard.

normal adj analogical, legitimate, natural, ordinary, regular, usual; erect, perpendicular, vertical.

notable adj distinguished, extraordinary, memorable, noted, remarkable, signal; conspicuous, evident, noticeable, observable, plain, prominent, striking; notorious, rare, well-known. * n celebrity, dignitary, notability, worthy.

note vb heed, mark, notice, observe, regard, remark; record, register; denote, designate. * n memorandum, minute, record; annotation, comment, remark, scholium; indication, mark, sign, symbol, token; account, bill, catalogue, reckoning; billet, epistle, letter; consideration, heed, notice, observation; celebrity, consequence, credit, distinction, eminence, fame, notability, notedness, renown, reputation, respectability; banknote, bill, promissory note; song, strain, tune, voice.

noted adj celebrated, conspicuous, distinguished, eminent, famed, famous, illustrious, notable, notorious, remarkable, renowned, well-known.

nothing n inexistence, nihilism, nihilist, nonentity, nonexistence, nothingness, nullity; bagatelle, trifle.

notice vb mark, note, observe, perceive, regard, see; comment on, mention, remark; attend to, heed. * n cognisance, heed, note, observation, regard; advice, announcement, information, intelligence, mention, news, notification; communication, intimation, premonition, warning; attention, civility, consideration, respect; comments, remarks.

notify vb advertise, announce, declare, publish, promulgate; acquaint, apprise, inform.

notion n concept, conception, idea; apprehension, belief, conceit, conviction, expectation, estimation, impression, judgement, opinion, sentiment, view.

notoriety n celebrity, fame, figure, name, note, publicity, reputation, repute, vogue.

notorious adj apparent, egregious, evident, notable, obvious, open, overt, manifest, patent, well-known; celebrated, conspicuous, distinguished, famed, famous, flagrant, infamous, noted, remarkable, renowned.

nourish vb feed, nurse, nurture; maintain, supply, support; breed, educate, instruct, train; cherish, encourage, foment, foster, promote, succour.

nourishment n aliment, diet, food, nutriment, nutrition, sustenance.

novel adj fresh, modern, new, rare, recent, strange, uncommon, unusual. * n fiction, romance, story, tale.

novice n convert, proselyte; initiate, neophyte, novitiate, probationer; apprentice, beginner, learner, tyro.

nude adj bare, denuded, exposed, naked, uncovered, unclothed, undressed.

nuisance n annoyance, bore, bother, infliction, offence, pest, plague, trouble.

nullify vb abolish, abrogate, annul, cancel, invalidate, negate, quash, repeal, revoke.

numb vb benumb, deaden, stupefy. * adj benumbed, deadened, dulled, insensible, paralysed.

number vb calculate, compute, count, enumerate, numerate, reckon, tell; account, reckon. * n digit, figure, numeral; horde, multitude, numerousness, throng; aggregate, collection, sum, total.

numerous adj abundant, many, numberless.

nuptial adj bridal, conjugal, connubial, hymeneal, matrimonial.

nuptials npl espousal, marriage, wedding.

nurse vb nourish, nurture; rear, suckle; cherish, encourage, feed, foment, foster, pamper, promote, succour; economize, manage; caress, dandle, fondle. * n auxiliary, orderly, sister; amah, au pair, babysitter, nanny, nursemaid, nurserymaid.

nurture vb feed, nourish, nurse, tend; breed, discipline, educate, instruct, rear, school, train. * n diet, food, nourishment; breeding, discipline, education, instruction, schooling, training, tuition; attention, nourishing, nursing.

nutrition *n* diet, food, nourishment, nutriment.

nutritious *adj* invigorating, nourishing, strengthening, supporting, sustaining.

O

oaf *n* blockhead, dolt, dunce, fool, idiot, simpleton.

oath *n* blasphemy, curse, expletive, imprecation, malediction; affirmation, pledge, promise, vow.

obdurate *adj* hard, harsh, rough, rugged; callous, cantankerous, dogged, firm, hardened, inflexible, insensible, obstinate, pigheaded, unfeeling, stubborn, unbending, unyielding; depraved, graceless, lost, reprobate, shameless, impenitent, incorrigible, irreclaimable.

obedience *n* acquiescence, agreement, compliance, duty, respect, reverence, submission, submissiveness, subservience.

obedient *adj* compliant, deferential, duteous, dutiful, observant, submissive, regardful, respectful, submissive, subservient, yielding.

obese *adj* corpulent, fat, fleshy, gross, plump, podgy, portly, stout.

obey *vb* comply, conform, heed, keep, mind, observe, submit, yield.

obfuscate *vb* cloud, darken, obscure; bewilder, confuse, muddle.

object[1] *vb* cavil, contravene, demur, deprecate, disapprove of, except to, impeach, oppose, protest, refuse.

object[2] *n* particular, phenomenon, precept, reality, thing; aim, butt, destination, end, mark, recipient, target; design, drift, goal, intention, motive, purpose, use, view.

objection *n* censure, difficulty, doubt, exception, protest, remonstrance, scruple.

obligation *n* accountability, accountableness, ableness, responsibility; agreement, bond, contract, covenant, engagement, stipulation; debt, indebtedness, liability.

obligatory *adj* binding, coercive, compulsory, enforced, necessary, unavoidable.

oblige *vb* bind, coerce, compel, constrain, force, necessitate, require; accommodate, benefit, convenience, favour, gratify, please; obligate, bind.

obliging *adj* accommodating, civil, complaisant, considerate, kind, friendly, polite.

oblique *adj* aslant, inclined, sidelong, slanting; indirect, obscure.

obliterate *vb* cancel, delete, destroy, efface, eradicate, erase, expunge.

oblivious *adj* careless, forgetful, heedless, inattentive, mindless, negligent, neglectful.

obnoxious *adj* blameworthy, censurable, faulty, reprehensible; hateful, objectionable, obscene, odious, offensive, repellent, repugnant, repulsive, unpleasant, unpleasing.

obscene *adj* broad, coarse, filthy, gross, immodest, impure, indecent, indelicate, ribald, unchaste, lewd, licentious, loose, offensive, pornographic, shameless, smutty; disgusting, dirty, foul.

obscure *vb* becloud, befog, cloud, darken, eclipse, dim, obfuscate, obnubilate, shade; conceal, cover, discover, hide. * *adj* dark, darksome, dim, dusky, gloomy, lurid, murky, rayless, shadowy, sombre, unenlightened, unilluminated; abstruse, blind, cabbalistic, difficult, doubtful, enigmatic, high, incomprehensible, indefinite, indistinct, intricate, involved, mysterious, mystic, recondite, undefined, unintelligible, vague; remote, secluded; humble, inglorious, nameless, renownless, undistinguished, unhonoured, unknown, unnoted, unnoticed.

obsequious *adj* cringing, deferential, fawning, flattering, servile, slavish, supple, subservient, sycophantic, truckling.

observant *adj* attentive, heedful, mindful, perceptive, quick, regardful, vigilant, watchful.

observation *n* attention, cognition, notice, observance; annotation, note, remark; experience, knowledge, note.

observe *vb* eye, mark, note, notice, remark, watch; behold, detect, discover, notice, perceive, see; express, mention, remark, say, utter; comply, follow, fulfil, obey; celebrate, keep, regard, solemnize.

obsolete adj ancient, antiquated, antique, archaic, disused, neglected, old, old-fashioned, obsolescent, out-of-date, past, passé, unfashionable.

obstacle n barrier, check, difficulty, hindrance, impediment, interference, interruption, obstruction, snag, stumbling block.

obstinate adj cross-grained, contumacious, dogged, firm, headstrong, inflexible, immovable, intractable, mulish, obdurate, opinionated, persistent, pertinacious, perverse, resolute, self-willed, stubborn, unyielding, wilful.

obstruct vb bar, barricade, block, blockade, block up, choke, clog, close, glut, jam, obturate, stop; hinder, impede, oppose, prevent, stop; arrest, check, embrace, interrupt, retard.

obstruction n bar, barrier, block, blocking, check, difficulty, hindrance, impediment, obstacle, stoppage; check, clog, embarrassment, hindrance, interruption, obturation.

obtain vb achieve, acquire, attain, bring, contrive, earn, elicit, gain, get, induce, procure, secure; hold, prevail, stand, subsist.

obtrusive adj forward, interfering, intrusive, meddling, officious.

obvious adj exposed, liable, open, subject; apparent, clear, distinct, evident, manifest, palatable, patent, perceptible, plain, self-evident, unmistakable, visible.

occasion vb breed, cause, create, originate, produce; induce, influence, move, persuade. * n casualty, event, incident, occurrence; conjuncture, convenience, juncture, opening, opportunity; condition, necessity, need, exigency, requirement, want; cause, ground, reason; inducement, influence; circumstance, exigency.

occasional adj accidental, casual, incidental, infrequent, irregular, uncommon; causative, causing.

occupation n holding, occupancy, possession, tenure, use; avocation, business, calling, craft, employment, engagement, job, post, profession, trade, vocation.

occupy vb capture, hold, keep, possess; cover, fill, garrison, inhabit, take up, tenant; engage, employ, use.

occur vb appear, arise, offer; befall, chance, eventuate, happen, result, supervene.

occurrence n accident, adventure, affair, casualty, event, happening, incident, proceeding, transaction.

odd adj additional, redundant, remaining; casual, incidental; inappropriate, queer, unsuitable; comical, droll, erratic, extravagant, extraordinary, fantastic, grotesque, irregular, peculiar, quaint, singular, strange, uncommon, uncouth, unique, unusual, whimsical.

odds npl difference, disparity, inequality; advantage, superiority, supremacy.

odious adj abominable, detestable, execrable, hateful, shocking; hated, obnoxious, unpopular; disagreeable, forbidding, loathsome, offensive.

odorous adj aromatic, balmy, fragrant, perfumed, redolent, scented, sweet-scented, sweet-smelling.

odour n aroma, fragrance, perfume, redolence, scent, smell.

offence n aggression, attack, assault; anger, displeasure, indignation, pique, resentment, umbrage, wrath; affront, harm, injury, injustice, insult, outrage, wrong; crime, delinquency, fault, misdeed, misdemeanour, sin, transgression, trespass.

offend vb affront, annoy, chafe, displease, fret, gall, irritate, mortify, nettle, provoke, vex; annoy, molest, pain, shock, wound; fall, sin, stumble, transgress.

offender n convict, criminal, culprit, delinquent, felon, malefactor, sinner, transgressor, trespasser.

offensive adj aggressive, attacking, invading; disgusting, loathsome, nauseating, nauseous, repulsive, sickening; abominable, detestable, disagreeable, displeasing, execrable, hateful, obnoxious, repugnant, revolting, shocking, unpalatable, unpleasant, repugnant; abusive, disagreeable, impertinent, insolent, insulting, irritating, opprobrious, rude, saucy, unpleasant. * n attack, onslaught.

offer vb present, proffer, tender; exhibit; furnish, propose, propound, show; volunteer; dare, essay, endeavour, venture. * n overture, proffering, proposal, proposition, tender, overture; attempt, bid, endeavour, essay.

offhand adj abrupt, brusque, casual, curt, extempore, impromptu, informal, unpremeditated, unstudied. * adv carelessly, casually, clumsily, haphazardly, informally, slapdash; ad-lib, extemporaneously, extemporarily, extempore, impromptu.

office n duty, function, service, work; berth, place, position, post, situation; business, capacity, charge, employment, function, service, trust; bureau, room.

officiate vb act, perform, preside, serve.

officious adj busy, dictatorial, forward, impertinent, interfering, intermeddling, meddlesome, meddling, obtrusive, pushing, pushy.

offset vb balance, counteract, counterbalance, counterpoise. * n branch, offshoot, scion, shoot, slip, sprout, twig; counterbalance, counterpoise, set-off, equivalent.

offspring n brood, children, descendants, issue, litter, posterity, progeny; cadet, child, scion.

often adv frequently, generally, oftentimes, repeatedly.

ogre n bugbear, demon, devil, goblin, hobgoblin, monster, spectre.

old adj aged, ancient, antiquated, antique, archaic, elderly, obsolete, olden, oldfashioned, superannuated; decayed, done, senile, worn-out; original, primitive, pristine; former, preceding, preexisting.

omen n augury, auspice, foreboding, portent, presage, prognosis, sign, warning.

ominous adj inauspicious, monitory, portentous, premonitory, threatening, unpropitious.

omission n default, failure, forgetfulness, neglect, oversight.

omit vb disregard, drop, eliminate, exclude, miss, neglect, overlook, skip.

omnipotent adj almighty, all-powerful.

onerous adj burdensome, difficult, hard, heavy, laborious, oppressive, responsible, weighty.

one-sided adj partial, prejudiced, unfair, unilateral, unjust.

only adj alone, single, sole, solitary. * adv barely, merely, simply.

onset n assault, attack, charge, onslaught, storm, storming.

ooze vb distil, drip, drop, shed; drain, exude, filter, leak, percolate, stain, transude. * n mire, mud, slime.

opaque adj dark, dim, hazy, muddy; abstruse, cryptic, enigmatic, enigmatical, obscure, unclear.

open vb expand, spread; begin, commence, initiate; disclose, exhibit, reveal, show; unbar, unclose, uncover, unlock, unseal, untie. * adj expanded, extended, unclosed, spread wide; aboveboard, artless, candid, cordial, fair, frank, guileless, hearty, honest, sincere, openhearted, single-minded, undesigning, undisguised, undissembling, unreserved; bounteous, bountiful, free, generous, liberal, munificent; ajar, unclosed, uncovered; exposed, undefended, unprotected; clear, unobstructed; accessible, public, unenclosed, unrestricted; mild, moderate; apparent, debatable, evident, obvious, patent, plain, undetermined.

opening adj commencing, first, inaugural, initiatory, introductory. * n aperture, breach, chasm, cleft, fissure, flaw, gap, gulf, hole, interspace, loophole, orifice, perforation, rent, rift; beginning, commencement, dawn; chance, opportunity, vacancy.

openly adv candidly, frankly, honestly, plainly, publicly.

operate vb act, function, work; cause, effect, occasion, produce; manipulate, use, run, work.

operation n manipulation, performance, procedure, proceeding, process; action, affair, manoeuvre, motion, movement.

operative adj active, effective, effectual, efficient, serviceable, vigorous; impor-

tant, indicative, influential, significant.
* n artisan, employee, labourer, mechanic, worker, workman.

opinion n conception, idea, impression, judgment, notion, sentiment, view; belief, persuasion, tenet; esteem, estimation, favourable judgment.

opinionated adj biased, bigoted, cocksure, conceited, dictatorial, dogmatic, opinionative, prejudiced, stubborn.

opponent adj adverse, antagonistic, contrary, opposing, opposite, repugnant. * n adversary, antagonist, competitor, contestant, counteragent, enemy, foe, opposite, opposer, party, rival.

opportune adj appropriate, auspicious, convenient, favourable, felicitous, fit, fitting, fortunate, lucky, propitious, seasonable, suitable, timely, well-timed.

opportunity n chance, convenience, moment, occasion.

oppose vb combat, contravene, counteract, dispute, obstruct, oppugn, resist, thwart, withstand; check, prevent, obstruct, withstand; confront, counterpoise.

opposite adj facing, fronting; conflicting, contradictory, contrary, different, diverse, incompatible, inconsistent, irreconcilable; adverse, antagonistic, hostile, inimical, opposed, opposing, repugnant. * n contradiction, contrary, converse, reverse.

opposition n antagonism, antimony, contrariety, inconsistency, repugnance; counteraction, counterinfluence, hostility, resistance; hindrance, obstacle, obstruction, oppression, prevention.

oppress vb burden, crush, depress, harass, load, maltreat, overburden, overpower, overwhelm, persecute, subdue, suppress, tyrannize, wrong.

oppression n abuse, calamity, cruelty, hardship, injury, injustice, misery, persecution, severity, suffering, tyranny; depression, dullness, heaviness, lassitude.

oppressive adj close, muggy, stifling, suffocating, sultry.

option n choice, discretion, election, preference, selection.

optional adj discretionary, elective, nonobligatory, voluntary.

opulent adj affluent, flush, luxurious, moneyed, plentiful, rich, sumptuous, wealthy.

oral adj nuncupative, spoken, verbal, vocal.

oration n address, declamation, discourse, harangue, speech.

orbit vb circle, encircle, revolve around. * n course, path, revolution, track.

ordain vb appoint, call, consecrate, elect, experiment, constitute, establish, institute, regulate; decree, enjoin, enact, order, prescribe.

order vb adjust, arrange, methodize, regulate, systematize; carry on, conduct, manage; bid, command, direct, instruct, require. * n arrangement, disposition, method, regularity, symmetry, system; law, regulation, rule; discipline, peace, quiet; command, commission, direction, injunction, instruction, mandate, prescription; class, degree, grade, kind, rank; family, tribe; brotherhood, community, class, fraternity, society; sequence, succession.

orderly adj methodical, regular, systematic; peaceable, quiet, well-behaved; neat, shipshape, tidy.

ordinary adj accustomed, customary, established, everyday, normal, regular, settled, wonted, everyday, regular; common, frequent, habitual, usual; average, commonplace, indifferent, inferior, mean, mediocre, second-rate, undistinguished; commonplace, homely, plain.

organization n business, construction, constitution, organism, structure, system.

organize vb adjust, constitute, construct, form, make, shape; arrange, coordinate, correlate, establish, systematize.

orgy n carousal, debauch, debauchery, revel, saturnalia.

origin n beginning, birth, commencement, cradle, derivation, foundation, fountain, fountainhead, original, rise, root, source, spring, starting point; cause, occasion; birth, heritage, lineage, parentage.

original adj aboriginal, first, primary, primeval, primitive, primordial, pristine; fresh, inventive, novel; eccentric, odd, peculiar. * n cause, commencement, origin, source, spring; archetype, exemplar, model, pattern, prototype, protoplast, type.

originate vb arise, begin, emanate, flow, proceed, rise, spring; create, discover, form, invent, produce.

ornament vb adorn, beautify, bedeck, bedizen, decorate, deck, emblazon, garnish, grace. * n adornment, bedizenment, decoration, design, embellishment, garnish, ornamentation.

ornate adj beautiful, bedecked, decorated, elaborate, elegant, embellished, florid, flowery, ornamental, ornamented.

orthodox adj conventional, correct, sound, true.

ostensible adj apparent, assigned, avowed, declared, exhibited, manifest, presented, visible; plausible, professed, specious.

ostentatious adj boastful, dashing, flaunting, pompous, pretentious, showy, vain, vainglorious; gaudy.

ostracize vb banish, boycott, exclude, excommunicate, exile, expatriate, expel, evict.

oust vb dislodge, dispossess, eject, evict, expel.

outbreak n ebullition, eruption, explosion, outburst; affray, broil, conflict, commotion, fray, riot, row; flare-up, manifestation.

outcast n exile, expatriate; castaway, pariah, reprobate, vagabond.

outcome n conclusion, consequence, event, issue, result, upshot.

outcry n cry, scream, screech, yell; bruit, clamour, noise, tumult, vociferation.

outdo vb beat, exceed, excel, outgo, outstrip, outvie, surpass.

outlandish adj alien, exotic, foreign, strange; barbarous, bizarre, queer, strange, uncouth.

outlaw vb ban, banish, condemn, exclude, forbid, make illegal, prohibit. * n bandit, brigand, crook, freebooter, highwayman, lawbreaker, marauder, robber, thief.

outline vb delineate, draft, draw, plan, silhouette, sketch. * n contour, profile; delineation, draft, drawing, plan, rough draft, silhouette, sketch.

outlive vb last, live longer, survive.

outlook n future, prospect, sight, view; lookout, watch-tower.

outrage vb abuse, injure, insult, maltreat, offend, shock, injure. * n abuse, affront, indignity, insult, offence.

outrageous adj abusive, frantic, furious, frenzied, mad, raging, turbulent, violent, wild; atrocious, enormous, flagrant, heinous, monstrous, nefarious, villainous; enormous, excessive, extravagant, unwarrantable.

outset n beginning, commencement, entrance, opening, start, starting point.

outspoken adj abrupt, blunt, candid, frank, plain, plainspoken, unceremonious, unreserved.

outstanding adj due, owing, uncollected, ungathered, unpaid, unsettled; conspicuous, eminent, prominent, striking.

outward adj exterior, external, outer, outside.

outwit vb cheat, circumvent, deceive, defraud, diddle, dupe, gull, outmanoeuvre, overreach, swindle, victimize.

overawe vb affright, awe, browbeat, cow, daunt, frighten, intimidate, scare, terrify.

overbalance vb capsize, overset, overturn, tumble, upset; outweigh, preponderate.

overbearing adj oppressive, overpowering; arrogant, dictatorial, dogmatic, domineering, haughty, imperious, overweening, proud, supercilious.

overcast vb cloud, darken, overcloud, overshadow, shade, shadow. * adj cloudy, darkened, hazy, murky, obscure.

overcome vb beat, choke, conquer, crush, defeat, discomfit, overbear, overmaster, overpower, overthrow, overturn, overwhelm, rout, subdue, subjugate, vanquish; conquer, prevail.

overflow vb brim over, fall over, pour over, pour out, shower, spill; deluge, inundate, submerge. * n deluge, inundation, profusion, superabundance.

overhaul vb overtake; check, examine, inspect, repair, survey. * n check, examination, inspection.

overlook vb inspect, oversee, superintend,

supervise; disregard, miss, neglect, slight; condone, excuse, forgive, pardon, pass over.

overreach *vb* cheat, circumvent, deceive, defraud, diddle, dupe, outwit, swindle, trick, victimize.

override *vb* outride, outweigh, pass, quash, supersede, surpass.

overrule *vb* control, govern, sway; annul, cancel, nullify, recall, reject, repeal, repudiate, rescind, revoke, reject, set aside, supersede, suppress.

oversight *n* care, charge, control, direction, inspection, management, superintendence, supervision, surveillance; blunder, error, fault, inadvertence, inattention, lapse, miss, mistake, neglect, omission, slip, trip.

overt *adj* apparent, glaring, open, manifest, notorious, patent, public, unconcealed.

overthrow *vb* overturn, upset, subvert; demolish, destroy, level; beat, conquer, crush, defeat, discomfit, foil, master, overcome, overpower, overwhelm, rout, subjugate, vanquish, worst. * *n* downfall, fall, prostration, subversion; destruction, demolition, ruin; defeat, discomfiture, dispersion, rout.

overturn *vb* invert, overthrow, reverse, subvert, upset.

overture *n* invitation, offer, proposal, proposition.

overwhelm *vb* drown, engulf, inundate, overflow, submerge, swallow up, swamp; conquer, crush, defeat, overbear, overcome, overpower, subdue, vanquish.

overwrought *adj* overdone, overelaborate; agitated, excited, overexcited, overworked, stirred.

own¹ *vb* have, hold, possess; acknowledge, avow, confess; acknowledge, admit, allow, concede, confess.

own² *adj* particular, personal, private.

P

pace *vb* go, hasten, hurry, move, step, walk. * *n* amble, gait, step, walk.

pacify *vb* appease, conciliate, harmonize, tranquillize; allay, appease, assuage, calm, compose, hush, lay, lull, moderate, mollify, quell, quiet, smooth, soften, soothe, still, tranquillize.

pack *vb* compact, compress, crowd, fill; bundle, burden, load, stow. * *n* bale, budget, bundle, package, packet, parcel; burden, load; assemblage, assembly, assortment, collection, set; band, bevy, clan, company, crew, gang, knot, lot, set, squad.

pact *n* agreement, alliance, bargain, bond, compact, concordat, contract, convention, covenant, league, stipulation.

pagan *adj* heathen, heathenish, idolatrous, irreligious, paganist, paganistic. * *n* gentile, heathen, idolater.

pain *vb* agonize, bite, distress, hurt, rack, sting, torment, torture; afflict, aggrieve, annoy, bore, chafe, displease, disquiet, distress, fret, grieve, harass, incommode, plague, tease, trouble, vex, worry; rankle, smart, shoot, sting, twinge. * *n* ache, agony, anguish, discomfort, distress, gripe, hurt, pang, smart, soreness, sting, suffering, throe, torment, torture, twinge; affliction, anguish, anxiety, bitterness, care, chagrin, disquiet, distress, dolour, grief, heartache, misery, punishment, solicitude, sorrow, trouble, uneasiness, unhappiness, vexation, woe, wretchedness.

painful *adj* agonizing, distressful, excruciating, racking, sharp, tormenting, torturing; afflicting, afflictive, annoying, baleful, disagreeable, displeasing, disquieting, distressing, dolorous, grievous, provoking, troublesome, unpleasant, vexatious; arduous, careful, difficult, hard, severe, sore, toilsome.

pains *npl* care, effort, labour, task, toilsomeness, trouble; childbirth, labour, travail.

painstaking *adj* assiduous, careful, conscientious, diligent, hardworking, industrious, laborious, persevering, plodding, sedulous, strenuous.

paint *vb* delineate, depict, describe, draw, figure, pencil, portray, represent, sketch; adorn, beautify, deck, embellish, ornament. * *n* colouring, dye, pigment, stain;

cosmetics, greasepaint, make-up.

pair vb couple, marry, mate, match. * n brace, couple, double, duo, match, two-some.

pal n buddy, chum, companion, comrade, crony, friend, mate, mucker.

pale vb blanch, lose colour, whiten. * adj ashen, ashy, blanched, bloodless, pallid, sickly, wan, white; blank, dim, obscure, spectral. * n picket, stake; circuit, enclosure; district, region, territory; boundary, confine, fence, limit.

pall n cloak, cover, curtain, mantle, pallium, shield, shroud, veil.

pall vb cloy, glut, gorge, satiate, surfeit; deject, depress, discourage, dishearten, dispirit; cloak, cover, drape, invest, overspread, shroud.

pallid adj ashen, ashy, cadaverous, colourless, pale, sallow, wan, whitish.

palpable adj corporeal, material, tactile, tangible; evident, glaring, gross, intelligible, manifest, obvious, patent, plain, unmistakable.

palpitate vb flutter, pulsate, throb; quiver, shiver, tremble.

paltry adj diminutive, feeble, inconsiderable, insignificant, little, miserable, petty, slender, slight, small, sorry, trifling, trivial, unimportant, wretched.

pamper vb baby, coddle, fondle, gratify, humour, spoil.

pang n agony, anguish, distress, gripe, pain, throe, twinge.

panic vb affright, alarm, scare, startle, terrify; become terrified, overreact. * n alarm, consternation, fear, fright, jitters, terror.

pant vb blow, gasp, puff; heave, palpitate, pulsate, throb; gasp, languish; desire, hunger, long, sigh, thirst, yearn. * n blow, gasp, puff.

parable n allegory, fable, story.

parade vb display, flaunt, show, vaunt. * n ceremony, display, flaunting, ostentation, pomp, show; array, pageant, review, spectacle; mall, promenade.

parallel vb be alike, compare, conform, correlate, match. * adj abreast, concurrent; allied, analogous, correspondent, equal, like, resembling, similar. * n con-formity, likeness, resemblance, similarity; analogue, correlative, counterpart.

paramount adj chief, dominant, eminent, pre-eminent, principal, superior, supreme.

paraphernalia n accoutrements, appendages, appurtenances, baggage, belongings, effects, equipage, equipment, ornaments, trappings.

parasite n bloodsucker, fawner, flatter, flunky, hanger-on, leech, spaniel, sycophant, toady, wheedler.

pardon vb condone, forgive, overlook, remit; absolve, acquit, clear, discharge, excuse, release. * n absolution, amnesty, condonation, discharge, excuse, forgiveness, grace, mercy, overlook, release.

parentage n ancestry, birth, descent, extraction, family, lineage, origin, parenthood, pedigree, stock.

parity n analogy, correspondence, equality, equivalence, likeness, sameness, similarity.

parody vb burlesque, caricature, imitate, lampoon, mock, ridicule, satirize, travesty. * n burlesque, caricature, imitation, ridicule, satire, travesty.

part vb break, dismember, dissever, divide, sever, subdivide, sunder; detach, disconnect, disjoin, dissociate, disunite, separate; allot, apportion, distribute, divide, mete, share; secrete. * n crumb, division, fraction, fragment, moiety, parcel, piece, portion, remnant, scrap, section, segment, subdivision; component, constituent, element, ingredient, member, organ; lot, share; concern, interest, participation; allotment, apportionment, dividend; business, charge, duty, function, office, work; concern, faction, interest, party, side; character, cue, lines, role; clause, paragraph, passage.

partial adj component, fractional, imperfect, incomplete, limited; biassed, influential, interested, one-sided, prejudiced, prepossessed, unfair, unjust, warped; fond, indulgent.

participate vb engage in, partake, perform, share.

particle n atom, bit, corpuscle, crumb,

drop, glimmer, grain, granule, iota, jot, mite, molecule, morsel, mote, scrap, shred, snip, spark, speck, whit.

particular adj especial, special, specific; distinct, individual, respective, separate; single, special; characteristic, distinctive, peculiar; individual, intimate, own, peculiar, personal, private; notable, noteworthy, special; circumstantial, definite, detailed, exact, minute, narrow, precise; careful, close, conscientious, critical, fastidious, nice, scrupulous, strict; marked, notable, odd, peculiar, singular, strange, uncommon. * n circumstance, detail, feature, instance, item, particularity, regard, respect.

parting adj breaking, dividing, separating; final, last, valedictory; declining, departing. * n breaking, disruption, rupture, severing; detachment, division, separation; death, departure, farewell, leave-taking.

partisan adj biased, factional, interested, partial, prejudiced. * n adherent, backer, champion, disciple, follower, supporter, votary.

partition vb apportion, distribute, divide, portion, separate, share. * n division, separation; barrier, division, screen, wall; allotment, apportionment, distribution.

partner n associate, colleague, copartner, partaker, participant, participator; accomplice, ally, coadjutor, confederate; companion, consort, spouse.

partnership n association, company, copartnership, firm, house, society; connection, interest, participation, union.

parts npl abilities, accomplishments, endowments, faculties, genius, gifts, intellect, intelligence, mind, qualities, powers, talents; districts, regions.

party n alliance, association, cabal, circle, clique, combination, confederacy, coterie, faction, group, junta, league, ring, set; body, company, detachment, squad, troop; assembly, company, gathering; partaker, participant, participator, sharer; defendant, litigant, plaintiff; individual, one, person, somebody; cause, division, interest, side.

pass¹ vb devolve, fall, go, move, proceed; change, elapse, flit, glide, lapse, slip; cease, die, fade, expire, vanish; happen, occur; convey, deliver, send, transmit, transfer; disregard, ignore, neglect; exceed, excel, surpass; approve, ratify, sanction; answer, do, succeed, suffice, suit; deliver, express, pronounce, utter; beguile, wile.

pass² n avenue, ford, road, route, way; defile, gorge, passage, ravine; authorization, licence, passport, permission, ticket; condition, conjecture, plight, situation, state; lunge, push, thrust, tilt; transfer, trick.

passable adj admissible, allowable, mediocre, middling, moderate, ordinary, soso, tolerable; acceptable, current, receivable; navigable, traversable.

passage n going, passing, progress, transit; evacuation, journey, migration, transit, voyage; avenue, channel, course, pass, path, road, route, thoroughfare, vennel, way; access, currency, entry, reception; act, deed, event, feat, incidence, occurrence, passion; corridor, gallery, gate, hall; clause, paragraph, sentence, text; course, death, decease, departure, expiration, lapse; affair, brush, change, collision, combat, conflict, contest, encounter, exchange, joust, pass, skirmish, tilt.

passenger n fare, itinerant, tourist, traveller, voyager, wayfarer.

passionate adj animated, ardent, burning, earnest, enthusiastic, excited, fervent, fiery, furious, glowing, hot-blooded, impassioned, impetuous, impulsive, intense, vehement, warm, zealous; hotheaded, irascible, quick-tempered, tempestuous, violent.

passive adj inactive, inert, quiescent, receptive; apathetic, enduring, long-suffering, nonresistant, patient, stoical, submissive, suffering, unresisting.

past adj accomplished, elapsed, ended, gone, spent; ancient, bygone, former, obsolete, outworn. * adv above, extra, beyond, over. * prep above, after, beyond, exceeding. * n antiquity, heretofore, history, olden times, yesterday.

pastime n amusement, diversion, entertainment, hobby, play, recreation, sport.

pat¹ vb dab, hit, rap, tap; caress, chuck, fondle, pet. * n dab, hit, pad, rap, tap; caress.

pat² adj appropriate, apt, fit, pertinent, suitable. * adv aptly, conveniently, fitly, opportunely, seasonably.

patch vb mend, repair. * n patch, repair; parcel, plot, tract.

patent adj expanded, open, spreading; apparent, clear, conspicuous, evident, glaring, indisputable, manifest, notorious, obvious, public, open, palpable, plain, unconcealed, unmistakable. * n copyright, privilege, right.

path n access, avenue, course, footway, passage, pathway, road, route, track, trail, way.

pathetic adj affecting, melting, moving, pitiable, plaintive, sad, tender, touching.

patience n endurance, fortitude, long-sufferance, resignation, submission, sufferance; calmness, composure, quietness; forbearance, indulgence, leniency; assiduity, constancy, diligence, indefatigability, indefatigableness, perseverance, persistence.

patient adj meek, passive, resigned, submissive, uncomplaining, unrepining; calm, composed, contented, quiet; indulgent, lenient, long-suffering; assiduous, constant, diligent, indefatigable, persevering, persistent. * n case, invalid, subject, sufferer.

patron n advocate, defender, favourer, guardian, helper, protector, supporter.

pattern vb copy, follow, imitate. * n archetype, exemplar, last, model, original, paradigm, plan, prototype; example, guide, sample, specimen; mirror, paragon; design, figure, shape, style, type.

pause vb breathe, cease, delay, desist, rest, stay, stop, wait; delay, forbear, intermit, stay, stop, tarry, wait; deliberate, demur, hesitate, waver. * n break, caesura, cessation, halt, intermission, interruption, interval, remission, rest, stop, stoppage, stopping, suspension; hesitation, suspense, uncertainty; break, paragraph.

pawn¹ n cat's-paw, dupe, plaything, puppet, stooge, tool, toy

pawn² vb bet, gage, hazard, lay, pledge, risk, stake, wager. * n assurance, bond, guarantee, pledge, security.

pay vb defray, discharge, discount, foot, honour, liquidate, meet, quit, settle; compensate, recompense, reimburse, requite, reward; punish, revenge; give, offer, render. * n allowance, commission, compensation, emolument, hire, recompense, reimbursement, remuneration, requital, reward, salary, wages.

peace n calm, calmness, quiet, quietness, repose, stillness; accord, amity, friendliness, harmony; composure, equanimity, imperturbability, placidity, quietude, tranquillity; accord, agreement, armistice.

peaceable adj pacific, peaceful; amiable, amicable, friendly, gentle, inoffensive, mild; placid, peaceful, quiet, serene, still, tranquil, undisturbed, unmoved.

peaceful adj quiet, undisturbed; amicable, concordant, friendly, gentle, harmonious, mild, pacific, peaceable; calm, composed, placid, serene, still.

peak vb climax, culminate, top; dwindle, thin. * n acme, apex, crest, crown, pinnacle, summit, top, zenith.

peculiar adj appropriate, idiosyncratic, individual, proper; characteristic, eccentric, exceptional, extraordinary, odd, queer, rare, singular, strange, striking, uncommon, unusual; individual, especial, particular, select, special, specific.

peculiarity n appropriateness, distinctiveness, individuality, speciality; characteristic, idiosyncrasy, individuality, peculiarity, singularity, speciality.

pedantic adj conceited, fussy, officious, ostentatious, over-learned, particular, pedagogical, pompous, pragmatical, precise, pretentious, priggish, stilted.

pedigree adj purebred, thoroughbred. * n ancestry, breed, descent, extraction, family, genealogy, house, line, lineage, race, stock, strain.

peer¹ vb gaze, look, peek, peep, pry, squinny, squint; appear, emerge.

peer² n associate, co-equal, companion, compeer, equal, equivalent, fellow, like, mate, match; aristocrat, baron, count, duke, earl, grandee, lord, marquis, noble, nobleman, viscount.

pelt¹ *vb* assail, batter, beat, belabour, bombard, pepper, stone, strike; cast, hurl, throw; hurry, rush, speed, tear.

pelt² *n* coat, hide, skin.

pen¹ *vb* compose, draft, indite, inscribe, write.

pen² *vb* confine, coop, encage, enclose, impound, imprison, incarcerate. * *n* cage, coop, corral, crib, hutch, enclosure, paddock, pound, stall, sty.

penalty *n* chastisement, fine, forfeiture, mulct, punishment, retribution.

penetrate *vb* bore, burrow, cut, enter, invade, penetrate, percolate, perforate, pervade, pierce, soak, stab; affect, sensitize, touch; comprehend, discern, perceive, understand.

penetrating *adj* penetrative, permeating, piercing, sharp, subtle; acute, clearsighted, discerning, intelligent, keen, quick, sagacious, sharp-witted, shrewd.

penetration *n* acuteness, discernment, insight, sagacity.

penitent *adj* compunctious, consciousstricken, contrite, regretful, remorseful, repentant, sorrowing, sorrowful. * *n* penance-doer, penitentiary, repentant.

penniless *adj* destitute, distressed, impecunious, indigent, moneyless, pinched, poor, necessitous, needy, pensive, poverty-stricken, reduced.

pensive *adj* contemplative, dreamy, meditative, reflective, sober, thoughtful; grave, melancholic, melancholy, mournful, sad, serious, solemn.

people *vb* colonize, inhabit, populate. * *n* clan, country, family, nation, race, state, tribe; folk, humankind, persons, population, public; commons, community, democracy, populace, proletariat; mob, multitude, rabble.

perceive *vb* behold, descry, detect, discern, discover, discriminate, distinguish, note, notice, observe, recognize, remark, see, spot; appreciate, comprehend, know, understand.

perceptible *adj* apparent, appreciable, cognizable, discernible, noticeable, perceivable, understandable, visible.

perception *n* apprehension, cognition, discernment, perceiving, recognition, seeing; apprehension, comprehension, conception, consciousness, discernment, perceptiveness, perceptivity, understanding, feeling.

peremptory *adj* absolute, authoritative, categorical, commanding, decisive, express, imperative, imperious, positive; determined, resolute, resolved; arbitrary, dogmatic, incontrovertible.

perennial *adj* ceaseless, constant, continual, deathless, enduring, immortal, imperishable, lasting, never-failing, permanent, perpetual, unceasing, undying, unfailing, uninterrupted.

perfect *vb* accomplish, complete, consummate, elaborate, finish. * *adj* completed, finished; complete, entire, full, utter, whole; capital, complete, consummate, excellent, exquisite, faultless, ideal; accomplished, disciplined, expert, skilled; blameless, faultless, holy, immaculate, pure, spotless, unblemished.

perfection *n* completeness, completion, consummation, correctness, excellence, faultlessness, finish, maturity, perfection, perfectness, wholeness; beauty, quality.

perform *vb* accomplish, achieve, compass, consummate, do, effect, transact; complete, discharge, execute, fulfil, meet, observe, satisfy; act, play, represent.

performance *n* accomplishment, achievement, completion, consummation, discharge, doing, execution, fulfilment; achievement, act, action, deed, exploit, feat, work; composition, production; acting, entertainment, exhibition, play, representation, hold; execution, playing.

perfume *n* aroma, balminess, bouquet, fragrance, incense, odour, redolence, scent, smell, sweetness.

perfunctory *adj* careless, formal, heedless, indifferent, mechanical, negligent, reckless, slight, slovenly, thoughtless, unmindful.

perhaps *adv* haply, peradventure, perchance, possibly.

peril *vb* endanger, imperil, jeopardize,

risk. * n danger, hazard, insecurity, jeopardy, pitfall, risk, snare, uncertainty.

perilous adj dangerous, hazardous, risky, unsafe.

period n aeon, age, cycle, date, eon, epoch, season, span, spell, stage, term, time; continuance, duration; bound, conclusion, determination, end, limit, term, termination; clause, phrase, proposition, sentence.

periodical adj cyclical, incidental, intermittent, recurrent, recurring, regular, seasonal, systematic. * n magazine, paper, review, serial, weekly.

periphery n boundary, circumference, outside, perimeter, superficies, surface.

perish vb decay, moulder, shrivel, waste, wither; decease, die, expire, vanish.

perishable adj decaying, decomposable, destructible; dying, frail, mortal, temporary.

permanent adj abiding, constant, continuing, durable, enduring, fixed, immutable, invariable, lasting, perpetual, persistent, stable, standing, steadfast, unchangeable, unchanging, unfading, unmovable.

permissible adj admissible, allowable, free, lawful, legal, legitimate, proper, sufferable, unprohibited.

permission n allowance, authorization, consent, dispensation, leave, liberty, licence, permit, sufferance, toleration, warrant.

permit vb agree, allow, endure, let, suffer, tolerate; admit, authorize, consent, empower, license, warrant. * n leave, liberty, licence, passport, permission, sanction, warrant.

perpetrate vb commit, do, execute, perform.

perpetual adj ceaseless, continual, constant, endless, enduring, eternal, everenduring, everlasting, incessant, interminable, never-ceasing, never-ending, perennial, permanent, sempiternal, unceasing, unending, unfailing, uninterrupted.

perplex vb complicate, encumber, entangle, involve, snarl, tangle; beset, bewilder, confound, confuse, corner, distract,

embarrass, fog, mystify, nonplus, pother, puzzle, set; annoy, bother, disturb, harass, molest, pester, plague, tease, trouble, vex, worry.

persecute vb afflict, distress, harass, molest, oppress, worry; annoy, beset, importune, pester, solicit, tease.

persevere vb continue, determine, endure, maintain, persist, remain, resolve, stick.

persist vb continue, endure, last, remain; insist, persevere.

persistent adj constant, continuing, enduring, fixed, immovable, persevering, persisting, steady, tenacious; contumacious, dogged, indefatigable, obdurate, obstinate, pertinacious, perverse, pigheaded, stubborn.

personable adj comely, good-looking, graceful, seemly, well-turned-out.

personal adj individual, peculiar, private, special; bodily, corporal, corporeal, exterior, material, physical.

perspective n panorama, prospect, view, vista; proportion, relation.

perspire vb exhale, glow, sweat, swelter.

persuade vb allure, actuate, entice, impel, incite, induce, influence, lead, move, prevail upon, urge; advise, counsel, convince, satisfy; inculcate, teach.

persuasion n incitement, inducement, influence; belief, conviction, opinion; belief, conviction, creed, doctrine, dogma, tenet; kind, sort.

persuasive adj cogent, convincing, inducing, inducible, logical, persuading, plausible, sound, valid, weighty.

pert adj brisk, dapper, lively, nimble, smart, sprightly, perky; bold, flippant, forward, free, impertinent, impudent, malapert, presuming, smart, saucy.

pertinent adj adapted, applicable, apposite, appropriate, apropos, apt, fit, germane, pat, proper, relevant, suitable; appurtenant, belonging, concerning, pertaining, regarding.

perturb vb agitate, disquiet, distress, disturb, excite, trouble, unsettle, upset, vex, worry; confuse, disturb.

pervade vb affect, animate, diffuse, extend, fill, imbue, impregnate, infiltrate, penetrate, permeate.

perverse *adj* bad, disturbed, oblique, perverted; contrary, dogged, headstrong, mulish, obstinate, pertinacious, perversive, stubborn, ungovernable, intractable, unyielding, wayward, wilful; cantankerous, churlish, crabbed, cross, cross-grained, crusty, cussed, morose, peevish, petulant, snappish, snarling, spiteful, spleeny, surly, testy, touchy, wicked, wrong-headed; inconvenient, troublesome, untoward, vexatious.

perversion *n* abasement, corruption, debasement, impairment, injury, prostitution, vitiation.

perverted *adj* corrupt, debased, distorted, evil, impaired, misguiding, vitiated, wicked.

pessimistic *adj* cynical, dark, dejected, depressed, despondent, downhearted, gloomy, glum, melancholy, melancholic, morose, sad.

pest *n* disease, epidemic, infection, pestilence, plague; annoyance, bane, curse, infliction, nuisance, scourge, trouble.

pestilent *adj* contagious, infectious, malignant, pestilential; deadly, evil, injurious, malign, mischievous, noxious, poisonous; annoying, corrupt, pernicious, troublesome, vexatious.

petition *vb* ask, beg, crave, entreat, pray, solicit, sue, supplicate. * *n* address, appeal, application, entreaty, prayer, request, solicitation, supplication, suit.

petrify *vb* calcify, fossilize, lapidify; benumb, deaden; amaze, appal, astonish, astound, confound, dumbfound, paralyse, stun, stupefy.

petty *adj* diminutive, frivolous, inconsiderable, inferior, insignificant, little, mean, slight, small, trifling, trivial, unimportant.

petulant *adj* acrimonious, captious, cavilling, censorious, choleric, crabbed, cross, crusty, forward, fretful, hasty, ill-humoured, ill-tempered, irascible, irritable, peevish, perverse, pettish, querulous, snappish, snarling, testy, touchy, waspish.

phantom *n* apparition, ghost, illusion, phantasm, spectre, vision, wraith.

phenomenal *adj* marvellous, miraculous, prodigious, wondrous.

philanthropy *n* alms-giving, altruism, benevolence, charity, grace, humanitarianism, humanity, kindness.

philosophical, philosophic *adj* rational, reasonable, sound, wise; calm, collected, composed, cool, imperturbable, sedate, serene, stoical, tranquil, unruffled.

phlegmatic *adj* apathetic, calm, cold, cold-blooded, dull, frigid, heavy, impassive, indifferent, inert, sluggish, stoical, tame, unfeeling.

phobia *n* aversion, detestation, dislike, distaste, dread, fear, hatred.

phrase *vb* call, christen, denominate, designate, describe, dub, entitle, name, style. * *n* diction, expression, phraseology, style.

physical *adj* material, natural; bodily, corporeal, external, substantial, tangible, sensible.

pick *vb* peck, pierce, strike; cut, detach, gather, pluck; choose, cull, select; acquire, collect, get; pilfer, steal. * *n* pickaxe, pike, spike, toothpick.

picture *vb* delineate, draw, imagine, paint, represent. * *n* drawing, engraving, painting, print; copy, counterpart, delineation, embodiment, illustration, image, likeness, portraiture, portrayal, semblance, representation, resemblance, similitude; description, representation.

picturesque *adj* beautiful, charming, colourful, graphic, scenic, striking, vivid.

piece *vb* mend, patch, repair; augment, complete, enlarge, increase; cement, join, unite. * *n* amount, bit, chunk, cut, fragment, hunk, part, quantity, scrap, shred, slice; portion; article, item, object; composition, lucubration, work, writing.

pierce *vb* gore, impale, pink, prick, stab, transfix; bore, drill, excite, penetrate, perforate, puncture; affect, move, rouse, strike, thrill, touch.

piety *n* devotion, devoutness, holiness, godliness, grace, religion, sanctity.

pile¹ *vb* accumulate, amass; collect, gather, heap, load. * *n* accumulation, collection, heap, mass, stack; fortune, wad; building, edifice, erection, fabric, pyramid, skyscraper, structure, tower; reactor, nuclear reactor.

pile² n beam, column, pier, pillar, pole, post.

pile³ n down, feel, finish, fur, fluff, fuzz, grain, nap, pappus, shag, surface, texture.

pilfer vb filch, purloin, rob, steal, thieve.

pilgrim n journeyer, sojourner, traveller, wanderer, wayfarer; crusader, devotee, palmer.

pilgrimage n crusade, excursion, expedition, journey, tour, trip.

pillar n column, pier, pilaster, post, shaft, stanchion; maintainer, prop, support, supporter, upholder.

pilot vb conduct, control, direct, guide, navigate, steer. * adj experimental, model, trial. * n helmsman, navigator, steersman; airman, aviator, conductor, director, flier, guide.

pinch vb compress, contract, cramp, gripe, nip, squeeze; afflict, distress, famish, oppress, straiten, stint; frost, nip; apprehend, arrest; economize, spare, stint. * n gripe, nip; pang, throe; crisis, difficulty, emergency, exigency, oppression, pressure, push, strait, stress.

pine vb decay, decline, droop, fade, flag, languish, waste, wilt, wither; desire, long, yearn.

pinnacle n minaret, turret; acme, apex, height, peak, summit, top, zenith.

pious adj filial; devout, godly, holy, religious, reverential, righteous, saintly.

pirate vb copy, crib, plagiarize, reproduce, steal. * n buccaneer, corsair, freebooter, marauder, picaroon, privateer, seadog, sea-robber, sea-rover, sea wolf.

pit vb match, oppose; dent, gouge, hole, mark, nick, notch, scar. * n cavity, hole, hollow; crater, dent, depression, dint, excavation, well; abyss, chasm, gulf; pitfall, snare, trap; auditorium, orchestra.

pitch vb fall, lurch, plunge, reel; light, settle, rest; cast, dart, fling, heave, hurl, lance, launch, plunge, send, toss, throw; erect, establish, fix, locate, place, plant, set, settle, station. * n degree, extent, height, intensity, measure, modulation, rage, rate; declivity, descent, inclination,

slope; cast, jerk, plunge, throw, toss; place, position, spot; field, ground; line, patter.

piteous adj affecting, distressing, doleful, grievous, mournful, pathetic, rueful, sorrowful, woeful; deplorable, lamentable, miserable, pitiable, wretched; compassionate, tender.

pithy adj cogent, energetic, forcible, powerful; compact, concise, brief, laconic, meaty, pointed, short, sententious, substantial, terse; corky, porous.

pitiable adj deplorable, lamentable, miserable, pathetic, piteous, pitiable, woeful, wretched; abject, base, contemptible, despicable, disreputable, insignificant, low, paltry, mean, rascally, sorry, vile, worthless.

pitiful adj compassionate, kind, lenient, merciful, mild, sympathetic, tender, tenderhearted; deplorable, lamentable, miserable, pathetic, piteous, pitiable, wretched; abject, base, contemptible, despicable, disreputable, insignificant, mean, paltry, rascally, sorry, vile, worthless.

pitiless adj cruel, hardhearted, implacable, inexorable, merciless, unmerciful, relentless, remorseless, unfeeling, unpitying, unrelenting, unsympathetic.

pity vb commiserate, condole, sympathize. * n clemency, commiseration, compassion, condolence, fellow-feeling, grace, humanity, leniency, mercy, quarter, sympathy, tenderheartedness.

place vb arrange, bestow, commit, deposit, dispose, fix, install, lay, locate, lodge, orient, orientate, pitch, plant, pose, put, seat, set, settle, situate, stand, station, rest; allocate, arrange, class, classify, identify, order, organize, recognize; appoint, assign, commission, establish, induct, nominate. * n area, courtyard, square; bounds, district, division, locale, locality, location, part, position, premises, quarter, region, scene, site, situation, spot, station, tract, whereabouts; calling, charge, employment, function, occupation, office, pitch, post; calling, condition, grade, precedence, rank, sphere, stakes, standing; abode, building, dwelling, habitation, mansion, residence, seat; city, town, village; fort, fortress, stronghold; paragraph, part, passage, portion; ground, occasion, opportunity, reason, room; lieu, stead.

placid *adj* calm, collected, composed, cool, equable, gentle, peaceful, quiet, serene, tranquil, undisturbed, unexcitable, unmoved, unruffled; halcyon, mild, serene.

plague *vb* afflict, annoy, badger, bore, bother, pester, chafe, disquiet, distress, disturb, embarrass, harass, fret, gall, harry, hector, incommode, irritate, molest, perplex, tantalize, tease, torment, trouble, vex, worry. * *n* disease, pestilence, pest; affliction, annoyance, curse, molestation, nuisance, thorn, torment, trouble, vexation, worry.

plain *adj* dull, even, flat, level, plane, smooth, uniform; clear, open, unencumbered, uninterrupted; apparent, certain, clear, conspicuous, evident, distinct, glaring, manifest, notable, notorious, obvious, open, overt, palpable, patent, unmistakable, transparent, visible; explicit, intelligible, perspicuous, unambiguous, unequivocal; homely, ugly; aboveboard, blunt, crude, candid, direct, downright, frank, honest, ingenuous, open, openhearted, sincere, single-minded, straightforward, undesigning, unreserved, unsophisticated: artless, common, natural, simple, unaffected, unlearned, unsophisticated; absolute, mere, unmistakable; clear, direct, easy; frugal, homely, simple; artless, natural, simple, unaffected, unlearned; unadorned, unfigured, unornamented, unvariegated. * *n* grassland, plateau, prairie, steppe.

plan *vb* arrange, calculate, concert, delineate, devise, diagram, figure, premeditate, project, represent, study; concoct, conspire, contrive, design, digest, hatch, invent, manoeuvre, machinate, plot, prepare, project, scheme. * *n* chart, delineation, diagram, draught, drawing, layout, map, plot, sketch; arrangement, conception, contrivance, design, device, idea, method, programme, project, proposal, proposition, scheme, system; ca-

bal, conspiracy, intrigue, machination; custom, process, way.

plane *vb* flatten, even, level, smooth; float, fly, glide, skate, skim, soar. * *adj* even, flat, horizontal, level, smooth. * *n* degree, evenness, level, levelness, smoothness; aeroplane, aircraft; groover, jointer, rabbet, rebate, scraper.

plant *vb* bed, sow; breed, engender; direct, point, set; colonize, furnish, inhabit, settle; establish, introduce; deposit, establish, fix, found, hide. * *n* herb, organism, vegetable; establishment, equipment, factory, works.

plaster *vb* bedaub, coat, cover, smear, spread. * *n* cement, gypsum, mortar, stucco.

plastic *adj* ductile, flexible, formative, mouldable, pliable, pliant, soft.

platitude *n* dullness, flatness, insipidity, mawkishness; banality, commonplace, truism; balderdash, chatter, flummery, fudge, jargon, moonshine, nonsense, palaver, stuff, trash, twaddle, verbiage.

plausible *adj* believable, credible, probable, reasonable; bland, fair-spoken, glib, smooth, suave.

play *vb* caper, disport, frisk, frolic, gambol, revel, romp, skip, sport; dally, flirt, idle, toy, trifle, wanton; flutter, hover, wave; act, impersonate, perform, personate, represent; bet, gamble, stake, wager. * *n* amusement, exercise, frolic, gambols, game, jest, pastime, prank, romp, sport; gambling, gaming; act, comedy, drama, farce, performance, tragedy; action, motion, movement; elbowroom, freedom, latitude, movement, opportunity, range, scope, sweep, swing, use.

playful *adj* frisky, frolicsome, gamesome, jolly, kittenish, merry, mirthful, rollicking, sportive; amusing, arch, humorous, jolly, lively, mirthful, mischievous, roguish, sprightly, vivacious.

plead *vb* answer, appeal, argue, reason; argue, defend, discuss, reason, rejoin; appeal, beg, beseech, entreat, implore, petition, sue, supplicate.

pleasant *adj* acceptable, agreeable, delectable, delightful, enjoyable, grateful, gratifying, nice, pleasing, pleasurable, prepossessing, seemly, welcome; cheerful, enlivening, good-humoured, gracious, likable, lively, merry, sportive, sprightly, vivacious; amusing, facetious, humorous, jocose, jocular, sportive, witty.

please *vb* charm, delight, elate, gladden, gratify, pleasure, rejoice; content, oblige, satisfy; choose, like, prefer.

pleasure *n* cheer, comfort, delight, delectation, elation, enjoyment, exhilaration, joy, gladness, gratification, gratifying, gusto, relish, satisfaction, solace; amusement, diversion, entertainment, indulgence, refreshment, treat; gratification, luxury, sensuality, voluptuousness; choice, desire, preference, purpose, will, wish; favour, kindness.

pledge *vb* hypothecate, mortgage, pawn, plight; affiance, bind, contract, engage, plight, promise. * *n* collateral, deposit, gage, pawn; earnest, guarantee, security; hostage, security.

plentiful *adj* abundant, ample, copious, full, enough, exuberant, fruitful, luxuriant, plenteous, productive, sufficient.

plenty *n* abundance, adequacy, affluence, amplitude, copiousness, enough, exuberance, fertility, fruitfulness, fullness, overflow, plenteousness, plentifulness, plethora, profusion, sufficiency, supply.

plethora *n* fullness, plenitude, repletion; excess, redundance, redundancy, superabundance, superfluity, surfeit.

pliable *adj* flexible, limber, lithe, lithesome, pliable, pliant, supple; adaptable, compliant, docile, ductile, facile, manageable, obsequious, tractable, yielding.

plight *n* case, category, complication, condition, dilemma, imbroglio, mess, muddle, pass, predicament, scrape, situation, state, strait.

plight *vb* avow, contract, covenant, engage, honour, pledge, promise, propose, swear, vow. * *n* avowal, contract, covenant, oath, pledge, promise, troth, vow, word; affiancing, betrothal, engagement.

plod *vb* drudge, lumber, moil, persevere, persist, toil, trudge.

plot *vb* connive, conspire, intrigue, machinate, scheme; brew, concoct, contrive,

devise, frame, hatch, compass, plan, project; chart, map. * *n* blueprint, chart, diagram, draft, outline, plan, scenario, skeleton; cabal, combination, complicity, connivance, conspiracy, intrigue, plan, project, scheme, stratagem; script, story, subject, theme, thread, topic.

plot *n* field, lot, parcel, patch, piece, plat, section, tract.

pluck *vb* cull, gather, pick; jerk, pull, snatch, tear, tug, twitch.

pluck *n* backbone, bravery, courage, daring, determination, energy, force, grit, hardihood, heroism, indomitability, indomitableness, manhood, mettle, nerve, resolution, spirit, valour.

plump *adj* bonny, bouncing, buxom, chubby, corpulent, fat, fleshy, full-figured, obese, portly, rotund, round, sleek, stout, well-rounded; distended, full, swollen, tumid.

plump *vb* dive, drop, plank, plop, plunge, plunk, put; choose, favour, support * *adj* blunt, complete, direct, downright, full, unqualified, unreserved.

plunder *vb* desolate, despoil, devastate, fleece, forage, harry, loot, maraud, pillage, raid, ransack, ravage, rifle, rob, sack, spoil, spoliate, plunge. * *n* freebooting, devastation, harrying, marauding, rapine, robbery, sack; booty, pillage, prey, spoil.

ply *vb* apply, employ, exert, manipulate, wield; exercise, practise; assail, belabour, beset, press; importune, solicit, urge; offer, present.

ply *n* fold, layer, plait, twist; bent, bias, direction, turn.

pocket *vb* appropriate, steal; bear, endure, suffer, tolerate. * *n* cavity, cul-de-sac, hollow, pouch, receptacle.

poignant *adj* bitter, intense, penetrating, pierce, severe, sharp; acrid, biting, mordacious, piquant, prickling, pungent, sharp, stinging; caustic, irritating, keen, mordant, pointed, satirical, severe.

point *vb* acuminate, sharpen; aim, direct, level; designate indicate, show; punctuate. * *n* apex, needle, nib, pin, prong, spike, stylus, tip; cape, headland, projection, promontory; eve, instant, mo-

ment, period, verge; place, site, spot,
stage, station; condition, degree, grade,
state; aim, design, end, intent, limit, object, purpose; nicety, pique, punctilio, trifle; position, proposition, question, text,
theme, thesis; aspect, matter, respect;
characteristic, peculiarity, trait; character, mark, stop; dot, jot, speck; epigram,
quip, quirk, sally, witticism; poignancy,
sting.

point-blank *adj* categorical, direct, downright, explicit, express, plain, straight.
* *adv* categorically, directly, flush, full,
plainly, right, straight.

pointless *adj* blunt, obtuse; aimless, dull,
flat, fruitless, futile, meaningless, vague,
vapid, stupid.

poise *vb* balance, float, hang, hover, support, suspend. * *n* aplomb, balance, composure, dignity, equanimity, equilibrium,
equipoise, serenity.

poison *vb* adulterate, contaminate, corrupt, defile, embitter, envenom, impair,
infect, intoxicate, pollute, taint, vitiate.
* *adj* deadly, lethal, poisonous, toxic. * *n*
bane, canker, contagion, pest, taint, toxin, venom, virulence, virus.

poisonous *adj* baneful, corruptive, deadly, fatal, noxious, pestiferous, pestilential, toxic, venomous.

poke *vb* jab, jog, punch, push, shove,
thrust; interfere, meddle, pry, snoop. * *n*
jab, jog, punch, push, shove, thrust; bag,
pocket, pouch, sack.

policy *n* administration, government,
management, rule; plan, plank, platform,
role; art, address, cunning, discretion,
prudence, shrewdness, skill, stratagem,
strategy, tactics; acumen, astuteness,
shrewdness, wisdom, wit.

polish *vb* brighten, buff, burnish, furbish,
glaze, gloss, scour, shine, smooth; civilize, refine. * *n* brightness, brilliance,
brilliancy, lustre, splendour; accomplishment, elegance, finish, grace, refinement.

polite *adj* attentive, accomplished, affable, chivalrous, civil, complaisant, courtly, courteous, cultivated, elegant, gallant,
genteel, gentle, gentlemanly, gracious,
mannerly, obliging, polished, refined,
suave, urbane, well, well-bred, well-
mannered.

politic *adj* civic, civil, political; astute, discreet, judicious, long-headed, noncom-
mittal, provident, prudent, prudential, sagacious, wary, wise; artful, crafty, cunning, diplomatic, expedient, foxy, ingenious, intriguing, Machiavellian, shrewd,
skilful, sly, subtle, strategic, timeserv-
ing, unscrupulous, wily; well-adapted,
well-devised.

political *adj* civic, civil, national, politic,
public.

pollute *vb* defile, foul, soil, taint; contaminate, corrupt, debase, demoralize, deprave, impair, infect, pervert, poison,
stain, tarnish, vitiate; desecrate, profane;
abuse, debauch, defile, deflower, dishonour, ravish, violate.

pollution *n* abomination, contamination,
corruption, defilement, foulness, impurity, pollutedness, taint, uncleanness,
vitiation.

pomp *n* display, flourish, grandeur, magnificence, ostentation, pageant, pageantry, parade, pompousness, pride, show,
splendour, state, style.

pompous *adj* august, boastful, bombastic, dignified, gorgeous, grand, inflated,
lofty, magisterial, ostentatious, pretentious, showy, splendid, stately, sumptuous, superb, vainglorious.

ponder *vb* cogitate, consider, contemplate, deliberate, examine, meditate,
muse, reflect, study, weigh.

poor *adj* indigent, necessitous, pinched,
straitened; destitute, distressed, impecunious, insolvent, moneyless, penniless,
poverty-stricken, reduced, seedy; emaciated, gaunt, spare, lean, lank, shrunk,
skinny, spare, thin; barren, fruitless, sterile, unfertile, unfruitful, unproductive,
unprolific; flimsy, inadequate, insignificant, insufficient, paltry, slender, slight,
small, trifling, trivial, unimportant, valueless, worthless; delicate, feeble, frail,
infirm, unsound, weak; inferior, seedy,
shabby, valueless, worthless; bad, beggarly, contemptible, despicable, humble,
inferior, low, mean, paltry, pitiful, shabby, sorry; bald, barren, cold, dry, dull,

feeble, frigid, languid, mean, meagre, prosaic, prosing, spiritless, tame, vapid, week; ill-fated, ill-starred, luckless, miserable, pitiable, unfortunate, unhappy, unlucky, wretched; deficient, imperfect, inadequate, insufficient, meagre, scant, small; faulty, unsatisfactory; scanty, thin; feeble, flimsy, weak.

popular *adj* lay, plebeian, public; comprehensible, easy, familiar, plain; acceptable, accepted, accredited, admired, approved, favoured, liked, pleasing, praised, received; common, current, prevailing, prevalent: cheap, inexpensive.

port¹ *n* anchorage, harbour, haven, shelter; door, entrance, gate, passageway; embrasure, porthole.

port² *n* air, appearance, bearing, behaviour, carriage, demeanour, deportment, mien, presence.

portable *adj* convenient, handy, light, manageable, movable, portative, transmissible.

portent *n* augury, omen, presage, prognosis, sign, warning; marvel, phenomenon, wonder.

portion *vb* allot, distribute, divide, parcel; endow, supply. * *n* bit, fragment, morsel, part, piece, scrap, section; allotment, contingent, dividend, division, lot, measure, quantity, quota, ration, share; inheritance, share.

portray *vb* act, draw, depict, delineate, describe, represent, paint, picture, sketch, pose, position.

pose *vb* arrange, bewilder, confound, dumbfound, embarrass, mystify, nonplus, perplex, place, puzzle, set, stagger; affect, attitudinize. * *n* attitude, posture; affectation, air, facade, mannerism, pretence, role.

position *vb* arrange, array, fix, locate, place, put, set, site, stand. * *n* locality, place, post, site, situation, spot, station; relation; attitude, bearing, posture; affirmation, assertion, doctrine, predication, principle, proposition, thesis; caste, dignity, honour, place, rank, standing, status; circumstance, condition, phase, place, state; berth, billet, incumbency, place, post, situation.

positive *adj* categorical, clear, defined, definite, direct, determinate, explicit, express, expressed, precise, unequivocal, unmistakable, unqualified; absolute, actual, real, substantial, true, veritable; assured, certain, confident, convinced, sure; decisive, incontrovertible, indisputable, indubitable, inescapable; imperative, unconditional, undeniable; decided, dogmatic, emphatic, obstinate, overbearing, overconfident, peremptory, stubborn, tenacious.

possess *vb* control, have, hold, keep, obsess, obtain, occupy, own, seize.

possession *n* monopoly, ownership, proprietorship; control, occupation, occupancy, retention, tenancy, tenure; bedevilment, lunacy, madness, obsession; (*pl*) assets, effects, estate, property, wealth.

possible *adj* conceivable, contingent, imaginable, potential; accessible, feasible, likely, practical, practicable, workable.

post¹ *vb* advertise, announce, inform, placard, publish; brand, defame, disgrace, vilify; enter, slate, record, register. * *n* column, picket, pier, pillar, stake, support.

post² *vb* establish, fix, place, put, set, station. * *n* billet, employment, office, place, position, quarter, seat, situation, station.

post³ *vb* drop, dispatch, mail. * *n* carrier, courier, express, mercury, messenger, postman; dispatch, haste, hurry, speed.

posterity *n* descendants, offspring, progeny, seed; breed, brood, children, family, heirs, issue.

postpone *vb* adjourn, defer, delay, procrastinate, prorogue, retard.

posture *vb* attitudinize, pose. * *n* attitude, pose, position; condition, disposition, mood, phase, state.

potent *adj* efficacious, forceful, forcible, intense, powerful, strong; able, capable, efficient, mighty, powerful, puissant, strong; cogent, influential, powerful.

potential *adj* able, capable, inherent, latent, possible. * *n* ability, capability, dynamic, possibility, potentiality, power.

pound¹ *vb* beat, strike, thump; bray, bruise, comminute, crush, levigate, pulverize, triturate; confound, coop, enclose, impound.

pound³ n enclosure, fold, pen.

pour vb cascade, emerge, flood, flow, issue, rain, shower, stream.

poverty n destitution, difficulties, distress, impecuniosity, impecuniousness, indigence, necessity, need, neediness, penury, privation, straits, want; beggary, mendicancy, pauperism, pennilessness; dearth, jejuneness, lack, scantiness, sparingness, meagreness; exiguity, paucity, poorness, smallness; humbleness, inferiority, lowliness; barrenness, sterility, unfruitfulness, unproductiveness.

power n ability, ableness, capability, cogency, competency, efficacy, faculty, might, potency, validity, talent; energy, force, strength, virtue; capacity, susceptibility; endowment, faculty, gift, talent; ascendancy, authoritativeness, authority, carte blanche, command, control, domination, dominion, government, influence, omnipotence, predominance, prerogative, pressure, proxy, puissance, rule, sovereignty, sway, warrant; governor, monarch, potentate, ruler, sovereign; army, host, troop.

powerful adj mighty, potent, puissant; able-bodied, herculean, muscular, nervous, robust, sinewy, strong, sturdy, vigorous, vivid; able, commanding, dominating, forceful, forcible, overpowering; cogent, effective, effectual, efficacious, efficient, energetic, influential, operative, valid.

practicable adj achievable, attainable, bearable, feasible, performable, possible, workable; operative, passable, penetrable.

practical adj hardheaded, matter-of-fact, pragmatic, pragmatical; able, experienced, practised, proficient, qualified, trained, skilled, thoroughbred, versed; effective, useful, virtual, workable.

practice n custom, habit, manner, method, repetition; procedure, usage, use; application, drill, exercise, pursuit; action, acts, behaviour, conduct, dealing, proceeding.

practise vb apply, do, exercise, follow, observe, perform, perpetrate, pursue.

practised adj able, accomplished, experienced, instructed, practical, proficient, qualified, skilled, thoroughbred, trained, versed.

pragmatic adj impertinent, intermeddling, interfering, intrusive, meddlesome, meddling, obtrusive, officious, over-busy; earthy, hard-headed, matter-of-fact, practical, pragmatical, realistic, sensible, stolid.

praise vb approbate, acclaim, applaud, approve, commend; celebrate, compliment, eulogize, extol, flatter, laud; adore, bless, exalt, glorify, magnify, worship. * n acclaim, approbation, approval, commendation; encomium, eulogy, glorification, laud, laudation, panegyric; exaltation, extolling, glorification, homage, tribute, worship; celebrity, distinction, fame, glory, honour, renown; desert, merit, praiseworthiness.

prank n antic, caper, escapade, frolic, gambol, trick.

pray vb ask, beg, beseech, conjure, entreat, implore, importune, invoke, petition, request, solicit, supplicate.

prayer n beseeching, entreaty, imploration, petition, request, solicitation, suit, supplication; adoration, devotion(s), litany, invocation, orison, praise, suffrage.

preach vb declare, deliver, proclaim, pronounce, publish; inculcate, press, teach, urge; exhort, lecture, moralize, sermonize.

precarious adj critical, doubtful, dubious, equivocal, hazardous, insecure, perilous, unassured, riskful, risky, uncertain, unsettled, unstable, unsteady.

precaution n care, caution, circumspection, foresight, forethought, providence, prudence, safeguard, wariness; anticipation, premonition, provision.

precede vb antedate, forerun, head, herald, introduce, lead, utter.

precedence n advantage, antecedence, lead, pre-eminence, preference, priority, superiority, supremacy.

precedent n antecedent, authority, custom, example, instance, model, pattern, procedure, standard, usage.

precept n behest, bidding, cannon, charge, command, commandment, decree, dictate, edict, injunction, instruction, law, mandate, ordinance, ordination, order, regulation; direction, doctrine, maxim, principle, teaching, rubric, rule.

precinct n border, bound, boundary, confine, environs, frontier, enclosure, limit, list, march, neighbourhood, purlieus, term, terminus; area, district.

precious adj costly, inestimable, invaluable, priceless, prized, valuable; adored, beloved, cherished, darling, dear, idolized, treasured; fastidious, overnice, over-refined, precise.

precipitate vb advance, accelerate, dispatch, expedite, forward, further, hasten, hurry, plunge, press, quicken, speed. * adj hasty, hurried, headlong, impetuous, indiscreet, overhasty, rash, reckless; abrupt, sudden, violent.

precipitous adj abrupt, cliffy, craggy, perpendicular, uphill, sheer, steep.

precise adj accurate, correct, definite, distinct, exact, explicit, express, nice, pointed, severe, strict, unequivocal, well-defined; careful, exact, scrupulous, strict; ceremonious, finical, formal, prim, punctilious, rigid, starched, stiff.

precision n accuracy, correctness, definiteness, distinctness, exactitude, exactness, nicety, preciseness.

precocious adj advanced, forward, overforward, premature.

precursor n antecedent, cause, forerunner, predecessor; harbinger, herald, messenger, pioneer; omen, presage, sign.

predatory adj greedy, pillaging, plundering, predacious, rapacious, ravaging, ravenous, voracious.

predicament n attitude, case, condition, plight, position, posture, situation, state; conjecture, corner, dilemma, emergency, exigency, fix, hole, impasse, mess, pass, pinch, push, quandary, scrape.

predict vb augur, betoken, bode, divine, forebode, forecast, foredoom, foresee, forespeak, foretell, foretoken, forewarn, portend, prognosticate, prophesy, read, signify, soothsay.

predominant adj ascendant, controlling, dominant, overruling, prevailing, prevalent, reigning, ruling, sovereign, supreme.

predominate vb dominate, preponderate, prevail, rule.

pre-eminent adj chief, conspicuous, consummate, controlling, distinguished, excellent, excelling, paramount, peerless, predominant, renowned, superior, supreme, surpassing, transcendent, unequalled.

preface vb begin, introduce, induct, launch, open, precede. * n exordium, foreword, induction, introduction, preamble, preliminary, prelude, prelusion, premise, proem, prologue, prolusion.

prefer vb address, offer, present, proffer, tender; advance, elevate, promote, raise; adopt, choose, elect, fancy, pick, select, wish.

preference n advancement, choice, election, estimation, precedence, priority, selection.

preferment n advancement, benefice, dignity, elevation, exaltation, promotion.

pregnant adj big, enceinte, parturient; fraught, full, important, replete, significant, weighty; fecund, fertile, fruitful, generative, impregnating, potential, procreant, procreative, productive, prolific.

prejudice vb bias, incline, influence, turn, warp; damage, diminish, hurt, impair, injure. * n bias, intolerance, partiality, preconception, predilection, prejudgement, prepossession, unfairness; damage, detriment, disadvantage, harm, hurt, impairment, injury, loss, mischief.

preliminary adj antecedent, initiatory, introductory, precedent, precursive, precursory, prefatory, prelusive, prelusory, preparatory, previous, prior, proemial. * n beginning, initiation, introduction, opening, preamble, preface, prelude, start.

prelude n introduction, opening, overture, prelusion, preparation, voluntary; exordium, preamble, preface, preliminary, proem.

premature adj hasty, ill-considered, precipitate, unmatured, unprepared, unripe, unseasonable, untimely.

premeditation n deliberation, design, forethought, intention, prearrangement, predetermination, purpose.

premise vb introduce, preamble, preface, prefix. * n affirmation, antecedent, argument, assertion, assumption, basis, foundation, ground, hypothesis, position, premiss, presupposition, proposition, support, thesis, theorem.

premium n bonus, bounty, encouragement, fee, gift, guerdon, meed, payment, prize, recompense, remuneration, reward; appreciation, enhancement.

premonition n caution, foreboding, foreshadowing, forewarning, indication, omen, portent, presage, presentiment, sign, warning.

preoccupied adj absent, absentminded, abstracted, dreaming, engrossed, inadvertent, inattentive, lost, musing, unobservant.

prepare vb adapt, adjust, fit, qualify; arrange, concoct, fabricate, make, order, plan, procure, provide.

prepossessing adj alluring, amiable, attractive, bewitching, captivating, charming, engaging, fascinating, inviting, taking, winning.

preposterous adj absurd, excessive, exorbitant, extravagant, foolish, improper, irrational, monstrous, nonsensical, perverted, ridiculous, unfit, unreasonable, wrong.

prescribe vb advocate, appoint, command, decree, dictate, direct, enjoin, establish, institute, ordain, order.

presence n attendance, company, inhabitance, inhabitancy, nearness, neighbourhood, occupancy, propinquity, proximity, residence, ubiquity, vicinity; air, appearance, carriage, demeanour, mien, personality.

present[1] adj near; actual, current, existing, happening, immediate, instant, living; available, quick, ready; attentive, favourable. * n now, time being, today.

present[2] n benefaction, boon, donation, favour, gift, grant, gratuity, largesse, offering.

present[3] vb introduce, nominate; exhibit, offer; bestow, confer, give, grant; deliver, hand; advance, express, prefer, proffer, tender.

presently adv anon, directly, forthwith, immediately, shortly, soon.

preservation n cherishing, conservation, curing, maintenance, protection, support; safety, salvation, security; integrity, keeping, soundness.

preserve vb defend, guard, keep, protect, rescue, save, secure, shield; maintain, uphold, sustain, support; conserve, economize, husband, retain. * n comfit, compote, confection, confiture, conserve, jam, jelly, marmalade, sweetmeat; enclosure, warren.

preside vb control, direct, govern, manage, officiate.

press vb compress, crowd, crush, squeeze; flatten, iron, smooth; clasp, embrace, hug; force, compel, constrain; emphasize, enforce, enjoin, inculcate, stress, urge; hasten, hurry, push, rush; crowd, throng; entreat, importune, solicit. * n crowd, crush, multitude, throng; hurry, pressure, urgency; case, closet, cupboard, repository.

pressure n compressing, crushing, squeezing; influence, force; compulsion, exigency, hurry, persuasion, press, stress, urgency; affliction, calamity, difficulty, distress, embarrassment, grievance, oppression, straits; impression, stamp.

prestige n credit, distinction, importance, influence, reputation, weight.

presume vb anticipate, apprehend, assume, believe, conjecture, deduce, expect, infer, surmise, suppose, think; consider, presuppose, suppose; dare, undertake, venture.

presumption n anticipation, assumption, belief, concession, conclusion, condition, conjecture, deduction, guess, hypothesis, inference, opinion, supposition, understanding; arrogance, assurance, audacity, boldness, brass, effrontery, forwardness, haughtiness, presumptuousness; probability.

presumptuous adj arrogant, assuming, audacious, bold, brash, forward, irreverent, insolent, intrusive, presuming;

foolhardy, overconfident, rash.

pretence n affectation, cloak, colour, disguise, mask, semblance, show, simulation, veil, window dressing; excuse, evasion, fabrication, feigning, makeshift, pretext, sham, subterfuge; claim, pretension.

pretend vb affect, counterfeit, deem, dissemble, fake, falsify, feign, sham, simulate; act, imagine, lie, profess; aspire, claim.

pretentious adj affected, assuming, conceited, conspicuous, ostentatious, presuming, priggish, showy, tawdry, unnatural, vain.

pretty adj attractive, beautiful, bonny, comely, elegant, fair, handsome, neat, pleasing, trim; affected, foppish. * adv fairly, moderately, quite, rather, somewhat.

prevailing adj controlling, dominant, effectual, efficacious, general, influential, operative, overruling, persuading, predominant, preponderant, prevalent, ruling, successful.

prevalent adj ascendant, compelling, efficacious, governing, predominant, prevailing, successful, superior; extensive, general, rife, widespread.

prevaricate vb cavil, deviate, dodge, equivocate, evade, palter, pettifog, quibble, shift, shuffle, tergiversate.

prevent vb bar, check, debar, deter, forestall, help, hinder, impede, inhibit, intercept, interrupt, obstruct, obviate, preclude, prohibit, restrain, save, stop, thwart.

prevention n anticipation, determent, deterrence, deterrent, frustration, hindrance, interception, interruption, obstruction, preclusion, prohibition, restriction, stoppage.

previous adj antecedent, anterior, earlier, foregoing, foregone, former, precedent, preceding, prior.

prey vb devour, eat, feed on, live off; exploit, intimidate, terrorize; burden, distress, haunt, oppress, trouble, worry. * n booty, loot, pillage, plunder, prize, rapine, spoil; food, game, kill, quarry, victim; depredation, ravage.

price vb assess, estimate, evaluate, rate,

value. * n amount, cost, expense, outlay, value; appraisal, charge, estimation, excellence, figure, rate, quotation, valuation, value, worth; compensation, guerdon, recompense, return, reward.

priceless adj dear, expensive, precious, inestimable, invaluable, valuable; amusing, comic, droll, funny, humorous, killing, rich.

prick vb perforate, pierce, puncture, stick; drive, goad, impel, incite, spur, urge; cut, hurt, pain, sting, wound; hasten, post, ride, spur. * n mark, perforation, point, puncture; prickle, sting, wound.

pride vb boast, brag, crow, preen, revel in. * n conceit, egotism, self-complacency, self-esteem, self-exaltation, self-importance, self-sufficiency, vanity; arrogance, assumption, disdain, haughtiness, hauteur, insolence, loftiness, lordliness, pomposity, presumption, superciliousness, vainglory; decorum, dignity, elevation, loftiness, self-respect; decoration, glory, ornament, show, splendour.

priest n churchman, clergyman, divine, ecclesiastic, minister, pastor, presbyter.

prim adj demure, formal, nice, precise, prudish, starch, starched, stiff, straitlaced.

primary adj aboriginal, earliest, first, initial, original, prime, primitive, primeval, primordial, pristine; chief, main, principal; basic, elementary, fundamental, preparatory: radical.

prime¹ adj aboriginal, basic, first, initial, original, primal, primary, primeval, primitive, primordial, pristine; chief, foremost, highest, leading, main, paramount, principal; blooming, early; capital, cardinal, dominant, predominant; excellent, first-class, first-rate, optimal, optimum, quintessential; beginning, initial, opening. * n beginning, dawn, morning, opening; spring, springtime, youth; bloom, cream, flower, height, heyday, optimum, perfection, quintessence, zenith.

prime² vb charge, load, prepare, undercoat; coach, groom, train, tutor.

primitive adj aboriginal, first, original, primal, primary, prime, primitive, primordial, pristine; antiquated, crude, old-fashioned, quaint, simple, unsophisticated; formal, grave, prim, solemn.

princely adj imperial, regal, royal; august, generous, grand, liberal, magnanimous, magnificent, majestic, munificent, noble, pompous, splendid, superb, royal, titled; dignified, elevated, high-minded, lofty, noble, stately.

principal adj capital, cardinal, chief, essential, first, foremost, highest, leading, main, pre-eminent, prime. * n chief, head, leader; head teacher; master.

principle n cause, fountain, fountainhead, groundwork, mainspring, nature, origin, source, spring; basis, constituent, element, essence, substratum; assumption, axiom, law, maxim, postulation; doctrine, dogma, impulse, maxim, opinion, precept, rule, tenet, theory; conviction, ground, motive, reason; equity, goodness, honesty, honour, incorruptibility, integrity, justice, probity, rectitude, righteousness, trustiness, truth, uprightness, virtue, worth; faculty, power.

print vb engrave, impress, imprint, mark, stamp; issue, publish. * n book, periodical, publication; copy, engraving, photograph, picture; characters, font, fount, lettering, type, typeface.

prior adj antecedent, anterior, earlier, foregoing, precedent, preceding, precursory, previous, superior.

priority n antecedence, anteriority, precedence, pre-eminence, pre-existence, superiority.

pristine adj ancient, earliest, first, former, old, original, primary, primeval, primitive, primordial.

privacy n concealment, secrecy; retirement, retreat, seclusion, solitude.

private adj retired, secluded, sequestrated, solitary; individual, own, particular, peculiar, personal, special, unofficial; confidential, privy; clandestine, concealed, hidden, secret. * n GI, soldier, tommy.

privilege n advantage, charter, claim, exemption, favour, franchise, immunity, leave, liberty, licence, permission, prerogative, right.

prize[1] vb appreciate, cherish, esteem, treasure, value.

prize[2] adj best, champion, first-rate, outstanding, winning. * n guerdon, honours, meed, premium, reward; cup, decoration, medal, laurels, palm, trophy; booty, capture, lot, plunder, spoil; advantage, gain, privilege.

probability n chance, prospect, likelihood, presumption; appearance, credibility, credibleness, likeliness, verisimilitude.

probable adj apparent, credible, likely, presumable, reasonable.

probably adv apparently, likely, maybe, perchance, perhaps, presumably, possibly, seemingly.

probation n essay, examination, ordeal, proof, test, trial; novitiate.

probe vb examine, explore, fathom, investigate, measure, prove, scrutinize, search, sift, sound, test, verify. * n examination, exploration, inquiry, investigation, scrutiny, study.

probity n candour, conscientiousness, equity, fairness, faith, goodness, honesty, honour, incorruptibility, integrity, justice, loyalty, morality, principle, rectitude, righteousness, sincerity, soundness, trustworthiness, truth, truthfulness, uprightness, veracity, virtue, worth.

problem adj difficult, intractable, uncontrollable, unruly. * n dilemma, dispute, doubt, enigma, exercise, problem, proposition, puzzle, riddle, theorem.

problematic adj debatable, disputable, doubtful, dubious, enigmatic, problematical, puzzling, questionable, suspicious, uncertain, unsettled.

procedure n conduct, course, custom, management, method, operation, policy, practice, process; act, action, deed, measure, performance, proceeding, step, transaction.

proceed vb advance, continue, go, pass, progress; accrue, arise, come, emanate, ensue, flow, follow, issue, originate, result, spring.

proceeds npl balance, earnings, effects, gain, income, net, produce, products, profits, receipts, returns, yield.

process vb advance, deal with, fulfil, handle, progress; alter, convert, refine, transform. * n advance, course, progress, train; action, conduct, management, measure, mode, operation, performance, practice, procedure, proceeding, step, transaction, way; action, case, suit, trial; outgrowth, projection, protuberance.

procession n cavalcade, cortege, file, march, parade, retinue, train.

proclaim vb advertise, announce, broach, broadcast, circulate, cry, declare, herald, promulgate, publish, trumpet; ban, outlaw, proscribe.

procrastinate vb adjourn, defer, delay, postpone, prolong, protract, retard; neglect, omit; lag, loiter.

procure vb acquire, gain, get, obtain; cause, compass, contrive, effect.

prodigal adj abundant, dissipated, excessive, extravagant, generous, improvident, lavish, profuse, reckless, squandering, thriftless, unthrifty, wasteful. * n spendthrift, squanderer, waster, wastrel.

produce vb exhibit, show; bear, beget, breed, conceive, engender, furnish, generate, hatch, procreate, yield; accomplish, achieve, cause, create, effect, make, occasion, originate; accrue, afford, give, impart, make, render; extend, lengthen, prolong, protract; fabricate, fashion, manufacture. * n crop, fruit, greengrocery, harvest, product, vegetables, yield.

product n crops, fruits, harvest, outcome, proceeds, produce, production, returns, yield; consequence, effect, fruit, issue, performance, production, result, work.

production n fruit, produce, product; construction, creation, erection, fabrication, making, performance; completion, fruition; birth, breeding, development, growth, propagation; opus, publication, work; continuation, extension, lengthening, prolongation.

productive adj copious, fertile, fruitful, luxuriant, plenteous, prolific, teeming; causative, constructive, creative, efficient, life-giving, producing.

profane vb defile, desecrate, pollute, violate; abuse, debase. * adj godless, heathen, idolatrous, impure, pagan, secular, temporal, unconsecrated, unhallowed, unholy, unsanctified, worldly; impure, polluted, unconsecrated, unhallowed, unholy, unsanctified; secular, temporal, worldly.

profess vb acknowledge, affirm, allege, aver, avouch, avow, confess, declare, own, proclaim, state; affect, feign, pretend.

profession n acknowledgement, assertion, avowal, claim, declaration; avocation, evasion, pretence, pretension, protestation, representation; business, calling, employment, engagement, occupation, office, trade, vocation.

proficiency n advancement, forwardness, improvement; accomplishment, aptitude, competency, dexterity, mastery, skill.

proficient adj able, accomplished, adept, competent, conversant, dextrous, expert, finished, masterly, practised, skilled, skilful, thoroughbred, trained, qualified, well-versed. * n adept, expert, master, master-hand.

profit vb advance, benefit, gain, improve. * n aid, clearance, earnings, emolument, fruit, gain, lucre, produce, return; advancement, advantage, benefit, interest, perquisite, service, use, utility, weal.

profitable adj advantageous, beneficial, desirable, gainful, productive, useful; lucrative, remunerative.

profound adj abysmal, deep, fathomless; heavy, undisturbed; erudite, learned, penetrating, sagacious, skilled; far-reaching, heartfelt, intense, lively, strong, touching, vivid; low, submissive; abstruse, mysterious, obscure, occult, subtle, recondite; complete, thorough.

profuse adj abundant, bountiful, copious, excessive, extravagant, exuberant, generous, improvident, lavish, overabundant, plentiful, prodigal, wasteful.

progress vb advance, continue, proceed; better, gain, improve, increase. * n advance, advancement, progression; course, headway, ongoing, passage; betterment, development, growth, improvement, increase, reform: circuit, procession.

prohibit vb debar, hamper, hinder, preclude, prevent; ban, disallow, forbid, inhabit, interdict.

prohibition n ban, bar, disallowance, embargo, forbiddance, inhibition, interdict, interdiction, obstruction, prevention, proscription, taboo, tabu, veto.

prohibitive adj forbidding, prohibiting, refraining, restrictive.

project vb cast, eject, fling, hurl, propel, shoot, throw; brew, concoct, contrive, design, devise, intend, plan, plot, purpose, scheme; delineate, draw, exhibit; bulge, extend, jut, protrude. * n contrivance, design, device, intention, plan, proposal, purpose, scheme.

projection n delivery, ejection, emission, propulsion, throwing; contriving, designing, planning, scheming; bulge, extension, outshoot, process, prominence, protuberance, salience, saliency, salient, spur; delineation, map, plan.

prolific adj abundant, fertile, fruitful, generative, productive, teeming.

prologue n foreword, introduction, preamble, preface, preliminary, prelude, proem.

prolong vb continue, extend, lengthen, protract, sustain; defer, postpone.

prominent adj convex, embossed, jutting, projecting, protuberant, raised, relieved; celebrated, conspicuous, distinguished, eminent, famous, foremost, influential, leading, main, noticeable, outstanding; conspicuous, distinctly, important, manifest, marked, principal, salient.

promiscuous adj confused, heterogeneous, indiscriminate, intermingled, mingled, miscellaneous, mixed; abandoned, dissipated, dissolute, immoral, licentious, loose, unchaste, wanton.

promise vb covenant, engage, pledge, subscribe, swear, underwrite, vow; assure, attest, guarantee, warrant; agree, bargain, engage, stipulate, undertake. * n agreement, assurance, contract, engagement, oath, parole, pledge, profession, undertaking, vow, word.

promising adj auspicious, encouraging, hopeful, likely, propitious.

promote vb advance, aid, assist, cultivate, encourage, further, help, promote; dignify, elevate, exalt, graduate, honour, pass, prefer, raise.

promotion n advancement, encouragement, furtherance; elevation, exaltation, preferment.

prompt vb actuate, dispose, impel, incite, incline, induce, instigate, stimulate, urge; remind; dictate, hint, influence, suggest. * adj active, alert, apt, quick, ready; forward, hasty; disposed, inclined, prone; early, exact, immediate, instant, precise, punctual, seasonable, timely. * adv apace, directly, forthwith, immediately, promptly. * n cue, hint, prompter, reminder, stimulus.

promptly adv apace, directly, expeditiously, forthwith, immediately, instantly, pronto, punctually, quickly, speedily, straightway, straightaway, summarily, swiftly.

prone adj flat, horizontal, prostrate, recumbent; declivitous, inclined, inclining, sloping; apt, bent, disposed, inclined, predisposed, tending; eager, prompt, ready.

pronounce vb articulate, enunciate, frame, say, speak, utter; affirm, announce, assert, declare, deliver, state.

proof adj firm, fixed, impenetrable, stable, steadfast. * n essay, examination, ordeal, test, trial; attestation, certification, conclusion, conclusiveness, confirmation, corroboration, demonstration, evidence, ratification, substantiation, testimony, verification.

prop vb bolster, brace, buttress, maintain, shore, stay, support, sustain, truss, uphold. * n brace, support, stay; brace, buttress, fulcrum, pin, shore, stay, strut.

propel vb drive, force, impel, push, urge; cast, fling, hurl, project, throw.

proper adj individual, inherent, natural, original, particular, peculiar, special, specific; adapted, appropriate, becoming, befitting, convenient, decent, decorous, demure, fit, fitting, legitimate, meet, pertinent, respectable, right, seemly, suitable; accurate, correct, exact, fair, fastidious, formal, just, precise; actual, real.

property *n* attribute, characteristic, disposition, mark, peculiarity, quality, trait, virtue; appurtenance, assets, belongings, chattels, circumstances, effects, estate, goods, possessions, resources, wealth; ownership, possession, proprietorship, tenure; claim, copyright, interest, participation, right, title.

prophecy *n* augury, divination, forecast, foretelling, portent, prediction, premonition, presage, prognostication; exhortation, instruction, preaching.

prophesy *vb* augur, divine, foretell, predict, prognosticate.

proportion *vb* adjust, graduate, regulate; form, shape. * *n* arrangement, relation; adjustment, commensuration, dimension, distribution, symmetry; extent, lot, part, portion, quota, ratio, share.

proposal *n* design, motion, offer, overture, proffer, proposition, recommendation, scheme, statement, suggestion, tender.

propose *vb* move, offer, pose, present, propound, proffer, put, recommend, state, submit, suggest, tender; design, intend, mean, purpose.

proposition *vb* accost, proffer, solicit. * *n* offer, overture, project, proposal, suggestion, tender, undertaking; affirmation, assertion, axiom, declaration, dictum, doctrine, position, postulation, predication, statement, theorem, thesis.

propriety *n* accuracy, adaptation, appropriation, aptness, becomingness, consonance, correctness, fitness, justness, reasonableness, rightness, seemliness, suitableness; conventionality, decency, decorum, demureness, fastidiousness, formality, modesty, properness, respectability.

prosaic *adj* commonplace, dull, flat, humdrum, matter-of-fact, pedestrian, plain, prolix, prosing, sober, stupid, tame, tedious, tiresome, unentertaining, unimaginative, unintentional, unromantic, vapid.

proscribe *vb* banish, doom, exile, expel, ostracize, outlaw; exclude, forbid, inter-

dict, prohibit; censure, condemn, curse, denounce, reject.

prosecute *vb* conduct, continue, exercise, follow, persist, pursue; arraign, indict, sue, summon.

prospect *vb* explore, search, seek, survey. * *n* display, field, landscape, outlook, perspective, scene, show, sight, spectacle, survey, view, vision, vista; picture, scenery; anticipation, calculation, contemplation, expectance, expectancy, expectation, foreseeing, foresight, hope, presumption, promise, trust; likelihood, probability.

prosper *vb* aid, favour, forward, help; advance, flourish, grow rich, thrive, succeed; batten, increase.

prosperity *n* affluence, blessings, happiness, felicity, good luck, success, thrift, weal, welfare, well-being; boom, heyday.

prosperous *adj* blooming, flourishing, fortunate, golden, halcyon, rich, successful, thriving; auspicious, booming, bright, favourable, fortunate, good, golden, lucky, promising, propitious, providential, rosy.

prostrate *vb* demolish, destroy, fell, level, overthrow, overturn, ruin; depress, exhaust, overcome, reduce. * *adj* fallen, prostrated, prone, recumbent, supine; helpless, powerless.

protect *vb* cover, defend, guard, shield; fortify, harbour, house, preserve, save, screen, secure, shelter; champion, countenance, foster, patronize.

protector *n* champion, custodian, defender, guardian, patron, warden.

protest *vb* affirm, assert, asseverate, attest, aver, avow, declare, profess, testify; demur, expostulate, object, remonstrate, repudiate. * *n* complaint, declaration, disapproval, objection, protestation.

prototype *n* archetype, copy, exemplar, example, ideal, model, original, paradigm, precedent, protoplast, type.

protract *vb* continue, extend, lengthen, prolong; defer, delay, postpone.

protrude *vb* beetle, bulge, extend, jut, project.

proud *adj* assuming, conceited, contended, egotistical, overweening, self-conscious, self-satisfied, vain; arrogant, boastful, haughty, high-spirited, highly strung, imperious, lofty, lordly, presumptuous, supercilious, uppish, vainglorious.

prove *vb* ascertain, conform, demonstrate, establish, evidence, evince, justify, manifest, show, substantiate, sustain, verify; assay, check, examine, experiment, test, try.

proverb *n* adage, aphorism, apothegm, byword, dictum, maxim, precept, saw, saying.

proverbial *adj* acknowledged, current, notorious, unquestioned.

provide *vb* arrange, collect, plan, prepare, procure; gather, keep, store; afford, contribute, feed, furnish, produce, stock, supply, yield; cater, purvey; agree, bargain, condition, contract, covenant, engage, stipulate.

provident *adj* careful, cautious, considerate, discreet, farseeing, forecasting, forehanded, foreseeing, prudent; economical, frugal, thrifty.

province *n* district, domain, region, section, territory, tract; colony, dependency; business, calling, capacity, charge, department, duty, employment, function, office, part, post, sphere; department, division, jurisdiction.

provision *n* anticipation, providing; arrangement, care, preparation, readiness; equipment, fund, grist, hoard, reserve, resources, stock, store, supplies, supply; clause, condition, prerequisite, proviso, reservation, stipulation.

provocation *n* incentive, incitement, provocativeness, stimulant, stimulus; affront, indignity, insult, offence; angering, vexation.

provoke *vb* animate, arouse, awaken, excite, impel, incite, induce, inflame, instigate, kindle, move, rouse, stimulate; affront, aggravate, anger, annoy, chafe, enrage, exacerbate, exasperate, incense, infuriate, irritate, nettle, offend, pique, vex; cause, elicit, evoke, instigate, occasion, produce, promote.

prudent *adj* cautious, careful, circumspect, considerate, discreet, foreseeing, heedful, judicious, politic, provident, prudential, wary, wise.

prudish *adj* coy, demure, modest, perjink, precise, prim, reserved, strait-laced.

prune *vb* abbreviate, clip, cut, dock, lop, thin, trim; dress, preen, trim.

pry *vb* examine, ferret, inspect, investigate, peep, peer, question, scrutinize, search; force, lever, prise.

public *adj* civil, common, countrywide, general, national, political, state; known, notorious, open, popular, published, well-known. * *n* citizens, community, country, everyone, masses, nation, people, population; audience, buyers, following, supporters.

publication *n* advertisement, announcement, blazon, disclosure, divulgement, divulgence, proclamation, promulgation, report; edition, issue, issuance, printing.

publicity *n* daylight, currency, limelight, notoriety, spotlight; outlet, vent.

publish *vb* advertise, air, bruit, announce, blaze, blazon, broach, communicate, declare, diffuse, disclose, disseminate, impart, placard, post, proclaim, promulgate, reveal, tell, utter, vent, ventilate.

pull *vb* drag, draw, haul, row, tow, tug; cull, extract, gather, pick, pluck; detach, rend, tear, wrest. * *n* pluck, shake, tug, twitch, wrench; contest, struggle; attraction, gravity, magnetism; graft, influence, power.

pulsate *vb* beat, palpitate, pant, throb, thump, vibrate.

pun *vb* assonate, alliterate, play on words. * *n* assonance, alliteration, clinch, conceit, paranomasia, play on words, quip, rhyme, witticism, wordplay.

punctual *adj* exact, nice, precise, punctilious; early, prompt, ready, regular, seasonable, timely.

puncture *vb* bore, penetrate, perforate, pierce, prick. * *n* bite, hole, sting, wound.

pungent *adj* acid, acrid, biting, burning, caustic, hot, mordant, penetrating, peppery, piercing, piquant, prickling, racy, salty, seasoned, sharp, smart, sour, spicy, stimulating, stinging; acute, acrimonious, cutting, distressing, irritating, keen, painful, peevish, piquant, poignant, pointed, satirical, severe, smart, tart, trenchant, waspish.

punish *vb* beat, castigate, chasten, chastise, correct, discipline, flog, lash, scourge, torture, whip.

punishment *n* castigation, chastening, chastisement, correction, discipline, infliction, retribution, scourging, trial; judgment, nemesis, penalty.

puny *adj* feeble, inferior, weak; dwarf, dwarfish, insignificant, diminutive, little, petty, pygmy, small, stunted, tiny, underdeveloped, undersized.

purchase *vb* buy, gain, get, obtain, pay for, procure; achieve, attain, earn, win. * *n* acquisition, buy, gain, possession, property; advantage, foothold, grasp, hold, influence, support.

pure *adj* clean, clear, fair, immaculate, spotless, stainless, unadulterated, unalloyed, unblemished, uncorrupted, undefiled, unpolluted, unspotted, unstained, unsullied, untainted, untarnished; chaste, continent, guileless, guiltless, holy, honest, incorrupt, innocent, modest, sincere, true, uncorrupt, uncorrupted, upright, virgin, virtuous, white; clear, genuine, perfect, real, simple, true; absolute, mere, sheer; attic, classic, classical.

purge *vb* cleanse, clear, purify; clarify, defecate, evacuate; deterge, scour; absolve, pardon, shrive. * *n* elimination, eradication, expulsion, removal, suppression; cathartic, emetic, enema, laxative, physic.

purify *vb* clean, cleanse, clear, depurate, expurgate, purge, refine, wash; clarify, defecate, fine.

puritanical *adj* ascetic, narrow-minded, overscrupulous, prim, prudish, rigid, severe, strait-laced, strict.

purity *n* clearness, fineness; cleanness, clearness, correctness, faultlessness, immaculacy, immaculateness; guilelessness, guiltlessness, holiness, honesty, innocence, integrity, piety, simplicity, truth, uprightness, virtue; excellence, genuineness, integrity; homogeneity, simpleness; chasteness, chastity, continence, modesty, pudency, virginity.

purpose *vb* contemplate, design, intend, mean, meditate; determine, resolve. * *n* aim, design, drift, end, intent, intention, object, resolution, resolve, view; plan, project; meaning, purport, sense; consequence, end, effect.

pursue *vb* chase, dog, follow, hound, hunt, shadow, track; conduct, continue, cultivate, maintain, practise, prosecute; seek, strive; accompany, attend, follow.

pursuit *n* chase, hunt, race; conduct, cultivation, practice, prosecution, pursuance; avocation, calling, business, employment, fad, hobby, occupation, vocation.

push *vb* elbow, crowd, hustle, impel, jostle, shoulder, shove, thrust; advance, drive, hurry, propel, urge; importune, persuade, tease. * *n* pressure, thrust; determination, perseverance; emergency, exigency, extremity, pinch, strait, test, trial; assault, attack, charge, endeavour, onset.

put *vb* bring, collocate, deposit, impose, lay, locate, place, set; enjoin, impose, inflict, levy; offer, present, propose, state; compel, constrain, force, oblige; entice, incite, induce, urge; express, utter.

puzzle *vb* bewilder, confound, confuse, embarrass, gravel, mystify, nonplus, perplex, pose, stagger; complicate, entangle.* *n* conundrum, enigma, labyrinth, maze, paradox, poser, problem, riddle; bewilderment, complication, confusion, difficulty, dilemma, embarrassment, mystification, perplexity, point, quandary, question.

Q

quail *vb* blench, cower, droop, faint, flinch, shrink, tremble.

quaint *adj* antiquated, antique, archaic, curious, droll, extraordinary, fanciful, odd, old-fashioned, queer, singular, uncommon, unique, unusual; affected, fantastic, farfetched, odd, singular, whimsical; artful, ingenious.

quake vb quiver, shake, shiver, shudder; move, vibrate. * n earthquake, shake, shudder.

qualification n ability, accomplishment, capability, competency, eligibility, fitness, suitability; condition, exception, limitation, modification, proviso, restriction, stipulation; abatement, allowance, diminution, mitigation.

qualify vb adapt, capacitate, empower, entitle, equip, fit; limit, modify, narrow, restrain, restrict; abate, assuage, ease, mitigate, moderate, reduce, soften; diminish, modulate, temper, regulate, vary.

quality n affection, attribute, characteristic, colour, distinction, feature, flavour, mark, nature, peculiarity, property, singularity, timbre, tinge, trait; character, characteristic, condition, disposition, humour, mood, temper; brand, calibre, capacity, class, condition, description, grade, kind, rank, sort, stamp, standing, station, status; aristocracy, gentry, noblesse, nobility.

qualm n agony, pang, throe; nausea, queasiness, sickness; compunction, remorse, uneasiness, twinge.

quandary n bewilderment, difficulty, dilemma, doubt, embarrassment, perplexity, pickle, plight, predicament, problem, puzzle, strait, uncertainty.

quantity n content, extent, greatness, measure, number, portion, share, size; aggregate, batch, amount, bulk, lot, mass, quantum, store, sum, volume; duration, length.

quarrel vb altercate, bicker, brawl, carp, cavil, clash, contend, differ, dispute, fight, jangle, jar, scold, scuffle, spar, spat, squabble, strive, wrangle. * n altercation, affray, bickering, brawl, breach, breeze, broil, clash, contention, contest, controversy, difference, disagreement, discord, dispute, dissension, disturbance, feud, fight, fray, imbroglio, jar, miff, misunderstanding, quarrelling, row, rupture, spat, squabble, strife, tiff, tumult, variance, wrangle.

quarrelsome adj argumentative, choleric, combative, contentious, cross, discordant, disputatious, dissentious, fiery, irascible, irritable, petulant, pugnacious, ugly, wranglesome.

quarter vb billet, lodge, post, station; allot, furnish, share. * n abode, billet, dwelling, habitation, lodgings, posts, quarters, stations; direction, district, locality, location, lodge, position, region, territory; clemency, mercy, mildness.

quell vb conquer, crush, overcome, overpower, subdue; bridle, check, curb, extinguish, lay, quench, rein in, repress, restrain, stifle; allay, calm, compose, hush, lull, pacify, quiet, quieten, still, subdue, tranquillize; alleviate, appease, blunt, deaden, dull, mitigate, mollify, soften, soothe.

quench vb extinguish, put out; check, destroy, repress, satiate, stifle, still, suppress; allay, cool, dampen, extinguish, slake.

query vb ask, enquire, inquire, question; dispute, doubt. * n enquiry, inquiry, interrogatory, issue, problem, question.

quest n expedition, journey, search, voyage; pursuit, suit; examination, enquiry, inquiry; demand, desire, invitation, prayer, request, solicitation.

question vb ask, catechize, enquire, examine, inquire, interrogate, quiz, sound out; doubt, query; challenge, dispute. * n examination, enquiry, inquiry, interpellation, interrogation; enquiry, inquiry, interrogatory, query; debate, discussion, disquisition, examination, investigation, issue, trial; controversy, dispute, doubt; motion, mystery, point, poser, problem, proposition, puzzle, topic.

questionable adj ambiguous, controversial, controvertible, debatable, doubtful, disputable, equivocal, problematic, problematical, suspicious, uncertain, undecided.

quick adj active, agile, alert, animated, brisk, lively, nimble, prompt, ready, smart, sprightly; expeditious, fast, fleet, flying, hasty, hurried, rapid, speedy, swift; adroit, apt, clever, dextrous, expert, skilful; choleric, hasty, impetuous, irascible, irritable, passionate, peppery, petulant, precipitate, sharp, unceremonious, testy, touchy, waspish; alive, animate, live, living.

quicken vb animate, energize, resuscitate, revivify, vivify; cheer, enliven, invigorate, reinvigorate, revive, whet; accelerate, dispatch, expedite, hasten, hurry, speed; actuate, excite, incite, kindle, refresh, sharpen, stimulate; accelerate, live, take effect.

quiet adj hushed, motionless, quiescent, still, unmoved; calm, contented, gentle, mild, meek, modest, peaceable, peaceful, placid, silent, smooth, tranquil, undemonstrative, unobtrusive, unruffled; contented, patient; retired, secluded. * n calmness, peace, repose, rest, silence, stillness.

quieten vb arrest, discontinue, intermit, interrupt, still, stop, suspend; allay, appease, calm, compose, lull, pacify, sober, soothe, tranquillize; hush, silence, still; alleviate, assuage, blunt, dull, mitigate, moderate, mollify, soften.

quit vb absolve, acquit, deliver, free, release; clear, deliver, discharge from, free, liberate, relieve; acquit, behave, conduct; carry through, perform; discharge, pay, repay, requite; relinquish, renounce, resign, stop, surrender; depart from, leave, withdraw from; abandon, desert, forsake, forswear. * adj absolved, acquitted, clear, discharged, free, released.

quite adv completely, entirely, exactly, perfectly, positively, precisely, totally, wholly.

quiz vb examine, question; peer at; banter, hoax, puzzle, ridicule. * n enigma, hoax, jest, joke, puzzle; jester, joker, hoax.

quotation n citation, clipping, cutting, extract, excerpt, reference, selection; estimate, rate, tender.

quote vb adduce, cite, excerpt, extract, illustrate, instance, name, repeat, take; estimate, tender.

R

race[1] n ancestry, breed, family, generation, house, kindred, line, lineage, pedigree, stock, strain; clan, family, folk, nation, people, tribe; breed, children, descendants, issue, offspring, progeny, stock.

race[2] vb career, compete, contest, course, hasten, hurry, run, speed. * n career, chase, competition, contest, course, dash, heat, match, pursuit, run, sprint; flavour, quality, smack, strength, taste.

rack vb agonize, distress, excruciate, rend, torment, torture, wring; exhaust, force, harass, oppress, strain, stretch, wrest. * n agony, anguish, pang, torment, torture; crib, manger; neck, crag; dampness, mist, moisture, vapour.

racket n clamour, clatter, din, dissipation, disturbance, fracas, frolic, hubbub, noise, outcry, tumult, uproar; game, graft, scheme, understanding.

radiant adj beaming, brilliant, effulgent, glittering, glorious, luminous, lustrous, resplendent, shining, sparkling, splendid; ecstatic, happy, pleased.

radiate vb beam, gleam, glitter, shine; emanate, emit; diffuse, spread.

radical adj constitutional, deep-seated, essential, fundamental, ingrained, inherent, innate, native, natural, organic, original, uncompromising; original, primitive, simple, uncompounded, underived; complete, entire, extreme, fanatic, fundamental, insurgent, perfect, rebellious, thorough, total. * n etymon, radix, root; fanatic, revolutionary.

rage vb bluster, boil, chafe, foam, fret, fume, ravage, rave. * n excitement, frenzy, fury, madness, passion, rampage, raving, vehemence, wrath; craze, fashion, mania, mode, style, vogue.

raid vb assault, forage, invade, pillage, plunder. * n attack, foray, invasion, inroad, plunder.

rain vb drizzle, drop, fall, pour, shower, sprinkle, teem; bestow, lavish, shower. * n cloudburst, downpour, drizzle, mist, shower, sprinkling.

raise vb boost, construct, erect, heave,

hoist, lift, uplift, upraise, rear; advance, elevate, ennoble, exalt, promote; advance, aggravate, amplify, augment, enhance, heighten, increase, invigorate; arouse, awake, cause, effect, excite, originate, produce, rouse, stir up, occasion, start; assemble, collect, get, levy, obtain; breed, cultivate, grow, propagate, rear; ferment, leaven, work.

ramble vb digress, maunder, range, roam, rove, saunter, straggle, stray, stroll, wander. * n excursion, rambling, roving, tour, trip, stroll, wandering.

rancid adj bad, fetid, foul, fusty, musty, offensive, rank, sour, stinking, tainted.

random adj accidental, casual, chance, fortuitous, haphazard, irregular, stray, wandering.

range vb course, cruise, extend, ramble, roam, rove, straggle, stray, stroll, wander; bend, lie, run; arrange, class, dispose, rank. * n file, line, row, rank, tier; class, kind, order, sort; excursion, expedition, ramble, roving, wandering; amplitude, bound, command, compass, distance, extent, latitude, reach, scope, sweep, view; compass, register.

rank[1] vb arrange, class, classify, range. * n file, line, order, range, row, tier; class, division, group, order, series; birth, blood, caste, degree, estate, grade, position, quality, sphere, stakes, standing; dignity, distinction, eminence, nobility.

rank[2] adj dense, exuberant, luxuriant, overabundant, overgrown, vigorous, wild; excessive, extreme, extravagant, flagrant, gross, rampant, sheer, unmitigated, utter, violent; fetid, foul, fusty, musty, offensive, rancid; fertile, productive, rich; coarse, foul, disgusting.

ransack vb pillage, plunder, ravage, rifle, sack, strip; explore, overhaul, rummage, search thoroughly.

ransom vb deliver, emancipate, free, liberate, redeem, rescue, unfetter. * n deliverance, liberation, redemption, release.

rapid adj fast, fleet, quick, swift; brisk, expeditious, hasty, hurried, quick, speedy.

rapture vb enrapture, ravish, transport. * n delight, exultation, enthusiasm, rhapso-

dy; beatification, beatitude, bliss, ecstasy, felicity, happiness, joy, spell, transport.

rare[1] adj sparse, subtle, thin; extraordinary, infrequent, scarce, singular, strange, uncommon, unique, unusual; choice, excellent, exquisite, fine, incomparable, inimitable.

rare[2] adj bloody, underdone.

rarity n attenuation, ethereality, etherealness, rarefaction, rareness, tenuity, tenuousness, thinness; infrequency, scarcity, singularity, sparseness, uncommonness, unwontedness.

rascal n blackguard, caitiff, knave, miscreant, rogue, reprobate, scallywag, scapegrace, scamp, scoundrel, vagabond, villain.

rash[1] adj adventurous, audacious, careless, foolhardy, hasty, headlong, headstrong, heedless, incautious, inconsiderate, indiscreet, injudicious, impetuous, impulsive, incautious, precipitate, quick, rapid, reckless, temerarious, thoughtless, unguarded, unwary, venturesome.

rash[2] n breaking-out, efflorescence, eruption; epidemic, flood, outbreak, plague, spate.

rate[1] vb appraise, compute, estimate, value. * n cost, price; class, degree, estimate, rank, value, valuation, worth; proportion, ration; assessment, charge, impost, tax.

rate[2] vb abuse, berate, censure, chide, criticize, find fault, reprimand, reprove, scold.

ratify vb confirm, corroborate, endorse, establish, seal, settle, substantiate; approve, bind, consent, sanction.

ration vb apportion, deal, distribute, dole, restrict. * n allowance, portion, quota, share.

rational adj intellectual, reasoning; equitable, fair, fit, just, moderate, natural, normal, proper, reasonable, right; discreet, enlightened, intelligent, judicious, sagacious, sensible, sound, wise.

raucous adj harsh, hoarse, husky, rough.

ravenous adj devouring, ferocious, gluttonous, greedy, insatiable, omnivorous, ravening, rapacious, voracious.

raving *adj* delirious, deranged, distracted, frantic, frenzied, furious, infuriated, mad, phrenetic, raging. * *n* delirium, frenzy, fury, madness, rage.

raw *adj* fresh, inexperienced, unpractised, unprepared, unseasoned, untried, unskilled; crude, green, immature, unfinished, unripe; bare, chaffed, excoriated, galled, sensitive, sore; bleak, chilly, cold, cutting, damp, piercing, windswept; uncooked.

ray *n* beam, emanation, gleam, moonbeam, radiance, shaft, streak, sunbeam.

reach *vb* extend, stretch; grasp, hit, strike, touch; arrive at, attain, gain, get, obtain, win. * *n* capability, capacity, grasp.

readily *adv* easily, promptly, quickly; cheerfully, willingly.

ready *vb* arrange, equip, organize, prepare. * *adj* alert, expeditious, prompt, quick, punctual, speedy; adroit, apt, clever, dextrous, expert, facile, handy, keen, nimble, prepared, prompt, ripe, quick, sharp, skilful, smart; cheerful, disposed, eager, free, inclined, willing; accommodating, available, convenient, near, handy; easy, facile, fluent, offhand, opportune, short, spontaneous.

real *adj* absolute, actual, certain, literal, positive, practical, substantial, substantive, veritable; authentic, genuine, true; essential, internal, intrinsic.

realize *vb* accomplish, achieve, discharge, effect, effectuate, perfect, perform; apprehend, comprehend, experience, recognize, understand; externalize, substantiate; acquire, earn, gain, get, net, obtain, produce, sell.

reality *n* actuality, certainty, fact, truth, verity.

really *adv* absolutely, actually, certainly, indeed, positively, truly, verily, veritably.

rear *adj* aft, back, following, hind, last. * *n* background, reverse, setting; heel, posterior, rear end, rump, stern, tail; path, trail, train, wake.

rear *vb* construct, elevate, erect, hoist, lift, raise; cherish, educate, foster, instruct, nourish, nurse, nurture, train; breed, grow; rouse, stir up.

reason *vb* argue, conclude, debate, deduce,

draw from, infer, intellectualize, syllogize, think, trace. * *n* faculty, intellect, intelligence, judgement, mind, principle, sanity, sense, thinking, understanding; account, argument, basis, cause, consideration, excuse, explanation, gist, ground, motive, occasion, pretence, proof; aim, design, end, object, purpose; argument, reasoning; common sense, reasonableness, wisdom; equity, fairness, justice, right; exposition, rationale, theory.

reasonable *adj* equitable, fair, fit, honest, just, proper, rational, right, suitable; enlightened, intelligent, judicious, sagacious, sensible, wise; considerable, fair, moderate, tolerable; credible, intellectual, plausible, well-founded; sane, sober, sound; cheap, inexpensive, low-priced.

rebel *vb* mutiny, resist, revolt, strike. * *adj* insubordinate, insurgent, mutinous, rebellious. * *n* insurgent, mutineer, traitor.

rebellion *n* anarchy, insubordination, insurrection, mutiny, resistance, revolt, revolution, uprising.

rebellious *adj* contumacious, defiant, disloyal, disobedient, insubordinate, intractable, obstinate, mutinous, rebel, refractory, seditious.

recall *vb* abjure, abnegate, annul, cancel, countermand, deny, nullify, overrule, recant, repeal, repudiate, rescind, retract, revoke, swallow, withdraw; commemorate, recollect, remember, retrace, review, revive. * *n* abjuration, abnegation, annulment, cancellation, nullification, recantation, repeal, repudiation, rescindment, retraction, revocation, withdrawal; memory, recollection, remembrance, reminiscence.

recapitulate *vb* epitomize, recite, rehearse, reiterate, repeat, restate, review, summarize.

receive *vb* accept, acquire, derive, gain, get, obtain, take; admit, shelter, take in; entertain, greet, welcome; allow, permit, tolerate; adopt, approve, believe, credit, embrace, follow, learn, understand; accommodate, admit, carry, contain, hold, include, retain; bear, encounter, endure, experience, meet, suffer, sustain.

recent *adj* fresh, new, novel; latter, modern, young; deceased, foregoing, late, preceding, retiring.

reception *n* acceptance, receipt, receiving; entertainment, greeting, welcome; levee, soiree, party; acceptance, admission, credence; admission, belief, credence, recognition.

reckless *adj* breakneck, careless, desperate, devil-may-care, flighty, foolhardy, giddy, harebrained, headlong, heedless, inattentive, improvident, imprudent, inconsiderate, indifferent, indiscreet, mindless, negligent, rash, regardless, remiss, thoughtless, temerarious, uncircumspect, unconcerned, unsteady, volatile, wild.

reckon *vb* calculate, cast, compute, consider, count, enumerate, guess, number; account, class, esteem, estimate, regard, repute, value.

reckoning *n* calculation, computation, consideration, counting; account, bill, charge, estimate, register, score; arrangement, settlement.

reclaim *vb* amend, correct, reform; recover, redeem, regenerate, regain, reinstate, restore; civilize, tame.

recline *vb* couch, lean, lie, lounge, repose, rest.

reclusive *adj* recluse, retired, secluded, sequestered, sequestrated, solitary.

recognition *n* identification, memory, recollection, remembrance; acknowledgement, appreciation, avowal, comprehension, confession, notice; allowance, concession.

recognize *vb* apprehend, identify, perceive, remember; acknowledge, admit, avow, confess, own; allow, concede, grant; greet, salute.

recoil *vb* react, rebound, reverberate; retire, retreat, withdraw; blench, fail, falter, quail, shrink. * *n* backstroke, boomerang, elasticity, kick, reaction, rebound, repercussion, resilience, revulsion, ricochet, shrinking.

recollect *vb* recall, remember, reminisce.

recollection *n* memory, remembrance, reminiscence.

recommend *vb* approve, commend, endorse, praise, sanction; commend, commit; advise, counsel, prescribe, suggest.

recommendation *n* advocacy, approbation, approval, commendation, counsel, credential, praise, testimonial.

reconcile *vb* appease, conciliate, pacify, placate, propitiate, reunite; content, harmonize, regulate; adjust, compose, heal, settle.

record *vb* chronicle, enter, note, register. * *n* account, annals, archive, chronicle, diary, docket, enrolment, entry, file, list, minute, memoir, memorandum, memorial, note, proceedings, register, registry, report, roll, score; mark, memorial, relic, trace, track, trail, vestige; memory, remembrance; achievement, career, history.

recover *vb* recapture, reclaim, regain; rally, recruit, repair, retrieve; cure, heal, restore, revive; redeem, rescue, salvage, save; convalesce, rally, recuperate.

recreation *n* amusement, cheer, diversion, entertainment, fun, game, leisure, pastime, play, relaxation, sport.

recreational *adj* amusing, diverting, entertaining, refreshing, relaxing, relieving.

recruit *vb* repair, replenish; recover, refresh, regain, reinvigorate, renew, renovate, restore, retrieve, revive, strengthen, supply. * *n* auxiliary, beginner, helper, learner, novice, tyro.

rectify *vb* adjust, amend, better, correct, emend, improve, mend, redress, reform, regulate, straighten.

rectitude *n* conscientiousness, equity, goodness, honesty, integrity, justice, principle, probity, right, righteousness, straightforwardness, uprightness, virtue.

recur *vb* reappear, resort, return, revert.

redemption *n* buying, compensation, recovery, repurchase, retrieval; deliverance, liberation, ransom, release, rescue, salvation; discharge, fulfilment, performance.

reduce *vb* bring, reduce; form, make, model, mould, remodel, render, resolve, shape; abate, abbreviate, abridge, attenuate, contract, curtail, decimate, decrease, diminish, lessen, minimize, shorten, thin; abase, debase, degrade, depress, dwarf, impair, lower, weaken; capture, conquer, master, overpower, overthrow, subject, subdue, subjugate, vanquish; impoverish, ruin; resolve, solve.

redundant *adj* copious, excessive, exuberant, fulsome, inordinate, lavish, needless, overflowing, overmuch, plentiful, prodigal, superabundant, replete, superfluous, unnecessary, useless; diffuse, periphrastic, pleonastic, tautological, verbose, wordy.

reel[1] *n* capstan, winch, windlass; bobbin, spool.

reel[2] *vb* falter, flounder, heave, lurch, pitch, plunge, rear, rock, roll, stagger, sway, toss, totter, tumble, wallow, welter, vacillate; spin, swing, turn, twirl, wheel, whirl. * *n* gyre, pirouette, spin, turn, twirl, wheel, whirl.

refer *vb* commit, consign, direct, leave, relegate, send, submit; ascribe, assign, attribute, impute; appertain, belong, concern, pertain, point, relate, respect, touch; appeal, apply, consult; advert, allude, cite, quote.

referee *vb* arbitrate, judge, umpire. * *n* arbiter, arbitrator, judge, umpire.

reference *n* concern, connection, regard, respect; allusion, ascription, citation, hint, intimation, mark, reference, relegation.

refine *vb* clarify, cleanse, defecate, fine, purify; cultivate, humanize, improve, polish, rarefy, spiritualize.

refined *adj* courtly, cultured, genteel, polished, polite; discerning, discriminating, fastidious, sensitive; filtered, processed, purified.

reflect *vb* copy, imitate, mirror, reproduce; cogitate, consider, contemplate, deliberate, meditate, muse, ponder, ruminate, study, think.

reflection *n* echo, shadow; cogitation, consideration, contemplation, deliberation, idea, meditation, musing, opinion, remark, rumination, thinking, thought; aspersion, blame, censure, criticism, disparagement, reproach, slur.

reform *vb* amend, ameliorate, better, correct, improve, mend, meliorate, rectify, reclaim, redeem, regenerate, repair, restore; reconstruct, remodel, reshape. * *n* amendment, correction, progress, reconstruction, rectification, reformation.

refrain[1] *vb* abstain, cease, desist, forbear, stop, withhold.

refrain[2] *n* chorus, song, undersong.

refresh *vb* air, brace, cheer, cool, enliven, exhilarate, freshen, invigorate, reanimate, recreate, recruit, reinvigorate, revive, regale, slake.

refuge *n* asylum, covert, harbour, haven, protection, retreat, safety, sanction, security, shelter.

refund *vb* reimburse, repay, restore, return. * *n* reimbursement, repayment.

refuse[1] *n* chaff, discard, draff, dross, dregs, garbage, junk, leavings, lees, litter, lumber, offal, recrement, remains, rubbish, scoria, scum, sediment, slag, sweepings, trash, waste.

refuse[2] *vb* decline, deny, withhold; decline, disallow, disavow, exclude, rebuff, reject, renege, renounce, repel, repudiate, revoke, veto.

regal *adj* imposing, imperial, kingly, noble, royal, sovereign.

regard *vb* behold, gaze, look, notice, mark, observe, remark, see, view, watch; attend to, consider, heed, mind, respect; esteem, honour, respect, revere, reverence, value; account, believe, consider, estimate, deem, hold, imagine, reckon, suppose, think, treat, use. * *n* gaze, look, view; attention, care, concern, consideration, heed, notice, observance; account, reference, relation, respect, view; affection, attachment, concern, consideration, deference, esteem, estimation, honour, interest, liking, love, respect, reverence, sympathy, value; account, eminence, note, reputation, repute; condition, consideration, matter, point.

regardless *adj* careless, disregarding, heedless, inattentive, indifferent, mindless, neglectful, negligent, unconcerned, unmindful, unobservant. * *adv* however, irrespectively, nevertheless, none the less, notwithstanding.

region *n* climate, clime, country, district,

division, latitude, locale, locality, province, quarter, scene, territory, tract; area, neighbourhood, part, place, portion, spot, space, sphere, terrain, vicinity.

register vb delineate, portray, record, show. * n annals, archive; catalogue, chronicle, list, record, roll, schedule; clerk, registrar, registry; compass, range.

regret vb bewail, deplore, grieve, lament, repine, sorrow; bemoan, repent, mourn, rue. * n concern, disappointment, grief, lamentation, rue, sorrow, trouble; compunction, contrition, penitence, remorse, repentance, repining, self-condemnation, self-reproach.

regular adj conventional, natural, normal, ordinary, typical; correct, customary, cyclic, established, fixed, habitual, periodic, periodical, usual, recurring, reasonable, rhythmic, seasonal, stated, usual; steady, constant, uniform, even; just, methodical, orderly, punctual, systematic, uniform, unvarying; complete, genuine, indubitable, out-and-out, perfect, thorough; balanced, consistent, symmetrical.

regulate vb adjust, arrange, dispose, methodize, order, organize, settle, standardize, time, systematize; conduct, control, direct, govern, guide, manage, order, rule.

regulation adj customary, mandatory, official, required, standard. * n adjustment, arrangement, control, disposal, disposition, law, management, order, ordering, precept, rule, settlement.

reign vb administer, command, govern, influence, predominate, prevail, rule. * n control, dominion, empire, influence, power, royalty, sovereignty, power, rule, sway.

rein vb bridle, check, control, curb, guide, harness, hold, restrain, restrict. * n bridle, check, curb, harness, restraint, restriction.

reject vb cashier, discard, dismiss, eject, exclude, pluck; decline, deny, disallow, despise, disapprove, disbelieve, rebuff, refuse, renounce, repel, repudiate, scout, slight, spurn, veto. * n cast-off, discard, failure, refusal, repudiation.

rejoice vb cheer, delight, enliven, enrapture, exhilarate, gladden, gratify, please, transport; crow, exult, delight, gloat, glory, jubilate, triumph, vaunt.

rejoin vb answer, rebut, respond, retort.

relate vb describe, detail, mention, narrate, recite, recount, rehearse, report, tell; apply, connect, correlate.

relation n account, chronicle, description, detail, explanation, history, mention, narration, narrative, recital, rehearsal, report, statement, story, tale; affinity, application, bearing, connection, correlation, dependency, pertinence, relationship; concern, reference, regard, respect; alliance, connection, nearness, propinquity, rapport; affinity, blood, consanguinity, cousinship, kin, kindred, kinship, relationship; kinsman, kinswoman, relative.

relax vb loose, loosen, slacken, unbrace, unstrain; debilitate, enervate, enfeeble, prostrate, unbrace, unstring, weaken; abate, diminish, lessen, mitigate, reduce, remit; amuse, divert, ease, entertain, recreate, unbend.

release vb deliver, discharge, disengage, exempt, extricate, free, liberate, loose, unloose; acquit, discharge, quit, relinquish, remit. * n deliverance, discharge, freedom, liberation; absolution, dispensation, excuse, exemption, exoneration; acquaintance, clearance.

relentless adj cruel, hard, impenitent, implacable, inexorable, merciless, obdurate, pitiless, rancorous, remorseless, ruthless, unappeasable, uncompassionate, unfeeling, unforgiving, unmerciful, unpitying, unrelenting, unyielding, vindictive.

relevant adj applicable, appropriate, apposite, apt, apropos, fit, germane, pertinent, proper, relative, suitable.

reliable adj authentic, certain, constant, dependable, sure, trustworthy, trusty, unfailing.

reliance n assurance, confidence, credence, dependence, hope, trust.

relief n aid, alleviation, amelioration, assistance, assuagement, comfort, deliverance, ease, easement, help, mitigation, reinforcement, respite, rest, succour, softening, support; indemnification, redress, remedy; embossment, projection, prominence, protrusion; clearness, distinction, perspective, vividness.

relieve vb aid, comfort, free, help, succour, support, sustain; abate, allay, alleviate, assuage, cure, diminish, ease, lessen, lighten, mitigate, remedy, remove, soothe; indemnify, redress, right, repair; disengage, free, release, remedy, rescue.

religious adj devotional, devout, godfearing, godly, holy, pious, prayerful, spiritual; conscientious, exact, rigid, scrupulous, strict; canonical, divine, theological.

relinquish vb abandon, desert, forsake, forswear, leave, quit, renounce, resign, vacate; abdicate, cede, forbear, forego, give up, surrender, yield.

relish vb appreciate, enjoy, like, prefer; season, flavour, taste. * n appetite, appreciation, enjoyment, fondness, gratification, gusto, inclination, liking, partiality, predilection, taste, zest; cast, flavour, manner, quality, savour, seasoning, sort, tinge, touch, twang; appetizer, condiment; flavour, taste.

reluctant adj averse, backward, disinclined, hesitant, indisposed, loath, unwilling.

rely vb confide, count, depend, hope, lean, reckon, repose, trust.

remain vb abide, continue, endure, last, stay; exceed, survive; abide, continue, dwell, halt, rest, sojourn, stay, stop, tarry, wait.

remainder n balance, excess, leavings, remains, remnant, residue, rest, surplus.

remark vb heed, notice, observe, regard; comment, express, mention, observe, say, state, utter. * n consideration, heed, notice, observation, regard; annotation, comment, gloss, note, stricture; assertion, averment, comment, declaration, saying, statement, utterance.

remarkable adj conspicuous, distinguished, eminent, extraordinary, famous, notable, noteworthy, noticeable, pre-eminent, rare, singular, strange,

striking, uncommon, unusual, wonderful.

remedy vb cure, heal, help, palliate, relieve; amend, correct, rectify, redress, repair, restore, retrieve. * n antidote, antitoxin, corrective, counteractive, cure, help, medicine, nostrum, panacea, restorative, specific; redress, reparation, restitution, restoration; aid, assistance, relief.

remiss adj backward, behindhand, dilatory, indolent, languid, lax, slack, slow, tardy; careless, dilatory, heedless, idle, inattentive, neglectful, negligent, shiftless, slack, slothful, slow, thoughtless.

remission n abatement, diminution, lessening, mitigation, moderation, relaxation; cancellation, discharge, release, relinquishment; intermission, interruption, rest, stop, stoppage, suspense, suspension; absolution, acquittal, discharge, excuse, exoneration, forgiveness, indulgence, pardon.

remorse n compunction, contrition, penitence, qualm, regret, repentance, reproach, self-reproach, sorrow.

remorseless adj cruel, barbarous, hard, harsh, implacable, inexorable, merciless, pitiless, relentless, ruthless, savage, uncompassionate, unmerciful, unrelenting.

remote adj distant, far, out-of-the-way; alien, far-fetched, foreign, inappropriate, unconnected, unrelated; abstracted, separated; inconsiderable, slight; isolated, removed, secluded, sequestrated.

removal n abstraction, departure, dislodgement, displacement, relegation, remove, shift, transference; elimination, extraction, withdrawal; abatement, destruction; discharge, dismissal, ejection, expulsion.

remove vb carry, dislodge, displace, shift, transfer, transport; abstract, extract, withdraw; abate, banish, destroy, suppress; cashier, depose, discharge, dismiss, eject, expel, oust, retire; depart, move.

render vb restore, return, surrender; assign, deliver, give, present; afford, contribute, furnish, supply, yield; construe, interpret, translate.

rendition n restitution, return, surrender;

delineation, exhibition, interpretation, rendering, representation, reproduction; rendering, translation, version.

renounce vb abjure, abnegate, decline, deny, disclaim, disown, forswear, neglect, recant, repudiate, reject, slight; abandon, abdicate, drop, forego, forsake, desert, leave, quit, relinquish, resign.

renovate vb reconstitute, re-establish, refresh, refurbish, renew, restore, revamp; reanimate, recreate, regenerate, reproduce, resuscitate, revive, revivify.

renown n celebrity, distinction, eminence, fame, figure, glory, honour, greatness, name, note, notability, notoriety, reputation, repute.

renowned adj celebrated, distinguished, eminent, famed, famous, honoured, illustrious, remarkable, wonderful.

rent[1] n breach, break, crack, cleft, crevice, fissure, flaw, fracture, gap, laceration, opening, rift, rupture, separation, split, tear; schism, separation.

rent[2] vb hire, lease, let. * n income, rental, revenue.

repair[1] vb mend, patch, piece, refit, retouch, tinker, vamp; correct, recruit, restore, retrieve. * n mending, refitting, renewal, reparation, restoration.

repair[2] vb betake oneself, go, move, resort, turn.

repay vb refund, reimburse, restore, return; compensate, recompense, remunerate, reward, satisfy; avenge, retaliate, revenge.

repeal vb abolish, annul, cancel, recall, rescind, reverse, revoke. * n abolition, abrogation, annulment, cancellation, rescission, reversal, revocation.

repeat vb double, duplicate, iterate; cite, narrate, quote, recapitulate, recite, rehearse; echo, renew, reproduce. * n duplicate, duplication, echo, iteration, recapitulation, reiteration, repetition.

repel vb beat, disperse, repulse, scatter; check, confront, oppose, parry, rebuff, resist, withstand; decline, refuse, reject; disgust, revolt, sicken.

repellent adj abhorrent, disgusting, forbidding, repelling, repugnant, repulsive, revolting, uninviting.

repent vb atone, regret, relent, rue, sorrow.

repentance n compunction, contriteness, contrition, penitence, regret, remorse, self-accusation, self-condemnation, self-reproach.

repentant adj contrite, penitent, regretful, remorseful, rueful, sorrowful, sorry.

repetition n harping, iteration, recapitulation, reiteration; diffuseness, redundancy, tautology, verbosity; narration, recital, rehearsal, relation, retailing; recurrence, renewal.

replace vb re-establish, reinstate, reset; refund, repay, restore; succeed, supersede, supplant.

replenish vb fill, refill, renew, re-supply; enrich, furnish, provide, store, supply.

replica n autograph, copy, duplicate, facsimile, reproduction.

reply vb answer, echo, rejoin, respond. * n acknowledgement, answer, rejoinder, repartee, replication, response, retort.

report vb announce, annunciate, communicate, declare; advertise, broadcast, bruit, describe, detail, herald, mention, narrate, noise, promulgate, publish, recite, relate, rumour, state, tell; minute, record. * n account, announcement, communication, declaration, statement; advice, description, detail, narration, narrative, news, recital, story, tale, talk, tidings; gossip, hearsay, rumour; clap, detonation, discharge, explosion, noise, repercussion, sound; fame, reputation, repute; account, bulletin, minute, note, record, statement.

repose[1] vb compose, recline, rest, settle; couch, lie, recline, sleep, slumber; confide, lean. * n quiet, recumbence, recumbency, rest, sleep, slumber; breathing time, inactivity, leisure, respite, relaxation; calm, ease, peace, peacefulness, quiet, quietness, quietude, stillness, tranquillity.

repose[2] vb place, put, stake; deposit, lodge, reposit, store.

reprehensible adj blameable, blameworthy, censurable, condemnable, culpable, reprovable.

represent vb exhibit, express, show; delineate, depict, describe, draw, portray, sketch; act, impersonate, mimic, personate, personify; exemplify, illustrate, image, portray, reproduce, symbolize, typify.

representation n delineation, exhibition, show; impersonation, personation, simulation; account, description, narration, narrative, relation, statement; image, likeness, model, portraiture, resemblance, semblance; sight, spectacle; expostulation, remonstrance.

representative adj figurative, illustrative, symbolic, typical; delegated, deputed, representing. * n agent, commissioner, delegate, deputy, emissary, envoy, legate, lieutenant, messenger, proxy, substitute.

repress vb choke, crush, dull, overcome, overpower, silence, smother, subdue, suppress, quell; bridle, chasten, chastise, check, control, curb, restrain; appease, calm, quiet.

reprimand vb admonish, blame, censure, chide, rebuke, reprehend, reproach, reprove, upbraid. * n admonition, blame, censure, rebuke, reprehension, reproach, reprobation, reproof, reproval.

reproach vb blame, censure, rebuke, reprehend, reprimand, reprove, upbraid; abuse, accuse, asperse, condemn, defame, discredit, disparage, revile, traduce, vilify. * n abuse, blame, censure, condemnation, contempt, contumely, disapprobation, disapproval, expostulation, insolence, invective, railing, rebuke, remonstrance, reprobation, reproof, reviling, scorn, scurrility, upbraiding, vilification; abasement, discredit, disgrace, dishonour, disrepute, indignity, ignominy, infamy, insult, obloquy, odium, offence, opprobrium, scandal, scorn, shame, slur, stigma.

reproduce vb copy, duplicate, emulate, imitate, print, repeat, represent; breed, generate, procreate, propagate.

reproof n admonition, animadversion, blame, castigation, censure, chiding, condemnation, correction, criticism, lecture, monition, objurgation, rating, rebuke, reprehension, reprimand, reproach, reproval, upbraiding.

repudiate vb abjure, deny, disavow, discard, disclaim, disown, nullify, reject, renounce.

repugnant adj incompatible, inconsistent, irreconcilable; adverse, antagonistic, contrary, hostile, inimical, opposed, opposing, unfavourable; detestable, distasteful, offensive, repellent, repulsive.

repulse vb check, defeat, refuse, reject, repel. * n repelling, repulsion; denial, refusal; disappointment, failure.

repulsion n abhorrence, antagonism, anticipation, aversion, discard, disgust, dislike, hatred, hostility, loathing, rebuff, rejection, repugnance, repulse, spurning.

repulsive adj abhorrent, cold, disagreeable, disgusting, forbidding, frigid, harsh, hateful, loathsome, nauseating, nauseous, odious, offensive, repellent, repugnant, reserved, revolting, sickening, ugly, unpleasant.

reputable adj creditable, estimable, excellent, good, honourable, respectable, worthy.

reputation n account, character, fame, mark, name, repute; celebrity, credit, distinction, eclat, esteem, estimation, fame, glory, honour, prestige, regard, renown, report, repute, respect.

request vb ask, beg, beseech, call, claim, demand, desire, entreat, pray, solicit, supplicate. * n asking, entreaty, importunity, invitation, petition, prayer, requisition, solicitation, suit, supplication.

require vb beg, beseech, bid, claim, crave, demand, dun, importune, invite, pray, requisition, request, sue, summon; need, want; direct, enjoin, exact, order, prescribe.

requirement n claim, demand, exigency, market, need, needfulness, requisite, requisition, request, urgency, want; behest, bidding, charge, claim, command, decree, exaction, injunction, mandate, order, precept.

rescue vb deliver, extricate, free, liberate, preserve, ransom, recapture, recover, redeem, release, retake, save. * n deliverance, extrication, liberation, redemption, release, salvation.

research vb analyse, examine, explore, inquire, investigate, probe, study. * n analysis, examination, exploration, inquiry, investigation, scrutiny, study.

resemblance n affinity, agreement, analogy, likeness, semblance, similarity, similitude; counterpart, facsimile, image, likeness, representation.

resemble vb compare, liken; copy, counterfeit, imitate.

resentful adj angry, bitter, choleric, huffy, hurt, irascible, irritable, malignant, revengeful, sore, touchy.

resentment n acrimony, anger, annoyance, bitterness, choler, displeasure, dudgeon, fury, gall, grudge, heartburning, huff, indignation, ire, irritation, pique, rage, soreness, spleen, sulks, umbrage, vexation, wrath.

reservation n reserve, suppression; appropriation, booking, exception, restriction, saving; proviso, salvo; custody, park, reserve, sanctuary.

reserve vb hold, husband, keep, retain, store. * adj alternate, auxiliary, spare, substitute. * n reservation; aloofness, backwardness, closeness, coldness, concealment, constraint, suppression, reservedness, retention, restraint, reticence, uncommunicativeness, unresponsiveness; coyness, demureness, modesty, shyness, taciturnity; park, reservation, sanctuary.

reserved adj coy, demure, modest, shy, taciturn; aloof, backward, cautious, cold, distant, incommunicative, restrained, reticent, self-controlled, unsociable, unsocial; bespoken, booked, excepted, held, kept, retained, set apart, taken, withheld.

reside vb abide, domicile, domiciliate, dwell, inhabit, live, lodge, remain, room, sojourn, stay.

residence n inhabitance, inhabitancy, sojourn, stay, stop, tarrying; abode, domicile, dwelling, habitation, home, house, lodging, mansion.

resign vb abandon, abdicate, abjure, cede, commit, disclaim, forego, forsake, leave, quit, relinquish, renounce, surrender, yield.

resignation n abandonment, abdication,

relinquishment, renunciation, retirement, surrender; acquiescence, compliance, endurance, forbearance, fortitude, long-sufferance, patience, submission, sufferance.

resist vb assail, attack, baffle, block, check, confront, counteract, disappoint, frustrate, hinder, impede, impugn, neutralize, obstruct, oppose, rebel, rebuff, stand against, stem, stop, strive, thwart, withstand.

resolute adj bold, constant, decided, determined, earnest, firm, fixed, game, hardy, inflexible, persevering, pertinacious, relentless, resolved, staunch, steadfast, steady, stout, stouthearted, sturdy, tenacious, unalterable, unbending, undaunted, unflinching, unshaken, unwavering, unyielding.

resolution n boldness, disentanglement, explication, unravelling; backbone, constancy, courage, decision, determination, earnestness, energy, firmness, fortitude, grit, hardihood, inflexibility, intention, manliness, pluck, perseverance, purpose, relentlessness, resolve, resoluteness, stamina, steadfastness, steadiness, tenacity.

resolve vb analyse, disperse, scatter, separate, reduce; change, dissolve, liquefy, melt, reduce, transform; decipher, disentangle, elucidate, explain, interpret, unfold, solve, unravel; conclude, decide, determine, fix, intend, purpose, will. * n conclusion, decision, determination, intention, will; declaration, determination, resolution.

resort vb frequent, haunt; assemble, congregate, convene, go, repair. * n application, expedient, recourse; haunt, refuge, rendezvous, retreat, spa; assembling, confluence, concourse, meeting; recourse, reference.

resource n dependence, resort; appliance, contrivance, device, expedient, instrumentality, means, resort.

resources npl capital, funds, income, money, property, reserve, supplies, wealth.

respect vb admire, esteem, honour, prize, regard, revere, reverence, spare, value, venerate; consider, heed, notice, observe. * n attention, civility, courtesy, consideration, deference, estimation, homage, honour, notice, politeness, recognition, regard, reverence, veneration; consideration, favour, goodwill, kind; aspect, bearing, connection, feature, matter, particular, point, reference, regard, relation.

respectable adj considerable, estimable, honourable, presentable, proper, upright, worthy; considerable, mediocre, moderate.

respectful adj ceremonious, civil, complaisant, courteous, decorous, deferential, dutiful, formal, polite.

respond vb answer, reply, rejoin; accord, correspond, suit.

responsible adj accountable, amenable, answerable, liable, trustworthy.

rest¹ vb cease, desist, halt, hold, pause, repose, stop; breathe, relax, repose, unbend; repose, sleep, slumber; lean, lie, lounge, perch, recline, ride; acquiesce, confide, trust; confide, lean, rely, trust; calm, comfort, ease. * n fixity, immobility, inactivity, motionlessness, quiescence, quiet, repose; hush, peace, peacefulness, quiet, quietness, relief, security, stillness, tranquillity; cessation, intermission, interval, lull, pause, relaxation, respite, stop, stay; siesta, sleep, slumber; death; brace, prop, stay, support.

rest² vb be left, remain. * n balance, remainder, remnant, residuum; overplus, surplus.

restive adj mulish, obstinate, stopping, stubborn, unwilling; impatient, recalcitrant, restless, uneasy, unquiet.

restless adj disquieted, disturbed, restive, sleepless, uneasy, unquiet, unresting, changeable, inconstant, irresolute, unsettled, unstable, unsteady, vacillating; active, astatic, roving, transient, unsettled, unstable, wandering; agitated, fidgety, fretful, turbulent.

restorative adj curative, invigorating, recuperative, remedial, restoring, stimulating. * n corrective, curative, cure, healing, medicine, remedy, reparative, stimulant.

restore vb refund, repay, return; caulk, cobble, emend, heal, mend, patch, reintegrate, re-establish, rehabilitate, reinstate, renew, repair, replace, retrieve, splice, tinker; cure, heal, recover, revive; resuscitate, revive.

restraint n bridle, check, coercion, control, compulsion, constraint, curb, discipline, repression, suppression; arrest, deterrence, hindrance, inhibition, limitation, prevention, prohibition, repression, restriction, stay, stop; confinement, detention, imprisonment, shackles; constraint, stiffness, reserve, unnaturalness.

restrict vb bound, circumscribe, confine, limit, qualify, restrain, straiten.

restriction n confinement, limitation; constraint, restraint; reservation, reserve.

result vb accrue, arise, come, ensue, flow, follow, issue, originate, proceed, spring, rise; end, eventuate, terminate. * n conclusion, consequence, deduction, inference, outcome; consequence, corollary, effect, end, event, eventuality, fruit, issue, outcome, product, sequel, termination; conclusion, decision, determination, finding, resolution, resolve, verdict.

resume vb continue, recommence, renew, restart, summarize.

résumé n abstract, curriculum vitae, epitome, recapitulation, summary, synopsis.

retain vb detain, hold, husband, keep, preserve, recall, recollect, remember, reserve, save, withhold; engage, maintain.

retainer n adherent, attendant, dependant, follower, hanger-on, servant.

retaliate vb avenge, match, repay, requite, retort, return, turn.

reticent adj close, reserved, secretive, silent, taciturn, uncommunicative.

retinue n bodyguard, cortege, entourage, escort, followers, household, ménage, suite, tail, train.

retire vb discharge, remove, shelve, superannuate, withdraw; depart, leave, remove, retreat.

retired adj abstracted, removed, withdrawn; apart, private, secret, sequestrated, solitary.

retirement n isolation, loneliness, privacy, retreat, seclusion, solitude, withdrawal.

retiring *adj* coy, demure, diffident, modest, reserved, retreating, shy, withdrawing.

retreat *vb* recoil, retire, withdraw; recede, retire. * *n* departure, recession, recoil, retirement, withdrawal; privacy, seclusion, solitude; asylum, cove, den, habitat, haunt, niche, recess, refuge, resort, shelter.

retribution *n* compensation, desert, judgement, nemesis, penalty, recompense, repayment, requital, retaliation, return, revenge, reward, vengeance.

retrieve *vb* recall, recover, recoup, recruit, re-establish, regain, repair, restore.

return *vb* reappear, recoil, recur, revert; answer, reply, respond; recriminate, retort; convey, give, communicate, reciprocate, recompense, refund, remit, repay, report, requite, send, tell, transmit; elect. * *n* payment, reimbursement, remittance, repayment; recompense, recovery, recurrence, renewal, repayment, requital, restitution, restoration, reward; advantage, benefit, interest, profit, rent, yield.

reveal *vb* announce, communicate, confess, declare, disclose, discover, display, divulge, expose, impart, open, publish, tell, uncover, unmask, unseal, unveil.

revel *vb* carouse, disport, riot, roister, tipple; delight, indulge, luxuriate, wanton. * *n* carousal, feast, festival, saturnalia, spree.

revelry *n* bacchanal, carousal, carouse, debauch, festivity, jollification, jollity, orgy, revel, riot, rout, saturnalia, wassail.

revenge *vb* avenge, repay, requite, retaliate, vindicate. * *n* malevolence, rancour, reprisal, requital, retaliation, retribution, vengeance, vindictiveness.

revenue *n* fruits, income, produce, proceeds, receipts, return, reward, wealth.

revere *vb* adore, esteem, hallow, honour, reverence, venerate, worship.

reverse *vb* invert, transpose; overset, overthrow, overturn, quash, subvert, undo, unmake; annul, countermand, repeal, rescind, retract, revoke; back, back up, retreat. * *adj* back, converse, contrary, opposite, verso. * *n* back, calamity,

check, comedown, contrary, counterpart, defeat, opposite, tail; change, vicissitude; adversity, affliction, hardship, misadventure, mischance, misfortune, mishap, trial.

revert *vb* repel, reverse; backslide, lapse, recur, relapse, return.

review *vb* inspect, overlook, reconsider, re-examine, retrace, revise, survey; analyse, criticize, discuss, edit, judge, scrutinize, study. * *n* reconsideration, re-examination, re-survey, retrospect, survey; analysis, digest, synopsis; commentary, critique, criticism, notice, review, scrutiny, study.

revile *vb* abuse, asperse, backbite, calumniate, defame, execrate, malign, reproach, slander, traduce, upbraid, vilify.

revise *vb* reconsider, re-examine, review; alter, amend, correct, edit, overhaul, polish, review.

revive *vb* reanimate, reinspire, reinspirit, reinvigorate, resuscitate, revitalize, revivify; animate, cheer, comfort, invigorate, quicken, reawaken, recover, refresh, renew, renovate, rouse, strengthen; reawake, recall.

revoke *vb* abolish, abrogate, annul, cancel, countermand, invalidate, quash, recall, recant, repeal, repudiate, rescind, retract.

revolt *vb* desert, mutiny, rebel, rise; disgust, nauseate, repel, sicken. * *n* defection, desertion, faithlessness, inconstancy; disobedience, insurrection, mutiny, outbreak, rebellion, sedition, strike, uprising.

revolution *n* coup, disobedience, insurrection, mutiny, outbreak, rebellion, sedition, strike, uprising; change, innovation, reformation, transformation, upheaval; circle, circuit, cycle, lap, orbit, rotation, spin, turn..

revolve *vb* circle, circulate, rotate, swing, turn, wheel; devolve, return; consider, mediate, ponder, ruminate, study.

revulsion *n* abstraction, shrinking, withdrawal; change, reaction, reversal, transition; abhorrence, disgust, loathing, repugnance.

reward vb compensate, gratify, indemnify, pay, punish, recompense, remember, remunerate, requite. * n compensation, gratification, guerdon, indemnification, pay, recompense, remuneration, requital; bounty, bonus, fee, gratuity, honorarium, meed, perquisite, premium, remembrance, tip; punishment, retribution.

rhythm n cadence, lilt, pulsation, swing; measure, metre, number, rhyme, verse.

rich adj affluent, flush, moneyed, opulent, prosperous, wealthy; costly, estimable, gorgeous, luxurious, precious, splendid, sumptuous, superb, valuable; delicious, luscious, savoury; abundant, ample, copious, enough, full, plentiful, plenteous, sufficient; fertile, fruitful, luxuriant, productive, prolific; bright, dark, deep, exuberant, vivid; harmonious, mellow, melodious, soft, sweet; comical, funny, humorous, laughable.

riches npl abundance, affluence, fortune, money, opulence, plenty, richness, wealth, wealthiness.

rid vb deliver, free, release; clear, disburden, disencumber, scour, sweep; disinherit, dispatch, dissolve, divorce, finish, sever.

riddle[1] vb explain, solve, unriddle. * n conundrum, enigma, mystery, puzzle, rebus.

riddle[2] vb sieve, sift, perforate, permeate, spread. * n colander, sieve, strainer.

ridicule vb banter, burlesque, chaff, deride, disparage, jeer, mock, lampoon, rally, satirize, scout, taunt. * n badinage, banter, burlesque, chaff, derision, game, gibe, irony, jeer, mockery, persiflage, quip, raillery, sarcasm, satire, sneer, squib, wit.

ridiculous adj absurd, amusing, comical, droll, eccentric, fantastic, farcical, funny, laughable, ludicrous, nonsensical, odd, outlandish, preposterous, queer, risible, waggish.

rig vb accoutre, clothe, dress. * n costume, dress, garb; equipment, team.

right vb adjust, correct, regulate, settle, straighten, vindicate. * adj direct, rectilinear, straight; erect, perpendicular,

plumb, upright; equitable, even-handed, fair, just, justifiable, honest, lawful, legal, legitimate, rightful, square, unswerving; appropriate, becoming, correct, conventional, fit, fitting, meet, orderly, proper, reasonable, seemly, suitable, well-done; actual, genuine, real, true, unquestionable; dexter, dextral, right-handed. * adv equitably, fairly, justly, lawfully, rightfully, rightly; correctly, fitly, properly, suitably, truly; actually, exactly, just, really, truly, well. * n authority, claim, liberty, permission, power, privilege, title; equity, good, honour, justice, lawfulness, legality, propriety, reason, righteousness, truth.

righteous adj devout, godly, good, holy, honest, incorrupt, just, pious, religious, saintly, uncorrupt, upright, virtuous; equitable, fair, right, rightful.

rightful adj lawful, legitimate, true; appropriate, correct, deserved, due, equitable, fair, fitting, honest, just, lawful, legal, legitimate, merited, proper, reasonable, suitable, true.

rigid adj firm, hard, inflexible, stiff, stiffened, unbending, unpliant, unyielding; bristling, erect, precipitous, steep, stiff; austere, conventional, correct, exact, formal, harsh, precise, rigorous, severe, sharp, stern, strict, unmitigated; cruel, sharp.

rigour n hardness, inflexibility, rigidity, rigidness, stiffness; asperity, austerity, harshness, severity, sternness; evenness, strictness; inclemency, severity.

rim n brim, brink, border, confine, curb, edge, flange, girdle, margin, ring, skirt.

ring[1] vb circle, encircle, enclose, girdle, surround. * n circle, circlet, girdle, hoop, round, whorl; cabal, clique, combination, confederacy, coterie, gang, junta, league, set.

ring[2] vb chime, clang, jingle, knell, peal, resound, reverberate, sound, tingle, toll; call, phone, telephone. * n chime, knell, peal, tinkle, toll; call, phone call, telephone call.

riot vb carouse, luxuriate, revel. * n affray, altercation, brawl, broil, commotion, disturbance, fray, outbreak, pandemonium, quarrel, squabble, tumult, uproar; dissipation, excess, luxury, merrymaking, revelry.

riotous *adj* boisterous, luxurious, merry, revelling, unrestrained, wanton; disorderly, insubordinate, lawless, mutinous, rebellious, refractory, seditious, tumultuous, turbulent, ungovernable, unruly, violent.

ripe *adj* advanced, grown, mature, mellow, seasoned, soft; fit, prepared, ready; accomplished, complete, consummate, finished, perfect, perfected.

ripen *vb* burgeon, develop, mature, prepare.

rise *vb* arise, ascend, clamber, climb, levitate, mount; excel, succeed; enlarge, heighten, increase, swell, thrive; revive; grow, kindle, wax; begin, flow, head, originate, proceed, spring, start; mutiny, rebel, revolt; happen, occur. * *n* ascension, ascent, rising; elevation, grade, hill, slope; beginning, emergence, flow, origin, source, spring; advance, augmentation, expansion, increase.

risk *vb* bet, endanger, hazard, jeopardize, peril, speculate, stake, venture, wager. * *n* chance, danger, hazard, jeopardy, peril, venture.

rite *n* ceremonial, ceremony, form, formulary, ministration, observance, ordinance, ritual, rubric, sacrament, solemnity.

ritual *adj* ceremonial, conventional, formal, habitual, routine, stereotyped. * *n* ceremonial, ceremony, liturgy, observance, rite, sacrament, service; convention, form, formality, habit, practice, protocol.

rival *vb* emulate, match, oppose. * *adj* competing, contending, emulating, emulous, opposing. * *n* antagonist, competitor, emulator, opponent.

roam *vb* jaunt, prowl, ramble, range, rove, straggle, stray, stroll, wander.

roar *vb* bawl, bellow, cry, howl, vociferate, yell; boom, peal, rattle, resound, thunder. * *n* bellow, roaring; rage, resonance, storm, thunder; cry, outcry, shout; laugh, laughter, shout.

rob *vb* despoil, fleece, pilfer, pillage, plun-

der, rook, strip; appropriate, deprive, embezzle, plagiarize.

robber *n* bandit, brigand, desperado, depredator, despoiler, footpad, freebooter, highwayman, marauder, pillager, pirate, plunderer, rifler, thief.

robbery *n* depredation, despoliation, embezzlement, freebooting, larceny, peculation, piracy, plagiarism, plundering, spoliation, theft.

robe *vb* array, clothe, dress, invest. * *n* attire, costume, dress, garment, gown, habit, vestment; bathrobe, dressing gown, housecoat.

robust *adj* able-bodied, athletic, brawny, energetic, firm, forceful, hale, hardy, hearty, iron, lusty, muscular, powerful, seasoned, self-assertive, sinewy, sound, stalwart, stout, strong, sturdy, vigorous.

rock[1] *n* boulder, cliff, crag, reef, stone; asylum, defence, foundation, protection, refuge, strength, support; gneiss, granite, marble, slate, etc.

rock[2] *vb* calm, cradle, lull, quiet, soothe, still, tranquillize; reel, shake, sway, teeter, totter, wobble.

rogue *n* beggar, vagabond, vagrant; caitiff, cheat, knave, rascal, scamp, scapegrace, scoundrel, sharper, swindler, trickster, villain.

role *n* character, function, impersonation, part, task.

roll *vb* gyrate, revolve, rotate, turn, wheel; curl, muffle, swathe, wind; bind, involve, enfold, envelop; flatten, level, smooth, spread; bowl, drive; trundle, wheel; gybe, lean, lurch, stagger, sway, yaw; billow, swell, undulate; wallow, welter; flow, glide, run. * *n* document, scroll, volume; annals, chronicle, history, record, rota; catalogue, inventory, list, register, schedule; booming, resonance, reverberation, thunder; cylinder, roller.

romance *vb* exaggerate, fantasize. * *n* fantasy, fiction, legend, novel, story, tale; exaggeration, falsehood, lie; ballad, idyll, song.

romantic *adj* extravagant, fanciful, fantastic, ideal, imaginative, sentimental, wild; chimerical, fabulous, fantastic, fictitious, imaginary, improbable, legendary, picturesque, quixotic, sentimental. * n dreamer, idealist, sentimentalist, visionary.

romp vb caper, gambol, frisk, sport. * n caper, frolic, gambol.

room n accommodation, capacity, compass, elbowroom, expanse, extent, field, latitude, leeway, play, scope, space, swing; place, stead; apartment, chamber, lodging; chance, occasion, opportunity.

roomy adj ample, broad, capacious, comfortable, commodious, expansive, extensive, large, spacious, wide.

root¹ vb anchor, embed, fasten, implant, place, settle; confirm, establish. * n base, bottom, foundation; cause, occasion, motive, origin, reason, source; etymon, radical, radix, stem.

root² vb destroy, eradicate, extirpate, exterminate, remove, unearth, uproot; burrow, dig, forage, grub, rummage; applaud, cheer, encourage.

rosy adj auspicious, blooming, blushing, favourable, flushed, hopeful, roseate, ruddy, sanguine.

rot vb corrupt, decay, decompose, degenerate, putrefy, spoil, taint. * n corruption, decay, decomposition, putrefaction.

rotten adj carious, corrupt, decomposed, fetid, putrefied, putrescent, putrid, rank, stinking; defective, unsound; corrupt, deceitful, immoral, treacherous, unsound, untrustworthy.

rough vb coarsen, roughen; manhandle, mishandle, molest. * adj bumpy, craggy, irregular, jagged, rugged, scabrous, scraggy, scratchy, stubby, uneven; approximate, cross-grained, crude, formless, incomplete, knotty, rough-hewn, shapeless, sketchy, uncut, unfashioned, unfinished, unhewn, unpolished, unwrought, vague; bristly, bushy, coarse, disordered, hairy, hirsute, ragged, shaggy, unkempt; austere, bearish, bluff, blunt, brusque, burly, churlish, discourteous, gruff, harsh, impolite, indelicate, rude, rugged, surly, uncivil, uncourteous, ungracious, unpolished, unrefined; harsh, severe, sharp, violent; astringent, crabbed, hard, sour, tart; discordant,

grating, inharmonious, jarring, raucous, scabrous, unmusical; boisterous, foul, inclement, severe, stormy, tempestuous, tumultuous, turbulent, untamed, violent, wild; acrimonious, brutal, cruel, disorderly, hard, riotous, rowdy, severe, uncivil, unfeeling, ungentle. * n bully, rowdy, roughneck, ruffian; draft, outline, sketch, suggestion; unevenness.

round vb curve; circuit, encircle, encompass, surround. * adj bulbous, circular, cylindrical, globular, orbed, orbicular, rotund, spherical; complete, considerable, entire, full, great, large, unbroken, whole; chubby, corpulent, full, plump, stout, swelling; continuous, flowing, full, harmonious, smooth; brisk, full, quick; blunt, candid, fair, frank, honest, open, plain, upright. * adv around, circularly, circuitously. * prep about, around. * n bout, cycle, game, lap, revolution, rotation, succession, turn; cannon, catch, dance; ball, circle, circumference, cylinder, globe, sphere; circuit, compass, perambulation, routine, tour, watch.

rouse vb arouse, awaken, raise, shake, wake, waken; animate, bestir, brace, enkindle, excite, inspire, kindle, rally, stimulate, stir, whet; startle, surprise.

rout vb beat, conquer, defeat, discomfit, overcome, overpower, overthrow, vanquish; chase away, dispel, disperse, scatter. * n defeat, discomfiture, flight, ruin; concourse, multitude, rabble; brawl, disturbance, noise, roar, uproar.

route vb direct, forward, send, steer. * n course, circuit, direction, itinerary, journey, march, road, passage, path, way.

routine adj conventional, familiar, habitual, ordinary, standard, typical, usual; boring, dull, humdrum, predictable, tiresome. * n beat, custom, groove, method, order, path, practice, procedure, round, rut.

row¹ n file, line, queue, range, rank, series, string, tier; alley, street, terrace.

row² vb argue, dispute, fight, quarrel, squabble. * n affray, altercation, brawl, broil, commotion, dispute, disturbance, noise, outbreak, quarrel, riot, squabble, tumult, uproar.

royal *adj* august, courtly, dignified, generous, grand, imperial, kingly, kinglike, magnanimous, magnificent, majestic, monarchical, noble, princely, regal, sovereign, splendid, superb.

rub *vb* abrade, chafe, grate, graze, scrape; burnish, clean, massage, polish, scour, wipe; apply, put, smear, spread. * *n* caress, massage, polish, scouring, shine, wipe; catch, difficulty, drawback, impediment, obstacle, problem.

rubbish *n* debris, detritus, fragments, refuse, ruins, waste; dregs, dross, garbage, litter, lumber, refuse, scoria, scum, sweepings, trash, trumpery.

rude *adj* coarse, crude, ill-formed, rough, rugged, shapeless, uneven, unfashioned, unformed, unwrought; artless, barbarous, boorish, clownish, ignorant, illiterate, loutish, raw, savage, uncivilized, uncouth, uncultivated, undisciplined, unpolished, ungraceful, unskilful, unskilled, untaught, untrained, untutored; awkward, barbarous, bluff, blunt, boorish, brusque, brutal, churlish, coarse, gruff, ill-bred, impertinent, impolite, impudent, insolent, insulting, rough, saucy, savage, uncivil, uncivilized, uncourteous, unrefined; boisterous, fierce, harsh, severe, tumultuous, turbulent, violent; artless, crude, inelegant, raw, rustic, unpolished.

rudimentary *adj* elementary, embryonic, fundamental, initial, primary, rudimental, undeveloped.

ruffian *n* bully, caitiff, cutthroat, hoodlum, miscreant, monster, murderer, rascal, robber, roisterer, rowdy, scoundrel, villain, wretch.

ruffle *vb* damage, derange, disarrange, dishevel, disorder, ripple, roughen, rumple; agitate, confuse, discompose, disquiet, disturb, excite, harass, irritate, molest, plague, perturb, torment, trouble, vex, worry; cockle, flounce, pucker, wrinkle. * *n* edging, frill, ruff; agitation, bustle, commotion, confusion, contention, disturbance, excitement, fight, fluster, flutter, flurry, perturbation, tumult,

rugged *adj* austere, bristly, coarse,

crabbed, cragged, craggy, hard, hardy, irregular, ragged, robust, rough, rude, scraggy, severe, seamed, shaggy, uneven, unkempt, wrinkled; boisterous, inclement, rude, stormy, tempestuous, tumultuous, turbulent, violent; grating, harsh, inharmonious, unmusical, scabrous.

ruin *vb* crush, damn, defeat, demolish, desolate, destroy, devastate, overthrow, overturn, overwhelm, seduce, shatter, smash, subvert, wreck; beggar, impoverish. * *n* damnation, decay, defeat, demolition, desolation, destruction, devastation, discomfiture, downfall, fall, loss, perdition, prostration, rack, ruination, shipwreck, subversion, undoing, wrack, wreck; bane, destruction, mischief, pest.

ruinous *adj* decayed, demolished, dilapidated; baneful, calamitous, damnatory, destructive, disastrous, mischievous, noisome, noxious, pernicious, subversive, wasteful.

rule *vb* bridle, command, conduct, control, direct, domineer, govern, judge, lead, manage, reign, restrain; advise, guide, persuade; adjudicate, decide, determine, establish, settle; obtain, prevail, predominate. * *n* authority, command, control, direction, domination, dominion, empire, government, jurisdiction, lordship, mastery, mastership, regency, reign, sway; behaviour, conduct; habit, method, order, regularity, routine, system; aphorism, canon, convention, criterion, formula, guide, law, maxim, model, precedent, precept, standard, system, test, touchstone; decision, order, prescription, regulation, ruling.

ruler *n* chief, governor, king, lord, master, monarch, potentate, regent, sovereign; director, head, manager, president; controller, guide, rule, straightedge.

rumour *vb* bruit, circulate, report, tell. * *n* bruit, gossip, hearsay, report, talk; news, report, story, tidings; celebrity, fame, reputation, repute.

rumple *vb* crease, crush, corrugate, crumple, disarrange, dishevel, pucker, ruffle, wrinkle. * *n* crease, corrugation, crumple, fold, pucker, wrinkle.

run vb bolt, career, course, gallop, haste, hasten, hie, hurry, lope, post, race, scamper, scour, scud, scuttle, speed, trip; flow, glide, go, move, proceed, stream; fuse, liquefy, melt; advance, pass, proceed, vanish; extend, lie, spread, stretch; circulate, go, pass, press; average, incline, tend; flee; pierce, stab; drive, force, propel, push, thrust, turn; cast, form, mould, shape; follow, perform, pursue, take; discharge, emit; direct, maintain, manage. * n race, running; course, current, flow, motion, passage, progress, way, wont; continuance, currency, popularity; excursion, gallop, journey, trip, trot; demand, pressure; brook, burn, flow, rill, rivulet, runlet, runnel, streamlet.

rupture vb break, burst, fracture, sever, split. * n breach, break, burst, disruption, fracture, split; contention, faction, feud, hostility, quarrel, schism.

rural adj agrarian, bucolic, country, pastoral, rustic, sylvan.

rush vb attack, career, charge, dash, drive, gush, hurtle, precipitate, surge, sweep, tear. * n dash, onrush, onset, plunge, precipitance, precipitancy, rout, stampede, tear.

ruthless adj barbarous, cruel, fell, ferocious, hardhearted, inexorable, inhuman, merciless, pitiless, relentless, remorseless, savage, truculent, uncompassionate, unmerciful, unpitying, unrelenting, unsparing.

S

sacred adj consecrated, dedicated, devoted, divine, hallowed, holy; inviolable, inviolate; sainted, venerable.

sacrifice vb forgo, immolate, surrender. * n immolation, oblation, offering; destruction, devotion, loss, surrender.

sacrilegious adj desecrating, impious, irreverent, profane.

sad adj grave, pensive, sedate, serious; dark, sober, sombre, staid; dejected, depressed, doleful, gloomy, melancholic, miserable, mournful, sorrowful.

saddle vb burden, charge, clog, encumber, load.

safe adj undamaged, unharmed, unhurt, unscathed; guarded, protected, secure, snug, unexposed; certain, dependable, reliable, sure, trustworthy; good, harmless, sound, whole. * n chest, coffer, strongbox.

safeguard vb guard, protect. * n defence, protection, security; convoy, escort, guard, safe-conduct; pass, passport.

sage adj acute, discerning, intelligent, prudent, sagacious, sapient, sensible, shrewd, wise; prudent, judicious, well-judged; grave, serious, solemn. * n philosopher, pundit, savant.

saintly adj devout, godly, holy, pious, religious.

sake n end, cause, purpose, reason; account, cause, consideration, interest, reason, regard, respect, score.

sale n auction, demand, market, vendition, vent.

salt adj saline, salted; bitter, pungent, sharp. * n flavour, savour, seasoning, smack, relish, taste; humour, piquancy, poignancy, sarcasm, smartness, wit, zest; mariner, sailor, seaman, tar.

salvation n deliverance, escape, preservation, redemption, rescue, saving.

same adj ditto, identical, selfsame; corresponding, like, similar.

sameness n identicalness, identity, monotony, oneness, resemblance, selfsameness, uniformity.

sample vb savour, sip, smack, sup, taste; test, try; demonstrate, exemplify, illustrate, instance. * adj exemplary, illustrative, representative. * n demonstration, exemplification, illustration, instance, piece, specimen; example, model, pattern.

sanctimonious adj affected, devout, holy, hypocritical, pharisaical, pious, self-righteous.

sanction vb authorize, countenance, encourage, support; confirm, ratify. * n approval, authority, authorization, confirmation, countenance, endorsement, ratification, support, warranty; ban, boycott, embargo, penalty.

sanctity n devotion, godliness, goodness, grace, holiness, piety, purity, religiousness, saintliness.

sanctuary n altar, church, shrine, temple; asylum, protection, refuge, retreat, shelter.

sane adj healthy, lucid, normal, rational, reasonable, sober, sound.

sanitary adj clean, curative, healing, healthy, hygienic, remedial, therapeutic, wholesome.

sarcastic adj acrimonious, biting, cutting, mordacious, mordant, sardonic, satirical, sharp, severe, sneering, taunting.

satirical adj abusive, biting, bitter, censorious, cutting, invective, ironical, keen, mordacious, poignant, reproachful, sarcastic, severe, sharp, taunting.

satisfaction n comfort, complacency, contentment, ease, enjoyment, gratification, pleasure, satiety; amends, appeasement, atonement, compensation, indemnification, recompense, redress, remuneration, reparation, requital, reward.

satisfy vb appease, content, fill, gratify, please, sate, satiate, suffice; indemnify, compensate, liquidate, pay, recompense, remunerate, requite; discharge, pay, settle; assure, convince, persuade; answer, fulfil, meet.

savage vb attack, lacerate, mangle, maul. * adj rough, sylvan, uncultivated, wild; rude, uncivilized, unpolished, untaught; bloodthirsty, feral, ferine, ferocious, fierce, rapacious, untamed, wild; beastly, brutal, brutish, inhuman; atrocious, barbarous, bloody, brutal, cruel, fell, hardhearted, heathenish, merciless, murderous, pitiless, relentless, ruthless, sanguinary, truculent; native, rough, rugged, uncivilized. * n aboriginal, aborigine, barbarian, brute, heathen, native, vandal.

save vb keep, liberate, preserve, rescue; salvage, recover, redeem; economize, gather, hoard, husband, reserve, store; hinder, obviate, prevent, spare. * prep but, deducting, except.

saviour n defender, deliverer, guardian, protector, preserver, rescuer, saver.

savour vb affect, appreciate, enjoy, like, partake, relish; flavour, season. * n flavour, gust, relish, smack, taste; fragrance, odour, smell, scent.

say vb declare, express, pronounce, speak, tell, utter; affirm, allege, argue; recite, rehearse, repeat; assume, presume, suppose. * n affirmation, declaration, speech, statement; decision, voice, vote.

saying n declaration, expression, observation, remark, speech, statement; adage, aphorism, byword, dictum, maxim, proverb, saw.

scan vb examine, investigate, scrutinize, search, sift.

scandalize vb offend; asperse, backbite, calumniate, decry, defame, disgust, lampoon, libel, reproach, revile, satirise, slander, traduce, vilify.

scandalous adj defamatory, libellous, opprobrious, slanderous; atrocious, disgraceful, disreputable, infamous, inglorious, ignominious, odious, opprobrious, shameful.

scanty adj insufficient, meagre, narrow, scant, small; hardly, scarce, short, slender; niggardly, parsimonious, penurious, scrimpy, skimpy, sparing.

scar vb hurt, mark, wound. * n cicatrice, cicatrix, seam; blemish, defect, disfigurement, flaw, injury, mark.

scarce adj deficient, wanting; infrequent, rare, uncommon. * adv barely, hardly, scantily.

scarcity n dearth, deficiency, insufficiency, lack, want; infrequency, rareness, rarity, uncommonness.

scare vb affright, alarm, appal, daunt, fright, frighten, intimidate, shock, startle, terrify. * n alarm, fright, panic, shock, terror.

scatter vb broadcast, sprinkle, strew; diffuse, disperse, disseminate, dissipate, distribute, separate, spread; disappoint, dispel, frustrate, overthrow.

scent vb breathe in, inhale, nose, smell, sniff; detect, smell out, sniff out; aromatize, perfume. * n aroma, balminess, fragrance, odour, perfume, smell, redolence.

sceptical *adj* doubtful, doubting, dubious, hesitating, incredulous, questioning, unbelieving.

schedule *vb* line up, list, plan, programme, tabulate. * *n* document, scroll; catalogue, inventory, list, plan, record, register, roll, table, timetable.

scheme *vb* contrive, design, frame, imagine, plan, plot, project. * *n* plan, system, theory; cabal, conspiracy, contrivance, design, device, intrigue, machination, plan, plot, project, stratagem; arrangement, draught, diagram, outline.

school *vb* drill, educate, exercise, indoctrinate, instruct, teach, train; admonish, control, chide, discipline, govern, reprove, tutor. * *adj* academic, collegiate, institutional, scholastic, schoolish. * *n* academy, college, gymnasium, institute, institution, kindergarten, lyceum, manège, polytechnic, seminary, university; adherents, camarilla, circle, clique, coterie, disciples, followers; body, order, organization, party, sect

schooling *n* discipline, education, instruction, nurture, teaching, training, tuition.

scintillate *vb* coruscate, flash, gleam, glisten, glitter, sparkle, twinkle.

scoff *vb* deride, flout, jeer, mock, ridicule, taunt; gibe, sneer. * *n* flout, gibe, jeer, sneer, mockery, taunt; derision, ridicule.

scold *vb* berate, blame, censure, chide, rate, reprimand, reprove; brawl, rail, rate, reprimand, upbraid, vituperate. * *n* shrew, termagant, virago, vixen.

scope *n* aim, design, drift, end, intent, intention, mark, object, purpose, tendency, view; amplitude, field, latitude, liberty, margin, opportunity, purview, range, room, space, sphere, vent; extent, length, span, stretch, sweep.

scorch *vb* blister, burn, char, parch, roast, sear, shrivel, singe.

score *vb* cut, furrow, mark, notch, scratch; charge, note, record; charge, impute, note; enter, register. * *n* incision, mark, notch; account, bill, charge, debt, reckoning; consideration, ground, motive, reason.

scorn *vb* condemn, despise, disregard, disdain, scout, slight, spurn. * *n* contempt,

derision, disdain, mockery, slight, sneer; derision, mockery, scoff.

scornful *adj* contemptuous, defiant, disdainful, contemptuous, regardless.

scoundrel *n* cheat, knave, miscreant, rascal, reprobate, rogue, scamp, swindler, trickster, villain.

scowl *vb* frown, glower, lower. * *n* frown, glower, lower.

scrap¹ *vb* discard, junk, trash. * *n* bit, fragment, modicum, particle, piece, snippet; bite, crumb, fragment, morsel, mouthful; debris, junk, litter, rubbish, rubble, trash, waste.

scrap² *vb* altercate, bicker, dispute, clash, fight, hassle, quarrel, row, spat, squabble, tiff, tussle, wrangle. * *n* affray, altercation, bickering, clash, dispute, fight, fray, hassle, melee, quarrel, row, run-in, set-to, spat, squabble, tiff, tussle, wrangle.

scrape *vb* bark, grind, rasp, scuff; accumulate, acquire, collect, gather, save; erase, remove. * *n* difficulty, distress, embarrassment, perplexity, predicament.

scream *vb* screech, shriek, squall, ululate. * *n* cry, outcry, screech, shriek, shrill, ululation.

screen *vb* cloak, conceal, cover, defend, fence, hide, mask, protect, shelter, shroud. * *n* blind, curtain, lattice, partition; defence, guard, protection, shield; cloak, cover, veil, disguise; riddle, sieve.

screw *vb* force, press, pressurize, squeeze, tighten, twist, wrench; oppress, rack; distort. * *n* extortioner, extortionist, miser, scrimp, skinflint; prison guard; sexual intercourse.

scrupulous *adj* conscientious, fastidious, nice, precise, punctilious, rigorous, strict; careful, cautious, circumspect, exact, vigilant.

scrutiny *n* examination, exploration, inquisition, inspection, investigation, search, searching, sifting.

scud *vb* flee, fly, haste, hasten, hie, post, run, scamper, speed, trip.

scuffle *vb* contend, fight, strive, struggle. * *n* altercation, brawl, broil, contest, encounter, fight, fray, quarrel, squabble, struggle, wrangle.

scurry vb bustle, dash, hasten, hurry, scamper, scud, scutter. * n burst, bustle, dash, flurry, haste, hurry, scamper, scud, spurt.

seal vb close, fasten, secure; attest, authenticate, confirm, establish, ratify, sanction; confine, enclose, imprison. * n fastening, stamp, wafer, wax; assurance, attestation, authentication, confirmation, pledge, ratification.

sear vb blight, brand, cauterize, dry, scorch, wither. * adj dried up, dry, sere, withered.

search vb examine, explore, ferret, inspect, investigate, overhaul, probe, ransack, scrutinize, sift; delve, hunt, forage, inquire, look, rummage. * n examination, exploration, hunt, inquiry, inspection, investigation, pursuit, quest, research, seeking, scrutiny.

searching adj close, keen, penetrating, trying; examining, exploring, inquiring, investigating, probing, seeking.

season vb acclimatize, accustom, form, habituate, harden, inure, mature, qualify, temper, train; flavour, spice. * n interval, period, spell, term, time, while.

seasonable adj appropriate, convenient, fit, opportune, suitable, timely.

secluded adj close, covert, embowered, isolated, private, removed, retired, screened, sequestrated, withdrawn.

seclusion n obscurity, privacy, retirement, secrecy, separation, solitude, withdrawal.

second[1] n instant, jiffy, minute, moment, trice.

second[2] vb abet, advance, aid, assist, back, encourage, forward, further, help, promote, support, sustain; approve, favour, support. * adj inferior, second-rate, secondary; following, next, subsequent; additional, extra, other; double, duplicate. * n another, other; assistant, backer, supporter.

secondary adj collateral, inferior, minor, subsidiary, subordinate. * n delegate, deputy, proxy.

secret adj close, concealed, covered, covert, cryptic, hid, hidden, mysterious, privy, shrouded, veiled, unknown, unrevealed, unseen; cabbalistic, clandestine, furtive, privy, sly, stealthy, surreptitious, underhand; confidential, private, retired, secluded, unseen; abstruse, latent, mysterious, obscure, occult, recondite, unknown. * n confidence, enigma, key, mystery.

secretive adj cautious, close, reserved, reticent, taciturn, uncommunicative, wary.

secure vb guard, protect, safeguard; assure, ensure, guarantee, insure; fasten; acquire, gain, get, obtain, procure. * adj assured, certain, confident, sure; insured, protected, safe; fast, firm, fixed, immovable, stable; careless, easy, undisturbed, unsuspecting; careless, heedless, inattentive, incautious, negligent, overconfident.

security n bulwark, defence, guard, palladium, protection, safeguard, safety, shelter; bond, collateral, deposit, guarantee, pawn, pledge, stake, surety, warranty; carelessness, heedlessness, overconfidence, negligence; assurance, assuredness, certainty, confidence, ease.

sedate adj calm, collected, composed, contemplative, cool, demure, grave, placid, philosophical, quiet, serene, serious, sober, still, thoughtful, tranquil, undisturbed, unemotional, unruffled.

sedative adj allaying, anodyne, assuasive, balmy, calming, composing, demulcent, lenient, lenitive, soothing, tranquillizing. * n anaesthetic, anodyne, hypnotic, narcotic, opiate.

sediment n dregs, grounds, lees, precipitate, residue, residuum, settlings.

seduce vb allure, attract, betray, corrupt, debauch, deceive, decoy, deprave, ensnare, entice, inveigle, lead, mislead.

seductive adj alluring, attractive, enticing, tempting.

see vb behold, contemplate, descry, glimpse, survey; comprehend, conceive, distinguish, espy, know, notice, observe, perceive, remark, understand; beware, consider, envisage, regard; experience, feel, know, suffer; consider, distinguish, examine, inspire, notice, observe; discern, look, penetrate, perceive, understand.

seek vb hunt, look, search; court, follow,

prosecute, pursue, solicit; attempt, endeavour, strive, try.

seem *vb* appear, assume, look, pretend.

segment *n* bit, division, part, piece, portion, section, sector.

segregate *vb* detach, disconnect, disperse, insulate, part, separate.

seize *vb* capture, catch, clutch, grab, grapple, grasp, grip, gripe, snatch; confiscate, impress, impound; apprehend, comprehend; arrest, capture, take.

seldom *adv* infrequently, occasionally, rarely.

select *vb* choose, cull, pick, prefer. * *adj* choice, chosen, excellent, exquisite, good, picked, rare, selected.

selection *n* choice, election, pick, preference.

self-conscious *adj* awkward, diffident, embarrassed, insecure, nervous.

self-control *n* restraint, willpower.

self-important *adj* assuming, consequential, proud, haughty, lordly, overbearing, overweening.

selfish *adj* egoistic, egotistical, greedy, illiberal, mean, narrow, self-seeking, ungenerous.

self-possessed *adj* calm, collected, composed, cool, placid, sedate, undisturbed, unexcited, unruffled.

self-willed *adj* contumacious, dogged, headstrong, obstinate, pig-headed, stubborn, uncompliant, wilful.

sell *vb* barter, exchange, hawk, market, peddle, trade, vend.

semblance *n* likeness, resemblance, similarity; air, appearance, aspect, bearing, exterior, figure, form, mien, seeming, show; image, likeness, representation, similitude.

send *vb* cast, drive, emit, fling, hurl, impel, lance, launch, project, propel, throw, toss; delegate, depute, dispatch; forward, transmit; bestow, confer, give, grant.

senile *adj* aged, doddering, superannuated; doting, imbecile.

senior *adj* elder, older; higher, preceding, superior.

sensation *n* feeling, sense, perception; excitement, impression, thrill.

sensational *adj* exciting, melodramatic,

startling, thrilling.

sense *vb* appraise, appreciate, estimate, notice, observe, perceive, suspect, understand. * *n* brains, intellect, mind, reason, understanding; appreciation, apprehension, discernment, feeling, perception, recognition, tact, understanding; idea, judgement, notion, opinion, sentiment, view; import, interpretation, meaning, purport, significance; good, judgement, reason, sagacity, soundness, understanding, wisdom.

sensible *adj* apprehensible, perceptible; aware, cognisant, conscious, convinced, persuaded, satisfied; discreet, intelligent, judicious, rational, reasonable, sagacious, sage, sober, sound, wise; observant, understanding; impressionable, sensitive.

sensitive *adj* perceptive, sentient; affected, impressible, impressionable, responsive, susceptible; delicate, tender, touchy.

sensual *adj* animal, bodily, carnal, voluptuous; gross, lascivious, lewd, licentious, unchaste.

sentence *vb* condemn, doom, judge. * *n* decision, determination, judgement, opinion; doctrine, dogma, opinion, tenet; condemnation, doom, judgement; period, proposition.

sentiment *n* judgement, notion, opinion; maxim, saying; emotion, tenderness; disposition, feeling, thought.

sentimental *adj* impressible, impressionable, over-emotional, romantic, tender.

separate *vb* detach, disconnect, disjoin, disunite, dissever, divide, divorce, part, sever, sunder; eliminate, remove, withdraw; cleave, open. * *adj* detached, disconnected, disjoined, disjointed, dissociated, disunited, divided, parted, severed; discrete, distinct, divorced, unconnected; alone, segregated, withdrawn.

sequel *n* close, conclusion, denouement, end, termination; consequence, event, issue, result, upshot.

sequence *n* following, graduation, progression, succession; arrangement, series, train.

serene *adj* calm, collected, placid, peaceful, quiet, tranquil, sedate, undisturbed, unperturbed, unruffled; bright, calm, clear, fair, unclouded.

serenity n calm, calmness, collectedness, composure, coolness, imperturbability, peace, peacefulness, sedateness, tranquillity; brightness, calmness, clearness, fairness, peace, quietness, stillness.

series n chain, concatenation, course, line, order, progression, sequence, succession, train.

serious adj earnest, grave, demure, pious, sedate, sober, solemn, staid, thoughtful; grave, great, important, momentous, weighty.

servant n attendant, dependant, factotum, helper, henchman, retainer, servitor, subaltern, subordinate, underling; domestic, drudge, flunky, lackey, menial, scullion, slave.

serve vb aid, assist, attend, help, minister, oblige, succour; advance, benefit, forward, promote; content, satisfy, supply; handle, officiate, manage, manipulate, work.

service vb check, maintain, overhaul, repair. * n labour, ministration, work; attendance, business, duty, employ, employment, office; advantage, benefit, good, gain, profit; avail, purpose, use, utility; ceremony, function, observance, rite, worship.

set¹ vb lay, locate, mount, place, put, stand, station; appoint, determine, establish, fix, settle; risk, stake, wager; adapt, adjust, regulate; adorn, stud, variegate; arrange, dispose, pose, post; appoint, assign, predetermine, prescribe; estimate, prize, rate, value; embarrass, perplex, pose; contrive, produce; decline, sink; congeal, concern, consolidate, harden, solidify; flow, incline, run, tend; (*with about*) begin, commence; (*with apart*) appropriate, consecrate, dedicate, devote, reserve, set aside; (*with aside*) abrogate, annul, omit, reject; reserve, set apart; (*with before*) display, exhibit; (*with down*) chronicle, jot down, record, register, state, write down; (*with forth*) display, exhibit, explain, expound, manifest, promulgate, publish, put forward,

represent, show; (*with forward*) advance, further, promote; (*with free*) acquit, clear, emancipate, liberate, release; (*with off*) adorn, decorate, embellish; define, portion off; (*with on*) actuate, encourage, impel, influence, incite, instigate, prompt, spur, urge; attack, assault, set upon; (*with out*) display, issue, publish, proclaim, prove, recommend, show; (*with right*) correct, put in order; (*with to rights*) adjust, regulate; (*with up*) elevate, erect, exalt, raise; establish, found, institute; (*with upon*) assail, assault, attack, fly at, rush upon. * adj appointed, established, formal, ordained; prescribed, regular, settled; determined, fixed, firm, obstinate, positive, stiff, unyielding; immovable, predetermined; located, placed, put. * n attitude, position, posture; scene, scenery, setting.

set² n assortment, collection, suit; class, circle, clique, cluster, company, coterie, division, gang, group, knot, party, school, sect.

setback n blow, hitch, hold-up, rebuff; defeat, disappointment, reverse.

settle vb adjust, arrange, compose, regulate; account, balance, close up, conclude, discharge, liquidate, pay, pay up, reckon, satisfy, square; allay, calm, compose, pacify, quiet, repose, rest, still, tranquillize; confirm, decide, determine, make clear; establish, fix, set; fall, gravitate, sink, subside; abide, colonize, domicile, dwell, establish, inhabit, people, place, plant, reside; (*with on*) determine on, fix on, fix upon; establish.

sever vb divide, part, rend, separate, sunder; detach, disconnect, disjoin, disunite.

several adj individual, single, particular, distinct, exclusive, independent, separate; different, divers, diverse, manifold, many, sundry, various.

severe adj austere, bitter, dour, hard, harsh, inexorable, morose, relentless, rigid, rigorous, rough, sharp, stern, stiff, straitlaced, unmitigated, unrelenting, unsparing; accurate, exact, methodical, strict; chaste, plain, restrained, simple, unadorned; biting, bitter, caustic, cruel, cutting, harsh, keen, sarcastic, satirical, sharp, trenchant; acute, afflictive, distressing, extreme, intense, sharp, stringent, violent; critical, exact, hard, rigorous.

sew *vb* baste, bind, hem, stitch, tack.

shabby *adj* faded, mean, poor, ragged, seedy, threadbare, worn, worn-out; beggarly, mean, paltry, penurious, stingy, ungentlemanly, unhandsome.

shackle *vb* chain, fetter, gyve, hamper, manacle; bind, clog, confine, cumber, embarrass, encumber, impede, obstruct, restrict, trammel. * *n* chain, fetter, gyve, hamper, manacle.

shade *vb* cloud, darken, dim, eclipse, ofuscate, obscure; cover, ensconce, hide, protect, screen, shelter. * *n* darkness, dusk, duskiness, gloom, obscurity, shadow; cover, protection, shelter; awning, blind, curtain, screen, shutter, veil; degree, difference, kind, variety; cast, colour, complexion, dye, hue, tinge, tint, tone; apparition, ghost, manes, phantom, shadow, spectre, spirit.

shadow *vb* becloud, cloud, darken, obscure, shade; adumbrate, foreshadow, symbolize, typify; conceal, cover, hide, protect, screen, shroud. * *n* penumbra, shade, umbra, umbrage; darkness, gloom, obscurity; cover, protection, security, shelter; adumbration, foreshowing, image, prefiguration, representation; apparition, ghost, phantom, shade, spirit; image, portrait, reflection, silhouette.

shadowy *adj* shady; dark, dim, gloomy, murky, obscure; ghostly, imaginary, impalpable, insubstantial, intangible, spectral, unreal, unsubstantial.

shake *vb* quake, quaver, quiver, shiver, shudder, totter, tremble; agitate, convulse, jar, jolt, stagger; daunt, frighten, intimidate; endanger, move, weaken; oscillate, vibrate, wave; move, put away, remove, throw off. * *n* agitation, concussion, flutter, jar, jolt, quaking, shaking, shivering, shock, trembling, tremor.

shaky *adj* jiggly, quaky, shaking, tottering, trembling.

shallow *adj* flimsy, foolish, frivolous, puerile, trashy, trifling, trivial; empty, ignorant, silly, slight, simple, superficial, unintelligent.

sham *vb* ape, feign, imitate, pretend; cheat, deceive, delude, dupe, impose, trick. * *adj* assumed, counterfeit, false, feigned, mock, make-believe, pretended, spurious. * *n* delusion, feint, fraud, humbug, imposition, imposture, pretence, trick.

shame *vb* debase, degrade, discredit, disgrace, dishonour, stain, sully, taint, tarnish; abash, confound, confuse, discompose, disconcert, humble, humiliate; deride, flout, jeer, mock, ridicule, sneer. * *n* contempt, degradation, derision, discredit, disgrace, dishonour, disrepute, ignominy, infamy, obloquy, odium, opprobrium, reproach, scandal; abashment, chagrin, confusion, humiliation, mortification; disgrace, dishonour, reproach, scandal; decency, decorum, modesty, propriety.

shameful *adj* atrocious, base, disgraceful, dishonourable, disreputable, heinous, ignominous, infamous, nefarious, opprobrious, outrageous, scandalous, vile, villainous, wicked; degrading, indecent, scandalous, unbecoming.

shameless *adj* assuming, audacious, bold-faced, brazen, brazen-faced, cool, immodest, impudent, indecent, indelicate, insolent, unabashed, unblushing; abandoned, corrupt, depraved, dissolute, graceless, hardened, incorrigible, irreclaimable, lost, obdurate, profligate, reprobate, sinful, unprincipled, vicious.

shape *vb* create, form, make, produce; fashion, form, model, mould; adjust, direct, frame, regulate; conceive, conjure up, figure, image, imagine. * *n* appearance, aspect, fashion, figure, form, guise, make; build, cast, cut, fashion, model, mould, pattern; apparition, image.

share *vb* apportion, distribute, divide, parcel out, portion, split; partake, participate; experience, receive. * *n* part, portion, quantum; allotment, allowance, contingent, deal, dividend, division, interest, lot, proportion, quantity, quota.

sharp *adj* acute, cutting, keen, keen-edged, trenchant; acuminate, needle-shaped, peaked, pointed, ridged; acute, apt, astute, canny, clear-sighted, clever, cunning, discerning, discriminating, ingenious, inventive, keen-witted, penetrating, perspicacious, quick, ready, sagacious, sharp-witted, shrewd, smart, subtle, witty; acid, acrid, biting, bitter, burning, high-flavoured, high-seasoned, hot, piquant, poignant, pungent, sour, stinging; acrimonious, biting, caustic, cutting, harsh, keen, mordant, pointed, sarcastic, severe, tart, trenchant; cruel, hard, rigid, severe; acute, afflicting, distressing, excruciating, intense, keen, painful, piercing, poignant, severe, shooting, sore, violent; biting, nipping, piercing, pinching; ardent, eager, fervid, fierce, fiery, impetuous, strong, violent; high, piercing, shrill; attentive, vigilant; keen, penetrating, piercing, severe; close, exacting, shrewd. * *adv* abruptly, sharply, suddenly; exactly precisely, punctually.

sharpen *vb* edge, intensify, point.

shatter *vb* break, burst, crack, rend, shiver, smash, splinter, split; break up, derange, disorder, overthrow.

shave *vb* crop, cut off, mow, pare; slice; graze, skim, touch.

sheen *n* brightness, gloss, glossiness, shine, spendour.

sheer¹ *adj* perpendicular, precipitous, steep, vertical; clear, downright, mere, pure, simple, unadulterated, unmingled, unmixed, unqualified, utter; clear, pure; fine, transparent. * *adv* outright; perpendicularly, steeply.

sheer² *vb* decline, deviate, move aside, swerve. * *n* bow, curve.

shelter *vb* cover, defend, harbour, hide, house, protect, screen, shield, shroud. * *n* asylum, cover, covert, harbour, haven, refuge, retreat, sanctuary; defence, protection, safety, screen, security, shield; guardian, protector.

shield *vb* cover, defend, guard, protect, shelter; repel, ward off; avert, forbid, forfend. * *n* aegis, buckler, escutcheon; bulwark, cover, defence, guard, protection, rampart, safeguard, security, shelter.

shift *vb* alter, change, fluctuate, move, vary; chop, dodge, gype, swerve, veer;

contrive, devise, manage, plan, scheme, shuffle. * *n* change, substitution, turn; contrivance, expedient, means, resort, resource; artifice, craft, device, dodge, evasion, fraud, mask, ruse, stratagem, subterfuge, trick, wile; chemise, smock.

shifty *adj* tricky, undependable, wily.

shimmer *vb* flash, glimmer, glisten, shine. * *n* blink, glimmer, glitter, twinkle.

shine *vb* beam, blaze, coruscate, flare, give light, glare, gleam, glimmer, glisten, glitter, glow, lighten, radiate, sparkle; excel. * *n* brightness, brilliancy, glaze, gloss, polish, sheen.

shiny *adj* bright, clear, luminous, sunshiny, unclouded; brilliant, burnished, glassy, glossy, polished.

shipshape *adj* neat, orderly, tidy, trim, well-arranged.

shirk *vb* avoid, dodge, evade, malinger, quit, slack; cheat, shark, trick.

shiver¹ *vb* break, shatter, splinter. * *n* bit, fragment, piece, slice, sliver, splinter.

shiver² *vb* quake, quiver, shake, shudder, tremble. * *n* shaking, shivering, shuddering, tremor.

shock *vb* appall, horrify; disgust, disquiet, disturb, nauseate, offend, outrage, revolt, scandalize, sicken; astound, stagger, stun; collide with, jar, jolt, shake, strike against; encounter, meet. * *n* agitation, blow, offence, stroke; assault, brunt, conflict; blow, clash, collision, concussion, impact, percussion, stroke.

shoot *vb* catapult, expel, hurl, let fly, propel; discharge, fire, let off; dart, fly, pass, pelt; extend, jet, project, protrude, protuberate, push, put forth, send forth, stretch; bud, germinate, sprout; (*with* **up**) grow increase, spring up, run up, start up. * *n* branch, offshoot, scion, sprout, twig.

shore¹ *n* beach, brim, coast, seabord, seaside, strand, waterside.

shore² *vb* brace, buttress, prop, stay, support. * *n* beam, brace, buttress, prop, stay, support.

short *adj* brief, curtailed; direct, near, straight; brief, compendious, concise, condensed, laconic, pithy, terse, sententious, succinct, summary; abrupt, curt, petulant, pointed, sharp, snappish, uncivil; defective, deficient, inadequate, insufficient, niggardly, scanty, scrimpy; contracted, desitute, lacking, limited, minus, wanting; dwarfish, squat, undersized, vertically challenged; brittle, crisp, crumbling, friable. * *adv* abruptly, at once, forthwith, suddenly.

shortcoming *n* defect, deficiency, delinquency, error, failing, failure, fault, imperfection, inadequacy, remissness, slip, weakness.

shorten *vb* abbreviate, abridge, curtail, cut short; abridge, contract, diminish, lessen, retrench, reduce; curtail, cut off, dock, lop, trim; confine, hinder, restrain, restrict.

shoulder *vb* bear, bolster, carry, hump, maintain, pack, support, sustain, tote; crowd, elbow, jostle, press forward, push, thrust. * *n* projection, protuberance.

shout *vb* bawl, cheer, clamour, exclaim, halloo, roar, vociferate, whoop, yell. * *n* cheer, clamour, exclamation, halloo, hoot, huzza, outcry, roar, vociferation, whoop, yell.

shove *vb* jostle, press against, propel, push, push aside; (*with* **off**) push away, thrust away.

show *vb* blazon, display, exhibit, flaunt, parade, present; indicate, mark, point out; disclose, discover, divulge, explain, make clear, make known, proclaim, publish, reveal, unfold; demonstrate, evidence, manifest, prove, verify; conduct, guide, usher; direct, inform, instruct, teach; explain, expound, elucidate, interpret; (*with* **off**) display, exhibit, make a show, set off; (*with* **up**) expose. * *n* array, exhibition, representation, sight, spectacle; blazonry, bravery, ceremony, dash, demonstration, display, flourish, ostentation, pageant, pageantry, parade, pomp, splendour, splurge; likeness, resemblance, semblance; affectation, appearance, colour, illusion, mask, plausibility, pose, pretence, pretext, simulation, speciousness; entertainment, production.

showy *adj* bedizened, dressy, fine, flashy, flaunting, garish, gaudy, glaring, gorgeous, loud, ornate, smart, swanky, splendid; grand, magnificent, ostentatious, pompous, pretentious, stately, sumptuous.

shred *vb* tear. * *n* bit, fragment, piece, rag, scrap, strip, tatter.

shrewd *adj* arch, artful, astute, crafty, cunning, Machiavellian, sly, subtle, wily; acute, astute, canny, discerning, discriminating, ingenious, keen, knowing, penetrating, sagacious, sharp, sharp-sighted.

shriek *vb* scream, screech, squeal, yell, yelp. * *n* cry, scream, screech, yell.

shrill *adj* acute, high, high-toned, high-pitched, piercing, piping, sharp.

shrink *vb* contract, decrease, dwindle, shrivel, wither; balk, blench, draw back, flinch, give way, quail, recoil, retire, swerve, wince, withdraw.

shrivel *vb* dry, dry up, parch; contract, decrease, dwindle, shrink, wither, wrinkle.

shroud *vb* bury, cloak, conceal, cover, hide, mask, muffle, protect, screen, shelter, veil. * *n* covering, garment; grave clothes, winding sheet.

shudder *vb* quake, quiver, shake, shiver, tremble. * *n* shaking, shuddering, trembling, tremor.

shuffle *vb* confuse, disorder, intermix, jumble, mix, shift; cavil, dodge, equivocate, evade, prevaricate, quibble; make shift, shift, struggle. * *n* artifice, cavil, evasion, fraud, pretence, pretext, prevarication, quibble, ruse, shuffling, sophism, subterfuge, trick.

shun *vb* avoid, elude, eschew, escape, evade, get clear of.

shut *vb* close, close up, stop; confine, coop up, enclose, imprison, lock up, shut up; (*with* **in**) confine, enclose; (*with* **off**) bar, exclude, intercept; (*with* **up**) close up, shut; confine, enclose, fasten in, imprison, lock in, lock up.

shy *vb* cast, chuck, fling, hurl, jerk, pitch, sling, throw, toss; boggle, sheer, start aside. * *adj* bashful, coy, diffident, reserved, retiring, sheepish, shrinking, timid; cautious, chary, distrustful, heedful, wary. * *n* start; fling, throw.

sick *adj* ailing, ill, indisposed, laid-up, unwell, weak; nauseated, queasy; disgusted, revolted, tired, weary; diseased, distempered, disordered, feeble, morbid, unhealthy, unsound, weak; languishing, longing, pining.

sicken *vb* ail, disease, fall sick, make sick; nauseate; disgust, weary; decay, droop, languish, pine.

sickly *adj* ailing, diseased, faint, feeble, infirm, languid, languishing, morbid, unhealthy, valetudinary, weak, weakly.

side *vb* border, bound, edge, flank, frontier, march, rim, skirt, verge; avert, turn aside; (*with* with) befriend, favour, flock to, join with, second, support. * *adj* flanking, later, skirting; indirect, oblique; extra, odd, off, spare. * *n* border, edge, flank, margin, verge; cause, faction, interest, party, sect.

sift *vb* part, separate; bolt, screen winnow; analyse, canvass, discuss, examine, fathom, follow up, inquire into, investigate, probe, scrutinize, sound, try.

sigh *vb* complain, grieve, lament, mourn. * *n* long breath, sough, suspiration.

sight *vb* get sight of, perceive, see. * *n* cognizance, ken, perception, view; beholding, eyesight, seeing, vision; exhibition, prospect, representation, scene, show, spectacle; consideration, estimation, knowledge, view; examination, inspection.

sign *vb* indicate, signal, signify; countersign, endorse, subscribe. * *n* emblem, index, indication, manifestation, mark, note, proof, signal, signification, symbol, symptom, token; beacon, signal; augury, auspice, foreboding, miracle; omen, portent, presage, prodigy, prognostic, wonder; symbol, type; countersign, password.

signal *vb* flag, glance, hail, nod, nudge, salute, sign, signalize, sound, speak, touch, wave, wink. * *adj* conspicuous, eminent, extraordinary, memorable, notable, noteworthy, remarkable. * *n* cue, indication, mark, sign, token.

significant *adj* betokening, expressive, indicative, significative, signifying; important, material, momentous, portentous,

weighty; forcible, emphatic, expressive, telling.

signify *vb* betoken, communication, express, indicate, intimate; denote, imply, import, mean, purport, suggest; announce, declare, give notice of, impart, make known, manifest, proclaim, utter; augur, foreshadow, indicate, portend, represent, suggest; import, matter, weigh.

silence *vb* hush, muzzle, still; allay, calm, quiet. * *interj* be silent, be still, hush, soft, tush, tut, whist. * *n* calm, hush, lull, noiselessness, peace, quiet, quietude, soundlessness, stillness; dumbness, mumness, muteness, reticence, speechlessness, taciturnity.

silly *adj* brainless, childish, foolish, inept, senseless, shallow, simple, stupid, weak-minded, witless; absurd, extravagant, frivolous, imprudent, indiscreet, nonsensical, preposterous, trifling, unwise. * *n* ass, duffer, goose, idiot, simpleton.

similar *adj* analogous, duplicate, like, resembling, twin; homogeneous, uniform.

similarity *n* agreement, analogy, correspondence, likeness, parallelism, parity, resemblance, sameness, semblance, similitude.

simmer *vb* boil, bubble, seethe, stew.

simple *adj* bare, elementary, homogeneous, incomplex, mere, single, unalloyed, unblended, uncombined, uncompounded, unmingled, unmixed; chaste, plain, homespun, inornate, natural, neat, unadorned, unaffected, unembellished, unpretentious, unstudied, unvarnished; artless, downright, frank, guileless, inartificial, ingenuous, naive, open, plain, simple-hearted, simple-minded, sincere, single-minded, straightforward, true, unaffected, unconstrained, undesigning, unsophisticated; credulous, fatuous, foolish, shallow, silly, unwise, weak; clear, intelligible, plain, understandable, uninvolved, unmistakable.

simplicity *n* chasteness, homeliness, naturalness, neatness, plainness; artlessness, frankness, naivety, openness, simplesse, sincerity; clearness, plainness; folly, silliness, weakness.

simultaneous *adj* coeval, coincident, concomitant, concurrent, contemporaneous, synchronous.

sin *vb* do wrong, err, transgress, tresspass. * *n* delinquency, depravity, guilt, iniquity, misdeed, offence, transgression, unrighteousness, wickedness, wrong.

since *conj* as, because, considering, seeing that. * *adv* ago, before this; from that time. * *prep* after, from the time of, subsequently to.

sincere *adj* pure, unmixed; genuine, honest, inartificial, real, true, unaffected, unfeigned, unvarnished; artless, candid, direct, frank, guileless, hearty, honest, ingenuous, open, plain, single, straightforward, true, truthful, undissembling, upright, whole-hearted.

sinful *adj* bad, criminal, depraved, immoral, iniquitous, mischievous, peccant, transgressive, unholy, unrighteous, wicked, wrong.

sing *vb* carol, chant, hum, hymn, intone, lilt, troll, warble, yodel.

singe *vb* burn, scorch, sear.

single *vb* (*with* out) choose, pick, select, single. * *adj* alone, isolated, one only, sole, solitary; individual, particular, separate; celibate, unmarried, unwedded; pure, simple, uncompounded, unmixed; honest, ingenuous, simple, sincere, unbiassed, uncorrupt, upright.

singular *adj* eminent, exceptional, extraordinary, rare, remarkable, strange, uncommon, unusual, unwonted; exceptional, particular, remarkable, unexampled, unparalleled, unprecedented; strange, unaccountable; bizarre, eccentric, fantastic, odd, peculiar, queer; individual, single; not complex, single, uncompounded.

sinister *adj* baleful, injurious, untoward; boding ill, inauspicious, ominous, unlucky; left, on the left hand.

sink *vb* droop, drop, fall, founder, go down, submerge, subside; enter, penetrate; collapse, fail; decay, decline, decrease, dwindle, give way, languish, lose strength; engulf, immerse, merge, submerge, submerse; dig, excavate, scoop out; abase, bring down, crush, debase, degrade, depress, diminish, lessen, lower, overbear; destroy, overthrow, overwhelm, reduce, ruin, swamp, waste. * *n* basin, cloaca, drain, sewer.

sinner *n* criminal, delinquent, evildoer, offender, reprobate, wrongdoer.

sip *vb* drink, suck up, sup; absorb, drink in. * *n* small draught, taste.

sire *vb* father, reproduce; author, breed, conceive, create, father, generate, originate, produce, propagate. * *n* father, male parent, progenitor; man, male person; sir, sirrah; author, begetter, creator, father, generator, originator.

sit *vb* abide, be, remain, repose, rest, stay; bear on, lie, rest; abide, dwell, settle; perch; brood, incubate; become, be suited, fit.

site *vb* locate, place, position, situate, station. * *n* ground, locality, location, place, position, seat, situation, spot, station, whereabouts.

situation *n* ground, locality, location, place, position, seat, site, spot, whereabouts; case, category, circumstances, condition, juncture, plight, predicament, state; employment, office, place, post, station.

size *n* amplitude, bigness, bulk, dimensions, expanse, greatness, largeness, magnitude, mass, volume.

sketch *vb* design, draft, draw out; delineate, depict, paint, portray, represent. * *n* delineation, design, draft, drawing, outline, plan, skeleton.

sketchy *adj* crude, incomplete, unfinished.

skilful *adj* able, accomplished, adept, adroit, apt, clever, competent, conversant, cunning, deft, dexterous, dextrous, expert, handy, ingenious, masterly, practised, proficient, qualified, quick, ready, skilled, trained, versed, well-versed.

skill *n* ability, address, adroitness, aptitude, aptness, art, cleverness, deftness, dexterity, expertise, expertness, facility, ingenuity, knack, quickness, readiness, skilfulness; discernment, discrimination, knowledge, understanding, wit.

skim *vb* brush, glance, graze, kiss, scrape, scratch, sweep, touch lightly; coast, flow, fly, glide, sail, scud, whisk; dip into, glance at, scan, skip, thumb over, touch upon.

skin vb pare, peel; decorticate, excoriate, flay. * n cuticle, cutis, derm, epidermis, hide, integument, pellicle, pelt; hull, husk, peel, rind.

skip vb bound, caper, frisk, gambol, hop, jump, leap, spring; disregard, intermit, miss, neglect, omit, pass over, skim. * n bound, caper, frisk, gambol, hop, jump, leap, spring.

skirmish vb battle, brush, collide, combat, contest, fight, scuffle, tussle. * n affair, affray, battle, brush, collision, combat, conflict, contest, encounter, fight, scuffle, tussle.

skirt vb border, bound, edge, fringe, hem, march, rim; circumnavigate, circumvent, flank, go along. * n border, boundary, edge, margin, rim, verge; flap, kilt, loose part, overskirt, petticoat.

slack vb ease off, let up; abate, ease up, relax, slacken; malinger, shirk; choke, damp, extinguish, smother, stifle. * adj backward, careless, inattentive, lax, negligent, remiss; abated, dilatory, diminished, lingering, slow, tardy; loose, relaxed; dull, idle, inactive, quiet, sluggish. * n excess, leeway, looseness, play; coal dust, culm, residue.

slacken vb abate, diminish, lessen, lower, mitigate, moderate, neglect, remit, relieve, retard, slack; loosen, relax; flag, slow down; bridle, check, control, curb, repress, restrain.

slander vb asperse, backbite, belie, brand, calumniate, decry, defame, libel, malign, reproach, scandalize, traduce, vilify; detract from, disparage. * n aspersion, backbiting, calumny, defamation, detraction, libel, obloquy, scandal, vilification.

slanderous adj calumnious, defamatory, false, libellous, malicious, maligning.

slant vb incline, lean, lie obliquely, list, slope. * n inclination, slope, steep, tilt.

slap vb dab, clap, pat, smack, spank, strike. * adv instantly, quickly, plumply. * n blow, clap.

slapdash adv haphazardly, hurriedly, precipitately.

slash vb cut, gash, slit. * n cut, gash, slit.

slaughter vb butcher, kill, massacre, murder, slay. * n bloodshed, butchery, carnage, havoc, killing, massacre, murder, slaying.

slay vb assassinate, butcher, dispatch, kill, massacre, murder, slaughter; destroy, ruin.

sleek adj glossy, satin, silken, silky, smooth.

sleep vb catnap, doze, drowse, nap, slumber. * n dormancy, hypnosis, lethargy, repose, rest, slumber.

sleeping adj dormant, inactive, quiescent.

sleepy adj comatose, dozy, drowsy, heavy, lethargic, nodding, somnolent; narcotic, opiate, slumberous, somniferous, somnific, soporiferous, soporific; dull, heavy, inactive, lazy, slow, sluggish, torpid.

slender adj lank, lithe, narrow, skinny, slim, slight, spindly, thin; feeble, fine, flimsy, fragile, slight, tenuous, weak; inconsiderable, moderate, small, trivial; exiguous, inadequate, insufficient, lean, meagre, pitiful, scanty, small; abstemious, light, meagre, simple, spare, sparing.

slice vb cut, divide, part, section; cut off, sever. * n chop, collop, piece.

slick adj glassy, glossy, polished, sleek, smooth; alert, clever, cunning, shrewd, slippery, unctuous. vb burnish, gloss, lacquer, polish, shine, sleek, varnish; grease, lubricate, oil.

slide vb glide, move smoothly, slip. * n glide, glissade, skid, slip.

slight vb cold-shoulder, disdain, disregard, neglect, snub; overlook; scamp, skimp, slur. * adj inconsiderable, insignificant, little, paltry, petty, small, trifling, trivial, unimportant, unsubstantial; delicate, feeble, frail, gentle, weak; careless, cursory, desultory, hasty, hurried, negligent, scanty, superficial; flimsy, perishable; slender, slim. * n discourtesy, disregard, disrespect, inattention, indignity, neglect.

slim vb bant, lose weight, reduce, slenderize. * adj gaunt, lank, lithe, narrow, skinny, slender, spare; inconsiderable, paltry, poor, slight, trifling, trivial, unsubstantial, weak; insufficient, meagre.

slimy *adj* miry, muddy, oozy; clammy, gelatinous, glutinous, gummy, lubricious, mucilaginous, mucous, ropy, slabby, viscid, viscous.

sling *vb* cast, fling, hurl, throw; hang up, suspend.

slink *vb* skulk, slip away, sneak, steal away.

slip¹ *vb* glide, slide; err, mistake, trip; lose, omit; disengage, throw off; escape, let go, loose, loosen, release, . * *n* glide, slide, slipping; blunder, error, fault, lapse, misstep, mistake, oversight, peccadillo, trip; backsliding, error, fault, impropriety, indiscretion, transgression; desertion, escape; cord, leash, strap, string; case, covering, wrapper.

slip² *n* cutting, scion, shoot, twig; piece, streak, strip.

slippery *adj* glib, slithery, smooth; changeable, insecure, mutable, perilous, shaky, uncertain, unsafe, unstable, unsteady; cunning, dishonest, elusive, faithless, false, knavish, perfidious, shifty, treacherous.

slipshod *adj* careless, shuffling, slovenly, untidy.

slit *vb* cut; divide, rend, slash, split, sunder. * *n* cut, gash.

slope *vb* incline, slant, tilt. * *n* acclivity, cant, declivity, glacis, grade, gradient, incline, inclination, obliquity, pitch, ramp.

sloppy *adj* muddy, plashy, slabby, slobbery, splashy, wet.

slouch *vb* droop, loll, slump; shamble, shuffle. * *n* malingerer, shirker, slacker; shamble, shuffle, stoop.

slovenly *adj* unclean, untidy; blowsy, disorderly, dowdy, frowsy, loose, slatternly, tacky, unkempt, untidy; careless, heedless, lazy, negligent, perfunctory.

slow *vb* abate, brake, check, decelerate, diminish, lessen, mitigate, moderate, modulate, reduce, weaken; delay,detain, retard; ease, ease up, relax, slack, slacken, slack off. * *adj* deliberate, gradual; dead, dull, heavy, inactive, inert, sluggish, stupid; behindhand, late, tardy, unready; delaying, dilatory, lingering, slack.

sludge *n* mire, mud; slosh, slush.

sluggish *adj* dronish, drowsy, idle, inactive, indolent, inert, languid, lazy, listless, lumpish, phlegmatic, slothful, torpid; slow; dull, stupid, supine, tame.

slumber *vb* catnap, doze, nap, repose, rest, sleep. * *n* catnap, doze, nap, repose, rest, siesta, sleep.

slump *vb* droop, drop, fall, flop, founder, sag, sink, sink down; decline, depreciate, deteriorate, ebb, fail, fall, fall away, lose ground, recede, slide, slip, subside, wane. * *n* droop, drop, fall, flop, lowering, sag, sinkage; decline, depreciation, deterioration, downturn, downtrend, subsidence, ebb, falling off, wane; crash, recession, smash.

slur *vb* asperse, calumniate, disparage, depreciate, reproach, traduce; conceal, disregard, gloss over, obscure, pass over, slight. * *n* mark, stain; brand, disgrace, reproach, stain, stigma; innuendo.

sly *adj* artful, crafty, cunning, insidious, subtle, wily; astute, cautious, shrewd; arch, knowing, clandestine, secret, stealthy, underhand.

smack¹ *vb* smell, taste. * *n* flavour, savour, tang, taste, tincture; dash, infusion, little, space, soupçon, sprinkling, tinge, touch; smattering.

smack² *vb* slap, strike; crack, slash, snap; buss, kiss. * *n* crack, slap, slash, snap; buss, kiss.

small *adj* diminutive, Lilliputian, little, miniature, petite, pygmy, tiny, wee; infinitesimal, microscopic, minute; inappreciable, inconsiderable, insignificant, petty, trifling, trivial, unimportant; moderate, paltry, scanty, slender; faint, feeble, puny, slight, weak; illiberal, mean, narrow, narrow-minded, paltry, selfish, ungenerous, unworthy.

smart¹ *vb* hurt, pain, sting; suffer.

smart² *adj* active, agile, brisk, fresh, lively, nimble, quick, spirited, sprightly, spry; effective, efficient, energetic, forcible, vigorous; adroit, alert, clever, dexterous, dextrous, expert, intelligent, quick, stirring; acute, apt, pertinent, ready, witty; chic, dapper, fine, natty, showy, spruce, trim.

smash vb break, crush, dash, mash, shatter. * n crash, debacle, destruction, ruin; bankruptcy, failure.

smear vb bedaub, begrime, besmear, daub, plaster, smudge; contaminate, pollute, smirch, smut, soil, stain, sully, tarnish. * n blot, blotch, daub, patch, smirch, smudge, spot, stain; calumny, defamation, libel, slander.

smell vb scent, sniff, stench, stink. * n aroma, bouquet, fragrance, fume, odour, perfume, redolence, scent, stench, stink; sniff, snuff.

smile vb grin, laugh, simper, smirk. * n grin, simper, smirk.

smoke vb emit, exhale, reek, steam; fumigate, smudge; discover, find out, smell out. * n effluvium, exhalation, fume, mist, reek, smother, steam, vapour; fumigation, smudge.

smooth vb flatten, level, plane; ease, lubricate; extenuate, palliate, soften; allay, alleviate, assuage, calm, mitigate, mollify. * adj even, flat, level, plane, polished, unruffled, unwrinkled; glabrous, glossy, satiny, silky, sleek, soft, velvet; euphonious, flowing, liquid, mellifluent; fluent, glib, voluble; bland, flattering, ingratiating, insinuating, mild, oily, smooth-tongued, soothing, suave, unctuous.

smother vb choke, stifle, suffocate; conceal, deaden, extinguish, hide, keep down, repress, suppress, stifle, smoke, smoulder.

smudge vb besmear, blacken, blur, smear, smut, smutch, soil, spot, stain. * n blur, blot, smear, smut, spot, stain.

smug adj complacent, self-satisfied; neat, nice, spruce, trim.

smutty adj coarse, gross, immodest, impure, indecent, indelicate, loose, nasty; dirty, foul, nasty, soiled, stained.

snag vb catch, enmesh, entangle, hook, snare, sniggle, tangle. * n knarl, knob, knot, projection, protuberance, snub; catch, difficulty, drawback, hitch, rub, shortcoming, weakness; obstacle.

snap vb break, fracture; bite, catch at, seize, snatch at, snip; crack; crackle, crepitate, decrepitate, pop. * adj casual, cursory,

hasty, offhand, sudden, superficial. * n bite, catch, nip, seizure; catch, clasp, fastening, lock; crack, filip, flick, flip, smack; briskness, energy, verve, vim.

snare vb catch, ensnare, entangle, entrap. * n catch, gin, net, noose, springe, toil, trap, wile.

snarl¹ vb girn, gnarl, growl, grumble, murmur. * n growl, grumble.

snarl² vb complicate, disorder, entangle, knot; confuse, embarrass, ensnare. * n complication, disorder, entanglement, tangle; difficulty, embarrassment, intricacy.

snatch vb catch, clutch, grasp, grip, pluck, pull, seize, snip, twich, wrest, wring. * n bit, fragment, part, portion; catch, effort.

sneak vb lurk, skulk, slink, steal; crouch, truckle. * adj clandestine, concealed, covert, hidden, secret, sly, underhand. * n informer, telltale; lurker, shirk.

sneer vb flout, gibe, jeer, mock, rail, scoff; (with at) deride, despise, disdain, laugh at, mock, rail at, scoff, spurn. * n flouting, gibe, jeer, scoff.

snip vb clip, cut, nip; snap, snatch. * n bit, fragment, particle, pice, shred; share, snack.

snooze vb catnap, doze, drowse, nap, sleep, slumber. * n catnap, nap, sleep, slumber.

snub vb abash, cold-shoulder, cut, discomfit, humble, humiliate, mortify, slight, take down. * n check, rebuke, slight.

snug adj close, concealed; comfortable, compact, convenient, neat, trim.

snuggle vb cuddle, nestle, nuzzle.

so adv thus, with equal reason; in such a manner; in this way, likewise; as it is, as it was, such; for this reason, therefore; be it so, thus be it. * conj in case that, on condition that, provided that.

soak vb drench, moisten, permeate, saturate, wet; absorb, imbibe; imbue, macerate, steep.

soar vb ascend, fly aloft, glide, mount, rise, tower.

sob vb cry, sigh convulsively, weep.

sober vb (with up) calm down, collect oneself, compose oneself, control oneself, cool off, master, moderate, simmer down. * *adj* abstemious, abstinent, temperate, unintoxicated; rational, reasonable, sane sound; calm, collected, composed, cool, dispassionate, moderate, rational, reasonabler, regular, steady, temperate, unimpassioned, unruffled, well-regulated; demure, grave, quiet, sedate, serious, solemn, sombre, staid; dark, drab, dull-looking, quiet, sad, sombre, subdued.

sociable *adj* accessible, affable, communicative, companionable, conversable, friendly, genial, neighbourly, social.

social *adj* civic, civil; accessible, affable, communicative, companionable, familiar, friendly, hospitable, neighbourly, sociable; convivial, festive, gregarious. * *n* conversazione, gathering, get-together, party, reception, soiree.

society *n* association, companionship, company, converse, fellowship; the community, the public, the world; elite, *monde*; association, body, brotherhood, copartnership, corporation, club, company, fellowship, fraternity, partnersnip, sodality, union.

sodden *adj* drenched, saturated, soacked, steeped, wet; boiled, decocted, seethed, stewed.

soft *adj* impressible, malleable, plastic, pliable, yielding; downy, fleecy, velvety, mushy, pulpy, squashy; compliant, facile, irresolute, submissive, undecided, weak; bland, mild, gentle, kind, lenient, tender; delicate, tender; easy, even, gentle, quiet, smooth-going, steady; effeminate, luxurious, unmanly; dulcet, fluty, gentle, mellifluous, melodious, smooth. * *interj* hold, stop.

soften *vb* intenerate, mellow, melt, tenderize; abate, allay, alleviate, appease, assuage, attemper, balm, blunt, calm, dull, ease, lessen, make easy, mitigate, moderate, mollify, milden, qualify, quell, quiet, relent, relieve, soothe, still, temper; extenuate, modify, palliate, qualify; enervate, weaken.

soil¹ *n* earth, ground loam, mould; country, land.

soil² *vb* bedaub, begrime, bemire, besmear, bespatter, contaminate, daub, defile,

dirty, foul, pollute, smirch, stain, sully, taint, tarnish. * *n* belmish, defilement, dirt, filth, foulness; blot, spot, stain, taint, tarnish

sole *adj* alone, individual, one, only, single, solitary, unique.

solemn *adj* ceremonial, formal, ritual; devotional, devout, religious, reverential, sacred; earnest, grave, serious, sober; august, awe-inspiring, awful, grand, imposing, impressive, majestic, stately, venerable.

solicit *vb* appeal to, ask, beg, beseech, conjure, crave, entreat, implore, importune, petition, pray, press, request, supplicate, urge; arouse, awaken, entice, excite, invite, summon; canvass, seek.

solicitous *adj* anxious, apprehensive, careful, concerned, disturbed, eager, troubled, uneasy.

solid *adj* congealed, firm, hard, impenetrable; compact, dense, impermeable, massed; cubic; firm, sound, stable, stout, strong, substantial; firm, just, real, sound, strong, substantial, true, valid, weighty; reliable, safe, sound, trustwirothy, well-established.

solidarity *n* communion of interests, community, consolidation, fellowship, joint interest, mutual responsibility.

solidify *vb* compact, congeal, consolidate, harden, petrify.

solitary *adj* alone, companionless, lone, lonely, only, separate, unaccompanied; individual, single, sole; desert, deserted, desolate, isolated, lonely, remote, retired, secluded, unfrequented. * *n* anchoret, anchorite, eremite, hermit, recluse, solitaire, solitarian.

solution *n* answer, clue, disentanglement, elucidation, explication, explanation, key, resolution, unravelling, unriddling; disintegration, dissolution, liquefaction, melting, resolution, separation; breach, disconnection, discontinuance, disjunction, disruption.

solve *vb* clear, clear up, disentangle, elucidate, explain, expound, interpret, make plain, resolve, unfold.

sombre *adj* cloudy, dark, dismal, dull, dusky, gloomy, murky, overcast, rayless, shady, sombrous, sunless; doleful, funereal, grave, lugubrious, melancholy, mournful, sad, sober.

some *adj* a, an, any, one; about, near; certain, little, moderate, part, several.

somebody *n* one, someone, something; celebrity, VIP.

something *n* part, portion, thing; somebody; affair, event, matter, thing.

sometime *adj* former, late. * *adv* formerly, once; now and then, at one time or other, sometimes.

sometimes *adv* at intervals, at times, now and then, occasionally, somewhiles; at a past period, formerly, once.

somewhat *adv* in some degree, more or less, rather, something. * *n* something, a little, more or less, part.

somewhere *adv* here and there, in one place or another, in some place.

song *n* aria, ballad, canticle, canzonet, carol, ditty, glee, lay, lullaby, snatch; descant, melody; anthem, hymn, lay, poem, psalm, strain; poesy, poetry, verse.

soon *adv* anon, before long, by and by, in a short time, presently, shortly; betimes, earth, forthwith, promptly, quick; gladly, lief, readily, willingly.

soothe *vb* cajole, flatter, humour; appease, assuage, balm, calm, compose, lull, mollify, pacify, quiet, sober, soften, still, tranquillize; allay, alleviate, blunt, check, deaden, dull, ease, lessen, mitigate, moderate, palliate, qualify, relieve, repress, soften, temper.

sordid *adj* base, degraded, low, mean, vile; avaricious, close-fisted, covetous, illiberal, miserly, niggardly, penurious, stingy, ungenerous.

sore *adj* irritated, painful, raw, tender, ulcerated; aggrieved, galled, grieved, hurt, irritable, painted, tender, vexed; afflictive, distressing, severe, sharp, violent. * *n* abscess, boil, fester, gathering, imposthume, pustule, ulcer; affliction, grief, pain, sorrow, trouble.

sorrow *vb* bemoan, bewail, grieve, lament, mourn, weep. * *n* affliction, dolour, grief, heartache, mourning, sadness, trouble, woe.

sorrowful *adj* afflicted, dejected, de-

pressed, grieved, grieving, heartsore, sad; baleful, distressing, grievous, lamentable, melancholy, mournful, painful, sad; disconsolate, dismal, doleful, dolorous, drear, dreary, lugubrious, melancholy, piteous, rueful woebegone, woeful.

sorry *adj* afflicted, dejected, grieved, pained, poor, sorrowful; distressing, pitiful; chagrined, mortified, pained, regretful, remorseful, sad, vexed; abject, base, beggarly, contemptible, despicable, low, mean, paltry, poor, insignificant, miserable, pitiful, shabby, worthless, wretched.

sort *vb* arrange, assort, class, classify, distribute, order; conjoin, join, put together; choose, elect, pick out, select; associate, consort, fraternize; accord, agree with, fit, suit. * *n* character, class, denomination, description, kind, nature, order, race, rank, species, type; manner, way.

so-so *adj* indifferent, mediocre, middling, ordinary, passable, tolerable.

soul *n* mind, psyche, spirit; being, person; embodiment, essence, personification, spirit, vital principle; ardour, energy, fervour, inspiration, vitality.

sound[1] *adj* entire, intact, unbroken, unhurt, unimpaired, uninjured, unmutilated, whole; hale, hardy, healthy, hearty, vigorous; good, perfect, undecayed; perfect, sane, well-balanced; correct, orthodox, right, solid, valid, well-founded; legal, valid; deep, fast, profound, unbroken, undisturbed; forcible, lusty, severe, stout.

sound[2] *n* channel, narrows, strait.

sound[3] *vb* resound; appear, seem; play on; express, pronounce, utter; announce, celebrate, proclaim, publish, spread. * *n* noise, note, tone, voice, whisper.

sound[4] *vb* fathom, gauge, measure, test; examine, probe, search, test, try.

sour *vb* acidulate; embitter, envenom. * *adj* acetose, acetous, acid, astringent, pricked, sharp, tart, vinegary; acrimonious, crabbed, cross, crusty, fretful, glum, ill-humoured, ill-natured, ill-tempered, peevish, pettish, petulant, snarling, surly; bitter, disagreeable, unpleasant; austere, dismal, gloomy, morose, sad, sullen; bad, coagulated, curdled, musty, rancid, turned.

source *n* beginning, fountain, fountainhead, head, origin, rise, root, spring, well; cause, original.

souvenir *n* keepsake, memento, remembrance, reminder.

sovereign *adj* imperial, monarchical, princely, regal, royal, supreme; chief, commanding, excellent, highest, paramount, predominant, principal, supreme, utmost; efficacious, effectual. * *n* autocrat, monarch, suzerain; emperor, empress, king, lord, potentate, prince, princess, queen, ruler.

sovereignty *n* authority, dominion, empire, power, rule, supremacy, sway.

sow *vb* scatter, spread, strew; disperse, disseminate, propagate, spread abroad; plant; besprinkle, scatter.

space *n* expanse, expansion, extension, extent, proportions, spread; accommodation, capacity, room, place; distance, interspace, interval.

spacious *adj* extended, extensive, vast, wide; ample, broad, capacious, commodious, large, roomy, wide.

span *vb* compass, cross, encompass, measure, overlay. * *n* brief period, spell; pair, team, yoke.

spare *vb* lay aside, lay by, reserve, save, set apart, set aside; dispense with, do without, part with; forbear, omit, refrain, withhold; exempt, forgive, keep from; afford, allow, give, grant; preserve, save; economize, pinch. * *adj* frugal, scanty, sparing, stinted, chary, parsimonious, sparing; emaciated, gaunt, lank, lean, meagre, poor, thin, scraggy, skinny, rawboned; additional, extra, supernumerary.

sparing *adj* little, scanty, scarce; abstemious, meagre, scanty, spare; chary, economical, frugal, parsimonious, saving; compassionate, forgiving, lenient, merciful.

spark *vb* scintillate, sparkle; begin, fire, incite, instigate, kindle, light, set off, start, touch off, trigger. * *n* scintilla, scintillation, sparkle; beginning, element, germ, seed.

sparkle *vb* coruscate, flash, gleam, glisten, glister, glitter, radiate, scintillate, shine, twinkle; bubble, effervesce, foam, froth. * *n* glint, scintillation, spark; luminosity, lustre.

sparse *adj* dispersed, infrequent, scanty, scattered, sporadic, thin.

spasmodic *adj* erratic, fitful, intermittent, irregular, sporadic; convulsive, paroxysmal, spasmodical, violent.

spatter *vb* bespatter, besprinkle, plash, splash, sprinkle; spit, sputter.

speak *vb* articulate, deliver, enunciate, express, pronounce, utter; announce, confer, declare, disclose, mention, say, tell; announce, celebrate, declare, make known, proclaim, speak abroad; accost, address, greet, hail; declare, exhibit, make known; argue, converse, dispute, say, talk; discourse, hold forth, harangue, mention, orate, plead, spout, tell, treat.

speaker *n* discourse, elocutionist, orator, prolocutor, spokesman; chairman, presiding officer.

special *adj* specific, specifical; especial, individual, particular, peculiar, unique; exceptional extraordinary, marked, particular, uncommon; appropriate, especial, express, peculiar.

speciality *n* particularity; feature, forte, pet subject.

species *n* assemblage, class, collection, group; description, kind, sort, variety; (*law*) fashion, figure, form, shape.

specific *adj* characteristic, especial, particular, peculiar; definite, limited, precise, specified.

specify *vb* define, designate, detail, indicate, individualize, name, show, particularize.

specimen *n* copy, example, model, pattern, sample.

speck *n* blemish, blot, flaw, speckle, spot, stain; atom, bit, corpuscle, mite, mote, particle, scintilla.

spectacle *n* display, exhibition, pageant, parade, representation, review, scene, show, sight; curiosity, marvel, phenomenon, sight, wonder.

spectator *n* beholder, bystander, looker-on, observer, onlooker, witness.

spectre *n* apparition, banshee, ghost, goblin, hobgoblin, phantom, shade, shadow, spirit, sprite, wraith.

speculate *vb* cogitate, conjecture, contemplate, imagine, meditate, muse, ponder, reflect, ruminate, theorize, think; bet, gamble, hazard, risk, trade, venture.

speculative *adj* contemplative, philosophical, speculatory, unpractical; ideal, imaginary, theoretical; hazardous, risky, unsecured.

speech *n* articulation, language, words; dialect, idiom, language, locution, tongue; conversation, oral communication, parlance, talk, verbal intercourse; mention, observation, remark, saying, talk; address, declaration, discourse, harangue, oration, palaver.

speed *vb* hasten, hurry, rush, scurry; flourish, prosper, succeed, thrive; accelerate, dispatch, expedite, hasten, hurry, quicken, press forward, urge on; carry through, dispatch, execute; advance, aid, assist, help; favour, prosper. * *n* acceleration, celerity, dispatch, expedition, fleetness, haste, hurry, quickness, rapidity, swiftness, velocity; good fortune, good luck, prosperity, success; impetuosity.

speedy *adj* fast, fleet, flying, hasty, hurried, hurrying, nimble, quick, rapid, swift; expeditious, prompt, quick; approaching, early, near.

spell[1] *n* charm, exorcism, hoodoo, incantation, jinx, witchery; allure, bewitchment, captivation, enchantment, entrancement, fascination.

spell[2] *vb* decipher, interpret, read, unfold, unravel, unriddle.

spell[3] *n* fit, interval, period, round, season, stint, term, turn.

spellbound *adj* bewitched, charmed, enchanted, entranced, enthralled, fascinated.

spend *vb* disburse, dispose of, expend, lay out, part with; consume, dissipate, exhaust, lavish, squander, use up, wear, waste; apply, bestow, devote, employ, pass.

spendthrift *n* prodigal, spender, squanderer, waster.

spent *adj* exhausted, fatigued, played out, used up, wearied, worn out.

sphere *n* ball, globe, orb, spheroid; ambit, beat, bound, circle, circuit, compass, department, function, office, orbit, province, range, walk; order, rank, standing; country, domain, quarter, realm, region.

spherical *adj* bulbous, globated, globous, globular, orbicular, rotund, round, spheroid; planetary.

spice *n* flavour, flavouring, relish, savour, taste; admixture, dash, grain, infusion, particle, smack, soupçon, sprinkling, tincture.

spicy *adj* aromatic, balmy, fragrant; keen, piquant, pointed, pungent, sharp; indelicate, off-colour, racy, risqué, sensational, suggestive.

spill *vb* effuse, pour out, shed. * *n* accident, fall, tumble.

spin *vb* twist; draw out, extend; lenthen, prolong, protract, spend; pirouette, turn, twirl, whirl. * *n* drive, joyride, ride; autorotation, gyration, loop, revolution, rotation, turning, wheeling; pirouette, reel, turn, wheel, whirl.

spine *n* barb, pricle, thorn; backbone; ridge.

spiny *adj* briery, prickly, spinose, spinous, thorny; difficult, perplexed, thorny, troublesome.

spirit *vb* animate, encourage, excite, inspirit; carry off, kidnap. * *n* immaterial substance, life, vital essence; person, soul; angel, apparition, demon, elf, fairy, genius, ghost, phantom, shade, spectre, sprite; disposition, frame of mind, humour, mood, temper; spirits; ardour, cheerfulness, courage, earnestness, energy, enterprise, enthusiasm, fire, force, mettle, resolution, vigour, vim, vivacity, zeal; animation, cheerfulness, enterprise, esprit, glow, liveliness, piquancy, spice, spunk, vivacity, warmth; drift, gist, intent, meaning, purport, sense, significance, tenor; character, characteristic, complexion, essence, nature, quality, quintessence; alcohol, liquor.

spirited *adj* active, alert, animated, ardent, bold, brisk, courageous, earnest, frisky, high-mettled, high-spirited, high-strung, lively, mettlesome, sprightly, vivacious.

spiritual *adj* ethereal, ghostly, immaterial incorporeal, psychical, supersensible; ideal, moral, unworldly; divine, holy, pure, sacred; ecclesiastical.

spit[1] *vb* impale, thrust through, transfix.

spit[2] *vb* eject, throw out; drivel, drool expectorate, salivate, slobber, spawl, splutter. * *n* saliva, spawl, spittle, sputum.

spite *vb* injure, mortify, thwart; annoy, offend, vex. * *n* grudge, hate, hatred, ill-nature, ill-will, malevolence, malice, maliciousness, malignity, pique, rancour, spleen, venom, vindictiveness.

spiteful *adj* evil-minded, hateful, ill-disposed, ill-natured, malevolent, malicious, malign, malignant, rancorous.

splash *vb* dabble, dash, plash, spatter, splurge, swash, swish. * *n* blot, daub, spot.

splendid *adj* beaming, bright, brilliant, effulgent, glowing, lustrous, radiant, refulgent, resplendent, shining; dazzling, gorgeous, imposing, kingly, magnificent, pompous, showy, sumptuous, superb; brilliant, celebrated, conspicuous, distinguished, eminent, famous, glorious, illustrious, noble, pre-eminent, remarkable, signal; grand, heroic, lofty, noble, sublime.

splendour *n* brightness, brilliance, brilliancy, lustre, radiance, refulgence; display, éclat, gorgeousness, grandeur, magnificence, parade, pomp, show, showiness, stateliness; celebrity, eminence, fame, glory, grandeur, renown; grandeur, loftiness, nobleness, sublimity.

splinter *vb* rend, shiver, sliver, split. * *n* fragment, piece.

split *vb* cleave, rive; break, burst, rend, splinter; divide, part, separate, sunder. * *n* crack, fissure, rent; breach, division, separation.

splutter *vb* sputter, stammer, stutter.

spoil *vb* despoil, fleece, loot, pilfer, plunder, ravage, rob, steal, strip, waste; corrupt, damage, destroy, disfigure, harm, impair, injure, mar, ruin, vitiate; decay, decompose. * *n* booty, loot, pillage, plunder, prey; rapine, robbery, spoliation, waste.

sponge *vb* cleanse, wipe; efface, expunge, obliterate, rub out, wipe out.

sponger *n* hanger-on, parasite.

spongy *adj* absorbent, porous, spongeous; rainy, showery, wet; drenched, marshy, saturated, soaked, wet.

sponsor *vb* back, capitalize, endorse, finance, guarantee, patronize, promote, support, stake, subsidize, take up, underwrite. * *n* angel, backer, guarantor, patron, prompter, supporter, surety, underwriter; godfather, godmother, godparent.

spontaneous *adj* free, gratuitous, impulsive, improvised, instinctive, self-acting, self-moving, unbidden, uncompelled, unconstrained, voluntary, willing.

sport *vb* caper, disport, frolic, gambol, have fun, make merry, play, romp, skip; trifle; display, exhibit. * *n* amusement, diversion, entertainment, frolic, fun, gambol, game, jollity, joviality, merriment, merry-making, mirth, pastime, pleasantry, prank, recreation; jest, joke; derision, jeer, mockery, ridicule; monstrosity.

spot *vb* besprinkle, dapple, dot, speck, stud, variegate; blemish, disgrace, soil, splotch, stain, sully, tarnish; detect, discern, espy, make out, observe, see, sight. * *n* blot, dapple, fleck, freckle, maculation, mark, mottle, patch, pip, speck, speckle; blemish, blotch, flaw, pock, splotch, stain, taint; locality, place, site.

spotless *adj* perfect, undefaced, unspotted; blameless, immaculate, innocent, irreproachable, pure, stainless, unblemished, unstained, untainted, untarnished.

spouse *n* companion, consort, husband, mate, partner, wife.

spout *vb* gush, jet, pour out, spirit, spurt, squirt; declaim, mouth, speak, utter. * *n* ajutage, conduit, tube; beak, gargoyle, nose, nozzle, waterspout.

sprain *vb* overstrain, rick, strain, twist, wrench, wrick.

spray[1] *vb* atomize, besprinkle, douche, gush, jet, shower, splash, splatter, spout, sprinkle, squirt. * *n* aerosol, atomizer, douche, foam, froth, shower, sprinkler, spume.

spray² *n* bough, branch, shoot, sprig, twig.

spread *vb* dilate, expand, extend, mantle, stretch; diffuse, disperse, distribute, radiate, scatter, sprinkle, strew; broadcast, circulate, disseminate, divulge, make known, make public, promulgate, propagate, publish; open, unfold, unfurl; cover, extend over, overspread. * *n* compass, extent, range, reach, scope, stretch; expansion, extension; circulation, dissemination, propagation; cloth, cover; banquet, feast, meal.

spree *n* bacchanal, carousal, debauch, frolic, jollification, orgy, revel, revelry, saturnalia.

sprig *n* shoot, spray, twig; lad, youth.

sprightly *adj* airy, animated, blithe, blithesome, brisk, buoyant, cheerful, debonair, frolicsome, joyous, lively, mercurial, vigorous, vivacious.

spring *vb* bound, hop, jump, leap, prance, vault; arise, emerge, grow, issue, proceed, put forth, shoot forth, stem; derive, descend, emanate, flow, originate, rise, start; fly back, rebound, recoil; bend, warp; grow, thrive, wax. * *adj* hopping, jumping, resilient, springy. * *n* bound, hop, jump, leap, vault; elasticity, flexibility, resilience, resiliency, springiness; fount, fountain, fountainhead, geyser, springhead, well; cause, origin, original, principle, source; seed time, springtime.

springy *adj* bouncing, bounding, elastic, rebounding, recoiling, resilient.

sprinkle *vb* scatter, strew; bedew, besprinkle, dust, powder, sand, spatter; wash, cleanse, purify, shower.

sprinkling *n* affusion, baptism, bedewing, spattering, splattering, spraying, wetting; dash, scattering, seasoning, smack, soupçon, suggestion, tinge, touch, trace, vestige.

sprout *vb* bourgeon, burst forth, germinate, grow, pullulate, push, put forth, ramify, shoot, shoot forth. * *n* shoot, sprig.

spruce *vb* preen, prink; adorn, deck, dress, smarten, trim. * *adj* dandyish, dapper, fine, foppish, jaunty, natty, neat, nice, smart, tidy, trig, trim.

spry *adj* active, agile, alert, brisk, lively, nimble, prompt, quick, ready, smart, sprightly, stirring, supple.

spur *vb* gallop, hasten, press on, prick; animate, arouse, drive, goad, impel, incite, induce, instigate, rouse, stimulate, urge forward. * *n* goad, point, prick, rowel; fillip, goad, impulse, incentive, incitement, inducement, instigation, motive, provocation, stimulus, whip; gnarl, knob, knot, point, projection, snag.

spurious *adj* bogus, counterfeit, deceitful, false, feigned, fictitious, make-believe, meretricious, mock, pretended, sham, supposititious, unauthentic.

spurn *vb* drive away, kick; contemn, despise, disregard, flout, scorn, slight; disdain, reject, repudiate.

spurt *vb* gush, jet, spirt, spout, spring out, stream out, well. * *n* gush, jet, spout, squirt; burst, dash, rush.

spy *vb* behold, discern, espy, see; detect, discover, search out; explore, inspect, scrutinze, search; shadow, trail, watch. * *n* agent, detective, double agent, mole, scout, secret emissary, undercover agent.

squabble *vb* brawl, fight, quarrel, scuffle, struggle, wrangle; altercate, bicker, contend, dispute, jangle, wrangle. * *n* brawl, dispute, fight, quarrel, rumpus, scrimmage.

squad *n* band, bevy, crew, gang, knot, lot, relay, set.

squalid *adj* dirty, filthy, foul, mucky, slovenly, unclean, unkempt.

squander *vb* dissipate, expend, lavish, lose, misuse, scatter, spend, throw away, waste.

square *vb* make square, quadrate; accommodate, adapt, fit, mould, regulate, shape, suit; adjust, balance, close, make even, settle; accord, chime in, cohere, comport, fall in, fit, harmonize, quadrate, suit. * *adj* four-square, quadrilaterial, quadrate; equal, equitable, exact, fair, honest, just, upright; adjusted, balanced, even, settled; just, true, suitable. * *n* four-sided figure, quadrate, rectangle, tetragon; open area, parade, piazza, plaza.

squeal *vb* creak, cry, howl, scream, screech, shriek, squawk, yell; betray, inform on. * n creak, cry, howl, scream, screech, shriek, squawk, yell.

squeamish adj nauseated, qualmish, queasy, sickish; dainty, delicate, fastidious, finical, hypercritical, nice, overnice, particular, priggish.

squeeze vb clutch, compress, constrict, grip, nip, pinch, press; drive, force; crush, harass, oppress; crowd, force through, press; (with out) extract. * n congestion, crowd, crush, throng.

squirm vb twist, wriggle, writhe.

squirt vb eject, jet, splash, spurt.

stab vb broach, gore, jab, pierce, spear, stick, transfix, transpierce; wound. * n cut, jab, prick, thrust; blow, daggerstroke, injury, wound.

stable adj established, fixed, immovable, immutable, invariable, permanent, unalterable, unchangeable; constand, firm, staunch, steadfast, steady, unwavering; abiding, durable, enduring, fast, lasting, permanent, perpetual, secure, sure.

staff n baton, cane, pole, rod, stick, wand; bat, bludgeon, club, cudgel, mace; prop, stay, support; employees, personnel, team, workers, work force.

stage vb dramatize, perform, present, produce, put on. * n dais, platform, rostrum, scaffold, staging, stand; arena, field; boards, playhouse, theatre; degree, point, step; diligence, omnibus, stagecoach.

stagger vb reel, sway, totter; alternate, fluctuate, overlap, vacillate, vary; falter, hesitate, waver; amaze, astonish, astound, confound, dumbfound, nonplus, pose, shock, surprise.

stagnant adj close, motionless, quiet, standing; dormant, dull, heavy, inactive, inert, sluggish, torpid.

stagnate vb decay, deteriorate, languish, rot, stand still, vegetate.

staid adj calm, composed, demure, grave, sedate, serious, settled, sober, solemn, steady, unadventurous.

stain vb blemish, blot, blotch, discolour, maculate, smirch, soil, splotch, spot, sully, tarnish; colour, dye, tinge; contaminate, corrupt, debase, deprave, disgrace, dishonour, pollute, taint. * n

blemish, blot, defect, discoloration, flaw, imperfection, spot, tarnish; contamination, disgrace, dishonour, infamy, pollution, reproach, shame, taint, tarnish.

stake¹ vb brace, mark, prop, secure, support. * n pale, palisade, peg, picket, post, stick.

stake² vb finance, pledge, wager; hazard, imperil, jeopardize, peril, risk, venture. * n bet, pledge, wager; adventure, hazard, risk, venture.

stale adj flat, fusty, insipid, mawkish, mouldy, musty, sour, tasteless, vapid; decayed, effete, faded, old, time-worn, worn-out; common, commonplace, hackneyed, stereotyped, threadbare, trite.

stalk¹ n culm, pedicel, peduncle, petiole, shaft, spire, stem, stock.

stalk² vb march, pace, stride, strut, swagger; follow, hunt, shadow, track, walk stealthily.

stall¹ n stable; cell, compartment, recess; booth, kiosk, shop, stand.

stall² vb block, delay, equivocate, filibuster, hinder, postpone, procrastinate, temporize; arrest, check, conk out, die, fail, halt, stick, stop.

stalwart adj able-bodied, athletic, brawny, lusty, muscular, powerful, robust, sinewy, stout, strapping, strong, sturdy, vigorous; bold, brave, daring, gallant, indomitable, intrepid, redoubtable, resolute, valiant, valorous. * n backer, member, partisan, supporter.

stamina n energy, force, lustiness, power, stoutness, strength, sturdiness, vigour.

stammer vb falter, hesitate, stutter. * n faltering, hesitation, stutter.

stamp vb brand, impress, imprint, mark, print. * n brand, impress, impression, print; cast, character, complexion, cut, description, fashion, form, kind, make, mould, sort, type.

stampede vb charge, flee, panic. * n charge, flight, rout, running away, rush.

stand vb be erect, remain upright; abide, be fixed, continue, endure, hold good, remain; halt, pause, stop; be firm, be resolute, stand ground, stay; be valid, have force; depend, have support; rest;

bear, brook, endure, suffer, sustain, weather; abide, admit, await, submit, tolerate, yield; fix, place, put, set upright; (*with* **against**) oppose, resist, withstand; (*with* **by**) be near, be present; aid, assist, defend, help, side with, support; defend, make good, justify, maintain, support, vindicate; (*naut*) attend, be ready; (*with* **fast**) be fixed, be immovable; (*with* **for**) mean, represent, signify; aid, defend, help, maintain, side with, support; (*with* **off**) keep aloof, keep off; not to comply; (*with* **out**) be prominent, jut, project, protrude; not comply, not yield, persist; (*with* **up for**) defend, justify, support, sustain, uphold; (*with* **with**) agree. * *n* place, position, post, standing place, station; halt, stay, stop; dais, platform, rostrum; booth, stall; opposition, resistance.

standard *adj* average, conventional, customary, normal, ordinary, regular, usual; accepted, approved, authoritative, orthodox, received; formulary, prescriptive, regulation. * *n* canon, criterion, model, norm, rule, test, type; gauge, measure, model, scale; support, upright.

standing *adj* established, fixed, immovable, settled; durable, lasting, permanent; motionless, stagnant. * *n* position, stand, station; continuance, duration, existence; footing, ground, hold; condition, estimation, position, rank, reputation, status.

standpoint *n* point of view, viewpoint.

standstill *n* cessation, interruption, stand, stop; deadlock.

staple *adj* basic, chief, essential, fundamental, main, primary, principal. * *n* fibre, filament, pile, thread; body, bulk, mass, substance.

star *vb* act, appear, feature, headline, lead, perform, play; emphasize, highlight, stress, underline. * *adj* leading, main, paramount, principal; celebrated, illustrious, well-known. * *n* heavenly body, luminary; aserisk, pentacle, pentagram; destiny, doom, fate, fortune, lot; diva, headliner, hero, heroine, lead, leading lady, leading man, prima ballerina, prima donna, principal, protagonist.

stare *vb* gape, gaze, look intently, watch.

stark *adj* rigid, stiff; absolute, bare, downright, entire, gross, mere, pure, sheer, simple. * *adv* absolutely, completely, entirely, fully, wholly.

starry *adj* astral, sidereal, star-spangled, stellar; bright, brilliant, lustrous, shining, sparkling, twinkling.

start *vb* begin, commence, inaugurate, initiate, institute; discover, invent; flinch, jump, shrink, startle, wince; alarm, disturb, fright, rouse, scare, startle; depart, set off, take off; arise, call forth, evoke, raise; dislocate, move suddenly, spring, startle. * *n* beginning, commencement, inauguration, outset; fit, jump, spasm, twitch; impulse, sally.

startle *vb* flinch, shrink, start, wince; affright, alarm, fright, frighten, scare, shock; amaze, astonish, astound.

starvation *n* famine, famishment.

starve *vb* famish, perish; be in need, lack, want; kill, subdue.

state *vb* affirm, assert, declare, explain, expound, express, narrate, propound, recite, say, set forth, specify, voice. * *adj* civic, national, public. * *n* case, circumstances, condition, pass, phase, plight, position, posture, predicament, situation, status; condition, guise, mode, quality, rank; dignity, glory, grandeur, magnificence, pageantry, parade, pomp, spendour; body politic, civil community, commonwealth, nation, realm.

stately *adj* august, dignified, elevated, grand, imperial, imposing, lofty, magnificent, majestic, noble, princely, royal; ceremonious, formal, magisterial, pompous, solemn.

statement *n* account, allegation, announcement, communiqué, declaration, description, exposition, mention, narration, narrative, recital, relation, report, specification; assertion, predication, proposition, pronouncement, thesis.

station *vb* establish, fix, locate, place, post, set. * *n* location, place, position, post, seat, situation; business, employment, function, occupation, office; character, condition, degree, dignity, footing, rank, standing, state, status; depot, stop, terminal.

stationary *adj* fixed, motionless, permanent, quiescent, stable, standing, still.

stature *n* height, physique, size, tallness; altitude, consequence, elevation, eminence, prominence.

status *n* caste, condition, footing, position, rank, standing, station.

stay *vb* abide, dwell, lodge, rest, sojourn, tarry; continue, halt, remain, stand still, stop; attend, delay, linger, wait; arrest, check, curb, hold, keep in, prevent, rein in, restrain, withhold; delay, detain, hinder, obstruct; hold up, prop, shore up, support, sustain, uphold. * *n* delay, repose, rest, sojourn; halt, stand, stop; bar, check, curb, hindrance, impediment; interruption, obstacle, obstruction, restraint, stumbling block; buttress, dependence, prop, staff, support, supporter.

steady *vb* balance, counterbalance, secure, stabilize, support. * *adj* firm, fixed, stable; constant, equable, regular, undeviating, uniform, unremitting; constant, persevering, resolute, stable, staunch, steadfast, unchangeable, unwavering.

steal *vb* burglarize, burgle, crib, embezzle, filch, peculate, pilfer, plagiarize, purloin, peculate, poach, shoplift, thieve; creep, sneak, pass stealthily.

stealthy *adj* clandestine, furtive, private, secret, skulking, sly, sneaking, surreptitious, underhand.

steam *vb* emit vapour, fume; evaporate, vaporize; coddle, cook, poach; navigate, sail; be hot, sweat. * *n* vapour; effluvium, exhalation, fume, mist, reek, smoke.

steamy *adj* misty, moist, vaporous; erotic, voluptuous.

steel *vb* case-harden, edge; brace, fortify, harden, make firm, nerve, strengthen.

steep[1] *adj* abrupt, declivitous, precipitous, sheer, sloping, sudden. * *n* declivity, precipice.

steep[2] *vb* digest, drench, imbrue, imbue, macerate, saturate, soak.

steer *vb* direct, conduct, govern, guide, pilot, point.

stem[1] *vb* (*with* **from**) bud, descend, generate, originate, spring, sprout. * *n* axis, stipe, trunk; pedicel, peduncle, petiole, stalk; branch, descendant, offspring, progeny, scion, shoot; ancestry, descent,

family, generation, line, lineage, pedigree, race, stock; (*naut*) beak, bow, cutwater, forepart, prow; helm, lookout; etymon, radical, radix, origin, root.

stem[2] *vb* breast, oppose, resist, withstand; check, dam, oppose, staunch, stay, stop.

step *vb* pace, stride, tramp, tread, walk. * *n* footstep, pace, stride; stair, tread; degree, gradation, grade, interval; advance, advancement, progression; act, action, deed, procedure, proceeding; footprint, trace, track, vestige; footfall, gait, pace, walk; expedient, means, measure, method; round, rundle, rung.

sterile *adj* barren, infecund, unfruitful, unproductive, unprolific; bare, dry, empty, poor; (*bot*) acarpous, male, staminate.

stern[1] *adj* austere, dour, forbidding, grim, severe; bitter, cruel, hard, harsh, inflexible, relentless, rigid, rigorous, severe, strict, unrelenting; immovable, incorruptible, steadfast, uncompromising.

stern[2] *n* behind, breach, hind part, posterior, rear, tail; (*naut*) counter, poop, rudderpost, tailpost; butt, buttocks, fundament, rump.

stew *vb* boil, seethe, simmer, stive. * *n* ragout, stewed meat; confusion, difficculty, mess, scrape.

stick[1] *vb* gore, penetrate, pierce, puncture, spear, stab, transfix; infix, insert, thrust; attach, cement, glue, paste; fix in, set; adhere, cleave, cling, hold; abide, persist, remain, stay, stop; doubt, hesitate, scruple, stickle, waver; (*with* **by**) adhere to, be faithful, support. * *n* prick, stab, thrust.

stick[2] *n* birch, rod, switch; bat, bludgeon, club, cudgel, shillelah; cane, staff, walking stick; cue, pole, spar, stake.

sticky *adj* adhesive, clinging, gluey, glutinous, gummy, mucilaginous, tenacious, viscid, viscous.

stiff *adj* inflexible, rigid, stark, unbending, unyielding; firm, tenacious, thick; obstinate, pertinacious, strong, stubborn, tenacious; absolute, austere, dogmatic, inexorable, peremptory, positive, rigorous, severe, straitlaced, strict, stringent, uncompromising; ceremonious, chilling, constrained, formal, frigid, prim, punctilious, stately, starchy, stilted; abrupt, cramped, crude, graceless, harsh, inelegant.

stifle *vb* choke, smother, suffocate; check, deaden, destroy, extinguish, quench, repress, stop, suppress; conceal, gag, hush, muffle, muzzle, silence, smother, still.

stigma *n* blot, blur, brand, disgrace, dishonour, reproach, shame, spot, stain, taint, tarnish.

still *vb* hush, lull, muffle, silence, stifle; allay, appease, calm, compose, lull, pacify, quiet, smooth, tranquillize; calm, check, immobilize, quiet, restrain, stop, subdue, suppress. * *adj* hushed, mum, mute, noiseless, silent; calm, placid, quiet, serene, stilly, tranquil, unruffled; inert, motionless, quiescent, stagnant, stationary. * *n* hush, lull, peace, quiet, quietude, silence, stillness, tranquillity; picture, photograph, shot.

still *adv, conj* till now, to this time, yet; however, nevertheless, notwithstanding; always, continually, ever, habitually, uniformly; after that, again, in continuance.

stimulate *vb* animate, arouse, awaken, brace, encourage, energize, excite, fire, foment, goad, impel, incite, inflame, inspirit, instigate, kindle, prick, prompt, provoke, rally, rouse, set on, spur, stir up, urge, whet, work up.

stimulus *n* encouragement, fillip, goad, incentive, incitement, motivation, motive, provocation, spur, stimulant.

sting *vb* hurt, nettle, prick, wound; afflict, cut, pain.

stingy *adj* avaricious, close, close-fisted, covetous, grudging, mean, miserly, narrow-hearted, niggardly, parsimonious, penurious.

stink *vb* emit a stench, reek, smell bad. * *n* bad smell, fetor, offensive odour, stench.

stint *vb* bound, confine, limit, restrain; begrudge, pinch, scrimp, skimp, straiten; cease, desist, stop. * *n* bound, limit, restraint; lot, period, project, quota, share, shift, stretch, task, time, turn.

stipulate *vb* agree, bargain, condition, contract, covenant, engage, provide, settle terms.

stir *vb* budge, change place, go, move; agitate, bestir, disturb, prod; argue, discuss, moot, raise, start; animate, arouse, awaken, excite, goad, incite, instigate, prompt, provoke, quicken, rouse, spur, stimulate; appear, happen, turn up; get up, rise; (*with* up) animate, awaken, incite, instigate, move, provoke, quicken, rouse, stimulate. * *n* activity, ado, agitation, bustle, confusion, excitement, fidget, flurry, fuss, hurry, movement; commotion, disorder, disturbance, tumult, uproar.

stock *vb* fill, furnish, store, supply; accumulate, garner, hoard, lay in, reposit, reserve, save, treasure up. * *adj* permanent, standard, standing. * *n* assets, capital, commodities, fund, principal, shares; accumulation, hoard, inventory, merchandise, provision, range, reserve, store, supply; ancestry, breed, descent, family, house, line, lineage, parentage, pedigree, race; cravat, neckcloth; butt, haft, hand; block, log, pillar, post, stake; stalk, stem, trunk.

stockstill *adj* dead-still, immobile, motionless, stationary, still, unmoving.

stocky *adj* chubby, chunky, dumpy, plump, short, stout, stubby, thickset.

stoic, stoical *adj* apathetic, cold-blooded, impassive, imperturbable, passionless, patient, philosophic, philosophical, phlegmatic, unimpassioned.

stolen *adj* filched, pilfered, purloined; clandestine, furtive, secret, sly, stealthy, surreptitious.

stolid *adj* blockish, doltish, dull, foolish, heavy, obtuse, slow, stockish, stupid.

stomach *vb* abide, bear, brook, endure, put up with, stand, submit to, suffer, swallow, tolerate. * *n* abdomen, belly, gut, paunch, pot, tummy; appetite, desire, inclination, keenness, liking, relish, taste.

stone *vb* free from stones, stein; brick, cover, face, slate, tile; lapidate, pelt. * *n* boulder, cobble, gravel, pebble, rock; gem, jewel, precious stone; cenotaph, gravestone, monument, tombstone; nut, pit; adamant, agate, flint, gneiss, granite, marble, slate, etc.

stony *adj* gritty, hard, lapidose, lithic,

petrous, rocky; adamantine, flinty, hard, inflexible, obdurate; cruel, hard-hearted, inexorable, pitiless, stony-hearted, unfeeling, unrelenting.

stoop vb bend forward, bend down, bow, lean, sag, slouch, slump; abase, cower, cringe, give in, submit, succumb, surrender; condescend, deign, descend, vouchsafe; fall, sink. * n bend, inclination, sag, slouch, slump; descent, swoop.

stop vb block, blockade, close, close up, obstruct, occlude; arrest, block, check, halt, hold, pause, stall, stay; bar, delay, embargo, hinder, impede, intercept, interrupt, obstruct, preclude, prevent, repress, restrain, staunch, stay, suppress, thwart; break off, cease, desist, discontinue, forbear, give over, leave off, refrain from; arrest, intermit, quiet, quiten, terminate; lodge, stay, tarry. * n halt, intermission, pause, respite, rest, stoppage, suspension, truce; block, cessation, check, hindrance, interruption, obstruction, repression; bar, impediment, obstacle, obstruction; full stop, point.

stoppage n arrest, block, check, closure, hindrance, interruption, obstruction, prevention.

store vb accumulate, amass, cache, deposit, garner, hoard, husband, lay by, lay in, lay up, put by, reserve, save, store up, stow away, treasure up; furnish, provide, replenish, stock, supply. * n accumulation, cache, deposit, fund, hoard, provision, reserve, stock, supply, treasure, treasury; abundance, plenty; storehouse; emporium, market, shop.

storm vb assail, assault, attack; blow violently; fume, rage, rampage, rant, rave, tear. * n blizzard, gale, hurricane, squall, tempest, tornado, typhoon, whirlwind; agitation, clamour, commotion, disturbance, insurrection, outbreak, sedition, tumult, turmoil; adversity, affliction, calamity, distress; assault, attack, brunt, onset, onslaught; violence.

stormy adj blustering, boisterous, gusty, squally, tempestuous, windy; passionate, riotous, rough, turbulent, violent, wild; agitated, blustering, furious.

story n annals, chronicle, history, record;

account, narration, narrative, recital, record, rehearsal, relation, report, statement, tale; fable, fiction, novel, romance; anecdote, incident, legend, tale; canard, fabrication, falsehood, fib, fiction, figure, invention, lie, untruth.

stout adj able-bodied, athletic, brawny, lusty, robust, sinewy, stalwart, strong, sturdy, vigorous; courageous, hardy, indomitable, stouthearted; contumacious, obstinate, proud, resolute, stubborn; compact, firm, hardy, solid, staunch, strong, sturdy; bouncing, burly, chubby, corpulent, fat, jolly, large, obese, plump, portly, stocky, strapping, thickset.

stow vb load, pack, put away, store, stuff.

straggle vb rove, wander; deviate, digress, bafdaboutt, ramble, range, roam, rove, stray, stroll, wander.

straight adj direct, near, rectilinear, right, short, undeviating, unswerving; erect, perpendicular, plumb, right, upright, vertical; equitable, fair, honest, honourable, just, square, straightforward. * adv at once, directly, forthwith, immediately, straightaway, straightway, without delay.

straightaway, straightway adv at once, directly, forthwith, immediately, speedily, straight, suddenly, without delay.

straighten vb arrange, make straight, neaten, order, tidy.

strain[1] vb draw tightly, make tense, stretch, tighten; injure, sprain, wrench; exert, overexert, overtax, rack; embrace, fold, hug, press, squeeze; compel, constrain, force; dilute, distill, drain, filter, filtrate, ooze, percolate, purify, separate; fatigue, overtask, overwork, task, tax, tire. * n stress, tenseness, tension, tensity; effort, exertion, force, overexertion; burden, task, tax; sprain, wrench; lay, melody, movement, snatch, song, stave, tune.

strain[2] n manner, style, tone, vein; disposition, tendency, trait, turn; descent, extraction, family, lineage, pedigree, race, stock.

strand vb abandon, beach, be wrecked, cast away, go aground, ground, maroon, run aground, wreck. * *n* beach, coast, shore.

strange *adj* alien, exotic, far-fetched, foreign, outlandish, remote; new, novel; curious, exceptional, extraordinary, irregular, odd, particular, peculiar, rare, singular, surprising, uncommon, unusual; abnormal, anomalous, extraordinary, inconceivable, incredible, inexplicable, marvellous, mysterious, preternatural, unaccountable, unbelievable, unheard of, unique, unnatural, wonderful; bizarre, droll, grotesque, odd, quaint, queer, peculiar; inexperienced, unacquainted, unfamiliar, unknown; bashful, distant, distrustful, reserved, shy, uncommunicative.

stranger *n* alien, foreigner, newcomer, immigrant, outsider; guest, visitor.

strangle *vb* choke, contract, smother, squeeze, stifle, suffocate, throttle, tighten; keep back, quiet, repress, still, suppress.

strap *vb* beat, thrash, whip; bind, fasten, sharpen, strop. * *n* thong; band, ligature, strip, tie; razor-strap, strop.

stratagem *n* artifice, cunning, device, dodge, finesse, intrigue, machination, manoeuvre, plan, plot, ruse, scheme, trick, wile.

strategic *adj* calcuated, deliberate, diplomatic, manoeuvering, planned, politic, tactical; critical, decisive, key, vital.

stray *vb* deviate, digress, err, meander, ramble, range, roam, rove, straggle, stroll, swerve, transgress, wander. * *adj* abandoned, lost, strayed, wandering; accidental, erratic, random, scattered.

streak *vb* band, bar, striate, stripe, vein; dart, dash, flash, hurtle, run, speed, sprint, stream, tear. * *n* band, bar, belt, layer, line, strip, stripe, thread, trace, vein; cast, grain, stripe, tone, touch, vein; beam, bolt, dart, dash, flare, flash, ray, stream.

stream *vb* course, flow, glide, pour, run, spout; emit, pour out, shed; emanate, go forth, issue, radiate; extend, float, stretch out, wave. * *n* brook, burn, race, rill, rivulet, run, runlet, runnel, trickle; course, current, flow, flux, race, rush, tide, tor-

rent, wake, wash; beam, gleam, patch, radiation, ray, streak.

strength *n* force, might, main, nerve, potency, power, vigour; hardness, solidity, toughness; impregnability, proof; brawn, grit, lustiness, muscle, robustness, sinewy, stamina, thews; animation, courage, determination, firmness, fortitude, resolution, spirit; cogency, efficacy, soundness, validity; emphasis, energy, force, nerve, vigour; security, stay, support; brightness, brilliance, clearness, intensity, vitality, vividness; body, excellence, potency, spirit, virtue; force, impetuosity, vehemence, violence; boldness, energy.

strengthen *vb* buttress, recruit, reinforce; fortify; brace, energize, harden, nerve, steel, stimulate; freshen, invigorate, vitalize; animate, encourage; clench, clinch, confirm, corroborate, establish, fix, justify, sustain, support.

strenuous *adj* active, ardent, eager, earnest, energetic, resolute, vigorous, zealous; bold, determined, doughty, intrepid, resolute, spirited, strong, valiant.

stress *vb* accent, accentuate, emphasize, highlight, point up, underline, underscore; bear, bear upon, press, pressurize; pull, rack, strain, stretch, tense, tug. * *n* accent, accentuation, emphasis; effort, force, pull, strain, tension, tug; boisterousness, severity, violence; pressure, urgency.

stretch *vb* brace, screw, strain, tense, tighten; elongate, extend, lengthen, protract, pull; display, distend, expand, spread, unfold, widen; sprain, strain; distort, exaggerate, misrepresent. * *n* compass, extension, extent, range, reach, scope; effort, exertion, strain, struggle; course, direction.

strict *adj* close, strained, tense, tight; accurate, careful, close, exact, literal, particular, precise, scrupulous; austere, inflexible, harsh, orthodox, puritanical, rigid, rigorous, severe, stern, strait-laced, stringent, uncompromising, unyielding.

strife *n* battle, combat, conflict, contention, contest, discord, quarrel, struggle, warfare.

strike vb bang, beat, belabour, box, buffet, cudgel, cuff, hit, knock, lash, pound, punch, rap, slap, slug, smite, thump, whip; impress, imprint, stamp; afflict, chastise, deal, give, inflict, punish, smite; affect, astonish, electrify, stun; clash, collide, dash, hit, touch; surrender, yield; mutiny, rebel, rise.

stringent adj binding, contracting, rigid, rigorous, severe, strict.

strip¹ n piece, ribbon, shred, slip.

strip² vb denude, hull, skin, uncover; bereave, deprive, deforest, desolate, despoil, devastate, disarm, dismantle, disrobe, divest, expose, fleece, loot, shave; plunder, pillage, ransack, rob, sack, spoil; disrobe, uncover, undress.

strive vb aim, attempt, endeavour, labour, strain, struggle, toil; contend, contest, fight, tussle, wrestle; compete, cope, struggle.

stroke¹ n blow, glance, hit, impact, knock, lash, pat, percussion, rap, shot, switch, thump; attack, paralysis, stroke; affliction, damage, hardship, hurt, injury, misfortune, reverse, visitation; dash, feat, masterstroke, touch.

stroke² vb caress, feel, palpate, pet, knead, massage, nuzzle, rub, touch.

stroll vb loiter, lounge, ramble, range, rove, saunter, straggle, stray, wander. * n excursion, promenade, ramble, rambling, roving, tour, trip, walk, wandering.

strong adj energetic, forcible, powerful, robust, sturdy; able, enduring; cogent, firm, valid.

structure vb arrange, constitute, construct, make, organize. * n arrangement, conformation, configuration, constitution, construction, form, formation, make, organization; anatomy, composition, texture; arrangement, building, edifice, fabric, framework, pile.

struggle vb aim, endeavour, exert, labour, strive, toil, try; battle, contend, contest, fight, wrestle; agonize, flounder, writhe. * n effort, endeavour, exertion, labour, pains; battle, conflict, contention, contest, fight, strife; agony, contortions, distress.

stubborn adj dogged, headstrong, inflexible, intractable, mulish, obdurate, obstinate, perverse, positive, refractory, ungovernable, unmanageable, unruly, unyielding, willful; constant, enduring, firm, hardy, persevering, persistent, steady, stoical, uncomplaining, unremitting; firm, hard, inflexible, stiff, strong, tough, unpliant, studied.

studious adj contemplative, meditative, reflective, thoughtful; assiduous, attentive, desirous, diligent, eager, lettered, scholarly, zealous.

study vb cogitate, lubricate, meditate, muse, ponder, reflect, think; analyze, contemplate, examine, investigate, ponder, probe, scrutinize, search, sift, weigh. * n exercise, inquiry, investigation, reading, research, stumble; cogitation, consideration, contemplation, examination, meditation, reflection, thought, stun; model, object, representation, sketch; den, library, office, studio.

stunning adj deafening, stentorian; dumbfounding, stupefying.

stunted adj checked, diminutive, dwarfed, dwarfish, lilliputian, little, nipped, small, undersized.

stupendous adj amazing, astonishing, astounding, marvellous, overwhelming, surprising, wonderful; enormous, huge, immense, monstrous, prodigious, towering, tremendous, vast.

stupid adj brainless, crass, doltish, dull, foolish, idiotic, inane, inept, obtuse, pointless, prosaic, senseless, simple, slow, sluggish, stolid, tedious, tiresome, witless.

sturdy adj bold, determined, dogged, firm, hardy, obstinate, persevering, pertinacious, resolute, stiff, stubborn, sturdy; athletic, brawny, forcible, lusty, muscular, powerful, robust, stalwart, stout, strong, thickset, vigorous, well-set.

style vb address, call, characterize, denominate, designate, dub, entitle, name, term. * n dedication, expression, phraseology, turn; cast, character, fashion, form, genre, make, manner, method, mode, model, shape, vogue, way; appellation, denomination, designation, name, title; chic, elegance, smartness; pen, pin, point, stylus.

stylish adj chic, courtly, elegant, fashionable, genteel, modish, polished, smart.

suave adj affable, agreeable, amiable, bland, courteous, debonair, delightful, glib, gracious, mild, pleasant, smooth, sweet, oily, unctuous, urbane.

subdue vb beat, bend, break, bow, conquer, control, crush, defeat, discomfit, foil, master, overbear, overcome, overpower, overwhelm, quell, rout, subject, subjugate, surmount, vanquish, worst; allay, choke, curb, mellow, moderate, mollify, reduce, repress, restrain, soften, suppress, temper.

subject vb control, master, overcome, reduce, subdue, subjugate, tame; enslave, enthral; abandon, refer, submit, surrender. * adj beneath, subjacent, underneath; dependent, enslaved, inferior, servile, subjected, subordinate, subservient; conditional, obedient, submissive; disposed, exposed to, liable, obnoxious, prone. * n dependent, henchman, liegeman, slave, subordinate; matter, point, subject matter, theme, thesis, topic; nominative, premise; case, object, patient, recipient; ego, mind, self, thinking.

sublime adj aloft, elevated, high, sacred; eminent, exalted, grand, great, lofty, noble; august, eminent, glorious, magnificent, majestic, noble, stately, solemn, sublunary; elate, elevated, exhilarated, raised.

submission n capitulation, cession, relinquishment, surrender, yielding; acquiescence, compliance, obedience, resignation; deference, homage, humility, lowliness, obeisance, passiveness, prostration, self-abasement, submissiveness.

submissive adj amenable, compliant, docile, pliant, tame, tractable, yielding; acquiescent, long-suffering, obedient, passive, patient, resigned, unassertive, uncomplaining, unrepining; deferential, humble, lowly, meek, obsequious, prostrate, self-abasing.

submit vb cede, defer, endure, resign, subject, surrender, yield; commit, propose, refer; offer; acquiesce, bend, capitulate, comply, stoop, succumb.

subordinate adj ancillary, dependent, inferior, junior, minor, secondary, subject, subservient, subsidiary. * n assistant, dependant, inferior, subject, underling.

subscribe vb accede, approve, agree, assent, consent, yield; contribute, donate, give, offer, promise.

subsequent adj after, attendant, ensuing, later, latter, following, posterior, sequent, succeeding.

subside vb settle, sink; abate, decline, decrease, diminish, drop, ebb, fall, intermit, lapse, lessen, lower, lull, wane.

subsidiary adj adjutant, aiding, assistant, auxiliary, cooperative, corroborative, helping, subordinate, subservient.

subsidize vb aid, finance, fund, sponsor, support, underwrite.

subsidy n aid, bounty, grant, subvention, support, underwriting.

substance n actuality, element, groundwork, hypostasis, reality, substratum; burden, content, core, drift, essence, gist, heart, import, meaning, pith, sense, significance, solidity, soul, sum, weight; estate, income, means, property, resources, wealth.

substantial adj actual, considerable, essential, existent, hypostatic, pithy, potential, real, subsistent, virtual; concrete, durable, positive, solid, tangible, true; corporeal, bodily, material; bulky, firm, goodly, heavy, large, massive, notable, significant, sizable, solid, sound, stable, stout, strong, well-made; cogent, just, efficient, influential, valid, weighty.

subterfuge n artifice, evasion, excuse, expedient, mask, pretence, pretext, quirk, shift, shuffle, sophistry, trick.

subtle adj arch, artful, astute, crafty, crooked, cunning, designing, diplomatic, intriguing, insinuating, sly, tricky, wily; clever, ingenious; acute, deep, discerning, discriminating, keen, profound, sagacious, shrewd; airy, delicate, ethereal, light, nice, rare, refined, slender, subtle, thin, volatile.

subtract vb deduct, detract, diminish, remove, take, withdraw.

succeed vb ensue, follow, inherit, replace; flourish, gain, hit, prevail, prosper, thrive, win.

success *n* attainment, issue, result; fortune, happiness, hit, luck, prosperity, triumph.

successful *adj* auspicious, booming, felicitous, fortunate, happy, lucky, prosperous, victorious, winning.

succession *n* chain, concatenation, cycle, consecution, following, procession, progression, rotation, round, sequence, series, suite; descent, entail, inheritance, lineage, race, reversion.

succinct *adj* brief, compact, compendious, concise, condensed, curt, laconic, pithy, short, summary, terse.

sudden *adj* abrupt, hasty, hurried, immediate, instantaneous, rash, unanticipated, unexpected, unforeseen, unusual; brief, momentary, quick, rapid.

sue *vb* charge, court, indict, prosecute, solicit, summon, woo; appeal, beg, demand, entreat, implore, petition, plead, pray, supplicate.

suffer *vb* feel, undergo; bear, endure, pocket, staunch, support, sustain, tolerate; admit, allow, indulge, let, permit.

sufferance *n* endurance, inconvenience, misery, pain, suffering; long-suffering, moderation, patience, submission; allowance, permission, toleration.

sufficient *adj* adequate, ample, commensurate, competent, enough, full, plenteous, satisfactory; able, equal, fit, qualified, responsible.

suffocate *vb* asphyxiate, choke, smother, stifle, strangle.

suggest *vb* advise, allude, hint, indicate, insinuate, intimate, move, present, prompt, propose, propound, recommend.

suggestion *n* allusion, hint, indication, insinuation, intimation, presentation, prompting, proposal, recommendation, reminder.

suit *vb* accommodate, adapt, adjust, fashion, fit, level, match; accord, become, befit, gratify, harmonize, please, satisfy, tally. * *n* appeal, entreaty, invocation, petition, prayer, request, solicitation, supplication; courtship, wooing; action, case, cause, process, prosecution, trial; clothing, costume, habit.

suitable *adj* adapted, accordant, agreeable, answerable, apposite, applicable, appropriate, apt, becoming, befitting, conformable, congruous, convenient, consonant, correspondent, decent, due, eligible, expedient, fit, fitting, just, meet, pertinent, proper, relevant, seemly, worthy.

sulky *adj* aloof, churlish, cross, cross-grained, dogged, grouchy, ill-humoured, ill-tempered, moody, morose, perverse, sour, spleenish, spleeny, splenetic, sullen, surly, vexatious, wayward.

sullen *adj* cross, crusty, glum, grumpy, ill-tempered, moody, morose, sore, sour, sulky; cheerless, cloudy, dark, depressing, dismal, foreboding, funereal, gloomy, lowering, melancholy, mournful, sombre; dull, gloomy, heavy, slow, sluggish; intractable, obstinate, perverse, refractory, stubborn, vexatious; baleful, evil, inauspicious, malign, malignant, sinister, unlucky, unpropitious.

sully *vb* blemish, blot, contaminate, deface, defame, dirty, disgrace, dishonour, foul, smirch, soil, slur, spot, stain, tarnish.

sultry *adj* close, damp, hot, humid, muggy, oppressive, stifling, stuffy, sweltering.

sum *vb* add, calculate, compute, reckon; collect, comprehend, condense, epitomize, summarize. * *n* aggregate, amount, total, totality, whole; compendium, substance, summary; acme, completion, height, summit.

summary *adj* brief, compendious, concise, curt, laconic, pithy, short, succinct, terse; brief, quick, rapid. * *n* abridgement, abstract, brief, compendium, digest, epitome, precis, résumé, syllabus, synopsis.

summit *n* acme, apex, cap, climax, crest, crown, pinnacle, top, vertex, zenith.

summon *vb* arouse, bid, call, cite, invite, invoke, rouse; convene, convoke; charge, indict, prosecute, subpoena, sue.

sundry *adj* different, divers, several, some, various.

sunny *adj* bright, brilliant, clear, fine, luminous, radiant, shining, unclouded, warm; cheerful, genial, happy, joyful, mild, optimistic, pleasant, smiling.

superb *adj* august, beautiful, elegant, exquisite, grand, gorgeous, imposing, magnificent, majestic, noble, pompous, rich, showy, splendid, stately, sumptuous.

superficial *adj* external, flimsy, shallow, untrustworthy.

superfluous *adj* excessive, redundant, unnecessary.

superintend *vb* administer, conduct, control, direct, inspect, manage, overlook, oversee, supervise.

superior *adj* better, greater, high, higher, finer, paramount, supreme, ultra, upper; chief, foremost, principal; distinguished, matchless, noble, pre-eminent, preferable, sovereign, surpassing, unrivalled, unsurpassed; predominant, prevalent. * *n* boss, chief, director, head, higher-up, leader, manager, principal, senior, supervisor.

supernatural *adj* abnormal, marvellous, metaphysical, miraculous, otherworldly, preternatural, unearthly.

supersede *vb* annul, neutralize, obviate, overrule, suspend; displace, remove, replace, succeed, supplant.

supervise *vb* administer, conduct, control, direct, inspect, manage, overlook, oversee, superintend.

supple *adj* elastic, flexible, limber, lithe, pliable, pliant; compliant, humble, submissive, yielding; adulatory, cringing, fawning, flattering, grovelling, obsequious, oily, parasitical, slavish, sycophantic, obsequious, servile.

supplement *vb* add, augment, extend, reinforce, supply. * *n* addendum, addition, appendix, codicil, complement, continuation, postscript, postscript.

supply *vb* endue, equip, furnish, minister, outfit, provide, replenish, stock, store; afford, accommodate, contribute, furnish, give, grant, yield. * *n* hoard, provision, reserve, stock, store.

support *vb* brace, cradle, pillow, prop, sustain, uphold; bear, endure, undergo, suffer, tolerate; cherish, keep, maintain, nourish, nurture; act, assume, carry, perform, play, represent; accredit, corroborate, substantiate, confirm verify; abet, advocate, aid, approve, assist, back, befriend, champion, countenance, encourage, favour, float, held, patronize, re-

lieve, reinforce, succour, uphold, vindicate. * *n* bolster, brace, buttress, foothold, guy, hold, prop, purchase, shore, stay, substructure, supporter, underpinning; groundwork, mainstay, staff; base, basis, bed, foundation; keeping, living, livelihood, maintenance, subsistence, sustenance; confirmation, evidence; aid, assistance, backing, behalf, championship, comfort, countenance, encouragement, favour, help, patronage, succour.

suppose *vb* apprehend, believe, conceive, conclude, consider, conjecture, deem, imagine, judge, presume, presuppose, think; assume, hypothesize; believe, imagine, imply, posit, predicate, think; fancy, opine, speculate, surmise, suspect, theorize, wean.

suppress *vb* choke, crush, destroy, overwhelm, overpower, overthrow, quash, quell, quench, smother, stifle, subdue, withhold; arrest, inhibit, obstruct, repress, restraint, stop; conceal, extinguish, keep, retain, secret, silence, stifle, strangle.

supreme *adj* chief, dominant, first, greatest, highest, leading, paramount, predominant, pre-eminent, principal, sovereign.

sure *adj* assured, certain, confident, positive; accurate, dependable, effective, honest, infallible, precise, reliable, trustworthy, undeniable, undoubted, unmistakable, well-proven; assured, guaranteed, inevitable, irrevocable; fast, firm, safe, secure, stable, steady.

surfeit *vb* cram, gorge, overfeed, sate, satiate; cloy, nauseate, pall. * *n* excess, fullness, glut, oppression, plethora, satiation, satiety, superabundance, superfluity.

surly *adj* churlish, crabbed, cross, crusty, discourteous, fretful, gruff, grumpy, harsh, ill-natured, ill-tempered, morose, peevish, perverse, pettish, petulant, rough, rude, snappish, snarling, sour, sullen, testy, touchy, uncivil, ungracious, waspish; dark, rough, sullen.

surpass *vb* beat, cap, eclipse, exceed, excel, outdo, outmatch, outnumber, outrun, outstrip, override, overshadow, overtop, outshine, surmount, transcend.

surplus *adj* additional, leftover, remaining, spare, superfluous, supernumerary, supplementary. * *n* balance, excess, overplus, remainder, residue, superabundance, surfeit.

surprise *vb* amaze, astonish, astound, bewilder, confuse, disconcert, dumbfound, startle, stun. * *n* amazement, astonishment, blow, shock, wonder.

surrender *vb* cede, sacrifice, yield; abdicate, abandon, forgo, relinquish, renounce, resign, waive; capitulate, comply, succumb. * *n* abandonment, capitulation, cession, delivery, relinquishment, renunciation, resignation, yielding.

surround *vb* beset, circumscribe, compass, embrace, encircle, encompass, environ, girdle, hem, invest, loop.

survey *vb* contemplate, observe, overlook, reconnoitre, review, scan, scout, view; examine, inspect, scrutinize; oversee, supervise; estimate, measure, plan, plot, prospect. * *n* prospect, retrospect, sight, view; examination, inspection, prospect, reconnaissance, review; estimating, measuring, planning, plotting, prospecting, work-study.

survive *vb* endure, last, outlast, outlive.

susceptible *adj* capable, excitable, impressible, inclined, predisposed, receptive, sensitive, susceptible.

suspect *vb* believe, conclude, conjecture, fancy, guess, imagine, judge, suppose, surmise, think; distrust, doubt, mistrust. * *adj* doubtful, dubious, suspicious.

suspend *vb* append, hang, sling, swing; adjourn, arrest, defer, delay, discontinue, hinder, intermit, interrupt, postpone, stay, withhold; debar, dismiss, rusticate.

suspicion *n* assumption, conjecture, dash, guess, hint, inkling, suggestion, supposition, surmise, trace; apprehension, distrust, doubt, fear, jealousy, misgiving, mistrust.

suspicious *adj* distrustful, jealous, mistrustful, suspect, suspecting; doubtful, questionable.

sustain *vb* bear, bolster, fortify, prop, strengthen, support, uphold; maintain, nourish, perpetuate, preserve, support;

aid, assist, comfort, relieve; brave, endure, suffer, undergo; approve, confirm, ratify, sanction, validate; confirm, establish, justify, prove.

swallow *vb* bolt, devour, drink, eat, englut, engorge, gobble, gorge, gulp, imbibe, swamp; absorb, appropriate, arrogate, devour, engulf, submerge; consume, employ, occupy; brook, digest, endure, pocket, stomach, swap; recant, renounce, retract. * *n* draught, gulp, mouthful.

swamp *vb* engulf, overwhelm, sink; capsize, embarrass, overset, ruin, sink, upset, wreck. * *n* bog, fen, marsh, morass, quagmire, slough.

swarm *vb* abound, crowd, teem, throng. * *n* cloud, concourse, crowd, drove, flock, hive, horde, host, mass, multitude, press, shoal, throng.

sway *vb* balance, brandish, move, poise, rock, roll, swing, wave, wield; bend, bias, influence, persuade, turn, urge; control, dominate, direct, govern, guide, manage, rule; hoist, raise; incline, lean, lurch, yaw. * *n* ascendency, authority, command, control, domination, dominion, empire, government, mastership, mastery, omnipotence, predominance, power, rule, sovereignty; authority, bias, direction, influence, weight; preponderance, preponderation; oscillation, sweep, swing, wag, wave.

swear *vb* affirm, attest, avow, declare, depose, promise, say, state, testify, vow; blaspheme, curse.

sweep *vb* clean, brush; brush, graze, touch; rake, scour, traverse. * *n* amplitude, compass, drive, movement, range, reach, scope; destruction, devastation, havoc, ravage; curvature, curve.

sweeping *adj* broad, comprehensive, exaggerated, extensive, extravagant, general, unqualified, wholesale.

sweet *adj* candied, cloying, honeyed, luscious, nectareous, nectarous, sugary, saccharine; balmy, fragrant, odorous, redolent, spicy; harmonious, dulcet, mellifluous, mellow, melodious, musical, pleasant, soft, tuneful, silver-toned, silvery; beautiful, fair, lovely; agreeable, charming, delightful, grateful, gratifying, pleasant; affectionate, amiable, attractive, engaging, gentle, mild, lovable, winning; benignant, gentle, serene, soft; clean, fresh, pure, sound. * n fragrance, perfume, redolence; blessing, delight, enjoyment, gratification, joy, pleasure.

swell vb belly, bloat, bulge, dilate, distend, expand, inflate, intumesce, puff, swell, tumefy; augment, enlarge, increase; heave, rise, surge; strut, swagger. * n swelling; augmentation, excrescence, protuberance; ascent, elevation, hill, rise; force, intensity, power; billows, surge, undulation, waves; beau, blade, buck, dandy, exquisite, fop.

swift adj expeditious, fast, fleet, flying, quick, rapid, speedy; alert, eager, forward, prompt, ready, zealous; instant, speedy, sudden.

swindle vb cheat, con, cozen, deceive, defraud, diddle, dupe, embezzle, forge, gull, hoax, overreach, steal, trick, victimize. * n cheat, con, deceit, deception, fraud, hoax, imposition, knave, roguery, trickery.

swing vb oscillate, sway, vibrate, wave; dangle, depend, hang; brandish, flourish, wave, whirl; administer, manage, ruin. * n fluctuation, oscillation, sway, undulation, vibration; elbow-room, freedom, margin, play, range, scope, sweep; bias, tendency.

swoop vb descend, pounce, rush, seize, stoop, sweep. * n clutch, pounce, seizure; stoop, descent.

symbol n badge, emblem, exponent, figure, mark, picture, representation, representative, sign, token, type.

symbolic adj emblematic, figurative, hieroglyphic, representative, significant, symbolical, typical.

symmetry n balance, congruity, evenness, harmony, order, parallelism, proportion, regularity, shapeliness.

sympathetic adj affectionate, commiserating, compassionate, condoling, kind, pitiful, sympathetic, tender.

sympathy n accord, affinity, agreement, communion, concert, concord, congeniality, correlation, correspondence, harmony, reciprocity, union; commiseration, compassion, condolence, fellow-feeling, kindliness, pity, tenderness, thoughtfulness.

symptom n diagnostic, indication, mark, note, prognostic, sign, token.

symptomatic adj characteristic, indicative, symbolic, suggestive.

system n method, order, plan.

systematic adj methodic, methodical, orderly, regular.

T

table vb enter, move, propose, submit, suggest. * n plate, slab, tablet; board, counter, desk, stand; catalogue, chart, compendium, index, list, schedule, syllabus, synopsis, tabulation; diet, fare, food, victuals.

taboo vb forbid, interdict, prohibit, proscribe. * adj banned, forbidden, inviolable, outlawed, prohibited, proscribed. * n ban, interdict, prohibition, proscription.

tackle vb attach, grapple, seize; attempt, try, undertake. * n apparatus, cordage, equipment, furniture, gear, harness, implements, rigging, tools, weapons.

tact n address, adroitness, cleverness, dexterity, diplomacy, discernment, finesse, insight, knack, perception, skill, understanding.

tail vb dog, follow, shadow, stalk, track. * adj abridged, curtailed, limited, reduced. * n appendage, conclusion, end, extremity, stub; flap, skirt; queue, retinue, train.

taint vb imbue, impregnate; contaminate, corrupt, defile, inflect, mildew, pollute, poison, spoil, touch; blot, stain, sully, tarnish. * n stain, tincture, tinge, touch; contamination, corruption, defilement, depravation, infection, pollution; blemish, defect, fault, flaw, spot, stain.

take vb accept, obtain, procure, receive; clasp, clutch, grasp, grip, gripe, seize, snatch; filch, misappropriate, pilfer, purloin, steal; abstract, apprehend, appropriate, arrest, bag, capture, ensnare, entrap; attack, befall, smite; capture, carry off, conquer, gain, win; allure, attract, bewitch, captivate, charm, delight, enchant, engage, fascinate, interest, please; consider, hold, interrupt, suppose, regard, understand; choose, elect, espouse, select; employ, expend, use; claim, demand, necessitate, require; bear, endure, experience, feel, perceive, tolerate; deduce, derive, detect, discover, draw; carry, conduct, convey, lead, transfer; clear, surmount; drink, eat, imbibe, inhale, swallow. * n proceeds, profits, return, revenue, takings, yield.

tale n account, fable, legend, narration, novel, parable, recital, rehearsal, relation, romance, story, yarn; account, catalogue, count, enumeration, numbering, reckoning, tally.

talent n ableness, ability, aptitude, capacity, cleverness, endowment, faculty, forte, genius, gift, knack, parts, power, turn.

talk vb chatter, communicate, confer, confess, converse, declaim, discuss, gossip, pontificate, speak. * n chatter, communication, conversation, diction, gossip, jargon, language, rumour, speech, utterance.

talkative adj chatty, communicative, garrulous, loquacious, voluble.

tame vb domesticate, reclaim, train; conquer, master, overcome, repress, subdue, subjugate. * adj docile, domestic, domesticated, gentle, mild, reclaimed; broken, crushed, meek, subdued, unresisting, submissive; barren, commonplace, dull, feeble, flat, insipid, jejune, languid, lean, poor, prosaic, prosy, spiritless, tedious, uninteresting, vapid.

tamper vb alter, conquer, dabble, damage, interfere, meddle; intrigue, seduce, suborn.

tang n aftertaste, flavour, relish, savour, smack, taste; keenness, nip, sting.

tangible adj corporeal, material, palpable, tactile, touchable; actual, certain, embodied, evident, obvious, open, perceptible, plain, positive, real, sensible, solid, stable, substantial.

tangle vb complicate, entangle, intertwine, interweave, mat, perplex, snarl; catch, ensnare, entrap, involve, catch; embarrass, embroil, perplex. * n complication, disorder, intricacy, jumble, perplexity, snarl; dilemma, embarrassment, quandary, perplexity.

tap[1] vb knock, pat, rap, strike, tip, touch. * n pat, tip, rap, touch.

tap[2] vb broach, draw off, extract, pierce; draw on, exploit, mine, use, utilize; bug, eavesdrop, listen in. * n faucet, plug, spigot, spout, stopcock, valve; bug, listening device, transmitter.

tardy adj slow, sluggish, snail-like; backward, behindhand, dilatory, late, loitering, overdue, slack.

tarnish vb blemish, deface, defame, dim, discolour, dull, slur, smear, soil, stain, sully. * n blemish, blot, soiling, spot, stain.

tart adj acid, acidulous, acrid, piquant, pungent, sharp, sour; acrimonious, caustic, crabbed, curt, harsh, ill-humoured, ill-tempered, keen, petulant, sarcastic, severe, snappish, sharp, testy.

task vb burden, overwork, strain, tax. * n drudgery, labour, toil, work; business, charge, chore, duty, employment, enterprise, job, mission, stint, undertaking, work; assignment, exercise, lesson.

taste vb experience, feel, perceive, undergo; relish, savour, sip. * n flavour, gusto, relish, savour, smack, piquancy; admixture, bit, dash, fragment, hint, infusion, morsel, mouthful, sample, shade, sprinkling, suggestion, tincture; appetite, desire, fondness, liking, partiality, predilection; acumen, cultivation, culture, delicacy, discernment, discrimination, elegance, fine-feeling, grace, judgement, polish, refinement; manner, style.

taunt vb censure, chaff, deride, flout, jeer, mock, scoff, sneer, revile, reproach, ridicule, twit, upbraid. * n censure, derision, gibe, insult, jeer, quip, quirk, reproach, ridicule, scoff.

taut adj strained, stretched, tense, tight.

tawdry adj flashy, gaudy, garish, glittering, loud, meretricious, ostentatious, showy.

tax *vb* burden, demand, exact, load, overtax, require, strain, task; accuse, charge. * *n* assessment, custom, duty, excise, impost, levy, rate, taxation, toll, tribute; burden, charge, demand, requisition, strain; accusation, censure, charge.

teach *vb* catechize, coach, discipline, drill, edify, educate, enlighten, inform, indoctrinate, initiate, instruct, ground, prime, school, train, tutor; communicate, disseminate, explain, expound, impart, implant, inculcate, infuse, instil, interpret, preach, propagate; admonish, advise, counsel, direct, guide, signify, show.

teacher *n* coach, educator, inculcator, informant, instructor, master, pedagogue, preceptor, schoolteacher, trainer, tutor; adviser, counsellor, guide, mentor; pastor, preacher.

tear *vb* burst, slit, rive, rend, rip; claw, lacerate, mangle, shatter, rend, wound; sever, sunder; fume, rage, rant, rave. * *n* fissure, laceration, rent, rip, wrench.

tease *vb* annoy, badger, beg, bother, chafe, chagrin, disturb, harass, harry, hector, importune, irritate, molest, pester, plague, provoke, tantalize, torment, trouble, vex, worry.

tedious *adj* dull, fatiguing, irksome, monotonous, tiresome, trying, uninteresting, wearisome; dilatory, slow, sluggish, tardy.

teem *vb* abound, bear, produce, swarm; discharge, empty, overflow.

tell *vb* compute, count, enumerate, number, reckon; describe, narrate, recount, rehearse, relate, report; acknowledge, announce, betray, confess, declare, disclose, divulge, inform, own, reveal; acquaint, communicate, instruct, teach; discern, discover, distinguish; communicate, express, mention, publish, speak, state, utter.

temper *vb* modify, qualify; appease, assuage, calm, mitigate, mollify, moderate, pacify, restrain, soften, soothe; accommodate, adapt, adjust, fit, suit. * *n* character, constitution, nature, organization, quality, structure, temperament, type; disposition, frame, grain, humour, mood, spirits, tone, vein; calmness, composure, equanimity, moderation, tran-

quillity; anger, ill-temper, irritation, spleen, passion.

temporary *adj* brief, ephemeral, evanescent, fleeting, impermanent, momentary, short-lived, temporal, transient, transitory.

tempt *vb* prove, test, try; allure, decoy, entice, induce, inveigle, persuade, seduce; dispose, incite, incline, instigate, lead, prompt, provoke.

tenacious *adj* retentive, unforgetful; adhesive, clinging, cohesive, firm, glutinous, gummy, resisting, retentive, sticky, strong, tough, unyielding, viscous; dogged, fast, obstinate, opinionated, opinionative, pertinacious, persistent, resolute, stubborn, unwavering.

tend[1] *vb* accompany, attend, graze, guard, keep, protect, shepherd, watch.

tend[2] *vb* aim, exert, gravitate, head, incline, influence, lead, lean, point, trend, verge; conduce, contribute.

tendency *n* aim, aptitude, bearing, bent, bias, course, determination, disposition, direction, drift, gravitation, inclination, leaning, liability, predisposition, proclivity, proneness, propensity, scope, set, susceptibility, turn, twist, warp.

tender[1] *vb* bid, offer, present, proffer, propose, suggest, volunteer. * *n* bid, offer, proffer, proposal; currency, money.

tender[2] *adj* callow, delicate, effeminate, feeble, feminine, fragile, immature, infantile, soft, weak, young; affectionate, compassionate, gentle, humane, kind, lenient, loving, merciful, mild, pitiful, sensitive, sympathetic, tender-hearted; affecting, disagreeable, painful, pathetic, touching, unpleasant.

tense *vb* flex, strain, tauten, tighten. * *adj* rigid, stiff, strained, stretched, taut, tight; excited, highly strung, intent, nervous, rapt.

tentative *adj* essaying, experimental, provisional, testing, toying.

term *vb* call, christen, denominate, designate, dub, entitle, name, phrase, style. * *n* bound, boundary, bourn, confine, limit, mete, terminus; duration, period, season, semester, span, spell, termination, time; denomination, expression, locution, name, phrase, word.

terminal *adj* bounding, limiting; final, terminating, ultimate. * *n* end, extremity, termination; bound, limit; airport, depot, station, terminus.

terminate *vb* bound, limit; end, finish, close, complete, conclude; eventuate, issue, prove.

termination *n* ending, suffix; bound, extend, limit; end, completion, conclusion, consequence, effect, issue, outcome, result.

terms *npl* conditions, provisions, stipulations.

terrible *adj* appalling, dire, dreadful, fearful, formidable, frightful, gruesome, hideous, horrible, horrid, shocking, terrific, tremendous; alarming, awe-inspiring, awful, dread, dreadful; great, excessive, extreme, severe.

terrify *vb* affright, alarm, appal, daunt, dismay, fright, frighten, horrify, scare, shock, startle, terrorize.

terror *n* affright, alarm, anxiety, awe, consternation, dismay, dread, fear, fright, horror, intimidation, panic, terrorism.

test *vb* assay; examine, prove, try. * *n* attempt, essay, examination, experiment, ordeal, proof, trial; criterion, standard, touchstone; example, exhibition, proof; discrimination, distinction, judgement.

testify *vb* affirm, assert, asseverate, attest, avow, certify, corroborate, declare, depose, evidence, state, swear.

testimonial *n* certificate, credential, recommendation, voucher; monument, record.

testimony *n* affirmation, attestation, confession, confirmation, corroboration, declaration, deposition, profession; evidence, proof, witness.

testy *adj* captious, choleric, cross, fretful, hasty, irascible, irritable, quick, peevish, peppery, pettish, petulant, snappish, splenetic, touchy, waspish.

text *n* copy, subject, theme, thesis, topic, treatise.

texture *n* fabric, web, weft; character, coarseness, composition, constitution, fibre, fineness, grain, make-up, nap, organization, structure, tissue.

thankful *adj* appreciative, beholden, grateful, indebted, obliged.

thaw *vb* dissolve, liquefy, melt, soften, unbend.

theatrical *adj* dramatic, dramaturgic, dramaturgical, histrionic, scenic, spectacular; affected, ceremonious, meretricious, ostentatious, pompous, showy, stagy, stilted, unnatural.

theft *n* depredation, embezzlement, fraud, larceny, peculation, pilfering, purloining, robbery, spoliation, stealing, swindling, thieving.

theme *n* composition, essay, subject, text, thesis, topic, treatise.

theoretical *adj* abstract, conjectural, doctrinaire, ideal, hypothetical, pure, speculative, unapplied.

theory *n* assumption, conjecture, hypothesis, idea, plan, postulation, principle, scheme, speculation, surmise, system; doctrine, philosophy, science; explanation, exposition, philosophy, rationale.

therefore *adv* accordingly, afterward, consequently, hence, so, subsequently, then, thence, whence.

thick *adj* bulky, chunky, dumpy, plump, solid, squab, squat, stubby, thickset; clotted, coagulated, crass, dense, dull, gross, heavy, viscous; blurred, cloudy, dirty, foggy, hazy, indistinguishable, misty, obscure, vaporous; muddy, rolled, turbid; abundant, frequent, multitudinous, numerous; close, compact, crowded, set, thickset; confused, guttural, hoarse, inarticulate, indistinct; dim, dull, weak; familiar, friendly, intimate, neighbourly, well-acquainted. * *adv* fast, frequently, quick; closely, densely, thickly. * *n* centre, middle, midst.

thief *n* depredator, filcher, pilferer, lifter, marauder, purloiner, robber, shark, stealer; burglar, corsair, defaulter, defrauder, embezzler, footpad, highwayman, housebreaker, kidnapper, pickpocket, pirate, poacher, privateer, sharper, swindler, peculator.

thieve *vb* cheat, embezzle, peculate, pilfer, plunder, purloin, rob, steal, swindle.

thin *vb* attenuate, dilute, diminish, prune,

reduce, refine, weaken. * *adj* attenuated, bony, emaciated, fine, fleshless, flimsy, gaunt, haggard, lank, lanky, lean, meagre, peaked, pinched, poor, scanty, scraggy, scrawny, slender, slight, slim, small, sparse, spindly.

thing *n* being, body, contrivance, creature, entity, object, something, substance; act, action, affair, arrangement, circumstance, concern, deed, event, matter, occurrence, transaction.

think *vb* cogitate, contemplate, dream, meditate, muse, ponder, reflect, ruminate, speculate; consider, deliberate, reason, undertake; apprehend, believe, conceive, conclude, deem, determine, fancy, hold, imagine, judge, opine, presume, reckon, suppose, surmise; design, intend, mean, purpose; account, believe, consider, count, deem, esteem, hold, regard, suppose; compass, design, plan, plot. * *n* assessment, contemplation, deliberation, reasoning, reflection.

thirst *n* appetite, craving, desire, hunger, longing, yearning; aridity, drought, dryness.

thirsty *adj* arid, dry, parched; eager, greedy, hungry, longing, yearning.

thorough *adj* absolute, arrant, complete, downright, entire, exhaustive, finished, perfect, radical, sweeping, unmitigated, total; accurate, correct, reliable, trustworthy.

thought *n* absorption, cogitation, engrossment, meditation, musing, reflection, reverie, rumination; contemplation, intellect, ratiocination, thinking, thoughtfulness; application, conception, consideration, deliberation, idea, pondering, speculation, study; consciousness, imagination, intellect, perception, understanding; conceit, fancy, notion; conclusion, fancy, idea, judgement, motion, opinion, sentiment, supposition, view; anxiety, attention, care, concern, consideration, deliberation, provision, solicitude; design, expectation, intention, purpose.

thoughtful *adj* absorbed, contemplative, deliberative, dreamy, engrossed, introspective, pensive, philosophic, reflecting, reflective, sedate, speculative; attentive, careful, cautious, circumspect, considerate, discreet, heedful, friendly, kindhearted, kindly, mindful, neighbourly, provident, prudent, regardful, watchful, wary; quiet, serious, sober, studious.

thoughtless *adj* careless, casual, flighty, heedless, improvident, inattentive, inconsiderate, neglectful, negligent, precipitate, rash, reckless, regardless, remiss, trifling, unmindful, unthinking; blank, blockish, dull, insensate, stupid, vacant, vacuous.

thrash *vb* beat, bruise, conquer, defeat, drub, flog, lash, maul, pommel, punish, thwack, trounce, wallop, whip.

thread *vb* course, direction, drift, tenor; reeve, trace. * *n* cord, fibre, filament, hair, line, twist; pile, staple.

threadbare *adj* napless, old, seedy, worn; common, commonplace, hackneyed, stale, trite, worn-out.

threat *n* commination, defiance, denunciation, fulmination, intimidation, menace, thunder, thunderbolt.

threaten *vb* denounce, endanger, fulminate, intimidate, menace, thunder; augur, forebode, foreshadow, indicate, portend, presage, prognosticate, warn.

thrift *n* economy, frugality, parsimony, saving, thriftiness; gain, luck, profit, prosperity, success.

thrifty *adj* careful, economical, frugal, provident, saving, sparing; flourishing, prosperous, thriving, vigorous.

thrill *vb* affect, agitate, electrify, inspire, move, penetrate, pierce, rouse, stir, touch. * *n* excitement, sensation, shock, tingling, tremor.

throng *vb* congregate, crowd, fill, flock, pack, press, swarm. * *n* assemblage, concourse, congregation, crowd, horde, host, mob, multitude, swarm.

throw *vb* cast, chuck, dart, fling, hurl, lance, launch, overturn, pitch, pitchfork, send, sling, toss, whirl. * *n* cast, fling, hurl, launch, pitch, sling, toss, whirl; chance, gamble, try, venture.

thrust *vb* clap, dig, drive, force, impel, jam, plunge, poke, propel, push, ram, run, shove, stick. * *n* dig, jab, lunge, pass, plunge, poke, propulsion, push, shove, stab, tilt.

thump vb bang, batter, beat, belabour, knock, punch, strike, thrash, thwack, whack. * n blow, knock, punch, strike, stroke.

tickle vb amuse, delight, divert, enliven, gladden, gratify, please, rejoice, titillate.

ticklish adj dangerous, precarious, risky, tottering, uncertain, unstable, unsteady; critical, delicate, difficult, nice.

tidy vb clean, neaten, order, straighten. * adj clean, neat, orderly, shipshape, spruce, trig, trim.

tie vb bind, confine, fasten, knot, lock, manacle, secure, shackle, fetter, yoke; complicate, entangle, interlace, knit; connect, hold, join, link, unite; constrain, oblige, restrain, restrict. * n band, fastening, knot, ligament, ligature; allegiance, bond, obligation; bow, cravat, necktie.

tight adj close, compact, fast, firm; taut, tense, stretched; impassable, narrow, strait.

tilt vb cant, incline, slant, slope, tip; forge, hammer; point, thrust; joust, rush. * n awning, canopy, tent; lunge, pass, thrust; cant, inclination, slant, slope, tip.

time vb clock, control, count, measure, regulate, schedule. * n duration, interim, interval, season, span, spell, term, while; aeon, age, date, epoch, eon, era, period, term; cycle, dynasty, reign; confinement, delivery, parturition; measure, rhythm.

timely adj acceptable, appropriate, apropos, early, opportune, prompt, punctual, seasonable, well-timed.

timid adj afraid, cowardly, faint-hearted, fearful, irresolute, meticulous, nervous, pusillanimous, skittish, timorous, unadventurous; bashful, coy, diffident, diminish, modest, shame-faced, shrinking, retiring.

tinge vb colour, dye, stain, tincture, tint; imbue, impregnate, impress, infuse. * n cast, colour, dye, hue, shade, stain, tincture, tint; flavour, smack, spice, quality, taste.

tint n cast, colour, complexion, dye, hue, shade, tinge, tone.

tiny adj diminutive, dwarfish, lilliputian,

little, microscopic, miniature, minute, puny, pygmy, small, wee.

tip[1] n apex, cap, end, extremity, peak, pinnacle, point, top, vertex.

tip[2] vb incline, overturn, tilt; dispose of, dump. * n donation, fee, gift, gratuity, perquisite, reward; inclination, slant; hint, pointer, suggestion; strike, tap.

tire vb exhaust, fag, fatigue, harass, jade, weary; bore, bother, irk.

tiresome adj annoying, arduous, boring, dull, exhausting, fatiguing, fagging, humdrum, irksome, laborious, monotonous, tedious, wearisome, vexatious.

tissue n cloth, fabric; membrane, network, structure, texture, web; accumulation, chain, collection, combination, conglomeration, mass, network, series, set.

title vb call, designate, name, style, term. * n caption, legend, head, heading; appellation, application, cognomen, completion, denomination, designation, epithet, name; claim, due, ownership, part, possession, prerogative, privilege, right.

toast vb brown, dry, heat; honour, pledge, propose, salute. * n compliment, drink, pledge, salutation, salute; favourite, pe.

toil vb drudge, labour, strive, work. * n drudgery, effort, exertion, exhaustion, grinding, labour, pains, travail, work; gin, net, noose, snare, spring, trap.

token adj nominal, superficial, symbolic. * n badge, evidence, index, indication, manifestation, mark, note, sign, symbol, trace, trait; keepsake, memento, memorial, reminder, souvenir.

tolerable adj bearable, endurable, sufferable, supportable; fair, indifferent, middling, ordinary, passable, so-so.

tolerance n endurance, receptivity, sufferance, toleration.

tolerate vb admit, allow, indulge, let, permit, receive; abide, brook, endure, suffer.

toll[1] n assessment, charge, customs, demand, dues, duty, fee, impost, levy, rate, tax, tribute; cost, damage, loss.

toll[2] vb chime, knell, peal, ring, sound. * n chime, knell, peal, ring, ringing, tolling.

tomb n catacomb, charnel house, crypt, grave, mausoleum, sepulchre, vault.

tone vb blend, harmonize, match, suit. * n

note, sound; accent, cadence, emphasis, inflection, intonation, modulation; key, mood, strain, temper; elasticity, energy, force, health, strength, tension, vigour; cast, colour, manner, hue, shade, style, tint; drift, tenor.

too adv additionally, also, further, likewise, moreover, overmuch.

top vb cap, head, tip; ride, surmount; outgo, surpass. * adj apical, vest, chief, culminating, finest, first, foremost, highest, leading, prime, principal, topmost, uppermost. * n acme, apex, crest, crown, head, meridian, pinnacle, summit, surface, vertex, zenith.

topic n business, question, subject, text, theme, thesis; division, head, subdivision; commonplace, dictum, maxim, precept, proposition, principle, rule; arrangement, scheme.

topple vb fall, overturn, tumble, upset.

torment vb annoy, agonize, distress, excruciate, pain, rack, torture; badger, fret, harass, harry, irritate, nettle, plague, provoke, tantalize, tease, trouble, vex, worry. * n agony, anguish, pang, rack, torture.

tortuous adj crooked, curved, curvilineal, curvilinear, serpentine, sinuate, sinuated, sinuous, twisted, winding; ambiguous, circuitous, crooked, deceitful, indirect, perverse, roundabout.

torture vb agonize, distress, excruciate, pain, rack, torment.* n agony, anguish, distress, pain, pang, rack, torment.

toss vb cast, fling, hurl, pitch, throw; agitate, rock, shake; disquiet, harass, try; roll, writhe. * n cast, fling, pitch, throw.

total vb add, amount to, reach, reckon. * adj complete, entire, full, whole; entire, integral, undivided. * n aggregate, all, gross, lump, mass, sum, totality, whole.

touch vb feel, graze, handle, hit, pat, strike, tap; concern, interest, regard; affect, impress, move, stir; grasp, reach, stretch; melt, mollify, move, soften; afflict, distress, hurt, injure, molest, sting, wound. * n hint, smack, suggestion, suspicion, taste, trace; blow, contract, hit, pat, tap.

touchy adj choleric, cross, fretful, hot-tempered, irascible, irritable, peevish, petulant, quick-tempered, snappish, splenetic, tetchy, testy, waspish.

tough adj adhesive, cohesive, flexible, tenacious; coriaceous, leathery; clammy, ropy, sticky, viscous; inflexible, intractable, rigid, stiff; callous, hard, obdurate, stubborn; difficult, formidable, hard, troublesome. * n brute, bully, hooligan, ruffian, thug.

tour vb journey, perambulate, travel, visit. * n circuit, course, excursion, expedition, journey, perambulation, pilgrimage, round.

tow vb drag, draw, haul, pull, tug. * n drag, lift, pull.

tower vb mount, rise, soar, transcend. * n belfry, bell tower, column, minaret, spire, steeple, turret; castle, citadel, fortress, stronghold; pillar, refuge, rock, support.

toy vb dally, play, sport, trifle, wanton. * n bauble, doll, gewgaw, gimmick, knickknack, plaything, puppet, trinket; bagatelle, bubble, trifle; play, sport.

trace vb follow, track, train; copy, deduce, delineate, derive, describe, draw, sketch. * n evidence, footmark, footprint, footstep, impression, mark, remains, sign, token, track, trail, vestige, wake; memorial, record; bit, dash, flavour, hint, suspicion, streak, tinge.

track vb chase, draw, follow, pursue, scent, track, trail. * n footmark, footprint, footstep, spoor, trace, vestige; course, pathway, rails, road, runway, trace, trail, wake, way.

trade vb bargain, barter, chaffer, deal, exchange, interchange, sell, traffic. * n bargaining, barter, business, commerce, dealing, traffic; avocation, business, calling, craft, employment, occupation, office, profession, pursuit, vocation.

traditional adj accustomed, apocryphal, customary, established, historic, legendary, old, oral, transmitted, uncertain, unverified, unwritten.

traffic vb bargain, barter, chaffer, deal, exchange, trade. * n barter, business, chaffer, commerce, exchange, intercourse, trade, transportation, truck.

tragedy *n* drama, play; adversity, calamity, catastrophe, disaster, misfortune.

tragic *adj* dramatic; calamitous, catastrophic, disastrous, dreadful, fatal, grievous, heart-breaking, mournful, sad, shocking, sorrowful.

trail *vb* follow, hunt, trace, track; drag, draw, float, flow, haul, pull. * *n* footmark, footprint, footstep, mark, trace, track.

train *vb* drag, draw, haul, trail, tug; allure, entice; discipline, drill, educate, exercise, instruct, school, teach; accustom, break in, familiarize, habituate, inure, prepare, rehearse, use. * *n* trail, wake; entourage, cortege, followers, retinue, staff, suite; chain, consecution, sequel, series, set, succession; course, method, order, process; allure, artifice, device, enticement, lure, persuasion, stratagem, trap.

traitor *n* apostate, betrayer, deceiver, Judas, miscreant, quisling, renegade, turncoat; conspirator, deserter, insurgent, mutineer, rebel, revolutionary.

traitorous *adj* faithless, false, perfidious, recreant, treacherous; insidious, perfidious, treasonable.

tramp *vb* hike, march, plod, trudge, walk. * *n* excursion, journey, march, walk; grant, landloper, loafer, stroller, tramper, vagabond, vagrant.

trample *vb* crush, tread; scorn, spurn.

trance *n* dream, ecstasy, hypnosis, rapture; catalepsy, coma.

tranquil *adj* calm, hushed, peaceful, placid, quiet, serene, still, undisturbed, unmoved, unperturbed, unruffled, untroubled.

tranquillize *vb* allay, appease, assuage, calm, compose, hush, lay, lull, moderate, pacify, quell, quiet, silence, soothe, still.

transact *vb* conduct, dispatch, enact, execute, do, manage, negotiate, perform, treat.

transcend *vb* exceed, overlap, overstep, pass, transgress; excel, outstrip, outrival, outvie, overtop, surmount, surpass.

transfer *vb* convey, dispatch, move, remove, send, translate, transmit, transplant, transport; abalienate, alienate, assign, cede, confer, convey, consign, deed, devise, displace, forward, grant, pass, relegate, transmit. * *n* abalienation, alienation, assignment, bequest, carriage, cession, change, conveyance, copy, demise, devisal, gift, grant, move, relegation, removal, shift, shipment, transference, transferring, transit, transmission, transportation.

transform *vb* alter, change, metamorphose, transfigure; convert, resolve, translate, transmogrify, transmute.

translate *vb* remove, transfer, transport; construe, decipher, decode, interpret, render, turn.

transmit *vb* forward, remit, send; communicate, conduct, radiate; bear, carry, convey, radiate.

transparent *adj* bright, clear, diaphanous, limpid, lucid; crystalline, hyaline, pellucid, serene, translucent, transpicuous, unclouded; open, porous, transpicuous; evident, obvious, manifest, obvious, patent.

transpire *vb* befall, chance, happen, occur; evaporate, exhale.

transport *vb* bear, carry, cart, conduct, convey, fetch, remove, ship, take, transfer, truck; banish, expel; beatify, delight, enrapture, enravish, entrance, ravish. * *n* carriage, conveyance, movement, transportation, transporting; beatification, beatitude, bliss, ecstasy, felicity, happiness, rapture, ravishment; frenzy, passion, vehemence, warmth.

trap *vb* catch, ensnare, entrap, noose, snare, springe; ambush, deceive, dupe, trick; enmesh, tangle, trepan. * *n* gin, snare, springe, toil; ambush, artifice, pitfall, stratagem, trepan, toil.

trappings *npl* adornments, decorations, dress, embellishments, frippery, gear, livery, ornaments, paraphernalia, rigging; accoutrements, caparisons, equipment, gear.

trash *n* dregs, dross, garbage, refuse, rubbish, trumpery, waste; balderdash, nonsense, twaddle.

travel *vb* journey, peregrinate, ramble, roam, rove, tour, voyage, walk, wander;

go, move, pass. * n excursion, expedition, journey, peregrination, ramble, tour, trip, voyage, walk.

traveller n excursionist, explorer, globetrotter, itinerant, passenger, pilgrim, rover, sightseer, tourist, trekker, tripper, voyager, wanderer, wayfarer.

treacherous adj deceitful, disloyal, faithless, false, false-hearted, insidious, perfidious, recreant, sly, traitorous, treasonable, unfaithful, unreliable, unsafe, untrustworthy.

treason n betrayal, disloyalty, lèse-majesté, lese-majesty, perfidy, sedition, traitorousness, treachery.

treasonable adj disloyal, traitorous, treacherous.

treasure vb accumulate, collect, garner, hoard, husband, save, store; cherish, idolize, prize, value, worship. * n cash, funds, jewels, money, riches, savings, valuables, wealth; abundance, reserve, stock, store.

treat vb entertain, feast, gratify, refresh; attend, doctor, dose, handle, manage, serve; bargain, covenant, negotiate, parley. * n banquet, entertainment, feast; delight, enjoyment, entertainment, gratification, luxury, pleasure, refreshment.

treatment n usage, use; dealing, handling, management, manipulation; doctoring, therapy.

treaty n agreement, alliance, bargain, compact, concordat, convention, covenant, entente, league, pact.

tremble vb quake, quaver, quiver, shake, shiver, shudder, tremble, vibrate, wobble. * n quake, quiver, shake, shiver, shudder, tremor, vibration, wobble.

tremendous adj alarming, appalling, awful, dreadful, fearful, frightful, horrid, horrible, terrible.

tremor n agitation, quaking, quivering, shaking, trembling, trepidation, tremulousness, vibration.

trend vb drift, gravitate, incline, lean, run, stretch, sweep, tend, turn. * n bent, course, direction, drift, inclination, set, leaning, tendency, trending.

trespass vb encroach, infringe, intrude, trench; offend, sin, transgress. * n en-

croachment, infringement, injury, intrusion, invasion; crime, delinquency, error, fault, sin, misdeed, misdemeanour, offence, transgression; trespasser.

trial adj experimental, exploratory, testing. * n examination, experiment, test; experience, knowledge; aim, attempt, effort, endeavour, essay, exertion, struggle; assay, criterion, ordeal, prohibition, proof, test, touchstone; affliction, burden, chagrin, dolour, distress, grief, hardship, heartache, inclination, misery, mortification, pain, sorrow, suffering, tribulation, trouble, unhappiness, vexation, woe, wretchedness; action, case, cause, hearing, suit.

tribulation n adversity, affliction, distress, grief, misery, pain, sorrow, suffering, trial, trouble, unhappiness, woe, wretchedness.

tribute n subsidy, tax; custom, duty, excise, impost, tax, toll; contribution, grant, offering.

trice n flash, instant, jiffy, moment, second, twinkling.

trick vb cheat, circumvent, cozen, deceive, defraud, delude, diddle, dupe, fob, gull, hoax, overreach. * n artifice, blind, deceit, deception, dodge, fake, feint, fraud, game, hoax, imposture, manoeuvre, shift, ruse, swindle, stratagem, wile; antic, caper, craft, deftness, gambol, sleight; habit, mannerism, peculiarity, practice.

trickle vb distil, dribble, drip, drop, ooze, percolate, seep. * n dribble, drip, percolation, seepage.

tricky adj artful, cunning, deceitful, deceptive, subtle, trickish.

trifle vb dally, dawdle, fool, fribble, palter, play, potter, toy. * n bagatelle, bauble, bean, fig, nothing, triviality; iota, jot, modicum, particle, trace.

trifling adj empty, frippery, frivolous, inconsiderable, insignificant, nugatory, petty, piddling, shallow, slight, small, trivial, unimportant, worthless.

trill vb shake, quaver, warble. * n quaver, shake, tremolo, warbling.

trim vb adjust, arrange, prepare; balance, equalize, fill; adorn, array, bedeck, decorate, dress, embellish, garnish, ornament; clip, curtail, cut, lop, mow, poll, prune, shave, shear; berate, chastise, chide, rebuke, reprimand, reprove, trounce; balance, fluctuate, hedge, shift, shuffle, vacillate. * *adj* compact, neat, nice, shapely, snug, tidy, well-adjusted, well-ordered; chic, elegant, finical, smart, spruce. * *n* dress, embellishment, gear, ornaments, trappings, trimmings; case, condition, order, plight, state.

trip *vb* caper, dance, frisk, hop, skip; misstep, stumble; bungle, blunder, err, fail, mistake; overthrow, supplant, upset; catch, convict, detect. * *n* hop, skip; lurch, misstep, stumble; blunder, bungle, error, failure, fault, lapse, miss, mistake, oversight, slip, stumble; circuit, excursion, expedition, jaunt, journey, ramble, route, stroll, tour.

triumph *vb* exult, rejoice; prevail, succeed, win; flourish, prosper, thrive; boast, brag, crow, gloat, swagger, vaunt. * *n* celebration, exultation, joy, jubilation, jubilee, ovation; accomplishment, achievement, conquest, success, victory.

triumphant *adj* boastful, conquering, elated, exultant, exulting, jubilant, rejoicing, successful, victorious.

trivial *adj* frivolous, gimcrack, immaterial, inconsiderable, insignificant, light, little, nugatory, paltry, petty, small, slight, slim, trifling, trumpery, unimportant.

troop *vb* crowd, flock, muster, throng. * *n* company, crowd, flock, herd, multitude, number, throng; band, body, company, party, squad; company, troupe.

trouble *vb* agitate, confuse, derange, disarrange, disorder, disturb; afflict, ail, annoy, badger, concern, disquiet, distress, disturb, fret, grieve, harass, molest, perplex, perturb, pester, plague, torment, vex, worry. * *n* adversity, affliction, calamity, distress, dolour, grief, hardship, misfortune, misery, pain, sorrow, suffering, tribulation, woe; ado, annoyance, anxiety, bother, care, discomfort, embarrassment, fuss, inconvenience, irritation, pains, perplexity, plague, torment, vexation, worry; disturbance, row;

bewilderment, disquietude, embarrassment, perplexity, uneasiness.

troublesome *adj* annoying, distressing, disturbing, galling, grievous, harassing, painful, perplexing, vexatious, worrisome; burdensome, irksome, tiresome, wearisome; importunate, intrusive, teasing; arduous, difficult, hard, inconvenient, trying, unwieldy.

truce *n* armistice, breathing space, cessation, delay, intermission, lull, pause, recess, reprieve, respite, rest.

truck *vb* barter, deal, exchange, trade, traffic. * *n* lorry, van, wagon.

true *adj* actual, unaffected, authentic, genuine, legitimate, pure, real, rightful, sincere, sound, truthful, veritable; substantial, veracious; constant, faithful, loyal, staunch, steady; equitable, honest, honourable, just, upright, trusty, trustworthy, virtuous; accurate, correct, even, exact, right, straight, undeviating. * *adv* good, well.

trust *vb* confide, depend, expect, hope, rely; believe, credit; commit, entrust. * *n* belief, confidence, credence, faith; credit, tick; charge, deposit; charge, commission, duty, errand; assurance, belief, confidence, expectation, faith, hope.

trustworthy *adj* confidential, constant, credible, dependable, faithful, firm, honest, incorrupt, upright, reliable, responsible, straightforward, staunch, true, trusty, uncorrupt, upright.

truth *n* fact, reality, veracity; actuality, authenticity, realism; cannon, law, oracle, principle; right, truthfulness, veracity; candour, fidelity, frankness, honesty, honour, ingenuousness, integrity, probity, sincerity, virtue; constancy, devotion, faith, fealty, loyalty, steadfastness; accuracy, correctness, exactitude, exactness, nicety, precision, regularity, trueness.

truthful *adj* correct, reliable, true, trustworthy, veracious; artless, candid, frank, guileless, honest, ingenuous, open, sincere, straightforward, true, trustworthy, trusty.

try *vb* examine, prove, test; attempt, essay; adjudicate, adjudge, examine, hear;

purify, refine; sample, sift, smell, taste; aim, attempt, endeavour, seek, strain, strive. * n attempt, effort, endeavour, experiment, trial.

trying adj difficult, fatiguing, hard, irksome, tiresome, wearisome; afflicting, afflictive, calamitous, deplorable, dire, distressing, grievous, hard, painful, sad, severe.

tug vb drag, draw, haul, pull, tow, wrench; labour, strive, struggle. * n drag, haul, pull, tow, wrench.

tuition n education, instruction, schooling, teaching, training.

tumble vb heave, pitch, roll, toss, wallow; fall, sprawl, stumble, topple, trip; derange, disarrange, dishevel, disorder, disturb, rumple, tousle. * n collapse, drop, fall, plunge, spill, stumble, trip.

tumult n ado, affray, agitation, altercation, bluster, brawl, disturbance, ferment, flurry, feud, fracas, fray, fuss, hubbub, huddle, hurly-burly, melee, noise, perturbation, pother, quarrel, racket, riot, row, squabble, stir, turbulence, turmoil, uproar.

tumultuous adj blustery, breezy, bustling, confused, disorderly, disturbed, riotous, turbulent, unruly.

tune vb accord, attune, harmonize, modulate; adapt, adjust, attune. * n air, aria, melody, strain, tone; agreement, concord, harmony; accord, order.

tuneful adj dulcet, harmonious, melodious, musical.

turbulent adj agitated, disturbed, restless, tumultuous, wild; blatant, blustering, boisterous, brawling, disorderly, obstreperous, tumultuous, uproarious, vociferous; disorderly, factious, insubordinate, insurgent, mutinous, raging, rebellious, refractory, revolutionary, riotous, seditious, stormy, wild, violent.

turmoil n activity, agitation, bustle, commotion, confusion, disorder, disturbance, ferment, flurry, huddle, hubbub, hurly-burly, noise, trouble, tumult, turbulence, uproar.

turn vb revolve, rotate; bend, cast, defect, inflict, round, spin, sway, swivel, twirl, twist, wheel; crank, grind, wind; deflect,

divert, transfer, warp; form, mould, shape; adapt, fit, manoeuvre, suit; adapt, alter, change, conform, metamorphose, transform, transmute, vary; convert, persuade, prejudice; construe, render, translate; depend, hang, hinge, pivot; eventuate, issue, result, terminate; acidify, curdle, ferment. * n cycle, gyration, revolution, rotation, round; bending, oil, deflection, deviation, diversion, doubling, flection, flexion, flexure, reel, retroversion, slew, spin, sweep, swing, swirl, swivel, turning, twist, twirl, whirl, winding; alteration, change, variation, vicissitude; bend, circuit, drive, ramble, run, round, stroll; bout, hand, innings, opportunity, round, shift, spell; act, action, deed, office; convenience, occasion, purpose; cast, fashion, form, guise, manner, mould, phase, shape; aptitude, bent, bias, faculty, genius, gift, inclination, proclivity, proneness, propensity, talent, tendency.

tussle vb conflict, contend, contest, scuffle, struggle, wrestle. * n conflict, contest, fight, scuffle, struggle.

tutor vb coach, educate, instruct, teach; discipline, train. * n coach, governess, governor, instructor, master, preceptor, schoolteacher, teacher.

tweak vb, n jerk, pinch, pull, twinge, twitch.

twin vb couple, link, match, pair. * adj double, doubled, duplicate, geminate, identical, matched, matching, second, twain. * n corollary, double, duplicate, fellow, likeness, match.

twine vb embrace, encircle, entwine, interlace, surround, wreathe; bend, meander, wind; coil, twist. * n convolution, coil, twist; embrace, twining, winding; cord, string.

twinge vb pinch, tweak, twitch. * n pinch, tweak, twitch; gripe, pang, spasm.

twinkle vb blink, twink, wink; flash, glimmer, scintillate, sparkle. * n blink, flash, gleam, glimmer, scintillation, sparkle; flash, instant, jiffy, moment, second, tick, trice, twinkling.

twirl vb revolve, rotate, spin, turn, twist, twirl. * n convolution, revolution, turn, twist, whirling.

twist *vb* purl, rotate, spin, twine; complicate, contort, convolute, distort, pervert, screw, twine, wring; coil, writhe; encircle, wind, wreathe. * *n* coil, curl, spin, twine; braid, coil, curl, roll; change, complication, development, variation; bend, convolution, turn; defect, distortion, flaw, imperfection; jerk, pull, sprain, wrench; aberration, characteristic, eccentricity, oddity, peculiarity, quirk.

twitch *vb* jerk, pluck, pull, snatch. * *n* jerk, pull; contraction, pull, quiver, spasm, twitching.

type *n* emblem, mark, stamp; adumbration, image, representation, representative, shadow, sign, symbol, token; archetype, exemplar, model, original, pattern, prototype, protoplast, standard; character, form, kind, nature, sort; figure, letter, text, typography.

typical *adj* emblematic, exemplary, figurative, ideal, indicative, model, representative, symbolic, true.

typify *vb* betoken, denote, embody, exemplify, figure, image, indicate, represent, signify.

tyrannical *adj* absolute, arbitrary, autocratic, cruel, despotic, dictatorial, domineering, high, imperious, irresponsible, severe, tyrannical, unjust; cruel, galling, grinding, inhuman, oppressive, severe.

tyranny *n* absolutism, arbitrations, autocracy, despotism, dictatorship, harshness, oppression.

tyrant *n* autocrat, despot, dictator, oppressor.

U

ubiquitous *adj* omnipresent, present, universal.

ugly *adj* crooked, homely, ill-favoured, plain, ordinary, unlovely, unprepossessing, unshapely, unsightly; forbidding, frightful, gruesome, hideous, horrible, horrid, hideous, loathsome, monstrous, shocking, terrible, repellent, repulsive; bad-tempered, cantankerous, churlish,

cross, quarrelsome, spiteful, surly, spiteful, vicious.

ultimate *adj* conclusive, decisive, eventual, extreme, farthest, final, last. * *n* acme, consummation, culmination, height, peak, pink, quintessence, summit.

umbrage *n* shadow, shade; anger, displeasure, dissatisfaction, dudgeon, injury, offence, pique, resentment.

umpire *vb* adjudicate, arbitrate, judge, referee. * *n* adjudicator, arbiter, arbitrator, judge, referee.

unabashed *adj* bold, brazen, confident, unblushing, undaunted, undismayed.

unable *adj* impotent, incapable, incompetent, powerless, weak.

unaccommodating *adj* disobliging, noncompliant, uncivil, ungracious.

unanimity *n* accord, agreement, concert, concord, harmony, union, unity.

unanimous *adj* agreeing, concordant, harmonious, like-minded, solid, united.

unassuming *adj* humble, modest, reserved, unobtrusive, unpretending, unpretentious.

unbalanced *adj* unsound, unsteady; unadjusted, unsettled.

unbecoming *adj* inappropriate, indecent, indecorous, improper, unbefitting, unbeseeming, unseemly, unsuitable.

unbelief *n* disbelief, dissent, distrust, incredulity, incredulousness, miscreance, miscreancy, nonconformity; freethinking, infidelity, scepticism.

unbeliever *n* agnostic, deist, disbeliever, doubter, heathen, infidel, sceptic.

unbending *adj* inflexible, rigid, stiff, unpliant, unyielding; firm, obstinate, resolute, stubborn.

unbridled *adj* dissolute, intractable, lax, licensed, licentious, loose, uncontrolled, ungovernable, unrestrained, violent, wanton.

uncanny *adj* inopportune, unsafe; eerie, eery, ghostly, unearthly, unnatural, weird.

uncertain *adj* ambiguous, doubtful, dubious, equivocal, indefinite, indeterminate, indistinct, questionable, unsettled; insecure, precarious, problematical; capricious, changeable, desultory, fitful, fluctuating, irregular, mutable, shaky, slippery, unreliable, unsettled, variable.

unchecked *adj* uncurbed, unhampered, unhindered, unobstructed, unrestrained, untrammelled.

uncommon *adj* choice, exceptional, extraordinary, infrequent, noteworthy, odd, original, queer, rare, remarkable, scarce, singular, strange, unexampled, unfamiliar, unusual, unwonted.

uncomplaining *adj* long-suffering, meek, patient, resigned, tolerant.

uncompromising *adj* inflexible, narrow, obstinate, orthodox, rigid, stiff, strict, unyielding.

unconditional *adj* absolute, categorical, complete, entire, free, full, positive, unlimited, unqualified, unreserved, unrestricted.

uncouth *adj* awkward, boorish, clownish, clumsy, gawky, inelegant, loutish, lubberly, rough, rude, rustic, uncourtly, ungainly, unpolished, unrefined, unseemly; odd, outlandish, strange, unfamiliar, unusual.

unctuous *adj* adipose, greasy, oily, fat, fatty, oleaginous, pinguid, sebaceous; bland, lubricious, smooth, slippery; bland, fawning, glib, obsequious, oily, plausible, servile, suave, smooth, sycophantic; fervid, gushing.

under *prep* below, beneath, inferior to, lower than, subordinate to, underneath. * *adv* below, beneath, down, lower.

underestimate *vb* belittle, underrate, undervalue.

undergo *vb* bear, endure, experience, suffer, sustain.

underhand *adj* clandestine, deceitful, disingenuous, fraudulent, hidden, secret, sly, stealthy, underhanded, unfair. * *adv* clandestinely, privately, secretly, slyly, stealthily, surreptitiously; fraudulently, unfairly.

undermine *vb* excavate, mine, sap; demoralize, foil, frustrate, thwart, weaken.

understand *vb* apprehend, catch, comprehend, conceive, discern, grasp, know, penetrate, perceive, see, seize, twig; assume, interpret, take; imply, mean.

understanding *adj* compassionate, considerate, forgiving, kind, kindly, patient, sympathetic, tolerant. * *n* brains, comprehension, discernment, faculty, intellect, intelligence, judgement, knowledge, mind, reason, sense.

undertake *vb* assume, attempt, begin, embark on, engage in, enter upon, take in hand; agree, bargain, contract, covenant, engage, guarantee, promise, stipulate.

undertaking *n* adventure, affair, attempt, business, effort, endeavour, engagement, enterprise, essay, move, project, task, venture.

undo *vb* annul, cancel, frustrate, invalidate, neutralize, nullify, offset, reverse; disengage, loose, unfasten, unmake, unravel, untie; crush, destroy, overturn, ruin.

undue *adj* illegal, illegitimate, improper, unlawful, excessive, disproportionate, disproportioned, immoderate, unsuitable; unfit, unsuitable.

undying *adj* deathless, endless, immortal, imperishable.

unearthly *adj* preternatural, supernatural, uncanny, weird.

uneasy *adj* disquieted, disturbed, fidgety, impatient, perturbed, restless, restive, unquiet, worried; awkward, stiff, ungainly, ungraceful; constraining, cramping, disagreeable, uncomfortable.

unending *adj* endless, eternal, everlasting, interminable, never-ending, perpetual, unceasing.

unequal *adj* disproportionate, disproportioned, ill-matched, inferior, irregular, insufficient, not alike, uneven.

unequalled *adj* exceeding, incomparable, inimitable, matchless, new, nonpareil, novel, paramount, peerless, pre-eminent, superlative, surpassing, transcendent, unheard of, unique, unparalleled, unrivalled.

unexpected *adj* abrupt, sudden, unforeseen.

unfair *adj* dishonest, dishonourable, faithless, false, hypocritical, inequitable, insincere, oblique, one-sided, partial, unequal, unjust, wrongful.

unfaithful *adj* derelict, deceitful, dishonest, disloyal, false, faithless, perfidious, treacherous, unreliable; careless, negligent; changeable, faithless, inconstant, untrue.

unfeeling adj apathetic, callous, heartless, insensible, numb, obdurate, torpid, unconscious, unimpressionable; adamantine, cold-blooded, cruel, hard, merciless, pitiless, stony, unkind, unsympathetic.

unfit vb disable, disqualify, incapacitate. * adj improper, inappropriate, incompetent, inconsistent, unsuitable; ill-equipped, inadequate, incapable, incompetent, unqualified, useless; debilitated, feeble, flabby, unhealthy, unsound.

unfold vb display, expand, open, separate, unfurl, unroll; declare, disclose, reveal, tell; decipher, develop, disentangle, evolve, explain, illustrate, interpret, resolve, unravel.

ungainly adj awkward, boorish, clownish, clumsy, gawky, inelegant, loutish, lubberly, lumbering, slouching, stiff, uncourtly, uncouth, ungraceful.

uniform adj alike, constant, even, equable, equal, smooth, steady, regular, unbroken, unchanged, undeviating, unvaried, unvarying. * n costume, dress, livery, outfit, regalia, suit.

union n coalescence, coalition, combination, conjunction, coupling, fusion, incorporation, joining, junction, unification, uniting; agreement, concert, concord, concurrence, harmony, unanimity, unity; alliance, association, club, confederacy, federation, guild, league.

unique adj choice, exceptional, matchless, only, peculiar, rare, single, sole, singular, uncommon, unexampled, unmatched.

unison n accord, accordance, agreement, concord, harmony.

unite vb amalgamate, attach, blend, centralize, coalesce, confederate, consolidate, embody, fuse, incorporate, merge, weld; associate, conjoin, connect, couple, link, marry; combine, conjoin, join; harmonize, reconcile; agree, concert, concur, cooperate, fraternize.

universal adj all-reaching, catholic, cos-mic, encyclopedic, general, ubiquitous, unlimited; all, complete, entire, total, whole.

unjust adj inequitable, injurious, partial, unequal, unfair, unwarranted, wrong, wrongful; flagitious, heinous, iniquitous, nefarious, unrighteous, wicked, wrong; biased, partial, prejudiced, uncandid, unfair.

unknown adj unappreciated, unascertained; undiscovered, unexplored, uninvestigated; concealed, dark, enigmatic, hidden, mysterious, mystic; anonymous, incognito, inglorious, nameless, obscure, renownless, undistinguished, unheralded, unnoted.

unlimited adj boundless, infinite, interminable, limitless, measureless, unbounded; absolute, full, unconfined, unconstrained, unrestricted; indefinite, undefined.

unmanageable adj awkward, cumbersome, inconvenient, unwieldy; intractable, unruly, unworkable, vicious; difficult, impractical.

unmitigated adj absolute, complete, consummate, perfect, sheer, stark, thorough, unqualified, utter.

unnatural adj aberrant, abnormal, anomalous, foreign, irregular, prodigious, uncommon; brutal, cold, heartless, inhuman, unfeeling, unusual; affected, artificial, constrained, forced, insincere, self-conscious, stilted, strained; artificial, factitious.

unprincipled adj bad, crooked, dishonest, fraudulent, immoral, iniquitous, knavish, lawless, profligate, rascally, roguish, thievish, trickish, tricky, unscrupulous, vicious, villainous, wicked.

unqualified adj disqualified, incompetent, ineligible, unadapted, unfit; absolute, certain, consummate, decided, direct, downright, full, outright, unconditional, unmeasured, unrestricted, unmitigated; exaggerated, sweeping.

unreal adj chimerical, dreamlike, fanciful, flimsy, ghostly, illusory, insubstantial, nebulous, shadowy, spectral, visionary, unsubstantial.

unreserved adj absolute, entire, full, unlimited; above-board, artless, candid, communicative, fair, frank, guileless, honest, ingenuous, open, sincere, single-minded, undesigning, undissembling; demonstrative, emotional, open-hearted.

unrighteous adj evil, sinful, ungodly, unholy, vicious, wicked, wrong; heinous, inequitable, iniquitous, nefarious, unfair, unjust.

unripe adj crude, green, hard, immature, premature, sour; incomplete, unfinished.

unrivalled adj incomparable, inimitable, matchless, peerless, unequalled, unexampled, unique, unparalleled.

unroll vb develop, discover, evolve, open, unfold; display, lay open.

unruly adj disobedient, disorderly, fractious, headstrong, insubordinate, intractable, mutinous, obstreperous, rebellious, refractory, riotous, seditious, turbulent, ungovernable, unmanageable, wanton, wild; lawless, obstinate, rebellious, stubborn, ungovernable, unmanageable, vicious.

unsafe adj dangerous, hazardous, insecure, perilous, precarious, risky, treacherous, uncertain, unprotected.

unsaid adj tacit, unmentioned, unspoken, unuttered.

unsavoury adj flat, insipid, mawkish, savourless, tasteless, unflavoured, unpalatable, vapid; disagreeable, disgusting, distasteful, nasty, nauseating, nauseous, offensive, rank, revolting, sickening, uninviting, unpleasing.

unsay vb recall, recant, retract, take back.

unscrupulous adj dishonest, reckless, ruthless, unconscientious, unprincipled, unrestrained.

unseasonable adj ill-timed, inappropriate, inopportune, untimely; late, too late; ill-timed, inappropriate, unfit, ungrateful, unsuitable, untimely, unwelcome; premature, too early.

unseasoned adj inexperienced, unaccustomed, unqualified, untrained; immoderate, inordinate, irregular; green; fresh, unsalted.

unseeing adj blind, sightless.

unseemly adj improper, indecent, inappropriate, indecorous, unbecoming, un-comely, unfit, unmeet, unsuitable.

unseen adj undiscerned, undiscovered, unobserved, unperceived; imperciptible, indiscoverable, invisible, latent.

unselfish adj altruistic, devoted, disinterested, generous, high-minded, impersonal, liberal, magnanimous, self-denying, self-forgetful, selfless, self-sacrificing.

unsettle vb confuse, derange, disarrange, disconcert, disorder, disturb, trouble, unbalance, unfix, unhinge, upset.

unshaken adj constant, firm, resolute, steadfast, steady, unmoved.

unshrinking adj firm, determined, persisting, resolute, unblenching, unflinching.

unsightly adj deformed, disagreeable, hideous, repellent, repulsive, ugly.

unsociable adj distant, reserved, retiring, segregative, shy, solitary, standoffish, taciturn, uncommunicative, uncompanionable, ungenial, unsocial; inhospitable, misanthropic, morose.

unsound adj decayed, defective, impaired, imperfect, rotten, thin, wasted, weak; broken, disturbed, light, restless; diseased, feeble, infirm, morbid, poorly, sickly, unhealthy, weak; deceitful, defective, erroneous, fallacious, false, faulty, hollow, illogical, incorrect, invalid, questionable, sophistical, unsubstantial, untenable, wrong; deceitful, dishonest, false, insincere, unfaithful, untrustworthy, untrue; insubstantial, unreal; defective, heretical, heterodox, unorthodox.

unsparing adj bountiful, generous, lavish, liberal, profuse, ungruding; harsh, inexorable, relentless, rigorous, ruthless, severe, uncompromising, unforgiving.

unspeakable adj indescribable, ineffable, inexpressible, unutterable.

unstable adj infirm, insecure, precarious, top-heavy, tottering, unbalanced, unballasted, unsafe, unsettled, unsteady; changeable, erratic, fickle, inconstant, irresolute, mercurial, mutable, unsteady, vacillating, variable, wavering, weak, volatile.

unsteady adj fluctuating, oscillating, unsettled; insecure, precarious, unstable;

changeable, desultory, ever-changing, fickle, inconstant, irresolute, mutable, unstable, variable, wavering; drunken, jumpy, tottering, vacillating, wavering, wobbly, tipsy.

unstrung adj overcome, shaken, unnerved, weak.

unsuccessful adj abortive, bootless, fruitless, futile, ineffectual, profitless, unavailing, vain; ill-fated, ill-starred, luckless, unfortunate, unhappy, unlucky, unprosperous.

unsuitable adj ill-adapted, inappropriate, malapropos, unfit, unsatisfactory, unsuited; improper, inapplicable, inapt, incongruous, inexpedient, infelicitous, unbecoming, unbeseeming, unfitting.

unsuited adj unadapted, unfitted, unqualified.

unsurpassed adj matchless, peerless, unequalled, unexampled, unexcelled, unmatched, unparagoned, unparalleled, unrivalled.

unsuspecting adj confiding, credulous, trusting, unsuspicious.

unswerving adj direct, straight, undeviating; constant, determined, firm, resolute, staunch, steadfast, steady, stable, unwavering.

untamed adj fierce, unbroken, wild.

untangle vb disentangle, explain, explicate.

untenable adj indefensible, unmaintainable, unsound; fallacious, hollow, illogical, indefensible, insupportable, unjustifiable, weak.

unthinking adj careless, heedless, inconsiderate, thoughtless, unreasoning, unreflecting; automatic, mechanical.

untidy adj careless, disorderly, dowdy, frumpy, mussy, slatternly, slovenly, unkempt, unneat.

untie vb free, loose, loosen, unbind, unfasten, unknot, unloose; clear, resolve, solve, unfold.

until adv, conj till, to the time when; to the place, point, state or degree that; * prep till, to.

untimely adj ill-timed, immature, inconvenient, inopportune, mistimed, premature, unseasonable, unsuitable; ill-considered, inauspicious, uncalled for, unfortunate. * adv unseasonably, unsuitably.

untiring adj persevering, incessant, indefatigable, patient, tireless, unceasing, unfatiguable, unflagging, unremitting, unwearied, unwearying.

untold adj countless, incalculable, innumerable, uncounted, unnumbered; unrelated, unrevealed.

untoward adj adverse, froward, intractable, perverse, refractory, stubborn, unfortunate; annoying, ill-timed, inconvenient, unmanageable, vexatious; awkward, uncouth, ungainly, ungraceful.

untroubled adj calm, careless, composed, peaceful, serene, smooth, tranquil, undisturbed, unvexed.

untrue adj contrary, false, inaccurate, wrong; disloyal, faithless, false, perfidious, recreant, treacherous, unfaithful.

untrustworthy adj deceitful, dishonest, inaccurate, rotten, slippery, treacherous, undependable, unreliable; disloyal, false; deceptive, fallible, illusive, questionable.

untruth n error, faithlessness, falsehood, falsity, incorrectness, inveracity, treachery; deceit, deception, error, falsehood, fabrication, fib, fiction, forgery, imposture, invention, lie, misrepresentation, misstatement, story.

unusual adj abnormal, curious, exceptional, extraordinary, odd, peculiar, queer, rare, recherché, remarkable, singular, strange, unaccustomed, uncommon, unwonted.

unutterable adj incommunicable, indescribable, ineffable, inexpressible, unspeakable.

unvarnished adj unpolished; candid, plain, simple, true, unadorned, unembellished.

unveil vb disclose, expose, reveal, show, uncover, unmask.

unversed adj inexperienced, raw, undisciplined, undrilled, uneducated, unexercised, unpractised, unprepared, unschooled; unskilful.

unwary adj careless, hasty, heedless, imprudent, incautious, indiscreet, precipitate, rash, reckless, remiss, uncircumspect, unguarded.

unwelcome adj disagreeable, unacceptable, ungrateful, unpleasant, unpleasing.

unwell adj ailing, delicate, diseased, ill, indisposed, sick.

unwholesome adj baneful, deleterious, injurious, insalubrious, noisome, noxious, poisonous, unhealthful, unhealthy; injudicious, pernicious, unsound; corrupt, tainted, unsound.

unwieldy adj bulky, clumsy, cumbersome, cumbrous, elephantine, heavy, hulking, large, massy, ponderous, unmanageable, weighty.

unwilling adj averse, backward, disinclined, indisposed, laggard, loath, opposed, recalcitrant, reluctant; forced, grudging.

unwise adj brainless, foolish, ill-advised, ill-judged, impolitic, imprudent, indiscreet, injudicious, inexpedient, senseless, silly, stupid, unwary, weak.

unwittingly adv ignorantly, inadvertently, unconsciously, undesignedly, unintentionally, unknowingly.

unwrap vb open, unfold.

unwrinkled adj smooth, unforrowed.

unwritten adj oral, traditional, unrecorded; conventional, customary.

unyielding adj constant, determined, indomitable, inflexible, pertinacious, resolute, staunch, steadfast, steady, tenacious, uncompromising, unwavering; headstrong, intractable, obstinate, perverse, self-willed, stiff, stubborn, wayward, wilful; adamantine, firm, grim, hard, immovable, implastic, inexorable, relentless, rigid, stiff, stubborn, unbending.

upheaval n elevation, upthrow; cataclysm, convulsion, disorder, eruption, explosion, outburst, overthrow.

uphill adj ascending, upward; arduous, difficult, hard, laborious, strenuous, toilsome, wearisome.

uphold vb elevate, raise; bear up, hold up, support, sustain; advocate, aid, champion, countenance, defend, justify, maintain, support, sustain, vindicate.

upon prep on, on top of, over; about, concerning, on the subject of, relating to; immediately after, with.

uppermost adj foremost, highest, loftiest, supreme, topmost, upmost.

upright adj erect, perpendicular, vertical; conscientious, equitable, fair, faithful, good, honest, honourable, incorruptible, just, pure, righteous, straightforward, true, trustworthy, upstanding, virtuous.

uproar n clamour, commotion, confusion, din, disturbance, fracas, hubbub, hurly-burly, noise, pandemonium, racket, riot, tumult, turmoil, vociferation.

uproarious adj boisterous, clamorous, loud, noisy, obstreperous, riotous, tumultuous.

uproot vb eradicate, extirpate, root out.

upset vb capsize, invert, overthrow, overtumble, overturn, spill, tip over, topple, turn turtle; agitate, confound, confuse, discompose, disconcert, distress, disturb, embarrass, excite, fluster, muddle, overwhelm, perturb, shock, startle, trouble, unnerve, unsettle; checkmate, defeat, overthrow, revolutionize, subvert; foil, frustrate, nonplus, thwart. * adj disproved, exposed, overthrown; bothered, confused, disconcerted, flustered, mixed-up, perturbed; shocked, startled, unsettled; beaten, defeated, overcome, overpowered, overthrown; discomfited, distressed, discomposed, overcome, overexcited, overwrought, perturbed, shaken, troubled, unnerved. * n overturn, revolution; capsize, overthrow, overturn; confutation, refutation; foiling, frustration, ruin, thwarting, frustration.

upshot n conclusion, consummation, effect, end, event, issue, outcome, result, termination.

upside down adj bottom side up, bottom up, confused, head over heels, inverted, topsy-turvy.

upstart n adventurer, arriviste, parvenu, snob, social cimber, yuppie.

upturned adj raised, uplifted; retroussé.

upward adj ascending, climbing, mounting, rising, uphill. * adv above, aloft, overhead, up; heavenwards, skywards, up.

urbane adj civil, complaisant, courteous, courtly, elegant, mannerly, polished, polite, refined, smooth, suave, well-mannered.

urge *vb* crowd, drive, force on, impel, press, press on, push, push on; beg, beseech, conjure, entreat, exhort, implore, importune, ply, press, solicit, tease; animate, egg on, encourage, goad, hurry, incite, instigate, quicken, spur, stimulate. * *n* compulsion, desire, drive, impulse, longing, wish, yearning.

urgency *n* drive, emergency, exigency, haste, necessity, press, pressure, push, stress; clamorousness, entreaty, insistence, importunity, instance, solicitation; goad, incitement, spur, stimulus.

urgent *adj* cogent, critical, crucial, crying, exigent, immediate, imperative, important, importunate, insistent, instant, pertinacious, pressing, serious.

usage *n* treatment; consuetude, custom, fashion, habit, method, mode, practice, prescription, tradition, use.

use *vb* administer, apply, avail oneself of, drive, employ, handle, improve, make use of, manipulate, occupy, operate, ply, put into action, take advantage of, turn to account, wield, work; exercise, exert, exploit, practise, profit by, utilize; absorb, consume, exhaust, expend, swallow up, waste, wear out; accustom, familiarize, habituate, harden, inure, train; act toward, behave toward, deal with, handle, manage, treat; be accustomed, be wont. * *n* appliance, application, consumption, conversion, disposal, exercise, employ, employment, practice, utilization; adaptability, advantage, avail, benefit, convenience, profit, service, usefulness, utility, wear; exigency, necessity, indispensability, need, occasion, requisiteness; custom, exercise, habit, handling, method, practice, treatment, usage, way.

useful *adj* active, advantageous, available, availing, beneficial, commodious, convenient, effective, good, helpful, instrumental, operative, practical, profitable, remunerative, salutary, suitable, serviceable, utilitarian; available, helpful, serviceable, valuable.

useless *adj* abortive, bootless, fruitless, futile, idle, ineffective, ineffectual, inutile, nugatory, null, profitless, unavail-

ing, unprofitable, unproductive, unserviceable, valueless, worthless; food for nothing, unserviceable, valueless, waste, worthless.

usher *vb* announce, forerun, herald, induct, introduce, precede; conduct, direct, escort, shepherd, show. * *n* attendant, conductor, escort, shepherd, squire.

usual *adj* accustomed, common, customary, everyday, familiar, frequent, general, habitual, normal, ordinary, prevailing, prevalent, regular, wonted.

usurp *vb* appropriate, arrogate, assume, seize.

utility *n* advantageousness, avail, benefit, profit, service, use, usefulness; happiness, welfare.

utilize *vb* employ, exploit, make use of, put to use, turn to account, use.

utmost *adj* extreme, farthest, highest, last, main, most distant, remotest; greatest, uttermost. * *n* best, extreme, maximum, most.

utter¹ *adj* complete, entire, perfect, total; absolute, blank, diametric, downright, final, peremptory, sheer, stark, unconditional, unqualified, total.

utter² *vb* articulate, breathe, deliver, disclose, divulge, emit, enunciate, express, give forth, pronounce, reveal, speak, talk, tell, voice; announce, circulate, declare, issue, publish.

utterance *n* articulation, delivery, disclosure, emission, expression, pronouncement, pronunciation, publication, speech.

V

vacant *adj* blank, empty, unfilled, void; disengaged, free, unemployed, unoccupied, unencumbered; thoughtless, unmeaning, unthinking, unreflective; uninhabited, untenanted.

vacate *vb* abandon, evacuate, relinquish, surrender; abolish, abrogate, annul, cancel, disannul, invalidate, nullify, overrule, quash, rescind.

vagabond *adj* footloose, idle, meandering, rambling, roving, roaming, strolling, vagrant, wandering. * n beggar, castaway, landloper, loafer, lounger, nomad, outcast, tramp, vagrant, wanderer.

vagrant adj erratic, itinerant, roaming, roving, nomadic, strolling, unsettled, wandering. * n beggar, castaway, landloper, loafer, lounger, nomad, outcast, tramp, vagabond, wanderer.

vague adj ambiguous, confused, dim, doubtful, indefinite, ill-defined, indistinct, lax, loose, obscure, uncertain, undetermined, unfixed, unsettled.

vain adj baseless, delusive, dreamy, empty, false, imaginary, shadowy, suppositional, unsubstantial, unreal, void; abortive, bootless, fruitless, futile, ineffectual, nugatory, profitless, unavailing, unprofitable; trivial, unessential, unimportant, unsatisfactory, unsatisfying, useless, vapid, worthless; arrogant, conceited, egotistical, flushed, high, inflated, opinionated, ostentatious, overweening, proud, self-confident, self-opinionated, vainglorious; gaudy, glittering, gorgeous, ostentatious, showy.

valiant adj bold, brave, chivalrous, courageous, daring, dauntless, doughty, fearless, gallant, heroic, intrepid, lion-hearted, redoubtable, Spartan, valorous, undaunted.

valid adj binding, cogent, conclusive, efficacious, efficient, good, grave, important, just, logical, powerful, solid, sound, strong, substantial, sufficient, weighty.

valour n boldness, bravery, courage, daring, gallantry, heroism, prowess, spirit.

valuable adj advantageous, precious, profitable, useful; costly, expensive, rich; admirable, estimable, worthy. * n heirloom, treasure.

value vb account, appraise, assess, estimate, price, rate, reckon; appreciate, esteem, prize, regard, treasure. * n avail, importance, usefulness, utility, worth; cost, equivalent, price, rate; estimation, excellence, importance, merit, valuation, worth.

vandal n barbarian, destroyer, savage.

vandalism n barbarism, barbarity, savagery.

vanish vb disappear, dissolve, fade, melt.

vanity n emptiness, falsity, foolishness, futility, hollowness, insanity, triviality, unreality, worthlessness; arrogance, conceit, egotism, ostentation, self-conceit.

vanquish vb conquer, defeat, outwit, overcome, overpower, overthrow, subdue, subjugate; crush, discomfit, foil, master, quell, rout, worst.

vapour n cloud, exhalation, fog, fume, mist, rack, reek, smoke, steam; daydream, dream, fantasy, phantom, vagary, vision, whim, whimsy.

variable adj changeable, mutable, shifting; aberrant, alterable, capricious, fickle, fitful, floating, fluctuating, inconstant, mobile, mutable, protean, restless, shifting, unsteady, vacillating, wavering.

variance n disagreement, difference, discord, dissension, incompatibility, jarring, strife.

variation n alteration, change, modification; departure, deviation, difference, discrepancy, innovation; contrariety, discordance.

variety n difference, dissimilarity, diversity, diversification, medley, miscellany, mixture, multiplicity, variation, kind, sort.

various adj different, diverse, manifold, many, numerous, several, sundry.

varnish vb enamel, glaze, japan, lacquer; adorn, decorate, embellish, garnish, gild, polish; disguise, excuse, extenuate, gloss over, palliate. * n enamel, lacquer, stain; cover, extenuation, gloss.

vary vb alter, metamorphose, transform; alternate, exchange, rotate; diversify, modify, variegate; depart, deviate, swerve.

vast adj boundless, infinite, measureless, spacious, wide; colossal, enormous, gigantic, huge, immense, mighty, monstrous, prodigious, tremendous; extraordinary, remarkable.

vault¹ vb arch, bend, curve, span. * n cupola, curve, dome; catacomb, cell, cellar, crypt, dungeon, tomb; depository, strongroom.

vault² vb bound, jump, leap, spring; tumble, turn. * n bound, leap, jump, spring.

veer vb change, shift, turn.

vegetate vb blossom, develop, flourish, flower, germinate, grow, shoot, sprout, swell; bask, hibernate, idle, stagnate.

vehement adj furious, high, hot, impetuous, passionate, rampant, violent; ardent, burning, eager, earnest, enthusiastic, fervid, fiery, keen, passionate, sanguine, zealous; forcible, mighty, powerful, strong.

veil vb cloak, conceal, cover, curtain, envelop, hide, invest, mask, screen, shroud. * n cover, curtain, film, shade, screen; blind, cloak, cover, disguise, mask, muffler, screen, visor.

vein n course, current, lode, seam, streak, stripe, thread, wave; bent, character, faculty, humour, mood, talent, turn.

velvety adj delicate, downy, smooth, soft.

vend vb dispose, flog, hawk, retail, sell.

venerable adj grave, respected, revered, sage, wise; awful, dread, dreadful; aged, old, patriarchal.

veneration n adoration, devotion, esteem, respect, reverence, worship.

vengeance n retaliation, retribution, revenge.

venom n poison, virus; acerbity, acrimony, bitterness, gall, hate, ill-will, malevolence, malice, maliciousness, malignity, rancour, spite, virulence.

venomous adj deadly, poisonous, septic, toxic, virulent; caustic, malicious, malignant, mischievous, noxious, spiteful.

vent vb emit, express, release, utter. * n air hole, hole, mouth, opening, orifice; air pipe, air tube, aperture, blowhole, bunghole, hydrant, plug, spiracle, spout, tap, orifice; effusion, emission, escape, outlet, passage; discharge, expression, utterance.

ventilate vb aerate, air, freshen, oxygenate, purify; fan, winnow; canvas, comment, discuss, examine, publish, review, scrutinize.

venture vb adventure, dare, hazard, imperil, jeopardize, presume, risk, speculate, test, try, undertake. * n adventure, chance, hazard, jeopardy, peril, risk, speculation, stake.

verdict n answer, decision, finding, judgement, opinion, sentence.

verge vb bear, incline, lean, slope, tend; approach, border, skirt. * n mace, rod, staff; border, boundary, brink, confine, edge, extreme, limit, margin; edge, eve, point.

verify vb attest, authenticate, confirm, corroborate, prove, substantiate.

versatile adj capricious, changeable, erratic, mobile, variable; fickle, inconstant, mercurial, unsteady; adaptable, protean, plastic, varied.

versed adj able, accomplished, acquainted, clever, conversant, practised, proficient, qualified, skilful, skilled, trained.

version n interpretation, reading, rendering, translation.

vertical adj erect, perpendicular, plumb, steep, upright.

vertigo n dizziness, giddiness.

verve n animation, ardour, energy, enthusiasm, force, rapture, spirit.

very adv absolutely, enormously, excessively, hugely, remarkably, surpassingly. * adj actual, exact, identical, precise, same; bare, mere, plain, pure, simple.

vestige n evidence, footprint, footstep, mark, record, relic, sign, token.

veteran adj adept, aged, experienced, disciplined, seasoned, old. * n campaigner, old soldier; master, past master, old-timer, old-stager.

veto vb ban, embargo, forbid, interdict, negate, prohibit. * n ban, embargo, interdict, prohibition, refusal.

vex vb annoy, badger, bother, chafe, cross, distress, gall, harass, harry, hector, molest, perplex, pester, plague, tease, torment, trouble, roil, spite, worry; affront, displease, fret, irk, irritate, nettle, offend, provoke; agitate, disquiet, disturb.

vexation n affliction, agitation, chagrin, discomfort, displeasure, disquiet, distress, grief, irritation, pique, sorrow, trouble; affliction, annoyance, curse, nuisance, plague, torment; damage, troubling, vexing.

vibrate vb oscillate, sway, swing, undulate, wave; impinge, quiver, sound, thrill; fluctuate, hesitate, vacillate, waver.

vice n blemish, defect, failing, fault, imperfection, infirmity; badness, corruption, depravation, depravity, error, evil, immorality, iniquity, laxity, obliquity, sin, viciousness, vileness, wickedness.

vicinity *n* nearness, proximity; locality, neighbourhood, vicinage.

vicious *adj* abandoned, atrocious, bad, corrupt, degenerate, demoralized, depraved, devilish, diabolical, evil, flagrant, hellish, immoral, iniquitous, mischievous, profligate, shameless, sinful, unprincipled, wicked; malicious, spiteful, venomous; foul, impure; corrupt, debased, faulty, impure; contrary, refractory.

victim *n* martyr, sacrifice, sufferer; prey, sufferer; cat's-paw, cull, cully, dupe, gull, gudgeon, prey, puppet.

victimize *vb* bamboozle, befool, beguile, cheat, circumvent, cozen, deceive, defraud, diddle, dupe, fool, gull, hoax, hoodwink, overreach, swindle, trick.

victor *n* champion, conqueror, vanquisher, winner.

victorious *adj* conquering, successful, triumphant, winning.

victory *n* achievement, conquest, mastery, triumph.

view *vb* behold, contemplate, eye, inspect, scan, survey; consider, contemplate, inspect, regard, study. * *n* inspection, observation, regard, sight; outlook, panorama, perspective, prospect, range, scene, survey, vista; aim, intent, intention, design, drift, object, purpose, scope; belief, conception, impression, idea, judgement, notion, opinion, sentiment, theory; appearance, aspect, show.

vigilant *adj* alert, attentive, careful, cautious, circumspect, observant, unsleeping, wakeful, watchful.

vigorous *adj* lusty, powerful, strong; active, alert, cordial, energetic, forcible, vehement, vivid, virile, strenuous; brisk, hale, hardy, robust, sound, sturdy, healthy; fresh, flourishing; bold, emphatic, impassioned, lively, nervous, piquant, pointed, severe, sparkling, spirited, trenchant.

vigour *n* activity, efficacy, energy, force, might, potency, power, spirit, strength; bloom, elasticity, haleness, health, heartiness, pep, punch, robustness, sound-

ness, thriftiness, tone, vim, vitality; enthusiasm, freshness, fire, intensity, liveliness, piquancy, strenuousness, vehemence, verve, raciness.

vile *adj* abject, base, beastly, beggarly, brutish, contemptible, despicable, disgusting, grovelling, ignoble, low, mean, odious, paltry, pitiful, repulsive, scurvy, shabby, slavish, sorry, ugly; bad, base, evil, foul, gross, impure, iniquitous, lewd, obscene, sinful, vicious, wicked; cheap, mean, miserable, valueless, worthless.

vilify *vb* abuse, asperse, backbite, berate, blacken, blemish, brand, calumniate, decry, defame, disparage, lampoon, libel, malign, revile, scandalize, slander, slur, traduce, vituperate.

villain *n* blackguard, knave, miscreant, rascal, reprobate, rogue, ruffian, scamp, scapegrace, scoundrel.

vindicate *vb* defend, justify, uphold; advocate, avenge, assert, maintain, right, support.

vindictive *adj* avenging, grudgeful, implacable, malevolent, malicious, malignant, retaliative, revengeful, spiteful, unforgiving, unrelenting, vengeful.

violate *vb* hurt, injure; break, disobey, infringe, invade; desecrate, pollute, profane; abuse, debauch, defile, deflower, outrage, ravish, transgress.

violent *adj* boisterous, demented, forceful, forcible, frenzied, furious, high, hot, impetuous, insane, intense, stormy, tumultuous, turbulent, vehement, wild; fierce, fiery, fuming, heady, heavy, infuriate, passionate, obstreperous, strong, raging, rampant, rank, rapid, raving, refractory, roaring, rough, tearing, towering, ungovernable; accidental, unnatural; desperate, extreme, outrageous, unjust; acute, exquisite, intense, poignant, sharp.

virile *adj* forceful, manly, masculine, robust, vigorous.

virtual *adj* constructive, equivalent, essential, implicit, implied, indirect, practical, substantial.

virtue *n* chastity, goodness, grace, morality, purity; efficacy, excellence, honesty, integrity, justice, probity, quality, rectitude, worth.

virtuous adj blameless, equitable, exemplary, excellent, good, honest, moral, noble, righteous, upright, worthy; chaste, continent, immaculate, innocent, modest, pure, undefiled; efficacious, powerful.

virulent adj deadly, malignant, poisonous, toxic, venomous; acrid, acrimonious, bitter, caustic.

visible adj perceivable, perceptible, seeable, visual; apparent, clear, conspicuous, discoverable, distinct, evident, manifest, noticeable, obvious, open, palpable, patent, plain, revealed, unhidden, unmistakable.

vision n eyesight, seeing, sight; eyeshot, pen; apparition, chimera, dream, ghost, hallucination, illusion, phantom, spectre.

visionary adj imaginative, impractical, quixotic, romantic; chimerical, dreamy, fancied, fanciful, fantastic, ideal, illusory, imaginary, romantic, shadowy, unsubstantial, utopian, wild. * n dreamer, enthusiast, fanatic, idealist, optimist, theorist, zealot.

vital adj basic, cardinal, essential, indispensable, necessary; animate, alive, existing, life-giving, living; essential, paramount.

vitality n animation, life, strength, vigour, virility.

vivacious adj active, animated, breezy, brisk, buxom, cheerful, frolicsome, gay, jocund, light-hearted, lively, merry, mirthful, spirited, sportive, sprightly.

vivid adj active, animated, bright, brilliant, clear, intense, fresh, lively, living, lucid, quick, sprightly, strong; expressive, graphic, striking, telling.

vocation n call, citation, injunction, summons; business, calling, employment, occupation, profession, pursuit, trade.

vogue adj fashionable, modish, stylish, trendy. * n custom, fashion, favour, mode, practice, repute, style, usage, way.

voice vb declare, express, say, utter. * n speech, tongue, utterance; noise, notes, sound; opinion, option, preference, suffrage, vote; accent, articulation, enunciation, inflection, intonation, modula-

tion, pronunciation, tone; expression, language, words.

void vb clear, eject, emit, empty, evacuate. * adj blank, empty, hollow, vacant; clear, destitute, devoid, free, lacking, wanting, without; inept, ineffectual, invalid, nugatory, null; imaginary, unreal, vain. * n abyss, blank, chasm, emptiness, hole, vacuum.

volatile adj gaseous, incoercible; airy, buoyant, frivolous, gay, jolly, lively, sprightly, vivacious; capricious, changeable, fickle, flighty, flyaway, giddy, harebrained, inconstant, light-headed, mercurial, reckless, unsteady, whimsical, wild.

volume n contortion, convolution, turn, whirl; book, tome; amplitude, body, bulk, compass, dimension, size, substance, vastness; fullness, power, quantity.

voluminous adj ample, big, bulky, full, great, large; copious, diffuse, discursive, flowing.

voluntary adj free, spontaneous, unasked, unbidden, unforced; deliberate, designed, intended, purposed; discretionary, optional, willing.

volunteer vb offer, present, proffer, propose, tender.

voracious adj devouring, edacious, greedy, hungry, rapacious, ravenous.

vote vb ballot, elect, opt, return; judge, pronounce, propose, suggest. * n ballot, franchise, poll, referendum, suffrage, voice.

vow vb consecrate, dedicate, devote; asseverate. * n oath, pledge, promise.

voyage vb cruise, journey, navigate, ply, sail. * n crossing, cruise, excursion, journey, passage, sail, trip.

vulgar adj base-born, common, ignoble, lowly, plebeian; boorish, cheap, coarse, discourteous, flashy, homespun, garish, gaudy, ill-bred, inelegant, loud, rustic, showy, tawdry, uncultivated, unrefined; general, ordinary, popular, public; base, broad, loose, low, gross, mean, ribald, vile; inelegant, unauthorized.

vulnerable adj accessible, assailable, defenceless, exposed, weak.

W

waft vb bear, carry, convey, float, transmit, transport. * n breath, breeze, draught, puff.

wag[1] vb shake, sway, waggle; oscillate, vibrate, waver; advance, move, progress, stir. * n flutter, nod, oscillation, vibration.

wag[2] n humorist, jester, joker, wit.

wage vb bet, hazard, lay, stake, wager; conduct, undertake.

wager vb back, bet, gamble, lay, pledge, risk, stake. * n bet, gamble, pledge, risk, stake.

wages npl allowance, compensation, earnings, emolument, hire, pay, payment, remuneration, salary, stipend.

wail vb bemoan, deplore, lament, mourn; cry, howl, weep. * n complaint, cry, lamentation, moan, wailing.

wait vb delay, linger, pause, remain, rest, stay, tarry; attend, minister, serve; abide, await, expect, look for. * n delay, halt, holdup, pause, respite, rest, stay, stop.

waive vb defer, forego, surrender, relinquish, remit, renounce; desert, reject.

wake[1] vb arise, awake, awaken; activate, animate, arouse, awaken, excite, kindle, provoke, stimulate. * n vigil, watch, watching.

wake[2] n course, path, rear, track, trail, wash.

wakeful adj awake, sleepless, restless; alert, observant, vigilant, observant, wary, watchful.

walk vb advance, depart, go, march, move, pace, saunter, step, stride, stroll, tramp. * n amble, carriage, gait, step; beat, career, course, department, field, province; conduct, procedure; alley, avenue, cloister, esplanade, footpath, path, pathway, pavement, promenade, range, sidewalk, way; constitutional, excursion, hike, ramble, saunter, stroll, tramp, turn.

wan adj ashen, bloodless, cadaverous, colourless, haggard, pale, pallid.

wander vb forage, prowl, ramble, range, roam, rove, stroll; deviate, digress, straggle, stray; moon, ramble, rave. * n amble, cruise, excursion, ramble, stroll.

wane vb abate, decrease, ebb, subside; decline, fail, sink. * n decrease, diminution, lessening; decay, declension, decline, decrease, failure.

want vb crave, desire, need, require, wish; fail, lack, neglect, omit. * n absence, defect, default, deficiency, lack; defectiveness, deficiency, failure, inadequacy, insufficiency, meagreness, paucity, poverty, scantiness, scarcity, shortness; necessity, need, requirement; craving, desire, longing, wish; destitution, distress, indigence, necessity, need, penury, poverty, privation, straits.

war vb battle, campaign, combat, contend, crusade, engage, fight, strive. * n contention, enmity, hostility, strife, warfare.

warble vb sing, trill, yodel. * n carol, chant, hymn, hum.

ward vb guard, watch; defend, fend, parry, protect, repel. * n care, charge, guard, guardianship, watch; defender, guardian, keeper, protector, warden; custody; defence, garrison, protection; minor, pupil; district, division, precinct, quarter; apartment, cubicle.

warehouse n depot, magazine, repository, store, storehouse.

warfare n battle, conflict, contest, discord, engagement, fray, hostilities, strife, struggle, war.

warlike adj bellicose, belligerent, combative, hostile, inimical, martial, military, soldierly, watchful.

warm vb heat, roast, toast; animate, chafe, excite, rouse. * adj lukewarm, tepid; genial, mild, pleasant, sunny; close, muggy, oppressive; affectionate, ardent, cordial, eager, earnest, enthusiastic, fervent, fervid, genial, glowing, hearty, hot, zealous; excited, fiery, flushed, furious, hasty, keen, lively, passionate, quick, vehement, violent.

warmth n glow, tepidity; ardour, fervency, fervour, zeal; animation, cordiality, eagerness, earnestness, enthusiasm, excitement, fervency, fever, fire, flush, heat, intensity, passion, spirit, vehemence.

warn vb caution, forewarn; admonish, advise; apprise, inform, notify; bid, call, summon.

warning *adj* admonitory, cautionary, cautioning, monitory. * *n* admonition, advice, caveat, caution, monition; information, notice; augury, indication, intimation, omen, portent, presage, prognostic, sign, symptom; call, summons; example, lesson, sample.

warrant *vb* answer for, certify, guarantee, secure; affirm, assure, attest, avouch, declare, justify, state; authorize, justify, license, maintain, sanction, support, sustain, uphold. * *n* guarantee, pledge, security, surety, warranty; authentication, authority, commission, verification; order, pass, permit, summons, subpoena, voucher, writ.

warrior *n* champion, captain, fighter, hero, soldier.

wary *adj* careful, cautious, chary, circumspect, discreet, guarded, heedful, prudent, scrupulous, vigilant, watchful.

wash *vb* purify, purge; moisten, wet; bathe, clean, flush, irrigate, lap, lave, rinse, sluice; colour, stain, tint. * *n* ablution, bathing, cleansing, lavation, washing; bog, fen, marsh, swamp, quagmire; bath, embrocation, lotion; laundry, washing.

waste *vb* consume, corrode, decrease, diminish, emaciate, wear; absorb, consume, deplete, devour, dissipate, drain, empty, exhaust, expend, lavish, lose, misspend, misuse, scatter, spend, squander; demolish, desolate, destroy, devastate, devour, dilapidate, harry, pillage, plunder, ravage, ruin, scour, strip; damage, impair, injure; decay, dwindle, perish, wither. * *adj* bare, desolated, destroyed, devastated, empty, ravaged, ruined, spoiled, stripped, void; dismal, dreary, forlorn; abandoned, bare, barren, uncultivated, unimproved, uninhabited, untilled, wild; useless, valueless, worthless; exuberant, superfluous. * *n* consumption, decrement, diminution, dissipation, exhaustion, expenditure, loss, wasting; destruction, dispersion, extravagance, loss, squandering, wanton; decay, desolation, destruction, devastation, havoc, pillage, ravage, ruin; chaff, debris, detritus, dross, husks, junk, matter,

offal, refuse, rubbish, trash, wastrel, worthlessness; barrenness, desert, expanse, solitude, wild, wilderness.

wasteful *adj* destructive, ruinous; extravagant, improvident, lavish, prodigal, profuse, squandering, thriftless, unthrifty.

watch *vb* attend, guard, keep, oversee, protect, superintend, tend; eye, mark, observe. * *n* espial, guard, outlook, wakefulness, watchfulness, watching, vigil, ward; alertness, attention, inspection, observation, surveillance; guard, picket, sentinel, sentry, watchman; pocket watch, ticker, timepiece.

watchful *adj* alert, attentive, awake, careful, circumspect, guarded, heedful, observant, vigilant, wakeful, wary.

watery *adj* diluted, thin, waterish, weak; insipid, spiritless, tasteful, vapid; moist, wet.

wave *vb* float, flutter, heave, shake, sway, undulate, wallow; brandish, flaunt, flourish, swing; beckon, signal. * *n* billow, bore, breaker, flood, flush, ripple, roll, surge, swell, tide, undulation; flourish, gesture, sway; convolution, curl, roll, unevenness.

waver *vb* flicker, float, undulate, wave; reel, totter; falter, fluctuate, flutter, hesitate, oscillate, quiver, vacillate.

wax *vb* become, grow, increase, mount, rise.

way *n* advance, journey, march, passage, progression, transit, trend; access, alley, artery, avenue, beat, channel, course, highroad, highway, passage, path, road, route, street, track, trail; fashion, manner, means, method, mode, system; distance, interval, space, stretch; behaviour, custom, fashion, form, guise, habit, habitude, manner, practice, process, style, usage; device, plan, scheme.

wayward *adj* capricious, captious, contrary, forward, headstrong, intractable, obstinate, perverse, refractory, stubborn, unruly, wilful.

weak *adj* debilitated, delicate, enfeebled, enervated, exhausted, faint, feeble, fragile, frail, infirm, invalid, languid, languishing, shaky, sickly, spent, strengthless, tender, unhealthy, unsound, wasted, weakly; accessible, defenceless, unprotected, vulnerable; light, soft, unstressed; boneless, infirm; compliant, irresolute, pliable, pliant, undecided, undetermined, unsettled, unstable, unsteady, vacillating, wavering, yielding; childish, foolish, imbecile, senseless, shallow, silly, simple, stupid, weak-minded, witless; erring, foolish, indiscreet, injudicious, unwise; faint, feeble, gentle, indistinct, low, small; adulterated, attenuated, diluted, insipid, tasteless, thin, watery; feeble, flimsy, frivolous, poor, sleazy, slight, trifling; futile, illogical, inconclusive, ineffective, ineffectual, inefficient, lame, unconvincing, unsatisfactory, unsupported, unsustained, vague, vain; unsafe, unsound, unsubstantial, untrustworthy; helpless, impotent, powerless; breakable, brittle, delicate, frangible; inconsiderable, puny, slender, slight, small.

weaken vb cramp, cripple, debilitate, devitalize, enervate, enfeeble, invalidate, relax, sap, shake, stagger, undermine, unman, unnerve, unstring; adulterate, attenuate, debase, depress, dilute, exhaust, impair, impoverish, lessen, lower, reduce.

weakness n debility, feebleness, fragility, frailty, infirmity, languor, softness; defect, failing, fault, flaw; fondness, inclination, liking.

wealth n assets, capital, cash, fortune, funds, goods, money, possessions, property, riches, treasure; abundance, affluence, opulence, plenty, profusion.

wear vb bear, carry, don; endure, last; consume, impair, rub, use, waste. * n corrosion, deterioration, disintegration, erosion, wear and tear; consumption; use; apparel, array, attire, clothes, clothing, dress, garb, gear.

wearisome adj annoying, boring, dull, exhausting, fatiguing, humdrum, irksome, monotonous, prolix, prosaic, slow, tedious, tiresome, troublesome, trying, uninteresting, vexatious.

weary vb debilitate, exhaust, fag, fatigue, harass, jade, tire. * adj apathetic, bored, drowsy, exhausted, jaded, spent, tired, worn; irksome, tiresome, wearisome.

wed vb contract, couple, espouse, marry.

wedding n bridal, espousal, marriage, nuptials.

weep vb bemoan, bewail, complain, cry, lament, sob.

weigh vb balance, counterbalance, lift, raise; consider, deliberate, esteem, examine, study.

weight vb ballast, burden, fill, freight, load; weigh. * n gravity, heaviness, heft, tonnage; burden, load, pressure; burden, consequence, efficacy, emphasis, importance, impressiveness, influence, moment, pith, power, significance, value.

weighty adj heavy, massive, onerous, ponderous, unwieldy; considerable, efficacious, forcible, grave, important, influential, serious, significant.

weird adj eerie, ghostly, strange, supernatural, uncanny, unearthly, witching.

welcome vb embrace, greet, hail, receive. * adj acceptable, agreeable, grateful, gratifying, pleasant, pleasing, satisfying. * n greeting, reception, salutation.

welfare n advantage, affluence, benefit, happiness, profit, prosperity, success, thrift, weal, wellbeing.

well¹ vb flow, gush, issue, jet, pour, spring. * n fount, fountain, reservoir, spring, wellhead, wellspring; origin, source; hole, pit, shaft.

well² adj hale, healthy, hearty, sound; fortunate, good, happy, profitable, satisfactory, useful. * adv accurately, adequately, correctly, efficiently, properly, suitably; abundantly, considerably, fully, thoroughly; agreeably, commendably, favourably, worthily.

wellbeing n comfort, good, happiness, health, prosperity, welfare.

wet vb dabble, damp, dampen, dip, drench, moisten, saturate, soak, sprinkle, water. * adj clammy, damp, dank, dewy, dripping, humid, moist; rainy, showery, sprinkly. * n dampness, humidity, moisture, wetness.

wheel vb gyrate, revolve, roll, rotate, spin, swing, turn, twist, whirl, wind. * n circle, revolution, roll, rotation, spin, turn, twirl.

whim *n* caprice, crochet, fancy, freak, frolic, humour, notion, quirk, sport, vagary, whimsy, wish.

whimsical *adj* capricious, crotchety, eccentric, erratic, fanciful, frolicsome, odd, peculiar, quaint, singular.

whine *vb* cry, grumble, moan, mule, snivel, wail, whimper. * *n* complaint, cry, grumble, moan, sob, wail, whimper.

whip *vb* beat, lash, strike; beat, flagellate, flog, goad, horsewhip, lash, scourge, slash; hurt, sting; jerk, snap, snatch, whisk. * *n* cane, crop, horsewhip, lash, scourge, switch, thong.

whirl *vb* gyrate, pirouette, roll, revolve, rotate, turn, twirl, twist, wheel. * *n* eddy, flurry, flutter, gyration, rotation, spin, swirl, twirl, vortex.

whole *adj* all, complete, entire, intact, integral, total, undivided; faultless, firm, good, perfect, strong, unbroken, undivided, uninjured; healthy, sound, well. * *adv* entire, in one. * *n* aggregate, all, amount, ensemble, entirety, gross, sum, total, totality.

wholesome *adj* healthy, healthful, helpful, invigorating, nourishing, nutritious, salubrious, salutary; beneficial, good, helpful, improving, salutary; fresh, sound, sweet.

wicked *adj* abandoned, abominable, depraved, devilish, godless, graceless, immoral, impious, infamous, irreligious, irreverent, profane, sinful, ungodly, unholy, unprincipled, unrighteous, vicious, vile, worthless; atrocious, bad, black, criminal, dark, evil, heinous, ill, iniquitous, monstrous, nefarious, unjust, villainous.

wide *adj* ample, broad, capacious, comprehensive, distended, expanded, large, spacious, vast; distant, remote; prevalent, rife, widespread. * *adv* completely, farthest, fully.

wield *vb* brandish, flourish, handle, manipulate, ply, work; control, manage, sway, use.

wild *adj* feral, undomesticated, untamed; desert, desolate, native, rough, rude, uncultivated; barbarous, ferocious, fierce, rude, savage, uncivilized, untamed; dense, luxuriant, rank; disorderly, distracted, frantic, frenzied, furious, impetuous, irregular, mad, outrageous, raving, turbulent, ungoverned, uncontrolled, violent; dissipated, fast, flighty, foolish, giddy, harebrained, heedless, illadvised, inconsiderate, reckless, thoughtless, unwise; boisterous, rough, stormy; crazy, extravagant, fanciful, grotesque, imaginary, strange. * *n* desert, waste, wilderness.

wilful *adj* cantankerous, contumacious, dogged, headstrong, heady, inflexible, intractable, mulish, obdurate, obstinate, perverse, pig-headed, refractory, selfwilled, stubborn, unruly, unyielding; arbitrary, capricious, self-willed; deliberate, intended, intentional, planned, premeditated.

will *vb* bid, command, decree, direct, enjoin, ordain; choose, desire, elect, wish; bequeath, convey, demise, devise, leave. * *n* decision, determination, resoluteness, resolution, self-reliance; desire, disposition, inclination, intent, pleasure, purpose, volition, wish; behest, command, decree, demand, direction, order, request, requirement.

willing *adj* adaptable, amenable, compliant, desirous, disposed, inclined, minded; deliberate, free, intentional, spontaneous, unasked, unbidden, voluntary; cordial, eager, forward, prompt, ready.

wily *adj* arch, artful, crafty, crooked, cunning, deceitful, designing, diplomatic, foxy, insidious, intriguing, politic, sly, subtle, treacherous, tricky.

win *vb* accomplish, achieve, acquire, catch, earn, effect, gain, gather, get, make, obtain, procure, reach, realize, reclaim, recover; gain, succeed, surpass, triumph; arrive, get, reach; allure, attract, convince, influence, persuade. * *n* conquest, success, triumph, victory.

wind¹ *n* air, blast, breeze, draught, gust, hurricane, whiff, zephyr; breath, breathing, expiration, inspiration, respiration; flatulence, gas, windiness.

wind² *vb* coil, crank, encircle, involve, reel, roll, turn, twine, twist; bend, curve, meander, zigzag. * *n* bend, curve, meander, twist, zigzag.

windy *adj* breezy, blowy, blustering, boisterous, draughty, gusty, squally, stormy, tempestuous; airy, empty, hollow, inflated.

wipe *vb* clean, dry, mop, rub. * *n* blow, hit, strike; gibe, jeer, sarcasm, sneer, taunt.

wisdom *n* depth, discernment, far-sightedness, foresight, insight, judgement, judiciousness, prescience, profundity, prudence, sagacity, sapience, solidity, sense, understanding, wiseness; attainment, enlightenment, erudition, information, knowledge, learning, lore, scholarship; reason, right, sense.

wise *adj* deep, discerning, enlightened, intelligent, judicious, penetrating, philosophical, profound, rational, seasonable, sensible, sage, sapient, solid, sound; erudite, informed, knowing, learned, scholarly; crafty, cunning, designing, foxy, knowing, politic, sly, subtle, wary, wily.

wish *vb* covet, desire, hanker, list, long; bid, command, desire, direct, intend, mean, order, want. * *n* behest, desire, intention, mind, pleasure, want, will; craving, desire, hankering, inclination, liking, longing, want, yearning.

wistful *adj* contemplative, engrossed, meditative, musing, pensive, reflective, thoughtful; desirous, eager, earnest, longing.

wit *n* genius, intellect, intelligence, reason, sense, understanding; brightness, banter, cleverness, drollery, facetiousness, fun, humour, jocularity, piquancy, point, raillery, satire, sparkle, whim; conceit, epigram, jest, joke, pleasantry, quip, quirk, repartee, sally, witticism; humorist, joker, wag.

witch *n* charmer, enchantress, fascinator, sorceress; crone, hag, sibyl.

witchcraft *n* conjuration, enchantment, magic, necromancy, sorcery, spell.

withdraw *vb* abstract, deduct, remove, retire, separate, sequester, sequestrate, subduct, subtract; disengage, wean; abjure, recall, recant, relinquish, resign, retract, revoke; abdicate, decamp, depart, dissociate, retire, shrink, vacate.

wither *vb* contract, droop, dry, sear, shrivel, wilt, wizen; decay, decline, droop, languish, pine, waste.

withhold *vb* check, detain, hinder, repress, restrain, retain, suppress.

withstand *vb* confront, defy, face, oppose, resist.

witness *vb* corroborate, mark, note, notice, observe, see. * *n* attestation, conformation, corroboration, evidence, proof, testimony; beholder, bystander, corroborator, deponent, eyewitness, onlooker, spectator, testifier.

witty *adj* bright, clever, droll, facetious, funny, humorous, jocose, jocular, pleasant, waggish; alert, penetrating, quick, sparkling, sprightly.

wizard *n* charmer, diviner, conjurer, enchanter, magician, necromancer, seer, soothsayer, sorcerer.

woe *n* affliction, agony, anguish, bitterness, depression, distress, dole, grief, heartache, melancholy, misery, sorrow, torture, tribulation, trouble, unhappiness, wretchedness.

wonder *vb* admire, gape, marvel; conjecture, ponder, query, question, speculate. * *n* amazement, astonishment, awe, bewilderment, curiosity, marvel, miracle, prodigy, surprise, stupefaction, wonderment.

wonderful *adj* amazing, astonishing, astounding, awe-inspiring, awesome, awful, extraordinary, marvellous, miraculous, portentous, prodigious, startling, stupendous, surprising.

word *vb* express, phrase, put, say, state, term, utter. * *n* expression, name, phrase, term, utterance; account, advice, information, intelligence, message, news, report, tidings; affirmation, assertion, averment, avowal, declaration, statement; conservation, speech; agreement, assurance, engagement, parole, pledge, plight, promise; behest, bidding, command, direction, order, precept; countersign, password, signal, watchword.

work *vb* act, operate; drudge, fag, grind, grub, labour, slave, sweat, toil; move, perform, succeed; aim, attempt, strive, try; effervesce, ferment, leaven, rise; accomplish, beget, cause, effect, engender, manage, originate, produce; exert, strain; embroider, stitch. * *n* exertion, drudgery, grind, labour, pain, toil; business, employment, function, occupation, task; action, accomplishment, achievement, composition, deed, feat, fruit, handiwork, opus, performance, product, production; fabric, manufacture; ferment, leaven; management, treatment.

worldly *adj* common, earthly, human, mundane, sublunary, terrestrial; carnal, fleshly, profane, secular, temporal; ambitious, grovelling, irreligious, selfish, proud, sordid, unsanctified, unspiritual.

worry *vb* annoy, badger, bait, beset, bore, bother, chafe, disquiet, disturb, fret, gall, harass, harry, hector, infest, irritate, molest, persecute, pester, plague, tease, torment, trouble, vex. * *n* annoyance, anxiety, apprehensiveness, care, concern, disquiet, fear, misgiving, perplexity, solicitude, trouble, uneasiness, vexation.

worship *vb* adore, esteem, honour, revere, venerate; deify, idolize; aspire, pray. * *n* adoration, devotion, esteem, homage, idolatry, idolizing, respect, reverence; aspiration, exultation, invocation, laud, praise, prayer, supplication.

worst *vb* beat, choke, conquer, crush, defeat, discomfit, foil, master, overpower, overthrow, quell, rout, subdue, subjugate, vanquish.

worth *n* account, character, credit, desert, excellence, importance, integrity, merit, nobleness, worthiness, virtue; cost, estimation, price, value.

worthless *adj* futile, meritless, miserable, nugatory, paltry, poor, trifling, unproductive, unsalable, unserviceable, useless, valueless, wretched; abject, base, corrupt, degraded, ignoble, low, mean, vile.

worthy *adj* deserving, fit, suitable; estimable, excellent, exemplary, good, honest, honourable, reputable, righteous, upright, virtuous. * *n* celebrity, dignitary, luminary, notability, personage, somebody, VIP.

wound *vb* damage, harm, hurt, injure; cut, gall, harrow, irritate, lacerate, pain,

prick, stab; annoy, mortify, offend. * *n* blow, hurt, injury; damage, detriment; anguish, grief, pain, pang, torture.

wrap *vb* cloak, cover, encase, envelope, muffle, swathe, wind. * *n* blanket, cape, cloak, cover, overcoat, shawl.

wreath *n* chaplet, curl, festoon, garland, ring, twine.

wreathe *vb* encircle, festoon, garland, intertwine, surround, twine, twist.

wreck *vb* founder, shipwreck, strand; blast, blight, break, devastate, ruin, spoil. * *n* crash, desolation, destruction, perdition, prostration, ruin, shipwreck, smash, undoing.

wrench *vb* distort, pervert, twist, wrest, wring; sprain, strain; extort, extract. * *n* twist, wring; sprain, strain; monkey wrench, spanner.

wrest *vb* force, pull, strain, twist, wrench, wring.

wrestle *vb* contend, contest, grapple, strive, struggle.

wretched *adj* afflicted, comfortless, distressed, forlorn, sad, unfortunate, unhappy, woebegone; afflicting, calamitous, deplorable, depressing, pitiable, sad, saddening, shocking, sorrowful; bad, beggarly, contemptible, mean, paltry, pitiful, poor, shabby, sorry, vile, worthless.

wring *vb* contort, twist, wrench; extort, force, wrest; anguish, distress, harass, pain, rack, torture.

wrinkle[1] *vb* cockle, corrugate, crease, gather, pucker, rumple. * *n* cockle, corrugation, crease, crimp, crinkle, crumple, fold, furrow, gather, plait, ridge, rumple.

wrinkle[2] *n* caprice, fancy, notion, quirk, whim; device, tip, trick.

write *vb* compose, copy, indite, inscribe, pen, scrawl, scribble, transcribe.

writer *n* amanuensis, author, clerk, penman, scribe, secretary.

wrong *vb* abuse, encroach, injure, maltreat, oppress. * *adj* inequitable, unfair, unjust, wrongful; bad, criminal, evil, guilty, immoral, improper, iniquitous, reprehensible, sinful, vicious, wicked; amiss, improper, inappropriate, unfit, unsuitable; erroneous, false, faulty, inaccurate, incorrect, mistaken, untrue. * *adv* amiss, erroneously, falsely, faultily, improperly, inaccurately, incorrectly, wrongly. * *n* foul, grievance, inequity, injury, injustice, trespass, unfairness; blame, crime, dishonesty, evil, guilt, immorality, iniquity, misdeed, misdoing, sin, transgression, unrighteousness, vice, wickedness, wrongdoing; error, falsity.

wry *adj* askew, awry, contorted, crooked, distorted, twisted.

XYZ

Xmas *n* Christmas, Christmastide, Noel, Yule, Yuletide.

X-ray *n* roentgen ray, röntgen ray.

xylograph *n* cut, woodcut, wood engraving.

yap *vb* bark, cry, yelp. * *n* bark, cry, yelp.

yard *n* close, compound, court, courtyard, enclosure, garden.

yarn *n* anecdote, boasting, fabrication, narrative, story, tale, untruth.

yawn *vb* dehisce, gape, open wide. * *n* gap, gape, gulf.

yearn *vb* crave, desire, hanker after, long for.

yell *vb* bawl, bellow, cry out, howl, roar, scream, screech, shriek, squeal.* *n* cry, howl, roar, scream, screech, shriek.

yelp *vb* bark, howl, yap; complain, bitch, grouse. * *n* bark, sharp cry, howl.

yet *adv* at last, besides, further, however, over and above, so far, still, thus far, ultimately.* *conj* moreover, nevertheless, notwithstanding, now.

yield *vb* afford, bear, bestow, communicate, confer, fetch, furnish, impart, produce, render, supply; accede, accord, acknowledge, acquiesce, allow, assent, comply, concede, give, grant, permit; abandon, abdicate, cede, forego, give up, let go, quit, relax, relinquish, resign, submit, succumb, surrender, waive. * *n* earnings, income, output, produce, profit, return, revenue.

yielding *adj* accommodating, acquiescent, affable, compliant, complaisant, easy, manageable, obedient, passive, submissive, unresisting; bending, flexible, flexile, plastic, pliant, soft, supple, tractable; fertile, productive.

yoke *vb* associate, bracket, connect, couple, harness, interlink, join, link, unite. * *n* bond, chain, ligature, link, tie, union; bondage, dependence, enslavement, service, servitude, subjection, vassalage; couple, pair.

young *adj* green, ignorant, inexperienced, juvenile, new, recent, youthful. * *n* young people, youth; babies, issue, brood, offspring, progency, spawn.

youth *n* adolescence, childhood, immaturity, juvenile, juvenility, minority, nonage, pupillage, wardship; boy, girl, lad, lass, schoolboy, schoolgirl, slip, sprig, stripling, youngster.

youthful *adj* boyish, childish, girlish, immature, juvenile, puerile, young.

zany *adj* comic, comical, crazy, droll, eccentric, funny, imaginative, scatterbrained; clownish, foolish, ludicrous, silly. * *n* buffoon, clown, droll, fool, harlequin, jester, punch..

zeal *n* alacrity, ardour, cordiality, devotedness, devotion, earnestness, eagerness, energy, enthusiasm, fervour, glow, heartiness, intensity, jealousness, passion, soul, spirit, warmth.

zealous *adj* ardent, burning, devoted, eager, earnest, enthusiastic, fervent, fiery, forward, glowing, jealous, keen, passionate, prompt, ready, swift, warm.

zenith *n* acme, apex, climax, culmination, heyday, pinnacle, prime, summit, top, utmost, height.

zero *n* cipher, naught, nadir, nil, nothing, nought.

zest *n* appetite, enjoyment, exhilaration, gusto, liking, piquancy, relish, thrill; edge, flavour, salt, savour, tang, taste; appetizer, sauce.

zone *n* band, belt, cincture, girdle, girth; circuit, clime, region.

Weights and Measures

Measurement of mass or weight

Imperial				Metric
16 drams	=	1 ounce (oz)	=	28.3495 g
16 oz	=	1 pound (lb)	=	0.45359 kg
100 lb	=	1 short hundredweight	=	45.3592 kg
112 lb	=	1 long hundredweight	=	50.8024 kg
2000 lb	=	1 short ton	=	0.9072 tonnes
2240 lb	=	1 long ton	=	1.01605 tonnes

Metric				Imperial
		1 milligram (mg)	=	0.015 grain (gr)
10 mg	=	1 centigram (cg)	=	0.1543 gr
10 cg	=	1 decigram (dg)	=	1.5433 gr
10 dg	=	1 gram (g)	=	0.0353 oz
10 g	=	1 decagram (dag)	=	0.353 oz
10 dag	=	1 hectogram (hg)	=	3.527 oz
10 hg	=	1 kilogram (kg)	=	2.205 lb
1000 kg	=	1 tonne (metric ton)	=	1.1023 short tons
			=	0.9842 long ton
			=	2204.62 lb

Square measure

Imperial		Metric
	1 square inch (sq in) =	6.4516 cm²
= 1 square foot (sq ft) =		0.0929 m²
9 sq ft	= 1 square yard (sq yd) =	0.8361 m²
30¼ sq yards	= 1 square perch =	25.2929 m²
40 sq perch	= 1 rood =	0.1012 ha
4 roods/4840 sq yds	= 1 acre =	0.4047 ha
640 acres	= 1 square mile (sq mi) =	2.5900 km²

Metric		Imperial
	1 square millimetre (mm²) =	0.00155 sq in
100 mm²	= 1 square centimetre (cm²) =	0.1550 sq in
100 cm²	= 1 square decimetre (dm²) =	15.500 sq in
100 dm²	= 1 square metre (m²) =	10.7639 sq ft
	=	1.196 sq yds
100 m²	= 1 square decametre (dam²) =	1076.391 sq ft
100 dam²	= 1 square hectometre (hm²) =	0.00386 sq mi
100 hm²	= 1 square kilometre (km²) =	0.3861 sq mi

100 m²	= 1 are =	119.6 sq yds
1000 m²	= 10 ares = 1 dekare =	1195.99 sq yds
10 000 m²	= 100 ares = 1 hectare (ha) =	2.471 acres

Cubic measure

Imperial   *Metric*

		1 cubic inch (cu in)	=	16.39 cm³
1728 cu in	=	1 cubic foot (cu ft)	=	0.02832 m³
27 cu ft	=	1 cubic yard (cu yd)	=	0.7646 m³

Metric   *Imperial*

1000 cubic millimetre (mm³) = 1 cubic centimetre (cm³) = 0.0610 cu in
1000 cubic centimetres (cm³) = 1 cubic decimtere (dm³) = 61.024 cu in
1000 cubic decimetres (dm³) = 1 cubic metre (m³)   = 35.3147 cu ft

Linear measure

Imperial   *Metric*

		1 inch (in)		25.4 mm
12 in	=	1 foot (ft)	=	0.3048 m
3 ft	=	1 yard (yd)	=	0.9144 m
2 yds	=	6 ft = 1 fathom (fm)	=	1.8288 m
5.5 yds	=	16.5 ft = 1 rod	=	5.0292 m
4 rod	=	22 yds = 66 ft =1 chain	=	20.12 m
10 chain	=	220 yds = 660 ft = 1 furlong (fur)	=	0.2012 km
8 fur	=	1760 yds = 5280 ft = 1 mile (mi)	=	1.609 km
3 mi	=	1 league	=	4.828 km

Metric   *Imperial*

		1 millimetre (mm)		0.03937 in
10 mm	=	1 centimetre (cm)	=	0.3937 in
10 cm	=	1 decimetre (dm)	=	3.937 in
10 dm	=	1 metre (m)	=	39.37 in
10 m	=	1 decametre (dam)	=	10.936 yds
10 dam	=	1 hectometre (hm)	=	109.36 yds
10 hm	=	1 kilometre (km)	=	0.6214 mi

Liquid measure

Imperial				Metric
4 fl oz	=	1 gill	=	0.1183 l
4 gills	=	1 pint (pt)	=	0.4732 l
2 pt	=	1 quart (qt)	=	0.9464 l
4 qt	=	1 gallon (gal)	=	3.7854 l

US and British equivalents

US	British
1 fluid ounce	1.0408 fl oz
1 pint	0.8327 pt
1 gallon	0.8327 gal

Metric				Imperial
10 millilitres (ml)	=	1 centilitre (cl)	=	0.02113 pt
10 cl	=	1 decilitre (dl)	=	0.2113 pt
10 dl	=	1 litre (l)	=	2.113 pt
			=	0.2642 gal
10 l	=	1 decalitre (dal)	=	2.642 gal
10 dal	=	1 hectolitre (hl)	=	26.42 gal
10 hl	=	1 kilolitre (kl)	=	264.17 gal

Temperature

Equations for conversion:

° Fahrenheit = ($9/5$ x x°C) + 32

° Centigrade = $5/9$ x (x°F-32)

° Kelvin = x°C + 273.15

Normal temperatures of the human body	36.9°C	=	98.4°F
Freezing point	0°C	=	32°F
Boiling point	100°C	=	212°F

Periodic Table

Group 1A	2A	3B	4B	5B	6B	7B	8	8	8	1B	2B	3A	4A	5A	6A	7A	0
H 1																	He 2
Li 3	Be 4											B 5	C 6	N 7	O 8	F 9	Ne 10
Na 11	Mg 12											Al 13	Si 14	P 15	S 16	Cl 17	Ar 18
K 19	Ca 20	Sc 21	Ti 22	V 23	Cr 24	Mn 25	Fe 26	Co 27	Ni 28	Cu 29	Zn 30	Ga 31	Ge 32	As 33	Se 34	Br 35	Kr 36
Rb 37	Sr 38	Y 39	Zr 40	Nb 41	Mo 42	Tc 43	Ru 44	Rh 45	Pd 46	Ag 47	Cd 48	In 49	Sn 50	Sb 51	Te 52	I 53	Xe 54
Cs 55	Ba 56	La* 57	Hf 72	Ta 73	W 74	Re 75	Os 76	Ir 77	Pt 78	Au 79	Hg 80	Ti 81	Pb 82	Bi 83	Po 84	At 85	Rn 86
Fr 87	Ra 88	Ac° 89															

Transition Elements

* Lanthanides	La 57	Ce 58	Pr 59	Nd 60	Pm 61	Sm 62	Eu 63	Gd 64	Tb 65	Dy 66	Ho 67	Er 68	Tm 69	Yb 70	Lu 71
° Actinides	Ac 89	Th 90	Pa 91	U 92	Np 93	Pu 94	Am 95	Cm 96	Bk 97	Cf 98	Es 99	Fm 100	Md 101	No 102	Lr 103

Element Table

Element	Symbol	Atomic Number	Relative Atomic Mass*
Actinium	Ac	89	{227}
Aluminium	Al	13	26.9815
Americium	Am	95	{243}
Antimony	Sb	51	121.75
Argon	Ar	18	39.948
Arsenic	As	33	74.9216
Astatine	At	85	{210}
Barium	Ba	56	137.34
Berkelium	Bk	97	{247}
Beryllium	Be	4	9.0122
Bismuth	Bi	83	208.98
Boron	B	5	10.81
Bromine	Br	35	79.904
Cadmium	Cd	48	112.40
Caesium	Cs	55	132.905
Calcium	Ca	20	40.08
Californium	Cf	98	{251}
Carbon	C	6	12.011
Cerium	Ce	58	140.12
Chlorine	Cl	17	35.453
Chromium	Cr	24	51.996
Cobalt	Co	27	58.9332
Copper	Cu	29	63.546
Curium	Cm	96	{247}
Dysprosium	Dy	66	162.50
Einsteinium	Es	99	{254}

Element	Symbol	Atomic Number	Relative Atomic Mass*
Erbium	Er	68	167.26
Europium	Eu	63	151.96
Fermium	Fm	100	{257}
Fluorine	F	9	18.9984
Francium	Fr	87	{223}
Gadolinium	Gd	64	157.25
Gallium	Ga	31	69.72
Germanium	Ge	32	72.59
Gold	Au	79	196.967
Hafnium	Hf	72	178.49
Helium	He	2	4.0026
Holmium	Ho	67	164.930
Hydrogen	H	1	1.00797
Indium	In	49	1114.82
Iodine	I	53	126.9044
Iridium	Ir	77	192.2
Iron	Fe	26	55.847
Krypton	Kr	36	83.80
Lanthanum	La	57	138.91
Lawrencium	Lr	103	{257}
Lead	Pb	82	207.19
Lithium	Li	3	6.939
Lutetium	Lu	71	174.97
Magnesium	Mg	12	24.305
Manganese	Mn	25	54.938
Mendelevium	Md	101	{259}
Mercury	Hg	80	200.59
Molybdenum	Mo	42	95.94

Element	Symbol	Atomic Number	Relative Atomic Mass*
Neodymium	Nd	60	144.24
Neon	Ne	10	20.179
Neptunium	Np	93	{237}
Nickel	Ni	28	58.71
Niobium	Nb	41	92.906
Nitrogen	N	7	14.0067
Nobelium	No	102	{255}
Osmium	Os	76	190.2
Oxygen	O	8	15.9994
Palladium	Pd	46	106.4
Phosphorus	P	15	30.9738
Platinum	Pt	78	195.09
Plutonium	Pu	94	{244}
Polonium	Po	84	{209}
Potassium	K	19	39.102
Praseodymium	Pr	59	140.907
Promethium	Pm	61	{145}
Protactinium	Pa	91	{231}
Radium	Ra	88	{226}
Radon	Rn	86	{222}
Rhenium	Re	75	186.20
Rhodium	Rh	45	102.905
Rubidium	Rb	37	85.47
Ruthenium	Ru	44	101.07
Samarium	Sm	62	150.35
Scandium	Sc	21	44.956
Selenium	Se	34	78.96
Silicon	Si	14	28.086

Element	Symbol	Atomic Number	Relative Atomic Mass*
Silver	Ag	47	107.868
Sodium	Na	11	22.9898
Strontium	Sr	38	87.62
Sulphur	S	16	32.064
Tantalum	Ta	73	180.948
Technetium	Tc	43	{97}
Tellurium	Te	52	127.60
Terbium	Tb	65	158.924
Thallium	Tl	81	204.37
Thorium	Th	90	232.038
Thulium	Tm	69	168.934
Tin	Sn	50	118.69
Titanium	Ti	22	47.90
Tungsten	W	74	183.85
Uranium	U	92	238.03
Vanadium	V	23	50.942
Xenon	Xe	54	131.30
Ytterbium	Yb	70	173.04
Yttrium	Y	39	88.905
Zinc	Zn	30	65.37
Zirconium	Zr	40	91.22

* Values of the *Relative Atomic Mass* in brackets refer to the most stable, known, isotope.

The Greek Alphabet

English Name	Capital	Lower Case	Sound
alpha	A	α	a
beta	B	β	b
gamma	Γ	γ	g
delta	Δ	δ	d
epsilon	E	ε	e
zeta	Z	ζ	z
eta	H	η	e
theta	Θ	θ	th
iota	I	ι	i
kappa	K	κ	k
lambda	Λ	λ	l
mu	M	μ	m
nu	N	ν	n
xi	Ξ	ξ	x
omicron	O	o	o
pi	Π	π	p
rho	Π	ρ	r
sigma	Σ	σ	s
tau	T	τ	t
upsilon	Ψ	υ	u
phi	Φ	φ	ph
chi	Ξ	χ	kh
psi	Ψ	ψ	ps
omega	Ω	ω	o

The International System of Units (SI units)

Quantity	Symbol	Unit	Symbols
acceleration	a	metres per second squared	ms^{-2} or m/s^2
area	A	square metre	$m2$
capacitance	C	farad	$F(1F = 1\ AsV^{-1})$
charge	Q	coulomb	$C(1C = 1\ As)$
current	I	ampere	A
density	ρ	kilograms per cubic metre	kgm^{-3} or kg/m^3
force	F	newton	$N(1N = 1\ kg\ ms^{-2})$
frequency	f	hertz	$Hz(1Hz = 1s^{-1})$
length	l	metre	m
mass	m	kilogram	kg
potential difference	V	volt	$V(1V = 1JC^{-1}$ or $WA^{-1})$
power	P	watt	$W(1W = 1Js^{-1})$
resistance	R	ohm	$\Omega\ (1\Omega = 1VA^{-1})$
specific heat capacity	c	joules per kilogram kelvin	$Jkg^{-1}\ K^{-1}$
temperature	T	kelvin	L
time	t	second	s
volume	V	cubic metre	$m3$
velocity	v	metres per second	ms^{-1} or m/s
wavelength	λ	metre	m
work, energy	W,E	joule	$J(1J = 1Nm)$

Useful prefixes adoped with SI units

Prefit	Symbol	Factor
tera	T	10^{12}
giga	G	10^9
mega	M	10^6
kelo	k	10^3
hecto	h	10^2
deda	da	10^1
deci	d	10^{-1}
centi	c	10^{-2}
milli	m	10^{-3}
micro	μ	10^{-6}
nano	n	10^{-9}
pico	p	10^{-12}
femto	f	10^{-15}
atto	a	10^{-18}

The Solar System

Planet	Diameter at the Equator km	Mass relative to the Earth[1]	Average distance from Sun km[6]	The planet's "year"
Mercury	44 840	0.054	57.91	87.969 days
Venus	12 300	0.8150	109.21	224.701 days
Earth	12 756	1.000	149.60	365.256 days
Mars	6790	0.107	227.94	686.980 days
Jupiter	142 700	317.89	778.34	11.86 years
Saturn	120 800	95.14	1427.01	29.46 years
Uranus	50 800	14.52	2869.6	84.0 years
Neptune	48 600	17.46	4496.7	164.8 years
Pluto	3500	0.1 (approx)	5907	248.4 years
Sun	1 392 000	332.958		
Moon	3476	0.0123		

[1] The mass of the Earth is 5.976×10^{24} kg